NORTHERN
ITALY

THE BLUE GUIDES

NORTHERN ITALY

FROM THE ALPS TO ROME

Edited by
ALTA MACADAM

Atlas and 58 Maps & Plans

ERNEST BENN LIMITED
LONDON AND TONBRIDGE

RAND McNALLY & COMPANY
CHICAGO, NEW YORK, SAN FRANCISCO

FIRST EDITION 1924
SECOND EDITION 1927
THIRD EDITION (From the Alps to Florence) 1937
FOURTH EDITION (From the Alps to Florence) 1953
FIFTH EDITION (From the Alps to Florence) 1960
SIXTH EDITION 1971
SEVENTH EDITION 1978

Published by Ernest Benn Limited
25 New Street Square, London EC4A 3JA
& Sovereign Way, Tonbridge, Kent

Rand McNally & Company
Chicago · New York · San Francisco

© Ernest Benn Limited 1978

Printed in Great Britain
ISBN *Library* 0-510-01604-9   0-528-84599-3 (USA)
ISBN *Paperback* 0-510-01603-0   0-528-84600-0 (USA)

PREFACE

This seventh edition of the Blue Guide to Northern Italy owes much to the previous edition edited by **Stuart Rossiter** whose successful rearrangement of the book to include the whole area from the Alps to Rome has remained virtually unchanged. The meticulous and imaginative hand of Stuart Rossiter is evident throughout, and the present editor, who worked as his assistant between 1970 and 1974 wishes to record her debt to him, and her gratitude for his continuing friendship and encouragement. Many of the earlier volumes in the series covering Northern Italy came out under the distinguished editorship of L. Russell Muirhead, the news of whose death in 1976 was received with great sorrow by all those who have since worked for the Blue Guides and tried to maintain his high standards.

Since the last edition perhaps the most important single change noticeable to the visitor which has taken place in Italy has been the closure of the historical centres of almost all the main cities to private motor traffic. This has meant the visitor can again appreciate to the full the individual atmosphere of each city and study its monuments with ease. Travellers by car are now expected to leave their vehicles outside the city centres (car parks are usually provided) and tour these areas on foot.

The motorway network in the North has been enlarged greatly in the last decade and now all the main centres can be reached by autostrade, which not only enables visitors on short stays to cover much greater distances, but also frees the old roads, which often pass through beautiful countryside, from heavy traffic. Despite the continuing problem of the reduction of opening times of museums and sometimes even their temporary closure, in many towns, such as Genoa, Modena, Bologna, Lucca, Florence, Prato, Sansepolcro, Perugia, and Grosseto, new museums have been opened since the last edition.

The gradual transformation of the Provinces into Regional administrative areas, with less dependence on Rome, may mean that local authorities will have more success in running museums and galleries and taking care of historical buildings, as the civic government of Turin has already demonstrated. Florence has shown great initiative in the restoration of her buildings and works of art since the Arno flooded its banks in 1966, and now virtually all her monuments and art treasures are again on view. The problems of Venice are beginning to be resolved, and restoration work is proceeding and the necessary precautions being taken to control the waters of the lagoon. During the preparation of this Guide news was received of the disastrous earthquake in the Friuli region north of Udine (which the editor experienced while travelling for the Guide in Trieste). It left nearly 1000 people dead and hundreds of thousands homeless. Reconstruction has been slow and hampered by the fact that earth tremors are still continuing.

The names of hotels and restaurants have not been included in this edition of the Guide. Italy is now well supplied with accommodation of every class in almost all small towns and villages as well as the big centres. The Provincial tourist boards publish a free annual list of hotels with details about prices and facilities, and help to travellers is readily available at the local tourist offices. General information about hotels and restaurants is given on p. 28 of this Guide.

The maps and plans, originally drawn for this book by **John Flower,** have been revised by him where necessary with his usual high standard of technical skill.

The editor has again been helped by numerous friends and official bodies in the preparation of the text. She would like to thank, in the first instance, the Italian State Tourist Office and *Count Sigmund Fago Golfarelli,* Head of the Foreign Publicity Department in Rome for his generous help and kindness, and *Mr. John Greenwood,* until recently the press Officer in London who was always ready with invaluable advice. The *Italian State Railways* greatly facilitated the editor's travel. The local tourist boards all over Northern Italy have always co-operated and supplied useful information. The Ente Provinciale del Turismo of Vicenza were particularly generous, and the editor would like to express her gratitude to the director, *Dr. Gianfranco Martinelli.* In Florence, both the Azienda Autonoma (particular thanks to *Dr. G. Boninsegni*) and the Ente Provinciale del Turismo, took great trouble on behalf of the Guide. *Philip Rylands* of King's College, Cambridge, kindly read the text on Venice and made many useful suggestions. Thanks are also due to *Giorgio Bonsanti* who checked the section on Modena and environs.

The editors have often been helped by the kindness of readers who have taken the trouble to point out errors or omissions in the text. Any further suggestions for the improvement of the Guide will always be welcomed.

CONTENTS

II   THE LAKES AND LOMBARDY

III   VENETIA

IV EMILIA

V TUSCANY AND NORTHERN LATIUM

VI THE MARCHES AND UMBRIA

MAPS AND PLANS

MAPS

TOWN PLANS

GROUND PLANS

ART IN NORTHERN ITALY, TUSCANY, AND UMBRIA

by ANDREW MARTINDALE
University of East Anglia

This brief account of Italian art is designed to do three things. First, it will draw the attention of the reader to the main stylistic changes which occurred in the major arts of architecture, sculpture, and painting. Second, mention will be made in passing of important examples of the varying styles and characteristics so that the reader will possess by the end an anthology of significant monuments. Third, some attempt will be made to indicate the relative importance of the different provinces which constitute Italy north of Rome. This last point is important. The traveller in northern Italy will quickly realize that the art has for much of its history a provincial basis. This is especially true of the Middle Ages. Medieval Lombard art is not like Venetian art; and this in turn is not like Roman art. Even so, with the coming of the High Renaissance this provincial character underwent a distinct change, in that Rome became the pre-eminent centre in the world of art. In the provinces, from c. 1470 onwards, art tended to reflect events in Rome; and at this point the interested traveller in northern Italy will be at a permanent disadvantage. Italian art of the 16C and 17C cannot be understood without an appreciation of the great works and monuments produced in Rome during this period. In international terms, the acknowledged artistic importance of Italy survived up to the middle of the 18C. Thereafter this importance, already long since rivalled by France and other countries, dwindled sharply and it was not until the 20C that Italy again achieved European importance.

Roman and Byzantine Art. Few large Italian towns lack visible evidence of their antique origins; major Roman remains are scattered through northern Italy—the great amphitheatre and the so-called Porta dei Borsari at Verona or the arch at Fano being among the more impressive examples. However, with the shift of the capital of the Empire from Rome to Constantinople (4C), Italian art in many important aspects became orientated towards the Eastern Mediterranean and remained predominantly so until the 13C. A few notable monuments of Byzantine art survive, especially in the group of churches in Ravenna, decorated with Byzantine mosaics (5C and 6C). In practice, Italian painting remained a provincial offshoot of Byzantine art down to the great pictorial developments in Rome c. 1275. Superb late instances of this fascination with Byzantine art are the 12C-14C mosaics in S. Marco, Venice. Still heavily influenced by Byzantine painting are the long series of 12C and 13C panel painting, especially those of Tuscany.

The Middle Ages. ARCHITECTURE. Lombardy produced some of the largest and most impressive Romanesque churches in Europe. The

11

material is invariably brick and certain obvious characteristics (for instance, the small external rows of blind arches known as 'Lombard arcading') had already appeared by the 9C. Thereafter, some particular features may be noted—broad screen-like façades, sometimes decorated with sculpture (Pavia, S. Michele 12C); external wall passages set behind arcading (Bergamo, S. Maria Maggiore and elsewhere); and large internal galleries over the aisles, usually called Tribune galleries (Pavia, S. Michele and Milan, S. Ambrogio). The largest churches (e.g. Cremona or Parma cathedrals) are enormous and extremely magnificent and are often dominated by vast bell-towers or *campanili*. Cremona campanile has a very elaborate spire. Developments in this type of architecture are hard to define since the buildings are seldom heavily decorated. However, in the late Gothic period (14C-15C) a fashion for moulded brick decoration is found (Mantua, S. Andrea, campanile and elsewhere). It is perhaps especially as examples of brick engineering on a gigantic scale that the greater churches catch the imagination.

The greatest immediate difference in Tuscany is one of material. Large amounts of marble were easily available and a façade such as that of S. Miniato al Monte, Florence (12C) relies almost entirely on coloured marble for its effect. The most influential Tuscan Romanesque building was Pisa cathedral and its façade (12C) with its superimposed rows of arcading and passages, became the model for countless other smaller churches. Romanesque forms survived well into the 13C and it may be some surprise to find that the rounded arcades of the nave of Siena cathedral are roughly contemporary with Amiens cathedral. Those of Orvieto cathedral are even later (begun 1290).

The development of a Gothic style of architecture in Italy was spasmodic and idiosyncratic. The spread of the Cistercian Order introduced a somewhat muted form of Burgundian Gothic architecture (see, for instance, S. Galgano near Siena) but this did not lead to the growth of a homogeneous Italian Gothic style. Gothic churches vary, as much as Romanesque ones, according to area. S. Croce and S. Maria Novella, Florence (late 13C) were probably influenced in plan by Cistercian precedents. S. Andrea, Vercelli (c. 1230) is notable for its capitals and attached columns which are obviously French in derivation. S. Giovanni e Paolo and the Frari church are the most impressive examples of Venetian Gothic. S. Petronio, Bologna (begun 1390) would have been one of the largest churches in Europe, had it been completed. In spite of the general aversion to the more elaborate forms of external and internal decoration, such as developed north of the Alps, there is one notable exception to the rule—Milan cathedral (begun c. 1386) heavily covered with tracery decoration and topped by innumerable pinnacles. The origins of this fashion were probably German and appear to stem from the Rhineland.

Italy is, of course, rich in medieval secular buildings. The Palazzo Ducale at Mantua (mainly 14-16C) is one of the largest, most rambling medieval palace complexes in Europe. Far more compact is the Doge's Palace, Venice (also mainly 14-16C). The Castello Sforzesco, Milan, and the Castello Estense, Ferrara, represent late and different types of private fortress. Important medieval fortified town-halls survive in the Palazzo Pubblico, Siena, and the Palazzo Vecchio, Florence (later much altered inside). Two small papal palaces are to be seen at Orvieto and Viterbo. Finally, S. Gimignano is famous for the survival of its medieval private defensive towers which give it a distinctive and memorable skyline.

SCULPTURE. The main development of Romanesque figure sculpture began in the early 12C. To the beginning of the century belong a series of Old Testament reliefs, placed across the façade of Modena cathedral. According to an inscription, they are by a mason called *Wiligelmo*. The quality of these reliefs is extraordinarily good. In spite of the rather stiff and formal conventions, the figures communicate in a convincing way, and it is still not clear where Wiligelmo learnt to carve. He had, however, a number of nothern Italian successors, including a mason who signed his name, *Niccolò,* and worked at Ferrara and Verona (c. 1130-40). Niccolò also carved reliefs on lintels, and from his circle come the large series of reliefs flanking the main portal of S. Zeno, Verona. Niccolò's work contains numerous points of interest, including the early use of carved figures to decorate the jambs of a portal.

Much of this figure sculpture decorated the exterior of churches. In Tuscany, external figure sculpture was generally confined to lintels over doors, and the first important named sculptor in Pisa left his name on a characteristic piece of Tuscan interior sculpture, a pulpit. This pulpit, originally in Pisa cathedral, is now in Cagliari (Sardinia). The sculptor's name was *Guglielmo* and the date 1162. The style is reflected in carving by other masons in and around Pisa (see S. Cassiano) and is a little disappointing being, if anything, over-ornate. However, it formed the basis of a flourishing line of masons, including the more concise work of *Gruamonte* (see Pistoia, S. Andrea).

Probably more considerable than any of these was the workshop of *Benedetto Antelami* which flourished at the end of the 12C and the beginning of the 13C. Something of Antelami's background can be deduced from clear stylistic and iconographic links with Provence. He worked chiefly in Parma and Borgo S. Donnino and his *chef d'oeuvre* was the baptistery at Parma with its three carved portals. These are important for their iconographic coherence. The programme is carefully worked out—perhaps for the first time in Italy—and includes doors dedicated to the Virgin and to the Last Judgement. Carved tympana are employed, and large standing figures (unusual in Italy) occur higher up on the façade.

Nevertheless, the first unequivocally Gothic sculptor was another Tuscan, **Nicola Pisano.** His work marks an enormous step in the development of a realistic figure style, and it is of interest that in pursuing this aim he borrowed heavily from antique art (see the pulpit, Pisa cathedral baptistery, 1259-60). A second pulpit in Siena cathedral is far less heavily antique and there are indications that he was borrowing more deliberately from the contemporary sculpture of France. These northern tendencies come out far more strongly in his son *Giovanni,* who is one of the most interesting 13C Italian artists. Giovanni's masterpiece should have been the façade of Siena cathedral but it was only completed many years after his death and in considerably altered form. From Giovanni's time, however, survive a number of large dramatically animated standing figures, which with their grimacing faces and twisting poses are among the most memorable Italian creations of the 13C. Also by Giovanni are two further pulpits—one in Pisa cathedral itself.

It is of some interest that the excellence of Tuscan masons was recognized outside Tuscany. Nicola Pisano's workshop produced the shrine of S. Dominic (S. Domenico, Bologna c. 1260-65, later much altered); and another protégé, *Arnolfo di Cambio,* became the chief sculptor in Rome, and was the author of one of the most splendid 13C tombs (in S. Domenico, Orvieto). *Tino da Camaino,* who probably learnt under Giovanni Pisano, eventually ended up in Naples; and another Tuscan, Giovanni di Balduccio, took a workshop north to work on the Shrine of St Peter Martyr in S. Eustorgio, Milan (1339). Thus the formative influence of the Pisano family can hardly be overrated.

Only one sculptor-architect stands apart—*Lorenzo Maitani,* who designed the west front of Orvieto cathedral. This was designed (c. 1310) as a most interesting combination of delicate relief and sparkling mosaic, and remains one of the most important medieval façades in Italy.

In fact there were few dramatic stylistic developments in the 14C, but it was a period of considerable formal inventiveness. Especially notable are a series of tombs to the Scaliger Lords of Verona, outside S. Maria Antica. The most elaborate and latest of these, to Cansignorio della Scala (died 1375), is from the workshop of the leading Lombard mason, *Bonino da Campione,* and is a memorable mass of niches, pinnacles, and crocketted gables.

PAINTING. The 'Byzantine manner' in Italian painting survived up to the end of the 13C. The means by which it changed are now unclear, but the important centre was Rome. It is enough to record here that **Giotto** (c. 1267-1337) was probably trained in Rome or by Roman artists, and that the Franciscan church at Assisi, where he may or may not have painted (it was at any rate decorated by Roman artists), remains the best place to see the development of an Italian Gothic style of painting.

Giotto was, of course, by birth a Florentine and some of his major works are in Florence (S. Croce). But the best preserved paintings are those in the Arena chapel, Padua (c. 1305-10). His importance as a painter can be gauged by his immense influence which includes not merely subsequent 14C Florentine painters but also artists north of the Appenines such as *Altichiero* (Padua and Verona). The only city to provide an effective challenge to Giotto was Siena. The great series of frescoes by *Simone Martini,* and *Ambrogio* and *Pietro Lorenzetti* (S. Francesco, Assisi and Palazzo Pubblico, Siena, c. 1230) although frequently drawing from Giotto for the figure style, generally contain far more incidental detail and are less serious and forbidding in tone. This predilection is already to be found in the work of *Duccio* (c. 1260-1318/19) whose masterpiece, the *Maestà* for Siena cathedral, is still to be seen in the Museo dell'Opera del Duomo there.

The International Style in Painting and Sculpture. The art of the period c. 1400 is normally termed 'International Gothic'. This derives from the fact that a particular figure style, compounded of flowing drapery and graceful forms, achieved a fashionable status on both sides of the Alps. Alongside this style went a liking for detailed realism and gay décor. It was a style to be found north of the Apennines in Milan and Venice and one of its chief exponents was *Gentile da Fabriano*

(c. 1370-1427) whose main surviving work is, however, now in Florence (the Uffizi). In spite of subsequent stylistic change, it might be argued that *Pisanello* (c. 1395-1455/6) really belongs to this group of painters. Florence of course had its own exponents of this style, the most famous being the painter *Lorenzo Monaco* (c. 1370-c. 1425; several works now in the Uffizi, Florence) and *Lorenzo Ghiberti* (1378-1455; see especially his first doors for the Florentine baptistery). With Ghiberti, however, one also reaches the beginning of the Florentine Renaissance.

The Early Renaissance in Florence. The changes which took place in Florentine art c. 1400-30 were of fundamental importance for the subsequent history of Western art. They were inspired partly by a reaction against the elegance and refinement of the International Style, partly by reverence for the art of antiquity, and partly by a new scientific interest in realistic portrayal. The three major figures are **Masaccio** the painter (1401-28), **Donatello** the sculptor (1386-1466), and **Brunelleschi** the architect (1377-1446). As yet there was little attempt at archæological exactitude in the use of antique motifs. Antiquity was seen much more as a source for ideas. With this went experiments in a new system of perspective construction, probably pioneered by Brunelleschi but codified by a further great Florentine architect *Alberti* (c. 1404-72). Major monuments of this early period include the Brancacci chapel of Masaccio (S. Maria del Carmine), Donatello's statues in Or San Michele, and Brunelleschi's church of S. Lorenzo. Many of the ideas of these artists were accepted and developed by subsequent painters and sculptors such as *Paolo Uccello* (1396/7-1475), *And. del Castagno* (?1423-57), *Filippo Lippi* (c. 1406-69) or *Luca della Robbia* (1400-82). It is, however, to be observed that the severity of Masaccio or the drama of Donatello do not appear to have been especially attractive and much of the subsequent art seems to be pitched in an appreciably lower key.

This is also true of the second half of the century which produced a number of artists of astonishing ability and virtuosity. The chief painters were *Ghirlandaio* (1449-94; see frescoes in S. Maria Novella, Florence) and *Botticelli* (c. 1445-1510) who both painted for the Medici family or their agents. The chief sculptors were two men of great ability. *Antonio Rossellino* (1427-c. 1479) and *Andrea Verrocchio* (c. 1435-88; many works in Florence). Of equal importance for the development of figure painting was the sculptor-painter *Antonio Pollaiuolo* (c. 1432-98) under whose influence two great artists emerged. The first, *Luca Signorelli* (c. 1441-1523), was the author of a major series of frescoes in the chapel of S. Brizio, Orvieto cathedral (begun 1499). The other far greater artist who had as his immediate master *Andrea Verrocchio,* was **Leonardo da Vinci** (1452-1519).

One further painter should be noted as probably the most distinguished offshoot of the early Florentine Renaissance—*Piero della Francesca* (c. 1415-92). He was trained in Florence, but worked most of his life in central Italy and the Marches, being closely connected with the court of Urbino. His most complete surviving work is now the fresco cycle in S. Francesco, Arezzo.

Brunelleschi's achievements were partially those of an engineer (the dome of Florence cathedral) and partly those of a designer (see also the church of S. Spirito, Florence). The classical motifs which he incorporated into his buildings were widely copied throughout the century. Alberti, already mentioned, probably possessed a more profound archæological appreciation of classical architecture (see the façade of the Rucellai Palace, Florence, or S. Francesco, Rimini) which he later carried to Mantua. A third architect, *Michelozzo* (1396-1472) was responsible for one of the most influential palace designs of the 15C, namely the Medici Palace, Florence.

Florentine ideas quickly spread outwards from Tuscany, artists visiting both Rome (*Fra Angelico*) and cities north of the Apennines. (*Masolino* painted at Castiglione d'Olona, near Milan, c. 1435; Michelozzo worked in Milan c. 1460; Donatello, Uccello, Castagno, and Filippo Lippi all visited the Veneto; Leonardo went to Milan c.1473.) This in turn affected the provincial northern schools.

The early Renaissance in the North of Italy. The two major political centres in North Italy were Milan and Venice. Both had flourishing local schools and each was influenced in a different way by Renaissance ideas. The stay of Leonardo in Milan (c. 1473-99) had in general a destructive effect since Leonardo's interests in tonal effects, complicated figure structure, and the problems of painting emotion ran counter to the tendencies of the local painters (especially *Foppa*, 1427/30-1515/16; see the two panels in the Accademia Carrara, Bergamo) and introduced a fashion which was never effectively assimilated but only imitated (for example, by *Boltraffio* 1467-1516, many of whose works are in Milan).

The Veneto was fortunate in producing two near-contemporary artists, each of whom moulded the ideas from Tuscany into an individual and influential style. The first, *Mantegna* (1431-1506), was trained in Padua; and his early work (see especially the altarpiece in S. Zeno, Verona, c. 1456-59) demonstrates a firm control of Tuscan ideas coupled with an ardent feeling for antique remains. Mantegna's skill as a painter secured for him the post of court artist to the Gonzagas at Mantua where the *Camera degli sposi* in the Castello (1474) still ranks as one of the outstanding pieces of European palace decoration. His influence as an observer of antique remains was probably equally important, directing the course of the subsequent Renaissance towards an ever more sensitive appreciation of Antiquity.

The second great artist of the late Quattrocento was *Giovanni Bellini* (c. 1435-1516)—brother-in-law of Mantegna and initially much influenced by him. Bellini dominated Venetian painting up to c. 1505. His portraits and Madonnas were much in demand and his altarpieces (see especially his S. Giobbe altar, Accademia, Venice) provided a canon to which other painters conformed. Not to be missed are his latest works, which are among the most memorable (see the altars in S. Zaccaria and S. Giovanni Evangelista, Venice). Giovanni's father, *Jacopo,* and brother, *Gentile,* were also eminent painters of large narrative paintings, some of which survive (Accademia, Venice). A more sensitive and attractive painter of the same genre was *Carpaccio* (c. 1470-1523/6. See the great cycle of paintings of S. Orsola, now in the Accademia, Venice).

The impact of Paduan and Venetian painting can be found in numerous North Italian centres. The most important was probably Ferrara, which had a court 'school' of its own dominated by the curious and mannered styles of *Cosmè Tura* (c. 1430-95), *Cossa* (1435/6-77) and

Ercole Roberti (c. 1448/55-96). This current style is well illustrated by the decorations in the Palazzo Schifanoia, Ferrara (completed in 1470). An extension of Paduan-Venetian influence is to be found in the Marches where the Venetian *Carlo Crivelli* spent much of his life (c. 1435-93. See especially the early altar at Massa Fermana, 1468).

The sculptors of the period were also much influenced by the archæological tendencies of Mantegna. One of the most famous, *Piero Buonacolsi,* was nicknamed *'Antico'* because much of his time he either made antique-looking bronze figures, or repaired real antiques for Isabella, the Marchesa of Mantua. Padua again produced some notable sculptors (see especially the bronze sculpture of *Riccio* and *Bellano* in the church of the Santo, Padua); and Venice attracted some remarkable marble sculptors (see the many works by the Lombardo family in Venice, and also in the Santo, Padua), one of whom, *Tullio Lombardo,* showed a striking sensitivity for the softer qualities of good classical sculpture.

The clarity which is to be found in much of this Quattrocento art is not so apparent in the architecture, which tended to be elaborate and over-ornate in appearance. The recovery of classical detail went ahead but there was much uncertainty about its effective use. Monuments to this confusion are the façade of the Certosa at Pavia (begun 1473 but never completed) and the Colleoni chapel at Bergamo (1470s). Milanese architecture also tended to elaboration and there was a continuation of the fashion, already mentioned, for moulded terracotta decoration. This is of some interest, since it is in this context that the greatest architect of the High Renaissance, Donato Bramante, first achieved fame. Bramante, before his departure to Rome (1499), had already worked for twenty years in Milan and his works tend to be ornate (see especially the ingenious church of S. Maria presso S. Satiro, Milan, begun c. 1483). One of the interesting effects of his later contact with Rome was that he immediately dropped this rather provincial aspect of his work.

The High Renaissance and Mannerism in Florence. The art of the High Renaissance is closely connected with the sustained patronage of three Popes—Julius II, Leo X, and Clement VII. Their reigns saw the establishment in Rome of a nucleus of brilliant artists who came to dominate art for the next half-century or more. Although none of the major figures was a Roman by birth, they all found Rome a congenial place in which to live and work. Their names are now household words—**Michelangelo**, from Florence (1475-1564), **Raphael**, originally from Urbino (1483-1520), and **Bramante** (1444-1514), from Urbino, although immediately from Milan (see above). But the first monuments of High Renaissance art are (or were) to be found in Florence. For between c. 1500 and c. 1507 Michelangelo, Raphael, and Leonardo (lately returned from Milan, see above) all lived here. It was largely the success of Julius II in forcing or persuading artists to work for him which caused what in retrospect can be see as one of the major 'population shifts' in the history of art.

The concerns of the High Renaissance were many, and it is misleading to see it as a monolithic 'movement'. Michelangelo's interests lay particularly in the recreation of an heroic figure style akin to the more grandiose monuments of Hellenistic art. This is already clear in the famous David and the unfinished St Matthew (both in the Accademia,

Florence). But Leonardo's interests were still especially bound up in complex figure-patterns and in the problems of portraying human emotion. And although none of his late work may now be seen in Italy, it made a deep impression on the young Raphael, who arrived in Florence from Perugia in 1504. Northern Italy is also somewhat denuded of the early work of Raphael but some examples are to be found in Florence.

The artists who went to Rome, c. 1505-7, found Bramante already installed there, supervising the first stages of one of the most gigantic architectural enterprises undertaken since the end of the Roman Empire—the rebuilding of St Peter's. Bramante's outstanding abilities were partly those of an engineer (his training in Lombardy must have stood him in good stead) and partly those of an artist able to manipulate mass and to devise a decoration consistent with the enormous surfaces involved. The result was the rebirth of classical architecture on a new scale.

Evidence of these developments outside Rome is not difficult to find. Michelangelo himself lived in Florence, 1516-30, and from this period dates the Medici chapel in S. Lorenzo. At the same time, a considerable body of artists remained working in Florence, assimilating the various interests that went to make up the High Renaissance. Chief among the painters was probably *Andrea del Sarto*, one of the great colourists of this period (1486-1531; see frescoes in the churches of the Scalzo and SS. Annunziata, Florence). His followers included *Pontormo* (1494-1556) and *Rosso Fiorentino* (1495-1540), many of whose works are still in Florence.

This process of assimilation is intimately linked with a stage of art usually called Mannerism. This was never an organized movement; it is, rather, a convenient word to describe the wide response to the major works of the great artists already mentioned. These ideas were worked out over a long period occupying a large part of the 16C, the fund of art being constantly enriched by the particular contributions of talented individuals. Florence remained important as the centre of Medici power and the first Grand Duke of Tuscany, Cosimo, numbered among his painters *Bronzino* (1503-72) and the historian *Giorgio Vasari* (1511-74). The decorations done for Cosimo in the Palazzo Vecchio, Florence, are among the best examples of this Mannerist court art. Another example of an artist decisively influenced by Roman art is *Parmigianino* (1503-40), whose work in Parma includes frescoes in the church of the Madonna della Steccata (paintings also in the Pitti Palace, Florence).

Harder to place is the painter *Correggio* (?1489-1534) whose main achievements consist of two magnificent dome paintings in the cathedral and the church of S. Giovanni Evangelista in Parma. Correggio may not have visited Rome but these enormous undertakings must certainly have been inspired by the great works of Raphael and Michelangelo. On a totally different scale and closer in feeling to Mantegna is his Camera di San Paolo in Parma.

Other provincial centres of importance might be mentioned briefly, reflecting as they did the Mannerist art of central Italy—as for instance Cremona, where a flourishing local school is found in the second half of the century (see especially S. Sigismondo, with its especially well-preserved decoration). But most important of all was probably Mantua, where court art from 1524 to 1546 came under the direction of Raphael's pupil, *Giulio Romano* (?1499-1546). Numerous buildings and schemes of decoration survive in Mantua, produced either by him or under his direction. A short distance from Mantua lies the tiny Gonzaga town of Sabbioneta, which is also rich in monuments reflecting the art of Mantua and also Venice.

In central Italy, the position of sculptors was analogous to that of the painters. Rome came to occupy a central position and most important figures spent some of their formative years there. This is true of one of the greatest sculptors of the first part of the century, *Jacopo Sansovino* (1486-1570). He began work in Florence (St Matthew, now in the Museo dell'Opera del Duomo) but soon moved to Rome, ultimately going to Venice (see below). Probably the true central Italian heir to Michelangelo was *Giovanni da Bologna* (1529-1608)—actually a Fleming called Jean de Boulogne who came to Italy c. 1555. He ultimately settled in Florence and worked for Cosimo I. Works of almost every description, from small bronzes (in the *Studiola,* Palazzo Vecchio) to colossal two- and even three-figure groups and a fountain (Boboli Gardens), survive in Florence to demonstrate his versatility (see also the Neptune Fountain, Bologna), and to provide a link between Mannerist sculpture at its most highly developed stage and the Baroque art of the 17C.

Venice in the 16C. Of all the great 15C centres of artistic production, Venice alone continued to preserve through the 16C some kind of independence of central Italy; so that Venetian art has in a special sense a recognizable character of its own which is not merely a provincial reflection of Rome. Many of the interests of High Renaissance Florence and Rome are apparent in the works of *Giorgione* (c. 1476-1510) and the young *Titian* (c. 1495-1576); but whereas in central Italy great importance came to be attached to anatomy, figure articulation, and draughtsmanship, in Venice these counted for little beside the manipulation of colour and tone. A number of important works survive in Venice (see the Accademia and many churches, especially the Frari) which demonstrate this moment of transition in Venetian art.

The development of High Renaissance ideas into what might be called a Mannerist style took comparatively long in Venice, since the penetration and absorption of the ideas themselves was slow, and to some extent resisted. Their impact was assisted among other things by the activities of *Giulio Romano* at Mantua, *Parmigianino* at Parma, by the work of *Pordenone* (1483/4-1539) in Venice itself (see the church of S. Rocco), and by the coming of *Jacopo Sansovino* from Rome (1527). Even so the greatest changes in Venetian art are apparent, not around 1500, but in 1540. These changes involve the later work of *Titian,* and the painting of *Veronese* (c. 1528-88) and *Tintoretto* (1518-94), the later sculpture of *Sansovino* and the work of *Vittoria* (1525-1608).

Evidence of change in Titian's work towards a more complicated and agitated figure style and more sombre colour palette is visible in the ceiling paintings now in S. Maria della Salute (c. 1542). This change of interest and technique is similar to the style developed by Tintoretto with its mighty figures and dramatic tonal contrasts (Venice contains innumerable masterpieces, but see especially the Scuola di San Rocco, 1564-88). Sculptural parallels to this painting are to be found in the giant figures of Mars and Neptune by Jacopo Sansovino (completed 1567,

Palazzo Ducale) and in the work of Vittoria (see S. Maria de'Frari and other churches).

Alongside this strongly characterized style must be set the far more obviously attractive work of Veronese, who is famous for his colourful and decorative narrative painting and ceilings (see the Accademia and especially S. Sebastiano, Venice). He continued the tradition of Pisanello, Carpaccio, and Gentile Bellini, and his work was immensely influential later on in the 18C.

The restrained and decorative beauty of Veronese's painting finds an architectural parallel in the work of his friend and collaborator, *Palladio* (1508-80). Palladio was famous both for his theoretical treatise on architecture, and also for his many country villas on the Venetian mainland. Among many, the Villa Maser still survives, designed by Palladio and decorated inside by Veronese. But the best centre for seeing Palladio's work is probably Vicenza. Palladio's work grows directly out of the architectural activities of Sansovino (for instance, Libreria di S. Marco and Loggetta, Venice), so that he has direct links with one of the most elegant and restrained artists of High Renaissance Rome.

Baroque Art. Italian art of the 17C is perhaps even more obviously dominated by Rome than that of the 16C. Moreover, since most Baroque art is, in a very obvious sense, something to be experienced, it is difficult for the traveller to do justice to it or to understand it without a visit there. All the greatest artists practised there—some of them almost exclusively. Among these must be mentioned *Gian Lorenzo Bernini* (1598-1680), whose major work is almost entirely in Rome and includes architecture and town planning, and sculptural schemes such as altars, tombs, and fountains; and *Algardi* (1595-1654) and *Duquesnoy* (1594-1643), his rivals in sculpture, who worked in a more restrained style. Besides Bernini, as architects, were *Borromini* (1599-1667) and *Pietro da Cortona* (1596-1669), the last being also a celebrated decorator. His ceilings and interior paintings form, in fact, an essential element in Roman Baroque art, together with those of *Gaulli* (1639-1709) and *Pozzo* (1642-1709).

PAINTING. Nevertheless, the contribution of the central and northern provinces was considerable. Many of the 'Roman' artists and architects were born in the north; and many of them subsequently maintained links with the towns and areas from which they came. In this respect, Bologna stands out as perhaps the most important centre in North Italian painting. Here, already in the later 16C, the art was dominated by the three **Carracci,** who, together, exercised a most important formative influence on the style of the 17C. Of these, Annibale (1560-1609), who was the most important, went to Rome in 1595, leaving Lodovico (1555-1619) to run the Academy which had been founded in 1585-86. All, however, were much in sympathy with the great artists of the first half of the 16C and with the great works of classical antiquity; and, by reinterpreting these, paved the way for a 'classical' revival which ran counter in some respects to the 'Baroque' tendencies found elsewhere. (Numerous examples of their works are to be found in and around Bologna.) They in turn produced followers who developed this classicism and idealism still further. Of these, *Guido Reni* (1575-1642) worked mainly in Rome and Bologna; and *Andrea Sacchi* (1599-1661) was in part trained in Bologna although his important work was all done in Rome. Another pupil, *Domenichino* (1581-1641) worked mainly in Rome and also in Naples.

The other great formative influence on 17C painting was **Michelangelo da Caravaggio** (1573-1610), born at Caravaggio near Milan. Although he went to Rome c.1590 and never returned north, his painting, which is full of strong colouring and chiaroscuro and portrays a dramatic unidealized world, formed a strong contrast to the Bolognese painting. He was much criticized in Rome (but patrons still bought his paintings) and some of the more important effects of his activities are to be seen either in the far south of Italy (Naples) or north of the Alps (see, for instance, Rubens and Rembrandt). However, his work exercised a pervasive influence throughout Italy and this can be easily detected in different ways in the paintings of *Guercino* (1591-1666) or *Orazio Gentileschi* (1563-1638; a Pisan by birth).

There are many areas of local activity in North and central Italy during this period, some of them disappointing. Of these the most obvious is Venice, dominated by the imitators of Tintoretto and Veronese. The brief appearance of two outsiders during the 1620s (*Domenico Feti*, 1589-1623, and *Giovanni Lys*, 1597-1629/30) offers a slight interlude. To the west, however, more considerable achievements are found. In Milan, an Academy was founded in 1621, and a flourishing local school existed, dominated by *G. C. Procaccini* (1574-1625), *Il Cerano* (c. 1575-1632), and *Il Morazzone* (1573-1626). Many works still exist by these artists in Milan cathedral (cycle of paintings of St Charles Borromeo) and in Milanese churches. In Genoa, too, a local Baroque school flourished led by *Bernardo Strozzi* (1581-1644) and *G. Assereto* (1600-49). Strozzi himself lived in Venice at the end of his life.

In fact, Genoa preserved throughout the century an interesting nucleus of talented painters. *G. B. Castiglione* (? before 1610-65) displayed an astonishing range of style (works in Genoese churches; he became court painter at Mantua in 1648) while the tradition of great fresco painting was kept alive into the 18C by *Domenico Piola* (1628-1723) and *Gregorio de Ferrari* (1647-1726; many examples in Genoa). Outside Genoa, isolated artists such as *Francesco Maffei* at Vicenza (c. 1600-60) displayed an unorthodox style which contrasted strongly with the mid-century Baroque classicism which seems to have developed in the wake of the Carracci. This tendency towards a rather dull academicism was occasionally disrupted by the visits of eminent outsiders from other parts of Italy. Thus Pietro da Cortona worked for a short time in Florence (Palazzo Pitti, 1643-47) and left some direct record of the Roman Grand Manner, to be reflected in the paintings of *Il Volteranno* (1611-89; numerous works in Florence). Important at a later stage was the activity of the Neapolitan *Luca Giordano* (1632-1705) who executed commissions both in Florence and Venice.

SCULPTURE AND ARCHITECTURE. In sculpture there was no city outside Rome to play a role equivalent to that of Bologna in painting. Nevertheless, in Florence, the tradition of Giovanni Bologna was carried on by his pupil *Pietro Tacca* (1577-1640) whose work includes parts of the monument to the Grand Duke Ferdinand I in Livorno and the tomb-sculpture in the sumptuous Cappella dei Principi, S. Lorenzo (Florence, mentioned below). Later examples of Florentine Baroque are to be seen in the work of *G. B. Foggini* (1652-1725—for instance, in

S. Maria del Carmine). Much 'local' Baroque is disappointing and it is worth noting that a number of first-class works by Roman-based sculptors exist in the north. In Piacenza stand two magnificent equestrian monuments to the Farnese by *Francesco Mochi* (1580-1654) and in S. Paolo, Bologna stands an altar group by *Algardi* (1595-1654). Work by Algardi is also to be found in S. Carlo, Genoa, but Genoa also produced one first-class Baroque sculptor who, trained in Rome, worked in Genoa: *F. Parodi* (1630-1702; various works in and around Genoa).

With a few exceptions the achievements in architecture were less spectacular than in painting. The rich and extravagant effects of some Roman work are well caught in Florence by the Cappella dei Principi (S. Lorenzo). *B. Bianco* (before 1590-1657) is probably the greatest Baroque architect of Genoa (see especially the University), while Milan is celebrated for *F. M. Ricchino* (1583-1658) whose work is to be seen in S. Giuseppe, the Palazzo di Brera and the Collegio Elvetico. In Venice, no visitor can miss the splendid S. Maria della Salute, the masterpiece of *B. Longhena* (1598-1682) standing at the entrance to the Grand Canal. But of all the exciting and impressive 17C architecture north of Rome, the greatest concentration is to be found in Turin, which had become the capital of Piedmont in 1563. The great developments in planning and architecture spread across the 17C into the 18C, and the most striking buildings are those of *G. Guarini* (1624-83) under whom Turin became one of the most stimulating centres of Baroque architectural design. Guarini was succeeded by two more great architects, *F. Juvarra* (1678-1736), of international renown, designed the great basilica at Superga and the 'Castello' of Stupinigi. *Bernardo Vittone* (1704/5-70) successfully combined the contrasting traditions of his two great predecessors and carried them far into the second half of the 18C.

Post-Baroque Art. With the 18C, the international importance of Italian art dwindled. Foreigners indeed came to Italy in unprecedented numbers. But Italy was now regarded particularly as a repository of *antique* art. The great developments in *contemporary* art happened elsewhere—mainly in France.

Nevertheless, one final brilliant flowering of Italian art took place in Venice; for here a group of artists, overthrowing much of the cumbrous tradition of the Baroque 18C, created a distinctive Italian Rococo style. Probably the initiator of the change was *Sebastiano Ricci* (1659-1734), but the greatest representative of this style was **Giambattista Tiepolo** (1696-1770), whose many works are to be found not only in Venice but also in Milan, and elsewhere in northern Italy. Alongside Tiepolo were many lesser masters among whose works the *vedute* of Venice by *Antonio Canaletto* (1697-1768) and *Francesco Guardi* (1712-93) are probably the best known. It is of interest that almost all the chief painters of Venice during that period travelled to foreign courts—such was the popularity of the Venetian style. Thus Venice, in this final phase, produced an art which was truly international.

It is, however, evident that in spite of isolated exceptions Italian art of the late 18C and 19C has not the central importance that it had held since the late 15C. The obvious exceptions would include the great neo-classical sculptor *Canova* (1757-1822), who possessed in his day an unequalled international reputation. But even so, the most interesting developments in Neo-classicism belong to France, Germany, and England. This pattern, in which Italy reflected rather than led Europe, was repeated through the 19C into the era of Art Nouveau where, once again, Italy produced a number of striking reflections of an international movement (see, for instance, the exciting and bizarre but little-known *Camera di Commercio,* Mantua 1914 by Aldo Andreani).

The greatest Italian contributions to European art since the time of Tiepolo undoubtedly came in the 20C. There is indeed one important Italian movement, Futurism, which began with a manifesto in 1909 and had a distinctive effect on the development of Cubism north of the Alps. The Futurists were above all concerned with art and its relevance to the 20C environment. Their impact was to some extent lessened by the death, during the First World War, of the most creative of them, *Umberto Boccioni* (1882-1916).

The attempt to relate art directly to their view of the character of 20C existence can also be seen in the visionary drawings of the Futurist architect, *Antonio Sant'Elia* (1888-1916; who likewise died during the First World War). Thereafter, Italian art has developed in step with northern art, frequently making important contributions. Notable was the work of the so-called *scuola metafisica* founded (c. 1917) by *Giorgio de'Chirico* (b. 1888) in which was produced a species of proto-Surrealist painting; and this account of Italian art may be ended by alluding to more recent achievements of Italian architects, especially of Pier Luigi Nervi (see, for instance, the Exhibition Hall, Turin, or the earlier Stadio Comunale at Florence).

GLOSSARY OF ART TERMS

AMBO (pl. *ambones*). Pulpit in a Christian basilica; two pulpits on opposite sides of a church from which the gospel and epistle were read.

AMPHORA. Antique vase, usually of large dimensions, for oil and other liquids.

ANTEFIX. Ornament placed at the lower corners of the tiled roof of a temple to conceal the space between the tiles and the cornice.

ANTIPHONAL. Choir-book containing a collection of *antiphonoe*—verses sung in response by two choirs.

ARCA. Wooden chest with a lid, for sacred or secular use. Also, monumental sarcophagus in stone, used by Christians and pagans.

ARCHIVOLT. Moulded architrave carried round an arch.

ATLANTES (or *Telamones*). Male figures used as supporting columns.

ATRIUM. Forecourt, usually of a Byzantine church or a classical Roman house.

ATTIC. Topmost storey of a classical building, hiding the spring of the roof.

BADIA, *Abbazia.* Abbey.

BALDACCHINO. Canopy supported by columns, usually over an altar.

BASILICA. Originally a Roman building used for public administration; in Christian architecture, an aisled church with a clerestory and apse, and no transepts.

BORGO. A suburb; street leading away from the centre of a town.

BOTTEGA. The studio of an artist: the pupils who worked under his direction.

BROCCATELLO. A clouded veined marble from Siena.

BROLETTO. Name often given to the town halls of North Italy.

BUCCHERO. Etruscan black terracotta ware.

BUCRANIA. A form of classical decoration—heads of oxen garlanded with flowers.

CAMPANILE. Bell-tower, often detached from the building to which it belongs.

CAMPOSANTO. Cemetery.

CANEPHORA. Figure bearing a basket, often used as a caryatid.

CANOPIC VASE. Egyptian or Etruscan vase enclosing the entrails of the dead.

CARYATID. Female figure used as a supporting column.

CAVEA. The part of a theatre or amphitheatre occupied by the row of seats.

CELLA. Sanctuary of a temple, usually in the centre of the building.

CHIAROSCURO. Distribution of light and shade, apart from colour in a painting; rarely used as a synonym for grisaille.

CIBORIUM. Casket or tabernacle containing the Host.

CIPOLLINO. Onion-marble; a greyish marble with streaks of white or green.

CIPPUS. Sepulchral monument in the form of an altar.

CISTA. Casket, usually of bronze and cylindrical in shape, to hold jewels, toilet articles, etc., and decorated with mythological subjects.

COLUMBARIUM. A building (usually subterranean) with niches to hold urns containing the ashes of the dead.

CONFESSIO. Crypt beneath the high altar and raised choir of a church, usually containing the relics of a saint.

CYCLOPEAN. The term applied to walls of unmortared masonry, older than the Etruscan civilization, and attributed by the ancients to the giant Cyclopes.

DIPTYCH. Painting or ivory tablet in two sections.

DUOMO. Cathedral.

EXEDRA. Semicircular recess in a Byzantine church.

EX-VOTO. Tablet or small painting expressing gratitude to a saint.

GIALLO ANTICO. Red-veined yellow marble from Numidia.

GONFALON. Banner of a medieval guild or commune.

GRAFFITI. Design on a wall made with iron tool on a prepared surface, the design showing in white. Also used loosely to describe scratched designs or words on walls.

GRISAILLE. Painting in various tones of grey.

HERM. (pl. *Hermæ*). Quadrangular pillar decreasing in girth towards the ground, surmounted by a bust.

HYPOGEUM. Subterranean excavation for the interment of the dead (usually Etruscan).

ICONOSTASIS. High balustrade with figures of saints, guarding the sanctuary of a Byzantine church.

IMPASTO. Early Etruscan ware made of inferior clay.

INTARSIA (or *Tarsia*). Inlay of wood, marble, or metal.

KRATER. Antique mixing-bowl, conical in shape with rounded base.

KYLIX. Wide shallow vase with two handles and short stem.

LOGGIA. Covered gallery or balcony, usually preceding a larger building.

LUNETTE. Semicircular space in a vault or ceiling, often decorated with a painting or relief.

MATRONEUM. Gallery reserved for women in early Christian churches.

METOPE. Panel between two triglyphs on the frieze of a temple.

NARTHEX. Vestibule of a Christian basilica.

NIELLO. Metalwork with an engraved and enamelled design.

NIMBUS. Luminous ring surrounding the heads of Saints in paintings; a square nimbus denoted that the person was living at that time.

PALAZZO. Any dignified and important building.

PALOMBINO. Fine-grained white marble.

PAVONAZZETTO. Yellow marble blotched with blue.

PAX. Sacred object used by a priest for the blessing of peace, and offered for the kiss of the faithful. Usually circular, engraved enamelled or painted in a rich gold or silver frame.

PERISTYLE. Court or garden surrounded by a columned portico.

PIETÀ. Group of the Virgin mourning the dead Christ.

PISCINA. Roman tank; a basin for an officiating priest to wash his hands before Mass.

PLAQUETTE. Small metal tablet with relief decoration.

POLYPTYCH. Painting or tablet in more than three sections.

PORTA DEL MORTO. In certain old mansions of Umbria and Tuscany, a narrow raised doorway, said to be for the passage of biers of the dead, but more probably for use in troubled times when the main gate would be barred.

PREDELLA. Small painting attached below a large altarpiece.

PRESEPIO. Literally, crib or manger. A group of statuary of which the central subject is the Infant Jesus in the manger.

PUTTO. (pl. *putti*). Figure of a child sculpted or painted, usually nude.

RHYTON. Drinking-horn usually ending in an animal's head.

SCACCIATO. Term used to describe the effect obtained in sculpture from the delicate use of the sculpting tool, describing a fine line rather than depth.

SCHOLA CANTORUM. Enclosure for the choristers in the nave of an early Christian church, adjoining the sanctuary.

SINOPIA. Large drawing on a wall made in preparation for painting a mural. It was done on the rough coat of plaster, and retraced in a red earth pigment called *sinopia* (because it originated from Sinope, a town on the Black Sea).

SITULA. Water-bucket.

STAMNOS. Big-bellied vase with two small handles at the sides, closed by a lid.

STELE. Upright stone bearing a monumental inscription.

STEREOBATE. Basement of a temple or other building.

STYLOBATE. Basement of a columned temple or other building.

TELAMONES, see *Atlantes*.

TESSERA. A small cube of marble, glass, etc., used in mosaic work.

TONDO. Round painting or bas-relief.

TRANSENNA. Open grille or screen, usually of marble, in early Christian church.

TRIPTYCH. Painting or tablet in three sections.

VILLA. Country house with its garden.

The terms QUATTROCENTO, CINQUECENTO (abbreviated in Italy '400, '500), etc., refer not to the 14C and 15C, but to the 'fourteen-hundreds' and 'fifteen-hundreds', i.e. the 15C and 16C, etc.

PRACTICAL INFORMATION

I APPROACHES TO NORTHERN ITALY

Throughout the year direct air services operate between London and Milan, Turin, Genoa, Venice, and Pisa (the nearest international airport to Florence). There are four scheduled flights a day to Rimini in summer, as well as numerous charter flights. Principal Italian towns and tourist resorts are linked with London by direct rail routes from Calais, Ostend, Dunkirk, and Boulogne. Car-sleeper trains run from Calais, Brussels, and Paris to Milan. The easiest approaches by road are the motorways through the Mont Blanc or St Bernard tunnels, or over the Brenner Pass. Scheduled to open shortly is the tunnel under Mont Cenis which will afford a faster approach to Piedmont. Steamer services operate all year from Southampton to Genoa.

Travel Agents. General information may be obtained from the Italian State Tourist Office, 201 Regent St., W.1., who issue free an invaluable *Traveller's Handbook* (revised c. every year). Travel Agents (most of whom belong to the Association of British Travel Agents) sell travel tickets and book accommodation, and also organize inclusive tours and charter trips to Italy. These include: *C.I.T.,* 10 Charles II St., S.W.1. (agents for the Italian State Railways), *Thomas Cook & Son,* 45 Berkeley St., W.1, and other branches, *American Express,* 9 Suffolk Place, S.W.1., etc.

Air Services between London and Italy are maintained by British Airways (Dorland House, Lower Regent St., S.W.1), Alitalia (251 Regent St., W.1.), and British Caledonian. Considerable reductions (c. 50%) can be obtained (in 1977) by booking one month in advance. All services have a reduced monthly excursion fare, and night flights are operated between Milan and London in summer at advantageous prices. Passengers between the age of 12 and 21 are entitled to a 25% discount, as well as students (up to the age of 26). The cost of transport between airports and town air terminals varies with the distance and must be paid in local currency.

Railway Services. The three most direct routes from Calais viâ Paris are: Marseille—Ventimiglia—Sanremo—Genoa (c. 22 hrs); Modane—Turin (c. 16 hrs); Lausanne—Domodossola—Milan (c. 16 hrs). All these services have sleeping cars (1st class: single or double compartment; 2nd class: 3-berth compartments) and couchettes (seats converted into couches at night: 1st class: four; 2nd class: six). Return fares for the journey from London are usually double the single fare. Information on the Italian State Railways from C.I.T., London.

Motoring. British drivers taking their own cars by any of the multitudinous routes across France, Belgium, Luxembourg, Switzerland, Germany, and Austria need only the vehicle registration book, a valid national driving licence (accompanied by a translation, issued free by the R.A.C., A.A., and E.N.I.T. offices), and an International Insurance Certificate (the 'Green Card'). A nationality plate (e.g. GB) must be affixed to the rear of the vehicle so as to be illuminated by the tail lamps. Motorists who are not owners of the vehicle must possess the owner's permit for its use abroad.

The continental rule of the road is to drive on the right and overtake on the left. The provisions of the respective highway codes in the countries of transit, though similar, have important variations, especially with regard to priority, speed limits, and pedestrian crossings. Membership of the *Automobile Association* (Fanum House, Leicester Square, London W.C.2), or the *Royal Automobile Club* (83 Pall Mall, London S.W.1) or the *Royal Scottish Automobile Club* entitles motorists to many of the facilities of affiliated societies on the Continent and may save trouble and anxiety. The U.K. motoring organizations are represented at most of the sea and airports, both at home and on the Continent, to assist their members with customs formalities.

Car Ferries are operated by British and French Railways from Dover to Calais, Boulogne, and Dunkirk and from Newhaven to Dieppe; also by Townsend Thorensen Ferries from Dover to Calais; by British Rail and Zeeland Steamship Co. from Harwich to Hook of Holland; by Belgian State Marine from Harwich to Ostend and from both Dover and Folkstone to Ostend. A hovercraft service operates from Ramsgate to Calais, and from Dover to Boulogne and Calais. In London full particulars are available from the A.A., R.A.C., or British Rail, all at the *Continental Car Ferry Centre,* 52 Grosvenor Gardens, S.W.1, and at Liverpool Street.

A **Car Sleeper Express** operates in summer from Boulogne and Paris to Milan.

Air Ferries for cars are run from Southend, Lydd, or Coventry to Calais, Le Touquet, Ostend, Rotterdam, etc.

Passports or Visitors Cards are necessary for all British travellers entering Italy and must bear the photograph of the holder. American travellers must carry passports. British passports valid for ten years are issued at the Passport Office, Clive House, Petty France, London S.W.1, or may be obtained for an additional fee through any tourist agent. No visa is required for British or American travellers to Italy.

Currency Regulations. The allowance permitted by the British Government for pleasure travel outside the sterling area per yearly period (beginning on 1 Nov) varies from time to time. In 1977 it is £500 for each person, all of which may be held in foreign notes. There are also frequent variations on the amount of sterling notes which may be taken out of Britain, and of Italian lire notes which may be taken in or out of Italy. Since there are normally strict limitations, the latest regulations should be checked before departure. At present, only 100,000 in lire notes can be taken in or out of Italy, and £100 in sterling notes can be taken in or out of Great Britain.

Money. The monetary unit is the Italian lira (plural: lire). The current exchange value is approximately 1500 lire to the £ sterling (870 lire to the U.S. dollar). There are coins of 5, 10, 20, 50, and 100 lire, and notes of

500, 1000, 2000, 5000, 10,000, 20,000, 50,000, and 100,000 lire. For some years there has been a shortage of small change in Italy, and 'mini-cheques' (for 50, 100, 150, and 200 lire) have been issued by the banks. These are now accepted in most places as valid currency.

Customs Regulations. The following articles are admitted without formality (beyond an oral declaration) for personal use (but may not be disposed of in Italy): camping equipment, fishing tackle, two cameras with 10 films each, one ciné camera with 10 films, one canoe or similar boat, sport equipment (skis, rackets, etc.), one portable typewriter, one gramophone with a 'reasonable' number of records, one tape-recorder with a 'reasonable' number of tapes, one portable radio set and one portable television set (subject to a licence fee to be paid at the Customs), one pram, one musical instrument, binoculars, one bicycle, sporting guns and 200 cartridges (a shooting permit is required and must be obtained beforehand from Italian Consulates). Other items essential for the owner's profession or trade. The duty-free allowance for U.K. residents going to or returning from Italy varies from time to time; information is obtainable from travel agents or at airports. Items bought in Italy, up to a maximum total value of 1 million lire, can be exported free of duty, but special permits are necessary (and the payment of a tax) for the exportation of antiques and modern art objects.

Police Registration. Police Registration is required within three days of entering Italy. For travellers staying at a hotel the management will attend to the formality. The permit lasts three months, but can be extended on application.

II HOTELS AND RESTAURANTS

Hotels and Pensions. Hotels in Italy are classified into five categories: De Luxe, First, Second, Third, and Fourth. Pensions are classified into three categories, First, Second, and Third. In country districts there will occasionally be found the modest *Locanda,* or inn graded below the fourth class. De Luxe hotels compare favourably with their counterparts in other countries, with private baths to all rooms; first-class hotels usually live up to their name, with baths in most rooms. In some localities the second-class hotels deserve upgrading; in others they may disappoint. The difference between third- and fourth-class hotels is mainly of size and number of public rooms, and either class may give first-rate accommodation and service. Pensions in most towns are usually clean and are to be recommended to visitors staying more than a few days in one place. However, those that provide board are entitled to impose half-pension terms.

In this Guide hotels have not been indicated in the text since it can now be taken for granted that almost every small centre in the country will be provided with adequate accommodation. Hotels and pensions of every class will be found in the larger towns. The Italian State Tourist Office publishes an annual Official List of all Italian hotels and pensions (*Annuario Alberghi*) which can be consulted at travel agents or E.N.I.T.

In Italy, each Provincial Tourist Board (*Ente Provinciale Turismo*) issues a free list of hotels giving category, price, and facilities, and local tourist offices help travellers to find accommodation on the spot, and they run booking offices at the main railway stations (i.e. Milan, Venice, and Florence). More detailed information about hotels and restaurants can be found in the guides to Italy published by Michelin (Hotel and Restaurant 'Red Guide', revised annually), the Touring Club Italiano ('Alberghi e ristoranti d'Italia', 'Nuova Guida Rapida', in Italian only), and others.

Charges vary according to class, season, services available, and locality. Every hotel or pension has its fixed charges agreed with the Provincial Tourist Board. In all hotels the service charges are included in the rates. V.A.T. is added in all hotels at a rate of 9% (14% in De Luxe hotels). However, the total charge is exhibited on the back of the door of the hotel room. The average prices in 1977 were as follows:

Hotel	Single Room	With Bath	Double Room	With Bath
De Luxe	12,000-18,000	21,000-42,000	22,500-30,000	37,000-60,000
1	9,000-13,500	13,500-24,000	15,000-25,500	21,000-33,000
2 or **P1**	7,500-12,000	10,500-18,000	12,000-18,000	13,500-22,500
3 or **P2**	6,000- 9,000	7,500-12,000	9,000-13,500	10,500-16,500
4 or **P3**	4,500- 6,000	6,000- 9,000	6,000- 9,000	9,000-13,500

ALBERGHI DIURNI ('day hotels'), in the larger towns, are establishments provided with bathrooms, hairdressers, cleaning services, rest and reading rooms and other amenities, but no sleeping accommodation. They are usually situated in or near the main railway station, open from 6 a.m. to midnight.

Youth Hostels. The Italian Youth Hostels Association (Associazione Italiana Alberghi per la Gioventù, Via Guidobaldo del Monte 24, Rome) has over fifty hostels situated all over the country. These can be used by Y.H.A. members, and the cost for simple accommodation is 1350 lire per night (in 1977). Details from the Youth Hostels Association, 29 John Adam Street, London W.C.2, and E.N.I.T.

Students' Hostels exist in many Italian towns and are available not only to students taking courses, but also to students visiting the country for holiday purposes. Application should be made to 'Casa dello Studente' in Bologna, Ferrara, Florence, Genoa, Milan, Modena, Parma, Pavia, Perugia, Pisa, Siena, and Urbino; and Casa Fusinato, Via Marzolo, Padua; Foresteria dell'Istituto di Ca' Foscari, Venice. The average cost is from 1500-2500 lire a night and meals taken at the University Canteens are from 1500-2500 lire. The 'Guide for Foreign Students' giving detailed information on students' hostels, students' facilities, etc., can be obtained from the Italian Ministry of Education, Viale Trastevere, Rome (500 lire).

Camping is very popular in Italy. The Local Tourist Bureau of the nearest town will give information and particulars of the most suitable sites. There are over 1200 official camping sites in Italy, and the usual charge (in 1977) is 1000 lire per person (500 lire for car). Full details of the sites are published by the Touring Club Italiano in 'Campeggi in Italia' (from C.I.T.). A list and location map can be obtained free from the Federazione Italiana del Campeggio at their headquarters, Casella Postale 649, Florence.

Restaurants. Italian food is usually good and inexpensive. The least pretentious restaurant often provides the best value. Prices on the menu do not include a cover charge (*coperto,* shown separately on the menu) which is added to the bill,. The service charge is now almost always automatically added at the end of the bill. Tipping is therefore not strictly necessary, but a few hundred lire are appreciated. The menu displayed outside the restaurant indicates the kind of charges the customer should expect. However, many simpler establishments do not offer a menu, and here, although the choice is usually limited, the standard of cuisine is often very high. The price for a meal (in 1977) per person, in a luxury restaurant can be from 8000-10,000 lire, in an average restaurant from 4000-7000 lire, and in a trattoria from 3000-5000. Lunch is normally around 1 o'clock, and is the main meal of the day, while dinner is around 8 or 9 o'clock.

Pizzas (a popular and cheap food throughout Italy) and other snacks are served in a *Pizzeria, Rosticceria* and *Tavola Calda.* A *Vinaio* often sells wine by the glass and simple food for very reasonable prices. Bars (which are open from early morning to late at night) serve numerous varieties of excellent refreshments which are usually taken standing up. The customer generally pays the cashier first, and presents a receipt to the barman in order to get served. It has become customary to leave a small tip of 50 lire for the barman. If the customer sits at a table he must not pay first as he will be given waiter service and the charge will be considerably higher. Black coffee (*caffè* or *espresso*) can be ordered diluted (*alto* or *lungo*), with a liquor (*corretto*), or with hot milk (*cappuccino*). In summer, many customers take cold coffee (*caffè freddo*), or cold coffee and milk (*caffè-latte freddo*).

Food and Wine. Characteristic dishes of the Italian cuisine, to be found all over the country, are included in the MENU given below. Many of the best dishes are regional specialities; these are given in a separate section at the end.

Antipasti, Hors d'oeuvre

Prosciutto crudo o cotto, Ham, raw or cooked
Prosciutto e melone, Ham (raw) and melon
Salame, Salami
Salame con funghi e carciofini sott'olio, Salami with mushrooms and artichokes in oil
Salsicce, Dry sausage
Tonno, Tunny fish
Fagioli e cipolle, Beans with onions
Carciofi o finocchio in pinzimonio, Raw artichokes or fennel with a dressing
Antipasto misto, Mixed cold hors d'oeuvre
Antipasto di mare, Seafood hors d'oeuvre

Minestre e Pasta, Soups and pasta

Minestre, zuppa, Thick soup
Brodo, Clear soup
Minestrone alla toscana, Tuscan vegetable soup
Spaghetti al sugo or *al ragu,* Spaghetti with a meat sauce
Spaghetti al pomodoro, Spaghetti with a tomato sauce
Tagliatelle, flat spaghetti-like pasta, almost always made with egg
Lasagne, Layers of pasta with meat filling and cheese and tomato sauce
Cannelloni, Rolled pasta 'pancakes' with meat filling and cheese and tomato sauce

Ravioli, Filled with spinach and ricotta cheese
Tortellini, Small coils of pasta, filled with a rich stuffing served either in broth or with a sauce
Agnolotti, Ravioli filled with meat
Fettuccine, Ribbon noodles
Spaghetti alla carbonara, Spaghetti with bacon, beaten egg, and black pepper sauce
Spaghetti alle vongole, Spaghetti with clams
Pappardelle alla lepre, Pasta with hare sauce
Gnocchi, A heavy pasta, made from potato, flour, and eggs
Risotto, Rice dish
Fagioli all'uccelletto, White beans in tomato sauce

Pesce, Fish

Zuppa di pesce, Mixed fish usually in a sauce (or soup)
Fritto misto di mare, Mixed fried fish
Fritto di pesce, Fried fish
Pesce arrosto, Pesce alla griglia, Roast, grilled fish
Pescespada, Sword-fish
Aragosta, Lobster (an expensive delicacy)
Calamari, Squid
Sarde, Sardines
Coda di Rospo, Angler fish
Dentice, Dentex
Orata, Bream
Triglie, Red mullet
Sgombro, Mackerel
Baccalà, Salt cod
Anguilla, Eel
Sogliola, Sole
Tonno, Tunny fish
Trota, Trout
Cozze, Mussels
Gamberi, Prawns

Pietanze, Entrées

Bisteccha alla fiorentina, Beef rib steak (grilled over charcoal)
Vitello, Veal
Manzo, Beef
Agnello, Lamb
Maiale (arrosto), Pork (roast)
Pollo (bollito), Chicken (boiled)
Costolette Milanese, Veal cutlets, fried in breadcrumbs
Costoletta alla Bolognese, Veal cutlet with ham, covered with melted cheese
Saltimbocca, Rolled veal with ham
Bocconcini, As above, with cheese
Ossobuco, Stewed shin of veal
Spezzatino, Veal stew, usually with pimento, tomatoes, onions, peas, and wine
Petto di pollo, Chicken breasts
Pollo alla cacciatore, Chicken with herbs and (usually) tomato and pimento sauce
Cotechino e Zampone, Pig's trotter stuffed with pork and sausages
Stracotto, Beef cooked in a sauce, or in red wine
Trippa, Tripe
Fegato, Liver
Tacchino arrosto, Roast turkey
Cervelli, Brains
Bollito, Stew of various boiled meats
Fagiano, Pheasant
Coniglio, Rabbit
Lepre, Hare
Cinghiale, Wild boar

Contorni, Vegetables

Insalata verde, Green salad
Insalata mista, Mixed salad
Pomodori ripieni, Stuffed tomatoes
Funghi, Mushrooms
Asparagi, Asparagus
Zucchine, Courgettes
Melanzane alla parmigiana, Aubergines in a cheese sauce

Spinaci, Spinach
Broccoletti, Tender broccoli
Piselli, Peas
Fagiolini, French beans

Carciofi, Artichokes
Peperoni, Pimentoes
Finocchi, Fennel
Patatine fritte, Fried potatoes

Dolci, Sweets

Torta, Tart
Monte Bianco, Chestnut flavoured
    pudding

Zuppa inglese, Trifle
Panettone, Milanese sweet cake
Gelato, Ice cream

Frutta, Fruit

Fragole con panna, Strawberries
    and cream
Mele, Apples
Pere, Pears
Arance, Oranges
Ciliegie, Cherries

Pesche, Peaches
Albicocche, Apricots
Uva, Grapes
Macedonia di frutta, Fruit salad
Fichi, Figs

Regional Dishes include:

Piedmont —	*Fonduta,* a hot dip with fontina cheese, milk, and egg yolks sprinkled with truffles and white pepper
	Bagna Cauda, a spicy sauce with garlic and anchovies used as a dip for raw vegetables
	Bolliti misti (con salsa verde), various boiled meats stewed together (with a green sauce made with herbs)
Lombardy —	*Risotto alla Milanese,* Rice in chicken broth (or white wine) with saffron
	Zuppa Pavese, Clear soup with poached eggs
Veneto —	*Fegato alla Veneziana,* Calf's liver thinly sliced fried with onions
	Baccalà alla vicentina, Salt cod simmered in milk
	Polenta, a maize flour cake served with a sauce as a pasta dish, or with sausages, game, fish etc.
Liguria —	*Pesto,* a sauce made of fresh basil, garlic, pine nuts, and cheese and served with pasta
Tuscany —	*Cacciucco alla livornese,* a stew of fish in a hot sauce
	Tortino di carciofi, Baked artichoke pie
	Baccalà alla livornese, Salt cod cooked in tomatoes, black olives and black pepper (an acquired taste)
	Castagnaccio, Chestnut cake with pine nuts and sultanas
Umbria —	*Porchetta,* Roast suckling pig with herbs, fennel, etc.

The wines are very regional, and though the best known (such as *Chianti, Orvieto, Valpolicella,* etc.) are available nationally, travellers will often find the local wine the best value for money. In Lombardy and Piedmont, the rather heavy red wines include *Barolo* and *Barbera.* Verona is the centre of the wines of the Veneto, somewhat lighter and more delicate in flavour, among the best of which are *Soave, Bardolino, Valpolicella, Pinot, Merlot,* and *Cabernet.* In Emilia, the sparkling red *Lambrusco* and *Sangiovese* are to be recommended and the white *Albana,* as well as the unusual *Fontanina* and *Malvasia di Maiatico.*

The most famous wine of central Italy is *Chianti* (the name is protected by law, and only those wines from a relatively small district which lies between Florence and Siena are entitled to the name 'Chianti Classico'). *Chianti Classico 'Gallo Nero'* (distinguished by a black cock on the bottle) is usually considered the best, but *Chianti 'Putto'* and *Chianti 'Grappolo'* are also very good. Other wines in Tuscany (where the red table wine is usually of better quality than the white) such as *Vino nobile di Montepulciano, Vernaccia* (white, from San Gimignano) *Aleatico* (a dessert wine from Elba), and *Brunello* (not cheap) are particularly good. In Umbria the white *Orvieto* is very popular. The Marches produce the dry, white *Verdicchio* in its distinctive bottle (excellent with fish).

III   TRANSPORT

Railways. The Italian State Railways (F.S.—Ferrovie dello Stato) run five main categories of trains. (1) *T.E.E.*, luxury first-class express trains running between the main Italian (and European) cities. A special supplement is charged and seat reservation is obligatory. (2) *Rápidi*, fast trains running between main towns. A special supplement is charged (approx. 30% of the normal single fare). Some *rápido* trains carry only first class and seats must be booked in advance. (3) *Espressi*, long-distance express trains (often international). They stop only at main stations and carry both classes. (4) *Diretti*, although not stopping at every station, are usually a good deal slower than the *Espressi*. (5) *Locali*, local trains stopping at all stations.

There are limitations on travelling short distances on the first-class express trains. Trains in Italy are usually crowded, especially in summer; seats can be booked from the main cities at the station booking office. Fares are still much lower than in England. A 'Biglietto Turistico di libera circolazione', obtainable only outside Italy, gives freedom of the Italian railways for 8, 15, 21 or 30 days. A 'Chilometrico' ticket is valid for 3000 kilometres (and can be used by up to five people at the same time).

RESTAURANT CARS are attached to most international and internal long-distance trains (lunch or dinner from 5000 lire). A lunch tray brought to the compartment (including three courses and wine, and costing 3000-4000 lire) is a convenient way of having a meal while travelling. Some trains now also have self-service restaurants. Also, snacks, hot coffee and drinks are sold throughout the journey from a trolley wheeled down the train. At every large station snacks are on sale from trolleys on the platform, and can be bought from the train window. Carrier-bags with sandwiches, drink, and fruit (*cestini da viaggio*), or individual sandwiches (*panini*) are available.

Tickets must be bought at the station before the journey, otherwise a fairly large supplement has to be paid to the ticket-collector on the train. Porters are entitled to a fixed amount for each piece of baggage; at present (1977) the tariff is 300 lire.

Coaches. Local buses abound between the main towns. The principal Italian coach companies which operate regular long-distance coach services include: *S.I.T.A.*, 30 Via Orti Oricellari, Florence; *Lazzi*, 47r Piazza Stazione, Florence; *Sadem*, Piazza Carlo Felice, Turin; and *Autostradale*, Piazza Castello, Milan. All details can be obtained from C.I.T., London, or at their local offices in Italy.

Air Services. Frequent internal flights are operated between most main towns. Reductions are granted for families and night travel.

Taxis. Before engaging a taxi it is advisable to make sure it has a meter in working order. Fares vary from city to city but are generally cheaper than London taxis. No tip is expected, but 100 lire or so can be given. A supplement for night service is charged.

IV MOTORING

Motorists intending to visit Italy will save much trouble by joining the *Automobile Association,* the *Royal Automobile Club,* the *American Automobile Association,* the *American Automobile Touring Alliance,* or other club accredited by the Automobile Club d'Italia (A.C.I.) or the Touring Club Italiano. Temporary membership of the A.C.I. can be taken out on the frontier or in Italy. The headquarters of the A.C.I. is at 8 Via Marsala, Rome. Concessions gained from membership include parking facilities, legal assistance, and discounts on tolls and car hire. Also, a free breakdown service is provided for foreign motorists by the *Soccorso A.C.I.*

It is obligatory to carry a red triangle in the car in case of accident or breakdown. This serves as a warning to other traffic when placed on the road at a distance of 50 metres from the stationary car. It can be hired from the A.C.I. for a minimal charge, and returned at the frontier. In case of breakdown, the nearest A.C.I. office can be contacted by telephone number 116. On the Autostrada del Sole (Milan-Rome), there is an emergency press button box on the right of the road every two kilometres.

Petrol Coupons. Foreign motorists in Italy with a vehicle registered outside the country are entitled to purchase a certain number of petrol coupons for c. 47% of the market price of petrol in Italy. The normal cost of petrol in 1977 is 500 lire per litre. Petrol coupons can be purchased only outside Italy or at the frontier and cannot be paid for in Italian currency. In Britain they are available from the A.A., C.I.T., R.A.C., and Barclays Bank. A maximum allowance of 400 litres is allowed for up to two visits to Italy a year. Unused petrol coupons can be refunded at the frontier or by the issuing office.

Car Hire. Self-drive is available in most Italian cities and the cost varies from about 7000 lire a day plus c.100 lire per km. upwards according to the size of the vehicle. Arrangements for the hire of cars in Italy can be made in this country through Alitalia or British Airways (in conjunction with their flights) or through any of the principal car-hire firms. It should be noted that travellers hiring cars in Italy are not entitled to petrol coupons.

Italian Motorways (Autostrade). Italy has the finest motorways in Europe. There are about 5500 kilometres of them and more are under construction. Tolls are charged according to the rating of the vehicle and the distance covered. Service areas are found on all autostrade, and there are speed limits on mountain sections, etc. On some motorways (including the Autostrada del Sole) cars with foreign number plates qualify for reduced tolls which correspond to the lowest tariff (applicable to motorcycles).

The Autostrada del Sole (Milan-Rome) continues to the S. The E. coast of Italy from Trieste to Bari is now served by autostrade. In the north, autostrade connect Milan, Turin, Modena, Padua, Verona, Venice, Bologna, and the other main cities, and the autostrada along the coast from Ventimiglia to Livorno has been completed.

Maps. The Italian Touring Club publishes several sets of maps including the *Carta Automobilistica d'Italia,* on a scale of 1:200,000. This is divided into 30 plates printed on 28 sheets, of which sheets 1-16 refer to the area dealt with in this guide. The sheets are on sale at all Italian Touring Club Offices and at many booksellers; in England they are obtainable at the R.A.C., the Map House, 54 Beauchamp Place, London S.W.3, and Stanford's, 12-14 Long Acre. A new series of larger maps on the same scale covers a number of tourist areas in the north, notably the Dolomites; Milan and environs; Turin, Milan, and the Ligurian coast; and the Paduan plain from Milan to the Adriatic. Less bulky is their *Carta Generale d'Italia,* on a scale of 1:500,000, covering the whole of Italy in four sheets. Special maps at 1:50,000 are also available for certain popular Alpine areas.

The *Istituto Geografico Militare* of Florence (14 Viale Strozzi) publishes a map of Italy on a scale of 1:100,000 in 272 sheets, and a field survey (levate di campagna) partly 1:50,000, partly 1:25,000, which are invaluable for the detailed exploration of the country, especially its more mountainous regions; the coverage is, however, still far from complete at the larger scales.

V   GENERAL HINTS

Season. The best season for a visit to the greater part of northern Italy is May and June, although there is always a risk of rain. The earlier spring months, though often dry and sunny, are sometimes unexpectedly chilly, with strong northerly winds. In Umbria and Tuscany, however, the green countryside is very beautiful in early spring before the main tourist season. The height of the summer is unpleasantly hot, especially in the Po valley and the larger towns, and in the low basin of Florence which is enclosed by hills. Winter days in Milan or Venice are sometimes as cold and wet as an English winter. Late September and October can be delightful, but are often marred by heavy rain. The Tuscan autumn is particularly lovely. A refuge from the summer heat can be found in the upper Alpine valleys of Piedmont, Lombardy, and in the Dolomites, while the winter sports season in the high Alpine resorts is becoming more popular every year and is extended even to midsummer in the high Alps. Seaside resorts are frequented from mid-June to mid-September; before and after this season many hotels are closed and the bathing-beaches are practically deserted.

Language. Familiarity with the Italian language will add greatly to the traveller's profit and enjoyment, but those who know no language but English and a little French or German can get along quite comfortably in the main tourist resorts. Even a few words of Italian, however, are a great advantage, and the attempt in itself will enlist the native courtesy of the Italian race to the assistance of the visitor in difficulties. German in readily spoken in most of the districts formerly occupied by Austria. Some hints for pronunciation follow.

Words should be pronounced well forward in the mouth, and no nasal intonation exists in Italian. Double consonants call for special care as each must be sounded.

Consonants are pronounced roughly as in English with the following exceptions: c and cc before e and i have the sound of ch in chess; sc before e and i is pronounced like sh in ship; ch before e and i has the sound of k; g and gg before e and i are always soft, like j in jelly; gh is always hard, like g in get; gl is nearly always like lli in million (there are a few exceptions, e.g. negligere, where it is pronounced as in English); gn is like ny in lanyard; gu and qu are always like gw and kw. S is hard like s in six except when it occurs between two vowels, when it is soft, like the English z or the s in rose; ss is always hard. Z and zz are usually pronounced like ts, but occasionally have the sound of dz before a long vowel.

VOWELS are pronounced much more openly than in Southern English and are given their full value. There are no true diphthongs in Italian, and every vowel should be articulated separately.

THE STRESS normally falls on the last syllable but one; in modern practice an accent-sign is written regularly only when the stress is on the last syllable, e.g. *città*, or to differentiate between two words similarly spelt but with different meaning: *e.g. e*—and; *è*—is. In this volume, to assist the traveller, a stress-accent has been placed on unfamiliar place-names where the foreigner might otherwise be misled; while in the index every place-name with a strictly irregular stress is given an accent.

Manners and Customs. Attention should be paid by the traveller to the more formal manners of Italians. It is customary to open conversation in shops, etc., with the courtesy of *buon giorno* (good day) or *buona sera* (good evening). The deprecatory expression *prego* (don't mention it) is everywhere the obligatory and automatic response to *grazie* (thank you). The phrases *per piacere* or *per favore* (please), *permesso* (excuse me), used when pushing past someone (essential on public vehicles), *scusi* (sorry; also, I beg your pardon, when something is not heard), should not be forgotten. A visitor will be wished *Buon appetito!* before beginning a meal, to which he should reply *Grazie, altrettanto.* This pleasant custom may be extended to fellow passengers taking a picnic meal on a train. Shaking hands is an essential part of greeting and leave-taking. In shops and offices a certain amount of self-assertion is taken for granted, since queues are not the general rule and it is incumbent on the inquirer or customer to get himself a hearing.

Photography. There are few restrictions on photography in Italy, but permission is necessary to photograph the interiors of churches and museums and may sometimes be withheld. Care should also be taken before photographing individuals, notably members of the armed forces and the police. Photography is forbidden on railway stations and civil airfields as well as in frontier zones and near military installations.

Churches are normally closed for a considerable period during the middle of the day (12 to 15, 16, or 17), although cathedrals and some of the large churches may be open without a break during daylight hours. Smaller churches and oratories are often open only in the early morning, but the sacristan may usually be found by inquiring locally. The sacristan will also show closed chapels, crypts, etc., and a small tip should be given. Some churches now ask that sightseers do not enter during a service, but normally visitors may do so, provided they are silent and do not approach the altar(s) in use. At all times they are expected to cover their legs and arms, and generally dress with decorum. An entrance fee is becoming customary for admission to treasuries, bell-towers, etc. Lights (operated by 100 l.coins) have now been installed in many churches to illuminate frescoes and altarpieces. In Holy Week most of the pictures are covered and are on no account shown.

Museums are usually open six days a week, the commonest closing day being Monday. Many museums are open from 9.30-16 on weekdays and 9.30-13 on Sundays and holidays. Most of the State museums have recently adopted standard opening hours for the summer and winter, namely 9-14 on weekdays, and 9-13 on Sundays and holidays. However, hours of admission are constantly being altered and shortened, and great care should be taken to allow enough time for variations in the hours shown in the text when planning to visit a museum. On Sundays and holidays, most museums are open in the mornings only, either free or at half price. Entrance fees vary from 100 to 250 lire.

MUSEUM CARDS are available (valid one year) from the R.A.C., C.I.T., or Barclays Bank, which, for 40p, will allow the visitor free entrance to all the State-owned museums. Students holding the International Student Identity Card issued by the National Union of Students are also entitled to free entrance to all State-owned museums.

Public Holidays. The number of Italian National Holidays when offices, shops, and schools are closed have recently been reduced. They are now as follows: 1 Jan (New Year), Easter Monday, 25 April (Liberation Day), 1 May (Labour Day), 15 Aug (Assumption), 1 Nov (All Saints' Day), 8 Dec (Conception), Christmas Day and 26 Dec (St Stephen). Each town keeps its Patron Saint's day as a holiday, e.g. Venice (25 April, St Mark), Florence, Genoa, and Turin (24 June, St John the Baptist), Bologna (4 Oct, St Petronius), Milan (7 Dec, St Ambrose).

Entertainments. The Opera season in Italy usually begins in December and continues until April or May. The principal opera houses in northern Italy are La Scala in Milan, La Fenice in Venice, and the Teatro Comunale in Florence. During the summer operas are performed in the open air in the Arena of Verona.

Annual MUSIC AND DRAMA FESTIVALS take place in many towns; among the most famous international festivals are the Festival of the Two Worlds in Spoleto (June and July), the Maggio Musicale Fiorentino in Florence (May and June), and the Drama Festival in the Roman Theatre at Verona (June-Sept). Details of their programmes are widely published in advance (*The Times,* etc.). Traditional festivals are celebrated in most towns and villages in commemoration of a local historical or religous event, and are often very spectacular. Among the most famous are the Palio in Siena (2 July and 16 August), and the Football Match in medieval costume in Florence (24 and 28 June).

Cinemas abound in all towns, and it is usual to tip the usher who shows you to your seat in theatres and cinemas.

Telephones and Postal Information. Stamps are sold at tobacconists and Post Offices. Correspondence can be addressed c/o the Post Office by adding "Fermo Posta" to the name of the locality. There are numerous public telephones all over Italy in bars, restaurants, kiosks, etc. These are usually operated by metal discs known as 'gettone', rather than coins, which are bought (50 lire each) from tobacconists, bars, some newspaper stands, and Post Offices.

Newspapers. The most widely read Northern Italian newspapers are the *Corriere della Sera* of Milan, the *Stampa* of Turin, *La Nazione* of

Florence, and *Il Resto del Carlino* of Bologna. Foreign newspapers are readily obtainable at central street kiosks and railway stations.

Working Hours. Government and business offices usually work from 8 or 9-13 or 14 five days a week. In the industrial towns of the north, however, the working day tends to be longer, with a short lunch break. Shops generally open from 8.30 or 9-13 and 15.30 or 16-19.30 or 20, although in the larger towns in the north shops sometimes close earlier and the lunch break is shorter. Banks are open from 8.30 to 13 or 13.20 every day except Saturdays and Sundays. Travellers' cheques can be changed at most hotels (at a slightly lower rate of exchange), and foreign money can be changed at main railway stations and airports.

Weights and Measures. The French metric system of weights and measures (recently adopted in the U.K.) is used in Italy with the French terms substantially unaltered. The *metro* is the unit of length, the *grammo* of weight, the *ara* of land-measurement, the *litro* of capacity. Greek-derived prefixes (deca, etto, kilo, miria) are used with those names to express multiples; Latin prefixes (deci, centi, milli) to express factions (kilómetro-1000 metri, millimetro-1000th part of a metro). For approximate calculations the metro may be taken as 39 inches and the kilometro as 5/8 of a mile, the litro as 1¾ pint, the ettaro as 2½ acres, 14 grammi as ½ oz, an 'etto' as 3½ oz, and a 'kilo' as 2¼ lbs.

EXPLANATIONS

TYPE. The main routes are described in large type. Smaller type is used for branch-routes and excursions, for historical and preliminary paragraphs, and (generally speaking) for descriptions of greater detail or minor importance.

ASTERISKS indicate points of special interest or excellence.

DISTANCES are given cumulatively from the starting-point of the route or sub-route in kilometres. Mountain heights have been given in the text and on the atlas in metres.

MAIN ROADS are designated in the text by N (meaning 'number'), instead of the more familiar Italian form S.S. ('Strada Statale'), followed by their official number.

POPULATIONS (approximated to the nearest hundred) have been given from the latest official figures (estimates of 1975 based on the census of 1971). They refer to the size of the Commune or administrative area, which is often much larger than the central urban area.

PLANS. Double-page town plans are gridded with numbered squares referred to in the text thus: (Pl. 1-16). On the ground plans of museums figures or letters have been given to correspond with the descriptions which appear in the text.

ABBREVIATIONS. In addition to generally accepted and self-explanatory abbreviations, the following occur in the guide:

A.A.	Automobile Association
Abp.	archbishop
A.C.I.	Automobile Club Italiano
Adm.	admission
Bp.	bishop
C	century
c.	circa
C.A.I.	Club Alpino Italiano
C.I.T.	Compagnia Italiana Turismo
cons.	consecrated
E.N.I.T.	Ente Nazionale per le Industrie Turistiche
E.P.T.	Ente Provinciale per il Turismo
exc.	except
fest.	*festa,* or festival (i.e. holiday)
gr.	gramme
incl.	including
kg.	kilogramme
km.	kilometre (s)
l.	lira (pl. lire); left
m	metre (s)
m.	sea miles
min.	minutes
Pal.	Palazzo
Pl.	plan
Pta.	Porta
P.za	Piazza
r.	right
R.A.C.	Royal Automobile Club
Rif.	Rifugio (mountain hut)
Rte	Route
SS.	Santi or Saints
Stn.	Station
T.C.I.	Touring Club Italiano
V.	Via (street)

For abbreviations of Italian Christian names, see p. 623; for glossary of art terms, see p. 24.

I PIEDMONT AND LIGURIA

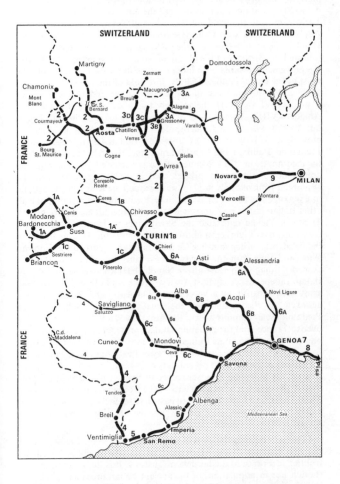

The ancient principality of **Piedmont**, the cradle of the Italian nation, with 4,541,000 inhabitants in an area of 25,399 sq. km., is divided into the modern provinces of Alessandria, Asti, Cuneo, Novara, Turin, and Vercelli, and the autonomous region of the Val d'Aosta. Physically the province occupies the upper basin of the Po, and, as its name implies, lies mainly 'at the foot of the mountains' which encircle it—the Pennine, Graian, Cottian, and Maritime Alps. The cultural relations of Piedmont

41

with France have always been very close, and the French language, used at the Court and Parliament of Turin down to the days of Cavour, still survives in the language of the people in many of the mountain glens.

Historically Piedmont combines the territories of the old marquessates of Ivrea and Monferrato and of the county of Turin; the name Piedmont does not occur until the 13C. In 1045 the territory of Turin came into the hands of the House of Savoy by the marriage of Adelaide of Susa with Otho (Oddone), son of Humbert the White-Handed, Count of Savoy, and the provincial history from then onwards followed the fortunes of the House of Savoy. These princes, faced with the movement towards civic independence in the 12-13C, did not, like most of the feudal families of Italy, lose hold of their lands, and in the 14C, under the guidance of the Green Count and the Red Count (Amadeus VI and VII), the princely house so gained in power that Amadeus VIII was made Duke of Savoy by the Emperor in 1391. Under him Vercelli was annexed, and the life of the province became orientated more towards Italy. In the 16C another period of activity began, under Emmanuel Philibert and Charles Emmanuel I, and Saluzzo was added to Piedmont. In 1714 Monferrato was included by treaty in the dominions of the Savoy princes, and in 1720 Victor Amadeus II, appointed King of Sicily in 1713, was awarded the Kingdom of Sardinia in exchange for the other island. The Piedmontese kingdom, like all other Italian states, was obliterated by the Napoleonic conquests, but the Treaty of Vienna reinstated the Savoy kings at Turin and gave them suzerainty over Liguria in addition. Victor Emmanuel II, who, thanks to the astuteness of his minister Cavour, had taken part in the Crimean War, and thus won the goodwill of France and England, found a powerful though expensive ally in Napoleon III when the second War of Italian Independence, against Austria, broke out in 1859. The Austrian army was crushed in a succession of defeats, and Lombardy was annexed to Piedmont after the final victory of Solferino. The Piedmontese dominions west of the Alps (Savoy and Nice) were handed over to France, and the remaining Italian provinces were added one by one to Victor Emmanuel's kingdom. In 1865 he transferred his capital from Turin to Florence, and the history of Piedmont became merged in the history of Italy. By the peace treaty of 1947 the districts of Tenda and Briga in the Maritime Alps were ceded to France, after a plebiscite; and this, with some minor adjustments of the frontier at the Montgenèvre, Mont Cenis, and Little St Bernard passes, reduced the provincial area by c. 140 sq. kilometres. At the same time the Val d'Aosta was granted a special measure of autonomy.

Liguria comprises the strip of land lying between the Mediterranean and the summits of the Maritime Alps and the Apennines from the frontier of France to the borders of Tuscany. It is the smallest in area, though not in population, of the ancient Italian provinces (1,867,000 inhab.; 5429 sq. km.) and is made up of the modern provinces of Genoa, Imperia, La Spezia, and Savona. It is fortunate in including two of the most favoured stretches of the Italian coastline—the Riviera di Ponente and the Riviera di Levante—respectively W. and E. of Genoa—where the mild winter climate encourages a luxuriant growth of vegetation, including palms, oranges, and lemons, and the cultivation of flowers in early spring is important.

The Ligurian people, occupying a territory that has always been easier of access by sea than by land, are noted seafarers, and they have thus been influenced by immigrations from overseas rather than by landward invasions. Traces of Punic and Greek relations are evident, superimposed on the rather primitive civilization of the native Ligurians (about whom little definite is known), and later Genoa became an important Roman seaport. Less exposed, on the whole, by its inaccessibility, to the incursions of the Gothic invaders of Italy, Liguria was all the more open to the attacks of the Saracenic corsairs of the later Middle Ages, and the medieval importance of Genoa sprang from the measures of organized defence taken against these pirates. The aristocratic republic of Genoa ruled the destinies of the whole seaboard from the 13C to the days of Napoleon, reaching its apogee as a colonizing power after the rival republic of Pisa had been crushed in 1290, but suffering a severe check at the hands of Venice in 1380. In the succeeding centuries Savona and the towns of the Western Riviera, jealous of Genoa, took advantage of the factious spirit of the times, and Liguria fell alternately into the power of Lombard, Piedmontese, and French overlords. The revival of local energy under Andrea Doria in the 16C was short-lived, and the 17-18C were a period of negligible activity. The Napoleonic campaigns of 1796 and 1799 resulted first in the creation of a 'Ligurian Republic' and then of the absorption of the province into the French Empire; but in 1815 Liguria was attached to the kingdom of Piedmont. Genoa played an important part in the history of the Risorgimento, and Ligurian vessels provided transport for Garibaldi's attack on Sicily in 1860. In the Second World War the coastal area, especially Genoa, suffered severely from air attack.

1   WESTERN PIEDMONT

A   Modane to Turin

ROAD, 113 km., crossing the Mont Cenis Pass.—22 km. *Lanslebourg.*—32 km. *Mont Cenis Pass.*—59 km. **Susa.**—99 km. *Rivoli.*—113 km. **Turin.**

From **Modane** village the N6 proceds viâ (22 km.) *Lanslebourg* (1399 m) to (32 km.) the Mont Cenis Pass or *Colle del Moncenisio* (2081 m). Overlooking the Lac du Mont-Cenis is (36 km.) the *Hospice du Mont-Cenis* (1925 m).

The Mont Cenis Pass is one of the historic passes over the Alps, crossed by Pepin the Short (755), Charlemagne (774), and Charles the Bald (877) and many other sovereigns with their armies. It is probable, however, that Hannibal crossed by the Col du Clapier (but see p. 77). The carriage road was constructed by Napoleon in 1803-13. The Italians attacked the pass in June 1940 but were unable to storm its defences. The hospice was founded by Louis the Debonair c. 815 at the instance of St Heldrad, abbot of Novalesa, and enlarged in 1811.

The former hotel at (39 km.) *Grand' Croix* is now the French frontier-post. The actual frontier, moved to this point from the pass itself in 1947, is c. 2 km. farther on, and the Italian frontier-post is at (50 km.) *Molaretto* (1139 m) below an abrupt zigzag.—59 km. Susa, see below.

RAILWAY, 106 km., viâ the Mont Cenis Tunnel, in 1½–2¼ hrs. Luggage and passports are checked at Modane or in the train. This route is followed by through trains from Paris to Rome.

Cars were first accepted for transit by train in 1935, and there is now a CAR-CARRIER SERVICE hourly in 20 min. No formalities other than normal customs inspection (at Modane); vehicles must be at Modane 30 min. before depature time, at Bardonecchia 15 min. before. The building of a road tunnel, parallel with the railway, has begun.—From Bardonecchia ROAD, 90 km., alongside the railway. N 335. 13 km. *Oulx.*—N 24. 36 km. **Susa.**—N 25. 76 km. *Rivoli.*—90 km. **Turin.**

The *Mont Cenis Tunnel* or *Tunnel du Fréjus*, which crosses the Franco-Italian frontier, begun in 1857 and finished in 1871 on the plans of the engineers Sommeiller, Grandis, and Grattoni, was the first great Transalpine tunnel and reaches a summit level of 1295 m. It had an immediate effect on world communications, speeding the transmission of mail from the East to northern Europe by several days, with Brindisi replacing Marseille as the transit port. Originally 12.2 km. long, the tunnel was realigned in 1881 and again after the Second World War and is now 12.8 km. long.

Bardonécchia (1311 m) is the first station in Italy. Here cars are off-loaded from the train. The old village (3200 inhab.), with good 15C stalls in its church, lies above the station in a wide basin at the junction of several valleys. Frequented for winter-sports by the Torinese it has a ski-school, numerous lifts, horse-drawn and motorized sledges, a skating rink, and an open-air swimming pool.

The most striking excursion is viâ (¾ hr. S.) *Mélezet* and (1¼ hr) *Pian del Colle* with its old frescoed chapel to (3 hrs) the *Vallée Etroite* in France, surrounded by fantastic broken peaks.—Other interesting little mountain churches are to be seen at *Millaures*, 3 km. E., and *Rochemolles*, 6½ km. N. A chair-lift ascends in two stages to 2026 m on *Monte Colomion* (2053 m; *View of the Pelvoux range).

Road and railway descend the picturesque glen of the Dora di Bardonécchia viâ (6 km.) *Beaulard* (1217 m) to 13 km. **Oulx** (1121 m), a scattered village and an important centre for mountain excursions. Here the road joins the N 24 coming down the Dora Riparia from the Montgenèvre pass and Cesana Torinese (11 km.; comp. Rte 1C).

Sauze d'Oulx (1510 m), or *Salice*, 5 km. S.E., with an old church, is a ski-ing resort, connected by cableway with Sportinia (2148 m) on a pleasant forest-clad plateau below Monte Triplex (2506 m).

Road and railway now follow the combined waters of the Dora down the Valle di Susa.—At (19 km.) *Salbertrand* the Waldensians defeated the French in 1689.—24 km. *Exilles*, with an old fort.—30 km. *Chiomonte* has two Romanesque churches, and an electric power-station on the river. The dolphin symbol which appears carved here and there recalls that this valley belonged to Dauphiny until transferred to Turin in 1713. It is frequented for winter sports (chairlifts).—On the following steep descent the road twice passes under the railway.

36 km. **Susa** (502 m), an interesting old town (7230 inhab.), stands at the junction of the main roads over the Montgenèvre and Mont Cenis passes on the Dora Riparia.

Susa, the Roman *Sergusio,* was the seat of the Gaulish chief Cottius who received the dignity of prefect from Augustus and gave his name to the surrounding *Cottian Alps* (Alpi Còzie). The town was burned in 1173 by Barbarossa in revenge for the repulse of an assault in 1168.

SAN GIUSTO, a cathedral since 1772, is a notable 11C church (W. front restored), with a fine massive tower. It has 13C stalls, and in the S. transept are an incomplete polyptych by *Macrino d'Alba* (with SS. Hugh of Lincoln and Hugh of Grenoble) and a wooden figure of a kneeling lady (16C). In the S.E. chapel is the *Triptych of

Rocciamelone, a Flemish brass of the early 14C (shown by a pupil of the adjoining Seminario), with the Madonna, SS. George and Joseph (?), and the donor.

The triptych was originally in a chapel on the summit of the *Rocciamelone* (3538 m; 8 hrs), which rises to the N.; it was carried there by Bonifacio Rotari, a Piedmontese nobleman, in fulfilment of a vow made in a Turkish prison in 1358. The mountain is now crowned by a bronze statue of the Virgin (1900) the goal of a pilgrimage on 4-5 August.

Passing under the 4C *Porta Savoia,* Via Archi ascends past the Parco d'Augusto to the **Arco d'Augusto,* an arch erected in 8 B.C. by Cottius in honour of Augustus, adorned with processional reliefs. Higher up is a double Roman arch, with remains of an aqueduct. Below a tower of the *Castle* of Countess Adelaide (11C; small museum) is Piazza della Torre, with the best of the medieval mansions of the town (13C). The tall Romanesque tower to the left is that of *Santa Maria Maggiore* (church destroyed), while S.W. of the town is the 13C church of *San Francesco,* with external wall-paintings.

Novalesa, a little over 8 km. N. of Susa, is at the end of the old Mont Cenis road, from where travellers used to cross the pass on mule-back. About 15 min. S.W. are the remains of the Benedictine abbey, founded in 726. The main church was rebuilt in 1712, but several Romanesque (11C) chapels survive, only one of them (St Eldrado), containing 13C frescoes, now serving as such.

The church of (4 km.) *Giaglione,* to the left of the Mont Cenis road, has remarkable external paintings of the 15C (Cardinal Virtues and Deadly Sins); and there are little mountain hotels at *Meana di Susa* (3 km. S.E.), with a station on the main railway, and at *Frais,* S. of Chiomonte (see above; cableway).

The road (alternative route on either bank of the Dora) descends the Valle di Susa, passing (44 km.) *Bussoleno,* with its 12C campanile, and the ruined castle of *San Giorio.*—The river is crossed at (52 km.) *Borgone.*—62 km. *Sant' Ambrogio di Torino.*—66 km. *Avigliana,* an ancient little town (4560 inhab.) with many fine old mansions of the 15C, is commanded by a ruined castle of the Counts of Savoy.

Here begins the ascent to the Sacra di San Michele, seen high up on the hill to the right, a favourite summer excursion from Turin. The road first ascends to (3½ km.) the isthmus between two small lakes, and then turns right for the ascent to (14 km.) the **Sacra di San Michele** (962 m), an abbey founded c. 1000 and suppressed in 1622. The buildings (open 9-12, 14-19), which stand on the end of the ridge of Monte Pirchiriano overlooking the valley from a height of 610 m (*View of the valley and the Alps), were enlarged in the 12C. The 154 rock-hewn steps of the *Scalone dei Morti* pass beneath the *Porta dello Zodiaco,* with Romanesque sculptures (1135) to reach the *Church,* a 12-13C building, with remains of older work and supported by massive substructures. The crypt contains tombs of the House of Savoy-Carignano.—The return may be made by mule-track direct to Sant'Ambrogio (1¼ hr; see above) or by a zigzag road S. over the *Colle Braida* (1007 m) to (11 km.) *Giaveno* (with skiing facilities), 31 km. W. of Turin viâ Orbassano (bus). For the road to *Viù,* see p. 57.

70 km. The **Abbey Church of *Sant'Antonio di Ranverso,* to the right of the road, is one of the most interesting buildings in Piedmont. Founded in 1188, it was extended in the 13-14C, while in the 15C the apse and the strange façade, with its sharply-gabled doorways and terra-cotta decorations, were added. The interior (open 10-12, 16-18 exc. Fri) has 15C frescoes and a polyptych of the Nativity by Def. Ferrari (1531) on the high altar. The tower and the little cloister are Romanesque.— 76 km. *Rivoli* once a favoured residence of the Counts of Savoy, is dominated by the unfinished *Castello* begun in 1712 on the site of an older castle destroyed in 1706. The Casa del Conte Verde (so called) is a

typical early 15C patrician house.—At 78 km. the road passes beneath the new ring road and continues into the centre of (90 km.) **Turin** as the Corso Francia.

B   Turin and Environs

TURIN, in Italian **Torino**, the chief town (1,200,000 inhab.) of Piedmont and the capital of the former kingdom of Sardinia, is one of the most important industrial centres of Italy, famous since 1899 as the site of the Fiat motor works. It stands on the Po at the confluence of the Dora Riparia in a plain at the foot of the Alps, whose summits are visible to the west, while to the east the foothills beyond the Po complete the panorama. The town itself is regularly built on a Roman plan consciously developed in the 17-18C. The centre of the city presents a remarkably homogeneous nineteenth century aspect, while trams still traverse the long straight streets, now closed to motor traffic. The city will be enhanced when the programme of cleaning the sombre façades has been completed. Although one of the least visited large towns in Italy, Turin also has notable artistic and archaeological collections.

Railway Stations. *Porta Nuova* (Pl. 9), the main station, for all services. *Porta Susa* (Pl. 1), a secondary station on the Milan, Domodóssola, and Aosta lines, at which all trains call; also for the line to Pont Canavese.—*Torino Céres* (Pl. 3), for Cirié, Lanzo, and Céres.

Airport, *Caselle,* 16 km. N., with services to Milan, Rome, London and Paris. Connecting bus terminates at Savet office, 10 Via P. Gobetti (Pl. 10).

Numerous **Hotels,** near the station, etc.

Post Office (Pl. 6), 10 Via Alfieri.

Information Office, *E.P.T.,* 222 Via Roma, and at Porta Nuova Station.

British Consulate, 1 Corso Vittorio Emanuele.—**United States Consulate,** 17 Via Alfieri.

Tramways. 5. *P.za Castello* to *Sassi* for the Superga cog-tramway. **6.** *Via Sacchi* (near Staz. Porta Nuova)—Via Venti Settembre—Via Garibaldi—P.za Statuto—*Corso Francia.*—**9.** *Via Sacchi*—Via Venti Settembre—Cathedral—*P.za della Repubblica.*—**Buses. 59.** *P.za Statuto*—Stazione Porta Susa—P.za Solferino—Stazione Porta Nuova—Corso Vitt. Emanuele—*Parco del Valentino* (Palazzo Torino Esposizioni).—**64.** *P.za Castello*—P.za San Carlo—*Staz. Porta Nuova.*—**67.** *P.za Arbarello*—P.za Solferino—Staz. Porta Nuova—*Cavoretto.*

Country Trolley-Bus. No. 6. *Corso Francia* to *Rivoli.*—**Country Buses** from various points to *Aosta;* to *Pinerolo, Sestriere,* and *Claviere;* to *Ivrea;* to *Milan;* to *Saluzzo* and *Cuneo;* and in season to mountain and Mediterranean resorts.

Amusements. THEATRES. *Regio,* P.za Castello, the opera-house; *Stabile di Torino,* 8 Via Rossini; *Carignano,* P.za Carignano; *Alfieri,* P.za Solferino; *Nuovo,* Palazzo Torino Esposizioni.—CONCERTS. *Auditorium della R.A.I.,* 15 Via Rossini; *Conservatoire Gius. Verdi,* 11 Via Mazzini.

GOLF COURSE at *Fiano,* 22 km. N.W.—SWIMMING. *Municipal Pool* (covered), 294 Corso Galileo Ferraris; open-air baths at *Lido di Torino,* 21 Via Villa Glori, on the right bank of the Po above Ponte Franco Balbis (beyond Pl. 13; bus 52 to P.za Zara), and many others.

History. The marriage of Countess Adelaide (d. 1090), heiress of a line of French counts of Savoy, to Oddone (Otho), son of Humbert 'the White-Handed', united the Cisalpine and Transalpine possessions of the House of Savoy, and Turin became their capital. After a period of semi-independence in the 12-13C, the city consistently followed the fortunes of the princely house of Savoy. In 1506-62 it was occupied by the French, but it was awarded to Duke Emmanuel Philibert 'the Iron-Headed' by the Treaty of Cateau-Cambrésis (1559). In 1639-40 and in 1706 it suffered sieges, being relieved on the latter occasion by the heroic exploit of Pietro Micca, a Piedmontese sapper, who exploded a mine and saved the beleaguered citadel at the cost of his life. From 1720 Turin was capital of the kingdom of Sardinia, and after the Napoleonic occupation (1798-1814) it became a centre of Italian nationalism, and the headquarters of Camillo Cavour (1810-61), a native of the town and the prime mover of Italian liberty. Silvio Pellico lived here from 1838 until his death in 1854. In 1861-65 it was the capital of Victor Emmanuel II (1820-78) as king of Italy. During the Second World War, Allied air raids caused heavy and scattered damage.—Besides Cavour and Victor Emmanuel II (as well as many other distinguished princes of the House of Savoy), Turin claims among its famous natives the mathematician Joseph Lagrange (1736-1813), the physicist Amedeo Avogadro (1776-1856), the politician, author, and painter Massimo d'Azeglio (1798-1866), and the sculptor Carlo Marochetti (1805-68). The ill-fated Princesse de Lamballe (1749-92), friend of Marie Antoinette, was also born at Turin. The artists known as the "Gruppo dei Sei" were influential in Turin from about 1928 until 1935; one of the them was Carlo Leví, born here in 1902 (d. 1975).

The centre of the civic life of Turin is included in the area lying between Corso Vittorio Emanuele, Corso Galileo Ferraris and its continuations, Corso Regina Margherita and Corso San Maurizio, and the Po. Roughly bisecting this area is the fashionable arcaded VIA ROMA (Pl. 6) which connects the main station with P.za Castello; and on either side of it and parallel with it are streets laid out at right angles.

Outside the main station is P.za Carlo Felice, with a garden, and halfway along Via Roma is the arcaded PIAZZA SAN CARLO (Pl. 6; begun 1640) a charming square, with the twin churches of San Carlo and Santa Cristina. The *Monument to Duke Emmanuel Philibert* (1838), whose equestrian figure ('el caval d'brôns') is shown sheathing his sword after the victory of St Quentin (1557), is considered the masterpiece of Carlo Marochetti.

At the end of Via Roma is the huge, rectangular, PIAZZA CASTELLO (Pl. 6, 7), planned in 1584, with a monument to the Duke of Aosta (d. 1931), by Eug. Baroni (1937), and war memorials by Vela (1859) and Canonica (1923). In the centre stands **Palazzo Madama,** the most imposing of the ancient buildings of Turin. This is a four-square castle of the 15C, one side of which has been replaced by a characteristic wing and façade of 1718-21, by Fil. Juvarra.

A castle was begun here after 1276 by William VII of Monferrato on the site of the Roman Porta Decumana, the E. gate of the Roman city. The palace takes its present name from the two regents, Maria Cristina, widow of Victor Amadeus I, and Giovanna Battista, widow of Charles Emmanuel II, both of whom were entitled 'Madama Reale', who resided here and 'improved' the old castle. The palazzo was the seat in 1848-60 of the Subalpine Senate and in 1861-65 of the Italian Senate.

Since 1935 the palace has housed the civic ***Museum of Ancient Art** (open daily 9-19; Sun 10-18; closed Mon and fest.). GROUND FLOOR. Romanesque and Gothic sculpture, in wood and stone, both religious and secular, from Piedmont and the Val d'Aosta, notably a fine ceiling from St-Marcel. The ground floor of a 16-sided tower of the Porta Decumana contains stained glass; in a room with a painted ceiling from a house near the cathedral are exhibited the Codice delle Catene, the illuminated 14C statutes of the city of Turin, and stallwork from the abbey of Staffarda (near Saluzzo) and elsewhere. Off the Great Hall, in the medieval N.E. tower of the main guard-room (unlocked by the custodian) are copies of the celebrated *Book of Hours of the Duc de Berry ('Les très riches Heures de Milan', c. 1450), illustrated by *Jan van Eyck,* and a late 15C missal of Card. Dom. della Rovere. Although owned by the museum the originals are rarely on display. Also here are paintings by *Def. Ferrari* (including a fine Madonna and Child, and a night scene of the Nativity).

The GREAT HALL displays the treasures of the collection: *Maestro della*

Trinità di Torino, The Holy Trinity; *Barnaba da Modena,* Madonna and Child, a large work; Greek and Roman jewellery; works by *Def. Ferrari* (notably St Michael); *Nerroccio di Landi,* Bust of St Catherine; tilework from Savona; *Macrino d' Alba,* Triptych; jewellery, including a gold ring (12C); a *Portrait of a man by *Antonello da Messina,* signed and dated 1476, one of his best and last works; various paintings by *Giov. Martino Spanzotti.* In the centre of the room: *Tino da Camaino,* Madonna and Child; *Ant. Vivarini,* Coronation of the Madonna; *Giov. Martino Spanzotti,* Madonna and Child with angels; *Pontormo,* St Michael; two books of drawings by *Juvarra;* the shield of Giov. Maria della Rovere painted by *Polidoro da Caravaggio* (1512). In the next room is Renaissance sculpture, including high reliefs, by *Bambaia,* for the tomb of Gaston de Foix, and the tombstone of Matt. Sanmicheli, from Calcineri (near Saluzzo); while in the basement of the S.W. tower of the Porta Decumana (part of an arch of which is visible) is preserved an 11C mosaic from Acqui cathedral.

The lift (or spiral staircase) in the S.W. tower ascends to the SECOND FLOOR in which is a remarkable collection of gilded and painted glass (verre églomisé; 15-19C) including a triptych by *Iacopino Cietario* (1460). Here also are the main collections of applied art, comprising ivories, enamels, glass, majolica (notably from Turin and Savona), textiles, bookbindings, etc.—On the FIRST FLOOR, beyond the Salone Centrale (the seat of the Senate; comp. above) are the Royal Apartments. Some of the furniture here dates from Charles Emmanuel II (d. 1675), but the fittings are mainly in early-18C style, with paintings by *V. A. Cignaroli* and sculptures by *Simon Troger* (Judgement of Solomon; 1741). The best of this series of rooms is frescoed by *Guidobono* (1714), with 18C tapestries of local weave, after Cignaroli.

In the N.W. corner of P.za Castello is the octagonal church of *San Lorenzo* (1634-87), formerly the Chapel Royal, with a superb Baroque *Interior by Guarini (c. 1667). Beyond it is P.za Reale (with a good grille of 1842), the approach to the **Palazzo Reale,** the former royal residence, by Amedeo di Castellamonte (1646-60). The roadway across the square leads to the P.za San Giovanni and the cathedral.

Visitors are admitted (9-12 or 12.30, and 14-16 or 15-17.30; Fri & fest. 9-12.30 only; closed Mon) to the state apartments, which are sumptuously decorated in the 18C style and contain historical paintings, Chinese porcelain, and statues of the Savoy princes.—The pleasant *Giardino Reale,* approached through the palace, is open free daily 9-dusk.

Between the royal palace and San Lorenzo is the sober *Palazzo Chiablese,* part of which is occupied by a *Museum of the Cinema* (adm 10-12, 15-18 or 18.30; Nov-May also 20.30-23, with projections; closed Mon), entered from No. 2 P.za San Giovanni.

At the right-hand corner of the royal palace is the Loggia from which Charles Albert proclaimed war against Austria in 1848, and under the arcade in P.za Castello is the entrance (No. 191) of the ***Royal Armoury,** or *Armeria Reale* (which has been closed for restoration since 1974).

Though not large, the collection contains some remarkable pieces by the great Bavarian and Austrian armourers and gunsmiths.—The entrance hall contains arms and ensigns of the Risorgimento period, weapons from Eritrea, souvenirs of Napoleon, etc.—Of the 57 suits of armour (21 equestrian) in the main gallery, 8 were made for the Martinengo family of Brescia. Among noteworthy exhibits (r. to l.) are: the suit of Don Felipe Guzman, nearly 2m high; etched and gilt armour; small arms, including a pistol of Charles V; sword, with a forged signature of Donatello; late-14C 'pig-faced' bascinet; shield with lantern for night service; uniform worn by Prince Eugene at the battle of Turin (1706); small *Shield (French or Flemish) associated with the court of Henri II; ceremonial armour of

Emmanuel Philibert. At the end: sword. with scabbard and cover, said to have belonged to St Maurice, actually of 13C work; Roman and Etruscan armour. Among the swords, one is said to be that of Alfonso d'Este; another is of the time of the Thirty Years' War; a third (two-handed), with contemporary shield, is of the reign of Henri IV; equestrian armour worn by Emmanuel Philibert at St Quentin (1557).

On the FIRST FLOOR is the *Royal Library* (for adm. apply to the director), with 150,000 volumes, 5000 MSS., and many miniatures and drawings, including a self-portrait of Leonardo da Vinci.

Beyond the armoury are the *Prefettura* (No. 201) and the new *Teatro Regio* rebuilt in 1973 after a disastrous fire in 1936 (remnants of the old theatre survive behind the modern buildings). The Viale Primo Maggio leads down through the Giardino Reale to Corso San Maurizio.

Across the square Via Garibaldi (Pl. 6) leads west. On the right the church of the *Trinità* (1590-1606), by Vitozzi, has a marble interior by Juvarra (1718). The carved confessionals are notable. In Via Porta Palatina, on the right, is the church of *Corpus Domini* (1607-71), also by Vitozzi, with a lavishly decorated interior by Bened. Alfieri. In this church, in 1728, Jean Jacques Rousseau abjured the Protestant faith. The church of the *Santi Martiri* (farther on, on the left), the most sumptuous in Turin, by Tibaldi, was begun in 1577; the high altar is by Juvarra, and the frescoed ceiling by Vacca and Gonin. The PALAZZO DI CITTÀ (Pl. 6), opposite (entered from Via Milano), begun in 1659 by Lanfranchi and finished a century later by Alfieri, is preceded by the monument to the 'Green Count', Amadeus VI (d. 1383), the conqueror of the Turks, by Pelegio Palagi (1853). The church of *San Domenico,* in Via Milano (Pl. 2), dates from 1354, its belfry from 1451; at the E. end of the S. aisle is a painting by Guercino (Virgin and SS. Catherine and Dominic).

To the right, by Via della Basilica, is the **Cathedral** (Pl. 7; *San Giovanni Battista*), built in 1491-98 for Abp. Dom. della Rovere by *Meo del Caprino* and other Tuscans, after three churches had been demolished to make way for it. The campanile (1468-70) was completed by Juvarra in 1720.

INTERIOR. Immediately to the right is the tomb of Jeanne de la Balme (d. 1478), with kneeling effigy and female 'weepers'; to the left are two Romagnano effigies: Marquis Antonio (d. 1479) and his son Bp. Amedeo (d. 1509), the latter by *Ant. Carlone*. In the second S. chapel is a *Polyptych by *Def. Ferrari*, with scenes from the life of SS. Crispin and Crispinian and pictures of mercantile life.

Behind the apse is the **Chapel of the Holy Shroud** *(Cappella della Santissima Sindone),* by *Guarino Guarini* (1668-94). Its walls, entirely lined with black marble, throw into effective contrast the white monuments erected in 1842 by Charles Albert to the memory of four of his ancestors. On the altar is the urn containing the Holy Shroud in which the body of Christ was wrapped after his descent from the Cross. This sacred relic is said to have been taken from Jerusalem to Cyprus, and thence to France in the 15C, and to have been brought to Turin by Emmanuel Philibert in 1578. The shroud, rarely exhibited, is kept in a silver casket within an iron box enclosed in a marble case. The keys are held respectively by the Abp. of Turin and the Chief of the Palatine Clergy.

Adjoining the campanile are the ruins of a *Roman Theatre,* and in the parallel Via Porta Palatina is the restored **Porta Palatina** (Pl. 7), the two-arched Porta Principalis Dextera of the wall of the Roman colony *Augusta Taurinorum,* flanked by two sixteen-sided towers.

Just beyond is the large P.ZA DELLA REPUBBLICA (Pl. 3), known locally as Porta Palazzo, the scene of a popular general market (and, on Saturdays, of the

"Balôn" antique market). From here Via Cottolengo leads to two noted charitable institutions of Piedmontese origin: the *Cottolengo*, founded for the aged infirm in 1828 by St Joseph Benedict Cottolengo (1786-1842), canon of the Corpus Domini (see above); and the *Istituto Salesiano*, established in 1846 by St John Bosco (1815-88) for the education of poor boys, where the basilica of *Maria Santissima Ausiliatrice*, by Spezia (1865-68), with the founder's tomb, is preceded by a monument to him (by Gaetano Cellini, 1920). The saint's modest apartment, where he died, may be seen at the back of the first courtyard.

To the N.W., off Via Giulio, is the **Consolata** (Pl. 2), a popular place of worship made up of the union of two churches by Guarini (1679), one oval, the other hexagonal, with a group of Baroque cupolas contrasting with the 11C campanile of the demolished church of Sant'Andrea. Against the apse-wall is a tower of the Roman wall.

In the hexagonal church is a venerated image of the Virgin; and in a chapel on the left of the altar are kneeling figures of Maria Teresa, wife of Charles Albert, and Maria Adelaïde, wife of Victor Emmanuel II, by Vincenzo Vela (1861).

Via della Consolata leads S. âcross the P.za Savoia to Via Garibaldi. At the end of the last is P.za dello Statuto, with a monument (1879) to the engineers of the Mont Cenis tunnel. To the S. of Via Garibaldi is the *Mastio* (Pl. 2), or keep of the old citadel (1564-68), the rest of which was demolished in 1857. It contains an artillery museum (open Sun & Tues 9-11.30; Thurs & Sat 9-11.30, 15-17.30).

To the S. of P.za Castello, and reached by the Galleria Subalpina, is *Piazza Carlo Alberto,* with a bronze equestrian statue of Charles Albert by Marochetti (1861). The **Palazzo Carignano** (Pl. 6) presents a façade of 1864-71 towards this square; the Baroque W. front, begun in 1679 by Guarini, overlooking P.za Carignano, is faced with brick.

This palace was the birthplace (1820) of Victor Emmanuel II, and the ground floor was used for the meetings of the lower house of the Subalpine Parliament (1848-59) and the Italian Parliament (1861-64). The upper floors contain the *Museo del Risorgimento* (adm. 9-18, Sun 9-12; closed Mon and fest.).—On the other side of the square is the *Biblioteca Nazionale* (removed here in 1974), with over 850,000 vols. and c. 5000 MSS. mainly from religious institutions in Piedmont.

To the S.W. of *Piazza Carignano,* in which is a monument by Albertoni (1859) to Vinc. Gioberti (1801-52), the philosopher, is the **Palazzo dell'Accademia delle Scienze** (Pl. 6), a rather gloomy structure built for the Jesuits by Guarini (1678), containing the Museum of Antiquities (on the ground floor, l.), the Egyptian Museum (on the ground floor and first floor), and the Picture Gallery (on the second floor). Adm. 9-14, Sun 9-13; closed Mon.

The **Museum of Antiquities** contains objects discovered mainly in Piedmont and Liguria. The main hall (in two sections) has four side-rooms. The exhibits are well labelled. *Section I:* Piedmontese material from the Stone Age up to the Barbarian invasions. Paleolithic instruments, Bronze Age swords, Iron Age helmets; Bronze Age implements, forks, compasses, surgical instruments, and statuettes; Vases in terra sigillata. *Side rooms:* Roman gold, silver, and bronze work, including two statuettes of a Faun and dancer; and the Marengo treasure discovered in 1928 with a silver bust of Emp. Lucius Verus; Roman glass.—*Section II:* Greek vases (Attic red- and black-figure ware); Roman statues and bas reliefs (copies of Hellenistic works); portrait busts. *Side rooms:* Etruscan and Cypriot collections.

The rich ***Egyptian Museum** is claimed to be second only to that of Cairo.

The real founder of this remarkable museum was Charles Felix, who in 1824 bought the collections of Bern. Drovetti, the trusted counsellor of Mohammed Ali. Later important acquisitions came from the expeditions of Schiaparelli (1903-20) and Farina (1930-37), notably at Ghebelein (Aphroditopolis), Qau el-Kebir (Antæopolis, near Assiut), and Heliopolis. The museum played a leading part in the rescue digs in Nubia before the completion of the Aswan high dam, and was rewarded with the **Rock Temple of Ellessya** (15C B. C.); this was transported by sea in sections viâ Genoa in 1967 and has been reconstructed complete with its bas-relief frieze showing Thothmes III.

The large sculptures are on the GROUND FLOOR: ROOM I. Colossal Pharaonic head (XI Dynasty); black diorite *Statue of Rameses II (1299-33 B.C.), statues of Amenhotep II (XVIII Dyn.), of Thothmes I (XVII Dyn.); Horemheb and his wife (XIX Dyn.); figures of Sekhmet, the lion-headed goddess, and of Ptah.—R. II. *Seated figure of Thothmes III (1496-22 B.C.); sarcophagus of the court official Khemneferbok (XXVI Dyn.); statue of Tutankhamen, with the god Amen-ra (XVIII Dyn.); sarcophagus-cover of Nefertari, queen of Rameses II. Another room (usually locked) contains the reconstructed Rock Temple of Ellessya (comp. above).

FIRST FLOOR. In ROOM I, round the walls are objects from the original collection. In the centre are the most important discoveries from Heliopolis (figure of the priest Meneptah; XXV Dyn.); Qau el-Kebir (objects of the III-VI Dyn., including fine wooden statuettes); and Ghebelein (tomb-gateway of the XIX-XX Dyn.; funeral boats of the Middle Kingdom).—The Mummy Room (II) contains mummies and mummy-cases, scarabs, amulets, Canopic vases, ushabti figures, and several copies of the funerary papyrus, the 'Book of the Dead'; in the middle window, fragments of a mummy-case inlaid with enamel.—R.III. Egyptian archæological material arranged chronologically, from the Predynastic to the Coptic periods. It gives an excellent idea of the evolution of Egypt over the centuries. This room contains, on the left, a reconstruction of a frescoed funerary chapel (XVIII Dyn.), and the reconstructed Tomb of Khaiè, director of the works at the Necropolis of Thebes, and his wife Meriè (XVIII Dyn.), with the furniture, food, cooking utensils, etc., found intact. Mummy and contents of the tomb of Princess Ahmose (XVII Dyn.). Cases of pottery, alabaster, and glass.—R. IV. Statuettes of animal deities, and religious documents; the Mensa Isiaca, in bronze with silver inlay, discovered at the Sack of Rome in 1527.—R. V. Objects showing the daily life of the Egyptians, clothes, furniture, and some interesting jewels.—R. VI contains commercial and literary papyri with architectural plans and plans of gold mines; a love-poem; the Royal Papyrus, with a list of the Kings of Egypt from the Sun to the XVII Dyn.; the Papyrus of the Palace Conspiracy (XX Dyn.). In the centre, writing materials, rolls of papyrus, etc.—R. VII. Mural paintings from the tomb of Iti at Ghebelein (c. 2100 B.C.); toilet and other domestic articles; Coptic art.

The *Galleria Sabauda on the second floor, had as a nucleus the collections of paintings made by the princes of the House of Savoy. Remarkably rich in Flemish and Dutch works, it is interesting also for its paintings by Piedmontese masters, some of them hardly represented elsewhere. The first group of rooms is devoted to the ITALIAN SCHOOLS generally.

ROOM I. 102. *Bernardo Daddi,* Coronation of the Virgin; 108. *Taddeo Gaddi,* Four doctors of the Church; *Fra Angelico,* 105. Madonna, 103,

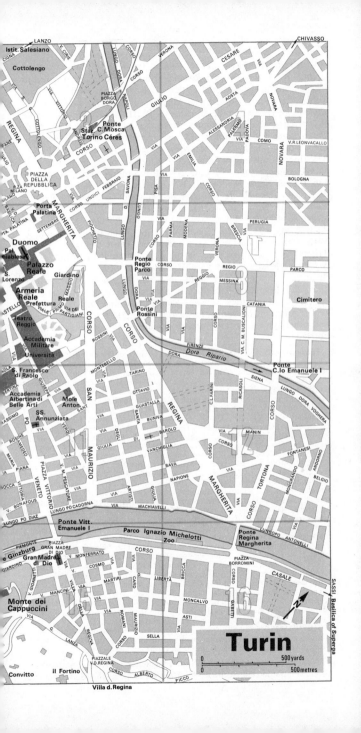

104. Angels; *Desiderio da Settignano,* Bas-relief of Madonna and Child.—R. II. 106. *Cosimo Rosselli,* Triumph of Chastity, a sequel to the painting in the National Gallery (London); 113. *Filippino Lippi,* Tobias; 115, 116. *Lor. di Credi,* Madonnas; *117. *Ant.* and *Piero del Pollaiuolo,* Tobias and the Archangel.—R. III. 141. *Paolino da Brescia,* Polyptych (school of Foppa; from San Lorenzo at Mortara); *Bergognone,* 135. Madonna, 134. SS. Ambrose and Augustine, and other works.—R. IV. 164. *Mantegna,* *Madonna and saints; *Savoldo,* 573. Holy Family and St Francis, 574. Adoration of the Shepherds.—R. V. 140. *Giampietrino,* SS. Catherine of Alexandria and Peter Martyr; 136. *Ces. da Sesto,* Madonna.—R. VI. *Bronzino,* Portrait of Eleonora da Toledo; *Daniele da Volterra,* Beheading of St John the Baptist; *Sodoma,* 56. Holy Family, *63. Madonna and four saints.—R. VII. 4. *Argenta,* Charles Emmanuel I as a child; 524. *Sammachini,* Andromeda; 124. *Giulio Campi,* Adoration of the Magi.—Beyond R. VIII, with 14C Piedmontese woodcarving (Two deacons, and the Trinity), across a vestibule, is the entrance to R. IX: 162. *Greg. Schiavone,* Madonna; 565. *Girol. da Santacroce,* St Jerome; 161. *Titian,* St Jerome; 578. *Moretto,* Madonna; 539. *Mazzuoli,* Nativity; 153. *Garofalo,* Disputa.—RR. X-XIII are devoted mainly to the 17C eclectics and romantics: *Salvator Rosa, Albani,* and *Pietro Bonzi;* 519. *G. C. Procaccini,* Madonna; *Fr. del Cairo,* 457. Martyrdom of St Agnes, and other typical works; *Pompeo Batoni,* Mythological scenes, and portraits.

The upper galleries (RR. XIV-XVIII; the Flemish and Dutch room; the French schools; and the Gualino Collection) have been closed since 1974 but are here described as they were arranged before their closure. R. XIV contains large Venetian works: *Veronese,* 572. The Queen of Sheba, 580. Christ in the house of the Pharisee; 564. *Palma Giovane,* Danaë (once ascribed to Veronese); 560. *Fr. Bassano,* Rape of the Sabines, and other paintings by the Bassano family.—R. XV. *Albani,* 489, 495, 500, 509. The Elements; 491. *Elis. Sirani,* Santa Francesca Romana.—R. XVI. 469. *Orazio Gentileschi,* Annunciation; 616. *Solimena,* Deborah; and several large saints by *G. B. Crespi.*—R. XVII (18C). *Bellotto,* 585. View of Turin, 582. Bridge over the Po; 598. *Seb. Ricci,* The Israelites in the wilderness; 589-593. *Guardi,* Venetian sketches; 594. *G. B. Tiepolo,* Triumph of Aurelian.—R. XVIII. 193. *Torinese Master of* 1499, Adoration of the Magi.

The FLEMISH AND DUTCH ROOM is a large room with screens, containing some fine primitives: 187. *Jan van Eyck,* St Francis; 192. *Flemish 16C Master,* Crucifixion; 194. *Barend van Orley,* Consecration of a king of France; 189. *Roger van der Weyden,* Visitation, with interesting landscape; *202. *Memling,* Passion scenes, painted with great animation, and in fine condition; 188. *Petrus Christus,* Madonna; 412. *Saenredam,* Interior of a synagogue; many charming small landscapes by *Paul Brill* and *Jan Brueghel;* 223. *Abr. Sellaert,* Procession of the Demoiselles du Sablon at Brussels; *Van Dyck,* *264. The children of Charles I, a masterpiece (1635), presented by Henrietta Maria to her sister Christina of Savoy, 279. The Infanta Isabella, Governess of the Netherlands; *405. *Paul Potter,* Four bulls; 377. *Gerard Dou,* At the window; 414. *Gasp. Vanvitelli,* Naples harbour; 433. *G. Griffier,* View of London (?) from the suburbs; 392. *Barend Fabritius,* Expulsion of Hagar; 362. *Cornelius Engelbrechstz,* Crucifixion (a triptych).—The other large room on this floor is devoted mainly to the FRENCH SCHOOLS, with examples of *Poussin, Claude,* and *Mignard;* also, 316-7. *A. Querfurt,* Camp scenes; 360. *Vigée-Le Brun,* Portrait of a girl; 357. *Subleyras.* An abbé; *Clouet,* *3. Marguerite de Valois, 2. Charles the Good; 331. *Corneille de Lyon,* Card. de Lenoncourt; 334-5. *Coypel,* Carle Van Loo and his wife.

The GUALINO COLLECTION, which occupies the remainder of this floor, contains good Italian and German paintings, ancient sculpture, Byzantine ivories, Chinese works (good 6C head), medieval furniture, and lace.

A stair descends to the lower floor, in which four rooms contain works of the PIEDMONTESE SCHOOL, A. *Macrino d'Alba,* 26. Madonna with saints and angel musicians, 31-34. Panels of a polyptych from San Francesco at Alba.—B. *Gaudenzio Ferrari*, 49. Madonna, 51. Deposition, 46. St Peter and a donor, 50. Crucifixion; 65. *Lanino*, Madonna; 39. *Giovenone*, Madonna and donors.—C. 35. *Defendente Ferrari*, Marriage of St Catherine; 52. *Vercelli Master* (15C), Adoration of the Magi; 29 bis. *Spanzotti*, Madonna with SS. Ubaldo and Sebastian (triptych).—D. 30 bis. *Def. Ferrari*, Donor, with SS. John the Baptist and Jerome; fragments of frescoes from destroyed churches; 21. *Barnaba da Modena*, Madonna and Child.

Opposite the Academy stands the large church of *San Filippo Neri*, rebuilt by Juvarra (c. 1714), with a 19C façade. From here Via Maria Vittoria (l.) leads to P.za Carlo Emanuele II (Pl. 10), in which is a monument to Cavour by Giov. Dupré (1873).

Via dell'Accademia Albertina on the left leads past the *Accademia Albertina di Belle Arti* (Pl. 11) to the arcaded VIA PO, the main street of the E. quarter of Turin. The Albertina contains a small picture gallery (open daily 10-12; Sun and fest. closed; apply to the Segreteria), principally interesting for drawings by Gaud. Ferrari and Lanino and paintings by Piedmontese masters. In Via Po, to the left, is the church of *San Francesco di Paola*, containing 17C sculptures by Tom. Carlone, and father along (No. 17) is the *University* (Pl. 7; 1714), with a brick façade facing Via Verdi.

The college, which has a chequered history dating back to the early 15C, has occupied its present site since 1720.

On the other side of Via Po, in Via Montebello, rises the **Mole Antonelliana** (Pl. 11), begun in 1863 as a synagogue by Aless. Antonelli, and finished by the municipality in 1897. The terrace (86 m; view) is reached by lift (10-12, 14.30-19.30; also 21-23 in summer; closed Mon); the spire, 167 m high, has been rebuilt since it lost its upper 47 m in a gale in 1953.

Via Po ends in the spacious P.za Vittorio Veneto (Pl. 11), beyond which Ponte Vittorio Emanuele I leads to the church of the *Gran Madre di Dio* (Pl. 15), built by Bonsignore in 1818-31, in imitation of the Pantheon at Rome, to celebrate the return from exile of Victor Emmanuel I (1814). The king's monument, by Gaggini, stands in front of the church. From Corso Moncalieri (r.) Via M. Giardino ascends to the wooded **Monte dei Cappuccini** (283 m; Pl. 15), on whose summit are a Capuchin church and convent, and the *Duke of Abruzzi Mountain Museum* (relief plans, etc., closed for restoration).

Below the Ponte Vittorio Emanuele I, on this bank, is the Parco Michelotti, with a small *Zoo* and Aquarium (Pl. 16; open 8-20).

Farther upstream, beyond the Ponte Umberto I, is the pleasant **Parco del Valentino** (Pl. 14, 13), laid out on the left bank of the Po and opened in 1856.

It contains a Botanic Garden and the *Castello del Valentino*, built in 1630-60 by Maria Cristina in the style of a French château and now occupied by the School of Architecture of the University. The reproduction of a *Medieval Village* and *Castle* (open except Mon & fest., 10-12, 15-17 or 18) was erected for the exhibition of 1884. The village (Borgo) shows types of old Piedmontese houses. The castle is modelled on various strongholds in the Val d'Aosta, etc. In the park, nearby, is the fine equestrian monument of Prince Amadeus, the masterpiece of Davide Calandra (1902). Boats may be hired for rowing on the river.

At the S.W. end of the park are the buildings of the *Turin Exhibition*, built in 1948 for the first Motor Show (held biennially in Nov). There are now five halls (used frequently for exhibitions), one of which is adapted in winter as a skating-rink.

Beyond the park the Corso Massimo d'Azeglio is prolonged as Corso Unità d'Italia, where (No. 40; 2 km. farther) stands the splendid *Carlo Biscaretti di Ruffia Motor Museum (adm. 9.30 or 10-12.30 & 15-17.30 or 19; closed Mon), founded in 1933 and moved here in 1960. The building, designed by Amedeo Albertini, contains an international collection of vehicles, admirably displayed and technically documented. Farther on still, overlooking the river, is the huge *Palazzo del Lavoro*, designed by Pier Luigi Nervi for the 1961 exhibition, now a study centre of the International Labour Office.

From P.za Castello it is a short ride by bus No. 64 to the **Galleria d'Arte Moderna** (Pl. 5; adm. 9-19, Sun 10-18; closed Mon & fest) in Via Magenta just off Corso Galileo Ferraris. This is one of the most important collections of 19C and 20C painting in Italy, with French artists well represented.

EXCURSIONS FROM TURIN

To SUPERGA, 8 km. TRAMWAY No. 5 from P.za Castello to *Sassi* and rack-railway from there to Superga in 16 min. The **Basilica of Superga** (open 9-12.30, 14-19 exc. Fri), crowning a hill-top (672 m) which commands a splendid *View, was built in 1717-31 by Victor Amadeus II in fulfilment of a thanksgiving vow for the deliverance of Turin in 1706. It is considered the masterpiece of Juvarra. The exterior, with its columned portico, its dome, and its two campaniles, is impressive.

In the *Crypt* (entrance to the left of the church) are the tombs of the Kings of Sardinia from Victor Amadeus II (d. 1732) to Charles Albert (d. 1849), and of other princes of Savoy. In the garden to the S. a monument to Humbert I shows an Allobrogian warrior swearing fealty to the dynasty.—Behind the basilica a plaque records the air disaster of 4 May 1949 in which 31 people, including the whole team of Turin Football Club, were killed.

TO MONCALIERI, 8½ km. (bus). **Moncalieri** (62,550 inhab.) lies just beyond the S.E. suburban limits of Turin across the Po. Its hill-top centre has industrial surroundings that almost double its population. The 15C *Castle,* much enlarged in the 17-18C, was the favourite residence of Victor Emmanuel II; and Victor Amadeus II (1732) and Victor Emmanuel I (1824) died here. The state apartments are open 9-12.30, 14.30-17.30 (winter: 9-12, 14-16; fest, Mon, & Fri, 9-12.30). In the principal square is the 14C church of *Santa Maria della Scala,* containing good stalls (1748) and Canonica's monument of Princess Clotilde (d. 1911).

To Stupinigi, see Rte 1C.

To the COLLE DELLA MADDALENA, 5 km. BUS from P.za Vitt. Veneto (Pl. 11). The route ascends S.E. past the *Villa della Regina* (once the residence of Marie-Anne d'Orléans, queen of Victor Amadeus II) to the *Colle della Maddalena* (766 m) the slopes of which have been laid out as a huge *Parco della Rimembranza,* with fine trees, for a War Memorial. A colossal bronze torch-bearing Victory, over 18 m high, by Edoardo Rubino (1928), stands below the summit. The *View is almost equal to that from Superga.

The VALLI DI LANZO are the Alpine valleys N.W. of Turin, less frequented than they deserve by visitors from beyond Piedmont, for their scenery is as fine as any in the western Alps. They are the heart of the *Graian Alps,* which lie between the valleys of the Dora Riparia and Dora Báltea.

RAILWAY from Turin c. every hr to *Lanzo* in 35-55 min, and *Céres* in 1-1½ hr.

The road leaves by P.za Repubblica (Pl. 3), Corso Giulio Cesare, and Corso Emilia (1.). To the l. (9 km.) is *Venaria,* with a royal hunting lodge built c. 1660, and restored by Juvarra in 1714-28. Part of the buildings are used as a barracks; the Galleria di Diana has been restored and is open on request.—13 km. _Caselle_, with the airport on the right.— Beyond (21 km.) _Ciriè_, where the Gothic Duomo has a good campanile and portal, the industrial area is left behind as the road ascends the Stura valley.—33 km. **Lanzo Torinese** (5580 inhab.) is a picturesque little place, with houses huddled round the 14C _Torre del Comune_. The old Turin road crosses the Stura below the town by the _Ponte del Diavolo_ (1378), a daring, single-arched bridge.—35 km. _Germagnano_ (488 m).

The VALLE DI VIÙ, which starts at Germagnano (bus to Margone), is watered by the S. branch of the Stura.—13 km. **Viù** (774 m) is a good centre for excursions. A hill-road runs S. over the _Colle del Lis_ (1311 m: two ski-lifts) to Rubiana and (34 km.) Avigliana (p. 45).—**Usseglio**, the highest commune in the valley, is strung out for 5 km. in a series of hamlets. It has skiing facilities. The chief hotels are at (28 km.) _Cortevicio_ (1265 m) whence a path leads in 4¼ hrs to the _Rifugio Cibrario_ (2615 m), the base for the ascent of the _Croce Rossa_ (3517 m) and other frontier peaks.—At (33 km.) _Margone_ (1410 m) the made-up road ends. A track continues to (38 km.) _Lago Malciaussià_ (refuge), and a path continues from there up the valley to (3½ hrs) _Founs d'Rumour_ (2649 m; Rifugio Tazzetti), from where the _Rocciamelone_ (3537 m) is ascended in 3 hrs (descent to Susa, see Rte 1A).

The main road goes on viâ (42 km.) _Pessinetto_ to (46 km.) **Céres** (689 m), the railway terminus, at the junction of the Val Grande and the Valle d'Ala. It is a summer resort.

The VALLE D'ALA, the central one of the three Lanzo valleys, is ascended by a bus from Céres to Balme, going on (15 July-15 Sept) to Piano della Mussa.—8 km. **Ala di Stura** (1079 m) is the chief village. A chair lift ascends to (1415 m) Pian Belfè. Other centres are (12 km.) _Mondrone_ (1230 m), near a fine gorge and waterfall of the Stura; and (15 km.) **Balme** (1431 m) with three ski-lifts, from where the rocky _Uia di Mondrone_ (2964 m) is ascended.—20 km. _Piano della Mussa_ (1720 m) is a lovely little basin at the head of the valley. The _Rif. Gastaldi_ (2659 m; 19 km), 2½ hrs farther on, is a base for the ascent of the _Bessanese_ (3604 m; 4½ hrs), on the French frontier.

The VAL GRANDE (bus from Céres to Forno), to the N., is the least frequented of the Lanzo valleys. The chief villages are (9½ km.) _Chialamberto_ (876 m), (13 km.) _Bonzo_, and (16 km.) _Groscavallo-Pialpetta_ (1069 m). The _Colle della Crocetta_ (2636 m) provides a fine walk N. from Pialpetta to (6 hrs) Ceresole Reale (p. 61).— 21 km. _Forno Alpi Gráie_ (1226 m), the uppermost village lies in a magnificent cirque of mountains. The _Rif. Paolo Daviso_ (2375 m), 3¼ hrs W., serves as an approach to the _Monte Levanna_ (central peak, 3503 m; 11 hrs) viâ the _Colle Girard_ (3078 m; 5½ hrs).

From Turin to _Aosta_, see Rte 2; to _Genoa_, see Rte 6; to _Milan_, see Rte 9; to _Ventimiglia and Nice_, see Rte 4.

C   Turin to Briançon

ROAD, 123 km.—N23. 10 km. _Stupinigi._—36 km. **Pinerolo.**—53 km. _Perosa Argentina._—69 km. _Fenestrelle._—91 km. **Sestriere.**—102½ km. _Cesana Torinese._ —N24. 109 km. _Claviere_ (frontier).—N94. 111 km. _Col du Montgenèvre._ —123 km. **Briançon.**

BUS daily from Turin (Via Buozzi) to _Briançon_ in 4¼ hrs; more frequently to _Pinerolo_ (¾ hr), _Perosa_ (1¼ hr) and _Sestriere_ (2½ hrs).

RAILWAY, viâ (25 km.) _Airasca_ (junction for Saluzzo and Cuneo), to _Pinerolo_, 38 km. in 35-60 min. (going on to Torre Péllice).

The Pinerolo road (N23) runs from Porta Nuova, past _Mirafiori_, with the main Fiat works, to (10 km.) **Stupinigi**, noted for the _Villa Reale_, a royal hunting-lodge laid out in 1729-30 by Juvarra on an ingenious and complicated plan, the property of the Mauritian Order. It is open 10-12.30, 15-18 (winter, 10-12.30, 14-17), closed Mon & Fri, and contains a _Museum of Furniture_. The rooms are adorned with ceiling-paintings by Carle Van Loo and others. It is surrounded by a fine park. The parish church contains the relics of St Hubert, patron of huntsmen (procession on 3 Nov).—23 km. *Airasca.*

36 km. **Pinerolo** (37,310 inhab.), the historic capital of the Princes of Acaia, ancestors of the House of Savoy, is beautifully situated at the foot of the hills where the Chisone and Lémina valleys merge into the Piedmontese plain. It is a commercial and industrial centre. In the centre of the old town is the restored Gothic *Cathedral.* Via Trento and Via Principi d'Acaia (r.), with ancient houses, ascend to the early 14C *Palace of the Princes of Acaia,* and the church of *San Maurizio,* reconstructed in 1470, with a fine campanile of 1336. It is the burial place of eight princes of Acaia (1334-1490). Via Ortensia di Piossasco descends from here to the Public Garden in which stands the *Waldensian Church* (1860).

The fortress of *Pignerol* (as it is called in French) was under French control in 1630-1706, and, thanks to its remoteness from Paris, was found convenient as a State prison. The 'Man in the Iron Mask' was held here from 1668 to 1678, and the Duc de Lauzun in 1671-81; while the chancellor Nicolas Fouquet died here in 1681 after 19 years' incarceration.

The **Vaudois Valleys** (*Valli Valdesi*). The valleys of the Chisone and the Péllice (described below) are inhabited mainly by the Protestant Waldenses or Vaudois. This sect found its origin in the S. of France about 1170, under the inspiration of Peter Waldo, a Lyons merchant who sold his goods and started preaching the gospel. His adherents were formally condemned by the Lateran Council in 1184 and persecution drove them to take refuge in these retired valleys of the Piedmontese Alps. About 1532 the Vaudois became absorbed in the Swiss Reformation. When renewed persecution broke out in 1655 under Charles Emmanuel II, assisted by the troops of Louis XIV, a strong protest was raised by Cromwell in England, and Milton wrote his famous sonnet. Still further persecution followed the Revocation of the Edict of Nantes (1685), but the remnant of the Vaudois, about 2600 in number, were allowed to retreat to Geneva. In 1698 Henri Arnaud led a band of 800 to the reconquest of their valleys, and a rupture between Louis XIV and Victor Amadeus of Savoy was followed by their recognition as subjects of Savoy, and tolerance began to prevail. Since the beginning of the 19C much interest has been taken in Protestant countries on their behalf, and an Englishman, Gen. Beckwith, helped them personally and built their church in Turin (1849). Since 1848 they have enjoyed complete religious liberty. Towards the close of the 19C large colonies emigrated to Sicily, Uruguay, and the Argentine Republic.

The road running S. from Pinerolo to (31 km.) *Saluzzo* (see Rte 4) passes (12½ km.) *Cavour* (bus), the ancestral home of the great statesman's family. Here Giov. Giolitti died in 1928. *Staffarda* (20 km.) has a fine Cistercian *Abbey, founded in 1135 and well restored.

Another interesting road from Pinerolo (railway as far as Torre Péllice) ascends the Péllice valley.—15½ km. **Torre Péllice** (518 m), the headquarters of the Waldensians (4800 inhab.), is a pleasant little town with some good 19C buildings, including a Waldensian church and college, and a museum illustrating their history. It also has ski facilities. To the N. extends the pleasant valley of *Angrogna.*—Futher up the main valley are (22 km.) *Villar Péllice* (664 m), and (25 km.) *Bobbio Péllice* (732 m), two little summer resorts.—A very fine walk ascends the valley above Bobbio to (c. 3 hrs) the long upland valley of *Pra,* beneath *Monte Granero* (3171 m; Rifugio Granero at 2355 m). The road runs as far as (6 km.) *Villanova,* skirting a long flood-embankment built with the aid of a grant from Cromwell.—From Pra the frontier may be crossed in summer by bridle-path over the *Colle della Croce* (2305 m) to La Monta and (5 hrs) *Abriès* in France.

Beyond Pinerolo the Briançon road ascends the Chisone valley.— 53 km. *Perosa Argentina,* a silk-working town, lies at the foot of the *Val Germanasca,* a Waldensian stronghold with talc deposits.

A bus ascends the valley viâ (8 km.) *Perrero* to (17 km.) *Prali* and (19 km.) *Ghigo* (1759 m), beyond which a chair-lift ascends to Cappello d'Envie (2556 m). A rough road continues to (21 km.) *Ribba,* whence a bridle-path (open in summer) crosses the *Colle Nuovo d'Abriès* (2635 m) to (7 hrs) *Abriès* in France.

63 km. *Villaretto* is the chief hamlet of Roreto, at the S. foot of the *Orsiera* (2878 m). Just beyond is a dramatic view of the remarkable fortifications built in 1727 by Charles Emmanuel III to defend (69 km.) **Fenestrelle** (1154 m), a little town frequented as a winter and summer resort. The tall sombre houses are surrounded by forests and dominated from the S. by the *Albergian* (3043 m), an easy climb of 6 hrs.

The plateau of *Pra Catinat* (1829-1981 m), a noted ski-ing ground, is reached by a winding road from the Dépôt di Fenestrelle, a little downstream; while a cableway leads up to the Agnelli Sanatoria, 152 m below. The road, often difficult, goes on over the *Colle delle Finestre* (2176 m) to Meana and (37 km.) *Susa* (Rte 1A).

80 km. *Pragelato* is noted for its Alpine flowers and for the honey they produce. It has become an important ski resort. The road now ascends more steeply, soon leaving the Chisone valley, and passes on the left the old village of Sestriere.

91 km. **Sestriere,** on the Colle di Sestriere (2030 m), is the most fashionable summer and winter alpine resort in Piedmont, with unusual 'tower-hotels'. The ski slopes in the neighbourhood are excellent.

Buses. Daily express service to *Turin,* and *Milan;* service to Cesana and *Oulx* (for the railway).

Cable Railways, hourly or oftener to *Monte Banchetta; Monte Sises;* viâ *Alpette* to *Monte Sises; to Fraitève.* There are also eighteen ski-lifts and a chair-lift for winter sports. Open air (heated) and covered swimming pools.—18-hole golf course.

The principal ski-runs are on the slopes of *Monte Banchetta* (2830 m) to the E., and the *Monte Sises* (2658 m) to the S.E., both spurs of the *Rognosa* (3280 m), a dull climb of 4 hrs. Much more rewarding is the easy ascent of the *Fraitève* (2701 m), 1¾ hr N.

From Sestriere to *Oulx,* see Rte 1A.

The descent from Sestriere passes (95 km.) *Champlas du Col,* and reaches the Dora Riparia valley at (102½ km.) **Cesana Torinese** (1361 m), a large red-roofed village with an old church, at the junction of the road to Oulx (Rte 1A). As another ski resort, it has numerous chair-lifts and ski-lifts.

A chair-lift rises to the *Colle La Bércia* (2236 m); while an interesting road ascends the valley running S. to (3 km.) *Bousson* (1489 m), with an old church. From here routes continue either S.W. to the *Rifugio Mautino* (2105 m) and thence over the *Col Bousson* (2153 m; open in summer) to Cervières and (7 hrs) *Briançon;* or E. to (6½ km.) *Sauze di Cesana* (1547 m), on the winding upland route to Sestriere. From Sauze the long and beautiful Ripa valley leads S.E. to (4½ hrs) the *Rif. Monte Nero* (2129 m) the base for the ascent of the *Punta Ramière* (3303 m) and other peaks. The *Val di Thures,* running S.E. from Bousson, offers another approach to the Ramière.

A zigzag ascent of the Piccola Dora valley leads to the frontier, with the Italian customs, at (109 km.) **Claviere** (1768 m), another frequented winter and summer resort, with fine easy ski-slopes.—Beyond the new frontier an easy slope leads up to (111 km.) the **Col du Montgenèvre** or **Monginevro** (1860 m), the frontier before 1947, where an obelisk commemorates the construction of the road by Napoleon. The French mountain-resort of *Montgenèvre,* with custom-house, is only 2 km. from Claviere.

A little to the S., and almost from a common source, rise the Dora, which flows through the Po into the Adriatic, and the Durance, flowing through the Rhone into the Mediterranean.

"Adieu, ma soeur, la Durance, nous nous séparons sur ce mont;
Tu vas ravager la Provence, moi féconder le Piémont."

The Mont-Genèvre *(Mons Janus)* is one of the oldest, as well as one of the lowest passes over the main chain of the Alps. It was crossed by the armies of Marius, Augustus, Theodosius, and Charlemagne; and again in 1494 by Charles VIII and his army, dragging with them 600 cannon. The present road was constructed under Napoleon in 1802-7. French armies entered Italy by it in 1818 and 1859; and in 1917-18 French reinforcements were sent to the Italian armies over the pass.

The descent leads by *La Vachette* to (123 km.) **Briançon** in France.

2   TURIN TO AOSTA, COURMAYEUR, AND CHAMONIX. THE GREAT ST BERNARD

AUTOSTRADA, A5, to **Aosta** (c. 10 km. shorter; see below).—The old ROAD (N 26) diverges l. from N 11 at (23 km.) *Chivasso* (comp. Rte 9) and strikes N.—36 km. *Caluso.*—46 km. *Strambino*, with a castle (11-14C).—56 km. **Ivrea.** Beyond Ivrea road and motorway are both confined in the valley. There is access from the motorway only to the main places; the old road has many sharp corners and traverses narrow village streets.—73 km. *Pont-St-Martin.*—87 km. *Verrès.*—98 km. **St-Vincent.**—101 km. *Châtillon.* The autostrada ends just before (125 km.) **Aosta**, where N 27 branches (r.) to the Great St Bernard Tunnel.—N 26. 156 km. **Pré-St-Didier.**—161 km. **Courmayeur.**—166 km. *Entrèves* (custom-house at the tunnel mouth).—181 km. **Chamonix-Mont Blanc.**—BUS services from Turin to Aosta in 3 hrs, with some international services through the tunnels.

RAILWAY to *Prè-St-Didier*, 161 km. in 3¼-5 hrs, usually with a change at (129 km.) *Aosta* (2-3 hrs).

The **Val d'Aosta**, the district which includes the main valley of the Dora Báltea and its numerous tributary valleys, is one of the most beautiful parts of Italy. The mountains which surround its head (Gran Paradiso, Mont Blanc, Matterhorn, and Monte Rosa), its glaciers, its forests, its pastures, and its unequalled view-points combine with its Roman remains and many feudal castles (only four of which, Verrès, Fénis, Isogne, and Sarre, are open to the public) to make it an area of great beauty and interest. It is divided into three parts by 'narrows' at Bard and Montjovet. The language most commonly spoken in the country is French, but Italian predominates in the towns and is everywhere understood. An interesting relic of the colonization of the valley from the Swiss Valais remains in the German dialect which still survives at Gressoney. Under the Italian Constitution of 1945 the valley was granted a statute of administrative and cultural autonomy, with a Regional Council of 35 members, sitting in Aosta.

The most important tourist centres are Gressoney, Cogne, Champoluc, Brusson, Breuil, Courmayeur, and St-Vincent, all of which have good hotels. The guides of Valtournanche and Courmayeur are world-famous and many have accomplished first ascents not only in Switzerland, but also in America and Africa and among the Himalayas. The roads are apt to be crowded in summer, including the two great arteries which offer an additional exit from the upper valley—the Great and Little St Bernard passes.

From Turin the old road and the motorway (10 km. shorter) both cross the low moraine ridge through which the Dora Báltea, farther E., cuts its way into the Po valley.—After (36 km.) *Caluso*, the Lago di Candia is visible on the right. Beyond a stretch of heavily wooded country the mountains come into view.—56 km. **Ivrea**, a pleasant old town (29,800 inhab.), was the Roman *Eporedia*, a bulwark in the 1C B.C. against the Salassian Gauls of the Upper Dora. In the Middle Ages its marquesses rose to high power, and Arduin of Ivrea was crowned King of Italy in 1002. Ivrea is well known for its carnival, held annually in February. The Olivetti typewriter factories were founded here in 1908, and it has expanded as an industrial centre.

On the approach from the S., *Ponte Nuovo* crosses the Dora Báltea. On the left is the *Ponte Vecchio,* a bridge of 1716 on older foundations. In the upper part of the town, approached by steep lanes, is the CATHEDRAL, of which two apsidal towers and the crypt date from the 11C. In the raised ambulatory is a row of columns taken from older buildings. On the left of the façade (1854) is a Roman sarcophagus. The sacristy contains two paintings by Defendente Ferrari. Behind the cathedral is the *CASTLE,* built by Aymon de Challant (1358) for Amadeus VI, the 'Green Count', with four tall angle towers, one of which was partially destroyed by an explosion in 1676. Formerly a prison, it is now being restored. The *Bishop's Palace,* also opening on the untidy old P.za Castello, has Roman and medieval fragments in its loggia. In P.za Carlo Alberto, the *Museo Civico* has oriental and archæological collections.

In the public park by the river, below the Dora bridges, is the Romanesque campanile (1041) of *Santo Stefano.*

Ivrea is the capital of the **Canavese,** the subalpine district extending from the level moraine ridge of the *Serra d'Ivrea,* to the E., up to the foot of the Gran Paradiso. The VALLE DE LOCANA, the chief valley of this district, is reached direct from Turin (Porta Susa) by railway or rail bus to (52 km.) *Pont Canavese* (see below). The railway serves (21 km.) *San Benigno,* which preserves the 11C campanile and other remains of the abbey of *Fruttuaria,* where Arduin of Ivrea died, a monk, in 1013.

The road from Ivrea (bus) joins the road from Turin opposite (23 km.) *Cuorgnè,* an ancient little town on the Orco, with many medieval houses, now somewhat suffocated by new industrial buildings. *Valperga,* 3 km. S., has a restored castle, near which is a charming little 15C church (frescoes). Above rises the *Santuario di Belmonte,* founded by Arduin, but rebuilt in the 14C.—29 km. *Pont Canavese,* the railway terminus, stands at the foot of the flowery Val Soana, which is served by a bus from Pont to *Ronco Canavese* (13 km.) and *Valprato* (16 km.).—Beyond Pont the road (bus to Noasca daily, to Ceresole in May-Oct) keeps close to the Orco, passing (33 km.) *Sparone.*—40 km. *Locana* (613 m), the last big village, has developed as a winter sports centre. The ascent becomes steeper and the outliers of the Gran Paradiso loom up on the right.—Above (54 km.) *Noasca* (1035 m), with its charming waterfall (above the houses to the right), the road enters a narrow gorge through which the Orco foams in a sequence of cascades, and after a tunnel the road emerges suddenly into the pastoral plain of Ceresole.—62 km. **Ceresole Reale** (1495 m), stands in a long upland basin, dominated by the peaks of the Levanna, whose natural beauty has been somewhat marred by the dam and reservoir of the Turin electric-power works. Ceresole was the scene in 1544 of a victory of the troops of Francis I over those of Charles V, when the young Coligny was knighted on the field. It is a good centre for excursions and has ski-ing facilities. A fine excursion crosses (16 km.) the *Col du Nivolet* (2841 m), where the road becomes a bridle-path, to (c. 32 km.) Pont Valsavaranche (see below). From the upland basin of Serrù (2393 m) this road lies within the National Park (p. 67).

Beyond (59 km.) *Montalto Dora,* with its well-restored 15C castle prominent on the right, begins the Val d'Aosta proper, whose slopes are covered with trellised vineyards. French-speaking territory is reached at (73 km.) *Pont-St-Martin* (343 m), an attractive town with a fine *Roman bridge (1C B.C.) on the Lys, and the ruins of a 12C castle.

For *Gressoney* and the *Val du Lys,* see Rte 3B.

Beyond (76 km.) *Donnaz* station, before the level-crossing, a row of old houses ends by a stretch of Roman road with a remarkable rock-hewn arch.—The road enters the narrow Gorge de Bard, through which in 1800 Napoleon passed unperceived with an army during the night. At the other end are the villages of *Hône* (l.) and *Bard* (r.), with its forbidding fortress (the train tunnels beneath its promontory), an 11C foundation largely reconstructed in the 19C, and now being restored. As an over-Liberal young officer, Cavour was despatched to this remote garrison by Charles Felix (1830-31).

To the left is the steep Ayasse valley, up which a bus runs to (15 km.) *Champorcher* (1315 m), a small resort. From here a bridle-path crosses (4 hrs) the *Finestra di Champorcher* (2838 m) to (7 hrs) Cogne (p. 67).

On the right (83 km.) is the church of *Arnaz*, revealed since its restoration in 1950-52 as the oldest in the region (c. 1000) with mural paintings (?15C); here also are a ruined castle and many tower-houses.— 87 km. **Verrès** (395 m) stands at the mouth of the Val d'Ayas. Its four-square *Castle* commands this valley (r. of road and railway), at the head of which can be glimpsed snow-capped mountains. A road leads up to the castle (open 9-12, 14-17 or 18; closed Tues) or a path ascends in 15 min. from P.za Chanoux. It was founded by the Challant family in 1380 and strengthened in 1536, and has sheer walls 30 m high. The *Castle of Issogne*, rebuilt by Georges de Challant in 1497-98, 10 min. S.W. of the station beyond the Dora, is a splendid example of the late-medieval residence (adm. as for Verrés, exc. closed Mon), with a notable series of frescoes, including scenes of everyday life (in the loggia), and fitted up with local furniture.

From Verrès to *Champoluc*, see Rte 3C; to *Valmériane*, see below.

Beyond (94 km.) *Montjovet* the road traverses another ravine.— 98 km. **St-Vincent** (434 m), situated amid groves of chestnuts, has been famous since 1770 as a health resort, and is a popular congress and excursion centre, with a casino. The old church has a 13C fresco in a niche outside the apse. Recent restorations have revealed its foundations on the baths of a Roman villa. The Romanesque interior has 13-16C frescoes. A funicular rises in 3 min. to the *Palazzo delle Fonti* (1960) where the mineral spring (*Fons Salutis*) gushes from the hill-side.

Pleasant walks may be made to the castle of *Montjovet* (615 m), ¾ hr downstream, and to (1¾ hr S.E.) *Emarese* (1048 m) above Montjovet, a village commanding a fine view. Some 244 m above the village is an ice-grotto. *Mont Zerbion* (see below) is easily ascended from St-Vincent in 5 hrs.

BUSES run all the year round from St-Vincent to the station, and to Châtillon; to the *Col de Joux*, for Brusson (Rte 3A); also in Aug to Breuil, Cogne, the Great and Little St Bernard, Gressoney, Champoluc, etc.

101 km.   **Châtillon** (549 m), the town (4490 inhab.) second in importance in the Val d'Aosta, preserves a number of 16-17C houses. In the district are quarries of green marble. The Marmore torrent (a waterfall is well seen on the left side of the valley), flowing down from the Valtournanche is here crossed by three bridges: the uppermost dates from 1766, while farther down is the Roman bridge, with another bridge immediately above it. The feudal castle of the Challant family was twice renovated in the 18C after damage by French troops (1706) and earthquake (1755).

On the opposite side of the Valtournanche is the hill crowned by (3 hrs) the chapel of *St-Evence* (1668 m), which affords a good view of the Matterhorn at the head of the Valtournanche. The descent may be made to Chambave viâ *St-Denis*, a village overhung by the ruined castle of *Cly* (1351).—The ruined castle of *Ussel* (1350) may be reached in 1 hr by crossing the Dora below the railway station.—For excursions in the Valtournanche, see Rte 3D.

ASCENTS. *Mont Zerbion* (2721 m), affording a fine panorama of Monte Rosa and the Val Challant, is easily reached in 5 hrs, viâ *Promiod* (1493 m) and the Val de Promiod, at the head of which the *Col de Portola* (2415 m) leads over to Antagnod and Perriasc (Rte 3C) in 4¼ hrs.— *Mont Barbeston* (2483 m) on the S.

side of the Val d'Aosta is likewise reached in 5 hrs viâ *Pontey* and the thickly wooded *Valmériane*. The *Col de Valmériane* (2281 m) gives access to the Val de Chalame, which may be descended to *Verrès* (see above) in 8 hrs viâ *Champ de Praz*.—From Châtillon to *Zermatt*. see Rte 3D.

106 km. *Chambave* (475 m), beneath the castle of Cly (see above), once noted for its wine (moscato). To the S. extends the lonely *Val Clavalité*, with the snowy *Pyramid of the Tersiva visible at its head. Just beyond, on the left, appears the *Castle of Fénis* (adm. as for Verrés, above), one of the finest in Piedmont, rebuilt c. 1340 by Aymon de Challant (being restored). The courtyard and the loggias have frescoes of saints and sages, with proverbs in Old French; the chapel is equally well decorated.—113 km. *Nus* (474 m), with the scanty ruins of its castle, lies at the mouth of the Val St-Barthélemy.

The wooded VAL ST-BARTHÉLEMY, 25 km. long, traversed by a bus (daily in July-Aug) for the first 13 km., leads to (16 km.) *Lignan* (1628 m), its principal village.

To the right is the 12C castle of *Quart* (725 m).—The valley expands into the fertile basin of Aosta, with a small airfield. A large steelworks S. of the town is very prominent.

125 km. **AOSTA** (579 m), surrounded by lofty snow-capped mountains at the junction of the Buthier and the Dora Báltea, is a town (39,000 inhab.) of great antiquity. The old centre, less than two kilometres square, is still enclosed by its Roman walls and contains many Roman and medieval survivals. Industrial expansion outside the walls detracts from the beautiful position and fine monuments of the town. Many of its inhabitants speak French rather than Italian.

Hotels, mostly within the walls.
Buses run all year to centres of the Val d'Aosta, also to *Turin*, and to *Milan;* and viâ the Great St Bernard tunnel to *Martigny*, and to *Courmayeur* and *Chamonix* (viâ the Mt Blanc tunnel).
Tourist Offices. *E.P.T.*, P.za Narbonne; *Azienda Autonoma*, P.za E. Chanoux.

History. Once the chief town of the Gallic Salassi, Aosta was captured by Terentius Varro in 24 B.C. and renamed *Augusta Prætoria;* and its centre still retains a Roman plan almost intact. The character of the later city, however, is Southern French rather than Italian, the architecture is essentially Burgundian, and the people speak a French dialect. Throughout the later Middle Ages town and valley owed allegiance to the great house of Challant, viscounts of Aosta, and latterly the dukedom was a cherished appanage of the house of Savoy. The most famous native of Aosta is St Anselm (1033-1109), Archbishop of Canterbury from 1093. St Bernârd of Menthon (d. c. 1081), founder of the famous Hospice, was Archdeacon of Aosta.

PIAZZA EMILE CHANOUX is the centre of the town, with the *Town Hall* (1837). From here Via Porte Pretoriane leads E. to the **Porta Prætoria,** a massive double gateway of three arches. On the left is the tall rear wall of the *Roman Theatre, comparable with that of Orange, with remains of the cavea and scena. Excavations are being carried out to the S. and W. Via Sant'Anselmo continues E. to the *Arch of Augustus, a triumphal arch erected in 23 B.C. to commemorate the defeat of the Salassi. This is decorated with ten Corinthian columns, and is fairly well preserved though rather disfigured by a roof of 1716. The Crucifixion below was added in 1540. Farther on, beyond the modern bridge over the Buthier, is a remarkable single-arched *Roman Bridge* (still in use) over a dried-up channel.

To the right, on the return, Via Sant'Orso leads to the priory and collegiate church of **Sant'Orso,** or *St-Ours,* founded by St Anselm, with a campanile finished in 1131 and an outré Gothic façade. Within are 16C stalls. Ottonian frescoes (early 11C) in the roof vaulting have recently been restored. They are shown by the sacristan (Tues-Fri 9.30-12, 14-18.30, Sat & Sun until 17.30; closed Mon). By means of platforms and walkways in the roof they can be seen at close range (some of the scenes show the miracles on Lake Gennesaret and at the Marriage at Cana; they were damaged in the 15C by the construction of the vault). In the crypt are 12 plain Roman columns. The venerable CLOISTER (adm. as for the

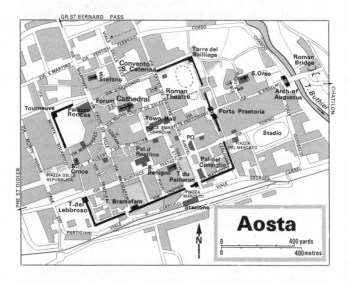

frescoes in the church) has fascinating *Capitals carved in white marble covered with a dark patina. At the top of unusually low columns, they can be examined with ease. The *Priory* (1494-1506), with an octagonal tower, has fine terracotta decoration. Opposite Sant'Orso excavations in the church of *St Laurent* (not yet reopened) have revealed an unusual palaeochristian church with four apses. In the lane behind the priory the *Archæological Museum* has been closed since 1973; it is being slowly transferred to new premises.

Via Sant'Orso continues beyond the church to meet Via Guido Rey which leads left to the *Torre del Baillage,* a 12C addition to the Roman walls, and a goal since 1707. Nearby, in the Convent of St Catherine (ring for adm.), are eight arches of the Roman *Amphitheatre,* a building once capable of holding 15,000 spectators. Some of the arches have been built into the wall of the convent; the others traverse the orchard.

The **Cathedral** (*San Giovanni Battista*), an ancient foundation preserving Romanesque campanili at the E. end, was rebuilt in the Gothic style, and given a sculptured W. portal in 1526, now framed within a neo-classical façade of 1848. In the choir are good mosaic pavements (12C and 14C), one with the Labours of the Months, the other with lively animals and the Tigris and Euphrates. Here also are good stalls (c. 1469) and, on the left of the apse, the tomb of Thomas II of Savoy (d. 1259). The ambulatory contains the tombs of two bishops (c. 1375 and 1431), of local workmanship.

The *Treasury* (adm. only with special permission) contains an ivory diptych of 406, and reliquaries of SS. Gratus and Jucundus, local patron saints; the Romanesque *Crypt* has antique columns. The cloister to the N. of the church dates from 1460.

In a sunken garden on the N.W. side of the cathedral are some remains of the *Roman Forum* with the base of a temple. From here there is access (daily 8-12, 14-18) to a splendid underground *Cryptoporticus* (perhaps used as a horreum). The double north walk, over 92 metres long, is particularly remarkable.

The ***Roman Walls**, forming a rectangle c. 732 m long and 572 m broad, are in best preservation on the S. and W. sides. Standing across the W. wall is the medieval *Torre del Lebbroso,* celebrated in Xavier de Maistre's tale, 'Le Lépreux de la Cité d'Aoste'. Near the *Torre Bramafam,* a relic (11C) of the lords of Challant, remains of the Porta Principalis Dextera have been unearthed; while the *Torre del Pailleron* stands in a garden near the station.

The road (bus) crossing the Dora Báltea by the Pont Suaz, S. of Aosta, ascends in rapid zigzags through the hamlets of Charvensod to (12 km.) *Péroulaz* (1364 m), also reached by cableway. From *Les Fleurs,* a little higher up, a chair-lift ascends to *Pila* (1914 m; 6 km. farther by road) with easy ski-slopes, connected by ski-lift with *Chamolé* (2310 m) on the N. slope of the ridge separating the main valley from the Val de Cogne.—The **Becca di Nona** (3142 m; 6 hrs; guide optional) is reached from Péroulaz by a track leading past the hermitage of *St-Grat* and over the *Col de Plan-Fenêtre* (2225 m) to (4 hrs) *Comboé* (2121 m), 2 hrs below the summit, on which is a statue of the Virgin. The *View of the Alps extends from Mont Blanc to the Mischabelhörner. The descent may be made viâ the *Col d'Arbolé* (2868 m) to (6 hrs) *Cogne.*—The ascent of **Mont Émilius** (3559 m; 9 hrs; guide desirable) is made viâ Comboé (see above), the *Lac d'Qrbolé* (2961 m), and the S. arête.—*Mont Fallère* (3061 m; 6½ hrs; guide desirable), to the N., is reached by an easy track viâ *Sarre* and the *Val Clusetta,* or viâ *St-Pierre* and *Verrogne* (see below). The descent may be made to Gignod. St-Oyen (see below), or the Combe de Vertosan and St-Nicolas (p. 67).

FROM AOSTA TO THE GREAT ST BERNARD, 34 km. by the old road to the pass (usually closed in Nov-May); 29 km. to the tunnel mouth. The road (N 27) affords striking views, including that of Aosta itself. Amidst a country of trellised vines and fields of maize is (4½ km.) *Variney* (785 m), where a road diverges to Valpelline. On the other side of the valley, 152 m below, lies Roisan.—8 km. *Gignod* (994 m) has a 15C church tower on the ruins of an ancient castle.—From (11 km) *Condemine* (1128 m) there is a magnificent view of the whole length of the Valpelline.—At (16 km.) **Étroubles** (1280 m), a quiet summer resort, the road crosses the stream and there is an impressive view up the valley, closed by the Grand Golliaz and the Aiguille d'Artanavaz.—18 km. *St-Oyen* (1376 m) may be taken as a base for the ascent of (5 hrs) *Mont Fallère* (3061 m) viâ the Col Flassin. A little farther on the road divides.

The left branch, following the infant Artavanaz through *St-Léonard,* becomes motorway, making a long loop to the W. before turning E., then N. beneath long snow galleries. The Italian custom-house is just below the tunnel mouth. The **Great St Bernard Tunnel,** built in 1958-64, is 5.8 km. long and rises slightly from the Italian side (1875 m) to the Swiss (1918 m).

The old road (r.), narrow and sometimes slippery, climbs through (22 km.) *St-Rhémy* (1632 m), a dreary village. From 1658 until 1915 the young men of Étroubles and St-Rhémy exercised the right to act as guides and snow-sweepers on the St Bernard road instead of serving in the army. To the N.W. is a view of the striking *Pain de Sucre* (2793 m). The old bridle-path, which keeps to the right side of the valley, saves walkers c. ½ hr. The Italian customs post on the Swiss border by a small lake, lies some distance beyond the Albergo Italia. Just beyond the frontier is (34 km.) the **Great St Bernard Hospice** (2469 m; post office), one of the highest habitations in Europe, a massive stone building on the summit of the pass, exposed to storms from the N.E. and S.W. On the N.W. it is sheltered by the *Chenalette* (2889 m), on the S.E. by *Mont Mort* (2867 m).

The Hospice was supposedly founded in the 11C by St Bernard of Menthon, archdeacon of Aosta, a native of Savoy, though the earliest known documents (1125) called it then after St Nicolas; by 1215 it was regularly manned by Austin canons from their mother-house at Martigny, and its riches, both in lands and money, increased steadily until the Reformation. The resources of the monks were severely taxed by Napoleon, who, though he made numerous donations to the Hospice, quartered a garrison of 40 men there for some months. Since 1925 the Hospice has been managed by 10 or 12 canons assisted by a number of lay brothers or 'marronniers'. In their rescue of snow-bound travellers the canon are assisted by the famous St Bernard dogs, a breed said to be a cross between the Pyrenean sheep-dog and the Newfoundland, although modern conditions have made their services much less important.

The pass of the **Great St Bernard* (2472 m) is more remarkable for its historical and religious associations than for its scenery, which, though interesting, is less impressive than that on most of the other great passes. Known and used by Celts and Romans, its ancient name was *Mons Jovis* (Mont Joux), from a temple of Jupiter Poeninus which once stood on the Plan de Jupiter, and it was only in the 12C that it acquired its present style. The pass was much frequented by pilgrims and clerics bound to or from Rome, and between 774 and 1414 it was crossed twenty times by the medieval emperors, including Frederick Barbarossa in 1162. In the campaigns of 1798-1800 many French and Austrian soldiers crossed the pass. The most famous passage was made by Napoleon, who, on 14-20 May 1800, led 40,000 troops by this route into Italy and a month later defeated the Austrians at the battle of Marengo. Each regiment occupied three days on the passage, halting the first night at Bourg-St-Pierre, the second at St-Rhémy or Étroubles, the third at Aosta.

The road, now Swiss No. 21, descends viâ (41 km.) *Bourg St Pierre* and (55 km.) *Orsières* to (61 km.) *Sembrancher* and (73 km.) **Martigny**.

The VALPELLINE, N.E. of Aosta, affords an unfrequented route to the foot of the Pennine Alps and is ascended by buses from Aosta. From (4½ km.) *Variney*, on the St Bernard road (see above), the road descends to cross the Buthier.—13 km. **Valpelline** (951 m) stands at the junction of the Val d'Ollomont with the main valley. In the former, 3 km. N., lies *Ollomont* (1336 m), with disused copper mines, and now an excursion centre. It lies at the foot of the *Col de Fenêtre* (2786 m), 5 hrs farther viâ Vaud and Balme, the uppermost group of chalets. Calvin escaped into Switzerland by this pass after an unsuccessful attempt at reforming the Aostans. Just off the path to the left is (2 hrs) the beautiful alpine basin of *By* (2042 m) beneath *Mont Vélan* (3709 m). Above it (5½ hrs) lies the *Rif. d'Amiante* (2964 m).

The narrow Valpelline road now ascends N.E. past a power station to (20 km.) *Oyace* (1367 m), high above the Buthier, with an old tower of the lords of the valley. To the S. towers the imposing *Monte Faroma* (3073 m).—The road continues beyond (26 km.) *Bionaz* (1600 m) to a dam, from where the arduous *Col de Luseney* (3265 m) leads into the Val St-Barthélemy in 6 hrs; the higher village of Chamin here was wiped out in 1952 by a landslide.—1½ hrs. *Prarayé* (1993 m), the uppermost hamlet in the valley, lies at the foot of two frontier passes into Switzerland, the *Col de Collon* (Refuge; 3130 m), and the *Col de Valpelline* (3562 m). On the way to the latter is the *Rifugio Aosta* (2850 m), on the Za-de-Zan Glacier, above which rises the *Dent d'Hérens* (4180 m). Unfrequented passes lead E. in 7½-10 hrs to Breuil and Valtournanche (Rte 3D).

The Courmayeur road, beyond *Sarre* with its 13C Castle rebuilt in 1710 (decorated with hunting trophies, open on request), reaches (133 km.) *St-Pierre* (661 m), with its restored castle on an isolated rock, affording a good view S. On the S. side is the castle (mainly 14C) of *Sarriod de la Tour*. The road on the right ascends in 8 km. to *St-Nicolas* (1126 m), a little summer resort.

To the S. extends the Val di Cogne, traversed by a road (N 507; bus from Aosta) through (1 km.) *Aymaville*, with its turreted castle (mostly 18C).—5 km. *Pondel* has a Roman bridge of 3 B.C. over the Grand'Eyvia.—21½ km. **Cogne** (1533 m) stands in a wide basin at the junction of the main valley with the Valnontey, which runs due S. to the Gran Paradiso. It is a favourite summer and winter resort, and has some of the most productive magnetite mines in the country.

Several easy passes lead W. into the Valsavaranche (8-9 hrs), notably the *Col de Lauson* (3301 m), reached viâ (4 hrs) the *Rif. Vitt. Sella* (2588 m). The finest ascent is that of the *Punta Tersiva* (3512 m; 7 hrs with guide), viâ the Grauson valley and *Ervillières;* more difficult are those of the *Grivola* (3969 m), 8½ hrs E., rewarded by a *View of the Val d'Aosta; the **Gran Paradiso** (4061 m), 12 hrs S. by the romantic *Valnontey*, with glaciers at its head, and in which is the 'Paradisia' alpine garden founded in 1955, and the *Gran San Pietro* (3692 m; 9½ hrs S.E.). The last is approached viâ (½ hr) *Champlong*, the basin of *Lillaz,* and the *Valeille.*—From Cogne to *Champorcher*, see p. 62.

The whole of the Gran Paradiso massif, extending from the E. ridge of the Val de Rhêmes (W.) to the upper Val Soana (E.), including the upper Valsavaranche, the Valnontey and the Valeille, and bounded on the S. by the N. side of the Locana valley, an area of 971 sq. km., is dedicated as the **National Park of the Gran Paradiso**, in which hunting, shooting, and digging up plants are rigorously prohibited. The park was started as a hunting preserve for Victor Emmanuel II in 1856; presented to the State by Victor Emmanuel III in 1919, it was established as a nature reserve in 1922. This is the only part of the Alps in which the ibex (stambecco) has survived in its natural state, and the chamois and Alpine marmot are common. The flowers are at their best in May-June. The construction of a power-reservoir on the Nivolet plateau has caused little disturbance. Ordinary visitors can find accommodation on the borders of the park and climbers are allowed to use the Alpine refuges on the Col du Nivolet, the Gran Paradiso (Rif. Vitt. Emanuele II), and the Grivola (Rif. Vitt. Sella). Permission to use the 'case' and 'casotti' of the park organization may be obtained from the Direzione del Parco N.G.P. in Turin.

136 km. **Villeneuve** (671 m), an unattractive village beneath the ruined 12C Châtel d'Argent, is the best starting-point for exploring the Valsavaranche and Val de Rhêmes. These twin valleys join the Val d'Aosta just W. of Villeneuve.

The **Valsavaranche**, to the E., is ascended by bus in summer viâ (4 km.) *Introd,* with its castle and medieval tithe barn. The bus terminus is at (17 km.) *Dégioz* (1541 m), but the road goes on to (20 km.) *Eaux-Rousses* (1666 m) and to (25 km.) *Pont Valsavaranche* (1946 m). Dégioz is connected with Rhêmes-Notre-Dame and with Cogne by several easy passes. A royal hunting road built by Victor Emmanuel II leads from Dégioz, over the Nivolet plateau and pass, to the Gran Piano di Noasca (2222 m) and, beyond several other passes, descends to Noasca (p. 61). Pont is a base for the ascent of the *Gran Paradiso* (see above; 6-7 hrs), reached viâ the *Rif. Vitt. Emanuele II* (2775 m).—From the head of the valley the Col du Nivolet leads viâ the Rifugio Città di Chivasso (2604 m) to Ceresole Reale (p. 61) in 6 hrs (road in construction).

The **Val de Rhêmes**, farther W., is ascended by bus in summer from Villeneuve to (9 km.) Rhêmes-St-Georges (1170 m) and (19 km.) *Rhêmes-Notre-Dame* (1676 m) in a charming upland basin. Passes lead E. into the Valsavaranche (across the Entrelor pass, 3007 m) and W. into the Valgrisanche. The striking peak at the head of the vale is the *Granta Parey* (3474 m; reached viâ the Rifugio Benevolo, 2285 m), but the most repaying ascent (c. 8 hrs) is that of *Mont Tout-Blanc* (3439 m) to the S.E.

141 km. *Arvier* (774 m), with the 13C Château de la Mothe, grows good wine and stands at the foot of the Valgrisanche.

The **Valgrisanche,** narrow and rocky in its lower reaches, and almost blocked by the castle-crowned rock of Montmajeur, is ascended by a bus in summer.—10 km. *Planaval* (1554 m), with a distant view of the Matterhorn, and (16 km.) *Valgrisanche* (1664 m), the bus terminus, with a fine campanile, are the principal centres. To the W. rises the *Rutor* (3486 m). A huge dam holds the waters of the *Lago di Beauregard,* a long power-reservoir, along which a track leads to *Surier,* 1½ hrs higher up. From here the *Col du Mont* (2632 m; bridle-path open in summer) leads across the frontier to Ste-Foy-Tarentaise in 7 hrs. At the head of the valley, 2 hrs more, is the *Rifugio Bezzi* (2281 m) dominated by the *Grande Sassière* (3756 m).

Passing *Avise* (r.), a pleasant village with three castles (10C, 12C, and 15C), the road threads the fine gorge of the Pierre-Taillée and, crossing the Dora (785 m), comes into view of Mont Blanc. On the opposite side of the river is seen the village of *Derby,* notable for its medieval houses.— 149 km. *La Salle.*—Beyond the 13C tower of Châtelard (r.) is (152 km.) **Morgex** (920 m), the principal village in the Valdigne, the upper valley of the Dora. The church has 6C elements.

156 km. **Pré-St-Didier** (1010 m) is a little holiday resort with an 11C church tower and chalybeate springs, at the junction of the Dora de la Thuile and the Dora Báltea. It is the terminus of the railway from Aosta and stands at the foot of the Little St Bernard Pass.

The *Tête de Crammont* (2737 m) is easily ascended in 4½ hrs from the Little St Bernard road, ½ hr along which a path ascends through larches on the right to within ½ hr of the summit. The *View is one of the most remarkable in the district. The whole of the Mont Blanc massif is visible, from the Aiguille des Glaciers in the S.W. to Mont Dolent in the N.E. Farther E. may be recognized Mont Vélan, the Grand Combin, the Matterhorn, and Monte Rosa; to the S.E. extends the lovely valley of Aosta, while farther S. is the enormous ice-field of the Rutor with the Grivola and Gran Paradiso behind.

FROM PRÉ-ST-DIDIER TO BOURG-ST MAURICE, 54 km. N 26 branches left and ascends in zigzags high above the gorge of the Dora de la Thuile, passing through two tunnels.—10 km. **La Thuile** (1440 m), a summer and winter resort in a pastoral basin amid wooded mountain-slopes. It has good ski-ing facilities.

From Grande Golette, at the foot of the Val des Chavannes (r.), a chair-lift ascends in two stages, on the left, to *Les Suches* (2149 m) and *Chaz Dura* (2560 m), affording access to remarkably fine ski-slopes. The best summer expeditions are the ascent of *Mont Bério Blanc* (3258 m), 6 hrs N. with guide, viâ the Val des Chavannes; and by the good track to (3¼ hrs S.) the *Lac du Rutor,* passing three fine waterfalls. The *Rutor* (3486 m) is climbed from the lake in 7 hrs, with guide.

Beyond the *Pont Serrant* (1650 m), high above the torrent, *Lac Verney* (2085 m; fine view of Mont Blanc from the shore; good fishing) can be seen on the right. At (22 km.) is the frontier, near which remains of a Roman posting-station and an old hospice have been found. Here is the Italian customs post. Just over the frontier is (23 km.) the **Little St Bernard Pass** (2188 m), on the watershed between the Dora Báltea and the Isère.

Nearby is the *Colonne de Joux* (Jupiter's Column) a Celtic or Roman monument of cipollino marble, with a statue of St Bernard added in 1886, and a little below it is an Iron Age stone burial circle just over 73 m in diameter, in which Gaulish and Roman coins have been discovered. The best view is gained from the *Belvedere* (2641 m; path to the left, 1 hr).

A gentle descent leads past the ruined *Hospice du Petit-St-Bernard* (2152 m), the medieval Hospitale Columnæ Jovis, founded c. 1000, which used to offer free hospitality to poor travellers. After war damage, it was ceded to France in 1947 and is now derelict. The monks, who depended for food on an estate near Paris, have mostly moved to Ycone, near Martigny (Switzerland). The Botanical Garden founded here in 1897 by Abbot Pierre Chanoux may be reconstituted. The descent goes on, through forest, to (51 km.) *Séez* (904 m), with the French custom-houses, and (54 km.) **Bourg-St-Maurice.**

A new superstrada (N 26 dir) ascends past the hamlets of *Pallusieux* (1108 m) and *Verrand* (1250 m), served by the old steep and winding road.

161 km. **Courmayeur** (1228 m), situated in a deep vale at the S. foot of the Mont Blanc range, is the Chamonix of Piedmont, but enjoys a much milder climate than its rival of Savoy. It is frequented in summer, by both alpinists and lovers of mountain scenery, and winter sports flourish. The winter season lasts from mid-Dec to mid-April.

Hotels, some seasonal, here, and many others in the near environs; and at Entrèves, La Palud, and Dolonne.
Golf course (9 holes; July-Aug) at Planpincieux in the Val Ferret (see below).—
Winter Sports. *Ski School* in winter in the village, in summer at the Rifugio Torino. Cableways from the village and from La Palud, see below.
Buses to *Planpincieux, Pré-St-Didier, Petit-St-Bernard, Chamonix, Cogne, Aosta, Morgex, St-Vincent, Turin* and *Milan.*
A cableway, passing above *Dolonne* to the W., ascends viâ *Plan Chécrouit* (1696 m) to the *Col de Chécruit* (1899 m), whence *Mont Chétif* can be reached on foot in 1½ hrs. The view of the abyss of the Allée Blanche, and of the Aiguille Noire de Peuterey, is impressive. The cable cars go on to *Creta d'Arp* (2755 m), affording another marvellous view of the chain of Mont Blanc.—The *Mont de la Saxe* (2358 m), N.E. of Courmayeur, is easily accessible in 3 hrs by bridle-path viâ Villair and Le Pré; the finest view of the Grandes Jorasses is obtained from the slightly higher *Tête Bernarde* (2534 m), the N.E. peak of this group.

FROM COURMAYEUR TO THE COL FERRET (Orsières), 5 hrs on foot. The road leads N. and reaches the long VAL FERRET at (3 km.) *Entrèves* (1300 m), a hamlet with a castle between the old road and the superstrada (see below).—3½ km. *La Palud* (1370 m), with the lower station of the Mont-Blanc cable railway (see below).—The road goes on viâ the chalets of (6 km.) *Planpincieux* (1448 m), between which and (10 km.) *La Vachey,* but beyond the stream, lies the golf course.—At (15 km.) the foot of the Triolet Glacier the road ends, and the ascent continues by a good bridle-path to (¾ hr) the *Pré-de-Bar* chalets (2060 m).—2¼ hrs. The **Col Ferret** (2533 m) lies on the Swiss frontier, between the Italian Val Ferret and the Swiss Val Ferret. The most interesting feature of the view is the long stretch of valley, including the whole of the Val Ferret and Val Veni leading up to the Col de la Seigne, 29 km. away. The Grandes Jorasses hide the summit of Mont Blanc, and on the Swiss side the Grand Combin and Mont Vélan are prominent.—The descent to *Orsières* in Switzerland takes 3¾ hrs.

FROM COURMAYEUR TO THE COL DE LA SEIGNE (Les Chapieux), 5 hrs on foot. The road crosses the Dora beyond Le Larzey and ascends the right bank, rounding Mont Chétif.—4 km. *Notre-Dame de la Guérison* commands a view of the Grandes Jorasses above Entrèves and the Val Ferret, and of the Brenva Glacier. The road ascends the VAL VENI, leaving on the right (6 km.) *Purtud* (1490 m), and traverses the forest of St-Nicolas. The road deteriorates at (9 km.) the inn of La Visaille (1658 m), above which towers the Aiguille Noire de Peuterey, with the Aiguille Blanche and the Dames Anglaises behind. A good track goes on to (1 hr) *Lac Combal* (1940 m), formed by the partial stoppage of the Dora by a moraine of the Miage Glacier; c. 91 m higher up to the right is the *Lac de Miage* in a wild setting at the foot of the glacier. The Val de l'Allée-Blanche (La Lex Blanche, 'lex' signifying a mountain pasture), the uppermost basin of the Dora valley, leads on viâ the Rifugio Elisabetta (2156 m) to (3 hrs) the **Col de la Seigne** (2512 m; refuge huts), on the French frontier, the water-shed between the basins of the Po and the Rhône. The *View is magnificent. The route on to (2 hrs) *Les Chapieux* lies in Switzerland.

Lac Combal is the starting-point of the most usual ascent of Mont Blanc from the Italian side (11½ hrs; guide essential) viâ the Miage Glacier and (3½ hrs) the *Refuge du Dôme* or *Rifugio Gonella* (3120 m), whence the route runs viâ the W. branch of the Glacier du Dôme and the *Col de Bionnassay* (3880 m). The night may be spent at (8½ hrs) the *Cabane Vallot* (4362 m), near the old and new observatories, beyond which the steepest part of the climb leads past the Bosses du Dromadaire and the Rochers de la Tourette.—11½ hrs **Mont Blanc** (4810 m), the highest mountain in western Europe, commands a view (too often obscured by clouds) remarkable for extent rather than for any feature of individual beauty, ranging from the Dauphiny Alps to the Bernina and from the Côte d'Or to the Apennines. The highest summit is in France.

FROM COURMAYEUR TO CHAMONIX BY CABLE RAILWAY, c. 1 hr. This *Traverse of the Mont Blanc massif is the most sensational excursion from Courmayeur. Its working depends, naturally enough, on the weather, but normally a car starts every hour from La Palud. Passengers going the whole way should be in possession of French money as well as a passport. The last car for the return leaves Chamonix at 16.45.

From La Palud (see above) the route ascends (all the year), with a break at the *Pavillon du Mont-Fréty* (2131 m; *View) to (¼ hr) the **Rifugio Torino** (3322 m). There are three ski-lifts serving the adjoining slopes, and a summer ski-school. A little higher is the **Col du Géant** (3369 m). It commands a magnificent panorama of the Graian Alps, to the S., and the S. side of the Pennine Alps, to the W. From the pass Chamonix is reached on foot in 6 hrs viâ Montenvers (not difficult, but guide essential).

The next stage of the railway leads to the *Punta Helbronner* (3462 m), which marks the frontier; thence the line goes on, across the magnificent expanse of the Vallée Blanche, to the Gros Rogon and (40 min.) the *Aiguille du Midi* station. The descent to *Chamonix* (55 min.) leads viâ the Plan des Aiguilles.

The superstrada bypasses Entrèves and La Palud (comp. above) and, beyond a short tunnel, reaches the Italian customs-post (1381 m) by the mouth of (166 km.) the **Traforo del Monte Bianco**, the world's longest road tunnel (11.6 km.), opened through the mountains in 1958-65. At the far end (1274 m) a brief zigzag descends to (181 km.) **Chamonix-Mont Blanc** in France.

3   NORTHERN PIEDMONT

A   From Domodóssola to Aosta

3½-4 days. ROAD to *Macugnaga*, 40 km. (bus 2-4 times daily in 2-2¼ hrs). BRIDLE-PATH to *Alagna*, 8 hrs, thence to *Gressoney-St-Jean*, 6½ hrs, thence to *Brusson*, 4 hrs, and thence to *St-Vincent*, 3 hrs; RAILWAY or BUS (27 km.) *Aosta* in c. 1 hr. This magnificent cross-country route for walkers, presenting no difficulty in fine weather, follows the S. side of the main massif of **Monte Rosa**. The nights may be spent at Macugnaga, Alagna, and Gressoney or Brusson.—Rima, Alagna, Gressoney, and Brusson are all connected by bus with the main railway system.

From Domodóssola to (9 km.) *Pallanzeno*, see Rte 10.—N 549 ascends rapidly from (12 km.) *Piedimulera* (248 m), affording a fine backward view of the Val d'Ossola, and soon enters the VALLE ANZASCA, down which flows the Anza amid scenery which combines the loveliness of Italy with the grandeur of Switzerland. After two short rock-tunnels, a distant view of Monte Rosa towers at the head of the valley.—16 km. *Castiglione d'Ossola* (514 m) lies near the foot of the *Valle della Segnara* (2 km. farther on).—The road descends to the level of the Anza, crossing the torrent of the Val Bianca, with its waterfalls, just before reaching (23 km.) *Pontegrande* (510 m).

Here a road on the left diverges for (½ hr) **Bannio-Anzino** (669 m), the chief village of the Valle Anzasca, with a picturesque campanile and a fine bronze figure of Christ (probably 16C Flemish). From Bannio the *Colle d'Orchetta,* W. of the *Cima di Capezzone* (2421 m), leads to (6½ hrs) *Fobello* (see Rte 9).

An alternative route into the Val Sesia starts from Pontegrande and ascends past Bannio to (3½ hrs) the *Alpe de Selle.* From here the path on the right crosses (4 hrs) the *Colle d'Egua* (2236 m), whence a short descent leads to (5½ hrs) *Carcóforo* (1303 m), in a wooded upland vale. Hence the Egua valley descends to (7 hrs) **Rimasco** (905 m), which is connected by road with Balmuccia (see Rte 9). At Rimasco the road ascends W. up the Val Sermenza.—At (8½ hrs) **Rima** (1417 m) the road ends and ascending a side valley to the W., it is possible to cross either the easy *Colle di Moud* (2323 m), 1½ hrs N. of *Monte Tágiaferro* (2964 m), or the *Bocchetta Moanda* (2419 m) to the S., reaching *Alagna* (see below) in 5 hrs more. The latter pass affords the finer views of Monte Rosa.—From Rima or Carcóforo to *Macugnaga,* see below.

From Pontegrande, or from *Vanzone,* 3 km. farther on, several passes afford access to the Val d'Antrona (p. 120) in 7-9 hrs.

30 km. *Ceppo Morelli* (753 m) has a remarkably steep bridge crossing the Anza. Above *Prequartera* the valley appears blocked by an enormous rock called the *Morghen,* which in fact divides the Valle Anzasca proper from the Macugnaga basin. The road runs through a narrow gorge and emerges at (35 km.) *Pestarena* (1154 m), the first hamlet of the commune of Macugnaga, where gold-bearing ore is worked.—At (37 km.) *Borca* (1202 m) begins the Colle del Turlo (see below), but it is preferable to go on to (40 km.) *Staffa,* the chief centre of the scattered commune of **Macugnaga** (1326 m). The valley is inhabited largely by the descendants of an Alemannic colony transplanted from the Valais in 1262-90. It is now a popular summer resort, famed for its wonderful prospect of Monte Rosa, of which the Macugnaga face is the most stupendous 'wall' in the Alps, and with the construction of ski-lifts has developed into an important winter-sports centre. The *Old Church* (late 13C; restored in 1580), above Staffa, preserves German characteristics in its S. door and chancel windows. The road ends at (41 km.) *Pecetto* (1399 m), the highest of the commune's hamlets.

From here a chair-lift ascends in two stages to the *Belvedere* (1932 m), or *Wengwald,* a fine viewpoint, as its name implies, above the wooded medial moraine of the Macugnaga Glacier. The return (3½ hrs; guide desirable) may be made by crossing the N. arm of the glacier to the chalets of *Jazzi,* and from there to *Fillar* (1981 m). Here the ascent traverses the glacier itself, emerging on the other side at the *Pedriola Alp* (2053 m; Rifugio Zamboni), from where a rough descent of 2-2½ hrs leads to Macugnaga viâ the chalets of Crosa and Rosareccio (where a cableway also descends to Pecetto).

There are ski-lifts above and below Pecetto, and a cableway from Staffa to the *Passo Monte Moro* (2868 m; Rif. Bionda).

ASCENTS (with guides). The *Pizzo Bianco* (3216 m), 5 hrs S.W., commands a fine view of Monte Rosa.—The *Cima di Jazzi* (3827 m) is ascended in 8 hrs viâ the *Eugenio Sella Refuge* (3150 m), 5½ hrs).—**Monte Rosa** itself (*Dufourspitze,* 4638 m) has been ascended from Macugnaga, but this route, though not unduly difficult for the expert, is one of the most dangerous in the Alps on account of its frequent avalanches. The *Marinelli Refuge* (3100 m), named in memory of a climber who lost his life in attempting this ascent, is easily reached in 6 hrs.

FROM MACUGNAGA TO ALAGNA VIÂ THE COLLE DEL TURLO, 8 hrs (guide useful).—This is at once the most arduous and the most uninteresting part of the journey, and travellers with time can make a detour to Rima, either from Pontegrande (see above), or else by the Colle del Piccolo Altare (see below). The bridle-path from Macugnaga (Staffa) crosses the Anza, and descends its right bank, joining the direct route from Borca (see above) at *Quarazza* (1304 m). Here begins the ascent of the Val Quarazza to the S.—At (2½ hrs) *La Piana* (1609 m), near the beautiful cascade of La Pissa, a path diverges on the left for Rima and Carcóforo, while a little farther up the valley the path to Rima over the *Colle del Piccolo Altare* (2630 m) bears off to the left. Monte Rosa is seen better from these passes (each c. 7 hrs from Macugnaga) than from the Turlo. The remainder of the ascent lies over rocks and debris and finally crosses a small snowfield before reaching (4½ hrs) the **Colle del Turlo** (2736 m), the pass between the *Corno di Faller* (3128 m), to the W., and the *Corno Piglimò* (2894 m). The descent on the S.W. side follows a former military road. At (6 hrs) the *Faller Alp* (1987 m), the steep descent into the Val Sesia begins. After the waterfall of the Acqua Bianca the floor of the valley is reached at (c. 7 hrs) the chapel of *Sant'Antonio* (1388 m). A road continues left passing (r.) the disused gold-mines of Creas.

8 hrs **Alagna Valsesia** (1183 m), a village at the head of the Val Sesia, has become fashionable as a summer resort. There is a chair-lift to the plateau of *Otro* (1673 m), a good ski-ground.

FROM ALAGNA TO GRESSONEY-LA TRINITÉ VIÂ THE COLLE D'OLEN, 7 hrs (guide not required). A well-marked path leads to the *Sevii Alp*, and an easy ascent continues to (2 hrs) the *Città di Mortara Refuge* (1999 m) and (4½ hrs) the **Colle d'Olen** (2871 m; *Rif. Città di Vigevano*) which commands a good view of the Graian Alps. About ¼ hr E. of the pass is the *Mosso International Scientific Institute*, built in 1905-07 at the instance of Angelo Mosso (1846-1910), the physiologist. From the *Corno del Camoscio* or *Gemshorn* (3026 m), ½ hr N., which commands a finer view of the grand line of snow peaks from Monte Rosa to the Gran Paradiso, a path descends S.W. to (7 hrs) the *Gabiet Alp* (2362 m), with two refuges. At (6¾ hrs) *Orsia* (1751 m; also reached by cableway from the Gabiet) the path reaches the Lys valley, which is descended to (7 hrs) Gressoney-la-Trinité (Rte 3B).—The journey can now be made more quickly by taking the *Funivia di Monte Rosa*, a cableway in three stages (viâ Bocchetta delle Pisse, with ski lifts), to *Punta Indren*, 1½ hr's walk due N. of the Corno di Camoscio (comp. above). Punta Indren is the starting-point for the ascent (via the new Linty Refuge) to the *Gnifetti Refuge* (3647 m; 1½ hrs) and the *Punta Gnifetti* (4561 m; Regina Margherita Refuge), reached in 5 hrs.

From Alagna to *Varallo* and *Novara*, see Rte 9; to *Rima* and *Rimasco*, see above.

FROM ALAGNA TO GRESSONEY-ST-JEAN VIÂ THE COLLE VALDOBBIA, 6½ hrs (guide not required).—This is the easiest route from the Val Sesia to the Val de Lys, but it is surpassed in interest and beauty by the higher Colle d'Olen (see above).—The Val Sesia is descended as far as (3 km.; ½ hr) *Riva Valdobbia* (Rte 9) where a turn to the right follows the Valle Vogna.—1 hr. *Ca' d'Ianzo* (1359 m).—From (2 hrs) *Peccia* (1532 m) the track ascends a side valley on the right.

From the head of the Valle Vogna a fine mountain walk leads on across three passes (*Colli del Maccagno*, 2495 m; *di Loozoney*, 2410 m; *della Mologna Grande*, 2446 m; *Rif. Rivetti*) and descends to (9½ hrs) *Piedicavallo* (Rte 9).

4½ hrs. The **Colle Valdobbia** (2479 m), between the *Cresta Rossa* (2986 m), to the N., and the *Corno Rosso* (2976 m), commands a fine view of the Gran Paradiso, to the S.W. A rapid descent follows.—6½ hrs. **Gressoney-St-Jean** (1385 m), see Rte 3B.

FROM GRESSONEY-ST-JEAN TO BRUSSON VIÂ THE COLLE DELLA RANZOLA. 4 hrs.—The well-marked but steep bridle-path ascends from the right bank of the Lys, opposite the Valdobbia path, and leaves on the left Castel Savoia, a favourite residence of Queen Margherita (d. 1926). A steep ascent leads to the Ranzola Alp (good view of the Val de Lys), and a little farther on (c. 2½ hrs) the **Colle della Ranzola** (2171 m), from which Mont Blanc is visible in clear weather. A much more extensive view is gained from the *Punta di Combetta* or *della Regina* (2390 m), ½

hr S. Another interesting ascent is that of *Monte Tiosè* (2647 m), 1¾ hrs
N.E. The latter is best reached from the chalets of *Prabarmasse* (1910 m),
below the pass on the W. side. The descent is gradual as far as (3¼ hrs)
Estoul (1812 m), a hamlet which commands a good view of the lower Val
Challant and of the castle of *Graines* (p. 74) not far below. From here a
steep zigzag path descends to (4 hrs) **Brusson** (1330 m), see Rte 3C.

FROM BRUSSON TO ST-VINCENT VIÂ THE COL DE JOUX, 2¼-3 hrs (Road,
22 km.). The road ascends through magnificent forests to (1¼-1½ hrs)
the **Col de Joux** (1638 m), which is not strictly a pass, but merely a
grassgrown plateau on the S.E. shoulder of *Mont Zerbion* (2721 m). It is
connected by road (bus) with St-Vincent.—1¾ hrs. *Amay* (1490 m)
affords a wonderful view of the upper Val d'Aosta.—2½ hrs. *Moron* has
an old church.—3 hrs. **St-Vincent,** and thence to *Aosta* (27 km.), see
Rte 2.

B   From Pont-St-Martin to Gressoney-la-Trinité

ROAD, 34 m. BUS 2-3 times daily (oftener in summer) in 1¼ hrs; through coaches
from Genoa and (in summer) Turin and Milan.

The **Val de Lys**, whose most important commune is Gressoney, contains the
largest and oldest of the German-speaking colonies which crossed over from Valais
in the Middle Ages. The people of this valley, who are mentioned as early as 1218,
were subjects of the Bishop of Sion, they have kept their language and customs
even more distinct from their Italian neighbours than have the people of Alagna or
Macugnaga, and both the attractive chalets ('rascards'), and the costume of the
women, which is brightly coloured and adorned with hand-made lace, argue a
Northern origin. Though politically Italian, and with a German-speaking
population, it is odd that the commune bears a purely French name.

Pont-St-Martin, see Rte 2.—7 km. *Lillianes* (655 m) and (10 km.)
Fontainemore (760 m) are surrounded by luxuriant chestnut groves.—
12 km. *Pont de Guillemore* is an old bridge spanning the Lys where it
plunges into a deep chasm.—14 km. *Issime* (939 m) and (18 km.) *Gaby*
(1032 m) are summer resorts, the former German speaking, the latter
with a Provençal patois. At Issime the church, rebuilt after 1567, has a
repainted Last Judgement by the brothers De Henricis on its façade.

From Issime the *Bec de Frudière* (3075 m) may be ascended in 7 hrs for the sake
of the *View. The final ascent starts from the *Col de Chasten* (2552 m), which
connects Issime with (6 hrs) *Quinçod.*—The *Colle della Vecchia* (2185 m) leads
from Gaby to Piedicavallo in 6½ hrs.

The road ascends the beautiful Val de Lys, of which (28 km.)
Gressoney-St-Jean (1385 m) is the principal village. It is a quiet summer
resort, frequented also in winter, with a chair-lift on the W. side to
Weissmatten (or Pra' Bianco; 2019 m).—At the end of the road is
(34 km.) the sister-village of **Gressoney-la-Trinité** (1628 m), a pleasant
mountaineering and ski-ing resort.

On the E. side of the valley a chair-lift rises to *Punta Iolanda* (2350 m), and a
cableway mounts to the Alpe Gabiet (p. 72). For the cross-country routes to
Alagna and Brusson, see Rte 3A.

PASSES. FROM GRESSONEY-ST-JEAN TO CHAMPOLUC, 6-7 hrs.—The
ordinary route ascends the valley to (35 min.) *Chemonal,* whence a well-marked
path ascends past the chalets of *Alpenzù Grande* (1666 m) and *Alpenzù Piccolo*
(1805 m), where the route from La Trinité is joined, for *Montil* (2480 m) and (4 hrs)
the *Colle di Pinter* (2780 m). The descent viâ the *Alpe Cunéaz* (2047 m) to (6½ hrs)
Champoluc (Rte 3C) is less well marked.—An alternative route (7 hrs) crosses (4
hrs) the *Passo di Mascognaz* (2947 m), below which a bridle-path leads to the *Alpe
Mascognaz* (1827 m) and *Champoluc* (Rte 3C).

FROM GRESSONEY-LA-TRINITÉ TO FIÉRY viâ the easy *Colle de la Bettaforca* (2676m; limited view), 5 hrs by bridle-path, starting up the main valley. The ascent begins at *Selbsteg* and passes (1½hrs) the chapel of *Sant'Amnna*. From (2¾hrs) the pass the descent is through (4¼hrs) *Résy* (2065m).—5 hrs. *Fiéry*, see Rte 3C.

ASCENTS. The *Testa Grigia* or *Grauhaupt* (3315m) is worth ascending (6½ hrs, with guide). From the Colle di Pinter (see above) the ascent mounts steeply to the N., and just below the summit there are some awkward rocks. The climb is rewarded by a stupendous mountain panorama, from the Monviso and the Maritime Alps to the S.W., past the Grivola and Gran Paradiso, to Mont Blanc, whose supreme height is plain from here. The Matterhorn, the Lyskamm, and Monte Rosa are near at hand to the N., while far off to the E. are the Alps of the Trentino.—Less hardy climbers may enjoy a similar view from the *Corno Vitello* or *Kalberhorn* (3057m), which is reached in 5 hrs (guide essential) viâ the Passo di Mascognaz (see above); easier still is the *Punta di Combetta* (2390m), S. of the Colle della Ranzola (see Rte 3A).

Higher ascents from Gressoney-la-Trinité are made viâ the *Gnifetti Refuge* (see p. 72). Farther W. (7 hrs), best reached viâ (3½ hrs) the *Bettolina Pass* (2896m) is the **Quintino Sella Refuge** (3601m), a base for the ascents, viâ (1½hrs) the *Felik-Joch* (4068m), of (2½ hrs) the *Castor* (4230m) and of the *Lyskamm* (W. peak; 4472m; 4½hrs).—From the Sella Refuge the Gnifetti Refuge may be reached in 5 hrs viâ the *Naso del Lyskamm* (4099m).

C   From Verrès to Brusson and Champoluc

27km. BUS twice daily to St-Jacques in 1¾ hrs (oftener in July-Aug); through coaches from Turin and Genoa in summer.

This route traverses the Evançon valley, known in its lower reaches as the **Val de Challant**, above Brusson as the **Val d'Ayas**. The latter has always been noted for its pine forests and for its massive wooden chalets.

Verrès, see Rte 2. The first steep ascent ends at (4km.) *Targnod* (724m).—5km. *Ville* (765m) is the centre of the commune of *Challant-St-Victor*.

The ruined castle (½ hr S.W.) was the original home of the Challant family (12-14C).—Ville is connected with (7 hrs) Issime by (4 hrs) the *Col de Dondeuil* (2345m), from which may be ascended the *Bec Torché* (3016m; 1 hr) and the *Bec de Vlou* (3032m; 1½ hrs), two splendid viewpoints.

7km. *Corliod* (1006m) and (9km.) *Quinçod* (1050m) are two hamlets of *Challant-St-Anselme*. To Issime by the Col de Chasten, see Rte 3B. Farther on, through a defile, can be seen on the left the *Tête de Comagna* (2098m).—13km. *Arcesaz* is dominated by the ruined castle of *Graines* (13C). The road now ascends in zigzags to (16km.) **Brusson** (1330m), a village made up of several hamlets well situated on the Evançon.

To *St-Vincent* and to *Gressoney*, see Rte 3A.

The road ascends the Val d'Ayas. On the left at (19km.) *Extrepieraz* (1378m) diverges the old bridle-road to Antagnod, above which rises the crest of Mont Zerbion.—At (24km.) *Periasc* (1500m) the road emerges in the basin of Ayas, whose slopes are dotted with numerous villages.

High up on the left are the hamlets of *Lignod* (1638m) and *Antagnod* (1710m), charmingly grouped round its conspicuous old campanile.

An easy ascent leads to (27km.) **Champoluc** (1570m), a select summer resort amid splendid forests, enjoying a fine view of Castor and Pollux and the other peaks at the head of the valley. To Gressoney-St-Jean, see Rte 3B. A cableway leads up to Saleri (2000m), and from there a chair lift rises between Monte Sarezza (2828m) and Testa Grigia (3315m; comp. above).

Above, Champoluc the road becomes rougher, and, beyond (3 km.) *Fracney* and (4 km.) **St-Jacques-d'Ayas** (1676 m), it degenerates into a bridle-path. A tablet commemorates the Abbé Gorret, a famous alpinist, for 21 years parish priest of St-Jacques. A direct path leads hence to the Bettaforca Pass (Rte 3B).—5 km. *Fiéry* (1878 m) is a peaceful hamlet at the upper end of the Val d'Ayas, where it divides into the *Val de Verra (N.E.)* and Val de Cortoz (N.W.). For Résy and the pass to Gressoney, see Rte 3B, to Breuil and Valtournanche, see Rte 3D.—Above the Verra Glacier rises the *Breithorn* (4171 m), more easily climbed from Breuil (Rte 3D) and farther E. are *Castor* and *Pollux* (4230 m and 4094 m). These may be climbed viâ the *Mezzalama Refuge* (3036 m) beside the Verra Glacier (6 hrs from Champoluc). To the W. of Fiéry rises the *Grand Tournalin* (3379 m), usually ascended from Valtournanche (Rte 3D).

D   From Châtillon to Valtournanche and Breuil

ROAD, 27 km. BUS twice daily in 1½ hrs. In summer innumerable coaches from Northern Italian towns.

The **Valtournanche,** just over 27 km. long, extending from the base of the Matterhorn to the Val d'Aosta, is noteworthy especially for the fine perspective of the great peak at its head, and for its broad pastoral plateaux which offer admirable ski-slopes.

Châtillon, see Rte 2.—2 km. *Champlong,* with remains of 14-15C aqueducts which formerly conveyed water to St-Vincent.—At (7 km.) *Antey-St-André* (1081 m), with the mother-church of the valley (12C campanile), the road crosses to the left bank of the Marmore.

On the high plateau, 9 km. W. by road (bus from Châtillon on weekdays in summer), lie the scattered hamlets of *Torgnon* (1478 m-1634 m), a quiet resort frequented by climbers among the little-known peaks overlooking the Val St-Barthélemy (p. 63).

Beyond (9 km.) *Fiernaz* the valley begins to narrow.—From (11 km.) *Buisson* a cable-car ascends to *Chamois* (1815 m; no road), a small ski resort with a ski lift up to Punta Fontana Fredda (2513 m).—At (14 km.) *Ussin* (1259 m) the valley widens again.—Beyond the Cignana, with a cascade on the left, at *Moulin-Dessous,* is (18 km.) **Valtournanche** (1528 m), the chief village of the valley, and frequented by skiers. The village square is charming; and outside the church is a tablet to the memory of Canon Georges Carrel of Aosta (d. 1870), one of the first to attract attention to the interest of the neighbouring peaks; others commemorate guides who perished on the High Alps.

PASSES. Fiéry (see above) may be reached in 5 hrs viâ (1½ hrs) the beautiful upland basin of *Cheneil* and the *Col de Nana* (2805 m). The *Col de Valcornère* (3147 m) leads N.W. in 6 hrs to Prarayé (p. 66).—ASCENTS. The *Grand Tournalin* (3379 m; 5 hrs) is ascended viâ *Cheneil* and the *Col Sud du Tournalin* (3100 m) between the Grand and Petit Tournalin. The descent may be made to Fiéry (see above). *Mont Roisetta* (3349 m; 5 hrs) rises farther N.

A pleasant path follows the hills above the left bank of the river viâ (1½ hrs) *Chamois* (comp. above) and (2¾ hrs) *Antey-la-Magdeleine* (1640 m), reaching Châtillon in 5 hrs.—Another path leads W. to *Falegnon* (1914 m), the *Lago Cignana* (2108 m), and up the Vallone Cignana, to (1½ hrs) the foot of the *Becca Sale* (3091 m). From the lake a path leading S. viâ (5 hrs) *Torgnon* (see above), offers a pleasant alternative return to Châtillon.

Higher up in the valley beyond the hamlet of *Crépin* is the entrance (r.) of the narrow Gouffre des Busserailles, made accessible by wooden galleries. After the chapel of *Notre Dame de la Garde* (1829 m) comes a narrow defile, from which the road emerges in the pastoral basin of (27 km.) *Breuil,* walled in on the N. and W. by the Matterhorn, the Dent d'Hérens, and the Château des Dames.

Breuil-Cervinia (2004 m) has in recent years become one of the most popular ski-ing resorts in Italy. Thanks to the great extension of its cable-railways affording access to the admirable ski-slopes on the Italian side of the main ridge of the Alps, 'winter' sport can be enjoyed in summer also. The surname 'Cervinia' is an addition of the 1920s. Its inhabitants are famous as mountain guides.

Golf Course (9 hols, 18 tees), below the village. Covered **Swimming Pool**, **Tennis**, and **Skating** in the village. **Ski-School** all the year round. **Ski Lifts** on the slopes to the N. and S.W. of the village; another from Plan Maison (see below). **Bob Sleigh Run.**—Cable Railway to Furggen and Plateau Rosà, see below.

Breuil is the starting-point of the cable ascending to the main frontier ridge on either side of the Theodule Pass. The first section ascends to *Plan Maison* (2600 m). Thence there are two branches: the left-hand branch leads to the crest of the *Furggen* ridge (3499 m); the right-hand branch ascends to *Cime Bianche* (2899 m), whence another car goes on up to the *Plateau Rosà* (3499 m), with ski-lifts in summer.

The **Breithorn* (4171 m) is an easy ascent of 1½-2 hrs from the last station, rewarded by a magnificent view extending from the Bernese Alps to the Gran Paradiso.

From Breuil were started most of the earliest attempts to scale the **Matterhorn** (4478 m; *Mont Cervin* or *Monte Cervino*), but the summit was not gained from this side by a direct route until 1867. The ascent may now be made by practised mountaineers in c. 12 hrs. A path leads to (2½ hrs) *L'Oriondé* (2885 m), with the Duca degli Abruzzi refuge-inn, from where the ascent follows the S.W. arête passing (6 hrs) the Rif. J.A. Carrel (3830 m), the *Pic Tyndall* (4241 m; named after Prof. Tyndall), and the precipitous rock walls beneath the summit, now fitted with ropes.—Other ascents are those of (3¼ hrs) the **Gran Sometta* or Cemetta (3167 m), reached either viâ the *Motta di Plété* (2889 m; 2 hrs E. by bridle-path) or viâ the upper Col des Cimes-Blanches; the *Château des Dames* (3488 m in 8 hrs) viâ the Col de Valcornère, and (10-11 hrs) the difficult *Pointe Sella* (3860 m) and *Pointe Giordano* (3876 m), peaks of the *Jumeaux*, viâ (3½ hrs) the *Jumeaux Refuge* (2803 m).—From Plateau Rosà a good route leads over the Col Supérieur des Cimes-Blanches (2980 m) to (4½ hrs) *Fiéry* (Rte 3C).

FROM BREUIL TO ZERMATT a rough track leads over pastures for 1½ hrs and rock and rubble for ¾ hr to *Les Fornets* (3077 m; Rif. Bontadini), at the foot of the Lower Theodule Glacier, where traces remain of the fort erected in 1688 by Victor Amadeus II to prevent the return of the exiled Waldenses. The track (guide advisable) ascends the glacier and reaches the **Theodule Pass** (3292 m; numerous ski-lifts), on the Swiss frontier, in c. 2½ hrs from Breuil. On the pass is the *Rif. Teodulo*. The awkward descent of the Upper Theodule Glacier leads to (8 hrs) *Zermatt.*

4   TURIN TO VENTIMIGLIA

ROAD, N20, 177 km., open all the year.—20 km. *Carignano.*—28 km. *Carmagnola.*—53 km. *Savigliano.*—86 km. **Cúneo.**—94 km. *Borgo San Dalmazzo.*—112 km. *Limone Piemonte.*—118 km. Tunnel (Italian customs).— 131 km. *Tende* (French customs).—150 km. *La Giandola.*—177 km. **Ventimiglia.**—The A6 AUTOSTRADA from Turin to Savona follows this route fairly closely up to (50 km.) *Fossano,* 14 km. S. of Savigliano.—BUSES several times daily from Turin to Cúneo viâ Saluzzo in 2¼-2½; also from Cuneo to Limone and from Limone to Tende to Breil.

RAILWAY. The line is at present open only as far as *Limone Piemonte,* 120 km., in 2¼-3½ hrs; to *Cúneo,* 88 km. in 1¼-2 hrs. There is a longer alternative route to Cúneo viâ Airasca and Saluzzo in 2-3 hrs (94 km.). The railway from Limone to Ventimiglia has still not been reopened; its repair has been planned for years. A bus (twice daily) at present replaces the train.

The initial tract of N20 is now a minor road, the main road (N393; c.

1 km. shorter) running to the E. near the right bank of the Po to rejoin N20 just before Carmagnola (see below).—19½ km. *Carignano,* on the old road, is an ancient lordship long associated with the royal house of Savoy. The Cathedral (1757-67) is the masterpiece of Bened. Alfieri. *Pancalieri,* 13 km. S.W. off the Saluzzo road, was the native place of David Rizzio (1533?-66).—28 km. *Carmagnola,* beyond the Po, was the birthplace of the condottiere Francesco Bussone (1390-1432), called 'Il Carmagnola'. The 'Carmagnole', a popular song in Paris during the French Revolution, was originally sung by strolling minstrels from Piedmont. The road bears right in the town.—At (39 km.) *Racconigi* is the royal palace (mainly 19C) in which Umberto of Savoy, the present claimant to the throne, was born in 1904.—46 km. *Cavallermaggiore.*— 53 km. **Savigliano** (19,210 inhab.) was, the birthplace of Giov. Schiaparelli (1835-1910), the astronomer.

Saluzzo (17,420 inhab.), the historic seat of a famous line of marquesses, 13 km. W. of Savigliano, is connected with it by railway, and with Cuneo by frequent buses. It was the birthplace of G. B. Bodoni (1740-1813), the famous printer, and of Silvio Pellico (1789-1854), the patriot author. The large *Cathedral* was built in 1481-1511. The ancient streets of the upper town lead up to the modernized *Castle.* Just below it is the church of *SAN GIOVANNI, erected in 1281 with a choir extension of 1472 containing good stalls and the tomb of Marquess Ludovic II (d. 1503), by Bened. Briosco. On the N. side are the cloister and chapter house, the latter with a monument of 1528. Farther along Via San Giovanni, the charming 15C *Casa Cavassa,* by Sammicheli, houses the small town museum. On the Cúneo road are the imposing 14C castles of *Manta* (4 km.) and *Verzuolo* (6 km.).—To *Pinerolo,* see p. 58.

The road continuing W. from Saluzzo ascends the upper valley of the Po; bus (coming from Cúneo) 5 times daily to Paesana, in connection with the Pinerolo-Crissolo bus.—At (34 km.) *Paesana* the hills close in. The road goes on past a by-road (l.) which mounts in steep curves to *Serre,* to (45 km.) *Crissolo* (1333 m), a summer and winter resort (chair-lift) standing at the base of the graceful pyramid of the **Monviso** (3841 m). The road ends at (52 km.) *Pian del Re* (2050 m), at the source of the Po. From here the ascent (8 hrs; with guide) leads viâ (2½ hrs) the *Rif. Quintino Sella* (2640 m) and (4½ hrs) the old *Upper Refuge* (3047 m) to the summit. From above Pian del Re the remarkable *Pertuis de la Traversette,* a tunnel pierced beneath the Col de la Traversette (2950 m), leads into the French valley of the Guil and Abriès. Originally dug by Marquess Ludovic II in 1478-80 for the use of merchants trading into Dauphiny, the tunnel has been many times blocked up. It was completely restored in 1907, but is now not usually traversable. The pass (7 hrs from Pian del Re to Abriès) is considered by some authorities to have been Hannibal's route over the Alps.

From Savigliano to *Mondovì,* see Rte 6C.

86 km. **Cúneo** (533 m), approached by a monumental viaduct over the Stura, is a regularly built provincial capital (56,070 inhab.) deriving its name from the 'wedge' of land at the confluence of the Gesso and the Stura. The huge arcaded p.za, the cathedral, and the public buildings were mostly rebuilt after the destructive but unsuccessful siege by Conti in 1744. On Tuesdays the square is the scene of a noted market for raw silk and chestnuts. Via Roma, with heavy arcades, is the main street of the old town. A tall square tower surmounts the former town hall. *San Francesco,* a secularized church of 1227, has a good portal (1481). Magnificent boulevards have replaced the former ramparts.

The Stura viaduct also carries the railway to the new station; from the old station (*Cúneo-Gesso*), below the town to the E., electric trains run to Borgo San Dalmazzo.—BUSES to Turin, the Western valleys, to Mondovì and Savona, and to Garessio and Imperia, start from the Largo Audifredi (Via Roma); to Ventimiglia and Nice from the central P.za Galimberti.

Cúneo is the gateway to the southern Cottian Alps approached by the Val Maira (or Macra) and the Val Varaita, to the N.W.; they are served by buses several times daily to Acceglio, Pradlèves, and Pontechianale.—The road (N22) up the VAL MAIRA leaves on the left at (12 km.) *Caráglio* the VAL GRANA, with the summer resort of *Pradléves* (510 m), 26 km. from Cúneo.—At (20 km.) *Dronero* (622 m), with a 15C bridge and market-hall, the road enters hill country.—The church of *San Costanza al Monte*, 4 km. N., preserves a notable 12C apse.—From (55 km.) **Acceglio** (1219 m) a poor road goes on to (6 km.) *Chiappera* (1591 m), the highest hamlet in the valley, beneath the *Brec de Chambeyron* (3389 m), on the frontier; while to the left at the Lago del Saretto begins the bridle-path over the *Col du Sautron* (2684 m) to *Larche* (6¼ hrs; see below).

The road up the VAL VARAITA begins at (23 km.) *Costigliole,* on the Saluzzo road. Thence it runs viâ (50 km.) *Sampeyre* (980 m) to (61 km.) **Casteldelfino** (1295 m), a village taking its name from a castle founded in 1336, once the centre of the Dauphins' Cisalpine territory.—To the N. of (68 km.) *Pontechianale* (1614 m), with a power reservoir, rises the Monviso (see above), ascended in 9 hrs. Above the village a track goes on to the *Col Agnel* (2699 m) on the frontier, leading in c. 7 hrs to Fontgillarde or La Monta in the Queyras. This was a route favoured by invading troops, and was crossed by Bayard in 1515 and by Philip, Duke of Parma, in 1743.

The *Certosa di Pesio* (1000 m), 26 km. S.E. of Cúneo (bus), is a 12C foundation greatly altered, in an attractive upland vale.

94 km. **Borgo San Dalmazzo** (631 m) is named after St Dalmatius, the apostle of Piedmont, martyred here in 304. Above it is the picturesque church of the Madonna di Monserrato.

A road (bus from Cúneo) runs S.W. up the valley of the Gesso viâ (10 km.) *Valdieri* (774 m) and thence by a side valley on the S. to (16 km.) *Entracque* (904 m), a quiet hill resort. In summer other buses ascend the main valley viâ (18 km) *Sant'Anna* (975 m) to (25 km.) the **Terme di Valdieri** (975 m), rebuilt in 1952-53, with hot sulphur springs, rather similar in their properties to those of Aix-les-Bains. A curiosity of the neighbourhood is a cryptogamic plant (*Ulva labyrinthiformis*) which grows in gelatinous masses over the rock down which the sulphur water flows; and this substance ('muffa') is applied to wounds and inflammations. The *Monte Matto* (3087 m; 5 hrs) to the N.W., and the *Punta dell'Argentera* (3300 m; 6 hrs; difficult) to the S.E., the highest peak of the Maritime Alps, may be ascended. A road is planned to connect Terme di Valdieri with Le Boréon in France.

FROM BORGO SAN DALMAZZO TO THE COLLE DELLA MADDALENA, 60 km., on N 21, ascending the wooded VALLE STURA. Bus daily from Cúneo to Pietraporzio, oftener to Vinadio; twice daily in summer to the Colle; also in June-Sept from Cúneo to the Terme di Vinadio.—17 km. *Demonte* (774 m) is the ancient capital of the valley.—27 km. *Vinadio* (899 m) has imposing 17C fortifications.— From (33 km.) *Pianche* (980 m) a road leads S. to (5 km.) the *Terme di Vinadio* (1274 m), with hot sulphur springs.—Beyond (42 km.) *Pietraporzio* (1247 m), with the Italian customs, the road traverses the striking defile of *Le Barricate* (stormed by Francis I in 1515), and reaches (49 km.) *Bersezio* (1625 m).—53 km. *Argentera* (1695 m) is the highest village and, beyond the *Lago della Maddalena* (1974 m), the summit is reached at (60 km.) the **Colle della Maddalena** (1995 m), or *Col de Larche,* an easy pass amid pastures noted for their varied flowers, and free from snow between mid-May and mid-October. Francis I passed this way on his invasion of Italy in 1515 and Napoleon decreed that 'the imperial road from Spain to Italy' should be carried over it. The descent leads viâ (7 km.) *Larche,* with the French custom-house, to (32 km.) *Barcelonette.*

Across the Gesso the road ascends the Val Vermenagna with the railway traversing a series of short tunnels and viaducts higher up.— 106 km. *Vernante* (797 m) faces a ruined castle across the valley.— 112 km. **Limone Piemonte** (998 m), the terminus of most trains (seasonal car-carriers to Tende), is a large village among open pastures, frequented for winter sports, with a 12-14C church. There are chair-lifts to the *Capanna Chiara* (1500 m; refuge) and to *Maire Buffe* for high-level excursions.—Above Limone the road ascends to 1321 m and enters a tunnel 3 km. long (customs-post at tunnel mouth), emerging at

1280 m. The *Colle di Tenda* (1909 m) above it (walkers only) marks the present frontier with France.

The districts of Tende and La Brigue, although parts of the County of Nice, were expressly reserved to Italy in the Franco-Italian treaty of 1860, by courtesy of Napoleon III, because a great part of the territory was a favourite hunting-ground of Victor Emmanuel II. In 1947 they were rejoined to the rest of the county by treaty, an act which was confirmed a month later by a local plebiscite resulting in a large majority in favour of France.

From the tunnel exit there is a striking view of the 20 hairpin bends below; the descent traverses two rocky gorges, between which is the lofty railway viaduct of Viévola.—Beyond (131 km.) **Tende**, or *Tenda* (815 m), with the French custom-house, the road (now Route Nationale 204) follows the Roia, threading magnificent gorges. On the r. at San Dalmazzo di Tende, a by-road leads towards *Monte Bego* (2873 m) where the Valle delle Meraviglie (reached by walkers) has 40,000 graffiti on a glazed wall from a Ligurian cult that survived from Palaeolithic times to the Iron Age.—150 km. *La Giandola*, just above *Breil* (or Breglio), where its more important branch leaves the valley for Nice.— The road continues to descend the Roia past Breil, 11 km. beyond which it passes again into Italy (more customs-posts).—177 km. **Ventimiglia.**

5   VENTIMIGLIA TO GENOA

ROAD, N 1, 163 km.—5 km. **Bordighera.**—17 km. **Sanremo.**—40 km. *Imperia (Porto Maurizio).*—43 km. *Imperia (Oneglia).*—65 km. **Alassio.**—72 km. **Albenga.**—82 km. *Loana.*—93 km. *Finale Ligure.*—103 km. *Spotorno.*—117 km. **Savona.**—127 km. *Varazze.*—152 km. **Pegli.**—163 km. **Genoa.**—BUSES at frequent intervals for the whole distance or parts of it.
AUTOSTRADA DEI FIORI (A 10) runs 'en corniche' farther inland among the foothills, with frequent long tunnels.
RAILWAY, 151 km. in 2¼–3¾ hrs; all trains stop at *Sanremo* and *Savona,* and all but the 'Ligure' at *Alassio.* Through sleeping-cars run on this route from Calais to Sanremo; through carriages from Marseille to Vienna, Spain to Rome, Ventimiglia to Amsterdam, etc.
The ***Riviera di Ponente,** that part of the Italian Riviera lying W. of Genoa, is less rugged than the Riviera di Levante (p. 105), but equally charming and luxuriant, with many frequented coast resorts, planted with palms, bougainvillaea, and exotic plants.

VENTIMIGLIA (26,900 inhab.), or **Vintimille,** with a flower market and good sea bathing, is divided by the Roia into an old town (W.) and a new town. In the old town (76 m) the restored 11-12C *Cathedral* has a portal of 1222, and a Madonna by Barnaba da Modena (3rd N. altar). It is adjoined by an 11C *Baptistery* incorporating Lombard remains of its predecessor. The church of *San Michele* also preserves 11C details, including its crypt; the stoups are fashioned from Roman milestones. The *Municipio* (10-12, 15-18, Sun 10-12), in the new town, houses finds from Ligurian *Albium Intemelium,* later Albintimilium on the Roman Via Aurelia, where Agricola spent his boyhood. Extensive remains of this, 15 min. E. of the town, include a *Theatre* of the 2C A.D.

An attractive coastal drive leads W. to (5 km.) *Mórtola Inferiore,* where the road divides; the upper road (r.) passes the *Giardini Hanbury* (adm. daily), a fine botanic garden founded in 1867 by Sir Thomas Hanbury and his brother Daniel. Here is exposed a section of Roman road; a tablet recalls famous travellers by this route. Beyond the cape on which the garden is laid out is the frontier village of *Grimaldi.* A lift descends to the beach at the *Balzi Rossi* ('red rocks'), in which are several caves where relics of Palaeolithic man were discovered in 1892 (small museum on the site). The international customs-post is at (8 km.) *Ponte San Luigi* above which stands the castle where Serge Voronoff (1866-1951) experimented with monkey-gland rejuvenation.—The main road, by the sea, passes in tunnels beneath the Giardini and enters France by the *Ponte San Ludovico*.

The flowery valleys of the Vallecrosia and the Nervia are ascended by buses from Ventimiglia. In the former is (16 km.) *Perinaldo*, birthplace of G. D. Cassini (1625-1712), the astronomer. In the Nervia valley are (9 km.) *Dolceacqua*, with a ruined castle of the Doria and a medieval bridge, and (24 km.) *Pigna*, picturesquely situated opposite the fortified village of *Castel Vittoria*.

5 km. **BORDIGHERA** (11,800 inhab.) is famous as a winter resort and had a large English colony. It is also a centre for the cultivation of flowers, and its citizens have the exclusive right of providing palmfronds for the papal services at St Peter's at Eastertide.

Post Office in the Station square.—*Azienda di Turismo*, Palazzo del Parco.
English Church, *All Saints'*, Via Regina Vittoria.
Buses to *Bordighera, Ventimiglia*, and *Nice;* to *Alassio* and *Genoa;* to *Cúneo*
Tennis Club, Via Stoppani.—*International Library*, 30 Via Roma.

The new town consists of two parallel thoroughfares, Via Vittorio Emanuele, near the shore, and Via Romana, higher up, with their connecting streets. In Via Romana the villa in which Margherita di Savoia died (1926) faces the Istituto Internazionale di Studi Liguri, with the *Museo Bicknell* (weekdays only, 10-12, 15.30-17.30), a good local natural history collection. The road ends on the E. in the *Spianata del Capo*, with the old town above (gates restored in 1960), and the Capo Sant'Ampelio below. Here the church was stripped inside in 1964 to reveal its Romanesque structure. Pleasant walks may be taken along the Lungomare W. to the Kursaal and to the E. to the palm-gardens known as the *Giardino Winter* and *Giardino Madonna della Ruota* ($\frac{1}{4}$-$\frac{1}{2}$ hr).

Via dei Colli affords splendid coastal views. In the Communal Cemetery in Valle di Sasso, N.E. of the town, is a *British Military Cemetery*, with 72 graves.—Among the inland excursions the most repaying is the ascent of *Monte Santa Croce* (350 m; *View), climbed in 20 min. from the Vallecrosia halt on the Ventimiglia bus route.

11 km. **Ospedaletti**, on a sheltered bay, is particularly favoured as a winter resort. The streets form the circuit for an annual motor-race (April). The town supposedly takes its name from a 14C hospice of the Knights of Rhodes, who were established at Porto Maurizio. They are unlikely to be commemorated in the name of *Coldirodi*, a village 6 km. inland (bus; panoramic road) where there is a Pinacoteca.—The road rounds the Capo Nero.

17 km. **SANREMO** is the largest summer and winter resort (64,700 inhab.) on the Italian Riviera; its villas and gardens lie in an amphitheatre between Capo Nero and Capo Verde, in a wide bay 8 km. across.

Post Office, 132 Via Roma.—**E.P.T.**, 1 Via Nuvoloni.
English Church. *All Saints'*, Corso Matuzia at the W. end of the town.
Buses to *Bordighera, Ventimiglia*, and *Nice;* to *Alassio* and *Genoa;* to *Cúneo* and *Turin;* to *Poggio;* to *Ceriana* and *Baiardo;* to *Coldirodi;* etc.
Golf Course (18 holes) on the San Rómolo road (4 km. N.); cable railway from the Corso degli Inglesi. *Tennis Club*, 18 Corso Matuzia. A *Harbour* for small boats is under construction.
Edward Lear (1812-88) spent his last years at Sanremo at the Villa Emily, now Villa Verde. Alfred Nobel (1833-96), the inventor, also died here, and here in 1878 Tchaikovsky finished his 4th Symphony and 'Eugen Onegin'. His empress, Maria Alexandrovna, consort of Alexander II, was here surrounded after 1874 by a Russian colony.

Via Matteotti, the main street of the modern town, leads S.W. past the gardens of the **Casino Municipale** (always open), with a celebrated evening restaurant and gaming rooms. From here the *CORSO DELL'IMPERATRICE, lined with magnificent palm-trees, leads to the *Giardino dell'Imperatrice*, in which is a monument to Garibaldi by Bistolfi. Along the shore in the other direction Via Nino Bixio leads to the Genoese fort of *Santa Tecla* (1755) and the mole of the *Harbour* (view).

High up on the left is LA PIGNA, the old town, with quaint narrow streets, steep flights of steps, tunnels, and arches. The *Duomo* (San Siro) is a 13C building enlarged in the 17C. Fine views of the town and the coast are obtained from the *Madonna della Costa*, a church of 1630 with a dome of 1775, and from the Corso degli Inglesi which passes the *Castello Devachan*, scene of an international conference of 1920.

Excursions may be made by cable railway (from Corso d. Inglesi) viâ San Rómolo to (7 km.) *Monte Bignone* (1309 m), the highest of the horseshoe of hills surrounding Sanremo; and by road to (4 km. E.) the *Madonna della Guardia*, a viewpoint overlooking Capo Verde; also up the Armea valley, viâ Poggio and Ceriana, to (24 km.) the picturesque village of *Baiardo* (899 m), partly ruined by an earthquake in 1887 but now a healthy mountain resort.

Beyond Sanremo the coast road rounds Capo Verde and passes (l.) *Bussana Nuova*, above which stands ruined *Bussana Vecchia*, deserted since the earthquake of 1887.—25 km. *Arma di Taggia* is a small bathing resort.

Taggia, the old village 3 km. up the pretty Argentina valley (bus from Sanremo), has a 15C Gothic church with a polyptych and other works by Lod. Brea, and a cloister incorporating older columns. The Dominican Convent preserves numerous works of art. A Roman bridge of 16 arches crosses the valley to Castellaro and the Santurio della Madonna di Lampedusa.

The road passes the small resorts of *Cipressa* and *San Lorenzo al Mare* and approaches the double town of **Imperia** (41,700 inhab.) created in 1923 by the fusion of Porto Maurizio, Oneglia, and adjoining villages to form a provincial capital.—40 km. **Porto Maurizio** is dominated by a large church (San Maurizio; 1781-1832) and has an old quarter of stepped streets. A bus connects it with (43 km.) **Oneglia,** an important centre of the olive-oil trade, at the mouth of the Impero torrent from which the province takes its name. Between the two towns are the Municipio and post office.

Oneglia was the birthplace of Andrea Doria (1466-1560), the Genoese admiral, of Edmondo De Amicis (1846-1909), the author, and of Jean Vieusseux (1779-1863; p. 448); and here in 1959 died Grock (Adrien Wettach), the great Swiss clown.

From Imperia (Oneglia) to *Ormea* and *Ceva*, see Rte 6C.

An ascent over Capo Berta leads to (48 km.) **Diano Marina,** another olive-growing town, with a sandy beach, frequented as a summer and winter resort.—50 km. *San Bartolomeo al Mare* is a modern resort with many hotels.—53 km. *Cervo* retains a picturesque air with a rich Baroque church.—Beyond (56 km.) *Marina di Andora* the road rounds the prominent Capo Mele (view N. to Alassio).—62 km. **Laiguéglia** is a quiet resort preserving old streets and an imposing 18C church.

An interesting walk ascends the old Roman road S.W. for (1 hr) *Castello di Andora* (94 m), a ruined castle with a late-13C church, the finest late-Romanesque building on the Riviera. A descent to the medieval bridge over the Merula leads to Andora (see above).

65 km. **ALASSIO** (14,000 inhab.), standing at the head of a wide and beautiful bay, facing nearly E., is noted for the luxuriance of its gardens, and is one of the most frequented Ligurian coast resorts. It enjoys an exceptionally mild winter climate and an excellent sandy beach.

English Church, *St John's,* services on Sun at 11 (at 10 in July-Sept), also at 8, Easter-Oct.
Buses frequently from P.za Libertà to *Albenga* and *Laigueglia;* hourly to *Nice* and to *Genoa.*—**Motor-Boat** trips in summer to the *Isola Gallinaria,* etc.
Olive Schreiner spent c. 6 months here in 1887-88, her longest sojourn in any one place during her stay in Europe (1882-89); and while wintering here in 1904 Elgar composed his overture 'In the South (Alassio)'.

Alassio preserves its old main street, a campanile of 1507, and the 16C *Torrione,* built for defence against Barbary pirates.

Pleasant hill walks may be taken inland to (1½ hrs) the *Madonna della Guardia* (586 m) or *Monte Pisciavino* (600 m); or N.E. along the old Roman road (beyond the railway) to (40 min.) the ruined medieval arch and the little chapel; *View above *Capo Santa Croce.*

The road ascends over Capo Santa Croce; out at sea is the *Isola Gallinaria,* to the N. of which were dredged up the Roman amphoræ now in Albenga.

Little remains of the once powerful Benedictine monastery here, which at one time owned most of the Riviera; but the cave is shown in which St Martin is said to have taken refuge c. 370 from his Arian persecutors.

72 km. **Albenga,** a fascinating old town (21,170 inhab.), was the Roman port *Album Ingaunum,* but is now 1 km. from the sea thanks to the shifting of the course of the Centa in the 13C. It preserves most of its medieval wall (on foundations of the 1C B.C.) and three 17C gates; also about a dozen 13-14C brick tower-houses, mostly well-restored.

In the centre of the town the elegant campanile (1391) of the cathedral forms a striking group with two other towers. The *Cathedral,* an early-14C enlargement of an 11C structure, with a galleried apse, was restored inside in 1964-66. The *Palazzo Vecchio del Comune* (1387 and 1421), incorporating a tall tower of c. 1300, houses the Civico Museo Ingauno (10-12, 15-18) with Roman and medieval remains including Albisola pharmacy jars. Steps descend to the level of the 5C *BAPTISTERY, ten-sided without and octagonal within, preserving a fine mosaic (5C or 6C) in its principal apse and 8C transennæ; the original roof was destroyed in 1900. Beyond the N. flank of the cathedral is the charming Piazzetta dei Leoni, with three lions of unknown provenance and the *Torre Costa del Carretto.* Behind the Bishop's Palace (16C) is the old *Palazzo Vescovile* with external frescoes (15C). The evocative Via Bernardo Ricci (the Roman decumanus) crosses Via delle Medaglie (cardo maximus) at the 13C *Loggia dei Quattro Canti.*

To the W. of the cathedral in P.za San Michele rises the 13C tower of the Palazzo Peloso-Cepolla, the rooms of which form the *Museo Navale Romano* (9-12, 15-19; winter 9-12, 14-18), containing wine amphoræ and marine fittings salved since 1950 from a Roman vessel sunk offshore. The church of *Santa Maria in Fontibus,* S. of the cathedral, has a Gothic doorway.

On the hill S.W. of the town and on the old Roman road leading to Alassio are considerable remains of Roman tombs, some damaged in 1944.

BUSES run frequently along the coast road; also to *Villanova d'Albenga,* a fortified outpost of Albenga, 6½ km. W.; and to *Campochiesa,* 4 km. N. beyond the Ponte Lungo, where in the 12-14C church are wall-paintings of the 13-16C including a Last Judgement (1446) inspired by the 'Divina Commedia'. Other services to *Calizzano* (see below), to *Garessio,* and to *Pieve di Teco* (see Rte 6C).

Alongside the Genoa road is the *Ponte Lungo,* a 13C (not Roman) bridge crossing the old bed of the Centa, in whose alluvial plain asparagus is grown all the year round.—77 km. *Ceriale* and (79 km.) *Borghetto Santo Spirito* are modest seaside resorts.—82 km. **Loano,** an old seaside town (13,250 inhab.) with palm-groves, has a town hall (1578), formerly the Palazzo Doria, containing a 3C mosaic pavement; and to the N. a Carmelite convent with a dignified church (1603-8) commanding a good view. No. 32 Via Cavour was the birthplace of Rosa Raimondi, Garibaldi's mother.

Inland, viâ Borghetto (see above), are the old hill-villages of *Toirano* (6 km.) and *Balestrino* (9 km.), the latter with a Del Carretto castle. The *Grotta della Básura,* 30 min. N. of Toirano off the Bardineto road, is a remarkable stalactite cavern (apply at Ente Grotte, Toirano), with the only footprints of Mousterian man so far discovered.—A bus runs viâ Toirano to (22 km.) *Calizzano,* a summer resort with a ruined castle of the Del Carretto.

85 km. **Pietra Ligure** is another old town (9800 inhab.) with a ruined Genoese fort and a church (San Nicola) by Fantone (1791). The fine modern seaside quarter is succeeded on the W. by shipyards, with the large Istituto Santa Corona (a sanatorium for Milan) behind.—91 km. *Borgio* is a modest bathing resort with the little Romanesque cemetery church of San Pietro to the W.—93 km. **Finale Marina,** with a large Baroque church, is the chief section of the town of *Finale Ligure* (14,300 inhab.). The Museum contains finds from local caves (see below) and the Capuchin church stands on an earlier Pieve (6-8C). Adjoining is **Finale Pia** where the church has a 13C campanile. Both are popular seaside resorts with numerous summer pensions.

The old village of *Finalborgo,* 2 km. inland from Finalmarina (bus every ½ hr), has a church with a fine octagonal campanile (13C). It contains a 16C tomb of the Del Carretto family, whose ruined castle commands the place from the N.W. To the N. of Borgo and in the hill W. of Marina are many limestone caves in which prehistoric remains have been found; and on the old Roman road which (to avoid the coastal cliffs) ascended the Valle di Ponci N. of Finale Pia and then descended the Val Quazzola to Vado are about a dozen Roman bridges (1C A.D.), five of them intact.

From (96 km.) *Varigotti* the road ascends the 'Malpasso' over the Capo di Noli, with fine views in both directions between tunnels and cuttings.—100 km. **Noli,** an important port in the Middle Ages, preserves its walls and three tall towers of brick, as well as many old houses. The church of *San Paragorio* (W. end), with a 15C porch, preserves its crypt, a 13C bishop's throne in wood, and a 'Volto Santo' Crucifix (12C) like that at Lucca. Dominating the town from the E. is the *Castello di Monte Ursino.*—103 km. *Spotorno* has a fine sandy beach.—Beyond the headland of *Bergeggi,* with its islet offshore, and another cape, is (113 km.) *Vado Ligure,* once a Roman port, now an industrial suburb of Savona with oil-discharging docks connected by pipeline with a refinery at Trecate (p. 115).

117 km. **SAVONA,** an important port and provincial capital (80,100 inhab.), consists of an old quarter, overlooking the inner harbour, surrounded by the regular and rather banal streets of the new town.

Ironfounding and shipbreaking are the chief industries and crystallized fruit is a local speciality.

History. The Gallo-Roman *Savo,* used as a Carthaginian depôt during the Second Punic War, was dependent on the port of Vada Sabatia (Vado) and was of little importance until the Crusades. Later, under the Alerami and the Del Carretto, it waged naval war against the Barbary pirates; but in 1528 its harbour was blocked by the jealous Genoese, who, in 1542, built a fort to keep the town in subjection. The fort survives to this day, mostly incorporated in the iron-foundry S. of the town, and here Mazzini was confined in 1830-31. In 1809-12 and in 1814 Pius VII was interned at Savona by order of Napoleon; and in the Second World War the town was shelled from the sea.

The main arcaded Via Paleócapa runs from the station to the harbour. On its N. side is the 16C church of *San Giovanni Battista,* containing an early Flemish triptych (behind the high altar) and, in the N.E. chapel, an Adoration of the Shepherds by Ant. Semino, and paintings by Ratti. Behind the church are the *Post Office* and the *Theatre* called after the native Gabriello Chiabrera (1553-1638), the 'Italian Ronsard'. At the seaward end, which has a terrace of pretty Art Nouveau houses with tiled façades, commanding the harbour, is the *Torre Pancaldo,* a 14C tower recalling Leon Pancaldo of Savona, Magellan's 'Genoese' pilot.

The port may be visited by motor-boat excursion on Sundays and holidays. From the quay an aerial ropeway transports carbon to factories at San Giuseppe di Cáiro (21 km.; p. 90).

Opposite San Giovanni the VIA PIA, with many fine stone doorways in the Genoese manner, leads into the old town. A right turn, through the colonnade of the Town Library, leads to the *Cathedral,* built in 1589-1605 (façade of 1886) to replace its medieval forerunner demolished to make way for the Genoese fort. The font (?12C) and choir-stalls (1495) are from the old building. Facing the cathedral is the *Palazzo Della Rovere,* begun by Giul. da Sangallo for Julius II but never finished; it now contains law courts. On the right of the cathedral is the *Sistine Chapel* (usually locked), erected by Sixtus IV (see below) in memory of his parents, and given a harmonious Baroque interior in 1764. It contains a fine marble tomb, by Mich. and Giov. De Aria, with figures of the two Della Rovere Popes, Sixtus IV and Julius II. Via Pia (r.) threads an archway to P.za del Mercato, where are the two *Torri del Brandale* (12C; restored) and the *Archivolto del Brandale,* on the old quay. Most of the quayside buildings were destroyed in the bombardment of 1941, and on the left appear two medieval tower-houses. Farther on is the portal of the house of Ansaldo Grimaldi (1552), brought from Genoa in 1957 and erected in the front of the house of Lamba Doria. In Via Quarda Superiore (the first street parallel with the quay) a small *Civic Art Gallery* (15-18, fest. 10-12, 15-18; closed Mon & Tues), on the fourth floor of the Palazzo Pozzobonello, contains a Calvary by Donato de'Bardi and a polyptych by Vinc. Foppa.

In the cemetery of *Zinola,* half-way to Vado, is a *British Military Plot,* with 104 graves, mostly from the wreck of the 'Transylvania', torpedoed off Savona in 1917.—About 6 km. N.W., with a station on the Turin railway, is the *Santuario di Nostra Signora della Misericordia,* with a 16C church, a favourite excursion from Savona and the goal of a pilgrimage on 18 March.

BUSES run frequently from the station to the harbour and to *Vado* or *Varazze:* to the *Santuario* (see above); and along the coast in both directions; and to *Cairo Montenotte;* twice daily to *Millésimo* and *Calizzano,* and to *Sassello;* daily to *Acqui, Alessandria,* and *Milan;* to *Alba;* and to *Turin* (see Rte 6C).

East of Savona the beaches are less attractive.—121 km. *Albisola Marina* is separated by a torrent from its twin bathing-place *Albisola Capo,* and noted for its pottery and as the birthplace of Julius II (Giuliano della Rovere; 1443-1513).

A road climbs viâ (2 km.) *Albisola Superiore* to (16 km.) the *Colle del Giovo* (516 m), and thence descends, past (23 km.) the summer resort of *Sassello,* to (59 km.) *Acqui* (Rte 6B).

124 km. *Celle Ligure,* a fashionable resort, was the birthplace of Sixtus IV (Fr. della Rovere; 1414-84), uncle of Julius II.—127 km. **Varazze,** a popular seaside resort (15,200 inhab.), is an old town retaining much of its rampart, at the N. corner of which is preserved the 10C façade of the original church of *Sant'Ambrogio.* The present church (1535) has a 13C campanile and contains Baroque altar-paintings; in the sacristy, polyptych by Giov. Barbagelata (1500). Jacobus de Varagine (1230-98), author of the 'Golden Legend', was born here.—134 km. *Cogoleto* is a small industrial town connected with the family of Columbus; and Tennyson halted here to pledge the explorer's memory.—137 km. *Arenzano* is another popular resort with fine gardens, kursaal, and sea-water baths.—At (147 km.) *Voltri,* an industrial suburb, the road reaches the boundary of 'Greater Genoa', and from here onwards is built up almost uninterruptedly.

At the *Santuario dell' Acquasanta* (1683-1710), c. 5 km. inland (frequent buses; station on the Genoa-Acqui railway), Maria Cristina of Savoy was married to Ferdinand II of the Two Sicilies in 1832.—To *Turin* viâ Acqui, see Rte 6B.

Beyond *Palmaro,* with a bathing beach, the road traverses *Pra,* with foundries.—152 km. **Pegli,** a favourite weekend resort of the Genoese, retains a few fine villas backed by pine-woods. Inland from the station is the *Villa Doria,* a pleasant public park with a 16C mansion housing the *Naval and Maritime Museum* (9.30-11.30, 14-17; closed Sun, Mon, & fest.), a good collection comprising 16-17C maps and globes; ship-models; and maritime prints and paintings including a portrait of Columbus ascribed to Rid. Ghirlandaio.—Much finer is the *Villa Durazzo-Pallavicini* (adm. as for Villa Doria, above), just to the E., a luxuriant garden commanding good views, and containing many scenic and architectural conceits of the 1840s, such as a partly underground lake, a 'Chinese' temple, etc. The mansion houses in 23 rooms the *Museum of Ligurian Archæology,* noteworthy for prehistoric finds from Ligurian cave-dwellings.

Sestri Ponente, with a petroleum port, to seaward of which on reclaimed land extends the airport of Genoa, and *Cornigliano* are industrial suburbs continuous with (158 km.) *Sampierdarena* beyond the mouth of the Polcevera, known for its old-established engineering and metallurgical works. At the Ansaldo works in 1854 was built the first Italian locomotive. The road cuts through the point on the W. side of the harbour of (163 km.) **Genoa** (Rte 7).

6   TURIN TO GENOA

A   Viâ Asti and Alessandria

ROAD, 175 km. N 10. 18 km. **Chieri** (by-pass, l.).—30 km. *Villanova.*—55 km. **Asti.**—91 km. **Alessandria.**—98 km. N 35 bis.—112 km. Novi Ligure (2 km. r.).—120 km. N 35 comes in on the left.—122 km. *Serravalle Scrivia.*—147 km. *Busalla.*—149 km. *Passo dei Giovi* (472 m).—175 km. **Genoa.**

AUTOSTRADA, A 21, to (94 km.) *Tortona,* where the A 7 autostrada continues S., joining this route at Serravalle and following it closely into Genoa.

RAILWAY, 169 km. in 1¾ hr-2½ hrs; to *Asti,* 56 km. in 30-60 min; to *Alessandria,* 91 km. in 1-1½ hrs. Through trains from Calais, Paris, and Rome run on this line.

N 10 leaves Turin by the Ponte Regina Margherita and the Corso Casale and turns S.E. into the hills. A tunnel takes the road under *Pino Torinese,* served by a hillier road (17 km., viâ Superga, p. 56), which this road joins in 15 km.—19 km. **Chieri,** served by bus and local train from Turin, is a pleasant little industrial town (31,100 inhab.), the old streets of which contain many fine old houses. The *CATHEDRAL, built in 1405-36, has one of the tallest of the pointed porches characteristic of Piedmontese Gothic. Its 13C baptistery has 15-16C frescoes and a polyptych after Spanzotti. During restoration work, the original walls and Roman remains beneath the floor, have been revealed. The church contains a marble altarpiece attrib. to Matt. Sanmicheli (S. transept); 15C choir stalls; and a small 9-10C crypt incorporating Roman work. The sacristy has good 16C woodwork. Beyond a *Triumphal Arch,* in the main street, much altered since its erection in 1580 in honour of Emmanuel Philibert, is the 14C church of *San Domenico,* which has a graceful campanile and fine capitals and mouldings. Farther on, in the Istituto Don Bosco (at the corner of Via Roma; adm. freely granted) are remains of a *Commandery of the Templars,* including part of the church, rebuilt in the 15C, with columns of reticulated brickwork.

A bus goes on (on an alternative road to Asti) to (12 km.) the hill-village of *Castelnuovo Don Bosco,* the home of St John Bosco. He was born at *Becchi,* 5 km. S., where a large Salesian pilgrimage church has been erected.—*Vezzolano* (p. 116) is 5½ km. N. of Castelnuovo.

At (30 km.) *Villanova d'Asti* begin the famous Asti vineyards as the road enters the Monferrato.

55 km. **ASTI,** a famous old Piedmontese city (80,000 inhab.) reached the zenith of its importance in the 13C, and was a possession of the house of Savoy from 1575. The district is noted for its wines, including Barbera, Nebbiolo, Grignolino, and Asti Spumante.

The ancient Palio of Asti, a costume pageant and horse race similar to that of Siena, was revived in 1967. It takes place in early September in a huge stadium in the S. part of the town. It provides an added attraction to the annual wine fair.

The W. approach from Piazza Torino leads into the long CORSO VITT. ALFIERI, the main street extending the whole length of the town. The *Torre San Secondo,* a Romanesque tower on a Roman base, serves as campanile for the church of Santa Caterina (1773). On the corner of P.za Cairoli the *Palazzo Alfieri,* birthplace of the poet Vittorio Alfieri (1749-1803), has collections and study rooms devoted to his work. The early 18C mansion was built by his cousin Bened. Alfieri. Beneath the adjoining Liceo is the 8C crypt of the destroyed church of

Sant'Anastasio (adm. on application) with fine capitals. A turning to the left leads to the CATHEDRAL, a dignified Gothic building of 1309-54, with a campanile of 1266, and a florid S. porch of c. 1470; the E. end was extended in 1764-69. At the W. end are two holy-water stoups made from Romanesque capitals supported by inverted Roman capitals, and a font likewise constructed of Roman material in the 15C. On the W. piers of the crossing are two 12-13C reliefs. The Baroque frescoes are by *Carlo Carlone* (c. 1760) and *Fr. Fabbrica* (nave; 1696-1700), and the inlaid stalls (1768) are noteworthy.

To the N.E., is a cloister (?11C), while to the left of that is the small church of *San Giovanni,* covering a 7C or 8C crypt, perhaps the original baptistery.—Farther to the N. Via Natta, in a quarter containing many 13-14C houses, leads to Via Giobert, which ends (l.) at the surviving portion of the town walls.

The road leading back from the cathedral to the Corso Alfieri crosses Via Carducci, No. 35 in which is the 15C *Palazzo Zoia.* At the corner of Via Giobert and the Corso a small municipal art gallery occupies the 18C *Palazzo De Bellino* (10-12, 16-19, closed Mon). The *Prefettura,* opposite, is of similar date.

The streets descending S. from the Corso still retain a number of crumbling tower-houses of the old Astigiano, nobility (Alfieri, Malabayla, Rocro, Solari, etc.); the *Pal. Malabayla,* in Via Mazzini, is a fine though dilapidated Renaissance mansion.

Farther on in the Corso is Piazza Roma, with the 13C *Torre Comentina,* beyond which Via Morelli leads (l.) to P.za Medici, with the *Torre Troyana,* the finest medieval tower in the city.

To the right, opposite Via Morelli, a short street leads to P.za San Secondo, with the large Gothic church of *San Secondo,* containing a fine polyptych by Gaud. Ferrari (just within the S.W. door), and covering a 6C crypt. From here Via Cavour leads on past the *Torre dei Guttuari* to the station. On the right (26 Via Venti Settembre) is the late-14C *Pal. Catena,* with terracotta decoration.

The Corso skirts the triangular P.za Alfieri (r.), with a statue of the poet, separated by a block of public offices from the public garden and P.za Emanuele Filiberto del Mercato. At the E. end of the Corso, 550 m farther, is the church of *San Pietro in Consavia* (1467), now, with its cloister, containing a small lapidary collection. This with the adjoining circular 10C *Baptistery* (earlier the church of the Order of St John of Jerusalem) are open daily exc. Mon, 10-12, 16-19.

There is a charming little Romanesque church (12-14C) at *Viatosto,* 4 km. N. of Asti; while from *Montechiaro* (16 km. N.W. by the road or railway to Chivasso) may be visited San Nazario (early 11C), 5 km. N.W. of the station, and San Secondo (11C) above *Cortazzone,* 8 km. S.W.—For Vezzolano, see p. 86.

Road and railway follow the Tanaro valley to (91 km.) **Alessandria,** a cheerful but uninteresting provincial capital (103,400 inhab.) that takes importance from a position almost equidistant from Turin, Milan, and Genoa. A rail centre, with felt-hat factories, it is mainly of 18-19C appearance.

It was founded by seven castellans of the Monferrato who rebelled against Frederick Barbarossa in 1168, and named their new city after Pope Alexander III. A curious old figure at the corner of the 18-19C *Cathedral* is said to depict the peasant Gagliaudo who by an ancient trick induced the Emperor to raise the siege of 1175.—The *Palazzo della Prefettura* (1773), by Bened. Alfieri, in the central P.za della Libertà, is the best of the city's mansions, but there are others here and in Via Guasco which leads N. to the 14-15C church of *Santa Maria di Castello.*

During recent restoration work, parts of the 6C church and medieval building have come to light.

Alessandria has direct rail communication with Alba, Acqui, Ovada, Novara, Vercelli, Milan, Pavia, and Piacenza.

The Genoa road crosses (101 km.) the battlefield of *Marengo,* where Napoleon defeated the Austrians on 14 June 1800, in a battle which he regarded as the most brilliant of his career, though Gen. Desaix fell on the field. The commemorative column was removed by the Austrians in 1814 and not brought back until 1922. A small Museum has been arranged in the Villa di Marengo (16-19; fest. 9.30-12, 16-19; winter: 14.30-17.30; fest. also 10-12; closed Mon).

At *Boscomarengo,* 9 km. S., is the remarkable church of Santa Croce, erected in 1567 by Pius V (d. 1572), a native of the village, as his mausoleum. His splendid tomb remains empty, however, as he is buried in Santa Maria Maggiore in Rome. The paintings include works by Giorgio Vasari.

Diverging from N 10 (which continues E. to Tortona; p. 175) N 35 bis (r.) crosses a plain to pass just E. of (112 km.) **Novi Ligure** (2 km. r.) a modern-looking town (32,300 inhab.) with a 12C castle-tower. The battle of Novi (15 Aug 1799), where the Austrians and Russians defeated the French, was avenged at Marengo (see above).

FROM NOVI TO GENOA VIÂ GAVI, 56 km., a pleasant alternative, shorter but hillier than the main road.—The road ascends S. to give a fine view of the castle of (10 km.) *Gavi,* an ancient little town with a good 13C church.—20 km. *Voltaggio* (341 m) is a summer resort in the upper Lemme valley. The road rises to 773 m, then descends rapidly on the Ligurian side, with fine views seaward.—41 km. *Pontedécimo,* and thence to Genoa, see below.

Beyond Novi this route joins N 35 from Milan (Rte 16) and ascends the narrowing valley of the Scrivia.—122 km. *Serravalle Scrivia* lies 2 km. N. of the excavations of the Roman town of *Libarna,* of which the decumanus maximus, the amphitheatre, and theatre have been exposed (flanking the railway).

From Serravalle the old 'camionale', one of Italy's earliest motorways, has doubled as part of the A7, the Autostrada dei Fiori (comp. Rte 16); it affords the most direct route into (173 km.) **Genoa.**

From (125 km.) *Arquata Scrivia,* on the old road, there are two railway lines to Genoa, running more or less parallel. The communal cemetery contains 94 graves of British soldiers.—The valley becomes more attractive on the approach to (141 km.) *Ronco Scrivia* (325 m), the first Ligurian village. The newer railway line plunges into the Giovi Tunnel, over 8 km. long. The road, beyond (147 km.) *Busalla* (359 m), ascends to (149 km.) the *Passo dei Giovi* (472 m), then descends in zigzags into the industrial Polcévera valley.—160 km. *Pontedécimo* (91 m) is within the territory of the city of Genoa; the road traverses an almost continuous series of industrial suburbs—*San Quirico, Bolzaneto,* and *Rivarolo* (with a view of the great viaduct that takes the coastal autostrada over the railway)—to join the coast road at *Sampierdarena.*—175 km. **Genoa,** see Rte 7.

B   Viâ Alba and Acqui Terme

ROAD, 202 km. To (27 km.) *Carmagnola,* see Rte 4.—47 km. *Bra.*—64 km. **Alba.**—87 km. *Cástino.*—115 km. *Bistagno.*—125 km. **Acqui Terme.**—148 km. *Ovada.*—186 km. *Voltri.*—202 km. **Genoa.** This is a roundabout route, traversing the characteristic Piedmontese hill country of *Le Langhe,* with many ruined castles. The partisans were active here in 1944-45.

AUTOSTRADA, A 26, from Ovada to Genoa.

RAILWAY to *Acqui Terme* viâ Asti (change), 102 km. in 2-2½ hrs. *Alba* is reached (not very frequently) in 1 hr direct from Turin viâ Bra. From Acqui to *Genoa,* 58 km. in 1¾ hrs.

From Turin to (27 km.) *Carmagnola,* see Rte 4. N 393 diverges left across the railway for (37 km.) *Sommariva del Bosco,* with a picturesque castle and (47 km.) **Bra,** a town of 25,400 inhab. with tanneries and a few old houses, birthplace of St Joseph Cottolengo (1786-1842). The museum preserves finds from Roman Pollentia.

At *Pollenzo,* 5 km. S.E., the church contains fine 15C stalls, brought from Staffarda.—The road running S. from Bra, following the railway to Savona, passes (7 km.) *Cherasco,* an ancient little town with a 13C church, a castle of 1348, and the Museo Adriani (good coins and medals).—25 km. *Dogliani* is a centre for exploring the vine-clad Langhe hills, noted for Barolo and Dolcetto wines. *Carrù,* 8 km. S.W. of Dogliani, is the birthplace of Luigi Einaudi (1874-1961), President of Italy in 1948-55.—33 km. *Murazzano.*—52 km. *Ceva,* see Rte 6C.

The road (N 231) turns E. to descend the valley of the Tánaro, on whose N. bank, opposite Alba, come in a road from Asti and alternative routes, shorter but hillier, from Carmagnola viâ Corneliano d'Alba and from Turin direct viâ Poirino and Canale (N 29).—64 km. **Alba,** with 31,000 inhab., one of the most important vine-growing centres of Piedmont, is noted also as the birthplace of the Emperor Pertinax (126-193) and of Macrino d'Alba, the early 16C painter. In the ancient town, with its decorated medieval houses and tall brick towers, the over-restored *Duomo* contains fine carved and inlaid stalls (c. 1500), and in the *Palazzo Comunale* are two good paintings, one by Macrino.—The road leaves the Tánaro and begins to climb. Beyond (87 km.) *Cástino* it enters the valley of the Bórmida di Millésimo, where the Acqui road turns left.—97 km. *Vésime.*

N 29 goes on up the valley from Castino to (2½ km.) *Cortemilia.* and thence either to Millésimo or on to the Acqui-Savona road. From Vésime a hill-road ascends in 11 km. to *Roccaverano,* a typical cheese-making townlet of the Langhe, with a church (1509-16) in a Bramantesque style and the tall round tower (1204) of its ruined castle.

At (115 km.) *Bistagno* the two branches of the Bórmida join, and the road descends their united stream.—125 km. **Acqui Terme** (165 m), the Roman *Aquæ Statiellæ,* is famous for its sulphurous waters and mud baths. In the middle of the town (22,900 inhab.) the sulphurous waters (75° C) bubble up beneath a little pavilion, known as *La Bollente* (1870). The Romanesque *Cathedral* has a fine portal beneath a 17C loggia, and preserves its triple apse of the 11C, a campanile completed in the 13C, and a spacious crypt. In the sacristy is a triptych by B. Robeus (15C Catalan). Behind the cathedral, in the public garden, are remains of the *Castle* of the Paleologi (with an archæological museum); while in the other direction the church of *San Pietro* has a fine 11C apse and octagonal campanile. On the other side of the Bórmida, near the Vecchie Terme, are four arches of a *Roman Aqueduct* and an open-air swimming-pool.

Acqui is also on the road and railway from Alessandria to Savona. The road to (74½ km.) Savona (N 30) ascends the valley of the Bórmida di Spigno, passing (25 km.) *Spigno* and (40 km.) *Dego.*—47 km. *Cairo Montenotte* recalls Napoleon's first victory in Italy (April 1796), won over the Austrians and Piedmontese at

Montenotte, c. 15km. E. *San Giuseppe di Cairo,* beyond, has large carbon works.—52km. *Cárcare,* and thence by N 29 to Savona, see Rte 6C.

At (148km.) *Ovada,* the A 26 autostrada from Alessandria to Genoa joins the route. Ovada, birthplace of St Paul of the Cross (Paolo Danei; 1694-1775), founder of the Passionist Order, stands at the foot of the last ascent, the summit of which (532 m) is reached in a short tunnel beneath the *Passo del Turchino.* The road descends rapidly to the coast at (186km.) *Voltri.* From there to (202km.) **Genoa,** see Rte 5.

C   Viâ Mondovì and Savona

ROAD, 207km. To (52km.) *Savigliano,* see Rte 4.—N28, 66km. *Fossano.*—88km. **Mondovì.** 111km. *Ceva.*—N28 bis. 133km. *Millésimo.*—At (141km.) *Cárcare N29 is joined.—161km.* **Savona.** Thence to **Genoa,** see Rte 5.

AUTOSTRADA, A 6, 127km. takes much the same route to Savona, where it joins A 10 (45km.) for Genoa (172km, by-passing Savona).

RAILWAY to Savona, 149km. in 2-3 hrs; to *Mondovì,* 83km. in 1-1¾hrs. Another route to Savona, viâ Bra, joining the above route at Ceva, is 3km. shorter (stopping trains only). From Savona to *Genoa,* see Rte 5.

From Turin to (52km.) *Savigliano,* 6km. beyond which N 28 branches left from the Cúneo road, see Rte 4.—66km. *Fossano* is noteworthy for its massive 14C castle and its Baroque churches.—88km. **Mondovì** is a pleasant town (21,900 inhab.), lying partly in the Ellero valley (Mondovì Breo, the modern town; 381 m) and partly on a hill (Mondovì Piazza; 558 m). A funicular (and road) ascend from the lower town to the upper, in which are the *Cathedral*(by Fr. Gallo; 1743-63), the gorgeous *Chiesa della Missione* (1678), with a 'trompe-l'oeil' vault-painting by And. Pozzo, and the *Belvedere* (*View), a garden laid out round an old tower. Mondovì was the scene of a victory of Napoleon in 1796, and was the birthplace of Giov. Giolitti (1842-1928). Five times prime minister from 1892 to 1921, he introduced universal suffrage into Italy.

Lurisia. a spa with radioactive springs, developed since 1928, lies 15 km. S.W. of Mondovì beyond Villanova, and is reached by bus from Mondovì or from Cúneo, 22 km. N.W.

Frabosa Soprana (892m). 16km. S. of Mondivì (bus), is locally famed as a summer and winter resort, with ski-lifts and chair-lift to *Monte Moro* (1760m). Ascents are made in the E. group of the Maritime Alps (Mongioie, 2630m; Mondolè, 2382m) with the aid of refuge-inns at *Prel* (1699m) and *Monte Balme* (1996m). A fairly hilly road runs S.E. to (10km.) *Bossea* in the Val Corsaglia (bus daily or oftener from Mondovì, 24km.), with stalacite *Caves.—*Pamparato* (817m) is a smaller hill resort, 21km. S. of Vicoforte (bus from Mondovì).

95km. *Vicoforte,* by-passed by the main road, has a large domed pilgrimage church, begun in 1596 by Vittozzi, continued after 1728 by Fr. Gallo, and completed in 1890.—111km. **Ceva** (370m) is an important road and railway junction.

FROM CEVA TO IMPERIA, N 28, 87km. Railway to Ormea, infrequently in 1 hr; bus thence in 2 hrs. The road follows the railway up the Tánaro valley.—11km. *Bagnasco* (485m), dominated by a ruined castle.—23km. *Garessio* (579m), a favourite summer resort, lies in a delightful situation among the hills, mainly along the side-road (bus) which here diverges for Albenga (37km.) viâ the *Colle San Bernardo* (957m).—35km. *Ormea* (732m), another pleasant hill-resort, with a ruined castle, is the beginning of a fine walk to (7 hrs N.) Frabosa (see above) viâ the Colla dei Termini (2006m) and Bossea.—42km. *Ponte di Nava* (818m). The road enters Liguria, passing (44km.) *Case di Nava,* and crosses the watershed at (46km.) the *Colle di Nava* (934m). *Monesi,* 16km. W., is a small winter-sporting centre on Monte Saccarello (2201 m).—After a descent to (56 km.) *Pieve di Teco* (244 m), this route crosses the inland road from Bordighera to Albenga. After another ascent to (64 km.) the *Colle San Bartolomeo* (621 m), the road descends the Impero valley, passing (79 km.) *Pontedássio*, with a spaghetti museum, to (87 km.) *Imperia* (Oneglia, see Rte 5).

The Savona road next reaches (133 km.) *Millésimo*, an old-walled village with a castle and quaint fortified bridge. A hilly road leading S. to Albenga (56 km.) passes (25 km.) *Calizzano* (p. 83).—At (141 km.) *Cárcare* the road from Acqui and Cairo comes in (p. 89).—Just beyond (148 km.) *Altare*, a small glass-making town, the road tunnels beneath the *Bocchetta di Cadibona* (435 m), a pass popularly regarded as marking the division between Alps and Apennines. The descent leads down the Letimbro valley, amid chestnut woods.—161 km. **Savona**, and thence to (207 km.) **Genoa**, see Rte 5.

7   GENOA

GENOA, in Italian **Génova** (804,000 inhab.), the most important port of Italy, is built on the irregular seaward slopes of an amphitheatre of hills. Preserving many relics of an ancient and honourable history, and adorned with the palaces, churches, and parks of its great maritime families, it well merits its title 'la superba'. The interesting old quarters clustered around the port, with their steep and narrow alleys of tall houses, contrast with the new suburbs sprawled across the hills behind. Genoa possesses a number of beautiful art collections.

Railway Stations. *P.za Principe* (Pl. 1), the central station for all services; *Brignole* (Pl. 12), formerly a subsidiary station for the Spezia and Pisa line, but now almost as busy as P.za Principe.

Steamer Quay. *Stazione Marittima* (Pl. 5), Ponte dei Mille and Ponte Andrea Doria.

Airport. *Cristoforo Colombo*, at Sestri Ponente (6 km. W.), built into the sea. Alitalia flights to London and Frankfurt (and internal services). British Caledonian flights to London (Gatwick). City Air Terminal, 188 Via XII Ottobre.

Hotels, near the station, Via Balbi, and near Piazza Fontane Marose.

Post Office. 1 Via Boccardo (P.za De Ferrari).

Information Offices. *E.P.T.* 11/4 Via Roma; Offices at: Stazione Principe, Stazione Brignole, and Airport.

British Consulate, Via XII Ottobre.

Theatres. *Teatro Margherita*, 16/A Via Venti Settembre (used by the opera company of the Teatro Carlo Felice, which has still not been rebuilt since its destruction in the war); *Sala Duse*, 6 Via Bacigalupo (P.za Corvetto); *Politeama Genovese*, 2 Via Bacigalupo.

City Transport. The buses most useful to the visitor are: **1.** *P.za Caricamento*—Sampierdarena—Pegli—*Voltri;* **3.** *P.za Caricamento*—Staz. Principe—Sampierdarena—*Pegli Lido;* **4.** *Staz. Brignole*—Corso A. Saffi—P.za Cavour—P.za Caricamento—P.za Principe—Via Cornigliano—*Sestri;* **15.** *P.za Caricamento*—P.za Tommaseo—Sturla—Quarto—Quinto—*Nervi;* **33.** *P.za Principe*—Circonvallazione a Monte—P.za Manin—P.za Corvetto—P.za De Ferrari—*Staz. Brignole;* **34.** *P.za Dinegro*—P.za Principe—P.za Nunztata—P.za Corvetto—P.za Manin—*Cimetero di Staglieno;* **36.** *Via Piave*—Corso Buenos Aires—P.za De Ferrari—P.za Corvetto—*P.za Corvetto*—*P.za Manin;* **42.** *P.za De Ferrari*—P.za Vittoria—Galleria Mameli—*Boccadasse.*

Country Buses in all directions from P.za della Vittoria and P.za Acquaverde (Staz. Principe); frequent service along the coast in both directions.

Motor Boats. Organized trips round the harbour (c. 1 hr), at 15 in winter or 16 in summer, from Ponte dei Mille, just W. of Staz. Marittima.—**Ferries** for *Sardinia* (Tirrenia and Canguro lines), and for *Sicily* (Grandi Tràghetti).

Funicular Railways. F. Largo della Zecca (Pl. 6) to *Castellaccio* (Righi) viâ S. Nicolò (Pl. 2); **H.** P.za Portello (Pl. 7) to *Corso Magenta.*—Rack Railway **(G)**

from Via del Lagaccio, near P.za Principe (Pl. 1) to *Granarolo.*—Lifts. **I.** Via XX
Settembre to *Corso A. Podestà* (Ponte Monumentale); **M.** Corso Magenta to *Via
Crocco;* **N.** P.za Portello to the *Castelletto.*

History. The position of Genoa at the northernmost point of the Tyrrhenian Sea
has given it a lasting maritime importance; and the original Ligurian inhabitants of
the site established early contact with the first known navigators of the
Mediterranean—the Phoenicians and the Greeks—and objects excavated have
proved the existence of a trading-post here in the 6C B.C. In the 3C B.C. Genoa
preferred to throw in her lot with Rome rather than with the invading
Carthaginians and the town, destroyed by the latter in 205 B.C.. was soon rebuilt
under the Roman prætor Sp. Cassius. Protected by its mountains, Genoa was
little affected by the barbarian invasions, and Roman connections were not
entirely severed until the arrival of the Lombards in 641. In the succeeding centuries
the raids of Saracen pirates spurred the Genoese to retaliation and the sailors of
Genoa not only withstood the pirates' attacks, but also captured their strongholds
of Corsica and Sardinia. The latter island was taken with the aid of Pisa, and its
occupation led to two centuries of war, which ended in the utter rout of the Pisans
at the Meloria (1284) and at Porto Pisano (1290). With this success began the
acquisition of Genoa's great colonial empire, which extended as far as the Crimea,
Syria, and North Africa; and important Genoese colonies were established in the
Morea. These advances, and the large profits made during the Crusades, led to a
collision with the ambitions of Venice; and the subsequent war ended in the defeat
of the Genoese at Chioggia (1380). Meanwhile the internal politics of Genoa were
sufficiently turbulent. After the fall of the consuls in 1191 the power passed to the
podestà or mayors and the 'Capitani del Popolo' (1258-1340), with intervals of
submission to the Emperor Henry VII (1311-13) and to Robert of Anjou, King of
Naples (1318-35). In 1340 came the election of the first doge, Simone Boccanegra.
The continual strife between the great families—the Doria, the Spinola, and the
Fieschi—made Genoa an easy victim to the rising military powers in the 15C and a
succession of foreign masters followed. Charles VI of France (1396-1409) was
followed by the Marquess of Monferrato (1409-13) and Filippo Maria Visconti
(1421-35), under whom the Genoese inflicted a crushing defeat on the fleet of
Aragon at Ponza (1435). The domination of the Sforza (1466-99) was followed by a
further French conquest under Louis XII (1499-1512). In 1528, however, Andrea
Doria (1466-1560), the greatest of the Genoese naval leaders, formulated a
constitution for Genoa which freed the city from foreign rule, though it established
despotic government at home, and was followed (1547-48) by the insurrections of
Fieschi and Cibo. The conquests of the Turks in their oriental empire, the
transference of overseas trade with America to Atlantic ports, and the domination
of Spain, brought utter decadence to Genoa in the 17C, and in 1684 Louis XIV
entered the town after a bombardment. The Austrian occupation of 50 years later
was ended by a popular insurrection (5-10 Dec, 1746), which was started by the
action of a boy, Battista Perasso. In 1768 Genoa's last remaining colony, Corsica,
revolted under Paoli, and the Genoese sold their rights in the island to France. In
1796 Napoleon entered Genoa, and four years later the city was beleaguered by the
Austrians on land and the English at sea; but Masséna's stubborn defence was
relieved by the victory of Marengo. The Ligurian Republic, formed in 1802, soon
became a French province, but in 1815 Genoa was joined to Piedmont by the treaty
of Vienna, and speedily developed into a stronghold of the Risorgimento, with
Mazzini as the leading spirit, abetted by Garibaldi, the brothers Ruffini and their
heroic mother, the soldier patriot Nino Bixio (1821-73), and Goffredo Mameli
(1827-49) the warrior poet. The ill-fated expedition of Pisacane and Nicotera (June
1857) set forth from Genoa, and it was in Genoa that Garibaldi planned his
daredevil expedition with the 'Thousand' in 1860. Genoa, especially the old town,
was damaged by Allied air and sea bombardment in the Second World War.

Among the most famous natives of Genoa are Christopher Columbus (1447-
1506), the navigator; Nicolò Paganini (1784-1840), the violinist and composer; and
Giuseppe Mazzini (1805-72), the ideologist of the Risorgimento. Popes Innocent
IV (Sinibaldo Fiesco; d. 1254) and Innocent VIII (G. B. Cibo; 1432-92) were
Genoese. Aless. Stradella (1642-82), the composer, was murdered in Genoa by
assassins hired by the former lover of his Venetian wife.

Art. The architecture of medieval Genoa is characterized by the black-and-white
striped façades of the older churches and other buildings; and the earliest sculpture
came from the workshops of the Pisani and the Comacini. The Renaissance
brought the work of Galeazzo Alessi, the Perugian architect, while the 16C

sculpture of the Gaggini was followed by the work of the Carlone and the disciples of Bernini. The Genoese school of painting is said to derive from the Florentine Perin del Vaga, who was commissioned to decorate the Palazzo Doria in 1527. In 1607 Rubens visited Genoa, and in 1621 Van Dyck arrived and stayed on and off in the city for six years. Luca Cambiaso, Lazzaro Calvi, and G. B. Castello are the most illustrious names of the 16C, followed in the 17C by Bernardo Strozzi ('il Prete Genovese'), Bernardo and Valerio Castello, G. B. Castiglione, Fiasella, and the Piola brothers, and in the 18C by Magnasco, Baratta, and others.

I CENTRAL GENOA

The main thoroughfare leading, under various names, from the *Piazza Principe Station* (Pl. 1) to the central Piazza De Ferrari skirts the brow of the group of hills on which Genoa is built. To the right, below, is the labyrinth of the old town; to the left are the newer quarters on the hillside.

From Piazza Acquaverde, with its subways, bus-stations and Columbus monument (1862), VIA BALBI (Pl. 1, 6) leads downhill towards the centre. This street and its continuations contain many dignified old mansions, though the narrowness of the roadway detracts from the full effect of their external façades. On the right (No. 10) is the former **Palazzo Reale** (Pl. 6), designed c. 1650 for the Balbi family by G. A. Falcone and P. F. Cantone and remodelled in 1705 for the Durazzo by Carlo Fontana.

It is now occupied by the Departments of Fine Arts and Antiquities, and is officially known as Palazzo Balbi-Durazzo. From 1842 to 1922 it was the royal seat in Genoa and it contains several suites of sumptuously decorated rooms (temporarily closed to the public). On the upper floor the Gallery of Mirrors and the Ballroom are magnificent; and among the paintings are some charming portraits of royal ladies, a 16C Dutch series of Scenes from the life of St Agnes, and a Crucifixion by *Van Dyck*. Luca Giordano is represented by two large paintings, and there are characteristic works by *Dom. Parodi, Guidobono, Nuvolone* (Portrait of a lady), *Strozzi,* and *Guido Reni.*

Opposite, at No. 5, is a palace (1634-36) built as a Jesuit college by Bartolomeo Bianco, occupied by the *University* since 1803. A flight of steps flanked by lions (1704) leads to an imposing court whence another staircase ascends to the Aula Magna, in which are statues and reliefs by Giambologna (1579). The building houses the faculties of arts, law, and natural science; the library is in a former Jesuit church next door. No. 1, the *Palazzo Durazzo-Pallavicini,* also by Bart. Bianco, has a later double loggia. The *Palazzo Balbi-Senárega,* opposite (No. 4), is also by Bianco. On Piazza della Nunziata, beyond, stands the **Santissima Annunziata** (Pl. 6), a church rebuilt in 1591-1620, with a 19C portico. The domed interior is richly adorned with coloured marble and 17C Genoese paintings (G. B. Carlone, etc.). Via P. E. Bensa leads on to Largo della Zecca, in which is the entrance to the *Galleria Garibaldi,* a road-tunnel leading to P.za Portello and continued from there by the *Galleria. Nino Bixio* to P.za Corvetto.

To the right is VIA CAIROLI (Pl. 6), in which *Palazzo Balbi* (No. 18) has an imposing staircase by G. Petondi (1780). This street ends in Piazza della Meridiana with the *Pal. della Meridiana,* a good plain 16C building.

VIA GARIBALDI (Pl. 6, 7), which leads out of this piazza, is lined with some of the most magnificent of Genoese palaces. *Palazzo Bianco (No. 11; adm. 9.30-11.45, 14.30-17.30; Sun, Mon, & fest. closed) was so named because of its colour, although it has now darkened considerably. It was built for the Grimaldi c. 1565 by Orsolino and Ponzello and enlarged after 1711. It contains the collections presented to the State, with the palace, by the Duchess of Galliera in 1884. Only the outstanding pieces, with some later acquisitions, are on view; the remainder is accessible to students on application.

ROOM 1 (beyond Room 2). *Byzantine (13C) School,* Madonna and Child; *Barnaba da Modena,* Madonna of the Goldfinch; works by the *Brea* family (late 15-16C), including a Crucifixion by *Ludovico;* Byzantine embroidered altarcloth of the 13C (from the Cathedral).— ROOM 2. *Giov. Mazone,* Crucifixion; works by *Luca Cambiaso* (including the 'Madonna della candela').—SECOND FLOOR. R.3 (South Loggia). *Paolo Veronese,* Crucifixion; *Palma il Vecchio,* Madonna and Child with Saints; *Filippino Lippi,* Madonna and Child with Saints; *Pontormo,* Portrait of a Florentine gentleman.—ROOM 4. *Master of St John the Evangelist,* *Four scenes from the life of the Saint; *Hugo van der Goes,* *Christ blessing; *Joos van Cleve,* Madonna and Child; *Gerard David,* *Madonna 'della pappa', Madonna and Child, and Saints, Crucifixion; *Corneille de Lyon,* Portrait of a young man; *Jean Clouet,* Portrait of a gentleman; *Jan Provost,* St Peter, Annunciation, St Elisabeth; *Lucas Cranach the elder,* Portrait of a lady; *Flemish School* (early 16C), St Jerome.—R.5. *Jan Matsys,* Portrait of Andrea Doria, Madonna and Child; works by *Jan van Scorel.*—RR. 6 & 7. Works by *Van Dyck* and *Rubens,* who both came to Genoa in the early 17C.— ROOM 8. *David Teniers the younger,* Watchmen; *Jan Steen,* Hostelry party; *Jacob Ruysdael,* Landscape; *Jan van Goyen,* Landscape with rabbits.—R.9. *Simone Vouet,* David with the head of Goliath.—ROOM 10 (North Loggia), *Guercino,* God the father. ROOM 11. Works of the Spanish school, including *Murillo* (Flight into Egypt).

ROOMS 12-15 contain interesting paintings of the 17-18C Ligurian school, including works by *Bernardo Strozzi, Anton Maria Vassallo, Sinibaldo Scorza, Giovanni Andrea* and *Orazio De Ferrari, Domenico Fiasella,* and *Giov. Andrea Ansaldo.* The local collection is continued on the ground floor (across the courtyard) in RR. 16-20 (*Dom. Piola, Gregorio De Ferrari, Bart. Guidobono, Giov. Battista Gaulli, Il Baciccio, Valerio Castello, Giov. Benedetto Castiglione,* and *Aless. Magnasco*).

Almost opposite Palazzo Bianco is **Palazzo Rosso** (Pl. 6), also named from its colour, a magnificent building of 1671-77 erected for the Brignole family by Matteo Lagomaggiore and bequeathed to the city by the Duchess of Galliera in 1874. Admission 9.30-11.30, 14.30-17.30; Sun, Mon, & fest. closed.

It contains rooms frescoed by Genoese painters and a notable collection of works of art. FIRST FLOOR. R. 2. *Pisanello,* Portrait of a man; *Paris Bordone,* Portrait of a young man; *Bonifazio Veronese,* Adoration of the Magi; *Paolo Veronese,* Judith.—R. 3. *Titian,* Holy family.—R. 4. Works by *Mattia Preti* and *Caravaggio* (Ecce Homo).—R. 5. *Guercino,* Cleopatra; *Guido Reni,* St Sebastian.—RR. 6-10 contain works by the local Ligurian school.—SECOND FLOOR. RR. 13 & 14. *Portraits by *Van Dyck* (Geronima Brignole, the goldsmith Puccio and his son, Anton Giulio Brignole, Paolino Adorno Brignole). Also in ROOM 14: *Albrecht Dürer,* Portrait of a young boy; *Frans Pourbus the elder,* Viglius Von Aytta; *Rubens,* Christ carrying the Cross.—R. 15. *Murillo,* St Francis. The collection also includes Coins and medals (RR. 29-34), and Ligurian ceramic ware (RR. 36-39).

Immediately beyond Palazzo Rosso, on the left, is **Palazzo Tursi** (the

Municipio) begun in 1568 by the Ponsello brothers; the loggie were added in 1596 around the magnificent courtyard.

Visitors (admitted 9-12, 14-17) are shown the ex *Sala del Consiglio Generale* and the adjoining *Sala della Giunta* with Paganini's Guarnerius violin (1742). In the *Sala del Sindaco* (shown only when not in use) is preserved a bronze tablet inscribed with a decree (117 B.C.) delimiting the boundary between the Genuates and the Veturii, and three letters from Columbus.

Most of the other mansions in this street can be admired only from the outside, though the courtyards are usually accessible; notable among them are the late-16C *Palazzo Serra* or *Campanella* (No. 12) and *Palazzo Cattaneo-Adorno* (Nos. 8-10); the *Palazzo Podestà* (No. 7), begun by G. B. Castello in 1583, with a good stucco vestibule and a rococo grotto and fountain in the courtyard; *Palazzo Spinola* (No. 5), now a bank, with frescoes in the vestibule (the fine courtyard has been enclosed for use as a banking hall); *Palazzo Doria* (No. 6) of 1563, remodelled in 1684, with a charming little courtyard; *Palazzo Carrega Cataldi* (No. 4) by G. B. Castello (1558-60), now the Chamber of Commerce. *Palazzo Parodi* (No. 3) is by Alessi (1567), with a portal by Taddeo Carlone (1581); No. 2, the *Palazzo Gambaro*, now a bank, is by Ponzello (1565); No. 1, the *Palazzo Cambiaso*, also a bank, is by Alessi (1565).—The irregular P.za Fontane Marose has several fine mansions (*Palazzi Pallavicini*, No. 2, begun 1575; *Negone*, No. 4, rather later, altered c. 1750; and *Spinola dei Marmi*, No. 6, of the 15C, with a particoloured marble façade and statues of the family).

Via Venticinque Aprile leads south to PIAZZA DE FERRARI (Pl. 11), the busiest square in Genoa, with an abundant fountain. On the left, behind Rivalta's Garibaldi monument (1893), stands the neo-classical pronaos of the *Teatro Carlo Felice,* gutted in 1944 and still not rebuilt. Next to it is the *Accademia Ligustica di Belle Arti,* built by the same architect, Carlo Barabino, in 1827-31 (restored after war damage). An art gallery contains paintings by Ligurian artists (13-19C), including Perin del Vaga and Strozzi. Here also is the civic *Biblioteca Berio.* Farther on is the *Exchange;* on the right side of the Doge's Palace; and at the farther end the palazzo of the Società di Navigazione Italia. From the square issue Via Roma (N.E.) and Via Venti Settembre (S.E.).

Behind the offices of the Società Italia is the Baroque church of the **Gesù** (Pl. 11), built in 1589-1606 by Pellegrino Tibaldi and Gius. Valeriani; the façade was completed in 1892 to the original design. The sumptuous polychrome interior provides a fit setting for the paintings. These include an Assumption, by *Guido Reni* (3rd chapel on the right); a Circumcision (1608; high altar), and St Ignatius curing the sick (1620; 3rd chapel on the left), both by *Rubens.*—Surrounding the adjoining Piazza Matteotti is **Palazzo Ducale** (Pl. 11), the former residence of the Doges, now occupied by the Law Courts. The present building was begun in 1806 by Simone Cantone, but some 13C work is visible at the back (comp. p. 98). The vestibule with a cortile at either end (one with a 17C fountain) is attractive with remains of statues of the Doria family by Montorsoli and Taddeo Carlone. Excavations in the piazza in 1975 revealed an Imperial Roman house.

A little farther on stands the *Cathedral (San Lorenzo;* Pl. 10), a Romanesque building consecrated (unfinished) in 1118 and modified in the 13-14C and during the Renaissance. The façade was restored in 1934.

On the S. side of the church are Hellenistic sarcophagi, a 15C Grimaldi tomb, and the portal of *San Gottardo,* with Romanesque sculpture. The façade, approached by a flight of steps between two lions (1840), is

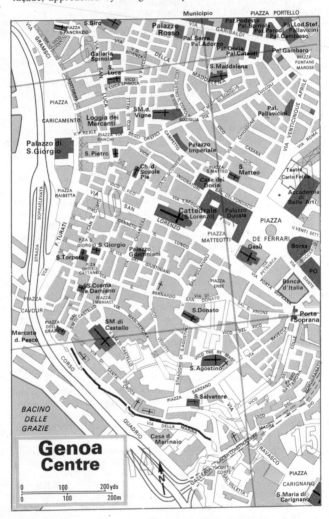

adorned with bands of particoloured marble: the three W. doorways approximate to the French Gothic style. The *Campanile* (being restored) was completed in 1522; the sundial at the corner is locally called 'L' Arrotino', i.e. 'The Knifegrinder'. On the N. side are more sarcophagi and the 12C portal of *San Giovanni.

The INTERIOR is plain and severe, with Corinthian columns. The nave roof was raised in 1550, and the cupola, by Alessi, added in 1567. The pulpit (1526) is by *Pier Angelo Scala* of Carona. In the South Aisle are: (1st altar) a marble Crucifixion of 1443, and a British naval shell that damaged the chapel without exploding in 1941; (3rd altar) the Virgin with saints, by *Luca Cambiaso;* and, to the right of the high altar, the *Vision of St Sebastian, by *Fed. Barocci* (1595). The stalls in the apse date from 1514-64. In the Lercari Chapel, to the left of the high altar, are wall and ceiling paintings by *Cambiaso* and *Bern. Castello.* The great *CHAPEL OF ST JOHN THE BAPTIST. on the N. side, has a richly decorated front by 15C sculptors from Bissone (Lugano). The interior is decorated with precious marble and designs by *Giov. D'Aria,* and with statues of Old Testáment characters by *Matteo Civitali,* and of John the Baptist and the Virgin by *And. Sansovino* (1504). Above the modern altar is a baldacchino (1532) by *da Corte* and *Della Porta.* The 13C sarcophagus, on the left, formerly held relics of the saint. In the adjoining chapel is the tomb of Giorgio Fieschi (d. 1461) by *Giov. Gaggini;* beyond the N. door is that of Luca Fieschi (c. 1336), in the manner of *Giov. Pisano.*

The sacristy, on the N. side of the church, leads to a series of vaults containing the Treasury (adm. 9.30-12, 15-17.30; closed Sun, Mon, & fest.). Here are a 1C Roman glass dish, said to have been used at the Last Supper; two copes, one of the mid-15C (but popularly assigned to Pope Gelasius), another of the mid-16C; the *Zaccaria Cross, a Byzantine work of the 10C refashioned in the 13C; the 11-12C reliquary of the Arm of St Anne, brought from Pera (Istanbul) in 1461; a 12C casket, perhaps given by Frederick Barbarossa in 1178; a silver-gilt casket for the ashes of St John the Baptist, by Teramo Danieli and Sim. Caldera (c. 1440); a chalcedony dish (? 1C) with the head of John the Baptist (a French 15C addition); the consecration Bull of Pope Gelasius II (1118); and many reliquaries, chalices, etc.

II   THE OLD TOWN AND THE HARBOUR

The Old Town, lying between the harbour, the Via Garibaldi, and the Via Venticinque Aprile, with its narrow lanes or 'carugi', some of which are less than 3 m wide, and its lofty houses, is, although damaged by war and flood, still a most interesting quarter of Genoa, and a walk through its narrow alleys gives an excellent insight into Genoese life. Many of the houses have charming gateways in white marble or black stone bearing the symbol of St George, patron of the city. The two itineraries given below include most of the points of interest.

From opposite the W. end of the cathedral the narrow Via Chiabrera (Pl. 10) leads S.W. Busts and reliefs decorate the portico of the 17C *Palazzo Giustiniani* (No. 6). From Via San Bernardo, on the right, Vico dei Giustiniani leads left to Piazza Embriaci (Pl. 10), in which No. 5, the *Casa Brignole Sale* (formerly Embriaci; 1580), has a Doric portal by Orsolino. The steep Salita della Torre degli Embriaci, passing a 12C tower embattled in 1923, ascends to *Santa Maria di Castello (Pl. 10), a Romanesque church with 15C Gothic additions, well restored. It occupies the site of the Roman castrum and preserves some Roman columns.

From the sacristy is the entrance to the Dominican convent of 1442, where the restored second cloister has 15C vault-paintings and a charming fresco of the Annunciation signed 'Iustus de Alemania 1451'. A Museum (closed for restoration) includes paintings by *Lod. Brea* formerly in the church.

The Salita Santa Maria di Castello and Via Santa Croce lead S.E. to the large Piazza Sarzano. This area was badly damaged in the war and is still in a partly derelict state. On the site of the bombed convent of *San Silvestro* (l.) interesting excavations have revealed the remains of the medieval Castello built above the pre-Roman walls of the ancient city.

The Stradone Sant'Agostino passes (r.) the Gothic church of **Sant'Agostino** (Pl. 14), begun in 1260, which preserves a fine campanile with graceful windows and spire. It has been closed for many years awaiting restoration. The Stradone ends beside **San Donato** (Pl. 10), a fine church consecrated in 1189 with a splendid polygonal campanile and a good doorway. The beautiful interior contains an *Adoration of the Magi, by Joos van Cleve (stolen in 1974, but recovered and to be returned here after restoration). Beyond San Donato, Via San Bernardo leads to the left, with several fine doorways and a good courtyard at No. 19 (*Palazzo Schiaffino*), while the Salita Pollaiuoli continues to Via Canneto il Lungo, a long lane with many fine doorways (at No. 23, remains of the *Palazzo Fieschi*). Via Canneto il Curto (l.) leads past the Piazzetta Stella (doorway at No. 5) to P.za San Giorgio, with the two small churches of *San Giorgio* and *San Torpete* (Pl. 10). Just to the S.W. is P.za Grillo Cattaneo, at No. 6 in which is a splendid portal by Tamagnino. From here the Vico dietro il Coro leads to *Santi Cosma e Damiano,* an 11C church with traces of an earlier building.

From San Giorgio (see above) Via Canneto il Curto or any parallel street leads back to Via San Lorenzo.

A SECOND ITINERARY THROUGH THE OLD TOWN starts between the Palazzo Ducale and the cathedral, following Via. T. Reggio. In this street is (r.) the old *Palazzo del Comune* (1291) with the *Torre del Popolo* (1307), now incorporated in the Ducal Palace. On the other side of the street are the 15C *Palazzetto Criminale* (now the City and Republic Archives) and (No. 12) the *Cloister of San Lorenzo* (restored). The Salita allo Arcivescovato (a few metres back) leads to Piazza San Matteo, with *San Matteo** (Pl. 11), the ancient church of the Doria family. Built in 1125, it has a striped black and white Gothic façade (1278) with inscriptions recounting the glorious deeds of the Dorias.

The interior (1543) contains sculptures by *Montorsoli* and *Silvio Cosini,* and paintings by *G. B. Castello* and *Cambiaso;* and in the crypt (apply to the sacristan) is the tomb of Andrea Doria, by Montorsoli. An archway on the left of the church leads to the cloister (1308-10) by *Magister Marcus Venetus,* with coupled columns, and notable capitals at the two W. corners.

The little piazza is surrounded by mansions of the Doria family; No. 15 is the *Casa di Lamba Doria* (13C); No. 17 the *Casa di Andrea Doria,* presented to the famous admiral by his native city in 1528 (inscription); No. 14, the *Casa di Branca Doria,* has a magnificent portal. Off Via Chiossone, in which No. 1 is another Doria house with a portal by Pace Gaggini, the ancient Vico della Casana leads to the left. The animated Via Luccoli (left again), with many good shops, crosses P.za Soziglia (with a cafe founded in 1828) to reach the fine Campetto (Pl. 10). *Palazzo Imperiale* (1560) here (No. 8) is a sumptuous building by G. B. Castello. The upper part of the façade is decorated with paintings and stucchi by Semini. In the crooked Via degli Orefici, No. 9 (47r) has a charming 15C marble relief of the Adoration of the Magi, and No. 7 a portal carved with the Labours of Hercules by the Della Porta. In Piazza

Banchi, at the end of the street, is the *Loggia dei Mercanti,* designed possibly by Alessi (1570-95), renewed in 1838 and now occupied by the Commercial Exchange. The restored church of *San Pietro di Banchi,* approached by steps, was designed by Lurago (1581) in the Tuscan manner. In Via Ponte Reale, leading down to the quays, a tablet marks the house where Daniel O'Connell, 'the Liberator', died in 1847.

Opposite the end of the Campetto (see above) a passage leads to **Santa Maria delle Vigne** (Pl. 10), a church refashioned after 1598 (good Baroque interior) with a façade of 1842. Parts of its Romanesque predecessors (10C and 12C) can be seen on the left side, including fragments of the cloister, the nave wall, and the five-spired campanile; here, too, is an interesting tomb. From the piazza in front Vico dei Greci leads W. to Vico Mele with many interesting houses: No. 16r has a black stone relief of St John the Baptist (15C); No. 6, the *Palazzo Serra,* has an imposing portal and a Gothic outside stair; No. 8 is also noteworthy. Vico Torre San Luca continues to (No. 1) **Palazzo Spinola,** a 15C mansion left to the State in 1958 with a rich art collection (temporarily closed, but normally open 9-14, exc. Sun & Mon). The paintings include works by *Van Dyck* (Young boy, a fragment; the four Evangelists), *Joos van Cleve* (Madonna), and *Guido Reni. Antonello da Messina's* Ecce Homo was removed several years ago for restoration. In Via della Posta Vecchia, parallel to the E., are many noble portals, especially at No. 16 (1531). Vico della Scienza (l.) leads into Piazza di Pellicceria (Nos. 1 and 3 are palaces of the Spinolas); from here Vico del Pelo leads to the picturesque Via della Maddalena. On the right the church of **Santa Maria Maddalena** (Pl. 11), rebuilt in 1588 by And. Ceresola, preserves five 14C statues on its modern façade (1911). The richly decorated interior contains paintings by Bern. Castello, G. B. Parodi, and other Genoese masters. Via della Maddalena leads back past a good portal (No. 39r), a courtyard at No. 29 (the house of Simone Boccanegra), and a tabernacle at No. 34.

VIA SAN LUCA (Pl. 6, 10) was the main street of the city in the Middle Ages, when it was the principal place of residence of the great Genoese families; it no longer pretends to elegance. The church of *San Luca,* to the left, has an interior decorated by Dom. Piola. In the other direction is **San Siro** (Pl. 6), a large church rebuilt by And. Ceresola and Dan. Casella (1586-1613), with a façade of 1821. Its predecessor was the first cathedral of Genoa before the 9C. The nave and apse are frescoed by *G. B. Carlone* and in the 5th chapel on the N. side is a Presepio by *Pomerancio.* From the other side of Via San Luca, Vico dell'Agnello leads viâ Piazza dell'Agnello (in which No. 6 is the *Palazzo Cicala* of 1542 by Bern. Cantone) to Piazza San Pancrazio. From here Vico San Pancrazio (r.) leads to P.za di Fossatello, beyond which is Via Lomellini, with a courtyard at No. 2 and a portal at No. 12. No. 13, **Casa Mazzini** (adm. 9.30-11.30, 14-17; closed Sun, Mon, & fest.) was the birthplace of Giuseppe Mazzini (1805-72). It now contains a small museum and library of the Istituto Mazziniano. On the left is *San Filippo Neri* (Pl. 6), with an adjacent *Oratory,* two good works of the 18C.

From P.za Fossatello Via del Campo (portals at Nos. 1,9, and 35r), leads to the Gothic arch of Porta dei Vacca (1155). From here the long and disreputable Via di Pré leads behind Palazzo Reale to the church of

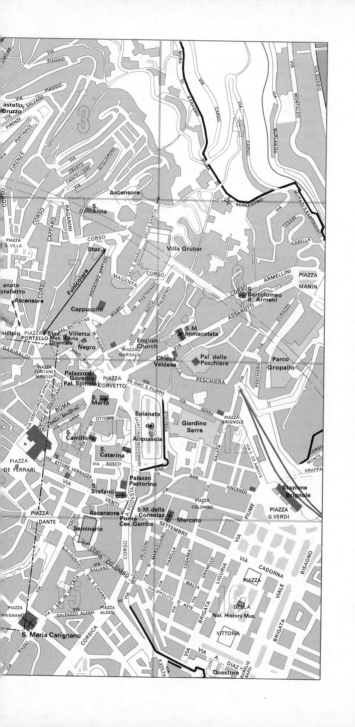

San Giovanni di Pré (Pl. 5), founded in 1180, with a severe interior (often restored) having an apse at each end, and a fine five-spired campanile.

The Salita San Giovanni ascends to Piazza Acquaverde and the station; below the church Piazza Commenda, with the loggia of the Commandery of the Knights of St John, affords access to the **Harbour,** along the great length of which runs the 'Sopraelevata', which distributes the motorway traffic to the city. A wall separates the main quay from the wharves and landing stages, and visitors are not admitted without a pass from the Ufficio dei Permessi at the Stazione Marittima (boat trips, see p. 91).

The old mole (Molo Vecchio, Pl. 9) was begun in 1257 by the Cistercian friars Oliverio and Filippo, and new works were undertaken in 1553 and 1642. An important extension of the harbour (1876-88) was due to the generous donation of 20 million lire by De Ferrari, Duke of Galliera. The Bacino della Lanterna and Bacino Sampierdarena unite Genoa with Sampierdarena. The harbour now occupies c. 1300 acres, of which two-thirds are water. It is principally important for its import trade in oil, coal, grain, and cotton. At the end of the Second World War it was full of mines and sunken ships, and most of the docks were badly damaged, but the efficiency of the port was re-established by 1950, since when new petrol quays have been constructed and the Cristoforo Colombo Airport (p. 91) built out over the water.

Via Gramsci ascends to Piazza Principe, with a monument to Galliera (1897), and the main approach to the *Stazione Marittima* (Pl. 5), beyond which is **Palazzo Doria Pamphilj** (Pl. 1), or *Palazzo del Principe,* composed of two buildings acquired by Andrea Doria in 1521 which were thrown into one by *Dom. Caranca* (1529); *Montorsoli* may have added the loggia (1543-47), towards the garden. Charles V and Napoleon were entertained here, and the composer Verdi after 1877. Part of the palace is now used as an international seamen's centre; but the frescoes by *Perin del Vaga* and the stuccoes by *Luzio Romano* and *Gugl. della Porta* can be seen in the vestibule and on the stairs. Conspicuous above the E. side of the harbour is the **Lanterna,** a lighthouse restored in 1543, which is the characteristic feature of the seaboard of Genoa.

In the other direction Via Gramsci passes the Custom House, the Harbourmaster's Office, and many warehouses, and ends at PIAZZA CARICAMENTO (Pl. 10), with a statue of Raff. Rubattino (1809-72), the shipowner who, against his will, supplied two vessels for Garibaldi's expedition. Here also stands the Gothic **Palazzo di San Giorgio* (Pl. 10), begun c. 1260 and extended in 1571. Once the palace of the Capitani del Popolo, it became in 1408 the seat of the famous Banco di San Giorgio. It is now occupied by the Harbour Board. Within is a typical courtyard with staircases restored in the 13C style and a two-storeyed portico. The Salone dei Capitani del Popolo and the Salone delle Compere are interesting (for adm. apply to the keeper).

From behind the Palazzo the long P.za Raibetta and Via Filippo Turati lead to Piazza Cavour (Pl. 10), at the foot of the *Old Mole* (see above), on which is the imposing *Porta Siberia* designed by Alessi and built by Ant. Roderio (1553). On the right in Piazza Cavour is the *Pescheria,* a modern building by Mario Braccialini. From here Corso Maurizio Quadrio, continued by Corso Aurelio Saffi, gradually ascends to Via Rivoli (Pl. 15), commanding a fine view of the harbour. For the new quarters of the town, see below.

III   EASTERN AND NORTHERN GENOA

From Piazza De Ferrari the wide and lively VIA VENTI SETTEMBRE and the short but broad VIA DANTE run S.E., the latter prolonged by a tunnel. Between them are the large Exchange and Post Office buildings. On the right, in Via Dante, is a little garden with the reconstructed 12C *Cloister of Sant'Andrea,* brought from a demolished convent. Above rises **Porta Soprana** (Pl. 11), a tall gateway of 1155 (restored).

Piazza Dante, with tower blocks, leads into Via Fieschi, which ascends above a rebuilt part of the city to the high-lying classical church of *Santa Maria Assunta di Carignano* (Pl. 15), begun by Alessi in 1552. The sculptures on the façade are by *Claude David,* and within on the dome-piers are four great Baroque statues of saints (1662-90), two by *Puget,* one by *Fil. Parodi,* and one by *David.* Via Rivoli goes on to Corso Saffi and the harbour (see above).

The arcaded Via Venti Settembre leads S.E. to the *Ponte Monumentale* (Pl. 11), officially *Ponte Cesare Gamba,* which carries Corso Andrea Podestà (lift). The area to the N. has been rebuilt on a completely new plan.

Via Venti Settembre beyond the bridge passes the fashionable church of **Santa Maria della Consolazione** (Pl. 11), by *Pier Ant. Corradi* (1681-1706) with a dome by *Sim. Cantone* (1769) and a front of 1864. It contains a 14C Crucifixion of the school of *Lorenzetti,* a Madonna, after *Della Robbia,* and, in the choir, a Descent from the Cross, in monochrome, by *Perin del Vaga.* Farther on is a large open space with the gardens of Piazza Verdi on the left (leading to the Brignole station) and Piazza della Vittoria on the right. In the centre of the latter is the *War Memorial* (1931), a triumphal arch by Marcello Piacentini; on the right of the square, in the Via Brigata Liguria, is the *Natural History Museum* (open Tues, Thurs, Sat, & Sun 14.30-17).

Corso Buenos Aires, the continuation of Via Venti Settembre, leads to Piazza Tommaseo, in which is a monument to Gen. Manuel Belgrano (1770-1820), liberator of the Argentine Republic, by Arnaldo Zocchi (1927). Steps mount to the Via F. Pozzo, rising below the *Villa Paradiso* (16C) to Via Albaro. Here at No. 1 is *Palazzo Saluzzo,* where Byron lived in 1822. Farther on to the left the Faculty of Engineering of the University occupies the splendid *Palazzo Cambiaso* (1548). Opposite stands the church of *San Francesco* (1324-87), beyond the E. end of which in P.za Leopardi is *Santa Maria del Prato,* a church restored in this century to its original appearance of 1172. Beyond Piazza Leonardo da Vinci, centre of the quarter of ALBARO, is the huge municipal swimming-pool above **Lido d'Albaro** frequented by bathers. Dickens lived at Villa Bellavista here in 1844 before moving into Genoa (see below). The return may be made along the sea front (Corso Italia) past the little church of *San Giuliano d'Albaro* (1240, enlarged in the 15C) and the buildings of the *Fiera Internazionale.*

Just before the Ponte Monumentale a ramp ascends to Piazza Santo Stefano, where the church of **Santo Stefano** (Pl. 11) has a particoloured front of the 13-14C and a 10C crypt. The choir-gallery of 1499 is the work of *Donato Benti* and *Bened. da Rovezzano.* On the S. wall is a Martyrdom of St Stephen by *Giulio Romano.* Viale Quattro Novembre ascends between the *Acquasola Gardens* (Pl. 11, 12) with fine trees and (l.) *Santa Caterina,* a church largely rebuilt in 1566, with a portal of 1521 by P. Ant. Piuma, and paintings by G. B. Castello and others.

Beyond, the road descends to PIAZZA CORVETTO (Pl. 11), an important centre, connected by tunnel with Piazza Portello. The Victor Emmanuel monument in the centre is by Barzaghi (1886). In front *Palazzo della Prefettura* occupies the 16C Palazzo Spinola. To the left Via Roma, with the parallel Galleria Mazzini, leads back to Piazza De Ferrari; the Salita Santa Caterina, with several 16C palazzi, leads to Piazza delle Fontane Marose.

Behind the Mazzini monument (by Costa, 1882), with its flight of steps, is the charming hillside garden of the Villetta Di Negro (Pl. 7), with busts of famous citizens. At the top of the hill in a beautiful quiet position, a fine new building houses the ***Museo d'Arte Orientale E. Chiossone** (adm. 9.30-11.30, 14-17; closed Sun, Mon, & fest.). This splendid collection of Japanese, Chinese, and Thai art was left to the Accademia Ligustica di Belle Arti by the painter Edoardo Chiossone (1832-98), and has been augmented during this century.

The objects are displayed to great advantage and are well catalogued and labelled. Interesting exhibitions from the collection are held every six months. The collection is especially notable for its Japanese works, and includes: large Chinese, Thai, and Japanese sculptures (12-18C); Japanese arms and armour; Kakemono paintings; a prehistoric section; ceramics and porcelain; theatrical masks; small bronzes, etc.

From Piazza Corvetto the long straight Via Assarotti leads N.E. to Piazza Manin passing (l; Pl. 8) the sumptuous church of the *Immacolata* (1864-73).

The turning nearly opposite leads up to Via San Bartolomeo, No. 5 in which is the *Villa Pallavicino delle Peschiere* (by Alessi, 1560-62), where Dickens stayed in 1845.

Piazza Manin is the starting place for a tour of the avenues known as the *CIRCONVALLAZIONE A MONTE*, described below. This thoroughfare, over 4 km. long (bus 33) commands a grand view of the city with its gardens and brightly coloured buildings. The lifts and funicular railways mentioned on p. 91 serve as intermediate approaches. Corso Carlo Armellini leads left out of the piazza, passing the church of *San Bartolomeo degli Armeni*, founded by refugee monks from Armenia in 1308, but completely rebuilt and incorporated into a secular structure. The altarpiece is a triptych by Turino Vanni (1415). On the right of the Corso Solferino is the *Villa Gruber*, incorporating a 15C tower. At the end of the Corso Paganini is the *Spianata Castelletto* with, just to the S., the Belvedere Montalto (view).

The Corso Carbonara (l.) leads down to the huge *Hospice* (Albergo dei Poveri; Pl. 2), begun in 1655 to designs of P. A. Corradi and others and finished a century later.—*Santa Maria del Carmine* (Pl. 6), below the hospice, preserves some remains of the original 14C church on this site.

From the Spianata the long Corso Firenze bends round the mock-antique Castel Micheli and reaches the church of *San Nicola da Tolentino* (Pl. 2), with a good interior (1597; restored), and statues of the Madonna by Tom. Orsolino (?) and Taddeo Carlone.

The funicular railway goes on up to *Castellaccio* or *Righi* (302 m) where terraces afford panoramic views of the city and its fortifications; the view is even better from a point c. 7 min. up the road towards the fort of Castellaccio and the Parco del Peralto.

Corso Firenze is continued by Corso Ugo Bassi, which passes (l.) the magnificent *Castello D'Albertis* (Pl. 1), a 19C reconstruction of a medieval Ligurian castle on the old bastion of *Monte Galletto*. The interior is being arranged as an Ethnographical Museum (adm. 9.30-11.30, 14-17; closed Sun, Mon, & fest.), with an exhibition of pre-Columbian art. From here Corso Ugo Bassi and its continuations wind down to the Salita della Provvidenza and the main railway station.

Via Ambr. Spinola ascends from Corso Ugo Bassi to Via Napoli, above which is the *Santuario d'Oregina* (1653), dedicated to Our Lady of Loreto, (bus 40 from Staz. Brignole). The church, which commands a fine view, is the object of a partriotic pilgrimage on 10 Dec in memory of the defeat of the Austrians on that date in 1746.—Farther W. Via Napoli (see above), crossing the Granarolo rack-railway, leads to the 14C church of *San Rocco*, with stucco work by Marcello Sparzo (c. 1600), and the basilica of *Gesù e Maria* (rebuilt in 1628), both containing 16-17C paintings. The San Rocco station of the rack-railway is about midway between the upper terminus at *Granarolo* (236m; view) and Piazza Principe (Pl. 1).

The **Staglieno Cemetery*, or *Camposanto di Staglieno*, in the Bisagno valley 3 km. N.W. of the city is reached by bus 48 or 34. The cemetery (open daily 8-17), covering nearly 400 acres with its galleries and gardens, was laid out in 1844-51 and gives an interesting idea of Genoese funerary sculpture during the last century. The conspicuous colossal statue of Faith is by Santo Varni; and near the upper gallery, in a clump of trees, is the simple tomb of Mazzini, surrounded by memorials of members of Garibaldi's 'Thousand'. There is a *British Military Cemetery* from the First and Second World Wars on the right of the avenue leading N. from the main entrance.

Excursions inland may be made to (21 km.) the hill-resort of *Casella* by electric railway from Piazza Manin (Pl. 8); and to the *Santuario della Guardia* (805m), a fine viewpoint, c. 11 km. N.W. of the centre (bus 63 from Cornigliano).

From Genoa to *Milan*, see Rte 16; to *Piacenza*, see Rte 38; to *Pisa*, see Rte 8; to *Turin*, see Rte 6; to *Ventimiglia*, see Rte 5.

8   GENOA TO PISA

ROAD, N 1, 190 km.—11 km. *Nervi.*—20 km. *Recco* (for *Camogli*, 2 km.).—28 km. *San Lorenzo della Costa* (for **Santa Margherita**, 3 km., and **Portofino**, 8 km.).—32 km. **Rapallo.**—43 km. *Chiávari.*—53 km. **Sestri Levante.**—71 km. *La Baracca* (for *Lévanto*, 15 km.).—113 km. **La Spézia.**—129 km. *Sarzana.*—140 km. *Avenza* (for *Carrara*, 4 km.).—147 km. *Massa.*—159 km. *Pietrasanta.*—167 km. *Viareggio.*—190 km. **Pisa.**—BUSES: frequent and fast services on all sections between Genoa and Spezia.

AUTOSTRADA '*Azzurra*', A12, 149 km. The section up to La Spezia has a succession of long tunnels with breathtaking glimpses of the coast in between.

RAILWAY, from *Genova-Brignole*, 162 km. in 2-3½ hrs; to *Rapallo*, 27 km. in c. ½ hr; to *La Spezia*, 87 km., in 1-1½ hrs. From *Piazza Principe* station the journey is c. 10 min. longer. Through-trains on this route between Paris, Turin, and Rome or Florence.

The first part of this route traverses the **Riviera di Levante**, a delightful strip of coast now threatened by indiscriminate new building. The landscape is diversified by olive-groves and villas amid gay gardens. By far the best views are gained from the road, as on the railway numerous tunnels cause frequent interruptions; the railway, however, follows the coast between Sestri and La Spezia, where the main road runs well inland. In the isolated **Cinque Terre** a coastal road is still under construction, the subject of much controversy since it is opening up this area also to speculative new building. All along this coast pollution is an increasing problem, and the fishing is deteriorating.

The old coastal road leaves Genoa by the Corso Italia and the eastern suburbs of Albaro and *Sturla.*—At (6½ km.) *Quarto dei Mille* a monument marks the starting-point of Garibaldi and the Thousand ('i Mille') on their expedition to Sicily (5 May 1860), which ended in the liberation of Italy.—Beyond (9½ km.) *Quinto al Mare* the Corso Europa, the main road from central Genoa viâ Brignole station comes in on the left.

11 km. **Nervi** is a favourite winter and summer resort, now included in the city of Genoa.

Post Office, 1 Viale Franchini.
Buses to *Genoa* (No. 15 to P.za Caricamento; No. 17 to P.za De Ferrari); frequent services to *Rapallo* and to *Recco* (going on to Uscio and Monleone); long distance services in summer to all parts.
Theatre, Teatro dei Parchi, with summer ballet festival. *Swimming Pool* by the shore.

The town was bombarded by Wm. Bentinck in 1814 and became the earliest winter resort of the Riviera di Levante in 1863.

The principal attractions of Nervi are the *Passeggiata Anita*

Garibaldi, a pleasant walk between the railway and the rock-bound shore; and the *Parco Municipale,* formed by the junction of the gardens of the Villa Gropallo and the Villa Serra. In the latter is the *Galleria d'Arte Moderna* (9.30-11.30, 14-17; closed Sun, Mon, & fest.), a large collection of modern Italian art. Farther E. is the charming park of the *Villa Luxoro* (adm. as for Modern Art Gallery above), with a small art gallery. The village of *Sant'Ilario,* 3km. inland, commands fine views.

The little seaside resorts which follow enjoy good views of the Portofino peninsula.—13km. *Bogliasco* is separated by a tunnel and viaduct from (15km.) *Pieve Ligure.*—16km. *Sori.*—20km. *Recco* is a little port noted for its hardy seamen in the Middle Ages and for clockmaking today. Rebuilt since its railway viaducts attracted air attacks in 1944, it has an interesting church (1951-60). The main road begins to climb inland across the base of the Portofino peninsula, but a coast road descends to the right for 1½km. to Camogli, rejoining the main road by a steep hill 4km. farther on.

Camogli, a picturesque little fishing port (7000 inhab.) descending steeply to a rocky shore, was famous for its merchant ships in the days of sail, its fleet having played a prominent part in the naval wars of Napoleon, of Louis-Philippe, and in the Crimea. The Blessing of the Fish (2nd Sun in May) and the 'Stella Maris' procession of boats to the Punta della Chiappa (1st Sun in Aug) are popular festivals. The Dragonara castle has an aquarium. Hourly motor-launch service in summer to Punta Chiappa and San Fruttuoso (see below).

A pleasant path leads S. from Camogli to (25min.) *San Rocco,* 14min. beyond which the path forks, the level left branch leading to the Semáforo Nuovo (see below), the right branch descending to (50 min.) the old church of *San Nicolò,* beyond which is (1¼hrs) the *Punta della Chiappa,* where the view is remarkable for the ever-changing colours of the sea. A rough-hewn altar on the point reproduces in mosaic a graffito found at San Nicolò.

24km. *Ruta* is a good centre for visiting the W. part of the Portofino peninsula, with buses to Camogli, Portofino Vetta, and on the main road.

A road (bus) leads S. in 1½km. to *Portofino Vetta* in a large park beneath the *Monte di Portofino (610m). This area is destined to become a protected area because of its natural beauty. From the summit there is a wonderful view of the Riviera from Alassio to La Spezia, the Apuan (S.E.) and Cottian Alps (W.), and, out at sea, Elba and (in exceptionally clear weather) Corsica. The bridlepath from Ruta to the Monte (1 hr) leads off beside a tunnel on the Rapallo road, rises to 427 m, then descends to a cross-roads.—The right-hand path leads to (1 hr) the *Semáforo Nuovo* (470m) on a cliff overlooking the sea.—The left path bears to the right at (10 min.) the *Pietre Strette* and descends steeply to (1¾hrs) *San Fruttuoso,* a picturesque little village with the Gothic church and cloister of an abbey founded before the 10C, and the grey *Torre dei Doria* (boat hourly from Camogli or Portofino, twice daily from Santa Margherita and Rapallo, in summer only). A bronze statue of Christ, by Galletti (1954), stands offshore, eight fathoms down, as protector of all those who work beneath the sea.—The left-hand path at Pietre Strette leads to (2 hrs from Ruta) Portofino.

The road to the right at Ruta descends to (½ hr.) San Rocco (see above).

The main road penetrates a short tunnel.—Beyond (28km.) *San Lorenzo della Costa,* where the church has a triptych by Quentin Matsys (1499), the road to Santa Margherita descends to the right (3km.; short cut by path).

Santa Margherita Ligure (12,800 inhab.), on the W. side of the Bay of Rapallo or Golfo Tigullio, is one of the most popular resorts of the Riviera. It is the point of departure for the excursion to Portofino.

Post Office, Via Gramsci, behind Lido hotel.

Buses to *Portofino* and *Rapallo* every 15 min.; to *Ruta* and to *Genoa* many times daily.—*Boat Trips* to Portofino, the Cinque Terre, and excursions in the gulf.

The pleasant road along the shore of Santa Margherita leads on S. to Portofino. At 3 km. it passes (r.) the former monastery of *La Cervara*, where Francis I of France was held prisoner after Pavia (1525), and where Gregory XI rested on the return of the papacy from Avignon to Rome (1377). Then, passing a modern castle on a point, it reaches (3½ km.) the tiny bay of *Paraggi*, at the mouth of its wooded glen.— 5½ km. **Portofino** is a romantic fishing village, situated partly on a small headland, partly in a little bay favoured by the English in the 19C, and now beloved of rich yachtsmen. A foreground of sea and a background of trees combine charmingly with the gay little houses. High above the village, towards the Capo, is the little church of *San Giorgio*, which is reputed to contain the relics of St George, brought by Crusaders from the Holy Land. In front of the church is the *Castle* (adm. 9-12, 15-18).

The classic excursions are to the **Capo*, a walk of ¼ hr over the hill of San Giorgio; to San Fruttuoso by bridle-path viâ Case del Prato; or to Portofino Vetta (see above; 1½-2 hrs on foot). Boat trips (20 min.) to S. Fruttuoso (see above).

The road from Santa Margherita to Rapallo (3 km.) passes *San Michele di Pagana*, where the church contains a fine Crucifixion by Van Dyck. Near by is the *Villa Spinola*, where the Italo-Yugoslav Treaty of Rapallo was signed in 1920.

32 km. **RAPALLO** (29,000 inhab.), in a sheltered position at the head of its gulf, is the best known holiday resort on the Riviera di Levante, and is popular both in summer and in winter. The mole of the new port under construction has blocked the view out to sea.

Post Office, Via Boccoleri.
English Church, *St George's*, W. of the town.
Buses frequently to *Genoa*, to *Santa Margherita*, to *Ruta*, to *San Maurizio*, to *Santa Maria del Campo*, and to *Chiávari*; daily to *La Spezia*, *Pisa*, and beyond; also to *Portofino*.
Golf Course (18 holes) and *Tennis* at Sant'Anna, N. of the town (bus). *Boat Trips* in the gulf.—*Procession* at Montallegro on 1-3 July.

The lovely surroundings are the main attraction of Rapallo, the only interesting buildings in the town being the *Collegiate Church* (1606), with its 20C adornments, and the restored *Castello*. The *Villino Chiaro*, on the coast road, was the home of Max Beerbohm (1872-1956) from 1910. The principal excursion is that to Santa Margherita and Portofino (see above).

A rope railway (c. 2 km.) and a winding road viâ *San Maurizio* (11 km.; bus twice daily) ascend inland to the sanctuary of *Montallegro*, where the 16C church contains frescoes by Nic. Barabino, and, over the high altar, the Byzantine painting of the Dormition of the Virgin, which legend declares was miraculously transported from Dalmatia. The summit of *Monte Rosa* (680 m), ¼ hr above the church, commands a splendid view.

A good path descends direct to Rapallo; or the walk may be extended to the S.E. viâ *Monte Castello* (662 m), the *Madonnetta* (439 m), and the beautiful pinewoods of *Sant'Andrea* (246 m) to the *Madonna delle Grazie* (185 m), above the road between Zoagli and Chiàvari (see below), c. 2¾ hrs from the sanctuary. The ruined convent of *Valle Christi* (13-16C) lies above the S. side of the Bogo valley, 2 km. N.W. of Rapallo: farther up the main valley are the ruined church of *San Tomaso* (1160) and the village of (4 km.) *Santa Maria del Campo*. The excursion may be prolonged by bridle-path W. to Recco (c. 1¾ hrs) or S.W. to Ruta (c. 1½ hrs).

Beyond Rapallo the road zigzags across a series of small valleys, one of the longest bends now avoided by a tunnel.—37 km. *Zoagli*, another resort, stands at the mouth of a narrow glen. The road now passes *Sant' Andrea di Rovereto*.—43 km. **Chiàvari** is a shipbuilding town (31,700 inhab.) with a quaint old main street and a sandy beach, at the mouth of the Entella. In the Istituto Internazionale di Studi Liguri (Via Vitt. Veneto) finds from a pre-Roman necropolis are exhibited.

Here Garibaldi, arriving in exile from the S., was arrested 'in the most polite and friendly manner possible' on 6 Sept 1849, since his forbears were native to the town. It was also the family home of Nino Bixio and Gius. Mazzini.

A road runs inland viâ *Carasco*, there diverging right from an alternative route to Genoa (67 km.; viâ the Valle Fontanabuona) to run N. up the Sturla valley past *Terrarossa*, popularly thought to be the home of Christ. Columbus' grandparents, to (12½ km.) *Borgonovo* (keep left) and (16 km.) *Borzonasca*, and thence over a pass into the Áveto valley.—43 km. *Rezzoâglio* and (58 km.) *Santo Stéfano d'Aveto* (1017 m) are quiet little summer resorts.

The right fork at Borgonovo (see above) takes the main road by corkscrew turns over (28 km.) the *Passo del Bocco* (956 m) into the Val di Taro.—61 km. *Bedónia*, beyond which at 69 km. the road joins that from Sestri (see below).—75 km. *Borgo Val di Taro.*

46 km. *Lavagna*, separated from Chiávari by the Entella bridge, has a long sandy beach, and is famous for its slate quarries. It was the birthplace of Innocent IV (Sinibaldo Fieschi; d. 1254). At San Salvatore, c. ½ hr up the valley, is the fine early Gothic church which he founded.—50 km.   *Cavi.*—53 km.   **Sestri Levante** (21,800 inhab.), delightfully situated at the base of a peninsula known as L'Isola, is a favourite resort in summer, with another fine beach. From Piazza Matteotti, with the 17C parish church, a street ascends past the restored Romanesque church of San Nicolò to the *Albergo dei Castelli,* rebuilt with antique materials (1925) on Genoese foundations, with a magnificent park (adm. 8-12, 16-20; winter 8-17), at the end of the peninsula. The *Pinacoteca Rizzi* (10 Via Cappucchini) is open June-Sept, Thurs & Sat 16-18; fest. 9-12, 16-18; Oct-May, 10-12, 14-16.

Monte Castellaro (255 m), c. 1 hr S.E., above the Punta Manara, commands a good view of the coast.

The road from Sestri to (65 km.) Borgo Val di Taro (bus) is a tortuous and steeply undulating link between Liguria and the Emilian plain. It runs E. at first, then N.—34 km. *Varese Ligure*, on the Vara, has a 15C castle of the Fieschi, well restored in 1965.—At (46 km.) the *Passo di Cento Croci* (1053 m; *View) the road enters Emilia and begins the descent into the Taro valley.—65 km. *Borgo Val di Taro*, and thence to Berceto and the Spézia-Parma road, see p. 371.

FROM SESTRI LEVANTE TO LA SPEZIA BY THE COAST ROAD (N 370), under construction for many years and still not complete. It is much discussed in relation to the new building which is taking place in its train which threatens the beauty of the coast. It is not yet open between Monterosso and Manarola (distances approx.) and closely follows the railway (many tunnels). 3 km. beyond Sestri this route branches right to pass above *Riva Trigoso*, with naval shipyards. A by-road serves (10 km.) *Moneglia*, a little seaside town with two old castles, the birthplace of Luca Cambiaso (1527-85), the painter, and (14 km.) *Déiva Marina*, both by-passed by N 370.—24 km. *Bonassola* is a quiet village in beautiful surroundings.—27 km. **Lévanto** a secluded bathing resort in a little bay, with lovely gardens, a fine swimming-pool and a good sandy beach, preserves remains of its old walls and has a 13-15C church.—The road avoids and the railway tunnels through Monte Vé (487 m).—39 km. *Monterosso al Mare*, which has a good church of 1300, is the first of the five attractive seagirt villages called the **Cinque Terre**, noted for their wine. The road (1977) ends here. The others are *Vernazza, Corniglia, Manarola*, and *Riomaggiore*, and all have interesting old churches. The villages were previously linked from Lévanto to Portovenere only by a network of *Footpaths, and before the advent of the railway had for centuries been accessible only by sea. Nowadays they tend to be crowded with trippers on Sundays. A railway tunnel 7 km. long connects Riomaggiore with La Spézia, while the road will thread two shorter tunnels.—66 km. *La Spézia*, see below.

Beyond Sestri the main road winds steeply up the *Passo del Bracco.*

The road passes to landward of the autostrada. The Vetta del Petronio rises prominently on the left.—From (63 km.) *Bracco* a road of 6 km. descends vertiginously to Moneglia (see above). After the summit-level of 620 m the road begins the descent to (71 km.) *La Baracca* at the junction of the road through pine-woods to Lévanto (15 km.).—In the Vara valley this road recrosses the autostrada just before (88 km.) *Borghetto di Vara,* then ascends a side-valley to the low pass of (105 km.) *La Foce* (241 m), which commands a fine prospect of La Spézia and its gulf.

113 km. **LA SPÉZIA,** at the head of its fine gulf, is one of the chief naval ports of Italy. A provincial capital (122,000 inhab.) and (since 1929) the seat of a bishop, the town forms a rectilinear L round a prominent hill. It makes a good centre for excursions.

Post Office, P.za Verdi.—**E.P.T.,** 47 Viale Mazzini.

Buses from below the Station (steps) to Via Chiodo and the quayside.—From P.za Chiodo: every ¼ hr to *Portovénere,* and to *Lérici,* going on less frequently to *Tellaro;* to *Sarzana* and *Carrara;* to *Sestri Levante;* to *Reggio Emilia;* from Via Rosselli, every 2 hrs to *Viareggio* and *Florence.*—*Steamers* from the Public Gardens to Portovenere and to Lérici and Fiascherino.

Teatro Civico, P.za Mentana.—*Swimming Pool,* Viale N. Fieschi.

The main Corso Cavour runs N.W. to S.E. through the town, passing the *Museo Archeologico Lunense* (10-12, 16-18; Sun 10-12), with Ligurian statue-stelae (Bronze and Iron Age) and Roman remains from Luni, and (l.) the rebuilt *Cathedral,* with a large polychrome terracotta by And. della Robbia. At the seaward end an equestrian statue of Garibaldi stands in the fine *Public Gardens* that extend between the busy Via Chiodo and the Viale Italia bordering the gulf. To the right, the P.za Chiodo commemorates the architect of the *Naval Arsenal,* the most important in Italy (1861-69; open day 19 March; weekdays by permit, apply at guardroom, passport), by the entrance to which is the *NAVAL MUSEUM (adm. daily 9-12, 15-18; contribution expected to orphans' fund), where models and relics collected since 1571 illustrate the marine history of Savoy and Italy. From here Via Chiodo runs N.E. to the Post Office, behind which rises the old citadel; farther on opens the huge PIAZZA ITALIA, enclosed by new administrative buildings, with the crypt of a new cathedral.

TO THE CASTELLAZZO, LA FOCE, AND BIASSA, fine round of 19 km., with splendid views, preferably made on foot. It may be divided into two walks by means of the trolley-bus to Chiappa, on the La Foce road.—The Via dei Colli ascends from the top of Via Spallanzani above the old castle to the Porto Castellazzo in the town wall. Beyond the gate a road leads gradually W. to (4 km.) *La Foce,* on the Genoa road (see above), which returns to the town (Chiappa trolley-bus). The walk may be continued by crossing the main road and taking the by-road which ascends S. and passes beneath the summits of *Monte Parodi* (666 m; fine view) and *Monte Verrúgoli* (740 m). The descent curves down to (15 km.) *Biassa* (358 m) and thence leads direct to Pegazzano (bus terminus) and (19 km.) *La Spézia.*

The *Gulf of Spézia* is nearly everywhere accessible by car, but is most pleasantly seen by steamer.

PORTOVÉNERE, at the extremity of the S. arm of the gulf, is reached either by steamer from the Public Gardens (¾ hr), or by bus (35 min.), passing the arsenal. From *Cadimare* the road goes on through the olive groves of *Fezzano,* with a good view of the arsenal with its ships and of the N. coast of the gulf with the Apuan Alps. Beyond the *Punta di Pezzino* opens the charming bay called the *Seno delle Grazie* on the opposite horn of which is the *Lazzaretto* built by the Genoese in the 17C. After many zigzags around numerous little capes and bays the island of Palmaria comes into sight, opposite Portovénere.—12 km. **Portovénere,** the ancient *Portus Veneris*, a dependency of Genoa since 1113, is a charming fortified village built on the sloping shore of the *Bocchetta*, the narrow strait (114 m wide) separating the *Isola Palmaria* from the mainland. On a rocky promontory at the S. end of the village the restored 6C and 13C church of *San Pietro* commands a splendid view of Palmaria and the lofty cliffs of the Cinque Terre. *Byron's Cave*, or the *Grotto Arpaia*, formerly beneath it, collapsed in 1932. It was from here that the poet started his swim across the gulf to San Terenzo to visit Shelley at Lérici (1822). In the upper part of the village is the beautiful 12C church of *San Lorenzo*, above which (steep climb) towers the 16C *Castello* (*View). Below the church steps descend to the characteristic *'Calata Doria'*, where tall houses rise from the sea. An excursion may be made by boat round the rugged island of *Palmaria*, visiting its caves. On the N. point is the old *Torre della Scuola*, built by the Genoese in 1606 and blown up by the English fleet in 1800. The island is noted for the gold-veined black 'portoro' marble. Farther out is the *Isola del Tino*, with remains of an 8C monastery.

LÉRICI, on the N. shore of the gulf, is reached from La Spézia either by steamer in ½–¾ hr, or by bus in 35 min. The road passes the shipyards of *San Bartolomeo* and *Muggiano* (bus terminus), and the foundry of *Pertúsola*, and, piercing the *Punta di Calandrello*, reaches the beautiful bay of Lérici. The fishing village of (8 km.) *San Terenzo*, with its castle, is on the nearer shore of the bay; here died Paolo Mantegazza (1831-1910), founder of the first pathological laboratory in Europe. A little farther along, on a small cape, is the *Casa Magni*, the last home of Shelley (1822), from which he embarked on the fatal sail to Leghorn. It is now a small Museum.—10 km. **Lérici**, is a sea-bathing and winter resort (14,300 inhab.), on the point beyond which is the *Castle* of the 12-16C which was taken by the Genoese from the Pisans. Before the modern Via Aurelia existed Tuscan coaches were embarked here by felucca for Genoa. A bus connects Lérici with Sarzana (7½ km.; see below) on the main road into Tuscany.—The coast road goes on above the little bays of *Fiascherino*, where D. H. Lawrence lived in 1913-14, to (14 km.) *Tellaro*, a medieval village rising sheer from the sea.

From La Spézia to *Parma* and to *Reggio Emilia*, see Rte 38.

From La Spézia the Pisa road traverses the N. suburb of Migliarina and then skirts the wide Magra valley, beyond which rise the Apuan Alps. It joins the road from Lérici, and crosses the river.

An alternative road (N 432) continues to (4 km.) *Améglia*, dominated by a 10C castle, then crosses the river lower down and hugs the shore all the way to Viareggio.

129 km. **Sarzana**, an ancient town (19,300 inhab.), the S.E. outpost of the Genoese Republic, retains its old fort and its town gates. The see of the Bp. of Luni, removed here in 1204, was absorbed in 1929 in that of La Spézia. The *Cathedral*, mainly 14-15C, contains a panel painting of the *Crucifixion, by Gulielmus, dated 1138; and, in the transept chapels, good 15C marble reliefs by Riccomanni. Famous natives are Tom. Parentucelli (Nicholas V, pope 1447-55), Dom. Fiasella (1589-1669), the painter, and Carlo Fontana (1865-1956), the sculptor. On a hill to the E. (20 min. walk) is the *Fortezza di Sarzanello*, a Castracani castle of 1322; and at *Fosdinovo*, 11 km. N.E., is a restored 13C castle of the Malaspina.—135 km. *Luni* station.

About 2 km. right are the scanty ruins of the ancient Etruscan and Roman town of *Luni*, which was once important enough to lend its name to the whole district (*Lunigiana*), but which was devastated in the 9-11C by corsairs and by malaria, and at last abandoned. In the museum (9-12, 14-17 or 18 exc. Mon) is an honorific inscription to M. Acilius Glabrio, who defeated Antiochus III at Thermopylae in 191 B.C.

High up among the Apuan Alps (l.) appear the first of the white marble quarries of Carrara as the road enters Tuscany.—140 km. *Avenza* is important as the road and railway junction for Carrara, 4 km. N.E. Near the bridge is a tower built by Castracani, tyrant of Lucca.

Carrara (70,200 inhab.), world-famous for its white marble, is a flourishing town with a good Romanesque *Duomo* altered in the 13C, when the attractive Gothic story was added to its façade. In the square are a house believed to have sheltered Michelangelo on his visits to buy marble, and a monument to Andrea Doria left unfinished by Baccio Bandinelli. The *Accademia di Belle Arti* occupies the old Malaspina castle and 16C palace.—The famous *Marble Quarries* in the Apuan Alps, which have been worked for over 2000 years, are well worthy of a visit. They produce 500,000 tons of marble a year, and over 300 quarries are now in use. They are best reached by bus from Carrara to Colonnata (6 times a day; 3 times on fest.) or to Fantiscritti (Ponte di Vara; weekdays only). It is interesting to follow up this visit by an inspection of the marble-sawing mills and sculpture workshops in the town. In Viale XX Settembre a modern building houses a permanent exhibition of marble quarrying and craftsmanship.

Marina di Carrara is a bathing-beach and marble port, 3 km. S.W. of Avenza (buses from Carrara) connected to *Marina di Massa,* a larger bathing resort with innumerable pensions, the lofty Torre Fiat and other industrial holiday colonies, which is 6 km. farther on along the shore.

The main road turns inland to (147 km.) **Massa,** a small provincial capital (64,700 inhab.) with marble quarries, pleasantly situated below the Apuan foothills. Massa was from 1442 to 1790 the capital of the Malaspina duchy of Massa-Carrara, and in the Piazza Aranci is the large *Palazzo Cybo Malaspina,* a 17C building given a charming courtyard by G. F. Bergamini. High above it is the 14-16C *Rocca,* where earlier Malaspina dukes entertained many distinguished guests. The *Duomo,* founded in the 15C but greatly altered, contains 16C Malaspina tombs.—155 km. *Querceta* is the junction for the roads to Serravezza (3 km. l.) and Forte dei Marmi (3 km. r.), both served by bus.

From *Serravezza,* a small town with a 16C cathedral and a town hall built by Duke Cosimo I of Tuscany, a bus goes on to (10 km.) *Levigliani,* a centre for climbing in the Apuan Alps.

Forte dei Marmi and its S.E. continuation *Marina di Pietrasanta* are elegant bathing resorts, with villas set in the pine-woods, severely damaged in a tornado in 1977, behind the (mostly private) beaches. A fine esplanade connects them with Marma di Carrara (N.W.) and Viareggio (S.E.).

159 km. **Pietrasanta** the chief town (25,700 inhab.) of the seaboard district of *Versilia,* has a most attractive old piazza, surrounded by fine buildings. The town was heavily battered in the Second World War during the fighting for the 'Gothic Line'. The *Cathedral* (1330), with a campanile of 1380, contains a pulpit and choirstalls by Lor. Stagi (1502-6), a font by Donato Benti (1509), and altar-furnishings by Ferd. Tacca (1649). Next door is the 14C church of *Sant'Agostino* (damaged); and opposite is the imposing doorway (1515) of the *Pretura.* Higher up is the 12C *Rocca.* The town is also famous for its marble.

Valdicastello, 3 km. E., was the birthplace of the poet Giosuè Carducci (1835-1907). Buses connect Pietrasanta with its Marina and with Seravezza and Pontestazzemese (see above).

167 km. **VIAREGGIO,** the most popular seaside resort (58,300 inhab.) on the W. coast of Italy, is frequented for its gently shelving beach of fine sand, for the pleasant parks and gardens which surround its hotels, and for the magnificent pine-woods in the neighbourhood.

Post Office, P.za Shelley.—*Information Bureau.* 5 Viale Carducci.

Buses from the station (circular service) along the sea-front (Viale Carducci) to *Lido di Camaiore* and *Forte dei Marmi;* also inland to *Camaiore;* from P.za Mazzini to *Pisa;* to *Lucca* and *Florence;* to *Spezia;* and to *Torre del Lago.*

The CARNIVAL held in February is one of the most famous in Italy.

A splendid double promenade, with a roadway and a footway, leads along the shore from the Giardini d'Azeglio to the Piazza Puccini. At the inner corner of the Giardini d'Azeglio is the Piazza Shelley, with a bust of the poet by Urbano Lucchesi (1894). Beautiful pine-woods extend along the shore in either direction from the town. The outer harbour is busy with boat-building and a 16C tower guards the inner basins where a new port is under construction.

Shelley and his friend, Lt. Williams, perished on 8 July, 1822, by the foundering of their little schooner 'Ariel' off Viareggio on a voyage from Leghorn to La Spezia. Their bodies, washed ashore on the beach of II Gombo (p. 505), N. of the mouth of the Arno, were there cremated in the presence of Trelawny, Byron, and Leigh Hunt. Shelley's ashes were collected and buried in the Protestant cemetery at Rome.

The fine road along the coast to Forte dei Marmi and Marina di Carrara (see above) passes (5 km.) the *Lido di Camaiore*, an extended bathing-resort.—Inland from Viareggio (11 km. N.) is the little town of *Camaiore*, with a pleasant old church and, in the little museum, a Flemish tapestry of 1516.

174 km. *Torre del Lago Puccini* has adopted the name of Giacomo Puccini (1858-1924), who made it his bohemian home and composed many operas by the *Lago di Massaciúccoli*, 1 km. E.—At 181 km. the autostrada to Florence diverges left, while this route crosses the Serchio.—190 km. **Pisa**, see Rte 44A.

9   TURIN TO MILAN

ROAD. (*a*) AUTOSTRADA (A4), 139 km., leaving the old road beyond the Stura bridge and keeping for the most part N. of the old road.—(*b*) VIĀ VERCELLI AND NOVARA, N 11, 144 km.—23 km. *Chivasso.*—41 km. *Cigliano.*—74 km. **Vercelli**.— 96 km. **Novara.**—117 km. *Magenta.*—144 km. **Milan.** (*c*) VIĀ MORTARA. 148 km.—23 km. *Chivasso.* N 31 bis.—71 km. **Casale.**—N 596 dir, N 494. **Mortara.**—113 km. *Vigévano.*—125 km. *Abbiategrasso.*—148 km. **Milan.**

RAILWAY, 153 km. in 1½-2 hrs; to *Vercelli*, 79 km. in 50-60 min.; to *Novara.* 101 km. in 1-1½ hr.

The N 11 leaves Turin as the Corso Giulio Cesare, crossing the Stura and branching right at the entrance to the motorway to traverse the long town of (11 km.) *Settimo Torinese.*—23 km. **Chivasso** is an important railway junction (26,500 inhab.). The 15C church, with a fine doorway, contains a Descent from the Cross, by *Defendente Ferrari* (1470-1535), a native of the town. In 3 km. more N 11 diverges left from N 31 bis (see p. 116).—41 km. *Cigliano,* N. of the motorway and beyond the Dora Báltea, is at the junction of the road to Biella.

FROM CIGLIANO TO BIELLA, N 593, N 143, 31 km. At (12 km.) *Cavaglià* this route crosses the Vercelli-Ivrea road, just N. of the A 5 motorway spur. The Lago di Viverone, 5 km. W., is locally frequented for swimming and water-sports.—At (17 km.) *Salussola* the church contains good 18C woodwork.—27 km. *Gagliánico* has a splendid castle, mainly 16C, with a well-decorated cortile.—31 km. **Biella**, on the Cervo, is a busy textile-making town (56,000 inhab.) divided into two portions, *Biella Piano* (410 m) and *Biella Piazzo* (475 m), connected by rack-and-pinion railway. In the lower town are the ill-restored Gothic *Cathedral* of 1402, with a neo-Gothic narthex of 1825; the interesting 10C *Baptistery;* the 13C Romanesque campanile of the demolished church of Santo Stefano; and the elegant Renaissance church of *San Sebastiano* (1504, with a 19C façade), which contains paintings by Lanino and notable stalls incorporating panels of an 11C reliquary. In the upper town are many 15-16C mansions, including the austere *Palazzo Cisterna* (late 16C), and the 13-16C church of *San Giacomo.* Across the Cervo, in the park of San Gerolamo, is the Villa Sella with a fine 15C cloister and the Istituto Nazionale di fotografia alpina (open 9-12, 15-18 exc. Sat & Sun).

A direct railway service viâ Santhià connects Biella with Turin or Vercelli; and buses run to Vercelli and Ivrea. The favourite excursion is by road (bus) to (12 km. N.W.) the *Santuario d'Oropa* (1181 m), a large hospice of three quadrangles, with a modest church by Juvarra, the most frequented pilgrimage resort in Piedmont, said to have been founded by St Eusebius in 369. A new church, with a large dome, begun in 1885 to a design by Ign. Galletti (1774), rises beyond the farthest quadrangle. Below the sanctuary a cable railway ascends from the valley in 10 min. to the Rifugio Mucrone; from here a walk of 20 min. leads to the *Lago del Mucrone* (1902 m), on the slope of *Monte Mucrone* (2335 m) which is climbed thence in 1½ hrs (good ski slopes; a cable railway also ascends to the summit). A chair-lift goes up from the lake to *Monte Camino* (2391 m), on the watershed E. of the Val de Lys.

From Biella a road (bus) ascends the Cervo valley viâ (7 km.) *Andorno Micca* and (15 km.) *Campiglia Cervo,* a little holiday resort, to (20 km.) **Piedicavallo** (1036 m), the highest village in the Cervo valley, connected by mountain passes with Gaby in the Val de Lys (see Rte 3 B) and with Rassa in the Valsesia (see p. 116).

Other points of interest near Biella are *Cándelo* (5 km. S.E.), with a remarkable Ricetto, or communal fortress and storehouse, built in the 14C as a refuge for the townsfolk; *Graglia* (9 km. W.), above which rises the *Santuario di Graglia* (247 m), a fine viewpoint, where mineral water springs have recently been utilized; and *Mosso Santa Maria* (19 km. N.E.) and *Trivero* (26 km.) made up of hamlets.

From Trivero the STRADA PANORAMICA ZAGNA (N 232; named after its originator) winds upwards to the W.—Beyond (4 km.) *Caulera* are splendid woods of rhododendrons. The views N. to Monte Rosa are very fine.—13 km. *Bielmonte* (1517 m) is a winter sports centre (chair-lift to Monte Marca, 1625 m).—24 km. *Rosazza,* in the Cervo valley (comp. above).

The Milan road soon recrosses the motorway and bypasses (54 km.) *Tronzano,* where a road on the left leads in 3 km. to *Santhià,* an important railway junction, whose name is a corruption of Sant'Agata. Here is a rice-growing district, in summer covered with water. Just to the N.W. the Great St Bernard motorway (A 5) joins the A 4.

74 km. **VERCELLI,** the largest rice-producing centre in Europe, is an interesting old town (55,900 inhab.). It was noted in the 16C for its school of painters, most famous of whom was Il Sodoma (Giov. Ant. Bazzi, 1477-1549). The wide Corso Garibaldi, on the W., skirts the old town from S. to N. To the left, in front of the station, is the basilica of ***Sant' Andrea** (1219-27), Romanesque but showing Cistercian Gothic elements very early for Italy. It was founded by Card. Guala Bicchieri with the revenues of the abbey of St Andrew, Chesterton (Cambs.) bestowed on him by his youthful ward, Henry III. The fine façade is flanked by two lofty towers connected by a double arcade, and the cupola is topped by a third tower. The detached campanile (1407), to the S.E., is in the same style. The interior has pointed arcades carried on slender clustered piers, with shafts carried up unbroken to the springing of the vaults. To the N. is a fine cloister with clustered columns and a chapter-house with a 16C vault on four columns.—Via G. Bicchieri leads to the **Cathedral,** with three cupolas, begun in 1572 to a design of Pellegrino Tibaldi, but preserving the Romanesque campanile of an older church.

In the S. transept, the octagonal chapel of the Blessed Amadeus IX of Savoy (d. in the castle 1472) contains his tomb and that of his successor Charles I (d. 1490); also a 12C Byzantine crucifix of hammered bronze.—The CHAPTER LIBRARY (adm. on application) includes the 4C Evangelistary of St Eusebius (in a 12C binding); some Anglo-Saxon poems (11C); the Laws of the Lombards (8C); and other early MSS, perhaps relics of the Studium, or early university which flourished here from 1228 for about a century.

Via del Duomo runs S. past the 18C church of Santa Maria Maggiore, behind which is the restored 13C *Castle,* to Via Gioberti. This leads (l.) to *San Francesco,* a restored church of 1292 containing a good St Ambrose, by Giovenone; behind its apse is the MUSEO BORGOGNA (Tues & Thurs 14.30-16.30, Sun 10.30-12.30; other days on request), whose twenty rooms of paintings include works by Sodoma, Def. and Gaudenzio Ferrari, Lanino, Giovenone, and Boniforte Oldoni.

Via Borgogna ends in the Corso Libertà, the main street of the old town. On the left is seen the Gothic *Torre dei Tizzoni;* on the right is *San Giuliano* with its Romanesque campanile. Nearly opposite, the *Palazzo Centori* (No. 87) has a delightful interior court arcaded in the Tuscan style (1496). Via A. G. Cagna leads left to the church of **San Cristoforo,** notable for the fine series of *Frescoes by *G. Ferrari* (1531-33), and for the *Madonna of the Pomegranate (1529), on the high altar, considered his masterpiece. The first street on the left, on the return, opens into P.za del Municipio, in which are the *Town Hall* and the church of *San Paolo* (begun c. 1260), containing a Madonna and saints by Lanino (covered). Across the Corso is P.za Cavour, the old market square, with the machicolated *Torre degli Angeli* rising above the roofs. To the right, in Via Gioberti, is the tall square *Torre di Città;* while in Via Verdi, to the N., the *Museo Leone* (Thurs & Sun 14.30-16.30) is a good archæological and historical collection in a building incorporating 15C and 18C palazzi.

Farther along the Corso, to the right opposite the Post Office, is P.za Zumaglini, the modern business centre of the town, with the banks and the Exchange.— Vercelli is connected by direct railways with Alessandria viâ Casale Monferrato; and with Pavia, viâ Mortara.

The road crosses the Sesia and Monte Rosa is seen to the N.— 96 km. **NOVARA,** a provincial capital (102,000 inhab.) and one of the oldest towns in Piedmont, is celebrated for its four battles, most important of which were the first (1500) when Lodovico il Moro was taken prisoner by the French, and the fourth (1849), when the Piedmontese were defeated by Radetzky's Austrians.

Post Office, Corso XX Settembre.—**E.P.T.,** 2 Corso Cavour.
Theatre, P.za Martiri della Libertà. Open-air *Swimming Pool,* W. of the station.

Novara preserves but few relics of antiquity. The most striking building is the church of *San Gaudenzio* (1577-1690), in part to a design of Pellegrino Tibaldi, on to which a tall slender cupola, with a spire 121 m high, was built by Antonelli (1840-88). The campanile (1763-96) is an attractive composition by Bened. Alfieri. Within (N. side) is a good polyptych by G. Feerari (1514) and (S. transept) the Baroque chapel of the patron saint. Nearby, in Palazzo Faraggiana, is an Ethnographical Museum and a Music Museum (adm. as for Museo Civico, below). To the S., across the main Corso Italia, is the *Broletto,* a group of well-restored buildings of the 13C, 15C, and 18C; here is installed the *Museo Civico* (8.30-12, 15-17 or 18; fest 9-12; closed Tues), the picture gallery of which contains paintings by Ferrari and Antonello da Messina. Across P.za della Repubblica rises the *Duomo,* rebuilt by Antonelli in 1863-65 but preserving its Romanesque *Baptistery.* P.za Martiri, just to the W., is ringed by the *Mercato,* the *Teatro Coccia,* and the remains of a *Castle* of the Sforza, with a park to the S. and W.

Novara is connected by road and direct railway with *Alessandria;* with *Arona,* on Lago Maggiore (Rte 11); with *Orta* (Rte 10B), viâ Borgomanero; and with *Varallo* (see below).

The Milan road by-passes *Trecate,* with its oil refinery, and crosses the Ticino to enter Lombardy.—117 km. *Magenta,* by-passed to the N., is famous for the victory of the French and Italians over the Austrians in 1859, which is commemorated by an ossuary and a monument to Marshal MacMahon.—144 km. **Milan,** see Rte 14.

FROM NOVARA TO VARALLO AND ALAGNA, 92 km.; bus or railway to *Varallo* in 1½-1¾ hrs; bus thence to *Alagna* in 1½ hrs.—This route, leading N.W., reaches the Sesia at (30 km.) *Romagnano,* a papermaking and cotton-spinning town, also on the Santhià-Arona railway. At *Gattinara,* 2½ km. S. beyond the river, known for its red wine, the parish church contains paintings by Lanino.—The road now enters the VALSESIA, a winding valley which affords an attractive approach to the high Alps from the S. It is famous for its lace, an important feature in the gala costumes of the villages in the upper valley. The lower valley is industrial, with manufacturers of paper, furniture, etc.—44 km. *Borgosesia* is the largest of several small cotton-spinning towns. *Valduggia,* 5 km. E. on the Orta road, was the birthplace of Gaudenzio Ferrari (1471-1546).—57 km. **Varallo Sesia** (450 m), the capital of the upper Valsesia, is a pleasant little town (8000 ınhab.). The church of *San Gaudenzio,* picturesquely placed at the head of a stairway, contains a polyptych by Gaudenzio Ferrari. The *Pinacoteca* (10-12, 15-18; winter on request) contains paintings by Valsesian artists including Gaud. Ferrari, Lanino, and Tanzio de Varallo. The chief sight of Varallo is the *SACRO MONTE, the ascent to which begins at the church of *Madonna delle Grazie,* which has a *Fresco of the Life of Christ, by G. Ferrari (1513) in 21 scenes.

The *Santuario* (608 m; reached on foot in 20 min. or by cable railway or road), or *Nuova Gerusalemme del Sacro Monte,* was founded c. 1486 by the Blessed Bern. Caimi, a Friar Minor. The building was started in 1493 but not completed until the late 17C. It is surrounded by 45 chapels intended to recall the various holy sites in Jerusalem, and these were adorned by contemporary artists of the Valsesia (Gaud. Ferrari, Tabacchetti, D'Enrico, Morazzone). Tabacchetti's best chapels are the Temptation (No. 38; with a Crucifixion by Ferrari) and Adam and Eve (No. 1); D'Enrico's is the Vision of St Joseph (No. 5). The *Basilica dell'Assunta* dates from 1641-49, with a façade of 1896.

A pleasant excursion on foot (or by car, 23½ km.) is from Varallo to *Pella* on the Lake of Orta (3½ hrs) viâ the *Madonna di Loreto* (frescoes by G. Ferrari and And. Solario), *Civiasco,* and *La Colma* (942 m).—In the great bend of the Sesia rises the *Becco d'Ovaga* (1630 m) climbed in 3 hrs by a marked path from Varallo viâ Crévola and the *Rif. Spanni,* near the summit.

The picturesque VAL MASTALLONE, leading N. from Varallo, is ascended by road (bus) to (18 km.) *Fobello* (881 m), above which lies (20 min.) *Cervatto* (1021 m), two small summer resorts. From Ponte delle Due Acque, 2 km. below Fobello, a road diverges r. for (20 km. from Varallo; bus) *Rimella* (1180 m), a scattered village retaining many traces in its dialect of the German-speaking colony from the Valais that migrated here in the 14C. Both Rimella and Fobello are connected by mountain passes with the Val Anzasca (Rte 3A).

Above Varallo the Valsesia is known as VALGRANDE, and at (67 km.) *Balmuccia* the Val Sermenza leads N. to Rimasco, for Rima and Carcóforo (see Rte 3A).—From (74 km.) *Scopello* (658 m) a chair-lift ascends to *Alpe di Mera* (1600 m), a winter-sports resort. The road turns N., passing the mouth of the *Val Rassa,* out of which passes lead to Piedicavallo (see p. 113).—Beyond (81 km.) *Campertogno* (815 m) the ascent becomes steeper, and from (83 km.) *Mollia* (881 m) there is a fine view of the Alagna basin backed by Monte Rosa.—90 km. *Riva Valdobbia* (1143 m) stands at the foot of the Colle Valdobbia, an important pass into the Gressoney valley.—92 km. **Alagna,** see Rte 3A.

An alternative ROAD FROM TURIN TO MILAN (148 km.; bus to Casále, and thence to Milan) diverges from the main road beyond (23 km.) *Chivasso* and follows the Po, with the Monferrato hills rising above the S. bank.—57 km. *Trino,* an ancient place, has been noted for its printers and binders since the 15C.—71 km. **Casale Monferrato** (43,700 inhab.), just off the main road, on the S. bank of the Po, is the chief town of the old duchy of Monferrato, whose princes of the Paleologno family held a famous court in 1319-1533. It is noted for its production of cement and artificial stone. The *Duomo,* consecrated in 1107, has an over-restored façade with flanking towers and a striking narthex. *San Domenico* is an early-Gothic church to which a fine Renaissance portal of 1505 has been added. The *Museo Civico* occupies the rococo Palazzo Treville (by G. B. Scapitta) in Via Mameli. On the ground floor is a collection of sculpture by Leonardo Bistolfi (1859-1933) and upstairs, paintings by Matteo da Verona, Moncalvo, etc. The Synagogue (1595) contains a *Jewish Museum* (fest. 10-12, 15.30-16.30; other days on request). Direct railways connect Casale with Turin, Mortara, Vercelli, Asti, and Alessandria.

The Monferrato hills are traversed by the roads from Casale and from Chivasso to Asti (42 km. and 52 km.). Just W. of the latter road (21 km. from Chivasso) is *Albugnano,* with the Benedictine **Abbey of Vezzolano* (1095-1189; open 7-12, 15-18.30), the finest group of Romanesque buildings in Piedmont, with remarkable sculptures, especially on the façade and the unusual rood-screen, and a cloister the W. side of which appears to be older than the church, while the S. side dates from 1600.

From the Casale-Asti road at *Serralunga* station (14 km. from Casale) a by-road diverges right (W.) for the **Santuario di Crea** (4½ km.), founded in 1590 on the site of the refuge of St Eusebius, Bishop of Vercelli in 340-70. In the church (13C, altered 1608-12) are a Madonna and saints, in fresco, by *Macrino d'Alba* (1503), and a triptych of 1474 with the donors, William VIII of Monferrato and his wife. The 23 main chapels of the sanctuary contain characteristic late-15C sculptures by *Tabacchetti* and paintings by *Caccia.* The highest chapel (del Paradiso) commands a good view over the Monferrato.—*Moncalvo,* 22 km. from Asti on the Casale road, has a good and typical Gothic church of the 14C (with paintings by the local artist, Gugl. Caccia), some houses of similar date, and a fragment of an old castle. The local vines are renowned.

Beyond Casale the road crosses the Sesia and enters Lombardy.—101 km. **Mortara** (15,200 inhab.), an important railway junction and the chief town of the *Lomellina,* retains the churches of *Santa Croce,* with paintings by Lanino, and *San Lorenzo* (Romanesque and Gothic), with pictures by Lanino and Procaccini.—111 km. **Vigévano** is an ancient silk-manufacturing town (68,200 inhab.) now famed for making shoes. Lodovico il Moro (1478-1500) and Francesco II Sforza (1522-35) were born here, and it preserves some beautiful Renaissance buildings. The **Piazza Ducale,* perhaps designed by Leonardo da Vinci (1494), is surrounded on three sides by graceful slender arcades; the *Duomo* (1532-1606), at one end, is interesting for its paintings by 16C Lombards. A Museum (opened by the sacristan) houses its rich treasury, which includes Flemish and local tapestries, illuminated codexes, and goldsmiths' work. The *Castello Sforzesco,* built about 1340, and enlarged in 1492, consists of a huge group of interesting buildings closed indefinitely awaiting restoration. It has a handsome tower and a loggia by Bramante. The *Museo Civico* has an archæological collection and a picture gallery.—About 4 km. S.E. is the large *Sforzesca,* designed by Gugl. da Camino for Il Moro in 1486.—Beyond the Ticino the road traverses the big agricultural market-town of (125 km.) *Abbiategrasso* (27,900 inhab.).—148 km. Milan, see Rte 14.

II THE LAKES AND LOMBARDY

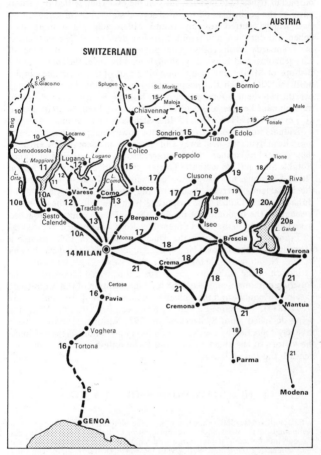

Lombardy, with Milan, the largest city in northern Italy, as its capital, has played an important part in the making of Italy. The province includes regions of remarkable diversity within its boundaries, extending as it does from the summits of the central Alps to the low-lying fertile plain of the Po. Some of the loveliest scenery in the country surrounds the great Italian Lakes (all of which, except Orta, are wholly or partly in Lombardy), while the southern part of the province is either industrialized or given over to intensive agriculture. The population of 8,837,700 is included within an area of 23,850 sq. km. and varies remarkably in density; the modern Lombard provinces are Bergamo, Brescia, Como, Cremona, Mantua, Milan, Pavia, Sondrio, and Varese.

117

In Roman times the centre of Cisalpine Gaul, Lombardy takes its present name from the Lombards or Longobards, one of the so-called barbarian tribes that invaded Italy in the 6C. They settled in various parts of the peninsula and founded several states, but for some reason that which centred roughly round Milan achieved a more than ephemeral duration, and retained the founders' name. The association of Lombardy with transalpine powers dates from the time of Charlemagne, and Lombardy, though actually under the control of the Bishops of Milan, remained nominally a part of the Germanic Empire until the 12C. Then the people of the great Lombard cities, having overthrown the temporal power of the bishops, formed themselves into the Lombard League, and defeated the Emperor, Frederick Barbarossa, at Legnano in 1176. Out of the citizens' organizations, however, individual families soon rose to despotic power, and for two centuries or more local dynasties held sway and were able, incidentally, by virtue of their control of finance, to encourage the arts within their dominions. Notable among them were the Torriani, Visconti, and Sforza at Milan, Pavia, Cremona, and Bergamo; the Suardi and Colleoni at Bergamo; the Pallavicini, Torriani, Scaligeri, and Visconti at Brescia; and the Bonacolsi and Gonzaga at Mantua. With the fall of the powerful Visconti at the beginning of the 15C the power of Venice encroached from the E., and in the 16C Lombard territory was invaded by the kings of France; in the outcome the Duchy of Milan in 1535 became a dependency of the Spanish Habsburgs, though Ticino and the Valtellina in the N. attached themselves to the Swiss Confederation. The extinction of the Habsburg line in Spain transferred Lombardy to the Austrian dominion, and, with the brief intervention of the Napoleonic Cisalpine Republic and the French kingdoms of Lombardy and of Italy (1797-1814), it remained a subject-province of Austria, the Valtellina being detached from Switzerland in 1797. National aspirations were savagely repressed by the Austrian military governors of the 19C until the victory of the allied French and Piedmontese brought Lombardy beneath the Italian flag in 1859.

10   (BRIG) DOMODÓSSOLA TO MILAN

FROM BRIG TO DOMODÓSSOLA, 65 km. The **Simplon Pass** (2009 m; *Passo del Sempione*) and the steep parts of its approaches are wholly on Swiss soil. The pass was only intermittently of importance until Napoleon chose it as the passage for his road connecting the Rhône Valley with the Northern Italian plain. The work, decided upon immediately after the passage of the St Bernard and the battle of Marengo (1800), was begun on the Italian side in 1800, on the Swiss side a year later, and was completed in 1805, this mountain section being the final achievement in the construction of the great highway extending 182 km. from Geneva to Sesto Calende.—About 1 km. below the summit on the S. side stands the *Simplon Hospice* (2001 m), built by Napoleon as barracks in 1811 and acquired by the monks of St Bernard in 1825.

In summer the Italian custom-house is at *Paglino,* just within (43 km.) the frontier; in winter it is at (47 km.) *Iselle.* N 33 descends the **Val Divedro,** past the mouth of the railway tunnel, to (52 km.) *Varzo* (568 m), a centre for the ascent of Monte Cistella (2575 m). A road (continued by a mule path) ascends the Val Cairasca (in 6 hrs) to *Alpe Veglia* (1753 m), a summer resort below *Monte Leone* (3552 m).—65 km. *Domodóssola* (see below).

The RAILWAY from Brig (40 km.) passes through the *Simplon Tunnel,* the longest rail tunnel in the world (19.8 km.), the first gallery of which was pierced in

1898-1905. Although a subsidiary gallery, connected by cross-shafts, formed part of the original construction, this was not enlarged to take a second track until 1912-21. The maximum elevation is only 705 m and the Simplon is thus the lowest of the great Alpine tunnels; but there are 2134 m of mountain overhead where the main ridge is pierced.—CAR CARRIER trains frequently between Iselle and Brig.

A Viâ Stresa

FROM DOMODÓSSOLA, N33, 125 km.—6½ km. *Villadóssola.*—20 km. *Cuzzago.*—30½ km. *Gravellona.* Thence along the shore of Lago Maggiore, viâ (42 km.) *Stresa.*—58 km. **Arona.**—67 km. *Sesto Calende.*—84 km. *Gallarate.*—125 km. **Milan.** From just beyond Sesto Calende the AUTOSTRADA (A 8) offers a faster approach (3 km. shorter) to Milan.

RAILWAY, 125 km. in 1¼-2¼ hrs; to *Stresa* (39 km.) in 30-50 min.; to *Arona* (56 km.) in 40-70 min. Through carriages on this route from Calais to Milan and Venice.

Domodóssola (271 m), the chief place of the Valle d'Ossola, at the foot of the Simplon Pass, is a characteristic little Italian town (20,500 inhab.), of Roman origin, with an old arcaded market-place. In the *Palazzo Silva* (with a frieze of 1519), near the market-place, is a *Museum of Antiquities.* The church of *SS. Gervaso e Protasio,* nearby, has an old porch (15C frescoes) and bronze doors of 1955. The wide Via Rosmini leads past the large Collegio Mellerio Rosmini, in which is the *Simplon Museum* (Museo Sempioniano), illustrating the construction of the tunnel; farther on Via Mattarella leads to an interesting 17C *Calvary* (view from the top). A monument in Piazza Liberazione (No. 9) commemorates Georges Chavez, the Peruvian airman, who was killed in his fall near Domodóssola, after having made the first flight over the Alps (29 Sept 1910).

The VALLE BOGNANCO, W. of Domodóssola, may be visited by bus in ½ hr to (8 km.) *Bognanco Fonti* (663 m), a popular little spa. Some buses go on in ½ hr (and a cable railway ascends) to (12½ km.) *Bognanco San Lorenzo* (980 m) where the road ends. San Lorenzo is connected with (6 hrs) *Antronapiana* by the *Passo del Fornalino* (2356 m).

FROM DOMODÓSSOLA TO THE SAN GIACOMO PASS, 55 km., bus twice daily in 2¼ hrs to Ponte di Formazza, 40 km. The scenery on the route is very spectacular. At San Michele or Ponte in the Val Formazza (see below) guides may be hired for excursions to the peaks round the Gries pass.

At (5 km.) the foot of the Val Divedro this route leaves the road and railway to the Simplon.—Near (13½ km.) *Crodo* (356 m) is a little spa, with iron springs.—The gorge of the Dévero is crossed to reach (19 km.) *Baceno* (685 m), where the double-aisled *Church* (14-16C) has frescoes by Ant. Zanetti. At the head of the Dévero valley (l.) is *Alpe Dévero* (1640 m), a pleasant fishing and winter-sports resort (ski-lift).—21 km. **Premia.**—26 km. *San Rocco* (754 m) has an ancient church.—At (30 km.) *Rivasco* are the great Conti works, which furnish electricity to Milan. The road traverses the most typical stretch of the VAL ANTIGORIO, with its vineyards, fig-trees, and chestnuts, and comes to (32 km.) *Foppiano* or *Unter Stalden* (933 m) the first German-speaking village. After twice crossing the Toce in the grand *Gola delle Casse,* the route enters the **Val Formazza,** an interesting region colonized in the Middle Ages by German-speaking families from the Valais.—35 km. *Alla Chiesa,* or *Andermatten* (1235 m), like Foppiano, is in the commune of **Formazza,** a series of picturesque hamlets extending through (39 km.) *Ponte,* the municipal centre (Italian customs) to the frontier. It is now a winter sports centre (chair-lift from Ponte).—45 km. *Cascata del Toce* (1661 m). The *****Falls of the Toce,** or *Cascata la Frua,* are among the grandest in the Alps, though they now function only on days when their source is not being tapped for hydro-electric power (June-Sept, fest. only). The stream spreads out like a fan in its descent and, gliding down a series of steps, forms an uninterrupted mass of white foam for over 300 m, while the perpendicular descent is about 143 m. The best view-points are a little footbridge close to the hotel, and a bend in the track leading to Domodóssola, 10 min. lower down.

The road deteriorates as it approaches (48 km.) *Riale* (1720 m) which lies at the junction of the routes to the Gries (footpath) and San Giacomo passes. The right-hand route passes (r.) a power-reservoir to reach (56 km.) the *Passo di San Giacomo* (2315 m). A bridle-path goes on across the Swiss frontier to (2 hrs) All'Acqua in the Val Bedretto.

FROM DOMODÓSSOLA TO LOCARNO, road, 48½ km. Railway, 51 km. in 40-70 min., closely following the road. The road crosses the Toce to reach (4½ km.) *Masera* (306 m) where there is an old church tower. Here is the entrance to the VAL VIGEZZO, frequented by artists since the 19C and known as the "Valle dei Pittori', which rises near (13 km.) *Druogno* to an indefinite watershed separating the W. and E. branches of the Melezzo.—17 km. **Santa Maria Maggiore** (815 m), the chief village of the valley, is finely situated in an upland basin, with a swimming pool, and is connected by bus with *Toceno, Vocogno,* and *Craveggia,* three pleasant villages across the torrent. The area has been opened up for skiers (cable railway to Piana di Vigezzo, 1724 m).—20 km. *Malesco* (760 m) stands at the divergence of a road to Cannobio (see p. 130).—23 km. *Re* (710 m) has a modern shrine of the Madonna, which attracts many pilgrims.—At (29 km.) the bold *Ponte della Ribellasca* (552 m; custom house) the road enters Switzerland.—Below (30 km.) *Cámedo* the valley is joined by innumerable side streams which give the district its name (Centovalli, the 'Hundred Valleys').—41 km. *Intragna* (369 m) is conspicuous by its lofty church tower. The village was the original home of the Gambetta family, whence the grandfather of Léon Gambetta emigrated to Genoa.—48½ km. *Locarno.*

From Domodóssola to *Macugnaga* and *Aosta,* see Rte 3A.

6½ km. **Villadóssola,** with a 12C campanile, lies at the S.E. foot of *Moncucco* (1899 m; 4 hrs), at the mouth of the Valle d'Antrona, which ascends on the right.

The VALLE D'ANTRONA. Bus daily from Domodóssola to Antronapiana in 1½ hr.—Beyond (8 km.) *Viganella* (582 m), with its graceful waterfall, the road crosses the Ovesca, and, as the valley widens, there is a view of the Punta di Saas rising at its head. From (12 km.) *San Pietro di Schieranco* (652 m), the Passo dei Salarioli leads S. to the Val Anzasca.—16 km. **Antronapiana** (902 m), charmingly situated among larch and fir woods, is the chief village of the valley frequented for trout-fishing. It offers some delightful excursions, best of which is the walk to (¾ hr) the beautiful little *Lago d'Antrona* (1083 m) formed in 1642 by a landslip from the *Cima di Pozzoli* (2546 m) to the N.

Beyond (9 km.) *Pallanzeno* this route leaves the Macugnaga road on the right to cross the Toce.—14 km. *Vogogna* has a 14C castle of the Visconti.—Beyond (20 km.) *Cuzzago* the road bears right to cross the railway and the Toce.

The road on the left bank of the river leads to (18 km.) Pallanza viâ (8 km.) *Mergozzo.*

25 km. *Ornavasso,* near the marble quarries of Candóglia, was colonized in the 13C by a Germanic immigration from the Valais.— 30½ km. **Gravellona Toce,** near the junction of the Strona and the Toce, has a small *Antiquarium* of Iron Age and Roman finds.—35 km. *Feriolo* is the junction with the road along the shore of Lago Maggiore.—38 km. *Baveno,* and thence to (42 km.) **Stresa,** see Rte 10A.

Beyond Stresa the road continues along the southern reach of the lake, where the scenery is less impressive and the villages less frequented than farther N. On the E. bank is the picturesque old church of *Arolo.*— 47 km. *Belgirate,* standing on a conspicuous headland, was the home of the five heroic brothers Cairoli, only one of whom, the statesman Benedetto (1825-89), survived the wars of Italian independence.— 49 km. *Lesa* is famous for its vineyards and orchards. The Palazzo Stampa here was a residence of Manzoni. At *Ispra,* on the opposite shore, is the first centre in Italy for nuclear studies.—54 km. *Méina.*

On the right above appears the colossal statue called San Carlone (see below).—58 km. **Arona,** an ancient town (16,700 inhab.) and an important railway junction, is the S. terminus of the steamer service. The lakeside promenade affords a good view of Angera. The palace of the Podestà dates from the 15C. In the upper town in the church of *Santa Maria* the Borromeo chapel contains an *Altarpiece (1511) of six panels by Gaud. Ferrari. The lunette over the main door has a charming 15C relief of the Holy Family. The neighbouring church of the *Santi Martiri* has a Madonna by Bergognone over the high altar.

To the N., above the Simplon road, stands the *San Carlone,* a colossal statue of San Carlo Borromeo (1538-84), archbishop of Milan, who was born in the castle that now lies in ruins above the town. The statue, 23 m high, standing on a 12 m pedestal, was erected in 1697 by a relative of the saint. The pedestal may be ascended by outside steps, and the statue itself by an internal stair.

The steamer to Stresa calls first at *Angera* (5 min.) beneath the chapel-crowned hill of San Quirico (412 m) on the Lombard side of the lake. Anciently a place of some importance, the town possesses a fine old castle of the Visconti, which passed to the Borromei in 1439, and was extensively restored in the 16-17C. This and other places on the E. bank are served by the Luino-Novara railway and connected by bus with Varese.

Beyond Arona the route curves round the S. end of the lake, leaving the Novara road on the right. Road and railway cross the Ticino by a two-storied bridge near its outflow from the lake.—67 km. **Sesto Calende,** on the left bank, is said to derive its name from its market day in Roman times—the sixth day before the Kalends. The Milan autostrada begins 4 km. farther on, running slightly to the N.E. of this road, while to the S., beyond (76 km.) *Somma Lombardo* with its Visconti castle, lies *Malpensa,* the intercontinental airport of Milan.—84 km. **Gallarate,** a cotton-spinning town (46,500 inhab.), is a junction for Varese (19 km.) and Laveno. The cathedral is modern (1856-60), but the church of San Pietro dates from the 12C, and there is a small Archæological Museum at 4 Via Borgo Antico.—90 km. **Busto Arsizio** (r.), another cotton town (82,100 inhab.), is also on the line from Novara to Bergamo. The church of *Santa Maria di Piazza* (1515-23) contains paintings by G. Ferrari and Luini.—At (95 km.) **Legnano,** an important manufacturing town (48,300 inhab.), a monument, visible from the railway, commemorates the battle here in which Barbarossa was defeated by the Lombard League in 1176. *San Magno* (1504) houses a polyptych by Luini and frescoes by Lanino. The *Museum* (10-12, 15-17; closed Mon) contains local Roman finds.—110 km. **Rho,** with a large oil-refinery and chemical works. Here the railway from Novara and Turin comes in.—125 km. **Milan,** see Rte 14.

B   Viâ Orta

ROAD, 132 km.—30½ km. *Gravellona.*—37 km. *Omegna.*—48 km. **Orta.**—60 km. *Borgomanero.*—75 km. *Sesto Calende.*—132 m. **Milan.**

RAILWAY, to *Borgomanero,* 60 km. in 1¼-2 hrs, continuing to Novara; to *Orla,* 47 km. in 60-80 min.

From Domodóssola to (30½ km.) *Gravellona Toce,* see above.—37 km. *Omegna,* a small manufacturing town (16,700 inhab.) at the N. end of the Lake of Orta, retains a few old houses, a medieval bridge, and the ancient town gate leading to the Valle Strona. A bus runs viâ Gravellona to Pallanza and Intra.

The upper VAL STRONA, which descends from the hills to the N.W., is a narrow winding glen, c. 20 km. long, ending at the *Laghetto di Capezzone* (2104 m), a lovely tarn beneath the *Cima di Capezzone* (2420 m).

On the right beyond (45 km.) *Pettenasco* is a view of the Sacro Monte, behind which Orta lies concealed.—48 km. **Orta San Giulio** is pleasantly situated on the lakeward side of a little peninsula. From the Piazza Principale, which enjoys a good view of the Isola San Giulio and the lake, a road passing the *Church of the Assumption,* with an 11C doorway, leads to the gateway of the SACRO MONTE, a low hill ascended in 20 minutes.

The *Sacro Monte (396 m), dedicated to St Francis of Assisi, has a single path flanked by 20 chapels in early-Renaissance style built between 1596 and 1670 (two are 18C and a 21st chapel is unfinished). In them frescoes and groups of life-size terracotta figures illustrate scenes in the life of the saint. The most interesting chapels are the 10th, 11th, 13th, 16th, and 20th, while the terrace of the 15th, and the campanile at the top, afford fine views. The frescoes are by G. C. Procaccini, A. M. Crespi, and the Fiamminghini; the sculptures by Dionigi Bussola, Mich. Prestinari, and Carlo Beretta.

The **Lake of Orta** (290 m), 8 m. long and about $\frac{3}{4}$ m. wide, a quiet sheet of water surrounded by mountains, is less visited by tourists than the larger lakes.

STEAMBOATS ply to (5 miin.) the *Isola San Giulio* and (20 min.) *Pella;* to (1 hr) *Oira* and (1$\frac{1}{4}$ hr) *Omegna.*
The *Isola San Giulio, opposite Orta, once shunned as the haunt of serpents and other noxious beasts, was purged of the pest in 390 by St Julius, the founder of the original island church. In 962 the island was defended by Willa, wife of Berengar II of Lombardy, against the incursions of the Emperor Otho the Great. Today the island contains villas belonging to the Milanese aristocracy. Within the interesting *Basilica* is a remarkable * *Pulpit* of Óira marble (11-12C), with quaint carvings. The white marble sarcophagus with Roman carvings, near the door, is said to be that of the traitor duke, Meinulphus, and now serves as an alms-box. Some of the chapels are decorated with 15C Lombard frescoes, one of which (Virgin and Child enthroned, with four saints), is attributed to Gaud. Ferrari. In the sacristy are a charter of Otho the Great giving thanks for his eventual capture of the island, and a whale's vertebra passing for a bone of one of the serpents destroyed by St Julius.

Just before the S. end of the lake, the road skirts a hill crowned by a restored Lombard tower.—Beyond (55 km.) *Gozzano* (linked by bus with Arona) is (60 km.) **Borgomanero.** The road straight ahead continues to (82 km.) Novara (p. 114). This route turns left for (75 km.) *Sesto Calende,* whence to (132 km.) **Milan,** see Rte 10A.

11   LAGO MAGGIORE

LAGO MAGGIORE (193 m) the *Lacus Verbanus* of the Romans, is the second largest lake in Italy (82 sq. m.; Lago di Garda, 143 sq. m.). Its total length, from Magadino to Sesto Calende, is 40 m., and its greatest breadth 3 m. between Baveno and Laveno; its greatest depth, off Ghiffa, is 372 metres. About one-fifth of the lake, at the N. end, belongs to Switzerland. The chief affluent is the Ticino, which flows in at Magadino and out at Sesto Calende. Other important feeders are the Maggia, which enters the lake at Locarno; the Toce or Tosa, which flows into the gulf of Pallanza, and is joined just before its inflow by the Strona, fed by the waters of the Lake of Orta; and on the E. side the Tresa, which drains the Lake of Lugano and enters Lago Maggiore at Luino. These numerous tributaries, fed mostly by mountain snows, subject the lake to sudden floods. The *tramontana* blows regularly from the N. in the early morning, followed after 10 by the *inverna* from the S. The *mergozzo* blows from the W. in the gulf of Pallanza, and the usually placid waters are sometimes lashed to fury by the *maggiora*.

Though the W. Italian bank has belonged to Piedmont since 1743, the history of the lake is bound up with its Lombard E. shore. Since the 15C the greatest power around the lake has been the Italian family of Borromeo, who still own the islands that bear their name and the fishery rights all over the lake.

STEAMER SERVICES. Frequent services of steamers ply up and down the lake, though only a few pass the frontier between Cannobio and Brissago. The central ports, Laveno-Verbania-Baveno-Stresa, are linked by additional services. In summer hydrofoils and a Swiss boat maintain direct services between Stresa and Locarno (passports necessary). Between Brissago and Locarno more frequent service in 50-60 min.

Approaches by Rail. FROM MILAN TO ARONA VIÃ SESTO CALENDE, 69 km. in c. 1 hr, see Rte 10A.

FROM MILAN (Porta Garibaldi) TO LUINO VIÃ GALLARATE, 91 km. in 1½ hr (irregularly), viâ Busto Arsizio and Besozzo.

FROM MILAN TO LAVENO VIÃ VARESE, 73 km., Nord-Milano railway in 1¼-1¾ hr; road parallel. *Milan,* see Rte 14.—22 km. **Saronno** is an industrial town (35,100 inhab.), noted for its macaroons. The sanctuary of the *Madonna dei Miracoli* (1498) by G. A. Amedeo and V. Seregni contains frescoes by Gaudenzio Ferrari, Luini, and others. From Saronno branch lines diverge for *Como* and for *Novara* and buses run to *Seregno.*—46 km. *Malnate.* About 8 km. S.W. of Malnate is **Castiglione Olona,** which was practically rebuilt by Card. Branda Castiglioni (1350-1443). In the piazza are the *Chiesa di Villa,* built and adorned by local masons and sculptors in the Florentine Renaissance style; and the *Casa dei Castiglioni,* with an interesting interior, where the cardinal was born and died. Among the frescoes is a view, by Masolino, of the Hungarian city of Veszprem, where the cardinal served as bishop in 1412-24. At the top of the hill is the *Collegiata,* replacing the family's feudal castle (c. 1428). It is decorated with *Frescoes by Florentine artists, notably the Life of the Virgin, in the semidome, by Masolino; here too is the tomb of the cardinal; while in the Baptistery, a little to the left (in a former tower of the castle; shown by the sacristan) are further frescoes by Masolino (life of St John the Baptist; 1435) and a font, with putti recalling those at San Giovanni in Brágora in Venice. 4 km. farther S., at *Castelseprio,* an old chapel contains some extraordinary mural paintings in an Oriental (Alexandrian) style, thought to date from the 7C or 9C. They were discovered by a partisan in the Second World War. The church lies among the ruins of a late Roman camp around which grew a small town that was destroyed in 1287.—51 km. **Varese,** see p. 130.

62 km. *Gavirate* on the N. shore of the **Lago di Varese,** 5¼ m. long, a sheet of water once famous for its quantity of fish, but now threatened with pollution. *Voltorre,* 2 km. S.E., on the shore of the lake, has an old monastery with an interesting Romanesque brick cloister. Boats ply from Gavirate to the *Isola Virginia* or *Isolino,* where a small museum contains objects found in lake dwellings.—69 km. *Cittiglio* is the terminus of a bus running N. through the Val Cuvia to Luino.—73 km. *Laveno,* see p. 128.

Approaches by road. The main road from the Simplon Pass to Milan (Rte 10) strikes the lake at Baveno and follows the W. bank to Sesto Calende. The upper half of the W. bank is followed by a good road from Bellinzona to Baveno viâ Locarno, while a secondary road follows the E. bank from Magadino to Laveno. These two are connected by a car-ferry between Intra and Laveno.

A STRESA AND THE CENTRE OF THE LAKE

STEAMER approx. hourly to Laveno, in c. 80 min.

STRESA (5155 inhab.), on the S. shore of the gulf of Pallanza, enjoys the most charming situation on the lake, and on that account is frequented not only by travellers, but also by Italian and foreign residents attracted by its pleasant villas and luxuriant gardens. It is also a conference centre.

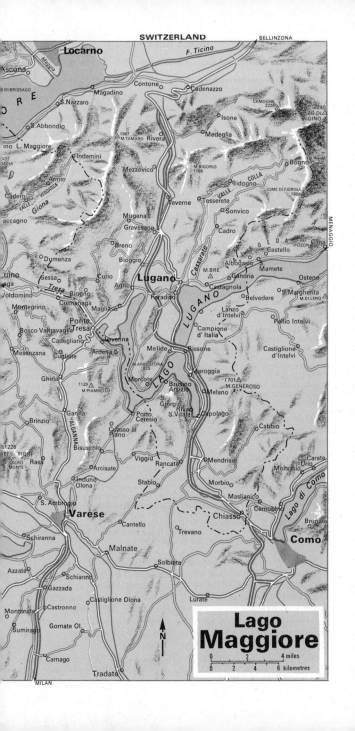

Lago Maggiore

Post Office, opposite the pier.—*Information Office,* Palazzo dei Congressi, Piazzale Europa.

Rowing Boats and Motor-boats for hire.—**Steamers,** see above; also to the Isole Boromee, and Santa Caterina (p. 128) in 15 min.

Buses to the *Mottarone,* to *Domodóssola,* to *Milan,* to *Novara,* to *Turin,* to *Locarno.*—Coach tours of the lakes in summer.

Golf Course (9 holes) at Vezzo.—*Swimming Pools* on the Baveno road.

The town and its surroundings abound in picturesque villas. Just N. of the church is the *Villa Ducale,* which belonged to Rosmini, who died there in 1855, and later to the Duchess of Genoa (d. 1912), mother of Queen Margherita. On the other side of the pier are *Villa Pallavicino* with a fine garden (March-Oct, 8.30-19) and small menagerie, and *Villa Vignola* (no adm.). Above the town to the S.E. is the *Collegio Rosmini,* which occupies the buildings of a convent of Rosminians, an order of charity founded by Antonio Rosmini (1797-1855), the philosopher. In the adjoining church is his monument, by Vela.

Pleasant walks may be taken among the woods on the hillside to the W. between Stresa and Levo.

FROM STRESA TO MONTE MOTTARONE, 21 km. (bus from the station or the pier in connection with main line trains or lake steamers), or Funicular from Stresa Lido. The road climbs in turns, touching (5 km.) *Vezzo* (483 m) and *Panorama* (view), near the gold course, and at 8 km., just before *Gignese* (which has an Umbrella Museum, open 9-12, 14-18), it branches right to (10 km.) *Alpino* (777 m) where the Giardino Alpinia (open May-Oct) has some 2000 species of plants. Beyond a wood and after a steep climb it joins a road from Orta (comp. below).— 20 km. *Mottarone* (1379 m), a winter sports centre, is 20 min. from the summit of *Monte Mottarone (1491 m).

The *View includes the whole chain of the Alps from Monte Viso in the W. to the Ortler and Adamello in the E., with the Monte Rosa group especially conspicuous to the N.W. Seven lakes are seen close at hand, and in clear weather Milan Cathedral can be distinguished standing out in the Lombard plain.—The descent may be made to (16 km.) *Orta* by road, or to (2½ hrs.) *Omegna* or (3 hrs.) *Baveno* by steep rough tracks.

The less interesting S. arm of the lake is described in Rte 10A.

On leaving Stresa all steamers touch at the *Isola Bella* and the *Isola dei Pescatori,* and the majority also at the *Isola Madre* (beyond Baveno; see below).

The *****Borromean Islands,** so named from the noble Italian family of Borromeo, to which all but the Isola dei Pescatori belong, are four islets at the mouth of the bay of Pallanza, noted for their wealth of vegetation and for the beauty of their surroundings. Stresa is perhaps the best centre for a visit to the group, though the *Isola Madre* lies nearer Pallanza and the *Isola dei Pescatori* nearer Baveno, both of which also have boat trips to the islands. The small *Isola San Giovanni* or *Isolino* (no adm.; see below), lies close to Pallanza. A combined ticket for the visit to the Isola Bella and Isola Madre may be obtained.

ROWING-BOATS from *Stresa,* see above; from *Pallanza,* see below. Circuits of the islands at fixed tariffs.—STEAMERS, see above.

Nearest to Stresa is the **Isola Bella,** the most famous of the isles. It was a barren rock, with a small church and a few cottages, until, with the architect Ang. Crivelli (d. 1630), Count Charles III Borromeo conceived its transformation in honour of his wife Isabella, from whom it takes its name. Renato II and his brother, Vitaliano II (d. 1690), brought it to its present appearance by constructing a palace, surrounded with terraced gardens, the soil for which had to be brought from the mainland; the palace was only finished in 1958.

The **Garden* consists of ten terraces, the lowest built on piles thrown out into the lake, and all decorated with statues, vases, and fountains, in an ornate style, and enhanced by the luxuriance of the rare exotic plants. The view of the lake and its surroundings is famous, as are also the white peacocks.

The *Palace* (adm. March-Oct, 9-12, 13.30-17.30) is decorated with fine furniture, tapestries, ancient weapons, and numerous landscapes by Tempesta, who sought refuge here when accused of the murder of his wife. The chapel contains family tombs by Giov. Ant. Amadeo and Bambaia, brought from demolished churches in Milan. The fine picture gallery (adm. only with special permission) contains works by Giov. Ant. Boltraffio, Bergognone, Paris Bordone, Lanino, and other Lombard artists.

Nearer Bavena lies the **Isola dei Pescatori** or *Isola Superiore,* occupied almost entirely by a fishing village.

3 m. **BAVENO** (4280 inhab.) is beautifully situated on the S. shore of the gulf of Pallanza opposite the Borromean Islands. Quieter than Stresa, it preserves a pleasant little square. The famous shore-road to Stresa, with a charming view of the Borromean Islands, is flanked by villas, among which is the Castello Branca (formerly Villa Clara), occupied by Queen Victoria in the spring of 1879.

To the N.W. of Baveno rises *Monte Camoscio (890 m), reached by a road ascending through the village of *Oltrefiume* and climbing the S. side of a large granite quarry.—A shady road mounting the hillside S. of Baveno leads in 1¼ hr to *Levo* (see above). *Monte Mottarone* (see above) may be ascended in c. 3 hrs from Baveno either viâ Levo, or by the right side of the Selva Spessa valley.

The **Isola Madre,** nearer to Pallanza, is the largest of the Borromean Islands, and, like the Isola Bella, has a splendid *Botanic Garden* (March-Oct, 9-12, 13-17.30) planted with exotic trees of even greater luxuriance; the rhododendrons are especially striking. The villa in the centre is surrounded by avenues which afford delightful glimpses of the mainland, especially towards Pallanza in the afternoon.

After leaving the island a few of the steamers call at (5½ m.) *Suna.*

6¾ m. **PALLANZA,** charmingly situated in full view of the Borromean Islands, is sun-baked in summer, but delightful in spring and autumn, and enjoys a mild winter climate. The flora of the neighbourhood is luxuriantly beautiful. In 1939 Pallanza and Suna were united with Intra to form the commune of **Verbania** (34,400 inhab.), a name derived, like the Latin name of the lake (Lacus Verbanus), from the vervain (verbena) which grows abundantly on its shores.

Post Office, P.za Gramsci.—*Information Office* on the lake shore.
Bus to *Intra* and to the station of *Verbania-Pallanza,* going on to *Omegna;* also to *Arona;* to *Locarno;* to *Milan;* to *Novara.*
Tennis Courts and Swmming on the shore between Pallanza and Suna.
Boats for hire at fixed charges.

The pleasant lake-front is planted with magnolias. Near the pier is the mausoleum, by Piacentini, of Marshal Cadorna (1850-1928), a native of Pallanza; and just inland is the market-place, with the *Municipio* and the modernized church of *San Leonardo* (16C), the tall tower of which was completed by P. Tibaldi in 1589. In the Palazzo Dugnani is a small local *Museum* (April-Oct, 10-12, 15-18; Nov-March, Sat & Sun 10-12, 14-16). The narrow Via Cavour leading N. from the market-place, is continued to (1 km.) the fine domed church of the *Madonna di Campagna,* which was begun in 1519 and contains frescoes in the cupola attrib. to B. Lanino, and others by C. Procaccini.

Intra may be reached by the pleasant lake-side road or (shorter) by the road passing behind the Punta della Castagnola. Between the two roads are the *Villa*

San Remigio, with fine gardens (open on holidays) and, farther on, the **Villa Táranto,** with remarkable *Botanical Gardens (open in April-Oct, 8.30-sunset). A Roman cippus is built into the wall of the church of *Santo Stefano,* just N. of the upper road.

A serpentine road diverging on the left just beyond Madonna di Campagna ascends to (9 km. from Pallanza) the top of *Monte Rosso* (693 m). The road goes on to (13 km.) *Cavandone,* from where a road returns to Pallanza viâ Suna.

The steamer passes the little *Isola San Giovanni* (with a villa that was once the summer home of Toscanini), then rounds the Punta della Castagnola.—9 m. **Intra,** a busy industrial town, lies between the mouths of the San Giovanni and San Bernardino torrents. To the N., close to the lake, are the beautiful private gardens of the *Villa Poss* and *Villa Ada.* A car-ferry (½-hourly) connects Intra with Laveno.

A bus runs to (10 km.) *Miazzina* (719 m), the best starting-point for the ascent of (5 hrs) *Monte Zeda* (2188 m). Another bus ascends N. from Intra, viâ (6 km.) *Arizzano* and (9 km.) *Bèe,* to (13 km.; 30 min.) **Premeno** (802 m), a favourite summer resort (with winter sports facilities also) commanding a fine view. Even better is the view from the higher *Pian di Sole* (949 m).

BUS from Intra viâ Pallanza to (9 km.) *Verbania-Pallanza* station and (19 km.) *Omegna;* to *Cannobio,* see below.

As the steamer crosses towards Laveno the prominent Rocca di Caldè, backed by Monte Támaro, comes into view. Behind Intra, with Monte Rosso to the E. of it, is Monte Órfano, and the snows of the Mischabelhörner and the Weissmies on the horizon. To the right Monte Mottarone rises above Stresa, with Monte Rosa in the distance on its right hand.

12 m. **Laveno Mombello,** an important port (9100 inhab.), was strongly fortified by the Austrians in 1849-59. It is noted for its ceramics, and ìs frequented for its good climate. Of its two stations that of the State Railways is c. 1 km. from the lake; the main Nord-Milano station for Varese and Milan adjoins the pier. A monument in the piazza by the waterside commemorates the Garibaldini who fell in an attempt to capture the town in 1859. The *Villa Pullè,* on the site of an Austrian fort, on the Punta di San Michele to the N.W., contains a small Garibaldian museum.

The *View from Laveno, which extends as far N. as Monte Rosa, the Mischabel group, and the Fletschhorn group, is best from the cableway to Poggio Sant'Elsa, from where it is 30 min. on foot to the *Sasso del Ferro (1062 m), the beautiful hill to the E. Still wider is the panorama from *Monte Nudo (1235 m), 2 hrs farther E.—A favourite excursion from Laveno (also made by boat) follows the shore past (2½ km.) *Cerro* to *Leggiuno* where the Oratory of SS. Primo e Feliciano (9C) has Roman foundations.—5½ km. *Santa Caterina del Sasso,* a 15C Carmelite convent (abandoned and closed to visitors) which stands in a commanding position above the lake and affords a good view of the gulf of Pallanza and the Borromean Isles.

FROM LAVENTO TO LUINO, by road (16½ km.), bus; also railway in 20 min.—At (5 km.) the road skirts a conical hill (380 m) crowned by the *Rocca di Caldè,* the 10C castle of the Marquesses of Ivrea, which was destroyed by the Swiss in 1518.— 8½ km. *Porto Valtravaglia.*—16½ km. *Luino,* see below. The road continues viâ (22 km.) *Maccagno* (see below) and (30 km.) *Pino sulla sponda del Lago Maggiore* which boasts the longest Italian place-name. Beyond the frontier (custom-house) it joins at 49 km. the main road from Locarno to Bellinzona.

From Laveno to *Milan* viâ Varese, see p. 123.

B   FROM INTRA TO LOCARNO BY ROAD

ROAD, 40 km. N 34 to the frontier, N 21 beyond; bus 7 times daily in 1¾-2½ hrs, more frequently to *Cannóbio* (20 km. in 40 min.).

Intra, see above. The road follows the lakeside.—4½ km. *Ghiffa,* a scattered village, centres on the fine Castello di Frino (now a hotel). The little 13C church of *Novaglio,* above the road, is a curious mixture of Lombard and Gothic architecture.—Above (8 km.) *Oggebbio,* another scattered village among chestnut groves, is the little oratory of *Cadessino,* with 15-16C frescoes. Ahead, across the lake, Luino comes into view, as, beneath *Oggiogno* high up on its rock, the road passes the favourite villa of the statesman Massimo d'Azeglio (1798-1866), where he wrote most of his memoirs.

11 km. **Cánnero Riviera,** a holiday resort lying in a sheltered and sunny position at the foot of *Monte Carza* (1118 m). Off the coast are two rocky islets (accessible by rowing-boat) on which stood the castles of *Malpaga* or Cánnero (12-14C), once the refuge of the five robber brothers Mazzarditi. The existing ruins date partly from a villa built by Ludovico Borromeo after 1414.

On the hill above the town is the church (14-15C) of *Carmine Superiore,* built on the summit of a precipice, and containing some good ceiling-paintings and a triptych of the 14C Lombard school.—*Monte Zeda* (2188 m) may be ascended from Cánnero in 6½ hrs.

The road rounds Punta d'Amore opposite Maccagno.—20 km. *Cannóbio,* see below. About 5 km. farther on is the frontier into Switzerland. The road goes on viâ (30 km.) *Brissago* and (36 km.) *Ascona* to (40 km.) **Locarno.**

C   FROM LUINO TO CANNOBIO (LOCARNO) BY STEAMER

Steamers in summer make the journey from Luino to Locarno; more ply (in 25 min.) from Luino to Cannobio including slower boats from the S. part of the lake (see p. 123).

Luino is the most important tourist centre on the Lombard side of the lake. A small industrial town (15,200 inhab.), it lies a little N. of the junction of the Tresa and Margorabbia, which unite to flow into the lake at Germignaga. Near the landing stage is a statue of Garibaldi, commemorating his attempt, on 14 Aug 1848, to renew the struggle against Austria with only 1500 men, after the armistice which followed the defeat of Custozza. The *Town Hall* occupies an 18C palazzo by Felice Soave. Luino is the probable birthplace of the painter, Bernardino Luini (c. 1490). An Adoration of the Magi attributed to him adorns the cemetery church of *San Pietro,* and the *Madonna del Carmine* has frescoes by his pupils (1540).

On the landward side of the town is the railway station (with custom-house), where the Swiss line from Bellinzona meets the Italian line from Novara (no through trains).

A bus runs via *Cremenaga* and from there along the Italian side of the frontier to (12 km.) *Ponte Tresa* (in 20 min.) on Lake Lugano.

From Luino to *Laveno,* see p. 128; to *Varese,* see p. 131.

About 3 m. N. of Luino *Maccagno Superiore* and *Maccagno Inferiore,* two little holiday resorts, at the narrowest point of the lake, lie on either side of the mouth of the Giona, which waters the Valle Vedasca. Above the second village is the picturesque Santuario della Madonnina, supported by two lofty arches, while higher still is an old watch-tower.

The *Lago Delio* (922 m; 2 hrs. N.E.), lies ½ hr E. of the summit of *Monte Borgna* (881 m) which has a good view of the lake.

Fifteen minutes to the N.W. across the lake **Cannóbio,** a busy place (5740 inhab.) of considerable antiquity, is the principal station of the 'torpediniere' or anti-smuggling launches. The *Santuario della Pietà,* near the pier, is in the style of Bramante; the dome and choir-vault are by Pellegrino Tibaldi (after 1571). The fine altar-painting is by Gaud. Ferrari. The *Town Hall,* called Il Parrasio, is a 13C building with 17C alterations.—Buses to *Locarno* and to *Intra,* see p. 128.

From Cannobio a bus runs daily to (½ hr) *Falmenta* in the Val Cannobina, and another to (1½ hr) *Finero.* The road, running inland from Cannobio, ascends the *Val Cannobina* to *Traffiume,* where a boat may be hired to visit the *Orrido di Sant'Anna,* a romantic gorge with a waterfall. From there it goes on viâ *Finero* and over the watershed (945 m) to *Malesco* in the Val Vigezzo, where it strikes the road and railway from Locarno to Domodóssola (p. 120).

12   THE LAKE OF LUGANO

Approaches. The most interesting approach from the south is the route viâ Varese and Ponte Tresa or Porto Ceresio (preferably the latter) going on to Porlezza and Menaggio; by this means it is only necessary to set foot on Swiss soil at Lugano where boats are changed. Travellers by road traverse Swiss territory from Ponte Tresa through Lugano to Gandria.

ROAD, 69 km. Autostrada direct to (56 km.) Varese, bearing right from the Sesto Calende branch (A 8) on the outskirts of Gallarate (37 km.).—From Varese Via René Vanetti joins the minor road (N 344) to (69 km.) *Porto Ceresio.*

RAILWAY FROM MILAN (*Porta Garibaldi*) to Porto Ceresio viâ Gallarate, 77 km., in 1½-2 hrs.

An alternative approach by rail may be made direct FROM MILAN (*Centrale*) TO LUGANO VIÂ COMO. 77 km. in 1-1½ hr, part of the main St Gotthard route. *Milan,* see Rte 14; thence viâ Monza to 46 km. *Como,* see Rte 13. The railway tunnels beneath Monte Olimpino and enters Switzerland from Lombardy.— 51 km. **Chiasso** (241 m), with the Swiss and Italian custom-house is important only as an international station. From here to (77 km.) **Lugano** the line skirts the lake, crossing it half way up on a causeway.

From Milan to (37 km.) *Gallarate,* see p. 121.—The Lago di Varese soon comes into view on the left.

56 km. **VARESE** is a flourishing town of 89,000 inhab., with footwear factories, whose pleasant surroundings are much frequented as a summer residence by the Milanese.

Railway Stations. *State Railway,* E., of the town, for Milan viâ Gallarate.— *Nord-Milano,* a few metres farther N., for Laveno and Milan viâ Saronno.

Post Office opposite Nord-Milano station.—**E.P.T.,** P.za Monte Grappa.

Buses from the State station to the *Sacro Monte;* from between the stations to *Gavirate,* etc., on the Lake of Varese; to *Luino* and *Angera,* on Lago Maggiore; to *Porto Ceresio* and *Ponte Tresa,* on the Lake of Lugano; etc.

Golf Course (18 holes) at Luvinate, 5 km. along the Laveno road.—*Indoor Swimming Pool,* S.W. of Public Gardens.—*Ice Skating* rink (open all year), swimming-pools and tennis courts, near the Bettole Hippodrome.

The principal street extends from Piazza Venti Settembre, near the stations, to Piazza Monte Grappa, rebuilt in modern style. A little to the N. an archway (r.) leads to the *Basilica of San Vittore,* built in 1580-1615 from the designs of Pell. Tibaldi, with a façade of 1795. It contains large works by Nuvolone and Luca Giordano, and highly elaborate woodcarving. The *Baptistery* behind dates from the 12C (for adm. apply to the sacristan); the detached 17C campanile (75 m) commands a fine view. From P.za Monte Grappa Via W. Marcobi leads to Via Luigi Sacco, in which is the *Palazzo Estense* (now the Municipio) built by

Francis III of Modena in 1766-72. The *Public Gardens,* formerly the duke's private grounds, command a good distant view of the Alps. Here Villa Mirabello houses the *Musei Civici* (9.30-12, 15-18; closed Mon) with interesting prehistoric finds from Lombardy, a Pinacoteca (Lombard 17-18C school), etc.

The favourite excursion from Varese is the ascent of the Sacro Monte and the Campo dei Fiori, easily combined in a single expedition. Buses ascend at frequent intervals from the State station viâ (4 km.) *Sant'Ambrogio Olona,* with an interesting church and (5 km.) *Prima Cappella* at the foot of the pilgrims' ascent to the Sacro Monte. Higher up the road divides. On the right the road winds up high above the valley to (8 km.) the *Sacro Monte* (880 m), a small village huddled on the hill-top round the Rococo pilgrimage church of *Santa Maria del Monte,* rebuilt in 16-17C. Flanking the broad cobbled path leading down to Prima Cappella are a statue of Moses and 13 shrines by Gius. Bernascone, with terracotta groups by Dionigi Bussola representing the Mysteries of the Rosary. There is a small Museum attached to the sanctuary.—The longer left branch above Prima Cappella ascends to (9½ km.) the *Monte delle Tre Croci* (1033 m) which commands a wonderful view. About 1 hr W. is the *Campo dei Fiori* (1226 m), with an even wider panorama.

Another interesting excursion may be made to Castiglione Olona and Castelseprio (13 km. S.; p. 123).

FROM VARESE TO PONTE TRESA (Lugano), 21 km., bus hourly. The road ascends the Valganna, the narrow valley of the Olona, passing the little *Laghetto di Ganna,* and beyond (11 km.) *Ganna,* the *Lago di Ghirla* (¾ m. long), both of which are favourite skating-grounds of the Milanese. To the right rises *Monte Piàmbello* (1129 m), a fine view-point for the Lake of Lugano.—At (14 km.) *Ghirla* the Lugano road keeps to the right, descending sharply to (21 km.) **Ponte Tresa,** which consists of an Italian village and a Swiss village separated by the Tresa, which here marks the frontier, entering a little land-locked bay of the lake. The bus goes on to *Lavena,* 1½ km. E., at the narrow entrance to the lake itself.—On the Swiss side of the Tresa the road continues to (32 km.) *Lugano.*

FROM VARESE TO LUINO, 24 km., bus hourly. This route follows the Lugano road (see above) to (14 km.) *Ghirla,* then turns left to follow the Margorabbia in its descent of the *Valtravaglia.* Below (19 km.) *Bosco Valtravaglia* the Val Cuvia road from Cittiglio (p. 123) comes in from the left. It reaches the lake at *Germignaga* just S.W. of (24 km.) *Luino.*

From Varese to *Laveno,* and to *Milan* viâ Saronno, see p. 123.

From Varese this route follows the Ponte Tresa road (see above) and immediately turns right beneath the railway to reach (60 km.) *Induno Olona,* at the foot of *Monte Monarco* (857 m).—Near (62 km.) *Arcisate,* in 1848, a handful of Garibaldini withstood for four hours an Austrian force of 5000. A road goes off to (r. 6 km. E.) *Viggiú,* a small holiday resort.—At (64 km.) *Bisúschio,* the 16C Villa Cicogna Mozzoni, frescoed by the school of the Campi brothers, is open to the public (15 April-Oct, 14-18; fest. 9-12, 14-18). A fine park surrounds the villa.— 69 km. **Porto Ceresio** stands on a wide bend in the lake at the foot of *Monte Pravello.* The railway terminates by the steamer quay.

The **Lake of Lugano** (270 m; *Lago di Lugano* or *Lago Ceresio*) is a very irregularly shaped sheet of water comprising three main reaches and the deep narrow bay of Capolago. Its total length from Porlezza to Agno is about 22 m.; its width is never more than 2 m. Of its area (20 sq. m.) rather more than half is politically Swiss; only the N.E. arm, the S.W. shore between Ponte Tresa and Porto Ceresio, and the enclave of Campione, nearly opposite Lugano, belong to Italy. The greatest depth (288 m) occurs off Albogasio. None of the streams which feed the lake are of much importance and the surface-level is therefore more constant than that of its larger neighbours. The waters of the lake drain into Lago Maggiore by the river Tresa, which flows out at Ponte Tresa. Except for the noontide *breva,* the lake is not exposed to periodic winds, but the tempestuous *caronasca* (named from Carona) occasionally sweeps the central reach from the W. The scenery of the shores, except for the bay of Lugano, is far wilder and more desolate than on the greater lakes; and grim mountains hedge in the N.E. arm between Gandria and Porlezza.

STEAMER SERVICES. Steamers of the Società Navigazione Lago di Lugano ply in summer 4-5 times daily between Porto Ceresio and Lugano; once daily between Italian Ponte Tresa and Lugano direct, and once viâ Porto Ceresio and Campine. Between Lugano and Porlezza there are three services on holidays; on weekdays one of these terminates at Osteno, two only continuing to Porlezza. In addition there are local services between Lugano and Campine, and Lugano and Capolago.—Tickets are taken on board and fares must be paid in Swiss currency. Luggage is checked on board the steamers. There are restaurants on board the afternoon steamers. Passports should be carried.

FROM PORTO CERESIO TO LUGANO, 9½ m., steamer in 70 min.—The boat leaves the quay with the less attractive W. arm of the lake on its left hand and Porto Ceresio itself on the right, and heads N.E. into Swiss waters.—2 m. **Morcote** is perhaps the most picturesque village on the lake, standing at the foot of *Monte Arbóstora* (839 m). Characteristic is the tall campanile of the pilgrimage-church of *Madonna del Sasso* (14C) which is adorned with 16C frescoes.—The steamer crosses to the opposite shore to touch at (3¼ m.) *Brusino Arsizio* below the chapel-crowned *Monte San Giorgio,* which divides the two S. arms of the lake. As the Capolago reach opens out to the right, Monte Generoso appears above the village of Maroggia.—5 m. *Melide,* frequented for its bathing beach, was the birthplace of Dom. Fontana (1543-1607), architect of the royal palace at Naples.—6 m. *Bissone,* at the E. end of the causeway that carries road and railway across the lake, was the birthplace of the sculptor Stefano Maderna (1576-1636). A monument on the shore commemorates him and many fellow-artists born here. The steamer passes under the causeway. On the right is seen the Baroque façade of the chapel of Madonna dei Ghirli.

7 m. **Campione d'Italia,** the centre (1950 inhab.) of a small Italian enclave, uses Swiss money and postal services. It has long been noted for its sculptors and architects; the chapel of St Peter (1327) is a good example of their work. In the parish church are some 15C reliefs and here is kept the key to the cemetery chapel of *Santa Maria dei Ghirli* with frescoes outside (Last Judgement; 1400) and within (14C). The village is visited for its Casino, with gaming-room and dancing (motor-launches from Lugano). A funicular railway mounts to Sighignola (1302 m).— The steamer steers close beneath the Punta San Martino at the foot of Monte San Salvatore, entering the bay on which Lugano stands.— 8¼ m. *Lugano-Paradiso* (see below). The view is delightful: Monte Brè, with its many villas, stands up boldly in the foreground, while more distant, at the head of the lake, are Monte Brenzone and the pointed Pizzoni; to their right, farther off, appear the Cima la Grona and the distant Legnone.

9½ m. **LUGANO** (276 m), the largest town (35,600 inhab.) of Canton Ticino, is charmingly situated at the mouth of the Cassarate torrent, between the commanding heights of Monte Brè (E.) and Monte San Salvatore (S.). The character of the old town, with its narrow streets and closely-packed dwellings, is thoroughly Italian, but all round it, on the shore and on the hills behind, has sprung up a new settlement of hotels and villas, giving the place a cosmopolitan air; the new buildings extend to the S. suburb of *Paradiso*.

Lugano was taken from Milan by the Swiss in 1512 and was ruled as a subject district until the dissolution of the old Swiss Confederation in 1798. It vigorously repulsed an attempt to bring it under Italian domination, choosing rather to remain 'free and Swiss'; and in 1803 became part of the new canton of Ticino. From 1848 to 1866 Lugano was Mazzini's headquarters during the struggle of the Italians to throw off the Austrian yoke in Lombardy.

The landing-stage faces the *Municipio* (1844-45), beyond which is the central PIAZZA DELLA RIFORMA. To the left narrow streets lead up to the *Cathedral,* which has a façade in the Lombard-Venetian style and three good portals, and to the short funicular that mounts to the *Railway Station.*

The RIVA, with its series of quays, extends along the entire lake-front, commanding beautiful views. Along it to the S. is the plain Franciscan church of **Santa Maria degli Angioli,** founded in 1499, which contains some remarkable *Frescoes by *Bernardino Luini* (d. 1532), the most striking being the huge Crucifixion (1529-30), occupying the great arch between the nave and the choir.

The funicular railway and the flight of steps, beside the church, ascend to Via Clemente Maraini, in which is the *English Church.*

In the other direction the Riva Giocondo Albertolli leads N.E., passing the Kursaal, to the pretty PARCO CIVICO, formerly the grounds of the Villa Ciani, in which are Vincenzo Vela's *Statue of 'La Desolazione', the figure of a mourning woman, and Antokolsky's 'Dying Socrates'. The mansion here is now a *Historical Museum.* Farther on, beyond the bathing-beach, more easily reached from the steamboat quay of *Lugano-Castagnola* (see below), stands the **Villa Favorita,** set in a delightful garden overlooking the lake. It houses a fine *Collection of pictures made by the Baron Heinrich Thyssen-Bornemisza (d. 1947). The rich collection of Italian masters includes works by Paolo Uccello, Giov. Bellini, Carlo Crivelli, Bramante (*Ecce Homo), Dom. Ghirlandaio, Vitt. Carpaccio, Filippino Lippi, Boltraffio, Titian, Veronese, and Caravaggio. The Flemish, Dutch, and German schools are well represented by Jan van Eyck (*Diptych), Gerard David, Frans Hals, Jan Steen, Vermeer, Hieronymus Bosch, Dürer, Cranach the Elder, and Holbein (Henry VIII). There are several characteristic El Grecos, and works by Ribera, Velazquez, Goya, Claude, Watteau, and Boucher. English paintings include examples by Gainsborough, Reynolds, and Romney.

FROM LUGANO TO PORLEZZA, 11 m. Steamer daily in 1½ hr.

The road (27 km.) connecting Lugano and Menaggio, viâ the N. shore of the lake and (15 km.) Porlezza, keeps high up above Gandria on the slopes of Monte Brè, and descends to the lake at *Oria,* the frontier station. A regular bus service runs between Oria, Menaggio, Tremezzo, and Como.

From the Lugano-Paradiso and Lugano-Centrale piers the steamer steers to (2½ m.) *Lugano-Castagnola.* The N. shore of the lake, studded with hotels and villas on the sunny slops of Monte Brè, is in strong contrast with the uninhabited S. bank.—5 m. *Gandria,* with picturesque houses along the lakeside, is the last Swiss village.

Re-entering Italian waters the boat reaches (5¾m.) *Santa Margherita* (custom-house) on the opposite bank, connected by a funicular railway with Belvedere di Lanzo (p. 139). It crosses once more to the N. bank and touches at (6¼m.) *Oria,* once the home of Antonio Fogazzaro (1842-1911), the author, passes *Albogasio,* and reaches (8 m.) the picturesque village of *San Mamette,* with a 12C campanile. Above stands *Castello,* finely placed at the mouth of the unfrequented Val Solda.—As it crosses to (9½m.) *Osteno* there is a fine view of the head of the lake, dominated on the N. by the *Monte dei Pizzoni* (1303 m), while ahead are the jagged *Monte Pidaggia* (1505 m) and the mountains of Lake Como. Close by are the Órrido, a narrow ravine accessible only by boat, and some stalactite caverns.—10¼ m. *Cima* lies close under the rocks of Pizzoni.—11 m. **Porlezza,** at the head of the lake, is the starting-point of a bus service to Mebagguio.

The VAL CAVARGNA, down which flows the Cuccio, descending from the N., is little visited, but affords access to many passes leading into the Cassarate valley behind Lugano, while from its upper end the *Pizzo di Gino* or *Menone* (2245 m) may be ascended.

The buses from Menaggio cross the Cuccio and passing the lovely *Lago del Piano* (279 m), ascend to (8 km.) *Grandola* (377 m), the road summit.—14 km. *Menaggio,* see p. 142.

13   COMO AND ITS LAKE

The **LAKE OF COMO** (199 m) is Virgil's *Lacus Larius,* from which is derived the alternative name of *Lago Lario.* The lake is formed of three long, narrow arms which meet at Bellagio, one stretching S.W. to Como, another S.E. to Lecco, the third N. to Cólico. Its total length is 31 m. from Como to Gera, its greatest breadth 2¾m. just N. of Bellagio, its greatest depth 410 m off Argegno, and its area 56 sq. m. The chief feeder is the *Adda,* which flows in at Cólico and out at Lecco. The lake is subject to frequent floods (last in 1976 when Como was inundated), and is swept regularly by two winds, the *tivano* (N. to S.), in the morning, and the *breva* (S. to N.) in the afternoon. It was for long a holiday retreat of the English: Wordsworth lived here in 1790, Shelley and Byron visited the lake, and D. H. Lawrence made it his home from 1925-27. It is now favoured particularly by the Milanese. The characteristic *lucie* fishing boats can still be seen, particularly around Lecco.

STEAMER AND HYDROFOIL SERVICES. A frequent service of steamers is maintained between Varenna, Menaggio, Bellagio, Tremezzo, and Como; and is extended to Colico once daily (twice on holidays). The service from Bellagio to Lecco runs once daily (2-3 times on holidays). In the central part of the lake a service runs between Bellano (or Varenna) and Lenno. A car ferry runs frequently between Bellagio and Varenna (in 15 min.), Bellagio and Cadenabbia (in 10 min.), and Cadenabbia and Varenna (in 30 min.). Fewer services in winter.

Approaches by Rail. FROM MILAN TO COMO BY THE MAIN ST-GOTTHARD LINE, 46 km. in 35-55 min. Trains depart from Centrale and (slower trains) from Porta Garibaldi stations.—To (10½ km.) *Monza,* see p. 166.—21 km. *Seregno* is a furniture-making town on the direct road from Milan to Erba.—34 km. *Cantù-Cermenate* is 4 km. W. of Cantù (p. 138). Beyond Como the Express trains go on to the frontier at (51 km.) *Chiasso,* for Lugano and the north.

FROM MILAN TO COMO VIĀ SARONNO, 46 km. Nord-Milano railway in ¾-1¼ hr. From Milan to (22 km.) *Saronno,* see p. 123.—From there with many intermediate stations to *Como-Lago.*

FROM MILAN TO LECCO AND CÓLICO, 90 km., see Rte 15.

FROM MILAN TO CANZO-ASSO, 52 km., Nord-Milano railway in 60-80 min. Part of the industrial district near (22 km.) *Séveso* was declared contaminated and evacuated in 1976 after a chemical leakage from a factory. In the wood of *Barlassina*, to the right, St Peter Martyr was murdered in 1252. In the fertile *Brianza*, a region with many imposing country houses is (35 km.) *Inverigo*, with a fine villa built by Luigi Cagnola (1813-33), now a children's home.—44 km. **Erba** on the Como-Lecco road, is a scattered community with an open-air theatre. In the Villa San Giuseppe at Crevenna an Archæological Museum is open on Wed and Sat 10-12, and Sun & fest. 16-18. The *Buco del Piombo,* a limestone cavern, lies 1 hr uphill to the N.W. It is open and illuminated from Easter-Oct on Sat 15-18, Sun & fest. 10-12, 14-18; in July and Aug daily 15-18.—52 km. *Canzo-Asso,* the terminus of the railway, is connected by bus with Bellagio (see p. 140).

Approaches by Road. FROM MILAN there is an AUTOSTRADA (A9) direct to (49 km.) *Como,* bearing right from the Lago Maggiore autostrada at 19 km.; the old main road (N35), 43½ km., runs viâ Séveso, leaving Milan by the Via Carlo Farini and the suburb of Affori.

COMO (213 m), beautifully situated at the S.W. extremity of the Lake of Como, is a manufacturing town (98,400 inhab.), the capital of the province which bears its name, and the seat of a bishop. Conspicuous to the N. is Monte Bisbino, while to the S. rises the tower of Baradello. The industry is the weaving of silk, long a domestic occupation, but nowadays mainly concentrated in large factories. The centre, nevertheless, preserves to a marked degree its Roman street plan.

Railway Stations. *San Giovanni* for State Railway trains to Milan, Lecco, and to Lugano and the rest of Switzerland. *Como-Lago* (on the lakeside; the most convenient station for visitors) and *Como-Borghi* for Nord-Milano trains to Milan viâ Saronno.

Hotels, near the water front.

Parking. The centre of the town is closed to traffic. Parking in P.za Volta, around the walls, and on the lakeside.

Post Office, Via Gallio. **E.P.T.,** 17 P.za Cavour; *Information Office,* Stazione Centrale (San Giovanni).

Buses and trolley-buses from P.za Matteotti for towns on the lake; and for *Bergamo.*—Country buses from P.za Cavour to *Cernobbio; Ponte Chiasso* (viâ Maslianico); *Cantù; Erba; Lanzo d'Intelvia* viâ Argegno; *Bellagio* viâ Nesso; *Côlico* viâ Menaggio; *Porlezza; Lecco;* etc.

Steamers on the lake, see below. *Rowing-Boats* and *Motor-Boats* for hire at P.za Cavour.

Swimming in summer at Villa Geno, on the E. shore, beyond the funicular station; and at Villa Olmo, on the W. shore.—*Golf Course* (18 holes) at Montofrano, 4 km. S.E. (Villa d'Este).—*Tennis* at Villa Olmo, and Cassate.

History. Originally a town of the Insubrian Gauls, Como was captured and colonized by the Romans in the 2C B.C. The town appears as a republic in the 11C, but in 1127 it was destroyed by the Milanese. Frederick Barbarossa, however, rebuilt it in 1155, and it secured its future independence by the Peace of Constance (1183). In the struggles between the Torriani and the Visconti Como fell to the latter in 1335, and became a fief of Milan. From then on it followed the vicissitudes of the Lombard capital. In March 1848 a popular rising compelled the surrender of the Austrian garrison, and the city was finally liberated by Garibaldi on 27 May 1859. Among the most famous natives ('Comaschi') are the Elder and the Younger Pliny (A.D. 23-79 and A.D. 62-120), Paulus Jovius (1483-1552), the historian, and Alessandro Volta (1745-1827), the physicist. Landor lived in Como in 1815-18, where he was unjustly suspected of spying on Queen Caroline (p. 139).

The centre of the life of Como is PIAZZA CAVOUR, a pleasant square with cafés and hotels, open to the lake and adjoining the steamer quay. In the delightful Giardini Pubblici, overlooking the lake, are the *Tempio Voltiano* (open 10-12, 15-18), erected in 1927, a classic rotonda containing the scientific instruments of Volta, charmingly displayed in old-fashioned show cases. The *War Memorial* was designed by Ant. Sant'Elia, himself killed in 1916.

A pleasant path continues round the shore to *Villa Olmo* (1780), built for the Odescalchi by Sim. Cantoni and set in a formal park; it is used as a congress hall, and for exhibitions and concerts.—In the other direction a drive leads along the shore to *Villa Geno,* with another park and bathing beach.

The short Via Plinio leads away from the lake to P.za del Duomo, in which are the cathedral (see below), the *Broletto* (1215; the old town hall), built in alternate courses of black and white marble, with a few red patches, and the *Torre del Commune* of the same period, used as a campanile since the addition of the top story in 1435 (partly rebuilt in 1927).

The *Cathedral (*Santa Maria Maggiore*), built entirely of marble, dates mainly from the late 14C, when it replaced an 11C basilica. The union of the Renaissance with Gothic architecture has here produced a remarkably homogeneous style.

The rebuilding, financed mainly by public subscription, was entrusted first to *Lor. degli Spazzi,* who, like his many successors, worked under the patronage of the Milanese court. The West Front (1460-90), designed by *Fiorino da Bontà,* and executed by *Luchino Scarabota* of Milan, is in a Gothic style, with a fine rose window, though the three doorways are unexpectedly round-arched. It is decorated with reliefs and statues (c. 1500) by *Tom.* and *Iac. Rodari* of Maroggia, and others. The seated figures (being restored) of the two Plinys on either side of the main doorway are probably by *Amuzio da Lurago.* The two lateral doorways, also decorated by the *Rodari,* are wonderful examples of detailed carving. The work of rebuilding continued through the 16C (choir) and 17C (transepts), and ended with completion of the dome in 1770 by *Fil. Juvarra.*

Interior. The cathedral is 87 m long, 58 m wide across the transepts, and 75 m high under the dome.—The aisled NAVE of five bays is covered with a groined vault and hung with 16C tapestries. On the W. wall is a Madonna from the old cathedral. Two lions at the W. end, now supporting stoups, are also survivals from the ancient basilica. A graceful little rotunda (16C) serves as baptistery. In the SOUTH AISLE are figures of saints and six reliefs of the Passion by *Tom. Rodari* (1492). Beyond the S. door (also well carved) are a bishop's tomb of 1347 and the Altar of Sant'Abbondio, finely decorated with gilded woodcarving, and flanked by a *Flight into Egypt by *Gaud. Ferrari,* and an *Adoration of the Magi by *Luini.* Farther on is a *Virgin and Child with four saints, with a celebrated angel-musician in front, also by *Luini.* Between the nave and aisle hangs a painted and embroidered standard of the Confraternity of S. Abbondio (1608-10). NORTH AISLE. 4th Altar, Deposition, finely carved by *Tom. Rodari* (1498); hanging in the nave, standard of Giov. Malacrida (1499). 3rd Altar. *Gaud. Ferrari,* *Marriage of the Virgin; *Luini,* Nativity. Just before the N. door is the sarcophagus of Giovanni degli Avogadri (d. 1293). At the second altar, between busts of Innocent XI and Bp. Rovelli, is a carving of the Madonna between St Louis and St Stephen, by *Tom. Rodari.*

In P.za Grimoldi, to the N., are the *Bishop's Palace* and *San Giacomo.* The church has Romanesque elements (columns, brickwork in aisles, apse and dome).—South-east of the cathedral is the *Teatro Sociale* built in 1811 by Gius. Cusi with a neo-classical façade.

Via Vittorio Emanuele leads S. from the cathedral to the 17C *Municipio;* opposite is the five-sided apse of the church of *San Fedele* (12C), which at one time served as cathedral. The angular N.E. doorway, with remarkable bas-reliefs, shows Byzantine influences. The interior, and the pretty Piazza to the W. should not be missed. Farther along the

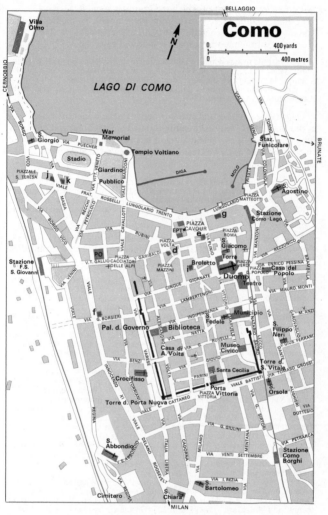

street on the left two good palazzi serve as *Museo Civico* (adm. 10-12, 14.30-17 or 17.30; Sun 9-12.30; closed Mon). The collection includes: Neolithic finds; a reconstructed ceremonial carriage of the Iron Age; recent archæological finds from Mandana; Assyrian and Egyptian antiquities; Roman urns and sarcophagi; Medieval fragments from churches (and casts of the statues of the two Plinys from the Cathedral); and material relating to the Risorgimento and the two World Wars. There is a pretty garden.

The second turning on the left off Via Giovio leads to the church of

Santa Cecilia, the front of which incorporates some Roman columns. Next door was the Liceo where Volta once taught. A fragment of the Roman wall may be seen in the courtyard of the school here. The *Porta Vittoria* is surmounted by a many-windowed tower of 1192.

Two other old towers remain on this section of the wall; that on the E. (r.) is the *Torre di San Vitale,* that on the S.W. the *Torre di Porta Nuova.* The Porta Vittoria is named in memory of the surrender of the Austrian garrison (1848), in the barracks immediately opposite. The *Garibaldi Monument,* by Vinc. Vela, in the P.za Vittoria, was erected in 1889.

Outside the gate, beyond an unattractive traffic-ridden area (see Plan) is the Basilica of *Sant'Abbondio,** isolated amidst industrial buildings near the railway. An 11C building, it has two graceful campanili and a finely decorated apse, well restored. It is dedicated to St Abondius, third bishop of Como.

The oldest church on this site was probably founded by St Felix in the 4C and received its present name on the death of Abondius in 469. The existing building consists of five aisles, despite its comparatively small size. In the apse are frescoes of the mid-14C by Lombard artists. The organ is also decorated with frescoes of this period by local artists.

Viale Varese (with the *Crocefisso,* a 16C sanctuary), or Via Alessandro Volta, in which is the house where the scientist lived and died (tablet) lead back towards the lake.

From Viale Geno a funicular railway ascends frequently to (7 min.) **Brunate** (713 m), 5 km. from Como by road. The village commands a fine view of Como and its lake. About ½ hr above Brunate is *San Maurizio* (871 m).
About 3 km. S. of Como (trolley-bus every 10 min.) is *Camerlata,* a suburb dominated by the 11-12C church of *San Carpoforo,* which may occupy the site of a 4C foundation of St Felix. In the sacristy is preserved St Felix's crozier, and a chapel in the crypt may locate his burial place. The *Monte Baradello* (432 m), above the church, is crowned by the conspicuous tower of **Castello Baradello,** the solitary remnant of a stronghold reconstructed by Barbarossa c. 1158 and destroyed by Charles V's Spaniards in 1527. In 1277 Napo Torriani and other members of his family were exposed here in cages after their defeat by the Visconti.
A trolley-bus goes on hourly to (10½ km.) **Cantù,** a pleasant town (35,300 inhab.) with lace and furniture industries. The *Parish Church* has a remarkably slender Romanesque campanile, and *San Teodoro* has a fine apse in the same style. At *Galliano,* 1 km. E., are the 10-11C basilica and baptistery of San Vincenzo. The church has a *Fresco cycle of 1007. Cantù has a station on the Lecco railway, but is 4 km. from Cantù-Cermenate station on the main line to Milan.
FROM COMO TO CERNOBBIO AND MASLIÁNICO, 8 km., trolley-bus every 20 min.—The line passes the Villa Olmo and at (4 km.) *Cernobbio* (see below) the route turns inland to ascend the valley of the Breggia to *Masliánico.* A short walk S. along the frontier leads to *Ponte Chiasso,* whence trolley-buses return to Como every 10 minutes.
FROM COMO TO LECCO, 30 km. by road (bus). The State Railway, 42 km., takes a more devious southerly route through Cantù, Oggiono, and Civate.—Via Dottesio leaves Como and traverses the Brianza, passing just N. of Montórfano (comp. p. 134.—13 km. *Erba,* see p. 135. On the right (15 km.) is the *Lago di Pusiano* with its poplar-grown islet. *Bosisio,* on its E. shore, was the birthplace of Giuseppe Parini (1729-99), the poet.—Farther on (20 km.) is the smaller *Lago d'Annone.* A road on the right leads to Annone (2½ km.) where the church has a magnificent carved-wood altarpiece of the 16C, and to *Oggiono* (5 km.), which has a polyptych by Marco d'Oggiono, Leonardo's pupil, in its church.—25 km. *Civate.* In the hills to the N. is (1 hr; steep climb) **San Pietro al Monte,** where the *Santuario* (keys at Civate church) consists of the partly ruined church of *San Pietro* and the triapsidal oratory of *San Benedetto,* both of the 10C. The former, with lateral apses, has 11-12C mural paintings and a remarkable baldacchino above the main altar.—30 km. *Lecco,* see p. 144.

FROM COMO TO CÓLICO, (55 m.) by the lake, steamer once or twice daily on holidays in 3-4 hrs; to *Bellagio*, (28½ m.), 6 times daily in 1½-2 hrs; to *Menaggio*, (31¼ m.), 6 times daily in 2-2½ hrs (frequent service between Como and Carate, and between Tremezzo, Bellagio, and Varenna). The Hydrofoil provides a much quicker service (with fewer stops) but is not recommended to the visitor who has time to enjoy the fine scenery. It traverses the Lake from Como to Cólico c. 4 times daily in 1¼ *hrs; to* Bellagio frequent service in 35 min; to Menaggio frequent service in 40 min.

The steamer keeps at first to the E. bank, rounding the Punta di Geno.—2 m. (W.) **Cernóbbio**, part holiday-resort, part lakeside village (8120 inhab.), lies at the foot of *Monte Bisbino* (1325 m), ascended hence in 3 hrs. The Hotel Villa d'Este (well seen from the lake as the boat leaves the dock) occupies a villa built in 1568 by the beneficent Card. Tolomeo Gallio (1527-1607), a native of Cernóbbio. In 1816-17 it was the home of the maligned Queen Caroline of England.—On the opposite bank is the scattered village of *Blevio,* with a villa that belonged to the dancer Taglioni (1804-84). At *Perlasca,* the northernmost hamlet of this village, was born Benedetto Odescalchi (1611-89), afterwards Innocent XI.—4 m. (W.) **Moltrasio,** with a 'lido', has a Romanesque church. Here at the Villa Salterio in 1831 Bellini composed the opera 'Norma'.—4¾ m. (E.) *Torno* is a medieval village with two old churches. In the bay to the E. is the *Villa Pliniana* (1570), named after an intermittent spring described in the letters of the younger Pliny (open 20 Aug-30 Oct, 15-18). Here in 1813 Rossini composed 'Tancredi'.—Almost continuous with Moltrasio are the villages of (5½ m.) *Urio,* with a tall Lombard campanile, and (5¾ m.) *Carate,* with attractive villas and gardens.

On the opposite bank, above *Riva,* with the pier of (7¼ m.) *Faggeto Lario,* stand the villages of *Molina, Lemma,* and *Palanzo,* high up on the slopes of *Monte Palanzolo* (1436 m), and farther on are (8 m.) *Pognana* and *Quarzano.* On the W. bank, at the narrowest portion of the lake, is (9½ m.) *Torriggia-Laglio.* Opposite lies the three-cornered village of (10 m.) *Careno,* with another tall campanile, and farther on is (11¼ m.) *Nesso,* at the mouth of the Orrido, a deep ravine with a waterfall.—12½ m. (W.) *Brienno* lies among chestnut groves.—15 m. (24 km.; W.) **Argegno,** where the high mountain ranges N.E. of the lake come into view. It lies at the foot of the fertile Val d'Intelvi.

A bus runs from Argeno via (6 km.) *Castiglione d'Intelvi,* (9 km.) *San Fedele* and (11 km.) *Pellio,* to (15 km.) **Lanzo d'Intelvi** (907 m), a summer resort, admirable for excursions on foot. The bus goes on to (17 km.) *Belvedere di Lanzo* (919 m), overlooking the Lake of Lugano, to which a funicular descends, reaching the shore at Santa Margherita (p. 134).

Beyond *Colonno* is (18 m.; W.) *Sala Comacina,* with a good Gothic campanile partly concealed by *Isola Comacina,* a favourite resort of political refugees during the disturbed medieval history of Lombardy. The island was captured and laid waste by the men of Como in 1169, but the ruins of some of its nine churches are still worthy of a visit. In 1917 it passed by inheritance to Albert, King of the Belgians, but was later handed over to the Academy of Milan as a rest-home for artists.—20½ m. (E.) *Lézzeno* is near the Grotta dei Búlberi, artificially darkened to resemble the Blue Grotto at Capri (accessible by boat).—22½ m. *Ossúccio,* where a Romanesque tower supports an elaborate Gothic belfry, lies between Comacina and the *Punta di Balbianello,* a headland on which stands the *Villa Arconati* (1790), once the home of Silvio Pellico (1788-1854), author of 'Le Mie Prigioni'. The park is open on Tues, 9-12, 14.30-17.30.

24 m. (W.) **Lenno** lies at the mouth of the Acquafredda, at the S. end of the Tremezzina. The parish church has an 11-12C crypt and an 11C octagonal baptistery adjoining. Here on the shore was the site of Pliny's villa 'Comedia', so-called from its lowly position as compared with the 'Tragedia' at Bellagio.—Beyond Lenno the steamer coasts the smiling *Tremezzina,* the fertile green shore dotted with villas and gardens, which extends along the foot of Monte di Tremezzo as far as La Maiolica, N. of Cadenabbia.—24¾ m. *Azzano.*

25½ m. **Tremezzo** and (25¾ m.) **Cadenabbia,** now almost continuous, are two immensely popular holiday resorts, consisting almost entirely of hotels and villas. Cadenabbia is officially only a hamlet in the parish of *Griante.*

English Church (*The Ascension*) at Cadenabbia; services in the season.
Tennis Courts and **Lido** at Cadenabbia.
Car Ferry, in summer, as required, from Cadenabbia to *Bellagio* (10 min.) and to *Varenna* (15 min.).

On the shady road between Tremezzo and Cadenabbia is the *Villa Carlotta (open April-Oct 8.30-18; March, 9-12, 14-16.30), built in 1747 by the Marchese Giorgi Clerici and surrounded by a magnificent park noted for azaleas and rhododendrons in May.

The collection of sculpture within includes Thorvaldsen's frieze of the Triumphal Entry of Alexander into Babylon, cast in plaster for Napoleon in 1811-12 and intended for the throne-room at the Quirinal. After the emperor's downfall the work was continued at the expense of Count Sommariva, who is represented, along with the artist, at the end of the frieze. The opening scenes of 'La Chartreuse de Parme' (1839) recall Stendhal's stay here as Sommariva's guest in 1818. Among works by Canova are Cupid and Psyche (a copy), the Repentant Magdalen, Palamedes, and other sculptures.—Near the water's edge is a little memorial chapel with a Pietà by Bened. Cacciatori.
At the *Villa Margherita,* on the shore just N. of Cadenabbia, staying with his publisher Ricordi, Verdi composed 'La Traviata' in 1853.
Cadenabbia lies in a sheltered position beneath the *Sasso di San Martino* (851 m; ascended in 3 hrs; walkers should be careful not to stray from the paths).—A fine climb ascends the successive summits of (5 hrs) *Monte Crocione* (1636 m), *Monte di Tremezzo* (5¾ hrs; 1764 m), and (6 hrs) *Monte Calbiga* (1697 m; *View, including the Valais Alps, Milan, and seven lakes).

Leaving Cadenabbia the steamer crosses the 'Centro Lago', the most beautiful part of the lake, to (27 m.; E.) *San Giovanni di Bellagio,* where the church contains an altarpiece by G. Ferrari. To the N. is *Loppia,* with a half-ruined church romantically placed beside a great grove of cypresses.

28½ m. (E.) **BELLAGIO** (3330 inhab.), ideally situated on a headland at the division of the lake, is also a very popular, though quieter, resort; and at the same time retains much of the picturesque aspect of an old Lombard town. There are local industries of silk-weaving and olive-wood carving.

Post Office, 10 Piazza Manzoni.
Buses to *Como, Lecco* and *Asso.*
Car Ferry in summer, as required, to *Cadenabbia* or *Varenna* (10 min.).

Lago di Como

0 — 3 miles
0 — 5 kilometres

The church of *San Giacomo,* in Via Garibaldi, to the left of the pier, has a 12C apse and capitals. The symbols of the Evangelists, on the reconstructed pulpit, were discovered during a restoration in 1907. At the *Casa Lillia* in 1837 was born Cosima Liszt. Above the town is (20 min.; bus from pier 10 min.) the *Villa Serbelloni* standing in a fine park (open in summer exc. fest. 10-16), and reputed to occupy the site of the younger Pliny's villa 'Tragedia', so-called by its owner in contrast with the low-lying 'Comedia' at Lenno, being raised above the lake as if on a cothurnus, the high buskin worn by tragic actors. It is now an international study centre.—On the road to Loppia is the *Villa Melzi-d'Eril* (adm. 9-12, 14-18) standing in a fine park.

Farther on are the *Villa Balzaretti,* with a mausoleum of the Gonzagas, and the fine gardens of the *Villa Trotti,* while on the crest of the ridge is the *Villa Giulia,* a frequent retreat of Leopold I, king of the Belgians. At present, however, visitors are not admitted to any of these lovely gardens.

FROM BELLAGIO TO ASSO VIÁ CIVENNA, 19 km.; bus in 1¼ hr.—The road ascends S., passing the cemetery and (l.) the Villa Giulia. At (6 km.) *Guello* a road on the right ascends in 8 km. to *Parco Monte San Primo,* whence a path goes on in 1½ hr. to *Monte San Primo* (1686 m).—8½ km. *Civenna.*—From (10½ km.) the chapel of *Madonna del Ghisallo* (754 m), the highest point of the road, is a *View of the Lake of Lecco (l.) with the two Grigne beyond, and of Bellagio behind.—11 km. *Magreglio* is another starting-point for the ascent of (3½ hrs) Monte San Primo (see above). The road descends the steep Valassina to (19 km.) *Asso* which is almost continuous with *Canzo,* the chief place in the valley.—Another bus goes along the W. bank of the Lake of Lecco, viá Limonta, Vassena, and Onno, and ascends the Valbrona to *Asso* (see above).

From Bellagio to *Lecco* by steamer, see p. 143.

31¼ m. **Menággio** is a cheerful little town (3290 inhab.) on the W. shore, much frequented by tourists.

Golf Course (18 holes) at Grándola, 3½ km. along the Porlezza road.
Lido, on the N. shore.

Menaggio has two piers; the principal one is near the Grand Hotel; the other. to the N.. is seldom used.

A pleasant walk crosses the Sangra river and ascends to (½ hr N.W.) *Laveno* (317 m), near the church of which is the *Villa Vigoni* (adm. on application), with a garden pavilion containing sculptures by Thorvaldsen. The *Villa Calabi* was the home of Massimo d'Azeglio (1798-1865), patriot and writer. From here the climb continues to (1½ hr) *Plesio* (600 m) and (2 hrs) *Madonna di Breglia* (785 m), above which the *Belvedere di San Domenico* (820 m) affords a wide view.—From the graveyard of Breglia an easy path ascends to the chapel of *Sant'Amate* (1621 m) on the crest of the ridge to the N.W., from which a walk of ½ hr S. leads to the *Cima la Grona* (1163 m), while 1½ hr N. of the chapel is *Monte Bregagno* (2107 m) commanding a wonderful view of the lake. The descent may be made to *Rezzónico* (see below).

Delightful drives may be taken along the shore from Menaggio to *Acquaseria* viá *Nobiallo,* with its leaning tower, and the tunnels in the *Sasso Rancio,* the 'orange rock' coloured by a ferruginous spring, or along the Tremezzina to *Cadenabbia.*

From Menaggio to *Porlezza* and *Lugano,* see Rte 12.

Opposite Menággio is (33½ m.) **Varenna,** pleasantly situated at the mouth of the Êsino, which descends from Monte Grigna. An Ornithological Museum here is open 10-12, 14.30-18, and the gardens of the *Villa Monastero* (a centre for scientific conventions) are open from 9-12, 14-17. The neighbouring quarries yield black marble and green lumachella or shell-marble. Above Varenna to the S. is the old castle of *Vezio,* said to have been founded by Queen Theodolinda, which commands a splendid *View. Car-ferry to Bellagio and Cadenabbia.

From Varenna a bus runs 4 times weekly up the right bank of the Ésino viâ *Perledo* (409 m) to (12½ km.) *Ésino* (907 m), with the Museo della Grigna (apply at Comune for the key), whence a path leads viâ *Cainallo* (1245 m) and the *Alpe di Moncódeno* (1685 m) to (6 hrs) the *Monza Refuge* (1808 m) and thence by a fatiguing slope to (8 hrs) the *Luigi Brioschi Refuge*, on the summit of ***Monte Grigna Settentrionale** (2410 m), a dolomitic peak commanding a wonderful view.—The descent may be made to *Mandello* (p. 144).

36½ m. (E.) **Bellano**, a town (3580 inhab.) with silk and cotton mills, lies at the mouth of the Pioverna, which, in its lower course, runs through a deep gorge. The restored church of *Santi Nazaro e Celso* is a good example of the 14C Lombard style. Tommaso Grossi (1790-1853) the poet, born here, is commemorated by a monument on the shore.

From Bellano a bus runs twice daily to (20 km. in 1 hr) *Premana*, viâ (8½ km.) *Taceno*, which adjoins the small spa of *Tartavalle*.—From Taceno another service runs four times daily to (26 km.; 1½ hr) *Lecco*. The route traverses the VALSÁSSINA, the valley of the Pioverna, which affords pleasant excursions and has ski-ing facilities (chairlift from Margno to 1456 m). Its principal village, *Introbio* (18 km. from Bellano) has cheese-factories. **Bárzio**, see p. 144.

39 m. (W.) *Acquaseria* lies at the foot of the Cima la Grona, while to the S. rises the Sasso Rancio. Farther N. on the same side is (40¼ m;) *Rezzónico*, with a castle, the cradle of the powerful family which bore its name and numbered Clement XIII among its famous sons.—41½ m. (E.) *Dervio*, with a ruined castle and an old campanile, is the best point for starting the ascent viâ *Sueglio* (4 km.) of the prominent *Monte Legnone* (2610 m; 7½ hrs; guide).—43 m. (W.) *Cremia*. Beside the pier is the old church of *San Vito*, with a fine Madonna and Angels by Ambr. Bergognone.—44 m. *Pianello* has a 12C church, and marble quarries.— 44¾ m. (W.) *Musso* is overlooked by the almost impregnable *Rocca di Musso*, the stronghold in 1525-32 of the piratical Gian Giacomo Medici, surnamed 'Il Medeghino', who levied tribute from the traders of the lake and the neighbouring valleys.—On the same (W.) bank is (45½ m.) *Dongo*, which, with Gravedona and Sórico, formed the independent *Republic of the Three Parishes* (Tre Pievi), that endured until the Spanish occupation of Lombardy. Mussolini was captured by partisans at Dongo in the spring of 1945 and was executed at Giulino di Mezzegra above Azzano (p. 140). The 12C church of Santa Maria in the adjacent hamlet of *Martinico* preserves an interesting doorway.

48½ m. (W.) **Gravedona** is the principal village (2830 inhab.) of the upper lake. The great square *Palazzo Gallio* or *del Pero*, with its four corner towers, was built c. 1586 by Pellegrino Tibaldi for Card. Tolomeo Gallio. To the S. is the church of *San Vincenzo*, with a very ancient crypt. Near by is the little 12C church of **Santa Maria del Tiglio*, with one eastern and two transverse apses. The W. tower, square in its lower stories, becomes octagonal higher up.—50 m. (W.) *Domaso*, at the mouth of the Livo, is overlooked by the chapel of Madonna di Livo. At the extreme N. end of the lake where the Mera flows in, are the villages of *Gera* and *Sórico*.—52½ m. (E.) *Piona* is the mouth of the land-locked bay called the *Laghetto di Piona*. The key of the little 12C cloister here is kept by the priest of *Olgiasca*, 1 m. S.W.—55 m. (E.) **Cólico** stands in a plain near the mouth of the Adda and is important mainly as the meeting-place of the routes over the Splügen and Stelvio passes.

From Cólico to *Lecco*, and to *Chiavenna* and *Tirano*, see Rte 15.

FROM BELLAGIO TO LECCO BY STEAMER, 14¼ m. in 80 min. (once daily, twice on Sat, 3 times on Sun). Leaving Bellagio the steamer crosses to the E. bank; on the left is the waterfall of Fiumelatte. It enters the lesser (S.E.) branch of the Lake of Como, usually called the *Lago di Lecco*.— 2½ m. (E.) *Lierna* lies at the foot of *Monte Palagia* (1549 m). Opposite, on the unfrequented W. bank, is (4¼ m.) *Limonta*, to the S. of which is (6¼ m.) *Vassena*. On the same bank is (7½ m.) *Onno*, connected by road through the Valbrona with Asso (p. 142).—8¾ m. (E.) **Mandello del Lario,** on the projecting delta of the Meria.

Mandello is an excellent starting-point for the ascent of the *Grigna Settentrionale* (2410 m; 7½ hrs) and of the *Grigna Meridionale* (2184 m). The *Buco di Grigna* (1802 m) leads between the two Grigne into the Valsássina (p. 143). The *Rifugio Rosalba* (4¼ hrs; 1724 m) is a halfway stage up the Grigna Meridionale; the *Rif. Elisa* (3¼ hrs; 1515 m) and *Rif. Bietti* (4¼ hrs; 1719 m) offer alternative approaches to the N. peak.

10½ m. (E.) *Abbadia Lariana* lies at the foot of the Grigna Meridionale. The W. bank of the lake, opposite, is uninhabited; at the foot of the steep *Monte Moregallo* (1276 m) are a few limekilns. On the approach to Lecco, *Monte Coltignone* (1474 m) rises on the left. On the right is *Malgrate,* beyond the mouth of the Ritorto, which drains the Lago d'Annone.

14¼ m. **Lecco,** is a manufacturing town (54,790 inhab.) standing at the S.E. end of the Lake of Como, at the outflow of the Adda. The *Ponte Azzone Visconti,* which spans the Adda, was built in 1336-38, but has lost most of its original character owing to subsequent enlargement. A monument by Confalonieri commemorates Alessandro Manzoni (1785-1873), the novelist, the scene of whose famous novel 'I Promessi Sposi' is laid partly around Lecco and Monte Resegone. His 18C villa is in Via Promessi Sposi, E. of the railway, and contains a small museum.

To the S. of the town the Adda expands to form successively the *Lago di Garlate* and the smaller *Laghetto di Olginate*. On the W. is the detached *Monte Barro* (922 m), a fine view-point. The ascent of the saw-shaped *Monte Resegone* (1875 m), which dominates Lecco from the E. may be made by cableway from the end of the road to Malnago to 1329 m; or by foot (4 hrs) viá the refuge huts Monzesi and Azzoni (1875 m). *Ballabio*, 8 km. N. of Lecco on the Valsássina road (buses from Lecco to Piani Resinelli, Barzio, and Introbio), is a good base for climbs (including rock-climbs) on the *Resegone* (reached from the road E. to the Valle Brembana) and on the *Grigna Meridionale* (2184 m) approached from Ballabio Inferiore viá Ballabio Superiore (l.) and the little climbing and ski-ing resort of *Piani Resinelli* (1257 m). Higher up are the *S.E.M.* (1329 m) and *Carlo Porta* refuges, whence marked paths ascend to the summit in 3 hrs. Beyond Ballabio the road crosses (11 km.) the *Colle di Balisio* (722 m) to enter the Valsássina.—17½ km. *Introbio,* see p. 143.

At the pass the road on the right leads to the holiday resorts of (12 km.) *Mággio* (770 m) and (5 km.) **Bárzio** (768 m). These serve as bases for ascents in the dolomitic *Corno Grande* range (1865 m). From Barzio a chair-lift mounts to *Piani di Bobbio* (1676-1768 m), a ski-ing centre; and from *Cremeno* between Móggio and Barzio, a road leads up to *Móggio* (890 m), the start of a track to (2 hrs) the *Rif. Castelli* (1649 m), another favoured winter-sports centre.

From Lecco to *Civate* and *Como,* see p. 138; to *Milan* and to *Tirano,* see Rte 15.

14   MILAN

MILAN, in Italian *Milano,* the famous capital of Lombardy, is the second largest town in Italy (1,722,000 inhab.) and is the principal commercial and industrial centre of the country. It has the appearance and characteristics of a busy modern city with a N. skyline punctuated by skyscrapers (*grattacieli*). At the same time it is a place of great historical and artistic interest, with a world-famous cathedral, many ancient churches, and magnificent art collections.

Main Railway Stations. *Centrale* (Pl. 4), Piazzale Duca d'Aosta, the largest station in Italy, for all main F.S. services (N.E. of the centre). The building was designed by U. Stacchini and built in 1925-31.—*Nord* (Pl. 10) for services of the Nord-Milano railway (Como, Novara, and Laveno viâ Saronno, etc).—*Porta Genova* (Pl. 13) for Mortara and Alessandria (connections on to Genoa).—*Porta Vittoria* (beyond Pl. 12) or *Porta Garibaldi* (Pl. 3) for car-sleeper expresses to Boulogne, Ostend, Brindisi, etc.—*Lambrate* (beyond Pl. 4) for Domodossola (Simplon express), Treviglio, Pavia, Bergamo, etc.

Airports at *Malpensa,* 45 km. N.W. and at *Linate,* 7 km. E., both for international and national flights. Bus service to city air terminal, Viale Luigi Sturzo 37 (next to Porta Garibaldi Station; Tram 33 or Metropolitana 2 from Central Station).

Hotels, between the Central Station and P.za d. Repubblica, and S. of the Duomo, etc.

Post Office (Pl. 10), Via Cordusio.—**E.P.T.,** Via Marconi 1 (P.za Duomo), with information offices at Central Station and Linate airport.—*Touring Club Italiano,* Corso Italia 10.

Parking. Most of the centre has now been closed to traffic; other areas are included in a 'green zone' where parking is prohibited between 8-9.30 and 14.30-16. Visitors are advised to park on the outskirts and make use of public transport.

Public Transport. Hourly tariff: a 100 l. ticket (in 1977) gives freedom of the system for 1 hr. Day tickets (500 l.) for unlimited travel are also available.

TRAMWAYS. The services most likely to be useful to the visitor are: **1.** *Central Station*—P.za Cavour—*P.za Scala*—Largo Cairoli—*Nord Station*—Corso Sempione; **4.** *P.za Repubblica*—Via Manzoni—P.za Scala—Via Legnano—Via Farini (for *Cimitero Monumentale*); **15.** Via Orefici (*Duomo*)—Corso Magenta (S.M. d. Grazie, for the *Cenacolo*); **19.** *Corso Sempione*—Nord Station—Via Broletto—Via Orefici (for *Duomo*)—Via Torino—Corso Porta Ticinese (for *San Lorenzo*).—BUSES. **50, 54.** Largo Augusto (Duomo)—Corso Magenta—Via Carducci (for *S. Ambrogio*)—Via S. Vittore; **60.** *Central Station*—Largo Cairoli—P.za Duomo—*Castello Sforzesco;* **61.** Corso Matteotti—P.za Scala—*Via Brera*—Via Solferino (for *San Marco*); **65.** *Central Station*—Via S. Gregorio—Corso Buenos Aires—Corso Venezia—P.za Fontana—Via Larga—*Corso Italia*—Porta Lodovico.

UNDERGROUND (**MM**: METROPOLITANA MILANESE). two lines (not yet completed). The most useful section to the tourist is (Line 1) Loreto—Lima—Porta Venezia—Palestro—San Bábila—Duomo—Cordusio—Cairoli (for *Castello Sforzesco*)—Cadorna (for *Nord Station*)—Conciliazione. Line 2 so far links Lambrate, Central, and Porta Garibaldi Stations (and is under construction as far as Milano Nord Station). Tickets (comp. above) at newspaper stands in every station (flat rate fare).

COACH TOURS of the city daily at 9 and 14.30 from Via Marconi (P.za Duomo).

Country Buses from Piazzale Cadorna to *Certosa di Pavia;* from Piazzale Medaglie d'Oro (Porta Romana) to *Melegnano* and *Lodi;* from P.za Castello for most other destinations in Northern Italy.

The **Opening times of Museums** are given daily in the 'Corriere della Sera' newspaper.

British Consulate, 7 Via San Paolo (off Corso Vittorio Emanuele).—**U.S. Consulate,** 32 P.za della Repubblica.—**English Church.** *All Saints,* Via Solferino.

Theatres. *La Scala,* P.za della Scala, the opera house, season in winter and spring; *Piccolo Scala,* Via Filodrammatici (at the side of the main theatre); *Piccolo Teatro,* 2 Via Rovello (Via Dante); *di Via Manzoni 'Renato Simoni',* Via Manzoni; *Odeon,* Via Santa Radegonda; *Lirica,* Via Larga; *Nuovo,* Largo San Bábila.

Sport. GOLF COURSE (27 holes) in the park at Monza (p. 166), and (18 holes) at Barlassina, Birago di Camnago.—TENNIS at Centro Polisportivo, Via Valvassori Peroni; Lido di Milano, Piazzale Lotto, etc.—SWIMMING POOLS (covered), 35 Viale Tunisia; Via Corelli (Parco Forlanini); 12 Via Sant'Abbondio and many others; (open air) *Romano,* 35 Via Ponzio; Lido di Milano, Piazzale Lotto, etc.—HORSE RACING at the Ippodromo San Siro, N.W. of the centre, with trotting course adjoining; also at Monza.—MOTOR RACING at Monza.

History. *Mediolanum,* a Celtic settlement which first came under the Roman power in 222 B.C., was of little importance until the later days of the Empire when with a population approaching 100,000 it rivalled Rome for primacy of the West. By the famous Edict of Milan in A.D. 313 Constantine the Great officially recognized the Christian religion, and the influence of the great bishop St Ambrose (340-397) was so profound that the adjective 'ambrosiano' has become synonymous with 'Milanese'. The Emp. Valentinian II died here in 392. Despite the slaughter of most of the male population by the Goths in 539, Milan rose to prominence again under its archbishops, and by the mid-11C it had developed into that type of early Italian city-state, the *Comune,* and was engaged in incessant strife with its neighbours—Pavia, Como, and Lodi. The vigorous emperor Barbarossa took advantage of the troubles to extend his power over Lombardy, and sacked Milan in 1158 and 1162, but his tyranny induced the Lombard cities to join together in the Lombard League, which beat Barbarossa at Legnano (1176) and, by the treaty of Constance (1183), won recognition of its independence. Powerful families now came into prominence and c. 1260 the Torriani rose to absolute power in Milan, only to be overthrown in 1277 by the Visconti, who ruled Milan until 1447. Under them, especially under Gian Galeazzo (1385-1402), the city increased in wealth and splendour, but the Visconti line died out in 1447, and after three republican years Francesco Sforza (the famous condottiere and defender of Milan against Venice), who had married Bianca, daughter of the last Visconti, proclaimed himself duke. He was succeeded by his son Galeazzo Maria, and then by his infant grandson Gian Galeazzo, under the regency of his mother Bona di Savoia. But the power was usurped by the child's uncle Lodovico 'il Moro', who brought great wealth and beauty to Milan thanks to his patronage of the fine arts. The expedition in 1494 of Charles VIII of France began a succession of foreign invasions. Between 1499 and 1535 Milan saw her dukes fall thrice from power, and passed alternately into the hands of the French and the Spaniards, finally becoming, under Charles V, capital of a province of the Empire. In 1713 it became Austrian, but in 1796 Napoleon entered its gates, proclaiming it three years later capital of the Cisalpine Republic, and again, after a brief occupation by the Austrians and Russians, capital of the Italian Republic (1802) and of the Kingdom of Italy (1805). The fall of Napoleon brought back the Austrians, who ruled the city with a tyranny against which the Milanese rebelled during the glorious 'Cinque Giornate' (18-22 March 1848). Milan at length found liberty on the entry of Victor Emmanuel II and Napoleon III after the battle of Magenta in 1859. Milan was bombed fifteen times in the Second World War; the worst air-raids were in Aug 1943, after which a great part of the city centre burned for several days.

Among famous natives of Milan are Cesare Beccaria (1738-94), philosopher and jurist, Alessandro Manzoni (1785-1873), Italy's classic novelist, Carlo Cattaneo (1801-69), patriot and scientific writer, and Felice Cavallotti (1842-98), radical dramatist and poet. Giuseppe Parini (1729-99), of Bosisio, the poet, and Cesare Cantù (1804-95), of Brivio, the historian, though born just outside the city, identified themselves with its literary life. The composers Verdi, Boito, and Giordano all died in Milan (1901, 1918, 1948).

Art. The most important relics of the Romanesque age of architecture are Sant'Ambrogio and San Lorenzo. The Cathedral is practically the only building of the Gothic age. But the wealthy and cultured court of the Sforzas attracted many great artists of the Renaissance, among them Filarete, Michelozzo, and Bramante, the architects, Amadeo the sculptor, and Bergognone and Foppa the painters. Milanese art, however, was completely transformed by the arrival in 1483 of the Tuscan, Leonardo; this great artist and the city he adopted were the centre of the new artistic and humanistic impulse that ended with the fall of Lodovico il Moro in 1499; but a host of pupils and disciples carried on his tradition of painting: Boltraffio, Cesare da Sesto, Marco d'Oggiono, Giampietrino, Salaino, And. Solario; and Luini and Gaudenzio Ferrari who formed schools of their own. Bambaia and Crist. Solari felt his influence in the world of sculpture. The inspiration died out in the 16C, and towards the end of the century Camillo and Giulio Procaccini introduced a new style of painting from Bologna, and Galeazzo

Alessi imported into architecture something of the dignity of Rome. The neo-classic buildings of Cagnola and Canonica are a noteworthy feature of the Napoleonic period, and some modern buildings continue the tradition of originality.

I   CENTRAL MILAN

Piazza del Duomo (Pl. 11) is the centre of the life of Milan. It is now closed to traffic (except for the W. end) although trams have been allowed to remain. The crowded Portici Settentrionali, along the N. side, are characteristic of the bustling atmosphere of the city. The equestrian statue of Victor Emmanuel II is by Ercole Rosa (1896).

The **Duomo*, the most magnificent Gothic building in Northern Italy, is a cathedral in the Northern Gothic style, but with very marked peculiarities of its own. The vast dimensions of the church are superseded only by those of St Peter's in Rome. The exterior is being slowly cleaned (and the stone replaced where necessary) so that the full effect of its remarkable sculptures can be appreciated.

It was begun c. 1386, on the site of an older church (recently revealed through excavations, comp. below), under Gian Galeazzo Visconti, who presented it with a marble quarry at Candoglia which still belongs to the Chapter. The design is attributed to the 'maestri comacini'—Simone da Orsenigo, Marco da Campione, and Giov. Grassi—who were aided by French, German, and Flemish craftsmen. In 1400 Filippino degli Organi was appointed master mason, and he was succeeded by Giov. Solari and his son Guiniforte, Giov. Ant. Amadeo, and (from 1567) Pellegrino Tibaldi, under whom the church was dedicated by St Charles Borromeo. The topmost spires were added in 1765-69, but the façade was not completed until 1813.

Exterior. The best view of the cathedral is obtained from the courtyard of the Palazzo Reale, on the S. side; but the most striking single feature is the apse, with its three huge windows.—The WEST FRONT (56 m high, 61 m wide), originally designed in the Baroque style by Tibaldi (c. 1567), was considerably altered by C. Buzzi (1645), who adopted a more Gothic plan, though preserving much of Tibaldi's work. It was only half finished when Napoleon crowned himself 'king of Italy' with the Iron Crown in 1805. He decreed that it should be completed at once, but rigidly restricted the cost, with the result that the upper half is a poor mock-Gothic creation. Plans to reconstruct it, mooted in 1886, were soon abandoned. The bronze door, with scenes from the Life of the Virgin, is by Lod. Pogliaghi (1906), and flanking this are doors (1950) by Franco Lombardi (S.) and Giannino Castiglioni (N.), dedicated to St Galdino and St Ambrose. The northernmost door is by Arrigo Minerbi (1948), with scenes relating to Constantine's edict establishing Christianity in the Roman Empire; the southernmost, by Luciano Minguzzi (1960), depicts the cathedral's history.

The huge cruciform **INTERIOR*, with double-aisled nave (48 m high), single-aisled transepts, and a pentagonal apse, has a forest of 52 tall columns, of which the majority bear circles of figures in canopied niches instead of capitals. The splendid effect is heightened by the stained glass of the windows. The pavement is by *Tibaldi*.—SOUTH AISLE: plain granite Sarcophagus of Abp. Aribert (d. 1045); above, a Crucifix, bas-relief in copper (11C); Sarcophagus (on pillars) in red marble of Abp. Ottone Visconti (d. 1295); Tomb of Marco Carelli, by *Filippino degli Organi* (1406), with six statues in canopied niches. Beyond two plaques with designs for the façade by G. Brentano (1886) is the small monument of Canon Giovanni Vimercati (d. 1548), with two fine portraits and a damaged Pietà by *Bambaia*. SOUTH TRANSEPT: Monument of Gian Giacomo Medici, by *Leone Leoni* (1560-63); altar of San Giovanni Bono (18C); Presentation of the Virgin, by *Bambaia,* and to the right, St Catherine, by *Cristoforo Lombardo;* statue representing St

Bartholomew flayed and carrying his skin, by *Marco d'Agrate* (1562). On the pendentives of the impressive DOME are medallions with busts of the Doctors of the Church, by *Crist. Solari* (1505). On the high altar is a large bronze ciborium by *Tibaldi*. The pulpits, organ, and choir-stalls are late 16C work; the screen between choir and ambulatory was designed by *Tibaldi*. A small door r. of the main altar leads down to the CRYPT and TREASURY (adm. 9-12, 15-18, exc. Mon).

Here are displayed some 5C ivory carvings; the evangelistary cover of Abp. Aribert; a small ivory bucket of the 10C; and a golden pax ascribed to Caradosso (praised by Cellini as the greatest artist of his kind). Also, croziers, pastoral crosses, etc.—The CRYPT has stucco reliefs by *Alessi* and *Tibaldi*, and contains the richly-robed body of St Charles Borromeo (pilgrimage on 4-11 Nov).

In the ambulatory is the fine doorway, with sculptural decoration by Hans von Fernach and Porrino and Giovannino De Grassi (1393), of the South Sacristy (which contains a statue of Christ at the column by C. Solari). Beyond (high up) is a statue of Martin V, the Pope who consecrated the high altar in 1418, by *Iacopino da Tradate* (1424), and the tomb of Card. Caracciolo (d. 1538), by *Bambaia*, and, farther on, a relief of the Holy Sepulchre (1389). Opposite is the doorway of the North Sacristy, by Giac. da Campione. In the middle of the NORTH TRANSEPT is the Trivulzio *Candelabrum, a seven-branched bronze candlestick nearly 5 m high, of French or German workmanship (13C or 14C).—NORTH AISLE. At the easternmost (8th) altar is a painting by *Barocci,* The Penance of Theodosius; 6th altar, Crucifix carried by St Charles during the plague of 1576; 5th altar, Renaissance shrine, by *Amadeo;* 3rd altar, Tomb of three archbishops of the Arcimboldi family; 2nd altar, Eight Apostles, marble reliefs (late-12C) from the former church of Santa Maria Maggiore; opposite is the Font, a Roman (?) porphyry urn, covered with a canopy by *Tibaldi*.

The entrance (9-17.30, winter 9-16.30; also lift, entered from outside the S. transept) to the ROOF is a small door in the corner of the S. transept, near the Medici tomb. The ascent provides a superb view of the sculptural detail of the exterior.

158 steps ascend to the roof of the transept from which can be seen a forest of pinnacles and flying buttresses. Walkways across the roof allow a close examination of the details of the carving, and magnificent views of the city beyond. At the angle facing the Corso is the Carelli Spire, the oldest pinnacle. From above the W. front it is possible to walk along the spine of the nave roof to the base of the Dome, by *Amadeo* (1490-1500), who planned also the four turrets but finished only that at the N.E. angle. Access to the S.W. turret has been suspended temporarily during restoration work, but normally it is open as far as the platform of the dome. From here another staircase, in the N.E. turret, ascends to the topmost gallery at the base of the central spire, surmounted by the Madonnina (108 m from the ground), a statue of gilded copper, nearly 4 m high. From this height there is a magnificent *View of the city, the Lombard plain, the Alps from Monte Viso to the Ortler (the outstanding peaks being the Matterhorn, Monte Rosa, the two Grigne, and Monte Resegone), and the Apennines.

Inside the W. front of the Cathedral is the entrance (open 10-12, 16-17, exc. Mon) to the excavations beneath the church carried out in the 1960s. Here can be seen a 4C octagonal Baptistery where St Ambrose baptised St Augustine in 387, and remains of the Basilica of S. Tecla (begun in the 4C). Material from the various periods (including Roman baths of 1C B.C.) is well labelled.

To the S. of the cathedral is the former **Palazzo Reale** (now used for exhibitions), presented to the municipality in 1919. It was entirely transformed in 1771-78, by Gius. Piermarini, and again in the 19C. Some of the masterpieces from the Brera (comp. p. 157) are to be removed here during restoration work. Opposite the S. transept of the cathedral is the new entrance to the MUSEO DEL DUOMO (adm. 10.30-12.30, 15-18 exc. Mon; Thurs 11-12.30, 15-17.30), recently rearranged in a wing of the palace.

The first rooms contain a splendid collection of sculpture from the exterior of the cathedral (including a statue of St George, by *Giorgio Solari*); a statuette in wood of the Madonna and Child, by *Bernardo da Venezia* (1392); stained glass of 14C-mid 15C. In R. 6 is a statue of a warrior (thought to be Galeazzo Maria Sforza) of the late 15C. R. 7. Paschal candlestick by *Lor. da Civate* (1447), Crucifix (c. 1040). R. 8. *Bened. Briosco* (attrib.), St Agnes; *Crist. Solari*, Job; *Unknown Master of 15C*, St Paul the Hermit (c. 1465); 16C Brussels tapestry; and other works by *Crist. Solari*. One room contains material relating to the famous choir school of the cathedral (founded in the 10-11C and developed by Franchino Gaffurio in the 15C.) The arrangement of the rest of the museum has not yet been completed.

Between the museum and the Archbishops' Palace, Via del Palazzo Reale affords a view of the apse and *Campanile of *San Gottardo* (formerly the palace chapel); the graceful campanile is by Fr. Pecorari (1330-36). In its present form the *Archbishops' Palace* is mainly the work of Tibaldi (1570 et seq.) with alterations by Piermarini (1784-1801).

From the N. side of P.za del Duomo the GALLERIA VITTORIO EMANUELE (Pl. 11) leads N. This huge glass-roofed shopping arcade, with cafès and restaurants, was designed (1865) by Gius. Mengoni, who fell from the top and was killed a few days before the inauguration ceremony in 1878. It emerges in PIAZZA DELLA SCALA, with a monument to Leonardo da Vinci (by P. Magni, 1872) surrounded by figures of his pupils, Boltraffio, Salaino, Cesare da Sesto, and Marco d'Oggiono. On the N.W. side of the square rises the **Teatro alla Scala** (Pl. 11), famous in operatic art.

The theatre was built in 1776-78 by Gius. Piermarini on the site of the church of Santa Maria della Scala, after the destruction by fire of the Regio Ducale Teatro. Works by Rossini, Donizetti, Bellini, and Verdi were first acclaimed here, and from the beginning of this century its reputation was upheld by the legendary figure of Toscanini (who led the orchestra again in 1946 when the building was reopened after serious war damage).—The *Piccola Scala* was opened here in 1955 for the performance of opera on a smaller scale, and chamber music concerts.— Under the portico, to the left of the theatre is the *Museo Teatrale* (adm. 9-12, 14-18; fest. 9.30-12.30, 14.30-18), with a valuable collection relating to theatrical and operatic history. From the museum the theatre may be visited.

On the S.E. side of the piazza is *PALAZZO MARINO (the *Palazzo Municipale*), with a good courtyard by Galeazzo Alessi (1553-58), and a façade by Beltrami (1886-92). Beyond is P.za San Fedele, in which are a statue of Manzoni and the church of *San Fedele*, begun by Tibaldi (1569) for St Charles Borromeo, and completed by Martino Bassi and Fr. Maria Richini, with an elaborate pulpit.

From the Scala the busy and fashionable VIA MANZONI (Pl. 7) leads N.E. towards P.za Cavour; at No. 29 (tablet) Verdi died in 1901. On the right, at No. 10 Via Morone, is the **Museo Poldi-Pezzoli** (Pl. 11), the former private house of G. G. Poldi-Pezzoli, bequeathed by him, with his art collection, to the city in 1879.

ADMISSION daily exc. Mon 9.30-12.30, 14.30-17; 1 April-30 Sept: fest. 9.30-12.30 only; and also Thurs 21-23 exc. in Aug).

The portrait of Poldi-Pezzoli in the entrance is by *Fr. Hayez.* On the ground floor the SALONE DELL'AFFRESCO (used for exhibitions), with Tiepoleso frescoes by *C. I. Carloni,* displays a Delft tapestry of 1602. The ARMOURY (being rearranged) has fine examples of antique and 14-17C arms and armour. Beyond, in the SALA DELL'ARCHEOLOGIA E DEI TAPPETI, are a fragment of Isfahan carpet (16C), a Tabriz carpet (c. 1560), antique vases, bronzes, silverware, and gold objects, an Ushak carpet (16C), and a prayer mat (Asia Minor; 18C).

An elliptical staircase, with landscapes by *Magnasco,* ascends to the main picture gallery on the FIRST FLOOR. In the vestibule, *Lor. Bartolini,* Bust of Rosa Poldi-Pezzoli. To the left are the SALETTE DEI LOMBARDI. In the first, *Vinc. Foppa,* Madonna; *Ambr. Bergognone,* Madonna; *Lombard painter* (c. 1460), Saints. In the second, *Vinc. Foppa* (?), Portrait; *And. Solario,* Rest on the Flight (with charming landscape); *Boltraffio,* Madonna; *Bernardino Luini,* Madonna. The third is devoted to *Luini* and the Lombard school. Beyond the vestibule is the ANTECHAMBER (or Sala degli Stranieri) with paintings by *Cranach* (Portraits of Luther and his wife), landscapes by *Theobald Michau,* a Brussels *Tapestry (c. 1500), and a 16C Venetian trousseau chest.—The SALETTA DEGLI STUCCHI contains porcelain from Saxony, Sèvres, and Capodimonte, etc.—SALONE DORATO. In the centre is a wonderful Persian carpet of 1522. *Mantegna,* *Madonna; *Giov. Bellini,* Pietà; *Botticelli,* *Madonna; *Piero della Francesca,* *St Nicholas of Tolentino; *Ant. Pollauolo,* *Lady of the Bardi family, one of the best-known portraits in Italy; *Guardi,* Venetian lagoon.

The three rooms beyond contain the collection of Emilio Visconti Venosta (including a portrait of Card. Ascanio Sforza by *Vinc. Foppa*); the Bruno Falck donation of antique clocks and scientific instruments; and a series of portraits (mostly by *Vittore Ghislandi* of Bergamo, 1655-1743).

Beyond the Salone Dorato and the Salette dei Stucci (r.) is the SALA NERA, so called from the decoration (partly preserved) in ivory and ebony: *Mariotto Albertinelli,* Triptych; *Flemish 16C School,* Annunciation, and Saints; *Luca Signorelli,* Mary Magdalen; Florentine table in marble intarsia.—The SALA DEI VETRI ANTICHI DI MURANO, as well as examples of glass (15-19C) from Murano, contains miniatures by Venetian and Florentine masters; *Lippo Memmi,* St Dorothy; *Bern. Daddi,* Crucifix. The two doors at the end lead in to the SALETTA DI DANTE (restored) decorated in the Art Nouveau style at the end of the 19C.—From the Sala Nera is the entrance to the SALA DELL'ARAZZO, with a battle-scene in tapestry, signed Franc. Springius. 1602. Also, *Sfonisba Anguissola,* Self portrait; *Guardi,* Landscapes; *Fr. Salviati,* Portrait of a boy.

Two rooms beyond have recently been opened to display paintings by *Gius. Ribera* and others; Islamic and Venetian metal work (15-18C); and arms and armour. Also here is a collection of sculpture including small bronzes of 16-17C, and a Hellenistic (2C B.C.) head of young Bacchus. The portrait of a lady is attrib. to *Palma il Vecchio.*

A small room off the Sala degli Arazzi contains a precious collection of ancient jewellery and goldsmiths' work, and Medieval religious bronzes and Limoges enamels. On easels (temporarily displayed here): *Cosimo Turà,* St Maurelius; *Carlo Crivelli,* St Sebastian, St Francis collecting Christ's blood; *Pietro Lorenzetti,* Madonna enthroned; *Vitale degli Equi,* Madonna and Child and SS. Catherine and Agnes.—SALA DEL SETTECENTO VENETO. Works by *Guardi, Canaletto, Bellotto,* and *G. B. Tiepolo.*—In the next room: *Fr. Bonsignori,* Head of a Saint; *Giov.*

Batt. Utili, Madonna and Child.—The SALETTA DEI VENETI has Venetian works including a Holy Family, by *Lor. Lotto.*

Via Morone, in which Manzoni met Balzac in 1837 and (at No. 1) he died in 1873 (small museum, open 9.30-12,30, 14-17.30; closed Sun & Mon), opens into P.za Belgioioso. Via Omenoni (r.) is named from the caryatids decorating the house of the sculptor Leone Leoni. Via San Paolo leads across the busy Corso Vitt. Emanuele to P.za Beccaria, with a monument to Cesare Beccaria (bronze copy of an original marble of 1871 by Gius. Grandi now in the Pal. di Giustizia). Here is the former *Tribunale* (originally Palazzo del Capitano di Giustizia) of 1586, restored as Police headquarters. Beyond is the Baroque church of *Santo Stefano Maggiore* (1584-95) with a later campanile, outside the predecessor of which Galeazzo Maria Sforza was murdered in 1476. The **Ospedale Maggiore** (Pl. 10), beyond, was built for Fr. Sforza in 1456 by Filarete, who was responsible for the fine terracotta decoration on the right wing. The façade and the decorative part of the cloister (r.) survived the war; the rest has been beautifully restored. The buildings are the headquarters of the *Università degli Studi,* founded in 1924.

The Natural Science schools of the University and other important educational institutions are in the *Città degli Studi,* which lies c.2 km. E. of Porta Venezia (tram 23 viâ Via Nino Bixio; or Metropolitana 2 to Piola sta.).—Opposite the Ospedale can be seen the 12C campanile of *Sant'Antonio Abate,* a church of 1582 with good 17C stalls. Adjoining (No. 5 Via Sant'Antonio) is a charming cloister of the early 16C.

In Largo Richini, at the S.W. end, is a colossal bust of Dr And. Verga (d. 1895), by Giulio Branca, and just beyond is **San Nazaro Maggiore** (Pl. 15), a basilica consecrated in 386, rebuilt after a fire of 1075 and altered c. 1578, but preserving much of its original wall and fragments of the dedication stone. Elegantly placed in front of the (S.W.) façade is the hexagonal *Trivulzio Chapel* (1518), with family tombs. In the *Chapel of St Catherine* (entered from the N. transept) is a large fresco representing the saint's martyrdom, by Bern. Lanino (1546). From the front of the church the busy Corso di Porta Romana (Pl. 15) returns towards the centre, ending in P.za Missouri.

In Via Unione, running N.W. out of P.za Missouri, No. 5 is a fine 16C palazzo (Palazzo Erba Odescalchi; now a police headquarters, adm. on request), with a good courtyard, and a remarkable elliptical spiral staircase (restored; attrib. to Bramante).

From the N.W. end of the Corso Via Mazzini continues to Via Falcone (l.) in which is the campanile (mid-11C) of the famous church of *San Satiro (Pl. 11). The church, entered from Via Torino, was rebuilt by Bramante from 1478, with the exception of the façade, which though begun by Gius. Ant. Amadeo in 1486 to Bramante's design was finished by Gius. Vandoni (1871). The T-shaped interior, by a clever perspective device and the skilful use of stucco, is given the appearance of a Greek cross; the rear wall is actually almost flat. At the end of the left transept is the *Cappella della Pietà,* dating from the time of Abp. Ansperto (868-881), altered at the Renaissance, with charming decoration and a terracotta Pietà, by Agost. De Fondutis. The eight-sided baptistery, off the right aisle, is a gem of Renaissance art, with terracottas by Fondutis from Bramante's design.

Via Spadari, almost opposite San Satiro, and Via C. Cantù (l.) go on to Piazza Pio XI. Here stands the **Biblioteca Ambrosiana** (Pl. 10), the notable library founded by Card. Fed. Borromeo and built by Lelio Buzzi in 1607-9. It has good art collections (adm. daily 9.30-17).

The **Pinacoteca**, on the first floor, is entered from the left side of the courtyard. The rooms, staircases, landings, etc., are numbered consecutively in Roman numerals. ROOM I. *Botticelli,* *Virgin and Child with angels; *Ghirlandaio,* Nativity; *Bergognone,* *Madonna enthroned with Saints; *Marco Basaiti,* The risen Christ.—R. II. Lombard sculpture of the 8-11C.—R. III. *Bambaia,* Fragments of the tomb of Gaston de Foix; Lombard frescoes (15C).—R. IV. *Maestro del Santo Sangue (attrib.),* Adoration of the Magi (triptych); *Bernart van Orley,* Madonna 'della Fontana'; 16C German portraits including works by *Hans Muelich;* Lombard and German bronzes; cases of clocks, jewellery, glass, and ivories.— R.V. Huge window by *Gius. Bertini* (1865) showing Dante with the MS. of the 'Divine Comedy'.—R. VI, *Jan Brueghel the Younger,* Fire, and Water, part of a series of the Four Elements painted for Card. Borromeo; all four were taken to France in 1796, where the other two still remain. *Hendrik Averkamps,* Games on the ice.

ROOM VII. *Luini,* Salvator Mundi, Madonna, Young St John; *Bramantino,* Adoration of the Child; a detached fresco and works by *Ant. Solario.*—R. VIII. *Bramantino,* Madonna with SS. Michael and Ambrose; *Luini,* *Holy Family, with St Anne and the young St John, from a cartoon by Leonardo; *Leonardo da Vinci,* *Portrait of a musician (Franchino Gaffurio?); *Ambr. De Predis (attrib.),* *Profile of a young lady, variously identified; *Marco d'Oggiono,* Madonna and Child with Saints.—R. IX. *Sodoma,* Holy Family.

ROOM X, a fine 17C chamber, provides a fit setting for *Raphael's* *Cartoon for the 'School of Athens', the only remaining cartoon of the fresco cycle in the Vatican.—R. XI. *G. B. Tiepolo,* Presentation in the Temple, Canonized bishop; *Caravaggio,* *Basket of fruit; *Barocci,* Nativity.—R. XII. In cases, Empire-period jewellery; portraits (sculpted) by *Thorvaldsen* and *Canova,* and (painted) by *Appiani.*—R. XIII. Venetian painters. *G. B. Moroni,* Cavalier (1554); *Titian,* Deposition. *Adoration of the Magi, painted (with assistants) for Henri II and Diane de Poitiers (1560; in original frame), Portrait of an old man in armour; *Veronese,* Holy Family, Tobias and the angel; *Iac. Bassano,* Adoration of the Shepherds, Annunciation to the Shepherds.—R. XIV, off the courtyard, displays 17C Mannerist paintings, including works by *Dan. Crespi.*

The Library (open 9-12, 14.30-16.30; Sat 9-12) contains about 750,000 vols, including 3000 incunabula, and 35,000 MSS. Among the most precious objects (of which copies only are normally shown) are Arabic and Syriac MSS; a Divine Comedy (1353); Petrarch's Virgil illuminated by *Simone Martini;* the 'Codice Atlantico', a collection of Leonardo's drawings on scientific and artistic subjects; a printed Virgil (Venice, 1470) and Boccaccio (1471). In the SALA DEL LUINI are a fresco of the Crown of Thorns, and portraits of the confraternity of Santa Corona (1521) by *Luini.*

To the N., centring on PIAZZA CORDUSIO (Pl. 11), with its banks and insurance offices, is the principal business quarter of Milan, with the Borsa (exchange), the Post Office, and the Banca d'Italia and other banks. In Via Mercanti, leading back to the Duomo, are (l.) *Palazzo dei Giureconsulti* (1560-64) and *Palazzo della Ragione* (r.), erected in 1228-33 with an upper story added in 1771. On its rear wall, in the peaceful P.za Mercanti, is a remarkable equestrian relief of 1233. In this piazza are also the Gothic *Loggia degli Osii* (1316) and the Baroque *Palazzo delle Scuole Palatine* (1645). Farther N. is *Palazzo Clerici* (Pl. 11), in the hall of which is a magnificent ceiling-painting by Tiepolo (1740).

II   THE CASTELLO SFORZESCO, THE CENACOLO, AND SANT'AMBROGIO

From P.za Cordusio (see above) the straight VIA DANTE (Pl. 10) leads to Largo Cairoli (monument to Garibaldi, by Ximenes, 1895) and Piazza Castello. In front stands ***Castello Sforzesco** (Pl. 6), the stronghold built by Francesco Sforza in 1451-66, on the site of a 14C castle of the Visconti destroyed under the 'Ambrosian Republic'. It now contains important art collections.

The designer of the castle was Giov. da Milano, but the decoration of the principal tower was entrusted to Filarete, the Florentine architect. The Castello was later enriched with works by Bramante and Leonardo; after a long period of use as barracks, it was restored by Luca Beltrami (1893-1904). Badly bombed in 1943, when two-thirds of the archives and many other treasures were lost, it was again carefully restored. It is square in plan; on the façade are three towers, the chief of which is the *Filarete Tower*, rebuilt in accordance with the supposed design of the original, destroyed by an explosion of powder in 1521. The picturesque P.za d'Armi, the main courtyard, contains fragments of old buildings from various parts of the city. Concerts are held here in summer. At the back on the left is the *Rocchetta*, which served as a keep, on the right is the *Corte Ducale*, the residential part, and in the centre is the *Torre di Bona di Savoia*.

From the charming courtyard of the Corte Ducale is the entrance to the **Museo d'Arte Antica** (adm. 9.30-12, 14.30-17.30). The collections are beautifully arranged and well labelled. Beyond the monumental 14C *Pusterla dei Fabbri*, ROOM I contains fragments from ancient churches and other Byzantine and Romanesque remains; late Roman sarcophagus, from Lambrate; marble portrait head (6C) supposedly of the Empress Theodora.—R. 2. Figure of Christ in wood from a 13C German Crucifixion; Tombs of Barnabò Visconti, by *Bonino da Campione* (1370-80), with a colossal equestrian figure, and of Regina della Scala, his wife.—In R. 3, beneath a Lombard frescoed ceiling (mid 15C), are remains of the façade of Santa Maria di Brera, by *Giov. di Balduccio* of Pisa; statues from the E. gate of the city by the same artist; tomb assigned to Bona di Savoia (14C).—R. 4, where the vault bears the arms of Philip II of Spain and Mary Tudor, contains further fragments of S.M. di Brera; *Sepulchral monument of the Rusca family, by a Lombard master (late 14C), from the church of S. Francesco in Como.

EAST WING. Beyond a small chapel (R. 5) with 14C Venetian sculpture, and a fragment of an English alabaster, R. 6 contains reliefs from the old Porta Romana, showing the triumph of the Milanese over Barbarossa (1171); bell from the Broletto of Milan.—R. 7, with frescoed escutcheons of the Dukes of Milan, is hung with tapestries. In the centre, the Gonfalon of Milan, designed by *Gius. Meda* (1566); *Stoldo Lorenzi* (1534-83), Statue of Adam.—The SALA DELLE ASSE (R. 8), at the N.E. corner of the castle, has frescoed decoration with ilex leaves, designed in 1498 by *Leonardo*, but much altered and restored.

A little doorway (r.; but usually kept locked) leads to two small rooms (9,10) over the moat containing Sforza portraits by *Luini* and panels in high relief by *Bambaia;* in the first room Lodovico il Moro is said to have mourned the death of his wife.

ROOM 11 (SALA DEI DUCALI), in the N. wing, is decorated with coats-of-arms showing the ancestry of Galeazzo Maria Sforza; it contains a relief by *Agost. di Duccio* from the Tempio Malatestiano at Rimini, and good 15C sculptures.—The former CHAPEL (R. 12) has restored frescoes by *Stef. de' Fedeli* and assistants (1466-76) and small relief panels of the same date. The Madonna and Child is a Lombard work of the late 15C, and the statue of the Madonna 'del Coazzone' is by *Pietro Solari*. Beyond is the Portico of the Elephant, so called from a faded fresco. The SALA DELLE COLOMBINE (r.; R. 13) has fresco decorations with the arms of Bona di Savoia, and sculpture by *Amadeo* and *Crist. Mantegazza*, including a marble tabernacle. The long SALA VERDE (R. 14) is divided by

Renaissance doorways salvaged from Milanese palazzi; that from the Banco Mediceo (1455) is by *Michelozzo;* the room contains tombs, armorial sculptures, and armour.—The SALA DEGLI SCARLIONI (R. 15) is on two levels. In the higher part are sculptures by *And. Fusina* (bishop's tomb of 1519) and *Bambaia*, *Effigy of Gaston de Foix, with fragments of his tomb (1525); below, the famous *RONDANINI PIETÀ, the unfinished last work of *Michelangelo*. Uncomfortably placed on a Roman altar, it is not enhanced by its setting. On the left is a fine bronze head of Michelangelo, by *Daniele da Volterra* (1564).

From the corner a wooden bridge leads out into the Corte Ducale across a subterranean court with a 16C fountain. It is necessary to return across the court to the entrance (see R. 1, above) where stairs lead up to the FIRST FLOOR and the COLLECTION OF APPLIED ARTS. RR. 34-35. Textiles (Hellenistic, Coptic, vestments, etc.).—R.36. MUSEUM OF MUSICAL INSTRUMENTS. This is a charming collection, with lutes, an outstanding group of wind instruments, a clavichord of 1503, a spinet played on by the 14-year-old Mozart, and a fortepiano by Muzio Clementi; there is also a rich collection of musical MSS and autographs. In R. 37, a ball court, are Vigevano's tapestries of the Months, from designs by *Bramantino* (c. 1503).—SECOND FLOOR. R. 27. Campionese sculpture (late 14C) from Monza.—R. 28. Wrought ironwork.—RR. 29-31. *Ceramics, Italian and foreign.—R. 32. Goldsmiths' work, enamels, ivories, and small bronzes.

The rest of the museum (RR. 16-26), including the Pinacoteca, has been closed since 1972. ROOMS 16-19 contain part of the Museum of Applied Arts, including frescoes, tapestries, ceilings, and furniture, arranged to give a progressive chronological impression of Lombard interiors of the 15-18C, incorporating a reconstructed room, decorated with 15C frescoes of the Story of Griselda, from the Castle of Roccabianca. The arrangement of the **Pinacoteca** may be altered when it is reopened. In the vaulted tower room (20): *554. *Mantegna* Madonna in glory (the 'Pala Trivulzio'; 1497); *Giov. Bellini*, 249. Portrait of a poet, 550. Madonna; *551. *Filippo Lippi*, Madonna and saints.—R. 21 contains paintings by *Bergognone;* also *Foppa*, 1. Martyrdom of St Sebastian, and others; *Bramantino*, Noli me tangere.—The little R. 22 has frescoes by *Lattanzio Gambara.*—R. 23. Venetian Schools: *Correggio*, 253. Madonna, *107. Portrait; *32. *Lor. Lotto*, Portrait; also good portraits by *Tintoretto*, *Boltraffio*, and *Bronzino.*—R. 24 Mannerists. *Pontormo*, Portrait of a youth. R. 25, over the portico contains the Belgioioso Collection of Flemish and Dutch masters.—The long R.26 contains 17C works, mainly Lombard, also *Van Dyck*, Henrietta Maria; *Guardi*, Seascape, etc.

In the arcaded *COURTYARD OF THE ROCCHETTA, in which both *Filarete* and *Bramante* had a hand, are the entrances to the Archæological Collection, and the Egyptian Museum. The **Egyptian Museum**, recently arranged in the basement of the Rocchetta contains an interesting and well displayed collection of objects dating from the Old Kingdom to the age of Ptolemy. It is divided in two sections: the first illustrates the funerary cult of ancient Egypt, with sarcophagi, mummies, and Books of the Dead (papyri). The second room exhibits household and personal objects, canopic vases, jewellery, funerary masks, stelæ, etc.—Most of the **Archæological Collection** has now been transferred to the Monastero Maggiore (comp. p. 157).—The corner tower, with the SALA DI LUCA BELTRAMI (frescoes, including one by Bramante) has been closed for several years.—In this courtyard, also, are the **Archivio Storico Civico** and the **Biblioteca Trivulziana** (with an oriental art centre); they are open to students from 9-12, 14-17, exc. on Sat. Elsewhere in the Castello are a medal collection (open to students only), and the Bertarelli Collection of prints and maps.

Beyond the Castello is the PARK (116 acres) crowded on holidays. Here is an *Aquarium* (9.30-12, 14-17; closed Mon; and Wed and Fri afternoons). Also the *Stadio Civico* (Pl. 6), a sports arena originally built by Canonica in 1806-7; a high view-tower (110m; lift) made of aluminium erected in 1936; a fine equestrian *Monument to Napoleon III*, by Fr. Barzaghi (1881), transferred from the Palazzo del Senato in 1927; and the *Palazzo dell'Arte* (Pl. 6), a hall for exhibitions (1957). At the farther end is the *Arco della Pace* (Pl. 5), by L. Cagnola (1807-38), a triumphal arch on the model of that of Severus at Rome, with statues and bas-reliefs. It was begun in honour of Napoleon I, but was dedicated to Peace by Ferdinand I of Austria on its completion. It marks the beginning of the *Corso*

Sempione, the historic Simplon Road, constructed by Napoleon's order (see p. 118).

From Piazzale Cadorna in front of the Nord station (Pl. 10) Via Boccaccio and Via Caradosso (l.) lead to **Santa Maria delle Grazie** (Pl. 9; closed 12-15), a church of brick and terracotta, with a very beautiful *Exterior. It was erected in 1466-90 to the design of *Guiniforte Solari,* and partly rebuilt by *Bramante* (1492-99) who is responsible for the striking choir and crossing and the W. portal.

Interior. In the 1st S. chapel is a fine tomb of the Della Torre family; in the 4th are frescoes by *Gaudenzio Ferrari* (1542); in the 5th are stucco bas-reliefs (late 16C) of angels. The apse has fine stalls of carved and inlaid wood. At the end of the N. aisle is the venerated *Chapel of Madonna delle Grazie.*

Bramante's *CHIOSTRINO and OLD SACRISTY (temporarily closed) which mark a significant step in the development of Renaissance architecture are entered from the N. aisle.

In the *Refectory* of the adjoining Dominican convent (entrance on the left of the façade: 10-15 on weekdays, and 9-13 on fest.) is Leonardo's world-famous *Cenacolo or **Last Supper,** painted in 1495-97. This is a tempera painting, not a true fresco, and the inferior durability of this technique, together with the dampness of the wall, has caused great damage to the picture, which had, in fact, considerably deteriorated by the middle of the 16C. It has been restored repeatedly, most recently in 1953. On the opposite wall is a large Crucifixion by *Donato da Montórfano* (1495), the fine preservation of which is a vindication of the lasting quality of true fresco-painting. At the bottom of the fresco, at either side, are the kneeling figures, now nearly effaced, of Lodovico il Moro and his wife Beatrice d'Este and their two children, added in 1497 by *Leonardo.*

Via B. Zenale and Via San Vittore (l.) lead to *San Vittore al Corpo* (Pl. 9), in part by Alessi, with good 16C choir-stalls. The old Olivetan convent (1507), which still contains a collection of frescoes by Luini, was rebuilt in 1949-53, after war damage, to house the **Leonardo da Vinci Museum of Science and Technology.** Admission daily, exc. Mon. 9.30-12, 14.30-17.

The vestibule contains frescoes of the 15C Lombard School. To the right in the FIRST CLOISTER are displayed ancient carriages and velocipedes. To the left is the *Library* (entered from No. 19 Via San Vittore; weekdays exc. Mon 9.30-12.30, 15-18.30), with the cinema beyond. A staircase mounts to the FIRST FLOOR. At the top (l.) is a room devoted to temporary exhibitions. On the right in the SALA DELLA BIFORA is the Mauro Collection of goldsmiths' work and precious stones; ahead the gallery is devoted to Cinematography. Rooms to the right demonstrate the evolution of the graphic arts (printing, typewriters, etc.). At the end of the gallery, to the right, is the long *GALLERIA LEONARDESCA, with models of machines and apparatus invented by Leonardo.

The rooms (r.) that border the first cloister are devoted to Time Measurement and Sound, including musical instruments with a reproduction of a lute-maker's shop. Off the middle of the Leonardo Gallery (r.) is the SALA DELLE COLONNE, formerly the conventual library. Three galleries round the second cloister illustrate the science of Physics, including electricity, acoustics, and nuclear reaction. Beyond the Astronomy gallery are rooms devoted to Optics and Radio and telecommunications (with memorials of Marconi).

The lower floor is devoted to Metallurgy, Petro-Chemical Industries, and Transport with a fine gallery of early motor-cars. External pavilions contain Railway Locomotives (from 'Bayard', one of Stephenson's engines supplied from Newcastle for the Naples-Portici line in 1843) and Rolling Stock; and aeroplanes and relics of aeronautical history. On the GROUND FLOOR is the **Civico Museo Navale Didattico,** founded in 1922, with navigational instruments and models of ships.—On the top floor is a *Modern Art Gallery* with works by De Nittis, Fattori, Gemito, Lega, Mancini, etc.

At the end of Via San Vittore (r.) stand the towers of the *Pusterla di Sant'Ambrogio,* one of the gates of the medieval city wall (restored); it contains a small museum of ancient arms.

The basilica of *Sant'Ambrogio (Pl. 10), the most interesting church in Milan, was the prototype of the Lombard basilica. Founded by St Ambrose, Bp. of Milan, it was built in 379-86 and enlarged in the 9C and again after 1038; in this church, hastily restored after use as a granary (following earthquake damage in 1177), the Emp. Henry VI married Constance of Sicily in 1186.

EXTERIOR. The splendid ATRIUM in front of the church dates in its present form from 1150, with older capitals; beneath its arcades lapidary fragments include the sarcophagus of Abp. Ansperto (d. 881). The façade of the church consists of a five-bayed narthex below, with five arches above, graduated to fit the gable. The great *Doorway* is made up of fragments from 8C and 10C buildings; the bronze doors belong to the 9C. The S. or Monks' campanile dates from the 9C, the higher Canons' campanile on the N. is a fine Lombard tower of 1128-44, crowned with a loggia of 1889.

INTERIOR. On the right is a statue of Pius IX (1880). On the left, beyond a bronze serpent of the 10C, a *Pulpit reconstituted from fragments saved after the vault collapsed in 1196; beneath it, a late-Roman Christian sarcophagus.—In the SOUTH AISLE: 1st chapel, fresco, Descent from the Cross, by *G. Ferrari;* 6th chap., Legend of St George, by *Lanino.* At the end of this aisle is the SACELLO DI SAN VITTORE IN CIEL D'ORO (light indicated), popularly 'Basilica Fausta', built in the 4C and altered later; the dome is covered with splendid 5C *Mosaics representing SS. Victor, Ambrose, etc.—In the 1st chapel (North Aisle) is a fresco of the Redeemer, by *Bergognone.*

In the SANCTUARY, under the dome, which was rebuilt in the 13C, is the great *Ciborium,* reconstructed at the same time; the shafts of the columns are probably of the time of St Ambrose, however, while the capitals are of the 9C. The four sides of the 13C baldacchino are decorated with reliefs in the Byzantine style. The altar has a magnificent and justly celebrated casing presented in 835 by Abp. Angilberto II, made of gold and silver plates sculptured in relief, with enamel and gems, the work of Volvinius, and representing scenes from the Lives of Christ and St Ambrose. In the apse are mosaics reset in the 10C and restored c. 1200, and the marble throne of St Ambrose.

The CRYPT contains the bodies of SS. Ambrose, Gervase, and Protasius in a shrine of 1897. From the E. end of the N. aisle a door admits to the *Portico della Canonica,* left unfinished by Bramante in 1499. A second side was added, following Bramante's plan, in 1955. The upper part houses the **Museo di Sant'Ambrogio** (adm. 10-12, 15-17; closed Tues, & Sat and fest. mornings). In it is the Treasury, containing a 12C cross; the Reliquary of the Innocents (early 15C); a missal of Gian Galeazzo Visconti (1395); two 15C monstrances, etc.—To the N. of the church is the *Monumento ai Caduti,* a striking war memorial erected in 1928. In the p.za is the *Università Cattolica,* founded in 1921, with two fine cloisters, Bramante's last work (1498) in Milan.

Via Sant'Agnese (Pl. 10), farther N., ends in Corso Magenta opposite *Palazzo Litta,* built by Fr. Maria Richini (1648), with a rococo façade added in 1752-63. On the right is the church of the **Monastero Maggiore**

(Pl. 10; usually closed) or *San Maurizio,* begun in 1503, perhaps by Dolcebuono, with a façade of 1574-81.

The harmonious *Interior is divided by a wall into two parts. The W. portion, originally for lay-worshippers, has small chapels below and a graceful loggia above and contains *Frescoes by Luini and his school (1522-29). 3rd S. chapel, frescoes by Luini himself; the life of St Catherine; on the dividing wall, SS. Cecilia, Ursula, Apollonia, and Lucia; and two lunettes. In the E. portion, formerly the nuns' choir (entered from the 4th N. chapel; apply to sacristan), are five more frescoes by Luini. A staircase behind the choir leads to the loggia, where are 26 fresco medallions containing half-length figures of holy virgins by *Boltraffio* (1505-10).— Two ancient towers, of Roman origin, can be seen from No. 2 Via Luini.

The adjacent nunnery (r.; entered from No. 15 Corso Magenta; 9.30-12.30, 14.30-17.30; closed Tues) houses a fine **Archæological Museum,** with collections relating to the history of Milan, finds from Cæsarea in the Holy Land, and a good display of antique vases.

Via Santa Maria alla Porta, on the right farther on, and Via Borromei (r.) lead to *Casa dei Borromei* (Pl. 10), one of the few surviving examples of early 15C domestic building in Milan, with a good second courtyard.

III   THE BRERA GALLERY WITH N. AND E. MILAN

From P.za Cordusio Via Broletto leads N. towards the 15C church of *Santa Maria del Carmine* (Pl. 7), with a façade completed in 1879, and a fine Baroque chapel S. of the choir. From here Via del Carmine leads to Via Brera, in which are (l.; No. 15) the Baroque *Palazzo Cusani* (1719), now the local military headquarters, and **Palazzo di Brera** (Pl. 7), begun by F. M. Richini in 1651, with a main portal by Piermarini (1780).

In the courtyard is a heroic bronze statue of Napoleon I, by *Ant. Canova* (1809), and between the columns of the arcades and on the landings of the main staircase are statues and busts of famous authors and artists. The Brera is regarded as the centre in Lombardy of art, literature, and learning, and in addition to the picture gallery it contains a *Library* (adm. 9-17, closed Sun and fest.), with c. 800,000 vols and pamphlets, including 2344 incunabula and 2000 MSS, the *Astronomical Observatory,* and the *Institute of Science and Letters.* The little piazza beside the palace contains a monument to the painter Hayez, by Barzaghi (1890).

The ****Pinacoteca** (adm. daily, exc. Mon, 9-14, fest 9-13), the famous picture gallery on the first floor, is one of the finest existing collections of North Italian painting. It is undergoing a lengthy restoration and rearrangement, and most of the rooms have been closed for several years. Some works may be temporarily removed to the Palazzo Reale (comp. p. 149). Some of the masterpieces, however, are at present exhibited in the order here described: *472. Raphael,* Marriage of the Virgin ('lo Sposalizio', 1504), the masterpiece of his Umbrian period; *510. Piero della Francesca,* Madonna with angels and saints and Federigo, Duke of Montefeltro; 476. *Ambr. Lorenzetti,* Madonna and Child; *475. Benozzo Gozzoli,* Miracle of St Dominic; *199. Mantegna,* The Dead Christ; *816. Scourging of Christ, the only known panel painting by *Bramante* (from Chiaravalle); *Riminese School.* Three panels with the story of St Colomba. *207. Carlo Crivelli,* Madonna della Candeletta; 214. *Giov. Bellini,* Pietà; 170. *Vittore Carpaccio,* St Stephen disputing with the Doctors (1514); 788. *Correggio,* Nativity; *289. Luini,* Madonna del Roseto.—945. *El Greco,* St Francis; 614. *Rembrandt,* Portrait of his sister; 679. *Rubens,* Last Supper.—100. *G. B. Moroni,* Antonio Navagero; 180. *Titian,* Count Antonio Porcia; 732. *Tintoretto,* Allegory; 136. *Iac. Bassano,* St Roch visiting the plague stricken; *Ann. Carracci,* The artist and his family; 402. *D. Crespi,*

Madonna and Saints; 781. *Pietro Longhi,* Family concert; 243. *Fr. Guardi,* The Grand Canal; 940. *Canaletto,* View of Venice; 230. *G. B. Tiepolo,* Battle.

The rest of the collection includes the following works (listed in no particular order). Lombard frescoes (14-16C); *19. *Vinc. Foppa,* Madonna and saints; 22-25. Saints, by *Bergognone.* 20. *Foppa,* St Sebastian; *Luini,* 47, 40, 49. St Ursula, St Thomas Aquinas, and St Sebastian; works by *Gaudenzio Ferrari.* Frescoes of the *School of Giovanni da Milano* (second half of 15C) from the Oratory at Mocchirolo near Lentate in Brianza; 968. *Ambr. Lorenzetti,* Madonna.

141. *Veronese,* Last Supper; 130. *G. B. Moroni,* Assumption; *Moretto,* 93. St Francis, *91. Madonna and saints; 179. *Palma Vecchio,* Three saints; *92. *Moretto,* Triptych; *Veronese,* 151. Baptism and Temptation of Christ, 241. Agony in the Garden, *140. Supper in the house of Simon; *149. *Tintoretto,* Descent from the Cross; 109. *Palma Vecchio,* Self-portrait; *143. *Tintoretto,* Discovery of the body of St Mark at Alexandria; *144. *Bonifazio,* Finding of Moses; *139. *Veronese,* SS. Anthony Abbot, Cornelius, and Cyprian; *Lor. Lotto,* 185, *184. Portraits; *Tintoretto,* 101. Young man, 142. St Helena with saints and donors.

165. *Bart. Montagna,* Virgin and saints; 157. *Martino da Udine,* St Ursula and her maidens; 167. *And. Previtali,* Coronation of the Virgin; 756. *Marco Basaiti,* Deposition; 158. *P. F. Bissolo,* Three saints; 116. *Giov. Cariani,* Madonna and saints; *175. *Cima da Conegliano,* Madonna and saints; *164. *Gentile and Giov. Bellini,* St Mark preaching at Alexandria; 176. *Cima,* St Peter between SS. Augustine and Nicholas of Bari; 160. *Michele da Verona,* Crucifixion; *Giov Cariani,* Resurrection.—223. *Stef. da Zevio,* Adoration of the Magi; 228. *Ant. Vivarini* and *Giov. d'Alemagna,* Polyptych; 799. *Iac. Bellini,* Madonna.

200. *Mantegna,* Pietà with saints (early work); *Carlo Crivelli,* 201. Madonna and saints (1482), 206. Crucifixion, *202, 203. Coronation of the Virgin (1493), with a Pietà in the lunette; *174. *Cima,* St Peter between St Paul and St John the Baptist; *Giov. Bellini,* 215. Madonna (1510), *216. Madonna (an early work); 219. *Cima,* St Jerome.—169. *Vitt. Carpaccio,* Marriage of the Virgin; 198. *Mantegna,* Madonna and cherubim; 171. *Vitt. Carpaccio,* Presentation of the Virgin.—942. *Girol. Savoldo,* Portrait; 164. *Paris Bordone,* Holy Family—. 105. *Paris Bordone,* Venetian lovers; 182. *Titian,* St Jerome; *183. *Lor. Lotto,* Portrait of a nobleman.

949, 950. *Bonifacio Bembo,* Fr. Sforza and Bianca Maria, his wife; *Defendente Ferrari,* 719, 718. Saints; *310. 'La Pala Sforzesca', a colourful Madonna with saints and donors, by a late 15C Lombard artist; *Bergognone,* 783, 259. Madonnas.—809. *Boccaccino,* Madonna; 279. *Bramantino,* Holy Family; *948. *Bart. Véneto,* Lady with a lute; 276. *Cesare da Sesto,* Madonna; 790. *Amb. De Predis,* Portrait of a man; 285. *Andrea Solario,* Madonna and saints; *319. *Boltraffio,* Portrait of the poet Casio; *282. *And. Solario,* Portrait of a man; 261. *Giampetrino,* Madonna.—275. *Cesare Magni,* Holy Family and Saint John; 286. *Sodoma,* Madonna; 281. *Boltraffio,* Two figures in adoration; 754. *Cesare da Sesto,* St Jerome; 277. *Gaud. Ferrari,* Madonna.—*Luini,* 314. Virgin between two saints, with the donor, Ant. Busti, and his family, *298. Virgin with saints.— Frescoes by *Bern. Luini,* brought from Santa Maria della Pace. 313. *Marco d'Oggiono,* Archangels casting out Satan; 321. *Gaud. Ferrari,* Martyrdom of St Catherine; *309. *Bramantino,* Crucifixion; *307. *Foppa,* Polyptych from S. Maria delle Grazie, Bergamo; *Bergognone,* 308. Assumption, 258. Saints.

376. *Cam. Procaccini,* Adoration of the shepherds; 398. *Nuvolone,* Family group; 403. *D. Crespi,* Last Supper; 380. *G. B. Crespi,* Madonna of the Roses; *G. C. Procaccini,* 343. Magdalen, 344. Annunciation; 392. *D. Crespi,* St Stephen.— 345. *G. C. Procaccini,* Marriage of St Catherine; 767. *Sofonisba Anguissola,* Self-portrait; 415. *D. Crespi* (?), Dead friar.

429. *Lor. Costa,* Adoration of the Magi; 819. *G. F. Maineri,* Head of St John the Baptist; *Correggio,* *427. Adoration of the Magi; 449, 449 bis. *Fr. Costa,* St John the Baptist and St Peter; 417. *Fil. Mazzola,* Portrait; 431, 433, 432. *Dosso Dossi,* St Sebastian, between St John the Baptist and St George (a portrait of Fr. d'Este).— 470. *Marco Palmezzano,* Coronation of the Virgin; 452. *Nic. Rondinelli,* St John the Baptist appearing to Galla Placidia; 428. *Ercole de' Roberti.* Madonna and saints; 469. *Marco Palmezzano,* Nativity; and paintings by the *Zaganelli* brothers.—435. *Scarsellino,* Virgin in glory, with the doctors of the Church; 439. *Garofalo,* Crucifixion; 448. *Francia,* Annunication; 422. *Girol. Mazzola,* St Thomas Aquinas; 430. *Nic. Pisano,* Madonna; 434. *Ortolano,* Crucifixion.

208, 210, 211. *Vitt. Crivelli,* Madonna and saints; *497, *Gentile da Fabriano,* Coronation of the Virgin (polyptych); 484. *And. di Bartolo,* 811. *Girol. di Giovanni,* 504. *L'Alunno,* Polyptychs; 481. *Gentile da Fabriano.* Madonna and angels. Frescoes by *Bramante* from Casa Panigarola. *Luca Signorelli,* 505. Madonna and saints; 477. Madonna; 508. *Tim. Viti,* Madonna; *476. *Luca Signorelli,* Scourging of Christ.

520. *Lod. Carracci,* Adoration of the Magi; 538. *Guido Reni,* SS. Peter and Paul; 598. *Luca Giordano,* Portrait of a chemist; 613. *Ribera,* St Jerome; 513. *Fr. Albani,* Dance of Cupids; 583. *Sassoferrato,* Madonna.—*Van Dyck,* 700. Amalia von Solms, 701. Madonna with St Anthony of Padua; 699. *Jordaens,* Abraham's sacrifice; landscapes by *Aless. Magnasco;* 632. *Maestro di Anversa del 1518,* Adoration of the Magi; 655. *Brueghel,* Village.—943. *Jan Steen.* Siesta; 607. *Salvator Rosa,* St Paul the Hermit; 951. *Reynolds,* Lord Donoughmore; 706. *Raphael Mengs,* Portrait of the singer Annibali. 235. 236. *Bern. Bellotto,* Views of La Gazzada, near Varese; 800. *Piazzetta,* Rebecca at the well; 780. *Pietro Longhi,* The dentist; 759. *Piazzetta,* Old man praying; 793. *G. M. Crespi,* Self-portrait. Portraits by *Fr. Hayez* of Manzoni, Rosmini, Rosmini, and Cavour.

The collection of MODERN AND CONTEMPORARY ART is to be arranged in Palazzo Citterio at No. 12 Via Brera.

Just behind the Brera in Via Borgonuovo is the *Museo del Risorgimento* (No. 23; open 9.30-12.30, 14.30-17.30; closed Mon).

The church of **San Marco** (Pl. 7), N. of the Brera, dates from 1254, but the interior was wholly altered in the Baroque period, while the front, except for the doorway and three statuettes of the 14C, dates from 1873.

Inside are 16C frescoes and paintings by the *Procaccini.* Beneath the 3rd arch in the left aisle is an interesting fresco, attrib. by some scholars to *Luini.* In the S. transept is the tomb of the Blessed Lanfranco da Settala (d. 1264), ascribed to *Giov. di Balduccio,* with six sarcophagi in the same manner. On the walls are detached frescoes from the Campanile (13C Lombard school).

The church of **San Simpliciano** (Pl. 6; being restored), to the W., dedicated to the successor of St Ambrose in the episcopal chair, was probably founded by St Ambrose himself in the 4C and, despite the alterations of the 12C, stands, save for the façade and the apse, largely in its original form. Eighteen huge window embrasures have been revealed since 1945. The interior contains the Coronation of the Virgin, a fine apse-fresco by Bergognone, masked by the towering altar.—In the area farther N. (tram 4) is the *Cimitero Monumentale* (Pl. 2), with a central pantheon, or 'famedio', containing the tombs of Manzoni and Cattaneo.

From San Marco Via Fatebenefratelli leads to the *Archi di Porta Nuova,* a gate reconstructed in 1171, with sculptures by a follower of Giov. di Balduccio (14C). From here Via Manzoni leads back to the centre and Via Filippo Turati and Via Vittor Pisani to the station, through a regularly built part of the town with several skyscrapers, among which the Pirelli building (34 stories; over 122 m high) stands out for its clean lines.—From P.za Cavour, outside the gate, with a monument to Cavour by Tabacchi (1865), is the entrance to the GIARDINI PUBBLICI (Pl. 8), notable for their fine trees.

The gardens contain monuments to distinguished citizens, a small *Zoo,* and, on the farther side, a *Planetarium.* Nearby, facing Corso Venezia, is the *Natural History Museum* (Pl. 8; adm. 9.30-12.30, 14 or 14.30-17 or 17.30; exc. Mon.)—In Via Palestro, S. of the Park, is the 18C VILLA REALE, once occupied by the regent Eugène Beauharnais and by Marshal Radetzky, who died there in 1858. It now contains an important **Gallery of Modern Art** (adm. 9.30-12, 14.30-17.30 exc. Tues) with Lombard paintings of 19C and 20C; and (2nd floor) the Carlo Grassi bequest of 19C French and 18C Italian works. Its masterpieces were twice stolen in 1975, but the paintings have now been recovered. They include works by *Corot, Gauguin, Van Gogh, Bonnard, Boudin, Cezanne, Millet, Renoir, Sisley; De Nittis, Fattori, Signorini, Segantini, Balla,* and *Boccioni.* A pavilion displays contemporary works as well as temporary exhibitions.

From the Giardini Via Marina leads S.W. to *Palazzo del Senato,* now the *State Archives* (Pl. 8), a fine Baroque building by Mangone and Richini, originally occupied by the Collegio Elvetico, for Italian-speaking Swiss seminarists.—Opposite, Via Sant'Andrea leads back

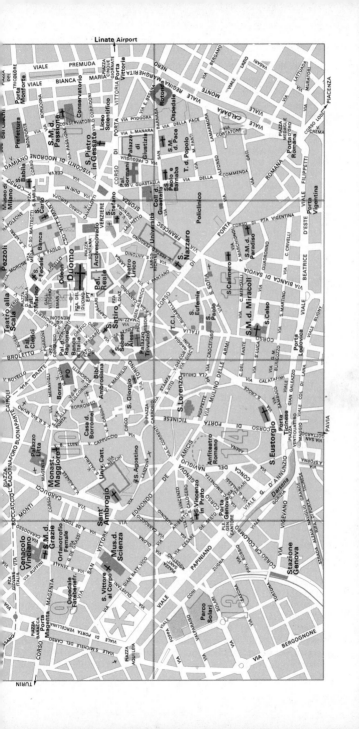

towards the centre. At No. 6 in this street the 18C *Palazzo Morando* houses two interesting collections (both open daily exc. Mon, 9.30-12.30, 14.30-17.30).

On the upper floor is the **Museo di Milano,** with a sequence of paintings, drawings, prints, etc., depicting the changing face of Milan from the mid-16C onwards. On the ground floor is the **Museo di Storia Contemporanea,** a collection regarding especially the two World Wars.

Via Sant'Andrea ends in Via Monte Napoleone, with its fashionable shops, which leads (r.) to Via Manzoni.

CORSO VITTORIO EMANUELE (Pl. 11), with its hotels, theatres, and shopping arcades, leads N.E. from behind the Duomo through a newly built area. On the left is the classic portico of the round church of *San Carlo* (1832-47), and on the right, at the beginning of CORSO VENEZIA, is *San Babila* (Pl. 12), a much-restored 12C church. At No. 11 Corso Venezia is the monumental gateway of the former *Seminary* (1564), with huge caryatids; opposite is *Casa Fontana,* now *Silvestri* (No. 10), with interesting terracotta work of c. 1475. The Corso, with fine mansions of the 18-19C, goes on to the Giardini Pubblici, the Piazzale Oberdan, and the modern area E. of the station.

From San Babila (see above) Corso Monforte continues E. to the *Prefettura,* and Via Conservatorio leads r. to reach the church of **Santa Maria delle Passione** (Pl. 12), founded c. 1485, with an octagonal dome by Crist. Solari (1511-30), and a Baroque front by Rusnati (1692-1729).

In the S. transept is a Descent from the Cross, by *Luini;* just to the E. is the monument of Abp. Daniele Birago, founder of the church, by *And. Fusina* (1495). The N. transept contains a Last Supper by *Gaud. Ferrari.* The frescoes in the sacristy are by *Bergognone* (c. 1505).

Entered from Via Chiossetto, a turning off Via Corridoni, farther S., is **San Pietro in Gessate** (Pl. 12), a Gothic church built c. 1475. In the S. aisle is a detached fresco of the funeral of St Martin, by *Bergognone.* The CAPPELLA GRIFI (N. transept) has remains of frescoes of the Story of St Ambrose, by *Butinone* and *Zenale* (1490). The N. aisle also has fragments of 15C frescoes.

Opposite San Pietro, in the Corso di Porta Vittoria, is the huge *Palazzo di Giustizia* (1932-40).—At the E. end of the Corso is the *Monument of the Cinque Giornate,* by Gius. Grandi (1883-91), covering the remains of those who fell during the 'Five Days' of March 1848, and a little to the S. of that is the curious 17C *Rotonda* (Pl. 16), the old mortuary of the Ospedale Maggiore popularly known as *Foppone,* now a children's garden.

IV   SOUTHERN MILAN

One of the busiest thoroughfares of southern Milan is CORSO ITALIA (Pl. 15), prolonging Via Mazzini beyond P.za Missori. Amongst modern buildings to the left, the ruined apse and crypt of the long-lost church of *San Giovanni in Conca* have been revealed (Via Albricci). On the right, farther on, is the building of the *Touring Club Italiano,* with a statue of the founder, L. V. Bertarelli (1927). On the left are the churches of *Sant'Eufemia,* rebuilt in a Lombard Gothic style in 1870, and *San Paolo Converso* (1549-80), the latter an attractive building containing pictures by Giul. and Ant. Campi. Farther S. stands *Santa Maria presso San Celso** (Pl. 15), a church begun by Dolcebuono in 1490 with a plain façade by Alessi and Martino Bassi (1570-72). The fine atrium is by Cesare Cesariano.

In the dark Interior the pictures are difficult to see. At the end of the S. aisle is a *Holy Family, by *Paris Bordone* (light on left); on the dome-piers are statues of the Virgin and St John the Evangelist, by *Ann. Fontana,* and of Elijah and St John the Baptist, by *Stoldo Lorenzi.* The inlaid choir-stalls, by *Alessi,* are beautiful. In the ambulatory are a Baptism of Christ (5th chapel), by *G. Ferrari,* and the Conversion of St Paul (9th chapel), by *Moretto.* In the W. chapel of the N. aisle is Christ in the Manger, by *Bergognone,* and (next chapel), a fresco of the Madonna and Saints dating from the early 15C. In the S. aisle is the entrance to the Romanesque church of **San Celso** (10C), with a façade reconstructed in 1851-54 and a graceful campanile. In the well-restored interior are fine capitals and a 14C fresco of the Madonna.

From Porta Lodovica, at the end of Corso Italia, Viale Gian Galeazzo leads W. to *Porta Ticinese* (Pl. 14), an Ionic gateway by Cagnola (1815), to the N.E. of which is the church of *Sant'Eustorgio* (Pl. 14), as interesting as Sant'Ambrogio and more attractive in its variety. It was well restored in 1958-59.

The 11C church was rebuilt save for the apse in the 12-13C, and the façade reconstructed in 1863-65. The three 15C chapels on the S. side, the apse, the slender campanile (1297-1309), and the graceful Portinari chapel are well seen from the outside. To the left of the façade is a 16C open-air pulpit.

The long and low INTERIOR, with aisles and apse, is typical of the Lombard basilicas, but an important series of chapels was added on the S. side in the 15C. The 1st chapel (with good sculptural detail) contains the tomb of Giac. Brivio, by *Tom. Cazzaniga* and *Bened. Briosco* (1486); in the 2nd is the tomb of Pietro Torelli (d. 1416); 4th chap., Tomb of Stef. Visconti (d. 1327), probably by *Giov. di Balduccio,* fresco fragments, and a 15C painted Crucifix; 6th chap., Tomb of Uberto Visconti (14C). In the S. transept is the CHAPEL OF THE MAGI, where the relics of the Magi were preserved until their transfer to Cologne in 1164 (some were returned to Milan in 1903). It contains a huge Roman sarcophagus that held the relics, and on the altar are reliefs of 1347. On the high altar also are 14C reliefs.—Entered from the Confessio, with nine slender monolithic columns, beneath the raised apse is the *CAPPELLA PORTINARI (1462-68), a gem of the Renaissance, built for Pigello Portinari and dedicated to St Peter Martyr. In the drum of the dome is a graceful choir of angels with festoons, in coloured stucco. The frescoed scenes of the life of St Peter Martyr are by *Vincenzo Foppa* (1466-68). In the centre is the *Tomb, borne by eight Virtues, of St Peter Martyr (Pietro da Verona, the inquisitor, murdered in 1252), by *Giov. di Balduccio* (1339).

Corso di Porta Ticinese leads N. past the arches of the ancient *Porta Ticinese* (c. 1330; with a tabernacle by Balduccio), and 16 Corinthian columns (*Colonne di San Lorenzo*), the remains of a porticus erected in the 4C, restored in the Middle Ages and again in 1954-5. On the right is **San Lorenzo Maggiore** (Pl. 14), a church founded in the 4C. It was rebuilt after the collapse of the vault in 1103 and again in 1574-88 by Martino Bassi (who, however, preserved the original octagonal form and much of the original masonry) and has four heavy square towers. The façade dates from 1894.

The spacious domed INTERIOR is surrounded by an ambulatory beneath a gallery. In the chapel of Sant'Aquilino (opening off the S. side; apply to the sacristan) the lower part dates from the 5C, the upper part from the 11-12C, and the door-jambs have been brought from a Roman building. It contains an early Christian sarcophagus and remarkable survivals of 5C mosaics, and covers an undercroft which was part of a Roman bath-house.

Corso di Porta Ticinese ends at the *Carrobbio* (Pl. 10), the Roman and early medieval centre of Milan. Via Torino continues N.E. past (l.) *San Giorgio al Palazzo* (Pl. 10), a church with a chapel decorated by Luini, and farther on the round church of *San Sebastiano* (1577), now a war memorial chapel.

Via Lupetta, opposite the last, leads to *Sant'Alessandro* (Pl. 11), with a good Baroque interior, and the 17C *Palazzo Trivulzio*, which contains in its courtyard a doorway from a destroyed mansion by Bramante.

The *British Cemetery* for the Second World War is reached by following Via Novara (beyond Pl. 9) for 7 km. then turning right (Via Cascina Bellaria) for the suburban village of *Trenno* (Metropolitana 1 to P.za De Angeli, then bus 72 towards Trenno; 25 min. in all).

Also reached by Via Novara (bus 72) or (more directly) by Via Monte Rosa (Metropolitana 1 to Piazzale Lotto) is the sports area of SAN SIRO. Here is the hippodrome and the controversial *Palasport* Stadium opened in 1976 and capable of holding 14,500 spectators.

V EXCURSIONS FROM MILAN

The abbey of CHIARAVALLE, rather unattractively situated c. 9 km. S. of Milan is reached either by tramway No. 13 to Piazzale Corvetto, then bus 77 to within 3 min. walk of the abbey; or from Rogoredo station on the Pavia or Lodi railway (20 min. walk alongside the Pavia line).

The Cistercian **Abbazia di Chiaravalle** was founded by St Bernard in 1135 and named after his own abbey of Clairvaux. The brick church (now a parish church), consecrated in 1221, has an imposing tower, of which the lower portion is original, while the upper tiers were added in the 14C. The interior was extensively altered in the 17C, but preserves inside the lantern some frescoes by French painters of the 13-14C; the other frescoes are the work of the *Fiammenghini* (1614), except that at the top of the night-stairs (S. transept), which is by *Luini* (1512). The carved stalls in the nave are by *Garavaglia* (1645). The sacristan shows the *Cemetery*, which contains tombs of the 13C; the remains of the *Chapter House*, with interesting graffiti; and two walks of the 13C *Cloister*.

The CERTOSA DI PAVIA stands just off the Milan-Pavia road at the limit of the park that, in the middle ages, extended N. from the Castello Visconteo (p. 174). It is most easily visited from Pavia (8 km.; bus or train in 10 min.), but is conveniently reached from Milan by coach excursion (leaving from P.za Castello at 14.30 on Sat & fest.; Jan-March, and Oct-Dec, fest. only) in 45 min. (return fare includes guide and entrance fee); or by road to (25 km.) *Torre del Mangano*, whence a turning on the left leads in 1 km. to the Certosa. On Sunday it is a popular excursion and tends to be crowded.

The ***Certosa di Pavia**, one of the famous buildings of Italy, is a Carthusian monastery founded by Gian Galeazzo Visconti in 1396 as a family mausoleum. The building was entrusted to the Campionese masons of Milan cathedral and the builders of the castle of Pavia. The monastery proper was finished in 1452, the church in 1472, under the Sforzas, with the exception of the façade which dates from the 16C. The Certosa is open from 9 to 16.30 or 18.30 (closed on major national holidays); visitors are conducted in parties.

From the entrance, facing W., a vestibule, with frescoed saints by *Luini,* leads through to the great garden-court in front of the church. On the left are the old pharmacy and food and wine stores; on the right the prior's quarters and the so-called *Palazzo Ducale,* rebuilt in the Baroque style by Richini to house distinguished visitors.

The sculptural and polychrome marble decoration of the ***West Front** of the church, of almost superabundant richness, marks the height of the artistic achievement of the Quattrocento in Lombardy; it was begun in 1473 and worked upon up to 1499 by *Crist.* and *Ant. Mantegazza* and *Giov. Ant. Amadeo,* then in the 16C *Cristoforo Lombardo* continued the upper part in simplified form, though it was never completed. On the lowest order of the façade are medallions of Roman emperors; above, statues and reliefs of Prophets, Apostles, and Saints, by the

Mantegazza; and Scenes from the Life of Christ by *Amadeo.* The *GREAT PORTAL was probably designed by *Gian. Crist. Romano* and executed by *Bened. Briosco,* the sculptor also of the bas-reliefs representing the Life of the Virgin and of four large reliefs: the Foundation of the Carthusian Order, 1084; Laying the First Stone of the Certosa, 27 Aug, 1396; Translation to the Certosa of the body of Gian Galeazzo, 1 March, 1474; Consecration of the Church, 3 May, 1497. On each side are two very rich *Windows, by Amadeo. The upper part, by *Crist, Lombardo* (1540-60), is decorated with 70 statues of the 16C by Lombard masters. The rest of the exterior is best seen from the N.E.

The *Interior is purely Gothic in plan, but Renaissance decorative motives appear towards the E. end; the chapels opening off the aisle were expensively redecorated and provided with notable Baroque grilles in the 17-18C, and only traces remain of the original frescoes and glass. NORTH AISLE. 1st chapel: Lavabo by the *Mantegazza* (1470).—2nd chap.: Altarpiece by *Perugino* (1499) of which only the panel representing God the Father is original.—4th chap.: Massacre of the Innocents, by *Dionigi Bussola,* the best of the Baroque altar-reliefs.— 6th chap.: *St Ambrose and four saints by *Bergognone* (1492).—NORTH TRANSEPT. In the centre, *Tomb statues of Lodovico il Moro and Beatrice d'Este, by *Crist. Solari* (1497), brought from S. Maria delle Grazie in Milan in 1564. The frescoes include Ecce Homo (over the small W. door) and Coronation of the Virgin (N. apse), by *Bergognone;* and two *Angels by *Bramante,* on either side of the window, above.—The OLD SACRISTY is entered through a doorway (by *Amadeo*) with medallion-portraits of the Dukes of Milan: it contains good 17C presses and a remarkable ivory *Altarpiece, with nearly 100 figures, after *Baldas. degli Embriachi* (early 15C); the vault is notable.

The CHOIR contains carved and inlaid *Stalls (1498), frescoes by *Dan. Crespi* (1629), and a sumptuous late 16C altar.—Another door by *Amadeo,* with medallions of the Duchesses of Milan, admits to the LAVATORIUM. Within is a finely-carved lavabo by *Alberto Maffiolo* of Carrara; on the left, *Madonna, a charming fresco by *Luini.*—SOUTH TRANSEPT: *Tomb of Gian Galeazzo Visconti, by *Gian Crist. Romano* (1493-97; the Madonna is by *Bened. Briosco,* the sarcophagus by *Galeazzo Alessi,* the figures of Fame and Victory by *Bern. da Novate;* two *Candelabra by *Fontana.* The fresco by *Bergognone,* above, depicts Gian Galeazzo, with his children, presenting a model of the church to the Virgin; higher up, two Angels by *Bramante.* Over the altar, a Virgin with St Charles and St Bruno, by *G. B. Crespi.* The doorway into the little cloister is by the *Mantegazza.*—NEW SACRISTY: Altarpiece, the Assumption, by *And. Solari,* completed by *Bern. Campi;* the 16C illuminated choir-books are notable. The CHAPTER HOUSE is entered through a charming little court, perhaps the work of *Bramante.* Its rooms contain reliefs by the *Mantegazza* and after *Amadeo.*—The pretty *LITTLE CLOISTER, with its garden, has terracotta decorations in the Cremonese manner, by *Rinaldo De Stauris* (1465).—The GREAT CLOISTER, with 122 arches, also has terracotta decoration by *De Stauris* (1478). On three sides are 24 cells, each with a decorative doorway, two rooms, and a little garden below, and a bedroom and loggia above.— The REFECTORY has ceiling frescoes by *Ambr.* and *Bern. Bergognone,* a reader's pulpit, and a little fresco of the Madonna by the *Zavattari* (1450). From the little cloister the church can be re-entered by a beautiful little *Door adorned with a Madonna by *Amadeo* (1466).— SOUTH AISLE: over the door from the transept, Madonna, by

Bergognone.—3rd chap.: *Bergognone,* *St Syrus, first bishop of Pavia, and other saints; unrestored ceiling-frescoes by *Iac. de' Mottis* (1491).—4th chap.: *Bergognone,* Crucifixion.—6th chap.: Risen Christ and saints, by *Macrino d'Alba* (signed; 1496), and Evangelists, by *Bergognone.*—7th chap.: good Baroque work by *C. Procaccini;* lavabo by the *Mantegazza.*

MONZA, 15½ km. N.E. of Milan, is best reached by BUS from Via Jacini near Nord station or P.za Quattro Novembre, beside the Central sta., in 20 min.; the road (leaving Milan by Viale Sarca, entirely built up, traverses the industrial suburb of *Sesto San Giovanni* (97,700 inhab.). Railway from Porta Garibaldi station, frequent services in 10-15 min.

Monza, nowadays a busy but agreeable industrial community (119,500 inhab.), manufacturing felt hats and cheap carpets, and internationally known to motor-racing enthusiasts, is a Lombard city of great age with a cathedral many centuries older than that of Milan.

The approach from Milan reaches Largo Mazzini just beyond the station. Via Italia leads past the church of *Santa Maria in Strada* (1357), with a terracotta front. On the left are a huge war memorial and the *Municipio.* In P.za Roma at the end is the *Arengario,* the brick town hall of 1293, with a tall battlemented tower and a balcony for public announcements. An *Archæological Museum* in the Salone (used also for exhibitions) is open weekdays 15-20 (fest. 10-13, 15-20; closed Mon). Via Napoleone leads back (r.) to the CATHEDRAL a 13-14C building on the site of a church founded by Theodolinda, queen of Lombardy, c. 595. The fine parti-coloured marble *Façade (in poor repair) by *Matt. da Campione* (1390-96; restored), has a bold doorway and rose-window, and is flanked by a brick campanile (1606). The interior also contains work by *Matteo,* including the organ gallery in the nave and the relief of an imperial coronation in the S. transept. The chapel on the left of the high-altar contains the plain tomb of Theodolinda and is decorated with frescoes (suffering from humidity) by the *Zavattari* (1444) depicting the story of her life. Enclosed in the altar is the famous *Iron Crown of Lombardy (shown with the contents of the Treasury, see below) used at the coronation of the Holy Roman Emperors since 1311, and containing a strip of iron said to have been hammered from one of the nails used at the Crucifixion (comp. Meredith's 'Song of Theodolinda'). The last emperors crowned with it were Charles V (at Bologna), Napoleon and Ferdinand I (at Milan).

The **Museo Serpero** (9-11.30, 14.30-17 exc. Mon; fest. 10-11.30, 15-16.30) houses the rich *Treasury.* Here are the personal relics of Theodolinda, including her silver-gilt **Hen and Chickens,* supposed to represent Lombardy and its seven provinces, her votive cross and crown, and a book-cover with a dedicatory inscription; also 6-7C silk embroideries; a 9C ivory diptych with St Gregory and David; and a processional cross given to Theodolinda by St Gregory (altered in the 15C and 17C).—Below the cathedral to the left is a brick gate-tower of its precinct.

Beyond the Arengario Via Carlo Alberto leads to P.za Citterio, beyond which Viale Regina Margherita leads to the decayed *Villa Reale* (by Piermarini, 1777-80), a residence presented by the King to the State in 1919, and now housing a small Civic Art Gallery of 19C paintings (April-Oct, 9-17.30 exc. Mon). In its splendid *Park* farther on, on the right, are the famous *Autodromo* (adm. 8-19), the motor race-track of Milan (10 km.), the horse race-course of Mirabello, and an 18-hole golf course. From behind the Villa an avenue leads to the *Cappella Espiatoria* (Expiatory Chapel), erected by Victor Emmanuel III on the spot where his father Humbert was assassinated on 29 July, 1900.—*Desio,* 7 km. N.W. of Monza, was the birthplace of Achille Ratti (1857-1939), afterwards Pope Pius XI.

15   MILAN TO TIRANO AND BORMIO

ROAD, 203 km. Superstrada to (56 km.) **Lecco,** where it joins N 36 (comp. below). 78 km. **Varenna.**—97 km. **Cólico.** N 38.—138 km. **Sondrio.**—155 km. *Tresenda.*—165 km. **Tirano.**—179 km. *Grosio.*—203 km. **Bormio.**—AUTOPULL-MAN to *Bormio Bagni* in 4¾ hrs daily; in summer also to *Bormio* (4½ hrs) and on viâ the *Stelvio Pass* to *Bolzano* (11 hrs).

RAILWAY TO SONDRIO (From Centrale or Porta Garibaldi station), 130 km. in 2¼-4 hrs. Connecting light railway or bus thence in ½ hr to *Tirano* and bus only (1¼ hr) *Bormio.*

The old road from Milan (N 36; 3 km. shorter) passes through (15 km.) *Monza* (see above) and (26 km.) *Usmate,* descending into the Adda Valley to skirt *Lago di Garlate.*

The superstrada crosses over the A 4 motorway and passes to the W. of Monza, through the low hills of the Brianza (p. 135), avoiding the small towns with which the region is dotted.—27 km. *Carate Brianza* (2 km. E.), a textile town visited for the remarkable *Church and baptistery at *Agliate,* on the opposite bank of the Lembro. Traditionally thought to have been founded in 881 by Ansperto, Bp of Milan, it probably dates from the 10-11C. The road passes between Lago di Pusiano and Lago di Annone to join the road from Como (comp. p. 134).—56 km. **Lecco** (Rte 13).—N 36 now skirts the whole E. side of Lake Como; the first 6 km., as far as Abbadia, have been made into dual carriageway, part of a controversial scheme to make the road into a superstrada as far as Cólico. The work, begun in 1962, has encountered serious difficulties (including several landslides with fatal accidents) as well as local opposition, and may finally be abandoned. The places along the lakeside are described in detail in Rte 13.—The *Views of the lake on the left are delightful.—66 km. *Mandello del Lário* commands a view of the Grigne up the Meria valley on the right.—76 km. *Fiumelatte,* with a curious periodic waterfall (on the right).—The landscape becomes less austere on the approach to (78 km.) *Varenna.* The road traverses several tunnels.—82 km. *Bellano.*—Beyond (90 km.) *Dorio* the road skirts the small bay of Piona, and at (97 km.) **Cólico** (Rte 13) touches the shore of the Lake of Como for the last time.

FROM CÓLICO TO CHIAVENNA (Splügen and Maloja Passes) N 36, 27 km.; railway in ½ hr following a similar course to the road. This route diverges to the left after 3½ km. from the Tirano road to cross the Adda and the partly marshy *Piano di Spagna.* Just before the river on the left can be seen the ruins of the *Forte di Fuentes,* built by the Spaniards in 1603 and destroyed in 1798 by the French. The road now skirts the *Lago di Mezzola,* separated from the Lake of Como by the silt brought down by the Adda.—13 km. *Novate Mezzola.* On the left is the little *Pozzo di Riva,* an expansion of the Mera, beyond which the road enters the *Piano di Chiavenna. Samólaco* to the left indicates by its name ('summus lacus') the point to which the Lake of Como extended in Roman times. The valley becomes wilder and is confined by black and tawny rocks. Ahead on the right appears the *Pizzo Stella* (3162 m).—27 km. **Chiavenna** (326 m), the Roman *Clavenna,* perhaps so named because it was the key (clavis) of the Splügen, Septimber, and Julier passes, is a charmingly situated town (7500 inhab.) in the fertile valley of the Mera. Above the turreted *Palazzo Balbiani* rises the *Paradiso* (view), a rock on the slopes of which are botanic gardens, and an archæological collection. The church of *San Lorenzo* dates from the 16C, and has a massive detached campanile. The octagonal baptistery contains a font of 1156, and in the treasury is a gold Pax of 12C German work.

The MALOJA ROAD (bus to St Moritz) leads E., ascending the VAL BREGAGLIA, the fertile upper valley of the Mera, to cross the frontier well before the pass. Many traces of a Roman road can be seen from the parallel mule-track.

The hamlets form part of the commune of *Piuro,* a once thriving town that was overwhelmed by a landslide in 1618. To the left at (5 km.) *Santa Croce* can be seen its old campanile.—7½ km. *Villa di Chiavenna* is the last Italian village. The Italian and Swiss custom-houses are passed before (10 km.) *Castasegna* (681 m), the first Swiss village. Thence the road (N 3) continues by a series of zigzags over (32 km.) the **Maloja Pass** (1817 m) into the Upper Engadine and (49 km.) St Moritz.

The SPLÜGEN ROAD from Chiavenna (N 36; coach daily in summer to Splügen in 3 hrs) is remarkable for its daring hairpin bends and long snow-galleries.—At (4 km.) *San Giacomo* (571 m) a bold bridge crosses over an effluent of the Liro.— Beyond (7½ km.) *Gallivaggio,* with its tall white campanile against a background of chestnut woods and precipices, the barren valley is strewn with fallen reddish rocks. The first tunnel emerges at (13 km.) **Campodolcino** (1103 m), a summer and winter resort in a small grassy plain. A cableway mounts to the snow-fields of *Motta* (1725 m), whence Madésimo (see below) is an hour's walk. Motta is connected by mule track with the *Rifugio Chiavenna* (2½ hrs) and, viâ the *Passo d'Angeloga* (2391 m), with the lonely *Val di Lei* (c. 4 hrs), the only portion of Italian territory of which the waters flow into the Rhine.—Surmounting ten steep bends and a tunnel the road passes a grand waterfall (best view from a projecting terrace) and crosses the *Val Scalcoggia* into (17½ km.) *Pianazzo* (1401 m). In this sunless valley (2 km. r.; bus from Chiavenna in 1½ hr) lies **Madésimo** (1533 m), a resort offering fine ascents in summer of the frontier peaks (*Pizzo d'Émet,* 3211 m; *Pizzo Spadolazzo,* 2948 m) and extensive snow-fields on the *Pizzo Groppera* (2948 m; cable railway) in winter (ski and sledge lifts; ski-school; skating rink).

The old road diverges left in the Gola del Cardinello, abandoned in 1834 on account of its dangerous position, and climbs through long snow galleries.— 21 km. The *Cantoniera di Teggiate* provides a good sight of the Liro ravine, while from (24 km.) *Stuetta* there is a grand view (l.) of the Pizzo Ferrè (with its fine glacier) and the Cima di Baldiscio.—28 km. *Montespluga* (1905 m) is situated in a desolate basin filled by a hydro-electric storage reservoir.—30 km. The **Splügen Pass** (*Passo Spluga;* 3274 m) lies on the narrow frontier-ridge (customs posts) between the mighty Pizzo Tambò (W.; 3274 m) and the Surettahorn (E.). The pass was known to the Romans, and the route from Clavenna (Chiavenna) to Curia (Coire) is mentioned in the Antonine itinerary. The most famous crossing of the pass, however, was that of Marshal Macdonald in 1800, when despite stormy weather and bad snow conditions he succeeded in conveying an army of infantry, cavalry, and artillery from Splügen to Chiavenna between 26 Nov and 6 Dec to guard the left flank of Napoleon's Army of Italy, losing 100 men and over 100 horses in the snow. The pass is usually obstructed in Nov-May.—A series of steep zigzags leads down to (39 km.) *Splügen.*

The Tirano road from Colico keeps close to the railway, ascending the Valtellina (see below), the upper vale of the Adda.—104 km. *Delebio* is a starting point for the ascent of *Monte Legnone* (2610 m) to the S.— 113 km. **Morbegno** (255 m) is a pleasant little town (9400 inhab.) at the lower end of the Bitto forge, just S. of the Adda. The church of San Lorenzo, E. of the town, was begun in 1418.

A bus climbs the *Valle del Bitto* viâ *Pedesina* to (17 km.) *Gerola Alta,* with skiing facilities. At the end of the road (22 km.) a chair lift ascends to Monte Ponterànica (1824 m). At the head of the W. arm of the valley rises the *Pizzo dei Tre Signori* (2554 m) so called from its position on the boundaries of the old lordships of Milan, Venice, and the Grisons.—The *Passo di San Marco* (1986 m; mule track) leads from the head of the left branch of the valley to Mezzoldo in the Valle Brembana (7 hrs; p. 180).

The road crosses the Adda to reach the station of (120 km.) *Ardenno-Masino.*

The stern VAL MÁSINO, diverging N., ascends to (17 km.) the Bagni del Másino (bus from Morbegno in 60 min.).—9 km. *Cataéggio* (791 m). The road winds upwards amid colossal boulders, one of which, the Sasso Remenno, is crowned by a chapel.—13 km. *San Martino* (926 m) lies at the junction of the Valle di Mello (r.) with the main valley. It is the best base for the ascent of ***Monte della Disgrazia** (3678 m; 10 hrs; guide essential), accomplished viâ (5 hrs) the *Rifugio Cesare Ponti* (2557 m).—The *Passo di San Martino* or *di Mello* (2991 m) at the head of the valley leads over to (12 hrs) *Chiareggio* above Chiesa (see below). The Valle di Zocca, joining the Valle di Mello from the N., leads up to the *Rifugio Allievi* (2280 m) from which the most attractive ascent is that of (4 hrs) the *Cima di Castello* (3400 m; view).

To the left of S. Martino in the Valle dei Bagni are (14 km.) the **Bagni del Másino** (1171 m), a quiet therapeutic establishment in a sheltered site with baths and hotel. From here the Valle Porcellizzo may be ascended to (4½ hrs) the *Rifugio Gianetti* (2533 m) whence the *Pizzo Cengalo* (3374 m) may be climbed in 4 hrs. Lower climbs may be made from the *Rifugio Omio*, 2 hrs W. of Bagni.

138 km. Sondrio the capital (23,400 inhab.) of the Valtellina, stands at the mouth of the Mállero, here canalized to control its floods. The *Museo Valtellinese di Storia e Arte* in Palazzo Quadrio is open daily, exc. Mon, Sat & Sun, 14.30-18.

The **Valtellina** or *Veltlin,* the upper valley of the Adda, is famous for the production of wines (Grumello, Sassella, etc). The vines on the steep hillsides are trained to grow on frames. The valley has had a chequered history, but has a high cultural tradition. In the 14C it passed into the power of Milan, but in 1512 it was united to the Grisons. The Reformation took a firm hold here, and in 1620, at the instigation of the Spanish governor of Milan, the Catholic inhabitants of the valley ruthlessly massacred the Protestants on the day of the Holy Butchery (Il Sacro Macello; 19 July). Twenty years of warfare followed, but in 1639 the valley was regained by the Grisons, who held it until Napoleon's partition of 1797, since when it has followed the fortunes of Lombardy.

FROM SONDRIO TO THE VAL MALENCO (frequent buses).—The road ascends the Mállero.—10 km. *Torre Santa Maria* (796 m), at the mouth of the picturesque Torreggio torrent.—14 km. **Chiesa** (1000 m) lies at the junction of the Val Malenco and the Val Lanterna, dominated on the W. by Monte della Disgrazia (see above; usually ascended from the other side) and on the N. by the snowy mass of the Bernina. Above to the N.W. is *Prímolo;* high up on the other side of the valley is *Caspoggio* (1150 m), now nearly as important as a ski-ing resort.—Some buses continue to (26 km.) *Chiareggio* a climbing centre at the head of the Val Malenco, whence a track goes over the *Passo del Muretto* (2562 m; frontier-post) to Maloja. Others take the Val Lanterna, viâ *Lanzada,* to *Franscia* (11 km.). The *Pizzo Scalino* (3339 m) to the E., affording a fine view of the Bernina range, may be ascended hence in c. 6 hrs. The central massif of the Bernina, rising to 4068 m, marks the frontier. Ascents (mostly difficult) are made from the *Rifugio Marinelli* (2804 m), above the head of the Scerscen valley, whence in summer the frontier may be passed, over the Scerscen glacier, to (10 hrs) Sils.—The *Lago del Palù* (1925 m) at the foot of *Monte Nero* (2912 m) is easily reached by cable-car from Chiesa. Another cableway ascends Monte Motta (2336 m). From Caspóggio a chair-lift climbs part way (1720 m) up Monte Palino (2686 m).

To the S. of Sondrio rises the *Corno Stella* (2620 m) a famous view-point, best ascended from Carona in the Valle Brembana (Rte 17).

The large building on the left above (144 km.) *Tresivio* is a sanatorium.—146 km. *Ponte in Valtellina.* The town, 2½ km. N., at the foot of the Val Fontana, has a 14-16C church, with a fresco by Luini and a bronze ciborium of 1578. A monument commemorates the astronomer Giuseppe Piazzi (1746-1826), a native of the town and discoverer of the first àsteroid.—At (154 km.) *Tresenda* the important road over the Passo dell'Aprica ascends on the right.

On the left is **Teglio** (776 m), once the principal place in the valley to which it gave its name (Val-Teglina). The *Palazzo Besta* (1539) and the church of *Santa Eufemia* (late 15C) are interesting. The chapel of *San Pietro* has an 11C campanile.

FROM TRESENDA TO ÉDOLO, 29 km. bus 4 times daily (coming from Tirano) in 1½ hr. The steep ascent makes a long loop to the N.E., with fine views of the Valtellina.—Just beyond (12 km.) the *Passo dell'Aprica* (1181 m) is the centre of **Aprica,** a scattered summer and winter resort (chair-lifts, cableways, ski-lifts, skating, covered swimming pool). The road descends viâ (21 km.) *Corteno Golgi* to (29 km.) *Édolo,* see Rte 19.

165 km. Tirano (430 m), with 8760 inhab., is the terminus of the

Bernina and Valtellina railways, and a starting-point for the ascent of the Stelvio Pass. The old town, on the left bank of the Adda, contains historic mansions of the Visconti, Pallavicini, and Salis families. Tirano was one of the chief sufferers in the massacre in the Valtellina in 1620.— About 1 km. N. (bus every ½ hr) is the pilgrimage church of *Madonna di Tirano,* begun in 1505, in the style of Bramante, with a fine doorway by Scala of Carona. The richly stuccoed interior has a large organ of 1617. Outside is a painted fountain of 1780.

The BERNINA ROAD AND RAILWAY from Tirano to St Moritz cross the frontier into Switzerland at (3 km.) *Campocologno,* with electric works that supply the Bernina Railway; but Italian is the language spoken all the way up to the Bernina Pass.—At (17 km.) *Poschiavo* (1013 m) the chief place in the valley, are many old houses. Above it the road and railway separate, the former climbing to (37½ km.) the **Bernina Pass** (2330 m), which the latter avoids by a tunnel. Before the summit a road branches (r.) to cross back into Italy at the *Furcola di Livigno* (2328 m); Livigno, 17 km., see p. 171. Just beyond the pass is the *Bernina Hospice* (2304 m) whence the descent leads viâ (50 km.) *Pontresina* to (58 km.) *St Moritz.*

Between Tirano and Bormio the Stelvio road crosses the Adda four times. Near (168 km.) *Sernio* a landslip from Monte Masuccio (2816 m) in 1807 fell into the Adda and formed a lake extending to (172 km.) *Tovo di Sant'Agata.*—174 km. *Mazzo di Valtellina* (560 m). The church of Santo Stefano, with a portal carved by Bernardino Rodari (1508), and the Casa Lavizzari contain paintings by Valorsa (see below).—At (176 km.) *Grosotto* (615 m), with its 15C houses, is the electric power station of the city of Milan. The Santuario della Madonna, erected in the 17C as a thank-offering for the defeat of the Swiss Protestants in 1620, has a noteworthy choir. The road crosses the Roasco, which descends from the Val Grosina.—179 km. **Grósio** (660 m), a large village (4700 inhab.), was the birthplace of Cipriano Valorsa (fl. c. 1550), 'the Raphael of the Valtellina', whose paintings adorn nearly every church in the valley. On the left is the ruined castle of the Visconti-Venosta, a mansion belonging to whom (restored) still stands in the village with other 15-16C houses. To the left opens the *Val Grosina.*—At (184 km.) *Bolladore* (850 m), cut off from sunlight for two months in winter, can be seen above, on the left, the village of *Sóndalo,* with its large sanatorium amid pine woods.—Beyond (189 km.) *Le Prese Nuove* the road enters the defile named the Serra di Morignone.—194 km. *Sant'Antonio Morignone.*—At (197 km.) *Ponte di Cepina* (1122 m) the valley expands again and in front can be seen the windings of the road over the Stelvio.

Cepina (1139 m), on the other side of the Adda, has a curious ossuary, closed by a wrought-iron grille of local workmanship (1737).

On the approach to the plain of Bormio, the town, with its old houses and steeples, backed by a magnificent circle of mountain peaks, makes a striking picture.

203 km. **Bormio** (920 m) once the seat of a count, is an ancient town (4060 inhab.), whose many ruined towers and picturesque old houses with carved doorways and painted façades recall its once prosperous transit trade between Venice and the Grisons. Of the numerous churches, *San Vitale,* near the entrance to the town, was founded in the 12C, but the most noteworthy is the *Crocifisso,* on the S. side of the Frodolfo, which is decorated with 15C and 16C frescoes. The painting of the Crucifixion by Agost. Ferrari dates from 1476. The *Castello dei Simoni* contains a small museum.

Bormio is an attractive centre for mountain walks and well equipped for a long season of winter sports, with a ski-school and jumps, a cableway and many lifts to the main ski-fields, and a skating-rink. There is also a large covered swimming pool.

About 3 km. above Bormio on the Stelvio road are the **Bagni di Bormio**, a well-known bathing establishment with warm springs (tennis-courts, thermal swimming pool, mud baths, etc.). Some remains of the Roman baths are visible. To the E. of Bormio extend the *Val di Zebrù* and *Val Furva*. In the latter is (12 km.) **Santa Caterina** (1718 m), a quiet resort equipped for summer climbing and winter ski-ing (bus in ¾ hr). A fine road runs S. from Santa Caterina over (13 km.) the bleak *Passo de Gávia* (2621 m) to (30 km.) *Ponte di Legno* in the Val Camónica; while to the E. is the Valle del Forno, with a track leading to (3¾ hrs) the *Pizzini Refuge* (2705 m). Two hours higher up is the *Gianni Casati Refuge* (3267 m), a favourite base for ascents in the Ortler-Cevedale group, notably of *Monte Cevedale* (3780 m; 2 hrs) and the *Gran Zebrù* (3859 m; 3¼ hrs).

A remarkable road ascends the Valdidentro, W. of Bormio, and the Valle Viola Bormina with *Arnoga*, to (25 km.) the *Passo di Foscagno* (2291 m; Italian custom-house) beyond which lies the duty-free zone of the VALLE DI LIVIGNO. Watered by the Spöl (good trout fishing) and one of the few portions of Italian territory N. of the Alpine watershed, it has recently been developed as a winter sports centre (cableways, chairlifts, and ski school).—39 km. **Livigno** is a long straggling village, now a ski resort, connected bv road (excursion in summer from Bormio to St Moritz, 13 hrs) with the Bernina Hospice, and with Zernez, both in Switzerland.—From Viera, the lowest hamlet in the valley, the return to Bormio (c. 7 hrs) may be made on foot viâ the *Alpisella Pass* (2285 m), the source of the Adda, and (4 hrs) *San Giacomo di Fraele*, whence a road skirts two artificial lakes, then descends the Scale di Fraele to the Valdidentro.

For the road to the *Stelvio Pass* and *Merano*, see Rte 26.

16   MILAN TO GENOA

ROAD, N 35, 157 km. leaving Milan by the Porta Ticinese, 26 km. *Torre del Mángano*.—34 km. **Pavia**, entered by the Viale Brambilla and quitted by the Ponte Libertà.—55 km. *Castéggio*. whence to Tortona N 35 is coincident with N 10.—66 km. **Voghera**.—82 km. **Tortona**.—102 km. *Serravalle Scrívia*. Thence to (157 km.) **Genoa**, see Rte 26.

The AUTOSTRADA DEI FIORI (A 7), 143 km. leaves Milan just outside the Porta Ticinese and passes well W. of Pavia.—Beyond (71 km.) *Tortona*, it follows the Scrivia running roughly parallel to N 35 all the way.

RAILWAY, 150 km.; expresses in 1½-2¼ hrs; to *Pavia*, 39 km. in 25 min.; to *Tortona*, 82 km. in 1-1¼ hr. This route is followed by international expresses from Austria and Germany to the Italian and French rivieras.

From Milan (Porta Ticinese) the road follows the Naviglio di Pavia, a canal begun by Galeazzo Visconti, through a fertile well-watered plain, skirting (16 km.) *Binasco* with its castle.—26 km. *Torre del Mángano*. To the left is the road to the Certosa di Pavia (1¼ km.; p. 164).

34 km. **PAVIA** is an old provincial capital (87,780 inhab.) on the Ticino, noted for its university and fine medieval churches. It still preserves a number of feudal tower houses. Its development as an important industrial and agricultural centre has led to indiscriminate new building outside the limits of the historical centre.

Post Office. P.za Leonardo da Vinci.—**E.P.T.** 1 Corso Garibaldi.—*Theatre.* Fraschini, Strada Nuova.

Bus Station, 17 Viale Matteotti; services to *Lodi*, to *Milan*, etc.

History. Originating in the Roman *Ticinum* about 220 B.C., Pavia became capital of the Lombards in the 6C, and appears under the name *Papia* in the 7C. In the church of San Michele were crowned Charlemagne (774), Berengar, the first king of Italy (888), Berengar II (950), and Frederick Barbarossa (1155). The commune took the Ghibelline side against Milan and Lodi, and afterwards passed to the Counts of Monferrato and, from 1359 onwards, to the Visconti. On 24 Feb

1525, in the adjacent commune of Mirabello, was fought the *Battle of Pavia*, in which Francis I was defeated and made prisoner by Charles V. It was of this battle that Francis wrote to his mother "Madame, tout est perdu fors l'honneur". The ramparts which still surround the city are of 17C Spanish work. Pavia is the birthplace of Lanfranc (1005-89), the first archbishop of Canterbury under the Normans, of Pope John XIV (d. 984), and of Girolamo Cardano (1501-76), the physician and mathematician. The name of the P.za Petrarca recalls Petrarch's visits to his son-in-law here.

The STRADA NUOVA, the main street of Pavia, prolongs the old Milan road straight through the town to the Ticino bridge, and is crossed at right angles by the second main thoroughfare (Corso Cavour, Corso Mazzini) in true Roman style.

Off Corso Cavour opens the arcaded P.za Vittoria (l.), its market now relegated below ground to make room for parked cars. Here the *Broletto* (12C and later) has a façade of 1563. To the right is the **Cathedral,** begun in 1488 from designs by Crist. Rocchi, G. A. Amadeo, and G. G. Dolcebuono, afterwards modified by Bramante, Leonardo, and Fr. di Giorgio. The immense cupola was not added until 1884-85 and the façade was completed in 1933. The rest of the exterior remains unfinished. The imposing interior contains a Madonna and Saints by *Carlo Sacchi* (N. transept), a Madonna of the Rosary, by *Carlo Soriani* (S. transept) and a painting by G. B. Crespi on the W. wall. To the left of the church rises the *Torre Civica* (78 m), the campanile of two demolished Romanesque churches (traces of which are still visible), with a bell-chamber by Pell. Tibaldi (1583). Via dei Liguri leads S. to the 12C church of *San Teodoro* with its octagonal cupola-tower. Inside, the remarkable 15-16C frescoes include a View of Pavia (W. wall) in c. 1520, by Bern. Lanzani, showing the many towers to which it owed its name 'the city of a hundred towers', and the Life of St Theodore (Sanctuary) attrib. to Lanzani. The crypt runs crossways beneath the Sanctuary and extends beyond the walls. From here Via Porta Pertusi descends past modern buildings to the picturesque covered *Bridge,* across the Ticino.

The original bridge built in 1351-54 on Roman foundations and roofed in 1583, collapsed in 1947 as a result of bomb-damage. The present one, a few metres farther E., is on a different design, as is the chapel replacing the 18C bridge-chapel.
The 12C church of *Santa Maria in Betlem,* in the transpontine suburb, has a façade with faience plaques; the plain Romanesque interior was well restored in 1953.

Via. Sev. Capsoni leads E. from the Strada to ***San Michele,** the finest church in Pavia, consecrated in 1155, with an octagonal cupola. The elaborately ornamented front has profusely decorated triple portals and sculptured friezes (the sandstone in which they are carved has been sadly consumed). The portals of the transept and the galleried apse are also interesting. The interior is similar to that of S. Pietro in Ciel d'Oro (comp. p. 174), while the gallery above the nave recalls that of Sant'Ambrogio in Milan. There is fine sculptural detail in many parts of the interior, particularly on the *Capitals. In the crypt is the tomb of Martino Salimbeni (d. 1463), by the sch. of *Amadeo.*

Corso Garibaldi leads E. to the much altered Lombard church of *San Primo;* while to the S. (viâ Via S. Giovanni) is the *Collegio Borromeo,* founded by St Charles Borromeo in 1561 and built in 1564-92 largely by Pellegrino Tibaldi; the river façade was added in 1808-20.

Farther N. in the Strada Nuova is the **University,** the successor of a famous school of law, the ancient 'Studio' at which Lanfranc is said to

have studied. The school was made a university in 1361 by Galeazzo II
Visconti, and is now particularly renowned for its faculties of law and
medicine. The buildings were extended by Piermarini in 1771-79 to
incorporate existing work of 1533. In the left-hand court is a statue of
Volta, the most distinguished alumnus. The adjoining courts of the
former Ospedale di San Matteo (1499), to the E., now form the Collegio
Fraccaro; the chapel houses the *Archæological Museum*.

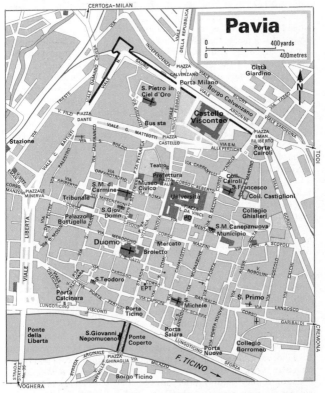

In the corner of P.za Leonardo are the *Torri,* three ancient tower-houses of the
noble families of Pavia, and beneath the square a 12C crypt (roofed over; for the
key, apply at Commune) thought to belong to the destroyed church of
Sant'Eusebio. To the N.E. in Corso Cairoli rises the late-Romanesque church of
San Francesco d'Assisi (1238-98) with a restored Gothic façade. The Renaissance
building to the E. was readapted to its original purpose when the *Collegio Cairoli*
was founded in 1948. Farther on in Via San Martino (No. 18), the *Collegio
Castiglione-Brugnatelli* (for women) occupies a 15C college building. The college
Chapel (shown on request) has restored 15C frescoes attrib. to Bonifacio Bembo
and others. A bronze statue of Pope Pius V, by Nuvolone (1692) faces the **Collegio
Ghislieri,** his foundation. The square is closed by the façade of *San Francesco da
Paola,* by Giov. Ant. Veneroni, beyond which lie the *Botanic Gardens.* Via Scopoli
returns W., past *Santa Maria delle Cacce* (16C cloister in adjacent school), to the
Palazzo Mezzabarba, a lively Baroque building (by Veneroni, 1730) now the
Municipio. The church of *Santa Maria Canepanova,* at the corner of Via Sacchi

and Via Mentana, is a graceful octagonal building begun by Giov. Ant. Amadeo in 1507, perhaps to a design by Bramante; it has a pretty little cloister.

At the N. end of the Strada Nuova a wide esplanade precedes the **Castello Visconteo,** the grim square fortress built by Galeazzo II Visconti in 1360-65. Of the corner turrets, in which the founder housed his great collections of literature and art, two alone remain. Freed in 1921 from four centuries of military occupation, the restored interior (adm. 10-12, 15-17; in winter, 10-12, 14-16), with a splendid arcaded courtyard, will eventually house all the collections of the Museo Civico. Already transferred is the *Archæological Museum,* containing well-arranged fragments from Roman Pavia (including a rich collection of Roman glass), as well as sculptures and inscriptions from Lombard royal tombs. In the medieval section are mosaic pavements, good sculptures, capitals, and reconstructed portals from destroyed 11-12C churches. A damascened saddle of 9C or 10C workmanship found in the Ticino during the reconstruction of the bridge, recently recovered after its theft, is no longer displayed. Here also are a huge wooden model of the cathedral made by Fugazza in 1497-1519, and a Museo del Risorgimento with relics of the Pavese Cairoli brothers (comp. p. 120). The Pinacoteca (awaiting transfer from the Museo Civico Malaspina, comp. below) is to be housed on the first floor.

Via Griziotti leads N.W. to the Lombard church of *San Pietro in Ciel d'Oro,* consecrated in 1132, and named from its former gilded vault, mentioned by Dante in his Paradiso (X, 128; quoted on the façade). The single portal in the handsome façade is asymmetrically placed, and the buttress on the right is made broader than that on the left in order to contain a stairway. The fine Romanesque interior, restored in 1875-99, has good 'bestiary' capitals. The altarpiece is the *Arca di Sant'Agostino,* one of the great sculptured shrines of Italy, executed c. 1362 by Campionese masters influenced by the Pisan Giov. di Balduccio, with a galaxy of statuettes, and bas-reliefs illustrating the story of the saint. It is supposed to contain the relics of St Augustine (d. 430), removed from Carthage during the Arian persecutions. The large crypt contains the remains of the Roman poet and statesman Boëthius (476-524), executed by Theodoric on a charge of treason.

A little to the S. in P.za Petrarca, No. 2 houses the **Museo Civico Malaspina** (adm. 10-12, 15-17; winter 10-12, 14-16; to be removed to the Castello, see above). The most precious works in the collection were stolen in 1970: a *Madonna and Child by Giovanni Bellini,* and a *Madonna and Child with the young St John by Correggio;* these have since been recovered, but the Portrait of a condottiere by *Ant. da Messina* is still missing. Other paintings include: *Ambr. Bevilacqua,* Madonna and Child; *Boltraffio,* Portrait of Dr Cesare de' Milio, *Portrait of a lady; Vinc. Foppa,* Madonna and Child with Saints; *Bergognone,* Christ carrying the Cross; *Lor. Veneziano,* St Augustine; *Hugo van der Goes,* Madonna and Child; *Luca di Leyda,* Madonna in prayer; *G. B. Tiepolo,* Head of an oriental. Also, detached frescoes from local churches, and a small collection of ivories, ceramics, enamels, bronzes, and miniatures. The fine collection of prints and engravings has already been transferred to the Castello.

Farther on is the large red brick church of **Santa Maria del Carmine,** begun in 1390, which has an attractive façade adorned with terracotta statues and an elaborate rose-window. The harsh colour of the glass does not enhance the interior. On some of the nave pillars are frescoes by local 15C painters. The charming lavabo in the sacristy (S. transept) is by *Amadeo*. Via Venti Settembre returns to Corso Cavour, crossing Via Mascheroni in which (r.) is the little Lombard campanile of *San Giovanni Domnarum.* In Corso Cavour is a 15C tower (at No. 17) and the Bramantesque *Palazzo Bottigella* (No. 30), with fine brick ornament.

The Corso Manzoni prolongs the Corso Cavour to the railway, beyond which are (5 min.) the church of *San Salvatore,* reconstructed in 1467-1511, with good frescoes by Lanzani, and (10 min. farther) *San Lanfranco,* formerly *San Sepolcro,* a 13C building containing the fine cenotaph (by Amadeo; 1498) of the beautiful Lanfranc, who is buried at Canterbury, and traces of 13C frescoes (r. wall of nave) including one showing the murder of St Thomas Becket at Canterbury. One of the cloisters retains some terracotta decoration also by Amadeo.

On the road (and railway) from Pavia to (42 km.) *Casalpusterlengo* (Rte 38) is (14 km.) *Belgioioso,* with the well-preserved medieval castle (open April-Sept, 14-sunset), where Francis I was imprisoned immediately after the battle of Pavia.

Other branch railways (slow trains) connect Pavia with *Alessandria,* viâ (31 km.) *Lomello,* the ancient capital of the Lomellina interesting for its medieval monuments, including S. M. Maggiore (11C) and its Baptistery (5C; upper part rebuilt in the 8C); with *Mortara* (fine churches), and *Vercelli;* and with (32 km.) *Stradella,* for Piacenza.

Beyond Pavia the road crosses the Ticino and farther on the Po. It diverges from the railway to join the Piacenza-Alessandria road (N 10) at (55 km.) *Castéggio.*—58 km. *Montebello.* On the left a monument marks the site of two battles: the victory of the French over the Austrians in 1800; and the Franco-Italian success of 1859, the first battle of that campaign.—66 km. **Voghera,** an important industrial centre (43,100 inhab.) and railway junction, has a 12C church (*SS. Flavio e Giorgio;* now the Cavalry memorial chapel) on the E. side, and a *Castle* of the Visconti on the S.

A road (bus) ascends the Stáffora valley to the S.E.—9 km. **Sálice** is a little spa with iodine-impregnated waters (season May-Oct).—Just beyond (21 km.) Ponte Nizza, a by-road (l.) leads to the *Abbazia di S. Alberto di Butrio,* founded in the 11C. Three Romanesque churches here have 15C frescoes.—29 km. *Varzi* is noted for its salami. The road goes on over the *Passo del Pénice* (1149 m; with ski-ing facilities) to (56 km.) *Bóbbio* (p. 367) on the road from Piacenza to Genoa.

The road crosses into Piedmont just before (82 km.) **Tortona,** another industrial town (29,800 inhab.), with a church, *Santa Maria Canale,* of the 13-15C, and a *Castle* dismantled by Napoleon. The *Museo Romano* in the 15C Palazzo Guidobono contains relics of ancient Dertona, including the sarcophagus of Elio Sabino (3C A.D.).—Direct roads and railways run from here to Alessandria and to Novi Ligure (the latter offering an alternative route to Genoa), but this route goes straight through the town, keeping to the left bank of the river Scrivia.—90 km. *Villalvérnia.* Farther on the road crosses the river to join the road from Novi short of (102 km.) *Serravalle Scrivia.* Thence to (157 km.). **Genoa,** see Rte 6.

17   MILAN TO BERGAMO

AUTOSTRADA, A4, 52 km., leaving Milan by the Viale Zara to join the motorway N.E. of the city (it is c. 10 km. farther by the main autostrada entrance N.W. of the centre). This is the busiest section of the Milan-Venice motorway. The views of the Alps on the left and later of the Valley of the Adda are fine. Bergamo is entered by Via San Giorgio.—BUS every ½ hr from P.za Castello.

DIRECT ROAD, N 11, 525, 49 km. viâ Gorgonzola.

RAILWAY, 54 km. in 1 hr viâ Treviglio Ovest. Another route runs viâ Monza and Carnate-Usmate, where a change is usually necessary (51 km. in 1¼ hr).

The direct road (N 11) leaves Milan as Corso Buenos Aires and Via Palmanova, traversing a level plain.—19 km. *Gorgonzola* and its district are noted for the manufacture of 'Bel Paese' as well as for the creamier veined cheese named from the town.—At (23 km.) *Villa Fornaci*, N 525 keeps straight on to cross the Adda at (31 km.) *Váprio*, while 8 km. farther on the motorway crosses overhead. The towers of the village churches are crowned by statues of saints: *San Colombano*, just S. of Váprio, is a charming little 11-12C church.

49 km. **BERGAMO**, a beautiful and interesting old city (130,000 inhab.), stands just below the first foothills of the Alps, between the valleys of the Brembo and the Serio. It is divided into two sharply distinguished parts: BERGAMO BASSA, with the station and the principal hotels and shops; and BERGAMO ALTA (366 m), the old town with its varied and attractive skyline crowning a steep hill. Bergamo is the centre of an important textile industry, mainly cotton and silk.

Hotels, nearly all in Bergamo Bassa.

Post Office, Via Locatelli.—**E.P.T.** Viale Vittorio Emanuele; *Azienda Autonoma*, 3 Via Tasso.—**Theatre.** *Donizetti* (Piano Festival, held jointly with Brescia, in April and June).

Local buses from the Station to the Funicular and to Bergamo Alta, etc.— **Funicular Railway** from the end of Viale Vittorio Emanuele to the Upper Town.— **Bus Station** in Piazzale Marconi: services to *Brescia;* to *Como;* to *Edolo;* to *Iseo;* to *Milan;* to the Bergamesque valleys (comp. p. 180).

History. Bergamo appears as a free commune in the 12C, but like other North Italian towns it soon became involved in the quarrels of the noble families. In the 14C the Visconti and the Torriani disputed possession of the city and in 1408-19 Pandolfo Malatesta was its overlord. Another period of Visconti rule ended in 1428, when Venice extended its sway thus far into Lombardy. Bergamo remained a Venetian possession until the fall of the Republic in 1797, and until 1859 it was part of the Austrian dominion. The Bergamasques played a prominent part in the Risorgimento and furnished the largest contingent to Garibaldi's 'Thousand'. Its most famous citizens were Bart. Colleoni, the 15C condottiere, and Gaetano Donizetti (1798-1848), the composer. G. B. Moroni (c. 1525-78), Palma Vecchio (c. 1480-1520), and probably Lor. Lotto (1480-1556), painters of the Venetian School, were born in the neighbourhood.

The broad avenues and pleasant squares of the LOWER TOWN were laid out by Marcello Piacentini in the first decades of this century; they give it a remarkable air of spaciousness. The principal thoroughfare consists of Viale Giovanni XXIII and its continuation, Viale Vittore Emanuele. Beyond Porta Nuova with its two little Doric 'temples' Viale Giovanni XXIII crosses the monumental **Piazza Matteotti,** which is made up of Piazza Cavour, with gardens, and PIAZZA VITTORIO VENETO, designed by Piacentini (1929), with arcades and the *Torre dei Caduti* as a war memorial. On the right the wide promenade known as the 'SENTIERONE' leads past (r.) the *Teatro Donizetti* to the church of *San Bartolomeo*, whose large altarpiece by Lor. Lotto (1516) has been removed. Higher up Viale Vitt. Emanuele is the lower station of the funicular to the UPPER TOWN. Above to the left stands the marble *Porta San Giacomo*.

From the upper station the narrow old Via Gómbito climbs past the 12C *Torre di Gómbito* (52 m) to PIAZZA VECCHIA, with a pretty fountain.

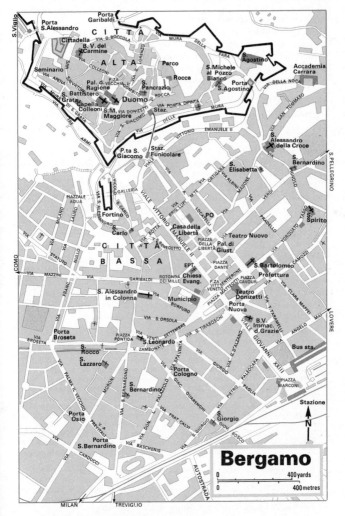

Bergamo

the centre of the old town. On the right is *Palazzo Nuovo* (1611), opposite which rises *Palazzo della Ragione,* rebuilt in 1538-43, bearing a modern Lion of St Mark, with, to the right, the massive *Torre del Comune* (12C; ascent by lift, 9-12, 14-30-18 exc. Tues). Beyond the arcades of Palazzo della Ragione lies the small PIAZZA DEL DUOMO, crowded with fine buildings.

The CATHEDRAL, altered in 1689, has a 19C west front. Its interesting history is summarized in an inscription on the S.W. pier of the crossing. The Baroque transeptal altars have statues by *And. Fantoni;* the painting on the 1st S. altar is by *Previtali,* and that on the 1st N. altar by *Moroni.* The charming little BAPTISTERY, opposite, by Giov. da Campione (1340), stood originally inside Santa Maria Maggiore. Between them rises the church of Santa Maria Maggiore (see below), against which is built the *Colleoni Chapel, by *Amadeo* (1476), a celebrated work of the Renaissance. The charm of the exterior detail is scarcely marred by the overlavish decoration and certain architectural weaknesses. Within are the *Tombs of Bart. Colleoni (d. 1476; see above) and his young daughter Medea (d. 1470), both by Amadeo, except for the equestrian statue of the condottiere, which is by *Sisto Siry* of Nuremberg (1501). The tomb of Medea was transferred in 1842 from the country church of Basella, on the Crema road. The remaining decoration of the chapel is 18C work, including some excellent marquetry seats, ceiling-frescoes by *Tiepolo,* and a Holy Family by *Angelica Kauffmann* (left side of apse).

*Santa Maria Maggiore, a Romanesque church, begun by *Maestro Fredo* in 1137, has beautiful details both inside and out. The N. porch (Campionese; 1353), facing the P.za del Duomo, the apses, the sacristy door (N.E.; 1375), the S. porch, by *Giov. da Campione* (1360), and the slim campanile (1436) are all excellent. The Baroque interior, which is hung with 16C Florentine tapestries, contains, in the S. aisle, the tomb of Card. Longo (1319); in the N. aisle, a Baroque confessional, by *Fantoni.* Against the W. wall is a monument to Donizetti (see above) by *Vela;* and, at the entrance to the choir, are two 16C pulpits with fine bronze rails and six bronze candelabra. The splendid intarsia choir-stalls (1522-55) are by various artists. In the N. transept are interesting 14C frescoes (including a scene in a smithy, and the Last Supper).

Between the Colleoni Chapel and the Baptistery a passageway leads through the *Curia Vescovile* (with frescoes of 13-14C), out past the *Tempietta di S. Croce* (probably dating from 11C, but altered in the 16C) into Via Arena. This leads past the *Istituto Musicale Donizetti* (No. 9; small museum of souvenirs) to Via San Salvatore (r.) and the *Cittadella* in which are arranged the Museo di Scienze Naturali (open 9-12, 14-16 exc. Tues) and the Museo Archeologico (open Sat, Sun, Mon, & Wed, 10-12, 15-17). Beyond the courtyard is the *Porta Sant'Alessandro.* From outside the gateway a bus (the funicular railway is out of action) ascends in 10 min. to **San Vigilio** (461 m), a fine view-point; still wider views may be obtained from the *Castello* (497 m), with remains of a Venetian fortress, or the *Bastia* (511 m). The new *Botanic Garden* on Colle Aperto is reached by Via Costantino Beltrami. From the Citadel, Via Colleoni leads back through the town, past the *House of Colleoni* (Nos. 9-11), bequeathed by the condottiere to a charitable institution. Via Gómbito continues to the Mercato delle Scarpe and the funicular to the lower town.

Other places of interest in the old town include the *Casa dell'Arciprete* (No. 11 Via Donizetti), a Renaissance mansion of 1520; and the *Rocca,* the ruins of a Visconti and Venetian castle (14C). It is surrounded by a Park of Remembrance which commands fine views of the towers of the Citta Alta and of the countryside all around. On the esplanade is a *Museo del Risorgimento.*

The most pleasant (and easiest) way of reaching the Galleria dell' Accademia Carrara from the upper town is by foot (c. 15 min.). Via Porta Dipinta descends to *Porta Sant'Agostino,* outside which is a good view of the Venetian walls (begun in 1561). From here Via della Noca (l.;

pedestrians only) leads downhill to the *Galleria dell'Accademia
Carrara* (adm. 9.30-12.30, 14.30-17.30 exc. Tues). The Academy and
Gallery were founded in 1780 by Count Giacomo Carrara, and the
splendid collection of paintings has since been augmented. The Venetian
school is particularly well represented.

SECOND FLOOR. ROOM I. *Paolo di Giovanni Fei*, Portable altar; works by *Ant.
Vivarini; Jacopo Bellini*, Madonna and Child.—R. II. *Aless. Baldovinetti*, Self
portrait (fragment of a fresco); *Botticelli* (and his School), several works including
a Portrait of Giuliano de' Medici; *Pesellino*, Story of Griselda (2 panels); *Bened. da
Maiano*, Angel (terracotta); *School of Fra Angelico*, Madonna of Humility;
Pisanello, *Portrait of Lionello d'Este; *Lor. Monaco*, Man of sorrows; *Neroccio di
Landi*, *Madonna and Child.—R. III. *Gentile Bellini*, *Portrait of a man; *Giov.
Bellini*, Madonna and Child; *And. Mantegna*, *Madonna and Child; *Marco
Basaiti*, the Redeemer; *G. F. Bembo*, Portrait of a man; *Lazzaro Bastiani* (attrib.)
Portrait of a man; *Vitt. Carpaccio* (attrib.), Six Saints; (on screen) *Giov. Bellini*,
Madonna and Child, and Madonna di Alzano. *Carlo Crivelli*, Madonna and
Child.—R. IV. *Lor. Costa*, St John the Evangelist; *Vinc. Foppa*, St Jerome; and
works by *Bergognone*.—R. V. *Vinc. Catena*, Supper at Emmaus; *And. Previtali*,
Madonna and Child.—R. VI. *Lor. Lotto*, Portrait of Lucina Brembati, three
predella panels, and several other works; *Giov. Cariani*, Portrait of Giov. Bened.
da Caravaggio; *Titian*, Orpheus and Euridice, Madonna and Child.
Room VII. *Tintoretto*, Portrait of an old man; works by *Garofolo* and *Paris
Bordone; Raphael*, *St Sebastian; works by *And. Solario*.—R. VIII. *Marco
Basaiti*, Portrait of a man; *Florentine Master of 16C* (formerly attrib. to
Pontormo), Portrait of a boy (Baccio Bandinelli?); small work attrib. to *Lor. di
Credi; Ghirlandaio*, Madonna and Child.—R. IX. *Portraits by *G. B. Moroni*.—
R. X. *Dürer*, Calvary, (workshop of Dürer) St Sebastian; *François Clouet*,
*Portrait of Saint Marsault; *Holbein the elder* (attrib.), Christ carrying the Cross;
and other works by Flemish, German, French, and Spanish masters.—R. XIII.
Dutch and Flemish works. *Rubens* (old copy), Martyrdom of St Agnes; *Ant.
Palamedesz*, Portrait of a girl; works by *Brueghel the elder*. R. XIV. *Longhi* and
Fr. Zuccarelli. R. XV. *G. B. Tiepolo*, and *Guardi*.

The centre of the town may be reached by Via San Tomaso and the
traffic-ridden Via Pignolo which descends steeply, passing many fine 16-
18C palazzi (No. 80 was once the house of Tasso's family) and the church
of *San Bernardino*, where the *Altarpiece is a good work by Lor. Lotto
(Madonna and saints; 1521). The church of *Santo Spirito*, whose
dignified interior (1521) contains a Madonna and saints by Lotto (4th S.
altar), St John the Baptist and other saints by Previtali (1st N. altar), and
a polyptych by Bergognone (2nd N. altar) stands on the corner of Via
Torquato Tasso, which leads back to the Sentierone.

Outside the church of *Sant' Alessandro in Colonna* a column made up of antique
fragments is said to mark the site of the martyrdom of St Alexander (297).
The *Castle of Malpaga*, 13 km. S.E. of Bergamo (bus, going on to Cremona),
dates from the 13C and 1470, and was the country home of Bart. Colleoni, who
died there in 1475. It contains frescoes attributed to Fogolino (c. 1520).
The road and railway from Bergamo to *Lecco* (33 km. in 45-60 min.) pass
(14 km.) *Pontida*, where the Benedictine abbey is famous as the traditional
meeting-place of the cities that first formed the Lombard League (Milan,
Bergamo, Brescia, Cremona, Mantua) in 1167. The upper cloister, probably by P.
Isabello, is noteworthy. *Sotto il Monte*, S. of Pontida (on the S. side of Monte
Canto), was the birthplace in 1881 of Angeló Roncalli, later Pope John XXIII.—
27 km. *Somasca* gave name to the Somascan order, whose founder, St Jerome
Emiliani (1481-1537), died here.

THE BERGAMASQUE VALLEYS

FROM BERGAMO TO PIAZZA BREMBANA, 38 km.; bus hourly in 70 min. At (9 km.) *Villa d'Almè* on the Brembo, a road leads across the river to the romanesque church of *San Tomè*, and on to *Almenno*, with another interesting church. The main road follows the Bremo valley. On the left is the *Valle Imagna* (bus to Sant'Omobono, 13 km.).—18 km. *Zogno* is the chief place in the lower Valle Brambana.—From (20 km.) *Ambria* a road on the right ascends to *Serina* (ski-ing facilities), the birthplace of Palma il Vecchio (polyptych in the sacristy of the church), and ends at *Oltre il Colle* (16 km.; bus from Bergamo), a summer resort.—23 km. *San Pellegrino* (village).—24 km. **San Pellegrino Terme** (355 m) is a favoured summer resort whose lithino-alkaline waters have become the Italian synonym for table waters. A funicular railway ascends to *San Pellegrino-Vetta*, a fine view-point.—29 km. *San Giovanni Bianco* (599 m) stands at the mouth of the Val Taleggio (noted for its cheese), the fine gorge of the Enna, at the head of which (bus) are the resorts of *Sottochiesa* and *Olda* (11 km.).—38 km. **Piazza Brembana** (510 m) is a summer resort and a base for excursions in the mountains.

Above Piazza the valley divides, both branches affording access to numerous little climbing and winter-sports resorts, all served by buses in the season. To the N., on the Brembo Occidentale, is (10 km.) *Mezzoldo* (835 m), whence a rough road crosses the *Passo di San Marco* (1896 m) to Morbegno (p. 168).—To the right of the Mezzoldo road is (9 km.) *Piazzatorre* at 850 m., a ski resort, with a chair-lift to Monte Tórcola (1789 m).

Another fine road runs N.E. up the *Val Fondra*, the valley of the Brembo Orientale. From (3½ km.) *Ponte di Bordogna* a zigzag road ascends (r.) in 5½ km. to *Roncobello* (1090 m), a well situated resort.—11 km. *Branzi*, in a pleasant basin, is noted for its cheese.—15 km. *Carona* (1300 m), is the base for the easy ascent (4 hrs) of the *Corno Stella* (2620 m), which commands a magnificent view of the Alps from the Bernese Oberland to the Ortler.

From Branzi another road climbs N. to (9 km.) **Fóppolo** (1545 m), the most developed of the Bergamasque mountain resorts, with a funicular railway from the road-end to the hotels, and chair-lifts up to the ski-fields. It is another base for the Corno Stella (see above), and the *Passo di Dordona* (2080 m) offers an easy mountain route into the Valtellina (5½ hrs to San Pietro Berbenno.). *San Simone* (2000 m), W. of Fóppolo, is also frequented by skiers.

FROM BERGAMO TO LÓVERE (VALLE CAVALLINA), 41 km. bus in 1¾ hr. SERIANA, the principal valley in the Bergamasque Alps, is mainly industrial, with many silk and cotton mills and cement works. The upper reaches, however, are unspoilt.—The road reaches the Serio at (6½ km.) *Alzano Lombardo*.—10 km. *Nembro* and (12½ km.) *Albino* are industrial villages. **Selvino**, a pleasant hill resort has become an important ski-ing centre. 11 km. N. of Nembro, it is connected by funicular railway with Albino. *Bondo Petello*, a hamlet above Albino, was the birthplace of G. B. Moroni, the painter.

From (18 km.) *Gazzaniga* a side-valley (r.) may be ascended for **Gandino** (5½ km.), an ancient little town, the birthplace of Bart. Bon the elder, sculptor, and G. B. Castello, painter. It preserves a medieval rampart gate and the *Basilica (1423), with a Baroque interior, including a notable bronze balustrade of 1590. A Museum displays the treasury and ancient textiles. There is also a chair-lift ascending to the Formico plateau (ski-ing; see below).—34 km. **Clusone** (720 m) is a small resort. The town hall has a 16C clock; and on the small *Oratorio del Disciplini* is a frescoed 'Dance of Death' (1485). A bus goes on up the valley (l.) viâ (12 km.) *Gromo*, a summer and winter-sports resort (road up to Spiazzi, 1200 m) to (23 km.) *Valbondione* (890 m), a scattered village in a barren mountain-basin. A road continues to *Lizzola* (chair-lift to Rambasi, 1599 m).

From Clusone a good road leads N.E. viâ (8 km.) *Castione della Presolana* to (14½ km.) the *Passo della Presolana* (1286 m), a favourite holiday resort (ski-ing), from which the *Pizzo della Presolana* (2521 m) is ascended in 4 hrs. A by-road from Bratto leads in 8 km. part way up *Monte Pora* (1879 m), recently developed as a ski resort.—The road descends into the Valle di Scalve and at (22½ km.) *Dezzo* joins the road from the Val Camónica (Rte 19).—31 km. *Schilpario* (1125 m), is another summer and winter resort among pine trees in the Valle di Scalve.—The road beyond crosses (43 km.) the *Passo del Vivione* (1798 m) and desends into the Val Camónica. 75 km. *Edolo*, see Rte 19.

FROM BERGAMO TO LÓVERE (VALLE CAVALLINA), 41 km. bus in 1¾ hr. Following the Tonale road (N 42), this route crosses the Serio at (4½ km.) *Seriate*, and bears left.—14 km. *Trescore Balneario* is a small watering-place with sulphur and mud baths. A chapel in the Suardi villa at Novale (shown on application) contains frescoes by Lotto (1524).—From (24 km.) *Casazza* a bus ascends (W.) to the small spa of *Gaverina*. Just beyond is the *Lago di Endine*, 3¾ m. long.—26 km. *Spinone*. At (39 km.) the mouth of the Valle Borlezza the road reaches the Lago d'Iseo.—41 km. *Lóvere*, see Rte 19.—The return may be made by the Val Borlezza and (17 km.) Clusone.

FROM BERGAMO TO BRESCIA, 50 km., railway in 1 hr. The uninteresting route passes (22 km.) *Palazzolo sull'Oglio*, and joins the main line from Milan at (32 km.) *Rovato*. The autostrada and the ordinary road run more or less parallel with the railway.

From Bergamo the LAGO D'ISEO (Rte 19) is reached by road, viâ Seriate, to (27 km.) *Sárnico* (bus in c. 1 hr), the starting-point of the steamers, at the foot of the lake.

18   MILAN TO BRESCIA AND VERONA

AUTOSTRADA, 162 km.; to *Brescia* (98 km.), passing near Bergamo (see Rte 19). ROAD, N 11, 158 km. 23 km. *Villa Fornaci;* keep right.—35½ km. *Treviglio.*— 41 km. *Caravággio.*—67 km. *Chiari.*—72 km. *Coccáglio.*—93 km. **Brescia,** beyond which the route is almost identical with that of the railway.—121 km. *Desenzano.*—134 km. *Peschiera.*—158 km. **Verona,** entered by the Porta San Zeno.

RAILWAY, 148 km. in 1¼-1¾ hrs; to *Brescia,* 83 km. in ¾-1¼ hr; to *Desenzano,* 111 km. in c. 1¼ hr.

From Milan to (23 km.) *Villa Fornaci,* where the Bergamo road continues straight on, see Rte 17. This road branches right to (29½ km.) *Cassano d'Adda,* the scene of many battles, on the Adda. Ezzelino da Romano was slain in battle here in 1259. *Rivolta d'Adda,* 6 km. S. beyond the river, has a good church of 1088-99.—35½ km. **Treviglio,** an agricultural and industrial centre (26,800 inhab.), is an important railway junction. The Gothic church of *San Martino* contains a fine polyptych by Zenale and Butinone (1485). *Santa Maria delle Lagrime* is a Renaissance building with another triptych by Butinone. Here in 1915, while in hospital with jaundice, Mussolini was married (probably bigamously) to Donna Rachele.

41 km. *Caravággio,* with a sanctuary of the Blessed Virgin (church of 1575; by Pellegrino Tibaldi), was the birthplace of the painters Michelangelo Amerighi da Caravaggio (1573-1610) and Polidoro Caldara (1495-1543).—At (46 km.) *Mozzánica* the road crosses the Serio and, beyond (59 km.) Calcio, the Oglio.—67 km. *Chiari* has a small Pinacoteca in its library.—At (72 km.) *Coccáglio* the Bergamo road comes in on the left.—74 km. *Rovato* is connected by railway-bus with Iseo and with Soncino and Cremona.

93 km. **BRESCIA,** a lively town (215,700 inhab.) of great historical and artistic importance, is situated at the mouth of the Val Trompia (149 m) and commanded by its old castle. Necessary reconstruction in the centre both before and since the war has been pleasantly accomplished. It is the centre of an exceptionally comprehensive network of bus services.

Hotels, near P.za d. Vittoria and the station.
Post Office, P.za della Vittoria.—**E.P.T.,** Corso Zanardelli.

Town Bus No. 5 from the Station to the centre (viâ Via Mazzini).—**Country Buses** from the Bus Station, near the railway station (some services also stop again in the town at Via Vittorio Emanuele and Porta Venezia). Frequent services to most towns in the province; to *Toscolano,* and *Gargnano;* also to *Gardone Val Trómpia,* every ½hr; frequently to *Bergamo* and *Lecco;* to *Parma;* to *Cremona;* to *Iseo* and *Édolo;* to *Desenzano, Sirmione,* and *Verona;* to *Milan;* to *Piacenza* and *Genoa,* etc.

Theatre. *Teatro Grande,* with seasons of opera, plays. and concerts (and a Piano Festival, held jointly with Bergamo, in April & June).—*Swimming Pools* N. of the town, and at the Stadio Comunale, Viale Piave.

History. The Roman colony of *Brixia* emerges again into prominence under the 8C Lombard king Desiderius, who was born in the neighbourhood. The city was a member of the Lombard League, but in 1258 it fell a prey to the tyrant Ezzelino da Romano. The customary family overlordships followed, with the Lombard Torriani and Visconti, the Veronese Scaligeri, and Pandolfo Malatesta playing prominent parts. From 1426 to 1797 Brescia enjoyed prosperity under Venetian suzerainty. Between 1509 and 1516 it was twice captured by the French under Gaston de Foix, the ruthless pillage after its second fall being mitigated by the generosity of Bayard, who lay wounded in the town for some days. The bravery of its citizens was again proved in March 1849, when the town held out for ten days against the Austrian general, Haynau (nicknamed the 'hyæna of Brescia'). The town suffered a great deal from bombing in the Second World War.—Among famous natives are the painters Vincenzo Foppa (? 1427-1515), Romanino (1485-1566), and Moretto (1498-1554); the Benedictine monk Arnold of Brescia (d. 1155), who preached against the worldliness of the church and was hanged at Rome; the mathematician Tartaglia (Nic. Fontana; 1506-59); and Tito Speri (1825-50), leader of the 1849 revolution and most famous of the martyrs of Belfiore.

From Milan the main road continues into the town as Corso Garibaldi; from the autostrada or the station the entrance to the city is by Corso Martiri della Libertà. The central PIAZZA DELLA VITTORIA, by Marcello Piacentini (finished in 1932) is a cold square built in grey marble and white stone. On the E. side is the red marble *Arengario,* a rostrum for public speaking adorned with bas-reliefs of notable events in Brescian history, by Ant. Maraini (1886-1963). At the N. end is the parti-coloured *Post Office.*

Just to the W. is the church of *Sant'Agata,* built c. 1438-72. In the attractive interior is a large fresco of the Crucifixion (1475; attrib. to Andrea Bembo).

An archway under the *Monte di Pietà* (with a loggia of 1484, and an addition of 1597), behind the Post Office, leads to thhe harmonious PIAZZA DELLA LOGGIA. On the left rises the *Loggia,* a beautiful Renaissance building with exquisite sculptural detail.

The ground floor was built between 1492 and 1508, the upper story between 1554 and 1574; architects who directed the building included Lodovico Beretta, Sansovino, Galeazzo Alessi, and And. Palladio. It was restored in 1914.—On the right of the Loggia is a fine 16C portal.

Above the N.E. corner of the square rises the *Porta Bruciata,* a fragment of the oldest city wall. The arcade at the E. end was the scene in 1974 of one of the most brutal political murders in modern Italian history when 8 people lost their lives and over 100 were injured (plaque). Beneath the *Torre dell' Orologio* (c. 1547) a passageway leads to P.za del Duomo, with a handsome row of buildings lining its E. side. The **Duomo,** begun in 1604 by *G. B. Lantana* on the site of the old 'summer cathedral' of San Pietro de Dom, has a cupola (1825) 82 m high. The bust of Card. Querini over the main entrance is by *Ant. Calegari.* In the middle of the N. aisle, above the new bishop's throne, are four panels by *Romanino.* By the 3rd S. altar is the fine tomb (1510) of SS. Apollonius and Philastrius, bishops of Brescia. A passage leads to the Romanesque *Rotonda or *Duomo Vecchio,* a circular building of the early 12C with a central rotunda supported on eight pillars. The choir is a 15C addition. Over the high altar is an *Assumption by *Moretto.* In front of the choir, glass in the pavement shows remains of the walls and mosaic pavement of Roman Baths of the Republican era excavated in 1975. Also here is a mosaic fragment of the apse of the 8C *Basilica di San Filastrio,* burned in 1097 with the exception of the crypt which preserves many miscellaneous columns and traces of frescoes. Other fragments of the mosaic pavement can be seen beneath the floor on the W. side of the rotunda. At the W. end of the upper gallery is the red marble *Sarcophagus of Bp. Berardo Maggi (d. 1308), by a Campionese sculptor.

On the right, tomb of Bp. Lambertino Baldovino (d. 1349), also Campionese, while on the left is that of Bp. De Dominicis (d. 1478). The S. transept altarpiece is a curious fresco of the Flagellation (15C); facing it, Translation of the patron saints from the castle to the cathedral, an elaborate work by *Fr. Maffai.* The ancient stairs which led up to the bell tower (destroyed in 1708) survive.—The contents of the TREASURY are displayed only on the Friday preceding Good Friday. They include a Byzantine cross-reliquary and the 'Croce del Campo', both late 11C.

At No. 3 Via Mazzini, behind the new cathedral, is the *Biblioteca Queriniana,* founded by Card. Querini in 1750 (adm. Tues-Sat 8.30-12, 14.30-19). Among the treasures exhibited are a 6C evangelistary, with silver letters on purple vellum, and a Concordance of the Gospels, by Eusebius (11C).

On the left of the Duomo Nuovo is the **Broletto,** a typical Lombard town hall of 1187-1230, now serving as the Prefettura. The exterior preserves the original appearance; within one loggia is a Baroque addition. Beyond the sturdy battlemented *Torre del Popolo* (11C), the N. part of the Broletto incorporates the little church of *Sant' Agostino,* the W. front of which has early-15C terracotta ornamentation, with two lion gargoyles.

Via dei Musei leads to P.za del Foro with remains on the E. of porticoes of the *Forum.* On the N. side are the imposing remains of the *Capitoline Temple* erected by Vespasian (A.D. 73), now housing a **Museum of Roman Antiquities** (adm. 9-12 and 14-17 or 15-18; closed Mon). The temple stands on a lofty stylobate approached by steps, fifteen of which are original, and has a hexastyle pronaos of Corinthian columns with a colonnade of three columns on each side, behind. The three cellæ were probably dedicated to the Capitoline Trinity (Jupiter, Juno, and Minerva). Beneath it is a Capitolium (unlocked by custodian) of the Republican era (after 89 B.C.) with mosaics of small uncoloured tesseræ. On the right is the Roman *Theatre,* whose shape can be appreciated, while it still awaits clearing and excavation.

In the cellæ are inscriptions and mosaics; the bronzes, ceramics, and glass are in a modern building behind. Most notable is the famous *Winged Victory, a bronze statue nearly 2m high, probably the chief figure of a chariot group from the roof of the Capitol. With it are six bronze heads, portions of a chariot and horse, the captive Regulus, etc., from the same group, discovered along with the statue in 1826. The statue appears to be a Venus of the Augustan age (type of the Venus of Capua) remodelled as a Victory under Vespasian. Also outstanding are an Italic bronze helm and pottery (7-5CB.C.); a fine Greek amphora (c. 510 B.C.); Gaulish silver horse-trappings (3C B.C.); and a fine marble head of an athlete (5C B.C.).

Farther on in Via dei Musei is the former church of *Santa Giulia* (16C) now occupied by the ***Museum of Christian Antiquities** (entrance through the W. door, at No. 4 Via G. Piemarta, left; open 9-12, 15-18, or 14-17). On the right a case contains the * *Cross of Desiderius* (mid-8C), presented to the convent of Santa Giulia by Desiderius, King of the Lombards. It is of wood overlaid with silvergilt and set with over 200 gems and cameos; on the lower arm are three portraits on gold-leaf under glass, probably of the 3C. In an adjoining case is an *Ivory Coffer, with scriptural scenes in relief (4C). Both the cross and the coffer have been removed temporarily to the Pinacoteca but are to be returned here. The case in the centre contains other early *Ivories; the Querini Diptych (5C), with Paris and Helen (?) on each leaf; the consular Diptych of Manlius Boëthius (5C); leaf of the Diptych of the Lampadii, with circus scenes (late 5C); and Lombardic gold jewellery. Other cases contain 13-14C ivories; Renaissance medals and plaquettes, including examples by *Briosco, Moderno, And. Riccio, Vittoria, Pisanello,* and *Caradosso.* The frescoes in the nave (late 16C) and choir (early 16C) have been restored. In the choir, Tomb of Count Marcantonio Martinengo (d. 1526) from the Chiesa del Cristo (see below), with bronze and marble reliefs by *Maffeo Olivieri;* and a marble group by *Vittoria;* on the right, intarsia lectern, by *Raff. da Marone* (1520). In a side room on the right, Murano glass, Limoges enamels, and Deruta and other maiolica.

From the apse can be seen (through a glass window) the Byzantine basilica of **San Salvatore,** a 9C rebuilding of the original Benedictine nunnery, founded by Desiderius, in which Ermengarde, daughter of Lothair I, and many other royal and noble ladies were sisters. Thirteen columns from Roman buildings support the nave, and the S.W. chapel contains frescoes by *Romanino.* In the crypt are 42 columns of varying origin. While excavations continue admission (by the stairs outside the transept door) is granted only by special request.

A wing of the nunnery has been adapted as a *Galleria d'Arte Moderna* (entrance at 81 Via dei Musei; closed for restoration since 1975, but normally open during the same hours as the Museum of Christian Antiquities). Here are works by Canova, Fr. Hayez, Signorini, Lega, Mafai, etc. Off the cloister is the 12C chapel of *Santa Maria in Solario* (opened by the custodian of the Museum of Christian Antiquities), its square undercroft, of Roman material, has a cippus for a central column.

Via G. Piamarta ascends to the castle: on the left is the *Chiesa del Cristo,* with good terracotta decoration (15C) and a marble doorway of the 16C. The **Castello,** on the Cydnean hill (mentioned in Catullus, and now pierced by a road-tunnel), was rebuilt by the Visconti in the 14C and contains a *Museum of the Risorgimento,* surrounded by a pleasant garden (small *Zoo*). The cylindrical *Torre della Mirabella* commands a fine view. A Museum of Arms and Armour is to be opened here, while the Museum of Natural History is to be moved to new premises in Via Crocifisso di Rosa (N. of the castle).

In the other direction Via A. Gallo leads S., past the site (No. 3 P.za Lebus) of the Roman *Curia* (fragments of which can be seen below ground level and on the façade of the house), to the church of **San Clemente** (if closed ring at No. 6 Vicolo S. Clemente) which contains the grave of Moretto (modern bust).

Moretto, 2nd S. altar, SS. Lucy, Cecilia, Agnes, Barbara, and Agatha; high altar, Madonna in glory; N.altars: Abraham and Melchizedek, Marriage of St Catherine, St Ursula and her maidens; *Romanino.* 1st S. altar, The risen Christ. In Via Trieste, a few metres to the left, is *Santa Maria Calchera* (open for services only) containing a painting by Romanino, the Communion of St Apollonius (2nd S. altar). In the square is a monument to Tartaglia, by Contratti.

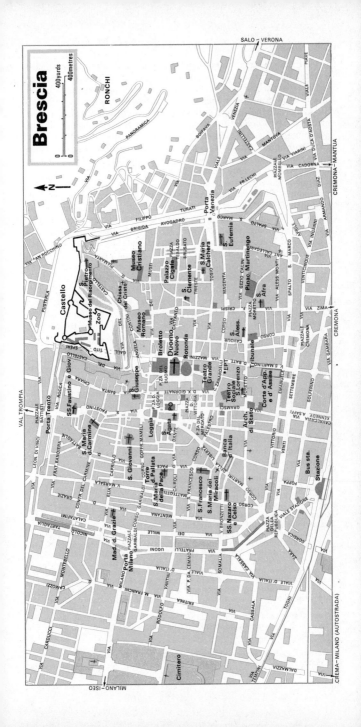

Via F. Crispi leads across Corso Magenta to P.za Moretto, in which is a statue of Moretto. On the left is the **Pinacoteca Tosio-Martinengo** (adm. as for the Roman Museum), a collection of paintings and frescoes in which the local schools are well represented. Among the early works is St George and the dragon, of the 15C Brescian school, with a charming medieval city. *Foppa,* *Standard of Orzinuovi, a double-sided painting, Madonna and saints; *Moretto,* Christ and the angel, *St Nicholas of Bari, with a delightful Virgin and Child, Salome (a portrait of Tullia d'Aragona), Portrait of a nobleman; *Romanino* is represented by several works, notably three portraits, *Moroni* also by several fine portraits, and there are good examples of *Ferramola* (lunette of the Madonna), *Civerchio, Savoldo* (Nativity), *Lattanzio Gambara* (Self-portrait), *Callisto Piazza* and the unusual genre painter *Giac. Ceruti*(fl. 1724-38). Notable among paintings of other schools are: *Raphael,* The Redeemer blessing, and an *Angel, fragments of the Coronation of St Nicholas of Tolentino, painted for Città di Castello; *Clouet,* Henri III; *Tintoretto,* An old nobleman; *Lor. Lotto,* Adoration of the Shepherds; and works by *Francia* and *Bramantino.* A portrait by *Sofonisba Anguissola,* and a charming likeness of Maria Martinengo, by *G. B. Cigola* (1769-1841) are among the later works. Outstanding in the fine array of drawings (which are shown only with special permission) is a *Deposition by *Giov. Bellini.* On the ground floor is an exhibition of 15C illuminated MSS. from S. Francesco and the Duomo (opened on request) and the Print room with works by *Jacopo Filippo d'Argento* and others.

Sant'Afra, just to the S., rebuilt since the war, has a Transfiguration by Tintoretto in the apse.

Via Moretto leads back towards the centre of the town passing (r.) the church of *Sant'Alessandro,* with an Annunciation, perhaps by Iacopo Bellini, and a Deposition, by Civerchio (1st and 2nd S. altars), and (l.) the 17C *Palazzo Martinengo-Colleoni,* now the Criminal Courts. Via San Martino della Battaglia leads right to CORSO ZANARDELLI, a busy promenade, with the arcades of the *Teatro Grande* (entered from Via Paganora), founded in 1709, rebuilt in 1863, but with a façade of 1782.

Corso Palestro, its continuation, continues to the church of **San Francesco,** built in 1254-65, with a good façade. The plain and solemn interior has many interesting frescoes. SOUTH AISLE. Ist Altar. *Moretto,* St Margaret of Cortona, St Francis, and St Jerome; between the 2nd and 3rd altars: Giottesque fresco of the Entombment (with a scene of monks above, dating from mid-14C); between the 3rd and 4th altars: 14C frescoes including a charming frieze of angels. Over the main altar, Madonna and Saints by *Romanino,* in a frame of rich workmanship by *Stef. Lamberti*(1502). The choir contains good stalls. In the middle of the N. aisle is an elaborately decorated chapel (15-18C). The fine Cloister (1394) is reached through the Sacristy (good view of the Campanile; upper story rebuilt).—Just to the S., in Corso Martiri is *Santa Maria dei Miracoli,* rebuilt since the war but preserving intact an elaborate Renaissance façade of 1488-1560. Opposite is the 17C *Palazzo Martinengo Villagna,* attrib. to Stef. Carra. In Via Fratelli Bronzetti, on the right, is the 16C side doorway of the church of **Santi Nazaro e Celso,** an 18C building, noteworthy for its paintings. Over the high altar is a *Polyptych, the Risen Christ, Annunciation, and Saints, by *Titian* (1522), while *Moretto* is represented by a Transfiguration (3rd S. altar) and a Coronation of the Virgin (2nd N. altar).

From San Francesco Via della Pace leads N. to the massive 13C *Torre della Pallata.* Nearby is **San Giovanni Evangelista** which has a good Renaissance doorway, also (3rd S. altar) a Massacre of the Innocents (1530) and (in the apse) a

*Madonna and saints, by Moretto. In the Corpus Domini chapel (N. side) are a Descent from the Cross by Civerchio, and good paintings of the Evangelists by Moretto and Romanino. In the Baptistery (N.W.), *Holy Trinity and four saints by Francia. Farther N. *Santa Maria del Carmine,* a 14C building with a fine façade and a 15C portal, contains paintings by Foppa and his school; while, at the W. end of Via Capriolo, is the *Madonna delle Grazie* by Lod. Barcella (1522); the 15C doorway comes from another church. The delightful rococo *Interior (1617) has an exuberance of stucco reliefs and frescoes covering its barrel vault and the domes in the side aisles, in contrast with the plain columns of the nave. A 16C courtyard affords access to a venerated sanctuary rebuilt in the 19C, and covered with charming ex-votoes.

From the Viale Bornata c. 3 km. E. of the town a cableway rises to *Monte Maddalena* (875 m), a noted view-point, also reached by the Strada Panoramica (see plan; stiff climb).

EXCURSIONS FROM BRESCIA

To the *Lake of Iseo* and *Édolo,* see Rte 19.

For LAKE GARDA a bus runs ½-hourly, following the Verona road to (9½ km.) *Treponti,* then turning left on N45 bis for (27½ km.) *Tórmini.* Thence it descends to the lake-shore at (32 km.) *Salò,* going on viâ *Gardone Riviera* to (40 km.) *Toscolano* and hourly to (46 km.) *Gargnano* (see Rte 20).

FROM BRESCIA TO THE LAKE OF IDRO AND TIONE; road, 98 km. Bus twice daily to Tione; frequently to Vestone.—To (27½ km.) *Tórmini,* see above. Thence the road ascends the VAL SABBIA, watered by the Chiese.—33 km. *Vobarno* has old-established iron-foundries.—At (43 km.) *Barghe* this route joins a shorter road from Brescia viâ Caino.—48 km. *Vestone,* a large village, has vestiges of three old castles.—At (53 km.) *Pieve Vecchia* a road diverges right to *Idro* village and this road continues to the **Lake of Idro** (*Lacus Eridius*), 6 m. long and ½ m. wide, surrounded by steep and rugged mountains. Its waters are utilized for hydroelectric power; and it is renowned for its trout. The road follows the W. bank. Beyond (59 km.) *Anfo* it traverses the old castle of that name, founded by the Venetians in 1486 but largely rebuilt.—63 km. *Sant'Antonio,* where the church has a 14C fresco cycle, is connected by road with *Bagolino* (9 km.), a mountain village (718 m) finely situated on the Cáffaro, and thence by minor road viâ the *Passo di Croce Domini* (29 km.; 1895 m) with Breno (46 km.; p. 191).—68 km. *Ponte Cáffaro,* beyond the head of the lake, marks the old international frontier. High up on the left is the castle of *Lodrone.*—At (72 km.) *Ca Rosso* a road on the right leads to the Val di Ledro and Riva (Rte 20). The left branch ascends the VALLI GIUDICARIE, watered by the Chiese.—77 km. *Condino,* the principal place in this valley, has a 15C church.—84 km. *Creto* lies at the foot of the wild *Val Daone* (l.), which penetrates into the heart of the Adamello group. Near (89 km.) *Roncone* the road crosses the watershed (838 m) and descends to (98 km.) *Tione,* on the road from Malè to Trento (Rte 24).

Another bus from Brescia ascends the VAL TRÓMPIA frequently to (19 km.) *Gardone Val Trómpia,* where the production of light arms and sporting guns continues the once flourishing fire arms industry begun in this valley in the 15C. About six times daily the bus goes on the (34 km.) *Bóvegno* and (40 km.) **Cóllio** (838 m), both summer resorts, with opportunities for winter sports on Monte Pezzeda (1653 m; cableway and chair-lift).—43 km. *San Colombano* (923 m), the bus terminus, is similarly equipped. A fine new road continues to (52½ km.) the *Passo del Maniva* (1670 m), beyond which it deteriorates as it negotiates the Passo di Croce Domini (see above).

FROM BRESCIA TO MANTUA, road 67 km. bus in 1¾ hr. At (20 km.) *Montichiari* this route bears left from the Parma road.—28 km. *Castiglione delle Stiviere* was once a fief of the Gonzagas, and the birthplace of St Louis Gonzaga (1568-91). The Museo Storico Aloisiano has paintings by Fr. Bassano, Fed. Barocci, etc.—50 km. *Góito,* where the road crosses the Mincio and the Via Postumia, was the scene of a victory of the Piedmontese over the Austrians (1848) and the birthplace of the troubadour Sordello (? 1200-1266), mentioned by Dante.—67 km. *Mantua,* see Rte 21.

FROM BRESCIA TO PARMA, road 98 km.; railway in 2¼ hrs, following a parallel route.—To (20 km.) *Montichiari,* see above.—26 km. *Carpenedolo.* On the right, between this village and the station of *Calvisano,* Prof. R. S. Conway located the site of Virgil's birthplace, the ancient village of Andes.—42 km. *Asola* preserves its old walls, and (55 km.) *Canneto sull'Oglio* has a massive tower of its former castle. At (57½ km.) *Piádena* the road crosses the Cremona-Mantua railway (Rte 21).—67 km. *San Giovanni in Croce* has a castle of 1407 remodelled with a graceful loggia in the 16C.—75 km. *Casalmaggiore* is notable for its embankments along the Po, which is crossed on a long bridge after the main Mantua-Parma road is joined. From here to (98 km.) *Parma*, see Rte 39.

FROM BRESCIA TO CREMONA, road 49 km.; parallel autostrada (A 21); railway in 1 hr. The left fork at 10 km. leads in 3 km. to *Montirone* (2 km. from its station), where the beautiful *Palazzo Lechi* (1738-46), by Ant. Turbino, is completely unspoilt and has magnificent *Stables of c. 1754. It contains paintings by Carlo Carloni, and was visited by Mozart in 1773 and Napoleon in 1805.—The chief intermediate town is (27 km.) *Verolanuova* (3½ km. W. of the main road), where the church contains two large paintings by G. B. Tiepolo, in excellent condition.—*Gottolengo*, 18 km. E. of Verolanuova and 34 km. S. of Brescia, was the main residence in 1746-56 of Lady Mary Wortley Montagu.

FROM BRESCIA TO CREMA (50 km.) the road passes the suburban church of *Chiesanuova*, notable for its charming *Nativity by Foppa, runs beneath the autostrada, and crosses the plain.—29 km. *Orzinuovi* has imposing remains of the Venetian ramparts designed by Sammicheli.—Beyond the Oglio bridge is (33 km.) *Soncino*, where the *Castle (adm. 10-12, 15-18), built by Galeazzo Maria Sforza (1473), is among the best preserved in Lombardy.—50 km. *Crema*, see p. 199.—From Brescia to *Bergamo*, see p. 181.

Beyond Brescia the mountains gradually recede. At (101 km.) *Rezzato,* the park of the Villa Fenaroli has been given over to an open-air museum of statuary. On the left a road leads to Salò.—115 km. *Lonato,* with a castle (reconstructed in its 15C form), built by the Visconti, was the scene of French victories over the Austrians in 1509, 1706, and 1796, the last an early success of Napoleon's. The castle houses a small museum and fine library. Farther on road and railway afford good views of Lake Garda and the Sirmione peninsula.—121 km. **Desenzano del Garda.** The main road passes close to the station above the town and steamer-pier (Rte 20), to which a bus descends in connection with the trains.—124 km. *Rivoltella.*

A road on the right just beyond leads in 4 km. to the tower (74 m high) of *San Martino della Battaglia,* which commemorates Victor Emmanuel's victory over the Austrian right wing on 24 June 1859. The interior (open 8-12, 14-18 or 19; winter 9-12, 13.30-17.30; closed Mon) contains sculptures and paintings relating to the campaign, and there are good views from the summit. At *Solferino,* 8 km. S., Napoleon III, in alliance with Victor Emmanuel, crushed the rest of the Austrian army on the same day. A memorial was unveiled in 1959 in honour of J. H. Dunant, who, horrified by the sufferings of the wounded, took the first steps to found the Red Cross. The tower of Solferino was erected probably by the Scaligiers. The low moraine-hills S. of the Lake of Garda, thrown up by the ancient glacier of the Adige, have been the theatre of many battles; during Prince Eugene's campaign in the War of the Spanish Succession (1701-6), during Napoleon's enterprises (1796-1814), and during the Wars of Italian Independence (1848-49, 1859, and 1866).

Beyond the junction with a road left for Sirmione, this road enters Venetia.—134 km. **Peschiera del Garda,** an ancient fortress, one of the four corners of the Austrian 'quadrilateral' (p. 204), stands at the outflow of the Mincio from the Lake of Garda. The impressive fortifications, (well seen from the road and railway), begun by the Venetians in 1553, were strengthened by Napoleon and again by the Austrians. They fell to the Piedmontese after a prolonged siege in 1848.—The hills to the S. of (140 km.) *Castelnuovo di Verona* were the scene of the two Italian defeats of *Custoza* (1848 and 1866).—The road descends to the plain before reaching (158 km.) **Verona** (Rte 23).

19 BRESCIA TO EDOLO

RAILWAY, 103 km. in 2-3½ hrs, closely following the ROAD (101 km.; bus in c. 3 hrs), which leaves Brescia by the Porta Milano and diverges from the Bergamo road at (6 km.) *Mandolossa.*

After traversing the fertile foothills of the Brescian Alps, planted with vineyards and gardens, called 'Ronchi', the road reaches the *Torbiere,* a large peat-moss at the S. end of the Lake of Iseo, where traces of pile-dwellings have been found.—23 km. **Iseo** (197 m), stands on the S. bank of the lake which bears its name. The church tower was built by Count Giacomo Oldofredi (1325), whose tomb is built into the façade alongside. Inside is a painting of St Michael by Fr. Hayez.

The **Lake of Iseo,** an expansion of the Oglio, 15 m. long and 3 m. wide, was the *Lacus Sebinus* of the Romans. The wooded island of *Monte Isola* which it contains is 2 m. long, and the largest island in any Italian lake. Lóvere, Iseo, and Pisogne are the chief holiday resorts on its banks, which have suffered less from modern development than those of the more famous lakes.

STEAMERS, 5 times daily between Sárnico and Lóvere, call at piers on both sides of the lake (more frequent service between Sàrnico and Tavernola); some additional services link interim ports; also local service Castro-Lóvere-Pisogne.

Sárnico, where the steamer starts, stands at the outflow of the Oglio and is served by railway bus from Palazzolo sull'Oglio (12 km.; p. 181) and by bus from Bergamo. It is frequented by motor-boat racing enthusiasts. To the N. rise the barren slopes of *Monte Brenzone* (1333 m), beneath which the W. bank is lined with villas. The boat calls at *Clusane* on the E. bank before re-crossing to the W. bank for *Predore,* which is noted for its vines. A ruined tower of the old castle is conspicuous.—The next call is made at (½ hr) *Iseo* (see above).—The steamer now turns N., with Monte Isola in front, and the Punta del Corno on the left. A call is made at the island pier of *Sensole* before *Sulzano* (see below) on the E. bank, and at *Peschiera Maráglio,* on the island, before touching at *Sale Marasino* (see below). It returns to the N. shore of the island at *Carzano* and *Siviano,* from where a pleasant walk of an hour skirts the W. shore of the island to the *Rocca Martinengo,* a half-ruined castle.—1½ hr. *Tavérnola Bergamasca,* on the W. bank, has its campanile built on to an old castle-tower. The slower boats now return to Siviano before continuing viâ Marone (see below). On the approach to (2½ hrs) *Riva di Solto* there is a fine view up the Valle Camónica northwards to the Adamello mountains. The black marble quarries here furnished marble for the columns of St Mark's in Venice. On the left are seen two little bays called the Bogn di Zorzino and Bogn di Castro, with curiously distorted rock-strata.—*Castro* has quarries and an old-established iron foundry.—2¾ hrs *Pisogne* (see below).

3 hrs **Lóvere,** at the N. extremity of the lake, is the principal tourist resort on its shores. It is reached most conveniently by steamer, or by bus from Pisogne (see below) or from Bergamo or Clusone (Rte 17). To the N. of the town is the church of *Santa Maria in Valvendra* (1473-83) which contains frescoed decoration and stalls (16C) and organ-shutters decorated outside by Ferramola and inside by Moretto (1518).

To the S. on the lake-shore is the GALLERIA DELL'ACCADEMIA TADINI (adm. May-Nov, 10-12, 15-18 or 14.30-17), which contains a few interesting paintings (Madonna, by *Iac. Bellini;* Monks in a cave, by *Magnasco;* Madonna enthroned and Baptism of Jesus by *Civerchio*), and in the garden the cenotaph of Faustino Tadini (d. 1799), by *Canova.*

A pleasant walk ascends above the town to the *Altipiano di Lóvere*(990 m), with some attractive country villas, and to (2½ hrs) *Bóssico,* among meadows and pinewoods. Thence a zigzag road descends to (6½ km.) *Sóvere* on the Clusone road, 6½ km. from Lóvere.

The railway and road beyond Iseo skirt the E. bank of the lake.— 26 km. *Pilzone* lies beneath the Pizzo dell'Orso (1001 m).—28 km. *Sulzano* is a starting-point for visiting Monte Isola. On the right is Monte Rodondone (1143 m). 31½ km. *Sale Marasino* has a conspicuous church.—34½ km. *Marone,* a large village, is the base for the ascent of *Monte Guglielmo* (1949 m), the culminating point of the range between the lake and the Val Trompia.

The ascent leads viâ (8 km.) *Zone* and the Rifugio Monte Guglielmo (key at Zone) to the summit (3½ hrs from Zone; fine view). The descent may be made to the Val Trompia at Lavone (5½ hrs), below Bóvegno.

The view is interrupted by tunnels as the road rounds the Corna dei Trenta Passi (1248 m).—44½ km. **Pisogne** is a large timber-growing and weaving village, principally notable as being the nearest station to Lóvere (bus in connection with the trains). Noteworthy are the church of *Santa Maria della Neve,* with frescoes by Romanino, and the 14C *Torre del Véscovo.* A winding road leads up to *Faíne* (9 km.; 825 m) and *Palot* (1031 m; ski-lift). From Pian Camuno a road ascends in 18 km. to the chair-lift for *Monte Campione* (1762 m), a new ski resort.—The road now leaves the lake to enter the lovely VAL CAMÓNICA, the upper course of the Oglio.

Taking its name from the Camuni, a Rhætian tribe, the valley has always been noted for its pastoral and agricultural riches; chestnut woods are an important source of wealth, both nuts and timber being exported. Wine and cheese are extensively produced, but the ironworks that were established here in the Middle Ages have dwindled in importance and the principal works nowadays are the generating stations for hydro-electric power. The extreme upper end, below the Tonale Pass, suffered severely in the First World War. Remarkable prehistoric rock carvings can be seen throughout the valley, especially in the area around Capo di Ponte (see below).

The first village of importance is (55 km.) **Darfo** (216 m) where a bridge crosses the Oglio. On the other bank is *Corna,* now the most important part of the township, with the railway station and an ironworks at the junction of the road from Bergamo viâ Lóvere (Rte 17). In the parish church of Darfo is a fine Entombment, attributed to Palma Giovane.—56½ km. **Boário Terme,** a mineral spa, stands at the junction of the Valle d'Ángolo road. Good local wines are made at Erbanno, 1 km. N. Rock carvings (B.C. 2200-1800) may be seen at Corni Freschi and Crape.

FROM BOARIO TO DEZZO AND SCHILPARIO (Valle di Scalve), road, 24 km. ascending the Valle d'Angolo (bus).—3 km. *Ángolo* enjoys a very fine view of the triple-peaked Pizzo della Presolana. Farther on the road enters the *Gorge of the Dezzo,* a narrow chasm with overhanging cliffs.—The torrent and its falls have been almost dried up by hydro-electric works.—15 km. *Dezzo,* on the road from Bergamo to Édolo, and (24 km.) *Schilpario,* see Rte 17.

62 km. *Esine* (1½ km. r.) has churches with good frescoes.—66 km. *Cividate Camuno* (r.) is the site of the ancient Roman capital of the valley; it preserves a few antique remains and a much more conspicuous medieval tower. Above it rises the tower of a former convent. Local finds are displayed in the Museo Archeologico della Valcamonica.

A winding road ascends W. viâ Malegno to (10 km.) *Borno* (899 m), a summer resort among pine woods in the Trobiolo valley, beneath the *Corna di San Fermo* (2326 m). Between Borno and *Cogno* is the convent of the Annunziata (1 hr), with two 15C cloisters.

Road and railway cross the Oglio and reach (70 km.) **Breno,** the chief town in the valley (5540 inhab.), an excellent centre for excursions. It is dominated by the ruins of its medieval *Castle* (9C and later). The *Parish Church* has a fine granite campanile and frescoes by Giov. Pietro da Cemmo and Romanino. The *Museo Camuno* merits a visit.

FROM BRENO TO THE LAKE OF IDRO, 46 km., mountain road.—5 km. *Bienno* (445 m) has two churches with frescoes. The road ascends to the E., passing Campolaro and the ski slopes of *Bazena* (1972 m; Rifugio Tassara). Thence (at 18 km.) by the Passo di Croce Domini to the head of the *Lake of Idro*, the *Passo Maniva* and *Collio*, see p. 187).

Above Breno the dolomitic peaks of the Concarena (2549 m) rise on the left and the Pizzo Badile (2435 m) on the right. The villages are mostly high up on the slopes of the foothills on either side.—80 km. **Capo di Ponte** came to prominence with the discovery here in the Permian sandstone of tens of thousands of rock engravings from Neolithic to Roman times (B.C. 14), now the feature of the *Parco delle Incisioni Rupestri*. The Naquane rock here has 900 figures carved in the Iron Age.

This is the nearest station to *Cimbergo-Paspardo* (838-945 m), a scattered commune affording fine views of the Concarena. The road passes *San Salvatore,* a Lombard church of the early 12C. An easier road leaves the valley-road 6½ km. downstream.—About 2 km. from Capo di Ponte, overlooking the river, is the church of * *San Siro*, dating from the 11C with earlier portions.

86 km. *Cedégolo,* with a church entirely frescoed by Ant. Cappello (17C), stands at the foot of the lovely Val Saviore, leading up to the Adamello mountain group, including *Cevo* (1024 m) and *Saviore dell'Adamello* (1210 m), 10 and 13 km. up the valley.

Ascents in the Adamello group may be started from the *Rifugio Prudenzini* (2234 m), 4½ hrs N.E. of Saviore; while above the s. side of the valley lies the *Lago d'Arno* (3 hrs; 1792 m), a lovely little mountain tarn. *Monte Adamello* (3555 m) is an easy though fatiguing alpine ascent from the refuge (6 hrs).

The road from Schilpario (p. 180) comes in on the r. as the valley opens out again and commands fine views of Monte Aviolo and other peaks of the Baitone group to the N.E.—98 km. *Sónico,* on the hill to the right among chestnut woods, has a large hydro-electric station.

A fine excursion leads up the Valle Malga viâ the chestnut woods of *Rino* to the *Lago di Baitone* (2247 m) and the lake-studded basin in which lies the *Rifugio Franco Tonolini* (2437 m, 5 hrs). Thence the *Corno delle Granate* (3111 m; *View) may be climbed in 2½ hrs; the *Punta di Premassone* (3070 m; *View), rather more easily in the same time.

101 km. **Édolo** (690 m), chief place (4330 inhab.) in the upper Val Camónica, is the terminus of the railway and stands on the Aprica-

Tonale road connecting the Valtellina with the Tyrol. The surroundings are beautiful, but the mountains are rather too distant for convenient ascents.

For the road to the *Aprica Pass* and *Tirano*, see p. 169.

FROM ÉDOLO TO THE TONALE PASS AND MALÈ, N42 (61 km.), bus twice daily, in winter once (weather permitting); more frequently to Ponte di Legno. The road follows the right bank of the Oglio nearly all the way, but crosses momentarily to the left bank at (5 km.) *Incúdine.*—9½ km. *Vezza d'Oglio* (1080 m), stands in a magnificent position at the confluence of two tributary valleys—the Val Grande on the N., the Val Paghera on the S. At the head of the latter rises the Corno Baitone; a road ascends the valley to (4 km.) the *Cascata di Paghera,* and is continued by a track to (7 km.) the *Lago d'Aviolo,* a reservoir.—The *Corno Tremoncelli* (2834 m), 6-7 hrs N., offers a fairly hard ascent, and commands a fine view of the Bernina and Adamello mountains, to the N.W. and S.E.

15 km. *Temù* (1149 m) is a resort for winter sports on Monte Calvo (chair-lift to 1958 m, and then ski-lifts), and for climbers the starting-point for the *Rifugio Garibaldi* (2542 m), 5 hrs S. at the head of the Val d'Avio, noted for its lake and its waterfalls. Glacier excursions may be made from the refuge. The *Adamello* (see above) may be ascended in c. 4½ hrs.

The valley becomes more and more attractive; above the road to the left is *Villa d'Allegno,* dominated by the scanty ruins of a castle; on the right above the pretty hamlet of Poia is seen the modern castle of Belpoggio.—19 km. **Ponte di Legno** (1260 m), the chief resort of the region with summer and winter seasons, stands in a wide open basin with excellent ski-slopes and a chair-lift ascending S. to an old fort (1847 m) on the Corno d'Aola. To the N. the Val di Pezzo is followed by the road to Bormio (p. 170), while to the S. and S.E. the Adamello and Presanella groups are conspicuous, notably the *Cima Salimmo* (3130 m) in the former, and the *Castellaccio* (3028 m), the N.W. spur of the latter.

The road now zigzags through woods up the flank of *Monte Tonale* (2694 m) and passes a large sanatorium.—29 km. The **Tonale Pass** (1884 m), on the former Austro-Italian frontier, separating Lombardy from the Trentino, is a wide opening between the Presanella foothills, or Monticelli, and the lower peaks to the left. To the W. of the pass a cable-car gives access to the snowfields of Presena, to the S., where skiing is possible in summer; and beyond the pass, numerous lifts operate on the slopes of Monte Tonale, to the N. A winged Victory marks the War Cemetery adjoining the road.—The road descends the Val Vermiglio, the upper reach of the Val di Sole.—39 km. *Pizzano* (1218 m).—44 km. **Fucine** (978 m) stands at the junction of the Val Vermiglio and Val di Peio, with the ruined castle of *Ossana* rising to the S.

In the latter valley, to the N., are the little summer resorts of *Cógolo* (6 km.) and **Peio Terme** (9 km.), both served by bus from Édolo. The latter is magnificently situated at a height of 1379 m in a pastoral valley and is the centre for important ascents among the mountains to the N.W. A cable-car and chair-lift rise to 2350 m below the *Rifugio Vioz* (3536 m) to the N.N.W., reached by foot in 6½ hrs. It is the base for the ascent of **Monte Vioz* (3644 m; 7 hrs), presenting no difficulty to expert climbers. **Monte Cevedale* (3764 m), the highest of this group, is climbed in 10½ hrs viâ the *Rifugio Cevedale* (4½ hrs; 1397 m) at the head of the Val della Mare, the first part of which is traversed (from Cogolo) by an unmade-up road (9½ km.). A good view of the whole range is gained from the *Civa di Boai* (2683 m), an easy climb of 4 hrs S. of Peio.

The main road descends the Val di Sole, which now widens, with many villages and hamlets scattered along the slopes.—46 km. *Pellizzano* lies on the opposite side of the river Noce.—49 km. *Mezzana* is a ski resort (chair-lift and cable-car from Marilleva).—52 km. *Mastellina,* (811 m), the home of the family of the painter Guardi (tablet on his father's house), lies opposite *Almazzago,* with its Romanesque belfry. The road from Tione and Trento soon comes in on the right.—61 km. *Malè,* see Rte 24.

20   LAKE GARDA

*LAKE GARDA (Lago di Garda; 65 m), the Roman *Lacus Benacus,*
is the largest and one of the most beautiful of the Italian lakes (33 m.
long, 2-11 m. wide; 143 sq. m. in area). The narrow N. part, between
towering cliffs, offers wild and romantic scenery; the broad basin to
which the lake widens in the S. is encircled by pleasant hills. The only
important stream flowing into the lake is the Sarca, descending from the
Trentino; the outlet is the Mincio. The predominant winds (which may
swell into violent storms) are the *sover,* from the N. in the morning, and
the *ora,* from the S. in the afternoon.

Wildfowl abound, and fish (though depleted by netting) are fairly
numerous. The winter climate is mild, and the summer heat tempered by
refreshing breezes. The olive is much cultivated, and plantations of
oranges and lemons as well as vineyards flourish on the shores. The W.
bank belongs to Lombardy, the E. bank to Venetia, and the N. extremity
to the Trentino. The lake is much frequented by German holiday-
makers, especially since the opening of the autostrada from the
Brennero.

Approaches. The 'Serenissima' Autostrada (A4; Turin-Milan-Venice) skirts the
S. end of the lake, with exits at *Desenzano, Sirmione,* and *Peschiera.* The
Autostrada (A12) from the Brennero viâ Bolzano and Trento runs close to the E.
side of the lake, with exits at *Lago di Garda Nord* and *Lago di Garda Sud.*
Desenzano and Peschiera are both stations on the main railway line from Milan to
Verona (Rte 18) and are connected by steamer and bus with ports on both banks.
Gargnano and *Salò* have bus connections with Brescia; *Bardolino* and *Garda* with
Verona; *Riva* with Trento (connecting with the main railway from Trento to
Verona at Rovereto), Brescia, and Desenzano.

Road round the Lake, 143 km. The magnificent road encircling the lake is
known as *La Gardesana* (*Occidentale* on the W. bank, *Orientale* on the E.) This
remarkable engineering feat entailed the blasting of a passage for the roadway
through many kilometres of solid rock, and the construction of c.80 tunnels. The
views are necessarily interrupted, but they are perhaps all the more striking for
that, and the expedition by car or bus, at least from Gardone to Riva, is one that
should not be missed.

Intermediate distances: Desenzano-Salo, 20 km.; Salo-Riva, 44 km.; Riva-
Peschiera, 65 km.; Peschiera-Desenzano, 14 km.

Bus Services: by the Gardesana Occidentale from *Peschiera* viâ *Desenzano*
(20 min.) to *Riva* several times daily; by the Gardesana Orientale from *Peschiera* to
Riva in 95 min.; more frequently from Lazise and Garda (c. hourly; all services
originating in Verona).

Steamer Services (including a paddle-steamer built in 1901). In summer two
services daily between Desenzano and Riva in 4½ hrs, calling only at ports on the
W. bank as far as Gargnano; hydrofoil service 4 times daily in 2 hrs (with fewer
stops); reduced services in winter. More frequent steamer services between
Desenzano and Maderno (in 1 hr 50 min.). Car ferry between Maderno and Torri di
Benaco in ½ hr. A service runs between Sirmione, Peschiera, and Garda (and a
boat or hydrofoil runs c. every hr. between Desenzano and Sirmione). Tickets
allowing free circulation on the lake services for specific periods may be purchased.
Tours of the lake in the afternoons in summer are also organized. All information
from the offices of the 'Navigazione sul Lago di Garda', 2 P.za Matteotti,
Desenzano sul Garda.

A   From Desenzano to Riva by the West Bank

(The kilometre distances are by road.)

Desenzano del Garda (69 m), the usual starting-point for excursions
on the Lago di Garda, is a lively little town (19,100 inhab.) connected
with its station (Rte 18) by bus. From the steamer quay a bridge crosses

an inlet used as a harbour for small boats, behind which is the main Piazza Giuseppe Malvezzi, with pretty arcades, and a monument to St Angela Merici (1474-1540), foundress of the Ursuline order. A road leads r. out of the piazza to the parish church with a *Last Supper by Gian Dom: Tiepolo. Just to the W., reached by Via Crocifisso, is an excavated area with a *Roman Villa* (adm. 9.30-12, 15-19; closed Mon) with polychrome 4C mosaics, and an Antiquarium. Close by, traces of a Basilica have been found.

The ROAD FROM DESENZANO TO SALÒ, N572, 20 km. at first skirts the lake.— 4 km. *Lonato Lido.* On the by-road (l.) to Lonato (1 km.; Rte 18) is the Abbey of *Maguzzano,* founded for Benedictines in the 10C and occupied by Trappists in 1903-38.—The road leaves the lake and its many camping sites and crosses the hilly district of *Valtenesi;* on the right is a view of the lake and the castle of Moniga.— 20 km. *Salò,* see below.

On the right as the steamer leaves the pier (following the route taken by Tennyson in 1880) can be seen the curious promontory of Sirmione, 3½ km. long and in places only 119 metres wide.

Sirmione, near the end of the promontory, is a spa, with warm sulphur springs (La Boiola) that rise in the lake. Wealthy Romans favoured Sirmione as a summer residence, and Catullus, who had a villa here, speaks of "Peninsularum, Sirmio, insularumque ocelle". It is now virtually given over to tourism with numerous large hotels.

Buses hourly to *Brescia* and *Verona;* to *Desenzano, Peschiera,* etc.
Boats for hire on the lake (with guide), and for water-skiing.--*Bathing Lido* on E. side of the peninsular; swimming off rocks on W. side.

The 15C church of *Santa Maria Maggiore* preserves some antique columns. The picturesque 13C *Rocca Scaligera* (adm. 9-13, 15.30-18.30; winter 9-14; fest. 9-13; closed Mon), where Dante is said to have stayed, was a stronghold of the Scaliger family, lords of Verona. The massive central tower, 29 m high, commands a good view. A road leads N. from Via della Repubblica to *San Pietro in Mavino,* a Romanesque church of 8C foundation, retaining early frescoes. At the end of the headland are the so-called GROTTE DI CATULLO (8 or-9 dusk; closed Mon), really the romantic ruins of a large Roman villa set amidst olive groves with a splendid view out over the lake. The frescoes date from the 1C B.C.

The steamer provides a striking view of the promontory as it leaves Sirmione; it then steers N.W. skirting the *Rocca di Manerba,* a headland once crowned by a castle. Then it passes through the narrow channel between the romantic headland of Punta San Fermo and the *Isola di Garda* on which is the Villa Borghese (no adm.) with a 19C palazzo in the Venetian Gothic manner. The boat turns S.W. to enter the Gulf of Salò, and passes *Porto Portese,* the landfall for *San Felice del Benaco* (3½ km.).

20 km. **Salò** (10,600 inhab.), the Roman *Salodium,* and the birthplace of Gaspare Bertolotti, or da Salò (1540-1609), generally considered to be the first maker of violins, is perhaps the most beautiful spot on the lake. It gave name to Mussolini's short-lived puppet republic of 1944. The Gothic cathedral (*Annunziata*) has a good Renaissance portal (1509). In the interior are paintings by Romanino (Madonna and Child, in the Baptistery), a polyptych by Paolo Veneziano (W. end of N. aisle), and a carved wooden tabernacle with ten statues in niches (15C) in the Sacristy. The *Palazzo Fantoni* is the seat of the Biblioteca Ateneo, which

has its origins in the Accademia degli Unanimi founded by G. Maione in 1560. The fine library has over 25,000 vols. many of great historical interest.

Between Salò and Gargnano extends the *Riviera Bresciana, a succession of villages linked by villas and hotels, and set in cedar and olive groves. The steamer passes close to *Barbarano* with the *Palazzo Martinengo* (adm. on written application), built in 1577 by the Marchese Sforza Pallavicino, the Venetian general.

24 km. **Gardone Riviera** and (25 km.) **Fasano Riviera,** now practically continuous, make up a frequented winter resort in the most sheltered situation on the lake. They enjoy an unusually mild winter climate, and the parks and gardens are embellished with rare trees. Gardone offers a good centre for excursions in the hilly hinterland of the Riviera, which soon becomes mountainous.

At Gardone di Sopra (above the Grand Hotel), which has an old campanile, is the *Vittoriale degli Italiani* (8-18.30; winter 8-12, 14-18) where Gabriele d'Annunzio died (1863-1938). The complex of gardens and memorials to the martial poet includes his villa (temporarily closed after recent thefts), an open-air theatre, concert-hall, and Museum. From *Mornaga,* to the W., there is a descent direct (red marks) to the *Piccolo Righi* (190 m; ½ hr). Another road from Gardone di Sopra (blue marks) ascends in 1½ hr to the chapel of *San Michele.* Other excursions may be made to the *Barbarano Gorge* (green marks), starting from the bridge over the river; while *Monte Pizzócolo* (1583 m), the highest of the neighbouring peaks, may be ascended in c. 5 hrs via Fasano di Sopra and Sanico.

28 km. **Toscolano-Maderno** (another resort) situated on the delta of the Toscolano, which is more fertile than it is picturesque, and backed by rocky hills, was the chief Roman settlement (*Benacum*) of the Riviera Bresciana. A frequent car-ferry crosses the lake to Torri (see Rte 20B). In Maderno, on the S. side, the 12C Romanesque church of *Sant' Andrea* shows remains of Roman and Byzantine architecture, especially in the decoration of the pillar capitals, doors and windows; an older church seems to have been incorporated in the building. In Toscolano, behind the church of Santi Pietro e Paolo (good 16C wood-carvings), are the *Santuario della Madonna del Benaco,* with 15C frescoes and remains of a Roman villa.

A winding road ascends from Toscolano to *Gaino* (301 m), a finely situated village, whence steep paths lead down (l.) into the Toscolano valley and (r.) to Cecina on the coast road.

33 km. *Bogliaco,* the next steamer halt, has a 9-hole golf course. The *Villa Bettoni* (adm. on application) contains a collection of 17-18C works of art.—36 km. **Gargnano** is notable for the 13C church and cloister of San Francesco.

The Valle Toscolana, a centre of paper-making from 15C-early 20C, is best visited by road from Gargnano or on foot from Gaino (see above). The road passes (12 km.) the hydro-electric *Lago di Valvestino* and descends to the remote villages of the Valvestino, ending at (25 km.) *Magasa.*

FROM GARGNANO TO LIMONE by the inland road, 33 km. This road soon diverges uphill (l.) from the 'Gardesana' and gradually winds its way up to the shelf which carries the scattered commune of *Tignale* (10 km.)—*Oldesio* (465 m) is connected with the pier of Tignale by a steep footpath. Beyond it is a curious view of the lake shore almost vertically beneath, and of Monte Baldo opposite.—12 km. **Gárdola** (555 m) is the chief village of Tignale. The *Madonna di Monte Castello* (691 m; 20 min.) commands the finest *View of the whole lake. The road leads to the right, just before Gardola, with Monte Castello on the right, and then gradually recedes from the lake.—From (14 km.) *Prabione* a track descends to the Porto di Campione.—After crossing (20 km.) the Torrente di San Michele this route leaves on the right a road back to the 'Gardesana' and reaches (25 km.) *Vesio* (625 m), the highest village in the commune of Tremósine (see below). Turning again towards the lake the road descends viâ (27 km.) *Voltino* to (33 km.) *Limone* on the lake shore (see below).

Beyond Gargnano the lake narrows considerably and the W. shore becomes a rocky wall through which the Gardesana road tunnels.— Beyond (42 km.) *Porto di Tignale,* connected by footpath with Tignale (see above), the mighty cliff of the Monte di Castello is conspicuous, with the chapel on its S. peak.—46 km. *Campione* stands on the delta of a torrent and has a large cotton mill.

A very fine *Road ascends, with many tunnels, viaducts, and sharp curves to (5 km.) **Pieve di Tremósine** (413 m) a village on a steep cliff descending into the lake, commanding a fine *View. Two roads go on to the upper village of Vcsio (see above), that viâ Villa being preferable (6 km.).

The terraced lemon and lime gardens become more noticeable on the approach to (54 km.) **Limone sul Garda,** which takes its name from its lemon plantations, said to be the first in Europe.

For the inland road to Gargnano, see above.—An interesting walk ascends the Valle del Singol to the *Passo di Bestana* (1269 m; on the old frontier) and the *Lago di Ledro* (5½ hr; see below).

Beyond the next point, the characteristic outline of the Sperone comes into view and the lower end of the lake is lost to sight. The mountains on the left, rising abruptly from the lake, are separated by the gorge of the Ponale, with waterfalls and a power station. The windings of the road up the gorge are well seen, and the N. end of the lake, with the isolated Monte Brione, offers a splendid panorama.

65 km. **Riva,** the Roman *Ripa,* a lively and agreeable little town (13,000 inhab.), and the most important place on the lake, is sheltered by Monte Rochetta to the W. Riva lay in Austrian territory until 1918, and the surrounding heights were strongly fortified. The town was spared by the Italian artillery during the advance of 1915, but it suffered considerably in the course of the campaign.

Post Office, Viale San Francesco.
Buses to **Trento** viâ *Le Sarche* and viâ *Rovereto;* to *Ponte Arche* and *Molveno;* to *Desenzano* by the W. shore; to *Peschiera* by the E. shore.
Boats for hire on the lake and for water-skiing.

The centre of the old town is P.za Tre Novembre, in which are the austere 13C *Torre Apponale,* the *Palazzo Pretorio* (1370), the *Palazzo Comunale* (1475), and some medieval porticos. In P.za della Rocca, encircled by water, stands the much altered 12C *Castle.* In the courtyard are Roman and medieval sarcophagi. Within, the *Museo Civico* (adm. March-Sept, 9-18) contains collections of archæology, armour and locally printed works, including a Talmud of 1558. On the road to Arco, is the church of the *Inviolata,* begun in 1603 by an unknown Portuguese, with a graceful Baroque interior.

A chair-lift (or on foot in 30 min.) ascends to the *Bastione* (view) a round tower built by the Venetians in 1506, and dominated by the craggy Monte Rocchetta (1521 m).
The chief short excursions from Riva are those to *Arco* (see below) and to *Tórbole* (see below).—The *Cascata del Varone* is approached by road viâ (3 km. N.) *Varone,* whence the waterfall, in its gorge, is 1 km. N.W. From Varone a road continues to (8 km.) *Tenno,* with its castle, and (12 km.) the turquoise-blue *Lago di Tenno.* From the lake the road goes on to (26 km.) *Ponte delle Arche* (Rte 24).
It is 4 km. from Riva by road along the shore, skirting the crescent-shaped

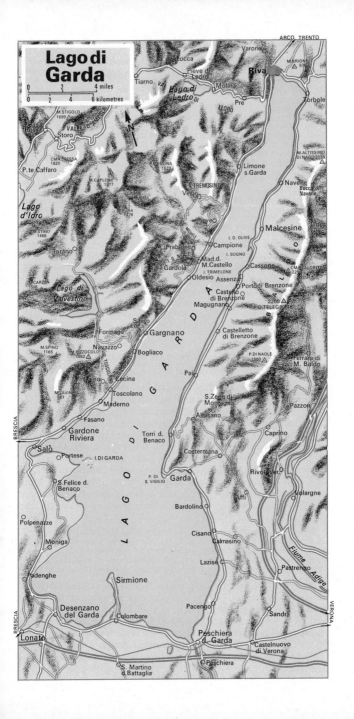

Monte Brione (376 m), to **Tórbole**, a summer resort near the mouth of the Sarca. Tórbole played a part in the war of 1439 between the Visconti and the Venetians, when fleets of warships were dragged overland by teams of oxen and launched into the lake. Goethe stayed here in 1786. To the S. rise the steep spurs of the Monte Baldo.

FROM RIVA TO THE LAGO DI LEDRO AND THE LAGO D'IDRO, 40 km. This route follows the road on the W. bank of the lake for a short distance, then diverges uphill to the right by the *PONALE ROAD*, which also tunnels through the cliffs of the Rocchetta and the Sperone. It soon reaches the mouth of the Val di Ledro near the not very impressive falls of the *Cascata del Ponale,* reached also by boat or by the Gardesana road. It turns inland up the valley for (10 km.) the *Lago di Ledro* (1¾ m. long), at the further end of which is *Pieve di Ledro* (660 m).—17 km. *Bezzecca.*—At (20 km.) *Tiarno di Sopra* the road crosses the watershed (745 m) and descends the Valle d'Ámpola, a steep gorge with frequent waterfalls. Just beyond (25 km.) the little lago d'Ámpola, an unmade road (l.) leads in 12 km. to the Passo di Tremalzo (1894 m) with a chair-lift and refuges. A tortuous road descends from there to Vesio (see above).—33 km. *Storo* and *Casa Rossa* (bus to Idro) in the Valli Giudicarie, 5 km. above Ponte Cáffaro on the Lago d'Idro (see Rte 18).

From Riva to *Molveno,* see Rte 24; to *Rovereto,* see Rte 23.

About 6 km. N.E. of Riva by road is the little health resort of **Arco** (91 m) in the valley of the Sarca (11,300 inhab.). Arco is the birthplace of the painter Giovanni Segantini (1858-99), whose monument by Bistolfi stands in the Giardino Pubblico. The *Assunta* is a handsome church in the Palladian style, and the former palazzo of the Counts, to the left, is a good 16C building. The *Castle* of the counts of Arco, on a rocky height (½ hr) commands a fine *View of the valley of the Sarca and the lake.

B   From Riva to Peschiera by the East Bank

(Kilometric distances are by road; for buses etc. see the beginning of the route.)

Beyond (4 km.) *Tórbole* (see above) the E. side of the lake is bounded by the almost inaccessible cliff of *Monte Altissimo di Nago* (2079 m), the N. peak of the Baldo range, which provides a dignified background for the Venetian shore of Lake Garda. Its peaks are best ascended from the Adige valley (see Rte 23).—13 km. *Navene* (no pier), a poor hamlet on this inhospitable shore, gives name to the *Bocca di Navene* (1430 m; 4 hrs by mule track), the only pass of importance across the Monte Baldo chain.—17 km. **Malcésine,** the seat of the Veronese Captains of the Lake in the 16-17C, preserves their old palazzo as a town hall. More conspicuous is the 13-14C castle of the Scaligers, restored by Venice in the 17C and housing a small Museum (adm. Apr-Oct, 9-18 or 19). The tower affords a fine *View.

A cableway mounts to the ski-slopes of Monte Baldo (1748 m). The *Punta del Telegrafo* (2201 m), the chief peak of the range, is a simple though tiring climb of c. 6 hrs. A pleasant walk of c. 2 hrs among the olive-grown slopes above the town ascends from the Navene road, 15 min. N. of Malcesine, to *Palazzina,* and then turns S. to the *Altipiano delle Vigne,* re-entering Malcesine from the S.

The coast becomes less wild farther S. past the islets of Olivo and Sogno, the village of *Cassone* (no pier), and the island of *Trimelone,* which bears the remains of a castle.—24 km. *Assenza* with the small 14C church of San Nicolò di Bari (13-14C frescoes), is in the commune of **Brenzone.**—25 km. *Porto di Brenzone.*—27 km. *Magugnano* is the seat of the commune.—Beyond the Romanesque church of San Zeno (early 12C) and (33 km.) *Pai* there is a magnificent view of the opposite shore of the lake.

39 km. **Torri del Benaco,** the Roman *Castrum Turrium* and the chief town of the Gardesana after the 13C, preserves a fine castle of the Scaligers dating from 1383 and a church with 15C frescoes. Its red and yellow marbles are locally famous. A frequent car ferry crosses to Maderno (see Rte 20A).

Torri is the landing point for (9 km.) *San Zeno di Montagna* a mountain resort high above the lake (582 m) reached by a zigzag road.

The steamer rounds (44 km.) the *Punta di San Vigilio,* the lovelist headland on the E. shore, on which are the little church of *San Vigilio* among cypress groves, and the *Villa Guarienti* (1540), possibly by Sammicheli.

46 km. **Garda** once a fortified town, and still retaining some interesting old houses, lies at the head of a deep bay. Famous under both Romans and Longobards, it had origins yet more ancient, as testified by an early necropolis on the outskirts. In the *Castle,* now gone, on Monte Garda, to the S.E., Queen Adelaide was held prisoner by Berenger II (c. 960), and Julius Caesar Scaliger (1484-1558) was born. The altar chapel of *Santa Maria Maggiore* preserves porch columns of its predecessor.

Short excursions may be made to the *Rocca,* the site of the old castle; to the *Eremo dei Camaldolesi* (309 m; 40 min.) the church of which houses a painting by Palma Giovane (the descent may be made to Bardolino); and to San Vigilio (see above). Garda is connected by bus (every hour, in 1 hr) with Verona.

The hills become lower and the view less romantic as the broad basin at the foot of the lake opens out.—51 km. **Bardolino,** another ancient place retaining some commercial importance, gives name to a well-known wine. A tower and two gates remain from an old castle of the Scaligers. The tiny Carolingian church of San Zeno retains its 9C form and, beyond, *San Severo* is 12C with contemporary frescoes. The shore becomes uninteresting on the approach to (53 km.) *Cisano,* a small village whose church retains a Romanesque façade and campanile.— 56 km. *Lazise,* retaining part of its medieval wall, has been succeeded by Bardolino as the chief port on this shore. A castle of the Scaligers (with Venetian additions) and the 16C Venetian custom house attest to its former importance, and form a charming group on the lake front. San Nicolò is a 12C church with 16C additions (14C frescoes).—66 km. **Peschiera** is on the main road and railway from Milan to Verona (Rte 18).

21 FROM MILAN TO CREMONA AND MANTUA

ROAD, 151 km., leaving Milan by the Porta Vittoria and the Corso Ventidue Marzo; immediately beyond the railway turn right on N 415.—44 km. **Crema.**— 83 km. **Cremona,** entered by Pta Milano and left by Pta Venezia.—N 10, 113 km. *Piádena.*—151 km. **Mantua,** entered by the Corso Vittorio Emanuele.

RAILWAY, 149 km. in 2¼-3 hrs; to *Clemona,* 86 km., in 1½ hr. The line follows the Via Emilia (Rte 38) viâ Lodi to Casalpusterlengo, then branches at *Codogno,* where a change is sometimes necessary (three through trains daily).—Another line viâ *Treviglio* (comp. Rte 18) to *Cremona* (99 km.; through trains) takes longer but serves *Crema* (56 km.) in 1¼-2 hrs; Crema to Cremona in 1 hr.

This route leaves Milan by the Linate airport road, from which, immediately beyond the railway, the Crema road, N 415, diverges right.—At (25 km.) *Bisnate* the Adda is crossed.—44 km. **Crema,** a town of 33,900 inhab. on the W. bank of the Serio, was in the Venetian dominion from 1454 to 1797. The *Cathedral,* in the Campionese style (1284-1341), has a fine tower, and the piazza in front of it is surrounded by Renaissance buildings, including the 16C *Palazzo Pretorio* with an archway leading to the main street, the pleasant ex-convent of SANT' AGOSTINO houses the library and *Museo Civico* (Sun 10-12, or on application at the library), where is displayed burial armour from Lombard tombs discovered in 1963 at Offanengo, N.E. of the town. The *Refectory,* restored as a concert hall, has frescoes by Giov. Pietro da Cemmo. *Santa Maria della Croce,* 2 km. N., is a handsome church (1493-1500), after Bramante, by Giov. Battagio.

To *Soncino* and *Brescia,* see Rte 18.

55 km. *Castelleone* has a 10C tower and the 15C church of Santa Maria di Bressanoro (2 km. N). The direct road by-passes the centre and runs straight across the plain to Cremona, while the old road (5 km. longer) passes through *Soresina,* now more industrial than agricultural, and *Casalbuttano.*

83 km. **CREMONA** is a busy and cheerful city (82,700 inhab.) notable for its many ancient brick buildings, survivals of the age of the Lombard city-states. It is an important agricultural market.

Hotels near the Duomo and P.za Roma.
Post Office, Via Verdi.—**E.P.T.,** 2 Galleria del Corso.
Theatre, *Ponchielli,* Corso Vittorio Emanuele.—A Festival of stringed instruments is held in October every 3 years (next in 1979).
Trolley-Buses from the Station to the P.za Roma.—*Local Buses* trom P.za Marconi to *Casalmaggiore* and most places in the province.—**Country Buses** from the same to *Milan;* to *Mantua;* to *Brescia;* to *Bergamo;* to *Piacenza;* and to *Soncino.* Also less frequently to *Fidenza* and *Salsomaggiore Terme;* and to *Genoa.* Once daily to *Padua, Venice* and *Trieste.*
History. Founded by the Romans as a colonia in 218 B.C., *Cremona* became an important fortress and road junction on the Via Postumia. Its decline after a siege and sack in A.D. 69 ended in destruction by the Lombards in 603. Cremona re-emerges as a city-state in 1098, warring as usual with its neighbours—Milan, Brescia, and Piacenza. In 1334 it was taken by Azzone Visconti of Milan, and remained from then on under Milanese domination; being given in dowry to Bianca Maria Visconti on the occasion of her marriage to Fr. Sforza in 1441, it enjoyed a century of patronage and prosperity.—Among Cremonese painters may be mentioned Boccaccio Boccaccino and his son Camillo, the Campi family, and G. B. Trotti; but Cremona is more celebrated for its terracotta sculpture work, and above all for the manufacture of violins; the most renowned makers being Andrea Amati (fl. 1550-80), Nicolò Amati (1596-1684), Ant. Stradivari (Stradivarius; 1644-1737), and Gius. Guarneri (Joseph Guarnerius; 1683-1745). The composer Claudio Monteverdi (1567-1643) is another famous native.

Corso Garibaldi descends to the centre from the station. On the left is the church of *San Luca* (closed) with a 15C façade adorned with the terracotta ornament typical of Cremona; adjoining is a little octagonal chapel in the Renaissance style of 1503. On the right (No. 178) *Palazzo Raimondi* of 1496 has frescoes on its curved cornice. It is the seat of the Scuola di Liuteria, and the centre of musical activity in Cremona. Farther on stands *Palazzo del Popolo* or *Cittanova* (1256), the headquarters of the popular, or Guelph party in the days of the free commune of Cremona; it is adjoined by the *Palazzo Trecchi* with a 'Gothic' façade of 1843-44. Opposite rises **Sant'Agata,** with a classical façade of 1845-48 by Luigi Voghera and a Romanesque campanile. Inside, on the r., is the Trecchi tomb by G. C. Romano (1502-5), and (3rd

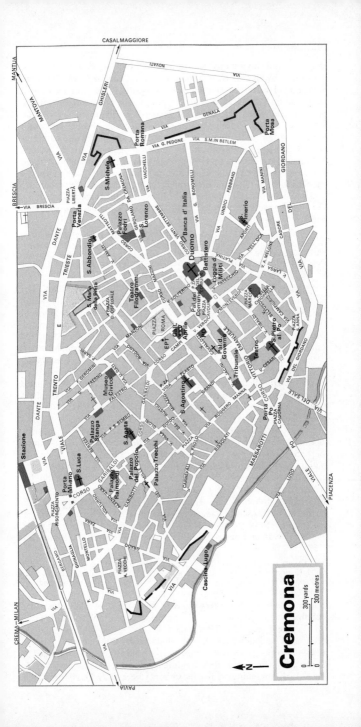

chapel in S. aisle) a panel illustrating the life of the saint (painted on both sides) by an unknown master of the 13C ('Maestro della Tavola di S. Agata'). The frescoes of the Life of St Agatha, on the sanctuary walls, are by Giulio Canipi (1536). Farther on along the Corso a detour may be made to the right by Via Milazzo and Via Plasio, to visit *Sant' Agostino, a 14C church with a good tower and notable terracotta ornamentation. In the interior are some good sculptures and paintings (4th S. chap., Annunciation, by Galeazzo Campi; 5th S. chapel, *Madonna and Saints, by Perugino), and interesting though damaged 15C frescoes in the vault and lunettes on the upper part of the wall of the chap. to the r. of the main altar, and in the 3rd S. chapel (where there are also two detached fresco portraits of Francesco and Bianca Sforza). Via Cavallotti, to the left beyond Sant'Agostino, leads back to the main street.

At the opposite corner is the monumental *National Insurance Building* (1935), traversed by the Galleria Venticinque Aprile, and beyond that is P.za Roma, a pleasant little park. Here may be seen the statue of the native composer Amilcare Ponchielli (1834-86), and the tombstone of Stradivarius salvaged from the church of San Domenico (demolished 1878).

*PIAZZA DEL COMUNE is the centre of the life of Cremona. The Romanesque *Torrazzo (13C) claims to be the highest medieval tower in Italy (110 m.; view; being restored). The *Bertazzola,* a double loggia of the Renaissance (1497-1525), stretches across the front of the cathedral. Beneath its arcades some sculptures are immured, including the sarcophagus of Folchino Schizzi (d. 1357), by Bonino da Campione, and that of Andrea Allia (1531), by Pedoni (beyond the main doorway).

The *Duomo is a splendid Romanesque basilica of 1107, consecrated in 1190 and finished considerably later. The W. front (1274-1606), varied but picturesque, is noteworthy for the rose-window of 1274; the main door is flanked by four statues of prophets. The exterior of the transepts is fine. The interior is remarkable especially for the *Frescoes (early 16C; difficult to see without strong light) on the walls of the nave and apse by *Boccaccino, Bambo, Altobello Melone, Romanino, Pordenone,* and *Bernardino Gatti.* Five 17C Brussels tapestries adorn the nave. The two pulpits have reliefs by *Pietro da Rho* or *Amadeo* (c. 1482). In the first S. chapel: *Pordenone,* SS. Peter and Dominic presenting a member of the Schizzi family to the Virgin. At the entrance to the N. transept, tomb of Monsignor Bonomelli, by *Trentacoste* (1931), and in the middle E. chapel of the transept, Pietà, an original composition by *Ant. Campi;* at the end, reliefs by *Amadeo* (1481). The choir has inlaid stalls by *G. M. Platina* (1490), and on the E. wall is a huge Assumption, by *Bern. Gatti* (1575).

In the crypt is the tomb of SS. Peter and Marcellinus, by *Briosco* (1560), while the Treasury (usually kept locked) contains two fine processional crosses. Some curious 12C mosaics in the old *Camposanto,* S. of the Duomo, are shown by the cathedral sacristan on request.

The octagonal **Baptistery** (closed since 1975), a plain Lombard building, with a dark interior, was planned by Teodosio Orlandino (1167). The *Loggia dei Militi* dates from 1292 (good windows) and has been restored as a war memorial. *Palazzo del Comune was rebuilt in 1206-45 but preserves an older tower (the windows have been spoiled by alterations). On the first floor landing is a fine Renaissance doorway. In the Sala della Giunta is a marble chimneypiece by G. G. Pedoni (16C).

Another room contains three violins made by Stradivarius and the Amati family.

Corso Venti Settembre and Via Gerol. da Cremona lead to the church of *San Michele,* founded perhaps in the 7C, and rebuilt after a fire in 1113. The exterior of the apse, the 12C columns in the nave and the rough-hewn capitals in the original crypt (now a war sanctuary) are interesting.—On the other side of Via Matteotti is the little church of *Sant'Abbondio,* to which is attached the *Loreto Chapel* containing a 15C Florentine Madonna in marble. The dignified Corso Matteotti leads back to the centre past *Palazzo Fodri* (c. 1500; now a bank), the finest of many old mansions in this street, decorated with terracotta friezes and over-restored frescoes.

Corso Vittorio Emanuele leads from P.za Cavour towards the river. Off its S. side is the monastic church of **San Pietro al Po,** sumptuously adorned with 16C paintings and stuccoes.

In Via Ugolani Dati, a turning on the right off Via Palestro, which leads back to the station, is the **Museo Civico** (adm. 10-12, 14-17, Sun 10-12), housed in Palazzo Affaitati (1561), with a fine 18C staircase. The paintings include (R. I) frescoes from demolished churches; (R. IX) *Gius. Arcimboldi* (c. 1530-93), 'Scherzo con Ortaggi', a remarkable surrealist portrait. In R. XXII some carved wooden panels in high relief show the craftsmanship of *Giac. Bertesi* (1642-1710). From R. XXIII, with medieval ivories, stairs descend to the ARCHÆOLOGICAL SECTION. where there is an excellent map of Roman Cremona, good geometric pavements, helmets, and the front of a legionary's strong-box. Also here are terracotta friezes and wrought iron work. The same room gives access up stairs to the TESORO DEE DUOMO, with 28 illuminated antiphonaries (1476-96) and a sacristy cupboard with 29 intarsia-work doors by G. M. Platina (1477). The Stradivarius Museum is housed here temporarily before its removal to the Scuola di Liuteria in Palazzo Raimondi (comp. p. 200). No. 36 Via Palestro is the *Palazzo Stanga,* with a Baroque front and a handsome courtyard, probably by Pietro da Rho; and at the top of the street the Istituto Tecnico has a fountain and bronze memorial to martyrs of freedom.

About 20 min. walk E. of Cremona along the bus route to Casalmaggiore is the *Church of **San Sigismondo,** where Fr. Sforza was married to Bianca Visconti (1441). The present building was started in 1463 in celebration of the event; its nave is covered with frescoes by the brothers Campi. Bern. Gatti and Cam. Boccaccino are likewise well represented here.

Cremona is connected by railway with *Treviglio,* and with *Brescia* (see Rte 18), and also with *Piacenza* and *Fidenza* (Rte 39).

Beyond Cremona the Mantua road, leaving the railway on the right, runs straight for 18 km., then turns abruptly S.E. Leaving on the right *Torre de' Picenardi* with its 16-18C villa, it crosses the road and railway from Brescia to Parma at (113 km.) *Piádena.* Here a small museum includes finds from the supposed site of *Bedriacum,* scene of a battle in A.D. 69 in which the generals of Vitellius defeated Otho.—The road passes N. of (123 km.) *Bózzolo,* with its 14C tower and palace of the Gonzagas, and crosses the Oligo near (128 km.) *Marcaria.*

151 km. **MANTUA,** in Italian *Mántova,* is an ancient and rather sombre city (66,000 inhab.) of the highest historical and artistic importance. It is surrounded on three sides by the Mincio ("smooth-sliding Mincius"), which widens out to form a sluggish lake of three reaches, Lago Superiore, Lago di Mezzo, and Lago Inferiore; the river itself, however, is not a special feature of the city. Mantua is a centre of the silk trade, and is interesting especially for its memorials of the great

days of the Gonzagas. Many of the roads of the old town are still cobbled.

Post Office, P.za Martiri.—**E.P.T.,** P.za Mantegna.

Buses from Porta Belfiore for towns in the province, and for *Milan.*

History. Virgil was born on Mantuan territory (comp. p. 188) about 70 B.C. and some of the town's earliest recorded history is due to the poet's interest in his native place. Mantua became a free community about 1126, and was afterwards dominated by the Bonacolsi and Gonzaga families, the latter of whom made it a brilliant centre of art and civilization (*Mantova la Glorisa*), especially in the reigns of Lodovico III (1444-78), Giovanni Francesco II (1484-1519), husband of Isabella d'Este, the greatest lady of her time (d. at Mantua, 1539), and Federigo II (1519-40). Giovanni delle Bande Nere, mortally wounded in a skirmish outside Mantua in 1526, is believed to have been buried in Santo Spirito. The sack of the city by Imperial troops in 1630 hastened its decline and the duchy came to a miserable end in 1708, when Mantua passed to the Austrians, who fortified it as the S.W. corner of their 'quadrilateral'. It held out against Napoleon for eight months in 1796-97, and was retaken by the Austrians in 1799. The town was again Austrian from 1814 to 1866. It suffered damage from the air in 1944.—Among the artists who flourished at the court of the Gonzagas were Leon Battista Alberti, Luca Fancelli, Pisanello, Mantegna, and Giulio Romano. Sordello (?1200-66) and Baldassare Castiglione (1478-1529) were born on Mantuan territory, and Giov. Batt. Spagnolo (1448-1516), or Mantuanus, the poet, the "good old Mantuan" of 'Love's Labour's Lost,' was a native of the city. The success of Monteverdi's 'Orfeo' at court in 1607 was the first landmark in the history of opera. The popularity of Verdi's 'Rigoletto' has endowed several Mantuan localities with spurious associations.

The approach from the W. (or the railway station) follows Corso Vittorio Emanuele through P.za Cavallotti into Corso Umberto I, the latter typical of the old city, with its dark and heavy porticoes narrowing as it enters P.za Marconi. In P.za Cavallotti is the handsome *Teatro Sociale* (1822). Just beyond P.ZA MARCONI, where several important streets converge is P.za Mantegna.

Here stands the unfinished basilica of **Sant'Andrea,** in the main a Renaissance building designed by *Alberti* and executed after his death by *Luca Fancelli* (1472-94); the dome was added by *Juvarra* in 1732 and the brick campanile of 1413 is a survival from an earlier church. A notable marble frieze surrounds the W. door. The finely proportioned *Interior contains frescoes, in the S. chapels (1534-70), by *Bened. Pagni* and *Rinaldo Mantovano,* pupils of Giulio Romano. The first chapel on the N. side (ring for sacristan) contains the tomb of *Andrea Mantegna* (1431-1506), with his bust in bronze, thought to be a self portrait. The painting of the Holy Family is also attrib. to him, while the Baptism of Christ is probably by his son Francesco. The frescoes, designed by Mantegna, were executed by his pupils, including *Correggio*. In the next chapel is a Madonna, by *Lor. Costa*. In the N. transept are the Andreasi-Gonzaga tomb, and that of Pietro Strozzi, an ingenious work of 1529, while the S. transept contains the Tomb of Giorgio Andreasi, by *Prospero Clementi* (1549).

The neighbouring P.za delle Erbe, crowded on market-days, contains a 15C house (No. 26), and the *Rotonda di San Lorenzo,* a small round church founded in 1082 and restored in 1908. The interior (open 10-12, 16-18; winter, 10-11, 15-14) has two orders of columns and faded frescoes (11-13C) in the dome. The PALAZZO DELLA RAGIONE is a building partly of the early 13C with 14-15C additions including a conspicuous clock-tower. The four-square *Broletto* (1227), with its corner-towers, separates this square from P.za del Broletto. On the farther side of the building and contemporary with it is a quaint figure of Virgil sculpted in the 13C, portraying the poet at the rostrum wearing his doctors' hat. Connected to the Broletto by an archway is the *Arengario*, a little 13C building with a loggia.

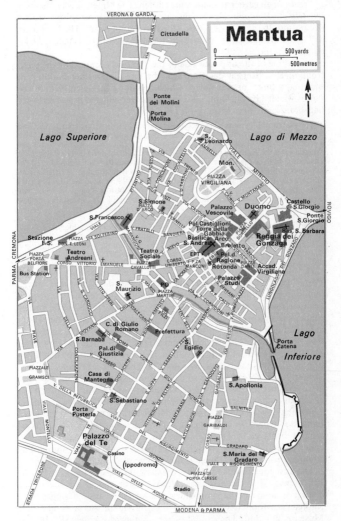

Another archway admits to the huge, cobbled P.za Sordello, on the left of which rise two grim battlemented palaces of the Bonacolsi family, who ruled Mantua before the Gonzagas. Above the first rises the *Torre della Gabbia*, from which protrudes an iron cage where condemned

prisoners were exposed. The next (*Pal. Castiglioni*) dates from the 13C.
Beyond that is the Baroque *Bishop's Palace.* The **Duomo,** at the end, has
a Baroque façade of 1756, a dismal failure designed to add apparent
height to the building. The broad brick campanile and part of the S. side
are relics of an earlier Romanesque church. The *Interior was designed
by *Giulio Romano* (1545) and is covered with exquisite stucco
decoration. In the S. aisle is a 6C Christian sarcophagus. The *Cappella
dell'Incoronata, a charming work in the style of *Alberti,* is reached by a
corridor off the N. aisle.

The whole of the opposite side of the piazza is occupied by the plain
front of the ***Reggia dei Gonzaga,** the most interesting building in
Mantua, a huge fortress-palace which remains a fitting emblem of the
power wielded by the Gonzagas. Visitors are conducted in parties every
half-hour, daily exc. Mon, 9–14, fest. 9–13.

The vast rambling mass of the Reggia is divided into three main parts: the *Corte
Vecchia,* or main front wing, the *Corte Nuova,* and the *Castello.* The Corte
Vecchia, or Ducal Palace proper, overlooking P.za Sordello, consists of the low
'Magna Domus', founded by Guido Bonacolsi c.1290, and the higher Palazzo del
Capitano, built a few years later by the Commune; the Gonzagas altered the
windows of the façade in the Gothic style, and it was restored to its original 15C
appearance at the beginning of this century. After the sack of Mantua in 1630 a
large part of the palace fell into decay; its restoration, begun in 1902, was
completed in 1934. The Castello, the 'keep' built in the 14–15C, overlooks the lake
and is connected with the rest of the palace by drawbridges only. The Corte Nuova,
next to the castle, was planned mainly by Giulio Romano in the 16C. The *Teatro di
Corte,* farther along P.za Sordello, at present serving as a vegetable market, and
the palatine Basilica of *Santa Barbara* (see below), complete the group.

Parts of the palace are often closed, and the order of the visit may be changed.
The room numbers given below refer to the Plan p. 207.

A 16C staircase ascends to the first floor. Here the long *Corridoio
Passerino* (Pl. 1) is decorated with portrait medallions of the Gonzaga
family from 1328 to 1708, sculptured coats-of-arms, etc. Off the corridor
are a series of rooms (the *Appartamento Guastalla;* Pl. 2–7). The former
chapel has a large ruined fresco of the Crucifixion (14C); another room
has a painting of a battle in 1494 between the Bonacolsi and Gonzagas in
P.za Sordello, by Dom. Morone, and the 15C tomb effigy of Margherita
Malatesta (the wife of Francesco I). In the last room (Pl. 7) are displayed
sinopie of Arthurian scenes, by Pisanello. The *Sala del Pisanello* (Pl. 8;
formerly *Sala dei Principi*) is so-called from a splendid *Mural painting
discovered in the 1960s showing a battle tournament. The unfinished but
vivacious composition is one of the masterpieces of Pisanello. Forming
a border along the top of the painting is the heraldic crest of the House of
Lancaster which would suggest a date of about 1436. The suits of
armour displayed here (found in the Santuario di S. Maria delle Grazie,
comp. p. 209) are strikingly similar to those depicted in the painting. The
adjoining room (Pl. 9) displays the sinopie of the painting.

The next four rooms form the APPARTAMENTO DEGLI ARAZZI (Pl. 10–
13), renovated in the neo-classical style at the end of the 18C. They
contain what are perhaps the oldest known *Tapestries, designed after
Raphael's cartoons (Acts of the Apostles) now in the Victoria and Albert
Museum, London. The ceiling of the *Sala dello Zodiaco* (Pl. 14) has
delightful frescoes by Lor. Costa il Giovane (1580). To the left is the
Salone dei Fiume (Pl. 15) with a view of the 16C "hanging garden".
Beyond the Sala dello Zodiaco is the *Sala dei Falconi* (Pl. 16). The
Saletta dei Mori, with a fine ceiling, gives access to the *Corridorio dei*

Mori (Pl. 18) hung with works by Dom. Feti. The ceiling is by pupils of Giulio Romano. On the door post of the *Galleria degli Specchi* (Pl. 19) is a notice signed by Claudio Monteverdi concerning the musical evenings held here. The frescoes are by Anton Maria Viani, and the bust of Maria Gonzaga by the school of Bernini. The *Salone degli Arcieri* (Pl. 20), with curious frescoes of horses, contains works by

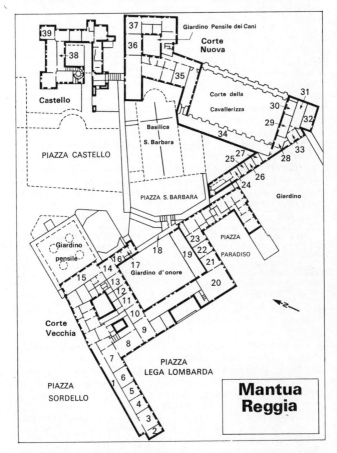

Tintoretto (Nativity of the Virgin), Rubens (the Gonzaga family; reassembled from fragments), and Dom. Feti (Miracle of the loaves and fishes).

The APPARTAMENTO DUCALE (Pl. 22-23), arranged by Duke Vincenzo I shortly after 1600, has been closed since 1974. The rooms contain interesting frescoes and carved and gilded ceilings.—The following rooms, (Pl. 24-37), reached by stairs from the Corridoio dei Mori, are also usually closed. The *Appartamento delle Metamorfosi* (Pl. 24-27) has a ceiling by the school of Viani. Beyond the *Appartamento Estivo* (Pl. 28-33) is the *Galleria degli Imperatori* (or *della Mostra*, Pl. 34) with a magnificent ceiling, built by Viani for the ducal collections, and containing original busts of Roman Emperors. The view of the Corte della Cavallerizza is attractive. Among the next series of rooms (Corte Nuova) the *Sala di Troia* (Pl. 35), with frescoes by Giulio Romano and his pupil Rinaldo Mantovano, and the *Giardino Pensile dei Cani* (restored) are noteworthy; also the *Appartamento del Tasso*, the alleged lodging of Torquato Tasso when the Gonzaga received him on his flight from Ferrara; the *Salone dei Quattro Marchesi* (Pl. 37), with a 5C Greek relief of a Dying Man; and the *Sala del Capitano* (Pl. 36), with a fine Hellenistic *Torso of Aphrodite.

The CASTLE proper (1390-1400) has a fine exterior, formerly covered with frescoes. The design of the loggia of the courtyard, built by Luca Fancelli, is attributed to Mantegna. A spiral ramp leads up to a room (Pl. 38) with 15C copies of Mantegna's frescoes of the Triumph of Julius Caesar (now at Hampton Court). Beyond other rooms with detached frescoes is the *Camera degli Sposi (Pl. 39; marriage chamber), one of the most celebrated works of the Renaissance. Its series of magnificent frescoes by Mantegna, painted in 1465-74, illustrate the life of Marquess Lodovico and his wife Barbara of Brandenburg. In the frieze to the left of the group representing the arrival of Card. Francesco Gonzaga is the supposed self-portrait of the painter. The guide also shows the quaint *Casetta dei Nani* on a mezzanine floor, a series of miniature apartments and stairs built for the dwarfs of Duke Vincenzo. The *Appartamento d'Isabella d'Este* (closed for restoration) has frescoed lunettes, her study, and her music room, decorated with musical motifs inlaid in wood, by the Della Molla brothers.

The Sculpture collection including a fine Attic stele and a *Caryatid of the 5C B.C. is displayed in the Corte Nuovo (closed since 1974).

The *Basilica Palatina di Santa Barbara,* has a handsome campanile by Bertani (1562-65); in the largest of the chapels is a Martyrdom of St Barbara, by Dom. Brusasorci.

Via Accademia leads from the Broletto to *P.za Dante* (monument to the poet) in which is *Palazzo degli Studi,* containing the town library. In the same square is the *Accademia Virgiliana,* built by Piermarini in 1767, with the * *Teatro Scientifico* by Ant. Bibiena (restored in 1972; open for concerts, etc., and 9-12, 15-18, exc. Sun & fest.). Mozart gave the inaugural concert in 1770 at the age of thirteen, during his first visit to Italy. A tablet on No. 17 Via Ardigò marks the residence of St Louis Gonzaga (1583), and in Via Pomponazzo are several handsome courtyards (Nos., 31, 27, 23).

On the left of the central P.za Martiri, a little park, above Giulio Romano's *Fish Market* alongside the river, contains an old brick campanile. The main Via Princ. Amedeo leads S.; on the right, at No. 18 Via Carlo Poma, is *Giulio Romano's House,* designed by himself. The *Palazzo di Giustizia* opposite (No. 7), with bizarre monster caryatids, is also his work. Via Acerbi continues S. to the ducal church of *San Sebastiano* (1460; in poor repair) built by Alberti in the form of a Greek cross. It now contains the sarcophagus of the Martyrs of Belfiore (shot in 1851-52) and serves in addition as a Memorial for the two World Wars. Opposite is *Mantegna's House* (ring for adm. 9-12). It was built to Mantegna's design by Giov. da Padova in 1466-73 as a studio and private museum. Beyond Porta Pusterla and a public garden is the *Palazzo del Te* (open 9-12.30, 15-18, fest. 9-13; winter, 9.30-12.30, 14-16; fest. 9.30-13; closed Mon), a summer residence of the Gonzagas, named either from the T-shape of the avenues approaching it, or from the lindens (tigli) that once shaded it. It owes its importance to the decorative design carried out by *Giulio Romano* and his pupils (including *Primaticcio,* who executed part of the stucco work). The most interesting of the rooms are the *Camera dei Cavalli*, with portraits of Gonzaga's horses; the *Camera di Psiche*, rich in frescoes illustrating the story of Psyche from Apuleius; the *Camera di Fetonte*, illustrating the fall of Phæton; and the *Sala dei Giganti*, a remarkably bold composition (frescoes by Rinaldo Mantovano).

At the foot of the garden is the little *Casino della Grotta*, with charming stuccoes by Giulio Romano and Primaticcio. A wing of the palace houses a small civic *Museum of Modern Art.*—In an unattractive part of the town to the S.E. (comp the Plan) is the restored romanesque church of *Santa Maria di Gradaro*, with a good Gothic portal. The adjoining conventual buildings surround a fine cloister.

Virgil is commemorated in Mantua by the spacious P.ZA VIRGILIANA with fine trees and a grandiose monument of 1927. The neighbouring church of *San Leonardo* contains a Madonna and saints over the high altar (partly hidden by the organ), a fine example of Francia, and, in the adjoining chapel of San Gottardo, a fresco of the Reedemer and saints, by Lor. Costa.—In Via Fernelli, farther S., is the church of *San Simone*, with a tablet (W. wall) to the Admirable Crichton who was buried here after being killed in a brawl in 1582. From the neighbouring *Chiesa della Vittoria* (deconsecrated), built by Francesco IV Gonzaga to celebrate the harrying of Charles VIII at Fornovo and despoiled by military occupation in the 18C, Napoleon seized Mantegna's Madonna for the Louvre. Farther W., across P.za Carlo d'Arco, is the Gothic church of *San Francesco* (1304; rebuilt 1954), revealed when the Arsenal that formerly engulfed it was destroyed in 1944. The campanile, S. transept, and W. front are original, and inside are interesting remains of contemporary frescoes.

Another interesting church is *Santa Maria delle Grazie*, 7 km. W. (Asola bus from Porta Leona, founded by Fr. Gonzaga in 1399 and containing the tomb of Baldassare Castiglione (d. 1529), by Giulio Romano (?).

FROM MANTUA TO MODENA, 72 km. by road (N413), railway viâ Suzzara in 1-1¾ hr. Outside Porta Virgilio is the *Bosco Virgiliano*, a wood planted in 1930. extending as far as *Piétole*, 8 km. S.E., a village regarded by some as the birthplace of Virgil (but comp. p. 188). The road crosses the new autostrada (A 22) which links the Brenner with Emilia, and then the Po.—22 km. **San Benedetto Po** grew up round the Benedictine abbey of *Polirone*, a house protected by the Countess Matilda of Canossa (1046-1115), whose tomb here is still extant. The church was rebuilt in 1539-42 by Giulio Romano, and three cloisters remain of the partly ruined monastery.—A by-road on the right farther on leads to *Gonzaga* (15 km.), the ancestral home of the famous ducal family.—54 km. **Carpi**, a hosiery and shirt-making town (58,200 inhab.), was a seigniory of the Pio family (1327-1525), famous as patrons of literature and the arts. Their *Castle*, in the handsome *Piazza, houses the Museo Civico (open Sun in June-Sept, 10-13, 15-17; in other months on application). The *Duomo*, built by Baldassare Peruzzi (1514) contains terracottas and sculptures by Begarelli and Clementi. The churches of *Santa Maria di Castello* (Romanesque remains), *San Nicolò* (1493-1529; wrongly attributed to Peruzzi), the *Crocifisso* (Madonna by Begarelli), and *San Francesco* (tomb of Marco Pio attributed to Iac. della Quercia) are also of interest.—72 km. *Modena*, see Rte 38.

FROM MANTUA TO VERONA. 38 km.; railway in c. ¾ hr. The only place of importance on this route is (22½ km.) *Villafranca di Verona* which preserves a castle of the Scaligers (1202) and gives name to the armistice of 11 July 1859, concluded between Napoleon III and Francis Joseph.

From Mantua to *Monsélice*, see p. 355; to *Parma*, see p. 371.

III VENETIA

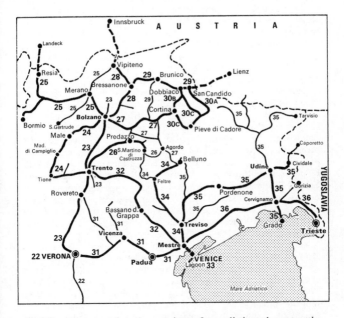

Venetia today comprises three regions of very distinct character: the *Véneto* or *Venezia Euganea* (4,277,500 inhab.; 18,365 sq. km.), with the provinces of Belluno, Padua, Rovigo, Treviso, Venice, Verona, and Vicenza; and two autonomous regions, *Trentino-Alto Ádige,* formerly *Venezia Tridentina* (866,400 inhab.; 13,613 sq. km.), the mountain territory of the Upper Adige valley and South Tyrol, the modern provinces of Bolzano and Trento; and *Friuli-Venezia Giulia* (1,244,500 inhab.; 7844 sq. km.), at the N.E. corner of the Adriatic, consisting of the provinces of Udine, Trieste, and Gorizia.

The *Véneto* consists approximately of the territory occupied by the Venetians in the 14C and early 15C when the dominion of the Milanese Visconti was tottering to its fall. Until then Venice had confined her interests mainly to maritime affairs, while the fortune of the landward cities had followed a line more like that of Lombardy. Verona, Padua, Vicenza, and Treviso in the 12C formed the Veronese League in imitation of the Lombard League, and with the same end of checking the power of the Emperor. Then had come the age of the great families, a relief after the depredations of the piratical Ezzelino da Romano, who terrorized the Adige valley in the early 13C. The Scaligeri in Verona and Vicenza, the Carraresi in Padua and Vicenza, and the Da Camino in Treviso held their little courts, brilliant in literature and art, for about a century, only to fall at last before the might of the Milanese Visconti. Meanwhile, however, the rising Turkish power had checked Venetian expansion in the East, and, with energy still unabated, the seafarers sought new expansion inland; the fall of the Visconti afforded the opportunity; and many cities, notably Treviso and Padua, came willingly into the Venetian fold, preferring the protection of the wealthy Republic to the chances of civic independence. By 1420 the whole territory from Verona to Udine and from Belluno to Padua acknowledged the Lion of St Mark. Further extensions of the Doges' dominion—to Bergamo in the west, Rimini in the south, and Fiume in the east—excited the jealousy of the powers beyond the Alps, and the League of Cambrai (1508) put an end to Venice's imperial ambitions. But for 300 years the Venetian dominions in Italy remained united. The Napoleonic invasion of Italy saw the dismemberment of Venetia; Venice itself and Venetia east of the Adige was ceded to Austria in 1797, while the western portion also fell to the same power in 1814, after a brief union with the Cisalpine Republic. In 1859 an armistice stayed the progress of Victor Emmanuel at the Lombard frontier, and it was not until the Austrian defeat by the Prussians in 1866 that Venetia was able by plebiscite to throw in her lot with the Piedmontese kingdom. In the Second World War the province suffered considerably from air attack, notably at Treviso, and from German destructiveness at Verona. German resistance had practically collapsed by the time the Allied armies reached Venetia; and Udine was entered on the last day of the fighting in Italy—1 May, 1945.

Venezia Tridentina—since 1947 officially known as *Trentino-Alto Ádige,* a semi-autonomous region—is another totally different territory; in place of the marshy lagoons and fertile hills of the Véneto, the countryside is a labyrinth of deep valleys and snow-clad mountain ranges. Most characteristic among the mountains of this region are the fantastic pinnacles of the *Dolomites,* the strangely shaped limestone mountains disposed in irregular groups between the Ádige and Piave valleys. The province of Trento is almost entirely Italian speaking, while in that of Bolzano the native language of Ladin, has, except in the more remote valleys, been overlaid by the official language of the ruling power—German until 1918, and, since then, Italian or German. The two provinces represent respectively the old ecclesiastic principalities of Trent and Bressanone, or Brixen, both of which in the Middle Ages paid nominal allegiance to the Empire. In the 14-15C the prince-bishops held the balance between the rising power of Venice, on the S., and the Counts of Tyrol, on the N., while in the 16C, under the great bishops Clesio of Trent and Madruzzo of Bressanone, the valleys were practically independent. The decay of local powers prevailed here as elsewhere in the 17-18C and the Trentino and Southern Tyrol became more closely attached to the Empire. During Napoleon's campaigns the region was transferred first to Austria, then (in 1803) to Bavaria; the insurrection of Andreas Hofer in 1809 led to a return to Austria in 1814. Austrian mis-government in the 19C caused great discontent in the Trentino, and a movement for absorption into Venetia, but in 1866 Prussia discountenanced the abandonment of any Austrian territory beyond the Véneto proper, and the Triple Alliance (Germany, Austria, and Italy) of 1882 appeared to confirm Austrian possession of the territory. The denunciation of the alliance by the Italians in 1915 and the successful outcome of the First World War brought the Trentino under Italian sway, and the extension of the frontier northward to the strategic line of the Brenner was an inevitable consequence, though the mountain warfare in the region produced little result for either side. In the Second World War the road and railway over the Brenner Pass, the main channel of communication between Italy and Germany, was heavily attacked from the air.

Venezia Giulia, the easternmost portion of Venetia, is a province with a chequered career. Historically, its west part had as its centre the patriarchate of Aquileia, where an important Roman city, largely destroyed in the barbarian invasions, had risen again in the 7C in rivalry with its daughter-city on the isle of Grado. The *Friuli* also (the present province of Udine, formerly in Véneto proper) came within the patriarchs' dominion. In 1420 the Friuli, with the mountainous country of Carnia to the N. and the city of Aquileia was absorbed by the Venetian power. Trieste meanwhile, an independent commune under her bishops, had been in continual rivalry with Venice for the seaborne trade of the Adriatic. Sometimes, with the aid of the warlike counts of Gorizia, or the dukes of Austria, Trieste held the upper hand, but on more than one occasion the Venetians captured the port. The Istrian coast generally owed allegiance to Venice, while the hinterland and Gorizia belonged to the vassals of Austria. In the war against Austria in 1507-16 the Venetians at first made important conquests, but outside intervention forced them to withdraw their frontier W. of Aquileia. Throughout the 16C disturbed conditions on the Istrian coast were fomented by the raids of Liburnian pirates nominally subject to Austria, and the power of Venice was frittered away in fruitless small operations. The outcome of the Napoleonic Wars here was the short-lived Kingdom of Illyria, which extended from Isonzo to Croatia, but was shattered in 1813-14 by an Austrian army and a British fleet; and from 1815 to 1918 the whole region fell under Austro-Hungarian dominion. In the First World War prolonged and fierce fighting took place fluctuating between the valleys of the Isonzo and the Piave, the Italians ultimately achieving success with the aid of the British and French detachments. The frontier was extended E. and S. to include the whole of Istria (including Fiume, after much negotiation), with the adjacent isles and Dalmatian Zara.

Towards the end of the Second World War, the Allied forces, advancing eastwards in May 1945, met Marshal Tito's Yugoslav forces at Cividale del Friuli and Monfalcone; and on 2 May the New Zealanders arrived at Trieste, where the occupying German force surrendered to General Freyberg. Italian and Yugoslav claims to the liberated territory came at once into conflict, and on 12 June the administration of Trieste, which had been occupied by the Yugoslavs, was taken over by Allied Military Government. In July 1946, all territory E. of the so-called 'French Line' was ceded by Italy to Yugoslavia, the ceded areas including the E. suburbs of Gorizia and all Istria S. of Cittanova. The region around Trieste, including the coast from Monfalcone to Cittanova with a portion of the hinterland, was established as a free territory—neutral and demilitarized—by the Treaty of Paris on 10 Feb 1947. At the same time the province of Udine was transferred from the Véneto to Venezia Giulia and the new region, under the title *Friuli-Venezia Giulia,* was granted special measures of autonomy. A more rational adjustment of the frontier at Gorizia was undertaken in 1952, and in 1954 Trieste finally returned to Italian rule while the remainder of Istria was incorporated in Yugoslavia.

22   VERONA

VERONA, surnamed 'La Degna', is a supremely beautiful and attractive city (271,400 inhab.) pleasantly situated on the rapid Ádige, at the foot of the Monti Lessini. Among the cities of Venetia it is second only to Venice for the interest of its monuments, and it is especially notable for the quantity of its Roman remains. Its modern commercial activity is in great part due to its position at the junction of two main arteries of transport: from Germany and Austria to Central Italy, and from Turin and Milan to Venice and Trieste.

Railway Stations. *Porta Nuova* (Pl. 13) for all main line services.—*Porta Vescovo* (beyond Pl. 12) is served by slow trains on the line to Vicenza and Venice.

Theatres. Opera is presented in the ARENA (15 July—29 August). Booking office: Ente Autonomo Arena di Verona. P.za Bra 28. *Drama festival,* including Shakespeare, in the ROMAN THEATRE (July-August).

E.P.T., Via C. Montanari 14 (Pl. 10). *Information Office,* Galleria Liston, P.za Brá.—**Post Office** (Pl. 7), P.za Viviani.

Trolley-buses from *Porta Nuova Station* viâ P.za Brà to *Porta Vescovo,* and viâ P.za Erbe and Teatro Romano to *San Giorgio.*—**Buses** traverse the city (No. **4** from Porta Nuova to Castelvecchio; No. **7** viâ P.za Erbe and Castelvecchio to San Zeno).—**Country buses** from P.za Brà, P.za Cittadella and P.za Isola. *Tramlines* to Domegliara, Grezzana, S. Bonifacio, and Tregnano.

History. The settlement of the Euganean tribes on this site became a Roman colony in 89 B.C. and, favoured by its position (then as now at the crossing of important traffic-routes), Verona flourished under the Roman emperors. Theodoric the Ostrogoth continued the favour bestowed on the city; and the Lombard king, Alboin, was murdered here, in his favourite residence, by his wife Rosamunda (573). Of the Frankish emperors, Pepin, son of Charlemagne, and Berengar I (who died here in 924) chose it as their seat. The free commune established here in 1107 united with Padua, Vicenza, and Treviso to form the Veronese League, the model of the Lombard League. Though always in sympathy with the Empire in its struggles against the Papacy, Verona resented Germanic attempts at conquest, defeated Barbarossa in 1164, and shared in the Lombard victory of Legnano in 1176. Family feuds within the city (on which the story of Romeo and Juliet is based) led to the calling in of the savage leader Ezzelino da Romano, who established a tyranny lasting from 1231 to his death in 1259. In 1260 Mastino della Scala, the podestà, established his position as overlord of Verona, and his family held sway in the city until 1387, throughout the most brilliant period of Veronese history. Dante found a refuge in the Ghibelline city under Bartolomeo (nephew of Mastino) in 1301-4, and in the reign of Cangrande I (1311-29) Verona reached its highest pitch of magnificence. After the fall of the house of Scaliger, Gian Galeazzo Visconti became tyrant of the city, but in 1405 Verona placed itself under the ægis of St Mark. John Evelyn, who visited Verona in 1646, called it "one of the delightfulest places that ever I came in". In 1796 it was occupied by the French. Armed protest against the invader (the '*Pasque Veronesi*', 1797) was avenged by the destruction of much of the city, and Verona was several times exchanged between France and Austria by the treaties of the early 19C, until it was finally awarded to Austria in 1814. During the Wars of Independence it formed the strongest point of the Austrian 'Quadrilateral' (along with Peschiera, Mantua, and Legnago), but in 1866 it was united with the Italian kingdom. During the Second World War the city suffered considerably from bombing, and the bridges were all blown up.

Among the famous Veronese are Catullus (87-47 B.C.), Vitruvius (1C B.C.), the physician Girolamo Fracastoro (1483-1553), and the dramatist Scipione Maffei (1675-1755), besides the artists named below.

Art. The wonderful church of San Zeno marks Verona as a centre of architecture in the Romanesque period, and the churches and palaces of later days are not unworthy of their magnificent predecessor. Fra Giocondo and Sammicheli were accomplished builders of the Renaissance, the latter renowned especially as a military architect. Sculpture at Verona is best represented by Pisanello, the medallist, and by Fra Giov. da Verona, the woodcarver. Veronese painting reaches individuality with the schools of Altichieri and Iac. d'Avanzo in the early 15C; and in later years the influences of Mantegna and especially of Venice were felt. Giov. Badile, Stef. da Zevio, and Pisanello first distinguished Veronese art and among their successors were Fr. Bonsignori, Dom. and Fr. Morone, Girolamo dai Libri (a skilful illuminator), Liberale, Fr. Torbido, Bonifazio Veronese, Ant. Badile, and most famous of all, Paolo Caliari, called Il Veronese (1528-88). The town walls erected by Sammicheli (c. 1523) on the lines of the older ramparts of the Scaligers, are the earliest example of the new military engineering that was later developed by Vauban.

I THE CENTRE

The focus of the life of Verona is the large and busy PIAZZA BRÀ (Pl. 10). Corso Porta Nuovo (from the Station) enters it under the *Portoni della Brà* (1389) which once carried a covered way joining the Castelvecchio (p. 219) to the Visconti citadel: a pentagonal tower of the latter survives behind the *Gran Guardia* a heavy Doric building begun in 1610 which commands the W. side of the piazza. On the corner of Via Roma is the *Museo Lapidario Maffeiano* (1714), the oldest collection of its kind in Europe, with Greek, Etruscan, and Roman inscriptions. This has been closed for several years awaiting transfer to new premises; students are admitted on request by the custodian. Closing the S.E. corner is the *Palazzo Municipale* by Barbieri (1838). The E. side is entirely occupied by the *Arena, the third largest Roman amphitheatre in existence after the Colosseum and that at Capua (adm. daily exc. Mon, 9-12, 15-18.30 in summer; 9-12, 14.30-17.30 in winter). Its interest is lessened, however, by lack of access to the sub-vaults.

Built originally c. A.D. 100, this amphitheatre is in excellent preservation, especially in the interior, and has been many times restored. Of the outermost arcade, however, which measured 152 by 123 metres, only four arches, preserving their simple decoration, were left standing by the earthquake of 1183; the inner arcade (138 by 109 metres) of two orders superimposed is almost complete. The present circumference is made up of 74 arches (80 at the Colosseum), and the floor of the arena is 73 metres long by 44 metres wide. The 44 stone stages of the cavea, restored in the 16C after medieval quarrying, provide space for 22,000 spectators; the topmost stages afford a fine view of the city. Goldoni's first successful play, 'Belisario', was produced here in 1834. The performance here of 'Aïda' in 1913 set a new standard for the production of operatic spectacle; opera season, see p. 214.— At the back of the Arena, on the E., is a fragment of the *Wall of Galerius;* also the church of *San Nicolò,* to the E. front of which has been added the Ionic façade of San Sebastiano, a church destroyed in 1945.

A wide promenade, known as the 'LISTON' borders the N.W. side of P.za Brà and is lined with fashionable cafés and restaurants. Beyond the *Palazzo Malfatti* (No. 16), by Sammicheli (1555), it leads into VIA MAZZINI (Pl. 7; commonly called Via Nuova), an elegant street closed to wheeled traffic. The Hotel Accademia (r.) occupies an 18C palazzo by Cristofoli; farther on (l.) is a good 15C Renaissance house. At the end, in Via Cappello (r.), also barred to traffic, is the so-called *Casa di Giulietta* (adm. 9-12, 15-18.30 in summer, and 9-12, 14.30-17.30 in winter), a restored 13C house once an inn with the sign 'Il Cappello' and thus identified with the Capulets.

The spacious interior (restored) is particularly interesting for its painted walls and fine wood ceilings (top floor). Shakespeare's play of Juliet Capulet (Cappello or Cappelletti) and Romeo Montague (Montecchi) is founded on a tale by Luigi da Porto, a 16C novelist. The legend of a feud between the two families is apocryphal; indeed, it is probable that the clans were in close alliance.

The picturesque and irregular *Piazza delle Erbe* (Pl. inset) occupies the site of the Roman forum and now serves as a general market. In a line along the centre of the piazza rise the *Colonna Antica,* a Gothic column with a stone lantern; the *Capitello,* a tribune of four columns of uncertain date; a fountain of 1368, with a Roman statue called 'Madonna Verona'; and the *Colonna di San Marco* (1523), with a Venetian lion (1886) replacing the original destroyed after the 'Pasque Veronesi' (see above).

The *Casa dei Mercanti,* on the W. side, founded by Alberto della Scala (1301) but now mainly a 17C building, houses the Chamber of Commerce. It bears a Madonna by Girol. Campagna (1595). The statue in the adjoining piazzetta commemorates the victims of an Austrian bomb that fell on this site in 1915. In the N.W. corner is the *Torre del Gardello* (1370), and on the N. is the Baroque *Palazzo Maffei* (1668). The *Casa Mazzanti,* on the E., once a palace of the Scaligeri, was reduced to its present size in the 16C and has a quaint frescoed façade (much faded). On the same side is the *Domus Nova* (rebuilt in 1659), joined by the *Arco della Costa* (from a whale's rib hung beneath the vault) to the great **Palazzo della Ragione,** founded before 1193 but much altered, with its main façade on this square rebuilt, except for the heavy *Torre delle Carceri,* in the 19C. The 12C *Torre dei Lamberti* (84 m; adm. daily exc. Mon 9-12.30, 14.30-18.30. Lift or stairs: *View) was completed with a lantern in 1464, and the Romanesque courtyard given a monumental Gothic staircase in 1446-50.

The Arco della Costa leads into the dignified *Piazza dei Signori, the centre of medieval civic life, with a monument to Dante. An arch joins the N. wing of the Pal. della Ragione (with two boxes for denunciations) to the *Palazzo del Capitano* (now the *Tribunale,* or law courts) with a gateway by Sammicheli (1530-31) and a crenellated tower. In the courtyard is a bizarre portal by Miglioranzi (1687). In the opposite corner of the piazza, through an archway (crowned with a statue of Scipione Maffei, 1756) is the back of the Casa Mazzanti with a curious outside walkway and stair. Here, too, is a Renaissance well-head. Beyond another arch, with a statue of Fracastoro (1559) is the *Loggia del Consiglio, an elegant Renaissance building of 1493.

The design has been wrongly attributed to Fra Giocondo. The twin windows are by *Dom. da Lugo* and *Matt. Panteo,* and the statues of famous sons of Verona in Roman times by *Alb. da Milano* (1493). Above the door an inscription records Verona's faithfulness to Venice and their mutual affection: "Pro summa fide summus amor MDXCII."

At the end is the *Prefettura,* originally (like the Tribunale) a palace of the Scaligeri, now restored in the original 14C style. The passage between the Prefettura and the Tribunale leads to the little early-Romanesque church of *Santa Maria Antica* with its 12C campanile. Outside are the *Tombs of the Scaligers (adm. 9-12, 15-18.30, winter: 9-12, 14.30-17.30), which are both historically interesting and illustrative of a century of Veronese architecture.

Over the side doorway of the church is the tomb of Cangrande I (d. 1329), by *Bonino da Campione* (the equestrian statue is a copy; original in the Castelvecchio, comp. p. 219). The other tombs are enclosed by a magnificent wrought-iron grille of the 14C, in which the ladder, emblem of the Della Scala, is many times repeated. Against the wall of the church is the plain tomb of Mastino I the first of the Scaliger dynasty, assassinated in 1277 in the P.za dei Signori. On the left of the entrance is the tomb of Mastino II (d. 1351) and in the opposite corner that of Cansignorio (d. 1375), both elaborate monuments by *Bonino,* with recumbent and equestrian figures. At the back of the enclosure is the tomb of Giovanni (d. 1359) by *Andreolo de' Santi;* nearby is the sarcophagus of Bartolomeo (d. 1304) with bas-reliefs.

The Gothic house at the corner of the Via delle Arche Scaligere is called *Romeo's House* and is doubtless as authentic as that of Juliet.

The church of ***Sant' Anastasia** (Pl. 3; open 7-12, 15-17), to the N., is a fine example of Gothic brickwork of two periods, 1290-1323 and 1423-81. The W. front is unfinished, but the double W. door is famous; to the right are two sculptured panels from a series of the life of St Peter Martyr. The graceful tower supports an eight-sided spire.

The INTERIOR is remarkable for the short space between the springing of the vault and the apex of the arcade; the fine architectural detail throughout has been revealed to advantage by recent cleaning. The holywater stoups are upheld by two life-like crouching figures, known as the 'Gobbi' (hunchbacks). The 1st S. altar is the Fregoso monument (1565), a fine marble composition by *Danese Cattaneo*. At the 3rd altar are frescoes by *Liberale* and *Benaglio* (attrib.); the 6th chapel has finely wrought door-jambs by *Pietro da Porlezza*: the sculptured Entombment is attrib. to *Bart. Giolfino.*—In the SOUTH TRANSEPT. Virgin and saints by *Girol dai Libri.*—The SANCTUARY contains the grandiose tomb (1424-29) of Cortesia Serego, general of Ant. della Scala, attr. to *Giov. di Bartolo;* it is surrounded by a delightful carved frame and frescoes by *Michele Giambono*. Opposite is a large fresco of the Last Judgement. On the jambs of the *Pellegrini Chapel, to the right, are four Apostles, by the School of *Mantegna,* and inside are two good Gothic family tombs and 24 terracotta reliefs of the life of Christ, by *Michele da Firenze;* also the effigy of Wilhelm von Bibra (d. 1490), ambassador of Cologne to the Vatican. The outermost chapel on the r. has frescoes by *Altichieri*. To the l. of the sanctuary, beyond a chapel with 15C frescoes, is the entrance to the SACRISTY, in which are fine stalls of 1490-93, 15C stained glass, and the gonfalon of the Millers' and Bakers' guild. Here, too, is displayed the celebrated fresco of *St George at Trebizond, by *Pisanello* (detached from inside the church).—In the NORTH AISLE the 5th chapel contains a 14C fresco of the Virgin with SS. Peter and Dominic. The organ (1705) stands over the N. door. At the sumptuous 4th altar is the Descent of the Holy Ghost, by *Giolfino* (1518), and around it are eight statues of saints and the Redeemer; at the 2nd, Christ in glory, by the same; above the 1st, frescoes by *Franc. Morone*.

Beyond the Gothic tomb of Guglielmo Castelbarco (d. 1320), above the former convent-gate, is the little 14C church of *San Pietro Martire* (usually closed), containing a fresco of the Annunciation (1514) by G. M. Falconetto. In the Via Emilei, just to the left, the *Palazzo Forti,* where Napoleon lodged in 1796-97, now houses the *Galleria d'Arte Moderna* and the *Museo del Risorgimento* (adm. 9-12.30, 14.30 or 15-18 or 18.30). Via Ponte Pietra leads to the Ádige (view). The *Ponte Pietra,* blown up in 1945 but rebuilt in 1958 on the old lines by dredging the material (part-Roman, part-medieval) from the river, is guarded by a medieval gateway. Beyond Piazza Bròilo the *Bishop's Palace* (Vescovado) has a façade of 1502; over the portal is a graceful Madonna attributed to Fra Giovanni da Verona. The attractive courtyard, with curious Romanesque capitals, is dominated by the Torrione di Ognibene (1172).

The ***Duomo** (Pl. 3), whose reconstruction was begun in 1139, is Romanesque below and Gothic above, while the apse is a charming composition in the classical manner. The S. porch, of the 12C, has a sculpture of Jonah and the whale. The W. entrance, another fine 12C porch, is guarded by statues of the Paladins, Roland (identified by the name carved on the sword) and Oliver. The campanile, continued above its Romanesque base by Sammicheli, was given its bell-chamber by Ettore Fagiuoli in 1924-27.

INTERIOR. The spacious NAVE has clustered pillars with curious capitals and pointed arches. Round each chapel is a charming framework of sculptured pilasters and architectural fretwork. The first three chapels on either side are decorated with architectural frescoes by *Falconetto* (1503). In the SOUTH AISLE the 2nd chapel contains the Adoration of the Magi by *Liberale,* with a Deposition, by *Giolfino,* above; by the nave pillar is a Romanesque marble stoup. Beyond the magnificent organ is the tomb-slab of Pope Lucius III, who died in Verona in 1185. Hanging above is a large Crucifix (early 15C). At the end is the *Cappella Mazzanti, with sculptured pilasters by *Dom. da Lugo* (1508); it contains the tomb of St Agatha (1353) by a Campionese master. The choir-screen by *Sammicheli* (1534) bears a Crucifixion with the Virgin and St John by *Giambattista da Verona.* The frescoes on the choir-vault are by *Torbido* (1534); the organ, on the left, has panels painted by *Fel. Brusasorci.* In the NORTH AISLE the 3rd chapel contains a polyptych by *Fr. Morone* and *Ant. Brenzoni* (1533); in the 1st chapel are the Nichesola tomb and an altar-frame both by *Sansovino* (1527), the latter enclosing the *Assumption, a much darkened work by *Titian.*

On the N. side of the cathedral is the Cortile Sant'Elena, where the charming Romanesque cloister (with a double arcade on one side) preserves fragments of 6C mosaic pavement. Opposite is the church of *Sant'Elena,* beneath which and to the E. excavations (adm. Fri, Sat & Sun 10-12, 15-17) have revealed the church of *Santa Maria Consolatrice,* the 8C cathedral, itself a replacement of an earlier basilica. The tombs of two early bishops have come to light. Beyond is SAN GIOVANNI IN FONTE its Romanesque baptistery, with 9C capitals and a huge font hewn from a single block of marble.—In P.za del Duomo is the *Chapter Library* (No. 21; open weekdays 10-12), founded by the archdeacon Pacificus (778-846) and containing many precious texts, while opposite the S. door of the cathedral a seated 14C figure of St Peter surmounts the doorway of *San Pietro in Archivolto.*

The Stradone Arcidiacono Pacifico leads from the piazza past *Palazzo Paletta* (No. 6; with an elaborate portal) to Via Garibaldi, which leads to the left. On the right are two twisted columns of pink marble from the demolished church of Santa Maria Novella. In Via San Mammolo, behind, is the charming Gothic doorway of the *Palazzo Miniscalchi.* Beyond this Via Fr. Emilei leads to the right past the Venetian-Gothic *Palazzo Franchini* (No. 20) to reach *Sant'Eufemia* (Pl. 7), a church of 1262, rebuilt in 1375, with fine tombs on the exterior. In the disproportionately long interior, the first chapel on the N. has a painting of Saints by *Moretto;* that S. of the choir contains frescoes by *G. F. Caroto,* Via Adua leads hence to the Roman gateway called the **Porta dei Borsari** (Pl. 6, 7), a double archway surmounted by two stages of windows and niches, through which passed the decumanus. It preserves only the outer front, though Roman masonry can be traced in the adjacent buildings. The gate is certainly older than the inscription affixed to it by Gallienus in A.D. 265. In the piazza outside the gate No. 1 is a typical Renaissance house (the frescoes have almost entirely disappeared), the home of the Giolfino family of artists.

To the right Via Diaz leads to *Ponte della Vittoria,* a stately bridge rebuilt since 1945, with four equestrian groups, by Salazzari and Bianchini, as a memorial of the First World War. The little Pilastrino dell'Agnello (16C) was erected by the Wool Guild.

Beyond the gateway extends CORSO CAVOUR (Pl. 6). No. 2 is the Baroque *Palazzo Carlotti* (1665). No. 11, a Renaissance palazzo of excellent design, now houses part of the Museo Civico di Storia Naturale. No. 10 is the Venetian Gothic *Casa Pozzoni.* Farther on (l.) is the church of the *Santi Apostoli* (1194), with a Romanesque tower, apse, and cloister. From the sacristy stairs lead down to *Santi Tosca e Teuteria,* a domed cruciform shrine (5C), consecrated in 751 as a Baptistery, and reduced again to burial chapel by Bevilacqua (two tombs and a relief) in 1427. No. 19 is * *Palazzo Bevilacqua,* an unusually ornate work by Sammicheli (1530); opposite is the finely restored Romanesque church of * *San Lorenzo* (c. 1110). In its two cylindrical W.

towers were approaches to the matroneum. *Palazzo Portalupi* (No. 38; 1802-4) is occupied by the Banca d'Italia. No. 44, *Palazzo Canossa* (1530-37; restored) by Sammicheli, has an 18C screen.

Riva San Lorenzo, behind, is a good viewpoint for the *Ponte Scaligero* or *Ponte Merlato,* built by Cangrande II (1354-76) and approached through the S. wing of the castle. Blown up in 1944, it was rebuilt, mainly with the original materials, and reopened in 1951. In the piazzetta is the **Arco dei Gavi,** a Roman arch of the 1C A.D. erected, astride the road, in honour of the family of the Gavii, demolished in 1805, and reconstituted from the fragments in 1932.

The **Castelvecchio* (Pl. 6), begun by Bevilacqua for Cangrande II in 1354, was used by the Venetians first as a citadel and after 1759 as a military college. From 1796, under French, Austrians and Italians, it served as barracks until 1923. After restoration it was inaugurated as a museum in 1925 by Victor Emmanuel III. Here in 1944 Mussolini's puppet Republican government staged Ciano's trial. One wing was later damaged by bombing. In 1956-64 the structure was thoroughly restored and the museum imaginatively recreated. Adm. 9-12, 15-18.30; winter, 9-12, 14.30-17.30.

From the drawbridge, across the courtyard, is the entrance to the Napoleonic E. wing. ROOM I. Sarcophagus (1179) depicting SS. Sergius and Bacchus; archivolt carved in relief, Christ between SS. Peter and Paul; male figure (13C) attrib. to Brioloto; lapidary inscription dated 979; in a niche, Lombard gold burial ornaments and small marble coffer of early-Christian workmanship.—In R. II, which affords a fine view of the bridge, begins the 14C SCULPTURE: St Cecilia, St Catherine, from destroyed churches.—R. III. Fragmentary relief; Madonna, after the manner of Giov. Pisano.—R. IV. Relief of the Virgin, from a sarcophagus; the Two Maries; *Crucifixion, from the hospital of Tomba. R. V. A glass panel in the floor shows Romanesque sub-structures incorporated into the castle. 15C SCULPTURE: two tabernacle panels; six low relief panels of the Prophets; *St Martin (1436); in the centre, St Peter enthroned.—A terrace opens on the *Porta del Morbio.*

Beyond the fortress wall is the entrance to the main KEEP (1370), or *Mastio,* guarding the approach road to the bridge which passes between the two parts of the fortress.—From R. VI (with 14C bells) a stair mounts to R. VII which is to display Lombard weapons. A bridge leads across to the REGIA proper. R. VIII (l.). Frescoes: Crucifixion, and Madonna (both 13C); Cavalry battle (fragment), from the Scaliger palace (mid-14C); the 'Via Trezza *Treasure', found in 1938, notably a jewelled gold star.—R. IX. Frescoes, including a 14C Madonna and Child; also sinopie of the sch. of *Altichiero.*—R. X. *Turone,* Polyptych of the Trinity (1360), his only signed work, and other attributed works; *Tom. da Modena,* SS. James and Anthony with a nun; *Sch. of Altichiero,* Boi Polyptych, from the Zanardi Boi Chapel at Caprino Veronese.—R. XI. Statute-book of the Chamber of Commerce (15C, with miniatures); *Iac. Bellini,* St Jerome in the Desert, Madonna dell'Umiltà, and the risen Christ; *Stef. da Zevio,* Madonna del Roseto; *Pisanello,* *Madonna della Quaglia; *Nic. di Pietro Gerini,* SS. Gregory and Bartholomew; *Michele Giambono,* Madonna del latte.—R. XII (l.) Flemish painters.

R. XIII, a long gallery overlooking the Adige, contains paintings of the school of Bressanone; *Iac. Bellini,* Crucifixion (signed but injudiciously restored); *Giov. Badile,* Polyptych; Madonna with SS. Martin and George, the so-called 'Ancona Fracanzani' (1428); also Madonnas and processional crosses of the 15C.

UPPER FLOOR. R. XIV. Veronese school (Mocetto and *Giolfino*).—R. XV, at the far end, *Carlo Crivelli,* Madonna della Passione; *Mantegna,* Holy Family, and Christ carrying the Cross.—R. XVI, works by *Liberale,* including coffer with the Triumph of Love and Chastity.—R. XVII. *Bonsignori.*—R. XVIII. *Fr. Morone* and *Fr. dai Libri.*—R. XIX. *Giov. Bellini,* two *Madonnas.*—A covered passage leads back to the Keep, where R. XX is to display the sumptuous grave-clothes taken from the tomb of Cangrande I in 1921. A second bridge leads to the upper floor of the Napoleonic wing; from the battlements the curve of the river is admirably seen and from the belvedere the *Equestrian figure of Cangrande I (14C), an evocative work strikingly displayed.

ROOM XXI. *Cavazzola,* *Passion scenes (1517) and four saints from the church

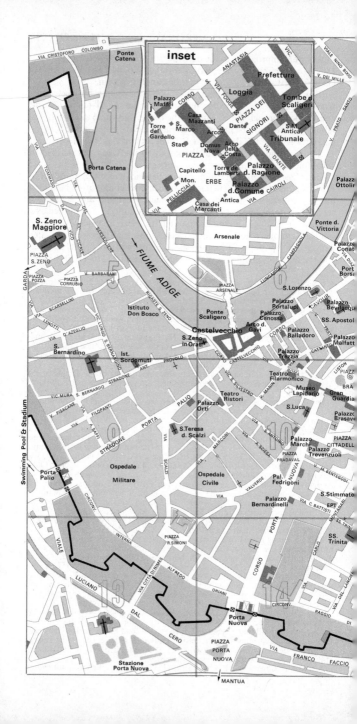

Verona

TRENTO

Porta S.Giorgio

S. Giorgio in Braida

S.Stefano

VIA S. ALESSIO

Vescovado

Palazzo dei Canonici

Duomo

Ponte Pietra

Teatro Romano

Castel S.Pietro

Museo Archeol.
S.Libera

S. Giovanni in Valle

Ponte Garibaldi

Palazzo Zamboni

Palazzo Paletta

Gall. d'Arte Moderna

Liceo

S. Anastasia

S. Chiara

S. Zeno in Monte

Palazzo Fumanelli

Palazzo Miniscalchi

S.Pietro Martire

Palazzo Forti

Palazzo Franchini

S. Benedetto

Prefettura

Casa di Romeo

Mercato Coperto

S.Maria in Organo

S.ufemia

Loggia see inset

PIAZZA ERBE

Tribunale

Pal. Ragione

PIAZZA INDIPENDENZA

Palazzo Giusti

Ponte Nuovo

Seminario

Palazzo Guerrieri

Teatro Nuovo

PO

Palazzo Mosconi

Casa di Giulietta

Bibl. Comun.

S.Tomaso

SS. Nazaro e Celso

Palazzo Arvedi

S.Maria d.Scala

SM. del Paradiso

Palazzo Diamanti

S.Nicolò

Palazzo Murari Bra

Ponte Navi

Arena

Palazzo Donzellini

Palazzo Tedeschi

S.Fermo Maggiore

Palazzo Giuliari

S.Paolo

Palazzo Travella

Dogana

Palazzo Pompei

Ist. Don Mazza

Pal. Municipale

S.Pietro Incarn.

Palazzo Sagramoso

VIA CAMPO FIORE

Palazzo Da Lisca

S.Fermo Minore

V. S. FRANCESCO

PZA D'ARMI DI CAMPO FIORE

Palazzo Dalla Torre

Porta Vittoria

Bastione Campo Marzo

Ponte Aleardi

Tomba di Giulietta

Cimitero Monumentale

N

Ponte S.Francesco

Verona

0   300 yards
0   300 metres

VICENZA

of San Bernadino; *G. F. Caroto,* Boy with a drawing; Benedictine monk.—R. XXII. Further works by *Caroto,* including The artist and his wife; also *Girol. dai Libri,* Holy Family with rabbits, Madonnas.—R. XXIII. *Paolo Veronese,* Descent from the Cross (c. 1565), Bevilacqua altarpiece (c. 1548); *Tintoretto,* Manger scene; *Seb. del Piombo* (attrib.), St Dorothy; *Lor. Lotto* (?), Portrait of a man (sometimes ascribed to Titian).—R. XXIV. *Brusasorci* (attrib.), Portrait of Pase Guarienti (in restoration; formerly attrib. to Veronese).—R. XXV. *Marcantonio Bassetti,* Portraits.—R. XXVI. Works by *Giandomenico* and *Giov. Batt. Tiepolo.*

Via Roma leads back to P.za Brà. On the right *Palazzo Carli,* once the residence of Marshal Radetzky, the Austrian commander, continues a military rôle as NATO Headquarters Allied Land Forces, Southern Europe. Here in 1859 the Emp. Francis Joseph ratified the peace of Villafranca (comp. p. 209).

II   THE WESTERN AND SOUTHERN QUARTERS

It is practicable to combine this and the following section by car.

From Piazza Erbe or the Castelvecchio, bus No. 7 ascends to Piazza San Zeno, in a popular quarter of the town. The walk along the Rigaste (quay) passes the little 13C church of *San Zeno in Oratorio* (restored). The church of ****San Zeno Maggiore** (Pl. 5; open 6-12.30, 14-19.30) is one of the most beautiful of the Romanesque churches of Northern Italy. It dates in the lower part from 1120-38 and was completed c. 1225; the apse was rebuilt in 1386-98.

EXTERIOR. The piazza is dominated by the brick **Campanile,* built in 1045-1149, and by the *Torre del Re Pipino* (c. 1300), N. of the church, supposed to be a relic of the 9C palace of Pepin, but really a fragment of the former abbey. The magnificent circular window in the upper part of the W. front, by Brioloto (c. 1200), depicts the Wheel of Fortune. The rich *Porch,* supported on marble lions, is decorated with sculptures by Nicolò, and on either side of the doorway are scriptural and allegorical scenes by Nicolò and Guglielmo, including the *Hunt of Theodoric,* in which the Emperor pursues a stag headlong to the devil. In the tympanum is St Zeno trampling the devil and above is a charming row of twin arches, continued round the S. side. The 11C doors (enlarged in the 12C) are decorated with rude bronze * *Reliefs* of biblical subjects.—The little church of *San Prócolo* (r.; closed) is partly 9C work.

The spacious basilican INTERIOR, as simple as it is impressive, has a nave separated from its aisles by simple and compound piers and covered by a trifoliate wooden ceiling (1386). Some of the capitals are from Roman buildings. On the W. wall to the left of the entrance hangs a 15C Crucifix. The large porphyry bowl in the N.W. corner is of Roman origin; the 15C stalls, near by, once adorned the apse. In the S.W. corner is the large font of pink marble (12C). The walls are frescoed in layers of varying date (13-15C). The 2nd S. altar is made up of 'knotted' columns of red marble on a lion and a bull (? from an older porch).

In the raised presbytery are a further series of very old frescoes (scribbled over). On the balustrade are statues of Christ and the Apostles (c. 1250). Above the high altar, in its original frame, is a *Triptych by *Mantegna,* the Madonna with angel musicians and eight saints, the figures influenced by Donatello. The panels of the predella are copies of the originals, now in the Louvre. The frescoes on the walls include two of the sch. of *Altichieri* (1397): the Crucifixion (l.; over the sacristy door) and Monks presented to the Virgin (over the S. arcade). In the N. apse is a painted figure of St Zeno (14C) and to the left is a statue of St Proculus (1392).

The spacious *Crypt,* supported by 49 Romanesque columns brought from other buildings, contains the tomb of St Zeno (1889) and other saints and bishops, including (it is said) SS. Cosmas and Damian. The sarcophagus of St Lucillus has good reliefs.—On the N. side of the church is the charming *Cloister,* with coupled columns, built in 1123, but altered in the 14C. On the E. side is *St Benedict's Chapel,* with four columns made up of ill-assorted fragments; on the N. side is a projecting lavatorium; on the S. side are tombs, including that of Farinata degli Uberti (d. 1348) and of members of the Scaliger family.

To the S. of San Zeno is the church of **San Bernardino** (Pl. 9), an interesting example of the transition from Gothic to Renaissance (1451-66). It is preceded by a frescoed cloister; over the convent entrance (l. of the church door) is a fresco of the saint by *Cavazzola.* On the high altar is a triptych by *Benaglio,* inspired by Mantegna's triptych (see above). South side. 1st chap. entirely frescoed by *Giolfino,* including some views of Verona; 4th chap., Crucifixion, by *Fr. Morone;* and the *Cappella Pellegrini,* a refined work of the Renaissance (1557), by *Sammicheli.* North side. Organ (1481), with SS. Bernardine and Francis on the doors, by *Dom. Morone;* Baroque altar-frame by *Bibbiena.* From the cloister (ring at convent door; donation) may be visited the *Sala Morone,* the former library, frescoed by Dom. Morone and his pupils (1503).

In the *Porta Palio* (Pl. 9), farther S. (1542-57), Sammicheli's skill in combining structural beauty with military strength is notable. Still farther S., near the station, is the *Porta Nuova,* a plainer work by the same artist (1535-40).

Via C. Battisti leads right from the Corso Porta Nuova to the Romanesque church of the *Trinità* (Pl. 14). Farther E. in a 19C cloister off Via del Pontiere is shown a 14C tomb called the *Tomb of Juliet.* A modern bust near it commemorates Shakespeare.

III   THE EASTERN AND NORTHERN QUARTERS

From Via degli Alpini (Pl. 11), behind the Municipio, the Stradone Maffei leads to the left. On the right of it is *Palazzo Ridolfi* (restored as the Liceo Scientifico), where the great hall is frescoed by Brusasorci (meeting of Charles V and Clement VII at Bologna, 1530). Beyond the church of *San Pietro Incarnario,* built on Roman foundations with a 14C campanile, the Stradone San Fermo, lined with palazzi, leads to *San Fermo Maggiore** (Pl. 7), really one church on top of another. The lower building retains Benedictine characteristics of 1065-1138, the upper one was largely rebuilt by the Friars Minor c. 1313 in a Gothic style (the different architectural styles are well seen from outside the E. end).

EXTERIOR. The partly Romanesque façade has a round-headed door, to the left of which is the tomb of A. Fracastoro (d. 1368), the physician of the Scaligeri. On the N. side a 15C porch protects a fine portal of 1363. The smaller apses and the campanile date from before the rebuilding.

INTERIOR. The aisleless nave, adorned with 14C frescoes, is roofed by a very fine wooden ceiling (1314). The main doorway has a Crucifixion, attr. to Turone, in the lunette. To the right is a fresco of the Martyrdom of four Franciscans in India; and to the left of the first altar, Angels, a fresco by *Stef. da Zevio.* The marble pulpit (1396), and the tomb of the donor, Barnaba Morano (1412), in the adjoining chapel are by *Ant. da Mestre.* The 3rd S. altar, beyond a 16C tomb borne by oxen, has a painting by *Fr. Tórbido.*

The CHOIR has a screen of 1573 and a fresco (1320) above the triumphal arch depicting Gugl. di Castelbarco offering the church to Prior Gusmerio. In the N. apse, Saints, by *Liberale.* On the N. side of the nave are a chapel (apply to the sacristan) containing the *Tomb of the Torriani (Girolamo and Marcantonio) by *And. Briosco* (c. 1516); the *Lady Chapel,* with the Madonna and saints, a vigorous work by *Caroto* (1528); and at the W. end the Brenzoni Mausoleum, by *Giov. di Bartolo* (1439), with an Annunciation by *Pisanello* above.—From the S. side of the choir the Lower Church may be visited, an interesting Romanesque work. On the S. side are two cloisters, recently rebuilt, with 16-17C frescoes.

Via Leoni, passing the damaged remains of the Roman *Porta dei Leoni* (1C A.D.), is continued by Via Cappello (p. 215) past the *City Library* (400,000 vols.)

towards P.za delle Erbe. Just off Via della Stella (l.) is the church of *Santa Maria della Scala,* with an apse and campanile of 1324 and a good Gothic tomb (1430; in the S. apse).

From behind San Fermo the *Ponte Navi,* once a bridge of boats, crosses the Ádige. To the right, overlooking the river, is *Palazzo Pompei* (Pl. 12), a fine early work by Sammicheli (c. 1530) housing the *Museo Civico di Storia Naturale* (adm. 9-12.30, 14.30 or 15-17.30 or 18 exc. Fri), notable for its collections of fossils found in the locality. Ahead, Via San Paolo (with some fine palazzi) leads to SAN PAOLO (Pl. 12), a church reconstructed in 1763 and rebuilt since 1944. It contains (2nd S. altar) St Anne, the Madonna, and saints, by *Girol. dai Libri* and (chap. to r. of main altar) *Madonna and saints by *Veronese;* also (high altar) a similar subject by *Giov. Caroto* (1516).

To the E. is **Santi Nazaro e Celso** (Pl. 8), a church built in 1463-84 near the site of a 10C shrine of the two saints, with a pretty forecourt.

The NORTH TRANSEPT, or Chapel of St Blaise (S. Biagio), the saint's burial-place, is noteworthy for its paintings: the altarpiece is by *Girol. dai Libri;* on the inside of the entrance arch is an Annunciation by *Cavazzola;* and on the walls are scenes from the life of the Saint, interesting frescoes by *Montagna* (suffering from humidity). In the SACRISTY is a triptych by *Fr. dai Libri,* three parts of a polyptych by *Montagna,* and 15C inlaid cupboards. Over the 2nd N. altar is a Madonna with saints, the masterpiece of *Ant. Badile.*

Via Muro Padri continues towards the celebrated **Giusti Gardens** (No. 2 Via Giardino Giusti; 8.30-18.30 daily), the 16C hillside pleasance of the contemporary Palazzo Giusti, praised by Coryat and Evelyn. A path leads up through the wood to a tower (with a spiral staircase) which gives access to the upper terraces. Via Carducci leads back towards the *Ponte Nuovo,* overlooking which is *San Tomaso Cantuariense* (St Thomas Becket), with a fine W. front and rose window of 1493. It contains Sammicheli's tomb (1884) and a painting of three saints by Girol. dai Libri (4th N. altar). The Interrato dell'Acqua Morta leads to the busy bus-station, facing which stands **Santa Maria in Organo** (Pl. 4), a church perhaps of 7C foundation which received its present form from Olivetan friars in the late 15C. The façade is partly early Gothic, partly Renaissance, and the graceful campanile, ascribed to *Fra Giovanni da Verona,* dates from 1525-33.

The interior is frescoed all over: in the nave are Old Testament scenes by *G. F. Caroto* (r.) and *Nic. Giolfino* (l.), while outside the S. transept are other works by *Caroto, Fr. Torbido,* and *Cavazzola* (Annunciation); within is an altarpiece (Santa Francesca Romana) by *Guercino.* From the apse of the N. transept (with a delightful Palm Sunday figure of Christ on an ass from the mid-13C) is the entrance to the *SACRISTY, notable for its stalls and cupboards, inlaid by *Fra Giovanni.* The walls are frescoed with portraits of monks by *Franc. Morone,* Fra Giovanni designed also the *STALLS, (inlaid with street scenes and musical instruments), the lectern, and candelabrum in the main apse. The crypt (shown by the sacristan; entered from the sacristy passage) preserves ancient capitals and a 14C relief over the altar.—A large Renaissance cloister of the adjoing convent may be seen to the left of the church.

The street ascending beyond S. Maria leads to *San Giovanni in Valle,* a charming church rebuilt in the 12C with materials from an earlier structure. The crypt contains two good early-Christian sarcophagi (4C) and part of a small cloister survives.

Farther N., overlooking the river, is the ***Roman Theatre** (Pl. 4; adm. 9-12, 15-18.30; 9-12, 14.30-17.30 in winter; closed Mon), founded under Augustus and enlarged later. The cavea with its rows of seats and the arches that supported them, and the two entrances have been uncovered;

the upper tiers command a splendid *View. In the ruins of the cavea is the little church of *Santi Siro e Libera* (920, altered 14C). At the back of the theatre a lift gives access to the convent building above, now an *Archæological Museum*. The well-arranged collection includes Hellenistic bronzes, well-preserved glass, sculpture (torsos; head of the young Augustus), mosaic fragments, and, in the cloister, sepulchral monuments. From the windows are good views of the theatre. Excavations continue near the entrance to the theatre. High above stands the *Castel San Pietro*, where the Austrians built their barracks on the foundations of a Visconti castle destroyed by the French in 1801.

Just beyond the Ponte Pietra is **Santo Stefano** (Pl. 3), a venerable church rebuilt in the 12C. Round the apse (with a stone episcopal throne) runs a curious gallery, with 8C capitals. The 1st S. chapel is a good Baroque work; on the l., the Forty Martyrs, by *Orbetto*. To the left of the sanctuary are frescoes by *Stef. da Zevio* (Annunciation) and *Altichiero* (Coronation of the Virgin). On the entrance arch above both transepts are charming frescoes of angel musicians (being restored). In the vaulted crypt is a raised semicircular gallery with capitals, etc., brought from older buildings.—Across the river are the cathedral, the battlemented tower of the bishops' palace, and the pretty little loggia of the chapter library.

The large church of **San Giorgio in Braida** (Pl. 3) was begun in 1477 on the site of a 12C church. The bold cupola was designed by *Sammicheli*, who also began the unfinished campanile. The façade is of the 17C.

The aisleless nave, with side chapels, is notable for numerous fine paintings (although some of them are difficult to see). Above the W. door, *Iac. Tintoretto*, Baptism of Christ.—SOUTH CHAPELS: 3rd, *Dom. Tintoretto*, Descent of the Holy Ghost; 4th, *F. Brusasorci*, Three Archangels.—Beside the minstrels' gallery, *Romanino*, St George before the Judge.—At the entrance to the sanctuary, *G. F. Caroto*, Annunciation.—The Sanctuary has a balustrade with bronze figures of saints: the two huge paintings are by *P. Farinati* (Miracle of the Loaves), and *Brusasorci* (Manna in the Desert). In the Apse, Sammicheli's fine altar incorporates *Veronese*, *Martyrdom of St George, a masterpiece of colour and design. North side, below the organ, *Moretto*, *Female saints; beside it, *Romanino*, Martyrdom of St George; 4th chap. *Girol. dai Libri*, *Virgin enthroned between St Zeno and St Laurence Giustiniani—above another Sammicheli altar; 3rd, *Caroto*, SS. Roch and Sebastian, and the Transfiguration; 1st, *Caroto*, St Ursula and her companions.

In the walls opposite the church opens the *Porta San Giorgio* (1525) by Sammicheli, beyond which a short walk through a little public garden leads to the Ponte Garibaldi.

At *San Michele Extra*, 4km. along the Vicenza road, is the *Madonna di Campagna*, a round church with a peristyle, probably designed by Michele Sammicheli (1484-1559), who was born in the village.

The **Valpolicella**, a district famous for its wine and its marble, is reached from Verona by road (trolley-bus) from the Porta San Giorgio, keeping N. of the main road to Trento. The chief village is (14 km.) *San Pietro in Cariano*, which preserves the old Vicariate, the seat of the Venetian district magistrates.—18 km. *Sant'Ambrogio* has quarries of 'rosso di Verona'. The *Church of *San Giorgio*, 3 km. N.E., dates from the 7C and has a 13C cloister.—20 km. *Domegliara*, on the main road, is the trolley-bus terminus.

The **Monti Lessini**, N. of Verona, have recently become frequented for winter sports, and several roads run up along the valleys of the *Tredici Comuni*, a high-lying district occupied by the descendants of Germanic settlers who migrated here in the 13C. Their dialect has practically died out. Buses run from Verona bus station to (13 km.) *Negrar*, with the 15C Villa Bertoldi and the charming gardens (1783-96) of the Villa Rizzardi, at Poiega, near by; (32 km.) *Sant'Anna d'Alfaedo*, with a local museum, and (35 km.) *Fosse,* two good walking-centres. Also (from Pta. Vescovo) up the Val Pantena, passing just W. of *Santa Maria in Stelle,* with a Roman hypogeum, to (11 km.) *Grezzana* (Romanesque campanile) and (34 km.) **Bosco Chiesanuova,** the main resort of the Lessini. On the N.E. side of the Corno d'Aquilio, above *Fosse,* is the *Spluga della Preta,* a remarkable pothole in the limestone, the depths of which (850 m) were descended in 1963.

Monte Baldo, the chain of hills separating the Ádige valley from Lake Garda, is reached from Verona by bus from the P.za Brà. Beyond (20 km.) *Domegliara* (see above) the road crosses the Adige and the route forks, the left-hand road descending to (35 km.) *Bardolino* and (38 km.) *Garda,* on Lake Garda (see Rte 20).—The right-hand branch mounts the Tasso valley to (34 km.) **Caprino Veronese.** Thence a twisty road, bedevilled by motor-rallies in Aug, goes on to (10 km.) *Spiazzi,* and (14 km.) *Ferrara di Monte Baldo* (856 m), the best starting-point for the ascent of the mountain. The *Punta del Telégrafo* (c. 2110 m; Refuge), the most conspicuous peak, with the best view, is climbed by a good path in 3¼ hrs; the *Cima Valdritta* (2218 m; 4¾ hrs) has a more restricted prospect. The descent to Lake Garda (see p. 198) is much steeper.

FROM VERONA TO BOLOGNA, 114 km. by direct railway in 1½-2¼ hrs. The main road (N12) follows the railway as far as Mirandola, then diverges viâ Modena.—19 km. *Isola della Scala* (9989 inhab.) is the junction for Rovigo.— 31 km. *Nogara* is also on the railway from Mantua to Monselice and Padua.— Lombardy is entered just short of (46 km.) *Ostiglia* (8072 inhab), where the road crosses the Po.—48 km. *Révere,* opposite, preserves an old palace of the Gonzagas, with a charming courtyard.—56 km. *Poggio Rusco* is a junction for Ferrara. The road here begins to diverge from the railway, and (67 km.) **Mirandola,** the first town in Emilia, with 21,750 inhab., is 4 km. W. of its station (bus). It was a principality of the Pico family, the most famous member of which was Giovanni Pico (1463-94), noted for his wide learning, a typical figure of the Italian Renaissance. The former princely residence preserves a few characteristic details, and there are family tombs in the church of San Francesco. A bus follows the main road to Modena; but this route soon diverges left for (74 km.) *San Felice sul Panaro. Finale Emilia* (13 km. E.) has a 14C castle.—86 km. *Crevalcore* was the birthplace of Marcello Malpighi (1628-94), the physiologist.—94 km. *San Giovanni in Persiceto.*—114 km. *Bologna,* see Rte 39.

From Verona to *Brescia* and *Milan,* see Rte 18; to *Mantua,* see p. 209; to *Trento* and *Bolzano,* see Rte 23; to *Vicenza, Padua,* and *Venice,* see Rte 31.

23   VERONA TO TRENTO AND BOLZANO

ROAD, 150 km. N 12.—53 km. *Ala.*—69 km. **Rovereto.**—92 km. **Trento.** 100 km. *Lavis.*—107 km. *San Michele all'Ádige.*—131 km. *Ora.*—138 km. *Bronzolo.*— 150 km. **Bolzano.**
The AUTOSTRADA DEL BRÉNNERO links the Brenner Pass with Modena and the Autostrada del Sole. Between Verona and Bolzano it runs parallel with the road on the opposite bank of the Ádige.
RAILWAY, following almost the same route as the roads. To *Trento,* 92 km. in 1-2 hrs; to *Bolzano,* 148 km. in 1½-3 hrs. This route has through carriages from Rome, Florence, and Bologna to Munich, Hamburg and Copenhagen.

Verona, see Rte 22. The road leaves the city by the Porta San Giorgio and traverses the Valpolicella (p. 225).—At (20 km.) *Volargne,* the 15C Villa del Bene (ring for custodian), enlarged by Sammicheli in 1551, contains frescoes by Dom. Brusasorci. The roads, railway, river and canal are now penned between the vertical cliffs of the *Chiusa di Rivoli. Rivoli,* on the farther bank, gave Masséna his ducal title after the battle of 1797. The deep valley covered with woods and vineyards, here called VAL LAGARINA, lies between the long ridge of Monte Baldo, on the left, and the Monti Lessini on the right. Here begins the region of Trentino-Alto Adige. Across the river, a little before (48 km.) *Vo,* is seen the 14C castle of *Avio* (opened by custodian on request).—The pretty campanile of the little church of San Pietro in Bosco (13C frescoes, recently restored) marks the approach to (53 km.) *Ala,* with several Baroque palazzi. It lies at the head of Val Ronchi, at the end of which the Monte Lessini are visible.—Between (59 km.) *Serravalle* and (62 km.) *Marco,* both rebuilt since the First World War, lay the front line of 1916-18. On the right are the *Slavini di Marco,* formed by landslips from Monte Zugna.

69 km. **Rovereto** (204 m) at the mouth of the Vallarsa, is the chief town (31,600 inhab.) of the Val Lagarina. Here Paolo Orsi (1849-1925), the archæologist, was born and died. The Corso and P.za Rosmini commemorate Ant. Rosmini (1797-1855), the philosopher, another native. The *Cassa di Risparmio* in the piazza is a rebuilt 15C mansion. The *Municipio,* though much altered, retains some 15C portions. Nearby, the *Museo Civico* (9-11, 14.30-16; winter, mornings only; closed Mon), opened to the public in 1855, houses an archæological collection, and exhibits of local interest including a natural history section. The *Castle* (8-12, 14-19; Nov-March, 9-12, 14-18; closed Mon), enlarged in the 15C, contains a large WAR MUSEUM, the most important in Italy devoted to events of the First World War. The war is commemorated by the *Sacrario,* erected in 1938, on the summit of the so-called Castel Dante, rising S. of the town. Nearby is the *Campana dei Caduti,* the largest bell in Italy, which tolls every evening for the fallen of all nations.

FROM ROVERETO TO RIVA, 21 km.; bus in 1 hr. The road crosses the Ádige between the station and village of (7 km.) *Mori.* It ascends the valley of the Cameras to (11 km.) *Loppio,* then crosses a huge moraine with a fine view of the Adamello on the left.—16 km. *Nago* commands a splendid panorama of Lake Garda and of the Sarca valley into which the road descends.—17 km. *Tórbole* (p. 196).—21 km. *Riva.* see Rte 20.

From Rovereto to Monte Pasubio, Schio, and Vicenza, see Rte 31.

Beyond Rovereto the mountain views increase in grandeur. Monte Pasubio, with its oddly flat-topped spurs, is seen on the right.—75 km. *Calliano.* On the right rises the ruined castle of *Beseno* (being restored), with the Becco di Filadonna (2150 m) behind it, and on the left is the Monte Bondone ridge.—83 km. *Acquaviva.* Villa Fogazzaro was the home of Emp. Karl I in 1915-18. Beyond *Mattarello* with its orchards of fruit trees, modern tower blocks announce the approach to Trento.

92 km. **TRENTO,** the chief town (97,200 inhab.) of its province and of the autonomous region of Trentino-Alto Ádige, stands near the confluence of the Ádige with the Brenta which descends from the Val Sugana on the E. Spectacular mountain ranges encircle the town which presents a cheerful air. Though it remained in Austrian hands until 1918, it is a typically North Italian city and entirely Italian speaking.

Railway Stations. *State Railways,* P.za Dante. *P.za Centa* for the Malè railway (bus beyond Cles).

Post Office, Via Calepina.—*Assessorato Provinciale Turismo,* 27 Via San Marco; *Azienda Autonoma Turismo,* 4 Via Alfieri.

Bus Station, near the state railway station. with services to *Fai, Andalo,* and *Molveno;* to *Arco* and *Riva* (1½ hrs); to *Pinzolo* (2¼ hrs) going on to *Madonna di Campiglio* (3 hrs); to *Borgo Valsugana* (1 hr); to *Cavalese,* viâ Ora (going on to *Predazzo;* 2½ hrs), viâ Cembra, or viâ Segonzano; to *Moena, Pozza di Fassa,* and *Canazei.*

History. *Trent,* the Roman *Tridentum,* owed its importance throughout the Middle Ages to its position on the main road from the German Empire into Italy; and in the 10C the bishops of Trent acquired the special privileges from the Emperor (probably Conrad the Salic) which they held until 1796 practically without a break. Early in the 15C the citizens rose against the overwhelming power of the bishops, but local strife was stilled by the threat of a Venetian invasion, the Lion of St Mark having control of the Val Lagarina as far up as Rovereto (1416). The Tridentines sought aid from the Count of Tyrol, the Venetians were defeated in 1487, and in 1511 Austria established a protectorate over the Trentino. In the 16C the city rose to prominence under Bp. Bern. Clesio and Bp. Crist. Madruzzo, and during the episcopate of the latter the famous Council of Trent met here (1545-63). The last prince-bishop fled before the French in 1796, and the Austrians took possession of the town in 1813, holding it until 1918 through a century of grave discontent.

VIA ROMA and its continuation VIA MANCI, the chief street of the old town, runs E. and W. From its N. side, between the Baroque church of *San Francesco Saverio* and the *Palazzo Galasso,* built by the banker Georg Fugger in 1602, Via Alfieri runs N., across the old course of the Ádige, to the public gardens and the station. To the left is a good monument to Dante (1896), behind which rises the tower of the Romanesque church of *San Lorenzo,* a fine example of 12C monastic architecture.

In Via Belenzani, opening opposite San Francesco, is (l.) the 16C *Palazzo del Municipio,* with frescoes by Brusasorci in the Sala della Giunta (open only when meetings are in session). On the other side of the street are *Palazzo Geremia,* in the Venetian Renaissance style, and *Palazzo Salvadori;* the former has charming frescoes of the early 16C (recently restored) showing the emperor Maximilian, who stayed here in 1508-09, and members of his court. Vicolo Cólico (r.) leads to the graceful and simple Renaissance church of **Santa Maria Maggiore,** by *Ant. Medeglia* (1520). The great portal of the façade dates from 1535; on the S. side is a 16C Lombardesque portal. In the interior were held several sessions, including the last, of the Council of Trent. The *Organ Gallery, richly carved, is by *Vinc. Grandi* (1534).—Via Cavour, passing the old Municipio, leads to PIAZZA DUOMO, a pretty square with a handsome 18C Neptune fountain, the frescoed *Palazzo Cazuffi* (16C), and the *Torre Civica,* on the site of a Roman enceinte tower (one of the 'Trenta Torri' from which Trent is erroneously supposed to have taken its modern name). *Palazzo Pretorio,* once the episcopal palace, now houses the MUSEO DIOCESANO (adm. 9-12, 14-18; closed Wed afternoon), with a fine collection of paintings and sculpture from local churches, objects from the cathedral treasury, and a superb series of Flemish *Tapestries by P. van Aelst (1497-1532).

The ***Duomo,** a handsome and severe Romanesque building, entirely of marble, was begun by *Adamo d'Arogno* (d. 1212), and not completed until 1515. The exterior, with its galleries, is impressive, especially at the E. end, where the three apses and the *Castelletto* (the rear part of the adjoining Pal. Pretorio) are effectively grouped. In the solemn interior clusters of tall columns carry the arcades, surmounted by a diminutive clerestory, and unusual arcaded staircases lead up to the galleries. It contains numerous tombs of bishops and 13-14C frescoes in the transepts. The Crucifix before which the decrees of the Council of Trent were promulgated is preserved in a large chapel on the right side. The baldacchino beneath the cupola is modelled on that of St Peter's in Rome.

Via Calepina leads E. from behind the cathedral to the 18C *Palazzo Sardagna,* in which the *Museo Tridentino di Scienze Naturali* is being arranged, and the monumental *Post Office,* behind which Via Santissima Trinità ends at the small Baroque church of the Trinità. Via

Oss-Mazzurana leads N. from beside the Torre Civica, past the charming Renaissance *Palazzo Tabarelli* (No. 4; r.) to rejoin Via Manci. To the right is the picturesque *Cantone,* once the chief crossroads in the town.

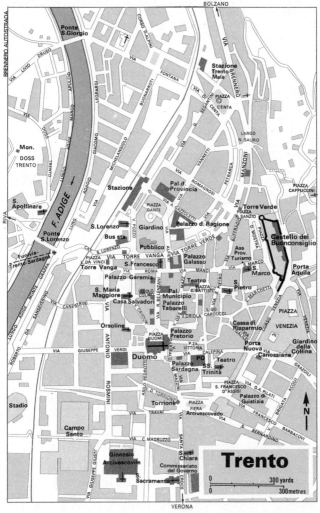

Via San Marco goes on to ***Castello del Buonconsiglio,** the stronghold of the medieval prince-bishops. The N. (l.) portion is the Castelvecchio, dating from the 13C; the S. portion is the Renaissance Magno Palazzo, built under Bp. Clesio in 1528-36. Adm. 9-12, 14-17 or 18.

The main entrance admits to the gardens, from which are visited the cells in which Cesare Battisti, Fabio Filzi, and Damiano Chiesa (three Italian patriots, born Austrian subjects) were imprisoned in 1916 before being shot as traitors in the adjoining fosse, where modest monuments mark the site of their death.

The ATRIUM, with a collection of bells, preserves frescoes in the vault by *Romanino*. From here stairs mount to the SECOND FLOOR. The GREAT HALL has a good ceiling and a chimneypiece by *Vinc. Grandi*. In adjoining rooms are a 17C organ from Riva, ecclesiastical sculpture, altarpieces, etc. The circular SALA DEGLI SPECCHI (unlocked by custodian) was transformed in the rococo style in the 18C (cases of small bronzes, porcelain, glass, etc.). Across the stairway the APARTMENT OF BERNARDO CLESIO contains an archæological collection, including the Tabula Clesiana, a bronze tablet with an edict of Claudius, dated the Ides of March, A.D. 46. From here a walkway (opened by the custodian) leads to the TORRE DELL'AQUILA with *Frescoes of the Months (c. 1400), with delightful contemporary rural scenes.

The First Floor (shown on request) has a collection of furniture, sculpture, and paintings displayed in a series of rooms with fine ceilings (by *Fogolino, Dosso Dossi*, and *Gerolamo Romanino*). Also here is the grim courtroom where the martyrs (see above) were condemned in 1916. The Chapel has terracotta decoration by *Zaccaria Zacchi* and an altarpiece by *Gerolamo Romanino*.—The LIBRARY contains a collection of 15C music manuscripts (French, German, and Italian).—The Castelvecchio, grouped round a picturesque courtyard at the N. end, contains a copious collection illustrating the Risorgimento and the First World War.

The *Torre Verde*, with its particoloured roof, formerly connected the castle with the town wall. Other relics of the ramparts are the *Torre Vanga* (c. 1210), and the *Torrione*, S. of the town.

Ponte San Lorenzo crosses the Ádige W. of the town. On the farther bank is the Romanesque and Gothic church of *Sant'Apollinare*. Behind it rises *Doss Trento* (307 m) an abrupt hill crowned on its N. summit by a circular colonnade commemorating Cesare Battisti (1875-1916; see above), a native of Trento. Nearby is the *Museo Nazionale degli Alpini* (9-12, 15-18; closed Mon) dedicated to the Alpine troops of Italy.—A precipitous road climbs S.W. to (7 km.) *Sardagna* (571 m; view; cableway from Ponte San Lorenzo) continuing up the N. ridge of *Monte Bondone*, the ski-slopes of whose crest are reached from the road by chair-lifts.—15 km. *Vaneze*, a small resort.—On (24 km.) the plateau of *Viotte* is a renowned alpine Botanic Garden. A cableway mounts to the summit of Monte Bondone (1875 m).

A road runs S.E. of Trento viâ (12 km.) *Vigolo Vattaro* (725 m; road l. to Lago di Caldonazzo 5 km. further, see below) and the imposing valley of the Centa, to (26 km.) **Lavarone** (1353 m), a scattered community on the pine-clad slopes of the Asiago plateau. The return may be made viâ *Folgaria*, a winter and summer resort, to Calliano on the N12. From there to Trento, see above.

FROM TRENTO TO THE LAGO DI CALDONAZZO, frequent bus service; local trains on Venice line to San Cristóforo and Caldonazzo in ½-¾ hr. N47, the Venice road, enters the ravine of the Férsine, in which the road is cut into the rock.—10 km. **Pérgine** (482 m), well placed on the saddle between the Brenta and Férsine valleys, has a restored castle and some interesting buildings. It is a good base for excursions in the Valle dei Mócheni to the N.E. viâ *Sant'Orsola* (10 km.), a small spa. The road bears right for (12 km.) *San Cristóforo* a popular bathing resort (water-skiing, etc.) at the N. end of LAGO DI CALDONAZZO. The road circles the lake viâ (on the E. shore) *Ischia* and *Tenna*, or follows the W. shore to meet the road (r.) from Vigolo Vattaro (see above) at (17 km.) *Calceránica* where the rustic Romanesque church (restored; 16C

frescoes) has an altar stone dedicated to the goddess Diana.—19 km.
Caldonazzo, another popular resort. *Lévico,* 3 km. N., see Rte 32.

From Trento to *Tione* and *Malè* (Bolzano) see Rte 24; to *San Martino di Castrozza,* see Rte 26; to *Venice* viâ Bassano, see Rte 32.

On the right beyond Trento is seen Monte Calisio, with lead mines dating from Roman times.—102 km. *Lavis* a vine-growing village, stands on the Avisio, at the foot of the Val di Cembra, up which runs a road to Cavalese (43 km.; p. 242) viâ *Cembra* (14 km.), where the church has 16C wall-paintings. On the left rises the *Paganella* (2098 m), reached in 8 min. by cableway.—110 km. *San Michele all'Ádige* is opposite the entrance of the spacious Val di Non (p. 234). The railway station is at Mezzocorona, on the right bank of the Ádige.—Beyond (118 km.) *Salorno* (with ruins of its castle on a precipitous rock), a German dialect becomes increasingly prevalent in the local speech.—133 km. *Ora.*

FROM ORA TO PREDAZZO, 36 km. The road zigzags up a steep side-valley.—13 km. *Fontanefredde,* from which a walk may be taken viâ *Redagno* (2 km. N.; 1556 m) to (2½ hrs) the *Passo degli Oclini* (1989 m) and (3½ hrs) the *Corno Bianco* (2317 m) a noted viewpoint.—16 km. *Passo di San Lugano* (1097 m), the summit level.—23 km. *Cavalese,* and from there to *Predazzo,* see Rte 26.

150 km. **BOLZANO,** in German *Bozen,* stands at the junction of the Tálvera and the Isarco (265 m), whose united stream flows into the Ádige about 3 km. S.W. With 107,100 inhab., it is the largest town in the upper basin of the Ádige, and has been the capital of a province since 1927. It has the character of a German rather than Italian town, and its population is mainly German speaking. The old town, with its low-pitched Tyrolean arcades and Gothic architecture has a somewhat grim aspect; it is surrounded by extensive modern suburbs. Bolzano is a splendid centre for excursions in the neighbourhood, with excellent transport facilities, though in summer the heat is apt to be oppressive.

Post Office, Via della Posta.—Information Bureaux of *E.P.T* and *Azienda Soggiorno* in P.za Walther. *Club Alpino Italiano,* 46 P.za Erbe.

Buses. No 3 traverses the town from the station to the Monumento della Vittoria (viâ P.za Walther and P.za Domenicani); No. 1 from the station to *Gries;* No. 9 from the coach station (Via Garibaldi, near the railway station) to *Merano.* Other services from coach station to *Ortisei* and *Plan;* to *Siusi;* to *Canazei* viâ *Nova Levante;* to *Belluno.*—Express services from P.za Walther: daily to *Brescia* (5 hrs) and *Milan* (6¾ hrs) viâ Trento, Riva, and Gardone; to *Trieste* (8½ hrs) viâ Brunico and Udine; to *Cortina* (3 hrs) viâ Dobbiaco; to *Vigo di Fassa* and *Passo Pordoi* (2¾ hrs); to *San Martino di Castrozza* (3 hrs).

Sport. *Swimming: Lido* (4 pools), Viale Trieste. *Skating* and *Ice-hockey,* at the Palazzo della Fiera, Via Roma. *Tennis* at the clubs in Via Martin Knoller and Virgolo.

Cable-Railway from Via Renon (near the station) to *Renon* (with connecting tramway to *Collalbo*); from Via Mayr Nusser (across the Isarco) to *Virgolo;* from Campiglo to *Colle;* and from Via Sarentino to *San Genesio* (from Bus No. 5 terminus).

History. A bridge is believed to have been thrown across the Isarco by Drusus somewhere in the neighbourhood of Bolzano, but nothing is known of a settlement here before the Middle Ages. Bolzano, as an important market, was a bone of contention between the bishops of Trent and the counts of Tyrol until 1531, when Bp. Clesio ceded it to the Counts. With the rest of Tyrol it was handed to Bavaria in 1805, but the rebellion of Andreas Hofer united it to Austria in 1809. In 1810-13 it was part of the Napoleonic kingdom of Italy, and from then until 1918 it was under Austrian dominion. It was damaged by bombing in the Second World War.

In the central P.za Walther, named after the minnesinger Walther von der Vogelweide, a statue of Drusus recalls his expedition of 38 B.C. against the Germanic tribes. On the S. side of the square is the **Duomo,** a

Gothic church of the 14-15C (restored since 1945) with a fine tower of 1501-19, by Johann Lutz, and a colourful roof. The former *Dominican Monastery,* a little to the W., has frescoes in the S. aisle, and in the Cappella di S. Giovanni (l. of apse; light on wall opposite entrance), with interesting Giottesque figures (1330-40). The Gothic cloister (entrance at No. 19) by F. Pacher and the Chapel of St Catherine (14-16C frescoes) survived the bombing which spoiled the rest of the church. To the N.E. is the unattractive Municipio, beyond which **Via dei Portici,** with its heavy low arcades, leads to the left. No. 39 on the left is the *Palazzo Mercantile,* or Chamber of Commerce, in an 18C mansion. From P.za delle Erbe (fruit market), at the end of the street, Via dei Francescani leads (r.) to the *Franciscan Church,* a 14C building (restored) with an attractive cloister on the N. side (interesting remains of frescoes). The fine carved wooden altarpiece by Giovanni Klocker (1500) has been removed for safety since its attempted theft. The N. wall of the church is decorated with an entertaining frieze of celebrated Franciscans (16C). Via Dr Streiter, to the S., is typical of old Bolzano.

Via del Museo leads from P.za delle Erbe to the Tálvera bridge; on the left is the *Museo Civico* (adm. 9-12, 15-17; closed Sun & fest.), an interesting collection of local antiquities and 'bygones'. To the right, beyond, extends the LUNGOTALVERA BOLZANO, a pleasant promenade on an embankment. On the right, below the promenade, is the *Castello Mareccio,* a 13C building with five later towers which now contains the provincial archives. Farther on is the *Fontana Laurino,* which commands a fine view, especially of the Catinaccio and Sciliar to the E.

The *Tálvera Bridge,* another fine view-point, leads across the river to the MONUMENTO DELLA VITTORIA, a triumphal arch by Marcello Piacentini (1928) adorned with sculptures by various artists and surrounded by gardens.

Corso Libertà leads on to the garden suburb of **Gries,** in whose main square stands a Benedictine monastery and abbey church. In Via Martin Knoller, N. of the square, the *Parish Church* (15-16C) contains another carved wooden altarpiece (1471-80), by Mich. Pacher and his school. Above the village rises the hill of *Guncinà* which can be climbed by the winding Passeggiata, beyond the church.

Another pleasant walk leads from the Municipio along the old Via dei Bottai to Via Andrea Hofer, with an old inn on the first corner. Farther N., across Via Cavour, is the Romanesque church of *San Giovanni.* Via Monte Tondo continues N. from Via Cavour past (r.) the 17C mansion of *Hortenberg.* From Via Sant'Osvaldo at the end of this street, a stepped ascent leads to the *PASSEGGIATA SANT'OSVALDO, a terrace walk, with views, which descends again to the N. end of the Lungotálvera promenade.

From the farther side of the Ponte Sant'Antonio (bus No. 5), which crosses the Tálvera 2 km. N. of the town, a cable railway ascends to *San Genesio Atesino* (1087 m), an old village with a fine view across the Val Sarentina, now frequented as a resort (ski-slopes).—On the S. side of the Isarco valley, reached by cableway or on foot (c. 2½ hrs) viá Castello di Campegno and Bagni di Sant'Isidoro, is **Colle** or *Colle di Villa* (1136 m), from where an easy footpath (½ hr) leads up to *Col dei Signori* (1180 m) a favourite summer and winter holiday centre for the people of Bolzano.

FROM BOLZANO TO COLLALBO, 12 km., cableway ascending the high plateau N.E. of Bolzano, with its *Views of the Dolomites.—The cableway starts from Via Renon and mounts to Soprabolzano, passing over vineyards.—On the right on the approach to (5 km.) *L'Assunta* some eroded earth-pyramids are seen.—(6 km.) **Soprabolzano** (1221 m) is a holiday resort with views extending to the Brenta and

Ortler groups. Here may be joined the rack railway from L'Assunta.—8 km. *Costalovara* has a small lake, on the road leading S. to Bolzano.—9 km. *Stella Renon* and (10 km.) *Colle Renon* are two scattered holiday resorts.—12 km. **Collalbo** (1154 m), the chief village of the plateau of *Renon*, is a good centre for short excursions. About ½ hr N. are the earth-pillars of Longomoso, the most remarkable of the many groups of erosion-pillars in the neighbourhood; and farther on (3½ hrs by a marked path) is the *Rifugio Corno di Renon* (2259 m), commanding a fine mountain view.—From Collalbo an easy path descends to Campodazzo in the Isarco valley.

FROM BOLZANO TO SARENTINO, 20 km., bus in 1½ hrs, the road mounts the narrow valley of the Tálvera, to the N. of Bolzano, and passes (r.) *Castel Róncolo* (1237), with frescoes in the interior (10-12, 15-19; closed Sun & Mon). Farther on (l.) are the ruins of *Castel Sarentino*. The road winds upward through an attractive gorge, with porphyry cliffs and two more ruined castles.—20 km. **Sarentino** (961 m), the chief place (6000 inhab.) in the Val Sarentina, is a fair centre for excursions (marked paths).

From Bolzano to the *Brenner* (Innsbruck), see Rte 28; to *Cortina* and *Pieve di Cadore*, see Rte 27; to *Merano* and *Bormio* (Stelvio Pass), see Rte 25; to *Tione* and *Trento* viâ Malè, see below.

24 BOLZANO TO MALÈ, TIONE, AND TRENTO

ROAD, 164 m.—25 km. *Passo della Méndola*.—34 km. *Cavareno*.—36 km. **Fondo**.—56 km. *Ponte di Mostizzolo*.—66 km. **Malè**.—71 km. *Dimaro*.—88 km. **Madonna di Campiglio**.—101 km. *Pinzolo*.—120 km. **Tione**.—132 km. *Ponte delle Arche*.—144 km. *Le Sarche*.—164 km. **Trento**.
BUSES. Daily service from Bolzano to *Madonna di Campiglio* in 3½ hrs (July-Sept). From Madonna di Campiglio to Tione and *Trento*, twice daily service all the year in 2¼ hrs. Summer service to *Malè* and from Malè to *Trento* viâ Dermulo (60 km. in 1½ hrs); and from Méndola and from Dermulo to Fondo.

This route through the W. part of Tridentine Venetia affords access to some of the finest country in the Italian Alps, including the Val di Non and Val di Sole and the Presanella and Brenta mountain-groups, forming part of the Adamello-Brenta national park. It connects also with the main roads from Lombardy: at Malè with the Tonale road from Édolo; at Tione with the Valli Giudicarie; and at Le Sarche with the road from the Lake of Garda.

From the Druso bridge at Bolzano the Méndola road bears to the left and crosses the Adige, beneath (4 km.) the hill of *Castel Firmiano* (being restored), an ancient stronghold said to have been founded in Roman times, and later the property of the bishops of Trento and the counts of Toggenburg.—At 7 km. a road (r.) leads to *San Paolo* (2 km.) with a fine Gothic and Renaissance church and notable bells, and to the ruined *Castle of Appiano* (8 km.), founded in the 12C, and still retaining a Romanesque chapel with murals.—10 km. *Appiano* is a scattered commune, with its principal centre at San Michele, on the main road. Several fine 17-18C houses here are in a Renaissance style peculiar to the district. The road ascends steeply across the face of the Mendelwand (good retrospective views of Bolzano). On the left, at 15 km. is a road leading down to *Caldaro* and thence past the Lago di Caldaro to Ora (14 km.).—A zigzag climb through woods ends at (25 km.) **Méndola** (1363 m), a beautifully situated resort (ski facilities) in the Passo della Méndola between the Penegal (N.) and Roen (S.), commanding a fine prospect of the Catinaccio and Látemar groups across the Ádige valley, and of the Brenta and Adamello to the S.W.

The *Penegal* (1737 m) is ascended by road; the *Roen* (2116 m) in 3 hrs by a marked track viâ the *Rifugio Oltrádige*, or by chairlifts.—A cableway descends from Médola to Sant'Antonio, near Caldaro (see above).

Passing above (29 km.) *Ruffrè,* the road turns left at (31 km.) *Belvedere.* About 2 km. N. is *Malosco* frequented, like (33 km.) *Ronzone,* for the sake of the mountain views.—34 km. *Cavareno.*

Here N43, leading S., affords a short cut to Trento.—3 km. *Romeno* was the birthplace of the 18C painter G. B. Lampi, whose frescoes adorn the church.—6 km. *Málgolo* has a fine medieval castle, well restored.—9 km. *Sanzeno,* a pleasant village with a large Gothic church, is the starting-point for a visit to the sanctuary of **San Romédio,* ¾ hr E., a pilgrim resort on a steep rock, consisting of five old chapels connected by steps, and a modern chapel. The two upper chapels are said to represent the hermitage occupied by the tutelary saint.—12 km. *Dermulo* is on the main road from Trento to Malè (see below).

The main road turns N. through (35 km.) *Sarnónico.*—36 km. *Fondo* (987 m) is a large village divided into two by a gorge.

The principal excursion is to *Monte Macaion* (1866 m), an easy walk of 3 hrs N.E., rewarded by a magnificent **View.*—*Castelfondo,* 5 km. N.W., beyond its battered old castle, is a pretty village from which the little-known valleys to the N. may be explored.

The road crosses the romantic Novella valley and descends to (42 km.) *Brez.*—Beyond (49 km.) *Revò* it descends from the plateau to (52 km.) a junction above the *Ponte San Gallo,* a bridge crossing the Lago di Santa Giustina. The left branch joins the main road coming from Trento.

FROM THE PONTE SAN GALLO TO SAN MICHELE ALL'ÁDIGE (Trento), 30 km. This road descends the lovely **VAL DI NON.* or *Anaunia,* with its woods and ruined castles.—4 km. *Cles* (658 m), the chief place in the valley, overlooks the hydro-electric Lago di Santa Giustina. The town, with 5500 inhab., has a good Renaissance church and old houses. To the N.E. rises *Castel Cles,* the ancestral home of the famous episcopal Clesio family, rebuilt in the 16C.

Monte Péller (2319 m) the N. peak of the Brenta group, may be climbed in 6 hrs by a marked path (and comp. below).
A good alternative road to Trento keeps to the W. of the main road.—4 km. *Tuenno.* The *Lago Tóvel,* 11 km. S.W., is a lovely lake in a deep valley beneath the Brenta range.—17 km. *Denno.*—At (21 km.) *Rocchetta* (see below) this route rejoins the main road.

The Cles-Trento railway follows the road closely. The Noce is crossed by the bridge of Santa Giustina, 143 m above the stream.—6 km. **Dermulo** stands at the junction of the valley road with the road to Méndola viâ Cavareno (N43d; see above). *Córedo* (831 m), 4 km. N.E. is a summer resort, with a 15C mansion of the bishops of Trento.—8 km. *Taio,* for the *Castello Bragher,* 2 km. N.E., the best preserved of the castles in the valley. Beyond the castle of *Ton,* high up on the left, is (19 km.) *Rocchetta,* where the valley appears closed by two huge crags. On the right is the upper road to Cles (see above); also a road to Molveno (p. 236). The valley opens out before (27 km.) *Mezzolombardo* (227 m), a centre of wine production.

A delightful road, starting about 1 km. N. of Mezzolombardo, ascends to (12 km.) **Fai** (960 m), a summer and winter resort. A cableway ascends from there to the *Paganella* (2098 m), a splendid viewpoint, from which a descent may be made W. to Ándalo (by chair-lift) and Molveno.

28 km. *Mezzocorona* lies mainly to the left. The road crosses the Ádige and joins the valley road at (30 km.) *San Michele all'Ádige* (p. 231).

Beyond the Ponte San Gallo the Tione road ascends the VAL DI SOLE, the upper glen of the Noce.—65 km. *Caldes,* with a restored castle.—66 km. **Malè** (738 m), the chief village in the valley, has bus connections with the railway from Trento to Cles, and chair-lifts to the ski-slopes of Monte Péller (see above).

A narrow road ascends the Val di Rabbi to (12 km.) **Rabbi Terme** (1195 m) a small spa and climbing centre. A good track crosses the *Passo di Rabbi* (2467 m) to (5 hrs N.) *Santa Gertrude* (p. 239). At the head of the valley (4 hrs N.W.) is the *Rifugio Dorigoni* (2436 m), for ascents on the S.E. side of the Ortler group.

At (71 km.) *Dimar* (766 m), the Tonale road (see Rte 19) to Edolo bears off to the right. This road ascends in zigzags amid pine-forests in the Val Meledrio viâ *Folgárida,* recently developed as a winter resort (chair-lifts etc.). Just beyond the summit-level (1682 m) is (87 km.) *Campo di Carlomagno,* another resort, commanding views of the Brenta group to the left. The road descends through forest.

88 km. **Madonna di Campiglio** (1522 m), the most frequented summer and winter resort in the western Trentino, stands in a wooded basin in the upper valley of the Sarca. It is the chief centre for ascents in the Brenta group, which lies to the E. The fashionable seasons are July-Aug and Dec-March. The winter sports facilities include a ski school, chair-lifts to the Spinale and Pradalago ski-slopes, ski-jump below the Spinale, and a skating rink.

The Brenta mountains, an isolated dolomitic group between Madonna di Campiglio and the Ádige valley, are for expert climbers only, but many easier excursions in their foothills are accessible to ordinary walkers, and the principal routes are marked by coloured signs.

Monte Spinale (2104 m), almost due E., is ascended in 2 hrs (chair-lift in 20 min.) by a well-marked path. The summit commands a splendid circular view of the Brenta, Adamello, Presanella, and Ortler mountains. The excursion may be continued by an easy track (1½ hrs), or funicular, to the *Rifugio Graffer* (2262 m), on the Passo del Grostè, from where the *Panorama extends to Monte Cevedale, 40 km. N.W.

Pleasant expeditions may be made to the *Lago di Nambino* (1¼ hrs N.W.); to the *Lago di Ritorto* (1½ hrs W.); and viâ Campo di Carlomagno to the *Lago delle Malghette* (2¼ hrs N.). The 'Giro delle Cascate' is a favourite walk of c. 4 hrs, visiting the magnificent *Val Brenta* and the *Vallesinella,* on the W. side of the main valley to the S. of Madonna di Campiglio.—A very fine longer expedition ascends the Val d'Agola (S.) to its head at the *Passo Bregn de l'Ors* (1835 m) and then down the wooded Val d'Algone to (7 hrs) *Sténico* (p. 236).

ASCENTS IN THE BRENTA GROUP (guides essential). From the Rifugio Graffer (see above) the chief ascent is the *Cima del Grostè* (2897 m; 2½ hrs), the northernmost main peak of the group. From the *Rif. Tuckett* (named after the English alpinist F. Tuckett, d. 1913) and the adjoining *Rif. Quintino Sella* (2271 m; 3½ hrs), the finest climb is the *Cima di Brenta* (3150 m; 3½ hrs). From the *Rif. Pedrotti* (2439 m.) and the *Rif. Tosa* a little farther on, at the head of the Val Brenta which ascends in three huge steps, the principal ascent is the *Cima Tosa* (3173 m.; 3¼ hrs), the loftiest in the group, not a very difficult climb for trained alpinists.

A steep and winding descent carries the road from the Campiglio basin down the Val di Nambino, with the Brenta group towering above the forest on the left.—Beyond (96 km.) *Sant'Antonio di Mavignola* (1123 m) the pines and larches gradually give way to chestnut-groves and the Val di Nambrone, and later the Val di Génova, open out on the right.

101 km. **Pinzolo** (770 m), splendidly situated at the junction of the two main upper valleys of the Sarca, is a large village (2800 inhab.) frequented mainly for ascents in the Presanella and Eastern Adamello

groups. The church of *San Vigilio*, to the N., is notable for its external fresco of the Dance of Death, by Sim. Baschenis (1539).

A similar painting (1519) by the same artist adorns the interior of the church of *Santo Stefano*, 3 km. up the **Val di Génova**. The magnificent valley 16 km. long, thickly wooded in parts, is the main approach to the Presanella and Adamello groups from the E. Several refuge-huts provide bases for the mountain ascents, for all of which guides are essential. The peaks and spurs on the S. side were the scene of some of the most difficult alpine fighting during the First World War. On the N. side of the valley, 5 km. from Pinzolo, is the *Cascata di Nardis*, a waterfall on the stream descending from the Nardis glacier.—The road passes the mouth of the Val Láres (l.) with another waterfall.—10 km. *Ragada* (1278 m), with a small war-cemetery. The road ends and a bridle-path goes on to (2 hrs) the *Pian di Bédole* (1578 m; Refuge) at the head of the valley. The steep path continues up the N. slopes to (2½ hrs more) the *Rifugio Città di Trento* (2480 m), well situated near a group of little glacier lakes. The principal ascents are those of *Monte Mandrone* (3281 m; 4½ hrs), the *Adamello* (3554 m; 7 hrs), and the *Presanella* (3556 m; 6½ hrs), the last reached viâ the Sella Freshfield, a col at the head of the Nardis glacier, named after the English alpinist Douglas Freshfield (d. 1929), who made the first ascent in 1864.

The *Rif. Giov. Segantini* (2371 m), c. 5 hrs N.W. of Pinzolo by the Val di Nambrone and the Val d'Ámola, is another starting-point for the ascent of the Presanella (see above: 5½ hrs).

The *Rif. Dodici Apostoli* (2488 m), c. 6 hrs E. of Pinzolo, is a base for climbs on the Cima Tosa and other peaks of the Brenta group. Chair-lifts ascend from Pinzolo to Dosso Sabion (2059 m).

The road descends the Val Rendena, the valley of the Sarca, now much wider and more populous. A narrow winding road branches left about 1 km. before (105 km.) *Caderzone* to bypass Tione and rejoin the Trento road beyond Saone (see below). The villages lower down the valley have suffered greatly from forest fires. The *Carè Alto* (3462 m) dominates the landscape on the right.—120 km. **Tione** (565 m), lies at the junction of the road to the Valli Giudicarie (p. 187) with that to Trento.

The Trento road turns E. and beyond (124 km.) *Saone* and the newly formed Lago Ponte Pia, enters the *Gola della Scaletta*, a narrow winding gorge of the Sárca.—132 km. **Ponte delle Arche** (398 m) is an important road centre, connected by bus with Riva (26 km. S.) and Molveno, as well as with Trento and Madonna di Campiglio.

Sténico (666 m), 4 km. N.W. has a medieval castle commanding a good view, and is connected with Madonna di Campiglio by a fine mountain walk (see above).

FROM PONTE DELLE ARCHE TO MOLVENO, 20 km. The road serves the scattered hamlet of *San Lorenzo in Banale*, passes the little *Lago di Nembia*, and then skirts the pleasant *Lago di Molveno*, 4 m. long. At its N. end is (20 km.) the frequented resort of **Molveno** (865 m), lying under the lee of the Brenta mountains, ascents in which, made from the Rif. Pradel (chair-lift), are rather tiring from this side.

Beyond Molveno the road goes on to (5 km.) *Ándalo* (1041 m), another resort with chair-lifts ascending to Paganella (see p. 231). From there the road continues viâ Fai or viâ (15 km.) *Spormaggiore* to Rocchetta and (24 km.) *Mezzolombardo* (see p. 234).

134 km. *Comano Terme* is a small spa treating skin complaints. Another fine gorge through the S. spurs of the Brenta group ends at (144 km.) *Le Sarche* to meet the main road from Arco and Lake Garda. The road leaves the Sarca valley and skirts the *Lago di Toblino*, with the picturesque *Castel Toblino* on a cape on the right. On the left farther on is the *Lago di Santa Massenza*.—151 km. *Vezzano*.—Beyond (155 km.) *Vigolo Baselga* which like Baselga di Vezzano (1 km. right), is another small spa, a road leads to *Terlago* (3 km.) with an old castle and charming little lake.—At (157 km.) the *Passo di Cádine* (495 m) the

watershed into the Ádige valley is crossed, and a little farther on is the entrance to the impressive gorge of the Buco di Vela.—At 160 km. is a turning for Sardagna and Monte Bondone (see Rte 23).—164 km. **Trento,** see Rte 23.

25   BOLZANO TO MERANO AND BORMIO

ROAD, N 38, 127 km.—29 km. **Merano.**—43 km. *Naturno.*—63 km. *Silandro.*—78 km. **Spondigna.**—80 km. *Prato allo Stelvio.*—86 km. *Gomagoi.*—91 km. *Trafoi.*—104 km. **Stelvio Pass.**—127 km. **Bormio.**

RAILWAY to *Spondigna,* 84 km. in 2½ hrs, halting 20 min. at *Merano* (32 km., ¾-1 hr) and continuing to *Málles* (9 km. farther) in 12 min. more.

BUSES daily (July-Sept) from Bolzano to the *Stelvio Pass* in 3¾ hrs (several services from Spondigna to the *Stelvio Pass* in 2 hrs); from the Pass to *Bormio* in 1 hr.; additional though services from Bolzano to Bormio (going on to Milan) in 4½-5 hrs, July-Sept.

From Bolzano N 38 crosses the Ponte Druso and ascends the left bank of the Ádige; the railway keeps close to the river. Fruit trees grow on the valley floor, while vineyards cover the lower slopes with woods above. The ruined Castel Casanova appears on a spur to the right on the approach to (10 km.) *Terlano.*—21 km. *Póstal* is connected by road and by bus from the station of Lana-Postal, with *Lana di Sopra* (5 km.), best visited from Merano (see below).

29 km. **MERANO** (320 m), in German *Meran,* lying on the right bank of the Passirio a little above its junction with the Ádige, is an ancient town (34,700 inhab.) famed as a climatic resort and spa. Together with *Maia Alta* and *Maia Bassa* (*Obermais* and *Untermais*) on the opposite bank of the torrent, it consists mainly of hotels, pensions, and villas set amid luxuriant vegetation in a sheltered valley. Spring and autumn are the fashionable seasons for visiting Merano; in summer the heat is oppressive, though Maia Alta is breezier. The inhabitants are mainly German speaking.

Numerous **Hotels and Pensions** (mostly open from April to October) in the town, and in Maia Alta and Bassa, many with gardens and swimming pools. Charges are raised during the high season (April-May, and Aug-Oct).

Post Office, Via Roma (beside the Ponte della Posta). *Azienda Autonoma di Soggiorno,* Corso Libertà.

Sanatoria. *Thermal Centre,* Via d. Terme; *Fonte San Martino,* N. of the town. *Institute of Physiotherapy,* in Via O. Huber.

Town Buses from the station to (1) *Maia Alta;* (2) *Maia Bassa* and *Sinigo;* (3) *Tirolo;* (4) *Funivia Avelengo.* Country Buses from P.za Rena to *Lana di Sopra;* to *Moso;* to *Santa Gertrude;* to *Fondo;* to *Madonna di Senales;* from P.za Rena to *Trieste;* to *Cortina d'Ampezzo;* to *Milan;* and viâ the Resia Pass to *Landeck.*—COACH TOURS in summer round *Lake Garda;* round the *Cinque Passi;* and to *Cortina* (Grand Tour of the Dolomites).

Amusements. *Teatro Puccini,* P.za del Teatro; *Casino di Cura* (Kursaal), Corso Libertà; *Race-course* at Maia Bassa; *Swimming Pools:* Via delle Terme (outdoor and indoor); Via Lido (outdoor).

History. Although it is probable the area was already inhabited in Roman times, the name *Meirania* appears for the first time in 857. After the town came into the possession of the Counts of Venosta in 1234 it gradually assumed importance so that by 1317 it was designated a municipality. A troubled yet unexciting history followed, and in the 19C it passed from French to Bavarian domination. In 1814, under Austrian rule, its favourable climate began to attract visitors. Since 1918 it has developed into one of the most celebrated climatic resorts in Italy. Radioactive springs are used in the Thermal centre.

The old main street of Merano is the dark and narrow VIA DEI PORTICI, which is approached from the station by Via Mainardo, from the river by Via delle Corse. Beneath its low arcades are excellent shops and on the N. side is the *Palazzo Municipale* (1930). Behind this is the *Castello Principesco* (adm. 9-12, 15-18; closed Sun), built by Archduke Sigismund in 1445-80 and containing contemporary furnishings. The arms of Scotland alongside those of Austria recall the marriage of Sigismund with Eleanor, daughter of James I of Scotland. Behind the castle, in Via Galilei, is the *Museo* (adm. 10-12, 16-18), with local collections.—At the end of Via dei Portici is the DUOMO, a Gothic church of the 14-15C, with a curious battlemented façade, a tall tower (83 m), 14-16C tomb-reliefs and wall-paintings on the S. side. Within are two 15C altarpieces by Martin Knoller. Behind the Duomo is a small octagonal Gothic chapel.

Via Leonardo da Vinci leads from the cathedral to the bank of the Passirio. To the right extends the cheerful Corso della Libertà, with the most fashionable shops.—Across the river, opposite the Post Office, lies the Gothic church of *Santo Spirito* (rebuilt 1473).—Alongside the N. bank of the river, run the *Passeggiate d'Inverno* and *Gilf*, sunny promenades that extend to the partly ruined *Castel San Zeno* (no adm.). A Roman bridge crosses to the shaded *Passeggiata d'Estate* on the other bank. The *Passeggiata Tappeiner*, on the hill above the town, passing the old *Torre della Polvere*, is another favourite walk.

ENVIRONS OF MERANO

The chief attraction of Merano is its delightful surroundings, made easily accessibly by good roads and frequent bus services.

The ROAD TO CASTEL TIROLO, a walk of 1¼ hrs to the N. (or bus No. 3 in 15 min) ascends over *Monte di Merano* to *Tirolo*, a village given over to tourism, especially favoured by Germans on walking holidays. It has a Gothic church. On the opposite side of a ravine (a walk of about 20 min. from the bus terminal) rises *Castel Tirolo (9-12, 14-17; Mon closed), the 12C castle of the counts of Tyrol which gave its name to the whole country round. With the abdication of Margaret Maultasch, the 'ugly duchess', in 1363, the castle and province passed to the Habsburgs. Damaged by a landslip in 1680, the castle was restored in 1904, and is remarkable above all for its superb position. It is now the property of the province. The Knights' Hall and the Chapel have sculptured Romanesque doorways, and the Throne Room commands a fine view.

TO SAN VIGILIO. Bus from P.za del Teatro to Lana di Sopra in 20 min.; cableway from there to the Giogo di San Viglilio (on the hour) in 22 min.—The route crosses the Ádige and runs viâ Marlengo and Cérmes; above the latter is the 13C castle of *Monteleone.*—7 km. *Lana di Sopra* (328 m) a resort, connected with the station of Lana-Postal by bus, stands at the mouth of the Val d'Ultimo. *Lana di Sotto*, to the S., has a 13C church. The cable railway ascends from Lana di Sopra to *San Vigilio* station (1485 m), from where a rough road goes on to (50 min.) **Monte San Vigilio** (1795 m), an excellent viewpoint, with an old chapel; and a chair-lift ascends to the Dosso dei Larici (1830 m).—For excursions in the Val d'Ultimo, see below.

TO AVELENGO. From its lower station (350 m) on the Rio di Nova, S.E. of Maia Alta (bus from P.za del Teatro), a cableway ascends hourly in 8 min. to the upper station (1245 m) at *Santa Caterina*, named after the 13C chapel near by. Thence a road crosses the ravine of the Sínigo and ascends to the plateau of **Avelengo** (1290 m), a winter-sports ground.

OTHER SHORT EXCURSIONS. The castle of *Scena* (594 m) on the hill 5 km. N.E. of Maia Alta (bus) is reached by road (5 km.) or in 1 hr on foot. The castle, a 14C building, restored by Archduke John of Austria in 1844, now belongs to Count Franz of Meran. Visitors are shown an armoury, rooms with Renaissance furniture, and (on application) the neo-Gothic tomb of Archduke John (d. 1859) and his wife. From near Scena a funicular ascends Monte Scena (1445 m), and from Verdins, at the end of the road, another one ascends to Masodi Sopra (Oberkirn; 1441 m).

A pleasant round crosses the Rametz bridge in Maia Alta and leads S. along the hillside to (c. 1½ hrs) *Castel Verruca* (727 m), a ruin commanding a fine view. Below it a footpath descends to *Castel del Gatto* (463 m), another ruin from which a road leads down to Rio di Nova and back to Maia Alta in c. 1 hr.

From Maia Alta the cable railway Ivigna ascends to (1905 m) *Meran 2000*, recently developed as a ski-resort (chair-lift to *S. Osvaldo;* refuge at 2302 m).

LONGER EXCURSIONS

FROM MERANO TO SANTA GERTRUDE, 42 km., bus 4-5 times daily in 2¼ hrs; a good road as far as Santa Valburga, thence rough road.—To (7 km.) *Lana di Sopra,* see above; this route turns right at the entrance to the village. The road ascends in zigzags to enter the VAL D'ULTIMO, the valley of the Valsura, now part of the Stelvio National Park.—20 km. *San Pancrazio* and (29 km.) *Santa Valburga* (1190 m) are the principal villages. The road ends at (42 km.) *Santa Gertrude* (1256 m), beautifully situated beneath the E. spurs of the Ortler range. Interesting passes lead N.W. into the Val di Martello (7-8½ hrs) and ascents are facilitated by the *Rif. Canziani* (2561 m), 3¼ hrs from Santa Gertrude.

FROM MERANO TO VIPITENO, N44, 58 km., bus in 2¼ hrs in summer, ascending the pastoral VAL PASSIRIA with its scattered villages. Beyond (5 km.) *Rifiano,* the fine gorge of the Val Masul is seen on the right. At (9 km.) *Saltusio* a new cable railway ascends to Rifugio Hirzer (Cervina; 1983 m), being developed as a ski-resort.—From (17 km.) *San Martino,* the road crosses the river to (18 km.) *Maso della Rena,* the birthplace of Andreas Hofer (1767-1810), the Tyrolese patriot, who led the successful insurrection of 1809 against Bavaria, the power to which the Tyrol had been awarded by the Treaty of Pressburg.—20 km. **San Leonardo in Passiria** (688 m), is the capital (2900 inhab.) of the valley, which here bends abruptly to the W.

An interesting road ascends the upper Val Passiria from San Leonardo to (9 km.) *Moso* and (16 km.) *Corvara in Passiria* (1419 m).

Beyond San Leonardo the Vipiteno road zigzags steeply up into the Váltina valley, from which another climb leads to the road summit at (41 km.) the **Passo di Monte Giovo** (2099 m), a good ski-ing centre. The descent, equally steep, leads at first through forest, but later the road commands good views of the Isarco valley and its tributaries.—58 km. **Vipiteno,** see Rte 28.

The Stelvio Road now begins the ascent of the **Val Venosta** or *Vintschgau,* the wide and fertile upper valley of the Ádige.—43 km. *Naturno* (554 m), a summer resort. The little Romanesque church of San Prócolo (9-12, 14-18; if closed apply at parish church) contains remarkable mural paintings (?9C).

The *Val di Senáles,* on the right beyond, is a long mountain valley, dominated from the N.E. by the mighty pyramid of the *Similáun* (3597 m), on the frontier. A road extends as far as (17 km.) *Vernago* (1700 m) on the lake of the same name, and is continued by a rough road to (26 km.) *Maso Corto* (2004 m), recently developed for winter sports (cablecar to Bella Vista, 2842 m). It is connected by the easy *Giogo Tasca* (2772 m) with the Silandro valley (6½ hrs). The chief ascent is that of the *Palla Bianca* or *Weisskugel* (3738 m), on the frontier.

51 km. *Castelbello* is dominated by its ruined castle.—57 km. *Laces* (1 km. l.), on the old road, S. of the river (now bypassed) is connected by cableway with *San Martino al Monte* (1736 m).—At (59 km.) the station of *Coldrano* (660 m) a road on the left ascends the Val Martello.

The road leads viâ (2 km.) *Morter,* with a triapsidal Romanesque church, and an aviary for falcons. The Castel Montani has been restored.—Beyond 11 km. *Ganda* is (26 km.) *Paradiso del Cevedale* (2088 m), a climbing and ski-ing resort, with ascents in the Ortler group. *Monte Cevedale* (see below) is ascended in 5½ hrs, with comparative ease, viâ the Rif. Casati. There are passes to Solda (W.; 6-7 hrs) and Santa Gertrude d'Ultimo (E.; 8 hrs). The upper end of the valley, with the Ortler group, forms the Stelvio National Park.

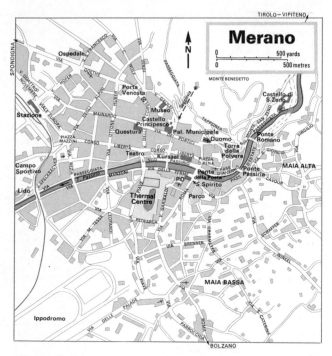

63 km. **Silandro** (722 m), with 5000 inhab., is the chief place in the valley, at the upper limit of the vine. It is being developed as a ski resort. Its tall church steeple is a prominent landmark, and its castles are picturesque.—68 km. *Lasa* is a marble-quarrying village.—77 km. **Spondigna** (885 m) is at the junction of the Stelvio Road with the road to Malles and the Resia Pass (see below).

The Stelvio Road crosses the wide Ádige valley to (79 km.) **Prato allo Stelvio** (915 m), another resort, at the foot of the Trafoi valley.—84 km. *Stelvio* on a height above the road.—86 km. *Gomagoi* (1267 m) lies at the foot of the Val di Solda.

The Solda road leads S. up this side valley to (12 km.) **Solda** (1907 m) one of the most important climbing centres in the upper Ádige and an excellent holiday centre as well for visitors of less active ambitions. The *Passeggiata di Montagna,* a walk laid out up and downstream, commands unequalled views of mountain and valley. It is also now favoured by ski-iers.

ASCENTS (guide essential). Bridle-paths connect Solda with three refuge-huts: the *Rif. Serristori* (2721 m), 1¾ hrs N.E., the *Rif. del Coston* (2661 m), 2¼ hrs S.W. and the *Rif. Città di Milano* (2581 m), 2¼ hrs S. A rather more difficult route leads to the *Rif. Payer* (3029 m), 3½ hrs W. From the Città di Milano hut *Monte Cevedale* (3769 m) is climbed in c. 5 hrs by way of the *Rif. Casati* (3266 m). The Payer hut is the base for the ascent of the ***Ortler** or *Ortles* (3905 m; 3¾ hrs), a magnificent viewpoint, famous as an Austrian strong-point throughout the First World War.

91 km. **Trafoi** (1543 m) is a summer and winter resort frequented for its panorama of the Ortler group. A chair-lift ascends to Rifugio Fórcola (2153 m). 4 km. farther up the Stelvio road (good viewpoint) an obelisk records the first ascent of the Ortler by Jos. Pichler in 1804.

A narrow road leads from Trafoi to the *Three Holy Springs,* the 'Tres Fontes' that gave the village its name. These are made to issue from the breasts of figures of Christ, the Virgin, and St John, in a little chapel, much visited by pilgrims.—The *Ortler* (see above) may be ascended from this chapel in 6-7 hrs.

The ascent to the pass is made by 48 serpentine loops hewn in the face of the ravine. To the left is the huge Madaccio Glacier, descending from the Ortler.—104 km. The **Stelvio Pass** (2758 m), the second highest road-pass in the Alps (12 m lower than the Col d'Iseran) is generally open only in June-October. On either side are hotels and it is frequented for summer ski-ing. Until 1918 this was the meeting-place of the frontiers of Italy, Switzerland, and Austria. The best viewpoint is (¼ hr N.) the *Pizzo Garibaldi* (2838 m), formerly named Dreisprachenspitze from the meeting of the districts where Italian, Romansch, and German are spoken. The descent on the W. side of the pass into the *Val Braulio* is rarely altogether free from snow.—At (99 km.) the *Quarta Cantoniera* (2489 m), with the Italian custom-house, the road to the *Umbrail Pass* or *Giogo di Santa Maria* (2502 m), crossing the Swiss frontier, diverges on the right for Santa Maria (14 km.) and Zernez (49 km.)

Below (110 km.) the *Terza Cantoniera* (2320 m) begins the descent of the Spondalunga ('long bank'), achieved by means of a striking series of zigzags. A wild defile protected by snow-galleries leads down to (118 km.) the *Prima Cantoniera* (1716 m), beyond which is the valley of the Adda.—127 km. **Bormio,** see Rte 15.

From Spondigna to Malles and Landeck

ROAD, 76 km. N 40 to the frontier; bus (July-Sept) in 1½-2 hrs from Merano; through service; railway to Malles only.

Spondigna, see above. Road and railway ascend the left bank of the Ádige.—4 km. **Sluderno** (921 m) is commanded by *Castel Cóira,* or *Churburg,* the 13C castle of the bishops of Coire, restored in the 16C by the Counts Trapp (interesting armoury).

From Sluderno an important road, followed by the bus from Merano to Zernez and Davos, leads W.—Beyond (3 km.) *Glorenza,* a typical old Tyrolean town, with 16C ramparts and three gates, begins the ascent of the Val Monastero (Münster-Tal), with the *Calven* gorge, where in 1499 the Swiss defeated the Austrians and won their practical independence of the Empire.—12 km. *Tubre* (1240 m), or *Taufers,* with the Italian custom-house, has a fine Romanesque church (good 13C frescoes).—Beyond (13 km.) the frontier is (15 km.) the village of *Münster* (1248 m), or *Müstair,* with the Swiss custom-house, in the canton of the Grisons.—25 km. **Santa Maria in Münstertal** (1375 m) stands at the junction of the Umbrail Pass road (see above). *Zernez,* for Davos and St Moritz, is 35 km. farther.

9 km. **Málles Venosta** (1051 m) is an old mountain town (4700 inhab.) with an attractive array of towers and steeples rising above its roofs. Most of the churches were rebuilt in the Gothic style, but *San Benedetto*

(key at No. 101 near by) is of the 9C or earlier (important Carolingian fresco cycle).

Above Malles the valley becomes steeper. The large Benedictine abbey of *Monte Maria* (mainly rebuilt in the 17-19C; frescoes of c. 1180), is conspicuous on the left on the approach to (11 km.) *Burgusio,* which has an old church-tower and a 13C castle. Just outside the town, the church of San Nicolò has Romanesque frescoes.—Beyond the little Lago della Muta lies (18 km.) the ancient village of *San Valentino alla Muta* (1470 m), with ski facilities (cableway to Alpe della Muta, 2120 m). The road now skirts the Lago di Resia formed from two smaller lakes by a dam.—23 km. *Curon Venosta* (1520 m), a pleasant summer resort at the foot of the Valle Lunga.—At the N. end of the lake, below the source of the Ádige, stands (26 km.) *Resia* (1525 m), the last Italian village, commanding a splendid view down the valley of the Ortler group. Both villages were rebuilt when their original sites were submerged. The frontier, with both custom-houses, lies 1 km. beyond the **Passo di Resia** (1507 m).—34 km. *Nauders* (1365 m), the first Austrian village, stands at the foot of the road from the Lower Engadine in Switzerland. The route descends into the Inn valley, which is followed to (76 km.) *Landeck.*

26   TRENTO TO SAN MARTINO DI CASTROZZA AND TO CORTINA

ROAD TO SAN MARTINO, 93 km.—53 km. *Cavalese.*—68 km. **Predazzo.**—93 km. **San Martino.**

ROAD TO CORTINA. 156 km. To *Predazzo,* as above.—78 km. *Moena.*—82 km. *San Giovanni,* and thence by the Pordoi and Falzárego passes to (156 km.) **Cortina,** see Rte 27.

BUS from Trento to San Martino in 4 hrs; viâ Borgo Valsugana, Passo del Brocon, and Fiera di Primiero in 5 hrs.

From Trento this route follows N 47 through the Férsina ravine for 5 km., then turns left.

At the crossroads a road (r.) ascends to the Valle di Pinè for (17 km. from Trento) *Baselga di Pinè* (969 m), a scattered commune and summer resort on the little Lago di Serráia. Farther up are the smaller resorts of (23 km.) *Bedollo* and (26 km.) *Brusago* (1103 m).

Beyond (16 km.) *Lases,* on a small lake, the road follows the Val di Cembra, the lower course of the Avisio. Farther on, beyond the erosion pillars (*pirámidi*) and the ruined castle of (23 km.) *Segonzano,* it skirts the artificial Lago di Stramentizzo, at the end of which it joins the road from Lavis (p. 231).—At (51 km.) *Castello di Fiemme* N48 comes in from Ora, and this route bears right to reach the summer and winter resort centre of (53 km.) **Cavalese** (998 m), the chief village in the *Val di Fiemme,* the middle course of the Avisio. Like many of the valleys of the Pyrenees, this glen has preserved something of medieval independence, and the 'Magnifica Comunità', installed in the ancient palace of the bishops of Trento, still administers the valuable communal lands, though justice is no longer dispensed at the stone table in the municipal park. The Gothic parish church has a marble portal and an attractive little courtyard. A cableway ascends to *Cermis* (1980 m) to the S., scene of a tragedy in 1976 when it failed leaving 42 dead.

Carano is a little spa 4 km. W.—A mountain road leads N. viâ (2 km.) *Varena*, a small health resort with hay-baths, to (9 km.) the *Passo di Lavazè* (1805 m), below the W. slopes of Látemar, whence a precipitous descent leads in 9 km. to the Bolzano road at Pontenova.

59 km. *Tésero*, where frescoes of Sabbath-breakers adorn the church of San Rocco, stands at the foot of the pretty *Val di Stava*, traversed by a road at the end of which (7 km.) are several ski-lifts.—From (61 km.) *Panchià* a road crosses the river for the Val Cavelonte.—62 km. *Ziano* (ski facilities).

68 km. **Predazzo** (1018 m; chair-lifts etc.), has a school for Alpine Frontiersmen (Guardia di Finanza). The *Museo Comunale* contains a collection of local geological specimens.

FROM PREDAZZO TO SAN GIOVANNI (Cortina), 14 km. N 48 ascends the Avisio valley with fine views of the mountains in front.—10 km. *Moena* (1184 m), is a cheerful village resort with a fine view of the Catinaccio and Sella ranges to the N.W. and N.E. A good path ascends to (2 hrs W.) the *Passo di Costalunga* (for Carezza, see p. 245).—To *Belluno, see* Rte 27.

Beyond the Ladin-speaking Val di Fassa, the road from Bolzano and Carezza is joined.—14 km. *San Giovanni*, and thence to *Cortina*, see Rte 27.

The San Martino road (N 50), from Predazzo, sharply ascends the Val Travignolo to the E.—Beyond (69 km.) *Bellamonte* (1372 m), becoming narrow, it twists high above a ravine.—76 km. *Panevéggio* (1515 m) has been rebuilt since 1918.

FROM PANEVÉGGIO TO FALCADE, 18 km., a cross-country road with fine views. On the left rises the *Cima Bocche* (2745 m), the chief peak of the range separating this from the San Pellegrino valley.—8 km. *Passo di Valles* (2033 m) is on the old Austro-Italian frontier, in the heart of the war zone of 1917.—18 km. Falcade, see Rte 27.

A series of broad curves, with splendid views, brings the road up to (85 km.) the **Passo di Rolle** (1970 m), a wide saddle with excellent ski-slopes, dominated by the Cimon della Pala. A steeper series of hairpin curves leads down through conifers on the S. side.

93 km. **San Martino di Castrozza** (1444 m), the most frequented summer and winter resort in the Southern Dolomites, lies in an ample basin of the Cismon valley, with wooded slopes leading up to the towering peaks of the Pale di San Martino.

Buses all the year to Fiera di Primiero and *Feltre* in 1½ hrs; from mid-July to mid-Sept to *Trento* in 4 hrs, to Predazzo and *Bolzano* in 3 hrs.
Winter Sports. Ski-slopes at Passo di Rolle (see above; chair-lifts), on the Col Tognola, to the W. (cableway and chair-lift), and at Pez Gaiard (ski-lift); bobsleigh run; skating rink.

The terraced village of San Martino, which arose round a small priory and hospice dating from the 15C, was demolished, except for the church, by the Austrians in 1915. It is a first-class climbing centre and also provides many easy excursions and wooded walks in the nearer environs.

The principal short excursions are marked by coloured signs; they include: the ascent of *Col Fosco* (1529 m), ½ hr S.W. of the village; the *Val Cigolera*, 2 hrs up and down, S. of that hill; the *Forcella* and *Lugo di Caláita* (1646 m), a walk of

c. 2 hrs, which may be prolonged to (4½ hrs) *Canale San Bovo* (p. 331); and the rougher climb to the *Passo del Colbricon*(1938 m; 2 hrs) and thence to *Paneveggio* (3¼ hrs).—Another bridle route to Canale San Bovo leads S.W. from the Val Cigolera over the Alpe Tognola to (4¾ hrs) *Caoria* (p. 331).

ASCENTS. The easiest ascent (guide advisable) is that of *Monte Cavallazza* (2325 m; 3 hrs) viâ the Colbricon Pass, rewarded by a splendid view of the Pale. For climbs among the *Pale di San Martino* themselves, guides are essential though practised climbers may follow the marked routes of the Club Alpino from refuge to refuge without further guidance.

The *Rifugio Pedrotti alla Rosetta* (2578 m), 3 hrs E. of San Martino, is the base for the ascent of the *Rosetta* (2743 m; ½ hr), the easiest of the peaks of the Pale. From San Martino a cableway and chair-lift rise almost to its summit. The *Cima di Vazzana* (3192 m) is a difficult climb of 3½ hrs.—The *Rifugio Mulaz* (2571 m), reached in c. 3 hrs from the Passo di Rolle, is a starting-point for the *Cima del Mulaz* (2906 m; 1 hr).—The *Rifugio Pradidali* (2278 m), to the S.E., is reached by a very fine mountain route of 3½ hrs. From this hut the ascent of the *Cima di Fradusta* (2939 m; 2½ hrs) is the most popular expedition.—A good high-level route (3 hrs) viâ the *Forcella di Miel* (2538 m) connects the Rif. Rosetta with the *Rifugio Treviso* (1623 m), at the head of the Val di Canali which ascends from Fiera di Primiero.

FROM SAN MARTINO TO AGORDO, (45 km.), part of a very fine circular road-route round the Pale di San Martino, returning viâ Cencénighe, Falcade, and Paneveggio.—It ascends the Cismon valley for 13 km. almost to Fiera di Primiero and then turns left to climb to (21 km.) the *Passo di Cereda* (1369m).—29 km. *Don* is the chief village in the wooded basin of *Gosaldo*.—33 km. *Forcella Aurine* (1299 m) commands a fine view of the Piz di Sagron to the S.W. The road descends into the Sarzana valley at (37 km.) *Frassenè* (1080m), a summer resort, from which the difficult *Croda Grande* (2849 m) is climbed (cableway to Rif. Scarpa, 1735 m).— 41 km. *Voltago* (858 m).—At (46 km.) *Agordo* the road and railway from Belluno come in, see p. 332.

From San Martino di Castrozza to *Fiera di Primiero* and *Feltre*, see p. 331.

27   BOLZANO TO CORTINA AND TO BELLUNO

ROAD TO CORTINA. 108 km.—20 km. *Nova Levante*.—28 km. *Carezza.*— 37 km. *Vigo di Fassa*.—39 km. **San Giovanni.**—51 km. **Canazei.**—63 km. *Passo Pordoi.*—72 km. *Arabba.*—79 km. *Pieve di Livinallongo.*—108 km. **Cortina.**

ROAD TO BELLUNO. 112 km. To *San Giovanni*, see above.—44 km. **Moena.**— 63 km. *Falcade.*—73 km. *Cencenighe.*—83 km. **Agordo.**—112 km. **Belluno.**

BUSES. The famous ***Strada delle Dolomiti** from Bolzano to Cortina, one of the most beautiful roads in the Alps, and a magnificent feat of engineering, is followed in summer by regular coach services, which for hurried travellers provide the best general idea of the Dolomite country. There is a daily express service (June-Sept) in 3 hrs, supplemented by an ordinary service (4½ hrs). Further buses run between Bolzano and Canazei. The summer service to *Belluno* (4-4½ hrs) terminates in winter at *Falcade* (3-3½ hrs).

Bolzano, see Rte 23. The Isarco is crossed by (3 km.) the *Ponte di Cardano*, dominated by its 13C castle, and passing beneath the two motorways the road enters the wild and romantic gorge of the *Val d'Ega*, perhaps most striking at the * *Ponte della Cascata*. Beyond a tunnel and another gorge the fantastic peaks of the Látemar range come into view on the right, with the *Cima della Valsorda* (2752 m) especially prominent.—16 km. *Ponte Nova* (872 m) is the junction of the road to the Passo di Lavazè and Cavalese (p. 242).—The Cantinaccio chain comes into view ahead on the approach to (20 km.) **Nova Levante** (1182 m), a winter sporting centre on the side of a wooded glen. A good path leads N. to Tíres (2¾ hrs) and a cableway rises to the Rif. Fronza (see below).—The Látemar soon appears at close quarters on the right, and the whole Catinaccio chain is seen on the left. The road skirts

(26 km.) the tiny green Lago di Carezza to reach (28 km.) *Carezza al Lago* (1609 m), frequented as a summer and climbing resort, with winter sports facilities. A chair-lift rises to the Rif. Paolina (2125 m).

The two most typical of the Dolomite mountain groups, with their characteristic battlemented skyline, may be climbed from Carezza (guides essential). To the S. rises the **Látemar** (Cimon del Látemar, 2842 m; 3½ hrs), ascended directly from the hotels; while the CATINACCIO, to the N. is approached viâ (2½ hrs) the *Rifugio Aleardo Fronza* (2339 m). The *Coronelle* (2781 m) is climbed thence in 2 hrs; the *Roda di Vael* (2806 m) in 2¼ hrs.

The road-summit is reached at (30 km.) the *Passo di Costalunga* (1745 m), offering a splendid view ahead of the Val di Fassa and the Marmolada and San Martino mountains, with the imposing Punta della Vallaccia between.—37 km. **Vigo di Fassa** (1382 m), the chief village in the Ladin-speaking Val di Fassa, and a winter sports resort, lies beneath the *Ciampediè* (1997 m; cableway to Rif. Ciampediè), a rocky spur of the Catinaccio c. 2 hrs N. The *Rif. Roda di Vael* (2280 m), 2¾ hrs W., is a base for higher climbs.—At the church of (41 km.) **San Giovanni** the road joins highway N48.

FROM SAN GIOVANNI TO BELLUNO. The road branches right to follow N48 S. to (44 km.) *Moena* (see p. 243), then turns E. on N346 to ascend the Val di San Pellegrino. A track ascends to Passo di Lúsia (2056 m; cableway in two stages). The road reaches the summit-level at (56 km.) the *Passo di San Pellegrino*. The *Rif. Taramelli* (2045 m), 2½ hrs N.W. of the pass, is a base for ascents on the S. side of the Marmolada (*Costabella*, 2759 m, 2½ hrs.).—The road descends steeply to (63 km.) *Falcade* (1297 m), a straggling village and now a ski resort.—68 km. *Canale d'Ágordo* (976 m), known until 1964 as Forno di Canale, lies at the foot of the long wild valley of *Garés*, a little-known approach to the Pale di San Martino.—71 km. *Celat* (971 m) is connected by bridle-path with the Val Pettorina (4 hrs. N.).—At the pleasant village of (73 km.) *Cencenighe* (773 m) this route meets the road from Alleghe and Cortina (see p. 246).—83 km. **Ágordo,** in the Cordévole valley, is an excellent centre for mountain drives, with a School of Mines and a 17C palazzo in the attractive main square.

From Ágordo to *Forcella Aurine* and *San Martino,* see p. 331.

Beyond Ágordo, the road continues S. through the magnificent gorge of the Canale d'Ágordo to (91 km.) *La Muda.*—The valley widens and enters the Piave basin, leaving, beyond (102 km.) *Mas,* the road to Feltre (r., 26 km.; see Rte 34).—112 km. **Belluno,** see Rte 34.

From San Giovanni, N48 turns N. up the Val di Fassa.—41 km. *Pozza* (1325 m) and (42 km.) *Pera* (1326 m) are both winter resorts and bases for ascents among the Catinaccio peaks and for the W. side of the Marmolada group.

The **Catinaccio** (see also above), especially famous for its marvellous colouring at sunrise (whence the German name *Rosengarten*), is approached by the Váiolet Valley, at the head of which is the *Gardeccia Refuge* (1948 m), reached by road from Pera in 2 hrs, and open in July-Aug and New Year week only. A path goes on to (1 hr more) the *Rif. del Vaiolet* (2243 m), above which rises the curious *Torri del Váiolet*, whose fantastic configuration is typical of the dolomitic mountains. The *Catinaccio di Antermóia* (3002 m), the highest peak in the group, is a difficult climb of 2½ hrs from the hut. It is also reached from the *Rif. Antermóia* (2497 m), 3½ hrs N.W. of Mazzin (see below) near an icy little lake.

On the E. side of the valley is the *Val di San Nicolò*, followed by a bridle-path over the *Passo di San Nicolò* (2362 m) to (3¾ hrs) the Rifugio Contrin (see below). To the S. of it rise the *Punta Vallaccia* (2637 m) and the *Costabella* (2759 m).

The Sasso Piatto and Sasso Lungo come into view as the road ascends the valley, and at (45 km.) *Mazzin* (1372 m) the Sasso di Pordoi rises ahead.—Beyond (46 km.) *Campestrin* and (47 km.) *Fontanazzo,* lies (49 km.) **Campitello,** an old-established climbers' resort (chair-lift to the Rodella; for the Sasso Piatto and Sasso Lungo, see p. 248).

51 km. **Canazei** (1465 m), standing in a hollow where the Dolomites Road leaves the Val di Fassa, is a centre for excursions in the Sella group to the N.E. and the Marmolada group to the S.E. It is well equipped with all the usual winter-sports facilities. The pyramidal Gran Vernel (3210 m) hides the Marmolada itself.

THE MARMOLADA, the largest and loftiest group of peaks in the Dolomites, is approached from this side by the Avisio and Contrin valleys. A road ascends the Avisio from Canazei to (2 km.) *Alba* (1517 m). A little above this a bridle-path on the right leads into the Val Contrin, at the head of which is the *Rif. Contrin* (2016 m).—The road goes on to the refuge-inn at (9 km.) *Pian Trevisan* (1717 m) and the *Rif. Castiglioni alla Fedáia* (2097 m) on the artificial *Lago di Fedáia,* 3 hrs from Canazei. For the continuation of the road (nearly complete) into the Val Pettorina, see below.—The *Marmolada* (3342 m), the highest peak in the Dolomites, may be climbed from the hut in 4½ hrs, with guide; but a chair-lift ascends from the S. side of the lake to the *Pian dei Fiacconi Refuge* (2520 m) whence an easy glacier path (chair-lift) goes on the *Punta del Rocca* (3309 m), with the small *Rif. Marmolada* (3258 m), E. of the main summit.
Ascents in the Sella group are best attempted from the Sella Pass (see p. 248).

From the steep hairpin turns above Canazei, the *View of the Sasso Lungo to the left and the Sella peaks ahead is more and more striking. This route joins (57 km.) the Passo di Sella road coming from Ortisei, and reaches the road summit at (63 km.) the **Passo del Pordoi** (2239 m), an open saddle, lying between the *Sass Beccè* (2534 m), on the S., and the rocky battlements of the *Sass Pordoi* (2950 m; chair-lift), on the N. A footpath to the left affords a better sight of the Marmolada; still more rewarding is the *View from the Belvedere (½ hr to the right), which may also be reached by chair-lift from Canazei.—A winding descent through high pastures brings the road into the Val Cordévole.—72 km. **Arabba** (1601 m) at the junction of the road to the Val Badia (Rte 29); its ski-slopes are on the Due Baite (chair-lift to La Mésola, 2734 m; funicular to Col Burz, 1943 m). The scattered parish of Livinallongo, is dominated from the E. by the *Col di Lana* (2452 m), the top of which was blown off by an Italian mine in 1916.—70 km. **Pieve di Livinallongo** (1475 m), the chief village of the district, enjoys fine views of the Civetta to the S. and the Pelmo to the S.E. The Col di Lana (see above) is climbed from here in 3 hrs.

FROM LIVINALLONGO TO AGORDO 35 km., bus in 1 hr. Following the Cortina road for 2 km. this route turns abruptly right, descending the Cordevole valley, in which are numerous war-cemeteries.—At 12 km. the road divides. On the right is the *Val Pettorina,* the main approach to the E. side of the Marmolada. The chief village in this valley is *Rocca Piétore,* 3 km. from Caprile, with an old church. From *Malga Ciapela* (1450 m; chair-lift for Marmolada, 3270 m), 6 km. farther on, beyond a fine gorge, the road turns N. and continues to the *Passo di Fedáia* (2057 m) and the *Rif. Feddia* (2004 m) at the end of the Fedáia lake (see above).
The left road leads viâ (14 km.) *Caprile* (1023 m), where an alternative road leads down the E. side of the Cordévole valley (viâ Andraz) to (18 km.) **Alleghe** (979 m), beside a small lake, the base for the difficult ascent of *Monte Civetta* (3220 m; 8 hrs) viâ the *Rif. Sonino* (2135 m), 3½ hrs E.—At the S. end of the lake (20 km.) *Masarè.*—26 km. *Cencenighe,* and thence to *Ágorrdo,* see p. 332.

The Cortina road beyond Pieve leaves the Cordévole and begins a long ascent.—84 km. *Andraz* lies below the road to the right. To the left, beyond a turning on the right for Caprile (see above), rises the ruined castle of Andraz. The Settsass and Monte Cavallo dominate the view on the left, with the Sasso di Stria in front.—94 km. The **Passo di Falzárego** (2105 m), between the *Sasso di Stria* (2477 m) and the Nuvolau ridge, was a hotly contested strongpoint in the First World War. To the left is the Lagazuoi massif, and farther on during the descent (r.), the strangely shaped Cinque Torri, with the Croda da Lago and Antelao behind them, and on the left the cliffs of the Tofane. The Bóite valley soon comes into view and the road zigzags down through the outlying hamlets of Cortina.—108 km. **Cortina,** see Rte 30.

28   BOLZANO TO INNSBRUCK VIÂ THE BRENNER PASS

ROAD, N 12, 125 km.—23 km. *Ponte Gardena.*—29 km. *Chiusa.*—40 km. **Bressanone.**—50 km. *Fortezza.*—72 km. *Vipiteno.*—78 km. *Colle Isarco.*—86 km. **Brennero** (frontier).—99 km. *Steinach.*—125 km. **Innsbruck.**
The Autostrada del Brennero follows this route.
RAILWAY, 134 km. in 2-3 hrs; to *Fortezza,* 48 km., in 1 hr. Through carriages run on this route to Innsbruck and Munich from Rome, Florence, and Venice.

The road and railway from Bolzano soon descend to the Isarco and follow its banks closely. The power-station of Cardano is on the left, the castle of Cornedo on the right.—9 km. *Prato all'Isarco* (315 m).

A road ascends on the right to (7 km.) *Tíres* (1028 m), and (10 km.) *Lavina Bianca* (1173 m), a summer resort beneath the W. side of the Catinaccio. The *Rif. Bergamo* (2134 m), 3 hrs E. by a good path, is the chief base for ascents.

Beyond Prato a road ascends (r.) to *Fiè* (7 km.; 880 m) and continues viâ *San Costantino* to **Siusi** (17 km.; see below).—N12 now enters a gorge in which lies (15 km.) *Campodazzo,* from which steep paths ascend to the Renon plateau. Beyond a quaint covered bridge it emerges from the gorge.—23 km. **Ponte Gardena** (470 m) or *Waidbruck,* is a road junction at the mouth of the Val Gardena. Above the town (20 min. walk) stands the 12C *Castle* of the Wolkenstein, with a good Gothic hall.

FROM PONTE GARDENA TO SIUSI, 11 km., bus. The road ascends S. above the left bank of the Isarco to (8 km.) *Castelrotto* (1060 m), an ancient village with a 17C town hall and an 18C belfry, now frequented for winter sports.—11 km. **Siusi** (998 m), or *Seis am Schlern,* is a well-known summer resort, frequented also for winter sports on the Alpe di Siusi. It lies on a broad terrace under *Monte Castello,* the N.E. spur of the Sciliar, in the forest beneath which is the ruined *Castelvecchio.*
Monte Pez (2564 m), the chief peak of the Sciliar, is ascended in 4 hrs by an easy path viâ (¾ hr) *Rázzes* (1205 m) and (3¾ hrs) *Rifugio Monte Pez* (2451 m). The outlying position of this height makes it a splendid viewpoint, and the dark chasm between its two N. spurs is impressive.—The **Alpe di Siusi,** a wide upland plateau to the E. is famous as a ski-ing ground in winter.

FROM PONTE GARDENA TO ORTISEI AND THE DOLOMITES ROAD, 37 km.

This route, ascending the Ladin-speaking *Val Gardena,* at first a narrow gorge, is served in summer by a bus from Bolzano to Corvara.

13 km. **Ortisei** (1234 m) or *St Ulrich,* the chief place (4100 inhab.) in the Val Gardena, is an excellent summer resort, with a ski-school in

winter. Cableways and lifts rise to the Alpe di Siusi, the Resciesa and the Seceda. The town is a centre for the manufacture of the wooden statuettes that adorn the local churches.

Buses to *Bolzano* and to *Plan;* in summer to *Milan;* to *Predazzo* and *Cavalese;* to *Canazei* and *San Martino di Castrozza;* to *Cortina;* to *Brunico;* etc.

In the central square is a *School of Woodcarving and Design,* which may be visited; and here also is a table showing the chief excursions in the neighbourhood. The 18C church contains good examples of local carving. The *Museo della Val Gardena* has a collection of local interest. To the N. side of the town are the wooded slopes of the Resciesa and to the S.E. the peaks of the Sasso Lungo dominate the view.

An even finer view is obtained from the Gothic church of *San Giácomo* (1 hr E.; cableway in 8 min. from the Santa Cristina road), which contains a fine carved altarpiece by Franz Unterberger (1750).—On the crest of the slopes S. of Ortisei (cableway) is the famous ski ground of the *Alpe di Siusi* (see above; c. 3 hrs). The mountains to the N. are climbed by aid of (2½ hrs or 19 min. by chair-lift) the *Rif. Resciesa* (2170 m).

The valley is now broader.—17 km. **Santa Cristina** (1428 m), another wood-carving village, is a popular winter-sports centre.

The magnificent **Sasso Lungo* (3181 m) and the *Sasso Piatto* (2955 m) are seen to the S. The *Rif. Vicenza* (2253 m), 2¼ hrs from Santa Cristina, is a base for these very difficult ascents.—To the N.E. of the village, in the Cisles valley, is (1¾ hrs) the *Rif. Firenze* (2037 m), the start for ascents in the *Odle* group (*Sass Rigais,* 3025 m) and for the *Punta del Púez Ovest* (2913 m).

20 km. **Selva di Val Gardena** (1563 m), or *Wolkenstein in Gröden,* a resort with similar attractions of those of Santa Cristina and well provided with cableways and ski-lifts, stands at the foot of the Vallunga, which penetrates the heart of the Púez and Gardenaccia mountains to the N.E.—22 km. *Plan Val Gardena* (1614 m). Beyond the ascent becomes steeper.—At (25 km.) *Plan de Gralba* (1810 m) a road to the Val Badia bears off to the left.

This spectacular road (N243) crosses (9 km.) the *Passo di Gardena* (2121 m), the saddle between the Pizzes da Cir (l.) and the N. wall of the Sella group. The open slopes on the N. side (chair-lift) are frequented for ski-ing. The zigzag descent passes a path on the r. leading to the *Rif. Pisciadù* (2585 m), for the N. peaks of the Sella group.—17 km. *Colfosco* (1645 m) has a splendid view of the frowning cliffs of the Sella across the valley.—At 19 km. this route joins the Val Badia road, c. 1 km. below Corvara p. 251).

The main road climbs between the Sasso Lungo and the Torri di Sella to (29 km.) the **Passo di Sella** (2213 m), an open saddle affording good ski-runs. The **View* on all sides is surpassed only by that from the *Rodella* (2387 m; refuge-hut, chair-lift), c. ¾ hr S.W., which is perhaps the finest in all the Dolomites, including nearly all the principal groups, with the Sasso Lungo (N.W.), Sella (N.E.), and Marmolada (S.E.) prominent near at hand.

Ascents in the Sasso Lungo group (viâ the Rif. Vicenza, 2 hrs) are all difficult; moderate climbers, with guide, can attempt the *Piz Boè* (3152 m), the loftiest of the Sella group, ascended in 4½ hrs viâ (3½ hrs) the *Rifugio del Boè* (2871 m).

The descent leads in zigzags beneath the *Piz Selva* (2940 m), leaving on the left the Boè track (see above).—At 37 km. this route joins the Dolomites Road (Rte 27), 5 km. above Canazei.

THE BRENNER ROAD above Ponte Gardena reaches (29 km.) **Chiusa** (523 m), or *Klausen*. This ancient little town is over-looked by the 17C buildings of the convent of Sabiona, built on the site of a Roman town of this name. Lower down is a 13C tower. The chapel of the Madonna di Loreto contains a precious treasury.—At 33 km. a bridge crosses the Isarco for the Funès valley.

The chief resorts in this valley are (2 km.) *Gudon* (720 m) with a 13C castle, (9 km.) *Funès-San Pietro* (1132 m), and (11 km.) *Santa Maddalena*. An easy path leads hence to the *Passo Poma* (2297 m; Rif. Genova) and the Badia valley at (7 hrs) Piccolino (p. 251).

40 km. **Bressanone** (559 m), in German *Brixen*, is an ancient episcopal city (16,200 inhab.), for many centuries the capital of an independent state in continual dispute with the counts of Tyrol. It stands at the confluence of the Rienza (coming from the Pusteria valley) with the Isarco and preserves many ancient buildings. The CATHEDRAL, completely rebuilt in the Baroque period (1745-54), contains some good carved alterpieces, and is adjoined by a Romanesque *Cloister* adorned with frescoes of the 14-15C. From the cloister is the entrance to the *Diocesan Museum* (adm. 9-12, 14-17, to be transferred to the Palazzo dei Principi Vescovi), notable for a collection of locally carved Presepi, or cribs, and for the cathedral treasury. In the *Baptistery*, an 11C building, was held the council instigated by Henry IV in 1080 to depose Hildebrand. It is decorated with interesting frescoes. To the N. of the cathedral is the 15C *Parish Church*, with a fine steeple (the 'White Tower'; table of excursions). The old houses in the square beside it and in the neighbouring arcaded Via dei Portici are typical.

The convent of *Novacella*, on the Pusteria road (Rte 29) is the most interesting short excursion; the fine 16C *Castle* of the Bishops at *Velturno* is 7 km. S.W.—A cableway ascends from S.E. of the town to *Sant' Andrea in Monte* (958 m) and *Valcroce* (2012 m) and thence by chair-lift to the *Rif. Plose* (2226 m), a fine viewpoint frequented for ski-ing. A bus runs viâ Sant'Andrea to (8 km.) *Éores* (1503 m) and (18 km.) *Pláncios* (1911 m), two resorts in the Éores valley. From Pláncios, a road (l.) leads to the Rif. Plose chair-lift (see above).

Above Bressanone the valley takes on a more alpine character; the road commands a fine view of the town and, farther on, of the Novacella convent on the right. At 44 km. the Pusteria road (Rte 29) bears off to the right.—45 km. *Varna* (l.; 671 m) with the ruins of a 13C castle, is on the road from the *Bagni di Scaléres* (1167 m), 6 km. W.—The road and railway from the Pusteria come in on the right by a small artificial lake on the approach to the fortifications (1833-38) that have given name to (51 km.) **Fortezza** (749 m), or *Franzensfeste*, an important railway junction. The valley remains generally very narrow.—Between (62 km.) *Múles* and (67 km.) *Campo di Trens* is the ruined Castel Guelfo (r.) and farther on two more castles (Castel Tasso and Castel Pietra) dominate the open vale of Vipiteno.

71 km. **Vipiteno** (948 m), or *Sterzing*, takes its Italian name from a Roman post established here. The town (5000 inhab.) owed its importance to the mines which were worked in the side-valleys until the 18C; it is now mainly important as a road-centre. The *Palazzo Comunale* (adm. granted), an attractive building of 1468-73, is the chief among the many old houses in the main street. At the end is the tall *Torre di Città*, around which are 15-16C *Mansions, many with battlements, built by the old mine-owning families. To the S. of the town, on the

Merano road, is the 16C *Parish Church,* and near by is the *Hospital,* another 16C building founded by the Teutonic Knights. A *Museum* (8.30-11.30, 14.30-18) contains works by Hans Mutscher (1458).

Monte Cavallo (1862 m; Refuge-hut), an easy climb of 3 hrs N.W. (cableway) is the best neighbouring viewpoint.

To the N.E. of Vipiteno extends the long *Val di Vizze* with several mountain inns, principally at (4 km.) *Prati* and (20 km.) *San Giacomo di Vizze* (1446 m), the highest village in the valley. The *Gran Pilastro* or *Hochfeiler* (3510 m), the highest of the Alpi Aurine or Zillertal Alps, stands on the frontier. 12 km. E.

To the W. of Vipiteno and approached from the Merano road is the VAL RIDANNA, the main avenue of access to the Alpi Breónie. On the left at (6 km.) *Stanghe* is the mouth of the impressive *Val di Racines.* The road goes on to (13 km.) *Ridanna* (1342 m), a quiet mountain hamlet visited by alpinists, and (17 km.) *Masseria,* with a chair-lift. Ascents are made from the *Rifugio Gino Biasi* (3190 m) and the *Rif. Cima Libera* (3148 m), 6 and 6½ hrs N.W. above the large Malavalle Glacier.

From Vipiteno to *Merano* by the Passo di Giovo, see p. 239.

The valley narrows and pine-forests clothe its higher slopes; on the right is seen Castel Strada.—77 km. **Colle Isarco** (1098 m), or *Gossensass,* a favourite summer resort and a good winter sports centre, stands at the foot of the wooded Val di Fléres, once famous for its silver mines.

The *Cima Bianca* (2716,), to the E., is a frequented viewpoint climbed in 4 hrs by a fair path (chair-lift to Rifugio Gallina, 1868 m). *Monte Cavallo* (see above), to the S.W., is reached in 3¼ hrs. From the glacier-fed *Val di Fléres* to the W., paths lead to (6 hrs) the *Rif. Cremona* (2423 m), and to (4¾ hrs) the *Rif. Tribulaun* (2368 m), beneath the dangerous *Tribulaun* (3097 m).

The railway makes a long detour into the Val di Fléres, but the road continues N.E.—83 km. *Terme del Brennero* (1309 m), a small spa surrounded by pine-forests.—86 km. **Brénnero** (1375 m), the last Italian village, with the custom-house and barracks, stands c. 230 metres S. of the stone pillar (1921) marking the frontier on the *Brenner Pass* (Passo di Brennero; 1375 m).

The lowest of the great alpine passes, the flat broad saddle of the Brenner, first mentioned with the crossing of Augustus in 13 B.C., was the main route of the medieval invaders of Italy.

Just beyond is the little *Brenner-See.*—92 km. *Gries am Brenner* (1254 m), with the Austrian custom-house.—99 km. *Steinach.*—104 km. *Matrei.*—125 km. **Innsbruck.**

29   BRESSANONE TO LIENZ VIÂ DOBBIACO

ROAD, N49, 109 km.—34 km. **Brunico.**—52 km. *Monguelfo.*—61 km. **Dobbiaco.**—66 km. *San Candido.*—73 km. *Passo Drava* (custom-house).—109 km. **Lienz.**

RAILWAY (from Fortezza, see Rte 28), 109 km., in 4 hrs; to *Dobbiaco,* 61 km. in 1½-2 hrs. Through trains continue to Vienna.

The **Pusteria,** the valley of the Rienza, which is traversed by the Italian portion of this route, is one of the most attractive districts in the Alto Ádige. In the gaily-coloured villages the churches have bulbous steeples, and often contain good local woodcarvings. The breadth of the valley allows splendid views of the mountains at the head of the side-glens on either hand. In the main valley German has replaced Ladin as the language of the people, but in the less accessible side-valleys the old dialects have been preserved.

Bressanone, see Rte 30. The Pusteria road soon diverges to the right from the Brenner road and passes (4 km.) the convent of **Novacella,** a picturesque group of buildings mainly of the 17-18C and surrounded by 15C fortifications, but including a Romanesque steeple and other older portions. The Baroque church contains carved altarpieces and gives access to the *Cloister* rebuilt in the 14C, with 14-15C frescoes. The Library and Picture Gallery contain old MSS and paintings of the local 15C school. The chapel of San Michele is a circular fortified building of the 12C rebuilt in the 16C.—Beyond (7 km.) *Sciaves* this route joins the road from Fortezza, with the castle of Rodengo above.—11 km. *Rio di Pusteria* stands at the foot of the Val di Valles, and commands a fine view downstream. Its ruined 16C barrier still spans the road beyond. A cableway ascends to the ski-slopes of *Maranza* (1414 m).—16 km. *Vandoies* (755 m). To the N. extends the Val di Fundres, leading up to (4½ hrs) the *Rif. Passo Ponte di Ghiaccio* (2545 m), usually approached from the Tures valley (see below).—Farther on the valley narrows and the road passes (25 km.) *Chienes,* opposite *Casteldarne* with its fine 16C castle. The convent of Castel Badia (in part restored as a hotel), with a 12C chapel, appears on the left on the approach (31 km.; r.) to *San Lorenzo di Sebato* (810 m), a village on the site of the larger Roman *Sebatum,* partly excavated. The 13C church contains good carvings.

FROM SAN LORENZO TO ARABBA, 44 km., an important north-to-south road through the Ladin-speaking Val Badia, down which flows the Gádera. Bus from Brunico, see below. The road follows the windings of the narrowing glen.—At (10 km.) *Longega* a fork on the left ascends a side-valley for 4 km. to *San Vigilio di Marebbe* (1193 m), a summer and winter resort (cable-car and chair-lift) with ascents from the head of the Val Marebbe. A track continues for 11 km. to Pederù (1540 m).—15 km. *Piccolino* (1115 m) commands a lovely view of the *Putia* (2875 m) above San Martino to the right.—Beyond (23 km.) Pederoa a road leads left to *La Valle* (2 km.), recently developed as a resort.—25 km. *Pedraces* (1315 m) stands below *San Leonardo in Badia,* the communal centre of the valley; both are frequented for winter sports (cableway to Croda Santa Croce, 1840 m).—28 km. **La Villa in Badia** (1483 m) is the chief centre of the valley for summer and winter holidays. Ski-ing is practised especially at *San Cassiano* (1537 m), 3 km. S.E., on the slopes of the *Varella* (3055 m).—33 km. **Corvara in Badia** (1568 m), at the junction of the Gardena Pass road to Ortisei (bus), is another resort. The towering *Sass Songher* (2665 m) dominates the valley from the N.W. and the Sella group is prominent to the S.W. As the road ascends the Marmolada comes into view ahead.—From (40 km.) the *Passo di Campolongo* (1875 m) the descent is rapid to (45 km.) *Arabba* on the Dolomites Road (Rte 27).

34 km. **Brunico** (830 m) or *Bruneck,* the picturesque capital (10,900 inhab.) of the Pusteria, stands in a small upland plain clad with firs, and overlooked by the castle of Bp. Bruno of Bressanone (1251). It is the native town of Mich. Pacher (c. 1430-98), whose sculptured wooden crucifixes adorn the churches of the region.

Buses to *Colfosco;* to *San Vigilio;* to *Campo Tures* and the Valle Aurina; to *Ortisei.* In summer to *Lago di Anterselva.* The Milan-Cortina and Innsbruck-Venice long-distance coach services pass through Brunico.

Brunico has some quaint old streets, but is principally attractive as an excursion centre. The finest local viewpoint is the *Plan di Corones* (2273 m; Refuge-hut), 3 km. S. viâ Riscone (or by cableway from Riscone); other excursions lead to *Castel Lamberto* (½ hr E.) overlooking the Rienza gorge, and to *Teodone* (½ hr N.E.) and Villa Santa Caterina (15C).

The level TURES VALLEY, running N. from Brunico, through which flows the Aurina river, affords access to a group of thickly wooded mountain glens lying beneath the peaks and glaciers of the Alpi Aurine on the frontier (bus). The lower valley is relatively uninteresting, but at (12 km.) *Molini di Tures* (856 m), the first of the important side-valleys (Val dei Molini) leads off to the W.—14 km. **Campo Tures** (874 m), or *Sand in Taufers*, is the chief centre in these valleys, and is commanded by the 13-15C castle of the barons of Tures. It is a noted climbing centre, and has winter sports facilities.—To the E. the Val di Riva leads in 12 km. to *Riva di Tures* (1598 m) for ascents among the *Vedrette Giganti*, a group of mountains noted for their numerous glaciers. The *Rifugio Roma* (2276 m) lies 2 hrs S.E.

The main Valle Aurina, above Campo Tures, passes (20 km.) *Lutago* (956 m) and turns N.E. The *Rif. Vittorio Veneto* (2922 m), 5 hrs N., with guide, lies beneath the Sasso Nero (3369 m), a splendid viewpoint.—Farther on are the villages of (28 km.) *Cadipietra,* (33 km.) *San Pietro* and (42 km.) *Casere,* the bus terminal respectively in winter and in summer, and (44 km.) *Pratomagno* (1623 m) the northernmost village in Italy. The peak of the *Vetta d'Italia* (2912 m) is the N. point of the frontier. The *Picco dei Tre Signori* (3498 m) farther E. marked the junction of the counties of Tyrol, Salzburg and Gorizia.

45 km. *Rasun,* to the left, lies opposite the scattered village of *Valdáora.* To the N. extends the long *Val di Anterselva* leading to the *Lago di Anterselva* (18 km.; 1642 m).—52 km. *Monguelfo* (1087 m), or *Welsberg,* a resort with a 12C castle, is at the foot of the Val Casies.— 57 km. **Villabassa** (1158 m), or *Niederdorf,* with some good 15-16C houses, is a starting-point for the excursion to the Lago di Braies.

The VAL DI BRAIES runs S. from the Pusteria for c. 6 km. and then divides. In the left branch are (2 km.) the *Bagni di Braies Vecchia,* and then (6 km.) *Prato Piazza* (1991 m), beneath the Croda Rossa (3146 m).—The right branch leads to (9 km.) *Braies Nuova* (1327 m) and (12 km.) the lovely ***Lago di Braies** (1493 m), a vividly green lakelet surrounded by pine woods and hemmed in by the crags of the *Croda del Becco* (2810 m) on the S. This peak affords a fairly easy and repaying climb of c. 5 hrs viâ (3¼ hrs) the *Rifugio Biella* (2295 m), with descents to Prato Piazza or Cortina.

61 km. **Dobbiaco** (1256 m), or *Toblach,* on the bleak saddle dividing the valley of the Rienza from the Danubian basin of the Drava, is divided into two distinct portions; Dobbiaco Nuovo, to the S. near the station, and Dobbiaco Paese, with a large church and a castle built in 1500 for the Emp. Maximilian I.

Buses to *Bolzano;* in summer to *Lago di Braies;* and to *Val Fiscalina.*

The gentle slopes around Dobbiaco provide excellent ski-ing grounds (chair-lift to Monte Rota, 1591 m). To the Lago di Dobbiaco and Cortina, see p. 258.

65 km. **San Cándido** (1175 m), or *Innichen,* with the Italian railway custom-house, is a frequented summer and winter resort on the Drava. The fine 13C collegiate *Church (tower 1326) is dedicated to SS. Candidus and Corbinian, who are depicted in the fresco above the S. door, by Mich. Pacher (d. 1498). The Crucifixion group above the high altar dates from c. 1200. For the Cadore road, see Rte 30.

At San Candido begins the Austrian Süd-Bahn, though the station at (71 km.) *Versciaco* is in Italian territory. The road custom-house and frontier are at (73 km.) *Passo Drava* (1113 m).—81 km. *Sillian,* with the Austrian railway custom-house.—111 km. **Lienz** (673 m).

30   THE CADORE AND CORTINA

The **Cadore,** through which this route passes, is the mountainous district surrounding the upper valley of the Piave and its western tributaries. Among its peaks it includes some of the most famous of the Dolomites, such as the Marmarole, Sorapis, Antelao, and Monte Cristallo. Until 1918 only the S.E. half of the district was Italian territory and the old frontier-line saw heavy mountain fighting. The Cadorini are mainly a Ladin-speaking people, with Ladin-Venetian dialects in the lower valleys; but German is everywhere understood from Cortina northwards.

A   From San Cándido to Pieve di Cadore

ROAD, N 52, N 51 bis, 60 km., bus to the Val Fiscalina.

From San Cándido (see above) the road ascends the VAL DI SESTO where many houses have the traditional balconies sheltered by a wide roof.—7 km. **Sesto** (1310 m), otherwise *Sexton,* and (9 km.) *San Giuseppe* (1339 m), rebuilt since the First World War, stand at the foot of the Val Fiscalina, a magnificent alpine valley between the Cima Undici and the Tre Scarperi, frequented by ski-iers.

Many fine mountain expeditions (guide advisable) are made from the *Rif. Zsigmondy-Comici* (2224 m), 4 hrs from Sesto above the head of the valley; or from the *Rif. Locatelli* (2405 m), farther W. below the Tre Cime di Lavaredo.—The rock-hewn *Strada degli Alpini* mounts in c. 5 hrs to the S., to the *Rif. Carducci* (2297 m), whence a track descends (4 hrs more) to Auronzo. See also p. 258.

At (15 km.) the *Passo di Monte Croce* (1636 m) begins the descent into the *Comélico Valley, with splendid views on the right of the Cadore Dolomites.—25 km. *Pádola* (1213 m) and (28 km.) *Candide* (1210 m) are two of the scattered villages that make up the commune of *Comélico Superiore.* The road makes a long loop to the left, and descends to (36 km.) **Santo Stéfano di Cadore,** the centre of the Comélico and a winter resort, where the Pádola flows into the Piave. For the road viâ Sappada to Tolmezzo, see Rte 35.

The Cadore road crosses the Piave and descends its wooded valley, which narrows into a gorge where the river has been dammed to form a power-reservoir. The road (difficult in winter as far as Cima Gogna; tunnel planned) penetrates a tunnel and crosses into the Ansiei valley, with a fine backward view of Monte Tudaio (2285 m).—At (46 km.) *Cima Gogna* (796 m) this route joins the road from Auronzo (Rte 30C). The road crosses the Piave at Treponti and again by (49 km.) the *Ponte Novo.*

The steep road on the left just above the bridge ascends through (6 km.) *Lorenzago* (880 m) to (14 km.) the *Passo della Mauria* (1295 m). Thence through Forni and Ampezzo to *Villa Santina* and *Tolmezzo,* see Rte 35.—*Vigo* and *Lággio* (944 m) are little summer resorts 4 km. N. of Ponte Novo.

At (50 km.) *Lozzo di Cadore* (753 m) the road crosses the Longiarin.— Beyond (54 km.) *Domegge* the Piave broadens to form the hydro-electric *Lago Centro Cadore.* Beyond is (57 km.) the Valley d'Oten, which separates the Marmarole from the Antelao. By the bridge stands the church of Il Molinà, below **Calalzo** (806 m), an industrial village that shares with Pieve the terminal station of the railway from the S.

60 km. **Pieve di Cadore** (878 m) is a pleasant summer and winter resort beneath the southern foothills of the Marmarole. The PALAZZO DELLA MAGNIFICA COMUNITÀ CADORINA (1525; adm. in summer 9-12, 15-19)

attests to its ancient importance as chief town of the Cadore. The modest birthplace (the year has long been in dispute) of the painter Titian (?1487-1576), with its museum (adm. in summer 9-12, 14-19; ring in winter) should not be confused with the 16C balconied house of his orator namesake. A Madonna with Saints by the artist hangs in the parish church (3rd altar on the left; recovered after its theft in 1971). The Casa di Babbo Natale in the *Park*, receives Italian mail addressed to Father Christmas.

Pozzale 2 km. above Pieve to the N.W., has a triptych by Carpaccio.—Calalzo may be made a starting-point for ascents of the Marmarole and Antelao, but these are more usually attacked from the Ansiei valley and San Vito di Cadore respectively (see below).

B   From Pieve di Cadore to Dobbiaco viâ Cortina

ROAD, N 51, 65 km.—20 km. *San Vito di Cadore.*—30 km. **Cortina.**—49 km. *Carbonin.*—65 km. **Dobbiaco.**

Pieve di Cadore, see above. The Cortina road runs S.W. leaving the Belluno road on the left at (1 km.) *Tai,* to cross into the Boite valley.—4 km. *Valle di Cadore* (820 m). A small power lake appears ahead as a long curve round the Vallesina valley affords a fine view of the Antelao (r.). The long villages of *Venás* and *Vodo* follow in succession as the road approaches (17 km.) *Borca di Cadore* (942 m) which faces the strangely-shaped Pelmo (see below). A summer resort, it has recently been developed also for ski-ing.—20 km. **San Vito di Cadore** (1011 m), lying beneath a semi-circle of mountains, with the Croda Marcora (3154 m) prominent to the N., is an excellent climbing and ski-ing centre, with a chair-lift to the Sennes plateau (1214 m).

The *Rifugio San Marco* (1823 m), c. 2 hrs E., is the base for the mighty peaks of the **Antelao** (3263 m), to the S.E., and the **Sorapis** (3205 m) to the N., each occupying 6½-7 hrs (guides essential).—The **Pelmo** (3168 m), 8 hrs S.W. across the valley, is ascended viâ (2½ hrs) the *Rif. Venezia* (1946 m).

21 km. *Chiapuzza.* The Tofane are soon prominent in front, with the Croda da Lago on the left, and farther on Monte Cristallo appears on the right above the Cortina basin.—28 km. *Zuel,* with the Olympic ski-jump (see below). The first scattered hamlets of Cortina are soon passed. 30 km. **CORTINA D'AMPEZZO** (1210 m at the church), deservedly the most popular holiday resort (8500 inhab.), both in winter and summer, in the Eastern Dolomites, lies in a sunny upland basin at the junction of the Bigontina and Bóite valleys. Venue of the 1956 Winter Olympic Games, it has unrivalled facilities for winter-sports; there are many comfortable hotels, and entertainments and excursions of every kind are available.

Numerous **Hotels** (some with swimming pools and tennis courts); prices raised at Christmas, in February, and July-Aug. Also at *Pocol, La Verra, Campo,* etc.
Buses to *Calalzo* for train connections to Milan; in the summer season several times daily to *Misurina;* to *Bolzano* viâ the Dolomites Road in 4½-6 hrs, going on to *Merano;* daily to *Bolzano* viâ the Val Gardena in 4¾ hrs; to *Dobbiaco* and *Lienz* in 3¼ hrs; to *Treviso* and *Venice* in 4 hrs; to *San Martino di Castrozza* and *Fiera di Primiero* in 5 hrs; to *Livinallongo,* and the *Rif. Marmolada* in 3 hrs; to *Milan* in 10 hrs.—Also many circular tours are organized varying in price and distance, including the trip to the *Grossglockner Pass* and back and the celebrated *Giro dei Cinque Passi,* a magnificent round trip through the Dolomites.

Winter Sports. On the bank of the Bóite, N. of the town, is the magnificent *Ice Stadium* (1956), with facilities for skating, curling, ice hockey, etc. Overlooking this, on the opposite bank is a *Bobsleigh Run* with sledge-hoist. On every side ski-slopes of graded difficulty are reached by aerial ropeway or by one of a dozen ski-lifts. chair-lifts or cable-ways; the Olympic ski-jump is at Zuel (see above). The *National Ski School* offers instruction privately or in groups, and hire of equipment.

The village of Cortina lies strung out along the Corso Italia, part of the main road up the Valle d'Ampezzo, or Bóite valley. The centre is the P.za Venezia, with the church, post office, tourist offices, and chief shops. A Museum contains paintings by Filippo de Pisis, who often stayed in Cortina. The view of the mountains on all sides is magnificent: to the W. are the Tofane, N.E. the precipice of the Pomagagnon masks Monte Cristallo, S.E. rise the broken spurs of the Sorapis, and the Becco di Mezzodì and Croda da Lago fill the horizon to the S. Cortina has few old buildings (a fire in 1976 destroyed virtually the last ones), but in the numerous surrounding hamlets are some fine old wooden houses, notably at *Alverà* and *Staolin,* near the Tre Croci road.

EXCURSIONS FROM CORTINA

The following ascents (cableways) should not be missed: *Pocol* (1539 m; from P.za Roma), above the Falzárego road, a splendid viewpoint with a large cemetery of the First World War; *Monte Faloria* (2123 m), above the town to the E. with its extension to the *Tondi di Faloria* (2327 m).

FROM CORTINA TO MISURINA (14 km.), a fine mountain drive which may be made part of a circular route viâ either Carbonin or Auronzo (comp. Rte 30C). The road ascends steeply E. up the Val Bigontina, passing the chalets of Alverà; the view widens rapidly, and the Antelao (r.) and Pelmo (behind) come momentarily into view.—8½ km. **Passo di Tre Croci** (1814 m), the highest point of the road, is visited for winter sports and for climbing. The Alpe Faloria on the right is a good ski ground.

The *Rif. Vandelli* (1926 m), 1½ hrs S. on the Lago del Sorapis, is a base for the difficult ascent of the Sorapis. To the N. a cable-way rises to the *Som Forca* (2213 m; chair-lift on to Forcella, 2989 m). The pass is traversed by a disused military road which descends the grim Val Grande to (c. 2¼ hrs) Ospitale (see below).

On the descent the curiously shaped peaks of the Cima Cadin are seen ahead, with the Tre Cime di Lavaredo to the left and the deep Ansiei valley to the right.—At 13 km. this route joins the road from Auronzo, with *Misurina* (see Rte 30C) 2 km. to the left.

ASCENTS FROM CORTINA. and ski-tours in winter (map obtainable at the tourist offices), are innumerable. A cableway rises from the town to Col Druscie (1779 m) and *Tofano di Mezzo* (3244 m). By foot, the *Castelletto Tunnel,* an excavation of 1916 at the S. end of the Tofane group, is easily reached in c. 3 hrs by a turning on the right of the Falzárego road. Above it is (4 hrs) the *Rifugio Cantore* (2545 m), whence the difficult *Tofana di Mezzo* (3244 m) is climbed in 3 hrs. The return from the hut may be made viâ the Astaldi path round the Forcella Pomedes to the *Rif. Duca d' Aosta* (2098 m), whence chair-lifts descend to the town by way of the *Col Druscié* (1779 m; refuge), a favourite ski-ing ground. An alternative for energetic walkers (c. 6 hrs) is to descend the long Val Travenanzes to the Dobbiaco road.—Other climbers' refuges reached from the Falzárego road are (3 hrs) the *Rif. Palmieri* (2046 m), at the foot of the *Croda da Lago* (2701 m), and (4½ hrs) the *Rif. Nuvolau,* on the summit of the *Nuvolau* (2575 m; chair-lift to *Rif. 5 Torri,* 2137 m).

CARBONIN

STRADA STATALE No.51
VIA CASTELLO
VIA MARANGONI

Stadio del Ghiaccio
(Olimpico)

VIA MARANGON
VIA ZUGLIO
VIA OTTÀ TIANA
CORSO ITALIA
STRADA STATALE No.48
CANTORE
VIA
Bus sta.
VIA MARCONI

VIA LACEDEL
CORSO ITALIA
Torrente Bottè
PO
PIAZZA
ROMA
Parrocchiale
PIAZZA
VENEZIA
MERCATO
ITALIA
VIA CANTORE

VIA DEI FRANCHI

Torrente Bigontina

Funivia — Belvedere

Mad.d.Difesa
VIA D.CAMPI
VIA OLIMPIA
VIA ROMA

Cortina

| 0 | 300yds |
| 0 | 300m |

V a l l e

P O

Chiave

Gadin

Maion

TOFANE

COL
DRUSCIE

Ronco

see
inset

Rif
Alp Adam

Gilardon

Val

Lacedel

Rif
A. Dibona

Mortisa

POCOL

Malghe
Fedarola

S

PASSO DI FALZAREGO

R.
Falzarego

Rio Costeana

	Funivia — Cable Rly
	Seggiovia — Chair Lift
	Sciovia — Ski Lift

SELVA DI CADORE

Environs of
Cortina

GRUPPO DEL CRISTALLO

VAL GRANDE

AGAGNON

Som Forca

Pso. di Tre Croci

MISURINA

STRADA

STRADA

Staolin

Torrente Bigontina

ocai

Alvera

Pecol

Cortina

FALORIA

b

ontina

AL

Rif.
Faloria

TONDI DI FALORIA

Colonna

lieto

AMPEZZO

Zuel

SORAPIS

0   1 mile
0   1 kilometre

N

S. VITO DI CADORE

FROM CORTINA TO CAPRILE BY THE GIAU PASS (30 km.; unmade-up road as far as Selva di Cadore), an interesting alternative to the Falzárego-Andraz route. This route leaves the Dolomites Road near the Pocol Hotel and ascends the wooded Costeana and Cernera valleys, across which is a wall built in 1753 to mark the boundary between the Ampezzano and the Cadore.—13 km. *Gino Ravà Ski Hut* (1969 m).—From (16 km.) the *Passo di Giau* (2233 m; refuge), a wide saddle of the Nuvolau, the road descends the Codalunga valley to (25 km.) *Selva di Cadore* (1335 m), where it joins the road from Longarone (Rte 34). Beyond is the descent into the Valle Fiorentina, above the opposite side of which are the scattered hamlets of *Colle Santa Lucia,* noted for its view of the Dolomites.—30 km. *Caaprile,* see p. 14½ 34.

From Cortina to *Bolzàno* by the Grand Dolomites Road, see Rte 27.

The Dobbiaco road ascends the Ampezzo valley, with the Tofane towering on the left above its wooded slopes, and the Pomagagnon rock-wall on the right. It makes a long detour round the hill of Podestagno, which is crowned by the remains of a castle, and leaves the Bóite near the ruins of Castel Sant'Uberto where the united Travenanzes and Fanes valleys come in on the left, opposite Monte Cadin (2367 m). The wooded Val Grande opens on the right on the approach to (42 km.) *Ospitale* to the N. of which towers the *Croda Rossa* (3146 m). To the right are the tiny Lago Nero and Lago Bianco.—46 km. *Cimabanche* (1529 m) is the highest point on the road.—48 km. **Carbonin** (1432 m), or *Schluderbach,* is the junction of the road from Auronzo (Rte 30C). Ascents in the *Cristallo* group to the S. are difficult and avalanches are frequent. The road turns N. and crosses what was approximately the front-line in 1916-17; the *Lago di Landro* (r.) enjoys a fine view S. of *Monte Cristallo* (2918 m).—61 km. *Lago di Dobbiaco* (1256 m) lies amid woods.—65 km. **Dobbiaco,** see Rte 29.

C   From Pieve di Cadore to Dobbiaco viâ Auronzo

ROAD, 66 km.—20 km. **Auronzo.**—45 km. *Misurina.*—50 km. *Carbonin.*— 66 km. **Dobbiaco.**

From Pieve di Cadore to (14 km.) *Cima Gogna,* see Rte 30A. This route leaves the Santo Stéfano road on the right and continues to ascend the tributary Ansiei valley. Soon it reaches the outskirts of Auronzo, which extends for 4 km. along the road, with a power-reservoir on the left.

20 km. **Auronzo** (864 m), with 3950 inhab., is commanded from the N. by the pointed Aiárnola. It is a centre for long excursions. A cablecar for skiers rises to *Monte Agudo* (1585 m).—Beyond the N.W. hamlets of Auronzo the wooded valley is thinly populated. Monte Popera, and the Croda dei Toni dominate the view on the right and the Marmarole peaks on the left. Beyond the spoil-heaps of some old zinc mines is the approach to the MARMAROLE, a fine dolomitic mass rising to 2932 m in the *Cimon del Froppa.*—After (34 km.) *Palus* (1112 m) the Sorapis and Cadin groups come into prominence, and on the left is the *Corno del Doge* (2615 m) shaped like a huge Doge's cap. The ascent becomes steeper, and the Tre Croci road from Cortina is joined.

44 km. **Lago di Misurina** (1737 m), one of the most beautifully situated lake in the Dolomites (although now sadly polluted) lies in the broad valley between the Cadin (E.) and the Cristallo group (W.), but the finest peaks in view are the Tre Cime di Lavaredo and the Sorapis, to the N.E. and S. respectively. Misurina is an excellent centre for winter sports

(especially skating) and some of the finest ascents in the Dolomites are made with guides, either from the hotels or from the climbers' refuges in the vicinity. A chair-lift rises to Col de Varda (2201 m).

Monte Piana (2324 m), 6 km. N. of Misurina by mountain-road, is a fine belvedere fiercely contested in 1916-17. The pyramid at its N. end commemorates the poet Carducci (1835-1907).—A still finer road, not always passable, leads N.E. to (7 km.) the *Rifugio Auronzo* (2320 m), at the foot of the beautiful *Tre Cime di Lavaredo* (Cima Grande, 2999 m, a difficult climb of c. 5 hrs). Thence a marked path goes on to a chapel and the *Rif. Lavaredo* whence a side path on the right leads to the *Bersaglieri Memorial, by Vitt. Ancona (1916). The main path continues past the *Lago di Lavaredo* and (2 hrs) the *Lago di Céngia* (artillery memorial) to (2½ hrs) the *Rif. Zsigmondy-Comici* (p. 253). From the Rif. Auronzo a track descends (r.) to the Ánsiei valley for (5 hrs) Auronzo; and from near the Lago di Lavaredo there is a route over the Forcella di Lavaredo to the Rif. Locatelli (p. 253; 1½ hrs from the Rif. Auronzo).

Beyond the lake soon begins a rapid ascent into the Valle Popena, and at (49 km.) *Ponte della Marogna* the road crosses the old frontier.— 50 km. **Carbonin,** and thence to (67 km.) *Dobbiaco,* see Rte 29.

31   VERONA TO VENICE

ROAD, 125 km., N 11 (PADANA SUPERIORE), leaving Verona by Via Venti Settembre (Pl. 8).—50½ km. **Vicenza,** entered by the Corso San Felice and left by the Porta Padova (or bypassed to the S.).—83 km. **Padua,** entered by the Porta Savonarola and left by the Via Belzoni (or bypassed to the N.).—89 km. *Ponte di Brenta.*—94 km. *Stra.*—104 km. *Mira.*—117 km. *Mestre.*—125 km. **Venice.**
The busy AUTOSTRADA, A 4 (SERENISSIMA), follows the same route and is 4 km. shorter.
RAILWAY, 119 km., in 1¼-1½ hrs; to *Vicenza,* 52 km., in 30-50 min.; to *Padua,* 82 km., in 45-60 min. Frequent service, mostly starting in Milan.

Leaving Verona, there is a view of the Madonna di Campagna on the right, and on the left the valleys of the Tredici Comuni (see above) leading up into the Monti Lessini.—11 km. *Vago. Zevio,* a fruit-growing town of Roman foundation, 5 km. S. on the Ádige, is the reputed home of the painter Stefano da Zevio.—15 km. *Caldiero* has hot springs (perhaps the Roman Fontes Junonis).

On the left is the road up the Val d'Illasi, at the head of which is the village of *Giazza* (29 km.) where a Germanic dialect is still spoken. An Ethnographical Museum has been opened here. On the way is (6 km.) *Illasi,* where the church has a fine frescoed Madonna by Stef. da Zevio, and there are two villas.

On the left farther on rises the fortified townlet of *Soave,* noted for its white wine, with battlemented walls, a conspicuous 14C castle (adm. 8-12, 15-19) of the Scaligers, and several old palazzi of the period.—At (22 km.) *Villanova,* an outlying part of *San Bonifacio* (r.), is the Romanesque abbey of San Pietro Apostolo (1131-39), many times restored.

At *Árcole,* 7 km. S., Napoleon defeated the Austrians under Alvinczy in Nov 1796.—At *Locara,* 5 km. farther along the main road, is the station for **Lonigo** (6 km. S.; bus), a little town (11,900 inhab.) at the foot of the Monti Bérici, where the *Town Hall* occupies a mansion of 1557. On the outskirts stands the *Rocca,* or *Villa Pisana* (1578; adm. only to park), a charming work by Scamozzi (recalling Palladio's Villa Rotonda; comp. p. 265) on the site of an old castle.

32 km. The *Villa da Porto* ('La Favorita') by F. A. Muttoni (1714-15; ring for adm.), is prominent to the right. The road traverses a wide valley

between the foothills of the Monti Lessini (l.) and the volcanic Monti Bérici.—33 km. *Montebello Vicentino* preserves some remains of a castle. On the right rise the ruins of the castle of *Brendola,* slighted in 1514; on the left opens the Val d'Agno, with the castles of Montecchio (see p. 266).—42 km. *Tavernelle.*

51 km. **VICENZA,** the city of Palladio, is a busy provincial capital (119,000 inhab.) with many beautiful buildings. It enjoys a pleasant situation beneath the foothills of the green Monti Bérici and is traversed by two sluggish little streams, the Retrone and the Bacchiglione. The streets, though narrow, are cheerful, and the Venetian dialect word *Contrà* or *contrada* replaces the more usual 'Via' in the older quarters of the town. Much of the centre has been rendered more peaceful since its closure to traffic.

Post Office, P.za Garibaldi.—**E.P.T.,** 5 P.za Duomo; *Information Office,* P.za Matteotti.

Buses from P.za Duomo to *Monte Bèrico;* from Campo Marzio and Viale Roma to *Asiago, Lonigo, Trento* viâ *Bassano* or *Rovereto, Recoaro, Este* and *Rovigo, Cittadella,* etc.; from P.za Matteotti to *Padua* and *Treviso.* The TRAMVIE VICENTINE company runs services (buses have now mostly replaced the trams) to *Bassano, Recoaro, Noventa, Marostica,* etc. from W. of the railway station.

History. The Roman municipium of *Vicetia,* the successor of a Gaulish town, was destroyed during the barbarian invasions, but rose to importance again in the later Middle Ages, and became in turn an episcopal city and a free commune, and a member of the Veronese League against Barbarossa (1164). Following the usual series of petty wars against its neighbours, Verona and Padua, Vicenza reached a certain stability under the Veronese Scaligers after 1314. In 1404 it joined itself to the Venetian dominion, and its chief architectural glories, both Gothic and Renaissance, date from the Venetian period. Like the rest of Venetia, it passed under Austrian dominion in 1813; the insurrection of 1848, though vigorous, was unsuccessful, but in 1866 Vicenza was united to the Italian kingdom. The town was bombed and the centre much damaged in the Second World War.

The greatest name in the history of Vicentine art is that of Andrea di Pietro (1508-80), nicknamed Palladio by his fellow-citizen the poet Gian Giorgio Trissino (d. 1615). He practically undertook the rebuilding of the town, and from him it is called the 'città di Palladio'. His work was carried on by Vincenzo Scamozzi (1552-1616). The most illustrious painter of Vicenza is Bartolomeo Montagna (1460-1523), a native of the province of Brescia; he was followed by his son Benedetto, by Giov. Buonconsiglio, and by Marcello Fogolino. Among other famous Vicentines are Ant. Pigafetta (1491-1534), the fellow-voyager of Magellan, Giac. Zanella (1820-88), the poet, and Ant. Fogazzaro (1842-1911), the novelist.

The road from Verona meets Viale Roma (coming from the station) at *Porta Castello.* The massive 11C tower here is a fragment of the Scaligers' stronghold, destroyed in 1819. On the right in P.za Castello, just inside the gate, are the three huge columns of *Palazzo Breganze,* probably designed by Palladio, and left unfinished by Scamozzi (c. 1600). Here begins the handsome CORSO PALLADIO, the principal street of Vicenza, notable for its many fine palaces. At the beginning, on the left, No. 13 is *Palazzo Bonin,* probably by Scamozzi; Nos. 38-40, the *Pal. Pagello,* is by O. Bertotti Scamozzi (1780). Beyond the Gothic *Pal. Thiene* (No. 47), No. 67, *Pal. Brunello,* is a charming example of 15C Venetian Gothic art. At No. 98 is the imposing **Palazzo del Comune,** formerly a private palazzo, begun by Scamozzi in 1592 and finished in 1662.

In the huge and dignified *PIAZZA DEI SIGNORI, behind the Municipio, is the majestic ***Basilica** (1549-1614), Palladio's masterpiece, with two open colonnaded galleries, Tuscan Doric below and Ionic above. The nucleus of the building is the 15C hall of the *Palazzo della Ragione* (adm. on application in the upper gallery), and the skill with which Palladio adapted a Renaissance shell to this Gothic core is especially notable. Its name 'Basilica' is derived from its original function as a place

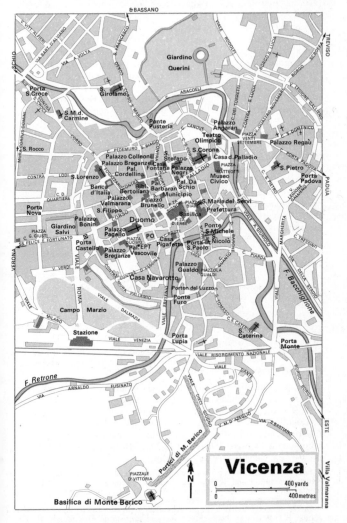

Vicenza

0   400 yards

0   400 metres

in which justice was to be administered. Near the N. corner rises the slender *Torre di Piazza* (12C), to which additional stories were added in 1311 and 1444. Facing the basilica are the brick *Loggia del Capitaniato* (1571) by Palladio, and the *Monte di Pietà,* in two parts (left, 1500; right;

1553-57) separated by the church of *San Vincenzo,* by Paolo Bonin (1614-17). Two graceful columns at the E. end of the piazza bear the Lion of St Mark (1464) and the Redeemer (1640). In the adjacent P.za delle Biade, *Santa Maria dei Servi,* a Gothic church of 1407 enlarged in 1490, has fine Renaissance altars and a late-15C cloister (S. side) with capitals of varying origin.

Piazza delle Erbe, behind the Basilica, is a quaint market square with a medieval prison-tower; and in the narrow streets to the S.W. are several old mansions, notably *Casa Pigafetta* (1481), in an early Renaissance style seemingly influenced by Spanish Gothic, and with a French motto. On the adjacent house a plaque records Ant. Pigafetta, one of Magellan's company in 1519-22. Contrà dei Proti (and its continuations to the W.) leads to Piazza del Duomo. Here is the *Palazzo Vescovile,* rebuilt after 1944, but preserving a charming courtyard-loggia (1494) by Bern. da Bissone.

The Gothic **Duomo,** largely rebuilt in the 14-16C, was practically destroyed in 1944; the façade (1467), the apse, and some chapels remained and it has been carefully rebuilt. The sturdy detached campanile (11C) stands on a ruined Roman building. North side: in the 4th chap., Madonna, by *Bart. Montagna* (removed for restoration in 1976); 5th chap., Coronation of the Virgin, with figures of painted stone, by *Antonino da Venezia* (1448) and two 16C tombs. South side: 5th chap., Polyptych, by *Lor. Veneziano* (1356; restored); 1st chap., 8C sarcophagus, and outside, pretty stoup. Beneath the crypt excavations (closed since 1973) have revealed part of a Roman street and considerable remains of a 9C double-aisled basilica, and of a still earlier cathedral.

From the E. end of the Duomo, Contrà Pasini leads S. past the two attractive *Case Arnaldi,* one Gothic, the other Renaissance. In the Contrà Carpagnon (left) is a house (No. 11) occupied by Frederick IV of Denmark in 1709. *Ponte Furo* crosses the little Retrone; there is a good view (left) of the Basilica and Torre di Piazza, and (right) of Monte Bérico. On the left (No. 2 Piazzetta Santi Apostoli) is the fine Gothic *Casa Navarotto* (14C). Leaving the *Portòn del Luzzo,* a 13C gateway, to the right, the street continues to Piazzola dei Gualdi with the two Renaissance *Palazzi Gualdo.* On the left, in Via Paolo Lioy, is the charming Gothic *Casa Caola.* The river may be recrossed by the hump-backed ** Ponte San Michele* (1620). At the end of Contrà Ponte San Michele is Contrà Piancoli with several interesting houses. Contrà delle Gazzolle leads back to the centre.

In Corso Palladio, beyond Palazzo del Comune, are *Palazzo da Schio* (No. 147; 15C Venetian Gothic, restored), known as the 'Ca' d'Oro', and (No. 163) the so-called *Casa del Palladio,* built by the architect for P. Cogollo. At the end, in the shaded P.za Matteotti is **Palazzo Chiericati,* an excellent specimen of Palladio's work (1550-57), in which is housed the ****Museo Civico** (9.30-12.30, 15-18.30; in winter: 9.30-12.30, 14.30-17.30; Sun 10-12.30; closed Mon).

Four rooms (l.) contain prehistoric finds from the province, including (R. III) a Venetic inscription, and (R.IV) objects from lake dwellings at Fimon.—RR. V-VI. Roman tombs and sculpture (head of Faun).—R. VII. Lombard relics (6-7C). In the courtyard, mosaic hunting-scene (4C).

On the SECOND FLOOR is the picture gallery; the friezes and ceilings are worth a glance. R.I. Works by *Paolo Veneziano* and *Battista da Vicenza.*—R. II. 878. *Giov. Mansueti,* Madonna and Child; 190. *Maineri,* Birth of St Thomas (or St Domenic); 297. *Memling,* Calvary.—R. III. 195. *Fr. and Bernardino Zaganelli,* Madonna in glory; 162. *Dom. Morone,* Scenes from the life of St Blaise; 179. *Marco Palmezzano,* The Dead Christ with Saints; 143. *Liberale da Verona,* Madonna in adoration of the Child; 178. *Bernardino Luini,* Adoration of the

Magi.—R. IV. *Bart. Montagna,* 335. Christ carrying the Cross, 4. Presentation of Christ in the temple, 6. Madonna and Saints (a large altarpiece), and other works. 44. *Carpaccio* (?), Madonna enthroned with Saints; *Cima,* Madonna with Saints.—R. V. 36. *Mansueti,* Madonna and Child with Saints; *Marcello Fogolino,* 34. Epiphany, 35. Saints.—R. VI. *Sansovino,* *Madonna and Child (terracotta) in its original wood frame.—R. VII. *74. *Tintoretto,* A miracle of St Augustine; 77. *Veronese,* Madonna and Child with Saints; 292. *Marcello Venusti,* Shepherds; 340. *Bernardino Licinio,* Portrait of a Fieramosca.—RR. VIII and IX. (l.). 17C works, including some by *Pietro Vecchia.*—R. X Paintings by *Jacopo Bassano* (including three Portraits, and Madonna with Saints); *743. *Brueghel the Elder,* Madonna and Child (with beautiful landscape), and scenes from the life of Christ around the border; 288. *Van Dyck,* Three ages of man.—R. XI *Fr. Maffei* (1626-60).—R. XII. 17C-18C artists, including *Pittoni.*—R. XIII. 18C. *Gius. Zais, Seb. and Marco Ricci,* etc.—R. XIV. *G. B. Tiepolo,* Immaculate conception. R. XV, the Great Hall (and the room beyond), has large works by *Luca Giordano* and *Bellucci,* and 17C civic paintings.

On the opposite side of the square is the *Territorio,* a defensive work transformed during the centuries with a tower rebuilt since the bombing. Within stands the *Teatro Olimpico (9-12.30 and 14-16 or 15-18.30; closed Mon; summer Sun closed at 17; best light in morning), the last work of Palladio (1580; finished by Scamozzi), a fascinating structure of wood and stucco with fixed scenery representing a piazza and streets in perfect perspective. The opening play, given by the Accademia Olimpica in 1585, was Sophocles' 'Oedipus Tyrannus'.

Just across the bridge over the Bacchiglione is P.za Venti Settembre with the 15C *Palazzo Angaran* (rebuilt), and in Contrà Venti Settembre is the fine *Palazzo Regaù* (15C Gothic). To the right is the 14C church of *San Pietro,* with a 15C brick cloister (apply at the hospice next door).

Contrà Santa Corona leads N. from the Corso to the Dominican church of **Santa Corona,** early Gothic in style (1261) with a Renaissance E. arm of 1482-89.

INTERIOR. N. side: 2nd altar, Glorification of St Mary Magdalen, by *Montagna;* 3rd, *B. Bassano,* St Anthony; 5th, *Giov. Bellini,* *Baptism of Christ, a superb late work, in a splendid altar of 1501; NORTH TRANSEPT. Derision of Christ, by *Tentorello* (late 14C; recently restored). The high altar (1669) is richly inlaid with marble. The choir stalls are finely inlaid (end of 15C). In the chapel N. of the sanctuary is the gold reliquary of the Holy Thorn (14C; rarely shown). A plaque on the nave pillar records the burial of Palladio here in 1580; his remains were later removed to the cemetery of Santa Lucia. To the S. of the choir is the THIENE CHAPEL, with two splendid Gothic family tombs (being restored in 1976). The chapel's altarpiece is by *G. B. Pittoni* (1723). The 4th S. chapel is sumptuously decorated by *G.B.* and *Aless. Maganza.* In the 3rd chapel is *Veronese's* *Adoration of the Magi, with superb colouring.

In the N. transept of the church of SANTO STEFANO (open early morning or late evening) to the W., is a beautiful painting of the *Madonna with SS. George and Lucy by *Palma Vecchio.* Opposite are the *Casa Fontana, the most successful Gothic building in the city, and the Renaissance *Palazzo Negri.* The *Palazzo della Banca Popolare,* or Pal. Thiene, to the left, has a courtyard and E. façade by Palladio (1558) and the main façade, with remains of frescoes, by Lor. da Bologna (1489) and a fine portal, in the Contrà Porti.

Also in *Contrà Porti are: (left) No. 8, the Gothic *Palazzo Cavalloni;* (right) No. 11, the dignified *Palazzo Porto Barbaran* (1570) by Palladio; No. 15, where Luigi Da Porto, author of the story of 'Romeo and Juliet' died in 1529; No. 17, *Palazzo Porto Breganze,* Gothic with a Renaissance doorway; No. 19, the magnificent 14C *Palazzo Colleoni Porto;* and No. 21, *Palazzo Iseppo Da Porto* (1552), by Palladio.

Contrà Riale runs S.W.; No. 12 (r.), the sumptuous *Palazzo*

Cordellina, is by Calderari (1776), and at No. 9 in the former 17C convent of San Giacomo is installed the fine *Biblioteca Civica Bertoliana.* To the right is the animated Corso Fogazzaro, in which, beyond the *Banca d'Italia* (Pal. Repeta; 1701-11), by Fr. Muttoni, stands the majestic 13C brick church of **San Lorenzo.** The W. front is the finest in Vicenza, with a splendid marble portal of the mid-14C, and sculptures in a good state of preservation although the church was secularized from 1797 to 1927.

INTERIOR (vista spoilt by the glass at the E. end). Above the door, Monument to Gen. Da Porto (1661), with a remarkable collection of military emblems. South Transept: Altar of the Trinity, with coloured reliefs (15-16C) and frescoes. On the N. side: against the W. wall, tomb of Scamozzi (d. 1616); 2nd bay, Volpe tomb, once ascribed to Palladio (1575); 3rd bay, remains of 14C frescoes (very ruined). The Choir and its flanking chapels contain interesting tombs, notably a fine Gothic tomb of the Da Porto family, on the left; opposite, Beheading of St Paul, a large fresco, by *Bart. Montagna.*

Santa Maria del Carmine, farther on, has good Renaissance sculptured details within; beyond is *Porta Santa Croce,* a well-preserved gateway of 1381.

In the opposite direction Corso Fogazzaro leads back to the Corso, passing *Palazzo Valmarana-Braga* (No. 16), by Palladio (1566).

Outside Porta Castello is the *Giardino Salvi,* with a 16C Palladian loggia and another by Longhena, ½ km. beyond which stands the remarkable church of **Santi Felice e Fortunato,** with a curious fortified campanile (1166), a fragmentary mosaic pavement, partly Constantinian, partly Theodosian, a Martyrion of the 4C, and parts of its cloister.

In the N.W. outskirts of the town (just within the walls) the church of *San Rocco* (comp. the Plan) preserves an elegant interior of the early Renaissance (if closed, ring at No. 22 Contrada Mure S. Rocco).

4 km. S. of the town, reached via Porta Castello, just by the autostrada, is the church of *Sant'Agostino.* It was built in 1322 on the site of an 8C chapel. Over the main altar, Polypytch by Battista da Vicenza (1404); 14C frescoes decorate the apse and nave walls.

MONTE BÉRICO AND THE VILLA ROTONDA

This excursion is a pleasant walk of c. 1 hr, rounding off the attractions of Vicenza (bus from P.za Duomo to Basilica). The green hillside of Monte Bérico has been preserved almost entirely from modern building. The Basilica, a pilgrim shrine, is apt to be crowded on Sunday, especially during September (Festival on 8 Sept).

The **Basilica di Monte Bérico** (*Madonna del Monte*), conspicuous from all parts of the town, is best reached via the Porta Lupia, S. of the town, and the *Portici,* a covered ascent with 150 arches and 17 chapels, designed by Fr. Muttoni (1746-78) and erected by various pious citizens or guilds. A fine view (E.) of the Villa Rotonda may be enjoyed from just below the basilica.

The BASILICA (closed 12.30-14.30) replaces a chapel built to commemorate two apparitions of the Virgin (1426-28); it was enlarged in 1476 and finally completely rebuilt, apart from the campanile, by Carlo Borella in 1688-1703. Lorenzo da Bologna's façade of 1476 has been re-erected alongside the present S. front. The interior contains (to the right of the altar) a *Pietà, by Bart. Montagna* (1500); from the Sacristy (l. of the altar) steps descend to the Gothic cloister where the refectory contains the *Supper of St Gregory the Great, by *Veronese*, repaired at the expense of the Austrian Emp. Francis Joseph after having been hacked to pieces by his soldiery in 1848 (recently restored).

The *Piazzale della Vittoria,* beside the church, built as a memorial of the First World War, commands a magnificent view of Vicenza, and of the mountains that once marked the front-line. From the Spianata del Cristo (half-way down the portico) a pretty lane (r.: Stradella S. Bastiano) leads downhill in c. 500 m to the **Villa Valmarana**, called *dei Nani* from the dwarfs adorning its wall (adm. Mon, Tues, Wed, 15.30-18.30; Thurs & Sat, 10-12.30, 15.30-18.30; Sun 10-12). It consists of the Palazzina, built in 1668, probably by Ant. Muttoni, and the Foresteria added by Fr. Muttoni. In both buildings are remarkable *Frescoes by *G. B. Tiepolo* and his son *Gian Domenico*.

The path on the r. beyond the villa leads to the ***Villa Rotonda** (*Capra*), the most famous of Palladio's villas (adm. to exterior only, daily 8-12, 15-19.30). Built as a belvedere for Cardinal Capra on a charming hill-top site, its central plan consists of a circular core (domed) within a cube. The four classical porches complete its symmetry. Begun c. 1551 by Palladio it was taken over at his death by Scamozzi and finished in 1606. It has been copied at Chiswick House, London and elsewhere.

The return may be made by the Via G. B. Tiepolo, descending from the Villa Valmarana to the Porta Monte, just above which is a charming little arch by Palladio (?) dated 1595.

THE VILLE VICENTINE

The two routes described below can each be travelled in a day from Vicenza and include some of the most spectacular villas in the environs of the city; others can be seen on the way to Verona (comp. p. 259), Recoaro (comp. below), and Padua (comp. p. 267). Many of the interiors of the villas are closed to the public (except with special permission), but the exteriors and gardens are often the most important features. Opening times change frequently and accessibility varies; it is therefore advisable to consult the E.P.T. office in Vicenza before starting a tour. The name of the villas changes with each new owner, but they generally carry also the name of the original proprietor.

ROUND TRIP FROM VICENZA TO THIENE AND MARÓSTICA, 63 km. N349 leads N. from Vicenza.—8 km. *Caldogno* (r.), with the Villa Caldogno-Nordera (1570; no adm.), designed by Palladio.—14 km. *Villaverla* has two fine villas: the Villa Verlato (1576 by Scamozzi), and the decayed Villa Ghellini (1664-79) by Pizzocaro.—At (20 km.) **Thiene** (18,600 inhab.) is the *Castello Porto-Colleoni* (1476?), an early castellated villa with a charming contemporary chapel adjoining (adm. 15 March-15 Oct 9-30-12, 15-18). N248 continues E. from Thiene past (25 km.) *Sarcedo* (l. of the road), with the Villa Capra (1764). Just beyond the Ástico, a road leads to *Lonedo di Lugo* (4 km. N.). Here the *Villa Godi-Valmarana* (open Tues, Sat, & Sun 14-18) is one of the earliest known works by Palladio (1540-42); it is frescoed by G. B. Zelotti. The small Modern Art Gallery has a representative collection of 19C Italian paintings, including works by Fr. Hayez, Tranquillo Cremona, the Indunno brothers, Segantini, De Nittis, Dom. Morelli, the "Macchiaioli" painters, G. Boldoni, etc. A Fossil Museum has local exhibits including a palm tree 5 metres high. The *Villa Piovene*, close by (adm. to garden only; ring), has a Palladian core, altered in the 18C by Muttoni.

28 km. *Breganze*, with several villas including the Villa Diedo-Malvezzi (1664-84, with additions).—37 km. **Maróstica**, a charming old fortified townlet preserving its Medieval *Ramparts. From the piazza, where a 14C battlemented castle serves as town hall, there is a fine view of the walls and the upper castle of the Scaligers (1372). The 'Partita a Scacchi', a chess match with human combatants, is played here in alternate years in early September (next in 1978). The match commemorates and reproduces a 'Duel' fought between Rinaldo da Angarano (white) and Vieri da Vallonara (black) for the hand of Lionora, daughter of Taddeo Parisio, the local Venetian governor. The herald's announcements are made in Venetian dialect. Bassano del Grappa lies 7 km. E., see p. 276.—N248 leads S. A by-road diverges left for *Nove* (3 km.), a ceramics centre with the Villa Macchiavello (restored 17C frescoes).—44 km. *Longa di Schiavon*. The Villa

Chiericati-Lambert (adm. only with special permission) has frescoes attrib. to Paolo Veronese.—At (49 km.) *Sandrigo*, the Villa Sesso was built by a follower of Palladio in 1570 and has contemporary frescoes. *Dueville* lies W. of the road beyond the Astico. Here are the Villa Da Porto 'dei Pilastroni', by Calderari (1770-76), and the *Villa Da Porto del Conte*, at Vivaro.—The road follows the river into (63 km.) **Vicenza**, past the *Villa Trissino* (no adm.) where Palladio worked as a young artist for his early patron, Gian Giorgio Trissino.

ROUND TRIP FROM VICENZA TO ORGIANO AND LONGARE, 84 km. This route traverses the 'Riviera Berica' S. of Vicenza. N11 leads W. from Vicenza. At (5 km.) *Olmo*, a by-road (2 km.) leads S.W. towards the autostrada and *Altavilla*, where the *Villa Valmarana* (1724) is being restored as a centre for research into the Italian theatre. North of Olmo (on the Monteviale road), *Villa Zileri* has a fine park with exotic trees. Visitors are admitted on request to see the frescoes by G. B. Tiepolo (1734; the earliest known by him outside Venice). At Sovizzo, to the W., *Villa Bissari Curti* (no adm.) has a garden with antique fragments and an amphitheatre.—Just before (13 km.) *Montecchio Maggiore*, the road passes the *Villa Cordellina-Lombardi*, by Massari, now owned by the province of Vicenza and used for conferences, courses, etc. It is particularly interesting for its fine frescoes (1754) by G. B. Tiepolo in the entrance hall. The picturesque village of Montecchio has two restored Scaliger castles, a legendary stronghold of the 'Montagues' of 'Romeo and Juliet'.—N500 leads S. to (27 km.) *Sarego*. The Villa da Porto 'La Favorita' is the work of Fr. Muttoni (1714-15).—29 km. *Lonigo*, with the Villa Pisani 'La Rocca' designed by A. Scamozzi in 1576.—38 km. **Orgiano**. Here the *Villa Piovene*, built by Muttoni in 1710, has a notable garden open to the public.—52 km. *Noventa Vicentina* where the town hall occupies the Villa Barbarigo (early 17C). Just to the E. of the town N247 leads back towards Vicenza viâ (75 km.) **Longare**. Here are three villas: Villa Trento (1645), and Villa Garzadori-da Schio, with frescoes attrib. to Dorigny. both open only by previous appointment; and the Villa Eolia (now a restaurant).—84 km. **Vicenza**.

FROM VICENZA TO RECOARO. 42 km., tramway in c. 1½ hrs. to (13 km.) *Montecchio*, see above. N246 ascends the Val d'Agno, leaving on the left the tramway to Chiampo.—19 km. *Trissino* (l.), with the Villa Marzotto, whose delightful park is open to visitors by previous appointment.—At (22 km.) *Castelgomberto* (r.) is the Villa Piovene da Schio of 1666 (chapel of 1614), with 18C additions (no adm.).—32 km. **Valdagno** (28,900 inhab.) has woollen mills. *Castelvecchio* (794 m), 6 km. W., is a summer resort in a pleasant situation.—42 km. **Recoaro Terme** (445 m) is a finely situated spa with ferruginous springs. The road goes on to (53 km.) *Valli del Pasubio* (see below), while a chair-lift ascends to *Recoaro-Mille* (1021 m) and *Monte Falcone* (1700 m), frequented by ski-iers.

FROM VICENZA TO ROVERETO. 72 km., railway viâ Thiene as far as Schio (32 km. in ¾ hr), bus thence in summer. The road runs viâ Isola Vicentina and Malo through spectacular countryside.—24 km. **Schio** is a well-situated town (36,400 inhab.) with wool manufactures. It has a cathedral begun in 1740, a good 15-16C church (*San Francesco*) and beyond it, on the Asiago road, an *Ossuary-Cloister*, with 5000 graves of soldiers who fell in 1915-18. Buses run to Thiene and in summer to Recoaro.—28 km. *Torrebelvicino*.—33 km. *Valli del Pasubio* (338 m) is at the junction of the road from Recoaro (see above).—At (42 km.) *Ponte Verde* a poor road on the right (28 km.) ascends to the Colle di Xomo and, (r.), **Monte Pasubio** (2235 m). The road ends about 150 m below the flat summit, which is easily reached thence in ½ hr. The massif was hotly contested in 1916-18 and a ring of boundary-stones defines the *'Zona Sacra'*, dedicated to those who fell here.—45 km. *Pian delle Fugazze* (1159 m), the highest point on the road, is 1½ km. from the *Sacello del Pasubio* (l.), an imposing war memorial with a battle museum. The descent is made through dolomitic country, amid villages rebuilt since the First World War.—72 km. *Rovereto*, see Rte 23.

FROM VICENZA TO ASIAGO, 55 km., railway to Thiene in ½ hr; bus thence in 1½ hrs; more frequently to Piovene. The autostrada from Vicenza to Trento is open as far as Rochetta, which is connected by superstrada to Asiago. From Vicenza to (20 km.) Thiene, see above.—Beyond (27 km.) *Chiuppano* the road ascends to the right in zigzags.—54 km. **Asiago** (998 m), rebuilt since 1919 (7050 inhab.), is near the centre of the plateau of the *Sette Comuni*, which enjoys a good climate, and is a favourite summer resort of the Milanese and Venetians. The inhabitants were of Germanic origin. Winter sports are practiced in the area, and there are good facilities. In the BATTLE OF ASIAGO (15-16 June 1918), the British XIV Corps was heavily engaged and the fallen rest in five cemeteries: *Barenthal, Granezza* and *Cavalletto*, S. of Asiago; and *Boscon* and *Magnaboschi*, E. and S. of *Cesuna*, to the S.W. The Italian dead lie in the Sacrario Militare, E. of the town, near the Astrophysical Observatory of Padua University.—*Gallio*, 4 km. E. on the mountain road to Primolano (42 km.; p. 277) is a summer and winter resort, with ski-lifts, etc.

Vicenza is connected by direct railway with (35 km.) *Castelfranco* (Rte 32) and (60 km.) *Treviso* (Rte 35); and with *Bassano* (p. 276) both by bus (viâ Maróstica: 37 km. in 55 min.) and railway (viâ Cittadella; 39 km. in 1 hr).

The Padua road passes (62 km.) the Villa Da Porto Rigo, by a follower of Palladio, in *Vancimuglio,* and, just short of (66 km.) *Grisignano di Zocco,* the Villa Ferramosca-Beggiato, by G. D. Scamozzi (c. 1560).

About 4 km. S.W., on either side of the Bacchiglione, are *Montegalda* and *Montegaldella,* the former with a 12C castle adapted as a villa in the 18C (closed for restoration), the latter with the 17C *Villa Campagnolo 'La Deliziosa',* embellished by Orazio Marinali (open Thurs & Sat 10-12).

83 km. **PADUA,** Italian **Pádova** (240,300 inhab.), is one of the most ancient and interesting cities in Italy. The arcaded streets of the old town, affording glimpses of the spherical domes of Sant'Antonio and Santa Giustina, and the many slow-running branches of the winding Bacchiglione, give the city a character all its own. The northern part of the city, rebuilt since war damage, is unattractive.

Post Office (Pl. 6), 5 Corso Garibaldi.—**E.P.T.,** Largo Europa (Pl. 6).

Town Buses traverse the principal streets. **1.** From the Station to the P.za Pedrocchi and S. Giustina.—**3.** From the Station to the P.za delle Erbe and Sant'Antonio.—COUNTRY BUSES from Via Trieste (Pl. 7) frequently to *Mestre* and *Venice;* to *Piove di Sacco* for Adria; to *Bassano;* to *Chioggia;* to *Monsélice* and *Este* or *Rovigo;* to *Treviso* viâ Noale to *Vicenza;* and to *Bologna;* from the Station to *Abano* and *Torreglia.*

Motor-Launch (*il Burchiello*) Wed, Fri & Sun in May-Sept, viâ the Brenta canal to *Venice* in c. 8 hrs with stops at Strà, Oriago, and Malcontenta (return from Venice by bus). Departure from Pontile Bassanello.

History. According to the Roman historian Livy (59 B.C.-A.D. 18), the most famous native of Padua (he was actually born at Téolo, in the Euganean Hills), *Patavium* was founded by the Trojan Antenor. At any rate it was an important settlement of the Euganei and Veneti, and received full Roman franchise in 89 B.C. After the barbarian invasions it rose again to prosperity under the Byzantine and Lombard domination, finally declaring itself an independent republic in 1164. In 1237-54 Ezzelino da Romano was tyrant of Padua, and the suzerainty of the Carraresi (1318-1405), though more auspicious, was ended by the Venetian conquest. From 1405 until the fall of Venice, Padua remained faithful to St Mark. The foundation of the University in 1222 attracted many distinguished men to Padua, including Dante and Petrarch, as well as innumerable students from England, earning for the city the surname of 'la Dotta' (the learned).

St Anthony of Padua (1195-1231), a native of Lisbon, driven, on a missionary journey, by a chance tempest to Italy, settled at Padua, where he preached and wrought miracles under the guidance of St Francis. He died at Arcella, 1½ km. N. of Padua, and was canonized in the following year. Famous natives include Bart. Cristofori (1655-1731; see p. 416); G. B. Belzoni (1778-1823), actor, engineer, and egyptologist; Ippolito Nievo (1831-61), the patriot novelist; and Arrigo Boito (1842-1918), the composer.

Art. Paduan painting was first inspired by Giotto's frescoes in the Cappella Scrovegni; but the birth of an individual school is especially connected with the name of Francesco Squarcione (1397-1468), who influenced a great number of disciples. Foremost among these was Andrea Mantegna (1431-1506), who, however, soon loosed himself from his master's control. The arrival of Donatello at Padua in 1443 opened a new horizon; and the native artists, notably Mantegna, were quick to range themselves behind him. From the beginning of the 16C the school of Padua is merged in the Venetian, and many Venetian artists worked in the city. The best known local painter was Aless. Varotari, known as Il Padovanino.—The Byzantinesque basilica of St Anthony and church of Santa Giustina appear not to have inspired a continuous tradition of building.

The centre of city life is Piazza Cavour (Pl. 6) and the adjacent piazzetta in which stands the large *Caffè Pedrocchi* (1831; left to the city in 1891), one of the most celebrated in Italy and famous in the 19C as a meeting-place for intellectuals. Via Otto Febbraio, part of the N.-S. artery of the city, leads shortly to the **University**, famous as a medical school nicknamed 'il Bo' (the ox) from the sign of an inn on whose site it stands. It was founded in 1222.

The façade dates from 1757, the tower from 1572; and the dignified courtyard (1552) by Andrea Moroni is embellished with armorial bearings and busts. Visitors are shown (week-days on application) the *Museum,* with Galileo's chair, etc. and the **Anatomical Theatre* (1594), the most ancient in Europe, built by the surgeon Fabricius, master of William Harvey who took his degree here in 1602. Thomas Linacre (1492) and John Caius (1539) likewise qualified here as doctors. Among the famous medical professors were Vesalius (1540) and Fallopius (1561), and Galileo was teacher of physics from 1592 to 1610, among his pupils being Gustavus Adolphus of Sweden.

Opposite the University the E. façade (1928-30) of the *Municipio* disguises a 16C building, by And. Moroni, that incorporates a tower of the 13C Palazzo del Podestà. Beyond the Municipio, separating P.za delle Erbe from P.za delle Frutta stands ***Palazzo della Ragione,** commonly called **Il Salone** (Pl. 10), a building of 1219, rebuilt in 1306 by *Fra Giovanni degli Eremitani.* The immense roof was reconstructed in 1756 after storm damage. A market now occupies part of the ground floor (and the adjoining piazze).

The entrance (9-12.30, 14-18.30 in summer, 9.30-12.30, 14.30-16.30 in winter; Sun & fest. 9.30-12.30) is by the right-hand staircase, towards the Municipio. The interior is one vast hall, 79 metres long, 27 metres wide, and 26 metres high. It contains a block of stone the 'pietra del vituperio', which once served as a stool of repentance for debtors, and a giant wooden horse, copied from that of Donatello (see below), made for a fète in 1466. On the walls are 319 frescoes of religious and astrological subjects, by *Giov. Miretto,* replacing the originals by Giotto which were destroyed by fire in 1420.

In P.za delle Frutta are remains of the *Palazzo Consiglio* (1283), with two good Byzantine capitals, and *Palazzo degli Anziani* (1285). Via San Clemente leads W. to P.ZA DEI SIGNORI, attractively enclosed by old buildings. To the left is the *Loggia della Gran Guardia,* a pretty Lombard edifice begun by Ann. Maggi (1496) and finished in 1523. On the W. side of the square *Palazzo del Capitanio* (1599-1605) occupies the site of the castle of the Carraresi, of which a 14C portico survives just off Via Accademia (at No. 11). The palazzo incorporates a tower, adapted in 1532 to accommodate an astronomical clock dating from 1344 (the oldest in Italy). Beyond the Arco dell'Orologio lies the Corte Capitaniato, where the buildings of the arts faculty, the LIVIANO (1939) incorporate the *Sala dei Giganti* with 14C frescoes (repainted in 1539). On the top floor is the *Museo di Scienze Archeologiche e d'Arte* (open Sat, exc. Aug, 15-18), containing a headless Athena (4C B.C.), a wax mould of Donatello, and plaster statuettes by Ammannati. From P.za Capitaniato, with a 16C Loggia and ancient acacias, the Corte Valaresso (fine staircase of 1607) leads under an arch of 1632 to P.za del Duomo.

The **Cathedral** (Pl. 9) was reconstructed in 1552 by And. da Valle and Agost. Righetti to a design, much altered, of Michelangelo. The

BAPTISTERY, a 13C Romanesque survival of an earlier church, is frescoed all over by *Giusto de'Menabuoi.*

In the ponderous interior, the most interesting parts are the SACRISTY and crypt, shown by the sacristan. The former contains four Saints, from a triptych by *Giorgio Schiavone,* and a Descent from the Cross, by *Iac. da Montagnana.* The TREASURY here contains illuminated *MSS. (12C and 13C), a Byzantine thurible of the 11C, a fine processional cross of 1228, and the large *Reliquary of the Cross, of silver gilt, with enamels, dating from c. 1440.

To the S. of the cathedral is the **Bishop's Palace,** with the *Museo Diocesano d'Arte Sacra* (open Tues, Wed, & Fri 10-11). Here are portraits of bishops by *Montagna,* one of Petrarch, and a chapel with the *Annunciation, a fresco by *Iac. da Montagna.* The adjoining *Chapter Library* preserves the treasury from the old cathedral at Monsélice. To the N. is the *Palazzo del Monte di Pietà* of the 13-14C, remodelled in 1530.—No. 31 in the neighbouring Via del Vescovado is the *Casa degli Specchi* or 'House of the Mirrors', so called from its facing of polished marble, an early 16C Lombardesque building by Ann. Maggi.

Via Dante, with several good palazzi, passes E. of the Romanesque church of *San Nicolò* and the *Teatro Verdi.* In Via Santa Lucia to the right are the church of *Santa Lucia* and the **Scuola di San Rocco** (Pl. 6), dating from 1480-1525 (adm. on application to the sacristan of Santa Lucia), an attractive Renaissance building containing *Frescoes illustrating the life of St Roch, mainly by *Dom. Campagnola* and *Gualtieri.* The modern P.za Insurrezione, beyond, is the centre of a rebuilt business quarter. Of the many old houses in Via S. Lucia, the so-called *Casa di Ezzelino,* on the right at the corner of Via Marsilio, is an interesting specimen of 12C work.

On the far side of P.za Garibaldi opens the *Porta Altinate,* a gateway of the 13C town wall. The Augustinian church of the **Eremitani,** to the N.E. (Pl. 6), was built in 1276-1306, the façade being added in 1360. It was almost completely destroyed by bombing in 1944, but has been rebuilt.

INTERIOR. On the N. side are two polychrome altarpieces by *Giov. Minello* and his school (early 16C), and the mausoleum of the law-professor Marco Benavides (1489-1582), by *Bart. Ammannati* (1546). There are Giottesque frescoes in the sanctuary and the N. chapel, and here and at the W. end are 14C tombs. The chapel on the S. of the apse contains all that remains of the CAPPELLA DEL MANTEGNA (light on right), the destruction of which was the greatest individual disaster to Italian art in the Second World War: behind the altar, Assumption; (l.) Martyrdom of St James (recomposed from the shattered fragments) and two fragmentary frescoes by *Giov. di Camerino;* (r.) Martyrdom of St Christopher (detached and removed to safety before the War). Mantegna worked on them between 1454 (when he was only 23) and 1457. Here, too, is a bas-relief of the Madonna, in the style of Donatello.

In a garden containing fragments of a Roman amphitheatre is the *Cappella degli Scrovegni (Pl. 6), or *Madonna dell'Arena,* built for Enrico Scrovegni in 1303 in expiation for his father's usury (comp. Dante, 'Inferno', xvii, 64-75). Adm. daily, exc. 25 Dec, 1 Jan, & Easter Day: 15 March-15 Oct, 9-12.30, 14-18.30; winter, 9.30-12.30, 13.30-16.30; fest. 9.30-12.30, 14-18. The interior is decorated with *Giotto's* famous **Frescoes, painted at the height of his power (1303-5) and last restored in 1887. They are arranged in three bands and depict the history of Christian redemption, beginning (end of the S. wall, on top) with the Expulsion of Joachim from the Temple, and ending (end of the N. wall, at the bottom) with the Descent of the Holy Ghost. On the entrance-wall is the Last Judgement. The bands at the end and separating the panels are adorned with busts of Saints and Doctors, and

Scenes from the Old Testament, mainly by Giotto's assistants; the ceiling medallions show Jesus, the Virgin, and the Prophets. The lowest range of paintings consists of allegorical figures of Virtues and Vices.— In the apse are frescoes by followers of Giotto; on the altar are statues of the Virgin and two saints, by *Giov. Pisano.* Behind the latter is the tomb of the founder, Enrico Scrovegni, by *Andreolo de'Santi.*

From P.za Garibaldi (comp. above) Via Altinate leads E. past *Palazzo Melandri* (No. 18), with a beautiful four-light window, and *San Gaetano,* a pleasant church by Scamozzi (1586), to **Santa Sofia,** the oldest church in Padua. Founded in the 9C on an earlier structure, it was rebuilt in the 11-12C in a Romanesque style recalling earlier churches of the Adriatic exarchate. The apse is remarkable.

From the Eremitani, Corso Garibaldi and Corso del Popolo continue N. to the Station. To the left Via Giotto and Via del Carmine lead to the church of the *Carmini* at the top of Via Dante (p. 269). The sacristan will show the adjacent **Scuola del Carmine** (1377), with frescoes by *Giulio* and *Dom. Campagnola,* notably the *Meeting of St Anne and St Joachim.—The road from the Carmini to the station passes the *Bastione della Gatta,* where the Paduans made a heroic resistance to the Austrians in the siege of 1509.—A little N. of the station (to the r. of the Castelfranco road) is the *Santuario dell'Arcella,* with a 19C church enclosing the cell where St Anthony died in 1231.

The Riviera dei Ponti Romani, from the Eremitani, meets Via San Francesco at the S.E. corner of the University. At their junction stands the alleged *Tomb of Antenor,* a marble sarcophagus erected in 1233 on short columns; another sarcophagus (1309) was set up here on the 2000th anniversary of Livy's birth. Straight ahead, beyond Via del Santo, are the 13C *Torre degli Zabarella* and the church of *San Francesco* (1416; restored), containing the monument of Pietro Roccabonella, natural philosopher, by Bart. Bellano and And. Riccio (1498; S.E. chapel).—Via del Santo leads S. to P.ZA DEL SANTO in which stands the equestrian *Statue of Gattamelata* (Erasmo da Narni, the Venetian condottiere, d. 1443), a masterpiece by *Donatello* (1453), and the first great Renaissance bronze cast in Italy.

The *Basilica of Sant'Antonio** (Pl. 11; open all day, 6.30-19 or 20), usually called simply *Il Santo,* was begun in 1232 as a temple for the tomb of St Anthony of Padua, and finished in the 14C.

EXTERIOR. The six spherical domes in the Byzantine manner, the cone of the central cupola, and the two minaret-like campanili give a curiously fantastic appearance to the church. The bronze doors (1895) and the frescoes of Franciscan saints in the portal are recent additions and the fresco above the principal doorway is a modern copy (comp. below).

The magnificent INTERIOR, though Gothic in plan and detail, is Byzantine in inspiration. It contains many important works of art. In the NAVE the first two piers on either side have holy-water stoups with statues of Christ, by *Aspetti* (l.) and St John the Baptist (r.), by *Tullio Lombardo;* against the next pair, tombs of Aless. Contarini (d. 1553), the Venetian general (l.) and Card. Bembo (on the inside of the pillar) who died in 1547, both by *Sammicheli* with busts by *Danese Cattaneo.* The former is an elaborate work, with statues by *Vittoria.*—On the S. side: 1st chapel, monuments of Erasmo Gattamelata (d. 1443), by *Bellano,* and of his son Giannantonio (d. 1455) by *P.Lombardo.* In the S. transept is the *CHAPEL OF ST FELIX, designed in 1372-77 by *Andriolo* and *Giov. De Santi,* with frescoes by *Altichieri* and *Avanzo.*—In the N. transept is the *CHAPEL OF ST ANTHONY,with the tomb (much revered) of St Anthony of Padua (d. 1231) behind the altar.

The chapel was designed by *Briosco* in 1500, begun by *Giov.* and *Ant. Minello,* and completed by *Falconetto* in 1546. High up on the entrance-screen are statues of the patron saints of Padua, among which that of St Justina, on the left, by Giov. Minello, is notable. The nine reliefs of the miracles of St Anthony which line the walls are (l. to r.) by Ant. Minello, Giov. Rubino and Silvio Cosini, Cattaneo and Girol. Campagna, Sansovino, Ant. Minello and Sansovino, Tullio Lombardo (two), G. M. Mosca and Paolo Stella, and Ant. Lombardo; Tiziano Aspetti made the statues on the altar (1593).

In the N. aisle are the Baroque tomb of Gen. Caterino Cornaro, by *Juste Le Court* (1674) and that of Ant. Roselli (d. 1466), by *Bellano;* and in the westernmost bay is a Madonna, by *Stef. da Ferrara* (?) facing the tomb of Ant. Trombetta (d. 1518), by *Briosco.*

The bronze doors of the CHOIR are by *Cam. Mazza* (1661), the four statues on the balustrade by *Aspetti* (1593). The 12 bronze *Reliefs of Old Testament scenes on the wall are by *Bellano* and *Briosco;* the decorations of the apse date from 1926. The magnificent *ALTAR (the sanctuary gates are unlocked on request by the uniformed custodians), sculpted by *Donatello* and his assistants in 1445-50, has suffered many vicissitudes and its present arrangements dates from 1895.

Below are twelve angel musicians; above is the Madonna enthroned surmounted by the *Crucifixion, between the six patron saints of Padua. On the other side is a Pietà, with four reliefs (two on each side) of *Miracles of St Anthony, and at the ends, the symbols of the Evangelists. Behind is a *Deposition in stone, and on the left a *Candelabrum, by *Briosco* (1507-15).—The chapel on the left of the sanctuary is a fragment of the 12C church of Santa Maria Mater Domini, which stood here before the basilica was built. It has 14C frescoes and interesting tombs. A Rococo chapel at the E. end of the ambulatory houses the *Treasury, containing more than 100 reliquaries.—The ceiling-painting in the SACRISTY, by *P. Liberi* (1615), shows the Entry of St Anthony into Paradise. In the adjoining *Chapter House* are fragmentary frescoes after *Giotto.*—To the S. of the church are four CLOISTERS (entered from the N. side of the church), with many tombstones and monuments. In the first cloister a modest slab on the N. side marks the burial-place of the entrails of Thomas Howard (1586-1646), earl of Surrey and Arundel, collector of the 'Arundel Marbles'; in the second a bust commemorates Gius. Tartini (1692-1770) who returned to die in Padua whence he had eloped in 1713 with a daughter of the Premazzone family. From here steps leads up (past the original steps reliefs from the base of the Gattamelata monument, comp. above) to the **Biblioteca Antoniana** (9-12, 14.30-17; Sat 9-12; closed Sun) which contains many MSS. and incunabula, including a MS. of sermons annotated in St Anthony's handwriting. The *Museo Antoniano* has been closed indefinitely: The fresco of SS. Anthony and Bernard adoring the monogram of Christ, by Mantegna (1452) from the lunette of the main W. door, is preserved in the *Presidenza* (First Cloister; sometimes shown on request).

In P.za del Santo are the **Oratorio di San Giorgio** and the **Scuola del Santo** (usually open during daylight hours). The *Oratory, originally the mausoleum of the Soranzo family, is entirely frescoed by *Altichieri* and *Iac. Avanzo* (Lives of St George, St Catherine, and St Lucy, 1378-84); in the Scuola are paintings (1510-12) of the Life of St Anthony, two of which are early works by *Titian.*

In the corner of the piazza is the *Museo Civico* (Pl. 14), awaiting transfer to a new site near the Cappella Scrovegni. It is open from 9-12.30, 15-17.30 exc. Mon & Sat afternoons; fest. 9.30-13.

FIRST FLOOR. ROOM I. Frescoes (very ruined) attrib. to *Pietruccio da Rimini,* from the Eremitani convent; *Paolo Veneziano,* Madonna and Child; *Giotto,* *Crucifix (from the Scrovegni Chapel); *Guariento,* Angel panels; *Michele Giambono,* Saints; *Fr. dei Franceschi,* Polyptych; *15C Paduan School,* Madonna and Child.—ROOM II. 15C tapestry from Arras; Faience ware.—Works by Paduan and Venetian painters of the 15C and early 16C: *Lor. Costa* (attrib.), The Argonauts; *Alvise Vivarini,* Portrait of a man; *Giov. Bellini* (attrib.), Madonna

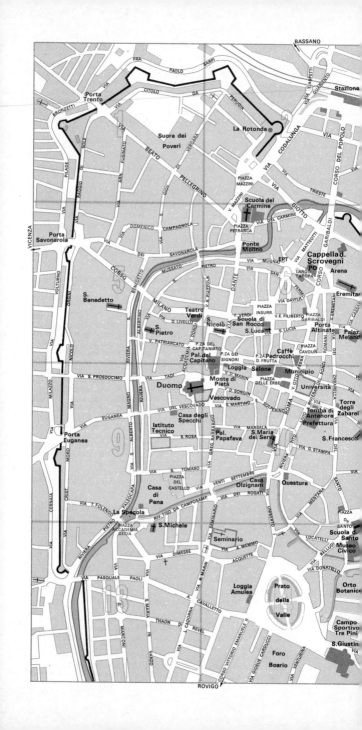

and St John the Baptist; *And. Previtali,* Madonna; *Giorgione,* two tiny paintings: *Leda and the Swan,* and *Figures in a landscape; Giov. Bellini,* Portrait of a young senator, St Catherine; *Palma Vecchio,* Portrait of a Poetess; *Titian,* Two cassone panels with mythological scenes.—Works by *Boccaccio Boccaccino; Fr. Torbido,* Portrait of a shepherd.—*Bonifazio Veronese,* Madonna and Saints.— R. III. *Veronese,* Last Supper; *Leandro Bassano,* several typical works.—R. IV. Works by *Padovanino,* and a fine collection of Venetian ceramics.—R. V. Works by *Pietro Liberti, Pietro Vecchia, Monsù Bernardo,* and *Onofrio Gabrielli.* Between this and R. VI, terracottas by *Briosco* and *Guido Mazzoni.*—R. VI, a large hall with a huge 15C tapestry has large works by *Campagnola,* Baptism of St Justina, Madonna and Saints; *Girol. del Santo,* Descent from the Cross; and works by *Giov. da Asola* and *Stef. dell'Arzere* (Calvary). *Palma Giovane,* Two magistrates of the Soranzo family, an allegory; *Tintoretto,* Jesus in the Pharisee's house (signed and dated); and *Veronese,* Martyrdom of St Justina; *Romanino,* Madonna enthroned; portraits by *Dom. Tintoretto* and *Leandro Bassano* (Doge Andrea Memmo).—RR. VIII-IX. Works by *Zais, G. B. Piazzetta,* and *Ant. Marini.*—R. X. *G. B. Tiepolo,* St Patrick casting out a devil; *Aless. Longhi,* Iac. Gradenigo (c. 1778), a typical Venetian of the decadence; *Pietro Longhi,* Geography lesson.—The SALETTE ROSSE and MUSEO BOTTACIN display miscellaneous paintings, sculpture, and faience ware.

On the other side of the vestibule is the MUSEO EMO CAPODILISTA, another eclectic collection of Venetian and Flemish works (16-18C); while the ground floor and cloister (part of the convent of Sant'Antonio) are occupied by a lapidary collection, a *Library* (200,000 vols.), and the civic and legal *Archives.*

Beyond the Museum is the **Botanic Garden** (Pl. 14; open weekdays in summer 14-18), the most ancient in Europe (1545), with some fine old trees and interesting hothouses. To the W. extends the wide Prato della Valle (Pl. 14), which includes the *Isola Memmia,* encircled by a canal bordered by statues of famous citizens, professors, and students of the University. On the W. side of the Prato is the *Loggia Amulea* (1861) with statues of Giotto and Dante by Vela (1865).

The Benedictine church of **Santa Giustina** (Pl. 14), designed by *Briosco* in 1502 but modified by its builder *And. Moroni,* recalls by its eight cupolas the exotic aspect of Sant'Antonio.

The huge cruciform interior is decorated in the Baroque manner, with altarpieces to match, and presents an epitome of 17C Venetian art. The fine inlaid *Choir-stalls are by the Norman *Riccardo Taurigny,* with the help of Vicentine craftsmen. In the apse is the Martyrdom of St Justina, a large painting by *Veronese* (1575). From the right of the choir a passage leads to the remains of an earlier church, including a 14C chapel, a 13C doorway, and a 15C choir with inlaid stalls. An adjoining chapel contains relics of the 5C (?) Oratory of St Prosdocimus, first bishop of Padua.

In Via Umberto I (Pl. 10), leading back from the piazza towards the centre, No. 30 is of the 13C and No. 4, *Casa Olzignani,* is a fine example of early Lombardesque architecture (1466). Across a bridge is Via Roma and (l.) the Gothic church of *Santa Maria dei Servi* (1372-92, restored 1930), with a fine doorway and a 16C portico. Inside are a frescoed Pietà by Iac. da Montagnana and the monument of the brothers De Castro, by Bart. Bellano, above the sacristy entrance. Via Marsala leads left to (No. 35) the Baroque *Palazzo Papafava,* now a police station.

Via G. Barbarigo, to the left beyond the palazzo, leads to the S.W. quarter, which contains some buildings of interest. Via Venti Settembre ends (r.) at P.za del Castello (Pl. 9), with some remains of the *Castle* (now a prison) built by Ezzelino da Romano; one tower is surmounted by an observatory ('La Specola'; 1767). Beyond the bridge, in the Riviera Tiso, is the *Oratorio di San Michele* (if closed, ring at No. 27), frescoed by Iac. da Verona (1397).

The railways from Padua to *Cittadella* (33 km.) and *Bassano* (48 km. in c. 1 hr), and to *Castelfranco* (31 km.) and *Montebelluna* (48 km. in 1 hr) diverge at (19 km.) *Camposampiero.*—The bus to *Carmignano,* starting from the Eremitani, serves (18 km.) the modern industrial town of *Piazzola sul Brenta,* with the imposing Villa

Camerini (in the Palladian style, with fine park; adm. on application), and (25 km.)
Isola Mantegna, the birthplace of Andrea Mantegna (1431-1506).
    From Padua to *Ábano* (for the Euganean Hills) and *Ferrara,* see Rte 37.

The autostrada and the main railway to Venice follow a dead straight
line across the plain towards Mestre. Much more interesting is the old
road along the Brenta, taken by the bus to *Fusina* (see below; boat
thence to Venice).

Diverging to the left from the autostrada feeder the road passes under
the motorway beyond (89 km.) *Ponte di Brenta,* on the right of which is
Noventa Padovana, with the *Villa Valmarana* (now a deaf and dumb
institution) and other villas. The whole road is lined by the beautiful
villas of the Venetian aristocracy, typified in English literature by
Portia's villa of Belmont.—95 km. **Stra** is notable for the *Villa Nazionale*
or *Pisani* (temporarily closed for restoration; normally open April-Sept
9-12.30, 15-18.30; winter 9-14; fest. 9-13), a fine example of the 18C
Venetian villa with *Frescoes by G. B. Tiepolo. It was bought from the
Pisani in 1807 by Napoleon, who presented it to Eugène Beauharnais;
and it was the scene of the first meeting of Hitler and Mussolini in 1934.
It is surrounded by a fine park (open 9-dusk).—The road skirts a
canalised branch of the Brenta (boat, Padua-Venice, in 8 hrs), past
Dolo, to the long village of (105 km.) **Mira,** one of the most attractive
places on the Brenta. Here the post office occupies the *Palazzo
Foscarini,* where Byron, between 1817 and 1819, wrote the fourth canto
of 'Childe Harold' and was visited by Thomas Moore. Here, too, he first
met Margherita Cogni, whom he called 'la bella Fornarina'. Just before
(109 km.) *Oriago,* is the *Villa Costanzo (Widmann-Foscari)* dating from
1719, but transformed in the 18C in the French Baroque style (adm.
Thurs & Sun 15-18).

A road diverges to the right beyond Oriago for *Malcontenta,* with the famous
*Villa Fóscari (adm. 1 May-30 Oct, Tues, Sat, & 1st Sun of month, 9-12), begun
c. 1560 by Palladio, with *Stables added after 1735; and (6½ km.) *Fusina,* on the
Venetian lagoon, where a boat leaves for Venice (35 min.; Zattere and Riva
Schiavoni).

The main road bears to the left for the important railway station of
(117 km.) **Mestre,** a dull town now incorporated in Venice which it has
outgrown (bus to Venice, Treviso, etc.).

Road and railway now cross the lagoon on parallel and connected
bridges more than 3½ km. long. The railway bridge dates from 1841-45,
the road bridge, or Ponte della Libertà, from 1931-32. On the right is
seen the commercial port of *Marghera,* built in 1919-28, with an oil
depot. Just before reaching Venice the road bridge diverges to the right
and ends at the Piazzale Roma (Pl. 5), alongside two multi-storey car
parks.—125 km. **Venice,** see Rte 33.

32   FROM VENICE TO TRENTO

ROAD. 150 km.—9 km. *Mestre.*—34 km. *Castelfranco.*—49 km. *Cittadella.*—
63 km. **Bassano.**—92 km. *Primolano.*—116 km. *Borgo Valsugana.*—121 km.
Roncegno.—130 km. *Lévico.*—139 km. *Pérgine.*—150 km. **Trento.**
    RAILWAY, following a similar course to the road, 157 km. in 3-3¾ hrs; to
Bassano, 60 km. in 1-1¾ hrs.

From Venice to (9 km.) *Mestre,* see Rte 31. The road runs N.W.
across the plain, passing (25 km.) *Piombino Dese,* with the Villa

Cornaro built for Doge Giorgio Cornaro by Palladio (1566-76) and containing stuccoes by Vittoria.—34 km. **Castelfranco Véneto** (27,900 inhab.), founded in 1199 by Treviso as a bulwark against Padua, is famous as the birthplace of Giorgione (Giorgio Barbarelli, 1478-1510). The old town, or 'Castello', is surrounded by a moat and a battlemented brick wall, one tower of which serves as a belfry. The main *Torre Civica* is the N. gate of the 'Castello'. In the centre is the classical *Cathedral* (1723-45) by Fr. Preti, which contains Giorgione's masterpiece, a *Madonna and Child with Saints (1504), in the chapel to the right of the presbytery (apply to sacristan). In the sacristy are frescoes by Veronese. The Casa Pellizzari, near the cathedral, containing frescoes possibly by Giorgione, is being converted into a small museum and art gallery. At Sant'Andrea, 4 km. S. W., the *Villa Corner-Tiepolo* (adm. Tues, Fri, Sat & Sun 9-18) has frescoes of the school of Veronese.—The road turns W. to (49 km.) **Cittadella** (16,700 inhab.), a picturesque walled *Town, the reply of the Paduans to Castelfranco. This route joins the road from Padua and turns N.—At (57 km.) *Rosà* the park of the 18C Villa Dolfin-Boldù may be visited by previous appointment. The Ca' Rezzonico, an early work by Longhena, comes into view on the approach to Bassano.

63 km. **Bassano del Grappa,** standing at the point where the Brenta emerges from the hills, is a cheerful little town (36,900 inhab.) with arcaded streets and a fine view N. from the old ramparts (Viale dei Martiri), on which stands a statue of Gen. Gaetano Giardino (1864-1935), defender of Monte Grappa in 1918.

It has been a dependency of Venice since the 15C, and the famous Da Ponte family of painters (notably Iacopo and Leandro) surnamed Bassano from this their native town, were prominent in Venetian art. Napoleon's victory over the Austrians here in 1796 was overshadowed by the campaign on Monte Grappa in 1917-18 (see below) in which the town suffered considerable damage. It was again damaged in the Second World War. Famous for its mushrooms, grappa, ceramics, and wrought-iron work, it has recently been developed as an industrial centre.

In the central P.za Libertà are the 18C church of *San Giovanni Battista* and the *Palazzo Municipale* (1582) with a fresco of St Christopher attributed to Iac. Bassano; the fresco (badly faded) on the building opposite is probably by his father, Francesco il Vecchio (dated 1522). The neighbouring P.za Garibaldi is dominated by the 13C *Torre di Ezzelino* and the campanile of the Gothic church of *San Francesco*. The *Museum* (adm. 10-12.30, 15-18.30; Sat & Sun 10-12.30) behind the latter in its former monastery (15C cloister), contains paintings by Iac. Bassano, casts and sketches by Canova, and a fine collection of the engravings for which Bassano was renowned in the 18C. Below P.za Libertà, the Piazzetta Monte Vecchio, with the old *Monte di Pietà* and a house frescoed by the Bassano and Nasocchio families (the frescoes have been removed for restoration), leads down to the *PONTE DEGLI ALPINI, a covered wooden bridge across the Brenta. Although many times rebuilt, it retains the form designed for it by Palladio in 1669. Beside it is a grappa distillery of 1769. At the N. end of the town are the ruins of the *Castello degli Ezzelini,* a tower of which serves as a belfry for the Duomo, a 15C church much restored. North of the cathedral, in the Salita Margnan, is the 15C Capuchin church of *San Sebastiano*.

About 4 km. E. of Bassano is *Romano d'Ezzelino*, with traces of the castle of the Ezzelini, most notorious of whom was Ezzelino III (1194-1259), the terror of the countryside.

Monte Grappa (1775 m). N. of Bassano, is ascended by road (31 km., bus in July-Sept in 2 hrs). It was the scene of heavy fighting between Austrians and Italians in 1917-18. On the summit are a votive chapel crowned by a figure of the Madonna, and a cemetery.

A road leads N.E. from Bassano to (18 km.) *Possagno,* the birthplace of Antonio Canova (1757-1822), the sculptor. Admission to his house and the Museum of casts 9-12, 15-18; in winter, 9-12, 14-17; fest. 9-12, 15-19. The *Tempio,* now the parish church, in which Canova is buried, was designed by himself.

The Trento road penetrates the hills by means of the so-called Canale di Brenta, a narrow valley which the railway negotiates with many tunnels.—92 km. *Primolano* (217 m), at the end of the Canale', is the junction of a road to Feltre (r.). The route enters the Valsugana and the Trentino.—101 km. *Grigno.*

From Grigno a road climbs to the holiday resorts (summer and winter sports) on the Tesino plateau: 10 km. *Castello Tesino,* 13 km. *Pieve Tesino,* and (27 km.) the *Passo del Brocon* (1616 m). Thence the road continues to (56 km.) *Imer* on the Feltre-Fiera di Primiero road (p. 331).

116 km. *Borgo Valsugana* (386 m) is the chief place in the valley. To the S.W. lies the Moggio valley, with the small resort of *Sella Valsugana*

From (121 km.) *Roncegno-Marter* station a road leads to *Roncegno* (535 m), a small chalybeate spa.—130 km. **Lévico** (506 m), another spa (5600 inhab.) with ferruginous waters, stands at the S.W. end of the Lago di Lévico. *Vetriolo Terme* (1500 m) lies 12 km. N.: it is a modern spa and winter sports centre (cablecar to Panarotta, 1819 m).

From Lévico to the Lago di Caldonazzo (3 km.), see p. 230.

139 km. *Pérgine* and thence to (150 km.) Trento, see Rte 23.

33   VENICE

VENICE, in Italian **Venézia,** with 364,550 inhabitants, stands on an archipelago of 117 islets or shoals, 2½ m. from the mainland and 1¼ m. from the open sea, whose force is broken by the natural breakwater of the Lido. The population of the commune includes Mestre; that of the historic centre being now only 137,000 compared with the 200,000 it had when the republic was at its zenith. A unique position, the grace of her buildings, the changing colours, and not least the total absence of wheeled transport, make Venice the most charming and poetic city in the world. The mother of soldiers, statesmen, philosophers, travellers, and artists, Venice bore unshaken the upheavals of the Middle Ages, and later was a rampart of Christendom against the Turks. Even in her decadence she preserved many reminders of an empire, the largest that Italy has known, save the Roman; and the construction in the 1930s of a large commercial harbour and oil refinery won back much of her pre-eminence in trade (although the consequences of pollution were disregarded). Alarm for the survival of the city which is gradually sinking and subject to periodic floods from exceptionally high tides (the 'acque alte') has been somewhat quelled since the construction of artesian wells and a new aqueduct and the control of the three entrances into the lagoon. A special law was passed in 1973 by the Italian government to safeguard the city, and committees funded from various countries have been working in conjunction with the Italian authorities for over ten years on the restoration of buildings.

Topography. The irregular plan of Venice is traversed by some 100 canals of which the *Grand Canal* divides the city into two unequal parts. The other canals, called *Rii* (sing. *rio*), with the exception of the *Cannaregio*, have an average breadth of 4-5 metres and are spanned by c. 400 bridges, mostly of brick or stone. The streets, nearly all very narrow, are called *Calle, Calletta,* or *Callesella;* a few are known as *Via, Ruga,* or *Stretto. Ramo* is a narrow alley usually connecting two wider ways; a *Sottopórtico* passes beneath buildings. A street alongside a canal is called *Fondamenta;* a *Rioterrà* is a street on the course of a filled-in rio. *Salizzada* was the name given to the first paved streets (1676). *Piscina* is a place where a pool formerly existed; *Lista* a lane which led up to an ambassador's palace. The only *Piazza* is that of St Mark; there are two *Piazzette,* one in front of the Doges' Palace, the other the Piazzetta dei Leoncini (now Giovanni XXIII). Other open spaces are called *Campo* or *Campiello,* according to their size. Names of streets and canals are written up in the Venetian dialect, which has made some curious corruptions (San Stae = Sant'Eustachio, San Marcuóla = Santi Ermágora e Fortunato, San Trovaso = Santi Gervasio e Protasio, etc.).—Notable features of some of the campi are the *Vere da Pozzo,* or well-heads, which surround the mouths of the old cisterns; the *Comígnoli* are the characteristic ornament of the house-tops; the *Altane* are the wooden balconies on which the ladies of the palaces used to take the air.—Houses are numbered consecutively throughout each of the six 'sestrieri' into which the city is divided (San Marco, Castello, Dorsoduro, San Polo, Santa Croce, and Cannaregio).

The city is supported on piles of Istrian pine, driven down about 7½ m to solid ground, and her buildings are fashioned in Istrian limestone, which withstands the corrosion of the sea. Her prosperity as a port is due to the diversion of silt-bearing rivers to N. and S. of the lagoon, still effected by channels dug in the 14-15C; and her very existence depends on the control of the eroding waters of the Adriatic, which are allowed to flow into the lagoon by only three channels (comp. p. 321). This work, under special supervision as early as the 12C, has been performed since 1501 by a board presided over by the Magistrato alle Acque. Despite these precautions, the city suffered the worst flood for nearly a century in 1966.

Gondolas are now almost exclusively used for pleasure (mostly by visitors) and not as a means of transport (although some ferries still operate across the Grand Canal; comp. below). Almost no noble Venetian families still maintain a private gondola. They are of ancient origin and peculiar build; the purpose of the curious toothed projection forward, called the *Ferro,* is uncertain. In 1562, in order to minimize the rivalry between noble houses, it was decreed that all gondolas should be painted black. The wooden shelter, or *Felze,* which used to be used to protect passengers in bad weather is now rarely seen. The cries of the gondoliers as they round a corner are peculiar to themselves. A small tip should be given to the *Ganzèr* armed with a boat-hook which pulls the gondolas to the shore and helps passengers to alight.

Railway Station (Pl. 1, 5), near the W. end of the Grand Canal. Public water-buses (*vaporetti*) and motor-launches (*motoscafi*), motor-boat taxis, and gondolas from the quay outside. Some of the motor-launch services (comp. below) and the taxis (unless specifically requested) for the Riva degli Schiavoni and the Lido, take the less attractive short cut by the Rio Nuovo avoiding the first bend of the Grand Canal.

Bus Station and **Multi-storey Car Parks** in the Piazzale Roma (Pl. 5). The vaporetti have a station adjoining the bus station. Car parking space in Piazzale Roma is very limited (especially in summer); more space (garage and open-air) is available in the Isola del Tronchetto (beyond Pl. 5; connected directly by motor-launch No. 3 in summer with Piazza San Marco). There are no free car parks.

Porters (distinguished by their badges) from the station or Piazzale Roma to the nearest landing-stage, 350 lire per piece; between any two points in the city: first piece 1,800 l.; 600 l. each extra. Tariffs are fixed.

Steamers anchor at the quays along the Riva degli Schiavoni or at the Zattere.— One of the most pleasant ways of arriving in Venice in summer is from Padua by the *'Burchiello'* motor-launch along the Brenta canal (in c. 8 hrs; comp. p. 267).

Airport. *Marco Polo* at Tessera (9 km.) near the Lagoon (N.E. of Mestre) for internal and international services. AIRPORT TERMINAL, Piazzale Roma (coach service to airport). Motor-boats to connect with British Airways, Alitalia, and Air France flights leave from the Giardinetti (Pl. 11). They are run by the Cooperativa San Marco Motoscafi (Tel. 35775). The trip takes c. 30 min. and costs 4000 l.

Car Ferry from *Piazzale Roma* to the *Lido* and *Punta Sabbioni.*

Hotels and Pensions all over the city, but accommodation can be difficult to find in summer and during the Biennale. Most of the hotels are near San Marco or the Rialto; others in quieter and often more attractive positions away from these two areas, and in the Dorsoduro. Prices are often raised from 1 June. Pensions usually impose half-pension terms; visitors requiring accommodation only should use hotels. Booking facilities at E.P.T. office on arrival at the Station.

Post Office (Pl. 7), Fondaco dei Tedeschi, near the Rialto, with Telephone exchange; *Telegraph Office* (Pl. 11), with branch P.O., P.za San Marco.

Information Bureaux. *E.P.T.,* 71f San Marco, at the Railway Station (with hotel booking service), and at the Venice exit from the Milan autostrada.— TRAVEL AGENCIES. *Wagons-Lits/Cooks,* Piazzetta Giovanni XXIII; *C.I.T.,* 48-50 P.za S. Marco, and Piazzale Roma; *American Express,* 1474 San Moisè.

British Consulate, 1051 Accademia.—ENGLISH CHURCH (St George's), Campo San Vio.

Water-Buses. Tickets can be bought at any landing stage; also books of tickets which have to be stamped before each journey. The tariff is 50 l. for one stop; 100 l. for two or more stops; on the diretto (faster service with fewer stops) the tariff varies between 150 l. and 200 l. Suitcases must be paid for. Most of the services run at frequent intervals (ev. 10 min.). The **'Vaporetti'** (220 pers.) are more comfortable and provide better views for the visitor than the smaller and faster **'Motoscafi'** (110 pers.). Services: **1.** 'Accelerato'. *Piazzale Roma—Stazione— Canal Grande—San Marco—Arsenale—Giardini—Lido,* with 19 stops in c. 1 hr (every 10 min. by day; also at night); **2.** 'Diretto'. *Rialto—Stazione—Piazzale Roma—Rio Nuovo—Canal Grande—Riva Schiavoni—Lido* (in summer to Casinò); **4.** *Piazzale Roma—Lido,* by the Grand Canal, stopping only at Rialto, Accademia, San Marco, San Zaccaria, and the Giardini (when the Biennale is open); **5.** 'Circolare sinistra' and 'circolare destra'. Two services provide a right circular and a left circular: *Riva Schiavoni* (Victor Emmanuel Mont.)—*Isola San Giorgio—Zitelle—Redentore—Sant'Eufemia—Zattere—San—Basilio—Silos— Santa Marta—Piazzale Roma—Stazione—Ponte delle Guglie—Ponte Tre Archi—Sant' Alvise—Madonna dell'Orto—Fondamente Nuove—Isola S. Michele* (Cimitero)*—Murano—Fondamente Nuove—Ospedale Civile—Tana Celestia* (Arsenale)*—Riva Schiavoni;* **6.** *Riva Schiavoni—Lido* (direct); **8.** *Riva Schiavoni—Giudecca—Sacca Fisola;* **9.** *Zattere—Giudecca* (near Sant'Eufemia); **10.** *Riva Schiavoni—Isola di San Lazzaro degli Armeni;* **11.** *Riva Schiavoni— Chioggia* (with connecting bus); **12.** *Fondamente Nuove—Murano—Mazzorbo— Burano—Torcello—Treporti;* **13.** *Fondamente Nuove—Isola di Sant'Erasmo;* **14.** *Riva Schiavoni—Sant'Elena—Lido—Punta Sabbioni.*

Summer only: **3.** *Tronchetto—San Marco;* **15.** *Riva Schiavoni—Punta Sabbioni* (direct); **18.** *Fondamente Nuove—Murano—Lido;* **20.** *Riva Schiavoni— San Lazzaro degli Armeni—Lido;* **28.** *Stazione—Piazzale Roma—San Zaccaria—Lido;* **25.** *Riva Schiavoni—San Pietro in Volta—Pellestrina— Chioggia.*

Traghetti (gondola ferries) cross the Grand Canal in several places, either straight (diretto) or diagonally (traversale). They are sometimes suspended without notice, but are a cheap and pleasant way of getting about in Venice. At present they run at Campo Santa Maria del Giglio; San Samuele and Palazzo Rezzonico; San Tomà; and near the Ca d' oro (for the market).

Gondolas (comp. above; principal stand at the Molo, facing the Piazzetta). For hire by the hour: 12,000 l. for 2 people for 1 hr; 15,000 l. for 3-6 people; each subsequent ½ hr, 7,500 l. Night surcharge (after 20) 25 per cent.

Taxis (motor-boats) charge by distance, i.e. from Piazzale Roma or the Station to the Rialto for 1-5 people, 6000 l; from Piazzale Roma or the Station to San Marco by the Grand Canal (for 1-5 people), 9400 l., etc. Hourly tariff for sight-seeing within the historical centre, 11,000 l.; outside the historical centre, 22,000 l.

Local Buses. From PIAZZALE ROMA to *Mestre* (Nos. 2, 4, 7, 8, 12, and 13); to *Marghera* (No. 6); to *Airport* (service AV); and to *Malcontenta* (MV). On the LIDO, from Piazzale Santa Maria Elisabetta to the *Casino* (service A); to *San Nicolò Airport* (A); to *Alberoni* (C).—COUNTRY BUSES from Piazzale Roma to *Padua, Bolzano, Merano, Cortina, Grado, Cáorle, lésolo Lido,* and *Abano Terme* (viâ Padua).

Theatres. *La Fenice* (Pl. 10), Campo San Fantin; *Ridotto,* Calle Vallaresso (Pl. 11). Open Air Theatres: *Palazzo Grassi* (Pl. 10); *Verde,* Isola di San Giorgio (Pl. 16).—CONCERTS are held in churches and the Palazzo Ducale in spring and summer.

Festivals. The feast of the *Redentore* (3rd Sun in July) is the most popular of these, when a bridge of boats unites the Zattere with the Giudecca; its vigil is

S.Alvise

Macelli
Pubblici

Mad. dell'Orto

Pal.
Mastelli

Casa

S. Giobba

Ghetto

Tempio
Israelitico

RIO TERRA S. LEONARDO

S. Marcuola

Palazzo
Labia

S.
Geremia

Pal.
Flangini

Scalzi

Staz. S. Lucia
F.S.

Ponte
degli
Scalzi

S.
Simeone
Piccolo

S.
Simeone
Grande

S. Marciliano

Pal.
Vendramin

S.
Vendramin
Calergi

Pal. Erizzo

Pal.
Soranzo
Barbarigo

S. Fosca

Palazzo
Giovanelli

Pal.
Correr

Pal.
Felice

Pal. Fond. d.
Giovanelli Turchi
S. Giov.
Decollato

Pal. Tron
Battaglia

Pal.
Foscarini
S.
Stae

Pal.
Pesaro
(Gall. Arte
Moderna)

Ca' d'
Oro

Pal. d.
Giust.

Pal.
Corner d.
Regina

S. Giacomo
dall'Orio

S.M. Mater
Domini

S.
Cassiano

Pal.
Querini

CAMPO
N. SAURO

Car
Park

PIAZZALE

ROMA

Giardino
Papadopoli

Pal.
Papadopoli

I Tolentini

Scuola
S.Giov.Evang.

S. Giov.
Evan.

Archivio
di Stato

S.
Rocco

Scuola
S.Rocco

Frari

CAMPO
S. AGOSTINO

CAMPO
S. STIN

Pal.
Soranzo

Pal. Corner
Mocenigo

CAMPO
S. POLO

S.
Polo

S.
Aponal

Pal.
Albrizzi

S.
Silvestro

Pal.
Papadopoli

Pal.
Bernardo

Pal.
Centani

Pal.
Grimani

Pal.
Grimani

S. Bened.

Teatro
Rossini

S.
Toma

Pal.
Pisani

Pal. Tiepolo
Persico

S.
Pantalon

Pal.
Civran

Pal.
Balbi

Pal.
Garzoni

Pal.
Corner
Spinelli

CAMPO S.
MARGHERITA

Ca' Foscari

Pal. Giustinian

Pal.Rezzonico

Pal.
Contarini
S. Michele
Barnaba

Scuola
Chiesa dei
Carmini

Pal. Cicogna

S.Raffaele
Arcang.

S. Sebastiano

Ognissanti

S.
Trovaso

Palazzo
Contarini
d. Figure

Pal.
Mocenigo

Pal Grassi

S.
Samuele

Pal.
Malipiero
Ca' d.
Duca

Pal.
Loredan

Pal.
Loredan

Pal.
Contarini
d.Scrighi

Pal.
Giustinian
Lolin

Pal
Moro-Lin

Pal.
Vitale

Pal.
Giustinian

Pal.
Cavalli

S.
Stefano

S.
Maurizio

Teatro
La Fenice

S.M.
Zobenigo

Pal.
Pisani

Pal.
Zaguri

Pal.
Barbaro

(Pref)

Pal.
Corner d.
Ca Grande

Ponte dell'
Accademia

Accademi
di Bella Arti

Pal.Da Mula

S. Agnese

Pal.
Nani

English
Church

Pal.
Loredan

Pal.
Dario

Pal.
Barbarigo

S.
Gregorio

Accademia
di Bella Arti

S. M. delle
Visitazione

Gesuati

Spirito
Santo

Venice

0   300 yards
0   300 metres

13

14

CANALE
DELLA
GIUDECCA

La Giudecca

N

Cimitero

ISOLA DI S. MICHELE

Sacche
della Misericordia

Scuola
Vecchia

Abbazia d.
Misericordia

Scuola
Nuova

S. Caterina

Gesuiti

Pal. Seriman

FONDAMENTE

S. Sofia

SS.
Apostoli

Pal.
sagredo

Pal.
Mich.d.Colonne

Pal.Valmarana

S.
Canciano

LARGA
G. GALLINA

NUOVE

escheria

Ca' Da
Mosto

S.M.d.
Miracoli

Pal.
Sanudo

Scuola di
S. Marco

Tribunale

S.Giac. d'
Rialto

S.Giov.e
Crisostomo

CAMPO
SAN
ZANIPOLO

SS.Giovanni
e Paolo

L'Ospedaletto

S. Francesco
d. Vigna

Pal. Camerlenghi

Ponte di
Rialto

Teatro
Malibran

BARBARIA D. TOLE

Scuola

CAMPO
S.BARTOLOMEO

Pal.
Manin

S.
Bart

S.
Lio

S.M.d.
Fava

S.M.
Formosa

Palazzo
Grimani

S.
Lorenzo

Pal.
Bembo

Pal.
Dandolo

Teatro
Goldoni

S.
Salvatore

Palazzo
Querini
Stampalla

Questura

S.Giorgio
d.Schiavoni

Luca

S.
Giuliano

S.Giov.
Nuovo

Pal.Trevisan

S.Giorgio
dei Greci

S.
Antonio

Pal. Cont.
d. Bovolo

Torre d.
Orologio

Pal.
Patriarcato

C. S. PROVOLO

CAMPO
BANDIERA
E MORO

S.
Martino

Fantin

MERCERIA

PROCURATIE
VECCHIE
S. MARCO

PIAZZA

Campanile

Prigioni
Pte d.
Sospiri

S.
Zaccaria

La Pieta

S.Giov.
in Bragora

S.
Moise

Mus.
Correr

Procuratie
Nuove

Libreria
Vecchia

PIAZZETTA

Palazzo
Ducale

RIVA

DEGLI

SCHIAVONI

EPT

Zecca

MOLO

Giardinetti

Bacino

Pal.Treves de'
Bonfili

Cap. di Porto

Pal.
Giustinian

Pal.
Tiepolo

CANALE

DI

S.

MARCO

Pal.
Contarini

PUNTA D. SALUTE

Semin.
Patriarc

Dogana di Mare

S. Maria
d.Salute

Bacino

S.Giorgio
Maggiore

Fondazione
Giorgio Cini

ISOLA DI S. GIORGIO
MAGGIORE

Canale della
Grazia

Teatro
Verde

Isola di S. Pietro

celebrated with aquatic concerts, fireworks, etc. The *Festa della Salute* (21 Nov), is usually celebrated by two bridges of boats, one opposite Santa Maria Zobenigo (Pl. 10), and one at the Dogana (Pl. 15). The *Regata Storica* (first Sun in Sept) starts with a procession in the Grand Canal and ends with races on the lagoon. Other 'Regate' (gondola races) and 'Serenate' (musical water-pageants after dark) occur at irregular intervals on the Grand Canal.—INTERNATIONAL EXHIBITIONS AND FESTIVALS (Film Festival, etc.), organized by the 'Biennale', are held at intervals throughout the summer. The BIENNALE (held in even years) is one of the most famous international exhibitions of Modern Art; it is held in the Giardini Pubblici (see p. 299) in permanent pavilions. Every other year smaller exhibitions are held in conjunction with the Biennale.

Admission to Churches and Museums. Opening times of churches and museums given in the text below, in force in 1977, may vary. A few of the less important churches are open for services only; the majority are open from 7.30 to 12. In the afternoon many remain closed until 16 or even 17 and close again at 19; some do not reopen at all in the afternoon. Many paintings in churches are difficult to see without a light which is sometimes provided (operated by 100 l. coin). Hours of opening of museums change constantly without warning; the F.P.T. office usually supplies a printed sheet with the current times.

History. The inhabitants of Aquileia and other cities of the Upper Adriatic who took refuge in the lagoons from the barbarian invasions (5-6C) decided to make their shelter a permanent abode when they saw the Lombard rule firmly established on the mainland. The patriarch of Aquileia migrated to Grado; Torcello became the commercial centre, Heraclea and later Malamocco the political. In the 6C and 7C the Venetian lagoon was subject to Byzantium and governed by 'maritime tribunes' who, though elected by the local nobility, were subject to the veto of the emperor. About 687 a 'dux' (doge) took the place of the tribunes; at first nominated by the emperor, after 726 he was elected, though subject to ratification from Byzantium until the 10C. After an ineffectual attempt by Pepin, son of Charlemagne, to capture the lagoon, the Venetians moved their capital to the islands round the Rialto (812). The political and commercial conquest of the East now began. By 1000 they had quelled the pirates of the Narenta and acquired the mastery of the Dalmatian coast; they prohibited a Norman landing on the Albanian coast; drew commercial profit from the Crusades; and established trading stations along the Balkan coast and as far E. as the Sea of Azov and Palestine. Though keeping aloof at first from Italian affairs, they joined the Lombard towns against Barbarossa; and Venice was the scene of the reconcilliation of the Papacy with the Empire in 1177. By the influence of Doge Enrico Dandolo the Venetians led the ships of the 4th Crusade to the conquest of Constantinople (1202-4) and the establishment of the Latin Eastern Empire, keeping for themselves the major part of the captured booty and territory. This outstanding success, capped by the conquest of the Cyclades and Crete, aroused the envy of Genoa; and in the war that ensued Venice was within an ace of destruction, but, thanks to the resource of Vittor Pisani, she crushed her adversaries at Chioggia (1380). Hardly had the danger from Genoa disappeared, when the rise of the Turks threatened a greater danger in the East. Venice became the chief bulwark of Christendom against the Ottoman power. At first she tried to come to terms, but after the fall of Constantinople in 1453 she lost piece by piece her Eastern empire—Negropont, Argos, Lépanto, Scútari, the Morea, and finally Cyprus, which had been ceded to Venice by Caterina Cornaro (Cornér) in 1489. The heroic stand of this last island ended in the torture and death of Bragadin, the gallant defender of Famagusta, on 17 Aug 1571.

The Venetian power, thus checked in the East, expanded rapidly on the Italian mainland. The conquest of the March of Treviso in 1338 was followed by the voluntary surrender of Feltre, Belluno, Vicenza, and Bassano. Padua and Verona fell in 1406, Udine and the Friuli in 1420, Bergamo and Brescia in 1428, Peschiera and Legnago in 1440, Ravenna in 1441, Crema in 1454, Rovigo in 1484, Cremona in 1499. All these conquests except Ravenna were retained until the fall of the Republic; but they were not won without a grim struggle directed especially during the long dogeship of Fr. Fòscari against Fil. Maria, last of the Visconti. Fòscari's spirit was at length broken by the evil conduct of his son Iacopo and, at the age of 84, he was forced to abdicate (1457). In the wars with the Visconti some of the most famous condottieri were engaged: Gattamelata, Colleoni, Fr. Sforza, and Carmagnola, the last of whom was unjustly beheaded for treason in 1432. Besides her permanent conquests Venice held brief sway over Rimini, Cesena, Imola, Rovereto, Gorizia, Trieste, and Fiume, and the extent of her power, rousing the jealousy of Europe, led to the formation of the League of Cambrai (1508). With almost all Europe against her, Venice lost a great part of her empire, but her skilful diplomacy sowed discord among the Allies, Pope Julius II came to her assistance, and by 1516 Venice had regained most of her Italian domains.

The discovery of America and the circumnavigation of the Cape robbed Venice of her pre-eminent commercial position, and the decadence of the Republic set in. The project to pierce the isthmus of Suez was checkmated by the war of 1508; and the victory over the Turks off Lépanto (1571), in which 111 of the 243 Christian vessels were Venetian, failed to compensate for the loss of Cyprus. However, in a dispute between the Republic and Pope Paul V over the rights of the civil power, the Pope, though he placed Venice under an interdict, was forced to yield, thanks largely to the able defence of her cause by Fra Paolo Sarpi. The war of Gradisca (1615-17), fomented by Austria, brought little good to the Republic and the defence of Crete against the Turks (1644-69) further exhausted her resources. The brief reconquest of the Morea in 1699 by Fr. Morosini endured only till 1718. In the 18C the power of the Republic was negligible; life was one continual carnival and the boundless wealth accumulated in happier days was idly frittered away. On 17 May 1797, Napoleon entered the city without trouble, and deposed the last of 120 doges, Lodovico Manin. By the treaty of Campo Formio (17 Oct 1797), Venice itself was ceded to Austria, and most of her terrestrial domain was united with the Cisalpine Republic. The treaty of Pressburg (26 Dec 1805), restored Venice to Italy, but, with the fall of Napoleon, the whole of Venetia reverted to Austria. The rising of 1848 led to the formation of a republic under Daniele Manin, which offered a heroic resistance to Austria until 21 Aug 1849, being subjected to the first air raid in history when bombs were dropped from balloons by means of pre-set fuses. In 1866 Venice was finally reunited to Italy. During the First World War 620 bombs were dropped upon the city, but the damage caused to artistic monuments, though considerable, was happily less than might have been feared.

The REPUBLICAN CONSTITUTION, at first democratic, gradually became oligarchic, the power being concentrated in the hands of a few families. The appointment of Councillors and Senators limited the power of the Doge, and the 'Serrata del Maggior Consiglio' (1297) rendered the power of the doge's council absolute. The rebellion of Querini and Tiepolo in 1310 against the serrata was quickly crushed, but led to the appointment of the *Council of Ten* for the punishment of crimes against the State. This council in 1355 beheaded the doge Marin Faliero, who had sought to turn his elective office into a despotic seigniory. At the height of its power the government of the Republic was thus constituted: the *Executive Power* lay with the Doge, six Councillors, and three leaders of the Quarantia (a tribunal of 40 members), who together constituted the 'Serenissima Signoria'; the *Legislative Power* was vested in the Maggior Consiglio, the Senate, and the Collegio, a sort of Parliamentary committee; the *Judicial Power* was managed by the Council of Ten, the Inquisitori di Stato, the Avogadori del Comun, the Quarantia (see above), the Signori di Notte, and other officials.

Among famous Venetians are Marco Polo (c. 1254-1324), the first European to travel in the Far East; Marin Sanudo the elder (1270-1343) and Fra Mauro (15C) the geographers; Marin Sanudo the younger (1466-1536) and P. Bembo (1470-1547), the humanists (the latter was appointed official historian of the city); John Cabot (1420-98) and Sebastian Cabot (1477-1537), who explored the coast of America from Hudson's Bay to Florida and were the first to touch the American mainland; Fra Paolo Sarpi (1552-1623), the writer (comp. above); Carlo Goldoni (1707-93), writer of comedies; and five popes: Gregory XII, Eugenius IV, Paul II, Alexander VIII, and Clement XIII. Aldus Manutius (1450-1516), the celebrated printer and inventor of italic type, went to Venice in 1490, the first dated book issuing from his press in 1494. Marshal Marmont (1774-1852) died in exile in Venice, and W. D. Howells was U.S. consul here in 1860-65. Frederick Rolfe, Baron Corvo, spent the last five years of his life in Venice and died here in 1913.

Native composers include Giov. Gabrieli (1557-1612) whose fame attracted Schütz as a pupil; Ant. Vivaldi (c. 1677-1741); Ermanno Wolf-Ferrari (1876-1948); and Gian. Fr. Malipiero (1882-1973). Monteverdi directed the music at St Mark's for thirty years until his death in 1643 when he was followed by his pupil Cavalli (1602-76), who came to Venice from Crema as a chorister, and here followed his master's operatic lead. Cimarosa died in exile in Venice in 1801. Venetian also was Lorenzo Da Ponte (1749-1838), Mozart's librettist. Benjamin Britten composed 'Curlew River' (1964) and much of 'The Prodigal Son.' (1968), during stays in Venice.

Besides the festivals mentioned on p. 281, the *Festa della Sensa* (Ascension) was formerly famous. On this occasion the doge used to sail in the 'Bucentaur' to the Porto del Lido, where he threw a ring into the sea, thus symbolizing the marriage of Venice with the Adriatic. The custom commemorated the conquest of Dalmatia in A.D. 1000, and acquired its later more magnificent trappings after the visit of Alexander III and the Emp. Frederick I in 1177.

Architecture and Sculpture. From the close relation of Venice with Byzantium and Grado, it was natural that the first inspiration of Venetian architecture was Byzantine; the semi-oriental splendour of Venetian taste was responsible for the peculiarities of the local Gothic, for the characteristics of the Venetian Renaissance and for the exuberance of the local Baroque. The Byzantine style, admirably expressed in the Basilica of St Mark, long held sway not only over architecture, but also over sculpture and painting, and in the coloured mosaics which survived even the triumph of mural painting. The incursion of Italian Romanesque after 1000 lasted little more than a century, for in the early 13C Gothic detail was applied to Romanesque forms (Santi Giov. e Paolo and the Frari), and soon after the undiluted Gothic appears, both in churches and palaces, with its unrivalled opportunities for ornament (Doges' Palace, Ca' d'Oro).

Sculpture at first progressed slowly in Venice, but late in the 14C Iacobello and Pier Paolo dalle Masegne, and others, some under the influence of the French Gothic style, aroused it from its lethargy. From the beginning of the 15C sculpture and architecture walked hand in hand. French and Tuscan craftsmen came to Venice and the art which they developed soon spread over Emilia, the Marches, and Dalmatia. Matteo de'Raverti, Giov. and Bart. Bon, and many other sculptor-architects produced work of such charm that the New Art did not oust the old Gothic until comparatively late. However, from 1460 onwards Renaissance influence gradually strengthened, under the influence of Fra Giocondo, Bart. Bon the younger, Rizzo, Pietro Solari, a Lombard from Carona, and others. To Pietro and his sons was due the inception of the style called *Lombardesco,* a tradition carried on by Lor. Bregno and Aless. Leopardi, the latter originally a goldsmith. Next came the period of massive builders—Sammicheli, Sansovino, Palladio, and Ant. da Ponte, the last a Venetian; and then the era of Baroque with Scamozzi, Aless. Vittoria, Gius. Sardi, and, greatest of all, Baldassarre Longhena. Baroque sculpture flourished under Danese Cattaneo, Girol. Campagna, Tiziano Aspetti, Giulio Dal Moro, and Vittoria. In the 17C architecture and sculpture alike declined into the error of exuberance. The inlaid furniture of And. Brustolon (early 18C) is unusually graceful and imaginative.

Painting. The 14C painters from Paolo (fl. 1332-58) to Iacobello Bonomo (fl. 1385), with Giov. da Bologna, did little more than adapt Gothic forms to Byzantine conventions. In 1365 the commission for decorating the hall of the Maggior Consiglio was given to the still old-fashioned Guariento, while the innovator Ant. Veneziano (fl. 1369), pupil of Agnolo Gaddi, was so little appreciated that he sought a wider field at Florence. In the 15C, however, Gentile da Fabriano and Pisanello were summoned to Venice (c. 1410-19) to continue the decoration of the palace, and their influence was at once acknowledged by Iacobello del Fiore, Mich. Giambono, and especially by Ant. Vivarini (1440-76). With the latter's school at Murano were associated his brother Bartolomeo, and son Alvise and Giov. d'Alemagna; among their pupils were Quirizio and Andrea da Murano. A more interesting painter was Iacopo Bellini (? 1405-70) who had studied at Padua the work of Squarcione, Mantegna, and Donatello. He laid the foundations of the great school of Venetian painting, perfected by his sons, Gentile (1429-1507), the great portraitist, who worked for a time for Mahomet II, and Giovanni (1430-1516) one of the greatest Venetian painters. Meanwhile, c. 1450, another definite artistic impulse displayed itself, with the imitators of Squarcione. Ant. da Negroponte was followed by Carlo Crivelli (fl. 1457-93), most of whose work, however, was done in the Marches. Another outside influence was that of Antonelló da Messina, whose pala for San Cassiano (since lost) was a revelation in technique; notable among his many admirers was Alvise Vivarini (after 1446-c. 1504). Among his successors were Marco Basaiti, Girol. Mocetto, Bart. Montagna, chief of the school of Vicenza and, less directly, the frank and exuberant Cima da Conegliano, Boccaccino, Buonconsiglio, Bonsignori, and last but perhaps greatest Lor. Lotto. Another school noted for its descriptive power included Laz. Bastiani, Bened. Diana, and the fresh and vivacious Vitt. Carpaccio (fl. 1482-1525).

The main current of Venetian painting followed the lead of the Bellini, and hosts of disciples emerged from the school of Giovanni. In the same chain come

Giorgione (Giorgio Barbarelli, 1478-1510), who raised Venetian painting to a high pitch of fame, and Titian (Tiziano Vecellio, ? 1480-1576), with whom came the highest renown. Around the rich genius of this master arose many disciples, themselves of high repute: Palma Vecchio, Bonifacio Veronese, Seb. del Piombo, Paris Bordone and Lor. Lotto, Dosso Dossi called 'the Ariosto of painting' from the scope of his imagination, Pordenone, and, greatest of all, Iac. Tintoretto (1518-94), who united Titian's colouring with Michelangelo's power of design. With Paolo Veronese (1528-88) clear atmosphere replaces the hot colouring of Titian and Tintoretto. Towards the close of the 16C the light of Venetian painting failed and the mannerists held sway—Palma Giovane, Dom. Tintoretto, and others, with the imitators of Veronese—his sons Carlo and Gabriele, his brother Benedetto, and G. B. Zelotti, best of his followers. The most outstanding painter of the 17C was Padovanino (1580-1648), in whose work still glows the light of Titian. Towards the 18C, a revival was felt, thanks to Seb. Ricci (1659-1734), Pellegrini (1675-1741), and the Rembrandtesque Piazzetta (1683-1754). More consonant with the easy life of the time were the delicate pastels of Rosalba Carriera, the clear detail of Canaletto (Ant. Canal, 1697-1768), the marine impressionism of Fr. Guardi (1712-93), and Bern. Bellotto (1720-80), nephew of Canaletto and sometimes given his name, and the amusing illustrations of Pietro Longhi; while over all shone the fertile imagination of G. B. Tiepolo (1696-1770), who was followed by his sons Gian Domenico and Lorenzo.

I   CENTRAL AND EASTERN QUARTERS

The **Piazza di San Marco** (Pl. 11), the piazza *par excellence*, is without an equal in the world. Surrounded on three sides by the dignified arcades of public buildings, bordered on the east by the façade of St Mark's, and paved with marble and trachyte from the Euganean Hills, it is of unrivalled charm, at all seasons, and however crowded or deserted. Napoleon commented that it was "the finest drawing-room in Europe". The famous pigeons of St Mark still flock to the square, and until recently were fed here at the public charge as in Republican days (they are now fed officially in the smaller campi of the city). The municipal band plays in the Piazza in summer.

Above the entrance to the Merceria (p. 299), at the N. corner of the piazza, rises the **Torre dell'Orologio,** by Mauro Coducci (1496-99), with wings attributed to P. Lombardo (1506). Above the great clock-face is a gilded figure of the Madonna, and above that are two bronze figures (1497), the 'mori' who strike the hours. The tower may be climbed to see the mechanism of the clock (No. 147, under the archway, 9-12, 15-18; fest. 9-12). The rest of the N. side is occupied by the arcades of the **Procuratie Vecchie,** reconstructed after a fire in 1512 by Gugl. Bergamasco and Bart. Bon the younger and Sansovino. These, the former residence of the Procurators who had charge of the fabric of St Mark's, are fronted by three open galleries, of which the lowest has 50 arches, the upper two 100.—Sansovino's church of San Geminiano, on the W. side, was pulled down in 1807 by Napoleon, who replaced it by the so-called *Ala Napoleonica* of the Palazzo Reale, a building by Gius. Soli (1810), the two lower floors of which copy the Procuratie Nuove, while on top is a heavy attic fronted by statues of Roman emperors.— The **Procuratie Nuove,** on the S., continue the design of the Libreria Vecchia which faces the Doges' Palace. Up to the tenth arch from the left they are the work of Scamozzi (1584-1616), and they were completed by Longhena c. 1640. They were a later residence of the Procurators (see above), and became a royal palace under Napoleon. In 1920 they were presented to the city by the royal family, and since 1923 they have been occupied by the **Museo Correr** (adm. 10-16, fest. 9-12.30; closed Tues), the city museum of art and history, which was founded by the wealthy citizen Teodoro Correr (1750-1830). The entrance is on the right of the central passage of the portico.

From the central door an imposing staircase mounts to a landing, where an antechamber leads to the SALONE NAPOLEONICO, once the ballroom and now a conference and exhibition hall.

The FIRST FLOOR is devoted to the **Historical Collections.** Loggia Napoleonica: old views and plans of Venice; engravings by *De Witt,* etc.—ROOM I. *Ant. Canova, Daedalus and Icarus,* marble group; models, and a (painted) Portrait of Amedeo Svaier.—R. II. Circular table with mythological scenes, of Wedgwood porcelain.—R. III. *L'Aliense,* Landing of Caterina Cornaro, queen of Cyprus (1489).—R. IV. Madonna enthroned between a Doge and Magistrates, high relief of 15C.—RR. V & VI. Documents and portraits of the Doges, and representations of their ceremonies.—R. VII. Elaborately carved bookcases of 17C, and a chandelier made in Murano.—RR. VIII-X. Robes and portraits, including St Justina with officials of the Republic by *Iac. Tintoretto,* and a Portrait of a Doge by *Lazzaro Bastiani.*—R. XI. Coins, a very complete collection from the 9C to the fall of the Republic; standards.

A passage (R. XII) leads to R. XIII, with mementoes of the Battle of Lépanto (1571); *Aless. Vittoria,* Bust of Francesco Duodo, in terracotta.—R. XIV. The Bucintoro (p. 284), including decoration from the vessel of 1729 by *Ant. Corradini.*—R. XV. The Arsenale.—R. XVI. Commerce and navigation; Persian and Chinese ceramics.—R. XVII. Arms and armour; 16C Flemish tapestry, Marriage of the Virgin.—R. XVIII. Eastern arms, notably a Persian shield of gold and silver (16C).—RR. XIX-XXIV are devoted to Fr. Morosini (Doge 1688-94) with his bust by *Fil. Parodi* and equestrian portrait by *Giov. Carbonico.*

On the SECOND FLOOR the **Museo del Risorgimento** (temporarily closed) continues the history of Venice to the present day. Of the fifteen rooms, RR. VI-X are concerned with 1848-49.

The **Quadreria,** or *Picture Gallery,* is arranged strictly chronologically. Room I. Byzantine period.—R. II. Triptychs and polyptych panels of the 14C, incl. works by *Paolo Veneziano.*—R. III. *Lor. Veneziano.*—R. IV. Gothic fragments and frescoes.—R. V. *Stef. Veneziano* and Gothic painters of the 14C.—R. VI. Gothic painters of the 15C: *Iacobello del Fiore,* Madonna; *Stefano da Zevio* (?), Angel musicians; *Fr. de' Franceschi,* Martyrdom; '*Master of the Jarves marriage-chest',* painted Frontal of a marriage-chest, with a story from Boccaccio.—R. VII. *Cosmè Tura,* *Pietà.*—R. VIII contains fine works of the Ferrarese school; and Madonnas by *Bart. Vivarini.*—R. IX. Gothic woodcarving.—R. X. Flemish painters: *Pieter Brueghel,* Adoration of the Magi.—R. XI. *Antonello da Messina,* *Pietà, painted during his short stay in the city c. 1476 (very ruined). Hugo van der Goes,* Crucifixion; *Dirk Bouts,* Madonna.—R. XII. Flemish and German painters: *Herri met de Bles,* Temptations of St Anthony; *Jos Amman von Ravensburg;* Saints; *Barthel Bruyn,* Portrait of a woman.—R. XIII. *Iac. Bellini.* Crucifixion; *Gentile Bellini,* Doge Giovanni Mocenigo; *Giov. Bellini,* Transfiguration; Madonna and Child; Portrait of a young Saint crowned with laurel leaves; Crucifixion; Pietà.—R. XIV. *Alvise Vivarini,* St Anthony of Padua.—R. XV. *Vitt. Carpaccio,* *Two Venetian courtesans (a well-known painting), St Peter Martyr.—R. XVI. Further works by *Carpaccio,* and by minor painters of the early 16C, including a Portrait of a Young Man in a red hat.— R. XVII. Works of the same period; *Giov. Dalmata,* Bust (Carlo Zen?); *Boccaccio Boccaccino,* Madonnas; *Lor. Lotto,* Madonna crowned by two angels. Cases of ivories and enamels.—R. XVIII. Greco-Venetian school.—RR. XIX-XXIII. Ceramics.

The last section of the museum has recently been opened to illustrate Venetian history by means of the minor arts. The exhibits include small bronzes (by *Tullio Lombardo, il Riccio, Aless. Vittoria,* and others); Madonna and Child a relief, by *Iac. Sansovino.*—Materials (17-18C), and lace.—Model of the Bucintoro; household objects; ladies' apparel; a display relating to gondolas. In the last two rooms are plans and maps, including a wood engraving (with the original block) of Venice in 1500 by *Iac. de' Barbari.*

In an isolated position at the corner of the Procuratie Nuove stands the **Campanile of St Mark,** over 98½ m high, first built in 888-912, and practically rebuilt by Bart. Bon in 1511-14. On 14 July 1902, it collapsed without warning. From the proceeds of a world-wide subscription an exact reproduction of the original was immediately begun under the direction of Luca Beltrami and Gaetano Moretti and opened on 25 Apr 1912.

The brick tower of the campanile is surmounted by a bell-chamber with four-light windows of Istrian stone, and a square story decorated with two winged lions and two figures of Venice beneath the symbol of Justice; the spire at the top is crowned by an angel weather-vane. The bell-chamber (adm. daily 9-21 incl. fest.), reached by a lift or by an easy sloping walk, commands a magnificent *View of the town and lagoon, the Euganean hills, and the Alps. Only one of the old bells survived the collapse of the tower; the others were presented by Pius X. Galileo experimented with his telescope from the top of the campanile in 1609.

At the base of the campanile is the *Loggetta, a masterpiece by Sansovino (1537-49), which was crushed by the fall of the tower, but has been carefully restored. It was originally a meeting-place of the 'nobili' or patricians, and later it was occupied by three military procurators. Its three arches, supported by twin columns, are surmounted by an ornate attic decorated with reliefs of Tritons and Nereids, and on either side of the arches are statues of Pallas, Mercury, Apollo, and Peace, all by Sansovino. The two admirable little bronze gates are by Ant. Gai (1735-37). Inside is a Madonna and Child, also by Sansovino; a charming work, it was recomposed (except for a young St John) from shattered fragments.—The three bronze *Pedestals* with sculptures in relief (by Aless. Leopardi, 1505) in front of the basilica support tall flagstaffs.

The **Basilica of St Mark (Pl. 11) stands high in importance among the churches of Christendom, not only in virtue of its sumptuous architecture, its artistic riches, and the splendour of its mosaics, but also because of its great antiquity and the history and legend that encompass it. Its inspiration is Byzantine, and the five domes of nearly equal circumference which cover it at once suggest the great churches of Constantinople. Its plan, indeed, is probably derived from the (destroyed) Church of the Apostles at Constantinople; but in it may be also seen that compromise between the centripetal shrine and the aisled basilica from which later developed the typical Western church-plan. The building is 76½ m long, including the atrium, and 62½ m across the transepts.

Admission to the BASILICA daily 6.30.19.30.— The TREASURY and PALA D'ORO (inclusive ticket) are open in summer from 10-17.30 (winter 10-15.30); fest. & Sun 14-16.30.—The LOGGIA on the façade, the GALLERIES, and the MUSEO MARCIANO are open 9.30-17.30 (winter 10-15.45).

History. Legend tells how St Mark the Evangelist, storm-tossed on a voyage to Aquileia, saw, near the islands of the Rialto, a vision of an angel who greeted him with the words "Pax tibi, Marce, Evangelista meus". This portent was fulfilled in 828 when Venetian merchants brought the body of St Mark from Alexandria and placed it in charge of Doge Giustiniano Partecipazio who caused the first church on this site to be built. Burned down in a popular rising (976) this church was replaced by Doge P. Orseolo, but the present form dates from a second rebuilding by Doge Dom. Contarini (1063-73). On its completion it was faced with marble from Ravenna, Sicily, Byzantium, and the East, and late in the 11C the mosaic decorations were begun in the Byzantine manner. These, however, have almost all been restored from the 16C onwards and some replaced by Tintoretto and others. Though the basilica has been a cathedral only since 1807 (it was formerly the chapel of the Doges' palace), the name and symbol of St Mark (a winged lion) have been emblematic of Venice since the earliest days of her history.

Exterior. The marvellous*FACADE,which changes colour as the light changes, is in two tiers, each of five semicircular arches. The two rows of columns which support the lower arches are of different kinds of marble, mostly from older buildings. In the recesses above and in the soffits of the arches are *Mosaics;* the five principal subjects (l. to r.) are: the Translation of the Body of St Mark to the Basilica (1260-70); Magistrates adoring the Body of the Saint (1728); Last Judgement (1836); Venice welcoming the Arrival of the Body; Removal of the Body from Alexandria (the two last by Pietro Vecchia, 1660). Around the portals are sculptured decorations of great interest and beauty, many of them fragments from earlier buildings. The central doorway is notable for the reliefs by Antelami (Virtues and Months; note especially May and August in the soffit). The central bronze door was brought from Byzantium. The S. door was cast by the Venetian goldsmith Bertuccio (1300).—Of the five arches of the upper tier only the central one contains a window; the other four are filled with mosaics (l. to r., Descent from the Cross, Descent into Hell, Resurrection, and Ascension), rearranged by Alvise Gaetano (early 17C) from designs by Maffeo da Verona. Surmounting the central arch is a statue of St Mark, by Nic. Lamberti (1415), and over the side-arches Warrior Saints; in the Gothic tabernacles are the Annunciation, the Archangel Gabriel, and the Evangelists (1385 et seq.). The famous *HORSES of bronze, with traces of the original gilding, are a Greek work of the time of Alexander, or just after, possibly from the Rhodian Chariot of the Sun at Delphi. They were part of Venice's share of the booty from Constantinople, taken from the hippodrome there in 1204. In 1798 they were carried off to Paris by Napoleon, where they remained until 1815; in 1917-19 they were removed for safety and again in 1940-45. One horse has been removed for restoration. At the S. corner of the gallery is a porphyry head (8C) said to be a portrait of Justinian II (d. 711).

The arcades of the SOUTH SIDE, which are surmounted by a 16C pediment, continue the design of the W. front. The bronze door admits to the baptistery. Between the windows of the upper storey is a Byzantine Madonna, in front of which two lamps are lighted nightly in fulfilment of a vow of a sea-captain. The two plain walls of the treasury, on the right, are adorned with marbles and fragments of ambones and plutei. In the corner are two sculptured groups in porphyry of the Tetrarchs, representing Diocletian and three other emperors, Egyptian works of the 4C. Near by are two isolated pillars, brought by Lor. Tiepolo from the church of St Saba at Acre; they are a rare example of 5C Greco-Syrian art. At the S.W. corner of the façade is the *Pietra del Bando* (Stone of Banishment), a stump of a column, also from Acre, from which the decrees of the Signoria were promulgated.

The impressive NORTH SIDE consists of four arches. Beneath the fourth is the Porta dei Fiori, with a Presepio in its lunette. Outside the projecting chapel of St Isidore is the tomb of Daniele Manin (d. 1857). In the Piazzetta Giovanni XXII (formerly dei Leoncini or di San Basso) is the *Palazzo Patriarcale* (1837-50). Just beyond the bridge behind it is the *Palazzo Trevisan* (early 16C).

The **Atrium** formerly surrounded the W. arm of the church on three sides, but the S. side of it is now walled off. Its slightly pointed arches, the earliest of their kind in Italy, support six small domes. The lower part of the walls is encased in marble; the upper part and the pavement are mosaic. The mosaics of the domes and arches, mainly original work of the 13C, depict (r. to l.): 1st Dome, Story of Genesis to the Death of Abel, probably the oldest mosaic in the series; under the 1st arch, the Flood; under the 2nd arch (l. of the door), Death of Noah and the Tower of Babel; 2nd Dome, Story of Abraham; 3rd-5th Dome, Story of Joseph; 6th Dome, Story of Moses. The *Columns of the fine INNER FAÇADE were either brought from the East or are fragments of the first basilica. Of the three doors, that on the right, the *Porta di San Clemente,* is said to have been a gift from the Emperor Alexius Comnenus. The rough damascening in silver dates from the 11C. The great door, the work of Leone da Molino (1113-18) is modelled on the other. The unrestored mosaics on the wall above represent the Evangelists, the Madonna and six Saints, and in the semi-dome is *St Mark in Ecstasy, rearranged from a cartoon of Titian's by the brothers Zuccato (1545). In the square space before the door are the Raising of Lazarus, the Crucifixion, the Descent from the Cross, and the Burial of the Virgin; on the pendentives are the Evangelists. The slab of red Verona marble with a white marble lozenge on the pavement according to tradition marks the spot where Barbarossa did obeisance before Alexander III. Against the outside wall are the tombs of Doge Vitale Falier (d. 1096) and his wife, made up of Byzantine fragments. In the apse beneath the 3rd dome is the tomb of Doge Bart. Gradenigo (d. 1342), by a Pisan sculptor; under the 6th is a bust of Pope John XXIII.

INTERIOR. Five great domes cover the Greek cross of the interior, alternating with barrel vaults; each of the four arms has vaulted aisles, in which the columns, with exquisitely foliated capitals, support a gallery fronted by a parapet of carved panels. The whole church is encased in marble below and in mosaic on a gold ground above; and the marvellous effects of light reflected from the rich hues of the mosaics are themselves an adequate reason for the church's surname 'Basilica d'Oro'. The *Pavement,* which has subsided in places, is supported on piles, and consists of a geometric mosaic of antique marble with representations of beasts, birds, etc.

In the WEST ARM or NAVE, in the lunette over the entrance, is a mosaic of Christ between the Virgin and St Mark, a classic example of Byzantine art (12C). In the archivolt of the great W. window (better seen from the atrium) are the Exaltation of the Cross, the Triumph of the Elect, and the Punishment of the Damned, impressively designed from cartoons by Tintoretto, Aliense, and Maffeo da Verona. In the archivolt of the entrance: Dream of St John, modern; Seven angels protecting the Seven Churches, Angel transfixing the Beast, both by the Zuccato brothers (1579); Mystic Repast of the Lamb, after Pordenone; the Madonna, and the Apocalypse, modern. In the dome: the Holy Ghost enthroned enlightening the Apostles; between the windows, the Converted Nations. In the inner archivolt; Judas's Kiss, the Crown of Thorns, Ecce Homo, the Crucifixion, the Marys at the Tomb, the Descent into Hell, the Doubting of St Thomas, antique mosaics of vigorous execution. All these were thoroughly restored in 1907-35. In the SOUTH AISLE is a stoup of Oriental porphyry.

Opposite is the entrance to the **Baptistery,** which with the Zen Chapel occupies the S. arm of the atrium. The Font, by Sansovino, has a lid with bronze reliefs of the school of Tiziano Minio and Desiderio Fiorentino; the statue of St John the Baptist, above, was executed by Segala (1575) from designs by Sansovino. Here are also the tombs of the Doges And. Dandolo (d. 1354) and Giov. Soranzo (d. 1328), and in front of the altar is the granite grave-slab of Iac. Sansovino (d. 1570), whose remains were transferred from the Seminario in 1929. On the altar is a 14C Baptism of Jesus between SS. George and Theodore (Byzantine). The roof has rather crude mosaics of the late 14C: Head of Christ, Nine Orders of Celestial Spirits, Virtues, Heavenly Powers; the Apostles ordained to baptize; Head of Christ with Prophets, and the Stable at Bethlehem; Life of St John the Baptist.— The adjoining *Cappella Zen* (closed for restoration) contains the bronze *Tomb of Card. G. B. Zen (d. 1501) started by Leopardi and Ant. Lombardo (1504) and finished by Lombardo and Paolo Savin (1521). Savin also designed the bronze altar. In the niches: five statues of the school of Antelami (12C); the vault-mosaics (13C, restored) relate the story of St Mark.

On the S. wall of the church are five rectangular mosaics of the Virgin and four Prophets; higher up, the Agony in the Garden, a perfect example of Venetian-Byzantine work. In the vault, Scenes from the lives of Apostles.—The NORTH AISLE contains a stoup of 'bardiglio' marble and the little *Chapel of the Crucifix,* with a pyramidal marble roof surmounted by a huge oriental agate and supported by six columns of precious marble with gilded Byzantine capitals. It contains a painted wooden crucifix brought from the East.—The five mosaic rectangles on the N. wall show a beardless *Christ with four prophets; above is the Glory of Paradise (17C); and in the vault, Death of St Peter, St Paul, and other Apostles.—The CENTRAL DOME (restored 1936) is adorned with mosaics of the purest Byzantine style. Round the central Ascension are the Virgin between two Angels, and the Apostles; between the windows, the 16 Virtues of Jesus; in the pendentives, the Evangelists, above the four Rivers of the Bible which typify them. At the spring of the pendentives are four gilded marble *Angels (10C Byzantine).

On the right of the NORTH TRANSEPT is the Lombardesque *Altar of St Paul.* In the vault-arches are the Last Supper, the Marriage at Cana, and Miracles of Jesus; in the dome, Life of St John the Evangelist; on the pendentives, Doctors of the Church; on the end wall, the Ancestry of the Virgin.—The *East Transeptal Aisle* contains the *Altar of Madonna Nicopoeia* (patroness of victory), with candelabra by Camillo Alberti (1520), a tabernacle supported by precious columns, and an icon from the sack of Constantinople. On the wall: the Institution of the Eucharist; above, Jesus expelling the usurers from the Temple, and other scenes from his life.—In the *West Transeptal Aisle* is the Gothic *Porta di San Giovanni* (which gives access to the Atrium, comp. above) with a mosaic lunette. In the aisle is a Greek marble stoup; on the wall, Susanna and the Elders, after Palma Giovane and Tintoretto; above, Dream of St Joseph, Flight into Egypt, Jesus among the Doctors; in the arch, Life of the Virgin, according to the apocryphal gospels. The *Chapel of the Madonna dei Màscoli* (1430), at the end of this aisle, has a carved Gothic altar attrib. to Giov. Bon. The vault *Mosaics of the Life of Mary (1430-50) are partly by Mich. Giambono; partly, however, they suggest the work of Iac. Bellini and Mantegna.—At the end of the transept the *Chapel of St Isidore* (1354-55; not always open) has a florid Gothic altar and vigorous mosaics in 14C style, depicting the history of the saint.

The SOUTH TRANSEPT is lighted by a fine rose window. On the left is the *Altar of St James,* a charming work in the 15C Lombardesque style. Beneath the inner arch: Scenes from the Life of Jesus. In the dome: Saints. Beneath the outer arch: Miracles of Jesus. The *West Transeptal Aisle* depicts the Prayers for and the Miraculous Discovery of the Body of St Mark, interesting especially for their reproduction of the interior of the basilica. Above (hard to see), Presentation of the Virgin in the Temple (17C).

The trefoil arch at the end of this aisle admits to the **Treasury** (adm. see p. 287; ticket should be retained for adm. to the Pala d'Oro), containing a rich store of booty from the sack of St Sophia in 1204. Most of its treasures were removed in 1797 and replaced in 1834. In the anteroom is a fine silver statuette of St Mark (1804). On the left is the *Sanctuary of Relics,* with many precious reliquaries, mostly Byzantine. On the right is the Treasury proper, containing four *Evangelistaries, the marble Chair of St Mark, two gilded silver altar-frontals, the sword of Fr. Morosini, vases, reliquaries, caskets, etc.

In the *East Aisle* of this transept, behind a screen, is the *Altar of the Sacrament,* with a tabernacle borne by columns of porphyry and pavonazzetto (purple marble). It is flanked by two candelabra (by Maffeo Olivieri, 1527). By the inner face of the left-hand entrance pilaster a square of marble and mosaic lit by a lamp marks the place where St Mark's body was hidden and where the saint appeared miraculously on 24 June 1094. On the wall are mosaics (reworked in 17C) of the Life of St Leonard the Hermit; in the vault, Miracles of Jesus (early 13C).

CHOIR. Against the E. pillars of the central dome are (r.) the *Pulpit of the Epistle,* where the newly elected doge showed himself to the people, and (l.) the *Pulpit of the Gospel,* consisting of two pulpits one above the other, supported by precious marble columns and surrounded by parapets of verde antico. It is crowned by a curious little Oriental-looking cupola.—The SANCTUARY is raised upon 16 little marble arches of fine workmanship, from the basilica of Orseolo. The imposing *Rood Screen,* with eight columns of dark marble, bears the great Rood, a work

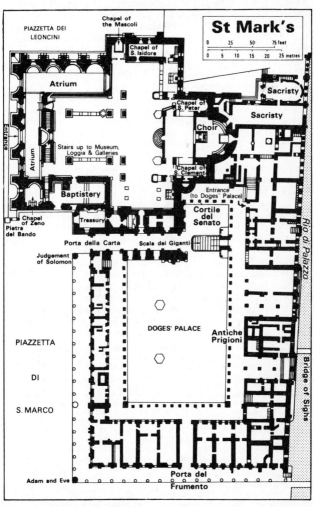

St Mark's

PIAZZETTA DEI LEONCINI

Chapel of the Mascoli

Chapel of S. Isidore

Atrium

Sacristy

Chapel of S. Peter

Sacristy

Choir

Atrium

Stairs up to Museum, Loggia & Galleries

Chapel of S. Clement

Baptistery

Entrance (to Doges' Palace)

Entrance

Chapel of Zeno

Cortile del Senato

Pietra del Bando

Treasury

Porta della Carta

Scala dei Giganti

Judgement of Solomon

Rio di Palazzo

PIAZZETTA

DI

S. MARCO

DOGES' PALACE

Antiche Prigioni

Bridge of Sighs

Adam and Eve

Porta del Frumento

in silver and bronze by Iac. di Marco Benato of Venice (1393), and marble statues of the Virgin, St Mark, and the Apostles by the Dalle Masegne (1394). Within the pilasters are the stalls reserved for magistrates and kings; on the parapet of the lower row are bronze reliefs by Sansovino (1537-44; miracles and martyrdom of St Mark), and below are intarsia benches.—The SOUTH CHOIR AISLE is entered by a transenna bearing statues of the Madonna and four female saints. On the left is a Gothic reliquary. The wall-mosaics depict the Life of St Clement the Pope (late 13C); in the vault, Capture of the Body of St Mark (13C). At the E. end is the *Chapel of St Clement* with a marble altarpiece (15-16C). Here tickets are shown for admission to the Sanctuary and Pala d'Oro. The baldacchino of the high altar is borne by four *Columns* of cipollino sculptured with New Testament Scenes which are extremely interesting both from an artistic and from a historic point of view. The two front columns are possibly of the early 6C; those behind are later Romanesque copies. On the marble balustrades are the four Evangelists by Sansovino. Over the altar (covering the back of the Pala d'Oro) has been placed an early-15C altarpiece. Behind this is the *Pala d'Oro, glowing with precious stones, enamel, and old gold. Made in 1105 for Doge Ordelaffo Falier, it was renewed by Doge P.Ziani in 1209, and finally enriched and enlarged in 1345.—The APSE, with two fine capitals from Orseolo's basilica, has three large niches. In the central one is an altar with six precious columns, including two of unusually transparent alabaster. The door in the left-hand niche (entrance to the sacristy) has bronze reliefs by Sansovino (Entombment, Resurrection, heads of the artist, of Aretino, and of Titian).

The mosaics in the archivolt of the choir arch depict the Adoration of the Magi, Annunciation, Resurrection, Presentation in the Temple, Baptism of Christ, after Tintoretto; in the dome, Christ holding a half-revealed Scroll, surrounded by the Virgin and 13 Prophets (12C); in the pendentives, Symbols of the Evangelists; in the apse, Christ in benediction (1506); between the windows, SS. Nicholas, Peter, Mark, and Hermagoras, patrons of the city (13C; restored). The mosaics of the wall and vault of the NORTH CHOIR AISLE are modern restorations (Lives of SS. Peter, Mark, and Hermagoras). It is separated from the transept by a transenna; outside of which, to the right, is a Gothic reliquary. The *Chapel of St Peter,* behind whose altar is the entrance to the sacristy, has two columns with superb Byzantine capitals.

In the charming Renaissance SACRISTY (usually closed), by Giorgio Spavento (1486-90) are decorative mosaics by the Zuccato and others after Titian and Padovanino, and inlaid cupboards. The CRYPT (rarely open), is supported by 50 ancient columns.

From a small door to r. of the main W. door (entered from the Atrium) is access to the **Loggia, Galleries, and the Museo Marciano** (adm., see p. 287). The LOGGIA on the façade commands a fine view of the Piazza and allows close examination of the bronze horses (comp. p. 288). The first room of the MUSEUM is to the l. at the top of the stairs. Here are displayed mosaic fragments, 16C illuminated choirbooks, and a double bass made by *Gaspare da Salò* in the second half of the 16C.—R. II. Cover for the Pala d'Oro painted by *Paolo Veneziano* and his sons *Luca* and *Giovanni* (1345).—R. III. Altar front of the Dead Christ between two angels and Symbols of the Evangelists, a Byzantine embroidery of the 11-12C; Persian carpets (16-17C); Lion of St Mark in gilded wood (16C).—Beyond the organ gallery (with access on to the loggia).—ROOM IV has a magnificent series of Tapestries with ten scenes from the life of Christ (c. 1420). Also four tapestries worked by *Giov. Rost* (1551) on a cartoon by Iac. Sansovino; marble fountain with marine carvings (2C A.D.), formerly the base of the stoup in the basilica; Christ and the Apostles by *Maffeo da Verona,* another case for the Pala d'Oro. The *GALLERIES offer a superb opportunity to study the mosaics.

The *Piazzetta* (Pl. 11), with the Doges' Palace on the left, and the Old Library on the right, extends from St Mark's to the Bacino di San Marco. Near the water's edge are two monolithic columns from the Levant, erected here at the end of the 12C; one bears a lion (Persian or

Assyrian; wings modern), the other a statue of St Theodore, the first patron of Venice.

The **Libreria Sansoviniana,** or *San Marco,* the masterpiece of *Sansovino* (begun 1536), was finished by *Scamozzi* (1582-88), and was considered by Palladio to be the most beautiful building since the days of antiquity. Beneath the portico are the entrances to the National Library, the Old Library itself, and the Archæological Museum.

The reading-rooms of the **Biblioteca Nazionale Marciana** (National Library of St Mark; adm. daily 9-16, Sat 9-13.30) are entered from No. 7. once the approach to the ancient Zecca, or Mint. Petrarch gave his books to Venice in 1362, but it was not until Card. Bessarione presented his fine collection of MSS. in 1468 that the library was formally founded. Today the library contains about 750,000 volumes and 13,500 MS. (many Greek).

The **Old Library** may only be seen by special permission from the Director. The main entrance at No. 13A (now kept locked) leads to a monumental staircase with stuccoes by *Vittoria* which mounts to an anteroom, with a *Fresco of Wisdom, by *Titian* on the ceiling. The Great Hall, restored in 1929, has 21 ceiling-medallions by various artists and ten paintings of Philosophers by *Tintoretto, Veronese,* and *And. Schiavone.* The exhibition of ancient books is now in a small adjoining room, and includes a late 14C Dante with illuminations, and evangelisteries dating back to the 9C. The precious *Grimani Breviary, illuminated by Flemish artists of c. 1500, is rarely shown. A room opening off the stair landing contains *Fra Mauro's Map, a celebrated world-map of 1459 drawn at San Michele di Murano (on the right is the bust of the author, perhaps by Bellano); the map of Hadji Mehemed of Tunis (c. 1560); Marco Polo's will; portulans; a MS. in Petrarch's hand; etc.

At No. 17 in the library portico is the entrance to the **Archæological Museum** (adm. 9-13.30), remarkable for its ancient Greek *Sculpture. Among the notable exhibits are: ROOM III. Triple herm of Hecate (archaistic style of 3C B.C.).—R. IV (in centre), 'Abbondanza Grimani' an original of the 5C B.C.; (r. of door), Athena, of the school of Pheidias; and a fine group of female statues (original Greek works).—R. V. Roman copy of the Apollo Lycius, perhaps after Praxiteles.— R. VI. Eros bending the bow of Heracles, after Lysippus; Dionysus and a Satyr, Roman copy of a Greek original; the Grimani altar with Bacchic scenes (1C B.C.).—A case in R. VII displays the Zulian cameo (Hellenistic, from Ephesus).— R. VIII. *Gallic Warriors, copies of a group presented by Attalus of Pergamum to Athens; Ulysses; and Leda and the swan.—RR. IX-X. Busts of Roman emperors and others, including Trajan, and *Vitellius (?), a remarkable portrait.—R. XI. Greek and Roman reliefs; Roman ivories and bronzes.—R. XII.-XIV. Reliefs and statuettes.—R. XV. Lapidary collection.—R. XVIII. Greek and Roman heads and torsos; Black Romano-Egyptian head.—R. XIX. Vases and small bronzes.— R. XX. Egyptian, Assyrian and Babylonian antiquities.

At the seaward end of the Piazzetta is the Molo, on the busy waterfront. To the right is the severe façade of the old *Zecca,* by Sansovino; beyond the Giardini a bridge communicates with the Calle Vallaresso where Harry's Bar, founded in the 1920s, continues to flourish as the city's most celebrated restaurant and cocktail bar.

The *Doges' Palace,** or *Palazzo Ducale* (adm. 8.30-18; 1000 l.), the former official residence of the doges and the chief magistrates, is the outward expression, with its strange mingling of square solidity and fanciful design, of the semi-oriental grandeur of the Serenissima.

Founded in 814, the palace was rebuilt after destructive fires in 976 and 1105, and remodelled in its present form in 1309 and 1404 (S. side) and in 1424-42 (W. side). After another conflagration in 1483, Ant. Rizzo began the chief interior façade and the Scala dei Giganti, and the work was continued by P.Lombardo, Giorgio Spavento, and Scarpagnino. Again burned in 1574 and 1577, it was restored by Ant. da Ponte, and the courtyard was completed in the 17C on the old lines by Bart. Monopola. The most memorable events in the palace after the fall of the Republic were the meetings of Daniele Manin's provisional government, held here in 1848-49.

The **Exterior,** in style a remarkably original form of Gothic, is lightened by an arcade of 36 columns of elegant design, surmounted by a loggia of 71 columns. Higher up, the pink and white marble façades are pierced by large windows; the balconied window on the S. front, by *P. P. Dalle Masegne* (1404), is balanced by a similar one (1536) facing the Piazzetta. Above the corner columns are high reliefs; at the S.E. corner, the Drunkenness of Noah, with St Raphael above; at the S.W. corner, Adam and Eve, with St Michael, all by Lombard artists of the 15C; while at the N.W. corner, above a capital with lawgivers of the ancient world, is the *Judgement of Solomon, attrib. to *Nanni di Bartolo,* with St Gabriel above. Next the basilica is the *Porta della Carta* (1438-42; temporarily covered during restoration work), an extremely graceful gateway by Bart. and Giov. Bon. It owes its name to the 'carte', or announcements of new laws, which used to be affixed here. The statues of Temperance and Fortitude betray the approach of the Renaissance. The group of Doge Fr. Fóscari and the Lion of St Mark is a reproduction (1885) of the original destroyed in 1797.

The *Cortile,** or main courtyard, is approached by a vaulted passage. The magnificent E. side was rebuilt after the fire by Antonio Rizzo (1483-98) and Scarpagnino (1546-53), while on the N. side are a Baroque façade by Monopola (1604-18) and the *Arco Fóscari* (early Renaissance with florid Gothic elements). On the side of the arch towards the court is a statue of the condottiere Fr. Maria I della Rovere, Duke of Urbino (1490-1538) by Giov. Bandini (1587) and (r.) a *Page by Ant. Rizzo (now replaced by a copy; original inside the palace).

In the centre of the courtyard are bronze *Well-Heads* (1556-59). The SCALA DEI GIGANTI, in the N.E. corner, decorated with a wealth of imagination and delicacy, is likewise by Rizzo (1484-1501). The colossal statues of Neptune and Mars are by Sansovino (1554). On the landing at the top the doges used to be crowned with the *corno ducale* or *zoia*. The smaller *Cortile dei Senatori,* beyond the stairway, is a charming Renaissance work by Spavento and Scarpagnino.

INTERIOR. The entrance is now in the left-hand corner of the courtyard (behind the Scala dei Giganti). The SCALA D'ORO, built in 1538-59, to the design of *Sansovino,* and decorated with stuccoes by *Vittoria* leads up to the **Primo Piano Nobile** (or second floor). A long gallery leads (r.) to the *Doges' Private Apartments* (open except when exhibitions are being mounted).

The first room is the SALA DEGLI SCARLATTI, or Robing Room, with a fine chimneypiece by Tullio and Ant. Lombardo (c. 1501), and, over the door, a *Bas-relief by *P. Lombardo,* Doge Leon Loredan at the feet of the Virgin. Opposite is a Madonna in coloured stucco (Padua; c. 1490). The ceiling by *Biagio* and *Pietro da Faenza* is admirably gilt and moulded (1506).—The walls of the SALA DELLO SCUDO are covered with maps and charts (1540).—Opposite the entrance is the *SALA GRIMANI, with a chimneypiece by *T.* and *A. Lombardo* and a ceiling decorated with rosettes. Here also are marble *Statues of Adam and Eve, by *Ant. Rizzo* (c. 1470) removed from the Arco Fóscari in the Cortile. The SALA FRIZZO, beyond, has a similar chimneypiece and a good ceiling, and contains a copy of a Pietà by Antonello da Messina (in the Museo Correr, comp. p. 286).—A passage with a Lombardesque ceiling leads to the SALA DEGLI STUCCHI (1741-52), which contains a painting by *Pordenone* (Christ borne by angels), and small works by *Tintoretto, Bonifazio, Bassano,* and *Salviati.* The SALA DEI FILOSOFI housed for a time Tintoretto's paintings of philosophers. On the staircase, above the door on the right: *Titian,* St Christopher, a fresco of 1524 (very ruined; light on r.).—The small rooms beyond, with chimneypieces by *T.* and *A. Lombardo,* have been arranged as a picture gallery. R. I. *Carpaccio,* Winged lion (1516); *Giov. Bellini,* Pietà; *Master of 14C,* Virgin in prayer.—R. II. *Works by *Hieronymus Bosch; Quentin Metsys,* Mocking of Christ.—Across the end of the Sala dello Scudo is the SALA DEGLI SCUDIERI, with a fine *Painting of Venice receiving the homage of Neptune by *G. B. Tiepolo* (removed from the Sala delle Quattro Porte where it was difficult to see), and paintings by *Tintoretto.*

The Scala d'Oro continues to the **Secondo Piano Nobile,** or third floor. At the top of the stairs is the ATRIO QUADRATO, where the fine wooden ceiling has a painting by *Tintoretto* with Justice presenting the Sword and the Scales to Doge Girol. Priuli.—On the right is the SALA DELLE QUATTRO PORTE by *Ant. da Ponte* (1575), after a plan of *Palladio* and *Rusconi.* On the right of the entrance, *Titian,* Doge Ant. Grimani before the Faith, probably finished by *Marco Vecellio,* Titian's nephew; *Giov. Contarini* (a pupil of Titian), Victory of the Venetians under Gattamelata at Verona (both temporarily removed for restoration); over the windows, photograph of Venice receiving the homage of Neptune by G. B. Tiepolo (comp. above). Paintings by the *Caliari* and *And. Vicentino.* The rich ceiling, by *Palladio,* has frescoes by *Tintoretto,* spoilt by restoration.—The ANTICOLLEGIO (Waiting Room), has a good ceiling by *Marco del Moro* with a ruined fresco by *Veronese,* and a fireplace by *Scamozzi;* opposite the window, *Veronese,* *Rape of

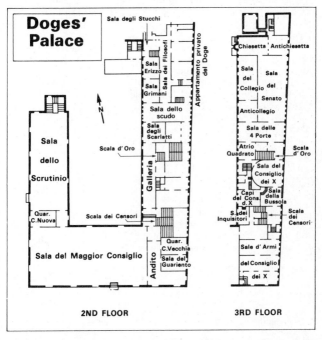

Doges' Palace

Sala degli Stucchi

Sala Erizzo
Sala dei Filosofi
Sala Grimani
Sala dello scudo
Sala degli Scarlatti

Appartamento privato del Doge

Sala dello Scrutinio

Scala d' Oro

Galleria

Sala del Maggior Consiglio

Quar. C.Nuova

Scala dei Censori

Andito

Quar. C.Vecchia
Sala del Guariento

Chiesetta Antichiesetta

Sala del Collegio
Sala del Senato

Anticollegio

Sala delle 4 Porte

Atrio Quadrato

Scala d' Oro

Sala del Consiglio dei X

Capi del Cons. d. X
Sala della Bussola

S. dei Inquisitori

Scala dei Censori

Sale d' Armi del Consiglio dei X

2ND FLOOR   **3RD FLOOR**

Europa; *Iac. Bassano,* Jacob's Return to Canaan; on the end walls (removed for restoration), *Tintoretto,* *Vulcan's Forge, Mercury and the Graces, *Bacchus and Ariadne, Minerva dismissing Mars. The SALA DEL COLLEGIO, where the doge and his councillors deliberated, is a treasure-house of art. The chimneypiece is by *Campagna.* The *Ceiling, by *Fr. Bello,* the finest in the palace, is doubly precious on account of the wonderful series of paintings by *Veronese* (c. 1577), with their superb colouring and skilful design; the most remarkable is that in the centre at the farther end: Justice and Pearce offering the Sword, the Scales, and the Olive-Branch to triumphant Venice. Over the entrance, *Tintoretto,* Doge And. Gritti before the Virgin; above the throne. *Veronese,* *Doge Seb. Venier offering thanks to Christ for the victory of Lépanto. Facing the fireplace, *Tintoretto,* Marriage of St Catherine, Doge Nic. da Ponte invoking the Virgin, Doge Alvise Mocenigo adoring Christ, three magnificent paintings.—The *SALA DEL SENATO, the seat of the doge and his senators, by *Da Ponte*, has another fine ceiling, by *Cristoforo Sorte* (1581), with Venice exalted among the Gods, by *Tintoretto*, as a centre-piece. Over the throne, *Tintoretto*, *Descent from the Cross—with Doges Pietro Lando and Marcantonio Trevisan adoring; on the left wall, *Palma Giovane*, Venice receiving the homage of subject cities presented by Doge Fr. Venier, Doge Pasquale Cicogna praying, and an Allegory of the league of Cambrai; *Tintoretto*, Doge P. Loredan praying to the Virgin; *Palma Giovane*, Doges Lor. and Girol. Priuli praying to Christ.—The door on the right of the throne admits to the ANTICHIESETTA (containing Seb. Ricci's cartoons for Dal Pozzo's 18C mosaics on the façade of St Mark's), next to which is the CHIESETTA,the doge's private chapel, with a Madonna by *Sansovino*.

From the Sala delle Quattro Porte a corridor leads into the SALA DEL CONSIGLIO DEI DIECI, the seat of the Council of Ten. The walls are adorned with historical paintings. In the right-hand farther corner of the ceiling is an *Old Man in Eastern costume with a Young Woman, by *Veronese*. In the centre of the left-hand side is: *Veronese*, Juno offering gifts to Venice, taken by Napoleon to Brussels in 1797 and returned in 1920. The originals of the central subject in this room and the next were taken to Paris in 1797.—The SALA DELLA BUSSOLA has a marble chimneypiece and, on the right of the farther door, a 'Bocca di Leone', an opening in which secret denunciations were placed.—On the right (usually closed) is the SALA DEI TRE CAPI DEL CONSIGLIO DEI DIECI,with a similar chimneypiece and two ceiling-paintings by *Veronese;* on the left is the SALETTA DEI TRE INQUISITORI, where the original ceiling-paintings by *Tintoretto* have been replaced.

From the landing outside the Sala della Bussola is the approach to the three SALE D'ARMI DEL CONSIGLIO DEI DIECI, the Council's private armoury, in which the state arms and armour were stored from the mid-16C until the fall of the Republic. These have been temporarily closed.

The anteroom, with its original gilded locks, contains a bust of Doge Seb. Venier, by *Aless. Vittoria*.—ROOM I. On the right at the end, Armour of Henri IV of France, presented by him to the Serenissima in 1603; two equestrian suits, that on the right called Gattamelata's though it is of 16C workmanship. In the centre, a richly decorated culverin (c. 1550). By the windows, page's armour found on the field of Marignano (1515). On the walls, two bronze busts of doges by *Tiziano Aspetti;* on the ceiling, Turkish standard taken at Lépanto.—ROOM II. On the right, between two 'pasha's tails', is a monument to Fr. Morosini (1687). At the other end, two early 'quick-firing' guns, one with twenty barrels, the other with a revolver mechanism.—ROOM III, named after Marcantonio Bragadin, contains parade helmets and breastplates, a bust of Bragadin by *Aspetti*, swords, pikes, etc., mainly of the 16C. On the left wall is a unique *Bascinet of the 14C, shaped like a bird's beak and made of a single piece.

The *Scala dei Censori* redescends to the Primo Piano Nobile. On the left is the ANDITO DEL MAGGIOR CONSIGLIO, with a good 16C ceiling and works by *Dom. Tintoretto*, off which are the *Sala della Quarantia Civil Vecchia* and the SALA DEL GUARIENTO, with the remains of a huge fresco of Paradise by *Guariento* (1365-67). To the r. is the *SALA DEL MAGGIOR CONSIGLIO, the seat of the governing body of the Republic, a fine hall 54m long, 25m wide, and 13½ high. One the entrance wall is *Paradise, by *Iac.* and *Dom. Tintoretto* (1587-90), the largest oil-painting in the world (7 x 22m). Beneath it was discovered in 1903 the remains of the fresco by Guariento mentioned above. On the other walls are large historical canvases, by *Tintoretto,* the *Bassani, Aliense, And. Vicentino, Palma Giovane,* and others. The frieze of 72 portraits of doges (from Obelerio Antenorio, c. 810, to Fr. Venier, d. 1556) is by *Tintoretto;* the space blacked in at the W. end takes the place of the portrait of Marin Faliero; an inscription records his execution. The *Ceiling is divided into 35 compartments of which the most noteworthy are the three central panels: *Palma Giovane,* Venice, welcoming the conquered Nations around her Throne; *Tintoretto,* Venice surrojnded by Gods gives an olive-branch to Doge Nic. da Ponte; and *Veronese,* *Venice surrounded by Gods and crowned by Victory, a masterpiece of light and colour. The balcony commands a fine view of the canal of St Mark, San Giorgio, and the lagoon.—The last door on the right admits to the *Sala della Quarantia Civil Nuova* and the SALA DELLO SCRUTINIO, where the votes of the Great Council for the new doge were recorded. The wall-paintings by *Vicentino, Marco Vecellio, Aliense, Tintoretto,* and others, record the victories of Venice. At the farther end is a triumphal arch in honour of Fr. Morosini; the frieze continues the series of portraits of the doges down to the last one, Lod. Manin. The rich ceiling has paintings by *Aliense, Fr. Bassano,* etc., descriptive of Venetian history. From the balcony there is a view of the Piazzetta.

A small door to the left of the throne in the Sala del Maggior Consiglio leads to the Bridge of Sighs and to the rooms which replace the prisons or *Piombi,* so called from their position beneath the leaden roof. Their miseries are described by Casanova, who escaped from them in 1775. Here also is the entrance to the *Pozzi,* eighteen dark dungeons in the two lowest storeys, reserved for the most dangerous criminals. The lowest of them, however, were not below the street level, and they were less terrible than the usual medieval prison.—The exit is through the *Sala dei Censori* and the *Sala dei Notai,* with works by Dom. Tintoretto, Leandro Bassano, and others.

The MOLO, or Quay, beneath the S. front of the palace, is the principal station for gondolas. At its E. end is the *Ponte della Paglia* which crosses the Rio di Palazzo. From this bridge may be seen the Renaissance E. front of the palace, and the famous **Bridge of Sighs** or *Ponte dei Sospiri,* a flying bridge in Istrian stone by Ant. Contino (c. 1600), named from the fact that it was used for the passage of prisoners from the Prigioni to be examined by the Inquisitors of State. The Prisons themselves are a severe construction begun by G. A. Rusconi (1560), continued by Ant. da Ponte (1589), and completed by Ant. and Tomasco Contino (1614).

The **Riva degli Schiavoni** (Pl. 12), beyond the Ponte della Paglia, now the favourite promenade of both Venetians and visitors, and the starting-point of many motor-launches and water-buses, was formerly the mooring-station for the trading vessels from Dalmatian and other Slavonic ports. Beyond the prison the Calle degli Albanesi leads to the *Aquarium* (open 9-19 exc., Tues; fest 9-20). Next is the Gothic façade (and disappointing modern extension) of the *Palazzo Dandolo,* the site of the Hotel Danieli since 1822. It numbers among its distinguished visitors George Sand, Alfred de Musset, Charles Dickens, Ruskin, Wagner, and Proust. Across the Ponte del Vin towers the Victor Emmanuel Monument by Ettore Ferrari (1887). At a house on the quay here (No. 4161) Henry James finished 'The Portrait of a Lady' in 1881.

The Sottoportico San Zaccaria leads inland to the pretty piazza and church of **San Zaccaria,** typical in showing a mixture of Gothic and Renaissance styles (1444-1515). It was begun by *Ant. Gambello,* and was completed after the

Renaissance by *Mauro Coducci*. Over the doorway is a statue of the patron saint by *Vittoria* (in poor condition). The campanile is in the 13C Byzantine style. The elegant interior has an aisled nave and a Gothic apse with a coronet of chapels. The aisle walls are entirely covered with 17-18C paintings. A door at the end of the S. aisle admits to the CHAPEL OF ST ATHANASIUS with stalls by *Fr. and M. Cozzi*. Over the altar, Birth of St John the Baptist, an early work by *Tintoretto;* (r. of altar), *Gian Dom. Tiepolo*, Flight into Egypt; (over door into the church), Crucifix, attrib. to *Van Dyck;* (r. wall), *Palma Vecchio* (attrib.), Madonna and Saints. The adjoining CHAPEL OF ST TARASIUS has three fine *Anconas, or altar-paintings, by *Ant. Vivarini* and *Giov. d'Alemagna* (1443), with ornate Gothic frames. In the fan vault are *Frescoes by *And. del Castagno* and *Fr. da Faenza* (1442; damaged); beneath are remains of a mosaic pavement (Romanesque-Byzantine, 12C). Steps lead down to the water-logged CRYPT (9C).—At the end of the N. aisle is the tomb of *Aless. Vittoria* (1528-1608), with a bust of the artist by himself (1595). Over the 2nd altar on this side is a *Madonna with four saints, by *Giov. Bellini* (1505).

Beyond the next bridge is *La Pietà* (temporarily closed for restoration), the church of an orphanage for girls, which achieved European fame for its music in the 17-18C. Vivaldi was violin-master in 1704-18 and concert-master in 1735-38. The church was sumptuously rebuilt in the present oval plan by Massari (1745-60) with galleries for choir and musicians, and a ceiling decorated by G. B. Tiepolo (1755). Across the next bridge Calle del Dose leads to the Campo Bandiera e Moro and the church of **San Giovanni in Brágora** (Pl. 12), rebuilt 1475. The interior contains: (N. aisle) Baptismal font (16C) where Vivaldi was baptised in 1678; *Alvise Vivarini*, Madonna and Child. In chap. at the end of this aisle, (r.) Triptych of the Madonna enthroned between SS. John the Baptist and Andrew, by *Bart. Vivarini*, and (l.) Triptych by *Fr. Bissola*. In the Sanctuary: over the altar, *Cima da Conegliano*, *Baptism of Jesus (1494); r. wall, *Paris Bordone*, Last Supper. At the end of S. aisle: *Alvise Vivarini*, The Risen Christ (1498); (over the sacristy door), 13C relief of the Madonna (Veneto-Byzantine); *Cima da Conegliano*, St Helena and Constantine (1502).—The Salizzada Sant'Antonino and the Fond. dei Furlani (r.) leads to the **Scuola di San Giorgio degli Schiavoni** (Pl. 12; open 9.30-12.30, 15.30-18.30; fest. 9.30-12.30; Mon closed), formerly the meeting-place of the Dalmatian Brotherhood with a façade by *Giov. De Zan* (1551). Inside the little room is entirely decorated with a delightful series of *Paintings by *Carpaccio* (1501-11) relating to the lives of SS. Jerome, Tryphon, and George, including an interior scene with St Augustine in his study having a vision of St Jerome's death, and St George slaying the dragon, justly one of his best known paintings.—The room upstairs has 17C decorations.

The orthodox Greek church of *San Giorgio dei Greci* (1539-61), to the S.W., has a leaning campanile (1587-92) and an iconostasis with late Byzantine figures, on a gold ground. Adjacent is a *Museum of Icons* (open 9.30-12.30, 15.30-18) with a fine collection (mostly 16-17C).

Beyond the Ponte Ca' di Dio the quay has been widened and extended. The next bridge crosses the Rio dell'Arsenale.

According to tradition, the great **Arsenal** was founded in 1104; it was enlarged from the 14-16C, and now occupies 32 hectares (80 acres). It gave its name (from the Arabic, 'darsina'a', meaning 'workshop') to all subsequent dockyards. At the height of Venetian prosperity it employed 16,000 workmen (comp. Dante's 'Inferno', xxi). It is surrounded by crenellated walls with towers, and the interior is best seen from motor-launch No. 5 which runs through the main canal (closed to private vessels) on its circular route of the city (comp. p. 279). The great Renaissance GATEWAY, to the left of the two entrance towers can be seen from the Fondamenta dell'Arsenale which can be followed a short way N. Recently restored, it was built in 1460 by Gambello, with 11C capitals and 16-17C additions; the statue of St Justina above is by Girol. Campagna. It is flanked by two colossal lions sent by Fr. Morosini from Piraeus as spoils of war and placed here in 1692. The larger one (which gave the name of Porta Leone to Piraeus) bears a Runic inscription carved in 1040 by Varangian guards from Byzantium sent to Athens to put down an insurrection; its fellow possibly stood on the road from Athens to Eleusis. The two smaller lions (r.), added in 1718 after the relief of Corfu, may have come originally from the Lion Terrace at Delos.

On the quay S. of the arsenal is the naval church of *San Biagio* (18C). Adjacent is the former Granary of the Republic which now houses the MUSEO STORICO NAVALE (adm. 9.30-12.30 & 14.30-16.30; Sun 9-12; closed Tues), containing arms and naval relics and a series of *Models, including one of the last 'Bucentaur' (1728), the gala ship used for the marriage of Venice with the sea. Across the next bridge the long broad Via Garibaldi leads E. through a popular quarter of the town past the Giardini Garibaldi and a street market to (15 min.) the Rio di Sant'Anna. A wooden bridge crosses the wide Canale di San Pietro with its busy boat yards to the *Isola di San Pietro* and **San Pietro di Castello** (closed 12-15 or 16.30), the cathedral of Venice from the 11C until 1807. The present Palladian church (after a design of 1557) contains, on the right, a marble throne from Antioch, with Cufic inscriptions, and a sumptuous high altar designed by *Longhena*. The Baroque Cappella Vendramin, in the N. transept, also designed by *Longhena*, has an altarpiece by *Luca Giordano*. The isolated campanile, by *Mauro Coducci*, dates from 1482-88, with a cupola of 1670. Across the canal can be seen the crenellated outer wall of the Arsenal.

The pleasant **Public Garden,** to the S. of Via Garibaldi, laid out in 1807, contains several monuments, and the pavilions of the *International Exhibition of Modern Art* (known as the 'BIENNALE' because it is held every second year; comp. p. 282). On its N. side is the graceful Renaissance church of *San Giuseppe di Castello*, with a good perspective ceiling and a painting of St Michael and a senator, by Tintoretto (1st S. altar). The sumptuous monument of Doge Marino Grimani (d. 1605) is by Scamozzi and Campagna.—Farther out is the island of *Sant'Elena*, with a modern quarter and the church of **Sant'Elena** (early 13C, rebuilt 1435), which was abandoned in 1807 but reopened in 1928. Over the principal door is a sculptured *Group by Ant. Rizzo (c. 1467), representing Adm. Vitt. Cappello kneeling before St Helena.

II   NORTH-WESTERN QUARTERS

The narrow, winding **Merceria** (Pl. 11) runs from the Torre dell'Orologio to the Rialto; it is the liveliest street in Venice and contains many well-stocked shops.

It diverges right for San Giuliano (San Zuliàn; Pl. 11), a church rebuilt in 1553 by *Sansovino* and *Vittoria*. The former was the sculptor also of the seated *Statue over the door which represents Tommaso Rangone, the scholar, founder of the church. The interior has a 16C ceiling with a painting of St Julian in glory by *Palma Giovane* and assistants. Over the 1st S. altar (above three Saints), Pietà, by *Paolo Veronese;* in chap. l. of high altar, Pietà, marble relief by *Girol. Campagna*. The 1st N. altarpiece (Madonna enthroned with Saints) is by *Boccaccio Boccaccino*.

Farther on in the Merceria is the church of **San Salvatore** (Pl. 7), the rebuilding of which, begun by *Giorgio Spavento* (1506), was continued by *Tullio Lombardo* after 1520 and finished by *Sansovino* in 1534; the Baroque façade, to a design of *Gius. Sardi,* was added in 1663.

Within, the plan of the dome and vaults is one of the best examples in Venice of the way in which problems of light and construction were solved at the height of the Renaissance. In the SOUTH AISLE, between the first two altars, Monument to And. Dolfin by *Giulio Del Moro* (1602); between the next two, Monument to Doge Fr. Venier (d. 1556) with statues of Charity and *Hope, sculpted by *Sansovino* when nearly 80 years old; over the 3rd altar (by *Sansovino*) is *Titian's* splendid *Annunciation, painted in 1566 (light; fee). In the SOUTH TRANSEPT, Tomb of Catherine Cornaro (Cornér), queen of Cyprus (d. 1510), by *Bern. Contino,* with good reliefs. Over the high altar a Transfiguration by *Titian* (c. 1560) screens a silver reredos, a chef d'oeuvre of Venetian goldsmith's work (14C). Titian's painting is lowered mechanically on request by the sacristan to reveal the altarpiece; the original silver gilt panels folded up for easy transportation (the upper and lower rows of sculpture are later additions). In the chapel to the N., Supper at Emmaus, by the school of Giov. Bellini (light in Sanctuary; fee).

The column outside the church commemorates Manin's defence of Venice in 1848-49. On the right is the CAMPO SAN BARTOLOMEO (Pl. 7), the most crowded centre of Venetian life, with a spirited statue, by Ant. dal Zotto (1883), of Goldoni, the dramatist of Venetian life. In the church of *San Bartolomeo* (rebuilt 1723; open 7.30-8.45) are paintings of four saints by Seb. del Piombo (1505).

To the right, reached by Calle della Bissa and Calle al Ponte Sant'Antonio is the church of **San Lio** (Pl. 7) dedicated to Pope Leo X. It contains a much darkened painting of St James, by *Titian* (1st l. altar), and the Gussoni Chapel (r. of high altar) by *P. and T. Lombardo,* with a fine Pietà.

On the left is the approach to the Rialto (see Section V) and farther on are the Fondaco dei Tedeschi, now the *Post Office,* and **San Giovanni Crisostomo** (Pl. 7), a Lombardesque church built by *Mauro Coducci* (1497-1504) in the form of a Greek cross.

The simple interior contains (N. transept) the Coronation of the Virgin, a bas-relief by *Tullio Lombardo.* The paintings have been removed for restoration: *SS. Christopher, Jerome, and Augustine, a good late work by *Giov. Bellini* (1513), and seven *Saints, the masterpiece of *Seb. del Piombo* (c. 1509).—On the right of the church is the *Corte Seconda del Milion,* with a Romanesque arch near the house of Marco Polo (No. 5858).

The Ponte San Giovanni Crisostomo and the Calle Dolfin continue to the church of the **Santi Apostoli** (Pl. 7), much rebuilt, which has a tall campanile of 1672.

The *Cappella Cornér* (2nd on the S. side) is a Lombardesque work (late 15C), attributed to Mauro Coducci. Over the altar is the Communion of St Lucy, by *G. B. Tiepolo* (c. 1748), and to the right and left are the tombs of Marco Cornér (attributed to *Tullio Lombardo*) and Giorgio Cornér (school of the Lombardi).

To the N. of the Apostoli, reached by Salizzada del Pistor, the Rioterrà dei Franceschi and Santi Apostoli, the Salizzada del Speziér, and the Salizzada Borgato and Seriman (No. 4851 is the fine Palazzo Contarini-Seriman, c. 1450), is the church of the *Gesuiti (Pl. 3; open 10-12, 17-19.30), rebuilt in 1715-30 by *Dom. Rossi,* with a Baroque façade by *Fattoretto.*

The imposing interior is ornamented with marble intarsia in imitation of frescoes and hangings. On the left is the *Martyrdom of St Laurence, by *Titian* (light on r.), a remarkable night scene; in the chapel N. of the over-decorated high altar is the monument to Doge Pasquale Cicogna, with a fine effigy by *Girol. Campagna.* In the Sacristy are paintings by *Palma Giovane.*

From the Campo dei Gesuiti, Fondamenta Zen leads r. to the disused church of Santa Caterina. From here Calle della Racchetta, and its continuation, Calle Doge Priuli return to the broad Strada Nuova (1872); opposite a few steps to the left is the Calle della Ca' d'Oro. The

*Ca d'Oro (Pl. 7), the most beautiful Gothic building in Venice, built in 1422-40 by *Matteo Raverti* and others for Marino Contarini, was presented to the State by Baron Giorgio Franchetti in 1915 along with his collections of paintings, antiquities, etc., which constitute the *Galleria Franchetti*. This is, at present, closed for restoration. When the gallery reopens the arrangement may have changed from the description given below. The name 'House of Gold' was derived from the rich painting and gilding which once adorned the façade overlooking the Grand Canal.

A small door beside the main gateway gives access to the charming little ENTRANCE COURT, beyond which is the MAIN COURTYARD, containing a fine *Well-head, by *Bart. Bon* (1427), adorned with figures of Charity, Justice, and Fortitude. Adjoining is the PORTICO, through which the house was approached from the canal, now containing examples of antique sculpture.

The FIRST FLOOR consists of an anteroom with an alcove, and a portico, extending towards the canal, with rooms on either side. ANTEROOM: Mantle said to have belonged to the Emperor Charles IV; in ROOM VI, the alcove on the right, with a rich ceiling, is *St Sebastian, by *Mantegna*, one of the last works of the painter (1506). The PORTICO, containing busts by *Aless. Vittoria*, ends in a loggia commanding a fine view of the Grand Canal.—ROOM I: *Carpaccio*, Death of the Virgin, Annunciation: bronze bust, called Bern. Scardeone (16C Paduan school); *And. Briosco*, Four reliefs of the Life of Santa Croce; *Ant. Vivarini*, Passion scenes (polyptych); *Lor. Veneziano*, Madonna enthroned, with saints, a polyptych in its original frame recovered from Austria in 1919, like the two paintings by Carpaccio mentioned above; small private altarpiece (16C Venetian) incorporating an Annunciation of German workmanship c. 100 years older. In the centre, bronze calf (16C Paduan school).—ROOM II contains a carved staircase, with remains of paintings, from a 15C Venetian house; also, *Paris Bordone*, Sleeping Venus.—ROOM III (nearest the canal on the other side of the portico): sculptures by *Tullio Lombardo* and *Vittoria*.—R. IV.: *Titian*, Venus; *Girol. Marchesi*, Madonna with angel musicians; *Iac. del Sellaio*, Madonna.—R. V: *Giov. Agost. da Lodi*, Pietà; *Giov. Bellini*(?) Madonna.

SECOND FLOOR. The ANTEROOM is decorated with a frescoed frieze of Bacchic scenes, in imitation of mosaic, by *M. Fogolino;* on the right, *Buonconsiglio*, The Lion of St Mark, with four saints. In the alcove (R. VII), *Van Dyck*, *Portrait of a nobleman of the Brignole family of Genoa; *Vittoria*, Bust of Marino Grimani (terracotta).—R. VIII (on the r. of the portico): *Palma Vecchio*, Madonna and two saints; *Palma Giovane*, Crucifixion, with St Mary Magdalene; 18C portraits, after Aless. Longhi.—R. IX has a fine ceiling from Verona; *Pontormo*, Girl carrying a lap-dog; *Bugiardini*, Sleeping Venus with a faun; *Filippino Lippi*, Nativity with angels.—R. X: *Signorelli*, Scourging of Christ; *Palmezzano*, Pieta (signed and dated 1529).—R. XI (opposite): *Bened. Rusconi*, Madonna enthroned, with saints, and two donors (Masters of the Mint; 1486); *Tintoretto*, Portrait of Niccolò Priuli; Assumption, and other Lombardesque reliefs; *Agnolo Gaddi*, Six apostles; *Dom. Tintoretto* Portrait of Paolo Paruta, the historian (d. 1598); also, the

Blind Beggar, a fine Chinese bronze, and, in the centre, a collection of Italian medals.

In the neighbouring *Palazzo Giusti* (1776), an annexe of the Ca' d'Oro, is a collection of Italian bronzes and pictures of the Flemish and Dutch schools (formerly in the Museo Archeologio and in the Accademia).

The Strada Nuova leads left to *San Felice* (Pl. 2), a church attributed to Sante Lombardo (1551-56). Farther on, beyond the splendid 15C façade (on the canal) of the *Palazzo Giovanelli,* is the Campo Santa Fosca, with a statue of Fra' Paolo Sarpi by Emilio Marsili (1892), overlooked by the equally splendid 15C façade of the *Palazzo Correr.*

To the right is Ponte Santa Fosca; on the right (No. 2400) is the noble Renaissance façade of *Palazzo Vendramin;* on the left, beyond the 17C Palazzo Diedo (attrib. to And. Tirali), across another canal, are the remains of the convent and church of *Santa Maria dei Servi,* destroyed in 1812. A pretty courtyard and Gothic doorway survive. The Calle Zancana, straight ahead, leads to the church of SAN MARCILIANO(Pl. 2), properly *San Marziale.* It contains St Martial and two saints, by *Tintoretto* (S. side; over-restored) and (sacristy) Tobias and the Archangel, a damaged work by *Titian* (c. 1540). The Fondamenta della Misericordia leads right past Palazzo Lezze (by Longhena, 1654) and then left, skirting the huge Scuola Nuova begun c. 1534 by Sansovino, to the *Scuola Vecchia* and *Abbazia della Misericordia* (Pl. 3), in a lonely corner of the town. The lunette from the Scuola Vecchia is in the Victoria and Albert Museum, London. The buildings are to be used as a restoration centre for works of art. The Sottoportico dell'Abbazia leads along Rio della Sensa, across a wooden bridge above an old boat yard, to Fondamento dei Mori. A tablet on No. 3399 marks the residence of Tintoretto from 1574 to his death in 1594. A quaint statue is affixed to its façade similar to the three 14C statues of Moors in the neighbouring Campo dei Mori. These are popularly supposed to be the Levantine merchants of the Mastelli family whose palazzo stands at the corner. At the upper end of the Campo a bridge crosses a canal (where funeral barges are usually moored) to reach the ***Madonna dell'Orto** (Pl. 2), formerly San Cristoforo, a church of Romanesque design with Gothic detail, recently restored.

The portal of 1460 shows the transition to Renaissance; the 15C Renaissance campanile is well preserved. The basilican Interior has fine Greek marble columns. It contains in the S. aisle, by the 1st altar, *Cima's* masterpiece of *St John the Baptist and four other saints (c. 1493). The *Contarini Chapel* (4th on the N. side) contains family busts (two by Vittoria), and, over the altar, St Agnes raising Licinius, a notable work by *Tintoretto;* on the S. wall is his *Presentation of the Virgin; in the 1st N. chapel, Madonna, by *Giov. Bellini* (c. 1478; temporarily removed for restoration). Two huge pictures, also by *Tintoretto,* adorn the choir, and in the chapel on the right a modest slab marks the painter's resting-place.

The Calle del Capitello, another turning on the right from the Fondamenta dei Mori (see above), leads to the late 14C church of **Sant' Alvise** (*San Luigi;* N. of Pl. 2). The paintings have all been removed while the church awaits restoration. They include a Crown of Thorns and Scourging (S. wall of nave), and, in the choir, a *Calvary (1743), all by *Tiepolo,* and eight little 15C tempera paintings (beneath the nuns' choir).

The area to the S.W. lies within the GHETTO, with its lofty houses and synagogues. Beyond it is the broad CANNAREGIO canal and the Lombardesque church of **San Giobbe** (Pl. 1; if closed ring at No. 620), built after 1450 by

Gambello and enlarged by P. Lombardo, with a fine doorway and a graceful campanile. On the right of the nave is a monument by *Claude Perrault* (1651) and, at the 4th altar, Three Saints, by *Paris Bordone*. In the Ante-Sacristy (r.), is a fragment of a late 14C oratory; the Sacristy has a 16C wooden ceiling, and (l. of the door into the Ante-Sacristy) a small painting in a fine frame of the Marriage of St Catherine by *And. Previtali*. At the end of the sacristy is the Cappella Da Mula with an Annunciation between SS. Michael and Anthony, a triptych by *Ant. Vivarini* and *Giov. d'Alemagna* (1440-50). The *CHOIR is a fine example of Lombardesque work, as is likewise the tomb slab of Doge Crist. Moro (d. 1471) and his wife Cristina Sanudo, in the pavement. The 2nd chapel on the N. side is the work of 15C Tuscans; in the vault are five large Della Robbia medallions. On the altar are statuettes of St John the Baptist, by *Rossellino*, and other saints, by his pupils. The statue of St Luke, in the 1st N. chapel, is by *Lor. Bregno*.

In the other direction the Cannaregio leads towards the Grand Canal, and is crossed near its mouth by the busy Ponte delle Guglie. Across the bridge (r.) is the church of **San Geremia** (Pl. 1), a clumsy building by *C. Corbellini* (1753-60). The interior is more successful and the fine campanile is among the oldest in Venice.

The relics of St Lucy (martyred in Syracuse in 304) were stolen from Constantinople in 1204 by Venetian crusaders; they were placed in this church when in 1863 Santa Lucia was demolished to make way for the railway station. A painting of her by *Palma Giovane* is preserved with a few relics and church vestments in a room to the r. of her chapel (unlocked on request). The painting of St Magnus crowning Venice (2nd S. altar) is by the same artist.—The *Palazzo Labia* in the square, begun by Andrea Cominelli (c. 1720) has frescoes by G. B. Tiepolo (shown on request; 9-12, 15-17).

The garish Lista di Spagna (given over to the tourist trade) leads to the church of the **Scalzi** (Pl. 1), formerly belonging to the Carmelites, a typical Baroque building by *Longhena* (1670-80) with a façade by Gius. Sardi.

The dark interior is profusely decorated with marbles and sculptures in the Baroque manner. The fanciful ceiling-fresco by *Tiepolo* was destroyed by a bomb in 1915 and is replaced by a modern painting (Council of Ephesus) by *E'¹ ·re Tito.* The 2nd S. chapel contains Tiepolo's frescoes of the Life of St Teresa (1725; in poor condition); on the altar is the Saint transfixed by the Angel, by *Baldi,* a follower of Bernini. The ceiling of the 1st N. chapel also has damaged frescoes by *Tiepolo.*

From San Geremia, across the Cannaregio, Rioterrà San Leonardo (with its market) and Rioterrà del Cristo (r.) lead to the church of **San Marcuola** (Pl. 2; *Santi Ermágora e Fortunato*), by *Giorgio Massari* (1728-36), with an unfinished façade towards the Grand Canal.

It contains paintings ascribed to Titian. The young Christ blessing, with SS. Catherine and Andrew (to the left, above the entrance); by *Tintoretto,* Last Supper (l. of the high altar); and several by *Fr. Migliori,* a little-known 18C Venetian.

III NORTH-EASTERN QUARTERS

Across Ponte San Giovanni Crisostomo (p. 300) the Salita San Canciano leads viâ the church of the same name to (r.) ***Santa Maria dei Miracoli** (Pl. 7), a beautiful and typical building by *Pietro Lombardo* (1481-89; recently restored).

In the lunette over the door in the admirably proportioned façade is a Madonna by *Giorgio Lascaris* (16C). The exterior has beautiful details. The nave vault is adorned with 50 panels bearing Heads of Prophets and Saints by *Pier Maria Pennacchi* (1528). On the raised choir and domed apse were lavished the full powers of *Pietro* and *Tullio Lombardo;* note especially the beautiful reliefs and, on the high altar, the charming Madonna by *Nic. di Pietro Paradisi* (1409).

From the Campo, Calle Castelli leads E. across Rio della Panada into Calle delle Erbe. Beyond Rio dei Mendicanti is the CAMPO SAN ZANI-PÓLO. Here on its fine pedestal, rises the equestrian *Statue of Bartolomeo Colleoni, the famous condottiere (c. 1400-75). This splendid monument, a masterpiece of grandeur and strong simplicity, was begun by *Verrocchio* in 1481, and finished, with the pedestal, by *Leopardi* (1489-96). During the First World War it accompanied the Horses of St Mark to Rome.

The church of *Santi Giovanni e Paolo (*San Zanipólo;* Pl. 8), the 'Pantheon of the Doges', disputes with the Frari the first place among the Gothic brick churches of Venice. It was begun by the Dominicans in 1246, though not consecrated until 1430, and was restored in 1921-26. The fine façade, with a doorway after *Ant. Gambello,* was never finished; against it are the tombs of three doges including the donor of the site.

The INTERIOR (96 m long; 43 m across the transepts), has lofty aisles separated by ten columns from the nave, and is notable for the slenderness of its arches and its luminous choir. Around the doorway is the colossal tomb of Doge Alvise Mocenigo (d. 1577) and his wife; to the left and right are the monuments to *Doges Pietro Mocenigo (d. 1476) by *P. Lombardo,* and Giovanni Mocenigo (d. 1485) by *T. Lombardo.*—In the SOUTH AISLE: tomb of Doge Raniero Zen (d. 1268); *Fr. Bissolo,* Madonna and eight saints; monument to Marcantonio Bragadin, the defender of Famagusta (1571), flayed alive by the Turks; *Giov. Bellini,* *Polyptych of the Life of St Vincent Ferrer, with a Pietà above (an early work). Beyond the huge monument (1708) to two Valier doges is the chapel of St Dominic with bronze reliefs by *Gius. Mazza* (1715-20), and a ceiling, the Saint in Glory, by *Piazzetta* (1727).—SOUTH TRANSEPT. The tomb. of Nic. Orsini (d. 1509), Prince of Nola, defender of Padua in 1508, has an ugly equestrian statue of gilded wood; at the 1st altar, *Lor. Lotto,* St Antonine (1542); above the next door, tomb of the condottiere Brisighella (d. 1510), by *Lor. Bregno.* The stained glass in the great window is from cartoons by *Bart. Vivarini, Cima,* and *Girol. Mocetto* (1473); 2nd altar, *Rocco Marconi,* *Christ and two saints.

NORTH AISLE: 1st chap., *Vittoria,* St Jerome, altar by *Gugl. Bergamasco;* then, poor monument to the Bandiera brothers, shot at Cosenza in 1844, and tomb of Gen. Baglioni (d. 1617); 2nd chap., Old copy of Titian's St Peter Martyr (see below); next come the tombs of *Doge Nic. Marcello (d. 1474), by *P. Lombardo,* *Doge Tom. Mocenigo (d. 1423), in a transitional style, by *Pietro di Nic. Lamberti* and *Giov. di Martino,* and several other tombs, including those of Alvise Trevisan, the scholar (d. 1528) and Doge Pasquale Malipiero (d. 1462), by *P. Lombardo.* Over the sacristy door are busts of Titian and the elder and younger Palma, and to the right of it Three Saints, from a polyptych by *Bart. Vivarini.*—NORTH TRANSEPT: Tomb of Leon. Prato (d. 1511), with a wooden equestrian statue; tomb of Agnese and Orsola Venier (d. 1411), a sumptuous Gothic work after the *Dalle Masegne,* commemorating the wife and daughter of Doge Ant. Venier (d. 1400), whose tomb, in a similar style, is above the adjoining door of the Chapel of the Rosary. On the wall adjoining is a monument to Doge Seb. Venier (d. 1578), who commanded the Venetian fleet at Lépanto, by *Ant. Dal Zotto* (1907).

The CHAPEL OF THE ROSARY (light; tee), erected in memory of the battle of Lépanto at the end of the 16C from the designs of Vittoria, was gutted in 1867 by a fire, in which perished Titian's St Peter Martyr and a Madonna and saints by Giov. Bellini, which had been placed there temporarily. It has undergone restoration since 1913 and has four ceiling-paintings by *Veronese*, and statues by *Vittoria* and *Campagna*.

CHOIR. On the right are the Gothic *Tomb of Doge Mich. Morosini (d. 1382), highly approved by Ruskin, and the Renissance tomb of Doge Leon. Loredan (d. 1521; wrongly dated), by *Grapiglia* (1572), with an effigy by *Campagna* and allegorical figures by *Danese Cattaneo*. On the left are the *Tomb of Doge Ant. Vendramin (d. 1478), a masterpiece of ornament by *Tullio Lombardo,* and the Gothic tomb of Doge Marco Corner (d. 1368), by *Nino Pisano*. In the outer chapel on the right, tomb of Sir Edward Windsor (d. 1574), ascribed to *Vittoria;* in the inner, altar-statue of St Mary Magdalen by *Bart. Bon the younger* (1524); in the outer chapel on the left, tombs of Iac. Cavalli (d. 1384) by *Paolo Dalle Masegne,* and of Doge Giov. Dolfin (d. 1361).

On the N. side of the campo is the **Scuola Grande di San Marco** (Pl. 7), one of the six great philanthropic confraternities of the Republic. The sumptuous façade by *P. Lombardo* and *Giov. Buora* (1487-90?), was finished by *Mauro Coducci* (1495). It is an original work of great charm with curious trompe l'oeil sculptures, by *Tullio Lombardo,* except for St Mark with the Brethren of the Scuola, ascribed to *Bart. Bon,* in the lunette of the doorway. The interior is now occupied by a hospital that extends to the lagoon, incorporating as its chapel *San Lazzaro dei Mendicanti* (1601-31), by Vinc. Scamozzi. Within (adm. on request 9-12), the hospital library has a fine coffered ceiling by Pietro and Biagio da Faenza, and the church a good early work (St Ursula) by Tintoretto. The Fondamentę Nuove, beyond, look out over the lagoon towards the cemetery island of San Michele and Murano.

Beyond the fine S. wall of San Zanipólo and a pretty well-head is the Baroque church of the *Ospedaletto,* by Longhena (1674). The Barbaria delle Tole continues E. towards the Rio di Santa Giustina. Beyond the church (now a school) a Calle left and then r. leads into the Campo of **San Francesco della Vigna** (Pl. 8; open 6-11, 16-19) a church designed by *Sansovino* (1534), with a façade by *Palladio* (1568-72) and two bronze statues by *Tiziano Aspetti*.

In the S. transept is the Virgin adoring the Infant Jesus, a sweet and harmonious composition by *Ant. da Negroponte* (c. 1450; removed for restoration). In the choir are the tomb of Doge Ant. Gritti (d. 1538) and, in the pavement, the fine tombstones of And. Bragadin (d. 1487) and Marcantonio Trevisan (d. 1554). The Giustinian Chapel on the left is beautifully adorned with sculptures by *P. Lombardo* and his school. From the N. transept is the entrance to the Cappella Santa, where a Madonna and saints by *Giov. Bellini* (1507) has still not been returned after restoration. From outside the chapel can be seen the 15C cloister. In the 3rd and 2nd chap. of the N. aisle: Chiaroscuri by *Tiepolo,* elaborate 18C sculptural friezes by *Temanza,* and three statues of saints by *Vittoria*. On the W. wall of the church, a Byzantine (13C) relief of the Madonna and Child, and a Triptych attrib. to *Ant. Vivarini* (removed for restoration).

The street nearly opposite the Ospedaletto (see above) leads towards the church of **Santa Maria Formosa** (Pl. 7), rebuilt by *Mauro Coducci* in 1492, and restored since 1916.

The campanile is in the Baroque style. Of the two façades, that towards the campo is of 1604; the other (1542) overlooks the canal. In the S. transept is a composite *Altarpiece by *Palma Vecchio* (c. 1520), notable especially for the majestic figure of St Barbara in the centre, typical of the Giorgionesque style of Venetian beauty; over the 2nd altar, on the S. side of the nave, is a triptych by *Bart. Vivarini* (1473).

To the N.W., near the junction of two canals, is the Calle del Paradiso, where the *Porta del Paradiso* bears a 14C relief of a Madonna with donors of the Fóscari and Mocenigo families and coats-of-arms. In the other direction the Ruga Giuffa leads out of the Campo S. M. Formosa; immediately on the left is the *Palazzo Grimani*, in the style of Sammicheli.

On the S. side of Santa Maria Formosa is the Campiello Querini from which a bridge crosses a small canal to the 16C **Palazzo Querini-Stampalia** (Pl. 7), the residence of the Patriarchs of Venice in 1807-50, now occupied by the Fondazione Querini-Stampalia, the bequest to the city of Count Giov. Querini (1869).

On the first floor is the LIBRARY open 14.30-20, 21-23.30; Sun 15-19), with over 230,000 vols. and 1100 MSS. The second floor is occupied by the **Picture Gallery** (adm. 10-12). On the left of the entrance-hall, with its busts and tapestries, ROOM I contains views of Venetian life in the 18C by *Gabriele Bella*, notably a painting of a game of tennis closely resembling modern lawn-tennis.—R. 2. *Catarino Veneziano* and *Donato Veneziano, Coronation of the Virgin* (1372); 15C *Venetian School*, Crucifixion.—R. 4 contains paintings by *Palma Giovane*.—R. 8. *Lorenzo di Credi, Adoration of the Virgin; Giov. Bellini, *Presentation in the Temple (a copy of a painting by Mantegna now in Berlin; photograph displayed), *Palma Vecchio, *Francesco Querini and *Paola Priuli Querini, two unfinished portraits (1528).—R. 9. *Fr. Rizzo, Adoration of the Magi; Paris Bordone, Holy Family; Palma Vecchio, Madonna and saints*; on an easel, *Vincenzo Catena*, *Judith.—RR. II-13. Paintings by *Pietro* and *Aless. Longhi*.—R. 15. Bedroom, with tapestries of 16C Flemish workmanship.—RR. 16, 17. Red and Green Drawing-rooms; *Tiepolo*, Procurator Giovanni Querini; lustres and mirrors.—R. 20. Dining room with Sèvres dinner service.

IV   THE GRAND CANAL

The *Grand Canal (*Canal Grande* or *Canalazzo*), 2½ m. long (including the Canale di Santa Chiara), 30-70 m wide, and with an average depth of 5 m, is the high road of Venice. In its course through the city, winding like an inverted S, it passes more than 100 marble palaces, Gothic or Lombardesque in style, and mostly dating from the 14-18C, though a few date back to the 12C. The wonderful views afforded by every turn of this splendid waterway are unequalled in the world. The posts or 'pali' in front of the palaces show the colours of the livery or 'divisa' of their proprietors.

The gondola is the ideal vessel from which to see the Grand Canal in all its glory; otherwise the slow vaporetto No. 1 ('accelerato'). In the itinerary which follows the most interesting buildings are marked R. or L., according as they appear on the right or left bank after starting from the Riva degli Schiavoni.

The stations (*pontili*) of the Vaporetti are: San Zaccaria (R.), San Marco (R.), Santa Maria della Salute (L.), Santa Maria del Giglio (R.), Accademia (L.), Ca' Rezzonico (L.), San Tomà (L.), Sant'Angelo (R.), San Silvestro (L.), Rialto (R.), Ca' d'Oro (R.), San Stae (L.), San Marcuola (R.), Riva di Biasio (L.), Ferrovia (R.; railway station), Piazzale Roma (L.; car park).

From the Riva degli Schiavoni the boats steer out into the Canale di San Marco passing the Palazzo Ducale, the Piazzetta, the Zecca, and the Giardinetti. Beyond the Rio del Palazzo Reale is the Lombardesque *Capitaneria di Porto*. The 15C Gothic *Palazzo Giustinian* (R.) houses the municipal tourist office.—On the Punta della Salute (L.) is the *Dogana di Mare*, a Doric construction by Gius. Benoni (1676-82), with a picturesque turret, and two telamones who support a gold globe on which is balanced a weathervane of Fortune; adjoining it is the Seminario Patriarcale.

The *Pal. Treves de' Bonfili* (R.), attributed to Monopola, contains statues of Hector and Ajax by Canova; the *Pal. Tiepolo* (now Hotel Europa) (R.) is a 17C building.—The charming little *Pal. Contarini-Fasan* (R.; 15C Gothic) has been fancifully called the 'House of Desdemona'.—Opposite is the church of *Santa Maria della Salute* (L.; Pl. 15), whose dome (see p. 320) is a dominating feature of the view from the Piazzetta.

The *Palazzi Manolesso-Ferro,* 15C Gothic spoilt by alterations, *Fini,* by Aless. Tremignon (1688), and *Pisani-Gritti,* another disfigured Gothic building (all R.), are now occupied by hotels. Opposite (L.) can be seen the apse (c. 1342) and cloister door of *San Gregorio.* Then follow three Gothic palaces; *Pal. Semitecolo* (L.), *Barbaro,* now *Wolkoff* (L.; 14C), and *Barbarigo* (R.).—The *Pal. Dario* (L.) is a Lombardesque building in varicoloured marble.—The *Pal. Corner* called **Ca' Grande** (R.; Pl. 10). a dignified edifice in the full Renaissance style, by *Sansovino* (1537), has a fine cortile, and is now occupied by the Prefecture. Facing it is the *Pal. Venier dei Leoni.* (L.; 1749), of which only the ground floor was built; within is a luxuriant garden. It is now occupied by the Peggy Guggenheim collection (comp. p. 320). In the red *Casa Biondetti* (L.) Rosalba Carriera (1676-1757) died. The *Pal. Da Mula,* later *Morosini* (L.; 15C Gothic) is followed by the *Pal. Barbarigo* (L.), occupied by the Venezia-Murano Co. with a mosaic façade designed by Giulio Carlini (19C). Beyond the Rio San Vio are the *Pal. Loredan,* now *Cini* (L.; 16C), and two *Palazzi Barbaro* (R.), one 17C (now Curtis), the other 15C Gothic.—The *Pal. Contarini-Dal Zaffo,* or *Manzoni Angaran* (L.), is a graceful Lombardesque building. The *Pal. Cavalli-Franchetti* (R), is a sumptuous 15C building, rebuilt c. 1890.

The boat passes beneath the wooden PONTE DELL' ACCADEMIA (c. 1930), with the Accademia (p. 315) set back on the left. The *Palazzo Giustinian-Lolin* (R.) is by Longhena (1623). The two *Palazzi Contarini degli Scrigni* (L.) are respectively by Scamozzi (1609), and in the 15C Gothic style.—The *Ca' del Duca* (R.) was begun by Bart. Bon for Fr. Sforza (15C), but building beyond the ground floor was forbidden (it is said) by the Republic. The Gothic *Pal. Loredan dell'Ambasciatore* (L.), a 15C palace with decorative marbles, was occupied by the Austrian ambassador in the 18C.—*Pal. Malipiero* (R.), rebuilt in 1622; *Pal. Contarini Michiel* (L.), Lombardesque (17C). Behind its campo (R.) appears the church of *San Samuele,* with a little Romanesque campanile.—The *Pal. Rezzónico* (L.; Pl. 10) by *Longhena* (begun c. 1660), with a story added by *Giorgio Massari* 1745), now contains the city's collection of 18C works of art (p. 318). The **Pal. Grassi** (R.), likewise by Massari (begun 1718), with a stair frescoed with carnival scenes by P. Longhi, is now an International Centre for Arts and Costume. Its rooms, furnished in period styles, contain examples of costumes and textiles from Egyptian times to the present day; temporary exhibitions are also held. The garden has been converted into an open-air theatre. Of the two fine *Palazzi Giustinian* (L.; 17C and 15C), the second was the residence of Wagner in 1858-59, when he wrote the second act of 'Tristan'. The beautifully proportioned *Ca' Fóscari* (L.; Pl. 10; 1428-37) is now the seat of the University Institute of Economics and Commerce; just beyond it is the busy Rio Fóscari, part of the short route to the station. The late Renaissance *Pal. Balbi* (L.) is by Aless. Vittoria (1582-90).—The *Pal. Moro-Lin* (R.), is of c. 1670 in a Tuscan style of the previous century; the *Pal. Da Lezze* (R.) has been altered from its original Gothic form; the *Pal. Civran-Grimani* (L.) is of the 17C.—The graceful building opposite (R.) is the *Pal. Contarini delle Figure,* in the Lombardesque style, ascribed to Scarpagnino (16C). Another Lombardesque palace is the *Pal. Giustinian Persico* (L.; beyond San Tomà landing-stage) of the 16C.—Opposite *Palazzo Tiepoletto* (L.; 15C) and *Palazzo Tiepolo* (16C) are four *Palazzi Mocenigo* (R.). The first was the residence of Emmanuel Philbert of Savoy (1574) and of Giordano Bruno (1592), who was betrayed by his host; in the third Byron wrote the beginning of Don Juan (1818) and entertained Thomas Moore. The graceful Gothic *Pal. Pisani Moretta* (L.), now *Giusti del Giardino,* is of the 15C; the *Pal. Barbarigo della Terrazza* (L.; on the corner of Rio S. Polo), after Bern Contino (1568-69), takes its name from its fine terrace over the canal. On the R. are the *Pal. Corner Gheltoff* (15-16C) and the *Pal. Garzoni* (15C).— Beyond the Rio San Polo are (L.) the *Pal. Cappello-Layard* (now Carnelutti; 15-16C), called after Sir Henry Layard (1817-94), the explorer of Nineveh; and the *Pal. Grimani,* a simple and elegant structure from the early 16C.—The Lombardesque *Pal. Corner-Spinelli (R.; Pl. 10) is by Mauro Coducci. The *Pal. Benzon* (R.) in the time of the Countess Marina Benzon (c. 1818) was the rendezvous of Venetian fashion and was visited by Byron, Moore, Canova, etc. The * *Pal. Bernardo* (L.) has a lovely Gothic façade (c. 1422); the *Pal. Donà della Madonnetta* (L.) is a Romanesque building dating from the 12-13C; the *Pal. Papadópoli* (L.) is a work of the best Renaissance period now attr. to Giangiacomo dei Grigi (16C).—The *Pal. Corner Contarini dei Cavalli* (R.) is an elegant Gothic work of c. 1450; the Pal. Grimani (R.; Pl. 10), now the seat of the Court of Appeal, is a masterpiece by Sammicheli (1556).—The *Pal. Businello* formerly *Giustinian* (L.) is a rebuilt Romanesque palace (17C). The 12-13C Romanesque *Palazzi Farsetti and *Loredan* (R.) are now occupied as the Town Hall. Next come the tiny Gothic *Pal. Dandolo* (R.), the 15C *Pal. Bembo* (R.), the probable birthplace of Pietro Bembo (1470-1547), and the *Pal. Manin* (R.), now the Banca d'Italia, by Sansovino (c. 1550). On the corner, bronze mont. to Mazzini (1951). The *Pal. Ravà* (L.; 1906), the last on this side before the Rialto, occupies the site of Petrarch's house and the palace of the Patriarchs of Grado.

The ***Ponte di Rialto** (Pl. 7), which crosses the canal at this point, was built by Ant. da Ponte in 1588-92 to replace the previous wooden bridge, which had in its turn superseded a bridge of boats in 1264. Its single arch, 48 m in span and 7½ m high carries a roadway divided into three lanes by two rows of shops. The boat passes between the **Fóndaco dei Tedeschi** (R.) and the **Pal. dei Camerlenghi** (L.). The former, once the warehouse of German merchants, was built in 1505 by Scarpagnino from the designs of Girolamo Tedesco, and is now occupied by the *General Post Office.* The latter, by Gugl. Bergamasco (1525-28), is an ornate building; it was once the seat of the lords of Exchequer.—The *Pal. Lion-Morosini* (R.) retains portions of an early 13C building.—The *Fabbriche Vecchie di Rialto* (L.) are by Scarpagnino (1522).—The *Fabbriche Nuove di Rialto* (L.), now the Assize Court, were built by Sansovino in 1552-55.

In front of them is the Erberia where, in the morning, boats put in laden with fruit and vegetables for market.—The *Ca' Da Mosto* (R.), Romanesque with Gothic features, was the birthplace of Alvise Cadamosto (1432-88), discoverer of the Cape Verde Islands; the *Pal. Michiel dalle Colonne* (R.) is a 17C building.—The *Pescheria* (L.), a graceful Gothic building (1907), is interesting to visit when the consignments of fish arrive; behind it is the 13C *Pal. Querini.*—The 14C *Pal. Sagredo* (R.), has a sumptuous 18C stair, and is adjoined by the 15C *Pal. Pésaro* (R.). The famous *Ca' d'Oro* (R.; Pl. 7), the most beautiful Gothic building in Venice, built by *Matteo Raverti* (1422-40) and others, now contains the *Franchetti Gallery* (see p. 301).—The *Pal. Fontana* (R.; 16C) was the birthplace of Clement XIII (C. Rezzonico, 1693-1769). The *Pal. Corner della Regina* (L.), by Dom. Rossi (1724), is now the 'Biennale' archive of contemporary art, and stands on the site of the birthplace of Queen Catherine Cornaro (1454-1510).—The enormous **Pal. Pésaro** (L.; Pl. 6), a fine Baroque building begun by *Longhena* in 1652 and completed c. 1710 by *Ant. Gaspari,* now contains the Gallery of Modern Art and the Oriental Museum (see p. 310). The *Pal. Gussoni Grimani della Vida* (R.) is ascribed to Sammicheli. The *Pal. Foscarini Giovanelli* (L.; 16C) was the birthplace of Doge Marco Foscarini (1695). The picturesque façade of *San Stae* (p. 310) faces the 16C *Pal. Barbarigo* (R.) which has almost lost its façade frescoes by Cam. Ballini. On the L. are the *Palazzi Priuli Bon* (Byzantine), *Duodo* (Gothic) and *Tron* (1590); on the R. the *Pal. Soranzo* (Lombardesque) and the *Pal. Erizzo alla Maddalena* (15C Gothic). The yellow *Pal. Marcello* (R.; 18C) was the birthplace of Bened. Marcello (1686-1739), the composer. Then come (L.) the *Pal. Belloni Battagià,* by Longhena (c. 1650), and the battlemented *Granaries* of the Republic.—The **Pal. Vendramin Calergi** (R.; Pl. 2), begun by Mauro Coducci and completed by the Lombardo, is the finest Lombardesque palace in Venice. Wagner died here on 13 Feb 1883; the commemorative inscription on the garden wall is by D'Annunzio. It is now the winter home of the Casino.

The **Fóndaco dei Turchi** (L.; Pl. 2) formerly the Turkish warehouse, is now a Natural History Museum (see p. 311). Beyond is the 15C Gothic *Pal. Dorigo Giovanelli* (L.). A little way beyond the church of *San Marcuola* (p. 303; R.) diverges the CANNAREGIO, the second largest canal in Venice. The *Palazzo Labia* (p. 303) can be seen on the canal, beyond the church of *San Geremia.*

At the church of the *Scalzi* (p. 303; R.), the boat passes under the PONTE DEGLI SCALZI (1934). On the right is the *Station,* on the left the lofty green dome and Corinthian portico of *San Simeone Piccolo.* Beyond the public *Giardino Papadópoli* (L.) is the mouth of the Rio Nuovo, a canal cut in 1933 as a short route from the station to the Piazza. Beyond it (L.) is the boat-station of Santa Chiara, behind which is the modern Piazzale Roma, the terminus of the road from the mainland.

The Fondamenta Santa Chiara, on the left at the end of the Grand Canal, leads to the former church of **Sant'Andrea della Zirada,** an early Gothic building containing a sumptuous altar by *Juste Le Court* (1679).

V   WESTERN QUARTERS

Across the Rialto Bridge (comp. p. 308) the Ruga degli Orefici leads down through the busy and colourful food market. The *Erberia,* where the fruit and vegetables are sold wholesale, is on the Grand Canal (between the Fabbriche Vecchie di Rialto and the Pal. dei Camerlenghi, see above). In the piazza (r.), amidst the stalls and barrows, is the little church of *San Giacomo di Rialto* (Pl. 7; open 10-12, 17-19), popularly thought to be the oldest foundation in Venice, in fact of the 11C and rebuilt in 1601. It preserves a few 11C Corinthian capitals. Across the square is the *Gobbo di Rialto* by Pietro da Salò (16C), a crouching figure which supports a flight of steps leading to a rostrum of Egyptian granite whence the laws of the Republic were proclaimed.—Signposts indicate the route for Palazzo Pésaro; on the way is *San Cassiano* (open 10-12, 16.30-19), an early foundation rebuilt except for the 12C campanile in the 17C. In the sanctuary are three paintings (light; fee) by Tintoretto: the *Crucifixion, Resurrection, and Descent into Limbo. The altar front was carved by Arrigo Mayring in 1696. Next to the sacristy is a pretty chapel decorated in 1746. Beyond, to the left, is **Santa Maria Mater Domini,** a Renaissance church probably after a design of *Giov. Buora* (1502-40) with a façade ascribed to *Sansovino.*

The pretty interior contains, in the 1st S. chapel, marble figures of saints by *Lor. Bregno* (1524) and *Ant. Minello;* over the high altar, Relief of the Madonna and Child (Florentine school). In r. transept, SS. Mark and John, statuettes by *Lor. Bregno;* in l. transept, Madonna in prayer, marble bas-relief (13C Byzantine). All the paintings have been removed for restoration; they include: *Vinc. Catena,* St Christina (1520); *Fr. Bissolo,* Transfiguration; *Bonifazio,* Last Supper; *Tintoretto,* *Invention of the Cross.

The Calle della Chiesa leads into the Sottoportico Tiossi and (l.) the Fondamenta Pésaro which ends at the courtyard of **Palazzo Pésaro** (Pl. 6), containing a Renaissance well-head from the Zecca. The great Renaissance palace contains the *Galleria Internazionale d'Arte Moderna* (1st and 2nd floors) and the *Museo Orientale* (2nd floor).

The **Gallery of Modern Art** (open 10-16; fest. 9.30-12.30) contains a good collection of paintings and sculptures, mostly purchased at the biennial art exhibitions. Rearrangements are frequent. Among the artists whose work is represented may be mentioned: *Ippolito Caffi, Medardo Rosso, Arturo Martini, Pio Semeghini, Guglielmo Ciardi, Fr. Messina, Emilio Greco, Fr. Hayez, Telemaco Signorini, Giov. Fattori, De Chirico, Carlo Carrà, Fil. de Pisis, Felice Casorati.—Rodin* (Casts of the Thinker and the Burghers of Calais), *Kandinsky, Paul Klee, Max Ernst, Gustave Klimt, Matisse,* and *Mirò.*
The **Museum of Oriental Art** (adm. 9-14; closed Mon), the bulk of whose collections were presented by Prince Henry of Bourbon-Parma, Count of Bardi, is devoted principally to Japanese and Chinese art, with specimens of Siamese and Javanese work. The Japanese paintings are especially interesting, and the lacquer-work and bronzes are of high quality. Notable also is the fine Khmer figure of Buddha (Cambodia; 12C).

Farther along the Grand Canal is the church of **San Stae** (*S. Eustachio;* Pl. 6), with a Baroque façade by *Dom. Rossi* (1709). It is at present closed for restoration and the numerous 18C paintings have been temporarily removed. To the S.W., in a secluded campo planted with plane trees, is the church of **San Giacomo dell'Orio** (Pl. 6), rebuilt in 1225, altered in 1532, but retaining its campanile.

The nave is covered by a beautiful 14C wooden *Roof. The Renaissance pulpit is of a type common in Belgium, but unusual in Italy. In the S. transept, stands a column of verde antico. Near the S. door is the entrance to the Sagrestia Nuova, which has a ceiling by *Veronese* (1577) and contains some good pictures: *Buonconsiglio,* Three saints; *Fr. Bassano,* John the Baptist preaching; *Veronese,* SS. Laurence, Jerome, and Prosper (1572; much restored); *Fr. Bassano,* Madonna with SS. John and Nicholas.—The main altarpiece (Madonna and four saints) is by *Lotto* (1546). A door on the left, beneath a 14C Madonna in relief, leads to the Sagrestia Vecchia, containing canvases by *Palma Giovane* (1575).

To the N. of San Giacomo on the Grand Canal (reached by Calle Larga and Fondamenta and Ramo del Megio) is the **Fóndaco dei Turchi** (Pl. 2), from 1621 the warehouse of the Turkish merchants. Once the most characteristic Romanesque palace (12-13C) in Venice it was virtually rebuilt after 1858. Here in 1562 Tasso stayed as a guest of the Duke of Ferrara. It now contains a NATURAL HISTORY MUSEUM (adm. 9-13.30, fest. 9-12) where the exhibits include an Ouranosaurus over 3½ m high and 7 m long and a giant crocodile nearly 12 m long, both found in the Sahara in 1973. There is also a lapidary collection.

To the W. of San Giacomo, viâ the Campo Nazario Sauro, is *San Simeone Grande* (open 8-11.30, 18-20). Over the high altar is a Last Supper by Tintoretto, and, in the chapel to l. of high altar, effigy of St Simeon (early 15C). In the sacristy is preserved a small painting of the Trinity attrib. to *Giov. Mansueti.*

South-east of San Giacomo the Calle del Tintor and the Rioterrà Primo and Secondo (r.) del Parrucchetta lead towards the *Campo San Stin.* From here the Calli del Tabacco and dell'Olio continue to the **Scuola di San Giovanni Evangelista** (Pl. 6), one of the six chief confraternities. The beautiful first court is attributed to *P. Lombardo* (1481); in the second court are the façade of the original foundation (1261), (l.) the Oratory, and (r.) the Scuola itself (façade of 1454). The interior of the Scuola (ring for adm., 9.30-12.30), partly in use as a restoration centre, has a double *Staircase, a work of great skill and elegance, by *Mauro Coducci* (1498). Out of the imposing 18C Salone (being restored) opens the *Oratorio della Croce* with the Reliquary of the Cross (1379), brought from Cyprus.

From the Campo San Stin (see above) the Calle della Chiesa leads to the ***Frari** (Pl. 6), properly the church of *Santa Maria Gloriosa dei Frari,* and dedicated to the Assumption. For architecture, historical sculpture, and painting it is the chief rival of San Zanipólo. Adm. 9 or 9.30-12, 14.30 or 15-18; fest. 14.30-18.

The original Franciscan church was begun c. 1250, continued on a new design in 1338, and finished c. 1443. It is built of brick in the Italian Gothic style and has a severe W. front; the majestic campanile dates from the second half of the 14C. The church faces S.W., but is here described as though it had the altar at the E. end.

The imposing *INTERIOR, 90 m long, is cruciform, with an aisled nave of 12 bays. On the right of the main door; Tomb of the Procurator Alvise Pasqualigo (d. 1528). Near the 1st pillar, Stoup, with a statue by *Girol. Campagna.* In the SOUTH AISLE, above the spot where the master is believed to be buried, is the Mausoleum of Titian, by L. and P. Zandomeneghi (1838-52), decorated with reliefs of Titian's four chief religious paintings in Venice, and a fifth (Visitation) no longer attributed to him. On the 3rd altar, *Statue of St Jerome by *Vittoria.* Beyond the 4th altar (with a Martyrdom of St Catherine, by *Palma Giovane*) is a monument to Bp. Marco Zen, of Torcello (d. 1641).—In the SOUTH TRANSEPT is the monument to Iac. Marcello (d. 1484), by *Pietro Lombardo* and others; on the right of the sacristy door is the funerary urn of Beato Pacifico, beneath an elaborate canopy, ascribed to *Nanni di Bartolo* and *Michele da Firenze,* in the florid Gothic of 1437; over the door, the fine tomb of Bened. Pésaro (d. 1503), by *Lor. Bregno,* with a statue of Mars by *Baccio da Montelupo;* on the left, the Gothic tomb of Paolo Savelli (d. 1405), with a gilt wooden equestrian figure.

In the SACRISTY is a charming little Lombardesque ciborium (r. of the entrance); over the altar, *Madonna and saints, by *Giov. Bellini* (1488), a perfect expression of the religious sentiment of this great and typical Venetian. A few steps lead down to the Chapter House (where part of the Treasury, and a lunette by *Paolo Veneziano* are displayed) which looks out onto the Palladian Cloister.

In the SOUTH CHOIR CHAPELS: 3rd chap., Polyptych by *Bart. Vivarini* (1482); 2nd chap., Two 14C tombs; 1st chap., *St John the Baptist, a statue in wood by *Donatello* (1438; recently restored). On the S. wall of the Sanctuary is the fine *Tomb of Doge Fr. Fóscari (d. 1457), a late Gothic mausoleum, by *Ant.* and *Paolo Bregno;* opposite is the sumptuous Renaissance *Tomb of Doge Nic. Tron (d. 1473), by *Ant. Rizzo*. Over the high altar of 1516 is an *Assumption by *Titian* (1518), celebrated among his masterpieces for its dramatic movement and its amazing colouring. In the NORTH CHOIR CHAPELS: 1st chap., *Bern. Licinio,* Madonna and saints; 2nd chap., Tomb of Melchiorre Trevisan (d. 1500), by *Lor. Bregno* (?); 3rd chap., *St Ambrose and eight other saints, begun by *Alvise Vivarini* and finished by *Marco Basaiti* (1503); on the floor a plain slab marks the grave of Monteverdi (date of birth incorrect); 4th chap., Tomb of Fed. Cornér, a gracious work of Tuscan provenance; font with statue of St John, by *Sansovino* (1554); on the altar, *St Mark and four other saints, by *Bart. Vivarini* (1474). The NORTH TRANSEPT contains a 15C carved bench-back of the German school.

The RITUAL CHOIR, which extends into the nave (an unusual arrangement in Italy), contains three tiers of *Stalls in carved and inlaid wood, by *Marco Cozzi* (1468). The Choir Screen is faced with marble and decorated with figures of Saints and Prophets in low relief; above are ten Apostles and a Crucifixion between the Virgin and St John the Evangelist, with Angels at the corners, an originally Gothic design completed in the Lombardesque style (1475).—In the NORTH AISLE is the Cappella Emiliani containing ten statues of the school of *Iacobello Dalle Masegne* (15C), and the tomb of Bp. Miani, with five similar statues. Near by is the monument to Iac. Pésaro (d. 1547), with a fine statue by an unknown hand. Over the Pésaro altar is the *Madonna di Ca'Pésaro, by *Titian* (completed in 1526; temporarily removed for restoration), a marvel of composition and colour. The mausoleum of Doge Giov. Pésaro (d. 1659), an elaborate Baroque work, is by *Longhena*. The Mausoleum of Canova (1827), by his pupils, reproduces Canova's design for a monument to Titian. Near the door is a monument to P. Bernardo (d. 1538), attributed to *Tullio Lombardo*.

The adjoining conventual buildings, with the Palladian cloister (comp. above) and another in the style of Sansovino, contain the STATE ARCHIVES, among the most famous in the world, and filling some 300 rooms. They provide a remarkable documentation of the Venetian Republic.

Beyond the interesting apse of the Frari is SAN ROCCO (Pl. 5), a church designed by *Bart. Bon* (1489) but almost entirely rebuilt in 1725 (façade of 1765-71). It contains scenes from the Life of St Roch (on the W. wall, nave, and in the choir) by *Tintoretto*. To the left is the *Scuola Grande di San Rocco** (9-13, 15.30-18.30; 1000 l.) begun for the important Confraternity of St Roch by *Bart. Bon* (1515), continued by *Sante Lombardo* (1524-27), and finished by *Scarpagnino* (1549), who added the splendid main façade, remarkable for its intentional asymmetry and its graceful ornament. The less imposing canal façade is likewise by *Scarpagnino*. Within are a fine staircase and several rooms containing statues by *Girol. Campagna* and good wood-carvings by *Fr. Pianta*, and 56 *Paintings of New Testament subjects, by *Tintoretto*, the range and variety of whose style can best be studied here (especially since their restoration). On the upper floor, to the left of the altar, is an *Annunciation by *Titian*, and in the Sala dell'Albergo the *Crucifixion (1565), a splendid painting by *Tintoretto*, with its companion paintings of Scenes of the Passion.

Beyond the Ponte della Scuola (first left, then right) is the church of **San Pantalon** (Pl. 9), the nave roof of which is covered by a huge painting by *Gian. Ant. Fumiani*. It also contains some good 18C paintings, and, in a chapel N. of the choir, the Coronation of the Virgin, by *Ant. Vivarini* and *Giov. d'Alemagna* (1444).

To the W. of San Rocco is the church of *San Nicolò da Tolentino* (Pl. 5), by Vinc. Scamozzi, with interesting 17-18C paintings and architecture. 3rd S. chap., *Bonifacio De'Pitati* (manner of), Banquet of Herod and the Beheading of St John the Baptist; S. transept, *Palma Giovane*, Madonna and Saints; Sanctuary (r. wall), *Luca Giordano*, Annunciation; outside the Sanctuary (l.), *Giov. Lys*, St Jerome visited by an angel; 3rd N. chap., *Palma Giovane*, Stories of St Cecilia.

From the Campo dei Frari, Calle Larga Prima leads to the church of *San Tomà* (Pl. 10). On the N. side of the church and on the walls of the 15C *Scuola dei Caleg heri* (i.e. Shoemakers) in the adjoining Campo, are some 15C reliefs. The Ponte San Tomà leads to the Calle dei Nómboli in which (No. 2793) is the *Palazzo Centani* (15C), the birthplace of Carlo Goldoni (1707-93), the comic playwright. It has a picturesque Gothic courtyard with a pretty well-head, and the interior (open 8.30-13.30 exc. Sun and fest.) contains Goldoni relics.

To the N.E., across Rio San Polo, is the church of **San Polo** (Pl. 6), with its admirable Gothic S. doorway and its isolated campanile of 1362. The exterior has been restored to its original Romanesque and Gothic form; on the E. end are little 12C reliefs. Inside is a Communion of the Apostles (W. wall) and an Assumption and Saints (1st r. altar), both by *Tintoretto*. On the high altar, Crucifix (Venetian, early 15C). The Conversion of St Paul in the apse is by *Palma Giovane*. On the walls of the sanctuary, four paintings of the Stations of the Cross, by *Gian. Dom. Tiepolo*. 2nd N. altar, *G. B. Tiepolo*, Virgin appearing to a Saint.— No. 1957, in the large campo, is the *Pal. Corner Mocenigo*, with a façade by Sammicheli (c. 1543); at Nos. 2169-71 is the large Gothic *Pal. Soranzo;* No. 2177 preserves fragments of the *Pal. Donà*. The Calle della Madonnetta leads N.E. to **Sant'Aponal** (*S. Apollinare;* Pl. 6; closed for restoration), rebuilt in the 15C, with a fine campanile, above the door of which is a 13C Lion of St Mark. To the left the Calle Bianca Cappello leads to the Ponte Storto, near which (No. 1280) is the birthplace of Bianca Cappello (c. 1560-87), the 'daughter of the Republic' and wife of Franc. Medici. Farther on, in the Campiello Albrizzi, is the 17C *Palazzo Albrizzi* (adm. by special permission only), which contains fine stuccoes framing allegorical works by P. Liberi (c. 1670).

The bustling Ruga Vecchia di San Giovanni leads from Sant'Aponal to the church of SAN GIOVANNI ELEMOSINARIO (Pl. 7), rebuilt by *Scarpagnino* in 1527-39, but preserving its campanile of 1398-1410. Over the high altar is a painting of the patron saint by *Titian* (c. 1535), and in the chapel on the right, SS. Catherine, Sebastian, and Roch, by *Pordenone* (1535).—Ruga degli Orefici returns to the Rialto.

VI   SOUTHERN QUARTERS: ACCADEMIA AND GIUDECCA

From the S.W. corner of P.za San Marco, Salizzada San Moisè leads shortly to SAN MOISÈ (Pl. 11), a Baroque church with an overcharged façade, by *Aless. Tremignon* (1668). It contains some good 17-18C paintings, and an extraordinary sculpted altarpiece which fills the apse. Inside the entrance is the grave of John Law (1671-1729), originator of the 'Mississippi Scheme', transferred from San Geminiano in 1808. The bridge beyond the church leads into the Calle Larga Ventidue Marzo (22 March 1848, the date of Manin's rebellion). From it the Calle del Sartor da veste diverges on the right for LA FENICE (Pl. 10), one of the most important theatres in Italy (1792; adm. granted to see the charming interior when rehearsals are not in progress). In this famous opera house many of Verdi's operas were first performed (including 'La Traviata' in 1853). In this century it saw the première of Stravinsky's 'The Rake's Progress' (1951) and Benjamin Britten's 'The Turn of the Screw'. The charming Renaissance church of *SAN FANTIN, by Scarpagnino (1507-49), has an apse by *Sansovino* (1549-63). The *Scuola di San Fantin* (now the seat of the Ateneo Veneto) contains paintings by Paolo Veronese and his school. The return towards the Calle Ventidue Marzo may be made around the Fenice building, passing its water-gate. Calle del Piovan leads to the church of **Santa Maria Zobenigo** (Pl. 10) or *del Giglio,* rebuilt by *Sardi* in 1680-83. On the pilasters of the façade are plans of Zara, Candia, Padua, Rome, Corfu, and Spálato; above are portraits of the Barbaro family, at whose cost it was rebuilt. The Cappella Molin (off the r. aisle; restored in 1975) displays the contents of the treasury and a Madonna and Child with the young St John, by *Rubens.* Beneath the organ in the presbytery are two paintings of the Evangelists by *Iac. Tintoretto.* Across the Rio di Santa Maria Zobenigo and the Rio Corner Zaguri is (l.; No. 2631) the Gothic *Pal. Zaguri* and (r.) the early 19C church of *San Maurizio.* Beyond is the spacious *Campo Morosini* (or Santo Stefano), in which is a statue of Nic. Tommaseo (1802-74), an eminent man of letters. On the left are the 17C *Palazzo Morosini* (Nos. 2802-3), the home of Fr. Morisini, and the *Pal. Loredan* (No. 2945), a late Renaissance building rebuilt by Scarpagnino (1536), occupied by the Istituto Veneto of Science and Arts. In the corner is the imposing 16-18C *Pal. Pisani,* now the Conservatory of Music.

The other end of the Campo Morosini is occupied by the early Gothic church of **Santo Stefano** (Pl. 10), erected in the 14C and altered in the 15C, with a fine brick façade and portal in the florid Gothic style (since restored).

The basilican INTERIOR, with three apses, has tall pillars alternately of Greek and red Veronese marble, and a fine tricuspid *Roof like that of the Eremitani in Padua. The tomb of Giacomo Surian (1493), on the W. wall, is a graceful Renaissance composition. The sepulchral Seal of Fr. Morisini, in the pavement of the nave, was cast by *Fil. Parodi* in 1694. The choir stalls of Gothic design are by *Marco* and *Fr. Cozzi* and *Leon. Scalamanzo* (1488). In the Sacristy are three paintings by *Iac. Tintoretto* (The Last Supper, Washing of the Feet, and Prayer in the Garden), and a Madonna and Saints by *Bonifazio.* In the cloister (l.) of 1532 is the tomb of Doge And. Contarini (d. 1382).

From the Campo Sant'Angelo, to the N.E., there is a view of the fine tower of Santo Stefano, the most oblique of the many leaning towers of Venice. In the campo is the Gothic house (No. 3584), once the Tre Stelle inn, in which the composer Dom. Cimarosa died in 1801.—Farther on in the same direction is the *Campo Manin* (Pl. 11), with a monument to the patriot Daniele Manin (p. 283). The Calle della Vida, beside the monument, and the Calletta Contarini del Bóvolo lead to the *Palazzo Contarini del Bóvolo* (No. 4299) celebrated for its graceful spiral staircase by Giov. Candi (c. 1499).

To the N., between Campo Santo Stefano and Campo Manin, is Campo San Benedetto. Here at No. 3958 is the grand 15C *Palazzo Pesaro degli Orfei*, now *Fortuny*. This was the home of the painter Mariano Fortuny (1871-1950) who here designed the famous Fortuny silks. The house (open weekdays 8.30-13.30) with a fine old wooden stair and loggia in the courtyard, has a remarkable 'fin de siècle' atmosphere and is filled with curios and the artist's own works.

The Calle delle Botteghe leads out of the Campo Morosini N.W. to the Salizzada San Samuele, in which is the house (No. 3337) where Paolo Veronese died in 1588. At the end (r.) is the *Pal. Grassi* (p. 307).

From the S. end of Campo Morosini, between the church of *San Vitale* and the gardens of Palazzo Cavalli the *Ponte dell' Accademia* crosses the Grand Canal. The ACCADEMIA DI BELLE ARTI (Pl. 10), occupying the church and convent of Santa Maria della Carità, contains the ****Galleria dell'Accademia,** by far the most important collection of Venetian paintings. It contains works of all periods from the 14C, and the 15C art of Giovanni Bellini, through the wonderful era of Titian, Tintoretto, and Veronese, down to Tiepolo and the 18C. Admission 9-14; fest. 9-13; closed Mon.

Stairs mount to ROOM I formerly the chapter house, with a superb wooden *Ceiling, ascribed to *Marco Cozzi* (1461-84) with paintings by *Alvise Vivarini* (Holy Father) and *Dom. Campagnola* (four Prophets). (From r. to left): *Paolo Veneziano,* *21. Coronation of the Virgin, and stories from the life of Christ and St Francis; 786. Madonna enthroned with angels; *Lor. Veneziano,* 9. Annunciation and four Saints; 650. Marriage of St Catherine and Saints; (in case) 25. *Iacobello Albergno,* Triptych with Crucifixion and Saints; 1000. *Stef. Veneziano,* Polyptych of the Apocalypse; 1. *Iacobello del Fiore,* Coronation of the Virgin in Paradise; *10. *Lor. Veneziano,* large Polyptych with the Annunciation, Saints, and Prophets. Left wall: 33. *Mich. Giambono,* Coronation of the Virgin in Paradise; 1236. *Ant. Vivarini,* Madonna and Child; (in centre) *18. Cross of St Theodore, 15C Venetian goldsmiths' work; 13. *Iacobello del Fiore,* Madonna of the Misericordia; 3. *Michele Giambono,* St James the Greater between other Saints; 5, 5a. *Lor. Veneziano,* SS. Peter and Mark.—On the end wall, between the entrance stairs, 15. *Iacobello del Fiore,* Justice between the archangels Michael and Gabriel.—On the back of the screen on the entrance to R. II, II. *Jacopo Moranzone,* Polyptych of the Assunta.

ROOM II contains a superb group of large altarpieces. 89. *Carpaccio,* The ten thousand martyrs of Mount Ararat (1510); 69. *Marco Basaiti,* The Prayer in the Garden; *38. *Giov. Bellini,* Sacred Conversation: Madonna enthroned with Saints (the 'Pala of San Giobbe'); *39. *Marco Basaiti,* Calling of the sons of Zebedee (1510); 815. *Cima da Conegliano,* Madonna 'of the Orange tree', between SS. Jerome and Stephen; 44. *Carpaccio,* Presentation of Christ in the Temple (1510); 611. *Cima,* Incredulity of St Thomas; 166. *Giov. Bellini* (and his School), Pietà; 36. *Cima,* Madonna enthroned with Saints.—ROOM III 70. *School of Giorgione,* Madonna with SS. Catherine and John the Baptist; *Cima,* 603, 604. Madonna with Saints, Deposition.

ROOM IV (l.) contains a group of exquisite small paintings: *610. *Giov. Bellini,* Madonna and Child between SS. Paul and George; 586. *Hans Memling,* Portrait of a young man; *Giov. Bellini,* *613. Madonna and Child between SS. Catherine and Mary Magdalene, *591. Madonna and Child; 628. *Cosmè Tura,* Madonna and Child; *835. *Iac. Bellini,* Madonna and Child; *47. *Piero della Francesco,* St Jerome in the desert; *588. *And. Mantegna,* St George; *583. *Giov. Bellini,* Madonna and Child blessing.—ROOM V 87. *Giov. Bellini,* Head of the Redeemer (fragment); *Giorgione,* *272. Old Woman, *915. 'La Tempesta'; *Giov. Bellini,* 595. Five allegories, *594. Madonna and Child, *596. Madonna 'degli Alberetti', *612. Madonna 'dei cherubini rossi', 883. Pietá, in a landscape, 881. Madonna and Child between St John the Baptist and a female Saint.

ROOM VI (the large room beyond R. III). *320. *Paris Bordone,* The fisherman presenting St Mark's ring to the Doge (fine architectural background); 210. *Iac. Tintoretto,* Madonna 'dei Camerlenghi', the treasurers of the Republic; *314. *Titian,* St John the Baptist; *291. *Bonifacio de' Pitati,* Dives and Lazarus the beggar.—R. VII (on the right). 303. *Bernardo Licinio,* Portrait of a lady; 299. *Giov. Cariani* (attrib.), Portrait; 912. *Lor. Lotto,* Gentleman in his study.—R. VIII contains paintings, by *Bonifacio de' Pitati* and his school, from the Palazzo dei Camerlenghi: 95. *Venetian School,* Visitation; *147. *Palma Vecchio,* Holy Family and two Saints; *Andrea Previtali,* 639. Christ-child in the manger, 640. Crucifixion; 737. *Gerol. Romanino,* Entombment.—R. IX. *Padovanino* (?), Tobias and the angel; 1035. *Titian,* Symbols of the Evangelists; 917. *Bonifazio,* God the Father, with the Piazza below.

ROOM X (through R. VI). 217. *Tintoretto,* Deposition; *203. *Paolo Veronese,* Christ in the House of Levi (1573), a splendid Venetian banquet-scene framed in a Palladian loggia; the figure in the foreground against the pillar on the left is the painter himself. The secular character of this painting brought Veronese into conflict with the Holy Office, and the name was changed from 'The Last Supper' to 'Christ in the House of Levi' before it was hung in the refectory of San Zanipólo. *Tintoretto,* *831. Transport of the body of St Mark, *42. Miracle of St Mark; 283. St Mark rescuing a Saracen; 245. *Titian,* Portrait of Procurator Iacopo Soranzo; 213. *Tintoretto,* Crucifixion; *400. *Titian,* Pietà.—ROOM XI. 652. *Iac. Bassano,* St Jerome; 45. *Paolo Veronese,* Allegory of Venice; *Tintoretto,* 41. Cain and Abel, 900. Creation of the animals, 43. Adam and Eve; 643. *Luca Giordano,* Deposition; 777. *Bernardo Strozzi,* Dinner in the house of the Pharisee; *G. B. Tiepolo,* 343. Frieze with the miracle of the bronze serpent (very ruined), 462. Discovery of the True Cross by St Helena; 751. *Luca Giordano,* Crucifixion of St Peter; *Veronese,* 37. Madonna enthroned with Saints, 260. Annunciation, 1324. Marriage of St Catherine.

CORRIDOR (R. XII), Landscapes, bacchanals and hunting-scenes by *Fr. Zuccarelli, Gius. Zais,* and *Marco Ricci.*—R. XIII is devoted to *Tintoretto, Andrea Schiavone,* and the *Bassano* family. Note especially the portraits by *Tintoretto:* *234. The Procurator And. Cappello, 233. Doge Alvise Mocenigo, 230, 237, 896, and 1012.—Off a gallery (R. XV) is R. XIV. 544. *Tiberio Tinelli,* Luigi Molin; 829. *Bern. Strozzi,* Doge Fr. Erizzo; 914. *Jan Liss,* Sacrifice of Isaac; and paintings by *Dom. Feti.*

Beyond is the door into R. XVI (r. of Corridor), with amusing mythological scenes by *G. B. Tiepolo*. ROOM XVIa (2nd r. off the Corridor). 453. *Dom. Pellegrini*, Bartolozzi the engraver; 478. *Aless. Longhi*, Tommaso Temanza; *483. *G. B. Piazzetta*, Fortune-teller; 1315. *Gius. Nogari*, Head of an old woman; 778. *Vittore Ghislandi*, Count Vailetti; 493. *Aless. Longhi*, Allegory.—R. XVII, on the left of the corridor, has a number of Venetian scenes, including works by *Canaletto* and *Guardi* (709. Isola di San Giorgio). Farther on, works by *G. B. Pittoni* and *Seb. Ricci* and *G. B. Tiepolo*, portraits by *Rosalba Carriera* and interiors by *Pietro Longhi*.—To the left is another corridor, R. XVIII, containing architectural scenes by *Moretti*, *Gaspari*, and *Joli;* 906. *Mengs*, Archæologist; on the right, statuettes by *Canova*.—To the left again is R. XIX. 600. *Boccaccio Boccaccino*, Marriage of St Catherine; *Marco Basaiti*, 68, 68a. SS. James and Anthony Abbot; 76. *Marco Marziale*, Supper at Emmaus; 90. *Carpaccio*, Meeting of SS. Anne and Joachim; *Marco Basaiti* (attrib.), 645. Portrait, 108. Dead Christ, 107. St Jerome; 589. *Antonello da Saliba*, Christ at the column; 599. *Agost. da Lodi*, The Washing of the feet.—On the left is R. XX., charming paintings from the Scuola di San Giovanni Evangelista (end of 15C and beginning of 16C), relating especially to the miracles of the relic of the Cross given in 1369 to the school by Filippo de'Masseri on his return from Jerusalem.

*566. *Carpaccio*, Cure of a lunatic by the Patriarch of Grado (interesting costumes and view of the old wooden Rialto bridge); 562. *Giov. Mansueti*, Healing of a sick child (interesting details of a Venetian interior); *Gentile Bellini*, 568. Recovery of the relic from the Canal of San Lorenzo (the first of the ladies on the left is Caterina Cornaro); 563. Healing of Pietro de' Ludovici by touching a candle in contact with the relic; *567. Procession of the relic, showing the piazza as it was in 1496; 565. *Benedetto Diana*, A child fallen from a ladder is miraculously saved; 561. *Lazzaro Bastiani*, Filippo de' Masseri offers the relic to the Chief Guardian of the Scuola di San Giovanni Evangelista; 564. *Giov. Mansueti*, The brothers fail in their attempt to carry the relic inside the church of San Lio, at the funeral of a companion who had disparaged it.

Beyond the corridor is R. XXI, which contains *572-580. *Carpaccio*, Legend of St Ursula, (1490-96), painted for the Scuola di Sant'Orsola. The series is almost contemporary with Memling's delicate miniature-like works at Bruges (1489), with which it is interesting to make a comparison.

576. Glory of St Ursula and her 11,000 Virgins; 572. The ambassadors of England demand the hand of Ursula, daughter of King Maurus of Brittany, for Hereus, son of their King Conon; on the right, Ursula's answer; 573. Dictating the conditions of the marriage (a delay of 3 years for Ursula to make a pilgrimage to Rome and the conversion of Hereus to Christianity); 574. Departure of the ambassadors to England and the reading of the conditions to Conon; 575. Hereus meets Ursula and Ursula leaves for Rome; *578. Dream of Ursula; an angel foretells her martyrdom; 577. Ursula, with Hereus and the 11,000 meets Pope Cyriac at Rome (view of Castel Sant'Angelo); 579. The pilgrims and the Pope reach Cologne; 580. The Huns, besieging Cologne, massacre the pilgrims; funeral of St Ursula.

From RR. XIX and XXII is the approach to R. XXIII (r.), the upper part of the church of the Carità. In the first part of the room: 822. *Laz. Bastiani*, St Veneranda enthroned; 54. *Giov. Bellini*, St Ursula and four saints; 27. *Bart. Vivarini* (?), Madonna enthroned. In the second part of the room: *B. Vivarini*, 581. Nativity, 607. Holy Family, 618. The Baptist; 28. *And. da Murano*. Polyptych, SS. Sebastian, Vincent, Roch, and Peter Martyr; in the lunette, Madonna della Misericordia; 100. *Laz. Bastiani*, The Cradle; *Giov. Bellini*, 734. Annunciation, 734A. St Peter; *B. Vivarini*, 825. St Ambrose and saints, 861. Polyptych, Nativity and saints. In the first chapel: 616. *School of Vivarini*, Madonna. In the apse: 621–621C. *Giov. Bellini* and his school, Polyptych, Nativity, St Sebastian, Polyptych, St Laurence and the Madonna. In the end chapel: 11. *Moranzone*, Virgin and saints; 104. *Laz. Bastiani*, Preaching of St Anthony; 103, 103A, 105. *Carlo Crivelli*, Saints. In the middle of the room: *B. Vivarini*, 584, 585. Two saints, 615. Madonna and saints.— R. XXIV is the former 'albergo' of the Scuola della Carità (fine ceiling of 1444): *626. *Titian*. Presentation of the Virgin (1538), painted for its present position. The solitary figure of the infant St Mary is charmingly graceful and the distant view of the mountains is a reminder of the artist's alpine home; *625. *Ant. Vivarini* and *Giov. d'Alemagna*, large Triptych (1466), also painted for this room; 606–608. *Montagnana*, Annunciation. The Reliquary of Cardinal Bessarione is 14-15C Byzantine workmanship.

North-West of the Accademia, across three canals, stands the church of *San Barnaba* (Pl. 9), by Lorenzo Boschetti (1749-76), with a 14C campanile; it contains a Holy Family, by Veronese, at the 3rd altar on the N. side. Across Rio San Barnaba (charming view along the Fondamenta del Squero from the bridge) the Fondamenta Rezzónico leads r. to the *Palazzo Rezzónico* (Pl. 10), begun by Longhena (c. 1660) and completed by Massari (1745).

The palace was the last home of Robert Browning and the small room on the first floor where he died in 1889 has been arranged as it was then. Whistler also occupied a room here in 1879-80. The palace contains the **Museo del Settecento Veneziano** (adm. 10-16; fest. 9.30-12.30; closed Friday), the city's collection of 18C art, displayed in rooms decorated in the most sumptuous 18C style. Stairs mount to the FIRST FLOOR. The SALONE DA BALLO has frescoes by *Pietro Visconti* and elaborate furniture carved by *And. Brustolon*.—ROOM 2 has a ceiling-fresco of the marriage of Ludovico Rezzonico by *G. B. Tiepolo*.—ROOM 3. Pastels and minatures by *Rosalba Carriera*.—In ROOM 4 are displayed 17C tapestries of Flemish manufacture.—ROOM 5. Ceiling fresco of the Allegory of Merit by *G. B. Tiepolo*. Beyond the 'PORTEGO' with a balcony over the Grand Canal and two statues of atlantes by *Aless. Vittoria*, R. 6 has another fine ceiling fresco ('Strength and Wisdom') by *G. B. Tiepolo* (removed for restoration). Across the passage the LIBRARY (7) has ceiling paintings by *Fr. Maffei*.—In R. 9 (good ceiling) is more furniture by *Brustolon*.—From the Portego (see above) stairs continue up to the SECOND FLOOR. Here a large has numerous paintings including: (on the wall in front of the entrance) *G. B. Piazzetta*, Death of Darius; *Jan. Liss*, Judith and Holofernes. In the room to the l. is another fine ceiling painting by *G. B. Tiepolo*, and an interesting series of small paintings by *Pietro Longhi* with contemporary scenes of Venetian life. The next two rooms have frescoes by *Gian Ant. Guardi*. Beyond is a charming bedroom and boudoir.—From the Prtego is the entrance to a series of rooms reconstructed from the Villa di Zianigo, the Tiepolo villa near Mira and decorated with *Frescoes by *Gian Dom. Tiepolo*, including 'The New World' (1791) and delightful scenes with clowns. The last room on this floor has two paintings by *Fr. Guardi*.—The THIRD FLOOR (temporarily closed) has a puppet theatre, an 18C pharmacy, costumes, etc.

Rio San Barnaba leads away from the Grand Canal to the church of the **Cármini** (Pl. 9; *Santa Maria del Carmelo*), a typical basilica of the 14C, with an early-16C façade. The N. portal has Byzantine reliefs. In the interior the nave is decorated with gilded wooden sculptural decoration beneath a frieze of 17-18C paintings. In the r. aisle (2nd altar), Adoration of the Shepherds, by *Cima* (c. 1509; light on altar); in the left aisle (2nd altar), SS. Nicholas, John the Baptist, and Lucy, by *Lotto* (1529). In the chap. to the r. of the main altar, Pietà, a bronze relief ascribed to *Fr. di Giorgio,* with portraits of Fed. da Montefeltro and Battista Sforza (c. 1474). The cloister now belongs to the adjoining School of Applied Art.

The *Scuola Grande dei Cármini* (adm. 9-12, 14-17), N.E. of the church is attributed to Baldass. Longhena (1668). An elaborate staircase with stucco decoration leads up to the Salone with a fine ceiling painting by G. B. Tiepolo (1739-44).

From the Campo in front of the church the Fondamenta del Soccorso follows the canal to the left; on the opposite bank, farther on, is the *Palazzo Cicogna,* formerly *Arian,* with an elaborate 14C Gothic window. Rio San Sebastiano diverges left; across the second bridge is the church of *San Sebastiano* (Pl. 9), rebuilt after 1506 by *Scarpagnino,* and decorated in 1555-70 by Paolo Veronese, who lived in the neighbouring Salizzada and is buried in the church. It has recently been well restored and is open 9-12, 16-19 (winter 15-17).

INTERIOR. In the panels of the beautiful ceiling (illuminated by the Sacristan; also seen from the Gallery, comp. below) is the *Story of Esther (1555-56) by *Veronese,* and Prophets, Apostles, and Evangelists, with charming decoration by *Benedetto Caliari.* Over the altar (r.), beneath the gallery, St Nicholas, by *Titian* (1563; a late work). In the church proper: SOUTH SIDE, 2nd altar, *Tullio Lombardo,* Madonna and Child with young St John, a marble group; beyond the 3rd altar, Tomb of Abp. Podocattaro of Cyprus (d. 1555), by *Sansovino.* In the CHOIR are *Paintings by *Veronese:* over the altar, Madonna and Child with St Sebastian (c. 1570); l. wall, St Sebastian encourages SS. Mark and Marcellian to martyrdom (c. 1565); r. wall, Second martyrdom of St Sebastian. The chap. to the N. of the choir has a majolica pavement of 1510, and in the floor in front is the tomb of Paolo Veronese (d. 1588) and of his brother Benedetto Caliari (d. 1598); on the wall is a bust of Paolo. The organ, by *Fr. Fiorentino* and *Dom. da Treviso* (1558), was designed by *Veronese* who painted the panels. Beneath it a door admits to the SACRISTY, with a panelled and painted ceiling, the earliest of Veronese's works in Venice (1555). The fine series of paintings (including a Resurrection) here are by *Brusasorci* and *Bonifazio.* From here a door leads to the stairs and corridor which end at the NUNS' CHOIR, with frescoes of the trial and martyrdom of St Sebastian by *Veronese* and his brother; the ceiling of the main church can also be seen well from here.—Over the 3rd N. altar, *Veronese,* Madonna, St Catherine, and a friar, said to be among his earliest works.

Beyond *San Raffaele Arcangelo* (just to the N.W.), with a sculptured Tobias, angel, and dog, over the main portal (and the same story, by Fr. and Giov. Ant. Guardi, on the organ), a bridge crosses the Rio dell'Angelo to an area traditionally inhabited by fishermen and sailors. Here the church of **San Nicolò dei Mendicoli** (W. of Pl. 9) has recently been beautifully restored. It was founded in the 7C and was subsequently rebuilt and restored many times. It has a detached campanile. The nave has interesting wood sculptures and paintings by *Alvise Dal Friso* and other pupils of Paolo Veronese. In the apse is a wooden statue of the titular Saint by the school of Bon. In the ceiling is a tondo of St Nicholas in glory by *Montemezzano.*

From San Sebastiano the ZÁTTERE, a series of quays lining the broad Canale della Giudecca, is soon reached. It has been planted with trees, and has fine views across to the Giudecca (comp. below) and of the large ships bound for the industrial port and oil refinery of Marghera conspicuous to the W. Just before the next bridge the Calle and Corte del Magazen lead to **San Trovaso** (Pl. 14; *Santi Gervasio e Protasio*), a church rebuilt in 1590. On either side of the choir, the last works of *Iac. Tintoretto,* completed by his son *Domenico* and others, are to be returned here after restoration. In the chapel on the left, Temptation of St Anthony, by *Tintoretto,* and St Chrysogonus on horseback, attrib.

to *Giambono* (removed for restoration); in the N. transept, which has an altar in Sansovino's style, is a Last Supper, by *Tintoretto.* The Rio San Trovaso, with its ancient balconied boat-house, is one of the busiest and most picturesque of the lesser canals of Venice; the *Palazzo Nani,* formerly Barbarigo, across the bridge, has a 15C façade.—Farther along the Zattere is the Renaissance church of *Santa Maria della Visitazione* (1493-1524), and a little farther the church of the **Gesuati** (Pl. 14; *Santa Maria del Rosario*), by *Massari* (1726-43). The fine ceiling (Story of St Dominic) is frescoed by *G. B. Tiepolo,* who painted also (over the 1st altar on the right) the *Virgin in Glory with SS. Rosa, Catherine of Siena, and Agnes of Montepulciano. 1st altar, opposite, Three saints, by *Seb. Ricci;* 3rd N. altar, Crucifixion, by *Tintoretto* (c. 1570); 3rd S. altar, Three Saints, by *G. B. Piazzetta.*

The long Zattere quay returns towards St Mark's past *Lo Spirito Santo* (Pl. 14; closed), a church of 1483, with a Renaissance façade, to *Santa Maria della Salute* (Pl. 15), a beautiful octagonal church built partly of Istrian stone and partly of brick cased in marble, by *Longhena* (1631-81) in thanksgiving for the deliverance of Venice from the plague; the dome is a dominant feature of the view from the mouth of the Grand Canal. It has recently been restored.

In the chapels opening off the circular aisle are (r.) three paintings by *Luca Giordano* and (l.) Descent of the Holy Ghost, a late work by *Titian.* The high altar, with its marble group of the Virgin casting out the plague, by *Juste Le Court,* and beautiful candelabrum by *And. Bresciano* (1570), is flanked by four columns from the Roman Theatre at Pola. The Great Sacristy contains three ceiling-paintings (Cain and Abel, Sacrifice of Isaac, David and Goliath) and an *Altarpiece (St Mark enthroned), all early works by *Titian,* the *Marriage at Cana, by *Tintoretto,* and many other paintings.

Across the rio to the W. is the triple apse (1342) of the former *Abbazia di San Gregorio* (now a restoration centre for paintings). Beyond two bridges is the *Palazzo Venier dei Leoni* (open April-Oct, Mon, Wed, and Fri 15-17). Here the *Peggy Guggenheim Collection** provides one of the most representative displays of modern art (after 1910) in Europe. Among artists represented in over 300 works are Picasso (6), Brancusi, Marc Chagall, Max Ernst (13, incl. two bronzes), Paul Klee (2), Salvador Dali (2), and Henry Moore (3).

On the E. of Santa Maria is the **Seminario Patriarcale** (visit by previous arrangement), containing an Oratory, with a Lombardesque altar, where Sansovino was originally buried; a cloister, with tombs and inscriptions, and a collection of sculpture; and on the upper floor, reached by a handsome staircase, the *Manfrediana Picture Gallery.*

Among the paintings are: Madonna by *Cima;* Apollo and Daphne, recognized since cleaning in 1955 as by the young *Titian; Dom. Beccafumi,* Penelope; Triptych with a central panel of the Kerchief of St Veronica, of the German School, and wings by *Filippino Lippi* (Christ with St Mary Magdalen, and with the Woman of Samaria); *Boltraffio* (or another follower of Leonardo), Holy Family. There are good portrait busts by *Vittoria* and *Canova.*

Either from the Zattere (near the church of the Gesuati) or from the Riva degli Schiavoni a vaporetto runs to the **Giudecca**, a southern industrial suburb of Venice, occupying eight islands. Originally called *Spinalunga* from its elongated shape, it owes its present name, perhaps, to the Jews of Venice, who are said to have been obliged to reside there at one time. Later on it was the site of aristocratic villas and pleasure-gardens.—Its most interesting building is the Franciscan church of the **Redentore,** the most complete and one of the most typical of *Palladio's* churches (1577-92), built in thanksgiving for the delivery of Venice from the plague of 1575-76. The interior is austere yet gracious. In the 1st chapel on the left is an Ascension, by *Tintoretto;* on the Baroque high altar (by Gius. Mazza) are fine bronzes by *Campagna* of the Crucifixion, St Francis, and St Mark. In the Sacristy (entered from the S. side of the church) are Madonnas by *Alvise Vivarini* (c. 1489), *Pasqualino,* and *Bissolo,* and other paintings.

From the pier a little E. of the Redentore or from the Riva degli Schiavoni a vaporetto plies to *San Giorgio Maggiore (Pl. 16; open 9-12.30, 14.30-19), one of the most conspicuous churches in Venice, standing on a separate islet.

The present building, rebuilt in 1565-80 by Palladio, and finished in 1610 by Sim. Sorella, stands on 10C foundations. The campanile (adm. 9-12.30, 14.30-17), raised in 1791 by Bened. Buratti on the lines of that of St Mark's, commands an extensive and characteristic *View of Venice, the Lagoon, the Adriatic, the Euganean Hills, and the distant Alps.

The cruciform interior, with its central dome, is dignified and simple. South Aisle: 2nd altar, Crucifix, ascribed to *Nic. Lamberti;* 3rd altar, School of *Tintoretto,* Martyrdom of SS. Cosmas and Damian. South Transept, School of *Tintoretto,* Coronation of the Virgin. The long Choir is entered between two candelabra by *Roccatagliata;* on the side walls, *Tintoretto,* *Last Supper (1594), *Shower of Manna; on the altar, *Campagna,* Bronze group of the Saviour on a globe borne by the Evangelists, and two angels. The Baroque *Stalls and lectern are by *A. van der Brulle,* a Fleming and *Gasp. Gatti* (1594-98). In chap. to l. of the high altar, *Tintoretto,* Resurrection and the Morosini family. North Transept, *Tintoretto* (and pupils), St Stephen. Stairs lead up to an upper chapel where the Conclave met in 1799-1800 (comp. below), with a tempera painting of St George and the Dragon by Vittore Carpaccio, a copy of his work in the Scuola di San Giorgio degli Schiavoni (comp. p. 298).

The adjoining Benedictine *Monastery was the scene in 1799-1800 of the Conclave that elected Pope Pius VII. After many years' use as barracks, it was in 1951-55 restored as the *Giorgio Cini Foundation,* an International Centre of Art and Culture. Visitors are shown the dormitory designed by *Michelozzo* and completed by *Giov. Buora* (1494-1533); a cloister (1579) and refectory (1560) by *Palladio;* and a fine staircase by *Longhena* (completed 1671). The library, also by *Longhena,* has 17C woodwork by *Pauc* and ceiling paintings by *Gherardi* and *Coli.* Count Cini's memorial to his son, killed in an air crash, also includes two boarding schools and an open-air theatre.

VII   ENVIRONS OF VENICE

The **Venetian Lagoon** (*Laguna Véneta*), separated from the Adriatic by the low and narrow sand-bar of the Lido, which is pierced by three channels, is a shallow expanse of water, 210 sq. m. in area. Rather more than half of this (115 sq. m.) is the *Laguna Morta,* under water only at high spring tides; the remainder is the *Laguna Viva,* perennially flooded. On some of the islands townships and monasteries were established in the Middle Ages, most of which are now decayed. The hauntingly beautiful but desolate lagoon today supports a few small fishing communities and market gardens, apart from the famous Lido and the glass manufactories of Murano. Motor-launches provide an excellent service between the main islands.

A. FROM VENICE TO THE LIDO; frequent service of vaporetti and motoscafi from the Station, the Riva degli Schiavoni, etc. (see p. 279); car-ferry from alongside Piazzale Roma.

The **LIDO**, near the N. end of the largest of the islands between the Lagoon and the Adriatic, has for more than sixty years been the most fashionable seaside resort in Italy, and has bequeathed its name to numberless bathing resorts all over the world. It consists of a group of luxurious hotels and villas bordering the long sandy beach, which is divided up into sections, each belonging (save at the extreme ends) to a particular hotel or bathing establishment.

Numerous **Hotels and Pensions** near the Viale S. Maria Elisabetta; luxury class establishments on the Lungomare Marconi.

Sea-Bathing. The big hotels on the sea-front have their own private beaches, and the other hotels and pensions share a bathing establishment on the Lungomare Marconi. Beach huts at some of these may be hired by the day. The public beaches are at the extreme N. and S. ends of the island, at S. Nicolò and Alberoni.

Golf Course (18 holes) at Alberoni, at the S. end of the island.—TENNIS COURTS at the larger hotels, and at Lungomare D'Annunzio.

Casinò Municipale open in summer (entrance fee, 5000 l.) with gaming rooms, night club, and theatre. Play (roulette, baccarat, etc.) begins at 15 and continues until about 2.30 in the morning.—PALAZZO DEL CINEMA, where the famous Film Festival has been held since 1936.

Buses from the landing-stage: **A** to the *Casinò* and the *Excelsior Hotel;* **C** and **11** to the *Città Giardino;* **C** also to *Malamocco* and *Alberoni.*

Airport (private planes) at *San Nicolò.*

Adjoining the landing-stage is *Santa Maria Elisabetta,* a church of 1627, whence the Gran Viale S. M. Elisabetta leads direct to the beach. Lungomare Marconi runs along the shore (r.) past the Grand Hotel des Bains, which provided the setting for Thomas Mann's 'Death in Venice' to the CASINÒ and PALAZZO DEL CINEMA. Just beyond is the Excelsior Palace Hotel with its landing stage on a canal (which also serves the Casinò; direct motor-launch services in summer from Riva degli Schiavoni). To the N. is *San Nicolò di Lido* (3 km.), with a little church where the doge attended mass after the marriage with the sea, which took place at the *Porto di Lido,* the channel at the N. end of the island.

The extension of the airport here in the 1930s obliterated the long disused *English Protestant Cemetery* (1684-1810); among the graves were those of Consul Joseph Smith (1682-1770), art-collector and diplomat, and his wife Catherine Tofts (d. 1756), the singer. The tomb-stones have been moved to a corner of the Catholic cemetery nearby. Opposite are the islands of *Le Vignole* (with the fine Forte Sant'Andrea, by Sammicheli) and *Sant'Erasmo,* both mainly occupied by market-gardens.

In summer vaporetti of service 20 from the Riva degli Schiavoni to the Lido call at SAN LÀZZARO DEGLI ARMENI, the seat since 1717 of an Armenian monastery founded by Peter of Manug, called Mechitar (the 'Consoler') and celebrated for its polyglot printing press. Visitors are shown the fine collection of manuscripts and books, and a small museum. The Treasury was damaged by a fire in 1975. Byron was a frequent visitor, and studied Armenian as a means of conquering his boredom. The island is also connected directly by service 10 (all the year) with Riva degli Schiavoni.

B. FROM VENICE TO MURANO, BURANO, AND TORCELLO. Regular services (comp. p. 279) from Fondamenta Nuove c. every hour. Excursion-steamer (more expensive) every afternoon in summer from the Riva degli Schiavoni, making the round trip in 4 hrs but allowing only a very brief stay at Torcello. Murano, and especially Burano have several good trattorie, while Torcello has one celebrated hotel and restaurant, and is a beautiful place to picnic (since it has no shops, food must be brought from Venice).

FROM VENICE TO MURANO the regular steamer touches first at the island of **San Michele,** on which are the *Cemetery* of Venice, with its cypress groves, and the Renaissance church of *San Michele,* by Mauro Coducci (1469-78), with an attractive interior. To the left of the entrance is the *Cappella Emiliani,* a charming little Renaissance building by Gugl. Bergamasco (c. 1530), containing three fine 16C reliefs.

In the Camaldulensian monastery which occupied the island from 1212 to 1810 Fra Mauro (d. 1459), the cartographer, was a monk. Silvio Pellico (1789-1854), the patriot author, was imprisoned here by the Austrians before being sent to the Spielberg; and G. P. R. James (1801-60), who died as British Consul in Venice, and the composer Wolf-Ferrari, are buried in the Protestant cemetery; Serge Diaghilev (1872-1929) lies in the Orthodox enclosure, and near him his composer protégé Igor Stravinsky (1882-1971; died in New York).

MURANO, about 1 m. from Venice, is a place of c. 7800 inhab., occupying five islets. Since 1292 it has been the centre of the Venetian glass industry, which under protective laws reached its zenith in the early 16C. After a period of decline it has now once more revived under the impulse of Ant. Salviati and others, though the modern products have little of the taste of former days. In 1441-50 Murano was the seat of a famous school of painters, headed by Ant. Vivarini and Giov. d'Alemagna. The regular boat service calls at three landing stages: Colonna, Faro, and Fondamenta Navagero. From Colonna, Rio dei Vetrai leads past numerous glass factories to (500m) SAN PIETRO MARTIRE, a Dominican Gothic church partly rebuilt in 1511 and restored in 1928. It contains (S. side) an Assumption (1510-13) and a *Madonna, with angels and saints, and Doge Agostino Barbarigo (1488), both by *Giov. Bellini.* The chap. to the l. of the presbytery has some good paintings by *Fr. da Santacroce, Nicolò Rondinelli,* and others. Above the door into the sacristy, St Jerome by *Paolo Veronese.* In the Sacristy is some elaborately carved panelling (1652-56) by *Pietro Morando.* In l. aisle, Deposition, by *Salviati.*

A bridge crosses the main Canale degli Angeli near the restored *Palazzo Da Mula,* one of the few traces of Murano's ancient splendour. To the r. Fondamenta Cavour leads to the MUSEO DELL'ARTE VETRARIA (adm. 10-16; fest. 9.30-12.30) in the Pal. Giustinian. This contains a splendid collection of glass from the oldest Egyptian to the present day. Noteworthy are the specimens of 15-16C Murano ware, and the Spanish and Bohemian glass.—A little farther on is the basilica of *Santa Maria e Donato,** a magnificent specimen of Ravennate Romanesque architecture, founded before 999 but remodelled in 1125-40, closed since 1974 for restoration. The *Apse has two rows of arches on twin columns, the lower arcade blind; the isolated campanile is striking. The columns of the nave have Byzantine capitals and support stilted arches; the splendid floor mosaic dates from 1140. In the N. aisle are a wooden relief of San Donato (1310), perhaps by *Paolo Veneziano,* a Madonna by *Laz. Bastiani* (1484), and a 14C polyptych of the Death of the Virgin. In the semi-dome of the apse is a Byzantine mosaic of the Virgin. The baptistery, entered beneath Bastiani's Madonna, contains a Roman sarcophagus, once used as a font.

The regular boat services (not the excursion boats) next touch at (5m.) *Mazzorbo* on its pretty canal, with a picturesque cemetery and the Gothic church of Santa Caterina. The islet was favoured for painting by Sir Winston Churchill. It is connected by bridge with Burano.

5¾ m. **Burano,** a cheerful little fishing village of great charm, with brightly painted houses and miniature canals. For long celebrated as the centre of the Venetian lace industry, the Scuola dei Merletti (Lacemaking school) was founded in 1872 to revive the industry which had decayed in the 18C. This was, however, closed in 1970, but many of the inhabitants still practice the art of lace-making and their products are sold in numerous shops on the island. The parish church contains a painting by Girol. da Santacroce behind the altar, a Crucifixion by G. B. Tiepolo in the N. aisle, and three charming small paintings by Giov. Mansueti in the Sacristy. Burano was the birthplace of Baldassare Galuppi (1706-85), 'il Buranello', the operatic composer, celebrated in verse by Browning.

San Francesco del Deserto, 20 min. S. by sándolo (on hire in Burano), an island in the most deserted part of the lagoon, is identified by its clump of cypresses. It is said to have been a retreat of St Francis in 1220 and now contains a little church, two charming cloisters, and beautiful gardens. Eleven friars live on the island.

6½ m. **TORCELLO**, though now a small group of houses in a lonely part of the lagoon, still preserves some lovely relics of its days of splendour, when, from the 5C to the 13C, it was the sea-girt stronghold of the people of Altinum, who were driven from the mainland by the Lombard invaders. At one time it is said to have had 20,000 inhabitants, but the rivalry of Venice and the malaria due to the marshes formed by the silting up of the Sile brought about its downfall.

A pleasant walk (c. 10 min.) leads along a canal from the landing-stage to the group of monuments. The *Cathedral (L'Assunta)*, founded in 639, is typical of Venetian Byzantine, and was altered in 864 and rebuilt in 1008. In the middle of the narthex which precedes the façade are remains of the 7C baptistery. The shutters of the windows on the S. side are formed of hinged stone slabs. The aisled basilican INTERIOR (open 9-19) has 18 marble columns with good capitals, and a superb pavement of 'opus Alexandrinum'. A Byzantine mosaic of the Last Judgement, probably reset in the 12C or 13C (and later restored) covers the W. wall. The marble pulpit and ambo on the N. side are made up from fragments from the earliest church. The iconostasis consists of four elaborately carved *Transennæ (9C), which are classic examples of late-Byzantine design, and, above columns (also with good capitals) are 15C paintings of the Virgin and Apostles. Higher up is a Gothic Crucifix in wood. Behind it is the choir, with a Synthronon (7C) in the apse, in which steps rise to the bishop's throne in the centre. Beneath the high altar is the Roman sarcophagus of the first Bp. of Altinum. In the semi-dome of the central apse, on a stark gold ground, is a mosaic of the *Madonna, one of the most striking figures ever produced in Byzantine art. Beneath are the Apostles, and on the arch, Annunciation. In the S. apse are more mosaics: Christ in benediction with Saints and angels, and a delightful vault decoration. Near the W. door is a stoup with strange carved animals. The tall detached CAMPANILE (no adm.) is a striking landmark in the lagoon.

The church of * *Santa Fòsca*, nearby, of the early 11C, is octagonal in plan, with a portico on five sides and a triple apse and wooden dome. The columns have Byzantine capitals. It has been drastically restored. On the grass, outside the Gothic Palaces of the Archives and Council, is a primitive stone seat known as 'Attila's chair'. The Palaces now contain the small *Museo dell'Estuario*, which includes Greco-Roman finds from Altinum, remains of a silver altarpiece from the Cathedral (10C), the embroidered banner of Santa Fosca (1366), and painted organ panels attr. to Veronese (adm. 10-12.30, 14-18 exc. Mon).
Some of the regular steamers go on to (8m) *Treporti*, S.E. of Burano.

C. FROM VENICE TO CHIOGGIA; motor-vessel in 2 hrs from the Riva degli Schiavoni, an interesting voyage through the 'Isole del Dolore' in the S. half of the Lagoon.—The boat passes between the islets of *San Sérvolo*

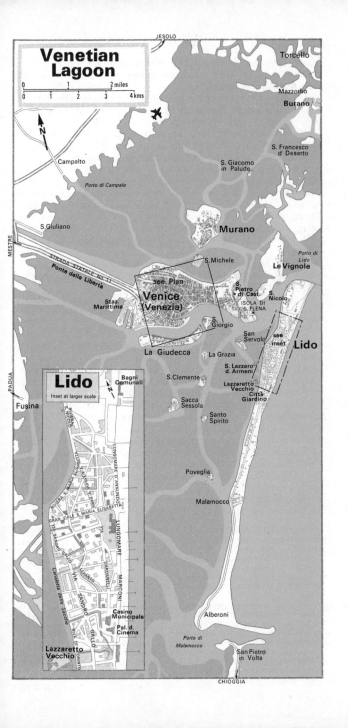

Venetian Lagoon

0   1   2 miles
0   1   2   3   4 kms

JESOLO

Torcello

Mazzorbo

Burano

Campalto

S. Francesco d' Deserto

Porto di Campalo

S. Giacomo in Palude

S. Giuliano

Murano

STRADA STATALE NO. 11
Ponte della Libertà

MESTRE

Porto di Lido

Le Vignole

S. Michele

see Plan

Venice (Venezia)

S. Pietro di Cast.

ISOLA DI S. ELENA

S. Nicolo

Staz. Marittima

S. Giorgio

San Servolo

see inset

Lido

La Giudecca

La Grazia

PADUA

S. Lazzaro d. Armeni

Fusina

S. Clemente

Lazzaretto Vecchio Città Giardino

Sacca Sessola

Santo Spirito

Lido
Inset at larger scale

Bagni Comunali

Poveglia

Malamocco

RIVIERA S. NICOLO

LUNGOMARE D'ANNUNZIO

GRAN VIALE S. MARIA ELISABETTA

VIA SANDRO GALLO

VIA LEPANTO

VIA DARDANELLI

LUNGOMARE MARCONI

Casino Municipale

Pal. d. Cinema

Canaretto delle Sacche

Alberoni

Lazzaretto Vecchio

Porto di Malamocco

San Pietro in Volta

CHIOGGIA

(l.) an asylum and *La Grazia* (r.) with an isolation hospital. Farther on are the islets of *San Clemente* (r.), another asylum where the 15C church has a fine series of Baroque monuments of the Morosini family, *Santo Spirito* (l.) the site of a famous monastery destroyed in 1656, and then *Poveglia* (the ancient *Popilia*), on the right, a verdant island now an old peoples' home.—5 km. *Malamocco*, a quiet fishing village lies towards the S. end of the island of the Lido. The ancient island of *Metamauco*, once the seat of the government of the Lagoon, was submerged c. 1107; the present village, nearer the mainland, has a good campanile and an old palace of the podestà.—7½ m. *Alberoni* is now a popular bathing resort, with the Lido golf course. Between it and the colourful fishing village of (10 m.) *San Pietro in Volta* the boat crosses the Porto di Malamocco, an entrance to the lagoon between the islands of the Lido and Pellestrina.—13½ m. *Pellestrina*, strung out along its narrow sand-bar, is a fishing village with a lace industry. On the left are seen the *Murazzi*, a great sea-wall undertaken in 1744-82 in two sections on either side of the Porto di Chioggia.

18½ m. **Chioggia,** the principal fishing port of Italy (52,500 inhab.), with many characteristic streets and alleys, is visited also for its bathing beach at Sottomarina (see below).

Always a loyal daughter of Venice, Chioggia suffered destruction at the hands of the Genoese in 1379; but the Venetians under Vittor Pisani succeeded immediately afterwards in shutting up the Genoese fleet in the harbour, and its subsequent surrender marked the end of the struggle between the two cities.

From the Piazzetta Vigo beside the quay, with its column bearing the Lion of St Mark, the Canale della Vena is crossed by the Ponte Vigo (1685) to reach the church of *San Domenico,* containing a St Paul, by Carpaccio (1520), and Christ crucified conversing with saints, ascribed to Tintoretto. From the Piazzetta Vigo the corso del popolo leads past the Romanesque campanile of *Sant' Andrea* and the so-called *Granaio,* a building of 1322 now serving as a market-hall, to the 19C Town Hall. Farther on, beyond San Giacomo and facing the little church of San Francesco (r.) is the family mansion of Rosalba Carriera, later occupied by Goldoni; then comes the early Gothic church of *San Martino,* and finally the piazza with the detached Romanesque *Campanile* (60 m) and the CATHEDRAL. The interior, reconstructed by Longhena after a fire in 1623, is notable for its rich marble decoration. The tree-planted piazza beyond has a marble balustrade overlooking the canal and adorned with 18C statues, one of which, a Madonna, is held in great reverence.

From San Giacomo the Calle San Giacomo leads across a long bridge to *Sottomarina,* a village of fishermen and market-gardeners with narrow houses closely wedged together. On the seaward side is the fine sandy beath with innumerable pensions and small hotels, and to the N. is the southern section of the Murazzi (see above).

At the end of the Corso is the Porta Garibaldi, some distance beyond which, on the right, is the station. To *Adria* and *Rovigo,* see p. 356.

D. FROM VENICE TO IÉSOLO: motor-launch in 40 min. from the Riva viâ the Lido to *Punta Sabbioni*, E. of Murano, in connection with a bus to (c. ½ hr) **Lido di Iésolo,** a popular bathing resort 9 m. long, between the old and new mouths of the Piave. The old village of *Iésolo,* formerly Cavazuccherina, 1 m. N. of the E. end, perpetuates the name of an early-medieval centre, known also as *Equilium,* the rival of Heraclea in the affairs of the lagoon (comp. p. 344). Here some remains of a Romanesque church survived until the Austrian offensive of June 1918.—The bus goes on to San Donà (Rte 36).

From Venice to *Bologna,* see Rte 37; to *Padua, Vicenza, Verona,* etc., see Rte 31; to *Trento,* see Rte 32; to *Treviso* and *Pieve di Cadore,* see Rte 34; to *Trieste,* see Rte 36; to *Udine* and *Tarvisio,* see Rte 35.

34   VENICE TO TREVISO, BELLUNO, AND PIEVE DI CADORE

ROAD, 158 km.—N 13. 30 km. **Treviso.** Leave by the Borgo Cavour and turn right, N348.—50 km. Turning for *Montebelluna* (2 km. l.).—85 km. **Feltre,** junction with the road from Trento.—N50. 115 km. **Belluno.**—123 km. *Ponte nelle Alpi.*—N51. 158 km. **Pieve di Cadore.**—The shortest road from Treviso to Ponte nelle Alpi (71 km.) runs viâ Conegliano and Vittorio Véneto (Rte 35). It is attractive but hilly and misses Feltre and Belluno.—The AUTOSTRADA (A27) follows this route as far as Vittorio Véneto.

RAILWAY, 160 km. Through trains daily by this route to *Calalzo-Pieve di Cadore* in 3½-4 hrs; on other trains carriages are changed at Treviso and Montebelluna. The route viâ Conegliano and Vittorio Véneto is shorter and quicker.

From the landward end of the Venice road bridge, the Mestre by-pass diverges right to join N13 north of the town beyond the motorway junction for Trieste. The road, with the railway on the left, drives due N. across the *Terraglio,* a plain once dotted with aristocratic Venetian villas, viâ (18 km.) *Mogliano Véneto* and (23 km.) *Preganziol.*

30 km. **TREVISO** is a bright and attractive provincial capital (91,100 inhab.) traversed by several branches of the Sile and the Cagnan. Many of its narrow streets are lined with arcades and the older houses often overhang the pavement and are decorated with exterior frescoes. New building following severe war-damage, avoiding extremes of preservation or innovation, has not robbed the old town of its character.

Post Office, Piazzale della Vittoria.—**E.P.T.,** Palazzo Scotti, 41 Via Toniolo.
Buses from the station to the P.za Indipendenza, etc.; also to Mestre and Venice.
Teatro Comunale, Corso del Popolo. Music Festival, Oct-Jan.
Airport (*San Giuseppe*) at Sant'Angelo (flights to Rome, Palermo, Bologna, etc.)

History. Treviso in the Middle Ages, as capital of the Marca Trevigiana, was well known for its hospitality to poets and artists, especially under the dominion of the Da Camino family (1283-1312). From 1389 to 1796 it was a loyal adherent of the Venetian dominion. During both world wars it suffered severely from air raids, notably on Good Friday, 1944, when half the city was destroyed in a few minutes. Treviso was the birthplace of the painters Pier Maria Pennacchi (1464-1514) and Paris Bordone (1500-71), and of Pope St Benedict XI (Nic. Boccasini, 1240-1303), a great Dominican.—The works of Tomaso da Modena, a brilliant successor of Giotto, are best studied in this city.

Travellers from Venice by road or rail enter the town by Via Roma and Corso del Popolo, crossing the Sile, with the Romanesque tower of *San Martino* (church modernized) on the left. Via Venti Settembre, bearing left, leads on to PIAZZA DEI SIGNORI, the animated centre of the town, where many streets converge. To the right here is *Palazzo dei Trecento* (restored), the 13C council house, and the adjoining *Palazzo del Podestà,* rebuilt in antique style in 1874-77, with a tall battlemented tower. Behind them is the *Monte di Pietà* (ring for adm. at No. 2), with the charming Renaissance Cappella dei Rettori.

The Calmaggiore, a busy arcaded street, goes on to P.za del Duomo, in which are the 12C *Baptistery,* conjoined with the *Campanile,* and the **Cathedral** (*San Pietro*), an attractive building with seven domes.

Founded in the 12C, the building underwent repeated alterations and extensions, down to the W. portico, added in 1836 (retaining two Romanesque lions). It was restored after severe war damage.

INTERIOR. 2nd S. altar, *Paris Bordone,* Adoration of the Shepherds. At the end of the S. aisle is the MALCHIOSTRO CHAPEL (light to r. of the altar), added in 1519, with frescoes by *Pordenone,* and an *Annunciation by *Titian* (being restored in 1976). In the vestibule of the chapel are the jambs of the 12C W. portal, the 'Madonna del Fiore', by *Girol. da Treviso il Vecchio* (1487), and the tomb of Bp. Castellano (1332). In the retro-choir, frescoes by *Lod. Seitz* (1880); on the right, tomb of Pope Alexander VIII (d. 1691), with a remarkable portrait-statue by *Giov. Bonazza;* on the left, *Monument of Bp. Zanetti (1486), by *P. Lombardo.* The Chapel of the Sacrament at the end of the N. aisle, contains the fine *Tomb of Bp. Franco (1501). The figure of St Sebastian, against the W. pillar of this aisle, is by *Lor. Bregno.* The interesting crypt, beneath the choir (apply to the sacristan) has a forest of columns from the 12C church and fragmentary mosaics.

The winding Vicolo del Duomo, behind the cathedral, affords a view of the picturesque Gothic Canons' Houses. Here, too, near the Episcopio, can be seen part of a circular Roman mosaic, recalling the motifs in the pavements of Aquileia.

Via Canova and Borgo Cavour prolong the Calmaggiore to the city wall. To the right in Via Cavour, beyond two pleasant cloistered courts, is *Casa Trevigiana* (adm. 10-12, 14-16 exc. Mon, and Sun and fest. p.m.; ring), a decorative building of the 14C (enlarged in the 16C) with a collection of applied art (including a remarkable display of wrought iron work). In the garden (removed from nearby) is the quaint 14C Municipio. In Borgo Cavour are the *Library* and **Museo Civico** (adm. 9-12, 14-16, fest. 10-12; closed Mon).

The ground floor (9 rooms and the cortile) contains (R. 1) the remarkable bronze ritual discs (5C B.C.) from Montebelluna and (R. 2) a unique collection of bronze sword-blades dredged from the Sile and its tributaries (Hallstatt period). The Roman relics include the tomb of a citizen of Tarvisium (Treviso) and statuettes from Oderzo. Early-Christian and Byzantine sculptures.

The PICTURE GALLERY is on the first floor. At the top of stairs, ROOM I (long gallery) displays 13-14C sculptures and numerous frescoes by local painters. Also, *G. B. Tiepolo,* Flora (detached fresco from Villa Corner at Merlengo); two 17C wood statues of Patriarchs (Venetian).—Four galleries overlooking a small cloister contain frescoes; a fine 14C statue of St Andrew from the Ospedaletto di Sant'Andrea; and the Virgin Annunciate, and *Story of the life of St Ursula, a splendid series of frescoes from Santa Margherita, by *Tomaso da Modena.* Also, *Girol. da Treviso* (or his workshop), Crucifixion.

ROOM 8. *Girol. da Treviso,* Resurrection; *Giov. Bellini* (with assistants), Madonna and Child; *Gerol. da Santacroce* (attrib.), Adoration of the Magi; *Cima da Conegliano,* Madonna and Child.—R. 9. *Lor. Lotto,* Portrait of a Dominican; *Titian,* Portrait of Sperone Speroni.—R. 10. Works by *Paris Bordone.*—R. 11. *Iac. Bassano,* Crucifixion, Three Saints.—R. 12. *Pordenone,* St Anthony Abbot.—R. 13. Frescoes of Pages attrib. to *Paolo Veronese* and his school and to *Bened. Caliari; Arminio Zuccato,* Mosaic.—The rest of the collection includes: *Gian Dom. Tiepolo,* Preaching of the Baptist; *Guardi,* View of Venice; *Pietro Longhi,* Portrait of a gentleman; Portraits by *Rosalba Carriera;* (R. 24) *Thos. Lawrence,* Portrait of Canova. Attractive among a host of later works are the sculptures and charcoal drawings by *Arturo Martini* (1889-1947).—Also in the museum (but not on display) are the prisms with which Newton made his experiments with the refraction of light, which passed into the hands of his disciple Count Algarotti.

At the end of the street is *Porta dei Santi Quaranta,* a town-gate of 1517. To the N. is the most interesting stretch of city wall, built by Fra Giocondo and others in 1509-18, the top of which has been laid out as a promenade almost as far as *Porta San Tomaso,* another fine gateway. The wall itself is better seen from the *Gardens* outside.

In the S.W. quarter is the large Dominican church of *San Nicolò, built in brick in the 13-14C, with a fine triple polygonal apse. The massive columns within are frescoed with *Saints by *Tom. da Modena* (St Agnes, on the N. side is especially charming). On the S. wall the 15C altars have good decoration. The huge fresco of St Christopher (1410) is attrib. to *Antonio da Treviso*. Above the high altar is a *Madonna and saints by *Marco Pensaben* (1521) and *Savoldo;* on the right is a memorial (1693) to St Benedict XI, the chief founder of the church; on the left the tomb of Agost. d'Onigo (c. 1500), with sculptures by *Ant. Rizzo,* and *Pages, frescoed by *Lor. Lotto.* The fine altarpiece in the chapel to the r. of the high altar has portraits of members of the Monigo commission attrib. to *Lotto.* On the walls are frescoes by the Sienese school (c. 1370; Adoration of the Magi, St Margaret of Hungary) and the contemporary Riminese school (votive image of the Madonna and

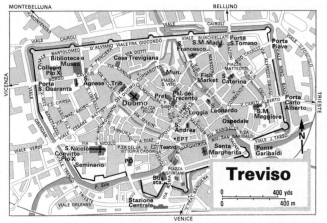

Saints). The chapel to the left of the presbytery has an altarpiece of the Risen Christ by *G. B. Bregno.* The 16C organ by *Gaetano Callido* was decorated by *Ant. Palma.*

The adjoining *Seminario* has two dignified cloisters and a chapter house containing delightful *Frescoes of leading Dominicans, by Tom. da Modena (1352; ring). Several interesting frescoes in the Byzantine style are temporarily stored here.

In Via Martiri della Libertà, leading N.E. from the Corso, is the *Loggia dei Cavalieri,* a Romanesque building of 1195. The Pass. del Molinetto leads left (opposite San Leonardo) to cross the Cagnan at the picturesque *Fishmarket;* Via San Parisio continues left to *San Francesco,* a large brick church of the 13C, restored in 1928 after many years' use as an army store. In the floor near the S. door is the tomb slab of Francesca, daughter of Petrarch, who died in childbirth in 1384; in the N. transept, that of Pietro Alighieri (d. 1364), the son of Dante; and, in the chapel to the left of the high altar, Madonna and saints, a fresco by Tom. da Modena (1351). Opposite the S. door is part of a huge fresco of St Christopher.

Santa Caterina (usually locked; key at the Comune), long deconsecrated but restored for the sake of its frescoes by Tomaso, stands a little E. of the Fishmarket (comp. above). Via Carlo Alberto leads to

Santa Maria Maggiore, a church of 1474 containing a tomb by Bambaia and a much-venerated Madonna originally frescoed by Tom. da Modena. The pleasant Riviera Garibaldi alongside the Sile returns towards the centre.

From Treviso to *Castelfranco* and *Vicenza,* see p. 267; to *Conegliano* and *Udine,* and to *Oderzo,* see Rte 35.

The Feltre road leaves Treviso by the Borgo Cavour, then bears right, crossing the Roman Via Postumia at (40 km.) *Postioma,* with the Montello in front.—49 km. A little to the left is seen **Montebelluna,** a modern town (23,900 inhab.) at the foot of the Montello, with a pleasant 17C church on a hill contrasting with the unattractive new cathedral below.

FROM MONTEBELLUNA TO ÁSOLO, 13 km., bus in 20 min. At (7 km.) *Maser,* at the foot of the hills of Asolo, is the *Villa Bárbaro, now *Villa Volpi,* built by Palladio in 1560-68 for Dan. Barbaro, patriarch of Aquileia. The house (adm. Tues, Sat, Sun, & fest. 15-18; in winter 14-17) contains brilliant frescoes by Veronese and stuccoes by Aless. Vittoria. In the grounds are a Carriage Museum and a fine Palladian *Temple.*—13 km. **Ásolo,** a charmingly situated town with interesting old houses, was presented by Venice to Queen Catherine Cornaro in exchange for her dominion of Cyprus and here in the *Castello* she lived in 1489-1509; the little museum (adm. 9-12 or 12.30, 14-16.30 or 18; closed Mon) in the 15C *Loggia del Capitano* contains memorials to her and of Browning, as well as paintings, sculpture, and archæological exhibits. From the name of this town Card. Bembo (who frequented Queen Catherine's court) coined the term 'asolare' (to gambol, amuse oneself at random), whence is derived 'Asolando', the name chosen by Robert Browning "for love of the place" for his last volume of poems (1899). Browning's first visit to Ásolo was in 1836, and it is the scene of his 'Pippa Passes', published five years later. Eleonora Duse (1850-1924), the actress, and Browning's son (1849-1912) are buried at Ásolo in the cemetery of Sant'Anna.—*Possagno* (p. 277) is 9 km. N.

The *Villa Emo at *Fanzolo,* 10 km. S.W. of Montebelluna, is open Sat, Sun, & fest. 15-18 (winter 14-17). Built by Palladio (1550-60) it has frescoes by G. B. Zelotti, and is well worth a visit.

Beyond Montebelluna rise (l.) the Colli Asolani with the castle of Ásolo, with Monte Grappa behind; to the right is the distant Monte Cavallo, then the nearer Monte Cesen shuts in the view.—57 km. *Cornuda.* The chapel of Santa Maria della Rocca crowns a prominent hill to the left. The road descends to the Piave and follows its right bank.—Opposite (64 km.) *Pederobba* is *Valdobbiádene* rebuilt since 1918. It has an ossuary containing the remains of Frenchmen who fell in Italy in the First World War. A road mounts to *Pianezze* (1070 m), with winter sports facilities (chair-lift to Monte Barbaria, 1465 m). The road from Valdobbiádene to Conegliano (34 km.; p. 333) is known as the 'Strada del Vino Bianco'.—Beyond (67 km.) *Fener* the valley narrows to form the Stretta di Quero; on the left rise the steep wooded slopes of Monte Tomático; on the right, as the road recedes from the Piave valley, is *SS. Vittore e Corona,* an interesting Romanesque church of 1100 beside a 15C monastery, a pleasant walk from Feltre (½ hr).

85 km. **Feltre** is an upland town (22,500 inhab.) whose ancient centre, largely rebuilt after a sack in 1509, rises above its modern extensions. Gateways survive at either end of the old main street, in which external frescoes by Morto da Feltre (? L. Luzzo, d. 1512) and his pupils adorn many houses, including the painter's own. Midway along Via Mezzaterra, opens *P.za Maggiore where stand the *Castle,* the *Municipio,* with a Palladian loggia (1558), and the *Palazzo Guarnieri.* A 16C Fountain by Tullio Lombardo stands in the forecourt of *San Rocco*

(1599). Via del Paradiso, with the 15C frescoed *Monte di Pietà* leads from the piazza to the *Museo Rizzarda,* notable for its superb wrought-iron work and housing the Galleria d'Arte Moderna. The *Museo Civico* (adm. 9-12, 15-16), within the E. gate, contains Roman and Etruscan remains, a portrait by Gentile Bellini, a triptych by Cima da Conegliano, and examples of Morto da Feltre's work. The masterpiece of Morto (a Transfiguration) is in the sacristy of the *Ognissanti,* beyond the gate. From the square a 16C stairway descends to the S. gate (1494) and to the *Cathedral,* which has a 15C apse and a campanile of 1392, heightened in 1690, and preserves a carved Byzantine cross of 542.

Pedavena 4 km. N., noted for its beer, is a centre for easy climbs to the Feltrino peaks.

FROM FELTRE TO SAN MARTINO DI CASTROZZA. N 50, 48 km., bus in 1 ½ hrs, a fine approach to the Southern Dolomites. This route follows the Primolano road to (6 km.) *Arten* and then bears right up the narrow and picturesque Cismon valley.—9 km. *Fonzaso.*—At (13 km.) *Ponte della Serra* it passes between two artificial lakes below (17 km.; l.) *Lamon.*—An attractive by-road on the left at 21 km. ascends the Val Cortella to *Canal San Bovo* (8 km.) and *Caoria* (14 km.; bridle-path to San Martino).—30 km. *Imer* stands at the foot of the attractive Val Noana (r.).—31 km. *Mezzano.* An important road ascends left in 5 km. to *Góbbera* (988 m) and thence down to Canal San Bovo (4 km. farther; see above). For its continuation to the Valsugana, see Rte 32.

35 km. **Fiera di Primiero** (710 m), with a Gothic church, is a resort with winter sports facilities. It stands at the confluence of the Cismon and Canali. Excursions in the Val Canali may be made to (1 hr) the ruined Castel Pietra, and (2½ hrs) the *Rifugio Treviso* (1630 m), a centre for ascents on the S. side of the Pale di San Martino.—Crossing the Cismon at (36 km.) *Siror,* another winter resort, the road ascends the left bank.—48 km. *San Martino di Castrozza,* see Rte 26.

From Feltre N 50 turns N.E. and descends again to the Piave valley. At (92 km.) *Busche* the road divides to follow both banks of the river to Belluno. At 3 km. along the right branch is *Lentiái,* where the unexpectedly fine church contains paintings by the Vecellio family, perhaps including Titian himself. From the left branch, *Monte Pizzocco* (2186 m), shaped like a doge's cap, comes into view on the left.—99 km. *Santa Giustina,* is an important agricultural centre on a fertile upland basin.—At 100 km. a by-road (l.) leads to *Lago di Mis* (11 km. N.), where the lofty road affording fine views of the dam threads the wild and rugged CANALE DEL MIS to the tiny hamlet of *Titelle* (22 km.).—At (104 km.) *Sédico,* the road to Ágordo and Cortina (see Rte 27) diverges; this route passes N. of the Villa Pagani-Gaggia where Hitler met Mussolini in July 1943. On the approach to Belluno, *Monte Pelf* (2501 m) becomes prominent at the head of the Ardo valley (l.).

115 km. **BELLUNO** is an old mountain capital (36,300 inhab.) splendidly situated above the junction of the Ardo and the Piave. It was the birthplace of Sebastiano Ricci (1659-1734), the painter, and of Pope Gregory XVI (1765-1846). The *Duomo,* by Tullio Lombardo (16C), was partly rebuilt after earthquakes in 1873 and 1936; the campanile by Juvarra (1743) is worth ascending for the view. In P.za del Duomo are the *Town Hall* (1838) and the *Palazzo dei Rettori,* now the Prefettura, a Renaissance building of 1492-96, to the right of which are the old town belfry and the *Museo Civico* (weekdays 9-12 on request), in a building of 1664. Beyond the last opens P.za del Mercato, with a fountain of 1410 and the *Monte di Pietá* (1501). Thence Via Mezzaterra, the main street of the old town, extends to the S. From it Vicolo San Pietro leads (l.)

to the church of *San Pietro,* with carved panels by Brustolon, and a high-altarpiece by Seb. Ricci. Via Santa Croce, farther down Via Mezzaterra (l.), leads to *Porta Rugo* (12C; restored 1622), commanding a splendid *View of the Piave valley and the Dolomites.—From the N. end of P.za Mercato a 16C gate admits to P.za Vitt. Emanuele. To the left opens the spacious main square of the modern town; to the right, Via Roma leads to *Santo Stefano,* a church of 1486 with a Roman sarcophagus outside the main portal. The lofty interior retains frescoes by Iac. da Montagnana (c. 1487; restored) and a fine wooden altarpiece by the Bellunese, And. di Foro (16C).

The *Alpe del Nevegal* (1030 m), 11 km. S. is a ski-resort; a chair-lift rises to the *Rif. Brigata Alpina Cadore* (1600 m), with a botanical garden near by. A mule track leads to the S.E. of the Nevegal viâ (3¼ hrs) the *Col Visentin* (Rif. A. Bristot; 1761 m), a magnificent viewpoint, to (5½ hrs) *Fadalto* (p. 333).

As the road leaves Belluno it crosses the Ardo with a good retrospect of the city. On the left rises *Monte Serva* (2132 m) and ahead, up the Piave valley, is the fine pyramid of *Monte Dolada* (1939 m).—123 km. *Ponte nelle Alpi* is at the junction of two routes to the Cadore from the S. The road turns N. and on the right, below the pyramidal *Pizzo Gallina* (1545 m), is the dam of the hydro-electric system of Piave-Santa Croce. Beyond *Monte Toc* (r.; 1921 m) it reaches (133 km.) *Longarone,* almost totally wiped out by a disastrous flood.

In 1963 a landslide from Monte Toc into the basin of the Vaiont dam caused a huge water displacement to sweep through the Piave valley, destroying five villages and killing 1899 people. The dam, 6 km. E., now largely filled with rubble and a scene of desolation, is reached viâ the spectacular *Gola del Vaiont.*
The *Valle di Zoldo,* traversed by the Maè and a narrow road (bus to Pecol), ascends N.W. towards the Pelmo massif. The local dialect approaches the Ladin of the Cadore valleys. The chief centre is (17 km.) *Forno di Zoldo* (810 m) at the junction of the Maè with several smaller torrents. Near by is the 15C church of *San Floriano,* containing a 13C stone triptych and an altarpiece by Brustolon. The church of *Zoppè di Cadore,* 8 km. N. beneath the Pelmo, has a Madonna by Titian. A good mountain road (20 km.) leads N. into the Ampezzo valley.—At (21 km.) *Dont* (935 m) is a monument to Andrea Brustolon (1662-1732), the woodcarver, whose work may be seen in many of the old village churches. The road on the left leads over the *Passo Duran* (1601 m) to (21 km.) Ágordo. Above Dont there is a splendid view of the Civetta (l.) and Pelmo (r.).—25 km. *Fusine* (1177 m) is the chief centre of the upper valley which is frequented for winter sports. *Monte Civetta* (3220 m) is ascended from here in 7½ hrs viâ the *Forcella d'Alleghe* and the *Rifugio Coldai* (2135 m; 3½ hrs). Another base for the ascent is (27 km.) *Pecol,* a small summer and winter resort, the terminus of the bus from Belluno.—The valley road now ascends to (33 km.) the *Forcella Staulanza* (1773 m), in full view of *Monte Pelmo* (3168 m), then descends rapidly to (42 km.) *Selva di Cádore,* (see p. 258).

136 km. *Castellavazzo,* dominated by the castle-tower of Gardona, commands a fine view of the mountains upstream.—141 km. *Ospitale,* named from an ancient hospice.—150 km. *Perarolo* stands at the confluence of the Bóite and the Piave; the railway makes a circuit of the side-valley high above the village, and Monte Antelao is prominent to the left. Farther on the valley opens out, and at (156 km.) *Tai* the road reaches the upland basin of Pieve di Cadore and joins the Cortina road. Hence to (158 km.) **Pieve di Cadore,** see Rte 30B.

35 FROM VENICE TO UDINE. THE FRIULI AND CARNIA

ROAD, 137 km. N 13. To (30 km.) *Treviso,* see Rte 34. Treviso is left by the Porta San Tomaso (alternative route to Codróipo, see below).—52 km. *Susegana.*— 58 km. **Conegliano** (by-pass, r.).—88 km. **Pordenone** (by-pass, l.).—113 km. *Codróipo* (by-pass, l.).—137 km. **Udine.**

AUTOSTRADA to Pordenone, 77 km., A4 (see Rte 36) to Portogruaro, then A28. To Udine, 129 km., A4 to Palmanova, then A23.

RAILWAY, 136 km. in c. 2 hrs. This is part of the international route between Italy and Austria viâ Villach, with through carriages viâ (230 km.), *Tarvisio* (frontier) from Marseille to Vienna, Rome to Vienna (and Moscow), Trieste to Munich, etc.

Many places in this region were severely damaged in the Friuli earthquake in May and September 1976. The epicentre was N.W. of Udine: the communes of Gemona, Tarcento, San Daniele, Maiano, and many others were devastated. Earth tremors continued for many months and the final toll was nearly 1000 dead, and over 70,000 homeless.

From Venice to (30 km.) **Treviso,** see Rte 34.

FROM TREVISO TO CODRÓIPO VIÂ ODERZO, 75 km. The route leaves Treviso by Via Carlo Alberto, and after 17 km., just beyond a huge battle memorial, crosses the Piave.—28 km. **Oderzo,** the Roman *Opitergium.* Finds exhibited in the Museo Civico (10-12 exc. Mon) include mosaics with hunting scenes and sculptural fragments. The Duomo, founded in the 10C, was rebuilt in Gothic style in the 14C.—At (36 km.) *Motta di Livenza* the 16C cathedral has a good façade. The road bears to the left beyond the town for (63 km.) *San Vito al Tagliamento,* the birthplace of Pomponio Amalteo (1505-88), the painter. The cathedral has a tall campanile, Romanesque below, Renaissance above, and contains some of Amalteo's works.—At 69 km. the route strikes the main road to Udine, and then turns right for (75 km.) *Codróipo* (see below).

From Treviso N13 continues due N., crossing the Piave at *Ponte della Priula,* with a votive temple commemorating the BATTLE OF THE PIAVE, where in 1918 the Italians withstood the last Austro-Hungarian attack and launched their successful counter-offensive. There are British war cemeteries at *Tezze* (8 km. E.) and at *Giávera* (9 km. W.).—58 km. **Conegliano** is a rapidly expanding wine-growing town (34,500 inhab.), noted also as the birthplace of the painter G. B. Cima (1460-1518), and has many attractive 16-18C houses. The Gothic *Cathedral* (14-15C) contains a fine altarpiece by Cima (1493); the adjacent guild hall ('Santa Maria dei Battuti') is covered with 16C frescoes (restored 1962). Above rises the ruined *Castello,* with a museum in one tower.

FROM CONEGLIANO TO PONTE NELLE ALPI (Belluno), 42 km., road (bus) and railway. The road turns N. 2½ km. E. of Conegliano.—13 km. **Vittorio Véneto** (31,000 inhab.), the town that gave its name to the final victory of the Italians in Oct 1918, consists of the lower industrial quarter of *Céneda* and the old walled town of *Serravalle* with many old houses and churches. Céneda has a museum relating to the battle in the former Town Hall (1537-38) and a dramatic memorial of 1968. In Serravalle the *Ospedale Civile* contains the chapel of San Lorenzo (10-12, 16-19) with 15C frescoes. In the *Loggia Serravallese* (1462) the Museum contains local archæological finds. paintings, frescoes etc. (it is open 9-12, 14-19 exc. Tues). The *Duomo* (1755) contains a fine altarpiece by Titian (Madonna with SS. Peter and Andrew; 1547). Vittorio is the starting-point for the *Bosco del Cansiglio,* a high-lying carstic plateau with forests of beech and fir (1120 m) to the E.; also for the road by the *Passo di San Boldo* (706 m) to Sédico (36 km. N.W.).

Beyond Vittorio the road ascends the Meschio valley passing three power-reservoirs.—27 km. *Fadalto* lies just below the *Lago di Santa Croce,* now a supply reservoir, which the road skirts. The *Col Visentin* (p. 332) is 4½ hrs S.W. by mule-track.—42 km. *Ponte nelle Alpi* (see Rte 34; l. for Belluno, r. for Pieve di Cadore).

75 km. *Sacile*, placidly reflected in the waters of the Livenza, was hit by the earthquake in 1976 when its 15C cathedral was damaged.— 88 km. **Pordenone** (*E.P.T.*, Viale Cossetti), a rapidly expanding town (51,900 inhab.) and the industrial centre of Friuli. It has recently been designated the chief town of a new province. Many of the buildings in the city, especially the newer ones, were severely shaken by the 1976 earthquake. It was the birthplace of the painter G. A. Sacchiense (1483-1539), called 'Il Pordenone'. The old centre consists mainly of one long winding Corso with arcades and some painted house fronts. At its S. end is the eccentric *Palazzo Comunale*, with a projecting clock tower in a Venetian Renaissance style (16C) at odds with the 13C Emilian Gothic core. The side towers were restored after earthquake damage. Nearby, in *Palazzo Richiere,* the MUSEO CIVICO was opened in 1970 (adm. 10-12.30, 15-18; closed Mon). The palace dates from the 15C and has fine painted wood ceilings and some remains of mural paintings.

Since the Friuli earthquake it has been used as a temporary home for paintings from damaged churches in the province, and from the Duomo (see below). Works from the latter include: *Pordenone*, Our Lady of Pity with SS. Joseph and Christopher and donors (1515); *Marcello Fogolino*, Madonna with SS. Blaise and Apollonia (1533), and St Francis of Assisi, St John Baptist and the Prophet David; *Pomponio Amalteo*, Flight into Egypt; and paintings by *Calderari*.—The permanent collection consists mainly of 16-18C works by regional artists: *School of Pordenone*, Head of a Friar; *Giov. Ant. Pordenone*, Finding of the True Cross; *Luca Giordano*, Judgement of Paris, etc.—On the Second Floor are 19-20C works by local artists including *Ant. Marsure* and *Michelangelo Grigoletti*.

The DUOMO (*San Marco*), with a Romanesque *Campanile and good W. portal by Pilacorte (1511), has been closed since the earthquake. Most of the paintings have been removed to the Pinacoteca (comp. above).—Just N. of the Corso (reached by Via Mercato) the church (deconsecrated) and conventual buildings of *S. Francesco* have been restored as a cultural centre. The exterior has notable brickwork decoration. Farther along the Corso, Via del Cristo leads N. to the *Chiesa del Cristo,* with a portal by Pilacorte. The interior has been stripped of its Baroque decoration to reveal its earlier origins. *San Giorgio* (16C), at the other end of the town, has a giant Tuscan column for campanile.

Maniago (26 km. N.), which once supplied Venice with daggers, now makes cutlery. The cathedral, rebuilt in 1468, and a market-hall, both frescoed by Amalteo, were damaged in 1976.

Beyond (103 km.) *Casarsa della Delizia* this route joins the road from San Vito (see above) and crosses the sandy bed of the Tagliamento on the long Ponte della Delizia.

Roads ascend both banks of the Tagliamento. Above the W. bank is (18 km.) *Spilimbergo*, where the Romanesque and Gothic cathedral containing paintings by Pordenone and stalls by Marco Cozzi, was severely damaged in 1976.—N463 follows the E. bank to (42 km.) *Gemona* (p. 343). The chief place on the way is (23 km.) *San Daniele del Friuli*, noted for ham. The town was devastated in the earthquake, but the frescoes (1487-1522) by Pellegrino da San Daniele in the church of Sant'Antonio Abate were miraculously saved.

113½ km. *Codróipo* was the Roman *Quadrivium*, on the Via Postumia. About 3 km. S.E. on the old Palmanova road is *Passariano* with the vast VILLA MANIN (by Giov. Ziborghi; c. 1738) that belonged to Lod. Manin, last of the Venetian doges. Exhibitions are held here, and since 1976 it has become a centre for the recuperation of works of art damaged in the Friuli earthquake. It was occupied by Napoleon in 1797 when he concluded the shameful treaty of *Campo Formio,* which sacrificed Venice to Austria. The village after which it is named is now called *Campofórmido,* 7 km. short of Udine on the main road.

137 km. **UDINE,** with 104,000 inhab., the historical centre of Friuli, became the focus of the rescue operations after the earthquake in 1976, which, however, left the city itself remarkably unharmed apart from the buildings on the Castle hill. It is the see of an archbishop, and has spinning and weaving mills and iron foundries. The old streets, mostly arcaded, fan out round the castle hill. Some splendid examples of Tiepolo's work are preserved in the city.

Post Office, Via Vittorio Veneto.—**E.P.T.,** 4 P.za Venerio.
Buses. No. 1 from the station viâ P.za Libertà to beyond Porta Gemona; No. 4 from P.za Libertà to Porta Venezia and S. Caterina. COUNTRY BUS STATION, Viale Europa Unita: services to *Cividale;* to *Aquileia* and *Grado,* to *San Daniele,* etc.

History. A Roman station called *Utina* is alleged to have occupied the site of Udine, and a 10C castle here is recorded as part of the domain of the patriarch of Aquileia. In the 13C Udine, appointed the seat of the patriarch, became the bitter rival of Cividale, but the attacks of the counts of Gorizia and Treviso (c. 1300) and of Philip of Alencon (c. 1390) unified the Friuli. In 1420, after nine years' resistance, Udine surrendered to Venice, the fortunes of which it followed thenceforth. It was occupied by Bernadotte in 1797, and by Massèna in 1805. In the First World War it was Italian G.H.Q. until Oct 1917, and then was held by the Austrians for a year. In the Second World War, after considerable damage from air-raids, it was entered by South African troops on 1 May 1945, the day before the official end of the campaign. The painter and architect Giov. da Udine (1487–1564) is the best-known native of the city.

PIAZZA DELLA LIBERTÀ, a picturesque square in the Venetian manner, is a worthy centre of the city. The particoloured **Palazzo del Comune,** or *Loggia del Lionello,* a typical Venetian Gothic building, dates from 1448–56 and was rebuilt after a fire in 1876; the statue of the Madonna at the corner is by Bart. Bon. Opposite is the Renaissance *Porticato di San Giovanni* (1533), with a chapel that has been converted into a war memorial, and the *Torre dell'Orologio,* by Giov. da Udine (1527; the 'mori' on the clock are modern). In the piazza are a fountain of 1542, two columns with the Lion of St Mark and Justice, and colossal statues of Hercules and Cacus from a demolished 18C palazzo. The statue of Peace (with a sarcastic inscription) commemorates the Treaty of Campo Formio.—The *Arco Bollani,* by Palladio (1556) serves as the entrance to the CASTLE HILL, access to which, however, has been suspended since the buildings were damaged in the earthquake.

The path leads up alongside a graceful Gothic portico (1487) and past the church of *Santa Maria di Castello* (13C) whose contemporary frescoes were badly damaged in 1976. The **Castle** was the seat of the patriarchs and Venetian governors; the present main building dates from 1517. It now houses the **Museo Civico,** the **Galleria d'Arte Antica e d'Arte Moderna,** and the **Museo del Risorgimento** (all the contents have been removed while the building is in restoration). Beside an archæological collection, the works of art include: *G. B. Tiepolo,* the 'Consilium in Arena'; *Canova,* Plaster sketch for a Crucifixion; *Pordenone,* Eternal Father; *Giov. Martini,* St Peter Martyr; *Pellegrino di San Daniele,* Annunciation; *Jacques Callot,* Udine in the 17C; *Carpaccio,* Christ and four angels; *Dom. da Tolmezzo,* Polyptych; works by *Ant. Carneo, Palma Giovane,* (Mauroner Collection) *Baciccia, Fra Galgerio, Marco* and *Seb. Ricci.* The classical and historical frescoes by *Amalteo* in the Sala del Parlemento Friulano were badly damaged in 1976.—On the esplanade, which commands a fine view of the Alps, the old (reconstructed) buildings include the *Casa della Contadinanza* containing an armoury (in restoration).

The **Duomo**, backing on to the busy Via Vittorio Véneto, was consecrated in 1335 and completed in the mid-15C. Much altered later,

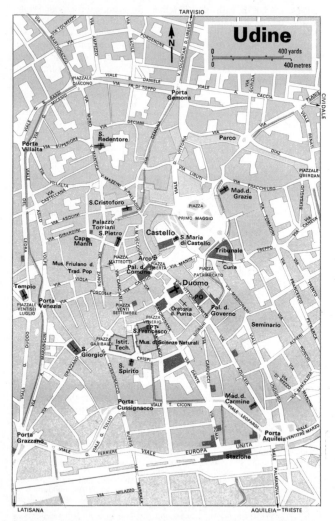

it retains a heavy octagonal campanile of 1441 above the 14C baptistery (entered from the church, see below). On the E. side (seen from Via Vittorio Véneto) are two statues (the Annunciation) of the 14C. By the door of the baptistery, on the N. wall of the church, is a blocked portal (in poor condition) dating from the late 13C. The brick W. front (late 14C) has been well restored.

INTERIOR. The transepts and choir, designed by *Dom. Rossi* and assistants (1678-1742), the frescoes by *Dorigny,* and the carved choir-stalls form an admirable Baroque ensemble. NORTH AISLE. 1st Chap. (light on right) *Giov. Martini* (1453-1535), St Mark and other Saints; 2nd Chap. *Pellegrino di San Daniele,* St Joseph. SOUTH AISLE. 1st Chap. *G. B. Tiepolo,* Holy Trinity; 2nd Chap. SS. Hermagoras and Fortunatus, also attrib. to *Tiepolo,* 4th chap. The Baroque altar encloses a small painting of the Risen Christ by *Tiepolo,* who also frescoed the walls. The elaborate organ in this aisle has paintings attrib. to *Pordenone* (1528).—From the apse a door (unlocked by sacristan) leads into a chapel with frescoes of the funeral of St Nicholas (1349) by *Vitale da Bologna,* recently discovered. Beyond the adjoining chapel, used as a store for detached frescoes and their sinopie, a door gives access to the 14C Baptistery. Here a charming 14C tomb carried by five caryatids contains the relics of SS. Hermagoras and Fortunatus.

The ORATORIO DELLA PURITÀ, on the S. side of P.za del Duomo, contains a frescoed and painted *Assumption, by *G. B. Tiepolo.*—Via Lovaria leads E. to the *Palazzo Arcivescovile* (ring at Curia; 9-13) with more *Frescoes by G. B. Tiepolo. On the stairs, Fall of the Angels; in the gallery, Old Testament scenes; in the Sala Rossa, Judgement of Solomon and four Prophets (in the lunettes). Another room is frescoed by Giov. da Udine.

The streets of old Udine, sometimes skirted by rushing streams, are well worth exploring, although the mural paintings on the house-fronts have now sadly all but disappeared. From P.za Libertà, Via Mercato Vecchio, Via Palladio (with the Palazzo Antonini, now the seat of the Banca d'Italia, by Palladio) and Via Gemona (comp. the Plan) are all within easy reach. Via P. Sarpi leads left off Via Mercato Vecchio past *San Pietro* with a good side portal, to P.ZA MATTEOTTI, a large arcaded market-place with attractive houses. The fountain was designed by Giov. da Udine (1542). Near the church of *San Giacomo,* with an early 16C Lombard façade, is a pretty well of 1486. A passageway leads from the piazzetta to Via Zanon with the tower of the 13C town wall and the Baroque *Cappella Manin.* In Via Viola, to the W. is the *Museo Friulano delle Arti e delle Tradizioni Popolari.* Farther S.E., in P.za Venerio, the church of *San Francesco,* was restored to its 13C appearance, for use as an auditorium. However, since the 1976 earthquake, it has become a store and restoration centre for the works of art salvaged from churches in the region. In Via Morpurgo, nearby, is the *Museo Friulano di Scienze Naturali,* with an interesting collection.

From P.za Libertà Via Manin leads N.E. through another town gate to the large P.za Primo Maggio. Here the 16C *Madonna delle Grazie,* a favourite votive church, has a cloister covered with ex-votos.

FROM UDINE TO GORIZIA. 36 km.; railway in 20-40 min. (through trains to Trieste in 1-1½ hrs).—23 km. *Cormons,* an ancient seat of the patriarchs of Aquileia, is the only intermediate place of importance.

FROM UDINE TO CIVIDALE, 17 km. Train every hour in 20 min. to *Cividale Stazione* and (most trains) *Cividale Città,* the end of the line (at the foot of the Corso, the most convenient for visitors). **Cividale del Friuli** is a very old town (11,300 inhab.) pleasantly situated at the point where the Natisone emerges into the plain. It was badly shaken in the earthquake of 1976.

Founded as *Forum Iulii,* perhaps by Julius Caesar, it gave its name to the *Friuli,* the first Lombard duchy to be formed in Italy. Later it was the capital of a free duchy of which Berengar I, afterwards King of Italy (888-924), was the most distinguished lord. From the 8C until 1238 Cividale was the chief seat of the patriarchs of Aquileia. It was the birthplace of Paulus Diaconus (Warnefride; 723-799), historian of the Lombards, and of Adelaide Ristori (1821-1906), the tragédienne (monument in P.za Giulio Cesare).

From the Città station and the main road from Udine, the Corso Alberto (closed to traffic) leads S. Beyond the pretty P.za Diacono, Corso Mazzini continues to the DUOMO (*S. M. Assunta*). It was begun in its present form in 1453 and continued in 1503-32 by Pietro Lombardo. In the austere interior the silver gilt *Altar (set within the Baroque high altar) is magnificent. On the N. wall is the sarcophagus of the Patriarch Nicolò Donato, by *Ant. da Carona;* above the W. door, equestrian monument to Marco Antonio di Manzano, killed in 1617 in the Turkish wars. At the end of the S. aisle hang fragments of a processional standard with the Annunciation, attrib. to *Giov. da Udine.* On the S. side is a small *Museo Cristiano* (opened by the sacristan) containing an octagonal *Baptistery (8C) reconstructed from Lombardic fragments, a marble Patriarchal throne (11C), and the altar of Duke Ratchis (744-49) with sculptured panels. Also, Lombardic sculptural fragments and interesting detached frescoes. In the *Treasury* is kept the great sword of Marquedo (Patriarch, 1368-81).

The ARCHÆOLOGICAL MUSEUM, across the square, has been closed since its damage in 1976. It contains numerous Roman remains and later material, but is especially famous for its early medieval treasures.

GROUND FLOOR. Sarcophagus of Duke Gisulphus (I or II; d. 568 or 610); the many precious relics which it contained are now on the floor above; Roman mosaic with Head of Oceanus; early Christian reliefs, one with a mermaid (8C); 12C sarcophagus, from the cathedral; wayside Madonna, a provincial 16C work; stone with the Lion of St Mark, commemorating the stubborn defence of Cividale in the siege of 1509. In the court, Jewish tombstones (13-18C). A noble staircase of 1530, with 16C frescoes and an altarpiece (Descent of the Holy Ghost) by *And. Vicentino,* ascends to the FIRST FLOOR. Here is the Chapter Library, with coins, Roman remains, etc. Central Room. Contents of a warrior's tomb, with his arms, gold and silver ornaments, and ivory chessmen; also the rare embroidered linen *Altar Cover (c. 1400) from San Pietro, with the Annunciation, Crucifixion, and Saints, popularly ascribed to the Blessed Benvenuta Boiani (d. 1292). Next room (6-9C). *Treasure of Duke Gisulphus (comp. above), including a fine bracteate cross (with portrait gems), a ring, and an enamelled fibula, all of gold. Also, gold ornaments, including a remarkable filigree disc. The end room contains the *Pax of Duke Ursus (c. 800), an ivory Crucifixion in a jewelled silver frame. Here are also the treasures of the cathedral and of S Maria in Valle, including the Grimani pax (mid-4C); ivy-leaf *Reliquary, apparrently a wedding gift from Philip II, prince of Taranto, to his bride (French; c. 1294); 10C ivory casket (Byzantine); silver cross of Patriarch Pellegrino II (c. 1200); processional cross of c. 900, in provincial style. Among the MSS. the following are outstanding: 'Bible of Aquileia' in 2 vols. (12C); *Psalter of Bp. Egbert of Trèves (977-93), and another of the 13C; both belonged to St Elizabeth of Hungary and were presented to the cathedral by her uncle Patriarch Berchtold von Andecht; History of the Lombards, by Paulus Diaconus (Montecassino; 8C). Triptych by *Pell. da San Daniele* (1501; his masterpiece) and *Girol. da Udine* (1539).

Palazzo Pretorio (in poor repair), closing the E. side of the square, was begun by Palladio in 1564. The *Palazzo Comunale* dates from the 13C, but it was virtually rebuilt in the 15-16C (and has a modern extension). Corso Ponte d'Aquileia leads down to the *Ponte del Diavolo* (15C; restored) crossing the impressive limestone gorge of the Natisone. From the N. side of the bridge Via Monastero Maggiore, once the main street of the town, leads E. At No. 2 (r.) are remains of the so-called

Ipogeo Celtico. Farther on the road passes through a Roman arch (note the medieval house on the left, in Stretta S. Maria di Corte) and, beyond Porta Patriarchale (surmounted by a Romanesque house) opens the Piazzetta S. Biagio on the banks of the Natisone. Here is the celebrated *TEMPIETTO (custodian at No. 17, Via Monastero Maggiore). This was part of a Lombardic church (8C) constructed of earlier fragments, and decorated with fine contemporary stucco reliefs of female saints; it contains a sarcophagus of Lombardic work, and 14C stalls. It was severely damaged in 1976 and is undergoing restoration. The church of *San Biagio* (key at No. 6 in the piazzetta) has a badly faded painted façade. The frescoes in the interior are particularly notable in the domed chapel in the S. aisle.

On the S. side of the town, beyond the *Porta San Pietro* (used by the Venetians as a magazine) is the church of *San Pietro,* with a good altarpiece by Palma Giovane.

From Cividale the road goes on up the Natisone valley, Slovene-speaking in its upper reaches, to (15 km.) *Stupizza,* the last Italian village. *Caporetto,* 15 km. farther on over the Yugoslav frontier, is memorable for the disaster to the Italian armies in Oct 1917.

FROM UDINE TO AQUILEIA AND GRADO, 48 km., N352, bus several times daily.—20 km. *Palmanova* is an old Venetian fortress built on a regular plan (1593), with symmetrical brick bastions, moated and grassgrown, and a hexagonal central piazza. The three chief gates are by Scamozzi, the Duomo by Longhena. Just to the S.W., the Udine autostrada joins the A4, under which this road soon passes.—At (29 km.) *Cervignano* it crosses the Venice-Trieste road (Rte 36).

37 km. **AQUILÉIA,** now a village of 3030 inhab., preserves magnificent and evocative remains of its great days both as a Roman city and as an early medieval capital. It is situated in a fertile plain. There are still large areas of the Roman city awaiting excavation.

History. Aquileia was founded as a Roman colony in 181 B.C. and soon rose to prominence. In 10 B.C. Augustus was in residence here and received Herod the Great. In A.D. 238 the 'Emperor' Maximinus was murdered by his troops when besieging the city, and in 340 Constantine II was slain on the banks of the Aussa (a little W.) by his brother Constans in their struggle for imperial power. The bishopric or patriarchate was founded soon after 313; but civil wars and barbarian incursions, culminating in the Lombard sack of 568, led to the transference of the see to Grado, which had become the foreport of Aquileia. After 606 there were two rival patriarchs, but in 1019 Poppo united the sees and rebuilt the basilica. Slow decadence, due to malaria, followed; in 1420 the civil power passed to Venice; the Austrians seized the place in 1509; and in 1751 the patriarchate was merged in the archbishoprics of Udine and Gorizia.

The approach road follows exactly the line of the Roman cardo. Car Park by the Basilica (if full, in the village by the post office). A whole day is needed to visit the site, Basilica, and two museums.

Admission times. The *Basilica* is open 8-12.30, 15-approx. 20. The *Archæological Museum* and *Crypt of the Basilica,* from 9-14, fest. 9-13. The *Excavations* are open from 8 to dusk. The *Palaeochristian Museum* is open 8.30-12.30, 15-18; winter, 8.30-12.30, 14-17; Sun & fest. 9-13; closed Mon.

The ****Basilica,** built soon after 313 by the first patriarch Theodore, was the scene of a historic council in 381, attended by SS. Ambrose and Jerome. It was extended soon afterwards and was reconstructed in its present form by the patriarch Poppo in 1021-31. A portico of the 11C extends from the W. front to the much altered remains of the *Baptistery.*

The tall *Campanile* (73 m) was built by Poppo; the upper part dates from the 14C, the bell-chamber and steeple from the 16C. On a Roman column facing it is a figure of the Capitoline Wolf, presented by Rome in 1919.

Within, the arcades surmounting the fine Romanesque capitals date from the patriarchate of Markward (1365-81), the nave ceiling from 1526. The huge mosaic **Pavement,* discovered at the beginning of this century, dates from Theodore's basilica. It portrays the vivid Story of Jonah amidst a great variety of fish, the Good Shepherd, a symbolic fight between a cock and a tortoise, the portrait heads of donors, etc. At the end of the S. aisle is the Gothic chapel of St Ambrose, built by the Torriani in 1298; it contains four family tombs (1299-1365) and a polyptych by Pellegrino da San Daniele (1503) in a fine frame; the S.E. chapel has a 9-10C transenna and a fresco of Christ blessing (14C), while the central Renaissance tribune and the altar to the right of it, with a good Pietà, are the work of Bernardino da Bissone. The high altar was carved by Seb. and Ant. da Ósteno (1498). In Poppo's apse are faded frescoes, with a dedicatory inscription (1031), showing the patriarch (with a model of the church), the Emperor Conrad II with Gisela of Swabia and Prince Henry (later Henry III) before the Madonna and six patron saints. The bishop's throne is probably somewhat earlier. In the N.E. chapel are interesting frescoes and a bas-relief with Christ between St Peter and St Thomas of Canterbury, sculptured soon after St Thomas' martyrdom in 1170. Outside the chapel is a bust of Christ (1916) by Furlan. In the N. aisle are fresco fragments (Madonna enthroned, 15C) and statuettes from a Deposition group. Near the W. end of the N. aisle is the *Santo Sepolcro,* an 11C reproduction of the Holy Sepulchre at Jerusalem.—The *Crypt,* beneath the presbytery has frescoes of great interest, thought to date from the mid-12C. They depict scenes from the life of Christ (including a fine Deposition), and of the Madonna, and scenes relating to SS. Hermagoras and Fortunatus.

The CRIPTA DEGLI SCAVI (adm. with same ticket as Museum, for opening times, see above) is entered from beside the Santo Sepolcro. It is remarkable for three levels of *Mosaics: those of a Roman house of the Augustan period (to the left on entering); the magnificent floor of a second basilica of the time of Theodore, encircling the foundations of Poppo's campanile; and parts of the floor of the late-4C basilica, as well as its column-bases.

Behind the church is the cypress-girt *Cimitero degli Eroi,* dedicated to the victims of the First World War.

The **Archæological Museum* (adm., see above) is reached by the main road (Via Giulia Augusta) and Via Roma (r.). It has a good collection of finds made in and around Aquileia.

On the GROUND FLOOR (and in the garden) are the larger sculptures and mosaic pavements of 2-4C. ROOM I. Busts of the Republican era, including the 'Old Man of Aquileia'; an inscription with the name of L. Manlius Acidinus, one of the city's founders; bas relief relating to the elevation of Aquileia to a Roman colony in the first century A.D.—R. II. Statues of Tiberius, Claudius, etc.—R. III. Finds from the necropolis; tomb stones, including one showing a smithy.—R. IV. Roman copies of Greek originals (Head of Jove, Venus, of the Medici type, etc.); Relief of the river god Æsontius (Isonzo).—FIRST FLOOR. R. V. Semi-precious gems (mostly of local make), cameos, intaglios (fine Farnese bull), objects in amber and gold (notably the golden flies, ornaments from a lady's veil).—R. VI. Egyptian fragments; Head of a Child (1C A.D.).—R. VII. Terracottas. R. VIII. Small

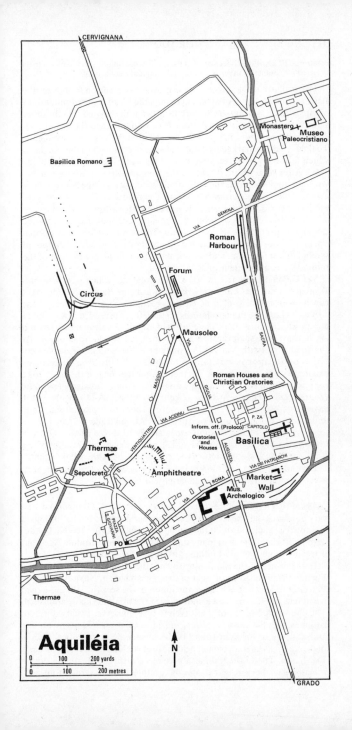

CERVIGNANA

Monastero
Museo
Paleocristiano

Basilica Romano

Via GEMINA

Roman
Harbour

Via SACRA

Forum

Circus

Mausoleo

Via GIULIA

Roman Houses and
Christian Oratories

Via ACIDINI

P. ZA
CAPITOLO

Inform. off. (Proloco)

Via AUGUSTA

Oratories
and
Houses

Basilica

VENTIQUATTRO

Via DEI PATRIARCHI

Thermae

Amphitheatre

Market

Sepolcreto

Wall

Via ROMA

Mus.
Archeologico

PIAZZALE
S. GIOVANNI

PO

Thermae

Aquiléia

| 0 | 100 | 200 yards |
| 0 | 100 | 200 metres |

N

GRADO

bronzes.—R. IX. Fine collection of *Glass, with some unique specimens.—On the floor above, domestic utensils, coins, and a lapidary collection.

The TOUR OF THE EXCAVATIONS is most easily made on foot. Near the Basilica, across Via dei Patriarchi (comp. the Plan) are the foundations of late Roman *Market-Halls,* with the town walls beyond. On the other side of the Basilica, reached from P.za Capitolo, are the remains of *Roman Houses and Christian Oratories* with superb mosaic pavements. To the E., clearly marked by a noble avenue of cypresses, is the *Via Sacra* which follows the Natissa stream N. along walls and colonnades of the 1-4C. After some 500 m it reaches the *Roman Harbour,* where a finely-wrought quay still skirts the sadly diminished waters of the Natissa, once a navigable river. Across Via Gemina a road leads past a group of modern houses to the former Benedictine Monastery of S. Maria in which are the remains of another large early-Christian *Basilica* (mosaic floor) and the *Museo Paleocristiano.* Temporarily closed, its normal opening times are given above. It contains a good collection of sarcophagi, transennæ, and mosaic panels. In the piazza in front of the monastery is a fragment of Roman road.

Via Gemina leads (r.) to Via Giulia Augusta, which passes several Roman monuments on its way back towards the Basilica. On the right can be seen a fine stretch of Roman road, and beyond, traces of the *Circus.* Behind the modern houses on the left of the road, a row of fluted composite columns mark the *Forum* of Aquileia (entrance just beyond the houses). The sculptural fragments include a fine Gorgon's head. At the road fork (with Via XXIV Maggio) is the *Grande Mausoleo,* an imposing (reconstructed) family tomb (1C A.D.), brought from its original site in the suburbs. Farther on, on the right of the main road (opposite the Basilica) is a large area still being excavated of *Roman Houses and Palaeochristian Oratories* (2-4C A.D.) with good pavements (especially W. of the vineyard). The polychrome mosaic floor under cover belonged to an oratory. Via Acidino leads W. past (l.) the scanty remains of the *Amphitheatre* and (r.) the site of the *Thermæ* towards the *Sepolcreto* (key at No. 17), a row of five family tombs of the 1-2C. Via XXIV Maggio returns S. to P.za Giovanni, the village square.

Beyond (41½ km.) *Belvedere* the causeway crosses the lagoon, with islets on either hand, to the island-city of Grado.

48 km. **GRADO** is a frequented seaside resort (10,200 inhab.) with a very popular sandy beach equipped with thermal and sand baths, joined to a town of ancient origin, the foreport of Aquileia after the 2C. Grado, despite its island site, was many times plundered in the Middle Ages, but it retains some fine old buildings in its narrow streets.

In the centre of the old fishing town is the ***Duomo** (SS. Ermagora e Fortunato) founded as the seat of the patriarchate of Nova Aquileia by Patriarch Elias after 568; after the union of the sees (p. 339) these rival patriarchs moved to Venice, and in 1451 the title was finally abolished. The church, a basilica of the Ravenna type, preserves twenty different columns with Byzantine capitals, and a fine 6C mosaic *Pavement. The ambo, made up of numerous 11C fragments, deserves notice. On the high altar is a Venetian pala of beaten silver (1372). In the apse is an early 15C fresco. The Cathedral has a precious treasury. Beneath the church remains have been revealed of a 4C oratory and hexagonal font.

The church of *Santa Maria delle Grazie,* a little to the left of the cathedral, is another basilica of the 6C or earlier on a small scale, with an even more miscellaneous assortment of ten columns, a restored marble transenna, and an apsidal bench and throne with passage behind. Excavation has revealed some good 6C floor-mosaics. Between the two churches is the restored *Baptistery,* also with 6C mosaics, approached by an avenue of sarcophagi. Remains of another early-Christian basilica have been found in the P.za della Vittoria, to the S.E.

A favourite excursion (motor-boat every afternoon in summer) is to the islet of *Barbana,* in the lagoon to the N.E., where a church, built in 1593 and rebuilt since 1918, with a venerated statue of the Virgin, is the goal of a yearly procession of boats (1st Sun in July).—Buses run at frequent intervals from Grado to Aquileia, going on to Udine or Gorizia.

FROM UDINE TO TARVISIO, 91km., N13, part of the main road to Vienna; railway, see p. 333. An autostrada from Udine to Tarvisio is planned. This route traverses the area devastated by the 1976 earthquake (comp. p. 333). The main road to Tarvisio runs N. from Udine, parallel with the railway. As far as (12km.) *Tricésimo* it is followed by frequent buses, some of which go on to *Tarcento,* a little town among the foothills, damaged in 1976, 4km. right of the road.—At 20km. N13 bears away to the left, by-passing *Artegna*(2km.) and **Gemona** (6km.), one of the worst hit towns in 1976 when over 300 people lost their lives. The monuments, including a fine Duomo and Palazzo del Comune, were all but destroyed.

At (27km.) *Taboga* this route is joined by the road from Casarsa (p. 334), on which, 2km. left, stands *Osoppo,* a medieval fortress strengthened by Napoleon, virtually wiped out in 1976. The main road now approaches the wide bed of the Tagliamento.—35km. *Venzone.* Its Medieval walls, beautiful Duomo of 1308, and fine old houses, were reduced to rubble by the earthquake.—Beyond the confluence of the Fella with the Tagliamento the road reaches (40km.) *Carnia* the junction for Tolmezzo and the Carnic Alps (see below), with the pyramidal *Monte Amariana* (1906m) prominent on the left.

N13 ascends the narrowing valley of the Fella and, beyond (45km.) the Valle d'Aupa (l.), in which is seen the old village of *Móggio Udinese* the road passes (48km.) *Resiutta,* at the foot of the Valle di Resia.—56km. *Chiusaforte* stands at the foot of the gorge, once fortified, from which it is named. The railway traverses a succession of tunnels high up on the E. side of the valley.—61km. *Dogna* stands at the foot of the Valle di Dogna, dominated by the Iôf di Montasio (2754m).—68½km. *Pontebba* was on the old Austro-Italian frontier, marked by the stream which traverses the village. The valley widens as the route enters the Valcanale, a Slovene-speaking region.—75km. *Bagni di Lusnizza* is a small sulphur spa.—79km. *Malborghetto-Valbruna* is the chief centre of the valley.—82km. *Ugovizza* has a few visitors, and Valbruna itself, in a valley to the S., has two hotels at the lower and upper ends of a cableway to *Monte Santo di Lussari*(1766m). The chief summer and winter resort here is (87km.) *Camporosso in Valcanale*(816m), where the road crosses the watershed and descends into the basin of Tarvisio, with waters flowing towards the Drava.—91km. **Tarvisio** (741m), the frontier station and Italian custom-house, with 6300 inhab. and two railway stations, is divided into an old lower town and a modern upper town. It stands at the junction of main roads to Vienna viâ Arnoldstein and Villach, to Ljubljana viâ Kranjska Gora, and to Caporetto. The last crosses the Yugoslav frontier at (14½km.) the *Passo del Predil* (1156m); at *Cave del Predil,* 3km. short of this, once noted for its lead and zinc mines, a road bears r. for the charming *Lago del Predil* or *Raibl-See,* dominated from the E. by *Monte Mangant*(2678m), where a road leads on to Chiusaforte (see above). Another excursion from Tarvisio is to the *Laghi di Fusine,* two charming little lakes 10km. S.E., off the Ljubljana road.—A chair-lift ascends from Tarvisio to the ski-slopes on the Monte Priesenig at 1289m; and climbers are catered for by several mountain refuges.

FROM UDINE TO THE CARNIC ALPS AND CADORE; railway to *Carnia* (c. 40 min.) in connection with bus thence to *Villa Santina* in 30 min. more.—To *Carnia,* see above. Thence road and railway ascend the left bank of the Tagliamento to (12km.) **Tolmezzo** (10,500 inhab.) the chief centre of Carnia, damaged in 1976 with a museum of local handicrafts.—From Tolmezzo a fine cross-country roads leads to (75km.) *Calalzo* (p. 253) viâ (19km.) *Villa Santina,*

(32 km.) *Ampezzo*, (46 km.) *Forni di Sotto*, and (55 km.) *Forni di Sopra*. All these are summer resorts, offering varied excursions among the little-known Carnic Alps. The descent into the Cadore valley beyond (64 km.) the *Passo della Máuria* (1295 m) is steep and winding.

The road running N. from Tolmezzo (bus) leads viâ (7 km.) *Cedarchis* and (16 km.) *Paluzza* to (23 km.) *Timau* (custom-house) and (33 km.) the *Passo di Monte Croce* (1362 m) on the Austro-Italian frontier. The descent leads to (45 km.) *Mauthen*, in the Ober-Gailtal.—On the right of the road, just beyond Cedarchis, are *Arta Terme* and *Piano d'Arta*, ½ hr higher up, two little summer resorts with mineral waters. Opposite them is the village of *Zuglio*, the ancient Forum Iulii Carnicum which guarded the Roman road over the pass. Above it (c. 1 hr) is the little church of San Pietro di Carnia, the oldest in the district (? 14C).

Paularo (648 m), a summer resort with some ancient chalets, is reached by road (14 km.) N.E. from Cedarchis up the Canale d'Incaroio; while another road to the W. connects Paluzza with Comeglians (16 km.; see below), with a branch to (10 km.) *Ravascletto* (950 m), on an open terrace, frequented both in summer and winter (chair-lift).

The Cadore can be reached also by road from Villa Santina by the Gorto valley, and thence viâ (14 km.) *Comeglians* (bus from Villa Santina), *Rigolaio* (18 km.) *Forni Avoltri* (26 km.) and (37 km.) *Sappada* (see below), a fine run of 50 km. to *Santo Stefano di Cadore* (p. 253); or (diverging before Comeglians) by a hilly road viâ Prato Carnico and the *Forcella Lavardet* (1542 m), again a distance of 50 km. to Santo Stefano.

Sappada (1217 m), recently much popularized as a summer and winter resort, extends for 4 km. along the uppermost valley of the Piave, from Cima Sappada at the E. end down to Palù and beyond. There are two chair-lifts, one rising S. from Cima, the other N. from Palù, eleven ski-lifts, and eight mountain refuges as well as tennis-courts; and there are daily bus services to Villa Santina, Calalzo, and San Candido.

36   VENICE TO TRIESTE

ROAD, 162 km. N 14.—37½ km. *San Donà di Piave*.—66 km. *Portogruaro*.—80 km. *Latisana*.—108 km. *Cervignano* (r. for *Grado*, 18 km.).—126 km. *Monfalcone*.—162 km. **Trieste** (158 km. by the coast road).

AUTOSTRADA, A 4, between Mestre and Monfalcone (119 km.), running farther N. all the way, shortens the total distance by 3 km.

RAILWAY, 157 km., several expresses daily in c. 2 hrs.

From the lagoon bridge of Venice N 14 turns E. skirting (12 km.) the airport of Venice (Marco Polo).—18 km. *Altino* (l.) represents the Roman *Altinum*, destroyed by Attila and the Lombards. It has a small Archæological Museum (closed Mon). The road crosses the Sile and leaves on the right the shortest road to Lido di Iesolo (p.   ) along the canal that carries the Sile's waters outside the Venetian lagoon. It reaches the *Piave*, a river famous as the line of Italian resistance after the retreat from the Caporetto (monument on the bridge) just before (37½ km.) *San Donà di Piave*, rebuilt since its ordeal in 1917-18.

A bus runs S. to (20 km.) *Lido di Iésolo* (p. 326) viâ (11 km.) *Eraclea*, a modern village (formerly Grisolera) on the Piave which has assumed the title of the ancient *Heraclea* (called after the emperor Heraclius), the episcopal and administrative centre of the lagoon in the 7-8C after the sack of Oderzo by the Lombards. The site was more probably at *Cittanova* (7 km. E. of San Donà) so called as having been again rebuilt in 727.

Beyond (41 km.) *Céggia* the road crosses the Livenza and there is a magnificent distant view of Monte Civetta and the Cadore Alps. Two kilometres beyond the river the main road to Caorle (21 km.) diverges (r.); Caorle is reached also by bus from San Donà or from Portogruaro in connection with trains.

Cáorle is a seaside resort with two beaches near the mouth of the Livenza. Founded by refugees from Concordia (see below). it was a bishop's see for twelve centuries and preserves a cathedral of 1048 with a fine detached round tower. Above the high altar is a celebrated Venetian pala of gilded silver.

66 km. **Portogruaro,** an old town (23,800 inhab.) at the junction of the main road from Treviso to Trieste, preserves its quaint streets with 14-15C houses (including the *Pal. Comunale*) and heavy arcades, and the slim campanile of its cathedral, which leans perceptibly. The *Museum* (9-12, 15-18; winter 9-14; fest. 9-13; closed Mon) contains finds from the Roman station of *Concordia Sagittaria.* The present village of Concórdia, 2 km. S., has a Gothic Duomo with a Romanesque campanile and baptistery; along the S. side excavations have revealed a 4C martyrium and a mosaic from a contemporary basilica. Excursions may be made to the N.W. of Portogruaro to see the fine Romanesque churches of two early Benedictine abbeys, at *Summaga* (6 km.) and *Sesto al·Réghena* (13 km.), recently restored, with 13-16C frescoes and 8C reliefs in the crypt.—At (80 km.) *Latisana,* where the parish church has a Baptism of Jesus by Veronese (1567), the road crosses the broad gravelly bed of the Tagliamento and thence follows the railway closely.

A road (N 354) leads S. along the river to **Lignano Pianeta, Sabbiadoro,** and **Riviera** forming a continuous planned pleasure resort with some 400 hotels and pensions along a sandy spit at the mouth of the Laguna di Marano. It is the second largest centre of tourism in Italy.—*Bibione* is another recently developed resort.

98 km. *San Giorgio di Nogaro* is connected by rail with Palmanova and Udine. Beyond the tiny Ausa river, the Austro-Italian frontier of 1866-1918, the countryside becomes more wooded.—At (108 km.) *Cervignano del Friuli,* also connected by rail with Udine, this route crosses the road (bus from Cervignano station) to Aquileia and Grado described on p. 339. Here also diverges the most direct road to Gorizia.

FROM CERVIGNANO TO GORIZIA, N 351, 28 km. Beyond (5 km.) *Ruda* the road crosses the motorway and approaches the W. bank of the Isonzo.—16 km. *Gradisca* is an old Venetian fortress still preserving many of its 15C watch-towers against the Turks and some good Baroque mansions. The county was ceded to Austria in 1511, and in 1615-17 was the occasion of the War of Gradisca, between Austria and Venice. Opposite rises Monte San Michele, a ridge hotly contested in the Carso campaign (museum).—The road crosses the Isonzo.

28 km. **Gorizia** (E.P.T., Galleria del Corso), with 43,600 inhabitants, is a provincial capital standing in an expansion of the Isonzo valley hemmed in by hills. After the fall of the independent counts of Gorizia in the 15C, the city fell into the hands of Austria, and it remained an Austrian possession almost continuously from 1509 to 1915. In the First World War it was the objective of violent Italian attacks in the Isonzo valley, and eventually was captured on 9 Aug 1916. Lost again in the autumn of 1917, it was finally taken in Nov 1918. The Treaty of Paris (Feb 1947) brought the Yugoslav frontier into the streets of the town, cutting off its E. suburbs, the subsidiary railway stations of Monte Santo and San Marco, and the old cemetery. The town, and the country on both sides, were threatened with complete ruin, but in 1952 more reasonable readjustments were made, including a ten-mile-wide zone in which local inhabitants may circulate freely.

The road passes the railway station on the way in to the town. The chief buildings of interest are towards the N. end. To the right of the *Post Office* in the main Corso G. Verdi is the central P.za della Vittoria in which are the handsome church of *Sant'Ignazio* (17-18C) and the *Prefettura.* Thence the old Via Rastello leads to the *Duomo,* a 14C building much restored, containing the treasury brought from Aquileia in 1752. Above it stands the Borgo Castello of the Venetians (1509); within its wards are the *Museo di Storia e Arte* (9 or 10-12, 15-18; closed Mon), the little church of Santo Spirito (1398), and the KEEP, a 12C castello of the counts of Gorizia, remodelled in 1508. The rampart walk commands a wide view. In the Baroque Palazzo Attems (1745) near the N. end of the main street is the *Museo della Guerra 1915-18* (adm. as above).—Across the river, 4 km. to the N.W. at *Oslávia,* a 'Gothic' castle holds the graves of 57,000 men of the 2nd Army who fell in 1915-18.

From Gorizia to *Udine,* see p. 337.—The *Bainsizza Plateau,* to the E., the scene of a brilliant Italian offensive in May-Aug 1917, is now Yugoslav territory.

At (114 km.) *Villa Vicentina* (2 km. l.) is a villa built by Elisa Bonaparte Baciocchi in 1815, where in 1869-70 Pasteur saved the silk industry of Italy, as he had that of France. The road crosses the Isonzo, and at (123 km.) *Ronchi dei Legionari* reaches the edge of the Carso and the region of the battle-front of 1915-17.

The town has a special place in Italian patriotic sentiment: here Gugl. Oberdan was arrested in 1882 and hence in 1919 D'Annunzio set out to occupy Fiume. It now has an important civil airport serving Udine, Gorizia, and Trieste (flights to London, Madrid, Frankfurt, Athens, etc.). The **Carso** (Germ. *Karst,* Slav. *Kras*), a curiously eroded limestone plateau, was the scene of the most violent struggles in the Austro-Italian campaign. Vast trenches and veritable caverns were easily constructed by widening the existing crevasses in its surface; and although large-scale operations were made difficult by the nature of the ground, immense concentrations of artillery were brought up by both sides for the defence of this key position. It was the Duke of Aosta's stand here with the 3rd Italian Army that averted complete disaster after Caporetto (Oct 1917).—The *Bora* (N.E. wind) sweeps the plateau with great fury at some seasons.

126 km. **Monfalcone,** an industrial town (31,000 inhab.) with large and conspicuous naval shipyards, has been completely rebuilt since 1918.

FROM MONFALCONE TO GORIZIA. Railway, 22 km.; frequent service to Gorizia Centrale in 20 min., going on to Udine. Bus, 4-8 times daily, in 35 min. The Udine road follows the railway past (3 km.) *Ronchi* (see above) which it leaves on the left. 6 km. *Redipuglia* has the huge war cemetery of the 3rd Army, with over 100,000 graves, including that of the Duke of Aosta (1869-1931), the heroic defender of the Carso.—At (9 km.) *Sagrado* the railway keeps to the left bank but the road crosses the Isonzo and turns right into (12 km.) *Gradisca,* whence to Gorizia, see above.

Outside the town the way divides. To the left is a road (N55) to Gorizia across the Carso; in the centre the main road (N202), an extension of the motorway with few intermediate exits, runs farther inland direct to (151 km.) *Poggioreale del Carso* (p. 351), whence alternative hilly spurs enter **Trieste** from the E. (162 km.) or S.E. (168 km.).—N14 keeps to the right along the coast.

At (132 km.) *San Giovanni al Timavo* it passes the mouth of the Timavo, which emerges here from an underground course of over 25 miles.—134 km. *Duino* is a fishing village with the ruined Castello Vecchio and the imposing Castello Nuovo.—137 km. *Sistiana,* on a delightful bay known to the Romans as Sextilianum. Here the coast road (fine sea views) bears to the right, viâ Miramare (see p. 351), for (158 km.) **Trieste.**

The old road (1½ km. farther) runs inland, through (4 km.) *Aurisina,* where the quarries of fine white stone have been worked since Roman times.—At (10½ km.) *Prosecco,* known for its wine, it turns right to descend into *Trieste.*

TRIESTE, the most important seaport of the northern Adriatic, although its commercial traffic has diminished in recent years, commands a pretty gulf backed by the low rolling hills of the Carso. It is an attractive provincial capital (270,100 inhab.), mainly modern in appearance, with lively streets, and a harbour of which the principal quays, unlike those of Genoa, are generally open. A few streets of the old town retain their character and the environs are pleasant. Trieste was the centre of Irredentism in Istria during the period of Austrian rule.

Airport at *Ronchi,* 35 km. N.W.; terminal at Stazione Centrale (Viale Miramare), coach in 60 min. International services daily to Athens, Brussels, Frankfurt, London, Madrid, etc.

Parking in the centre is particularly difficult; best on the Rive or near the cathedral.

Post Office, P.za Vittorio Veneto.—POLICE STATION (Questura), 6 Via Tor Bandena.

Tourist Offices. *E.P.T.,* Via G. Rossini; Information Offices at railway station and Molo Audace (April-Sept). *Azienda Autonoma,* Castello di San Giusto; Information Office, 4 P.za Unità d'Italia.

Local Buses from P.za Oberdan to *Barcola, Miramare, Grignano,* and *Sistiana;* to *Duino;* to *Prosecco;* to *Aurisina;* to *Opicina.* Other **Buses** from Staz. Largo Barriera Vecchia to *Muggia;* to *Koper, Piran, Porec,* and *Pula;* From main Bus Station in P.za della Libertà to *Muggia;* to *Sistiana;* to *Postojna* and *Ljubljana;* to *Rijeka;* to *Sežana;* to *Zagreb* and *Belgrade,* etc. Coaches to Venice, Milan, the Dolomites, etc.—RACK TRAMWAY from P.za Oberdan to *Opicina.*—TOUR of the city usually twice a week in summer from Tourist Office on Molo Audace; and weekly excursions to the Carso from the Molo Audace.

Steamers. International liners moor at the *Stazione Marittima;* to Grado from *Molo Pescheria;* to Muggia, Grignano, and Sistiana, steamers from *P.za Unità.* Regular steamer service for *Istria, Dalmatia,* and *Greece* (information at Molo Audace); less frequent service for *Venice.*—TOURS of the port and gulf by motor launch are organized in summer from Riva del Mandracchio.

Consulates. *British,* 2 Via Rossini; *American,* Via Valdirivo.—ENGLISH CHURCH. *Christ Church,* 11 Via San Michele.

Theatres. *Politeama Rossetti,* Viale Venti Settembre. *Teatro Comunale G. Verdi,* P.za Verdi (opera season in Nov-March, concerts in May & Oct). Open-air theatre (July-Aug) in the *Castle.*

Sport. GOLF COURSE, 9 holes, at Padriciano (6½ km. E.).—TROTTING RACES at Montebello stadium.—SEA BATHING. Riviera di Barcola; Grignano and Sistiana (sand); Duina (rocks).—SWIMMING POOL (covered), Riva Gulli.

History. The settlement of *Tergeste,* already an important outlet into the Adriatic for the produce of the middle Danube and its tributaries, was absorbed into the Roman dominion early in the 2C B.C. From the 9C to the 13C the city was ruled by its bishops, with various nominal overlords, and at the beginning of the 13C, with the rise of the independent Commune of Trieste, began also the age-long rivalry with Venice for the commerce of the Adriatic. The Venetians generally had the upper hand, and in 1382 Trieste came under the protection of the Austrian Emperor Leopold III. The strife with Venice, however, continued, and in 1463 Trieste, reduced to desperate straits by a blockade, was saved only by the intervention of Pius II. In 1470 Frederick III rebuilt the wasted city, but its latter-day prosperity dates from Charles VI, who declared it a free port in 1719, a privilege followed by further favours from Maria Theresa. Later emperors, however, though fostering the commerce of Trieste, paid less attention to its liberty of sentiment, and despite the increased prosperity brought about by the opening of the Suez Canal (1869) the Triestines leant more and more towards the cause of Italian unity. Italian troops entered Trieste in 1918 and the city, together with the Carso and Istria, was ceded to Italy by the Treaty of Rapallo in 1920. These territories fell in 1945 to Yugoslav forces and the Carso was incorporated into Yugoslavia. By the Italian peace treaty (1947) Trieste and Istria were created a Free Territory, with Anglo-American trusteeship of the city and a Yugoslav zone in Istria, until in 1954 the existing frontier was agreed at a further four-power conference in London. Trieste remains a free port.

Charles Lever (d. 1872) was British consul at Trieste from 1867 until his death, and he was succeeded by Sir Richard Burton, who also died here in 1890. J. J. Winckelmann (1717-68), the archæologist, was murdered at Trieste by a thief whose cupidity he had excited by displaying some ancient gold coins. James Joyce (1882-1941) lived in the city in 1905-14 and 1919-20.

The life of Trieste centres on the **Harbour,** fronted by the pleasant broad quay, or Riva, and always animated by the movement of ships. Its N. limit (beyond which extend the quays and warehouses of the Punta Franco) is marked by the *Canal Grande,* which serves as a mooring for small boats, the end of which is closed scenographically by the church of Sant'Antonio (see p. 350). Then beyond the Greek Orthodox church of

San Nicolò comes the *Molo Audace,* commemorating the name of the destroyer from which the first Italian troops landed on 3 Nov 1918. On the left, beyond the *Teatro Verdi* (museum, 10-13 exc. Mon), opens the handsome PIAZZA DELL'UNITÀ D'ITALIA (cafès) surrounded by the imposing Palazzi del Governo and del Comune and the huge offices of the Lloyd Triestino line. Here also is a statue of Charles VI and a bizarre fountain. The name of Riva Mandracchio is suggestive (Mandraki, in Greek 'sheepfold', commonly denotes an ancient galley port; comp. Rhodes, Kos, also Hvar). On the Molo Bersaglieri is the *Stazione Marittima;* trains bound for the station still run the length of the quay (although a railway tunnel is under construction beneath the city). Beyond the next jetty is the *Pescheria* with its spacious market hall open to the sea. Nearby is an *Aquarium* (daily 9-12, 15-18). In Piazza Venezia (l.) is the *Museo Revoltella* (9-13 exc. Mon; entrance at No. 27 Via Diaz) with a collection of 19C paintings displayed on the first floor. The later works of modern art are to be arranged in the adjacent palazzo. In P.za Attilio Hortis are the *Natural History Museum* (open daily 9-13) and the Public Library.

On a rise to the S.W. stands the *Museo Sartorio* (9 or 10-13, 14-18; closed Mon) with a collection of applied arts. Some paintings from the Museo di Storia ed Arte (see below) may be displayed permanently here. The villa also servés as an exhibition centre. Nearby, the *Villa Necker* was occupied by Jerome Bonaparte after 1815.—At the end of Riva Grumula, in Via Campo Marzio (comp. the Plan), is the MUSEO DEL MARE (9.30-12.30) with sections devoted to harbours, navigation, and fishing.

Via and Piazza Cavana and Via S. Sebastiano (all closed to traffic) penetrate the dwindling area of the old town. To the E., in Via del Teatro Romano, demolitions in 1938 revealed the remains of a *Roman Theatre* endowed in the late 1C by one Q. Petronius Modestus. Behind the theatre rises the hill of San Giusto, reached by narrow lanes and steps through the *Parco della Rimembranza,* or with a car by Via Capitolina.

On the hilltop, planted with trees and with a pleasant view out to sea, is the ***Cathedral of San Giusto** (closed 12-15), a venerable building of irregular plan and in several styles.

Between the 5C and the 11C two aisled basilicas arose, one dedicated to San Giusto, the other smaller, alongside it to the left, dedicated to Santa Maria Assunta. Still more to the left is a third Romanesque church, now the baptistery. In the 14C the two larger churches were made into one, and the whole dedicated to Justus, a Christian martyr who was hurled into the sea during the persecution of Diocletian.

EXTERIOR. The irregular façade incorporates five Roman Corinthian columns in its projecting campanile (1337), and the pillars of the main doorway are fragments of a Roman tomb, with six busts. Above the latter are three modern busts of bishops of Trieste (including Pope Pius II) and a splendid rose-window. Over the campanile door is a 14C statue of St Justus.

INTERIOR. The nave is made up of the N. aisle of San Giusto and the S. aisle of the Assunta and has a 14C roof. The central apse, disfigured in 1842, was restored on the 14C lines. The mosaic is by Guido Cadorin (1932). The Madonna on the wall is by B. Carpaccio (1540). The two aisles on the right preserve the dome of San Giusto and in the chapels are a polychrome Pietà (15C), a 14C Crucifixion on a gold ground, and the tomb of Don Carlos of Spain (d. 1855). The apse preserves its old choir-bench and some good Byzantine pillars and capitals between which are 13C frescoes (recently discovered) of the life of St Justus. The 13C *Mosaic above depicts Christ between SS. Justus and Servulus, and has

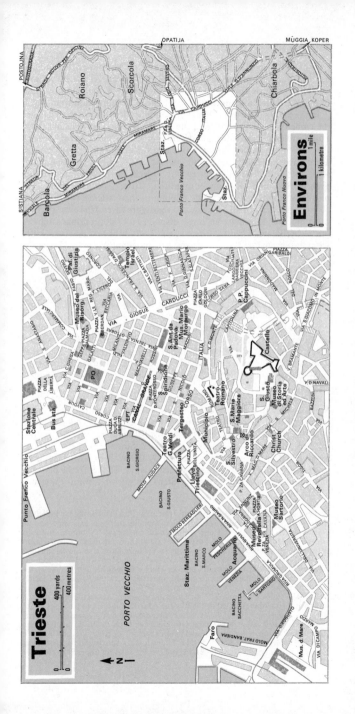

a beautifully decorated border. The apse of the Assunta on the left also has fine and well preserved mosaics (12-13C), while at the end of the outer left aisle is the good Renaissance grille of the treasury. The Baptistery (entered from the N. aisle) has a 9C immersion font.

In the piazza outside is a Venetian column (1560). Down the hill from the cathedral is the entrance to the **Museo di Storia ed Arte** and **Orto Lapidario** (9-13, exc. Mon), undergoing rearrangement. In the garden, the cenotaph of Winckelmann (see above) in a little chapel, stands among Roman altars, stelæ, and inscriptions, Egyptian and Gandhara sculptures, etc. The most interesting objects in the museum are the prehistoric and Roman antiquities from Tergeste and its neighbourhood, including finds relating to the Castellieri civilization, Roman glass and small bronzes, and red-figure vases. However, the two most precious objects are no longer displayed for safety reasons: a silver-gilt *Rhyton, in the form of a deer's head, and a bronze wine-vessel, both from Tarentum (5C B.C.). The paintings (including works by Magnasco and Tiepolo, a 14C Venetian triptych, and a Limoges enamel of the Last Supper) have been removed to the Museo Sartorio (comp. above).

To the left of the cathedral rises the castle, in front of which may be seen the paved floor and column bases (restored) of a large Roman *Basilica* of c. A.D. 100, and a good War Memorial of 1935. The 15-16C **Castello** (open during daylight hours) was begun by the Venetians in 1368 and later altered and enlarged by the Austrians. In summer plays are given in the courtyard. Part of the building houses the *Museo Civico* (9-13 or 14; closed Mon) with an interesting collection of arms and armour. The Cappella di S. Giorgio may also be visited. Exhibitions are held annually in the Sala del Capitano. There is a fine view from the ramparts.

The steep Via della Cattedrale descends to the ARCO DI RICCARDO, a vaulted Roman arch erected to honour Augustus in A.D. 33; its name survives from a belief now discounted that Richard I was confined here after his return from the Holy Land. Just below are (l.) the little church of *San Silvestro* (open Thurs & Sat 10-12, Sun at 11) of the 12C but remodelled in the 18C, now occupied by the Waldensians. The porch over the N. door supports the quaint campanile. To the r. is the Baroque church of *Santa Maria Maggiore*. Steps leads down towards the centre of the city.

Beyond the Capo di Piazza opens the triangular P.za della Borsa. On the left are the *Tergesteo* (1840), a classical building containing the stock exchange, and the *Borsa Vecchia* (1806), now the chamber of commerce. A bronze statue of Leopold I (1673) faces up the busy CORSO ITALIA, the main street with elegant shops, which leads to P.za Carlo Goldoni. In Via Imbriani (l.), before the square, is the small *Museo Morpurgo e Stavropoulos* (9-13, exc. Mon) with 19C collections. Beyond is the broad Via Giosuè Carducci which descends left to P.ZA OBERDAN, from which, at the end of Viale Regina Margherita, is seen the *Palazzo di Giustizia* (by E. Nordio; 1933); to the left is the *Museo del Risorgimento* (9-13, exc. Mon) in a fine palazzo by U. Nordio (1934), which incorporates the cell (open till dusk) of Guglielmo Oberdan, hanged in 1882 by the Austrians in the old barracks on this site. The *Synagogue* (1910), in Via San Francesco, is one of the finest in existence. From Piazza Oberdan Via Trenta Ottobre leads back to Piazza Sant'Antonio (formed by filling in part of the Canal Grande) before the coldly classical church of *Sant'Antonio* (1827-47). On the S. side of this square is *San Spiridione,* the Serbian church, with a fine interior (1868). From here Via Filzi continues S. to the Corso Italia.

EXCURSIONS FROM TRIESTE

The park of **Miramare** (open 9-one hour before sunset), beautifully situated above the Adriatic, 7 km. N.W. of Trieste, is a favourite resort of the Triestines. It is reached by motor-launch (¾ hr.) from the Molo Audace, or by bus from P.za Oberdan, or by railway. The road passes the *Faro della Vittoria,* a beacon erected in 1927 in memory of the victims of the First World War who died at sea. The white stone tower (adm. 9-13; lift) is by Arduino Berlam, the bronze Victory and the sailor are by Giov. Mayer. Beyond the bathing-resort of *Bárcola* are the park and **Castle** of Miramare, built in 1856-60 for Archduke Maximilian of Austria, who became Emperor of Mexico and was shot in 1867; its *Museo Storico* (9-14, fest. 9-13; closed Mon) contains a few souvenirs. In June-Sept son-et-lumière pageants are held nightly. The *Castelletto,* where Maximilian lived during the construction of the palace, houses a Gallery of paintings (adm. as Museo).—*Grignano,* a few minutes below the park to the N., is connected by steamer with Trieste (P.za Unità) and Sistiana (p. 346).

THE VEDETTA D'OPICINA AND THE GROTTA DEL GIGANTE, ½ day. The Opicina tramway from the P.za Oberdan runs to (5 km.) *Poggioreale* (360 m), whence a lane ascends to the *Vedetta* (396 m), a splendid viewpoint, with a panorama ranging from the Punta Salvore in Istria to the Carnic Alps. Another good viewpoint is the *Vedetta Italia,* ¾ hrs walk N.W. of Poggioreale.—7 km. **Villa Opicina** or *Opicina,* the terminus of the tramway, has also a station on the railway to Gorizia. Here a plaque on the Albergo Obelisco records Richard Burton's completion of the translation of the 'Thousand and one Nights.' *Borgo Grotta Gigante,* ½ hr N.W. on foot, may be more closely approached by taking the Prosecco bus from P.za Oberdan. The *Grotta del Gigante* (9-12, 14-17 or 19, closed Mon), ¼ hr's walk farther, is the largest single cave yet discovered in the Carso (238 m long, 137 m high); its stalactitic formations are famous.—*Monrupino* (421 m), 3 km. to the E., affords a superb view of the Carso plateau.

The road-route to Opicina follows the Via Fabio Severo and passes the buildings (1940-50) of the *University* founded in 1919.

TO MUGGIA, by steamer in summer from P.za dell'Unità in ½ hr, or by trolley-bus No. 20 (½ hr) from Largo Barriera Vecchia. The steamer rounds the Porto Franco and steers diagonally across the modern deep-sea harbour of Trieste engineered in the Vallone di Muggia. (In Istria 'vallone' means a wide bay, while 'val' or 'valle' is applied to the narrower fiords of the W. coast).

Muggia, a flourishing fishing-port (13,800 inhab.) of Venetian aspect, the only Istrian town remaining within Italy, lies at the base of the hill which bears the Roman and medieval settlement of Muggia Vecchia. The *Duomo* is a 13C foundation with a 15C Gothic façade, while the *Palazzo dei Rettori,* rebuilt after a fire in 1933, was once a palace of the patriarchs of Aquileia. An ascent of rather more than ½ hr leads to **Muggia Vecchia,** now in ruins except for the *Basilica,* a 9C building with an ambo of the 10C, transennæ in the Byzantine style, and remains of early frescoes.

By far the most interesting of the longer excursions that can be made by bus are across the Yugoslav frontier (passports) to the splendid **Caverns of *Postojna* (50 km.; Postumia) and to the *Basilica at *Poreč* (Parenzo); for both see the 'Blue Guide to Yugoslavia'.

IV EMILIA

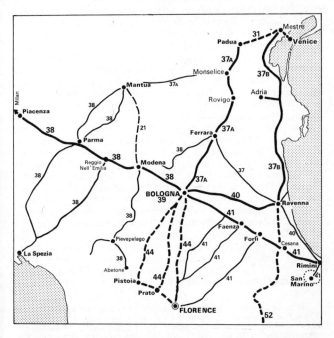

Emilia as the name of a district dates only from the Risorgimento (c. 1860) but its use is derived from the Via Æmilia, the great Roman road built by M. Æmilius Lepidus, that traverses the country from end to end. Emilia occupies the region between the middle and lower Po, the Apennines, and the Adriatic. Its area is 22,122 sq. km., with a population of 3,935,000. The modern provinces are those of Bologna, Ferrara, Forlì, Modena, Parma, Piacenza, Ravenna, and Reggio; and Bologna is the chief town. The eastern part of Emilia, coinciding roughly with the modern provinces of Ravenna and Forlì, is known as the *Romagna,* Extending as it does from the summits of the Apennines to the plain of the Po, Emilia has a very varied landscape. The mountain country, centring round the *Frignano,* is a region of chilly winters with periodic streams liable to sudden floods. All the principal towns except Ferrara and Ravenna lie along the line of the Via Æmilia at the foot of the mountains; the climate here is subject to extremes, and the summers are often unpleasantly hot.

The history of Emilia is a confused one. The *Romagna* in the E. followed a separate destiny. Ravenna was the capital of the Western Roman Empire from 402, after the fall of Rome, until it was taken by Odoacer, who, like his successor Theodoric, made it capital of a short-lived Gothic Empire. It was conquered by the Byzantines in 540, and was governed by Exarchs of the Eastern Empire for two centuries. In 757 the Romagna came into possession of the Popes, who maintained at least a nominal suzerainty here until 1860; in the 13-15C, however, the effective rule of the Da Polenta clan gave Ravenna a pre-eminent position in the world of learning. Parts of historic Romagna are now included in the modern provinces of Tuscany and the Marches.

The other districts of Emilia emerged disunited after the barbarian (Gothic, Lombard, Frankish) incursions of the 5-8C; and the cities spent themselves in internecine warfare. In the early Middle Ages Guelphs and Ghibellines held now one city, now another; but Piacenza and Parma later tended to be absorbed into the orbit of Milan, Ferrara felt the proximity of Venice, and Bologna was always open to incursions from the Papal dominions. The dominion of the Este family at Ferrara in the 13C extended over Modena and Reggio, while the Pépoli and Bentivoglio at Bologna, the Ordelaffi at Forli, and the Malatesta at Rimini held temporary local sway for varying periods up to the 16C. After the 16C wars the Papal power was firmly established in Romagna and at Ferrara and Bologna; while the Farnese family, descended from the son of Pope Paul III, made Modena the capital of a new duchy and the centre of a court of some pretensions. New dispositions followed the Napoleonic disturbances. The Empress Marie-Louise emerged as Duchess of Parma, with Piacenza and Tuscan Lucca subjoined; the rest of Emilia went to Austria, as successors of the Este dynasty, and Romagna remained papal land. In 1848 the ferment of the Risorgimento began to take effect; the ducal rulers were expelled, though only temporarily, from Parma and Bologna; in 1859 Carlo Farini announced the union of Emilia and Romagna with Piedmont, and in 1860 the union became effective.

Emilia, and especially the Romagna, played an important part in the Second World War. In 1944 Indian troops of the Eighth Army occupied San Marino on 20 Sept and Rimini fell to the Canadians on the 21st. Bad weather slowed down the campaign later in the year, but Cesena was taken on 21 Oct, Forlì on 9 Nov, Ravenna on 5 Dec, and Faenza on 16 Dec. After the advance to the Reno on 5 Jan, 1945, little progress was made until April, though the activities of the Romagnole partisans became increasingly harassing to the enemy. Between 1 and 9 April violent attacks were made on the Comacchio lagoon and across the Reno, and the stubborn resistance of Bastia and Argenta, aided by floods, delayed further advance for ten days; but the capture of Bologna on 21 April led to a rout; Modena, Reggio, Parma, and Piacenza were occupied in quick succession; and by 26 April the advance had reached Verona.

37   VENICE TO BOLOGNA AND TO RAVENNA

A   To Bologna

ROAD, 168 km. To (42½ km.) *Padua,* see Rte 31. N 16 leaves the city by the Corso Vitt. Emanuele.—63 km. *Monsélice.*—84 km. **Rovigo.**—121 km. **Ferrara.**—N 64. 168 km. **Bologna.**

AUTOSTRADA (152 km.), A 4 to Padua; then A 13 to Bologna.

RAILWAY, 160 km., several expresses daily in 1½-2¼ hrs; to *Ferrara,* 113 km. in 1-1½ hrs. Through carriages from Trieste to Rome run on this line.

From Venice to (42½ km.) *Padua,* see Rte 31. A short way beyond Padua a road to Mandria diverges on the right giving access to the *Euganean Hills.*

The road passes (r.) the *Villa Giusti,* where the armistice between Italy and Austria was signed on 3 Nov 1918.—Just short of (8 km.) Abano Terme Station, the road turns r. for (11 km.) **Abano Terme,** connected with Padua by bus, a thermal spa frequented since Roman times. The springs (80-87°C) are used mainly for baths, but Abano is principally noted for its mud therapy, effective especially in cases of rheumatism and arthritis.—*Monteortone,* 2 km. farther on, is another mud spa, with an interesting church built from 1435 to 1497, containing frescoes by Iac. da Montagnana.—5 km. N.W. is *Praglia,* with a Benedictine abbey and church (rebuilt 1490-1548), also by T. Lombardo. The refectory has paintings by Bart. Montagna and G. B. Zelotti, and the cloisters are beautiful.—14 km. *Montegrotto,* another small spa, with extensive remains of Roman baths, and a theatre.

Just before (19 km.) this road rejoins the N16, stands the curious castle of the *Cataio.* Built in 1570 by Pio Enea degli Obizzi, and afterwards the property of the dukes of Modena, it is now in private ownership. The frescoes by G. B. Zelotti on the first floor (permission to view them granted on request by the proprietor) depict the exploits of members of the Obizzi family, including one who attended Richard I of England to the Crusades, and another who perhaps fought for Edward III at Neville's Cross.

57 km. *Battaglia Terme* is yet another spa.—At *Valsanzibio,* 5 km. W., is the *Villa Barbarigo,* now Pizzoni Ardemagni, with a fine garden (1699) and maze.

64 km. **Monsélice** (17,800 inhab.) lies at the foot of a hill (*mons silicis*) with trachyte quarries and a ruined *Rocca.* The Castello, at the foot of the hill, dates from the 13-15C, and has a private museum of Medieval and Renaissance works of art (visible only with special permission). Via al Santuario continues up the side of the hill past the 13C *Duomo Vecchio* to the Villa Duodo (no adm.).—At *Arquà Petrarca* (6½ km. N.W.), Petrarch lived from 1370 until his death in 1374. His house (9-12.30, 13.30 or 14-16.30 or 19.30; ring), in a pretty setting, contains visitors' books with the signatures of Byron and Mozart. His plain marble sarcophagus, in front of the church, has an epitaph composed by himself.

FROM MONSÉLICE TO MANTUA. Road, 85 km.; bus in 2 hrs; railway, following the road, in 1¾-2¼ hrs.—9 km. **Este** (18,100 inhab.), the ancient *Ateste* (remains of which have recently come to light), and the cradle of the Este family who afterwards became dukes of Ferrara, was under Venetian dominion from 1405 to 1797. The huge battlemented *Castle* dates mainly from 1339 and encloses a Public Garden. Within its enceinte, in the *Palazzo Mocenigo* (16C), is the MUSEO NAZIONALE ATESTINO (adm. 9-12, 15-18, winter 9-14; fest. 9-13; closed Mon) a remarkable collection of pre-Roman and Roman antiquities, including the Benvenuti *Situla and remains of a temple of the Veneti; the Lex Rubria, a bronze tablet of 49 B.C.; and a fine *Medusa's Head, in bronze, of the 1C A.D.—Behind the castle are the fine park of the Villa Benvenuti, and the *Villa De Kunkler,* occupied by Byron in 1817-18, where Shelley composed his 'Lines written among the Euganean Hills'. The *Duomo* (rebuilt 1690-1708) contains a painting by G. B. Tiepolo. The Romanesque church of *San Martino* (1293) has a leaning campanile.—24 km. **Montagnana** (10,150 inhab.) preserves its medieval *WALLS intact, with two splendid fortified gate-castles, and has a Gothic *Duomo* with a portal attrib. to Sansovino. The *Palazzo del Municipio* is by Sammicheli. Just outside the walls to the E. is the *Palazzo Pisani,* built in 1565 to a design by Palladio.—Another Palladian villa can be visited at *Poiana,* 7½ km. N. of Montagnana.—40½ km. *Legnago* was once one of the fortresses of the 'Quadrilateral'.—49 km. *Cerea,* for the railway to Verona.—54½ km. *Sanguinetto* has an old castle, now the town hall.—61½ km. *Nogara* is on the route from Verona to Bologna.—84½ km. *Mantua,* see Rte 21.

The road now runs due S. crossing the Ádige.—84 km. **Rovigo** the growing chief town (51,500 inhab.) of the Polésine, the fertile strip of land between the lower Ádige and Po, has a *Cathedral* of 1696 and some towers of its old defences. In the central piazza are the *Palazzo Roncale* by Sammicheli (1555), the *Municipio* (16C, restored in 1765), the *Palazzo Roverella,* begun in the early 15C, and the PINACOTECA DEI CONCORDI (adm. 10-12, 16-19; Sat & Sun 10-12 only) which contains a few good pictures (*Quirizio da Murano,* Triptych of St Lucy; *Palma Vecchio,* Scourging of Christ, Madonna and saints; *Giov. Bellini,* Madonna; *Dosso Dossi,* SS. Benedict and Bartholomew, SS. Lucy and Agatha; *Tiepolo,* Portrait of Ant. Riccoboni). There is also an archæological section. The octagonal church ('La Rotonda') of the *Beata Vergine del Soccorso* by Fr. Zamberlan (1594-1602), pupil of Palladio, has a campanile by Longhena (1655). The Seminary in Viale Tre Martiri has a collection of 17-18C paintings shown on request.

The road E. from Rovigo to (66½ km.) *Chioggia* (p. 326; railway also in 1¼ hrs) passes (27½ km.) *Adria* (comp. Rte 37B).

The good Palladian *Villa Badoer* (1554-63) is situated 18 km. S.W. of Rovigo at *Fratta Polésine.*

At (96½ km.) *Polesella* the road reaches the Po, and follows its left bank. It crosses the Po to enter Emilia at (113½ km.) *Pontelagoscuro,* a river-harbour and industrial centre.

121 km. **FERRARA** (155,400 inhab.) situated in a fertile plain near the right bank of the Po, is principally famous as the residence of the Este dukes, whose court was one of the most illustrious of the Italian Renaissance, when 'Ferrara blades' rivalled the swords of Toledo. The S. part of the city retains many attractive cobbled streets and medieval houses, while the spacious streets and palaces to the N. are reminders of the succeeding æge. Extensive land-reclaiming operations in the environs have brought back to Ferrara much of its old prosperity. Since the closure of the centre to motor traffic, bicycles appear to be the most popular form of transport.

Post Office, Via Cavour.—**E.P.T.,** 22 Largo Castello.

Buses from the station to the centre, etc. COUNTRY BUSES from Via Cassoli (near the station) to *Bologna, Modena, Rovigo, Padua, Venice,* and (in summer) to the *Lidi Ferrarese.*

Parking. Largo Castello or P.za Repubblica.

Teatro Comunale, Corso Martiri d. Libertà (opera and concert season Nov-May). In summer concerts are held in the courtyards of various palazzi.

History. Originating probably as a refuge of the Veneti in the marshes of the Po, Ferrara first became important under the Exarchate of Ravenna (6C), but its main interest dates from the rise of the House of Este, the Guelphic family that established the earliest and one of the greatest of the North Italian principalities. Though the family had been of municipal importance for many years, their princely power dates in reality from the crushing defeat of the Ghibellines by Azzo Novello at Cassano in 1259. Ferrara remained under the sway of the Este dukes until 1598, and their court attracted a great concourse of poets, scholars, and artists, while trade and commerce flourished. Nicolò II (1361-88) gave hospitality to Petrarch; Alberto (1388-93) founded the university; Nicolò III (1393-1441) was the patron of Guarino da Verona and of Pisanello, and in his city (1438) the eastern Emp. John VI Palæologus met Pope Eugenius IV for the ecumenical council, later transferred to Florence; Lionello (1441-50) inaugurated the age of artistic pre-eminence that Borso (1450-71) continued; Ercole I (1471-1505) laid out new and spacious quarters of the city, to the extent that Ferrara has been called the first modern city in Europe; Alfonso I (1505-34), husband of Lucrezia Borgia, was the patron of Ariosto and Titian; Ercole II (1534-59) exiled his wife Renée, the daughter of Louis XII of France and the protectress of John Calvin, who lived for a while in Ferrara under the assumed name of Charles Heppeville; Alfonso II (1559-97) was the patron of Tasso and Guarini and began the reclamation of the marshes which still continues. In 1598 the city was annexed to the States of the Church on the pretext that Cesare d'Este, heir apparent to the duchy in a collateral line, was illegitimate, and the city decayed under 250 years of neglect. Ferrara suffered widespread bomb damage in the Second World War.

Ferrara had a productive school of painting, its leaders having been influenced in turn by the schools of Padua, Bologna, and Venice. The most eminent were Cosmè Tura, 'the Mantegna of Ferrara', Francesco del Cossa, Ercole de' Roberti, Lorenzo Costa, Dosso Dossi and his brother Battista Luteri, and Benvenuto Tisi, surnamed Il Garófalo, pupil of Raphael.—Ferrara was the birthplace of a great sculptor, Alfonso Lombardi (1497-1537), and of a great architect, Biagio Rossetti (c. 1447-1516), as well as of the reformer Girolamo Savonarola (1452-98), the poets Giambattista Guarini (1538-1612) and Fulvio Testi (1593-1646), and the composer Girolamo Frescobaldi (1583-1643).

In the centre of the city rises the magnificent *Castello Estense (Pl. 7; adm. 8.30-12.30, 15.30-18.30 or 14-17; fest. 9-13; closed Mon) the former palace of the dukes, a massive quadrilateral surrounded by a moat and approached by drawbridges. It houses the administrative offices of the province. The interior is being slowly restored.

Begun in 1385 by Bartolino Ploti for Duke Nicolò II, it was altered by Girolamo da Carpi (16C). Of the decorations by early Ferrarese masters which formerly adorned its rooms, the only important survivals are in the Sala dell'Aurora, the Salone and Saletta dei Giochi, and the Camerina dei Bacchanali (which are frescoed by *Cesare, Bastianino,* and *Camillo Filippi*). The Chapel of Renée de France, with marble decoration, was one of the few Calvinist chapels in Italy to survive the Counter-Reformation. In the dungeons (also shown) beneath the N.E. tower, Parisina, wife of Nicolò III, and her lover Ugo, his natural son, were imprisoned and slain; the cells were last used for political prisoners in 1943.

In the piazzetta on the W. side of the castle stands the chapel of *San Giuliano* (1405), its charming exterior unaffected by the reconstruction within.

The Corso Martiri leads S. along the E. side of the castle; on the right opens P.za della Repubblica, with a monument to the great reformer, Savonarola, by Galletti (1875). Beyond is the **Palazzo del Comune,** built for Azzo Novello (1243), considerably altered by Benvenuti and Rossetti, and skilfully restored in 1924. The bronze statues of Nicolò III and Borso, on the arch and column in front, are reproductions (by Zilocchi; 1926) of the 15C originals destroyed in 1796. The arcaded courtyard has a fine staircase by Benvenuti (1481).

The *Cathedral (Pl. 11), begun in 1135 by the architect Wiligelmo and the sculptor Nicolò, was almost complete by the end of the 13C. The very fine W. front is divided into three arcaded bays separated by buttresses beneath a low-pitched gable. The projecting great portal by Nicolò is crowned with an elaborate tribune (in restoration, 1976), probably by an early 13C Pisan sculptor, bearing a Last Judgement in high relief; within this stands a statue of the Madonna by Crist. da Firenze (1427). To the right is a statue of Alberto d'Este (1393). The N. side shows the original arcading; that on the S. is partly obscured by a portico of shops added in 1473. The massive campanile, S.E. of the church, was built from 1412 to 1514.

The interior, remodelled in 1712-18, is preceded by a narthex in which a fine 5C sarcophagus (the other dates from the 14C), and the original pilasters of the the main portal have been placed. In the 3rd chapel of the N. aisle is a Madonna and saints, by Garófalo (1524); in the 6th chapel a Coronation of the Virgin, a late work by *Francia*. In the N. transept are terracotta busts of Christ and the Apostles by *Alf. Lombardi*. In the S. transept are similar busts, a Martyrdom of St Laurence (over the altar), by *Guercino* (1629), and, facing the S. aisle, the *Altar of the Calvary, composed in 1673 from large bronze groups of statuary (15C; including the Virgin and St John, by *Nic. Baroncelli,* SS. George and

Maurelius, by *Giov. Baroncelli* and *Dom. Paris*). Below is the good effigy tomb of Bp Bovelli (d. 1954). In the apse is the Last Judgement, by *Bastianino* (1580-83).

The MUSEO DELLA CATTEDRALE (entered from the narthex up a long staircase) is open from 10-12, 15-17. It contains good Flemish tapestries and illuminated choir books; St George and an *Annunciation, by *Cosmè Tura*(1469), from the old organ-case; *Madonna of the Pomegranate, by *Iac. della Quercia* (1408); charming *Reliefs of the Months, from the old S. doorway; and an elaborate paliotto in gold thread.

To the N.E. of the cathedral (entrance 32 Via Cairoli) the *Seminario* occupies the 16C Palazzo Trotti, which contains two rooms frescoed by Garófalo (1519-20), with remarkable perspective effects.

In the piazza S. of the cathedral are the *Torre dell'Orologio* and a store that incorporates in its façade remnants of the 14C Palazzo della Ragione. At No. 7 Via San Romano are the Romanesque cloisters of the disused church of *San Romano* (being restored).

The attractive Via Voltapaletto, E. of the Cathedral, leads to the spacious church of *San Francesco,* partly rebuilt in 1494 by Biagio Rossetti. The frescoes above the arches (Franciscan saints) and on the vault are good Ferrarese work of the 16C. In the 1st chapel in the N. aisle the fresco of the seizure of Christ in the Garden (1524) by Garófalo has been detached and the sinopia exposed. In the 7th N. chap., Scarsellino, Rest on the Flight (recently restored). Via Savonarola continues to (No. 30) *CASA ROMEI (ring for adm.). Begun c. 1442 it retains two graceful courtyards, its original ceilings, and (in a room off the second courtyard) delightful contemporary mural paintings and a fine fireplace. The sculptures of the 13-15C have been collected from destroyed churches. Farther on, to the right, the church of *San Girolamo* (1712) faces the house (No. 19) where Savonarola passed the first twenty years of his life. Just behind San Girolamo is the church of *Corpus Domini* (key at 4A Via Pergolato), with a 15C façade and, in the nuns' choir, the tombs of Alfonso I and Il d'Este and of Lucrezia Borgia (d. 1519) and two of her sons. Via Savonarola ends at the severe *Palazzo Sarcco.*

To the left, Via Ugo Bassi leads to the Corso della Giovecca (see below), No. 174 in which is the *Palazzina di Marfisa d'Este* (9-12, 15-18; winter, 10-12.30, 15-18; fest 9-12). Built in 1559 it was restored in 1939. It has admirable ceilings and contemporary furniture, a supposed portrait of James I of England, and a damaged bust of Ercole I d'Este, by Sperandio. The 'grotto' in the garden is used for exhibitions.

To the right, Via Madama continues as Via Borgo Vado, where the church of *Santa Maria in Vado,* another work of Rossetti (1495-1518), has a handsome interior. Nearby, at No. 47 Via Borgo di Sotto, is the *Oratorio dell'Annunziata* (ring for adm. at No. 49, 10-12, 15-17) with 16C frescoes and a fine Resurrection of the 15C. In Via Scandiana (l.) No. 23 is **Palazzo di Schifanoia** (Pl. 12), begun in 1385, and enlarged in 1391, 1458, and in 1469 by Benvenuti and Rossetti. The *Salone dei Mesi* was decorated for Duke Borgo d'Este with delightful frescoes of the Months, one of the most renowned fresco cycles of the Renaissance of profane subjects. They were painted by *Fr. del Cossa, Ercole de' Roberti,* and other masters of the Ferrarese school. The other rooms are notable for their stucco ceilings. The contents of the MUSEO CIVICO (illuminated psalters, coins, medallions, and bronzes) are no longer on display. At the end of the street shady gardens crown the *Ramparts* (Pl. 16).

In Piazzale San Giorgio (4-5 min. on foot S. from the Porta Romana; Pl. 16), is the church of *San Giorgio,* which was the cathedral of Ferrara in the 7-12C, then rebuilt in 15C and partly renovated in the 18C. The campanile is by Rossetti (1485). Inside, in the choir, is the magnificent *Tomb of Lorenzo Roverella, physician to Julius II and afterwards Bishop of Ferrara, by Ambrogio da Milano and Ant. Rossellino (1475).

Via Venti Settembre leads back towards the centre. No. 152 is the *House of Biagio Rossetti,* and No. 124 is the *Palazzo di Lodovico il Moro* (Pl. 15), a masterpiece by *Rossetti,* which he left unfinished in 1503. There is an admirable courtyard and a ground-floor chamber decorated by *Garófalo.* Beneath a small loggia are displayed two remarkable archaic dug-out canoes from Comácchio (late Roman period). The Piano Nobile is occupied by the *MUSEO ARCHEOLOGICO NAZIONALE DI SPINA* (adm. 9-13, 15.30-18.30; winter 9-16; fest. 9-13; closed Tues). Opened in 1935, this contains a superb collection of objects discovered in the necropolis of Spina, near Comácchio, a Greco-Etruscan port that flourished in the 6C-3C B.C. The collection consists principally of vases, including many fine specimens of the 5C B.C., as well as ornate coloured ware of the 4C, of which the two rhytons in the shape of a mule's and a ram's head are striking examples. The most important items are displayed in the five rooms (10-14), with good ceilings, that overlook the garden; special mention may be made of a gold diadem (4C B.C.) and ear-rings.—Behind the Palace, off Via Beatrice d'Este, is the Convent of *Sant'Antonio in Polésine* (ring for adm. 9-12.30, 15-17) with some good 13C-15C frescoes (partly restored).

From the Palace, Via Mellone runs N.E. The first turning on the left, Via Carlo Mayr, leads back towards the centre. After some 500 m Via Gioco del Pallone diverges r. passing the house of Ariosto's family (No. 31). At No. 17 Via delle Scienze *PALAZZO PARADISO* houses the *Biblioteca Comunale Ariostea.* The building dates from 1391, and has a façade of 1610 by G. B. Aleotti. The courtyard contains Roman and Renaissance marbles, and in the library are the tomb of Ariosto, MS. pages of the 'Orlando Furioso', and autographs of Ariosto and Tasso.

A good idea of the old 15C city, with its well-preserved old houses and little churches, may be obtained from a stroll through the narrow lanes lying between Via Scienze and Via Borgo Vado (Pl. 11).

From the Castello the broad Corso della Giovecca leads E. On the left, No. 37 is a fragment of the old *Arcispedale Sant' Anna* where Tasso was confined as a lunatic in 1579-86; behind is a 15C cloister of the former Basilian convent. The *Palazzo Roverella* (No. 47) has a terracotta façade (1508) unusually elaborate for Ferrara. Just beyond it, Via Palestro leads N. to P.ZA ARIOSTEA (Pl. 7), with two Renaissance palaces, and a statue of Ariosto (19C) on a column which in turn has carried statues of Duke Ercole I, Pope Alexander VII, Liberty, and Napoleon. The *Certosa* (Pl. 3; 1452-61), straight ahead, has interesting cloisters, and is now occupied by the cemetery. The adjoining church of *San Cristoforo,* begun in 1498, probably by Rossetti, has good terracotta decoration.—Corso Porta Mare leads W. from P.za Ariostea past the Palazzina dei Cavalieri di Malta on the edge of the Parco Massari, which provides a fit setting for the *Museo Boldini* devoted to works by the Ferrarese painter Giovanni Boldini (1842-1931) and other local painters of the 19C. At the intersection with the Corso Ercole d'Este stand *Palazzo Sacrati,* with an elaborate 16C portal, and **Palazzo dei Diamanti** (Pl. 7) begun by Rossetti for Sigismondo d'Este c. 1492 and remodelled around 1565. It takes its name from the diamond

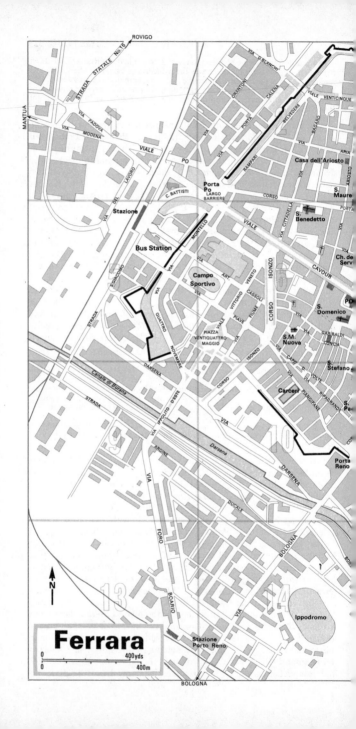

Ferrara

emblem of the Estes, repeated 12,600 times on its façade. It contains a **Pinacoteca,** especially notable for its paintings of the Ferrarese School. Closed since 1975, it is normally open 10-16, fest. 9.30-12.30 (closed Mon).

The outstanding works listed chronologically are: Frescoes from demolished churches and mansions, notably the *Apotheosis of St Augustine by *Serafino Serafini,* and SS. Christopher and Sebastian, of the school of *Piero della Francesca;* early Ferrarese paintings, including examples of *Cosmè Tura* (Story of San Maurelio, two tondi), *Fr. Cossa* (St Jerome), *Lor. Costa* and *Ercole Roberti.* The 16C Ferrara painters are copiously represented, especially *Dosso Dossi* and *Garófalo.* The *Madonna del Pilastro, and a large fresco of the Triumph of the Church over the Synagogue, both by *Garófalo,* and a fine polyptych by *Dossi,* should be noted, as well as a Crucifixion by *Gius. Mazzuoli. Scarsellino, Carlo Bononi,* and the Bolognese *Guercino* dominate the late 16C and early 17C. Paintings of other schools include: *Carpaccio,* Death of the Virgin; *Venetian School* (early 16C), The Tribute-money; and there are etchings and engravings.— In the Courtyard is a small lapidary collection. On the Ground Floor (entrance in Corso Ercole d'Este) is a *Museo del Risorgimento e Resistenza.*

The handsome Corso Ercole d'Este leads back to the castle, while Corso Porta Po runs W. towards the station. Just off Corso Ercole d'Este is the church of *Gesù,* which contains a *Pietà in terracotta by Guido Mazzoni (1485) notable for its realism. In Corso Porta Po is the Capuchin church of *San Maurelio,* with terracotta and wooden statues and bas-reliefs. No. 67 in the neighbouring Via Ariosto (r.) is the *Casa dell' Ariosto,* the house for himself by the poet, who died here in 1533.

The dreary plain E. of Ferrara (comp. Rte 37B) is traversed by roads and a privately-owned railway from Ferrara to (53 km.) *Codigoro,* viâ (33 km.) *Ostellato.* From Ostellato buses continue viâ *Comacchio* (22 km. farther; p. 363) to the coast, providing a means of visiting the site of Spina.
FROM FERRARA TO RAVENNA. 74 km.; branch railway, 74½ km. in 1-1¼ hrs. The twisting continuation of N16 crosses the reclaimed marshland, passing the little town of (35½ km.) *Argenta,* flooded by the Germans in the winter of 1944-45.—42 km. *Alfonsine,* another small town, was the centre of German resistance to the British Eighth Army's advance on the Po. The British Military Cemetery (78th Division) is c. 2 km. N.—74½ km. *Ravenna,* see Rte 40.
From Ferrara to *Modena,* see Rte 38.

The road to Bologna crosses the plain watered by the canalized Reno, on which stands (137 km.) *Malalbergo,* the only village of importance.— At (151 km.) *Ca' de' Fabbri,* a road leads right to Bentivoglio, where the Museo della Civiltà Contadina illustrates local peasant culture.— 168 km. **Bologna,** see Rte 39.

B   To Ravenna

ROAD, N 309, the new VIA ROMEA. 147 km. 51 km. *Chioggia.*—72 m. *Contarina.*—97 km. *Pomposa.*—116 km. *Porto Garibaldi.*—147 km. **Ravenna.**
The road, in parts a post-war revival of the long decayed Roman *Via Popilia,* runs dead flat and just above sea-level through an evocative landscape of lonely reclaimed marshes divided up by canals and canalized streams. The POLÉSINE, round the Po delta, is succeeded by the Valli di Comácchio, reclaimed from the drained lake. The whole region is much frequented by fishermen and by 'sportsmen' after duck and other birds. Though torrid in summer and damp in winter, the route affords the shortest E. approach to the Adriatic coastal resorts.

From Venice the road crosses the Ponte della Libertà, bears left and, just before the Autostrada entrance, left again on N309, soon crossing the Fusina road (p. 275). The industries of Marghera dominate the E. skyline. The road runs dead straight between the Taglio di Brenta and the Laguna Morta then joins the Padua-Chioggia road to cross the most southerly inlet of the Venetian Lagoon; striking *View of (51 km.) *Chioggia* (2 km. l.; see Rte 33). It crosses the mouth of the Brenta alongside the branch railway linking Chioggia with Rovigo.—At (62 km.) *Cavanella,* the Ádige is crossed, and the land becomes more intensely cultivated. Farther on the Po di Levante is also crossed.— 72 km. *Contarina* (8200 inhab.) and (73 km.) *Táglio di Po* (7970 inhab.), both industrial, lie N. and S. of the main channel of the Po. The delta of the Po has been made into a National Park.

Porto Tolle, 14 km. to the E., refines sugar and *Scardovari,* (29 km.), at the mouth of the Po, has important fisheries.

A diversion may be made W. from Contarina to (18 km.) **Adria,** the ancient capital (21,400 inhab.) of the Polésine, that gave its name to the Adriatic (to which it is now joined only by canal). The 17C church of *Santa Maria Assunta della Tomba* preserves an octagonal font of the 8C, and a terracotta Dormition of the Virgin (15C). The MUSEO ARCHEOLOGICO (9-12, 15-18, fest. 9-13; closed Mon) contains proof of the city's Greco-Etruscan origins (bronzes, vases, jewellery, etc.; 6-2C B.C.) and the famous iron chariot of a Gaulish chieftain (4C B.C.) found with the skeletons of its two horses. In 1938 excavations in the Etrusco-Roman necropolis brought to light blocks of masonry, probably foundations of a temple.

84 km. *Mésola,* just beyond the crossing of the Po di Goro, has a hunting lodge of Alfonso I d'Este (1583). On the right extends the *Grande Bonifica Ferrarese.* The once marshy country between Ferrara and the sea has many times been the subject of land-reclamation schemes. The first real efforts were due to Alfonso II d'Este, but the present scheme dates from 1872.—97 km. The Benedictine **Abbey of Pomposa,** founded in the 7-8C on what was then an island and gradually deserted in the 17C because of malaria. The *CHURCH (closed 12-14) dates from the 8-9C, and was enlarged in the 11C. It is preceded by an atrium with beautiful Byzantine sculptural decoration. The fine basilican interior (good capitals) is covered with charming 14C frescoes, some attrib. to *Vitale da Bologna* (including the Christ in glory in the apse). Most of the mosaic pavement survives. The monastic buildings include the CHAPTER HOUSE and REFECTORY. both with important frescoes of the Bolognese school. Guido d'Arezzo (c. 995-1050), inventor of the modern musical scale, was a monk here. The PALAZZO DELLA RAGIONE (abbot's justice-court) is a beautiful 11C building (altered in 1396). The fine campanile is 48 m high.

The road traverses fields were rice is cultivated, and approaches the sandy coast, passing between a line of seven developing resorts (*Lido delle Nazioni, Lido degli Estensi,* etc.) known as the 'Lidi Ferraresi' and (114 km.) *Comácchio,* 4 km. W., a curious town of canal-lined streets, most of whose 20,650 inhab. are engaged in the fishing and curing of eels. The fishing season is in Oct-Dec, when the huge shoals of eels rushing seawards are caught in special traps.

In the drained lagoon N.W. of Comacchio the burial-ground of the Greco-Etruscan city of **Spina** has yielded a large quantity of vases and other pottery, now at Ferrara. Founded c. 530 B.C. it was a port carrying on a lively trade with Greece, but it barely outlasted the 4C B.C. Part of the city itself was located by aerial survey in 1956 and excavations continue.

The road skirts the dwindling LAGO DI COMÁCCHIO, now more than two-thirds drained to the detriment of the egrets, herons, stilts, terns, and avocets that were once found in profusion. On the left the sea is hidden by the vast pinewoods of San Vitale.—Conspicuous industrial buildings on the sky-line announce the arrival at (147km.) **Ravenna,** see Rte 40.

38   MILAN TO BOLOGNA

ROAD, N9, 219km. 32km. *Lodi.*—52km. *Casalpusterlengo.* The road keeps to the right on leaving the town.—68km. **Piacenza,** whence the route follows the Roman Via Æmilia.—90½km. *Fiorenzuola.*—104½km. *Fidenza.*—127½km. **Parma.**—155km. **Reggio.**—180km. **Modena.**—193km. *Castelfranco.*—219km. **Bologna.**

The AUTOSTRADA DEL SOLE (A1) links Milan with Rome, with continuations to the S. It follows a course to Bologna roughly parallel to N9, but avoiding towns, it crosses the Po N.E. of Piacenza by a bridge with the longest prestressed concrete spans in Europe; thence it runs N. of the Via Æmilia as far as Modena where it crosses to the S. Beautifully engineered and constructed, the highway has convenient exits to all the main towns on the Via Emilia.

RAILWAY, 219km.; many expresses daily in 1¾-3 hrs. To *Piacenza,* 72km. in c. 1 hr; to *Parma,* 129km. in 1½-2 hrs; to *Modena,* 182km. in 2-2½ hrs.

The Via Emilia runs S.E. through the suburbs of Milan and crosses the railway at (6km.) *Rogoredo.*—18km. *Melegnano,* at one time known as *Marignano,* gives name to the battle of 14 Sept 1515, in which Francis I won a transient and delusive victory over the Swiss mercenaries of Massimiliano Sforza (among whom was numbered the young Zwingli); but at *Landriano,* 6½km. S.W., he was defeated in 1528. In the church of San Giovanni Battista is a Baptism of Christ by Bergognone.—At (24km.) *Tavazzano* a road on the right leads to Lodi Vecchio (see below).

32km. **Lodi,** an important centre (44,600 inhab.) for dairy produce, on the right bank of the Adda, was founded in 1158 by Frederick Barbarossa after the destruction of Lodi Vecchio (see below). At the bridge over the river here Napoleon repulsed the Austrians in 1796.

Here Maria Cosway (1759-1838), widow of Richard Cosway, and herself a painter, retired in 1821, to found the *Collegio delle Dame Inglesi,* where she is buried. It contains relics of the Cosways.

The Corso Adda and the Corso Vitt. Emanuele (coming from the station) meet in the large arcaded P.za della Vittoria. Here rise the *Broletto,* with an 18C façade and vestiges of the original 13C building, and the *Duomo,* with a 12C façade (altered in the Renaissance). Inside on the walls are fragments of 14C and 15C frescoes, and in the nave, a 13C gilt statue of San Bassiano. The 1st S. Chapel has a fine tomb by And. Fusina (1510). The *Museo Civico* in Corso Adda has an archæological section and a Pinacoteca (14-15C detached frescoes, paintings by Callisto Piazza, Cesare da Sesto, etc.).

In Via Incoronata (running N. from P.za della Vittoria) is the church of *INCORONATA. Constructed in 1488-94 by Giov. Battagio and G. G. Dolcebuono, this is a gem of Renaissance architecture. It has a well-preserved octagonal interior, with four fine paintings by Bergognone (in the chapel of St Paul, S. side), and others by Martino, Albertino, and Callisto Piazza ('Callisto da Lodi'), the last an imitator of Titian. The early 18C stalls are finely carved.

From the other side of P.za della Vittoria Via Marsala leads to *Sant'
Agnese* (l.), a 14C church with a good polyptych by Albertino Piazza.
From here Via Venti Settembre, with the fine *Pal. Varesi* at No. 43,
leads E. to *San Francesco* (1289), a church adorned with 14-15C
frescoes. In P.za Vitt. Emanuele, on the way to the station, are some
remains of a castle erected in 1370.

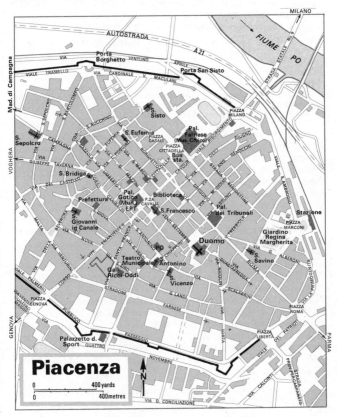

Lodi Vecchio (5 km. E.; 5400 inhab.), the Roman *Laus Pompeia*, mentioned by
Cicero, was a constant rival of Milan until its total destruction in 1158. Only the
church of *San Bassiano* (8C and 12C with 14C additions), dedicated to a 4C
bishop, was left standing.—At *Pandino*, 12 km. N., stands a 14C castle of the
Visconti.

At (52 km.) *Casalpusterlengo* (13,200 inhab.), the road to Cremona
diverges to the left.

FROM CASAL PUSTERLENGO TO CREMONA, 33 km., N234.—4½ km. *Codogno*
has some importance as an agricultural centre (15,200 inhab.) and as the junction
of the Cremona line with the main Milan-Bologna railway.—The road turns N. to
reach the swift-flowing Adda at (69½ km.) *Pizzighettone*, an old town (7140 inhab.)
preserving important remains of its old fortifications, including the Torrione, in

which Francis I was imprisoned after the battle of Pavia (1525). The church of San Bassano dates from the 12C, but has been greatly altered.—Thence to (33 km.) *Cremona* (see p. 200).

Near *Guardamiglio,* the road crosses over the Autostrada and traverses the Po on a long bridge to enter Emilia.

67½ km. **PIACENZA,** an important centre (109,000 inhab.) of internal trade, situated at the strategic point where the Via Æmilia touches the Po, possesses several fine churches. Its name (the French of which is *Plaisance*) is derived from the Latin *Palacentia*.

Post Office, 38 Via Sant'Antonino.—**E.P.T.,** Piazzetta dei Mercanti (near P.za Cavalli).

Buses from the station to the centre, etc.—COUNTRY BUSES from P.za Cittadella to *Cremona, Bologna,* and principal cities.

History. In Sant'Antonio were conducted the peace negotiations, ratified at Constance (1183), between Frederick Barbarossa and the Lombard League; but the most outstanding event in Piacenza's typical history was the plebiscite of 1848, by which she joined Piedmont, the first city so to do.

The centre of the old city is *Piazza Cavalli,* named from its pair of bronze equestrian **Statues* of dukes Alessandro (1625) and Ranuccio Farnese (1620) designed by Fr. Mochi, a pupil of Giambologna. Alessandro Farnese (1545-92) is better known as the 'Prince of Parma', governor of the Low Countries from 1578 till his death; Ranuccio was his son and successor in the dukedom. The ***Palazzo del Comune,** called 'Il Gotico', in the same square, is a fine Gothic building begun in 1280, in which brick, marble, and terracotta are harmoniously blended. Via Venti Settembre leads from the square, past *San Francesco,* a church begun in 1278 with a transitional façade and an E. procession path. The fine Gothic interior has a pretty apse. At the end of the street stands the ***Duomo,** an imposing Lombard Romanesque church (1122-1233), with two of its projecting W. porches supported by atlantes instead of the more usual lions. The 14C campanile is crowned by a gilded angel. Massive cylindrical pillars divide the nave and aisled transepts; the vault of the central octagon is adorned with frescoes by *Morazzone* and *Guercino.* On a nave pillar near the W. end are three votive frescoes (14C-15C); the transepts also have interesting frescoes. In the raised choir the high altar has a gilded reredos (1447), behind which are good stalls of 1471 with the organ set unusually above. The crypt has a forest of slender columns.

The apses and octagon, with their characteristic arcading, are well seen from the street behind the bishop's palace.

To the S.W. Via Chiapponi leads to the church of *Sant'Antonino* rebuilt in the 11C with an octagonal lantern tower, claimed to be the earliest of Italy, supported within on a group of massive pillars. The huge N. porch (called 'Paradiso') was added in 1350. A small Museum contains pergamenes, illuminated codexes, and 15-16C paintings.

Nearby is the *Teatro Municipale Verdi* (1803-10) with a little museum (ring for adm. at No. 17 Piazzale Plebiscito). Farther S.W. is the charming GALLERIA RICCI-ODDI, with a representative collection of Italian 19-20C painting (adm. 10-12, 15-17 or 18; winter, 10-12, 14-16; closed fest. & Mon). Artists represented include: Vito d'Ancona, Telemaco Signorini, Giov. Boldini, Giov. Fattori, Gius. Abbati, Vincenzo Cabianca, Fr. Hayez, Gerolamo Indunno, Vinc. Gemito, Ant. Mancini, Fil. Palizzi, Edoardo Dalbono, Dom. Morelli, and Ettore Tito.

Via Sant'Antonino, passing the Post Office, is prolonged by the busy Corso Garibaldi in which are (r.) the 12C front of *Sant'Ilario* (closed) and, at the end of the street, *Santa Brigida,* also 12C. A little to the left is *San Giovanni in Canale,* a 13C and 16C church well restored.

Via Campagna leads N.W. from beyond Santa Brigida to the *Madonna di Campagna,* a graceful Renaissance building by Alessio Tramello (1522-28), containing fine frescoes by Pordenone.

Via Sant'Eufemia leads N.E. past the church of *Sant'Eufemia,* with an early 12C front (restored); straight ahead is *San Sisto,* another pretty church by Tramello (1499-1511), preceded by a courtyard. It was for this church that Raphael painted his famous 'Sistine Madonna', sold by the convent to the elector of Saxony in 1754, and now at Dresden. On the N. choir pier is the monument of Duchess Margaret of Parma (1522-86), governor of the Netherlands in 1559-67; the fine stalls date from 1514.

Via Borghetto leads back towards the centre; on the left, in P.za Cittadella, is the huge plain **Palazzo Farnese,** begun by Duchess Margaret in 1558 and never completed; it is being restored to house the *Museo Civico.* In the archæological section is the famous 'Fegato di Piacenza', an Etruscan divination bronze representing a sheep's liver, marked with the names of Etruscan deities; the paintings include works by Botticelli, Bonifacio Veronese, Mattia Preti, etc. From P.za Cittadella Via Gregorio X, named after Pope Gregory X (Teobaldo Visconti of Piacenza, pope in 1271-76), leads to *Palazzo dei Tribunali,* a 15C building with a good sculptured doorway. In Via Roma, to the right, is the *Biblioteca Comunale Passerini-Landi* (adm. 9-12, 14.30-17.30) with over 170,000 vols, and 3000 MSS. (interesting psaltars and codexes). To the left in Via Roma is *San Savino,* a 12C church with two mosaics of the 13C or earlier.

At *San Lazzaro Alberoni,* c. 2½ km. S.E. of the town, the Collegio Alberoni has a gallery (adm. Sun 15-18) with 18 Flemish tapestries and a Christ at the Column by Antonello da Messina.—Interesting short excursions may be made to *Grazzano Visconti* (14 km. S.; bus in ½ hr), a village rebuilt in medieval style; and (viâ *San Giorgio Piacentino*) to *Velleia* (33 km. S.; bus), where the attractive ruins of a small Roman town, excavated in the 18C, stand amid rolling countryside.

Railways and N10 connect Piacenza with (32½ km.) *Cremona,* and with (58 km.) *Voghera* (for Alessandria or Genoa), and N45 leads to (145 km.) *Genoa* direct across the hills. On the last rather tedious route the main place of interest is (46 km.) *Bobbio,* noted for the learned monastery founded in 612 by the Irish saint Colombanus, who died here in 615. The Basilica, a 15-17C building, has a crypt with some traces of the primitive church and the tomb of St Colombanus (1480). The Museum contains a remarkable ivory Roman bucket with David in high relief (4C).

The route now follows the VIA ÆMILIA, a Roman road constructed in 187 B.C. by M. Æmilius Lepidus as a military thoroughfare from which to guard the newly-conquered lands of Cisalpine Gaul.—90½ km. *Fiorenzuola d'Arda,* with 14,600 inhabitants, was the birthplace of Giulio Alberoni (1664-1752), the gardener's son who rose to be a cardinal and the able minister of Philip V and Charles III of Spain. To the N. rise the huge refineries that extract petrol from the mineral oils, discovered in 1949, of *Cortemaggiore,* 6½ km. N. Production has diminished since 1960.

A pleasant road (bus to *Lugagnano;* 14½ km.) ascends the Arda valley.—9½ km. **Castell'Arquato,** a picturesque hill-town with double walls. In the pretty Piazza stand the *Palazzo Pretorio* of 1293 and the Romanesque *Collegiata* with a 14C cloister. A *Museo Geologico* houses local finds.

96 km. *Alseno.* About 4 km. left of the road is the abbey of *Chiaravalle della Colomba,* with a fine Romanesque church and a 13C Gothic *Cloister, with coupled columns, off which open the restored chapter-house and an octagonal chapel.

104 km. **Fidenza** (24,300 inhab.), known as *Borgo San Donnino* from the 9C to 1927, occupies the site of the Roman *Fidentia Iulia,* where St Domninus was martyred by the Emp. Maximian in 291. The *Cathedral,* built during the 13C, has a particularly fine porch with *Statues of David and Ezekiel from the workshop of Antelami.

On the road and railway to *Cremona* (40½ km. N.) the principal place is (15½ km.) *Busseto,* described (with excursions that may equally be made from Fidenza or Salsomaggiore) on p. 371.
Over 10 km. S.W. of Fidenza and connected with it by railway and by bus, lies **Salsomaggiore** (160 m.), one of the most frequented spas of Italy, with saline waters used in rheumatic, arthritic, and post-inflammatory disorders. From the Roman era until the mid-19C salt was extracted from the waters. The *Giardino Poggio Diana* has tennis-courts and a swimming pool.—*Tabiano,* 6½ km. S.E., is a smaller spa with sulphur springs beneficial to skin complaints.—*Sant'Andrea Bagni* is another spa in the pretty valley of the Dordone, 21 km. S.E. of Fidenza, reached viâ *Felegara* on the road and railway to Fornovo (p. 371).

116 km. *Castelguelfo* preserves a castle (no adm.) of the Ghibelline Pallavicini which was called the Torre d'Orlando until its capture in 1407 by the Guelph, Ottobono Terzi, who gave it its present name. The road crosses the Taro (view on the right).

127 km. **PARMA,** on the seasonal river Parma, is the second city of Emilia (177,400 inhab.), famous for its ancient buildings, the spires and domes of which give it a characteristic skyline, and for the paintings of Correggio. Parmesan cheese is a staple product of the surrounding country.

Post Office, Strada Pisacane.—**E.P.T.,** 5 P.za Duomo.
Buses from the station to P.za Garibaldi and Villetta (No. 1), etc. *Country Buses* from Viale Toschi to *Busseto, Montecchio, Fornovo, Salsomaggiore, Fidenza,* etc.
Teatro Regio, Via Garibaldi (famous for opera; also plays and concerts).—*Swimming Pools,* Viale Rustici, Viale Piacenza.

History. Little is known about the Roman station that was established here on the Via Æmilia, and Parma emerges in the early Middle Ages as a pawn in the struggles between the various lords who held sway over Emilia. In the strife between Pope and Emperor it was on the Ghibelline (Imperial) side, and in the 12-14C it had a republican constitution. From c. 1335 onwards, however, it was ruled by a succession of ducal families, the Visconti, Terzi, Este, and Sforza; in 1531 it became a papal dominion and in 1545 Paul III made it over, along with Piacenza, to his natural son Pier Luigi Farnese, with the title of duke. The house of Farnese, and their heirs, the Spanish house of Bourbon-Parma, held the duchy until 1801. In 1815 the Vienna Congress assigned Parma to the ex-empress Marie Louise, but in 1859 the widow of her son Charles III was obliged to hand it over to the King of Italy. It was heavily bombed in the Second World War.
Artistically Parma may be reckoned as subject to Lombardy until the arrival of Correggio c. 1520; and from him developed the Parmesan school of painting, including Parmigianino and Girol. Mazzola, as his most successful disciples.—Arturo Toscanini (1867-1957), the conductor, was born at No. 13 Borgo Rodolfo Tanzi and played in the orchestra of the Teatro Regio.

The main streets of the city meet at the central PIAZZA GARIBALDI with the *Municipio* (S. side) and *Palazzo del Governatore* (N. side), both of the 17C. Here also are monuments to Garibaldi and Correggio. To the N. is the church of the **Madonna della Steccata,** built in 1521-39 by Bern.

and Giov. Fr. Zaccagni, on the plan, it is said, of Bramante's original model for St Peter's at Rome. In the richly decorated interior (l. of the entrance) is the tomb, by Lor. Bartolini (1840), of Field-Marshal Count Neipperg (1775-1829), husband of Marie Louise. The decoration of the chapels as well as several fine tombs are excellent examples of the 16C style. Strada Cavour leads to Strada al Duomo which passes between the birthplace (r.) of Frate Salimbene (1221-c.1290), the chronicler, and the side of the *Archbishop's Palace*, whose well-restored façade shows successive additions of 1175 and 1234.

The handsome P.za Duomo is dominated by the *Duomo*, a splendid 11C church with a campanile (1284-94) and a projecting porch supported by two lions, with reliefs of the Months added around the arch in 1281. The nave is decorated with frescoes by pupils of Correggio (1555-70), and in the cupola is the celebrated *Assumption by *Correggio* (1520-30; access to the cupola to examine the fresco has been closed for several years during restoration works necessitated by the humidity which threatened the fresco). In the last chapel in the S. aisle is a Crucifixion with saints, by *Bern. Gatti;* the chapel opposite, in the N. aisle, contains interesting frescoes. On the W. wall of the S. transept is a *Deposition by *Benedetto Antelami* (1178).

The adjacent Romanesque *Baptistery* (9-12, 15-17.30 or 18), one of the finest in Italy, is a splendid octagonal building in red Verona marble, begun in 1196 by *Bened. Antelami*, who executed the three portals and the frieze that almost girdles the edifice. The interior has a magnificent series of 13C frescoes in the vault and lunettes, reliefs over the doors by Antelami, and a series of 14 *Statues of the months, and winter and spring, by Antelami (formerly in the wall niches). Immediately E. of the cathedral is the church of **San Giovanni Evangelista**, rebuilt in 1498-1510, with a façade of 1604-7, and containing in its dome a splendid fresco by *Correggio,* the *Vision of St John at Patmos (light in N. transept), as well as frescoes of St John writing, by the same painter (N. transept), and others by *Parmigianino* (1st and 2nd N. chapels).— The medieval *Farmacia di San Giovanni Evangelista* (entrance at No. 1 Borgo Pipa; 12.30-14) preserves its 16C decoration. *Sant'Antonio Abate,* to the S., was begun by F. Bibbiena in 1712, and finished in 1766.

On the other side of Strada Garibaldi, on the bank of the river, is the **Palazzo della Pilotta**, a gloomy and rambling pile built for the Farnese family in c. 1583-1622, but left unfinished; it was badly bombed and half of it demolished. Here are installed the important collections of the city (in the course of rearrangement), including the museum of antiquities, the large library, and the picture gallery containing Correggio's masterpieces. The *Museo Nazionale di Antichità* (adm. summer 9.30-13, 15-18, winter 10-16, fest. 10-13, Mon closed), founded in 1760, is interesting chiefly for the bronze and other objects excavated at Velleia (p. 367).

FIRST FLOOR. Classical sculpture (statues and architectural fragments which belonged to the Farnese, Gonzaga, and other collections, including a fine bronze head of a boy), Egyptian works, and medals. Objects excavated at Velleia (among which the famous Tabula Alimentaria, bronzes and statues). Greek, Italiot, and Etruscan pottery and small Etruscan funerary urns.

GROUND FLOOR. Prehistoric objects from the region around Parma: terracottas and other objects from the pile-dwellings of Parma and the lake-villages of Castione dei Marchesi, Castellazzo, etc. Works from the palæolithic and neolithic periods, as well as the Iron and Bronze Ages. Lapidary collection. Roman bronzes and architectural fragments. Goldsmiths' work from the region, and from Lombardy.—The TEATRO FARNESE, built of wood by *G. B. Aleotti* in 1618-28, was modelled on Palladio's theatre at Vicenza, but made use of movable scenery; it was almost entirely destroyed in the war, but has been partly reconstructed.—The PALATINE LIBRARY, adjoining, houses about 400,000 vols., with editions and matrices of G. B. Bodoni, the printer, whose office was in the palace in 1768-1813, and contains a fresco by *Correggio* (Coronation of the Virgin), from San Giovanni.

Opposite the library, on the second floor of the Palazzo, is the **Galleria Nazionale** (adm. summer 9.30-13, 15-18, winter 9.30-16, fest. 9-13; closed Mon), founded by Philip of Bourbon-Parma in 1752.

ROOM I. 15C-early 16C Emilian School. Paintings by *J. Loschi, C. Caselli, A. Araldi,* and *Francesco Francia.*—R. II. Detached frescoes by local artists.— R. III. Works by the Tuscans *B. Daddi* and *A. Gaddi,* the Venetian *Paolo Veneziano,* and the Emilian *Simone dei Crocifissi.*—R. IV. Tuscan paintings by *Spinello Aretino; Giovanni di Paolo,* the Redeemer and Saints; *Beato Angelico,* Madonna and Child with Saints.—R. V. *Works by *Cima da Conegliano* (Madonna and Child with Saints; Endymion, Apollo, and Marsyas); *Leonardo da Vinci,* *Head of a young girl (sketch); *Sebastiano del Piombo,* Clement VII.— R. VI. Works by *Garófalo,* and the Lombard and Roman schools.—R. VII. *Correggio,* *Madonna di San Gerolamo, Madonna della Scala (detached fresco).—R. VIII. *Anthony Mor,* Alessandro Farnese; *Correggio,* Deposition, Martyrdom of a Saint.—R. IX. *Murillo,* Job; *El Greco,* Healing of a blind man; *Correggio,* Madonna della Scodella ('Madonna of the Bowl').—In the oval hall (near the entrance): Portraits by *Frans Pourbus the Younger,* and works by *Anselmi.* Flemish masters exhibited here include *Paul Brill, Brueghel the Elder,* and *Van Dyck* (Clara Eugenia of Spain, Madonna and Child).—The long gallery has works by *Ann.* and *Lod. Carracci, Seb Ricci, Bern. Bertoldo, Zoffany,* and *Canaletto.*—The other rooms are closed for restoration: they contain works by *Parmigianino* (Marriage of St Catherine, Turkish slave); *Bronzino, Guercino, Holbein* (Erasmus), and numerous others.

The PRINTS AND DRAWINGS ROOM (with 23 drawings by *Parmigianino*) is opened on request. The SALA ICONOGRAFICA (portraits of the Dukes of Parma from the 16C to the 19C) and the SALONE FARNESE (contemporary art) have been closed.

In the former Convent of San Paolo (across P.za Marconi in Via Melloni) is the *Camera del Correggio** (open 9-12.30), the refectory of the abbess, frescoed by *Correggio* in 1518, at the order of the abbess of the day, with mythological scenes. The celebrated decoration of the vault has a most original design. The adjoining room is adorned with grotteschi and other frescoes by *Aless. Araldi* (1514).—Nearby, at No. 15 Via Garibaldi, is the *Museo Lombardi* (open 9.30-12.30, 15.30-17 or 18.30; fest 9.30-13.; Mon closed) with a collection relating to the empress Marie Louise of Austria.

On the other side of the river is the *Parco Ducale* in which is Palazzo Ducale (restored; adm. on request to the Carabinieri who now occupy the building). To the S., in Borgo Rodolfo Tanzi, is the birthplace of Toscanini, now a small museum relating to the conducter (adm. Mon, Fri, & Sat). The church of the *Annunziata,* in this part of the town, is an impressive Baroque building (1566), beyond which the graceful *Ospedale della Misericordia,* begun c. 1214 and enlarged in the 16C, houses the archives of the Duchy (open 9-14). About 1 km. to the S. in the *Villetta Cemetery* the embalmed body of Paganini rests beneath a classical canopy.—Also of interest is the *University,* in a 16C building ascribed to Galeazzo Alessi and Vignola, which has faculties of law and medicine and contains natural history collections.

The province is rich in feudal strongholds. Excursions may be made (buses) to *Montechiarúgolo* (16 km. S.E.), with a good castle of 1406 (no adm.) and *Montecchio Emilia* (2½ km. farther, across the Enza), which preserves parts of the **old** ramparts; or to *Torrechiara* (19½ km. S.) with its *Castle, the finest in the

province, built for Pier Maria Rossi (1448-60) and noteworthy for its 'golden
room'. It is open 9-13, 15.30-18.30; winter 9-13, 14-16; fest. 9-13; closed Mon. The
road continues beyond Torrechiara along the Parma river to Pastorello (31 km.)
where a by-road crosses the river and mounts to *Schia* (49 km.) with ski-ing
facilities on **Monte Caio** (1580 m).

The road to Busseto leaves the Via Æmilia at Castelguelfo (p. 368) and passes
(19½ km.) *Fontanellato* with a moated 13C *Castle of the Sanvitale family (open
10-12.30, 15.30-19; winter 9.30-12.30, 15-18; closed Mon), preserving furnishings
and a fresco (1533) by Parmigianino.—At (27½ km.) *Soragna* other 16C works of
art are preserved in the castle (open 9-12, 14 or 15-17 or 19; closed Tues) of the Meli
Lupi.—At (33 km.) *Róncole Verdi* is the humble birthplace of Gius. Verdi
(1813-1901), the composer. His house is open 9-12, 14 or 15-17 or 19 exc.
Monday.—38 km. *Busseto,* a charming little town, lordship of the Pallavicini in
the 10-16C, has a battlemented castle and many buildings adorned with terracotta
in the Cremonese manner. The Villa Pallavicino houses the Museo Civico. A road
continues N. of the town, passing the Villa di Sant'Agata (adm. April-Oct, 9-12,
15-19 exc. Mon; relics, incl. bust by Vinc. Gemito), built by Verdi in 1849, then
turns E. along the Po, making a slightly longer return (48½ km.) pasts the
fortresses of the Rossi family at *Roccabianca* and *San Secondo* (frescoes by the
Campi).

FROM PARMA TO LA SPEZIA, 124 km. by N62; railway, 120 km. in 2¾ hrs
(many tunnels). Beyond (10½ km.) *Collecchio* the road ascends the broad valley of
the Taro as far as (23 km.) *Fornovo di Taro,* a village noted as the scene of the
battle of 1495, in which the retreating Charles VIII of France defeated the
Milanese and Venetians. The Romanesque church has fine 13C sculptures on its
façade. [The railway here leaves the road and runs viá (61½ km.) Borgo Val di
Taro, traversing the Apennines by the Borgallo Tunnel, 8 km. long, and rejoining
the road at Pontrémoli.] The road ascends rapidly.—52½ km. *Berceto* (800 m) with
a 13C church.—Beyond (62 km.) *Passo della Cisa* (1039 m), the road summit, the
descent begins into the Magra valley.—80 km. *Pontrémoli* (236 m) lies among
chestnut-clad hills. In the church of San Francesco is a bas-relief attrib. to Agost.
di Duccio. The Museum in the castle displays the curious statue-stelæ of the
Linigiana cult. SS. Annunziata, S. of the town, has an interesting 16C interior.—
103 km. *Aulla,* beneath the picturesque 16C fort of Brunella. This route leaves the
Sarzana road and railway on the left, and crosses the Magra.—124 km. *La Spezia,*
see Rte 8.—For the road from Berceto and Borgotaro to Sestri Levante, see p.

FROM PARMA TO MANTUA (57½ km.); railway viá Piádena (where a change is
necessary) in 1½ hrs. N343 runs N. viá (16 km.) *Colorno,* which retains a ducal
palace of the Farnese, to cross the Po on a long bridge near *Casalmaggiore.*—
29 km. **Sabbioneta** has traces of its former glories under Vespasiano Gonzaga,
Prince of Bózzolo (1531-91). It is an excellent example of 16C town-planning, with
regular streets and fortifications. The *Palazzo Ducale* (1568) contains wooden
statues of the Gonzagas and fine ceilings and frescoes. In the *Incoronata* chapel is
the tomb of Vespasiano, by Della Porta, with his statue by Leone Leoni (1588).
The *Teatro Olimpico* (1590; restored), by Vinc. Scamozzi, resembles Palladio's
more famous example at Vicenza. The *Palazzo del Giardino,* built in 1584,
contains frescoed rooms by Campi and the school of Giulio Romano. The *Galleria
degli Antichi* connects the palace with Piazza Castello.—From here to Mantua, see
Rte 21.

An alternative route from Parma (68 km.) is the N62; railway viá Suzzara (where
a change is necessary) in 1½-2 hrs.—At (20½ km.) *Brescello* Sir Anthony Panizzi
(1797-1879), librarian of the British Museum, was born.—33½ km. **Guastalla**
(14,100 inhab.) was once the capital of a duchy of the Gonzagas. In the square is a
statue of Ferrante Gonzaga (d. 1457), the condottiere, by Leone Leoni. The
Basilica della Pieve, 10 min. beyond the railway, is an interesting Romanesque
church, restored in 1930.—The road leaves Suzzara on the right, and crosses the
Po at (55 km.) *Borgoforte.*—68 km. *Mantua,* see Rte 21.

Beyond Parma the Via Æmilia crosses the Enza just before
Sant'Ilario, with a good view of the mountains on the right.

153½ km. **REGGIO NELL'EMILIA** (now usually shortened to
'Reggio Emilia'), the large and flourishing centre (129,800 inhab.) of an
important agricultural area, is especially noted for the manufacture of
Parmesan cheese ('parmigiano-reggiano'). The *Regium Lepidi* of the

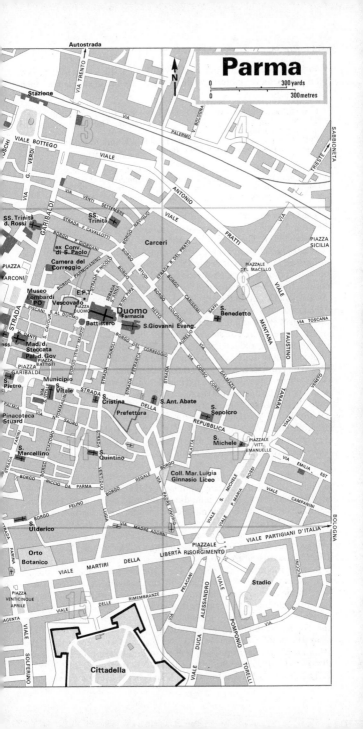

Romans, it is divided in two by the Via Æmilia; the S. part of the town retains a medieval pattern, while to the N. are broad streets and open squares.

Post Office, 3 Via Sessi (E. of P.za Cavour).—**E.P.T.,** 1 P.za Battisti.
Theatre. *Municipale,* P.za Cavour. Opera season, Dec–March; plays and concerts throughout the year.
Buses from the station to P.za Battista; from P.za Vittoria to *Modena, Mantua, Bologna, Ciano d'Enza, Montecchio, Boretto, La Spezia,* etc.

The most settled period of Reggio's turbulent history was under the Este domination (1409–1796).—Reggio was the birthplace of Lodovico Ariosto (1474–1533), and here in 1741 Horace Walpole quarrelled with Gray and was nursed by Joseph Spence through an attack of quinsy.

Via Emilia widens to form the little Piazza Battisti where the Albergo Posta and Ente Turismo occupy the restored *Palazzo del Capitano del Popolo* (1281). The **Duomo,** in the piazza adjoining to the S., is a Romanesque church, remodelled except for the apse and crypt. The unfinished façade was added in 1544 by *Prospero Spani* and the statues, notably Adam and Eve above the central door, are by him (1557). The curious tower bears a group of the Madonna and donors, in copper, by *Bart. Spani* (1522). In the 3rd chapel of the S. aisle is the tomb of Valerio Malaguzzi, uncle of Ariosto, by *Bart. Spani,* and in the E. chapels are (r.) the tomb of Bp. Rangone, and (l.) a marble ciborium, both by *Prospero Spani.* In the piazza is *Palazzo Comunale,* begun in 1414, where in 1797 the green, white, and red tricolour of the Revolution was proclaimed the national flag of Italy. The Sala del Tricolore, with a small museum, is shown on request. Behind the cathedral lie the market and the church of *San Prospero,* guarded by six red marble lions. It was rebuilt in 1514–27, with a choir (being restored) frescoed by Cam. Procaccini and fine inlaid stalls. In the broad Corso Garibaldi to the W. (reached viâ P.za Vittorio Emanuele and Via S. Pietro Martire), is the ornate but graceful church of *Madonna della Ghiara* (1597–1619), with a well-preserved interior decorated with frescoes and altarpieces by 17C Emilian painters.

To the N. of Via Emilia opens the huge P.za Cavour, bounded on the N. side by the elegant *Teatro Municipale* (1852–57; with a high theatrical reputation), and extending W. as P.za della Libertà. To the right, beyond a harrowing bronze monument (1958) to Resistance martyrs, are the MUSEI CIVICI (adm. Sun; during the week on request). From the vestibule (with fragments of mosaic pavements) are the entrances to the various collections. The *Museo Spallanzani* has a delightful natural history display (including a room of fossils). Another gallery has been arranged as a *Museo del Risorgimento e Resistenza.* The *Museo Chierici* consists of archæological material (including Etruscan finds), arranged for study purposes. The *Numismatic Collection* shows examples from the Reggio mint. In the basement (entrance in Via Secchi) the prehistoric collection is well displayed, with finds from the locality including a 5C treasure dug up in 1957 (fine gold fibula). The *Galleria Fontanesi,* with pictures by Emilian painters from the 15C to the 19C has been closed for restoration.

In the public garden behind the theatre has been erected the *Monument of the Concordii,* a Roman family tomb of c. A.D. 50 discovered in 1929 near Boretto, on the bank of the Po, 27½ km. N.W. of Reggio. To the S.W. rises the 'Gothick' spire of the *Galleria Parmeggiani* (closed for restoration), entered through a fine 16C Hispano-Moresque doorway brought from Valencia. The eclectic collections include medieval metal-work, 14-16C paintings of the Flemish and Spanish schools, a Christ Blessing by El Greco (recently restored), and an imaginative Abdication of Charles I of England by León y Escosura (1836-1902).

The best surviving palazzi (15-16C) are in Via Emilia towards the station (E.) and Via Roma leading N. from it. A frequent bus service (No. 7, and for the return No. 77) runs along the Modena road past the modern buildings of the asylum of *San Lazzaro*, a foundation dating back to the Middle Ages, to (2½ km.) *San Maurizio*, just beyond which is the *Mauriziano*, the country villa of the Malaguzzi family, where Ariosto often visited his relatives. Three frescoed rooms on the first floor have been restored to their appearance in the poet's time.

EXCURSIONS FROM REGGIO. About 16 km. N.E. is **Correggio** the birthplace of Antonio Allegri (1494-1534) surnamed Correggio, whose house still stands in Borgo Vecchio. The *Palazzo dei Principi*, begun c. 1500, contains a Head of Christ by Mantegna and 12 Flemish tapestries (16C). *San Quirino* (1513-87) built to a design attrib. to Vignola, is also of interest. The *Teatro Asioli* (18C) has recently been restored.—*Scandiano*, 13 km. S.E., is a picturesque little town, with the old castle of the Boiardi, famous among whom was the poet Matteo Maria Boiardo (1434-94). It was the birthplace of Abate Lazzaro Spallanzani (1729-99), the great experimental physiologist.—To the N. of Reggio is (17½ km.) *Novellara*, notable for a castle (now town hall) of the Gonzaga, dating in part from the 14C. It contains a small museum (open 9-12) with detached frescoes of 13-16C, and a remarkable series of ceramic jars made for a pharmacy in the 15-16C.

The road from Reggio to (25½ km.) *Ciano d'Enza* is the best approach to the castle of Canossa.—At (23 km.) *San Polo d'Enza* a by-road on the left ascends to (32½ km.) the ruined **Castle of Canossa** (adm. daily 9-12, 15-18.30), the home of the great Countess Matilda of Tuscany, famed for the submission of the Emperor Henry IV to Pope Gregory VII in 1077. Only the foundations of the castle of that time remain; the ruins above ground date from the 13C and later. The return may be made to Ciano (8 km.) viâ the castle of *Rossena*.

FROM REGGIO TO LA SPEZIA, 134 km.; bus twice daily in 5½ hrs. N63 ascends steadily to (27½ km.) *Casina*, beyond which a road on the left leads to *Carpineti* (9 km.), visited in summer (view from castle).—46 km. **Castelnovo ne' Monti** (702 m) is a pleasant hill resort. An easy ascent of 1½ hrs leads to the summit of the *Pietra di Bismántova*, a fine viewpoint, mentioned by Dante in the 'Purgatorio'.—66½ km. *Collagna* (830 m) stands among chestnut-woods.—From (77½ km.) the *Passo del Cerreto* (1261 m) the road descends rapidly.—96 km. *Fivizzano* (326 m) is a small Tuscan town enclosed in ramparts by Cosimo I Medici. The rapid descent continues into the Aulella valley and to (113 km.) *Aulla* (see p. 371)—134½ km. *La Spezia*, see Rte 8.

Beyond Reggio the Bologna road crosses the Rodano, leaves the Mauriziano (see above) on the left and reaches (167 km.) *Rubiera*, with its ruined castle, on the Secchia.

179 km. **MÒDENA,** a sombre town (177,600 inhab.), that has figured prominently in Italian history, is an important market for the produce of the rich plain at the foot of the Apennines. The Maserati motor-works are sited in the town, the Ferrari works outside on the Abetone road; conspicuous to the W. is the combined racing circuit (for motorcycles) and airfield (private planes).

Railway Stations. *FF.SS.*, for all main-line services (N.W. of Corso Vitt. Eman. II).—*Ferrovie Provinciali*, Viale Medaglie d'Oro (S.E. of the centre) for local trains to Fiorano and Sassuolo.

Post Office. 15 Via Emilia.—**E.P.T.**, 3 Corso Canal Grande.

Buses (and trolley-buses) link the stations with the centre.—*Country Buses* from the Bus Station (Viale Monte Kosica) to *Bologna, Cento, Ferrara*, etc.

Swimming Pools. Via Montecuccoli (indoor and outdoor).—*Horse Racing* (in April) at the *Ippodromo,* Via Ragazzi del '99 (S. of the town).

History. The Roman colony of *Mutina,* established in the 2C B.C. on a site already inhabited by Gauls and Etruscans, fell into decay under the Empire, and the present city dates its prosperity from the time of Countess Matilda of Tuscany (d. 1115), the loyal supporter of the Guelphs and the Pope's authority. After her death Modena became a free city and, in rivalry with Bologna, inclined more to the Ghibelline faction. In 1288 the Este family gained control of the city, and the duchy of Modena was created for Borso d'Este in 1452. It lasted until 1796, and was reconstituted in 1814-59 thanks to an alliance of the Estes with the house of Austria. Air-raid damage in the Second World War was mostly concentrated in an attack of May 1944.—Modena was the birthplace of the sculptors Guido Mazzoni (c. 1450-1518) and Antonio Begarelli (1498-1565), the former known as 'Il Modanino', of the physiologist Gabriele Falloppio (1523-63), and of Giov. Batt. Bononcini (1672-1750), Handel's rival in London. Mary of Modena (1658-1718), queen of James II of England, was the daughter of Alfonso IV d'Este.

Via Emilia forms the main thoroughfare of the city, and at its centre is P.za della Torre, in which rises the *Torre Ghirlandina (adm. weekdays 10-12.30, 15.30-19; if closed apply at Comune for key; closed fest.), the beautiful detached campanile of the cathedral, 96 m high and slightly inclined. Begun along with the cathedral, it was completed in 1319, and contains the bucket carried off by the Modenese in a raid on Bologna in 1325, commemorated in Tassoni's mock-heroic poem 'La Secchia Rapita'. The splendid Romanesque *Duomo (begun in 1099, completed in the 13C) stands on the site of the tomb of St Geminianus, patron of Modena. The sculptures on the main W. portal by *Wiligelmus* and on the S. side by his school, are well worth examining in detail (they have been covered during restoration work, but can be seen on application at the sacristy, Municipio, or E.P.T.). The plain bronze doors, recently installed, have been the subject of great controversy. The exterior of the apse is noteworthy; in the last arch on the S. side are four reliefs of the life of St Geminianus, by *Agost. di Duccio* (1442). The *Interior (closed 13-15.30) is of pale red brick, the Romanesque arcades having alternate slender columns and composite piers which support an early 15C vault. A *Tribuna and Ambo (illuminated by sacristan on request), supported on lions, form the approach to the raised choir. The coloured sculptures of Campionese workmanship represent the Evangelists (on the pulpit), the Washing of the Feet, the Last Supper, the Kiss of Judas, Christ before Pilate, the Via Dolorosa, and the Crucifixion. In the S. aisle are remains of 15C frescoes by local artists, and a terracotta Adoration of the Shepherds, by *Begarelli* (1527; restored 1976). In the semi-dome of the apse is a modern mosaic. On the r. wall of the choir are fresco fragments (Tuscan school, late 13C), and on the l. wall, four inlaid panels of the Evangelists, by Crist. da Lendinara (1477). In the N. aisle is an elaborately carved ancona attrib. to *Michele da Firenze* (restored 1977); the wood statue of S. Geminiano probably dates from the 14C. The Crypt (with interesting capitals) has a sculptured group by *Guido Mazzoni* (1480).

Near the left side of the Duomo is the **Museo Lapidario** (adm. 9-12, 15-18 on request). It contains about 100 Roman marbles, epigraphs, stelæ, and sarcophagi from the necropolis of Mútina; and medieval, Renaissance, and later sculpture. (For adm. apply at the Sacristy of the Duomo.)

The *Palazzo Comunale* in the P.za Grande, founded in the 12C, dates in its present form from a reconstruction of 1624. The Corso Canal Chiaro leads S.W. to the church of *San Francesco* (1244), which contains a fine *Descent from the Cross, by Begarelli (end of N. aisle). Rua del Muro (fine palazzi at Nos. 30 and 42) leads back to Via Emilia and the church of *Sant'Agostino* which has another rendering of the

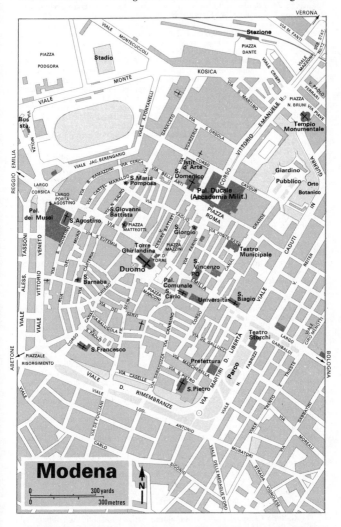

same subject by this sculptor. Next door is the **Palazzo dei Musei,** containing interesting art collections.

On the ground floor is the MUSEO DEL RISORGIMENTO (9-12.30; on Tues, Wed, & Fri also 16-19). In the courtyard is a collection of Roman sarcophagi, mosaics and architectural fragments.—On the first floor is the ARCHIVIO

STORICO (Mon-Sat 8-12.30; Tues & Fri also 15-18.30; closed fest.) and the **Biblioteca Estense** (9-14, Sat 9-13; closed Sun), with a fine exhibition of illuminated MSS., notably the *Bible of Borso d'Este, illuminated by *Taddeo Crivelli* and *Franco Russi;* a 14C edition of Dante; and the missal of Renée of France, by *Jean Bourdichon* (16C). On the floor above is the **Museo Civico** (adm. 9-12.30; on Tues, Wed, & Fri also 16-19; Sun 10-13, 15-18; closed Mon) a collection of local interest, part of it still displayed in a charming old-fashioned manner. It includes: 14C fresco from the Duomo; medieval sculptures; terracotta Madonna, by *Begarelli;* glass; weights and measures; scientific instruments; majolica; arms and armour; embroidered silks, textiles; applied arts. The Archæological section is still in the course of arrangement.

The **Galleria Estense** (adm. 9-14, fest. 9-13) is a fine collection of pictures formed by the Este family in the early 16C, notable especially for its examples of the 15-17C Emilian schools. It has recently been reopened and beautifully rearranged to include objects from the Museo Estense of applied arts. The rooms are not numbered, but the collection is displayed in roughly chronological order. VESTIBULE. Islamic ceramics, 16C Venetian enamels. Head of Jove (?), 2C A.D. Emilian romanesque sculpture. Small bronzes (Etruscan, Italic, Greek). At the end, marble *Bust of Francesco I d'Este, founder of the collection, by *Gian Lor. Bernini* (1652).

LONG GALLERY. Portable altars (*Venetian, late 14C, Tom. da Modena); Barnaba da Modena,* Madonna and Child with Saints, Crucifixion.—*Crist. da Lendinara,* Madonna and Child; *Agnolo* and *Bart. Erri,* Triptych (in restoration); *Cosmè Tura,* St Anthony of Padua; *Bart. Bonascia,* Pietà and symbols of the passion; *Bart. Erri,* Madonna and Saints (4 panels).—Works by *Fr. Bianchi Ferrari.*—Lombard, French, Spanish, and Byzantine sculptures in ivory and marble. Busts by *L'Antico* and *Tullio Lombardo.* Bronzes by *Il Riccio.—Fr. Botticini,* *Adoration of the Child; *Apollonio di Giovanni,* Story of Griselda; *Antoniazzo Romano,* Pietà; *Giuliano Bugiardini,* Birth of St John the Baptist.— Flemish works: *Albrecht Bouts,* St Christopher; *Joos van Cleve,* Madonna and Child and St Anne.—*Palma Vecchio,* *Portrait of a lady; *Cima da Conegliano,* Deposition; *Vinc. Catena,* Madonna and Child with Saints and donors.—Estense harp with rich painted decoration (end of 16C); *Gian Fr. Maineri,* Christ carrying the Cross; *Girol. da Carpi,* Portrait of a gentleman; *Dom. Panetti,* Madonna and Child (formerly attrib. to Garófalo).—At the end, *Correggio,* *Madonna Cámpori.* Sculptures by *Guido Mazzoni, Nicolò dell'Arca,* and *Ant. Begarelli* (large terracotta of the Madonna and Child).

There follow a series of small rooms. Works by *Girol. da Carpi* (Portrait of a man); *L'Antico,* Bust of Ceres; *Dosso Dossi,* Adoration of the Shepherds, Portrait of Alfonso I d'Este (with *Batt. Dossi),* Portrait of Hercules I d'Este (attrib.).— Ceramics from Urbino. *Fr. Duquesnoy,* Bust of a woman. Small bronzes by *Pietro Tacca, Giambologna,* and *Iac. Sansovino.*—Works by *Lelio Orsi, Giov. Gherardo delle Catene,* and *Marco Meloni.*—*Rosalba Carriera,* Portrait; *Velazquez,* Portrait of Francesco I d'Este; small works by *Bart. Schedoni.—Lelio Orsi,* Rape of Ganimede (ceiling); series of paintings by *Nicolò dell'Abate.—Mabuse,* Madonna and Child; *Hans Baldung Grien,* Head of an old man; *El Greco,* *Portable altar, a youthful work; *Pieter Brueghel the Younger,* Calvary; *Charles Le Brun,* Scenes from the life of Moses; *Rubens* (workshop), Adoration of the Magi; *Frans Pourbus,* Portrait of a woman.

The remainder of the collection is displayed in four large rooms. ROOM I. Paolo Veronese, 3 paintings of Saints; *Palma Giovane,* Adoration of the Magi (2 paintings); *Tintoretto,* Rape of Europa, Madonna and Child with Saints; *Bonifazio Veronese,* the Virtues; *Dom. Tintoretto,* Giving of the keys to St Peter.—R. II. *Carlo Cignani,* Flora; *Sassoferrato,* Madonna and Child; *Guercino,* Marriage of St Catherine; *Guido Reni,* Crucifixion; *Ann. Carracci,* Venus; *Lud. Carracci,* Assunta, Galatea; *Guido Reni,* St Roch in prison; *Lavinia Fontana,* Portrait; *Garòfalo,* Madonna enthroned with Saints.—R. III. Works by *Luca Ferrari* and *Guercino.*—R IV. Works by *Pomarancio* and *Daniele Crespi.* Huge canvases by *Giulio Cesare* and *Camillo Procaccini.* Seascapes by *Salvator Rosa.*

The **Galleria Cámpori,** also in this building, with a good collection of paintings chiefly of the 17-18C has been closed since 1970. In the GALLERIA CIVICA (adm. daily exc. Mon 11.30-12.30, 15.30-19; entrance on Viale Vittorio Veneto) frequent exhibitions are held.

Via N. Sauro leads N.E. off Via Emilia (comp. the Plan) to *Santa Maria Pomposa;* here is buried Lod. Ant. Muratori (1672-1750), provost of the church from 1716 and 'father of Italian history'. He lived and died in the adjacent house, now the *Museo Muratoriano* (apply to custodian of church 9-12), which preserves his autograph works and other momentoes. *San Giovanni Battista* contains a life-sized *Descent from the Cross by Guido Mazzoni (1476).—Via Ces. Battisti, on the left farther on, leads to the old church of *San Domenico* rebuilt in 1708-31 and (r.) the huge **Palazzo Ducale** (no adm.; now Accademia Militare), begun in 1634 for Francesco I on the site of the old Este castle. From the other side of the palace Corso Vittorio Emanuele leads towards the station; on the right is the imposing *Tempio Monumentale,* by A. Casanova and M. Barbanti (1923), a large church in the Romanesque style erected as a war memorial. In the public garden beyond is a Botanical Garden founded by Francesco III in 1772.

In the S.E. part of the town are the *University,* and the church of **San Pietro** (rebuilt in 1476), with a well ornamented brick front and a garishly decorated interior. It contains a notable Pietà, six statues in the nave, and a group of the Virgin and saints all by *Ant.* Begarelli, the latter completed by his nephew Lodovico for the master's tomb. In this church was buried also Alessandro Tassoni (1565-1635), author of 'La Secchia Rapita' (see above). Beyond the church is a pleasant park, with a war memorial (1926).—To the E. of the Pistoia road is the *Città dei Ragazzi,* or Boys' Town, founded by Father Rocchi; one of its houses was the gift of British ex-prisoners of war rescued by the founder in 1943-45.

FROM MODENA TO FERRARA, 74 km. (Highway N255); bus viá Crevalcore in 1½-2 hrs—9 km. *Nonántola,* with two 14C towers, is famous for its abbey, founded in 752 and rebuilt in brick in the 13C. The portal has reliefs by the school of Wiligelmus (1121). The church contains the tombs of Popes St Sylvester (in the choir) and Adrian III (in the crypt).—At (22½ km.) *San Giovanni in Persiceto* this route crosses the road from Bologna to Verona.—40½ km. **Cento** was the birthplace of Giovanni Fr. Barbieri, called Il Guercino (1591-1666), whose painting is well represented in the town picture gallery, and of Ugo Bassi (1801-49), a priest martyred in the cause of Italian freedom. The church of the *Rosario* contains a chapel built for Guercino and containing a fine Crucifixion by him, and above the town rises the 14C *Rocca.*—74 km. *Ferrara,* see Rte 37.

FROM MODENA TO ABETONE, 96 km., Highway 12, a fine road across the Apennines; bus.—Beyond (17½ km.) *Maranello* the ascent begins.—47 km. *Pavullo nel Frignano* (682 m) is the centre of the hilly Frignano, with a 19C residence of the dukes of Modena.—Rounding the hill on which stands the old castle of *Montecúccolo* (gutted) the road continues to climb past the old tower of *Montecénere,* with fine views, to (84½ km.) *Pievepélago* (781 m), an important road junction, connected by bus with Séstola (p. 487).—90½ km. *Fiumalbo* (935 m), with an old tower, is frequented for winter sports. It is the base for the ascent of *Monte Cimone* (2165 m; 5 hrs), the highest peak in the northern Apennines, which rises to the N.E. (rough track; from the summit, on a clear day, can be seen the E. and W. coasts of Italy). It is ascended part way from Séstola by funicular (comp. p. 487). The boundary between Emilia and Tuscany is crossed just short of the road summit.—96½ km. *Abetone,* and thence to Pistoia, see p. 492.

From Pievepélago a steep road to *Castelnuovo di Garfagnana* (45½ km.; p. 498), joins an alternative road from Modena (84½ km.), viá the Secchia valley, just below the *Foce delle Radici* (1529 m). A little below the pass on the Tuscan side is *San Pellegrino in Alpe,* with a museum illustrating the peasant life of the area.

From Modena to *Mantua* viá Carpi, see Rte 21; to *Mirandola,* see Rte 22.

Beyond Modena the Via Æmilia crosses the Panaro. To the left is the Forte Urbano, built by Urban VIII (1528) to mark the papal frontier of his time.—192 km. *Castelfranco Emilia.* On the approach to Bologna the Madonna di San Luca is seen on a hill to the right. The road crosses the Reno a little above the island on which Octavius, Mark Antony, and Lepidus met to form the Second Triumvirate (43 B.C.).—218 km. **Bologna,** see below.

39   BOLOGNA

BOLOGNA (489,600 inhab.), the capital of Emilia and one of the oldest cities of Italy, the seat of a famous university, is situated at the S. verge of the plain of the Po, at the N.E. foot of the slopes of the Apennines. The old town, built almost exclusively of brick, with arcaded streets, Romanesque and Gothic churches and handsome public monuments, is one of the most beautiful cities in northern Italy, often unjustly left out of the usual tourists' itinerary. The Bolognese school of painting is well represented in its picture gallery, and the museum is important for the study of Umbrian and Etruscan civilization. Bologna is famed for its gastronomy.

Post Office (Pl. 10), P.za Minghetti.—**E.P.T.**, 45 Via Marconi; information offices at the railway and bus stations.

Buses. No fare is charged before 9 and from 16.30 to 20. From the *Station* to P.za Maggiore, going on to the *Funivia di San Luca* (**21**); to *San Michele in Bosco* (**31**). From *P.za Galvani* to *San Mámalo* (**12**) and to *Certosa* (**43**). Nos. **12** and **18** from P.za Maggiore to the *Zona Fieristica*.—COUNTRY BUSES from P.za Venti Settembre; a comprehensive network which serves nearly all towns of interest in the region.—Daily TOUR OF THE CITY (9.15-12) in summer (on foot; no charge) is organized by the E.P.T. from Via 4 Novembre.

Airport at Borgo Panigale, 7 km. N.W. (Air Terminal, P.za XX Settembre).

Theatre. *Comunale.* Opera and Ballet season, Dec-April; concerts throughout the year. Plays and concerts in the new theatre in the Zona Fieristica.

Swimming Pools (open and indoor) at the Stadio Comunale and elsewhere.

History. *Felsina,* an important Etruscan city on the site of Bologna, was overrun by the Gauls in the 4C B.C. They named their settlement *Bononia,* and the name was retained by the Romans when they conquered the plain of the Po in 225-191 B.C. After the fall of the Western Empire, Bologna became subject to the Exarchs of Ravenna, and later formed part of the Lombardic and Frankish dominions. In the 11C it threw off the yoke of Ravenna, and in 1116 it was recognized as an independent commune by the Emperor Henry V. Its university first becomes prominent at about this time.

One of the foremost cities of the Lombard League (1167), it reached the summit of its glory after the peace of Constance (1183), and sided with the Guelphs, the papal party, against the Ghibellines, the emperor's party. In the ensuing contests the Bolognese won the fierce battle of Fossalta (1249). Enzo (1225-72), King of Sardinia, a natural son of the Emperor Frederick II, taken prisoner in the fight, was confined to Bologna for the remaining twenty-two years of his life. In 1325 the Bolognese were defeated in their turn at Zappolino (the scene of 'La Secchia Rapita'—see under Modena), but the papal legate sent to their assistance met no warm welcome, and c. 1337, Taddeo Pépoli, a popular champion, founded a lordship, held in turn by the Visconti, the Pépoli, and finally the ill-fated Bentivoglio, under the last of whom (Giovanni II Bentivoglio; 1463-1506) Bologna reached a high pitch of fame and prosperity. In 1506 Pope Julius II reconquered the city, and for three centuries Bologna was incorporated with the Papal States, save for a brief interval (1796-1814) when it was part of Napoleon's Cisalpine Republic. In 1814 Bologna was occupied by a British force under General Nugent, in support of the Austrians against Napoleon. Unsuccessful insurrections broke out in 1831 and 1848 (the latter inspired by the eloquence of Ugo Bassi), and from 1849 until the formation of the Kingdom of Italy in 1860 the town was held by an Austrian garrison. In the Second World War Bologna was for months the focal point of German resistance, but it escaped serious artistic damage. It was entered on 21 April 1945, by the Polish Second Corps.

Bologna, the seat of a bishop since the 3C, and of an archbishop since 1583, has contributed more prelates to the sacred college than any other city except Rome, and six of its natives have been popes: Honorius II, Lucius II, Gregory XIII, Innocent IX, Gregory XV, and Benedict XIV. Among painters born in Bologna may be mentioned Francesco Primaticcio (1504-70), the three Carracci (16C), Domenichino (1581-1641), Guido Reni (1577-1642), and Albani (1578-1660), the 'Anacreon of painting'. Other famous Bolognese are Card. Mezzofanti

(1774-1849), Ottorino Respighi (1879-1936), the composer, Luigi Galvani (1737-98), and Guglielmo Marconi (1874-1937), whose first experiments in the transmission of signals by Hertzian waves were made at his father's villa at Pontecchio. Giosuè Carducci, the poet, spent the last years of his life in a suburban villa. Charlotte Stuart (1753-89), only daughter of Charles Edward, the 'Young Pretender', died at Bologna, and was buried in San Biagio, a church destroyed in 1797.

Art. In the architecture of Bologna the predominant material has always been brick, for both constructional and decorative purposes, and the late-Gothic buildings of the 14C show the height to which skill in brick designing attained. In the 15C the forms of the Tuscan Renaissance came to Bologna, culminating in the Palazzo Bentivoglio, by Pagno di Lapo; and in the following century many great masters of the Renaissance—Formigine, Peruzzi, Vignola, and others—were at work in the city. The art of sculpture in Bologna is represented rather by masterpieces of visiting craftsmen, from Nic. Pisano to Giambologna, than by any strongly individual local school; but in painting, after a rather sparse early period up to the end of the 15C, when Marco Zoppo stands out as an interpreter of the Paduan style, Bologna claims a very distinctive school, though its productions were valued more highly a century ago than they are today. The wealthy court of the Bentivoglio attracted Cossa, Roberti, and Costa from Ferrara (c. 1490), and the last especially influenced Fr. Francia, the real founder of the Bolognese school, who had begun life as a goldsmith, and later came under the influence of Perugino. Costa's most faithful pupil was the Bolognese Amico Aspertini, while among Francia's numerous following was Timoteo Viti of Urbino. Another revival at the end of the 16C was fostered by the Carracci (Lodovico and his cousins Annibale and Agostino), who founded the 'Eclectic School', animated by a rebellion against formalism. Their influence extended into the 18C, through Albani, Guido Reni, Domenichino, and Guercino, to Carlo Cignani, Elisabetta Sirani, and their followers.

CENTRAL AND SOUTHERN QUARTERS

The centre of Bologna is the large and imposing open space made up of PIAZZA MAGGIORE (Pl. 11) and PIAZZA NETTUNO, which joins it at right angles. In the latter is the *Fontana del Nettuno,* or *del Gigante,* designed by Tom. Laureti, and adorned with an imposing figure of Neptune and other bronze sculptures by Giambologna (1566, restored in 1934). On the E. side of Piazza Nettuno is the PALAZZO DI RE ENZO, built in 1246, which was the prison of King Enzo (see above) from his capture at Fossalta in 1249 until his death in 1272. Adjoining, but facing Piazza Maggiore, is the PALAZZO DEL PODESTÀ, begun at the beginning of the 13C, but remodelled in 1484. The tower, pierced by an archway, is original. At the corners of the vaults beneath it are statues of the patron saints of the city (SS. Petronius, Florian, Eligius and Francis) by *Alf. Lombardi* (1525).

On the W. side of the piazza is the impressive **Palazzo Comunale,** part of which is the *Casa Accursio,* acquired by the Comune of Bologna in 1287, and altered by *Fieravante Fieravanti* in 1425-28. All the non-arcaded part and the court are of the latter date. The entrance gateway is by *Galeazzo Alessi* (c. 1555), and the bronze statue above it of Pope Gregory XIII (Ugo Buoncompagni of Bologna, the reformer of the calendar), is by *Alessandro Menganti* (1580). Above to the left, under a canopy, is a *Madonna in terracotta by *Nicolò dell'Arca* (1478). The tower was built in 1444.

INTERIOR (adm. 9-14 exc. Tues; Sun 9-12.30). The grand *Staircase* (1507) is ascribed to Bramante. The *Chamber of Hercules,* on the first floor, takes its name from the colossal terracotta statue by A. Lombardi; the Madonna del Terremoto ('of the earthquake') is attributed to Francia (1505). On the second floor is the *Sala Farnese,* containing frescoes by Cignani and other artists and a copper statue of

Pope Alexander VII by Dorastante d'Osio (1660). Here in 1515 Leo X received Francis I of France in secret; here also the Emp. Charles V was lodged in 1530. There follow fifteen rooms (with magnificent views of the city) which display Bolognese art of every period; the paintings include works by Jacopo di Paolo, Simone da Bologna, Francia, and Guercino.

In the S.W. corner of the piazza is the *Palazzo dei Notai,* or old College of Notaries, part of which was begun in 1381 by Berto Cavalletto and Lorenzo da Bagnomarino, and the rest completed by Bart. Fieravanti (1422-40). On the E. side is the *Palazzo dei Banchi* (1412), remodelled by Vignola (1565-68), once occupied by the moneylenders. Between these rises the immense incomplete façade of **San Petronio** (Pl. 11), the largest church in Bologna and one of the finest examples of Gothic brickwork in existence. Founded in 1390, on the designs of *Antonio di Vincenzo,* its construction went on until 1659, when the nave-vault was completed.

EXTERIOR. The church is orientated almost N. and S. In the unfinished façade (being slowly cleaned) are three canopied doorways, with reliefs illustrating Biblical history from the Creation to the time of the Apostles. The middle portal is remarkable for its *Sculptures by *Iac. della Quercia* (1425-38), including, under the arch, figures of the Madonna and Child with St Petronius (the St Ambrose, by *Varignana,* was added in 1510). The right- and left-hand doorways were designed by *Ercole Seccadenari* (1525) and sculptured by *Tribolo* and others.

INTERIOR. The great nave, 41 m high, is lighted by round windows, and is separated from the aisles by ten massive compound piers. The bare brick surfaces give the church a curious effect of emptiness. Excavations are being carried out in the nave.

SOUTH AISLE: 1st chapel, Madonna della Pace, by *Johannes Ferrabech* (German; late 14C) in an altarpiece by *Giac. Francia.*—2nd chap., polyptych by *Tom. Garelli* (1477), and early 15C frescoes.—3rd chap., frescoed polyptych of the school of the *Vivarini.*—4th chap., Crucifixion, by *Giac. Francia,* and further 15C frescoes; the stained glass is by *Jacob of Ulm* (1466).—8th chap., *Carved and inlaid stalls, by *Raff. da Brescia* (1521).—9th chap., Statue of St Anthony of Padua, attrib. to *Iac. Sansovino;* Miracles of the Saint, monochrome works by *Girol. da Treviso* (1526).—10th chap., Transenna of the 15C.—11th chap., on the left, Assumption, bas-relief by *Tribolo* (1537).—The choir contains carved stalls by *Agost. de' Marchi* (1468-77; restored). Before the high altar Charles V was crowned emperor in 1530 by Clement VII.

NORTH AISLE. At the E. end is a small MUSEUM (adm. 10-12, 16-18; closed Tues and Sat p.m.), including various designs for the completion of the façade, and a 16C model of the church on the projected cruciform plan. In the 3rd chapel (from the E. end), St Michael, by *Denys Calvaert;* Barbazzi monument, by *Vinc. Onofrio* (1479).—4th chap., St Roch, by *Parmigianino.*—In front of the monument of Bp. Cesare Nacci, by *Onofrio* (1479) begins the meridian line, nearly 67 m long, traced in 1655 by the astronomer Cassini, in substitution for an earlier one of 1575. It has since been several times adjusted; a hole in the roof admits the sun's ray.—5th chap., Transenna of the 15C; *Altarpiece by *Lor. Costa* (1492), with the Madonna and SS. Sebastian, George, James, and Jerome; tomb of Felice Baciocchi and his wife Elisa Bonaparte by *Baruzzi* (1820).—6th chap., Assumption by *Scarsellino,* and a modern statue of Card. Giac. Lercaro, by *Giac. Manzù.* The wooden pulpit is ascribed to *Agost. de' Marchi.*—7th chap., *Altarpiece by an artist of the late 15C Ferrara school, the Martyrdom of St Sebastian, with donor; on the walls, Annunciation and Apostles, by the same hand. The stalls date from 1495, and in the pavement is enamelled tilework of Faenza majolica (1487).—The 8th chap. has another fine marble balustrade, a gilded polychrome altarpiece of the 15C and remarkable *Frescoes (Heaven and Hell), by *Iac. di Paolo* (early 15C). Above the clock, outside the chapel, is a huge fresco of St Christopher.—The 10th chap., is a good Baroque work by *Torreggiani* (1743-50), with a fine grille and the tomb of Benedict XIV. Outside the chapel, 15C fresco of St Bridget of Sweden, Christ enthroned, by *Lippo di Dalmasio,* and a Madonna and Saints attrib. to *Giovanni da Modena.*—Above the N. aisle portal, Adam and Eve, by *Alf. Lombardi.*

Via dell'Archiginnasio skirts the left flank of San Petronio. Beneath the Portico del Pavaglione is the **Museo Civico** (Pl. 11), which is especially notable for its Etruscan antiquities (adm. 9-14 exc. Mon; Sun & fest. 9-12.30).

Ground Floor. VESTIBULE: Roman tombs; well-head; torso of an Imperial statue; Roman mosaic floors.—COURTYARD (the former cloister of Santa Maria della Morte): Milestone from the Via Æmilia; blocks from Roman bridges; slab inscribed with an electoral programme. A door off the courtyard (l.) admits to the *Museo del Risorgimento* and an exhibition gallery. At the foot of the stairs, reached through a glass door (unlocked on request) a second courtyard has terracottas of the 14-15C.
First Floor. ROOM I: Remains from caves, lake dwellings, etc., in the neighbourhood of Bologna.—ROOM II: Prehistoric objects, comparatively arranged.—ROOMS III-V: *Egyptian Antiquities.*—ROOM VI: *Greek Antiquities,* including a *Head of Minerva, said to be a copy of the Athene Lemnia of Phidias; head of a Greek; Attic sepulchral bas-relief (5C B.C.); fragment of an Augustan relief, showing a figure with a ram's head; the 'Cup of Codrus', a fine red-figured Attic vase, etc.—ROOM VII: *Græco-Roman Antiquities.*—ROOM VIII: *Etruscan Antiquities,* including realistic terracottas from a temple at Civita Alba, near Sassoferrato (2C B.C.).—ROOM IX: Smaller Roman antiquities, including ivory reliefs, bronze statuettes, utensils, etc.

ROOM X. *Antiquities from the burial-grounds of Félsina, the Umbro-Etruscan predecessor of Bologna, and other Etruscan remains. In the first section, tombs from various Etruscan sites around Bologna. In the main section is tomb-furniture illustrating the development of the Umbrian (9-6C B.C.) and Etruscan (6C-mid-4C) civilization. The Umbrian tombs contain urns with scratched, painted, and (later) stamped geometric decoration, while the Etruscan tombs bear reliefs in sandstone, and contain Greek vases (the so-called 'Etruscan' ware) and various objects of daily use in bronze, bone, etc. Along the window-wall are vessels from the tombs, including the best Attic vases, and a bronze *Situla (5C B.C.), from the Certosa, with a ceremonial procession. In the left wing are objects showing relations with foreign races, and the oldest Umbrian tomb (? 9C B.C.), with contents of a Late Bronze Age type.

ROOM XI. Recent excavations, including finds from the necropolis of Giardini Margherita.—R. XII displays Gaulish tombs with weapons and ornaments, and Roman objects. Also, mosaic panel of 1C A.D. from Claterna.
The MEDIEVAL AND RENAISSANCE sections of the museum have been closed since 1960, awaiting rearrangement. The collection includes: armour (carved ivory saddle of German workmanship, 14C); Ceramics and glass vase of Murano ware with the Flight into Egypt and the Adoration of the Magi (early 15C); and two vessels made for the wedding of Giov. Bentivoglio and Ginevra Sforza (late 15C).—Majolica, including plates with the arms of Este-Gonzaga and the fable of

Myrrha, with the coronation of Charles V, with the Farnese arms, and with those of Leo X; also the Presentation of the Virgin, in Gubbio ware, by *Maestro Giorgio* (1542). Limoges enamels and ivories, including a Runic calendar of 1514; old musical instruments.—Sculptures of the 15-18C: bronze model of the Neptune fountain; St Michael and a bust of Innocent X, by *Algardi;* Gregory XIII (bust), by *Menganti;* Paul III (bust), attr. to *Zac. Zacchi* (16C); tombstones of Pier Canonici.—Sculptures of the 13-15C with numerous tombs or sarcophagi of scholars of the university. Also a St George and a Nativity of St John the Baptist, by *Iac. della Quercia;* statue of Boniface VIII, in beaten copper, by *Manno*(1301); Lombard crosses.—More than 100 choir-books (13-17C); medallions; two Byzantine mosaics. Magnificent *Cope of English embroidery (c. 1300).

Farther along the busy Portico del Pavaglione is the ARCHIGINNASIO (restored), transformed by Antonio Morandi (1562-65) to accommodate the university, which occupied the building until 1800. The courtyard, vestibule, corridors, and stairways are covered with escutcheons of former rectors and professors, in relief or fresco. On the upper floor are the *Biblioteca Comunale* (adm. 9-19.45; c. 600,000 vols; 12.000 MSS.), the *Teatro Antatomico* (rebuilt since 1950; adm. by request to the porter) by A.Levanti (1648-49), with two admirable wooden anatomical figures ('gli spellati') by Ercole Lelli (1735), and the *Museo Gozzadini,* containing Umbrian and other antiquities. In front of the building are a piazza and a monument commemorating Luigi Galvani (1737-98), the physicist.

Via Farini leads right to Via d'Azeglio, in which (l.), at Nos. 31-33, is the *Palazzo Bevilacqua (Pl. 10), a good example of the imported Tuscan style of 1474-82. The splendid courtyard is surrounded by a double colonnade. The Council of Trent held two sessions in this building in 1547, having moved to Bologna to escape an epidemic. At No. 54 is the church of *San Prócolo,* with a Romanesque façade and, in the lunette (much faded), a Madonna with two saints by Lippo Dalmasio. To the right farther on is the church of *Corpus Domini* or La Santa (1478-80), whose terracotta façade and Franceschini frescoes were irreparably ruined by bombing. Inside are preserved the relics of St Catherine de' Vigri (d. 1463), an erudite ascetic of Bologna regarded as a patron saint of painters.

Via Tagliapetre and Via Urbana (l.) lead from here to the *Collegio di Spagna (Pl. 14), founded by Cardinal Albornoz in 1365 for Spanish students—the last survivor of the many colleges, resembling those at Oxford and Cambridge, which existed at Bologna in the Middle Ages. Among its famous students were Ignatius Loyola and Cervantes. Visitors are sometimes granted admission during term time. The main building is by *Matt. Gattapone* (1365); the gateway is the work of *Andrea da Formigine* (1525). The handsome courtyard has a double gallery; the chapel has an altarpiece by *Marco Zoppo.*

Via Urbana and its continuation Via Marsili lead E. to the picturesque P.ZA SAN DOMENICO, in which are statues of St Dominic (1627) and the Madonna (1633) and the tombs of Rolandino de' Passeggeri (1300) and Egidio Foscherari (1289), with their original canopies restored. In the piazza rises also the church of *San Domenico (Pl. 15; closed 12-15.30), dedicated by Innocent IV in 1251 to St Dominic, founder of the order of Preaching Friars, who died here in 1221 two years after establishing the convent on this site. The church, several times enlarged, is interesting chiefly for the works of art in its interior, remodelled by *Carlo Fr. Dotti* (1728-31).

INTERIOR. 6th chapel (S. aisle), dedicated to St Dominic, was rebuilt in 1597-1605, and restored in 1843 and again in 1883 (if closed, apply to the sacristan). In the centre is the *ARCA DI SAN DOMENICO a masterpiece to which many artists contributed. The reliefs representing scenes from the saint's life are the work of pupils of *Nic. Pisano,* among whom *Fra Guglielmo da Pisa* and *Arnolfo di Cambio* (only very little of the work is by the master himself). The cover of the sarcophagus, with the statues upon it, and the light-bearing angel on the left, are by Nicolò da Bari (1469-73), who took the name of *Nicolò dell'Arca* from this tomb. The angel on the right and the figures of SS. Petronius and Proculus are youthful works of *Michelangelo* (1495). The subjects ornamenting the base of the tomb are by *Alf. Lombardi* (1532). Behind the tomb a reliquary by *Iac. Roseto* (1383) encloses the Saint's skull. In the apse of the chapel is the Glory of St Dominic, by *Guido Reni;* on the right of the entrance, St Dominic raising a dead child, by *Aless. Tiarini;* on the left, St Dominic burning heretical books, by *Lionello Spada.*—In the N. transept is an inscription (1731) marking the tomb of King Enzo. In the adjoining chapel is a 14C wall monument (altered in 16C) to Taddeo Pépoli, and a painted crucifix signed by *Giunta Pisano.*—CHAPEL OF THE RELICS (at the end of the transept): Tomb of the Beato Giacomo da Ulma (Jacob of Ulm), the painter on glass, who died at Bologna in 1491.— Chapel of the MADONNA DEL ROSARIO (opposite St Dominic's chapel); Mysteries of the Rosary, an altarpiece of fifteen paintings by *Calvaert, Cesi, Lod. Carracci* and *Guido Reni.* Reni and Elisabetta Sirani are buried in this chapel (inscription on the left wall). In the adjoining vestibule is the *Tomb of Aless. Tartagni, by *Francesco Ferrucci*(1477).

From the Sacristy (r. of high altar), with a fine door in marquetry, by *Fra Damiano,* there is access to the Choir, viâ a room (lit by sacristan) in which are displayed a *Bust of St Dominic (1474), a fine work in terracotta by *Nicolò dell'Arca,* and paintings, including *Lippo di Dalmasio,* Madonna del Velluto, and a detached fresco of Charity and St Francis by *Lod. Carracci.* The rest of the museum (upstairs), with church vestments, hangings, and books of anthems, has been closed.—The CHOIR has *Stalls in marquetry by *Fra Damiano da Bergamo* (1541-51). The large painting of the Magi is by *Bart. Cesi.*—A door opposite the sacristy admits to the charming CLOISTER OF THE DEAD, its fourth side closed by the exterior of the apse and chapel of San Domenico. Here is a much ruined fresco of the Holy Trinity by *Pietro Cianori.* Off the Chiostro Maggiore is *St Dominic's Cell* (closed for restoration, but normally shown by the sacristan).

To the S. of San Domenico, at the end of Via Garibaldi is the *Palazzo di Giustizia* occupying Palazzo Ruini, with an imposing Palladian façade and courtyard (1584).

Via Rolandino leads N. from P.za S. Domenico. On the left is the elegant *Casa Gradi* or *dei Carracci* (15-16C); No. 2, opposite, has a curious trompe l'oeil niche in the courtyard. P.za Calderini proceeds to Via Farini. No. 15 (r.) is the *Casa Saraceni,* a gracious building of the late 15C; and close by (l.), at Nos. 6-10 in Via Castiglione, is the imposing pile of the *Palazzo Pépoli,* begun by Taddeo Pépoli in 1344. Via Castiglione is worth exploring as far as the gate and the 15C *Casa Bolognesi* (No.47) adjoining, before taking the first alley to the left (Vicolo Monticelli), to reach **San Giovanni in Monte** (Pl. 11), a church of ancient foundation attributed to St Petronius, but in its present form a 13C Gothic building with extensive 15C additions. The façade is in the Venetian-Gothic style, with a great portal by *Dom. Berardi* (1474), and above it an eagle in painted terracotta by *Nic. dell'Arca.* Three of the N. chapels were destroyed by bombs.

The INTERIOR consists of a nave and aisles separated by columns partly decorated with frescoes by *Giac.* and *Giulio Francia.* Over the entrance door is a good stained-glass window, St John the Evangelist by *Fratelli Cabrini,* after a design by *Franc. Cossa*(1481). In the midst of the church rises a Romanesque cross on an inverted Roman pillar capital, with a figure of Christ in figwood attributed to *Alf. Lombardi.* In the 3rd chapel of the S. aisle is a painting (light on r.) of SS. Joseph and James, by *Guercino,* and the Martyrdom of St Laurence, by *Pietro Faccini;* in the 7th chap., *Madonna enthroned with saints, by *Lor. Costa* (1497; light on r.). The inlaid choir-stalls are by *Paolo Sacchi* (1523), and the busts of apostles above them, by *Zaccaria da Volterra.* The *Madonna in glory on the E. wall is another fine work by *Lor. Costa.* The N. transept is a splendid work of the school of *Bramante* (1515): it contains a poor copy of Raphael's St Cecilia (now in the Pinacoteca p. 390), enclosed in the original frame. To the right lies the body of the blessed Elena Duglioli Dall'Oglio (1472-1520), who commissioned the original

From the church a road descends to Via Santo Stefano. To the left are some fine 15-16C *Mansions, notably Nos. 9-11, the *Palazzo Bolognini-Amorini,* now *Salina* (begun in 1525), in the style of Formígine, and No. 18, *Casa Isolani* by Pagno di Lapo Portigiani (1455). In Via de' Pepoli (l.) the Palazzo Pepoli-Campogrande (with frescoes by Crespi and Creti) is to house 18C paintings from the Pinacoteca (comp. p. 390). The basilica of *Santo Stefano (Pl. 11) is an ancient and picturesque group of buildings (closed 12-15.30), dedicated as a whole to St Stephen the Martyr, and including the oldest ecclesiastical building in Bologna. Three churches are united in the façade facing the piazza: Santi Pietro e Paolo, San Sepolcro or the Calvario, and the Crocifisso, with a 12C pulpit on its front.

The CROCIFISSO, restored in 1924, contains a good Aldrovandi tomb of 1438, a terracotta Pietà of the 16C and, beneath the raised choir, a crypt with some 11C details and a jumble of capitals. From here is the entrance to the polygonal church of SAN SEPOLCRO, perhaps founded as a baptistery in the 5C, but dating in its present form from the 12C. It has a brick cupola and interesting architectural details. Adjoining the curious tomb of St Petronius, an imagined imitation of the Holy Sepulchre at Jerusalem, is a Romanesque pulpit with a 19C stair.—To the left again is the church of SANTI VITALE E AGRICOLA, a venerable building perhaps of the 5C, with massive columns and capitals, incorporating many fragments of Roman buildings. The three apses (rebuilt in the 8C and 11C) are lit by tiny alabaster windows. The altars in the side-apses are the original sarcophagi of the 4C martyrs, SS. Vitalis and Agricola.—From San Sepolcro is the entrance to the CORTILE DI PILATO (12C), an open court with colonnades; in the middle is 'Pilate's Bowl' (8C) bearing an obscure inscription relating to the Lombard kings Luitprand and Ilprand.—Beyond the court is the church of the TRINITÀ, an early 13C building with Romanesque columns and capitals, and the Cappella della Croce, rebuilt in 1927 on Romanesque foundations. A doorway on the E. side of the Cortile admits to the *CLOISTER, which has two charming 11C colonnades and is overlooked by the Romanesque campanile.

Above the Trinità a small MUSEUM, entered from the upper story of the cloister (9-12, 15-18) has paintings by *Simone de' Crocifissi, Lippo di Dalmasio, Iac. di Paolo,* etc., and the reliquary of St Petronius, by *Iac. Roseto* (1380).

Via Santo Stefano goes on to P.za di Porta Ravegnana, passing the *PALAZZO DELLA MERCANZIA, or Chamber of Commerce, perhaps the best-preserved example of ornamented Italian-Gothic in the city. It was built in 1382-84 from the plans of *Ant. di Vincenzo* and *Lor. da*

Bagnormarino, and has been several times skilfully restored, though the wing (1840), overlooking Via Castiglione, is not in harmony.

PIAZZA DI PORTA RAVEGNANA (Pl. 11), just beyond, with some old houses and the famous leaning towers, is one of the most attractive corners in Bologna; five main roads led hence out of the city, each one ending in a gate on the line of the old city wall. In the centre rise the 'Due Torri' or **Leaning Towers,** the most characteristic of all the buildings of Bologna, a reminder of the days when some 180 such towers adorned the city.

The ***Torre degli Asinelli,** built by the Asinelli family (1109-19), is 97½ m high and leans 1.23 m out of the perpendicular (to the W.). The masonry at the base was added in 1488. A flight of 500 steps leads up to the top (open every day 9-19).—The ***Torre Garisenda,** built by the Garisendi family at the same time as the other, was left unfinished owing to the subsidence of the soil, and was shortened for safety in 1351-60. It is now only 48 m high and leans 3.22 m out of the perpendicular (to the S.); but it was higher when Dante wrote the descriptive verses ('Inferno', xxxi, 136) inscribed at the base of the tower.—No. 1 in the piazza is the *Casa dei Drappieri* (1486-96), with a balcony added in 1620.

VIA RIZZOLI, one of the busiest streets in Bologna, returns direct to the centre; the subway beneath preserves Roman mosaics found during its construction. It is, however, worth while to make a detour S. by Via Castiglione and Via Clavature (r.) to visit the church of *Santa Maria della Vita,* rebuilt in 1687-90, containing a vigorous *Pietà in terracotta by Nic. dell'Arca (after 1485). In an oratory of the hospital administration on the first floor is a Death of the Virgin, a youthful work in terracotta by A. Lombardi.

EASTERN AND NORTHERN QUARTERS

From P.za di Porta Ravegnana (see above) the STRADA MAGGIORE, a busy and attractive thoroughfare, runs S.E. on the line of Via Æmilia. The church of **San Bartolomeo** (Pl. 11; l.) has a damaged but richly decorated portico by *Formígine* (1515). The cupola is being restored. The ornate interior is largely the work of *G. B. Natali* (1653-84). In the fourth chapel of the S. aisle is an *Annunciation by *Albani* (1632). The Madonna in the N. transept is by *Guido Reni.*

Farther on in the Strada Maggiore is a series of characteristic Bolognese mansions, of all periods from the 13C to the 19C, some of them restored. Among the finest are the *Casa della Fondazione Gioannetti* (No. 13), with Gothic windows and polychrome decoration; *Casa Gelmi* (No. 26), built for Gioacchino Rossini, the composer, from designs by F. Santini (1824-27); *Casa Isolani* (No. 19), a characteristic 13C dwelling-house; *Palazzo Sanguinetti* (No. 34) with a rich 16C cornice; *Casa Reggiani* (Nos. 38-40), a large 15C mansion with an arcaded court; and *Palazzo Davia-Bargellini* (No. 44), known as 'Palazzo dei Giganti' from two atlantes flanking the gateway. It has an imposing staircase (1730) and contains the *Museum of Industrial Art* (adm. 9-14, Sun 9-12.30; Tues closed) and the *Galleria Davia-Bargellini* with a few interesting paintings (Vitale da Bologna, Ant. Vivarini, Garófalo, etc.).

In Via Guerrazzi to the S. are (No. 13) the *Accademia Filarmonica,* founded in 1666, to which Mozart was elected in 1770 at the age of 14, and (No. 20) the *Flemish College* (1650).

Opposite the last opens *P.za dei Servi,* with its four porticoes, built in a consistent style at various periods from the 14C to 1855. These are the continuation of the arcades of the church of ***Santa Maria dei Servi,** begun in 1346 and enlarged after 1386, one of the most attractive Gothic buildings in Bologna.

INTERIOR (very dark). In the 4th chapel of the S. aisle, Paradise by *Denys Calvaert* (1602). Outside the 6th chap., Madonna and Child, a fragment of a fresco attrib. to *Lippo di Dalmasio*. The finely carved main altar is the work of *Giov. Ant. Montórsoli* (1558-61). The CHOIR (entered by a door off the ambulatory) contains good Gothic stalls (1450; completed in 1617). In the AMBULATORY (beginning on S. side): *Lippo di Dalmasio*, Polyptych of the Madonna enthroned with saints; *Vinc. Onofrio*, terracotta statue of the Madonna with SS. Lawrence and Eustace (1503). On the other side (N.), the Grati monument is by the same artist. The Madonna by *Cimabue*, formerly in the apse, has been removed for restoration. In the 6th chapel of the N. aisle: Annunciation, by *Inn. da Imola*, in a frame by *Formígine;* between the 2nd and 3rd chapels, elaborate monument to Card. Gozzadini (d. 1536), by *Giov. Zacchi.*

At No. 5 in Viale Carducci, on the right beyond Porta Maggiore, is the *Casa di Carducci* (open 9-12, Sun & fest. 9-13), where the poet Giosuè Carducci lived in 1890-1907. There is a collection of MSS., and a library of over 40,000 vols. Outside is a monument by L. Bistolfi (1928).

P.za Aldrovandi leads N. to Via San Vitale. A short distance to the left is the church of *Santi Vitale ed Agricola,* completely rebuilt in 1824, except for its 12C crypt. It is dedicated to two saints martyred under Diocletian in an adjoining street. Nearly opposite is *Palazzo Fantuzzi* (begun in 1517) with a curious front and a fine Baroque staircase. A little farther on Via Benedetto XIV leads right to P.za Rossini, in which are (r.) the *Conservatorio G. B. Martini,* where Rossini studied in 1806-10, with one of the most important music libraries in Europe (8.30-13; closed Sun & fest.), and (l.) *Palazzo Malvezzi de' Medici,* by Bart. Triachini (1560). On the right, in Via Zamboni, is the Romanesque church of *San Giacomo Maggiore (Pl. 7), begun in 1267 and enlarged in succeeding centuries (restored in 1915). The top of the façade has majolica decoration, and on either side of the canopied doorway are recesses for tombs.

INTERIOR. The aisleless NAVE is surmounted by a bold vault of unusually wide span. The side chapels are crowned by a terracotta frieze of statues and urns (by Pietro Becchetti, 1765). In the 5th chapel on the S. side, Madonna and saints, by *Bart. Passarotti* (1565); 7th, Marriage of St Catherine, by *Inn. da Imola,* in a frame by Formígine; 9th, St Roch comforted by an angel, by *Lod. Carracci;* the 11th was designed by *Pellegrino Tibaldi,* who also painted the frescoes.—Ambulatory, 3rd chapel: Polyptych, by *Lor. Veneziano* (1368), a part of which is now in the Brera in Milan, with Coronation of the Virgin, by *Iac. di Paolo* (1420), Crucifix on the side wall, signed *Simone* (1370).—The *CAPPELLA BENTIVOGLIO at the end of the N. aisle, was founded in 1445 by Annibale Bentivoglio, and enlarged by Giovanni II (restored in 1952-53). Its altarpiece is a *Virgin with four saints and two angel musicians, by *Fr. Francia* (c. 1488). The *Frescoes from the Apocalypse (in the lunette above the altar), of the Triumph of Death (l. wall), and the Madonna enthroned (r. wall) with charming portraits of Giovanni II Bentivoglio and his family, are all by *Lorenzo Costa.* On the right wall is a relief of Annibale I on horseback, by an Emilian artist (1458). The worn floor-tiles date from 1489. Opposite the chapel is the *Tomb of Anton Galeazzo Bentivoglio, one of the last works of *Iac. della Quercia* and assistants (1435).—In the adjacent oratory of SANTA CECILIA (shown on application) are interesting *Frescoes of the lives of SS. Cecilia and Valerian, by *Fr. Francia, Lor. Costa,* and their pupils, executed in 1504-6 by order of Giovanni II Bentivoglio. They have been detached and are slowly being returned after restoration.

Alongside the church is a handsome portico of 1477-81, decorated with terracotta, perhaps by Sperandio, and opposite are *Palazzo Salem* (No. 20), by Dom. Tibaldi (1577-87), containing frescoes by the Carracci, and *Palazzo Malvezzi-Campeggi* (No. 22), by Formígine, with a good courtyard. P.za del Teatro, behind the church, commands the best view of the fine brick campanile (1472). The *Teatro Comunale* by Ant. Bibbiena (1756; façade 1933), here occupies the site of the great palace of the Bentivoglio, which was destroyed in a riot in 1507 and left in ruins until 1763 ('il Guasto'). Beyond No. 25, now the *Casa dello Studente,* with a good 15C court, rise the buildings of the **University** (Pl. 8), installed since 1803 in the *Palazzo Poggi,* built by Pell. Tibaldi (1549). The courtyard is ascribed to Bart. Triachini. In the courtyard is a statue of Hercules, by Ang. Piò. The curious *Torre dell' Osservatorio* dates from 1725. The various schools of the university are in Via San Giacomo, beyond the main building, and in Via Irnerio, to the N.

The university ('Studio'), the oldest in Italy, was founded in the second half of the 11C, and was already famous a century later, especially after Irnerius, chief of the Glossators, had taught here between 1070 and 1100. He revived the study of the Roman system of jurisprudence, which his disciples spread over Europe, sending in 1144 to England Vacarius, founder of the law school at Oxford. In return, many Englishmen and Scotsmen served as rectors at Bologna. In the 14C Bologna acquired notoriety as the first school where dissection of the human body was practised; it taught Petrarch and started Copernicus on the study of astronomy; and in 1789 it became renowned for the discovery of galvanism (comp. p. 380). The number of its female professors is remarkable, among them being the learned Novella d'Andrea (14C), Laura Bassi (1711-88), mathematician and scientist, and mother of twelve, and Clotilde Tambroni, professor of Greek in 1794-1817.

The UNIVERSITY LIBRARY (No. 35 Via Zamboni, Oct-June, 9-19, Sat 9-14; July-Sept 9-14, Sat 9-12; closed 1-15 Sept and on Sun) contains over 800,000 vols and 9000 MSS. and autographs and has a fine 18C reading-room. Here Card. Mezzofanti (1774-1849), who spoke fifty languages and was called by Byron "the universal interpreter", was librarian, and his own library is added to the collection.

Nearly opposite is the *Accademia di Belle Arti,* installed in an old Jesuit college, with a handsome courtyard containing a good 16C well-head. In this building is the ***Pinacoteca Nazionale,** one of the most important collections of painting in northern Italy (adm. 9-14; Sun & fest. 9-12.30; closed Mon). The gallery has a representative collection of the Bolognese school, as well as works by artists who worked in Bologna (including Giotto, Raphael, and Perugino). Acquisitions have augmented the 17C and 18C works. The rooms, recently 'modernized', have no numbers but the paintings are arranged by period and school.

BOLOGNESE SCHOOL OF 14C. (two galleries). Several works by *Vitale da Bologna,* including *St George and the dragon; *Jacopino da Bologna,* Polyptych; *Giov. da Modena,* Crucifix; works by *Simone de' Crocifissi.*—In a small room off the second gallery: Works by *Giotto* and his school (fine polyptych); *Lor. Monaco,* Madonna enthroned; *Byzantine School (late 13C),* Three panels of the life of Christ.—Up a short flight of steps, beyond a room with local 14C works, the 15C BOLOGNESE SCHOOL begins, including two Crucifixes by *Michele di Matteo.*—The next three rooms display detached *Frescoes (and sinopie) by *Vitale da Bologna* and his pupils from Mezzaratta.—The most important works of the 15-16C are displayed in the Long Gallery. VENETIAN SCHOOL. *Ant. and Bart Vivarini,* Polyptych; *Cima da Conegliano,* *Madonna; *Marco Zoppo,* St Jerome.—FERRARESE

SCHOOL. *Fr. del Cossa,* *Madonna enthroned; *Ercole de'Roberti,* *St Michael Archangel, a Mary in mourning (fresco fragment); *Lor. Costa,* Madonna enthroned with saints, SS. Petronius, Francis, and Dominic.—BOLOGNESE SCHOOL. *Fr. Francia,* Annunciation and saints, *Felicini altarpiece, Dead Christ, two paxes; *Amico Aspertini,* Adoration of the Magi.—*Raphael,* *Ecstasy of St Cecilia; *Perugino,* Madonna and saints; *Giulio Romano* (?), St John the Baptist; *Franciabigio,* Madonna and Child; *Giuliano Bugiardini,* Madonna and Child with St John.—*Parmigianino,* Madonna and St Margaret; works by the 16C Emilian mannerists, including *Passarotti, Procaccini,* and *Tibaldi.*—15-16C FOREIGN SCHOOLS. Pseudo *De Bles,* Esther and Ahasuerus; *El Greco,* Last Supper, an early work.

Beyond a corridor hung with prints and drawings, steps descend into a room of mannerist paintings including works by *Bart. Passarotti* and *Guido Reni.*—In the adjoining room is a fine collection of works by the *Carracci,* including an Annunciation by *Annibale.*—At the bottom of another short flight of steps (which encircle a model by *Bernini* for his fountain of the four rivers in P.za Navona, Rome) is a room which displays works by *Guido Reni.*—To the left is a gallery of 17-18C paintings (*Fr. Albani* and *Guido Reni,* supposed portrait of his mother). The small rooms off the gallery contain works by *Guercino; Domenichino,* and *Albani; Crespi, Gandolfi, Creti,* etc. The hall at the end (used for lectures, etc.) is hung with six huge altarpieces: *Domenichino,* Martyrdom of St Agnes; *Lud. Carracci,* Birth of St John the Baptist; *Guercino,* St Bruno; *Fr. Albani,* Baptism of Christ; *Domenichino,* Madonna of the Rosary; *Lud. Carracci,* Transfiguration; *Carlo Cignani,* Madonna and Child with saints.—The return to the exit leads past a small room with frescoes by *Nicolò dell'Abate* from the Palazzo Zucchini-Solimei.

The rest of the collection of 18C paintings is to be housed in Palazzo Pepoli-Campogrande, see p. 386. The 19C works are being arranged in Villa delle Rose (p. 394).

Near the other end of Via Belle Arti is (No. 8) the majestic *Palazzo Bentivoglio,* built to a design perhaps of Triachini in 1550-60. From here Via Mentana (l.) leads to the basilica of SAN MARTINO (founded in 1217. It was remodelled in the mid-15C, and the façade rebuilt in 1879, and the apses restored in 1929.

It contains an Adoration of the Magi, by *Girol. da Carpi* (1st S. chap.), a charming Madonna and saints, by *Francia* (1st N. chap.), and an Assumption with the Apostles, by *Lor. Costa* (5th N. chap.). The attractive cloister of 1560 is used as an open-air cinema.

Via Marsala, in which No.12 is the *Casa Grassi* (late 13C), leads from San Martino to VIA DELL'INDIPENDENZA, the long main street, opened in 1888, that connects the centre of Bologna with the railway station.

On the right, towards the station, is the *Montagnola,* a public garden laid out around the mound formed over the ruins of the citadel of Galliera. Beyond it is *Porta Galliera* (1661), and on the other side of the railway is the *Sacro Cuore,* a large church in the Byzantine style (begun in 1877 and completed in 1912; the dome was rebuilt in 1934).

In the other direction Via dell'Indipendenza leads back to P.za Nettuno. On the left is the **Cathedral,** or *Chiesa Metropolitana,* dedicated to St Peter. Founded very early (probably before the 10C), it was rebuilt several times after 1605, and exists now in the form of a Baroque building of the 17C, though the elaborate W. front is by *Alf. Torreggiani* (18C). The nave is by *Floriano Ambrosini* from designs by *Giov. Magenta,* and the choir is the work of *Dom. Tibaldi* (1575). The crypt and the fine campanile (begun in 1184) are the sole remains of the Romanesque building, except for the two lions of red Verona marble (1220), inside the W. door, which once supported the porch, and the stoup at the E. end of the S. aisle, which has been hollowed out of an old capital.

In the second chapel of the S. aisle is preserved the skull of St Anne, presented in 1435 by Henry VI of England to Nicolò Albergati, better known as the Cardinal of Santa Croce. Above the inner arch of the choir is an Annunciation, frescoed by *Lod. Carracci,* and in the crypt (unlocked by the sacristan) are a 12C Crucifixion group carved in cedar-wood and a large terracotta group in the manner of *Alf. Lombardi.*

The area behind the cathedral is an interesting survival of medieval Bologna, with many old houses and remains of the towers erected by patrician families (in Via Altabella, Via Sant'Alò, Via Albiroli, etc.).

WESTERN QUARTERS

From Via dell'Indipendenza (see above), a little beyond the cathedral, Via Manzoni leads to the W. On the right in this streeet is the *Madonna di Galliera,* a church remodelled in 1479, with a fine Renaissance façade (restored in 1906, but in poor condition). Opposite are three *Palazzi Fava,* of which the first (now a hotel) dates from the 16C (with frescoes by the Carracci, Albani, and others), the second from 15C, and the third is of the early 14C. To the right extends Via Galliera, formerly the main N.-S. artery of the city and dubbed, from the splendour of its palazzi, the 'Grand Canal' of Bologna.

Via Porta Castello leads to the important VIA UGO BASSI, which ends at the long P.za Malpighi (l.). In the middle of the piazza is the *Colonna dell'Immacolata,* with a copper statue designed by Guido Reni; on the left is *Porta Nova,* one of the old city gates; and in the churchyard on the right are the conspicuous *Tombs of the Glossators,* Accursio (d. 1260), Odofredo (d. 1265), and Rolandino de' Romanzi (d. 1284), restored in 1904.

On the W. of the piazza is *San Francesco (Pl. 10), in many ways the most attractive church in Bologna, with its two towers and chapel-girdled apse. It is in a more or less French Gothic style, begun in 1236, completed early in 1263, but considerably altered since. It was skilfully restored after war damage. The façade (c. 1250), looking on to P.za San Francesco has 13-14C tiles in the pitch of the roof. The smaller of the two towers was completed in 1261; the larger and finer, the work of *Ant. di Vincenzo* (1397-c.1402; restored 1950), is surrounded by decorative terracotta.

The entrance is through the vestibule between the towers. In the N. aisle are the terracotta Tomb of Pope Alexander V, completed by *Sperandio* (1482); in the S. aisle is the Fieschi tomb (1492); and on both sides are several 16C monuments. The choir has fine carved stalls and a marble *Reredos by *Iacobello* and *Pier Paolo dalle Masegne* (1388-92), with busts of saints curiously perched on the pinnacles crowning the structure. In the E. chapel of the ambulatory hangs a Crucifix attrib. to *Pietro Lianori.*

At No. 23 Via dei Gombruti (off Via Portanova; see below) the 'Old Pretender' stayed during several visits to Bologna.

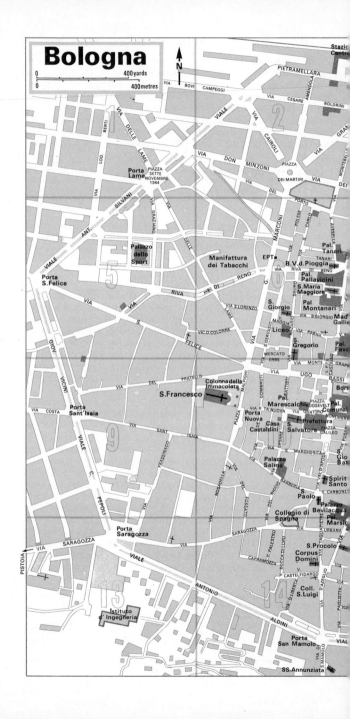

Via Portanova and its continuation Via Quattro Novembre lead E. from S. Francesco. On the right is *San Salvatore,* a classical church (the façade of which looks towards Via Battisti), by Giov. Magenta and Tom. Martelli (1605-23; restored), preserving a fine polyptych (Coronation of the Virgin) by Vitale da Bologna; and opposite is the *Casa Castaldini* (No. 13), with a good 15C courtyard, one of several interesting houses in this street. Others are the *Palazzo Marescalchi* (l.; No. 5), in the early 17C manner, and the enlarged *Palazzo della Prefettura* (r.) of 1561-1603, perhaps by Terribilia.—P.za Galileo adjoins P.za Roosevelt to the S., and Via Val d'Aposa continues past (No. 6) the charming *Façade of the *Spirito Santo,* a gem of terracotta ornament. Opposite the end of the street is *San Paolo,* another work of Giov. Magenta (1611), with a façade of 1636. From here Via Carbonesi and Via d'Azeglio return to the centre.

THE OUTSKIRTS OF BOLOGNA

To the S. of the town are the pleasant *Giardini Margherita.* By the entrance is the church of *Santa Maria della Misericordia,* enlarged in the 15C, with stained-glass windows by Francia in the 2nd and 6th S. chapels; the little church of the *Madonna del Baraccano,* farther along Viale Gozzadini, has a good fresco by Fr. Cossa behind the high altar.

On a hill to the S.W. (bus No. 31) stands the former Olivetan convent of **San Michele in Bosco** (134 m), commanding a splendid *View of Bologna. Here on 1 May 1860 took place the meeting between Cavour and Victor Emmanuel II at which approval was given for the sailing of the 'Thousand' to Sicily. The convent buildings are now occupied by an orthopædic hospital. The church (for adm. apply at the building on the right, rebuilt since 1437, and completed in the early 16C, has a façade ascribed to *Bald. Peruzzi* (1523) and a portal by *Giacomo Andrea da Ferrara* and *Bern. da Milano.* It contains the tomb of Armaciotto de' Ramazzotti, the condottiere, by *Alf. Lombardi* (1526).—The primitive church of *San Vittore,* on the next hill to the S. (at No. 40 Via San Mámolo) is of the 11C, enlarged in the 12C. It was altered in 1864, and partly restored afterwards. The cloister (r.) was rebuilt in the 15C.

Just outside the Porta San Mámolo (bus No. 12 from P.za Galvani or Via Rizzoli) stands the Observantine church of the *Annunziata,* beautifully restored. The Renaissance portico (visible from the road) precedes the austere basilica of c. 1475, constructed in the style of the century before. Via dell'Osservanza, opposite, ascends, with pleasant views, to the *Osservanza* convent. To the right, about 400 m. short of the convent, is the classical *Villa Aldini* (1811-16). Between Via dell'Osservanza and Via San Mámolo the park of *Villa Ghigi* has recently been opened to the public.—Bus No. 21 runs from the railway station viâ P.za Maggiore and Via Saragozza to the cable railway for the Madonna di San Luca. It passes the public park of Villa Spada and, just beyond, the entrance to *Villa delle Rose,* where the 19C works from the Pinacoteca (comp. p. 390) are being arranged. The cableway ascends (every ½ hr) to the sanctuary of the **Madonna di San Luca,** a famous viewpoint, which is connected with Porta Saragozza, just over 3 km. away, by a *Porticus of 666 arches (1674-1793). Where the porticus begins the ascent of the hill is the *Arco del Meloncello,* by C. F. Dotti (1718), formerly connected with the Certosa by another porticus. The sanctuary (290 m), built by Dotti in 1725-49, derives its name from one of the numerous paintings of the Virgin ascribed to St Luke, which is said to have been brought from Constantinople by a 12C pilgrim and is preserved above the high altar.—The return may be made by descending the porticus to Meloncello, and then diverging left to Porta Saragozza.

Over 1½ km. beyond Porta Sant'Isaia, on the left, is the *Stadio,* a huge sports stadium built in 1926, reached by bus No. 43. On the right is the *Certosa,* founded in 1334, suppressed in 1797, and consecrated in 1801 as the public cemetery of Bologna. The 14-16C church contains good marquetry stalls (1539) and frescoes by *Cesi* in its choir. Behind the church is the old cloister, and in the farther right-hand corner of this is the columbarium, with a statue of Murat, by *Vinc. Vela* (1865); beyond, to the left, is the tomb of Carducci. The Etruscan necropolis of Félsina (see the Museo Civico, p. 383) was discovered in the precincts of the Certosa in 1869

North East of the town (bus No. 12 or 18 from P.za Maggiore) lies the **Zona Fieristica** with permanent exhibition halls, a conference centre, and a theatre. The international Childrens' Book Fair is held annually in spring. Here, too, is the **Galleria d'Arte Moderna,** opened in 1975. On the top floor is a permanent collection of 20C works by artists from the region, most of which have been donated by the artists themselves. On the second floor frequent exhibitions are held; the ground floor is reserved for didactic purposes.

Off Via Æmilia (l.), 5km. S.E. of Bologna, is a *British Military Cemetry.* From Bologna to *Ferrara* and *Venice,* see Rte 37; to *Florence* viâ Pistoia or Prato, see Rte 43; to *Ravenna,* see below; to *Rimini,* see Rte 41; to *Verona,* see p. 226.

40   BOLOGNA TO RAVENNA

ROAD, N253, 76½ km.—25 km. *Medicina.*—51½ km. *Lugo.*—57 km. *Bagnacavallo.*—76½ km. **Ravenna.** Bus 5-6 times daily.

AUTOSTRADA. A14 to (34 km.) beyond Imola, where the A14 dir spur diverges for (61 km.) Ravenna.

RAILWAY in 1¼-2 hrs. The more direct route branches from the Rimini line at Castel Bolognese (good connection; several through trains daily); connection may also be made at Faenza with the Florence-Ravenna line (one through train from Bologna).

This route leaves Bologna by the Via and Porta San Vitale and traverses level country all the way.—25 km. *Medicina.*—44 km. *Massalombarda* takes its name from some Lombard fugitives who sought refuge here in 1251—51½ km. *Lugo* (34,700 inhab.) has a 14C castle and an arcaded market-place (1783-1889). This area was the scene of severe fighting in the winter campaign of 1944-45. *Fusignano,* 7 km. N., was the birthplace of Arcangelo Corelli (1653-1713), the composer, and *Cotignola,* 6 km. S.E., that of Attendolo Sforza (1369-1424), founder of the ducal family.—At (57 km.) *Bagnacavallo,* the native town of the painter Bart. Ramenghi (1484-1542), called 'Il Bagnacavallo', Allegra, infant daughter of Byron and Claire Clairmont, died in the Capuchin nunnery in 1821. The church of San Pietro in Silvis is a building of the Ravenna type probably dating from the early 7C. The recently restored frescoes in the apse are attributed to a Riminese master, c. 1323.

76½ km. **RAVENNA** is unique in western Europe for the profusion of its Byzantine remains. Now 10 km. from the sea, it was once a flourishing Adriatic port and the capital of the Byzantine exarchs, whose semi-oriental power is reflected by the magnificently coloured mosaics and imperial tombs. The cylindrical campanili of the 9-10C are characteristic of the city. The modern town (137,800 inhab.) is without distinction and is surrounded by extensive industrial suburbs.

Post Office, P.za Garibaldi.—**E.P.T.,** P.za San Francesco; *Azienda Autonoma,* Via Salara.

Buses traverse the town. Country services to *Marina di Ravenna, Punta Marina, Forlì, Rimini, Bologna, Cesena, Faenza;* and to *Venice,* and *Florence.*

History. The importance of Ravenna begins with the construction, by Augustus, of the imperial port of *Classis,* to which the town was united by the Via Cæsarea. Its greatest period, however, began with the 5C, when Honorius removed the imperial court from Rome to Ravenna. His sister, Galla Placidia, was the first to adorn the city with splendid monuments, and her example was followed by the Gothic kings Odoacer (473-93) and Theodoric (493-526). The capture of Ravenna by Belisarius in 540 led to a period of renewed prosperity under the Eastern Empire, and Justinian and his empress Theodora embellished the capital of the new Exarchate with unbounded magnificence. The inevitable decadence followed, and the province came into the hands of the Church in 757; sufficient vitality, however, was left for Ravenna to proclaim its independence as early as any town in Italy (1177). Another period of changing mastery followed, and in the 13-14C the city was governed by the Da Polenta family, distinguished for their hospitality to Dante. The unfortunate Francesca da Rimini was a daughter of this house. From 1441 to 1509 the domination of Venice brought revived prosperity to Ravenna, but the renewal of Papal domination and the sack of the city in 1512, after the battle between Louis XII of France and the Holy League outside its walls, marked the beginning of its final decay. In 1849 Garibaldi found a brief refuge in the pine-forest near the town, though his wife Anita died from the hardships of her flight from the Austrians; and in 1860 the city was finally united with the kingdom of Italy. It was captured from the Germans in Dec 1944. Since the war a busy industrial area has risen beyond the railway and the port is again flourishing.— Nicolò Rondinelli (1450-1510), the painter, was a native of Ravenna, and Byron lived here in 1819-21.

Art. Ravenna is unequalled in western Europe as a centre for the study of Byzantine architecture, sculpture, and mosaic. The plan of the churches had a widespread influence on later building, and the storyed capitals at San Vitale are equal to the finest work in Constantinople itself. The mosaics show a progressive movement from the naturalism of the earlier work inspired by classical ideals (Tomb of Galla Placidia, the Baptisteries, Sant'Apollinare in Classe) to the hieratic decorative quality of the purely Byzantine style (San Vitale; processional mosaics in Sant'Apollinare Nuovo).

In the central PIAZZA DEL POPOLO are two Venetian columns with bases (much worn) decorated by P. Lombardo (1483) now bearing statues of St Apollinaris and St Vitalis (1644). On the left of the crenellated *Municipio* is a portico of eight 6C columns (four bearing the monogram of Theodoric), which perhaps came from the church of Sant'Andrea destroyed in 1457. In the *Palazzo Guiccioli*, at No. 54 Via Cavour to the N.W., Byron lived with the Count and Countess Guiccioli, and wrote the end of 'Don Juan', 'Marino Faliero', and other poems. Just off the Via San Vitale, to the N. of this beyond a 17C archway, are the precincts of the church of ****San Vitale** (open all day 8.30-20), the most precious example of Byzantine art extant in western Europe.

Founded by Julianus Argentarius for Bp Ecclesius (521-34), the church was consecrated in 547 by Abp Maximian. The octagonal building is surrounded by a double gallery and surmounted by an octagonal cupola. The narthex, which stands obliquely to the church, was formerly preceded by an atrium; it can best be seen from the second cloister (see below).

The entrance is through the Renaissance south portal. The impressive INTERIOR is famous for its decoration in marble and mosaics. The remarkable plan—two concentric octagons with seven exedræ or niches and an apsidal choir—may have been suggested by SS. Sergius and Bacchus at Constantinople. The eight pillars which support the dome are encased in marble (largely renewed), and are separated by the exedræ with their triple arches. Higher up is the matroneum, or women's gallery, and above all is the dome, built, for lightness, of two rows of terracotta tubes laid horizontally and fitting into one another. The vault-paintings are of the 18C; the intended mosaic decoration was probably never executed. The modern pavement has been in great part removed to reveal the original floor.

The chief glories of the church are in the *CHOIR and *APSE. On the triumphal arch are mosaics of Christ and the Apostles with SS. Gervasius and Protasius, the sons of the patron saint. On either side are two constructions of antique fragments patched together in the 16-18C, including four columns from the ancient ciborium (the first on the left is of rare green breccia from Egypt). In the centre is the *Throne of Neptune,* a fragment of a Roman frieze. Within the arch, on either side, are two columns with lace-work capitals and impost-blocks bearing the monogram of Julius. In the lunettes are mosaics; on the right, Offerings of Abel and of Melchisedech; at the sides, Isaiah and the Life of Moses; on the left, Hospitality and Sacrifice of Abraham, at the sides, Jeremiah and Moses on the Mount. The upper gallery has magnificent capitals and mosaics of the Evangelists; and the vault-mosaics of Angels and the Paschal Lamb amid foliage are also very fine. The stucco decoration beneath the arches is beautiful. In the centre is the altar, reconstructed, with a translucent alabaster top (usually covered).

The apse has the lower part of its walls covered with marble inlay, a modern reconstruction from traces of the original plan. In the centre of the *Mosaic, in the semidome, Christ appears between two Angels who present St Vitalis and Bp Ecclesius (with a model of the church). On the side-walls are two fine processional pieces: on the left, *Justinian with a train of officials, soldiers, and clergy, among whom are Abp Maximian and Julianus Argentarius or Belisarius; on the right *Theodora with her court. In front of the apsidal arch are Jerusalem, Bethlehem, and two angels.

To the right of the apse, beyond an apsidal chamber, is the *Sancta Sanctorum,* containing two early sarcophagi. Farther on is the former entrance to the campanile (originally one of the staircase towers giving access to the matroneum); beneath an adjoining arch are some fine stuccoes. On the other side of the narthex (the former entrance to the church; best seen from the cloister outside, see below) is the second staircase tower, still preserving some original work, with a stair ascending to the matroneum.

From the N. side of San Vitale a pathway leads towards the charming ***Tomb of Galla Placidia,** a small cruciform building erected by the sister of Honorius towards the middle of the 5C. The plain exterior is decorated with blind arcades and pilasters. The interior, lit by alabaster windows, is famous for its magnificent *Mosaics, predominantly blue, especially interesting for the classic character of the figures and for their excellent state of preservation (although they are restored periodically).—Over the entrance is the Good Shepherd; in the opposite lunette, St Laurence with his gridiron; in the side lunettes, Stags quenching their thirst at the Holy Fount. The vaults and arches of the longer arm of the cross are decorated to represent rich hangings and festoons of fruit. In the shorter arm are four Apostles; the other eight are on the drum of the cupola. In the pendentives are the Evangelists, and, above all, the Cross in a star-strewn sky. The three empty sarcophagi are no longer considered to have held the remains of Placidia, Constantius, and Valentinian III; only one of them is of 5C workmanship.

Near the E. end of San Vitale (from where the terracotta frieze on the wall below the campanile can be seen) a little Renaissance portico admits to the **National Museum of Antiquities,** occupying two Renaissance cloisters and the surrounding rooms. It has been closed since 1970 for restoration and rearrangement (the adjoining convent of San Vitale is to be used as an extra wing of the museum). During restoration work the cloisters have remained open to visitors.

The FIRST CLOISTER contains Roman remains, including the Apotheosis of

Augustus, a Roman relief with idealized portraits of the imperial family. The SECOND CLOISTER, overlooking the narthex of San Vitale (comp. above) contains (in the centre) a statue of Clement XII (1738). The interesting sculptural fragments include a transenna and capitals of the 6C, and a well-head from Classe.

The contents of the museum include: a 6C group of Hercules and the Stag; *Glass from San Vitale; 15C paintings in tempera on wood in the Byzantine manner; precious *Fabrics from the tomb of St Julian at Rimini; the famous *Veil of Classis, with pictures of Veronese bishops of the 8-9C; Florentine embroidery of the school of Pollaiuolo; alabaster head, perhaps of Gaston de Foix, attr. to Tullio Lombardo; ivories, including a 6C *Diptych from Murano, evangelistary covers, etc; pottery and terracotta; Statue of Alexander VII (1699).

Nearly opposite the apse of San Vitale is the church of *Santa Maria Maggiore* (521-534, rebuilt 1671), preserving Byzantine capitals above Greek marble columns (the church, however, is usually locked).—Via G. Barbiani, on the other side of Via Cavour, leads S. to Via Cura, in which the small church of *Santi Giovanni e Paolo* (locked), rebuilt in 1758, retains a tiny 10C campanile.

To the S.E. of Via Cavour various streets (comp. the Plan) lead to P.za del Duomo viâ P.za Kennedy in which is the 18C *Palazzo Rasponi dalle Teste*. The **Cathedral**, founded early in the 5C by Bp Ursus, and often known as the *Basilica Ursiana*, was practically all destroyed in 1733 and immediately rebuilt. The columns of the central arch of the portico and those on either side of the central door are from the original church. The round campanile, many times restored, dates from the 10C.

In the nave is the 6C *Ambo of St Agnellus, pieced together in 1913. In the S. transept, two fine 6C sarcophagi; in the ambulatory, St Mark, a relief of 1492 ascribed to P. Lombardo.

Adjoining the cathedral is the octagonal ***Battistero Neoniano** (or *degli Ortodossi*), converted from a Roman bath-house, perhaps by Bp Neon (mid-5C), perhaps fifty years earlier. The plain exterior is decorated with vertical bands and small arches. Adm. 9-12, 14.30-18.

The remarkable interior is entirely decorated with mosaics and sculptural details which blend with the architectural forms. The original floor is now over 3 m below the present surface. Eight corner columns support arches decorated with mosaics of prophets. In the niches and on the wall-spaces which are arranged alternately beneath the arches are mosaic inscriptions and marble inlaid designs from the original Roman baths. Each arch of the upper arcade encloses three smaller arches; the stucco decoration is very fine. In the dome, built of hollow tubes, like that of San Vitale, are mosaics of the Baptism of Jesus (the old man with the reed represents the Jordan), the Apostles, the Books of the Gospel, and four Thrones, remarkable for their contrasting colours. The font is of the 12-13C. In the niches are a Byzantine altar and a pagan marble vase.

In the *Arcivescovado*, behind the cathedral, is the interesting **Museo Arcivescovile** (adm. 9-12, 14.30-18; fest. 9-13). The *Sala Lapidaria* contains fragments and mosaics from the original cathedral and from San Vitale; the marble pulpit from SS. Giovanni e Paolo (596); a 6C porphyry statue (? Justinian); and in the farthest room the famous *Ivory Throne of Maximian, an Alexandrine work of the 6C, carved with the story of Joseph, the Life of Christ, and figures of St John the Baptist and the Evangelists and a 6C Paschal calendar incised on marble.—The *Cappella Arcivescovile* (Oratorio di S. Andrea) is preceded by an atrium with a barrel vault covered with a delightful mosaic of birds. The chapel, built by Bp Peter II (494-519), contains good *Mosaics and the silver *Cross of St Agnellus (? 11C; many times restored). In an adjoining room is the so-called chasuble of St John Angeloptes, probably 12C work.

The **Biblioteca Classense** (entered from Via A. Baccarini), in a 16-17C building, contains a library with some valuable codexes, including an 11C text of Aristophanes.

In P.za San Francesco, to the N.E., is the church of **San Francesco,** built by Bp Neon in the 5C, remodelled in the 10C, but almost entirely rebuilt in 1793. The 10C campanile was restored in 1921. The interior has 22 columns of Greek marble. North aisle: Tomb of Luffo Numai, by *Tommaso Fiamberti* (1509); tombstone of Ostasio da Polenta (1396); and a 5C sarcophagus with Christ and the Apostles. The 1st chapel on the S. side is decorated by *Tullio Lombardo* (1525). The high altar is made from the 4C *Tomb of St Liberius. In the 9-10C Crypt (almost always flooded; light outside) can be seen the foundations of an earlier church with its mosaic pavement (in restoration).—On the left of San Francesco is the so-called *Braccioforte Mausoleum* (1480), containing several early Christian sarcophagi.

To the left again is the **Tomb of Dante** (open 9-12, 14.30-19), a building by *Cam. Morigia,* erected at the instance of Card. Luigi Gonzaga in 1780 to enshrine the older tomb by *Pietro Lombardo*(1483). This in turn covers the antique sarcophagus in which the poet's remains were originally interred in the old portico of San Francesco.

Exiled from Florence and harried by his political enemies, the poet found refuge, in 1317, with the Da Polenta family of Ravenna, and with them he spent his last years, finishing the Divine Comedy. He died on the night of 13-14 Sept 1321.

His effigy is by Pietro Lombardo, and the epitaph by Bernardo Canaccio (1357). The *Museo Dantesco,* approached by steps by the little (modern) memorial bell-tower, has been closed since 1970.—To the N. are two fine 15C Franciscan cloisters (restored).

At the corner of P.za San Francesco and Via Ricci stood *Palazzo Rasponi*, Byron's first home in Ravenna (1819); and farther S. is the 5C basilican church of *Sant'Agata Maggiore* (if closed, ring at door on r.), which has a squat round campanile completed in 1560, and contains Roman and Byzantine capitals, a 7C pulpit, and two Renaissance baldacchini.—Via Cerchio, to the left, ends opposite *Santa Maria in Porto*, a church begun in 1553, with a sumptuous façade by Morigia (1780). It contains fine stalls by Mariano (1576-93), and other French craftsmen, and (over the altar in the N. transept), a marble Byzantine relief called 'La Madonna Greca' (probably 11C). In the public gardens behind is the *Loggetta Lombardesca* (early 16C; recently restored).

Adjoining the church is the ex *Monastero dei Canonici Lateranensi* restored as the new seat of the **Accademia dei Belle Arti.** Its fine picture gallery (open 9-12, 15-18.30) is spaciously arranged around a pretty cloister in the well-lit rooms of the convent.

The collection includes: *Taddeo di Bartolo,* Annunciation; *Paolo di Giov. Fei,* Crucifixion; *Lor. Monaco,* Crucifixion; *Marco Palmezzano,* Nativity, Presentation in the Temple, etc.; *Bernardino Zaganelli,* Prayer in the Garden of Gethsemane; *16C Venetian school,* Last Supper (a tiny work); *Lud. Brea,* Madonna and Child; *Ant. Vivarini,* St Peter; *Gentile Bellini,* SS. Ludovic and Peter.—Works by *Luca Longhi, Nicolò Rondinelli, Fr. di Santacroce, Palma Giovane* (Creation of Man), and *Paris Bordone* (the Redeemer). The effigy of Guidarello Guidarelli, killed at Imola in 1501, is the work of *Tullio Lombardo* (1525).—The modern section includes works by *Armando Spadini, Felice Carena, Gius. Abbati,* and *Arturo Moradei.*

In Via di Roma, to the N., is the building known as *Palazzo di Calchi* or *degli Esarchi* (no adm.), perhaps a military post constructed by the exarchs to protect their own court against the townspeople. Beneath the arches are mosaic fragments from the Palace of Theodoric, nearer the railway, the foundations of which were excavated in 1908-14.

The church of *Sant'Apollinare Nuovo almost next door, one of the finest in Ravenna, was built by Theodoric in the early 6C; the mosaics are partly of this time, partly of the mid-6C.

Dedicated originally to Jesus and later to St Martin, the church passed from the Arians to the orthodox Christians under Abp Agnellus. Its present dedication dates only from the 9C. The façade with its portico was rebuilt in the 16C; adjacent is a fine 10C campanile of circular plan.

INTERIOR. The floor and the 24 Greek marble columns were raised in the 16C and are surmounted by a panelled ceiling of 1611; the arcades bulge noticeably to the N. Along the nave walls are two magnificent bands of *Mosaic; that on the N. side represents the port of Classis, with a procession of 22 virgin martyrs preceded by the Magi who offer gifts to the Infant Jesus seated on his mother's lap between four angels. On the S. side are Ravenna, showing the façade of Theodoric's palace, and a procession of 26 martyrs approaching Christ enthroned. Above, on either side, are 16 fathers of the Church, or prophets; higher still, 13 scenes from the Life of Christ. The stucco decoration beneath the arches is very fine. The Ambo in the nave dates from the 6C. In the apse, reconstructed in 1950, are the recomposed altar, transennæ, four porphyry columns, and a marble Roman chair.

At the corner of Viale Farini, leading to the station, is Piazza Anita Garibaldi, with a monument to the martyrs of the Risorgimento (with engaging lions). In Viale Farini is the church of **San Giovanni Evangelista** built by Galla Placidia in fulfilment of a vow made in 424 during a storm at sea. It was well restored after war damage.

Most of the façade and the first four bays were destroyed and the notable galleried apse, as well as the aisles, seriously damaged. The 10-14C campanile survives (leaning to the W.); two of the bells date from 1208. The main 14C portal has been reconstructed on the new wall which encloses the church precincts. Inside, some columns, with their capitals and impost blocks, are original. Round the walls are displayed mosaics from the 13C floor, their naïve designs illustrating episodes from the 4th Crusade. The carving on the 8C altar in the S. chapel is notable. In a chap. in the N. aisle are fragments of frescoes (on the vault and walls) of the 14C Riminese school.

To the left, beyond the cross-roads, is Via Paolo Costa. The first lane on the left (Via degli Ariani) leads to the church of *Santo Spirito* (usually locked), converted, like Sant'Apollinare, to the orthodox cult by Agnellus in the mid-6C. Fourteen columns and an ambo from the original church were retained after a rebuilding in 1543. In the same square is the BATTISTERO DEGLI ARIANI (now Santa Maria in Cosmedin; open 8-12, 14-19). It contains splendidly preserved *Mosaics (6C) of the Baptism of Christ and of the Apostles in the dome.—In Via P. Costa, No. 8 is the *Casa Stanghellini,* a charming 15C Venetian house, and at the end is the 12C *Torre Comunale.* From here Via G. Rossi (r.) leads to the church of *San Giovanni Battista,* with a cylindrical campanile; the interior, a 17C reconstruction, retains its ancient marble columns.

At the N. end of Via di Roma is *Porta Serrata* (1582). The Circonvallazione Rotonda leads E. through unattractive suburbs past the rugged bastions of the Venetian *Rocca di Brancaleone.* Beyond the railway (c. 20 min walk from the gate), in a clump of trees to the left of the road, is the **Mausoleum of Theodoric** (adm. 8.30-12, 14-19).

For those without a car, the Mausoleum is not very conveniently reached by bus (No. 2 from the station; infrequent service). The walk from Porta Serrata, along a busy trunk road, is not a pleasant one.

The unfinished building, begun by the great Ostrogoth himself, is of hewn stone without mortar and is crowned by a monolithic roof. For a time, until 1719, it was used as a monastic church (Santa Maria al Faro). The ten-sided lower story has a deep recess on every side. The upper floor, which is decorated with unfinished arcading, was approached by two 18C staircases, which collapsed in 1921. The monolithic cupola of Istrian limestone from Pola has a diameter of 11 m, and weighs about 300 tons. The crack, which is clearly visible, was probably the result of a harsh knock received during its installation. The problem of the methods of construction and the transport of the monolith is still unsolved. Inside is a porphyry bath which was used as the royal sarcophagus.

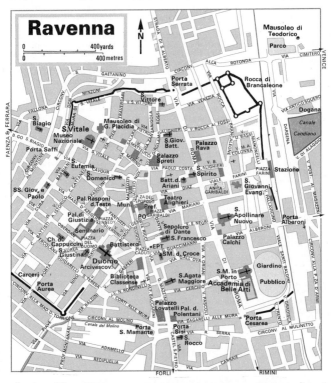

About 5 km. S. of Ravenna and reached either by rail (Classe station, on the Rimini line), or by road across the *Ponte Nuovo* (1736) and the site of Classis, is the basilica of *Sant'Apollinare in Classe* (open 7-12.30, 14-19.30), built for Bp Ursicinus by Julianus Argentarius in 535-38, and consecrated by Abp Maximian in 549. The narthex, which preceded the church, has been reconstructed. The magnificent late-10C *Campanile is the tallest and most beautiful of all the towers of Ravenna.

The impressive INTERIOR has 24 Greek marble columns with Byzantine bases and capitals. In the centre of the nave is the altar of Abp Maximian, restored in 1753. At the W. end of the church are eight columns from the two original ciboria, and in the aisles are inscriptions and sarcophagi of the 6C and subsequent centuries. The *Mosaics of the apse are extremely interesting, though much altered; in the centre, the

Transfiguration, with St Apollinaris in prayer below; at the sides, Sacrifices of Abel, Melchizedech, and Abraham, and Constantine IV granting privileges for the church of Ravenna to Abp Reparatus (7C); between the windows Bps Ursicinus, Ursus, Severus, and Ecclesius (6C). On the front of the arch are five rows of symbolic mosaics.

The Pineta di Classe, E. of the basilica beyond the railway, whose sylvan grandeur was sung by Dante and Byron, is now sadly diminished. Although designated a nature reserve it is threatened by the industrial development on the outskirts of Ravenna.

The road to the Marina (frequent buses in summer) follows the Candiano Canal which links the *Darsena* with the sea. In the busy suburb beyond the station is the polygonal church of *San Pier Damiano*, by Giov. Gandolfi (1958), with a striking hexagonal cupola and campanile.—13 km. *Marina d Ravenna*, a sandy bathing resort, has developed round the Porto Corsini (1736). Across the canal is *Marina Romea*, reached by bus by the Strada del Cimitero. *Garibaldi's Hut*, in the Pineta di San Vitale, off this road (c. 7 km. from Ravenna), may also be reached by ferry from the Marina road. This is a reconstruction of the hut where the great patriot lay in hiding in 1849; the original was burned in 1911.—The *Colonna dei Francesi* (1557), 4 km. S.W. along the Forlì road, marks the spot where Gaston de Foix fell mortally wounded in 1512 in the battle between the French and Julius II.—There is a *British Military Cemetery* 8 km. N.W. of Ravenna by the Ferrara road and a lane leading left to *La Tagliata*. About 2 km. farther on the Ferrara road, across the Lamone river, a road goes left for *Villanova* and a *Canadian Military Cemetery*.

FROM RAVENNA TO RIMINI, 52 km., N16 and railway parallel.—5 km. *Classe*, with the basilica of Sant'Apollinare (see above). 21 km. **Cérvia,** approached through pinewoods, is a small town (24,500 inhab.), built in 1698 on a regular plan and surrounded with walls round which has developed a large seaside resort and spa extending northwards as *Milano Maríttima* and southwards as *Pinarella*. The road crosses a stretch of salt-marshes with Cérvia and Cesenático located by conspicuous skyscrapers.—30 km. **Cesenático,** another popular bathing resort, is the port of Cesena, designed in 1502 by Leonardo da Vinci for Cesare Borgia, from which Garibaldi and his wife Anita set sail on their ill-omened flight towards Venice in Aug 1849.

Numerous summer hotels are also to be found in *Zadina Pineta,* its N. extension, and in *Valverde* and *Villamarina* on the way S. towards (35 km.) *Gatteo a Mare*. The road crosses the Rubicone, the fateful Rubicon which Cæsar crossed in defiance of Pompey in 49 B.C. From here the line of seaside resorts, with innumerable summer hotels, is virtually continuous for 30 km.; the main road runs a little farther inland to (52 km.) *Rimini, see Rte 41.*

41   BOLOGNA TO RIMINI

ROAD, 113 km., the S.E. section of the Via Æmilia (N9) almost flat and dead straight until Cesena with views of the Apennine foothills on the right; a nerveracking road recommended only for short distances between intermediate towns.—22 km. *Castel San Pietro.*—33 km. **Ímola.**—41 km. *Castel Bolognese.*— 49 km. **Faenza.**—63 km. **Forlì.**—71 km. *Forlimpópoli.*—82 km. **Cesena.**—96 km. *Savignano.*—113 km. **Rimini.**

AUTOSTRADA, A14, 113 km., almost parallel 3-5 km. to the N.

RAILWAY, 112 km., many expresses daily in 1¼-1½ hrs; to *Faenza,* 50 km. in 30-50 min. The line keeps parallel to and N. of the road.

Bologna, see Rte 39. The road leaves by the Porta Maggiore and proceeds S.E.—22 km. *Castel San Pietro* preserves a tower and gateway of its 13C castle.—33 km. **Ímola** (59,300 inhab.), on the Santerno, occupies the site of the Roman *Forum Cornelii,* founded by L. Cornelius Sulla in 82 B.C., and still preserves the main outlines of its Roman plan.—The Via Emilia divides the town in half, and the Via Appia, from the station, meets it at a double gate beneath a clock-tower, just W. of the central P.za Matteotti. In Via Emilia, to the W., are the *Palazzo Della Volpe* (1482) and the former convent of San Francesco, now containing the *Museum* and *Picture Gallery* (9-12.30, 14.30-18 or 15.30-19), which includes a Madonna with SS. Cassian and Peter Chrysologus, by Innocenzo Francucci (da Imola; 1494-1550), and a Science section. The street opposite leads to the *Cathedral,* entirely rebuilt in the 18C, containing the tombs of St Cassian, patron of the town (a teacher who was stabbed to death by the pens of his pupils), and St Peter Chrysologus, the eloquent archbishop of Ravenna (d. 450), a native of Imola. Farther S.W. rise the towers of the early-14C *Castle,* rebuilt by Gian Galeazzo Sforza, whose daughter Caterina married Girolamo Riario, lord of Imola, and held the fortress after his death until her defeat by Caesar Borgia (1500). It contains a collection of arms and armour.—To the left of Via Emilia may be noted *San Domenico* (Via Quarto, off V. Orsini), with its 14C brick portal, and the *Pretura* (68 Via Cavour, off the Via Appia), a fine palazzo of the Florentine Renaissance (1480). The 15C *Osservanza,* near Porta Montanara, contains works by Antonio da Imola. On the outskirts of the town rises the 12C campanile of *Santa Maria in Regola.*

A road runs from Imola to Florence, ascending the valley of the Santerno, and followed by a bus as far as Firenzuola.—26 km. *Castel del Rio* is dominated by the ruins of the 13C castle of the Alidosi and possesses a 16C palazzo (now the town hall) of the same family.—Beyond (32 km.) *Moraduccio* is a *British Military Cemetery* (l.).—47½ km. *Firenzuola,* a 14C Florentine colony, has a gateway at either end of its arcaded main street. The German 'Gothic' line was pierced by the taking of Firenzuola by the American Fifth Army in Sept 1944, after heavy fighting. The road ascends to the left, up a side valley, past *Rifredo,* to (58½ km.) the *Giogo di Scarperia* (882 m) on the Apennine watershed, then descends steeply with many turns into the Tuscan Mugello viâ (68 km.) *Scarperia,* with a Palazzo Pretorio of 1306.—74 km. *San Piero,* and thence to (98 km.) *Florence,* see p. 482.

41 km. *Castel Bolognese* (7230 inhab.) preserves only one tower of the castle built by the Bolognese in 1388 and destroyed by Cæsar Borgia in 1501.

It is the railway junction for Ravenna viâ Lugo, and is connected by road with *Riolo Terme,* a small summer spa (9 km. S.W.) with a castle enlarged by Caterina Sforza.

49 km. **FAENZA,** a pleasant old walled town (55,650 inhab.) on the Lamone, has long been famous for its manufacture of the glazed and coloured pottery known as majolica or 'faience'. The street names are indicated by faience plaques, and several houses have ceramic decoration. The town is divided into halves by the Via Æmilia (Corso Mazzini and Saffi).

History. From the early 13C until 1501 the powerful Manfredi family played a leading part in Faentine affairs, though their city was devastated in 1241 by Frederick of Hohenstaufen and again sacked in 1376 by Sir John Hawkwood, then in the papal service. In 1501 Cæsar Borgia took the town and slew the last of the Manfredi, and from 1509 Faenza was included in the States of the Church. It was damaged in the Second World War.—Evangelista Torricelli (1608-47), the inventor of the barometer, was born at Faenza.

The great period of Faentine majolica was 1450-1520, when the most famous of forty potteries was that of the brothers Pirotti (the Ca' Pirota). The earliest authenticated specimen is a votive plaque dated 1475, in the Cluny Museum at Paris, though its manufacture is documented in 1142. Baldassare Manara (first half of the 16C) and Virgilio Calamelli (Virgiliotto da Faenza; second half) are also distinguished names. The art had a second blossoming in the early 18C.

In the broad Viale Baccarini, which connects the station with the town, is the *Museo Internazionale delle Ceramiche* (daily 9.30-12.30, 15.30-17.30 or 18.30) a splendid and very full collection of Italian ceramics of all periods beautifully displayed and well labelled. On the lower floor are modern works from all countries, including pieces by Picasso and Matisse. The collection is complemented by a good library and photographic collection. Farther on is the *School of Ceramics* founded in 1916.

At the end of Corso Baccarini, Corso Mazzini (on the line of Via Æmilia) leads left to the centre of the town, formed by P.za della Libertà and P.za del Popolo, left and right of the Via Æmilia. In the former, with its fountain of 1619-21, is the **Duomo,** begun by *Giul. da Maiano* in 1474, a Renaissance building with an unfinished front.

The graceful interior (spoilt by its harsh colour) contains many works of art. South side, 1st chapel, Annunciation, relief by *Sperandio* (?; 1477), and Bosi monument by the local sculptor *Pietro Barilotti* (1542); 4th chap., Madonna and saints, by *Inn. da Imola;* 5th chap., sculptures by *Barilotti* and *Pietro Lombardo.* In the chapel to the l. of the apse (lights on r.) is the *Tomb of St Savinus (first bishop of Faenza, early 4C), with exquisite reliefs by *Bened. da Maiano* (1474-76).

In the picturesque arcaded P.za del Popolo are the old *Clock Tower,* by Aleotti (1606-7), the *Palazzo del Podestà* (partly of the 12C), and the *Municipio,* once the palace of the Manfredi. The local tourist office is beneath the last, in Voltone Molinella. Via Severoli leads right to the town **Museum and Picture Gallery** (adm. 9.30-12.30; 14.30-16.30 exc. Sat and Sun p.m.), with an interesting collection of works of art, some of which are listed below.

ROOM I. Sculptural fragments and Roman mosaics. *Romagnole School of 14C,* Polyptych; *Giov. da Rimini* (attrib.), Madonna and Child and saints; Crucifix carved by *Fra Damiano* of Bergamo; Madonna enthroned with saints, a large terracotta group sculpted by *Alfonso Lombardi.*—R. II. *G. B. Bertucci,* Triptych; good *Works by *Marco Palmezzano;* terracotta bust of an old man by *Lombardi.* The wood statue of St Jerome, once attrib. to *Donatello,* is now thought to be by his school.—R. III. Works by *Bertucci* and *Biagio d'Antonio da Firenze; Ferrarese School of 15C,* Madonna enthroned with saints.—R. IV. Bust of young St John, formerly attrib. to Donatello, is probably the work of *Ant. Rossellino; Biagio d'Antonio da Firenze,* Annunciation.—R.V. *Dosso* or *Battista Dossi,* Head of Mary Magdalene.—On the lower floor the 18C collection includes a watercolour by *Victor Hugo.*—The Modern Art collection has been removed to the nearby Palazzo Zauli Naldi (open mornings only), in Corso Matteotti. The works include two busts by *Rodin,* and paintings of the 'Macchiaioli' school.

Farther S.W. rises the 10C campanile of *Santa Maria Vecchia.*—In Borgo Durbecco, beyond the Lamone bridge, is the small Romanesque church of the *Commenda* (restored), with a remarkable fresco by Girol. Pennacchi the Younger (1533) in the apse. The next road to the right, beyond the Barriera, leads (½ km. farther) to a *British Military Cemetery.*

FROM FAENZA TO FLORENCE, 103 km.; railway, 120 km. in 2¼-2½ hrs. This interesting cross-country route ascends the Lamone valley.—12½ km. *Brisighella,* a spa in a pleasant site, is noted for its church, which contains fine Baroque stucco-work and a painting by Marco Palmezzano. The Museo Civico della Val Lamone displays local archæological material. Above the town stands a clock-tower erected in 1290 on a rocky spur, and a castle with two drum towers.—On the left, below the next railway bridge, is the curious *Pieve del Tho* (San Giovanni in Ottavo), a Romanesque church incorporating some Roman fragments.—25 km. *San Cassiano,* with 13C castle-ruins.—36 km. *Marradi* lies in a narrow stretch of valley. Its capture by the British 13th Corps in Sept 1944 made a breach in the German 'Gothic' line.—From (54 km.) *Colla di Casaglia* (913 m.) the road begins the descent into the Mugello.—72 km. *Borgo San Lorenzo,* and thence to (103 km.) *Florence,* see p. 482.

A railway connects Faenza with (30-35 min.) *Ravenna* viâ Granarolo.

63 km. **FORLÌ,** a flourishing provincial capital (109,300 inhab.) and agricultural centre, takes its name from the Roman *Forum Livii,* a station on the Via Æmilia, which bisects the town. Its urban architecture suffered under the influence of Mussolini, born nearby at Predappio.

E.P.T., Corse d. Repubblica.

Airport. *Ridolfi* at Ronco, c. 5 km. S.E. with internal flights (to Rome, Milan, and Sardinia).

In later years Forlì was ruled by the Ordelaffi family (1315-1500), but after the successful campaign of Cæesar Borgia it remained under the sway of Rome until the rise of the Italian kingdom in the 19C.—The Forlivese school of painting has Melozzo degli Ambrogi (1438-94) as its leader, with Marco Palmezzano as his chief disciple. Among other famous natives of the town are G. B. Morgagni (1682-1771), the anatomist, and Aurelio Saffi (1819-90), one of the builders of Italian liberty.

In the central piazza, named after Saffi, is the Romanesque church of **San Mercuriale** (12-13C but altered later) dedicated to the first bishop of Forlì. It has a fine contemporary *Campanile, 76 m high, a high relief of the school of Antelami above the W. door, and a graceful cloister, with an open loggia at either end. In the bold red-brick interior the S. and N. nave chapels have paintings by *Palmezzano* and architectural decoration by *Giac. Bianchi* (1536). In the S. aisle is the *Tomb, by *Fr. Ferrucci,* of Barbara Manfredi (d. 1466) wife of Pino II Ordelaffi, moved here from San Biagio (destroyed in 1944). Excavations beneath the apse have brought to light remains of the 11C church and crypt of 1176.—The *Palazzo del Municipio,* opposite the church, dates in its present form from 1459, and was altered in 1826.

Corso Garibaldi, with some 15-16C mansions, leads N.W. to the **Duomo** (r.), mainly a rich reconstruction of 1841, but preserving in its apse a huge tempera painting of the Assumption, the masterpiece of *Carlo Cignani* (1681-1706); the 2nd chapel in the N. aisle has a St Sebastian, by *Rondinelli.* The campanile, in P.za Ordelaffi, was formerly the watch-tower of the Orgogliosi, a rival family to the Ordelaffi.

At the S. end of the town is the **Rocca di Ravaldino** (1472-82; now a prison), where Caterina Sforza was besieged by Cæsar Borgia in 1499-1500. It was the birthplace of her famous son Giovanni delle Bande Nere (1498-1526).

In Corso della Repubblica, leading S.W. from P.za Saffi, the former hospital (1772) houses the **Museum and Picture Gallery** (adm. 9-14, fest. 10-13; closed Sat).

The Ground Floor contains finds from prehistoric sites at Vecchiazzano, Villanova, and San Varano; and Roman material from the province. On the 1st floor are the works of art, including: *Guercino,* Annunciation; *Ant.* and *Bern. Rossellino,* Tomb of 1458; Flemish tapestries; and several paintings by *Palmezzano,* including a fine *Annunciation, an early work inspired by Melozzo, and the Apostles' Communion. Noteworthy, also, are a Nativity and Agony in the Garden, both by *Fra Angelico.* There is a fine portrait (no longer believed to be Caterina Sforza) by *Lor. di Credi;* but *Melozzo* is represented only by a druggist's sign ('Il Pestapepe'). On the 2nd floor is the *Ethnographic Museum,* with interesting interiors, an Armoury, and Ceramics.

In the church of *Santa Maria dei Servi,* just to the S., the tomb of Luffo Numai (1502) has good reliefs by Tom. Fiamberti.

The south-eastern district of the town includes Piazzale della Vittoria, with a tall memorial column (1932). Viale d. Libertà connects the piazza with the station.

A bus runs 2 or 3 times daily from Forlì viâ the Corso Diaz and the Rabbi valley to (15 km.) **Predappio**, the birthplace of Benito Mussolini (1883-1945). The village, originally a hamlet called *Dovia* in the commune of *Predappio Alta* (2 km. farther on), received communal rank in 1925, and many new public buildings were erected. Attached to the cemetery, where Mussolini's remains were finally interred in 1957, is the little church of *San Cassiano in Appennino*, with some 10-11C portions (restored). Predappio was taken from the Germans by Poles of the Eighth Army in Oct 1944.

Other bus services connect Forlì with *Ravenna* (45 min.), with *Meldola* (12 km. S; 20 min.), and with *Florence* (daily; see below) viâ Rocca San Casciano, 1½ km. N. of which is a *British Military Cemetery*. There is another British Military Cemetery 3 km. S.W. of Forlì, on the right side of the road to Predappio, and an *Indian Military Cemetery* 2 km. N.E. on the right of the Ravenna road.

FROM FORLÌ TO FLORENCE (N67; bus), 119 km.—11 km. *Castrocaro Terme*, a small spa with alkaline and sulphurous waters, is dominated by its large ruined castle.—18 km. *Dovâdola* has an old castle and an 11C church.—28 km. *Rocca San Casciano* retains only fragments of its rocca.—55 km. *Passo del Muraglione* (907 m), on the watershed.—63 km. *San Godenzo* is noted for its *Abbey church, a massive Romanesque building founded in 1029 by Jacopo il Bavaro, Bp of Fiesole.—73 km. *Dicomano*, and from there to (119 km.) *Florence*, see Rte 43.

The main road goes on to (71 km.) *Forlimpópoli* where the castle of the Ordelaffi now contains a theatre.

Buses run hence to (6 km. S.) **Bertinoro**, an old-walled town on a hill, famous for its wine, with a 14C *Palazzo Comunale* and a *Rocca*, ercted in the 12C by the warlike Countess Aldruda Frangipane, and occupied later by the Mainardi, by the Ordelaffi, and by Cæsar Borgia. Excursions can be made to the 9C church of *Polenta*, 6 km. farther S., with the ruined castle from which sprang the famous Da Polenta clan of Ravenna.

82 km. **CESENA**, an ancient arcaded town (89,100 inhab.) on the Savio, enjoyed a period of brilliance under the Malatesta family (1379-1465). Pius VI (1717-99) and Pius VII (1742-1823) were born here. The town is a centre for the export of fruit and jam, and the European trotting championships are held in August on its racecourse. The *Biblioteca Malatestiana* (open 8-13, Mon 16-20), a lovely aisled basilica, built in 1447-52 by *Matt. Nuti* for Dom. Malatesta Novello (note his heraldic elephants), contains 340 valuable MSS. and 48 incunabula in original presses. Displayed are two Roman silver plates with banquet scenes in gold and niello. The *Cathedral*, begun in 1385, contains an altarpiece by Lor. Bregno (1514) and in the picture gallery in the *Municipio* are a Presentation by Francia, and two Saints, by Guercino. The *Rocca Malatestiana* (mainly 1466, restored), dominating the town from a wooded hill to the S., succeeds an earlier castle destroyed by Card. Albornoz in 1357. It is well seen from the attractive bridge (1772) that crosses the river S.W. of the town.

A *British Military Cemetery*, 2½ km. N.E. of Cesena, on the right of the road to Cervia, recalls the severe fighting in this area in Oct. 1944 by the Eighth Army. From Cesena to Bagno di Romagna, Bibbiena, and Sansepolcro, see Rte 52. Bus services connect Cesena with *Cesenático* (½ hr), and with *Cervia* (50 min.). on the coast (see Rte 37B).

Beyond Cesena, on a hill to the right, is the Madonna del Monte, a Benedictine abbey rebuilt in the 15-16C with a famous collection of ex-votos. Just before (96 km.) *Savignano sul Rubicone* the Rubicon is crossed on a Roman bridge dating from c. 186 B.C. The identification of the stream here, once known as the Fiumicino, with the Rubicon, was long a matter of doubt, but accords well enough with the evidence of the

Peutinger table.—102km. *Santarcángelo di Romagna* was the birthplace of Clement XIV (1705-74). On the right rises Monte Titano.

113km. **RIMINI** (124,500 inhab.), is the most frequented seaside resort on the Adriatic, and its dependent bathing-beaches, popular with German and British holiday-makers, extend along the shore in either direction. The old city, over a kilometre from the sea front, is separated from it by the railway. Standing at the seaward end of the Via Æmilia it preserves some Roman remains, but is above all famous for the Renaissance Tempio Malatestiano.

Post Office. Piazzale Giulio Cesare.—**E.P.T.**, outside the station.

Trolley-Buses from P.za Tre Martiri to the station and the shore, from where there are frequent services viâ Bellariva and Miramare to *Riccione.*—BUSES to *San Marino;* to *Ancona;* to *Cesena, Forlì* and *Faenza;* to *Cattolica;* to *Cervia* and *Ravenna,* etc.

Airport at Miramare, c. 6km. S. with summer services from all over Europe.

History. Rimini occupies the site of the Umbrian city of *Ariminum,* which became a Roman colony c.268 B.C. and was favoured by Julius Cæsar and Augustus. In the 8C, it became a papal possession, and after the struggles between the papal and imperial parties in the 12-13C, the Guelph family of Malatesta emerged as overlords. Malatesta di Verucchio (1212-1312), Dante's 'old mastiff', was the founder of a powerful dynasty of overlords, most famous of whom was Sigismondo (1417-68), a man of violent character and yet an enthusiastic protector of art and learning. His son, Giovanni the Lame, was the husband of the beautiful Francesca da Rimini (d. 1258), whose love for her brother-in-law Paolo inspired one of the tenderest passages in Dante's 'Inferno' ('we read no more that day'). Pandolfo (d. 1534) surrendered the town to Venice, but after the battle of Ravenna (1512) it fell again into papal hands. Rimini, bombarded from sea or air nearly 400 times, was the scene of heavy fighting between the Germans and the Eighth Army, and was captured by Canadians in Sept 1944.

The road from Bologna enters the old town by the **Ponte d'Augusto,** across the Marecchia, a bridge begun by Augustus in the last year of his life and finished by Tiberius (A.D. 21). The N. arch was rebuilt after the Goths destroyed it in order to cut Narses off from Rome in 552.

The church of *San Giuliano,* in the suburb beyond the bridge, contains a fine painting by Paolo Veronese, the Martyrdom of St Julian, and an interesting polyptych of the early 15C.

The Corso di Augusto leads from the bridge through the town. On the right is P.ZA CAVOUR with a 17C statue of Paul V and a fountain of 1543 incorporating Roman reliefs. The *Palazzo dell'Arengo* is a battlemented building of 1204. In the adjoining 14C *Palazzo del Podestà* the MUSEO DELLE ARTI PRIMITIVI has recently opened. It contains a remarkable ethnological collection from Africa, Oceania, and pre-Columbian America. To the S., behind the theatre, are the remains of the *Castello Sigismondo* (Rocca Malatestiano) which dates from 1446. It has been closed while excavation work is going on within its walls. To the left, in Via Sigismondo, is the Romanesque church of *Sant 'Agostino,* with a fine campanile and remarkable 14C frescoes by local artists (including Giov. da Rimini) in the sanctuary and adjoining chapel (being restored). In the Baptistery is preserved a 14C Crucifix.

From the other side of the Corso roads lead towards the Station and the sea. In Via Gambalunga is the *Biblioteca Gambalunga* which houses the **Pinacoteca** and **Museo Civico** (adm. 9-12). The prehistoric and archæological collection is in the course of rearrangement: it includes Etruscan tomb-furniture of the Villanovan period, with a remarkable axe-mould, and material found during excavations which are continuing in several parts of the city. The Roman section has mosaics and sculpture, and a collection of the coinage of Ariminum. The paintings include a *Pietà* by *Giov. Bellini*, Three Saints, by *Ghirlandaio*, and a Holy Family, by *Perin del Vaga* (in restoration).

In P.za Tre Martiri are the remains of a statue of Julius Cæsar and the little *Oratory of St Anthony* on the spot where the saint's mule miraculously knelt in adoration of the Sacrament. At the end of the Corso is P.za Giulio Cesare, in which stands the **Arco d'Augusto,** a single archway (c.27 B.C.; restored) with composite capitals, marking the junction of the Via Æmilia with the Via Flaminia.

Via Quattro Novembre leads from P.za Tre Martiri to the ****Tempio Malatestiano** (open 7–12, 15.30–19), one of the outstanding productions of the Italian Renaissance. Very seriously damaged in the fighting of 1944, it was carefully restored in time for its quincentenary. Since 1809 it has served as the cathedral of Rimini, with the title of Santa Colomba, transferred from the demolished old cathedral near the Castello.

The original building was a Franciscan church, built in the late 13C, which in 1450 Sigismondo Malatesta determined to transform into what can only be described as a combination of a religious edifice and a personal monument. The decline of his fortunes caused the suspension of the work in 1460, and the completion of the building is due to the Franciscans. Under Sigismondo the rebuilding of the interior was entrusted to *Matteo de'Pasti* and the exterior to *Leon Batt. Alberti,* while *Agost. di Duccio* executed the sculptures.

EXTERIOR. The front, inspired by the form of the Roman triumphal arch, is one of the masterpieces of *Alberti.* The upper part is incomplete. Each side is relieved by wide arches surmounting the stylobate, beneath which (on the S. side) are seven plain sarcophagi containing the ashes of eminent men who died in Rimini in the 15–16C.

INTERIOR. The spacious nave is flanked by a series of deep side chapels connected by sculptural decoration and closed by fine balustrades. The sculptural detail (including the vaults and window frames) is of the highest quality. On the right of the entrance is the tomb of Sigismondo, whose armorial bearings (the elephant and rose) and initials interlaced with those of Isotta (see below) recur throughout the church. SOUTH SIDE. 1st Chapel. Statue of St Sigismund supported by elephant's heads, and very low reliefs of angels (side walls), all works of *Agostino di Duccio.* In the niches, statues of the Virtues and armour-bearers. 2nd chap. (of the Relics) has a damaged *Fresco (inside, above the door) by *Piero della Francesca* (1451), representing Sigismondo kneeling before his patron, St Sigismund of Burgundy, and relics found in Sigismondo's tomb. 3rd chap. On the entrance arch, friezes of putti playing, and (over the altar), St Michael, by *Agostino.* Tomb of Isotta degli Atti, Sigismondo's mistress and later his third wife. The Crucifix (c. 1310) is now attrib. to *Giotto.* The 4th chap. has superb decoration representing the planetary symbols and signs of the Zodiac, also by *Agostino.* The 4th N. chapel, opposite, the masterpiece of *Agostino,* has reliefs representing the Arts and Sciences. The end chapels and presbytery do not belong to the original Malatesta building. The 3rd N. chap. has particularly charming putti. In the 1st chap. (of the Ancestors) are figures of Prophets and Sibyls, a tiny Pietà (15C, French), above the altar, and the Tomb of the Ancestors, with splendid reliefs by *Agostino.*

A little to the E. is the *Roman Amphitheatre,* of which only two brick arches remain above the foundations.

The **Marina di Rimini** consists of a magnificent sandy beach extending for several kilometres in either direction. In addition to the large hotels lining the seafront at Rimini, accommodation is available in more than a thousand hotels and pensions near the town and at the contiguous beaches of *Rivabella, Viserba, Torre Pedrera, Igea Marina,* and *Bellaria* to the N.W., and *Bellariva, Marebello, Rivazzurra,* and *Miramare* to the S.E.

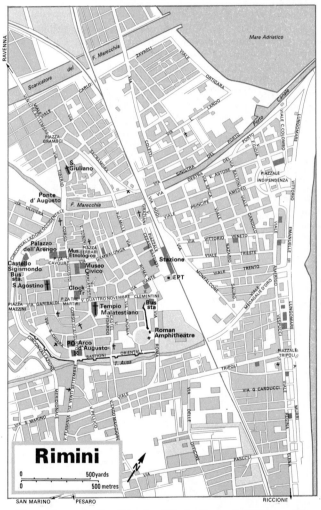

The sands are continued to the S.E. by those of **Riccione**, another internationally known resort (30,600 inhab.), beyond which again stands *Cattólica* with many more hotels.

A *Gurkha Military Cemetery* lies 3½ km. S. of Rimini on the San Marino road (r.).

A bus from Rimini (P.za Clementini) ascends the Marecchia Valley to (32 km.) *Novafeltria*, until recently called *Mercatino*, passing (14 km.) *Verucchio*, the attractive hill-town from which came the Malatesta clan, where the Collegiata has a Crucifixion (1404) by Nicolò di Pietro Paradisi. On the opposite hill rises the old Malatesta castle of *Scorticato*. Beyond Verucchio the road ascends the Marecchia valley to its head at (72 km.) the *Passo di Viamaggio* (987 m). The descent on the S.E. side leads into the Tiber valley on the road between Pieve Santo Stefano and Sansepolcro, see Rte 51.

From Rimini to *Ravenna*, see Rte 40; to *Pesaro, Ancona*, etc., see Rte 51.

SAN MARINO, S.W. of Rimini, is reached by a fast road (bus) from P.za Giulio Cesare, following a hilly course (27 km.). Cars are not permitted in the narrow streets of the town itself.

The little town (4500 inhab.) is interesting as being the capital of the diminutive REPUBLIC OF SAN MARINO (61 sq. km.; 19,600 inhab.), which has preserved its independence for more than sixteen centuries. It is said to have been founded c. 300 by Marinus, a pious stonemason from Dalmatia, who fled to the mountains to escape Diocletian's second persecution. The legislative power is vested in a Council General of 60 persons from whom 10 (the Congress of State) are chosen as an executive, and 12 as a Council that functions as a Court of Appeal; the chiefs of state are two 'regent captains' who hold office for six months (investiture 1 April and 1 Oct). San Marino has its own mint, postage stamps, police force, etc., and an army of about 1000 men. Most of its territory consists of the peaks and slopes of the limestone *Monte Titano* (739 m; *View). In the capital the church of San Francesco possesses a pinacoteca (St Francis by Guercino, and a Madonna and Child attrib. to Raphael). The *Palazzo del Governo* dates from 1894, and the three citadels (*Rocca, Cesta, Montale*) command a superb panorama of Rimini and the Adriatic. The principal market town of the Republic is *Borgomaggiore*, about 1½ km. lower down.

About 11 km. farther S.W. by a winding road is the fortress town of *San Leo*, where Cagliostro died in exile in 1794; here are two interesting 12C churches, one dedicated to Leo, the companion of Marinus (see above). The return to Rimini may be made by the Marecchia valley (see above).

V TUSCANY AND NORTHERN LATIUM

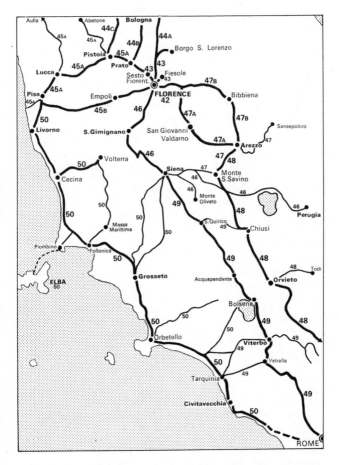

Tuscany is a mountainous region with an area of 22,991 sq. km. and a population of 3,566,000 lying between the Apennines and the Tyrrhenian Sea, bordered on the N. by Emilia and Liguria, on the E. by the Marches and Umbria, and on the S. by Latium. In the Tyrrhenian Sea, between the mainland of Italy and Corsica, are the islands of the Tuscan archipelago, chief of which is Elba. To the N. of the Arno, whose valley divides Tuscany into two unequal parts, it includes the main ridge and W. slopes of the Central Apennines. Here it is in the main a district of broken hills and irregular valleys, the only levels of any extent being the coastal strip, called *Versilia,* between Carrara and Livorno, and the plain between Florence and Pistoia. The so-called Apuan Alps, above the Versilian coast, are separated from the main chain of the Apennines by the deep vales of the Garfagnana and Lunigiana. Though southern Tuscany lies well to the W. of the main Apennine range, its only relatively flat areas are the Val di Chiana, S. of Arezzo, and the coastal *Maremma,* a once malarial region now largely drained. The region comprises the nine provinces of Arezzo, Firenze, Grosseto, Livorno, Lucca, Massa-Carrara, Pisa, Pistoia, and Siena. Tuscany is renowned for its fertility; it produces wines, olives, potatoes, and cereals. The mineral wealth includes mines of iron, copper, mercury, and antimony.

Tuscany derives its name from the inhabitants of ancient **Etruria,** known as *Tusci* or *Tyrrheni,* who probably landed at Tarquinii in the 8C B.C. In *Etruria Propria* they formed themselves into a CONFEDERATION of twelve principal cities, not yet certainly identified, but probably comprising Tarquinii, Veii, Caere (Cerveteri), Camars (Chiusi), Cortona, Perusia (Perugia), Vulci, Volsinii or Velsina (Orvieto), Vetulonia, Felathri (Volterra), Arretium (Arezzo), and either Rusellae or Falerii or Populonia. By the 6C or 5C *Etruria Circumpadana,* in the Po Valley, also had its confederation of twelve cities, with Felsina (Bologna) at the head. Etruria Propria was dealt its death-blow by the conquest of Veii by the Romans in 396 B.C., while the Gauls also invaded from the N. The Roman conquest was completed by the 3C B.C.

The Lombardic duchy of Tuscany, with its centre at Lucca, emerged out of the decay of the Roman Empire, and endured in a more or less stable form until the rise of the various civic states in the 12C and the Guelph-Ghibelline struggles. Florence, supporting the famous Countess Matilda, inclined to the Guelph, or papal, side; Siena, with Lucca, Pisa, and Pistoia were Ghibelline, and upheld the Emperor. By the beginning of the 15C Florence had established a hegemony in the province, the sea-power of her most dangerous rival, Pisa, having been shattered by the Genoese. The great age of Florence began in the 14C, with the artists and writers of the early Renaissance; and it continued under the rule of the famous Medici family, tyrants perhaps, but patrons of art and learning. Only Siena rivalled the position of Florence, and was victorious in a battle against the city and Clement VII in 1526. However, Cosimo de' Medici led Florence in a decisive battle against Siena in 1555, and from then on Medici rule endured, with only short interruptions, until 1737, when it was succeeded by Austrian grand-dukes of the House of Lorraine. Lucca meanwhile, alone of the other Tuscan cities, maintained its independence, and after the Napoleonic wars was incorporated in the Duchy of Parma. The Lorraine dynasty, restored at Florence after 1815, maintained a liberal form of government remarkable among the foreign rulers of Italy in the early 19C, but even so it was unable to maintain its position in the face of the rising will towards unity of the Italian people, and in 1860 Tuscany declared itself united to Piedmont, with Victor Emmanuel as king. In 1865 the capital of Italy was transferred from Turin to Florence, as a preliminary step towards its final triumphant establishment at Rome.

In the Second World War the Allies reached Tuscany in July 1944. The Germans retreated from Florence before the Eighth Army on 3 Aug, and the autumn was mainly occupied in the capture of the 'Gothic Line', the strong fortification erected by the Germans in the Tuscan

Apennines. The following months were spent in the hills above Bologna, and a strong German counter-attack from N. of Lucca on 19 Nov virtually put an end to the 1944 campaign here. In April 1945, the Allied attack was resumed; Massa was occupied on the 5th, and a strenuous advance through the Apennines to the N.E. led down to the Emilian plain and the capture of Bologna on the 21st, bringing about the final liberation of Tuscany.

Latium (*Lazio*), consists of five provinces: Frosinone, Latina, Rome, Rieti, and Viterbo, of which only the two last are included in this volume. They are, in addition, the least characteristic, sharing their common features rather with Umbria.

42   FLORENCE

FLORENCE, in Italian **Firenze,** has been famous for centuries as one of the principal centres of art and learning in Italy. In the later Middle Ages and the early Renaissance it was the intellectual capital of the peninsula, well meriting its designation 'the Italian Athens'. The city remains a treasury of art, not only on account of the priceless collections in its museums and galleries, but also by virtue of its rich endowment of medieval monuments and Renaissance buildings, in which it is rivalled by Rome alone. Today, Florence, with 465,000 inhabitants, is still one of the most beautiful cities in Italy, and the historical centre and the hills in the immediate vicinity have been largely preserved from new buildings, although much indiscriminate building has been allowed to take place since the War on the outskirts, especially in the plain towards Prato. It lies in a delightful position in a small basin enclosed by low hills (which accounts for its changeable climate and high temperatures in summer). It is important as the trading centre for the fertile valleys of Tuscany. It has for long been favoured as a residence by scholars, artists, and others from abroad. The river Arno, a special feature of the city, is a mountain torrent, subject to sudden floods and droughts.

Hotels and Pensions all over the city, and in the environs (particularly Fiesole). Booking Service at the Station.

Station. *Santa Maria Novella* (Pl. 6) for nearly all services; a few fast trains to the South depart from *Campo di Marte* (beyond Pl. 4).

Airport at *Peretola* (6 km. N.W.) for internal services to Milan and Rome. The nearest international airport to Florence is at *Pisa* (100 km. W.; comp. p. 499) with flights to London, Paris, and Frankfurt. Frequent connecting bus service from P.za Stazione (Lazzi and S.I.T.A. companies) in under two hours.

Parking. The centre of the city, between P.za del Duomo and the Arno, and Via Tornabuoni and Via del Proconsolo, is closed to traffic from 8 to 20. Parking at Fortezza da Basso, P.za del Carmine, etc; P.za Pitti, P.za Stazione, and P.za Libertà (these last three with hourly tariff).

Post Office. Via Pellicceria, Palazzo delle Poste (Pl. 7; open 8-20 for 'Poste Restante') with Telephone Office; also 53 Via Pietrapiana (Pl. 7).

Information Offices. *E.P.T.,* 16 Via Manzoni; *Azienda Autonoma di Turismo,* 15 Via Tornabuoni; *Informazioni Turistiche Nazionali,* Loggia Rucellai (Pl. 6).—TOURIST OFFICES. *C.I.T.,* 59 Via Cerretani, and 51 P.za Stazione; *Universalturismo,* 7 Via Speziali; *Eyre & Humbert,* 4 P.za Rucellai.

Bus Services (principal services only). **B.** *Fortezza da Basso—P.za San Marco— P.za Duomo—P.za Signoria*—Ponte alle Grazie—*P.za Pitti—P.za del Carmine— Porta Romana* (one of the most useful buses for the visitor, and the only one which traverses the whole of the centre of the city). **1.** *P.za Stazione*—Via Panzani—*P.za Duomo*—Via Cavour—*P.za Libertà,* etc; **7.** *P.za San Marco—Fiesole;* **10.** *P.za San Marco—Settignano;* **11.** *San Gervasio*—Via Cavour—*P.za Duomo*—P.za della Repubblica—Ponte alla Carraia—Porta Romana—*Due Strade;* 13 (red). *P.za Stazione*—P.za Duomo—*Viale dei Colli*—Porta Romana—Ponte della Vittoria—*P.za Stazione;* 17. San Gervasio—P.za Libertà—Stazione—Via Toselli—*Cascine;* 28. *Via Fiume* (Stazione)—*Sesto Fiorentino;* 29. *Via Fiume-Perétola* (airport); 31. *Via Magliabechi* (Santa Croce)—*Grássina* (Ugolino golf course); 32. *Via Magliabechi—Antella;* 33. *Via Magliabechi—Bagno a Ripoli;* 37. *P.za S Maria Novella*—Ponte alla Carraia—Porta Romana—Galluzzo—*Tavarnuzze.*

Country Buses from the E. or W. side of the Station (*Lazzi,* 47 P.za Stazione; *S.I.T.A.,* 15 Via S. Caterina da Siena, corner of the piazza); frequently to *Prato,* and to *Pistoia, Montecatini,* and *Pescia;* hourly to *L'Impruneta;* many times daily to *Empoli* and *Livorno;* to *Lucca, Viareggio,* and *La Spezia;* to *Poggio a Caiano* and *Carmignano;* to *Pontassieve;* to *Poggibonsi* and *Siena;* once or twice daily to *Bologna;* to *Volterra;* to *San Gimignano;* to *Arezzo;* to *Pisa;* to *Faenza;* to *Forlì* and *Rimini.*

Tours of individual monuments in the city, and of the villas and their gardens (in April, May, and June) in the environs are organized by the *Amici dei Musei di Firenze,* and the *Comitato delle Visite ai Giardini delle più belle ville fiorentine,* both in 10 Via del Proconsolo. Day trips by coach in the Tuscan countryside are organized by the *Associazione Toscana 'Agriturist',* run from the same office. The tours are announced in the local newspaper 'La Nazione'.

British Consulate, 2 Lungarno Corsini (Pl. 10); **United States Consulate,** Palazzo Canevaro, 38 Lungarno A. Vespucci (Pl. 5).—*English Church,* St Mark's (Pl. 10), 16 Via Maggio; *American Church,* St James's (Pl. 6), 13 Via Rucellai; *Christian Science Church,* 1 Via della Spada.

Institutes and Clubs. *British Institute,* 2 Via Tornabuoni (Italian language courses), with a library and reading room at 9B Lungarno Guicciardini. *Institut Français,* 2 P.za Ognissanti; *German Institute of Art History* (with fine consulting library), 44 Via Giuseppe Giusti; *Dutch Institute,* 5 Viale Torricelli; *Havard Center for Renaissance Studies* (with fine arts library), Villa I Tatti, Settignano; *Centro Linguistico Italiano 'Dante Alighieri',* 12 Via de' Bardi (Italian language courses); *Centro di Cultura per Stranieri* (Italian language courses) attached to the University of Florence, 52 Via Bolognese; *Centro di incontro per Stranieri,* Palazzo Strozzi; *Gabinetto Vieusseux* (large circulating library and reading rooms), Palazzo Strozzi; *Istituto Nazionale di Studi sul Rinascimento,* Palazzo Strozzi.—*A.C.I. (Automobile Club Italiano),* 36 Viale Amendola.

Concerts and Drama. *Teatro Comunale* (Pl. 5), 16 Corso Italia, symphony concerts and opera. Here is held the MAGGIO MUSICALE annual music festival (May-June; some concerts also in churches and the Pergola theatre).—*Pergola* (Pl. 7), 12 Via della Pergola, drama, and chamber music concerts (of high standing) organized by the *'Amici della Musica'* in Jan-April and Oct-Dec.—Chamber music concerts given by the *'Musicus Concentus'* are held in Santa Maria del Carmine (Salone Vanni) and the Auditorium of the Palazzo dei Congressi in Feb-April, and Oct-Nov.

Golf course (18 holes) at Ugolino, c. 11 km. S.E., beyond Grássina.—*Tennis,* Viale Michelangelo; Il Poggetto (Via Michele Mercati); the Cascine, etc.—*Swimming Pools* in the Cascine, Piazza Beccaria (covered), Lungarno Colombo, and others.

Popular Festivals and Exhibitions. *Scoppio del Carro,* on Easter Day, an annual religious festival held in and outside the Duomo; *Festa del Grillo,* on Ascension Day, a large fair in the Cascine where crickets are sold; 24 June, St John's Day, the patron Saint of Florence, a local holiday with fireworks at Piazzale Michelangelo. A football game in 16C costume is held in P.za Signoria three times during St John's week.—An Antiques Fair (the *Mostra Mercato Internazionale dell'Antiquariato*) is held biennially (next in 1979) in the autumn, in Palazzo Strozzi.

History. Excavations have proved the existence of an Etruscan settlement on the site of Florence; and of the Roman colony of *Florentia* founded in 59 B.C. to guard the Arno bridge, several mosaic floors and house-foundations have been discovered. The modern city, however, takes its rise from the Tuscan town that became of importance about the year 1000, when it supported the Margrave of Tuscany against the rebel city of Lucca. As early as 1115 it espoused the cause of the Pope when it led the League of San Genesio against the Emperor, and in the succeeding century it was torn by feuds arising from the murder of one of the Buondelmonti by the Amidei in 1215. At this time the names Guelph and

Ghibelline (derived from the German families of Wolf and Waiblingen or Hohenstaufen who were then contesting the Imperial crown) were assumed by the two rival parties in Florence, and afterwards they gradually came into use throughout Italy to denote (in a general way) the parties favouring the Pope (Guelph) and the Emperor (Ghibelline).

In 1246 the Ghibelline Uberti drove the Guelph Buondelmonti out of Florence, and the town was held by the Emperor Frederick II until his death in 1250. In the following years the Guelphs set up a popular government, conquered Pisa, Pistoia, and Siena, captured Arezzo, Volterra, and San Gimignano, and increased the trade and commerce of the city. In a renewed war against Siena the Florentines were defeated at Monteaperti (1260), but their city was spared through the generosity of Farinata degli Uberti. The victory of Campaldino (1289) gratified revenge and won back prestige, and the Guelphs were now firmly fixed in power. But the internal struggles were renewed, the new rival factions, known as Blacks and Whites, being led respectively by the Cerchi and Donati families. Charles of Valois, called in as peacemaker by Boniface VIII, favoured the Blacks and sent 600 Whites into exile (1303), among them being Dante, but the gates were shut against the Emperor Henry VII, and peace was restored for a time. In 1326 Walter de Brienne, Duke of Athens, seized the chief power, but he was expelled in 1343. During the ensuing struggles between nobles and people, among which the rising of 1378 of the Ciompi, or woolcarders, under Michele di Lando was especially notable, Cosimo de' Medici the elder gradually succeeded in making himself ruler of the city. Florence had meanwhile been prospering, and was now pre-eminent alike through the power of her arms, her wealth, her art, and her manufactures. At the Council of Florence in 1439-44 the Greek and Roman churches negotiated a union that lasted a brief fifteen years. Cosimo's wise and mild government was succeeded by the brief rule of Piero il Gottoso; then followed Lorenzo, who, having escaped the conspiracy of the Pazzi (26 April 1478), to which his brother Giuliano (father of Giulio, afterwards Pope Clement VII) fell a victim, concentrated the power in the hands of the partisan Council of Seventy. A great lord and munificent patron of the arts, Lorenzo (d. 1492) was surnamed Il Magnifico. His son Piero was driven out after his surrender to Charles VIII at Sarzana (1494), and the people, under the inspiration of the oratory of the Dominican Girolamo Savonarola, rebelled against the Medici, and a democratic Great Council held the reins of government. Savonarola was burned at the stake as a heretic (1498), but the Republic continued, and in 1502, under Piero Soderini, succeeded in retaking Pisa. The exhaustion which followed paved the way for the return of the Medici (Giuliano and Giovanni, afterwards Pope Leo X) in 1512, and, though they were banished by Charles V after his capture of Rome in 1527, that emperor made terms with the family, married his daughter, Margaret of Parma, to Alessandro de' Medici, great-grandson of Lorenzo the Magnificent, and appointed him Duke of Florence in 1530. The city, besieged by imperial troops and betrayed by Malatesta Baglioni, was overcome in spite of Michelangelo's new fortifications.

Alessandro, assassinated in 1537, was succeeded by a distant relative, Cosimo, son of the famous condottiere Giovanni delle Bande Nere and a distant descendant of Cosimo the Elder. This Cosimo received the title of Grand Duke from the Pope in 1569 and his line remained in power until the death of the last Medici in 1737. Previously, in 1735, the succession of Francis of Lorraine, afterwards Francis I of Austria, had been arranged by treaty, and Tuscany became an appanage of the Austrian imperial house. In 1799 the French expelled the Austrians, and, after an ephemeral appearance as the Kingdom of Etruria (1801-2) under the Infante Louis of Bourbon, the grand duchy was conferred in 1809 upon Elisa Bonaparte Baciocchi. The Bourbon restoration (1814) brought back the Lorrainers, whose rule, interrupted by the revolution of 1848, ended in 1859. In March 1860, Tuscany became part of united Italy and from 1861 to 1875 Florence was the capital of the Italian kingdom. Despite the efforts to prevent it by Gerhard Wolf, the wartime German consul (later made a freeman by grateful Florentines), all the bridges except the Ponte Vecchio were blown up by the Germans in the Second World War; the city was occupied by the Allies in August 1944, after considerable desultory fighting. In 1966, the Arno overflowed its banks and severely damaged buildings and works of art. This was treated as an international disaster, and most buildings have now been reopened after restoration.

Architecture. The glory of Florentine building begins towards the end of the 13C, when the finest works of the Gothic period were started (Santa Maria Novella, Santa Croce, and the Duomo, designed by Arnolfo di Cambio). Orsanmichele was reconstructed, the Palazzo Vecchio (attributed to Arnolfo) begun, and the palace of the Podestà (Bargello) erected, with other massive palaces, more fortresses than dwellings. In the 15C, Brunelleschi, who, with his friend Donatello, had studied the antiquities of Rome, transformed the aspect of Florence, and the influence of his art can be traced throughout the century. In his steps followed Donatello, Michelozzo, Giuliano da Sangallo, Giuliano and Benedetto da Maiano, Bernardo Rossellino, Cronaca, and Michelangelo himself. In the first half of the 16C, Michelangelo was the dominating spirit, and after him, Vasari. In the meantime Alberti had maintained a stricter classicism, and his example, followed by the builders of the 16C and 17C, was a main reason for the restraint shown in the Florentine Baroque.

Sculpture. In the 14C the chief Florentine sculptor was Orcagna, and in the 15C the outstanding figures were Ghiberti, famous for his Baptistery doors, and Donatello, the chief master of his age. Disciples of Donatello, whose masterpieces are spread wide throughout Northern Italy, were Agostino di Duccio, Bernardo and Ant. Rossellino, Desiderio da Settignano, Mino da Fiesole, Ant. del Pollaiuolo, Bened. da Maiano, and Verrocchio. Verrocchio, a painter as well as a sculptor, is famous for the equestrian figure of Colleoni at Venice, and was the master of Leonardo da Vinci. Less free and more classic was the work of Bened. da Rovezzano and Giul. da Maiano. In the next generation rose the mighty genius of Michelangelo, represented by his David and the Medici tombs; and alongside him arose the two Sansovinos, Andrea, and his pupil Iacopo, and Cellini with his marvellous workmanship. The last of the great Renaissance masters of Florence was Giambologna, but a fine tradition was maintained throughout the 18C and 19C.

Painting. In Cimabue, as early as the 13C, Florentine painting was already shaking itself free from the hieratic shackles of Byzantinism, but Giotto must be reckoned as the first modern painter, using nature as a model. Yet even his pupils, influenced no doubt by the Sienese school, retain traces of archaism, and it was not until the beginning of the 15C, when Masaccio, pupil of Masolino da Panicale, painted his frescoes in the Carmine, that the Renaissance in painting came fully to Florence. Once started, however, the flow was not to be stopped, and the two succeeding centuries provide a continuous stream of names famous in the annals of painting. Paolo Uccello, And. del Castagno, and Dom. Ghirlandaio were the early realists. Alongside them was the gentle mystic Fra Angelico, with his more sprightly disciple Benozzo Gozzoli. Pollaiuolo and Verrocchio distinguished themselves in painting as well as sculpture. Another group, with romantic ideals, has come to be regarded as specially Florentine—with the unique Botticelli, Filippino Lippi, most human of painters, and Piero di Cosimo. Fra Bartolomeo brought something of the robust colour of Venice to Florentine painting, and he was followed by And. del Sarto. The vivid portraits of Bronzino close the great age of Florentine painting, but individuality was maintained throughout the 17C.

Music. The change of style between Iacopo Peri's musical drama 'Dafne', performed in the Palazzo Corsi in 1597, and his 'Euridice', composed in 1600 to honour the marriage in Florence of Maria de' Medici to Henri IV of France, is generally held to mark the beginning of opera. The pianoforte was invented in Florence in 1711 by Bart. Cristofori (1655-1731). The composers Jean-Baptiste Lully (1632-87) and Luigi Cherubini (1760-1842) were natives of Florence.

Among the many other famous names that Florence has contributed to Italian culture the following may be cited: the poets Brunetto Latini (1212-94), master of Dante, Guido Cavalcanti (c. 1225-1300), the mighty Dante Alighieri (1265-1321), Luigi Pulci (1432-84), and Lorenzo de' Medici (1449-92); the historians Niccolò Machiavelli (1469-1527), Fr. Guicciardini (1482-1540), and Bern. Davanzati (1529-1606); Benvenuto Cellini (1500-71), whose memoirs rival his goldsmith's work; Amerigo Vespucci (1451-1512), the explorer; and Vincenzo Viviani (1622-1703), the pupil of Galileo. Petrarch, Leonardo, and Michelangelo were sons of Florentine fathers. Carlo Poerio died in Florence in 1867.

Anglo-American Associations. Florence was one of the principal goals of the 'Grand Tour' and throughout the 18-19C was visited by almost every traveller of note. Prince Charles Edward Stuart lived in the city in 1774-85, where he was known to Florentines as the Count of Albany. Florence Nightingale (1820-1910) was born in Florence. John Sargent, R.A. (1856-1925), son of a Boston physician, was likewise a native. Landor had several addresses in the city in 1821-28 before settling at Fiesole; while at the Villa Castiglione (3 km. beyond Porta S Niccolò) he met Lamartine, entertained Hazlitt, and was drawn by Bewick. He died in the Via della Chiesa behind the Carmine. Leigh Hunt lived here in 1823-25, for a time in the Via Magliabechi. Mark Twain finished 'Pudd'n-head Wilson' in 1892 at Settignano and later lived at Quarto in a villa earlier occupied by Jerome Bonaparte. Princess May of Teck, later Queen Mary, lived here with her family 'in exile' in 1884-85, mainly at the Villa I Cedri near Bagno a Rípoli.

I. THE DUOMO TO THE UFFIZI

The Duomo with its detached campanile and the Baptistery fill the PIAZZA DEL DUOMO and PIAZZA SAN GIOVANNI (Pl. 7); a comprehensive view of these impressive buildings is difficult in the confined space. However, the Cathedral, especially its southern flank, produces a memorable effect of massive grandeur, lightened by the colour and pattern of its marble. From the Piazza, which follows the shape of the Duomo, radiate numerous streets.

The **Duomo* (Pl. 7) or *Santa Maria del Fiore,* so called from the lily-flower in the city arms, was begun in 1296 by *Arnolfo di Cambio,* but was continued after 1357 according to a more imposing design by *Fr. Talenti.* The walls are encased in marble: white from Carrara, green from Prato, and red from the Maremma. The consecration of the church by Pope Eugenius IV took place in 1436. The competition for the design of the **CUPOLA (when various projects were presented including the suggestion that a huge mound of earth should be used to support the construction) was won by *Brunelleschi* and he started work in 1420. A feat of engineering skill, it was the first dome to be projected without the need for a wooden supporting frame to sustain the vault during construction. The pointed dome, built of huge bricks forming rings in a herring-bone pattern, was the largest and highest of its time. On the completion of the cupola in 1461 Brunelleschi was subjected to another competion as his ability to crown it with a lantern was brought into question. It is one of the masterpieces of the Renaissance, rising to the height of the surrounding hills (from which it is nearly always visible) and holding sway over the whole city.

EXTERIOR. The FAÇADE, erected to a third of its projected height by 1420, was demolished in 1587-88, and the present front was designed by Emilio De Fabris, and built in 1871-87. The bronze doors date from 1899-1903.—Building of the Cathedral was begun on the S. side. Here, high up above a doorway near the Campanile are 14C sculptures. Beyond is the PORTA DEI CANONICI, with fine sculptured decoration by *Lor. d'Ambrogio* and *Piero di Giovanni Tedesco* (1395-99). From here can be seen the gallery on the dome begun by *Baccio d'Agnolo* and abandoned by him in 1515 because of Michelangelo's stringent criticism.—On the N. side, the *PORTA DELLA MANDORLA has sculptures by *Giov. d'Ambrogio, Piero di Giov. Tedesco, Iac. di Piero Guidi,* and *Nic. Lamberti* (1391-1405). In the gable is an Assumption by *Nanni di Banco* (1414-21), and in the lunette an Annunciation in mosaic by *Dom.* and *Dav. Ghirlandaio* (1491). The busts in relief on the inside of the gable (difficult to see) of a prophet and sibyl are by *Donatello* (1422).

The INTERIOR (open 7-12, 14.30-19), c. 153 m long and c. 90 m wide across the transepts, is somewhat bare and chilly after the warmth of the colour of the exterior. The marble pavement was designed by *Baccio d'Agnolo, Fr. da Sangallo,* and others (1526-1660). Above the West Door, Mosaic of the Coronation of the Virgin attrib. to *Gaddo Gaddi. Ghiberti* designed the stained glass windows. The frescoes of angel musicians are by *Santi di Tito.* The huge clock, restored in 1973, uses the 'hora italica' method of counting the hours; the last hour of the day (XXIV) ends at sunset or Ave Maria (a system used in Italy until the

18C). *Paolo Uccello* decorated it and painted the four heads of prophets in 1443. The recomposed tomb of Antonio d'Orso, Bp of Florence (d. 1321) by *Tino da Camaino* includes a fine statue. Other fragments of the tomb are in the Bargello (comp. p. 435). The painting of St Catherine of Alexandria is by the School of *Bernardo Daddi.*

SOUTH AISLE. 1st Bay. A plain tomb slab marks the burial place of Brunelleschi in the Crypt of Santa Reparata beneath (discovered during excavations in 1972); on the wall is a bust of the architect by *Buggiano* (1446). *Nanni di Banco,* Statue of a Prophet (1408); *Benedetto da Maiano,* Bust of Giotto (1490; with an inscription by Politian). By the 1st pillar, is a graceful Stoup (c. 1380; the angel and basin are copies of the originals removed to the Museo dell'Opera del Duomo, comp. p. 422). Here is the entrance to the CRYPT OF SANTA REPARATA (adm. 9.30–11.45, 14.30–16.30; Sun. 9.30–11.45).

The extensive area of excavations (brought to light in 1972) is explained by a detailed model. Remains include: parts of the Roman edifices on the site of the primitive cathedral; the Paleochristian church of Santa Reparata (4-5C) with its mosaic pavement; and the reconstructions of the cathedral in the pre Romanesque and Romanesque periods (a pavement and some frescoes). Among the finds exhibited are Roman objects and the gilded bronze sword and spurs found in the tomb of Giovanni de' Medici buried here in 1351. Brunelleschi's tomb (comp. above) is also indicated.

Third Bay: Statue of Isaiah by *Ciuffagni* (1427) between two painted sepulchral monuments of Fra' Luigi Marsili and Card. Pietro Corsini, by *Bicci di Lorenzo.*—4th Bay: Bust of Marsilio Ficino by *And. Ferrucci* (1521).—Above the octagon the great dome soars to a height of 91 metres (without the lantern). It is frescoed by *Vasari* and *Fed. Zuccari* (the Last Judgement). The stained glass in the round windows of the drum was executed from cartoons by 15C artists. Against the pillars dividing the nave from the transepts stand eight 16C statues of Apostles: (clockwise from the nave) *Iac. Sansovino,* St James; *Vinc. de' Rossi,* St Thomas; *And. Ferrucci,* St Andrew; *Baccio Bandinelli,* St Peter; *Benedetto da Rovezzano,* St John; *Giov. Bandini,* St James the Less, St Philip; *Vinc. de' Rossi,* St Matthew. The marble Sanctuary by *Bandinelli* (1555) with bas-reliefs by himself and *Bandini,* encloses the High Altar, also by *Bandinelli,* with a wood crucifix by *Bened. da Maiano.*

Each of the three APSES is divided into five chapels. In the right and left apse are frescoes beneath the windows after Paolo Schiavo (c. 1440; heavily restored). Right Apse: 5th Chap. 'Madonna del Popolo', fragment of a Giottesque fresco. Above the entrance to the OLD SACRISTY, lunette of the Ascension by *Luca della Robbia.* The interesting interior is usually closed. Central Apse: 3rd Chap. On the altar, two graceful kneeling angels by *Luca della Robbia.* Beneath the altar, *Bronze reliquary urn, by *Ghiberti* with exquisite bas-reliefs. Over the door into the NEW SACRISTY is another fine relief by *Luca della Robbia* of the Resurrection. Together with *Michelozzo* and *Maso di Bartolomeo* he executed the beautiful bronze *Doors (1446-67). It was here that Lorenzo de' Medici took refuge on the day of the Pazzi conspiracy (see p. 415) in order to escape the death which befell his brother. The interior has been closed since 1972; the contents (to be returned here after restoration) include inlaid cupboards begun by *Ant.*

Manetti and others and continued by *Giuliano* and *Benedetto da Maiano* and a lavabo by *Buggiano*.

Left Apse. In the pavement (usually hidden by pews), Toscanelli's gnomon (c. 1450) for solar observations. In the 1st Chap., *Michelangelo's* *Descent from the Cross (c. 1550-53), intended for his own tomb. According to Vasari, the head of Nicodemus is a self-portrait. Unsatisfied with his work, the sculptor destroyed the arm and left leg of Christ, and his pupil, Tiberio Calcagni, restored the arm and finished the figure of Mary Magdalen. The figure of Christ is particularly remarkable. The adjoining chapel has a dossal painted on both sides (much ruined) by the School of Giotto.

A small door near the N. transept leads to the ascent of the dome (daily 8.30-11.30; 463 steps). The ascent is made between the double dome, giving an opportunity to examine its structure. From the cupola an incomparable *Panorama extends over the city to the hills beyond.

NORTH AISLE. 4th Bay. *Dom. di Michelino,* Dante with the Divina Commedia which illuminates Florence (1465); *Bicci di Lorenzo,* SS. Cosmas and Damian.—3rd Bay. *Bern. Ciuffagni,* King David (1434; designed for the old façade of the Cathedral). Beyond, two *Equestrian memorials to the famous condottieri, the English Sir John Hawkwood (Giovanni Acuto; d. 1394) who commanded the Florentine army from 1377 until his death, and Nic. Mauruzi da Tolentino (d. 1434). They are both frescoes imitating sculpture: the former by *Paolo Uccello* (1436) and the latter by *And. del Castagno* (1456).—2nd Bay, Bust of the organist Ant. Squarcialupi, by *Benedetto da Maiano* (1490; the epigraph is thought to be by Politian).—1st Bay. *Donatello* (attrib.), the prophet Joshua (traditionally thought to be a portrait of the Humanist Poggio Bracciolini), originally on the façade of the Duomo. On the 1st pillar, *Giov. del Biondo,* St Zenobius (late 14C).

The *Campanile (nearly 85 metres) the most individual belfry in Italy, was begun by *Giotto* in 1334, continued by *Andrea Pisano* (1343), and completed by *Fr. Talenti* in 1348-59. On the lowest story are two rows of bas reliefs (the originals are in the Museo dell'Opera del Duomo, comp. p. 422). The second story has a row of niches which contained statues of Prophets and Sibyls by Donatello and others (1415-36); these have also been removed to the Museo dell' Opera del Duomo and have been replaced by casts. Above are two stories, each with a pair of beautiful double-arched windows in each side, then the highest story, with large and triple-arched openings, and the cornice. The ascent of the tower (414 steps; adm. daily 8.30-12.30, 14.30-17, Sun. 14.30-17.30; winter: daily incl. Sun. 14.30-17, Sat. 8.30-12.30, 14.30-17), commands a succession of interesting views.

The *Baptistery of San Giovanni (Pl. 7: open 9-12.15, 14.30-17, Sun. 9-12.15, 14.30-15.45), one of the oldest and most revered buildings in Florence, is of uncertain date, between the 5C and 11C. It is octagonal in plan, and the outer casing, of green and white marble from Prato (11-13C), was the model for many similar schemes of decoration which are characteristic of Tuscan churches. The rectangular apse dates from the 13C and replaces an older semicircle. The cupola is concealed by a pyramid roof. The famous doors are bronze, with gilded bas-reliefs; the gold was discovered only after the doors had been removed for safety during the Second World War. Those on the N. and E. were designed by *Lorenzo Ghiberti* after a competition in which his work was preferred to that of many of the greatest artists of the Quattrocento, including Brunelleschi and Iac. della Quercia.

The *SOUTH DOOR, by *Andrea Pisano,* was erected in 1336 on the side facing the Duomo and moved to its present position in 1424. It has 28 compartments containing reliefs of the history of St John the Baptist and the theological and cardinal Virtues. The decorations of the bronze framing are by *Vitt. Ghiberti* (1452-64); over the doorway are bronze figures of the Baptist, the Executioner, and Salome, by *Vinc. Danti* (1571).

The *NORTH DOOR, by *Lorenzo Ghiberti* (1403-24), is again divided into 28 compartments, and the scenes of the Life of Christ, the Evangelists, and the Doctors, are contained within Gothic frames copied from the earlier *Pisano* doors. The bronze figures above are St John the Baptist preaching, the Levite, and the Pharisee, by *Fr. Rustici* (1506-11), from a design by *Leonardo* (mentioned by Vasari).

The **EAST DOOR is the celebrated work of *Ghiberti* (1425-52), said to have been called by Michelangelo the 'Gate of Paradise'. It is designed in 10 separate panels containing reliefs of scriptural subjects, in which the artist was assisted by *Michelozzo, Benozzo Gozzoli,* and others. The pictorial reliefs, no longer restricted to a Gothic frame, depict each episode with great conciseness, and the workmanship of the carving is masterly, with scenes in low relief extending far into the background. The subjects from above downwards, are: 1. The Creation and the Expulsion from Paradise; 2. Cain and Abel, 3. Noah's Sacrifice and drunkenness; 4. Abraham and the Angels and the Sacrifice of Isaac; 5. Esau and Jacob; 6. Joseph sold and recognized by his Brethren; 7. Moses receiving the Tables of Stone; 8. The Fall of Jericho; 9. Battle with the Philistines; 10. Solomon and the Queen of Sheba. In the framing are 24 very fine statuettes of Prophets and Sibyls, and 24 medallions with portraits of Ghiberti himself (the 4th from the top in the middle row on the left) and his principal contemporaries. The bronze door-frame is by Ghiberti also. Above the door the sculptural group of the Baptism of Christ, by *And. Sansovino,* and an Angel by *Innocenzo Spinazzi* (18C) were removed for restoration in 1975.

The harmonious INTERIOR, 25½ m. in diameter, is designed in two orders, of which the lower has Corinthian columns with gilded capitals, the upper a gallery with divided windows. The walls are in panels of white marble divided by bands of black, in the dichromatic style of the exterior. The beautiful pavement (1209) has niello decoration (especially notable near the font), recalling that of San Miniato (p. 474). On the right of the entrance is the font of 1371; on the right of the apse, the *Tomb of the antipope John XXIII (Baldassare Coscia, d. 1419), by *Donatello* and *Michelozzo.* On the left of the apse are two Roman sarcophagi; the statue of Mary Magdalen by Donatello has been removed to the Museo dell'Opera del Duomo (p. 422). The arch of the apse has mosaics, by the Franciscan *Iacopo* (1225-28), in the Byzantine style. The DOME is entirely lined with *Mosaics of the late 13C, representing stories from the Old and New Testaments, and the Last Judgement, with a gigantic figure of Christ in the centre (light operated by a coin).

On application to the Museo dell'Opera del Duomo (see below) visitors may ascend to the gallery, and visit the foundations of the Roman building which formerly stood on this site.

In the piazza, near the N. door of the baptistery, is the *Pillar of St Zenobius,* commemorating the elm which came into leaf when the body of the saint was carried by. Across the road, No. 7 is the *Casa dell'Opera di San Giovanni,* with a copy of a statuette of St John by Michelozzo (the original is now in the Bargello). Near the E. end of the

Duomo, No. 28 (red) was Donatello's studio (plaque). Nearby, No. 9 is the *Museo dell'Opera del Duomo (Pl. 7; adm. 9.30-16).

GROUND FLOOR. In the entrance hall, Lunette of the Madonna and Child, by *And. della Robbia;* bas-reliefs by *Baccio Bandinelli;* and a bust of Brunelleschi attributed to *Buggiano* or *Bandini.* The Vestibule beyond contains sculptures and

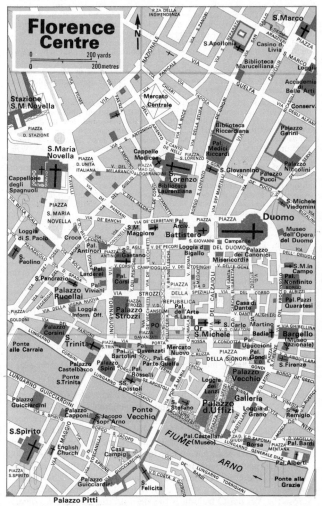

architectural fragments from the Duomo and a lunette of St Zenobius in terracotta, by *And. della Robbia* (1496).—ROOM I. The drawing (r.) of the old façade of the Duomo designed by Arnolfo di Cambio was made before its demolition in 1587 by *Bernardino Poccetti* (and is the most detailed illustration of it which has survived). On the wall opposite are numerous *Sculptures from the old façade by *Arnolfo di Cambio,* including a Madonna and Child, St Reparata, St Zenobius, the Madonna of the Nativity, and Boniface VIII. Opposite are the four seated Evangelists which were added to the lower part of the façade in the early 15C: *Bernardo Ciuffagni,* St Matthew: *Donatello,* *St John the Evangelist; *Nanni di Banco,* St Luke; *Nicolo di Piero Lamberti,* St Mark.—In the recess are sculptural fragments including an Etruscan cippus and a Roman sarcophagus. Two small rooms beyond were opened in 1977 to illustrate the technical aspects of *Brunelleschi's* architectural works. The display includes *Models of the cupola and lantern of the Duomo, and the appraratus he used in building them. Also, the death mask of the artist.—Beyond the angel and basin of the 14C Stoup from the Duomo (comp. p. 418) steps mount to ROOM II which displays antiphonals.—In the CHAPEL are reliquaries by *Pier Giov. di Matteo* and other artists of the 14-16C. The Madonna between SS. Catherine and Zenobius, above the altar, is by *Taddeo Gaddi* (1334).

On the Stair landing is *Donatello's* statue in wood of St Mary Magdalen (formerly in the Baptistery). Restored since flood damage, the original gilding has been returned to its surface.

FIRST FLOOR. ROOM I. To the left, *Cantoria by *Luca della Robbia* (the original panels are displayed beneath the reconstructed choir stall) and, opposite, *Cantoria by *Donatello.* Both were made in the 1430s and they are delightful works of superb workmanship. Around the walls, sixteen statues from the Campanile (comp. p. 419): *Donatello,* Bearded Prophet, Beardless Prophet, Abraham and Isaac (part of the modelling is attributed to *Nanni di Bartolo*); *Nanni di Bartolo,* Prophet; *Andrea Pisano* (attrib.), four Prophets; *Donatello,* St John the Baptist (attrib.), Habbakuk ('lo Zuccone'), 'Jeremiah'; *Nanni di Bartolo,* Abdia; *Andrea Pisano,* two Sibyls, David, and Solomon.—The adjoining Room exhibits the original *Bas-reliefs which decorated the lower story of the Campanile (see p. 419). Those by *Pisano* (many perhaps from Giotto's design) illustrate the Arts and Industries. The Planets, Virtues, Liberal Arts, and Sacraments, are by pupils of *Pisano* and *Orcagna.*

ROOM II. To the r., two Byzantine mosaic tablets thought to date from the early 14C; 27 needlework *Panels (in poor condition) from a liturgical tapestry with scenes from the life of St John the Baptist worked by the craftsmen of the Arte di Calimala (the Guild of Merchants of French cloth) from designs by *Ant. del Pollaiuolo; And. Pisano,* statuettes of Christ and St Reparata; *Nanni di Banco* (attrib.), statuettes of the Madonna and St Gabriel Archangel.—At the end of the room is the magnificent *ALTAR of silver-gilt by various Florentine artists of the 14-15C illustrating the history of St John the Baptist. The details merit close examination; they include a statuette of the Baptist by *Michelozzo,* reliefs of the Beheading of the Saint, by *And. del Verrocchio,* and of his birth, by *Ant. del Pollaiuolo.* The altar is surmounted by a silver *Cross by *Betto di Francesco* (1455), *Ant. del Pollaiuolo,* and probably other artists (Bernardo Cennini?). On the wall to the right, *Monte di Giovanni,* mosaic of St Zenobius (1505); *Pagno di Lapo Portigiani* (attrib.), bas-relief of the Madonna and Child; *Jacopo del Casentino* (attrib.), Processional painting of St Agatha (painted on both sides); *Tino da Camaino,* female bust; (above the door) *Bened. Buglioni,* Mary Magdalen in the Desert.

On the S. side of the Cathedral is the *Palazzo dei Canonici* with colossal statues of Arnolfo and Brunelleschi. Beyond is the *Misericordia,* the seat since 1576 of the Order thought to have been founded during the plague of 1326 to give medical care to the poor and attend to their burial. A charitable institution, the lay confraternity still continues its work of gratuitous help to those in need through some 2000 volunteers who are a characteristic sight of Florence in their black capes and hoods. The *Oratory* (left of the main door) contains an altarpiece by And. della Robbia, and a statue of St Sebastian by Bened. da Maiano. Across the Via dei Calzaiuoli is the elegant little *Loggia del Bigallo* (1352-58, attrib. to Alberto Arnoldi) originally a place where lost and deserted children were exposed. It now belongs to the Orfanotrofio del Bigallo; in the interior is the MUSEO DEL BIGALLO (No. 1 P.za San Giovanni; adm. 14-19 exc. fest.).

The Sala del Consiglio has a detached fresco of the Misericordia (1342; with a view of Florence), a fragment of another fresco formerly on the outside of the loggia, by *Nic. Gerini* and *Ambrogio di Baldese* (c. 1384); and a fresco cycle of the 14C with stories of Tobias. The relief of the Altoviti coat-of-arms is by *Desiderio da Settignano*. In a small room, two paintings of the Madonna of Humility, one by *Mariotto di Nardo,* the other by *Domenico di Michelino;* *Triptych by *Bern. Daddi,* an exquisite small work of 1333. In the inner part of the loggia: marble statues of the Madonna and Child with two angels, by *Alb. Arnoldi* (1359-64); predella by *Rid. Ghirlandaio* (one of the scenes shows the Misericordia, comp. above); detached fresco fragment (and sinopia) of the Redeemer, by the workshop of *Nardo di Cione,* and a painted Crucifix by the 'Maestro del Bigallo' (c. 1260).

The VIA DEI CALZAIUOLI, one of the main thoroughfares and shopping streets in the centre of Florence connects the Duomo with the Piazza della Signoria. To the right (reached by Via degli Speziali) is the sombre PIAZZA DELLA REPUBBLICA laid out at the end of the 19C after the demolition of the Mercato Vecchio and part of the ghetto. It occupies the site of the Roman forum. Beneath the heavy arcades (on certain days brightened by a flower market) is the central Post Office. Here are several cafés with tables outside including the Giubbe Rosse, the meeting place in the first decades of the century of artists and writers including De Chirico and Montale. The huge 'arcone' on the W. side of the piazza leads to Via Strozzi.—Farther along Via dei Calzaiuoli is (r.) the church of *Orsanmichele (Pl. 7; *San Michele in Orto*). Built as a market by *Fr. Talenti, Neri di Fioravante,* and *Benci di Cione* in 1337, the arcades were enclosed by huge three-light windows by *Simone Talenti* in 1380. These, in turn, were bricked up shortly after they were finished (but their superb Gothic tracery can still be appreciated). The upper story, completed in 1404, was intended (but probably never used) as a granary (for adm. see below). The statues of patron saints in the canopied niches on the pilasters were commissioned by the Arti Maggiori (or Greater Guilds) over a period of some two hundred years, and are an impressive testimony to the skill of the Florentine sculptors.

The statues, beginning at the Via dei Calzaiuoli and going round to the right are: St John the Baptist (1414-16), by *Ghiberti;* *Incredulity of St Thomas (1466-83), by *Verrocchio* (the tabernacle is the work of *Donatello* and formerly contained his St Louis of Toulouse now in the Museo dell'Opera di Santa Croce, comp. p. 441); St Luke (1601), by *Giambologna;* St Peter (1408-13), attrib. to *Donatello;* St Philip, Four crowned Saints (c. 1415), by *Nanni di Banco;* St George, by *Donatello* (copies of the original statue of 1417 and bas relief now in the Bargello, comp. p. 435); *St Matthew (1419-22), and *St Stephen (1428), by *Ghiberti;* St Eligius, by *Nanni di Banco;* St Mark (1411-13), by *Donatello;* St James, attrib. to *Niccolò Lamberti;* *Madonna, attrib. to *Giov. Tedesco;* and St John the Evangelist (1515), by *Baccio da Montelupo.*—Above the niches are medallions representing the lesser Guilds.

The dark INTERIOR (best light in the morning) is rectangular and has two aisles divided by square pillars painted with frescoes (restored) of the late 14C or early 15C. The magnificent Gothic *TABERNACLE by *And. Orcagna* (1349-59), is a masterpiece of all the decorative arts, ornamented with marble and coloured glass, as well as with statuettes and relief sculptures of the life of the Virgin. The painting on the altar of the *Madonna is by *Bern. Daddi.* Nearby is a statue of the Madonna and Child with St Anne, by *Fr. da Sangallo* (c. 1526).

Next to Orsanmichele stands the PALAZZO DELL'ARTE DELLA LANA (Pl. 7) built in 1308 (restored in 1905). It consists of the fortress-dwelling of the Compiobbiesi (afterwards occupied by the guild of wool merchants), and a small building to which is attached the picturesque Gothic shrine of *Santa Maria della*

Tromba (14C, formerly in the Mercato Vecchio). It contains a painting of the Madonna enthroned by Jacopo del Casentino. An overhead passageway (1569) gives access to the SALONI DI ORSANMICHELE, used for exhibitions.

On the other side of Via dei Calzaiuoli is the church of *San Carlo dei Lombardi* (1349-1404) with a severe (much ruined) façade. Within is a Deposition by *Niccolò di Pietro Gerini*.

The Via dei Calzaiuoli ends in the spacious ***Piazza della Signoria,** political and historical centre of Florence. Opposite rises the austere front of the Palazzo Vecchio, with the Loggia dei Lanzi on the right. The *Fountain of Neptune* (properly Fonte di Piazza) is by Bart. Ammannati and Giambologna (1563-75), with its colossal but rather flaccid god; the smaller more elegant bronze statues are by Vinc. Danti and others. A disc in the pavement in front of the fountain marks the place where Savanarola and his two companions were hanged and burned. Excavations in 1973 in the area of the piazza around the equestrian statue of Cosimo I by Giambologna (1594) revealed remains of the Roman city (2C A.D.) including baths. These have since been covered over.

The ***Palazzo della Signoria** or **Palazzo Vecchio** (Pl. 11; adm. 9-16, fest. 9-12; closed Sat) is a rectangular fortress-palace built by *Arnolfo di Cambio* (1298-1314), with later work by many 16C artists at the back and in the interior. The rusticated façade has graceful divided windows and a battlemented gallery, with a turret (1310) asymmetrically placed.

On the dissolution of the republican Signoria in 1532, the palace was occupied by the early Medici dukes, Cosimo I and Francesco, down to about 1587. In more recent times the Provisional Governments of 1848 and 1859 met here; and from 1865 to 1871 it housed the Chamber of Deputies and the Foreign Ministry of the Kingdom of Italy. Since 1872 it has been the seat of the municipal government.

On the steps are a copy of Donatello's Marzocco (now in the Bargello), the heraldic lion of Florence; *Judith and Holofernes, one of *Donatello's* last and most sophisticated works; David, a copy of the original by Michelangelo (now in the Accademia) which stood here from 1504 to 1873; and Hercules and Cacus, by *Bandinelli*.

The sombre CORTILE was reconstructed by *Michelozzo* (1470), the elaborate decorations being added in 1565 under the direction of *Vasari* on the occasion of the marriage between Francesco I and Joanna of Austria. In the centre is a fountain with a Putto and Dolphin, copy of the original by Verrocchio (now inside the Palazzo, see below). Beneath the arcade is a statue of Samson and a Philistine by *Pierino da Vinci*. In the large rectangular CAMERA DELL'ARME, the only room which survives from the 14C structure, occasional exhibitions are held. Beyond the Courtyard the GREAT DOUBLE STAIRCASE (by *Vasari*) leads up to the first floor.

The immense *SALONE DEI CINQUECENTO (or Sala del Consiglio), by *Cronaca* (1495) was built for the meetings of the Council of the Republic (addressed here in 1496 by Savanarola). The cartoons (later destroyed) by Michelangelo and Leonardo for the huge frescoes of the Battles of Anghiari and Cascina, which were to have decorated the walls, were frequently copied and studied by contemporary painters. The present name is derived from the meetings of the 500 deputies held here in 1865-71, when Florence was the capital of Italy. In the ceiling are paintings representing the history of Florence and of the Medici; on the walls are large frescoes, by *Vasari* and his assistants, of scenes from Florentine history, and paintings by *Ligozzi* and *Passignano*. Against the end wall (r.) is *Michelangelo's* *Victory, a strongly knit two-figure group probably executed for the tomb of Julius II in Rome. On either side, antique Roman statues. On the two long walls are displayed sculptures of the Labours of Hercules, by *Vinc. de' Rossi*. The door on the entrance wall, to the right (inconspicuous as it is usually kept closed, but adm. freely granted) gives access to the charming STUDIOLO DI FRANCESCO I. The harmonious decoration survives intact from the late 15C. It was created by Vasari and contains works by him, his pupils, *Bronzino* (the tondoes with portraits of Cosimo and Eleonora), *Giambologna, Ammannati, Vincenzo de' Rossi* (the statuettes in bronze), and others. A small staircase (usually closed) leads up to the richly decorated TESORETTO, also by *Vasari*.—The door opposite the Studiolo admits to the QUARTIERE DI LEONE X, decorated by *Vasari*, a series of rooms, with portraits of the Medici and scenes from their history, and a chapel. They are now occupied by the Mayor (Sindaco) and not open to visitors unless by special permission.

Also off the Sala dei Cinquecento (to the left of the dais) is a vestibule (the coved ceiling of which has painted grotesque decorations) hich leads in to the SALA DEI DUGENTO (open to visitors when not in use as Council chamber). This was reconstructed in 1472-77 by *Benedetto* and *Giuliano da Maiano* who also executed the magnificent ceiling. The name is derived from the Council of 200 citizens who first met here in 1441. On the walls are Florentine tapestries with the story of Joseph (1546-49) designed by *Bronzino, Salviati*, and *Pontormo*.

From the vestibule stairs ascend to the Second Floor (lift on the other side of the Sala dei Cinquecento). The *SALA DEI GIGLI has a ceiling by *Giul da Maiano*, a fresco of Roman notables and saints, by *Dom. Ghirlandaio*, and a richly carved doorway, with the *Baptist and putti by *Bened, da Maiano* (1480-81). A window of the old palace serves as a doorway in to the CANCELLERIA, the office of Niccolò Macchiavelli, who is here recorded in a fine bust (16C) and a painting attrib. to *Santi di Tito*. Here, too, is displayed the *Putto with dolphin, by *Verrocchio* the original removed from the courtyard below. The stone bas-relief of St George (c. 1270) used to decorate the Porta San Giorgio (comp. p. 472). In the adjacent GUARDAROBA *Dionigi Nigetti* designed the fine ceiling and cupboards, on the presses of which are 53 maps of great scientific and historical interest (late 16C). The huge globe was commissioned at the same period by Cosimo I. From here a door gives access to the Gallery (usually closed), a covered walk encircling the 13C part of the palace.—Beyond the Sala dei Gigli the SALA DELL'UDIENZA has another *Ceiling by *Giul. da Maiano*. The *Doorway is crowned by a statue of Justice by *Bened. da Maiano* (1476-78). The frescoes are by *Franc. Salviati* (c. 1550-60). Beyond a doorway over which is a dedication to Christ (1529) is the CAPPELLA DELLA SIGNORIA built in 1511 and painted by *Ridolfo Ghirlandaio*. A view of Piazza SS. Annunziata serves as background to the *Annunciation over the altar. In the passage beyond (with an old painted ceiling) parts of the ancient tower are visible. Here, too, are a mask of Dante and a detached fresco of the 14C.

The following rooms form part of the **Quartiere di Eleonora di Toledo**, the apartments of the wife of Cosimo I. They have notable tapestries (1643), 15C paintings, and ceilings by *Bernardo del Tasso* (note the views of the Piazze of Florence in the Camera di Gualdrada). In the Camera delle Sabine is a tondo of the Madonna and Child attrib. to *Lorenzo di Credi* and a Madonna and Child in the manner of And. del Sarto. Off the last room, the Camera Verde with grotesque decorations by *Ridolfo del Ghirlandaio*, is the *CAPPELLA DI ELEONORA by *Bronzino*, who also painted the altarpiece (Pietà, 1553).—A balcony leads across the end of the Sala dei Cinquecento. Here a painting of 1557 shows part of the lost Battle of Anghiari (comp. above). Beyond is the **Quartiere degli Elementi** (c. 1550) consisting of five rooms decorated by *Vasari* and his pupils, with some beautiful inlaid cabinets. From the LOGGIATO DI SATURNO a superb of view of Florence opens to the south-east. The little bronze demon is the work of *Giambologna*.

The *Alberghetto*, where Cosimo il Vecchio (1433) and Savonarola (1498) were imprisoned, and the TOWER (*View) have been closed to visitors since 1973. The **Quartiere del Mezzanino** (no adm.) contains numerous works of art including a Madonna and Child attrib. to *Masaccio* and a Portrait of a Gentleman by *Memling* (both stolen in 1971 but since recovered), and paintings by *Masolino, Bronzino, Rubens, Veronese, Seb. Ricci,* and *Tintoretto*. The **Collezione Loeser** has also been closed to the public. Left to the Commune of Florence in 1928 by the American art critic, it includes works of the Tuscan school from the 14C-16C.

The additions carried out in the 14-16C at the back of the Palazzo Vecchio can be seen from the Piazza della Signoria. No. 10 in the piazza is the *Tribunale di Mercatanzia* or Commercial Court, a fine building of 1359 (restored). The *Palazzo Uguccioni* (No. 7) has a stately façade (in poor repair) by Mariotto di Zanobi Folfi (1545). Above a bank at No. 5 is displayed the COLLEZIONE DELLA RAGIONE (adm. 10-16, Sun. 10-13; closed Tues) left to the city in 1970 by Alberto Della Ragione. The collection is representative of Italian art of the twentieth century (works by Severini, De Chirico, Morandi, Carrà, De Pisis, Casorati, Rosai, Mafai, Carlo Levi, Guttuso, and many others).

The *Loggia dei Lanzi (Pl. 11), so called because Cosimo I stationed a guard of German Lancers here, is properly known as the *Loggia della Signoria* since it was used for their public ceremonies. This graceful structure, by *Benci di Cione* and *Simone Talenti* (1376-81), with three lofty semicircular arches, anticipates the Renaissance. It was sometimes called *Loggia dell'Orcagna,* from a tradition that he designed it. Coloured reliefs of the Virtues, above, were added in 1384-89 by various artists.

It now displays important sculptures. On either side of the steps is a lion, that on the right being a Greek work, the other a 16C copy. Under the arch to the right, *Giambologna's* last work, the *Rape of the Sabines (1583). The dynamic composition foreshadows the sculpture of the Baroque period. To the left, *Perseus, *Benvenuto Cellini's* masterpiece in bronze, which stands on a pedestal of beautiful design, with statuettes and a bas-relief of Perseus rescuing Andromeda (copies; the originals are now in the Museo Nazionale, p. 434). Within the loggia are Hercules and the Centaur, by *Giambologna;* Ajax with the body of Patroclus, a copy of a Greek original of the 4C B.C.; and Rape of Polyxena, by *Pio Fedi* (1866). Against the back wall are Roman statues.

Between the Palazzo Vecchio and the Loggia dei Lanzi opens the long narrow PIAZZA DEGLI UFFIZI (Pl.11) which extends to the Arno. It is almost enclosed by the massive *Palazzo degli Uffizi (Pl. 11) built to a very original design by *Vasari* (1560-74) for Cosimo I to serve as government offices and an art gallery. It was completed, according to Vasari's project, by *Alf. Parigi the Elder* and *Bern. Buontalenti* (1574-80). The building now houses the famous Art Gallery and the Tuscan State Archives.

The *Archivio dello Stato,* on the 2nd floor, is entered by the 8th door under the left-hand colonnade. Founded in 1582, the archives occupy over 400 rooms and date back to the 8C. New quarters are being built for them in P.za Beccaria.

The ground floor of the *Palazzo della Zecca* is incorporated into the fabric of the building (r; the part without the colonnades). The famous 'florins', first issued in 1252, were minted here.

In Via della Ninna to the N. may be seen remains of the church of *San Piero Scheraggio* (comp. below).

The **Galleria degli Uffizi is the most important collection of paintings in Italy and one of the great art collections of the world. It is entered by the first door on the left under the colonnade. Admission daily exc. Mon 9-17, fest. 9-13.

The origins of the collection go back to Cosimo I. The galleries were enlarged and the collection augmented by Francesco I. The Medici dynasty continued to add numerous works of art in the following centuries: Ferdinand I brought sculptures from the Villa Medici in Rome; Ferdinand II inherited paintings by Raphael and Titian from Fr. Maria della Rovere of Urbino; and Cardinal Leopoldo began the collection of drawings and self-portraits. The last of the Medicis, Anna Maria Lodovica, widow of the Elector Palatine, through a family Pact (1737) settled her inheritance on the people of Florence. The huge collection was partly broken up during the last century when much of the sculpture went to the Bargello and other material was transferred to the Archæological Museum. This century many paintings formerly in the churches of Florence have been removed to the gallery for greater safety and ease of examination.

The following description includes only some of the most important paintings and sculptures (and asterisks have been used sparingly).

GROUND FLOOR. Beyond the ticket office is a room (not always open) which incorporates remains of the church of San Piero Scheraggio (11C) and an earlier church of the 9C, brought to light in 1971. Here are displayed a series of detached *Frescoes (c. 1450) by *And. del Castagno* of illustrious Florentines including Boccaccio, Petrarch, and Dante. These splendid monumental figures decorated a loggia of the Villa Pandolfini at Legnaia (and were later housed in the monastery of S. Apollonia). The room beyond (where the apse of the church has traces of primitive frescoes) displays (1977) recently restored works. In the adjacent rooms: *Fresco of the Annunciation by *Botticelli* (from the church of S. Martino), and a column of the church with a 14C fresco of St Francis.—There is a LIFT for the picture galleries. The STAIRCASE, lined with antique busts, leads up past the **Prints and Drawings Room** (open to students with special permission, 9-13). The collection is one of the finest in the world and is particularly rich in Renaissance and Mannerist works. *Exhibitions are held periodically.

On the SECOND FLOOR, the VESTIBULE (A) contains antique sculpture (statues of Hadrian and Augustus) and two dogs, well preserved Greek works, perhaps of the Pergamenian School. Beyond is the long U-shaped gallery lined with tapestries which provides a fitting setting for the collection of antique sculptures (mostly Hellenistic works). Opposite the windows overlooking the piazza are doors leading into the numerous galleries of paintings (the collection begins in Room 2, to the left).

EAST CORRIDOR. Room 1, to the right, has been closed to the public for many years. It contains two copies of the Doryphoros of Polykleitos. Outside is (77.) Hercules and the Centaur, a late Hellenistic work restored by G.B. Caccini in 1589. Also in this part of the corridor: Roman sarcophagi, and statues of an Athlete (100.) and a Guardian Deity (252.), both from classical Greek originals. Among the tapestries which stretch the whole length of the corridor, those with grotteschi on a yellow ground, by *Bachiacca*, are notable for the liveliness and imagination of the designs; and the 16C Flemish series (lives of Catherine de' Medici and Henri III) is interesting.

Room 2. TUSCAN SCHOOL OF THE 13TH CENTURY. Three huge *Paintings of the Madonna enthroned dominate the room, by *Cimabue* (8343.), showing the beginnings of freedom from Byzantinism (c. 1285); *Giotto* (8344.), with a new monumentality in the figures which was to become a characteristic of his school (c. 1310); and *Duccio di Boninsegna*, the 'Rucellai Madonna' (1285), the famous painting from S. Maria Novella. The *Polyptych of the Badia (Madonna and four Saints) is also by *Giotto*. Other works from the Florentine, Lucchese, and Pisan schools of the 13C include St Luke, by the *Maestro della Maddalena* (3493.).

Room 3. SIENESE SCHOOL OF THE 14TH CENTURY. 8346. *Ambr. Lorenzetti*, Presentation in the Temple (1342); two small panels: 3157. *Niccolò Bonaccorsi*, Presentation of the Virgin in the Temple, and 3475. *Simone de' Crocefissi*, Nativity. 8347. *Pietro Lorenzetti*, Panels of a Dossal with the Story of the Blessed Umiltà; *451-453. *Simone Martini*, Annunciation, one of the masterpieces of the Sienese school. The Saints are by his brother-in-law, *Lippo Memmi.* 8439. *Niccolò di Ser Sozzo Tegliacci,* Madonna and Child; *Amb. Lorenzetti*(painted for the church of S. Procolo): 61, 9411, 62. St Nicholas of Bari, Madonna and Child with Saints, and St Proculus (a triptych recomposed when the central panel was left to the Gallery by Bernard Berenson), *8348, 8349. Four scenes from the life of St Nicholas, restored in 1975. 445. *Pietro Lorenzetti,* Madonna in glory.

ROOM 4. FLORENTINE SCHOOL OF THE 14TH CENTURY.449. St Cecilia and eight scenes from her life, by an unidentified disciple of *Giotto;* 9258. *Iac. del Casentino,* Triptych of the Madonna enthroned, St Francis and Saints, and the Crucifixion; 3073. *Bernardo Daddi,* the Madonna between SS. Matthew and Nicholas (1328); 3515. *Nardo di Cione,* Crucifixion; 454. *Giottino* (?), Pietà; 3163. *Orcagna,* St Matthew with scenes from his life (1367-8, completed by his brother, *Jacopo di Cione*); 459. *Giovanni da Milano,* 10 panels of Saints, Martyrs, and Virgins.

ROOMS 5 AND 6. LATER GOTHIC SCHOOLS. 447. *Gherardo Starnina,* The Thebaid; 885. *Lor. Monaco,* Coronation of the Madonna (1413); *Gentile da Fabriano,* 887. Mary Magdalen, St Nicholas of Bari, St John and St George (1425; from the Quaratesi polyptych), *8364. Adoration of the Magi (1423); 464. *Agnolo Gaddi,* Crucifixion; *466. *Lorenzo Monaco,* Adoration of the Magi.—ROOM 7. FLORENTINE SCHOOL OF THE EARLY 15TH CENTURY. *Fra Angelico,* 1612. Coronation of the Virgin, 143. Madonna and Child; *884. *Dom. Veneziano,* Madonna enthroned with four Saints, in beautiful pastel colours; 8386. *Masaccio* and *Masolino,* Madonna and Child and St Anne. Masaccio added the Madonna and Child to his master's painting. *1615. *Piero della Francesca,* a panel with the portraits of Federico di Montefeltro and his duchess, Battista Sforza, with their allegorical triumph on the reverse (the detailed landscapes in transparent light are particularly beautiful). *479. *Paolo Uccello,* Battle of San Romano, painted (together with its companions, now in the Louvre and National Gallery, London) for Lorenzo il Magnifico's rooms in the Palazzo Medici-Riccardi, a brilliant exercise in perspective.—ROOM 8. (Above the door): *Paolo Uccello,* Nativity, a fresco (much ruined) from the church of S. Martino della Scala. 8351. *Filippo Lippi,* Predella of the Barbadori altarpiece (now in the Louvre); 483. *Aless. Baldovinetti,* Annunciation; 8354. *Filippo Lippi,* Madonna enthroned with Saints; 8355. *Franc. Pesellino,* predella of No. 8354. 487. *Aless. Baldovinetti,* Madonna and Child with Saints; 8356-7. *Filippo Lippi,* Annunciation and Saints; 3949. *Matteo di Giovanni,* Madonna and Child with Saints; 474. *Vecchietta,* Madonna and Child with Saints (1457). The large Tabernacle "del Madonnone" contains a sinopia of a fresco by *Lorenzo di Bicci. Filippo Lippi,* 8350. Adoration of the Child; *1598. Madonna and Child with two Angels (one of the most charming works by this artist), 8353. Adoration of the Child with St Bernard.

ROOMS 9-16 have been closed during rearrangement of the gallery. The masterpieces in them (by Botticelli and Leonardo) are temporarily displayed elsewhere in the gallery. A list of the major works (in no particular order) which will be in the rooms when they re-open is given below.

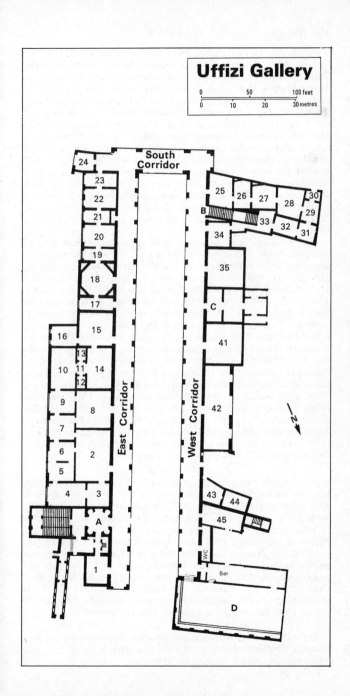

Uffizi Gallery

| 0 | 50 | 100 feet |
| 0 | 10 | 20 | 30 metres |

South Corridor

East Corridor

West Corridor

24
23
22
21
20
19
18
17
16
15
13
11
12
10
14
9
8
7
6
5
2
4
3
A
1

25 26 27 28 30
B 29
33 32 31
34
35
C
41
42
43 44
45
WC
Bar
D

N

POLLAIUOLO AND BOTTICELLI. *Piero del Pollaiuolo,* 495-9, 1610. Six
Virtues, 1492. Galeazzo Maria Sforza; *Sandro Botticelli:* 1606.
Fortitude (1470; one of a series representing the Virtues, destined for the
Tribunale della Mercanzia); *1487, *1484, Judith returning from the
camp of Holofernes, and the decapitated Holofernes in his tent; 1488.
Portrait of a man with a medal of Cosimo de' Medici; 1601. Madonna of
the Rose-bush (c.1470); and other Madonnas.—*Botticelli:* *1607.
Madonna with the Pomegranate (1487); *8360. Primavera, a
harmoniously grouped composition, with the three Graces to the left
united in dancing movement; *1609. Madonna of the Magnificat; **878.
Birth of Venus; this pagan subject (quite new to Florentine painting) is
treated with great freedom and energy; 1608. Annunciation; *882.
Adoration of the Magi (executed on his appointment as official court
painter, and including portraits of Medici courtiers with Lorenzo the
Magnificent, and a self-portrait on the extreme right); 29. Pallas and the
Centaur.

Filippino Lippi, 8652. St Jerome, 3246. Adoration of the shepherds;
Botticelli, *1496. Calumny (after 1487), a subject taken from Lucian's
account of a picture by Apelles, described in Alberti's work on painting;
8390. Salome, 8393. StAugustine with a boy on the seashore.—1485,
1711. *Filippino Lippi,* Portraits of an old man, and of the artist; 3094.
Lorenzo di Credi, Venus; 491-93. *Iac. del Sellaio,* Subjects from the
Book of Esther; 3154, 1502. *Bart. di Giovanni,* Miracles of St Benedict.

Hans Memling, 1100. Benedetto Portinari, 1090. St Benedict,
1101-2.Portraits, 1024. Madonna with angels; 1036, 8405. Pierantonio
Baroncelli and his wife, by an unknown Fleming; 1114. *Roger van der
Weyden,* Entombment.—*1065. *Nic. Froment,* Triptych with the
Raising of Lazarus; *Dom. Ghirlandaio,* 8387-88. Virgin enthroned with
saints, 881. Madonna with saints and angels, 1619. Adoration of the
Magi; *Filippino Lippi,* 1566. Adoration of the Magi, 1568. Madonna
(1486), painted for the Sala degli Otto in the Palazzo Vecchio; 8399. *Lor
di Credi,* Adoration of the Shepherds; *3191-93. *Hugo van der Goes,*
Adoration of the Shepherds, a celebrated triptych, brought to Florence
in 1476. On the wings are saints and members of the Portinari family.
*8359. *Botticini,* Tobias and the Archangel.

UMBRIAN SCHOOLS AND LEONARDO. *1435. *Perugino,* Madonna with
SS. John the Baptist and Sebastian, a typical work (1493); *Lor. di Credi,*
3244. Madonna with St John, 1597. Annunciation; *Luca Signorelli,*
1605. Holy Family, 502. Madonna, 3254. Crucifixion and saints
(c. 1480; painted partly by *Perugino*), 8369. The Trinity, with the
Madonna and saints; 8358. *Verrocchio,* Baptism of Christ (begun
c. 1470); according to Vasari and Albertini, the angel on the left was
painted by the young Leonardo; *Piero di Cosimo,* 3885. Madonna with
angel musicians, 1536. Perseus and Andromeda (1589), 506. Immaculate
Conception; *1594. *Leonardo da Vinci,* Adoration of the Magi
(unfinished).—*1618. *Leonardo,* Annunciation, painted in Verrocchio's
studio; 1490. Young man in a red hat, attr. to *Leonardo.*

ROOM 17, the SALA DELL'ERMAFRODITO (not always open) contains a
Sleeping Hermaphrodite, copy of a Greek original of the 2C B.C., and
small bronzes. Also a Triptych by *Mantegna.*

ROOM 18. The octagonal TRIBUNA (recently restored) was designed by *Buontalenti* (with a fine ceiling by *Bernardino Poccetti*) to display the most valuable pieces of the Medici collection, and particularly the statuary. The *Medici Venus, the most famous statue in the Uffizi, is a marble copy (probably of the 1C B.C.) of the Praxitelean Aphrodite of Cnidos, formerly in the Medici Villa in Rome. The other sculptures are: 230. 'Arrotino' (the knife-grinder), now thought to represent a Scythian as part of a group of Apollo and Marsias; 216. Wrestlers, a restored copy of a bronze original of the school of Pergamum; 220. Dancing Faun, a beautifully restored work; and 229. Apollino (Young Apollo) derived from an Apollo of Praxiteles.—Around the walls are a series of remarkable *Portraits: 28. *Bronzino,* Cosimo I; 783. *And. del Sarto,* Man with book; *Bronzino,* 748. Eleonora di Toledo, 1472. Medici princess, 1475. Don Giovanni de' Medici; 1508. *Rosso Fiorentino,* Angel musician; 1446. *Raphael,* Young St John; 1445. *Franciabigio,* Madonna del Pozzo; 1571. *Bronzino,* Don Francesco de' Medici (1553), 741., 736. Bartolomeo and Lucrezia Panciatichi; 2155. *Ridolfo del Ghirlandaio,* Young man; 3574. *Pontormo,* Cosimo il Vecchio; 1578. *Vasari,* Lorenzo il Magnifico; 1500. *Aless. Allori,* Bianca Cappello (?), a fresco.

ROOM 19. 1435. *Perugino,* Madonna with SS. John the Baptist and Sebastian (1493); 3282. *Lor. Costa,* St Sebastian; 1535. *Girol. Genga,* Martyrdom of St Sebastian; 1444. *Fr. Francia,* Portrait of Evangelista Scappi. *Perugino,* 1474. Portrait of a Young Man (attrib. also to Costa), 1700. Portrait of Francesco delle Opere (1494), 8375. 8376. Don Biagio Milanesi, Baldassarre, Vallombrosan monks. *Luca Signorelli,* 502. Madonna and Child, 1605. Holy Family.—ROOM 20. DÜRER AND THE GERMAN SCHOOL. 1459, 1458. *Cranach,* Adam and Eve (1528); 1083. *Jan Bruegel the Elder,* Calvary; *Dürer,* 8406. Calvary (a drawing in chiaroscuro, 1505), 1089, 1099. St James and St Philip the Apostles, 8433., 8432. Adam and Eve (old copies from Dürer), *1434. Adoration of the Magi (1504), 1086. Portrait of the artist's father (painted at the age of 19, the first known work by the artist). 1645. *Joos van Cleve,* Portrait of a young man; *Cranach,* 512. Portrait of Luther (1543), 1056. St George (a tiny work), 1631. Self-portrait (1550).—ROOM 21. 901. *Vittore Carpaccio,* Halberdiers; 902. *Cima da Conegliano,* Madonna and Child; *Giov. Bellini,* 1863. Portrait of a gentleman, *631. Sacred allegory, 943. Lamentation over the Dead Christ. *Giorgione,* 945. the Infant Moses brought to Pharoah, 947. Judgement of Solomon, 911. Warrior (the 'Gattamelata'; doubtfully attrib. to Giorgione).—ROOM 22 contains German and Flemish works. *Holbein,* 1120. Supposed Portrait of Thomas More (attrib. to his School), 1630. Self-portrait, 1087. Portrait of Sir Richard Southwell (1536). 1643, 1644. *Joos van Cleve the Elder,* Portrait of an unknown man and his wife, 1084. Mater dolorosa; *Gerard David,* 1152. Deposition, *1029. Adoration of the Magi.

ROOM 23. 3348. *Giov. Fr. Mainieri,* Christ bearing the Cross; 1454. *Bernardino Luini,* Herod; 738. *Sodoma,* Derision of Christ; 1441. *Raphael* (attrib.), Portrait of Elizabeth Gonzaga; *Correggio,* 1329. Madonna in glory; 1455. Rest on the Flight, 1453. Madonna in adoration of the Child.—ROOM 24 is occupied by the COLLECTION OF MINIATURES (15-18C), but it is not normally open.

The short SOUTH CORRIDOR commands good views of the river and P.za degli Uffizi. Sculptures: *Roman matron, seated; Ceres, the so-called 'Night' draped with black marble; Boy with a thorn in his foot, replica of the 'spinario' in the Capitoline Museum; *Pedestal for a candelabrum; Sarcophagus with the Fall of Phaeton and chariot-races; *Crouching Venus, and Seated Girl preparing to dance, both from Hellenistic originals of the 3C B.C.; Mars, Roman copy of a Greek original; imperial busts.—The sculpture is continued in the W. corridor: two *Statues of Marsyas, from Hellenistic originals of the 3C B.C.; Nereid on a sea-horse, Hellenistic; bust of Cicero; athletes, warriors, and gods; Laocoön, a copy by *Bandinelli* of the Vatican group.

ROOM 25. Opposite the entrance is the famous (1456.) *'Tondo Doni' of the Holy Family, the only finished painting by *Michelangelo*. It was painted for the marriage of Agnolo Doni with Maddalena Strozzi (1504-05) when the artist was 30 years old. The contemporary frame by Domenico del Tasso is also noteworthy. Also in this room: 1587. *Mariotto Albertinelli,* Visitation; 8455. *Fra Bartolomeo,* Apparition of the Virgin to St Bernard; 1482. *Raphael* (attrib.), Portrait of Perugino; 2152. *Rosso Fiorentino,* Moses defending the children of Jethro.—

ROOM 26. (RAPHAEL AND ANDREA DEL SARTO). *1557. *Andrea del Sarto,* Madonna of the Harpies (1517); *Pontormo,* 1480. Portrait of a lady, 1843. Portrait of a man; *Raphael,* 1447. Madonna del Cardellino (of the Goldfinch, 1506). Painted for the marriage of the artist's friend, Lor. Nasi, it was shattered by an earthquake in 1547, but carefully preserved and repaired by the owner. *40P. Leo X with the Cardinals Giulio de' Medici (afterwards Clement VII) and Luigi de' Rossi (1518-19), one of his most powerful portrait groups which was to influence Titian, painted shortly before his death. 1450. Portrait of Julius II, a replica of inferior quality of the painting in the National Gallery of London; 1706. Portrait of a man (self-portrait?); 8760. Portrait of Fr. Maria della Rovere. *Pontormo,* 1525. Martyrdom of St Maurice and the eleven Martyrs, 8379. St Anthony Abbot; 1583. *Andrea del Sarto,* St James and two children.

ROOM 27 (PONTORMO). 8381. *Franciabigio,* Portrait of a young man with gloves; 8377. *Bronzino,* Holy Family, painted for Bartolomeo Panciatichi; 8740. *Pontormo,* Supper at Emmaus; 3190. *Rosso Fiorentino,* Madonna and Child with Saints; *Pontormo,* 743. Portrait of the musician Fr. Dell'Ajolle, 3565. Portrait of Maria Salviati, widow of Giovanni dalle Bande Neri.—ROOM 28 is devoted to TITIAN. *1462. Flora; *1437. Venus of Urbino (1538), inspired by Giorgione's Venus; 942. Knight of Malta; 926. Fr. Maria della Rovere; 1431. Venus and Cupid (c. 1560; a late work). *Palma Vecchio,* 950. Madonna and Saints, 3256. Raising of Lazarus, 939. Judith.

ROOMS 29-31, at the end of this wing, are devoted to works of the 16C Emilian Schools including charming examples of *Parmigianino* (in particular the Madonna 'with the long neck'), *Girol. da Carpi, Mazzolino,* and *Dosso Dossi.* In ROOM 31 are also: 1481. *Lor. Lotto,* Head of a young boy; 1443. 'La Fornarina', a well-known portrait by *Seb. del Piombo* (formerly ascribed to Raphael and thought to be the portrait of his mistress); and 2183. *Titian,* Portrait of a sick man. Formerly attributed to Seb. del Piombo, its attribution to Titian was confirmed after its recent restoration. Beyond ROOM 32, with further examples of *Seb. del Piombo, Lotto* (Susannah and the Elders), *Paris Bordone, Romanino,* and other artists of the Venetian schools, a CORRIDOR (33) displays many small late-16C works.—ROOM 34. 1343. *Veronese,* St Agatha crowned; 1796. *Giulio Campi,* Portrait of a man; 1387. *Tintoretto,* Portrait of a man; 933. *Giov. Batt. Moroni,* 933. Portrait of a man with a book, 906. Count Pietro Secco Suardi (1563).

From the W. Corridor a door (B) gives access to the **Corridoio Vasariano** (adm. by appointment at the ticket office), recently reopened after restoration. It was built by Vasari in 1565, on the occasion of the marriage of Francesco de' Medici and Joanna of Austria, to connect the Uffizi with the Pitti Palace. The covered passage-way (which traverses the Ponte Vecchio) affords unique views of the city, and is hung with notable paintings including a celebrated collection of self-portraits. A series of rooms (with works by the Caravaggesque school, *Artemisia Gentileschi, Borgognone,* and *Ann. Carracci*) precede the entrance to the corridor proper. Here, displayed by regional Schools, are 17C works by *Guido Reni* (Susannah and the Elders), *Guercino* (Sleeping Endymion), *Dom. Feti, Domenichino, Marrata, Pietro da Cortona, Mattia Preti, Salvator Rosa, Carlo Dolci, Sassoferrato, Gius. Maria Crespi,* and *Sustermans.* There follow 18C paintings by *Vanitelli, Ricci, Tiepolo,* and others.—The collection of self-portraits begins, appropriately, with one by *Vasari.* Arranged chronologically they include works by *Agnolo, Taddeo,* and *Gaddo Gaddi, And. del Sarto, Bandinelli, Beccafumi, Bronzino, Pierino del Vaga, Santi di Tito, Cigoli,* etc. Beyond the centre of the Ponte Vecchio: *Salimbeni, Fed.* and *Taddeo Zuccheri, Bernini, Pietro da Cortona, Batoni, Luca Giordano, Salvator Rosa,* and *Gius. Maria Crespi.* On the Oltrarno the Corridor continues with 16-18C foreign self-portraits including *Pourbus, Rubens, Gerard Dou, Sustermans, Rembrandt, Van Dyck, Zoffany, Velasquez, Callot, Charles le Brun, Lely, Kneller, Hogarth, Romney,* and *Reynolds.* The corridor descends past a group of sketches to the collection of 19C self-portraits (*David, Delacroix, Corot, Ingres, Fattori, Millais, Benjamin Constant, Latour,* etc.). The corridor ends with a group of 17-18C portraits (mostly of royalty). Visitors are usually asked to leave the corridor by the Boboli Gardens (comp. p. 471).

ROOM 35. 969. *Iac Bassano,* Self-portrait; *Fed. Barocci,* Portrait of a lady, 798. Noli me tangere, 1438. Portrait of Fr. Maria II Della Rovere, 751. Madonna del Popolo; *Tintoretto,* 924. Portrait of a man with red hair, 921. Portrait of an Admiral, 914. St Augustine, 957. Portrait of Iac. Sansovino, 935. Portrait of an old man in a fur, 3085. Leda, 966. Portrait of a Gentleman; *El Greco,* SS. John the Evangelist and Francis; *Leandro Bassano,* Family concert.—Beyond the stairs down to the exit (C; comp. below), ROOM 41 contains some fine works by Rubens and Van Dyck. *Rubens,* The Risen Christ, 729. Henri IV entering Paris, 722. Henri IV at Ivry, two large pictures composing the first part of a cycle depicting the King's history, 792. Portrait of Philip IV of Spain, 779. *Portrait of Isabella Brandt. Van Dyck,* 726. Susterman's mother, 777. Margaret of Lorraine, 1439. Portrait of the Emperor Charles V, 1436. Portrait of John of Montfort. Also, 745. *Sustermans,* Portrait of Galileo Galilei; 3141. *Jacob Jordaens,* Portrait of an old lady.

The NIOBE ROOM (42) contains statues forming a group of Niobe and her Children, found in a vineyard near the Lateran in 1583, and transferred to Florence in 1775 from the Villa Medici in Rome. These are Roman copies of Greek originals of the school of Skopas (early 4C B.C.); many of the figures are wrongly restored and others do not belong to the group. The Medici Vase in the centre is a neo-Attic work acquired by Lorenzo de' Medici. The paintings include: 8419. *Piazzetta,* Susannah and the Elders; 3139. *G.B.Tiepolo,* Erection of an imperial statue; and works by *Fr. Guardi, Canaletto,* and *Aless. Longhi.*

ROOM 43. 1096. *Claude Lorraine,* Seascape; 1301. *Jan Steen,* Lunch-party; *Jacob Ruysdael,* two fine Landscapes, and other Dutch and Flemish works.— R. 44. Works by *Ann. Carracci* (including 799. Man with a monkey); 9283. *Mattia Preti,* Allegory of Vanity. *Rembrandt,* *3890. Self-portrait, *8435. Portrait of an old man, and *1871. Self-portrait as an old man. *Works by *Caravaggio* (5312. Young Bacchus, 1351. Medusa head, 4659. Sacrifice of Isaac).—R. 45 is used for exhibitions.

A door at the end of the Corridor (beyond a small Bar) gives on to the roof of the Loggia dei Lanzi (D), with a splendid view over the Piazza della Signoria.—A long flight of stairs (comp. above) lead down from the West Corridor to the exit. On the landing are two beautiful portraits of Maria Theresa by *Goya,* and the famous sculptured Boar, a copy of a Hellenistic original, and the model for the 'Porcellino' in the Mercato Nuovo.

II. EASTERN QUARTERS: MUSEO NAZIONALE
AND SANTA CROCE

From P.za della Signoria the short Via de' Gondi leads to the busy
PIAZZA SAN FIRENZE (Pl. 11) where seven streets converge and a
miscellany of buildings are assembled. The *Palazzo Gondi* (l.), by
Giuliano da Sangallo (1490-1501) faces the imposing Baroque façade of
San Firenze (1772-75), with the church of S. Filippo Neri and the Law
Courts. At the end of the piazza, the slender tower of the Badia (comp.
below) rises opposite the plain battlemented *Bargello (Pl. 11; *Palazzo
del Podestà*), begun in 1254, enlarged and altered many times, and
restored in 1857-65. The simple and severe tower at the left-hand angle is
earlier than 1254. The palace now contains the **Museo Nazionale**,
illustrative of all aspects of Italian art since the Middle Ages and
including the best existing collection of Tuscan sculpture (with notable
works by Donatello and Michelangelo). The entrance is at No. 4 Via del
Proconsolo (adm. 9-14 exc. Mon; fest. 9-13).

The museum came into being in 1859 when the collection of sculpture and
applied arts formerly in the Uffizi (comp. p. 426) was transferred here. In 1888 the
important Carrand Collection was left to the museum, and later acquisitions
included a large group of armour and a collection of fabrics.

GROUND FLOOR. To the right, the GREAT HALL has recently been
reopened. It contains works by Michelangelo and his School. To the left:
(in wall-case) *Rustici*, small sculpture of a Battle; *Andrea Sansovino*,
Madonna and Child (terracotta). In the centre, three superb works by
Michelangelo: *Bacchus drunk (a youthful work), *Tondo of the
Madonna and Child with the infant St John, a fine example of the
sculptor's scacciato technique, and *Bust of Brutus. *Rustici*, Madonna
and Child; Tondo with Madonna and Child and infant St John. Beyond
the door, *Jacopo Sansovino*, Bacchus; *Michelangelo*, *Apollo-David.
The statuettes, models, and replicas (in cases against the wall) by
followers of Michelangelo include works by *Pietro Francavilla, Tribolo,
Giambologna, Bart. Ammannati*, and *Vinc. Danti*. Beyond is a bust of
Cosimo I by Bandinelli.—In the second part of the hall: *De' Rossi*,
*Dying Adonis; *Bandinelli*, colossal statues of Adam and Eve;
Ammannati, Tomb statue of a warrior. Reliefs by *De' Rossi* are
displayed in wall-cases.—The group of *Works by *Cellini* include
Narcissus, Apollo and Hyacinth, a scale model for his statue of Perseus
(in the Loggia dei Lanzi, p. 426) and the relief (Perseus releasing
Andromeda) and bronze statuettes (Danae and Perseus, Mercury,
Minerva, and Jove) from the pedestal of this statue. *Vinc. Danti's* statue
representing Honour overcoming Deceit is exhibited near
Giambologna's Virtue repressing Vice. The bronze door of a cupboard
was made by *Vinc. Danti* for Cosimo I; his bust, by *Cellini* is nearby.
Beyond another bronze relief (Moses and the Serpent) by *Danti*, is a
bust of Michelangelo, by *Daniele da Volterra*.

A door leads out into the CORTILE, the finest part of the palace,
adorned with a large number of coats-of-arms of the former Podestà.
Under the colonnade, beginning on the left: *Vinc. Danti*, Cosimo I;
Niccolò di Pietro Lamberti, St Luke the Evangelist; *Tribolo*, Fiesole;
Ammannati, Six statues from a fountain intended for the Sala dei

Cinquecento (Pal. Vecchio); *Dom. Poggini*, Clio; *Giambologna*, Oceanus, from the Boboli gardens; *Vinc. Gemito*, Fisherboy (1877). Here, also, are displayed the *Cannon of St Paul, a wonderful piece of casting by *Cosimo Cenni* (1638), and a smaller cannon also by Cenni cast in 1620 (showing the planet Jove with its 4 satellites, discovered by Galileo in 1610).—Off the Cortile is the SALA DEL TRENCENTO containing sculptures from the old façade of the Duomo, fragments from the Badia, and statues by *Tino di Camaino, Arnolfo di Cambio, Simone Talenti,* and *Paolo di Giovanni.* The adjacent room is used for exhibitions.

The open stair-way in the courtyard mounts to the Loggia, called the VERONE. Here are displayed works by *Giambologna* including his frequently copied *Mercury, a female statue representing Architecture, and a life-like group of birds in bronze (Turkey, Eagle, etc.).

On the right the SALONE DEL CONSIGLIO GENERALE (1) provides a splendid setting for sculptural works by *Donatello* and his contemporaries. In the middle of the room is his Marzocco, the Florentine heraldic lion. On the end wall is the reconstructed niche from Orsanmichele (comp. p. 423) which contains *St George (1416), a magnificent rendering in marble of the saint as the young Champion of Christendom. The original *Bas-relief of St George and the Dragon is also to be placed here after restoration. Other works by *Donatello* include (r.): *Young St John, from the Casa Martelli; on the left, *David, in bronze (c. 1430); and (between the windows on the left) another *David, a charming early work (begun in 1408) in marble. Opposite: *Michelozzo* (attrib.), St John the Baptist; (in the centre of the room) *Desiderio da Settignano*, *Busts of a young woman and boy; *Donatello*, *Atys-Amorino (a mythological subject of uncertain significance); *Bonacolsi*, Cupid in bronze.—Around the walls (from the right of the entrance door): *Vecchietta*, St Bernard; *Luca della Robbia*, Lunette of the Madonna with Angels; *Donatello* (attrib.), Dancing Putto. The two trial *Reliefs of the Sacrifice of Isaac were executed by *Ghiberti* and *Brunelleschi* in competition for the second bronze doors of the Baptistery (comp. p. 420). In 1403 Ghiberti was given the commission, a decision reached by a narrow majority. The *Reliquary Urn (1428), beneath, is also by *Ghiberti.* There follow fine works by *Bertoldo:* statuette of Orpheus, and reliefs of a Roman battle scene, Pietà, Triumph of Bacchus, and the Crucifixion. The bust in coloured terracotta, traditionally thought to represent Niccolò da Uzzano, and the relief of the Crucifixion are attributed to the School of *Donatello;* the Bust of a Youth with a medallion at his neck, is instead, thought to be by the master's own hand. One of the fine Marriage-chests (early 15C), below, shows the procession of San Giovanni (with the Baptistery in the background). *Desiderio da Settignano*, Relief of Young St John, Madonna and Child; *Agostino di Duccio*, Madonna and Child with angels (relief); workshop of *Donatello,* Bearded head of a man, in bronze, and a marble relief of Madonna and Child; *Michelozzo,* a marble and terracotta relief of the Madonna and Child; *Luca della Robbia,* Madonna del Roseto, and Tondo of Madonna and Child; (below) the tomb statue of Mariano Sozzino by *Vecchietta.* On the short wall: *Luca della Robbia,* two reliefs of St Peter, Madonna and Child; *Michelozzo,* Young St John, from the Casa dell' Opera di S. Giovanni, Madonna and Child; *Luca della Robbia,* Madonna della Mela.

The SALA DELLA TORRE (II) contains seals and part of the LOUIS CARRAND COLLECTION, which is continued in the SALONE DEL PODESTA (III), and consists of tapestries, paintings, sculptures, ivories, etc., bequeathed by a wealthy Lyons art-collector (d. 1888). The collection includes also a large chimneypiece of 1478, arms and armour, Oriental tiles and textiles; statuettes, plaquettes, and other small bronzes, now in the Sala dei Bronzi (p. 437); Limoges enamels, including *Pastoral staves; processional crosses and jewellery; a bronze pax by *Moderno;* ivories from the Etruscan period onwards; an early Christian diptych; Byzantine ivories; a fragment of an Anglo-Saxon coffer (the rest is in the British Museum); jesters' staves (French 15C); the *Pastoral staff of St Ivo; Renaissance medals; and cameos from the Roman period onwards.

The walls of the CAPPELLA DEL PODESTA (IV) are covered with damaged frescoes, ascribed to *Giotto,* and somewhat arbitrarily restored in 1839-40. The triptych of the Madonna enthroned and Saints is attrib. to *Giov. Fr. da Rimini;* the embroidered altarcloth is the work of *Jac. Cambi* (15C; from S.M. Novella). The high lectern and stalls, by *Bern. della Cecca* (1493-98), were made for San Miniato. Display cases contain enamels and illuminated missals of the 14C and 15C.

From ROOM III is the entrance to the SALA DEGLI AVORI (VI). Here are crucifixes, Madonnas, and coffers one with polychrome reliefs. On the right: Case with Byzantine ivories; Norman ivory horn; Etruscan and Roman ivories; *Flabellum (French 9C). On the left: (1) Case with Spanish, Flemish, German, French, and Italian ivories.—(2) Case with Roman, Byzantine, Carolingian (9C), Anglo-Saxon, and Belgo-Rhenish reliefs.—(3) Medieval French and Italian Madonnas and crucifixes.—At the end, Burgundian chessboard with intarsia ornament and bas-reliefs.—The SALA DELLE OREFICERIE (VII) contains ecclesiastical ornaments in precious metals, etc. (chalices, processional crosses, predella of the old silver altar frontal from the Baptistery, silver bust of St Ignatius, pastoral staves).—The SALA DELLE MAIOLICHE (VIII) has a collection of majolica plates, vases, and bowls.

SECOND FLOOR, reached viâ the Sala degli Avori (see above). ROOM I. Round the walls are a number of unclassified enamelled terracottas by the *Della Robbia.* The earliest examples are by *Luca,* those of the following period by *Andrea* and *Giovanni.* In the centre of the room are cases of small bronzes by *Tribolo, Bandinelli, l'Antico, Briosco, Giambologna,* and others. Against the walls (r.): *Bernini,* *Bust of Costanza Bonarelli; *Cellini,* Ganymede, an antique statue adapted and restored; *Bernini,* Model in terracotta for a fountain in Pistoia; *Rustici,* large relief in white terracotta (Noli me tangere; in restoration); workshop of *Dom. Gagini* (the Sicilian sculptor), statue of the Madonna and Child; *Sansovino,* relief of the Madonna and Child (in papier mâché).—ROOM II. *Andrea della Robbia,* Boy's head, Madonna and Child, Portrait of an unknown woman, and another Madonna. In the centre, models in bronze for the Mercury and the Rape of the Sabines, by *Giambologna.*—On the left is the SALA DEL VERROCCHIO (III). On the right here are works by *Mino da Fiesole:* *Giov. di Cosimo de' Medici, two Madonnas, *Rinaldo della Luna, Piero il Gottoso, and a Tabernacle; *Tom. Fiamberti,* Madonna. In the middle of the room, *Ant. del Pollaiuolo,* *Hercules and Antaeus, an exquisite small work. *Bened. da Maiano,* a large high relief of the Coronation of Ferdinand of Aragon (with six musicians, recently acquired by the Museum); *Gian. Crist. Romano,* relief of Fed. da Montefeltro. In the centre: *Verrocchio,* *David. Works by *Rossellino,* on the end wall, include two reliefs of the Madonna and Child. The bust of *Pietro Mellini is by *Bened. da Maiano;* that of Battista Sforza by *Fr. Laurana;* and of Matteo Palmieri, by *Rossellino. Ant. del Pollaiuolo,* *Young Warrior, *Portrait of an unknown man; *Verrocchio,* bas-relief of the Madonna and Child, Bust of Piero di Lorenzo de' Medici, Resurrection, *Bust of a lady (with beautiful hands), Death of Fr. Tornabuoni-Pitti, a tomb-relief; *Matt. Civitali,* Faith, Portrait of a young lady.

From Room II there is access to the SALONE DEL CAMINO (VI) with a superb display of Renaissance *Bronzes, the most important collection in Italy. The statuettes, animals, plaquettes, candelabrum, etc. are the work of *Tacca, Tribolo, Bandinelli, L'Antico, Briosco, Caradosso, Giambologna, Leone Leoni,* and others. On the right of the door, *Iac. Sansovino,* Christ in glory; to the l., in front of the window, *Lod. Cigoli,* Anatomical figure. At the end, splendid *Chimneypiece by *Benedetto da Rovezzano.*—From Room I a door leads in to the SALA DELLE ARMI (VII) with a magnificent display of *Arms and armour from the Medici collections (well labelled) with saddles decorated with gold, silver, and ivory, a shield by Gaspare Mola (17C), and numerous sporting guns, dress armour, oriental arms, etc. Also, Bust in marble of Giovanni delle Bande Neri, by *Fr. da Sangallo,* and bronze bust of Ferdinando I, by *Pietro Tacca.*—The MEDAGLIERE MEDICEO has been closed to the public (adm. only with special permission). This huge collection of Italian medals was started by Lorenzo de' Medici. Among the most notable are those designed by *Pisanello.*

On the other side of the Via del Proconsolo is the **Badia Fiorentina** (Pl. 7), the church of a Benedictine abbey, founded in 978. It was enlarged in 1285 and the interior was almost entirely rebuilt by *Matt. Segaloni* in 1627.

The exterior of the Gothic apse, by *Arnolfo di Cambio,* is all that remains of the 13C church. The main portal (1495), with a Madonna in terracotta, by *Bened. Buglioni,* and the vestibule with a Corinthian portico are by *Bened. da Rovezzano.* From the other end of the portico there is a good view of the graceful campanile, Romanesque below (1310) and Gothic (1330) above.

The INTERIOR has a fine Baroque ceiling. To the right: tomb of Giannozzo Pandolfini, from the workshop of *Rossellino;* and a sculpted altarpiece of the Madonna and Saints (1464-69) by *Mino da Fiesole.* In the right transept, Tomb of Bernardo Giugni (d. 1460), also by *Mino.* In the left transept, *Tomb of Ugo (d. 1001), Margave of Tuscany and son of the foundress of the church, an exquisite work by *Mino* (1469-81). Above is a good painting by *Vasari* of the Assumption. Left of the entrance, *Madonna appearing to St Bernard, a large panel of great charm, by *Filippino Lippi* (c. 1485).

From the right side of the choir, which has early 16C stalls, a door gives access to the *Chiostro degli Aranci,* by Bern. Rossellino (c. 1434-36). The frescoes were detached and removed to the store-rooms of the Uffizi in 1973.

From the end of the entrance-portico steps lead down into Via Dante Alighieri which traverses an area traditionally associated with the Florentine poet (see plaque). At the end on the left rises the stark *Torre della Castagna* (1282); opposite is the little chapel of *San Martino del Vescovo* (open 10-12, 15-17, Sat 15-16; closed Sun & fest.), rebuilt in 1479. It contains charming 15C frescoes from the workshop of Ghirlandaio, of great interest for their portrayal of contemporary Florentine life. Here, too, are two notable paintings of the Madonna, one Byzantine, the other attrib. to Perugino. Across the street among a picturesque group of houses (restored) is the *Casa di Dante* (adm. 10-13, 15-18 exc. Wed; fest. 10-13), where the poet is said to have been born. It contains a collection of material (little of it original) relating to the poet.

On the other side of the Via del Proconsolo (see above) is *Palazzo Pazzi* (No. 10), attributed to Giul. da Maiano (1458; recently restored). The Pazzi coat-of-arms (removed from the exterior) is displayed in the vestibule which leads to a fine courtyard. Across Borgo degli Albizi rises

Palazzo Nonfinito, left unfinished by Buontalenti, Caccini, Scamozzi, and Cigoli. It is now the seat of the NATIONAL MUSEUM OF ANTHROPOLOGY AND ETHNOLOGY.

The BORGO DEGLI ALBIZI (Pl. 7) is one of the finest old streets in the city. Among the notable buildings are: another *Palazzo Pazzi* (No. 26, built by Ammannati in 1568); the *Palazzo Altoviti* (No. 18), called 'dei Visacci' from the carved figures of celebrated citizens; the *Palazzo Albizi* (No. 12; c. 1500); and the *Palazzo Alessandri* (No. 15; 14C, altered in the 18C). At the end is the quaint old P.za di San Pier Maggiore, with a 17C archway which is all that remains of the demolished church of that name. To the right Via Palmieri traverses several streets before reaching the dark little church of *San Simone* (12C) in which is a charming Gothic tabernacle (1363; l. of the high altar) with coloured terracotta decoration.

The curved layout of the Via Torta and the Via Bentaccordi, farther on, preserves the outline of the Roman amphitheatre. The corner house in the latter street, on the right was a youthful home of Michelangelo.

Any one of the streets on the left ends in the large PIAZZA SANTA CROCE (Pl. 11) with some fine old buildings. The *Palazzo Serristori* (No. 1) is perhaps by Baccio d'Agnolo; Giulio Parigi built the *Palazzo dell'Antella* (No. 21) in 1619 when the polychrome decoration was carried out in three weeks by Giov. di San Giovanni and his assistants. The monument to Dante was erected by Enrico Pazzi (1865).

The church of *Santa Croce (Pl. 11; closed 12.30-15), rebuilt in c. 1294 possibly by Arnolfo di Cambio, is the largest and most beautiful of the Franciscan churches. The white façade (covered for restoration for several years), with its inlay of dark marble, is by Nic. Matas (1853-63) from a design supposed to be by Cronaca; its cost was defrayed by an English benefactor, Francis Sloan (d. 1871). On the left is a picturesque 14C arcade.

The wide cruciform INTERIOR, 115½ metres long, with an open timber ceiling, is simple and impressive. In the pavement are many fine tomb-slabs. For five hundred years it has been the custom to bury or to erect monuments to notable citizens in this church; it is the burial place of Michelangelo, Macchiavelli, and Galileo. The interior was rearranged by *Vasari* in 1560 when the choir was demolished, some frescoes destroyed, and the side-altars added.

WEST WALL. In the round window the stained-glass Deposition was composed from a cartoon attrib. to Giov. del Ponte. Monuments here commemorate the 19C patriots Gino Capponi and G. B. Niccolini.

SOUTH AISLE, 1st pillar: *Madonna del Latte', a charming tomb-relief by *Ant. Rossellino* (1478); in front, *Tomb of Michelangelo (d. 1564), by *Vasari* (1570); beyond the 2nd altar, Cenotaph of Dante, by *Stef. Ricci* (1829); beyond the 3rd altar, Monument to Vittorio Alfieri (d. 1803), the tragic poet, by *Ant. Canova* (1810), erected at the charges of the Countess of Albany. In the pillar opposite, a small inlaid door gives access to the stair-way of the exquisite *Pulpit by *Bened. da Maiano* (1472-76), decorated with scenes from the life of St Francis, and four Virtues. Beyond the 4th altar, Monument to Nic. Machiavelli (d. 1527), by *Inn. Spinazzi* (1787); and beyond the 5th altar, large Renaissance *Tabernacle with an extremely fine relief of the

Annunciation, by *Donatello* (1428-33). Near the door, the *Tomb of Leonardo Bruni (d. 1444), the humanist, by *Bern. Rossellino* is one of the most harmonious examples of Florentine sepulchral art of the 15C. There follow the tombs of Gioacchino Rossini (d. 1868), the composer, and Ugo Foscolo (with a statue by *Ant. Berti*, 1936).

On the right of the SOUTH TRANSEPT the *CASTELLANI CHAPEL contains important frescoes by *Agnolo Gaddi* and assistants (among them probably Gherardo Starnina) of the late 14C. They depict (r.) the histories of St Nicholas and St John the Baptist and (l.) St Anthony Abbot and St John the Evangelist. On each wall is a terracotta statue of a saint by the Della Robbia. On the altar wall is a Crucifix of painted wood, by *Niccolò di Pietro Gerini*. Among the monuments is one to the Countess of Albany (d. 1824).—At the end of the transept is the BARONCELLI CHAPEL (now Giugni): on either side of the entrance arch, Prophets by *Taddeo Gaddi;* to the right, below, *Tomb of a member of the Baroncelli family (1327) with a Madonna and Child also by *Gaddi*. On the back wall (r.), Madonna of the Girdle, a large fresco by *Bastiano Mainardi,* and a statue of the Madonna and Child, by *Vinc. Danti*. The fine series of *Frescoes here, by *Taddeo Gaddi,* of the Life of the Virgin, include (to the left) one of the earliest known night scenes in fresco painting. The altarpiece of the Coronation of the Virgin (recently restored) is by *Giotto* and his workshop.

Next is a portal by *Michelozzo,* with an inlaid door, attributed to *Giov. di Michele,* leading into a corridor, also by *Michelozzo*. Another inlaid door, on the left, gives access to the *SACRISTY. Here are frescoes by 14C Florentines (including a Crucifixion by *Gaddi*), particularly fine inlaid cabinets (recently restored after serious flood damage) containing antiphonals, and a bust of Christ, by *Giov. della Robbia*. Its apse, the RINUCCINI CHAPEL, is closed by a Gothic grille (1371) and entirely covered with *Frescoes by *Giov. da Milano*, representing scenes from the lives of the Virgin and St Mary Magdalene (c. 1366; being restored). Over the altar is a polyptych by *Giov. del Biondo*.—Outside in the corridor, Deposition by *Aless. Allori,* and a monument to Lor. Bartolini (d. 1850), the sculptor. At the end is the MEDICI CHAPEL, also by *Michelozzo* (1434) with a door by *Giov. di Michele*. Within is a Madonna and Child with Saints, by *Paolo Schiavo,* and St John the Baptist, by *Spinello Aretino*. The terracotta *Altarpiece of the Madonna and Child, with angels and saints, is by *Andrea della Robbia* (c. 1480).—Remains of an old courtyard can be seen from a nearby room.

The CHAPELS AT THE EAST END are notable for their frescoes by Giotto and his school. The 1st chapel on the right is the VELLUTI CHAPEL (being restored), with fragmentary frescoes by a follower of Cimabue; the 3rd is the BONAPARTE CHAPEL (tomb of Charlotte Bonaparte, d. 1839, by *Lor. Bartolini*).—4th PERUZZI CHAPEL, with *Frescoes by *Giotto,* probably later than 1320 (repainted in 1841-63, but cleaned and restored in 1959). In the archivolt, eight heads of Prophets; in the vaulting, symbols of the Evangelists; on the r. wall, Scenes from the Life of St John the Evangelist (Vision at Patmos, Raising of Drusiana, Ascent into Heaven); on the l. wall, Scenes from the Life of St John the Baptist (Zacharias and the Angel, Birth of St John, Herod's Feast); on the end wall were four Saints.—5th, BARDI CHAPEL. Over the altar, St Francis and scenes from his life by a Florentine artist of 13C. The walls are entirely covered with *Frescoes by *Giotto* (after 1317; repainting removed), representing the history of St Francis. On the entrance arch, the saint receiving the stigmata; in the vault, Poverty, Chastity, Obedience, and the Triumph of St Francis; on the end wall, Franciscan saints; on the side walls the saint is seen (l.) stripping off his garments, appearing to St Anthony at Arles, dying; (r.) giving the Rule of the Order, being tried by fire, and, finally, appearing to Brother Augustine and Bishop Guido of Assisi.—6th Chapel (SANCTUARY). Over the altar, a large 14C polyptych, the Madonna and saints, by *Nic. Gerini*, and four Fathers of the Church, by *Giov. del Biondo* (1368); above is a fine Crucifix by the 'Master of Figline'. The frescoes by *Agnolo Gaddi* (c. 1380) depict (in the vault) Christ, the Evangelists, and St Francis, and (on the walls) the Legend of the Cross.—7th, TOSINGHI AND SPINELLI CHAPEL (now Sloan Chapel). On the exterior wall, Assumption of the Virgin, a repainted fresco of the 14C. On the altar, Polyptych by *Giov. del. Biondo* (1372). In the 8th chapel is a Pietà by *Libero Andreotti* (1926).—10th, BARDI DI LIBERTÀ CHAPEL. Altarpiece by *Giov. della Robbia*, and frescoes of the lives of St Lawrence and St Stephen, by *Bern. Daddi.*—11th, BARDI DI VERNIO CHAPEL. Frescoes of the *Life of St Sylvester, by *Maso di Banco* (after 1367), and a fresco (in 2nd niche) of the Deposition after *Taddeo Gaddi*. The altarpiece, by *Giov. del Biondo*, has been removed for restoration.

NORTH TRANSEPT. The central chapel here, another Bardi Chapel, contains the celebrated wooden *Crucifix, by *Donatello* (c. 1412). The story, told by Vasari, of Brunelleschi's complaint that it was a mere 'peasant on the cross' is now thought to be apocryphal. On the right is the Baroque Niccolini Chapel with polychrome marble decoration; on the left the Salviati Chapel, with *Lor. Bartolini's* Tomb of Princess Sofia Czartoryska (d. 1837).—At the corner of the transept and N. aisle, monument to the composer Luigi Cherubini (d. 1842; born at No. 22 Via Fiesolana, not far N. of the church). Just within the aisle, monument to Raffaello Morghen (d. 1833), the engraver.

Against the first pillar of the nave, monument to Leon Battista Alberti (d. 1472), an unfinished group by *Lor. Bartolini* (c. 1849). NORTH AISLE. *Monument to Carlo Marsuppini (d. 1453), by *Desiderio da Settignano,* inspired by the Bruni monument opposite; the tomb-slab of his father, Greg. Marsuppini, in the pavement, is also by *Desiderio;* monument to Vitt. Fossombroni (d. 1844) by *Bartolini;* monument to Donatello. In the pavement between the 4th and 5th altar is the tomb-slab of Lor. and Vitt. Ghiberti, and against the wall, between the 1st and 2nd altar, the tomb of Galileo Galilei (d. 1642), by *G. B. Foggini.*

On the right of the church is the entrance to the conventual buildings and the **Museo dell'Opera di Santa Croce** (open ev. day 9-12, 15-18; winter 9-12, 18-17; Sun 9-12). The attractive FIRST CLOISTER is a 14C work. The graceful Campanile, in the 14C style, is by *Baccani* (1865). On the right are a portico and loggia of the late 14C and at the end the *Cappella dei Pazzi by *Brunelleschi* (1443-46), one of the most beautiful and original works of the Renaissance period; in the frieze are small medallions with cherubs, by *Donatello* and *Desiderio*. The colonnade has a barrel vault and a shallow cupola with terracotta decoration by *Luca della Robbia*, by whom is also the St Andrew over the doorway; the door, of wood, is by the brothers *Da Maiano*. The INTERIOR has medallions of Apostles and Evangelists by *Luca della Robbia* and his school, and, in the small apse, decorations of the school of Donatello and a stained-glass window attributed to *Alessio Baldovinetti.*—Beyond a doorway by *Michelozzo,* is the *SECOND CLOISTER, by *Brunelleschi,* finished after his death in 1453 and recently well restored. Off the first cloister is the entrance to the REFECTORY. On the end wall, huge fresco (detached for restoration and now returned to its original position) by *Taddeo Gaddi*, with the Tree of the Cross and Last Supper. On the two long walls (below roundels with Saints) are detached fragments of the fresco by *Orcagna* of the Triumph of Death which used to decorate the church. On the entrance wall, Christ carrying the Cross and Crucifixion, two fine detached frescoes of the early 15C. *Cimabue's* famous Crucifix, which was almost completely destroyed in the flood of 1966 (the greatest single loss of a work of art) has been returned here after being partially restored. In a niche, *St Ludovic of Toulouse, a colossal gilded bronze statue by *Donatello* from Orsanmichele (the tabernacle is a cast).

To the left is the first of a series of rooms recently reopened containing detached frescoes and sculptures restored after flood damage. ROOM I. Stained glass fragments (14-15C) from the church; detached frescoes of the 15C of the Madonna and Child, one showing the young Madonna sewing, and one thought to be an early work by Paolo Uccello.—ROOM II, formerly a chapel (traces of late 13C decoration on the walls) has Della Robbian works. Two little passages lead into the first room overlooking the Second Cloister; the passage on the right has a fine detached fresco of a Cardinal.—ROOM III. Interesting sinopie (found during restoration work in the Cappella de' Pazzi) and fresco fragments.—ROOM IV. Sculptural fragments, including the reconstructed tomb of Gastone della Torre, by *Tino da Camaino*.—ROOM V. 17C works.—Other important works belonging to the museum are to be returned here after restoration.—In the colonnade, just before the exit from the cloister, is a memorial to Florence Nightingale.

To the right again is the **Biblioteca Nazionale** (Pl. 11; adm. 9-19; Sat 9-13), erected in 1911-35 to the plans of *Cesare Bazzani*. The National Library was formed from the collection bequeathed by Ant. Magliabechi (d. 1714), and opened in 1747 on the first floor of the Pal. della Dogana where it remained till removed in 1935 to its present home (founded 1911). To the original collection were joined the Biblioteca Palatina-Medicea (1771) and the library ('Palatina II') formed by Ferdinand III (1861), together with several monastic collections. It became a copyright library for books published in Florence in 1869. In 1966 it was extensively flooded to a height of 4½m above street level, when a third of the library's holding was damaged. Nearly 100 experts are still working full-time on the restoration of the books, a task which is expected to continue until the end of this century.

On the left side of Santa Croce is Via San Giuseppe, where, in the house next to the church, the Trollope family lived in 1843-45. Via delle Pinzóchere leads to the **Casa Buonarroti** (Pl. 11; adm. 10-16, fest. 9-13; closed Tues) a house in Via Ghibellina (No. 70) bought in 1508 by Michelangelo. It was later transformed (following plans drawn up by the master) by his only descendent, his nephew Leonardo. His son, Michelangelo, in turn made part of the house into a gallery in 1612. It is now a museum.

GROUND FLOOR (left of Vestibule). Sculptures by *Michelangelo;* Venus and two cupids, an early work, and an unfinished statue of a slave, probably for the tomb of Julius II. The other rooms on this floor contain part of the collection formed by Michelangelo Buonarotti the Younger at the beginning of the 17C. It includes antiques (two funerary stelæ from Fiesole); minerals; sculpture and majolica. The paintings include: Portraits of the Buonarotti family by *Aless. Allori; Guido Reni*(attrib.), Head of an old man; *Giov. di Francesco*, Predella with the story of St Nicholas of Bari; amorous scene attrib. to the youth of *Titian*. In the last room, among various portraits of Michelangelo, sculptured head by *Daniele da Volterra*.

FIRST FLOOR. Works by *Michelangelo*. *Madonna of the Steps, a marble bas-relief, his earliest work carved at the age of fifteen or sixteen; *Battle of the Centaurs and Lapiths, also a bas-relief; wax models; bas relief in stucco of the Crucifixion, and a wood model (the only one to survive) for a Crucifix (1562).—Architectural drawings (facsimiles of the originals owned by the museum) and a wood model for the façade of San Lorenzo.—Wooden *Crucifix from Santo Spirito first attrib. to Michelangelo in 1962, and figure drawings.—Colossal torso, also by the master, the model for a river god. Also, works derived from Michelangelo.

To the right Via Ghibellina continues across Borgo Allegri, where (at No. 83, and No. 96) Cimabue and Ghiberti lived. The Via dei Macci (l.)

leads N. to **Sant'Ambrogio** (Pl. 8), rebuilt in the late 13C (with a 19C façade).

INTERIOR. Several works of art have been removed after severe flood damage. The chapel on the left of the high altar (Cappella del Miracolo) contains a magnificent *Tabernacle by *Mino da Fiesole* (1481). In the pavement an inscription relates to Mino's burial (1488); Verrocchio's is recorded on a slab between the 3rd and 4th altars on the N. side. In the middle of this wall, a wooden figure of St Sebastian by *Leon. del Tasso* stands in a graceful niche, and, above the 4th arch, is an Annunciation after *Filippino Lippi*.

Borgo La Croce leads E. to P.za Beccaria and Via Gioberti continues towards (2 km.; bus 34 from the station) the Vallombrosan abbey of **San Salvi,** with a 14-16C church. In the refectory (entrance at No. 16 Via San Salvi) is the celebrated *Last Supper, by *Andrea del Sarto* (1519), a masterpiece of Florentine fresco, remarkable for its colouring (being restored after flood damage).

In Via Pietrapiana (l.) is the *Loggia del Pesce,* reconstructed in 1956 on this site from fragments of Vasari's original of 1568. Via Verdi leads back to P.za Santa Croce. Via de' Benci, with its old rusticated houses, continues towards the river. An archway on the right admits to P.za dei Peruzzi with 14C houses and towers. Farther on at the corner (l.) of the Borgo Santa Croce is another old tower-house, with the remains of the *Loggia degli Alberti* at its foot.

Among the ancient houses in the Borgo are: No. 6, the *Palazzo Serristori,* which has an elegant courtyard; No. 8, the *Casa Morra,* which belonged to Vasari and contains frescoes by him; No. 10, the *Palazzo Rasponi,* in the 15C style.
Via de' Neri, with its old houses, leads back from Via de' Benci to the Palazzo Vecchio. On the right, in Via di San Remigio, is the church of *San Remigio* (Pl. 11), with a 13C façade; on the left, at the corner of the Via Castellani, is the *Loggia del Grano,* a good Renaissance building by Giulio Parigi and his son Alfonso (1619), now occupied by a cinema.

At No. 6 Via de' Benci (l.) a palazzo (late 15C), formerly attrib. to Giul. da Sangallo, but now thought to be the work of Cronaca, houses the *Museo Horne** (ring for adm. Mon 9-14, Wed & Fri 16-18; visitors are conducted). The fine collection of paintings and the applied arts (notable furniture and majolica) was presented to the nation, along with the mansion, by the English art historian, Herbert Percy Horne (1864-1916). Many of the contents have been restored after damage in the 1966 flood. The important collection of drawings (Italian and English schools) is now housed in the Uffizi (comp. p. 427).

The courtyard has interesting capitals. In the ground floor rooms a Madonna and two angels by *Neri di Bicci* illustrates the extent to which a painting can be ruined by water. Also here, a stone bas-relief of the Madonna and Child, by *Jacopo Sansovino.*—FIRST FLOOR. Room I. *Dosso Dossi,* Allegory of Music; *Masaccio* (attrib.), Story of St Julian (much ruined); *Pietro Lorenzetti,* St Benedict, St Catherine of Alexandria, and St Margaret (fragment of a polyptych); *Benozzo Gozzoli,* Deposition, a crowded composition left unfinished at the death of the painter (the colours have darkened with time); *Simone Martini* (attrib.), Portable diptych of the Madonna and Child and Pietà. The small sculptures include works by *Bernini, Rustici,* and *Giambologna.*—Room II. *Bartolomeo della Gatta,* St Roch; *Domenico Beccafumi,* Mythological scene, Drunkenness of Noah; *Giotto,* *St Stephen (part of a polyptych); *Filippino Lippi,* the side of a marriage-chest with the Story of Esther, Crucifix (a late work, much faded).—Room III. *Bernardo Daddi,* Madonna and Child, Crucifixion (formerly a diptych); *Vecchietta,* wooden statue of St Paul; *Beccafumi,* Tondo of the Holy Family (with a contemporary frame); *Desiderio da Settignano,* Head of Young St John in relief (replica of a work in Museo Nazionale, p. 435).—SECOND FLOOR. Room I. *Ercole Roberti* (attrib.), St Sebastian; *Filippo Lippi,* Pietà (a pax); *School of Giotto,*

Madonna and Saints; *Ant. Rossellino,* bas-relief of the Madonna and Child; *School of Sodoma,* Scene from the Battle of Anghiari (of historical interest as a contemporary copy of Leonardo's fresco in the Palazzo Vecchio); *'Master of the Horne Triptych'* (14C Florentine), Triptych of Madonna and Saints; *School of Lor. Monaco,* Portable Crucifix; *Giov. dal Ponte,* St Francis and two nuns.— Room II. *Neri di Bicci,* Archangel Raphael, Tobias, and St Jerome.

Opposite the Museo Horne are the *Palazzo Bardi* (No. 3; 15C) and (No. 1) the *Palazzo Alberti,* typical of the best traditions of Renaissance simplicity, once the home of L. B. Alberti. The old PONTE ALLE GRAZIE (Pl. 11), destroyed in 1944, has been replaced by a bridge of modern design. From here Lungarno Gen. Diaz returns towards the centre, passing P.za Mentana (monument to those who fell at Mentana in 1867) and the **Palazzo Castellani* (Pl. 11), a typical nobleman's dwelling of the Middle Ages. In the palace (entered from No. 1 P.za dei Giudici) is the **Museo di Storia della Scienza** (adm. 10-13, 14-16, closed fest.). A large part of the collection was owned by the Medici. Many of the works have been restored after severe flood damage. The collection is well labelled.

GROUND FLOOR. Alchemist's studio; early bicycles; human weighing machines; water clock, etc.—FIRST FLOOR. Room I (mathematics). Various instruments, many constructed by Crist. Schissler (early 17C); Day and Night clocks; compasses, etc. which belonged to Vinc. Viviani, disciple of Galileo. In an adjacent room are quadrants (one of which belonged to Sir Robert Dudley) and sextants, many invented by Sir Robert, who was made Director of the Arsenal of Livorno by Ferdinand I.—ROOM II. Calculators of the 17C-19C; a compass used by Michelangelo; and an Arab globe of 1085.—R. III. Sun dials, and a fine collection of globes.—R. IV. Huge tolomaic sphere built by Ant. Santucci in 1588; barometers, astrolabes, etc.—R. V. The telescope through which Galileo discovered Jove and other instruments he used, and first editions of his works. An amusing set of thermometers, one used by Ferdinand II de' Medici to hatch eggs and to boil them.—R. VI. Large telescopes, one of which belonged to Torricelli, and microscopes.—RR. VII-VIII. Instruments used in optical experiments.— R. IX. Mechanical instruments made in the 18C by order of the Grand Duke Pietro Leopoldo I.

SECOND FLOOR (recently opened). ROOM I. 16C and 17C scientific instruments and the books that describe their manufacture or use; gnomons and astrolabes.— ROOM 2. Large burning lens made by Bened. Bregans of Dresden and given by him to Grand Duke Cosimo III (later used by Davy and Faraday to experiment with high temperature chemicals).—R. 3. Instruments concerning fluids and gases (fountains, pumps, pneumatic machines).—R. 4. Electrostatic machines. In a niche on the N. wall, large lodestone (of natural magnetic rock) given by Galileo to Ferdinand II de' Medici.—In the next two rooms, anatomical models by Gius. Ferrini in wax, for use in obstetrics, and, in the last room, the surgical instruments of Aless. Brambilla (1728-1800).—In the corridor, one of the first cylinder phonographs built in 1890 by Edison; acoustic horn designed by Vinc. Viviani; and the speaking trumpet of Grand Duke Ferdinand II.

III.   NORTHERN QUARTERS: ANNUNZIATA, SAN MARCO, SAN LORENZO

Via Ricásoli (Pl. 7), running N.E. from the Duomo, crosses Via de' Pucci, at the corner of which (l.) is the *Tabernacolo delle Cinque Lampade,* or Tabernacle of the Five Lamps, with a fresco (r.) by Cosimo Rosselli. Via de' Pucci leads to the right past the Palazzi Pucci (façade attrib. to Ammannati) to Via de' Servi. Here the church of *San Michelino* or *San Michele Visdomini* has a fine series of 16C altarpieces, including a Holy Family and Saints (1518) by Pontormo (2nd altar on r.). During restoration work frescoes by Mariotto di Nardo have come to light. Farther N. in Via de' Servi is the *Palazzo Niccolini* by Dom. di Baccio d'Agnolo (1550).

On the left side of Via Bufalini, the continuation of Via de' Pucci, is the **Hospital of Santa Maria Nuova** (Pl. 7), founded in 1288 by Folco Portinari, believed to be the father of Dante's Beatrice. The portico in front (1574-1612) is by *Bern. Buontalenti*. In the centre is the church of SANT'EGIDIO (c. 1420), with a cast of a terracotta by Dello Delli (1424) in the lunette above (original, see below). Within, immediately on the right, are the remains of the Portinari tomb. The marble tabernacle to the left of the high altar is by *Bern. Rossellino* (1450). A door to the r. of the church leads into a cloister, the oldest part of the hospital, with a Pietà by *Giov. della Robbia*. To the left of the church, in another old courtyard of the hospital, is the tomb slab of Monna Tessa, the servant of Portinari who induced him to found the hospital, and a fresco of Charity by *Giovanni da San Giovanni*. In the offices of the Presidenza, above (adm. only by special request) are the original terracotta lunette by *Dello Delli* (comp. above), a fresco of the Crucifixion, an early work by *And. del Castagno*, and a Madonna and Child by *And. della Robbia* (formerly in Sant'Egidio). The Salone di Martino V (sometimes shown on request) contains detached frescoes (formerly flanking the church doorway) of Martin V consecrating the church, by *Bicci di Lorenzo* (with its sinopia), and the same pope confirming its privileges, by *And. di Giusto* (repainted). Also a detached fresco of the Resurrection (damaged), recently discovered, attrib. to *Pietro Gerini*.

Via Portinari, opposite S. Maria Nuova, leads to Via dell'Oriuolo in which (l.; No. 24) is the entrance to the MUSEO DI FIRENZE COM'ERA (adm. 9-16, Sun 9-12; closed Thurs). Here in several rooms of the pretty old Convento delle Oblate is a collection of maps, paintings, and prints illustrating the life of the city since the 15C. Of particular interest are the prospect of the city, a 19C copy of the 'Catena' plan of 1470, and the topographical plans drawn by *Stefano Bonsignori* in 1584, and by *Giovanni Jacopo De' Rossi* in 1660. In the large hall are 17C and 18C prints including a fine series by *Giuseppe Zocchi*. Among the small views of the city are a group by *Telemaco Signorini*. The charming lunettes of the Medici villas are by *Giusto Utens* (1599). A large collection of lithographs (1863) by *Durand*, and the plans of *Gius. Poggi*, architect when Florence was the capital of Italy, complete the collection.—In Via della Pergola, on the E. side of the hospital, is the house (No. 59) where Cellini died. The *Teatro della Pergola*, on the site of a wooden theatre erected in 1656 by Ferdinando Tacca, dates in its present form from the 19C. Here plays and chamber music concerts are performed (comp. p. 414).—At No. 1 Via Bufalini a tablet marks the site of Ghiberti's workshop, where the Baptistery doors were cast; while Bened. da Maiano had his studio (1480-98) at the beginning of Via del Castellaccio.

Via de' Servi continues N. to cross Via degli Alfani. Here to the right, at the corner of Via del Castellaccio, is an octagonal building (called 'il Castellaccio' from its fortress-like air, or, officially, *Rotonda di Santa Maria degli Angeli*), begun by Brunelleschi after 1433 as a memorial to the soldier Fil. degli Scolari (d. 1424) and, after a period of use as a church, completed in 1959 as a lecture-hall. Behind are the buildings of the Faculty of Letters and Philosophy of the University. In the other direction (No. 78 Via Alfani) is the *Opificio delle Pietre Dure* founded in 1588. The craft of working semi-precious stones is still carried out here, and a Museum (open 9-13, exc. Sun & fest.) exhibits some masterpieces of inlay and mosaic, and the craftsmens' tools and materials. Via de' Servi ends in *PIAZZA DELLA SANTISSIMA ANNUNZIATA (Pl. 7), the most beautiful square in Florence, surrounded on three sides by porticoes.

On the right is the Spedale degli Innocenti; in front is the church of the Annunziata and the convent of the Servi di Maria, with five Gothic windows; to the left, the colonnade (modelled on the earlier one opposite) of the Confraternity of the Servants of Mary, by Antonio da Sangallo and Baccio d'Agnolo (1516-25); at the corner of Via de' Servi, the *Palazzo Riccardi-Mannelli*, formerly *Grifoni*, by Ammannati (1557-63). In the middle of the square are an equestrian statue of the Grand Duke Ferdinand I, by Giambologna (his last work, cast by P. Tacca in 1608), and two bronze fountains by Tacca and his pupils (1629).

The **Spedale degli Innocenti** (Pl. 7) established in 1421 as a foundling hospital, the first institution of the kind in Europe, is still operating as an orphanage. The children play in the delightful gardens which can be seen through the courtyard. The *Colonnade, by *Brunelleschi* (1419-26) is one of the first masterpieces of Renaissance architecture. In the spandrels between the arches are delightful *Medallions by *And. della Robbia* (c. 1487), each with a baby in swaddling-clothes against a bright blue ground (the end ones on each side are modern). The frescoes under the colonnades are by *Poccetti* (c. 1605), except that above the door of the church which is by *Giov. di Francesco* (1459). The church (open mornings only) contains an altarpiece by *Mariotto Albertinelli* and *Giov. Ant. Sogliani*. The convent buildings are being restored to their original design by Brunelleschi. The *FIRST CLOISTER, already restored, has a charming lunette of the *Annunciation by *And. della Robbia*. The oblong CHIOSTRO DELLE DONNE, to the right, is another beautiful work by Brunelleschi. From the left corner of the first cloister stairs mount to the PICTURE GALLERY (open 9.30-13, 14-17; fest. 9-13; closed Mon).

An interesting collection of detached frescoes are arranged in the rooms above the cloister: in a small room to the right, 14-15C Florentine frescoes, two sinopie by *Bicci di Lorenzo*, Crucifixion and Pietà by *Lor. Monaco*. In the galleries overlooking the cloister, Madonna and Child with two cherubs, by *Dom. Ghirlandaio* and his workshop; fragments of an Adoration of the Magi, by the school of Perugino, and large frescoes by *Aless. Allori*. Among the paintings on the floor above is the huge brilliantly coloured *Adoration of the Magi, by *Dom. Ghirlandaio* (predella by *Bart. di Giovanni*); *Neri di Bicci*, Coronation of the Madonna; *Botticelli* (attrib.), Madonna and Child with an angel (a youthful work, a copy from Filippo Lippi); *Luca della Robbia*, Madonna and Child in terracotta; *Piero di Cosimo*, Madonna and Child with Saints.

At the N.E. end of the square is the church of the *Santissima Annunziata* (Pl. 7), founded by the original members of the Servite Order in 1250, and rebuilt, along with the cloister, by *Michelozzo* and others in 1444-81.

Of the portico the central arch is ascribed to *Ant. da Sangallo*, the rest is by *Giov. Batt. Caccini* (1600). The middle door, over which is a lunette with an Annunciation in mosaic by *Dav. Ghirlandaio* (1509), admits to the **Atrium** (Chiostrino dei Voti), by *Manetti* (1447), from the design of Michelozzo. On the walls are interesting frescoes of the early 16C, gradually being detached and restored. From r. to l.: *Rosso Fiorentino*, Assumption (1517), an early work; *Pontormo*, *Visitation (1516); *Franciabigio*, Marriage of the Virgin (1513; the head of the Virgin was damaged by the painter himself in a fit of anger). Beyond a marble bas-relief of the Madonna and Child by Michelozzo, *Andrea del Sarto*, *Birth of the Virgin (1514; the central figure is Lucrezia del Fede, the painter's wife), and the Coming of the Magi (1511; removed for restoration) with his portrait in the right-hand corner. Here intervenes the great door, in front of which are two bronze stoups by *Ant. Susini* (1615). Beyond the door: *Alessio Baldovinetti*, *Nativity. The remaining frescoes, by *Cosimo Rosselli* (Vocation and Investiture of San Filippo Benizzi, 1476) and *And. del Sarto* (Scenes from the life of that Saint, 1509-10) have been removed for restoration.

The heavily decorated INTERIOR (open all day, 7-19), with a rich ceiling by *Pietro Giambelli* (1664-69) on a design by Volteranno, was otherwise considerably altered in the 17-18C. The huge *Tabernacle, at the W. end, by *Pagno di Lapo Portigiani* (1448-61), from a design by Michelozzo, has a bronze grille by *Maso di Bartolomeo,* and an incongruous 17C canopy. It protects a painting (concealed by a grille) of the Annunciation (14C), traditionally ascribed to a friar who was miraculously assisted by an angel. In the adjoining chapel (difficult to see) is a head of Christ, by *And. del Sarto.*

NAVE CHAPELS. Right side: 5th chapel, Monument to Orlando de' Medici, a delicate work by *Bern. Rossellino* (1456); 9th chap., Pietà, a sculptured group by *Baccio Bandinelli,* who is buried here (1559).—Left side: 1st Chapel, the Cappella Feroni by G.B. Foggini (1692), *St Julian and the Saviour, fresco by *And. del Castagno;* 2nd chap., fresco of the Holy Trinity with St Jerome, also by *Castagno;* 3rd chap., Last Judgement, fresco by *Aless. Allori;* 4th chap., *Perugino,* Assumption. From the N. transept is the entrance to the Sacristy built by *Pagno di Lapo,* from Michelozzo's design.

From the large circular SANCTUARY (closed 12.30-16.30), begun by Michelozzo and completed in 1477 by Leon Battista Alberti, radiate nine semicircular chapels. To the left of the great arch is the tomb of Bp. Angelo Marzi Medici, with a fine figure of the defunct by *Fr. da Sangallo* (1546). The dome-fresco, the Coronation of the Virgin, is by *Volterrano.* Beneath it is the high altar, with a silver ciborium by *Ant. Merlini* (1656), and, behind, the choir, which has stalls and two lecterns (15C English workmanship).—The 5th chapel from the right was reconstructed by *Giambologna* as his own tomb, and contains fine bronze reliefs and a bronze crucifix by him, and other works by his pupils; 6th, Resurrection, by *Bronzino,* and a statue of St Roch, by *Veit Stoss;* 7th, Madonna and saints, after *Perugino;* 9th, Miracle of St Manettus (one of the founders), by *Cristofano Allori,* and Birth of the Virgin, by *Aless. Allori.*

The CLOISTER OF THE DEAD, with its memorial stones and frescoes, is entered from outside the church, to the left of the portico. At the end of the entrance walk, over a door into the church, is the *Madonna del Sacco, a beautiful fresco by *And. del Sarto* (1525).—The CHAPEL OF ST LUKE, to the left, has since 1563 belonged to the Fraternity of Florentine artists, and is the burial-place of Cellini, Pontormo, Franciabigio, Bartolini, and many others. In its vestibule is a Crucifixion attributed to *Ant. da Sangallo.* A special Mass for artists is held on St Luke's Day. It has frescoes by *Pontormo, Santi di Tito,* and *Vasari.* In the niches are statues by *Giovanni dell'Opera, Vinc. Danti, Montorsoli,* and others.

At No. 9b P.za della SS Annunziata, in Palazzo della Crocetta, is the *Museo Archeologico** (Pl. 7; adm. 9-14, fest. 9-13), which includes one of the most important collections of Etruscan antiquities in existence. The **Etruscan Topographical Museum,** on the GROUND FLOOR, has been closed since 1966 after severe flood damage, and the entrance to the FIRST FLOOR is now on Via della Colonna (No. 38). Two rooms at the foot of the staircase display recently restored objects from the collections, including the famous *François Vase,* a krater painted by Klitias in Athens and decorated with six rows of paintings (c. 560 B.C.); it was restored, after being broken, by Pietro Zei.

The **Egyptian Museum.** ROOM I. Hathor in the form of a cow suckling the Pharaoh Horemheb (XVIII Dyn.); bust in red basalt of a Pharaoh of the XII Dynasty (19C B.C.).—ROOM II. Reliefs. Note the bas-reliefs with the plan of a tomb preceded by a courtyard (14C B.C.); craftsmen at work (7-6C B.C.); polychrome relief from the tomb of Seti I, representing the goddess Ma'at and Hathor, and the Pharaoh (c. 1292 B.C.); scribes recording objects (fragment; c. 1400 B.C.).—ROOM III. Sarcophagi, mummies, canopic vases, papyri.—ROOM IV. Sarcophagi.—ROOM V. Mummies, stelæ and Coptic fabrics.—ROOM VI.

Statuettes in limestone and wood; portrait of a young woman, of surprising vivacity, from the Flavian period; two admirable polychrome statuettes: maidservant preparing the yeast for the beer, and maid-servant kneading dough (2625-2475 B.C.).—ROOM VII. Statuettes of divinities; amulets; scarabs; plant ornaments.—ROOMS VIII. Very rare Hittite *Chariot in wood and bone from a Theban tomb of the 14C B.C.; vases, necklaces, sandals, and arms.

The **Etrusco-Greco-Roman Museum** at present occupies Rooms IX-XXII of the First Floor and the whole of the Second Floor. First Floor: Etruscan sculpture. ROOM IX. Urns with mythological subjects and from the heroic cycles of the Greek world; in the centre, marble sarcophagus from Tarquinia (4C B.C.) with tempera paintings of a battle between Greeks and Amazons.—ROOM X. Sculptured urns, sarcophagi, and statues; urn in the form of an Etruscan house; urn with banqueting and dancing scene; lid of a sarcophagus with an obese Etruscan.

Etruscan, Greek, and Roman bronzes. ROOM XI. Etruscan inscribed mirrors and decorative bronzes.—ROOM XII. Small Greek and Roman bronzes; Roman and Christian lamps; urn with the symbolic ship of the Church.—ROOM XIII. The *Idolino, a statue of a young athlete offering, a libation, a Greek original of the 5C. B.C. found at Pésaro in 1530; the base is of 16C workmanship. Torso of an athlete, original Greek of the 6-5C B.C.; *Horse's Head, probably from a Greek quadriga group.—ROOM XIV, the Long Gallery, contains a bronze Minerva from Arezzo, a copy of a 5C Greek work; the *Chimæra, also from Arezzo, an Etruscan work of the 5C B.C., a fantastical animal, with the body of a lion, the head of a ram (on its back), and a serpent's tail (restored); and the *Arringatore, or Orator, dedicated to Aulus Metullus by an Etruscan artist of the 4C or 3C B.C. (found near Perugia in 1566).—ROOM XV. Bronze fittings, arms, and various instruments; inscribed bronzes and seals, among them the well-known Seal of Magliano, which has a double inscription showing names of divinities and ritual prescriptions.

SECOND FLOOR. PREHISTORIC COLLECTION. In two rooms to the r.; objects of the Rinaldone culture, and finds from Campiglia d'orcia, Populonia, and Montemercano.—ITALIC AND MEDITERRANEAN COMPARISONS.—R. III. Examples of the civilization of Central Italy, including the bronze cap-shaped helmet, chased by Oppeano of Este.—R. IV. Cypriot ceramics and sculpture; antiquities from Asia Minor.—R. V. Cretan ware bronzes.—Vases and Terracottas. R. VI. Vases from Greece and Rhodes, including a huge amphora.—R. VII. Decorated ceramics of the various Greek factories under Oriental influence.—R. VIII. Primitive Italic and Etruscan vases of impasto and black bucchero ware of the 9-8C B.C.—R. IX. Etruscan vases of impasto and bucchero ware (7-6C B.C.).—R. X. Etruscan bucchero ware of the 6-5C B.C.

ROOMS XI-XII. GREEK VASES in painted terracotta, with Etruscan imitations, a series largely dating from the finest period of the art, and important for the perfection of the paintings (some of which may be assigned to the school of Polygnotos) and for the light they throw on Greek mythology.—ROOM XII contains two well-known vases from Populonia and various vessels.—ROOM XIII. Etruscan vases in imitation of the Attic, and Faliscan vases from Southern Italy.—ROOM XIV. Late Italic vases (3C-1C B.C.).—ROOM XV. Etruscan and Roman terracottas.

From Room VI is the entrance to RR. XVII and XVIII which contain reproductions of tomb frescoes of Etruria, and the Tomb of Larthia Scianti, in polychrome terracotta, with a reclining effigy of the deceased. The rooms beyond, with frescoed tombs from Orvieto and a complete gilt bronze armour, are normally kept closed.

The COIN ROOMS (ancient Greek and Roman coins, Medieval and modern Italian coins, especially from Tuscany) and the COLLECTION OF PRECIOUS STONES are visible only with special permission. The latter includes gems, cameos (head of Alexander the Great and Olympia), vitreous paste (*Unguent box of Torrita), silver (bowl with Bacchus, Pan, Ariadne, and Silenus; shield of Flavius Ardaburius Aspar), a silver situla from Chiusi, the *Mirror of Bomarzo, and the seal-ring of Augustus, in gold and jasper, found in his mausoleum.—A precious collection of Greek, Etruscan, and Roman sculpture is also on view to students with special permission.

In the same building is the INSTITUTE OF ETRUSCAN AND ITALIC STUDIES, with an extensive library.

Via della Colonna, beyond the museum, crosses Borgo Pinti in which (r.; No.56) is the CONVENT OF SANTA MARIA MADDALENA DEI PAZZI(Pl. 8; adm. 9-12, 17-19). The convent has been beautifully restored after severe flood damage. The church is preceded by a fine *Courtyard by *Giuliano da Sangallo,* with ionic capitals. Inside the church, with pretty lateral chapels, are 16C altarpieces. At the end on the right is the entrance to the crypt (lit by sacristan) which leads to the Chapter House of the monastery in which is the famous *Fresco of the Crucifixion and Saints by *Perugino* (1493-96), one of his masterpieces. Also here, Christ and St Bernard, a detached fresco and its sinopia, by his workshop.

No. 68 in Borgo Pinti is the *Palazzo Panciatichi Ximenes* begun by the *Sangallo brothers* (c.1499) and enlarged in 1605; and No.97 is *Palazzo della Gherardesca,* with a fine garden.

The street ends in Piazzale Donatello, on the right of which is the disused *English Cemetery* (Pl. 4), a garden shaded by cypresses, with the graves of A.H. Clough (1819-61), Elizabeth Barrett Browning (1809-61; tomb designed by Lord Leighton); W. S. Landor (1777-1864); Theodore Parker of Lexington (1810-60); and Jean Vieusseux (1779-1863), the well-known bibliophile.

Via Gino Capponi, behind the Annunziata, honours Gino Capponi (1792-1876), the statesman-historian, at whose home (r.) the poet Gius. Giusti died suddenly in 1850. On the opposite corner of Via Giusti is the house where Andrea del Sarto died; and, farther down, that where Mrs Mary Somerville, the mathematician, worked in 1850-60. At the next corner (l.) stands the *Palazzo San Clemente* (Pl. 4; formerly Guadagni), home of Charles Stuart in 1777-85, whence in 1780 the Countess of Albany fled to the near-by Convento delle Bianchette. The Prince's weather-vane may be plainly seen.

From the Annunziata Via Cesare Battisti leads N.W. to P.za San Marco, passing (r.) the *Military Geographical Institute.* On the left at the corner of Via Ricásoli, is the ACCADEMIA DI BELLE ARTE (founded in 1786), with its delicate *Loggia dell' Ospedale di San Matteo,* the oldest loggia in Florence (1416), reopened in 1935 after 150 years. The seven arches inspired Brunelleschi's Loggia degli Innocenti. Above the doors are two lovely *della Robbian* lunettes of the Madonna and Saints. The courtyard inside has very unusual columns. A tabernacle by *Giovanni da S. Giovanni,* with the Rest on the Flight into Egypt, is in the Sculpture Gallery. Farther down Via Ricásoli (No. 60) is the *Galleria dell'Accademia* (adm. 9-14, Sun & fest. 9-13). The entrance to the main hall is, at present, through the first room of the Pinacoteca (comp. below). On the walls of the main hall are Brussels and Florentine tapestries serving as a background for *Works by *Michelangelo:* The four corner figures, Prisoners or Slaves, intended for the tomb of Julius II; in the centre, St Matthew, unfinished, for Santa Maria del Fiore; beyond, *Pietà di Palestrina (1515-20; unfinished) from Santa

Rosalia, Palestrina. In the apse stands the famous *David (1501-3), hewn from a block of marble abandoned by another sculptor in the Cathedral workshop. The colossal figure is remarkable for its anatomical perfection and marked the sculptor as the master-artist of his age.

Seven rooms of the PINACOTECA are at present open. ROOM 1 (near the entrance). *Fra Bartolomeo,* Isaiah and Job; *Fr. Granacci,* Madonna and Child with Saints; *Mariotto Albertinelli,* Annunciation, Madonna enthroned with Saints; *Filippino Lippi,* St John the Baptist and St Mary Magdalene; *Fr. Botticini,* SS. Augustine and Monica; *Perugino* and *Fil. Lippi,* *Descent from the Cross; *Perugino,* Assumption with Saints; *Rid. Ghirlandaio,* Madonna and Child with SS. Francis and Mary Magdalene; *Albertinelli,* The Trinity; *Bart. di Giovanni,* St Jerome; *Fra Bartolomeo,* *Madonna enthroned with Saints and angels; *Fr. Granacci,* Virgin of the Sacred Girdle.—In the centre, the original plaster model for the Rape of the Sabines (comp. p. 426), by *Giambologna.*

ROOM 2. (On screen) 6004. Madonna and Child by a Florentine master c. 1420; 3160. *And. di Giusto,* Madonna and Child with angels; 8457. *Frontal of a marriage chest of the 15C, showing the Baptistery and elegant populace in period dress; 8508. *Mariotto di Cristofano,* Scenes from the life of Christ and of the Madonna; 171 dep. *'Master of the Castello Nativity',* Nativity (from Villa Castello, comp. p. 481. 1562. *Cosimo Rosselli,* Madonna and Child with Saints; 4632. *Filippino Lippi,* Annunciation (an early work; a copy from a painting by his father, Fra Filippo Lippi); 3162, 3164. *Mariotto di Cristofano,* Marriage of St Catherine, Resurrection; 8624. *Domenico di Michelino,* St Tobias and three arcangels.—R. 3. *3166. *Sandro Botticelli,* Madonna and Child with the young St John, and angels; 5381. Pupil of *Paolo Uccello* (attrib.), The Thebaids; *8637. *Alesso Baldovinetti,* Trinity and Saints (much ruined); 8654. *Perugino* or *Dom. Ghirlandaio* (attrib.), Visitation; 8623. *Seb. Mainardi* (attrib.), Pietà.—ROOM 4. *8661. *Lorenzo di Credi,* Adoration of the Child; *8456. *Botticelli* (attrib.), Madonna 'of the Sea'; 8663. *Raffaellino del Garbo,* Resurrection; 8631-33. *Cosimo Rosselli,* God the Father, Moses and Adam, David and Noah; 8627-29. *Bartolomeo di Giovanni,* Deposition, St Francis, and St Jerome; 1621. *Seb. Mainardi,* SS. Stephen, James, and Peter.

To the left of the apse: original plaster model for Virtue overcoming Vice, by *Giambologna.*—ROOM 5. 13C and early 14C Florentine works. 3345. *Crucifix, of the Sienese school; 8459. *Pacino di Buonaguida,* Tree of the Cross; (on screen) Russian works: 8466. *'Maestro della Maddalena',* Mary Magdalen with stories from her life.—R. 6. 3469. *Andrea Orcagna,* Madonna and Child with angels and saints; 8464. *Nardo di Cione,* Triptych with the Trinity and two Saints; works by the Gaddi brothers, and Bernardo Daddi and his school.—R. 7. *Jacopo di Cione,* Coronation of the Virgin; 8467. *Giovanni da Milano,* Pietà; 8581-8603. Scenes from the life of Christ and from the life of St Francis, by *Taddeo Gaddi* (from the Sacristy of Santa Croce).—Other rooms are still in the course of re-arrangement, and include later works by *Bronzino, Pontormo, Santi di Tito,* etc.

In the S. part of the building is the CONSERVATORIO MUSICALE LUIGI CHERUBINI (entrance at No. 80 Via degli Alfani), with a *Museum of Old Musical Instruments,* and a library of autograph compositions.

On the N. side of its pleasant piazza stands the church of **San Marco** (Pl. 3), founded in 1299, reconstructed by *Michelozzo* in 1437-52 and by *Giambologna* in 1588, with a façade by *Gioacchino Pronti* (1780).

INTERIOR. Over the entrance, Crucifix, on a gold ground, in the style of *Giotto.* Right side: 2nd altar, *Fra Bartolomeo,* Madonna and six saints; 3rd altar, Virgin in prayer, an 8C mosaic from Rome.—Between the 2nd and 3rd altars on the N. side are the graves of the scholar Pico della Miràndola (1463-94) and of the poet Politian (Ang. Ambrogini; 1454-94). To the left is the Chapel of St Antoninus, by *Giambologna,* frescoed by *Passignano;* the Chapel of the Sacrament, left of the choir, has good Baroque decoration. The Sacristy is by *Michelozzo.*

To the right of the church is the Dominican **Monastery of San Marco** now containing the *Museo dell'Angelico** (Pl. 3; adm. 9-14, fest. 9-13) famous for the frescoes of the 'Blessed' Fra Angelico. The monastery, the buildings of which were enlarged by *Michelozzo* (1437-52), is rich in memories of the painters Fra Angelico and Fra Bartolomeo, and of St Antoninus and Savonarola, all of whom lived within its walls.

Cloister of St Antoninus, by *Michelozzo*. In the lunettes are scenes from the life of the saint (Antonio Pierozzi, 1389-1459, Prior of San Marco in 1443 and Archbishop of Florence in 1445), by *Bernardino Poccetti* and other painters of the 16-17C. In the corners are frescoes by *Fra Angelico*: (at the end of the entrance walk) *St Dominic at the foot of the Cross; (above the door into the Lavatorium) Ecce Homo; (above the door into the Pilgrim's Hospice) Christ in pilgrim's garb welcomed by two Dominicans; (r. of entrance) St Thomas Aquinas. The convent bell, in the style of Donatello, has been placed in the cloister.

The PILGRIM'S HOSPICE has been closed for restoration since 1973, and all the works by Fra Angelico removed to the Great Refectory, with the exception of the famous *Tabernacle of the Linaioli or flax-workers (1433), with a large Madonna enthroned, with a fine frame designed by Lor. Ghiberti.

The LAVATORIUM contains a Madonna with St Anne and other Saints, in monochrome, by *Fra Bartolomeo;* a lunette of St Peter Martyr (and its sinopia) by *Fra Angelico* (detached from the cloister); and a Della Robbian tabernacle.— GREAT REFECTORY (provisional arrangement). Right wall and screens; *Fra Bartolomeo*, Last Judgement, a large detached fresco (very ruined); *Fra Angelico*, *Deposition (1436) of the Compagnia del Tempio; three little tabernacles from Santa Maria Novella: * Madonna della Stella, Annunciation and Adoration of the Magi, and Coronation of the Virgin; Pala di San Marco, with two scenes from the predella; *Deposition from Santa Trinità c. 1435 (the cusps are by Lor. Monaco). Left wall and screens; *Fra Angelico*, *Naming of St John and Baptist, Marriage and Death of the Virgin; 35 *Panels from the Life of Christ and the Virgin (from the Annunziata); *Last Judgement from Santa Maria Nuova; Madonna and Child with St John the Baptist and three Dominican Saints (an early work).—The end wall is decorated with a large fresco of Providence by *Giov. Ant. Sogliani* (1536).

CHAPTER HOUSE. *Crucifixion and saints, fresco by *Fra Angelico*. To the right a door gives access to a corridor with a wood crucifix from the church of San Marco attrib. to *Baccio di Montelupo*. At the end may be seen the CLOISTER OF ST DOMINIC (no adm.), also by *Michelozzo*. To the left, at the foot of the stairs, is the SMALL REFECTORY with a *Last Supper frescoed by *Dom. Ghirlandaio,* and Della Robbian terracottas.

FIRST FLOOR. The **Dormitory** consists of small monastic cells beneath a huge wood roof, each with their own vault and adorned with an intimate fresco by *Fra Angelico* and his assistants (1435-45); three principal hands have been identified as 'Master of Cell 2' (2, 4, 11 & 23-28), 'Master of Cell 31' (31-34), and 'Master of Cell 36' (36, 37). At the head of the staircase is the *Annunciation, justly one of the most famous works of the master. In the cells (beginning to the left): 1. *Noli me tangere'; 3. *Annunciation; 5. Adoration of the Child; 6. Transfiguration; 7. Crowning of Thorns in the presence of the Madonna and *St Dominic; 8. The Maries at the sepulchre; 9. Coronation of the Virgin. At the end of the next corridor are the rooms (12-14) occupied by Savonarola as prior, with some souvenirs of him, and his *Portrait, by *Fra Bartolomeo;* 24. Baptism of Christ; 25 (outside) Madonna and Saints; 31. Cell of St Antoninus, with souvenirs of him; 33. Fra Angelico's cell (?), with the Kiss of Judas; 34. Agony in the Garden, the Virgin and St Martha; 35. Communion of the Apostles; 38, 39. Cells occupied by Cosimo il Vecchio in retreat, with an Epiphany.—The light and delicate *LIBRARY, by *Michelozzo* (1441) contains illuminated choirbooks and psalters (15-16C).

On the right of San Marco are the administrative buildings of the *University* of Florence. The *Botanic Garden* (Pl. 3), adjacent, founded in 1545 by Cosimo I, has a museum.

From the N. side of P.za San Marco runs Via Cavour, in which, on the left, is the *Casino Mediceo*, built by Buontalenti (c. 1574) on the site of the Medici Gardens, where Cosimo il Vecchio and Lorenzo il Magnifico collected antique sculpture, and Bertoldo held a school of art. The building is now occupied by the Law Courts.—At No. 69, beyond, is the **Chiostro dello Scalzo** (Pl.3; closed for several years while the frescoes are detached and restored), a small arcaded courtyard of the early 16C, with admirable frescoes in monochrome, by *And. del Sarto* and *Franciabigio* (1514-26), depicting the history of St John the Baptist.

The street ends on the N. in the modern P.ZA DELLA LIBERTA, where stand two isolated archways, the *Porta San Gallo* (1284), one of the old city gates, and a *Triumphal Arch,* erected in 1739 to commemorate the entry of Francis II of Lorraine. Via di San Gallo returns S. At No. 74, on the left, is *Palazzo Pandolfini,* by Giov. Fr. and Aristotile da Sangallo (1516-20), from a design by Raphael. A little farther on are the church of *San Giovannino dei Cavalieri* (Pl. 3) with a *Crucifixion by Lor. Monaco, and, between Nos. 42 and 40, the *Loggia dei Tessitori,* part of the weavers' guild-house (c. 1500).

From P.za San Marco Via degli Arazzieri (the site of the Florentine tapestry factory) leads into Via Ventisette Aprile. Here on the left is the former convent of **Sant'Apollonia** (Pl. 3; in restoration, but adm. sometimes granted). Beyond the vestibule, with works by *Paolo Schiavo,* the refectory has a *Last Supper, a dramatic composition, the masterpiece of *And. del Castagno* (c. 1450). Above are equally fine frescoes (much ruined) also by him, of the Crucifixion, Deposition, and Resurrection. The sinopia is displayed on the opposite wall. Among his other works collected here are a Pietà, Crucifixion and Saints. The fresco of St Eustace with charming scenes from his life is attrib. to his school. The large Crucifix is by *Raffaello da Montelupo.*

The street endfs at the large PIAZZA DELL'INDIPENDENZA (Pl. 3), which has statues of Ricásoli and Peruzzi.

At the N. corner stands the *Villino Trollope,* home of the Trollope family in 1848-66, where the visiting Anthony wrote 'Doctor Thorne' in 1857. Later, when a pension, it sheltered Thos. Hardy (1887). Beyond the other side of the square lies the *Fortezza da Basso* (being restored; an exhibition centre), designed by Ant. da Sangallo the Younger for Aless. de' Medici in 1534-35. An avenue and gardens have been laid out on the glacis.
From here Bus No. 1 runs N.E. to Via Vittorio Emanuele II for the Museo Stibbert (an uninteresting walk of c. 2 km.). Situated on the *Colle di Montughi* with many other villas including the Villa Fabbricotti (No. 48) where Queen Victoria stayed in 1894, the **Villa Stibbert** was inherited from his Italian mother by Frederick Stibbert (1838-1906). A Garibaldian hero, he began a collection c. 1860 which he bequeathed with the villa to the British Government. The bequest was not taken up and the villa eventually passed to the city of Florence. Adm. daily exc. Thurs 9-16, fest. 9-12. The villa consists of a 14C house and one of the 15C joined together in 1884 by Stibbert by means of the great hall. The balcony here was a favourite seat of Queen Victoria (see above) who took pleasure in watching the work of alteration. The eclectic *Museum has a remarkably bizarre atmosphere with 64 rooms crammed with an extraordinary variety of objects. The most important part of the collections is the display of arms and armour, both ancient (Etruscan, Roman, Lombard, etc.) and medieval. Specially notable are an equestrian figure of a *Condottiere, with 15C armour; a cavalcade of 28 fully armed horses and knights of 16C (in the great hall); and five rooms of Asiatic armour. The most important paintings in the museum were stolen in 1977.

From the piazza Via Nazionale leads left; in Via Chiara, Cellini's birthplace overlooks the animated *Mercato Centrale* (open mornings only), a vast hall by Gius. Mengoni (1874), the principal food market in the town. Fruit and vegetables are sold outside to the N.E. In Via dell'Ariento is a picturesque open-air market (straw, leather-goods, clothing, etc.) open every day (except Monday in winter and Sat in summer), weather permitting. The stalls extend up to P.za San Lorenzo (comp. below). Via Nazionale next crosses Via Faenza. In this street, a few paces to the right (No. 42) is the *Cenacolo di Foligno* (ring for adm. 9-16 or 17), a fine fresco of the *Last Supper by Perugino. The works in the Galleria Feroni have been removed from here to the Uffizi for restoration. On the next corner (l.) the poet Lamartine, then a diplomatic secretary, lived in 1826-29.

In the other direction the Via Faenza leads to the P.za Madonna degli Aldobrandini, at the corner of which is the entrance to the **Medici Chapels** (Pl. 7; adm. 9-14, Sun 9-13). In the Crypt, built on a design by Buontalenti, remains of graffiti attrib. to Michelangelo were discovered in 1976 (not yet on public view). A staircase ascends to the huge CHAPEL OF THE PRINCES, the mausoleum of the Medici grand-dukes, begun by *Matt. Nigetti* (1604) on a plan by Giovanni de' Medici, natural son of Cosimo I. It is an octagon 28 m in diameter and is entirely lined with dark-coloured marbles and semi-precious stones. The mosaic arms of the 16 towns of Tuscany are notable. In the sarcophagi round the walls, from right to left, are buried Ferdinand II, Cosimo II, Ferdinand I, Cosimo I, Francis I. and Cosimo III. The second and third sarcophagi are surmounted by colossal statues in gilded bronze, by *Tacca*. The vault frescoes are by *Pietro Benvenuti* (1828). Behind the altar two treasuries contain the mitre of Leo X and reliquaries presented by Clement VII.

The passage to the left leads to the so-called *New Sacristy, built by *Michelangelo* in 1520-24 and 1530-33, and left unfinished. It balances Brunelleschi's Old Sacristy (see below) but was used from its inception as a funerary chapel for the Medici family. Not only is the chapel a masterpiece of Renaissance architecture in itself, but it contains the famous **Medici Tombs,** only two of which were executed out of the three or more originally projected.

To the left of the entrance is that of *Lorenzo II, Duke of Urbino (1492-1519), grandson of Lorenzo il Magnifico. The statue of the Duke shows him seated, absorbed in meditation, and on the sarcophagus below are the reclining figures of Dawn and Twilight. Opposite is the tomb of *Giuliano, Duke of Nemours (1478-1516), the third son of Lorenzo il Magnifico, with the Duke in classical armour. Beneath are figures of Day and Night; the last is the most admired of all these compositions, and was the last creation of Michelangelo before he left Florence in anger at the abolition of the Republic. At the end is the *Madonna, an unfinished group intended for the tomb of Lorenzo the Magnificent and his brother Giuliano; also figures of St Cosmas (by *Montórsoli*) and St Damian (by *Raff. da Montelupo*), the medical saints who were the patrons of the Medici.

Outside the chapels, to the right, is P.za San Lorenzo, with a street market, in which is a seated statue of Giovanni delle Bande Nere, by *Baccio Bandinelli* (1540). Above the pretty flank of the church rise the large dome of the Chapel of the Princes, the smaller cupola of the New Sacristy, and the campanile (1740). *San Lorenzo (Pl. 7; closed 12 or 12.30-15 or 15.30) is on the site of a basilica consecrated by St Ambrose in 393. Rebuilding, by order of the Medici, was begun by *Brunelleschi* (1425-46) and continued inside by *Ant. Manetti* (1447-60). *Michelangelo* designed a grandiose façade (models survive in the Casa

Buonarotti, comp. p. 441), but only the interior façade was ever built; the exterior remains in rough-hewn brick.

The solemn cruciform INTERIOR, with pulvins above the Corinthian columns and fine side chapels in pietra serena, is one of the earliest and most harmonious architectural works of the Renaissance. In the RIGHT AISLE (2nd chap.), *Rosso Fiorentino,* Marriage of the Virgin (1523); gothic tomb-slab of the organist Franc. Landini (1398). At the end of this aisle is a *Tabernacle by *Desiderio da Settignano,* of extremely fine workmanship. The two bronze *Pulpits in the nave were designed by *Donatello* c. 1460. These were his last works, and they were finished by his pupils *Bertoldo* and *Bellano.*

Beneath the dome three grilles in the pavement and a simple inscription with the Medici arms marks the grave of Cosimo il Vecchio 'Pater Patriae' (d. 1464). On the high altar is a crucifix by *Baccio da Montelupo.*—RIGHT TRANSEPT. 1st chap. (r.), 15C painting of the Madonna and Child with Saints, a Roman sarcophagus, and a fresco fragment of a female saint (attrib. to Nardo di Cione). In the chapel opposite is a monument (left) to the goldsmith Bernardo Cennini, who printed the first book in Florence in 1471.—LEFT TRANSEPT. 1st chap. l. of high altar, Madonna and Child, a charming statue in polychrome wood of the end of the 14C, and two paintings attrib. to *Raffaellino del Garbo* or his school. 2nd chap., School of Ghirlandaio, St Anthony Abbot, St Leonard, and St Julian.

Inlaid doors give access to the *Old Sacristy (1420-29), one of the earliest and purest monuments of the Renaissance. The vault is particularly noteworthy. The decorative details are mainly by *Donatello.* Above the frieze of cherubs' heads, the *Tondoes in the pendentives and lunettes depict the four Evangelists and scenes from the life of St John the Evangelist. Modelled in terracotta and plaster they are much discoloured and ruined, but are remarkable for their composition. On either side of the altar large lunettes with reliefs of SS. Cosmas and Damian and SS. Lawrence and Stephen crown the bronze *Doors with figures of the Apostles and Martyrs in animated discussion. The terracotta bust of St Lawrence is attrib. to Donatello also. On the altar is a triptych by the school of *Taddeo Gaddi,* below a wood crucifix of the 15C. The raised seats and presses are decorated with inlay. In the centre is the sarcophagus of Giovanni Bicci de' Medici (d. 1428) and Piccarda Bueri, the parents of Cosimo il Vecchio, by *Buggiano* (1434). Set in to the wall is the magnificent porphyry and bronze sarcophagus of his sons Giovanni and Piero de' Medici, by *Verrocchio* (1472). In the little chapel l. of the altar is a lavabo with fantastic creatures, by the workshop of Donatello.

In the last chapel in the left transept is a monument (1896) to Donatello (d. 1466; buried in the vault below) and an *Annunciation by *Filippo Lippi.* The marble sarcophagus of Niccolò Martelli is by the school of Donatello.—LEFT AISLE at the E. end is a huge fresco, the Martyrdom of St Lawrence, by *Bronzino.* The Cantoria is after Donatello.

The CLOISTER, entered from the left aisle or from the piazza, is a picturesque garden-court, with two graceful arcades in the style of Brunelleschi. A staircase adjoining the former entrance, near a statue of the historian Paolo Giovio, by *Fr. da Sangallo* (1560), ascends to the

Laurentian Library, or *Biblioteca Laurenziana* (Pl. 7) begun by *Michelangelo* in 1524 at the order of Clement VII to house the collection of MSS. made by Cosimo il Vecchio and Lorenzo il Magnifico.

The VESTIBULE and GREAT STAIRCASE were treated by the architect with great freedom, and their style has in it the germ of the Baroque. They were left unfinished by the designer, and the staircase was completed by *Vasari* in 1571. The great solemn LIBRARY (adm. 10-13, Sun & fest. closed), with its ceiling and furniture designed by *Michelangelo,* introduces quite a new form of architecture to Florence, contrasting with the light, graceful library of *Michelozzo* in S Marco (see p. 450). Here, and in adjoining rooms, exhibitions are held every year of the books and illuminated manuscripts which include: a 5C Virgil and many other classical texts of first importance; Syrian gospels of the 6C; the oldest MS. of Justinian's Pandects (6-7C); the Codex Amiatinus (from Monte Amiata), written in England in the 8C; a Choir Book illuminated by Lorenzo Monaco and Attavante, a Book of Hours which belonged to Lorenzo il Magnifico, the Città di Vita of Matteo Palmieri, with illuminations in the style of Pollaiuolo and Botticelli; and a Treatise on Architecture with MS. notes by Leonardo da Vinci. The library also owns the parchment of the Union of the Greek and Roman Churches, recording the abortive effort of the Council of Florence in 1439.

From the other side of the piazza Via Gori leads to Via Cavour, skirting the magnificent flank of *Palazzo Medici-Riccardi (Pl. 7; entrance on Via Cavour, 9-13, 15-17 exc. Wed; fest 9-12), now the seat of the Prefecture. This mansion was built for Cosimo il Vecchio by *Michelozzo* after 1444, and was the residence of the Medici until 1540. Under the Riccardi, who bought it in 1659, it was extended to the W. and N. in a similar style. The palace was the residence of Charles VIII of France (in 1494) and of the Emperor Charles V (in 1536).

The dignified COURTYARD, with Composite colonnades, is decorated with medallions ascribed to *Bertoldo* inspired by antique gems; some ancient sculptures, mainly Roman, are preserved here and in the pretty second court. On the right a door gives access to a staircase which leads up to the little CHAPEL, the only unaltered part of Michelozzo's work, with a beautiful ceiling and marble floor. It is painted with celebrated *Frescoes by *Benozzo Gozzoli* (1549-60), representing the Procession of the Magi to Bethlehem, the personages in which are portraits of the Medici, the gentlemen of their household, the Emp. John VI Palæologus and Joseph of Constantinople, and the painter himself, while the whole is a gay and vivid picture of the life of his day. On either side of the altar are lovely landscapes with angels, recalling those of the painter's master, Fra Angelico. The altarpiece is a contemporary copy of a Madonna by Filippo Lippi.

The next door on the right in the courtyard admits to the first-floor GALLERY, a Baroque loggia (1670-88) covered by a fresco of the Apotheosis of the second Medici dynasty, by *Luca Giordano* (1683).—The door on the left of the main gateway leads to the former private apartments of the Medici, now occupied by the MEDICI MUSEUM, a collection of portraits and memorials of the Medici family. This has been closed since 1966, but is to be reopened when the works have been restored.

Via de' Ginori, behind the palace, is an impressive street of old palaces, among which (No. 4) is the *Biblioteca Riccardiana e Moreniana* (Pl. 7), containing illuminated MSS. and incunabula. At No. 15 Raphael stayed while visiting Florence in 1505.

The busy Via de' Martelli continues the Via Cavour back to P.za del Duomo.

IV.   WESTERN QUARTERS: SANTA MARIA NOVELLA AND SANTA TRÍNITA.

From the N. side of P.za del Duomo Via de' Cerretani leads due W. On the left is the *Archbishop's Palace,* incorporating (in Piazzetta dell'Olio) the Romanesque front of the church of *San Salvatore.* Farther on is **Santa Maria Maggiore** (Pl. 7,6), a dark church rebuilt at the end of the 13C, with 13-14C frescoes, some by *Mariotto di Nardo*. The internal façade is to a design of *Buontalenti*. In the chap. 1. of the choir: *Madonna enthroned, a Byzantine relief in painted wood; (r.) a column which survives from the tomb of Brunello Latini (d. 1294), Dante's teacher, and (l.) the tomb (1272) of Bruno Beccuti, with fine reliefs and a figure of the defunct attrib. to *Tino da Camaino*. In the sanctuary, frescoes (very ruined) attrib. to a contemporary of Spinello Aretino.

Via Rondinelli, on the left, farther on, leads to P.za Antinori, in which is (r.) the *Palazzo Antinori,* in the style of Giul. da Maiano, one of the most beautiful small Renaissance palaces in Florence. Opposite, to the left, is the Baroque church of *San Gaetano* (Pl. 6), by Matt. Nigetti and Gherardo and Pier Francesco Silvani (1604-48), containing a painting by Pietro da Cortona, the Martyrdom of St Lawrence.

Beyond extends VIA TORNABUONI(Pl. 6, 10), the most elegant street in Florence, with some of the best shops, as well as many fine old mansions. No. 19 (r.) is the *Palazzo Larderel* (formerly *Giacomini*), ascribed to Giov. Ant. Dosio (1580); No. 16 is the *Palazzo Corsi,* with an interior court by Michelozzo; No. 15 is *Palazzo Viviani,* which once belonged to the Della Robbia. Farther on, on the left, is *Palazzo Strozzi* (Pl. 6; being restored), begun by *Bened. da Maiano* (1489), either from his own design or from one by Giul. da Sangallo, and continued by *Cronaca,* whose work was, however, interrupted in 1539. The side most nearly complete faces the P.za Strozzi. The palace is typical of the 15C town-mansion, half fortress and half palace, with all three stories of equal emphasis constructed with large rough blocks of stone. Cronaca's great cornice, suggested by antique examples, and the wrought-iron torch-holders and fantastic lanterns by *Caparra* should be noted. The palace is now the seat of the *Gabinetto Vieusseux* (lending library), and various learned institutes, and is used for exhibitions and conferences. A small *Museum* (open 9-13, 15-18, Sat 9-13) illustrates the history of the palace and preserves its original model. The elegant Courtyard is also by Cronaca.—Via della Vigna Nuova diverges right.

The corner palazzo (r.) was from 1613 the home of Sir Robert Dudley; and in the corner house (l.) George Eliot lived while gathering material for 'Romola'. Wordsworth stayed at No. 11 in 1835.

Farther along the street is the *Loggia dei Rucellai,* by L. B. Alberti (c. 1460). Opposite, at No. 20, is the *Palazzo Rucellai* (Pl. 6) by *Bern. Rossellino* (1446-51), from a design by *Alberti,* who departed entirely from the canons of style laid down by Brunelleschi. The street on the left of the palace leads to P.za di San Pancrazio, where the disused church of *San Pancrazio* (being restored) has a beautiful porch by Alberti. Close by is the *Cappella dei Rucellai,* entered from Via della Spada (closed for restoration; key normally with the porter of Palazzo Ruccellai), another admirable example of Alberti's style. Inside is an idealized model in marble of the Holy Sepulchre, also by Alberti.—From Via della Spada, Via del Moro continues N. At its junction with Via delle Belle Donne is the curious *Croce del Trebbio,* a column with a cross of 14C Pisan workmanship. Just to the left opens a large square, the PIAZZA DI SANTA MARIA NOVELLA.

The two obelisks were set up in 1608 to mark the ends of the course of the annual chariot race on 24 June (Palio dei Cocchi) that began to be held here in 1563. The race was revived in 1927 in the Cascine Park.—The *Loggia di San Paolo* (1489-96) on the S.W. side is a free copy of Brunelleschi's Loggia degli Innocenti, with terracottas by *And.* and *Giov. della Robbia.*

*Santa Maria Novella (Pl. 6; closed 12-15), on the N., was begun by the Dominican friars *Sisto* and *Ristoro* in 1278, and completed by *Iac. Talenti* c. 1348. The façade, begun c. 1300, was continued in 1456-70 by *Giov. Bertini* from designs by *Alberti* which include the main doorway and the upper half. The use of scrolls to connect the nave and aisles was an innovation that has since become familiar through its excessive employment in Baroque buildings. To the right of the façade, and along the right side of the church, is a long line of Gothic arcaded recesses, the 'avelli' or family-vaults of Florentine nobles.

The INTERIOR, 99 m long and 28 m wide, has Composite pillars between nave and aisles; the bays decrease in width as they approach the altar, with the object of increasing the apparent length of the church. The glass in the rose window above the W. door was designed by *And. di Bonaiuto* (c. 1365). To the r. of the door is a fresco of the Florentine school of the end of the 14C.

SOUTH AISLE. By the 2nd altar, Monument to the Blessed Villana de' Bitti (d. 1360) by *Bern. Rossellino* (1451). Beyond the 5th altar is the entrance to the CAPPELLA DELLA PURA (1474) with delicate Renaissance decoration (in poor repair) and a 14C fresco of the Madonna and Child and St Catherine (detached from an 'avello' outside the church) over the altar to the left. Over the main altar, wood Crucifix by *Baccio da Montelupo* (1501; temporarily removed for restoration).

TRANSEPTS AND CHOIR CHAPELS. RIGHT TRANSEPT: Bust of St Antonius in terracotta (15C); (above) Tomb of Bp. Aliotti (d. 1336), once attrib. to *Tino da Camaino*. To the left, Tomb of Fra' Aldovrando Cavalcanti (d. 1279) above the tomb of Joseph, Patriarch of Constantinople (who attended the Council of Florence in 1439, and died in the convent the following year), with a contemporary fresco of him. At the end of the transept is the CAPPELLA RUCELLAI. On the altar, marble *Statuette of the Madonna and Child, by *Nino Pisano*. On the l. wall, large painting of the Martyrdom of St Catherine, by *Giul. Bugiardini*. The bronze tomb slab of Fra' Lionardo Dati, in the floor, is the work of *Ghiberti* (1425). The walls have traces of 14C frescoes.—CAPPELLA DEI BARDI (2nd on r. of choir). Sculptural fragments of the 13C and 14-15C frescoes (attrib. to the Bolognese School).—CAPPELLA DI FILIPPO STROZZI (light on left). Exuberant *Frescoes by *Filippino Lippi* (c. 1497-1502), giving a foretaste of 16C Mannerism. They tell the story (r.) of St Philip the Apostle and (l.) St John the Evangelist. Filippino also designed the stained glass window. Behind the altar, *Tomb of Filippo Strozzi, by *Benedetto da Maiano* (1491-93).

SANCTUARY (light behind the altar). The paschal candlestick (r.) is attrib. to *Piero di Giovanni Tedesco* (late 14C). Above the altar, bronze Crucifix by *Giambologna*. The stalls and lectern are attrib. to *Baccio d'Agnolo*. The *Frescoes by *Dom. Ghirlandaio* (assisted by other artists, among them perhaps the young Michelangelo) are considered his best work; on the right, Life of St John the Baptist; on the left, Life of the Virgin; on the end wall, Coronation of the Virgin, St Dominic burning heretical books, Death of St Peter Martyr, etc. Many of the figures are portraits of the artist's contemporaries, and the whole cycle mirrors Florentine life in the late 15C.

The *CAPPELLA GONDI (1st on l. of the choir) has architectural decoration by *Giul. da Sangallo* (c. 1503). Above the altar is the celebrated crucifix carved by *Brunelleschi* in order to show Donatello how the Redeemer should be represented (comp. p. 440), his only sculpture to survive in wood.—CAPPELLA GADDI (being restored). Architectural decoration by *Giov. Ant. Dosio* (1575-77); Christ raising Jairus' daughter, by *Bronzino*.—At the end of the left transept is the CAPPELLA STROZZI, a completely preserved mid-14C Tuscan chapel, with celebrated *Frescoes by *Nardo di Cione* (c. 1357). These have been detached (except those on the end wall and entrance arch) and will be returned here after restoration. They represent (in the vault), St Thomas Aquinas and the Virtues; on the end wall, the Last Judgement; on the left wall, Hell, a pictorial commentary on Dante's 'Inferno'. The altarpiece (Christ giving the keys to St Peter and the book of wisdom of St Thomas Aquinas) is by *And. Orcagna* (1357). On the left is the SACRISTY, with a fine cross-vault by *Iac. Talenti* (1350). Here is a *Lavabo in terracotta with a charming landscape, by *Giov. della Robbia* (1498). On the wall (l.) Crucifixion, by *Vasari*. Above the entrance, painted *Crucifix (formerly on the W. wall of the church) an early work by *Giotto*.

NORTH AISLE. 6th altar. *Aless. Allori,* Saints; 4th altar, *Vasari,* Resurrection. Beyond the 3rd altar, *Fresco of the Trinity and the Virgin and St John the Evangelist with donors, a superb work by *Masaccio* (c. 1428), famous for its perfect composition and accurate perspective. To the left, a small painting (St Lucy with a donor) by *Davide Ghirlandaio*. The *Pulpit (from which Caccini denounced Galileo's astronomical theories) is by *Buggiano,* designed by his master Brunelleschi. Between the first two altars, Tomb of Ant. Strozzi (1524), by *And. Ferrucci,* with a Madonna by his pupil, *Silvio Cosini*.

To the left of the church is the entrance to the *CLOISTERS (adm. weekdays 9-16 exc. Fri; Sun 9-12), now state property. The Romanesque *CHIOSTRO VERDE (after 1350), so called from the green tone of its decoration, is an oasis of monastic calm. Eugenius IV transferred the Papal court here in 1434-43. The frescoes, also predominantly green in colour, have all been detached after serious damage in the flood of 1966 (comp. below).

Off the cloister opens the *Cappellone degli Spagnuoli (Pl. 6), or *Spanish Chapel,* originally the chapter house, by *Iac. Talenti* (after 1350), and assigned by Duchess Eleonora di Toledo to the Spanish members of her suite. It has two fine windows, and its walls and vault are entirely covered with colourful *Frescoes by *Andrea di Bonaiuto* and assistants (c. 1355). The subjects are: in the vault, the Resurrection, Ascension, Christ walking on the water, Descent of the Holy Ghost; altar wall, Via Dolorosa, Crucifixion, Descent into Hell; right wall, the Mission, Works, and Triumph of the Dominican Order; left wall, the *Triumph of St Thomas Aquinas, with a brilliant assemblage of personages symbolizing the Sciences and the Arts; entrance wall, Life of St Peter Martyr.

On the right of the Chapel is the entrance to the *Chiostrino dei Morti* (closed for restoration). The frescoes ascribed to Nardo di Cione (Scenes from the Life of the Virgin) and a Giottesque figure of St Thomas Aquinas, have been detached for restoration. From the left walk of the Chiostro Verde a passage leads to the large REFECTORY. At the end are preserved interesting frescoed *Lunettes (detached from the Chiostro Verde) by *Paolo Uccello:* to the l., Creation of Adam, of the animals, and the Creation and Temptation of Eve (c. 1430); to the r., the Flood and Sacrifice of Noah (c. 1446). Although much damaged, they are remarkable for their figure studies and perspective device. On the entrance wall, large fresco of the Manna in the Desert, by *Aless. Allori* surrounding a fresco of the Madonna enthroned, executed three centuries earlier. On the right wall, *Aless. Allori,* Last Supper. The imposing GREAT CLOISTER (no adm.) is visible through a glass door. The 16-17C frescoes here (except those by *Pontormo*) have been detached.

From the W. corner of the piazza the long Via della Scala (Pl. 6) leads N.W. On the left (No. 85) is the 17C *Palazzo Ginori-Venturi* (Pl. 6), adjoining which are the famous *Orti Oricellari* (closed). In these gardens, Bern. Rucellai (a corruption of Oricellari) collected the sculptures stolen at the fall of the Medici dynasty in 1494, and later refounded the Platonic Academy. From c. 1580 the villa was occupied by Bianca Cappello.—Just before No. 62 Via della Scala is a lunette by Giov. della Robbia in the façade of a former church. On the left at the end of the street the Viale Fratelli Rosselli leads to the *Porta al Prato* (Pl. 1), gateway of the city wall of 1284. To the left in Via del Prato is the *Palazzo Corsini* where Prince Charles Stuart lived in 1774-77. Just beyond the gate, on the right, opens the Piazzale Vittorio Veneto, with the *Victor Emmanuel Monument* by Emilio Zocchi (1890), and, opposite, a small fountain commemorating the diamond jubilee of Queen Victoria.

Here is the main entrance to the *Cascine (Pl. 5, 1; bus 17 from the P.za Stazione; or 13 from the Duomo to Porta al Prato). This huge public park skirts the Arno for 3½ km., and is traversed by two avenues. It was laid out by the Medici on the lands of a dairy-farm (*cascina*) and has been public since the 18C. In these gardens the 'Ode to the West Wind' was 'conceived and chiefly written' (1819), and on the Narcissus fountain here a tablet (1954) commemorates its composition. The park contains two race-courses, and various sports-grounds, including one for the traditional ball-game, the Giuoco del Pallone. In the central Piazzale delle Cascine is the *Institute of Forestry,* and at the far end is the monument of the Maharajah of Kolhapur, who died at Florence in 1870. From here the view is dominated by the fine new suspension bridge being built over the Arno.

The return from the Cascine to the P.za Ognissanti is best made by the Lungarno Amerigo Vespucci (Pl. 6).

The church of **Ognissanti** (Pl. 6) is reached from Via della Scala (S Maria Novella) by Via del Porcellana (l.) and Borgo Ognissanti (r.). Founded in 1256 and altered c. 1627, the church has a Baroque front, by *Nigetti* (1637), incorporating a terracotta Coronation of the Virgin ascribed to *Bened. Buglioni*. The church suffered severe flood damage in 1966.

INTERIOR. SOUTH SIDE: 2nd altar, frescoes by *Dom.* and *Davide Ghirlandaio,* including the Madonna della Misericordia who protects the Vespucci (Amerigo is supposed to be the young boy whose head appears between the Madonna and the man in the dark cloak). The family tombstone (1471) is on the left of the altar. 3rd altar, *Santi di Tito,* Madonna and Saints. The 17C pulpit has bas-reliefs by a pupil of *Bened. da Rovezzano*.—SOUTH TRANSEPT (1st altar on right), *Iac. Ligozzi,* San Diego healing the sick. In the adjacent chapel the round tombstone in the pavement marks the burial place of Filipepi (Botticelli). Over the altar at the end of the transept, wood Crucifix by *Veit Stoss.*—In the dome, above the presbytery, frescoes by *Giov. da San Giovanni* (1616-17). From the North Transept a door leads into the SACRISTY, with a Crucifix by the school of Giotto and detached frescoes by *Taddeo Gaddi* (*Crucifixion) and *Agnolo Gaddi* (attrib.). On the N. side of the church is a fresco (over the 2nd altar) attrib. to *Ridolfo del Ghirlandio*.

On the left of the church in the Convent (No. 38; 10-12, 16-18; or ring) may be seen a CLOISTER in the style of Michelozzo, with 17C frescoes, and the REFECTORY, containing a *Last Supper the masterpiece of *Dom. Ghirlandaio* (1480), and (r. wall) St Augustine, by *Botticelli,* and (l. wall)

St Jerome, by *Ghirlandaio*.—A small MUSEUM,off the cloister, has a 15C Madonna and Child in terracotta, and vestments, etc. from the sacristy.

From P.za Ognissanti (with the attractive 15C Palazzo Lenzi at No. 2) Lungarno Vespucci leads left along the river. Beyond P.za Goldoni is the *Ponte alla Carraia* (Pl. 6, 10), rebuilt by Ammannati in 1559, blown up in 1944, and replaced by a new bridge (a copy of the original) in 1952. In the Lungarno Corsini is the imposing *Palazzo Corsini,* by Gherardo Silvani (1648-56), containing the GALLERIA CORSINI, the most important private art collection in Florence which has been closed to the public for over ten years.

Among the fine paintings here are a series of Apollo and the Muses, painted for the ducal palace at Urbino by *Giov. Santi, Tim. Viti,* and others; Cartoon of Julius II, attr. to Raphael; Crucifixion, by *Giovanni Bellini;* Poetry, by *Carlo Dolci;* and Madonnas by *Signorelli, Pontormo, Filippino Lippi,* etc.

Farther along the Lungarno Corsini is the palazzo where Louis Bonaparte, ex-king of Holland and farther of Napoleon III, died in 1846. The 15C *Palazzo Castelbarco* (No. 2; formerly *Gianfigliazzi*) was beautifully restored in 1958 as the British Consulate. Here the Countess of Albany lived from 1793 until her death; here in 1803 died the dramatist Alfieri, her second husband; and here later she was joined by Xavier Fabre, the painter.—The next bridge is the **Ponte a Santa Trinita* (Pl. 10; *View), first built in 1252 and several times rebuilt after flood damage. The present bridge, opened in 1958, is an exact replica of the bridge by Ammannati (1569) destroyed in 1944. The statue of Spring (l.) by Pietro Francavilla was recovered from the Arno. To the left opens Via Tornabuoni (comp. p. 455) with the great ** Palazzo Spini-Ferroni* (1289), on the corner, the sternest of the medieval mansions of Florence. Opposite is *Santa Trínita* (Pl. 10; closed 12-15.30), a Vallombrosan church in the 11C, rebuilt in the 13C, and provided with a Baroque front by *Buontalenti* in 1593-94.

The fine INTERIOR has the austerity characteristic of Cistercian churches, and is one of the most successful Gothic buildings in Florence. On the entrance wall are remains of the Romanesque church. The church is unusually dark (best light in morning); each chapel has a light: the switches are inconspicuously placed to the left. On the outside arches of many of the chapels are remains of 14-15C frescoes (some restored); the most interesting are those by *Giov. del Ponte* outside the choir chapels. SOUTH AISLE. 1st chap., Wood Crucifix and detached fresco of the 14C; 3rd chap., Altarpiece of the Madonna enthroned with four Saints, by *Neri di Bicci.* On the walls, detached fresco and sinopia by *Spinello Aretino* (considerably ruined) found beneath a fresco by Lor. Monaco in the adjoining chapel. The 4th chap. is entirely frescoed by *Lor. Monaco;* the altarpiece of the Annunciation is also by him. 5th chapel, Pietà, fresco attrib. to *Giov. Toscani,* and a noble altar, by *Bened. da Rovezzano,* part of the tomb of St John Gualberto, founder of the Vallombrosans. The tomb of Onofrio Strozzi by *Lamberti*(1421), in the adjoining sacristy, is one of the earliest in the Renaissance style. Here are displayed detached frescoes of the 13C and 14C.

CHOIR CHAPELS. *SASSETTI CHAPEL with frescoes of the life of St Francis by *Dom. Ghirlandaio* (1483-86). The scene (St Francis receiving the Rule of the Order from Pope Honorius) in the lunette above the altar takes place in Piazza della Signoria and those present include: (in the foreground, r.) Lorenzo the Magnificent with Sassetti and his son, and, to his right, Antonio Pucci, On the stairs are Agnolo Poliziano with Lorenzo the Magnificent's sons, Piero, Giovanni, and Giuliano. In the Miracle of the boy brought back to life (beneath) is the Piazza Santa Trinita (with the old Romanesque façade of the church and the old Ponte S. Trinita). On the altar, the *Adoration of the Shepherds is also by *Ghirlandaio* (1485). The *Tombs of Fr. Sassetti and Nera Corsi, his wife, are attrib. to *Giul. da Sangallo*.—In the chap. to r. of the main altar, the painted crucifix is said to have bowed approvingly to St John Gualberto when he pardoned his brother's assassin. Over the main altar, Triptych of the Trinity, four Saints, and the Annunciation, by *Mariotto di Nardo* (removed since 1973 for restoration). The vault has scant remains of paintings by *Alesso Baldovinetti*. In the 2nd chap. l. of the altar, *Tomb of Bp. Benozzo Federighi*, by *Luca della Robbia* (1454-57), with exquisite painted tiles. On the walls are detached frescoes by *Giov. del Ponte*.

NORTH AISLE. 5th chap., *Mary Magdalen, statue in wood by *Desiderio da Settignano*, finished by *Benedetto da Maiano*.—4th chapel, detached fresco of St John Gualberto surrounded by Vallombrosian saints, by *Neri di Bicci*, and an altarpiece by *Bicci di Lorenzo* (in restoration).—3rd chap., Annunciation by *Neri di Bicci*, and the tomb of Giuliano Davanzati (1444) adapted from a Roman sarcophagus.—2nd chap., Annunciation and St Jerome by *Ridolfo Ghirlandaio*.—The Romanesque CRYPT (with remains of the earlier church) is shown by the sacristan (tip).

In P.za di Santa Trínita stands the *Column of Justice*, a granite monolith from the Baths of Caracalla at Rome, presented by Pius IV to Cosimo I in 1560. The porphyry figure of Justice, by Tadda (1581) has a bronze cloak added subsequently. No. 1 in the piazza is the *Palazzo Bartolini Salimbeni*, a fine work by Baccio d'Agnolo (1517-20), recently restored as the French Consulate.

Between this point and P.za della Signoria are to be found the most characteristic remains of medieval Florence. Borgo Santi Apostoli leads to Piazza del Limbo, with the church of the **Santi Apostoli** (Pl. 10), of the late 11C (restored 1938), with a 16C doorway, ascribed to *Bened. da Rovezzano*. The basilican interior has fine green columns; the first two capitals are from Roman baths. In the 1st chap. in the N. aisle is the sinopia of the fresco formerly on the façade by *Paolo Schiavo*. At the end of the aisle, *Tomb of Prior Oddo Altoviti, by *Bened. da Rovezzano*, and a fine *Tabernacle by *Giov. della Robbia*, with two sculpted panels below from the tomb of Donato Acciaiuoli (1333). On the altar is a painting by the school of Orcagna (in restoration). The altarpieces from the S. aisle, by Vasari, Pomerancio, etc. have been in restoration since 1966.

Farther along, the Borgo is lined by medieval mansions (No. 19 is the *Palazzo Rosselli del Turco*, by Baccio d'Agnolo, 1517) and fortified dwellings, between which are dark and narrow alleys. The road ends at the busy VIA POR SANTA MARIA (Pl. 11), which leads from the Ponte Vecchio to the Mercato Nuovo. The medieval houses here were destroyed in 1944. Opposite (in a little square opening off Vicolo S Stefano) is the old church of *Santo Stefano al Ponte*, with a 13C front. The dark Via delle Terme, where at No. 29 Marconi made early experiments, leads back to the left to reach the *Palazzo di Parte Guelfa* (Pl. 11; no adm.).

The palace, built in the early 14C as the official residence of the Captains of the Guelph Party was enlarged and beautified in the 15C by *Fr. della Luna* and *Brunelleschi* and later by *Vasari*, who added the charming little balcony in Via Capaccio. Incorporated in the palace is the church of *Santa Maria Sovrapporta* or *San Biagio*.—In the same piazza are the 15C *Palazzo Canacci* and the 13C *Palazzo Giandonati*, and in Via Capaccio is the Gothic house of the *Arte della Seta*, with the arms of the silk-weavers in the style of Donatello.

Vicolo della Seta leads N. from here to the LOGGIA DI MERCATO NUOVO (Pl. 11), built by G. B. del Tasso in 1547-51 for the sale of silk and gold and now a market-place for cheap lace, straw work, and leather. Here stands 'Il Porcellino', a bronze fountain by Tacca, copied from the antique figure of a boar in the Uffizi.—To the left, at No. 9 Via Porta

Rossa, is the **Palazzo Davanzati** built in the 14C for the Davizzi family, whose coat-of-arms, perhaps by Donatello, adorns the façade. It was later the residence of the historian Bernardo Davanzati (1529-1606). The antique ironwork is fine.

The palace provides a fit setting for the MUSEO DELL' ANTICA CASA FIORENTINA (open 9-14, closed Sun), which displays furnishings and fittings of the Florentine house of the 15-17C. In the pretty courtyard, detached fresco of courtiers (15C). On the stairs, fresco of the Madonna and Child of the Umbrian school. FIRST FLOOR. The *Salone* has a fine painted ceiling (14-15C). The Florentine works here include a good polychrome terracotta bust of the Madonna of the Annunciation. The adjoining room has pretty wall paintings.—*Salotto.* Workshop of Filippino Lippi, Adoration of the Child; head of a boy in bronze (15C).—*Sala dei Pavoni.* Rare Sicilian bed cover; Madonna and Child, after Ghiberti; and painted doors of a tabernacle by Neri di Bicci.—SECOND FLOOR. The *Salone* has a beautiful series of small *Tapestries designed by Bachiacca (1553). An adjoining room has paintings by a follower of Piero di Cosimo, the 'Maestro di Serumido'. The Marriage bedroom has pretty 14C frescoes.—On the floor above is the *Kitchen.*

From the piazza opposite Via de' Vecchietti leads N. to Via Strozzi.

V. SOUTHERN QUARTERS: THE OLTRARNO AND SAN MINIATO AL MONTE

The **Ponte Vecchio** (Pl. 11), the oldest bridge in Florence and one of the most famous in the world was rebuilt in 1345. Except in its middle section, where there is a small open 'piazzetta' with a bust of Benvenuto Cellini (1900), it is lined by jewellers' shops, the backs of which, supported on brackets, overhang the river; and these, with the covered passage from the Uffizi to the Pitti Palace which surmounts the whole, give the bridge its characteristic appearance. The old houses at either end were blown up in the retreat of 1944, and the shops had to be restored after they were damaged in 1966.

On the other side Via Guicciardini leads on to P.za Pitti (see p. 466). Borgo San Iacopo leads r., passing No. 17 the *Torre dei Marsili,* a fine 13C towerhouse, and (r.) *San Iacopo sopr'Arno* (Pl. 10), with a 12-13C Romanesque porch. In the Baroque interior, restored after flood damage, the romanesque columns have been revealed. Borgo San Iacopo ends in the busy P.za Frescobaldi. To the left of Ponte a Santa Trinita Lungarno Guicciardini follows the river to Ponte alla Carraia, passing the late 16C *Palazzo Capponi* (No.1) and the *Palazzo Lanfredini* (No.9), with a façade by Baccio d'Agnolo.

The Lungarno Soderini, beyond Ponte alla Carraia, leads past the Seminario Maggiore (No. 19) where a new Museo Diocesano is to be opened, to *San Frediano* (Pl. 10), a church with an imposing dome and a good campanile. At the end of the Lungarno is the *Torrino di Santa Rosa* (1324), connected by a stretch of medieval wall with the *Porta San Frediano* (Pl. 5, 9), a fine gateway by Andrea Pisano (1332).

From P.za Sauro, Borgo San Frediano runs W. through a popular quarter of the town, with numerous artisans' workshops. It is still the most characteristic part of Florence and the inhabitants speak with a strong local accent. Opening off the S. side of the Borgo is the irregular Piazza del Carmine with the bare façade of the church of the **Carmine** (Pl. 10; open 7-12, 15-18 or 19) built in 1268, almost completely destroyed by fire in 1771, and rebuilt by *Gius. Ruggieri* and *Giulio*

Mannaioni (1782); the sacristy and two chapels alone escaped the fire. One of these was, by good fortune, the *BRANCACCI CHAPEL, at the end of the right transept, which contains the masterpiece of *Masaccio,* a series of frescoes which greatly influenced the Renaissance in Florence. The most important development in painting since Giotto, these frescoes illustrate well Masaccio's understanding of the monumentality and colour in Giotto's figures, which he combines with a new realism and movement. The frescoes are arranged in two rows, begun by *Masolino da Panicale* (1424-25), continued by *Masaccio* (1426-27; he died, at the age of 27, in 1428), and completed by *Filippino Lippi* (1484-85). UPPER ROW (r. to l.): *Masolino,* Temptation of Adam and Eve; *Masolino* and *Masaccio,* St Peter, accompanied by St John, brings Tabitha to life, and heals a lame man; *Masaccio,* *St Peter baptizing; *Masolino,* St Peter preaching; *Masaccio,* *The Tribute money, the painter's masterpiece; *Expulsion from Paradise.—LOWER ROW: *Lippi,* *Release of St Peter from prison; SS. Peter and Paul before the proconsul; Crucifixion of St Peter; *Masaccio,* SS. Peter and John distributing alms; *St Peter, followed by St John, healing the sick with his shadow; St Peter enthroned, with portraits of friars. The next half of this panel, begun by *Masaccio* and finished by *Lippi,* shows St Peter raising the Emperor's nephew; *Lippi,* St Peter in prison visited by St Paul.

In the APSE of the church is the fine *Monument of Piero Soderini (d.1522), by *Bened. da Rovezzano;* and at the end of the left transept is the sumptuous CHAPEL OF SANT'ANDREA CORSINI (d. 1373) by *Gherardo Silvani* (1675-83), with marble reliefs by *G. B. Foggini.*—The Gothic SACRISTY contains interesting paintings and detached frescoes of 14C and 15C. The choir chapel is frescoed with scenes from the life of St Cecilia by a master influenced by Bicci di Lorenzo. A door in S. side of the church admits to the CLOISTER (early 17C; not always open in the afternoon) with a well. The rooms off the cloister display frescoes detached from the cloister buildings and church. In the first room, once part of the Refectory: *Aless. Allori,* Last Supper and monochrome frescoes. In 2nd room, detached frescoes from the Cappella di San Girolamo, by *Starnina; Fil. Lippi,* the Rule of the Order (partly destroyed); Crucifixion, a beautiful work by an unknown hand; *Giov. di Milano,* Madonna enthroned with Saints. In 3rd room (where concerts of the Musicus Concentus are held, comp. p. 414), detached frescoes from the Cappella della Passione attrib. to *Lippo Fiorentino.* On the end wall, remains of a Last Supper by *Fr. Vanni.*

In Via dell'Ardiglione, near by, to the E. of the church (comp. the Plan), a plaque on a little house just beyond the arch over the road, records the birthplace of Filippo Lippi in 1406.

Borgo San Frediano returns E., continued, across the handsome long Via de' Serragli, by Via Santo Spirito. To the right a school now occupies both the *Palazzo Rinuccini* (No. 39), and the *Palazzo Manetti* (No. 31), home of Horace Mann in 1740-86. Lord and Lady Holland lived in the neighbouring *Palazzo Ferroni* with G. F. Watts as their guest in 1844-47. VIA MAGGIO leads to the right at the end, passing (No. 26) the house built by the Grand Duke Francesco I for Bianca Cappello, who was first his mistress and afterwards his wife. Via dei Michelozzi, on the right, leads to the pretty P.za Santo Spirito, in which is the **Palazzo Guadagni,* ascribed to Cronaca, among the best of 15C Florentine mansions. The church of **Santo Spirito** (Pl. 10; open 7-12, 15.30-17.30 or 18.30) presents a bare façade to the square, with the Corsini chapel on the left, and Baccio d'Agnolo's slender campanile behind.

The *INTERIOR, one of the most brilliant creations of the Florentine

Renaissance, was begun by *Brunelleschi* (1444), continued and completed by *Ant. Manetti, Giov. da Gaiole* and *Salvi d'Andrea*(1481). The plan is a Latin cross, with vaulted aisles, a ceiled nave, and a cupola. The colonnade, whose 35 columns (including the 4 piers of the cupola) have Corinthian capitals with imposts above, is carried round the transepts and apse, forming un unbroken arcade. The interior façade, designed by *Salvi d'Andrea* (1483-87) has a round stained glass window designed by *Perugino*. Around the walls are 40 semicircular niches (numbered here from r. to l.) containing interesting works of art (very poorly lit; difficult to see on a dark day or late in the afternoon): 2. Pietà, copy by *Nanni di Baccio Bigio* (1549) of Michelangelo's work; 3. St Nicholas of Tolentino, polychrome wood statue probably from a model by *Iac. Sansovino,* and two angels painted by *Franciabigio;* 5. Coronation of the Virgin, by *Aless. Gherardini;* 8. Tobias and the Archangel, marble altarpiece by *Giov. Baratta* (after 1690).—11. Madonna del Soccorso, a 15C painting in the manner of Cosimo Rosselli; 12. Wood 14C Crucifix; 13. *Filippino Lippi,* *Madonna and Child, with the Infant St John, saints and donors (c. 1490); 15. Sarcophagus of Neri Capponi, attrib. to *Bern. Rossellino* (1458).—17. Virgin with Saints, in the style of Lor. di Credi; 18. *Maso di Bianco,* Polyptych with Madonna and Child and Saints; 20. *Aless. Allori,* Martyred Saints; 23. 15C *Florentine School,* Annunciation; 24. *School of Dom. Ghirlandaio,* Nativity.—25. *Raffaele dei Carli* (attrib.), Madonna and Saints; 26. St Monica, attrib. to *Franc. Botticini;* 27. *Cosimo Rosselli,* Madonna enthroned with two Saints; 28. The Cappella Corbinelli, with marble *Decoration by *And. Sansovino;* 29. The Trinity, attrib. to *Franc. Granacci;* 30. *Raffaele dei Carli* (attrib.), Madonna enthroned; 31. A similar subject by the same painter.—36. *Rid. and Michele Ghirlandaio,* Madonna with St Anne and other Saints.

The rich high altar is by *Caccini* (1599-1609).—At the 35th niche, under the organ, is the entrance to a *VESTIBULE, with 12 Corinthian pillars supporting a barrel vault elaborately coffered, designed by *Giul. da Sangallo,* and carried out by *Cronaca;* the adjoining *SACRISTY is an octagonal chamber with Corinthian pilasters, also designed by *Giul. da Sangallo,* and with a lantern and dome executed on a model of *Ant. Pollaiuolo* and *Salv. d'Andrea* (1495-96). From the vestibule is the entrance to the FIRST CLOISTER, by *Alfonso Parigi the Elder.* The SECOND CLOISTER, entered from the piazza (shown by sacristan), was built by *Ammannati* in the Doric style (1564-69). Off the cloister is the CAPPELLA CORSINI with the Gothic tombs of Tom. Corsini (d. 1366) and of Neri Corsini, Bp. of Fiesole (d. 1377), and a contemporary fresco of the Resurrection and two Saints.
To the left of the church, at No. 29, is the entrance to the REFECTORY (adm. 9-13, fest. 9-12; closed Mon), with a large *Fresco of the Last Supper by *And. Orcagna* (c. 1360; very ruined). Here, too, is displayed a charming collection of sculpture from the FONDAZIONE SALVATORE ROMANO, including two fine statuettes by *Tino da Camaino,* Romanesque fragments and primitive stone reliefs, and a portal of 1471 sculpted by *Natale di Ragusa.*

From the S. end of the piazza Via Mazzetta leads back to P.za San Felice. Here, at No. 9, is the 15C *Casa Guidi,* where Robert Browning and his wife lived from 1848 until her death in 1861 (inscription; open weekdays 16-19; visitors ring). **San Felice** (Pl. 10) is a Gothic church with a Renaissance façade by *Michelozzo* (1457).

INTERIOR. The first half of the nave contains a closed gallery supported by eight columns and a pretty vault. S. side: 1st altar, remains of a fresco of the Pietà, attrib. to *Nic. Gerini;* above the side door, large *Crucifix from the workshop of *Giotto;*

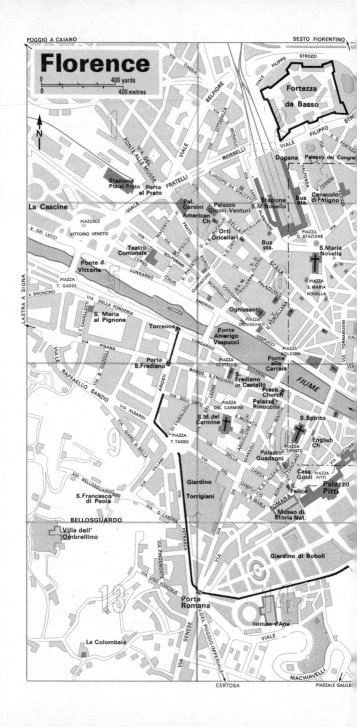

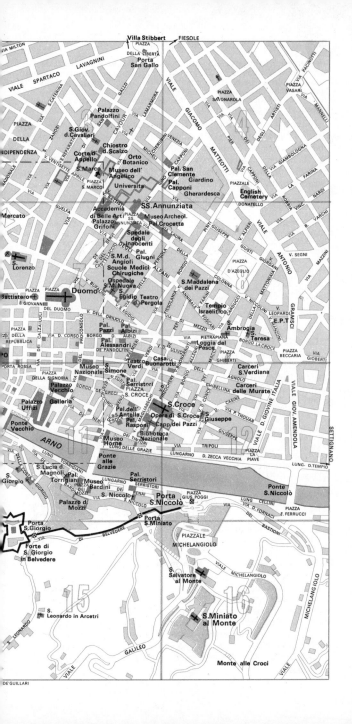

4th altar, Pietà, terracotta group attrib. to *Cieco da Gambassi;* 5th altar, Madonna and Saints by *Rid.* and *Mich. Ghirlandaio;* 6th altar, lunette fresco of the Virgin of the Sacred Girdle (late 14C Florentine). In the presbytery the altarpiece has a 15C Madonna and Child and two Saints of the 16C. N. side: 7th altar, fresco by *Giov. da San Giovanni* (the angels are by *Volterrano*); 6th altar, triptych by *Neri di Bicci* beneath a frescoed lunette of the 14C; 1st altar, triptych by a follower of *Botticelli.*

To the left is Piazza Pitti, No. 16 in which was the house of Paolo dal Pozzo Toscanelli (1397-1482), who was the greatest geographer of his time and conceived the project realized by Columbus. While staying at No. 21 in 1868 Dostoievsky wrote 'The Idiot'. The colossal ***Palazzo Pitti** (Pl. 10), a majestic palace, begun c. 1458, for the wealthy merchant Luca Pitti, by *Luca Fancelli* on a design by *Brunelleschi,* was left unfinished in 1465. Its imposing position results from excavations which artificially raised the site of the building.

In 1549 the palace was bought by Eleonora di Toledo, wife of Cosimo I, and enlarged by *Ammannati* (1558-70). Additions were made by *Giulio* and *Alfonso Parigi the Younger* (1620-40), following the original design. These greatly enlarged Brunelleschi's original façade, which was only half the present size. The various ruling families of Florence continued to occupy the palace, or part of it, until 1919, when Victor Emmanuel III presented the whole to the State.

The central door admits to the imposing ATRIUM, by Pasquale Poccianti (c. 1850), and to the Baroque COURT, by Ammannati (1558-70), the fourth side of which is formed by a terrace, with the *Fontana del Carciofo,* or *Artichoke Fountain,* by Susini and Fr. del Tadda, and beneath it the *Grotta di Mosè,* with another fountain and statuary.

Under the portico to the right is the entrance to the celebrated ****Galleria Pitti** (*Galleria Palatina*), founded 1640, a series of magnificently decorated apartments containing some 500 pictures, nearly all masterpieces of the 16-17C, still preserving to some extent the character of a private royal collection, the æsthetic arrangement of the rooms being considered rather than the chronological placing of the paintings. Many of the rooms are ornamented with elaborate ceilings and groups of decorative statuary.

Tickets are purchased off the courtyard, left of the stairs up to the gallery.
Admission to the six main rooms of paintings (numbered 1-6 on the Plan) is 9-14, exc. Mon; Sun & fest. 9-13. The other groups of rooms (numbered 7-15, and 16-26) of the Galleria Palatina have the same opening hours, but are sometimes closed for certain periods of the year. The *Appartamenti Monumentali* (ex Reale); numbered II-XIV) are generally open only on certain days of the week. The remaining rooms on the first floor (XV-XXII) are closed except for exhibitions, etc.—On the Second Floor, the *Galleria d'Arte Moderna* is open 9-14, exc. Mon; Sun & fest. 9-13. On the Ground Floor, the *Museo degli Argenti* is usually open on certain days of the week, and the *Museo delle Carrozze* is sometimes opened on request. Admission to the *Collezione Contini Bonacossi* in the Meridiana pavilion is usually granted on special request.
All the rooms are named as indicated in the description below; room numbers on the first floor have been given only to correspond with the Plan, p. 467.

The Grand Staircase by Ammannati ascends past (3rd landing) a statue, the 'Genio mediceo', by *Giambologna* to the entrance of the Galleria Palatina. The ANTICAMERA or SALA DEGLI STAFFIERI (A) contains statues by *Baccio Bandinelli* (Bacchus) and *Pietro Francavilla* (Mercury). The GALLERIA DELLE STATUE (B) is decorated with sculptures and Florentine tapestries by Pietro Fevère.—To the left is the SALA DELLE NICCHIE (1), in neo-classical style, which contains two seascapes by *Van der Velde the Elder,* and the Triumph of Galatea, by *Luca Giordano.* To the r. is the entrance to the first of the main rooms of paintings.

Palazzo Pitti
First Floor

Giardino di Boboli

Cortile dell Ammannati

PIAZZA

Cortile della Fama

The SALA DI VENERE (1) has the earliest ceiling (1641-42) of the fine group executed for the following four rooms by *Pietro da Cortona* and *Ciro Ferri*. *185, *Titian,* Concert (c. 1513; formerly attrib. to Giorgione, and at present removed for restoration); *4., 15. *Salvator Rosa,* Two large Seascapes; *9. *Rubens,* Ulysses in the Phæcian Isle, a companion to *14. Return from the hayfields (with a superb landscape); 8. *Guercino,* Apollo and Marsyas; *54. *Titian,* Portrait of Pietro Aretino; 84, *Bonifacio de' Pitati,* Sacred Conversation; *18. *Titian,* Portrait of a lady ('la bella'); 409. *Sebastiano del Piombo,* Baccio Valori.

SALA DI APOLLO (2). 150. *Anthony Van Dyck,* Charles I and Henrietta Maria; 270. *Guido Reni,* Cleopatra; 41. *Cristofano Allori,* St Julian; *81. *Andrea del Sarto,* Holy Family; 116. *Sustermans,* Portrait of Vittoria della Rovere; 50. *Guercino,* St Peter healing Tabitha; 237. *Rosso Fiorentino,* Madonna enthroned and Saints; 55. *Barocci,* Ferdinando, Prince of Urbino; 380. *Dosso Dossi,* St John the Baptist; *131. *Tintoretto,* Portrait of Vincenzo Zeno; 58. *Andrea del Sarto,* Deposition (1523); *Titian,* *92. Portrait of a Gentleman (c. 1540), *67. Mary Magdalen.

SALA DI MARTE (3). *83. *Tintoretto,* Portrait of Luigi Cornaro (in restoration); *82. *Anthony Van Dyck,* Portrait of Card. Guido Bentivoglio; *Titian,* 80. Portrait of Andrea Vesalio; *201. Portrait of Card. Ippolito de' Medici in Hungarian costume; *86. *Rubens,* Consequences of War, an allegory painted for Ferdinand II de' Medici (1638); 216. *Paolo Veronese,* Portrait of Daniele Barbaro (?); *Murillo,* 56, 63. Two paintings of the Madonna and Child; *Rubens,* *85. 'The Four Philosophers' (Rubens, his brother, Justus Lipsius, and Jan van Wouwer, with a bust of Seneca), 235. Holy Family; 256. *Fra Bartolomeo,* Holy Family.

SALA DI GIOVE (4). *110. *Giorgione* or *Giovanni Bellini,* Three Ages of Man; *245. *Raphael,* Veiled Woman (the 'Donna velata' or 'la Fornarina'), an exquisite late work; 370. *Piero del Pollaiuolo* (attrib.), Head of St Jerome; *Andrea del Sarto,* 123. Madonna with four Saints (unfinished), 124. Annunciation; *125. *Fra Bartolomeo,* St Mark; 149. *Bronzino,* Portrait of Guidobaldo della Rovere; 113. *Fr. Salviati,* The Fates; *64. *Fra Bartolomeo,* Deposition; 272. *Andrea del Sarto,* The Young St John the Baptist (1523; badly restored in the 19C); 219. *Perugino,* Madonna del Sacco; 156. *Guercino,* Madonna; 139. *Rubens,* Holy Family.

SALA DI SATURNO (5). *Raphael,* *151. Madonna della Seggiola (c. 1515), 158. Portrait of Card. Bernardo Dovizi da Bibbiena; 207. *Rid. del Ghirlandaio,* Portrait of a man (goldsmith); *Perugino,* 42. Mary Magdalen, *164. Deposition; *Raphael,* *59. Portrait of Maddalena Doni, in the pose of Leonardo's Gioconda, *174. Vision of Ezechial (a tiny work), 61. Portrait of Agnolo Doni, *165. Madonna del Baldacchino, a very large altarpiece of unusual design, 171. Portrait of Tommaso Inghirami; 166. *Ann. Carracci,* Head of a man; 172. *And. del Sarto,* Disputation on the Trinity; *178. *Raphael,* Madonna 'del Granduca' (c. 1504-05), showing the influence of Leonardo; 159. *Fra Bartolomeo,* The Risen Christ appearing to his Disciples.

SALA DELL'ILIADE (6), with a ceiling by *Sabatelli* of 1819 (with frescoes from the Iliad). 243. *Velazquez,* Equestrian portrait of Philip IV of Spain; 190. *Sustermans,* Portrait of Count Valdemar Christian of

Denmark; 187. *Fr. Pourbus the Younger,* Eleonora de' Medici; *Andrea del Sarto,* 225. Assumption (1526); *191. Assumption (1531; unfinished); *Artemesia Gentileschi,* 142. Mary Magdalen, 398. Judith; *Titian,* 200. Portrait of Philip II, *215. Portrait of Diego de Mendoza; 224. *Rid. Ghirlandaio,* Portrait of a young woman; 229. *Raphael,* Portrait of a lady ('la Gravida', c. 1506); 223. *Joos van Cleve* (attrib.), Portrait of a man; 391. *Pourbus,* Eleonora of Mantua.

The normal exit from the Gallery is through the VESTIBULE (C) which contains a fountain attrib. to *Fr. di Simone Ferrucci* (from the Villa di Castello), and a painting of St Sebastian by *Sodoma.* The GRAND STAIRCASE, a monumental work by *Luigi del Moro* (c. 1895-97) descends to the courtyard.

From the Sala di Venere (see above; Plan 1) there is access to the SALA DEL CASTAGNOLI (7), named after the artist who decorated it. It contains a magnificent mosaic *Table made in Florence in 1851 with Apollo and the Muses (bronze base of the four seasons by *Giov. Duprè*).

A door leads in to the SALA DELLE ALLEGORIE (or DEL VOLTERRANO; Pl. 8), with paintings and frescoes by *Volterrano:* 107. Love sleeping, 105. Mercenary love, 2578. Portrait of Antonio Baldinucci, 582. The Parson's jest; and works by *Giov. da S. Giovanni.* In the centre, statue of young Michelangelo, by *Emilio Zocchi* (1861).—SALA DELLE BELLE ARTI (9). Paintings by *Cigoli.*—SALONE D'ERCOLE (10), frescoes from the life of Hercules by *Pietro Benvenuti* (1828). In the centre is a huge Sèvres vase of 1784.—SALA DELL'AURORA (11). Paintings by *Empoli.* The SALA DI BERENICE (12) contains works by *Fr. Furini, Carlo Dolci,* and others.—SALA DI PSICHE (13). Fine works by *Salvator Rosa* (470. The Wood of the Philosophers, land- and seascapes, 133. Battle scene, and sketches on wood).—SALA DELLA FAMA (14). Flemish works (*Willem van Aelst, Jean Clouet,* etc.). The Vestibule and Bathroom (15) of Queen Maria Luisa (c. 1805) were designed in neo-classical style by *Gius. Cacialli.*

From the Sala del Castagnoli (see above) is the entrance to the SALA DELLA MUSICA (16) and the GALLERIA DEL POCCETTI (17), so named from the author of the frescoes in the vault. Paintings here include: *Rubens* 761, 324. Duke and Duchess of Buckingham; 249. *Pontormo,* Francesco da Castiglione; 408. *Peter Lely,* Cromwell; and landscapes by *Poussin.*—Beyond is the SALA DI PROMETEO (18). 604. *Marco Palmezzano,* Caterina Sforza; 359. *Beccafumi,* Holy Family; 182. *Pontormo,* The eleven thousand martyrs; 365. *Mariotto Albertinelli,* Holy Family; 167. *Baldassarre Peruzzi,* Dance of Apollo with the Muses; 364. *Iac. del Sellaio,* Madonna in adoration of the Child; 347. *Fr. Botticini,* Madonna and Child with angels; *343. *Filippo Lippi,* Tondo of the Madonna and Child, a charming composition, with scenes from the life of the Virgin in the background. 348. *School of Botticelli,* Madonna and Child with angels; 355. *Luca Signorelli,* Tondo of the Holy Family; *Botticelli,* 372. 353. Portrait of a man, and of a lady; 354. *Cosimo Rosselli,* Nativity.

Beyond the CORRIDOIO DELLE COLONNE (19) hung with small Flemish paintings (including some by *Cornelis van Poelenburgh*) is the SALA DELLA GIUSTIZIA (20). *Veronese,* 108. Portrait of Paolo Caliari, 186. Baptism of Christ; 494. *Titian,* Portrait of a Man; 121. *Giov. Batt. Moroni,* Portrait of a man; *Tintoretto,* 410, 65. Two portraits; *495. *Titian,* Vincenzo Mosti; 228. The Redeemer, an early work.—SALA DI FLORA (21). The 'Venus Italica' sculpted by *Canova,* and presented by Napoleon in exchange for the Medici Venus which he had removed to Paris. *Pontormo,* 379. Adoration of the Magi (in restoration), dep. 41. Portrait of a lady; 179. *Sebastiano del Piombo,* Martyrdom of

St Agatha (in restoration), 88, 87. *And. del Sarto,* Story of Joseph.—
SALA DEI PUTTI (22). Still-life paintings by *Rachel Ruysch* and others;
1165. Drawing of the Three Graces by *Rubens;* 453. *Salvator Rosa,*
Landscape.

From the Sala di Promoteo (18; see above) is the entrance to the SALA
DI ULISSE (23). 311. *Titian,* Alfonso I of Ferrara; 94. *Raphael,* Madonna
dell'Impannata (with the collaboration of his workshop); *School of
Moroni,* Portrait of a Man; 307. *And. del Sarto,* Madonna and Child
with Saints; 338. *Filippino Lippi,* Death of Lucrezia; 70. *Tintoretto,*
Portrait of Andrea Frizier, Grand Chancellor of Venice.—Beyond the
'Empire' bathroom (24) by *Cacialli,* is the SALA DELL'EDUCAZIONE DI
GIOVE (25). *96. *Crist. Allori,* Judith, with portraits of the artist, his wife,
and his mother-in-law; 183. *Caravaggio,* Sleeping Cupid, and works by
Carlo Dolci.—The *SALA DELLA STUFA (26), beyond, is beautifully
frescoed by *Pietro da Cortona* (1637-40; the Ages of the World) and
Matteo Rosselli (1622; Fames and the Virtues, on the ceiling). The
restored majolica pavement (Triumph of Bacchus, 1640) is by *Bened.
Bocchi.*

The other half of the palace is occupied by the **Appartamenti
Monumentali (ex Reali;** for opening times see p. 466), entered from the
Sala delle Nicchie (B; comp. above). This series of lavishly decorated
state apartments are notable particularly for their numerous portraits of
the Medici by Sustermans and a fine group of Gobelins tapestries.

The SALA VERDE (II) has a painting (formerly in the ceiling) of the Allegory of
Peace between Florence and Fiesole, by *Luca Giordano;* a table (1716), by *Giov.
Battista Foggini;* and a painting showing the studio of an artist (for long thought to
be that of Rubens), by *Cornelis de Baelheur.* The inlaid Cabinet was built for
Vittoria della Rovere in 1680.—The SALA DEL TRONO (III), and SALA CELESTE
(IV), contain portraits by *Sustermans* and *Frans Pourbus the Younger.*—The
CAPPELLA (V) has a Madonna by *Carlo Dolci* (in a rich frame by *Foggini*).—
SALA DEI PAPPAGALLI (VI). *School of Botticelli,* Madonna and Child with
angels; 764. *Titian,* Portrait of Giulia Varano. Cabinet in ebony and ivory by
Foggini. Fr. Pourbus the Younger, Elizabeth of France.—The SALA GIALLA (VII)
and the CAMERA DA LETTO DELLA REGINA MARGHERITA (VIII) contain a
magnificent series of hunting tapestries showing Louis XV.—The oval TOLETTA
DELLA REGINA (IX) is decorated in the Chinese style. The adjoining circular SALA
DI MUSICA DELLA REGINA (X) is usually kept closed.—From the Sala dei
Pappagalli (VI; see above) is the entrance to the APPARTAMENTI DI UMBERTO I,
four rooms (XI-XIV) lavishly decorated, with more portraits by *Sustermans.*—
The remaining series of rooms (XV-XXII) are normally kept closed and used only
for exhibitions. In the Sala Bianca (XV), or del Ballo, concerts are held.

On the floor above the Galleria Palatina is the **Galleria d'Arte Moderna** (for
opening times, see p. 466). The first series of rooms display works of the neo-
classical and romantic periods, including paintings by *Pompeo Batoni, Gaspare
Landi, François Fabre, Fr. Altamura,* and sculptures by *Giov. Duprè* and
Canova.—In the second wing: Works by *Stefano Ussi, Vinc. Cabianca, Odoardo
Borrani.*—Portraits by *Ant. Ciseri.*—Beyond the SALA DA BALLO (1825), with
two statues of the young Bacchus by *Giov. Duprè.* R. 13 has portraits by *Giov.
Fattori* and *Giov. Boldini, Ant. Puccinelli,* and *Vito d'Ancona.*—R. 14.
Landscapes by *Ant. Fontanesi, Serafino De Tivoli,* and *Andrea Markò.*—R. 15.
Works by *Cristiano Banti* and *Giov. Boldini.*—R. 16 contains the Diego Martelli
collection of Macchiaioli painters and the French school: works by *Gius. Abbati,
Giov. Boldini, Giov. Fattori, Silvestro Lega, Camille Pissarro, Telemaco
Signorini, Fed. Zandomeneghi.*—R. 17. Genre scenes by *Gius. Abbati, Adriano
Cecioni, Gius. De Nittis,* and *Giov. Fattori.*—R. 18. The Risorgimento. *Adriano
Cecioni,* Bust of Gius. Mazzini; Battle scenes by *Fattori* and *Silvestro Lega.*

The *Museo degli Argenti** (for opening times, see p. 466) is entered from the left
side of the courtyard. The entrance hall has tapestries and pictures relating to

Ferdinando I and Christine of Lorraine, and to Cardinal Leopoldo. The frescoes on the ceiling of the SALA DI GIOVANNI DI SAN GIOVANNI were begun in 1635 after the marriage of Ferdinando II and Vittoria della Rovere.—SALA DEL TRONO. Frescoes by the Bolognese *Angelo Michele Colonna* and *Agostino Mitelli* (1637-41). The cabinet, brought to Florence in 1628, was made in Augsburg.— Beyond the SALA DELL'UDIENZA PRIVATA, two more rooms contain tables of beautiful workmanship.—MEZZANINE. ROOM I. Cameo portraits of famous Florentines including Cosimo I by G. A. De Rossi (1557-62). Room 2. Picture in precious stones of Cosimo II in prayer (1617-27); *Jewellery collection of the last of the Medicis, the Electress Anna Maria.—Gold and silversmiths' work from the collection of Ferdinando II, including German ecclesiastical treasures of 14-15C.—Beyond a painted loggia, the last room, with a delightful frescoed vault, contains exotic and rare objects.

Off the right side of the courtyard (entered from the door to the left of the ticket office) is the *Cappella Reale,* frescoed by Luigi Ademollo, with vestments in the Sacristy.—Outside the entrance portico of the palace (l.) is the entrance on the piazza to the *Museo delle Carrozze* (adm. see p. 466), with a collection of carriages formerly in use in the Courts of Tuscany, Modena, and the two Sicilies, and dating from the 17-18C.

In the PALAZZINA DELLA MERIDIANA (adm., see p. 466) which was begun in 1776 by Gaspare Maria Paoletti, the *Collezione Contini-Bonacossi has recently been arranged. It includes a fine collection of Italian (and some Spanish) paintings, and furniture of 15-17C, majolica, etc. ROOM I. *Agnolo Gaddi,* Madonna and Child with Saints.—ROOM II. *Paolo Veneziano,* Two scenes from the life of St Nicholas.—ROOM III. *Bernardino Zenale,* St Michael arcangel, St Bernard; *Sassetta,* Madonna della Neve (altarpiece); *Defendente Ferrari,* Madonna and Child.—R. IV. *Giovanni Belini,* St Jerome in the desert; *Paolo Veronese,* Count Giuseppe da Porto and his son Adriano; *Vincenzo Catena,* Supper at Emmaus; *Gian Lorenzo Bernini,* Martyrdom of St Lawrence (sculpture).R. V. *Bramantino,* Madonna and Child with Saints; *Giov. Ant. Boltraffio,* Portrait of the poet Casio; *Cima da Coneglian,* St, Jerome in the deserts.—R. VI. *Fr. Goya,* Bull-fighter; El Greco, 'The tears of St Peter's'; *Diego Velazquez,* The water-carrier.—R.R. VII-IX. Della Robbian tondoes, statuettes by *Bambaia,* etc.—R. X. *Andrea del Castagno,* Madonna and Child with angels and Saints and two children of the Pazzi family (fresco from the castle of Trebbio).—R. XI. *Iac. Tintoretto,* Portrait of a man, Minerva, and Venus.

On the left of the palace is the entrance to the *Bóboli Gardens (Pl. 10,14), typical Italian gardens laid out for Cosimo I by Tribolo in 1550 on the hillside. They are open Nov-Feb, 9-16.30; March-April, and Sept-Oct, 9-17.30; other months, 9-18.30.

Near the entrance is the *Fontana di Bacco,* with a statue of Pietro Barbino, the dwarf of Cosimo I, by Valerio Cioli. Opposite the entrance is the fantastic *Grotta del Buontalenti,* four chambers by Buontalenti elaborately decorated with paintings and stucchi and statues (seen through a locked grille) including a fountain enclosed by cypresses and ilexes. From here the scenographic *Viottolone* descends Roman statues, to the first terrace. On the right is Ammannati's court with the Artichoke Fountain; on the left the *Amphitheatre,* surrounded by tiers of seats; in the centre are a large antique basin and an obelisk from Thebes. On the first platform are antique statues, among them a fine Ceres; on the second platform, a large fountain-basin, the *Lake of Neptune* in the middle of which is an island, with a bronze figure of Neptune by Stoldo Lorenzi (1565). A short detour to the left leads through romantic winding alleys overshawdowed by ilexes to the *Casino,* or Coffee-House (with a Bar), near some cypresses (view of Florence and Fiesole). On the last platform is a colossal figure of Abundance, by Giambologna and Tacca. To the right a double staircase leads up to the *Giardino del Cavaliere,* with the Monkey Fountain, by Tacca, on the promenade of the bastion constructed by Michelangelo (view of the fields and hills surrounding Florence). Here, in the Casino del Cavaliere, is the MUSEO DELLE PORCELLANE (adm. Tues, Thurs, Friday, & Sun, 9-14) with a beautifully displayed collection of Italian, German, and French porcelain including fine examples from the great factories, and the famous 'Alzate da ostriche'.

At the foot of the double stairs, another flight of steps descends between seated Muses and, at the end of a range of garden houses, is the *Prato dell'Uccellare,* enclosed by cypresses and ilexes. From here the scenographic *Viottolone* descends steeply between dark walls of evergreen. On each side and in the branching alleys are antique statues and 16-17C groups. The paths and little gardens to right and left with delightful vistas provide some of the most beautiful scenery in the park. At the bottom is the *Piazzale dell'Isolotto,* an open space bordered with high espaliers of ilex; a circular moat with fine sculptural decorations surrounds an island with a garden and a copy of Giambologna's Fountain of Oceanus (original in the Bargello). Beyond the Isolotto the Viottolone continues to the end of the gardens near the Porta Romana (comp. below). Here in the *Royal Stables* is the Istituto d'Arte, with a Museum of Plaster-casts. A path returns past the *Orangery* to leave the park at the Annalena gate on Via Romana.

From P.za Pitti Via Romana continues S.W. to the *Porta Romana* (Pl. 13,14), a massive gateway of 1326, passing (l.; No. 17) the *Palazzo Torrigiani,* known as 'La Specola' from the Observatory founded here by the Grand-duke Pietro Leopoldo. Here, in 1814, Sir Humphry Davy and Michael Faraday used Galileo's 'great burning-glass' to explode the diamond. It is now the seat of a ZOOLOGICAL MUSEUM (adm. Mon & Tues 9-12.30; Sat 14 or 15-17 or 18; and Sun 9-12) with a comprehensive natural history display, and a remarkable collection of anatomical models in wax, many made by Clemente Susini in 1775-1814.—In Via Foscolo, beyond the gate, is the 15C *Villa La Colombaia,* birthplace in 1820 of Florence Nightingale.

From P.za Pitti VIA DE' GUICCIARDINI (Pl. 10, 11) leads to the Ponte Vecchio, passing (No. 15) *Palazzo Guicciardini,* birthplace of Fr. Guicciardini (d. 1540), the Florentine historian; No. 16, the *Casa Campigli,* in which Machiavelli (d. 1527) lived and died, has been destroyed. On the right, in the piazzetta named after it, is the church of SANTA FELÍCITA (Pl. 10,11), last rebuilt by Ferd. Ruggieri in 1736. In the portico the tombs are of (r.) Card. Luigi Rossi (d. 1518), by *Raff. da Montelupo,* and (l. above) of Barduccio Chiericini (d. 1416). The fine interior is chiefly notable for the superb *Works by *Pontormo* in the Cappella Capponi (1st on r.), which include the altarpiece (Deposition), a fresco (recently detached and restored) of the Annunciation, and the tondoes in the cupola of the Evangelists (except St Mark, which is attrib. to *Bronzino*). These are considered among the masterpieces of 16C Florentine painting.—Over the 4th altar on the r. is a striking painting (the Martyrdom of the Maccabei brothers), by *Ant. Ciseri* (1863). Over the high altar, Nativity, by *Santi di Tito.*—The Sacristy (off the right transept) has a polyptych of the Madonna and Child with Saints, by *Taddeo Gaddi,* in its original frame; St Felicity and her seven children, by *Neri di Bicci,* a Crucifix attrib. to *Pacino di Bonaguida,* and two detached 14C frescoes of the Nativity and Annunciation, attrib. to *Niccolo di Pietro Gerini.*

A pleasant walk, beginning in the adjoining P.za de' Rossi, ascends the pretty Costa San Giorgio (Pl. 11) and then descends the picturesque lane of the Via di Belvedere (l.) to San Niccolò (see below). On the way up is the church of *San Giorgio sulla Costa* (or *Spirito Santo*) with a Madonna and Child with two angels, an early work by Giotto, and (No. 19) the *House of Galileo* where he was visited by Ferdinand II in 1620. On the left is *Villa Bardini,* with a fine park, recently left to the State. At the top is the attractive *Porta San Giorgio* (Pl. 15; c. 1260) with the copy of a relief of St George (1284; original in Palazzo Vecchio), and a fresco by *Bicci di Lorenzo.* Here is the entrance to the *Forte di Belvedere (Pl. 15), a huge fortress designed by Buontalenti (probably using plans drawn up by Don Giovanni de' Medici) in the shape of a six-pointed star, and built by Ferdinand I in 1590, ostensibly for the defence of the city but in reality to dominate the supposedly republican citizens. Entered from the Bóboli Gardens by a secret door, guarded night and day until 1850 by a sentry, it remained inaccessible to the public until 1958. From the ramparts (adm. 8-20) there is a splendid view in every direction, and the structure of defences may be examined. The interior is only opened for large exhibitions which are held here periodically.—From here the picturesque Via San Leonardo (see p. 475), continues to ascend.

At the S. end of Ponte Vecchio begins *VIA DE' BARDI (Pl. II), named after the family of which George Eliot's 'Romola' was a member. Among the old houses here destroyed in 1944 was the *Casa Ambrogi*, guest-house of Horace Mann, where Gray and Walpole stayed in 1740. The road diverges right from Lungarno Torrigiani and winds between a series of noble town houses. Adjoining No. 18 is the church of *Santa Lucia dei Magnoli* (open only for evensong), with a terracotta by Buglioni over the door, and within (1st altar left) St Lucy, by Pietro Lorenzetti, with an Annunciation at the sides, ascribed to Iac. del Sellaio. The street ends at the P.za dei Mozzi, with three 13C palazzi of the Mozzi family (r.). Nos 4 and 5 are the *Palazzi Torrigiani* (16C).

On the right side of the piazza is the Palazzo Bardini, now occupied by a fine collection of ancient works of art, known as the ***Museo Bardini** (Pl. 11; adm. 9-14 exc. Wed; fest 8-13), bequeathed to the city in 1923 by the antiquary Stef. Bardini. Many of the rooms have fine door-ways brought from demolished buildings.

From the atrium, beyond R. VI, is ROOM I, with Roman and Etruscan tombs, including a sarcophagus with Medusa's Head used again in the Middle Ages.—RR. II-IV contain leather, glass, and iron work, and a model of the Duomo.—RR. V-VIII contain notable Renaissance sculptural and architectural pieces.—RR. VII-VIII, formerly a courtyard, are now covered by a coffered ceiling with glass inserted in the panels. At the end is an important medieval arch between two fine sarcophagi; in front, *Charity, ascribed to *Tino di Camaino;* to the left, Pulpit with mosaic decoration in the Romanesque style of the South. Against the colonnaded wall is the fine Tomb of Riccardo Gattula (1417); also a well-head of red Veronese marble.—ROOM IX. (l. of the atrium) contains a 15C marble portal and two fine stone chimneypieces (that on the left from the bottega of *Desiderio da Settignano,* the other of Lombard work, with the Este coat-of-arms); on the left, a fountain-figure of a putto.—R. X. known as the crypt, is a large vaulted room with altar tombs and tomb-slabs; *Altarpiece, by *And. della Robbia;* relief, after Donatello.

A fine staircase leads up to the First Floor. RR. XI-XIII have been closed for rearrangement. They contain tournament-shields and parade-armour, as well as battle-armour; also a rare battle-lantern such as is depicted in the frescoes in the Sala dei Cinquecento (Pal. Vecchio).—R. XIV, facing the stair-head, contains plaster and other reliefs, including a polychrome Madonna ascribed to *Donatello;* also, a painted tondo attrib. to *Ambr. Lorenzetti.*—R. XV, the Salone, is notable for its 17C tapestries and portraits (including works by *Fr. Salviati*), and its furniture. Among the busts is one, at the end, of a *Girl with gilded hair. The central cases contain bronze medals, plaques, and statuettes. Also here, detached frescoes (from Palazzo Pucci) by *Giov. da San Giovanni,* and two tondoes by *Volterrano.*—R. XVI, a large hall furnished like a sacristy, with a fine chimneypiece and ceiling, contains a large Crucifix attrib. to a follower of Bernardo Daddi; *Michele Giambono,* St John the Baptist; *Giul. Bugiardini* (?), Madonna and Child; painted and gilded reliefs and statuettes.—R. XVII continues the collection of furniture and coloured statuettes, and in R. XVIII is the delightful *Virgin of the Annunciation, the loveliest object in the collection, a terracotta figure of a young girl in a flowered robe (Sienese, 15C); here also are other painted figures including St Catharine of Siena (Sienese, beginning of 15C), and St John (13C), and a painting of St Michael by *Ant. Pollaiuolo.*—R. XIX displays old musical instruments (including a spinet made in Rome in 1577).—On the upper floor the Galleria Corsi contains the artistic bequests of Alice and Arnaldo Corsi (1939).—From R. XVIII a small staircase descends to R. XX, the Sala del Crocifisso, named from a large realistic Crucifix (1387); here also are fine inlaid stalls (15C); 15-16C furniture, and a 17C wood model of Pisa Baptistery. The wood ceiling is notable.

Beyond P.za dei Mozzi *Via San Niccolò continues E. No. 99 is *Palazzo Strozzi-Ridolfi,* with a fine 14-15C courtyard. Farther on is the 14C church of SAN NICCOLÒ SOPR'ARNO (Pl. 11; open before 9.30 and for evensong), in the sacristy of which is the *Madonna della Cintola, a fresco attrib. to Piero del Pollaiuolo or Baldovinetti (1450) beneath a little shrine in the style of Michelozzo. Behind the church, on the Lungarno Serristori is the *Palazzo Serristori* (1515, rebuilt 1873), the home of the traitor Baglioni. At the end of Via San Niccolò is the massive *Porta San Niccolò* (1324). From here a flight of steps mount to the Piazzale Michelangelo.

VI.   SAN MINIATO AL MONTE
AND THE VIALE DEI COLLI

The church of *San Miniato* may be reached either on foot by the steps from Porta San Niccolò; or by bus No. 13 (red), from Piazza della Stazione. By car, it is approached from P.za Ferrucci viâ Viale Michelangelo (Pl. 16).
The *Viale dei Colli* is traversed by bus No. 13r.

The **Piazzale Michelangelo** (Pl. 16; 104 m) provides one of the most celebrated viewpoints in the world. From the balustrade there is a remarkable view of the city of Florence, and, beyond, the plain as far as Pistoia, and the peaks of the Apennines. The Monument to Michelangelo (1875) is made up of reproductions in bronze of some of the artist's famous marble statues in the city. The steps behind the Palazzina del Caffè (by Gius. Poggi) mount between cypresses to *San Salvatore al Monte,* a building of gracious simplicity (by Cronaca) called by Michelangelo his "bella villanella"—his pretty country maid. It has been closed awaiting much needed restoration.

*San Miniato al Monte** (Pl. 16), to the S. (reached by a monumental flight of steps, or by a winding road), one of the most beautiful and individual Romanesque churches in Italy, was begun by Bp. Hildebrand after 1018; the façade is 12C. Over the fine W. window is a large mosaic in a Byzantine style (13C) of Christ between the Virgin and St Minias, a 3C warrior-martyr.

The plain aisled INTERIOR (open 8-12.30, 14-19) is practically in its original state. Some of the capitals were brought from earlier Romanesque buildings in Florence and Fiesole; the very fine inlaid *Pavement dates from 1207. At the end of the nave, in front of the crypt, is an exquisite *Tabernacle by *Michelozzo* (1448), which formerly contained St John Gualberto's Crucifix, now at Santa Trínita; the terracotta decoration inside the vault is by *Luca della Robbia,* the paintings by *Agnolo Gaddi.* In the aisles are interesting remains of huge frescoes of 14-15C. The raised CHOIR has a fine transenna and magnificent *Pulpit faced with coloured marble. The carved and inlaid stalls are by *Giov. di Dom. da Gaiole* and *Fr. di Domenico* (*il Monciatto*) and date from 1466-70. Behind the altar in the semicircular apse is a Crucifix attrib. to Luca della Robbia; the imposing vault-mosaic (1297) representing Christ between the Virgin and St Minias and the symbols of the Evangelists was restored in 1491 by Aless. Baldovinetti. On the S. side is the SACRISTY (1387), frescoed by *Spinello Aretino;* in the vault are the Evangelists, on the lunettes the *Life of St Benedict. Here also are two Della Robbia statuettes and stalls like those in the choir.
In the N. aisle is the *CHAPEL OF THE CARDINAL OF PORTUGAL, by *Ant. Manetti* (1461-66), a pupil of Brunelleschi. This incorporates some of the best workmanship of the Florentine Renaissance. The exquisitely carved Tomb of Card. Iac. di Lusitania (1434-59) is by *Ant. Rossellino.* The ceiling has 5 terracotta medallions by *Luca della Robbia,* which are reflected in the inlaid floor below. The altarpiece of Three Saints, by *Ant.* and *Piero del Pollaiuolo* has been replaced by a copy (original in the Uffizi); in the lunette are two angels frescoed by the same artists. On the left wall, *Annunciation by *Baldovinetti.*
The large 11C CRYPT has beautiful columns, many of them with antique capitals. In their midst is the original 11C altar. The fine frescoes of Saints and Prophets (light to r. of altar) are by *Taddeo Gaddi.*—The CLOISTER, recently restored (open Mon, Thurs. & Sun 9.30-12) has frescoes by *Paolo Uccello* (1440) and a sinopia by *And. del Castagno.*

The *Campanile,* begun after 1523 from Baccio d'Agnolo's design was never finished. During the siege of Florence (1530) Michelangelo mounted two cannon here, and protected the building by a screen of mattresses from the hostile artillery. The *Bishop's Palace,* with well-designed twin windows, dates from 1295; it was enlarged in 1320 and later by Bp. Agnolo Ricásoli. The *Fortezza* originated in a hastily improvised defence-work planned by Michelangelo during the months preceding the siege. In 1553 Cosimo I converted it into a real fortress with the help of Fr. da Sangallo and others. It now encloses a cemetery.

The *Viale dei Colli,* a fine roadway 6 km. long, laid out by Gius. Poggi in 1865-70, is the most beautiful drive near Florence, and follows a winding course from the Porta San Niccolò (Pl. 12) to the Porta Romana (Pl. 13, 14). The walls, built by Michelangelo to protect his city, can be seen connecting the Forte di Belvedere with the two gates.

From Porta Romana, Viale Machiavelli mounts between gardens to Piazzale Galileo. Just beyond, to the left, *VIA SAN LEONARDO descends (one-way down) past villas and their gardens between olive groves behind high walls to Porta San Giorgio and the Forte di Belvedere (p. 472). It is one of the most beautiful and best-preserved roads in Florence. At the beginning, on the left, a plaque on No. 64 records the stay of Tchaikowsky here in 1878. Farther down (r.) is the 11C church of *San Leonardo in Arcetri,* which contains a celebrated *Pergamon of the early 13C removed from the demolished church of S. Piero a Scheraggio, with beautiful bas-reliefs. Over the high altar, *Lor. di Niccolò,* Triptych of the Madonna and Child with Saints. Other paintings include, Madonna of the Sacred Girdle with Saints, and an Annunciation with angels and Saints, both by *Neri di Bicci;* and Tobias and the angel, by the *Maestro di San Miniato.*

Via San Leonardo also leads r. from Viale Galileo; after a short distance Via Viviani branches left and ascends past the *Observatory* and the imposing 14C *Torre del Gallo* to reach the long village of **Pian de' Giullari.** No. 42, the *Villa il Gioiello,* was the house where the aged Galileo lived, practically as a prisoner, from 1631 until his death in 1642, and where he was visited by Torricelli, and possibly also Milton. The house and farm with lovely gardens have been restored.

The Viale Galileo continues to Piazzale Michelangelo (see above) and then descends to Ponte San Niccolò.

43   ENVIRONS OF FLORENCE

No city surpasses Florence in the number of beautiful excursions afforded by the country round it. The charm of the neighbouring villages is a fitting pendant to the gracious dignity of the town; and an excellent system of buses brings nearly every point of interest within easy reach.

A. FIÉSOLE is served by Bus no. 7 from P.za San Marco (Pl. 3) in 20 min. It is the goal of a favourite excursion by Florentines, especially in summer when its position makes it one of the coolest places in the neighbourhood of the city. Via Lamarmora and Viale Aless. Volta run N.E. out of Florence. The road soon ascends the hillside, with delightful views on either side. To the l. lies the 'Arrow Route' British Military Cemetery. A double curve precedes P.za San Domenico.

Walkers may reach this piazza, either by the Viale Volta and the Via delle Forbici, or by the Viale Don Minzoni, and the bank of the Mugnone, passing (r.) the *Villa Palmieri,* the traditional scene of one of the episodes in Boccaccio's 'Decameron'. On the right of the piazza a road runs to the *Villa Landor* (formerly Villa Gherardesca), the residence of Walter Savage Landor from 1829 until 1835, when he left his family here. The 'Valley of Ladies' described in the Decameron lies within the grounds. Emerson, Monckton Milnes, and N.P. Willis were among Landor's visitors here. The Villa is now used as an orphanage by the Ospedale degli Innocenti.

At (6½ km.) **San Domenico di Fiesole** the church dates from 1406-35; the portico (1635) and campanile (1611-13) were added by *Matteo Nigetti*. The interesting interior has nave chapels with fine Renaissance arches.

N. side: 1st Chap., *Fra Angelico*, *Madonna with angels and saints (c. 1430; the original predella is in the National Gallery, London): the architectural background was added by *Lor. di Credi* in 1501 (the picture has been removed since 1973 for restoration); 2nd chap., *Giov. Ant. Sogliano* (completed by *Santi di Tito*), Epiphany; 3rd chap., *Jacopo da Empoli*, Annunciation (1615). S. Side: 2nd Chap., *Lor. di Credi*, Baptism of Christ. On the high altar is a wooden tabernacle of 1613 (*Andrea Balatri*). In the adjoining Monastery, St Antoninus (Ant. Pierozzi, 1389-1450) and Fra Angelico (Guido di Pietro or Fra Giovanni da Fiesole, 1387-1455) first assumed the religious habit. The little CHAPTER HOUSE (ring at No. 4, r. of the church) contains a beautiful fresco of the *Crucifixion by *Fra Angelico* (c. 1430) and a detached fresco (with its sinopia) of the Madonna and Child, also by him.

The Via di Badia, descending to the left, leads in 5 min. to the ***Badia Fiesolana,** the cathedral of Fiesole until 1028, and later a Benedictine and Lateranensian house. The church was rebuilt under the direction of Cosimo il Vecchio in the 15C. The bare front incorporates the *Façade of the smaller Romanesque church. The plain cruciform *Interior (if closed, ring at adjoining convent) is in an imposing design in the style of Brunelleschi. The Refectory of the Convent contains a fresco by Giov. da San Giovanni (1629). In the conventual buildings the European University has been established (the first students were admitted 1976/77. The ascent from here to Fiesole by the old road or the new both lined with fine villas and beautiful trees, is a delightful walk affording lovely views.

8 km. **FIESOLE** (295 m), a little town (14,700 inhab.) on a thickly wooded hill overlooking the valleys of the Arno and the Mugnone, is the most attractive and interesting spot in the neighbourhood of Florence.

Fæsulæ, one of the chief cities of the Etruscan confederacy, probably dates from the 9-8C B.C., but is first mentioned in 283 B.C., when its people, in alliance with other Etruscans, were defeated by the Romans at Lake Vadimone. With the Roman occupation it became the chief town in Etruria, but the barbarian invasions led to the decay of the city and to its supersession by Florence as the capital of Tuscany.

The bus stops in the P.za Mino da Fiesole, called after the sculptor (c. 1430-84; born at Poppi in the Casentino) who made Fiesole his home. On the N. side of the piazza is the Romanesque ***Duomo,** a restored building of 1028, with 13-14C additions, and a machicolated campanile of 1213.

The sombre plain Interior (open 7-12, 14.30 or 15-18 or 19; best light in morning) has columns with fine antique capitals and a raised choir.—The CAPPELLA SALUTATI (r. of the choir) contains frescoes in the vault of Evangelists by *Cosimo Rosselli* and two of *Mino da Fiesole's* best works: the *Tomb of Bp. Leonardo Salutati (1465), and an *Altar-front. To the r. of the high altar, *School of Cosimo Rosselli,* Coronation of the Madonna, a crowded composition in bad condition, with a contemporary frame. Over the high altar is a large rich altarpiece by *Bicci di Lorenzo* (c. 1440); and the apse is frescoed by *Nicodemo Ferrucci* (late 16C). On l. of main altar, *Giovanni del Biondo,* Coronation of the Virgin (1372). In a nearby chapel is a fine marble altarpiece by *And. Ferrucci* (1493). The Sacristy contains a precious mitre (rarely shown). The Crypt is worth a visit.

On the E. side of the piazza are the old *Palazzo Pretorio,* with coats-of-arms of many podestà, and the church of *Santa Maria Primerana* (re-built in the 16-17C), containing Della Robbia terracottas and a bas-relief with the self-portrait of Fr. da Sangallo (1542).—The W. side of the piazza is occupied by the *Bishop's Palace* and the *Seminary,* both with fragments of the Etruscan acropolis wall in their gardens. Between them Via San Francesco rises steeply, passing (r.) the *Public Garden;* a terrace higher up commands a *View of Florence. Beyond (r.) the church of *Sant'Alessandro* (recently well restored) with fine Roman columns, and (l.) that of Santa Cecilia, is the top of the hill (345 m) where stood the Etruscan and later the Roman acropolis. It is now occupied by **San Francesco,** a church of c. 1330 with an attractive little rose-window. Inside is an Annunciation, attrib. to *Raffaellino del Garbo* (in restoration), and in the Franciscan friary are two charming cloisters (17C and 14C), some remains of the acropolis, and a missionary MUSEUM, rich in Far Eastern objets d'art (notable Chinese and Egyptian collections). A path through the shady gardens leads back down hill to the main square.

From P.za Mino the street behind the apse of the Duomo leads to the **Roman Theatre and Etruscan Museum** (adm. 9.30-12.30, 14-17; closed Mon; summer, 10-12, 15-19).

A terrace affords a good comprehensive view of the excavations, backed by the Mugnone valley and the dark cypresses of the hill of San Francesco. The ROMAN THEATRE, built at the time of Sulla, was enlarged by Claudius and Septimius Severus; the cavea, excavated in the hillside, is 34 m across and held 3000 spectators. On the right of the theatre are the THERMÆ, built under Sulla and enlarged by Hadrian, with three swimming basins and the usual chambers attached to a Roman bath. A terrace allows a fine view of a long stretch of ETRUSCAN WALLS with a gateway, which enclosed the city. On the other side of the theatre (to the N.W.) is a ROMAN TEMPLE (the basement is intact) and, on a lower level, remains of an Etruscan temple. Nearby are the two altars from the temples (the larger one is Roman).—The MUSEUM occupies a small Ionic temple (1912-14). Under the portico is a fragment from the frieze of one of the temples (1C B.C.). ROOM I. Etruscan Roman stelæ and urns. R. II. Vases of all periods from the foundation of Faesulæ to the early Christian epoch; in centre, lead cinerary urn (3-2C B.C.). R. III. Sculpture from various buildings in Fiesole; body of a Roman she-wolf in bronze (1C B.C.), still Etruscan in style, found in the capitol of Faesulæ; head of Claudius; torso of Dionysius, etc.

In Via Duprè, just to the r. of the entrance to the Roman Theatre is the **Museo Bandini** (adm. 10-12, 14-19; winter 9.30-12, 14-17).

GROUND FLOOR. Sculptural fragments from the Baptistery of Florence, Della Robbian works; two paintings (damaged) by the School of Ghirlandaio.—FIRST FLOOR. ROOM I. 1. *Bernardo Daddi* (attrib.), St John the Evangelist; 6. *School of Daddi,* Diptych, with the Annunciation, Crucifixion, and Adoration of the Magi (much ruined); 11. *Niccolò di Pietro Gerini,* Trinity; 12. *Jacopo di Cione,* Pietà with Saints (part of an altar); 14. *Bicci di Lorenzo,* Benediction and Visitation of the Camaldolense order; 17. St Catherine of Alexander; 18. *Agnolo Gaddi,* Madonna and four Saints; 19, 20. *Roger van der Weyden,* Two grisaille works; 21. *Neri di Bicci,* Adoration of the Child; 22. *Taddeo Gaddi,* Annunciation; Four small panels by *Niccolò di Tommaso;* 28. *Lor. Monaco,* Crucifixion. Beyond a case of small Byzantine ivories: *Niccolò di Buonacorso,* Annunciation; *Neri di Bicci,* Crucifix (painted on both sides); *Master of early 15C,* Crucifixion and Last Supper; 37. *Jacopo di Cione,* Madonna and donor; 38, 39. *Bicci di Lorenzo,* Celestial gerarchy.—ROOM II. 2. *Filippino Lippi,* Madonna and Child; *Jacopo del Sellaio,* 3. St Jerome in the desert. *4, 5, 6. Triumph of Divinity, Love and

Chastity, and Time; *7. *Lorenzo di Bicci,* St James the Aposle and St Nicholas; *Giov. da Ponte,* Four Saints.

In the Via Dupré is the entrance to the *Cemetery,* in which may be seen the tomb of Giovanni Dupré (1817-82), the sculptor, with a copy of his Pietà, and, against the hill of San Francesco, a large section of the Etruscan wall.

Among the delightful walks to be enjoyed in and around Fiesole may be mentioned that to (5 km.) the *Castello di Vincigliata* round the N. shoulder of *Monte Céceri.* The castle was built in 1031, and restored in 1855 by John Temple Leader, who was visited here by Gladstone and Queen Victoria.—Another good walk keeps straight on from the first sharp bend on the Florence road, passing (r.) the *Pensione Bencistà* and the *Villa Goerike,* where Arnold Böcklin, the Swiss painter, died in 1901, to (2½ km.) **Maiano,** the home of the brothers Benedetto and Giuliano da Maiano (1442-97 and 1432-90).

The return to San Domenico (p. 476) may be made by the steep old road to Florence, which passes the Convent of *San Girolamo* (15-17C) and the *Villa Medici* (adm. by owner's permission), built by Michelozzo in 1458-61, a favourite resort of Lorenzo the Magnificent and his friends.

B. SETTIGNANO, E. of Florence, may be reached from P.za San Marco (Pl. 3) by bus No. 10. By car it is best reached from Lungarno del Tempio (at Ponte San Niccolò, comp. p. 475) where the long straight Via del Campofiore and its continuation Via Lungo l'Affrico run N.E. After c. 1 km. Via Gabriele d'Annunzio diverges right for Settignano.

Beyond Coverciano Via Poggio Gherardo branches left from the main road for Maiano (see above) past (r.) a small road which leads shortly to the graceful 15C church of *San Martino a Mensola,* containing a triptych by Taddeo Gaddi, and other good pictures.

At (5 km.) *Ponte a Ménsola* Via Vincigliata leads left for *Villa I Tatti,* the home of Bernard Berenson (1865-1959) which he left to Harvard University as a Centre of Italian Renaissance Studies. A beautiful Italianate garden surrounds the villa which contains the late owner's library (open to students) and art collection (adm. by previous appointment; usually shown to small groups on Wed afternoons) with works by Dom. Veneziano, Signorelli, Giambono, Bernardo Daddi, Sassetta, Bergognone, Cima da Conegliano, and others. The pretty by-road continues up the hill through woods past the castles of Vincigliata and Poggio to (6 km.) Fiesole (see p. 476).

The road continues up to Settignano winding across the old road; both have fine views of the magnificent trees on the sky-line of the surrounding hills.—7½ km. **Settignano** (178 m), a cheerful village on a pleasant hill, is known for its school of sculptors, most famous of whom were Desiderio (1428-64) and the brothers Rossellino (Antonio Gamberelli, 1427-79, and Bernardo Gamberelli, 1409-64); and here, at the *Villa Buonarroti,* Michelangelo passed his youth. In the main piazza are a statue of Nic. Tommaseo, the patriotic writer, who died here in 1874, and the 16C church of the *Assunta* (restored in 1976), which contains a Della Robbia Madonna, a 16C pulpit, and a 15C ciborium. In the lower P.za Desiderio (view of Florence) is a monument to the sculptor. The 15C *Villa Gamberaia,* c. 1 km. S.E., has a magnificent garden.

The branch road sign-posted to Montebeni joins a pretty road to Fiesole (comp. above) at Vincigliata.

C. THE CERTOSA AND L'IMPRUNETA. Buses 37 and 36 run from the P.za Santa Maria Novella to (6 km.) the Certosa, and 37 continues on to (9 km.) Tavarnuzze; country bus hourly from S.I.T.A. Bus Station (Pl. 6) to (14 km.) L'Impruneta. Outside the Porta Romana the 37 bus turns to the left up the long Viale del Poggio Imperiale, lined with handsome villas and their gardens, and bordered by a splendid avenue of trees, and then to the right to reach the halt of (3 km.) *Gelsomino.*

From this stop it is a short walk back to the Viale which may then be followed up to *Poggio Imperiale,* a huge villa (permission to visit from the Istituto della SS Annunziata), confiscated by Cosimo I in 1565. It was enlarged in the 17-18C, and takes its present name from the Grand Duchess Maria Maddalena, a former proprietress. It is now a girls' school, and Princess Marie José of Belgium (later Queen of Italy) was a pupil here during the First World War.

Both buses continue along the Siena road, passing (r.) the thick cypresses of the *Cimitero Evangelico degli Allori,* formerly a cemetery only for Orthodox Greeks. A turn of the road reveals the picturesque hill of the Certosa.—5 km. *Galluzzo,* beside the Ema.—6 km. *Certosa.*

Immediately to the right of the road rises the *Colle di Montaguto* (110 m) on which stands the **Certosa del Galluzzo** or *di Val d'Ema* (adm. 9-12, 14.30-17), founded in 1342 by the Florentine Niccolò Acciaiuoli, High Steward of the kingdom of Naples. In 1958 the Carthusians were replaced by Cistercians, their first reappearance in the area since their expulsion by the Grand Duke of Tuscany 176 years earlier. A new road ascends to the car park. Visitors are conducted by a monk.

The spacious courtyard dates from 1545. The CHURCH and the fine stalls in the *Monk's Choir* (1591) are being restored. Beneath the *Lay Brethren's Choir* is a chapel with the magnificent *Tomb-slab of Card. Agnolo II Acciaiuoli, formerly attrib. to Donatello and now thought to be the work of Fr. da Sangallo. Also here are three other pavement tombs of the Acciaiuoli family, and the Gothic monument to the Founder, Niccolò Acciaiuoli (d. 1365). The extensive conventual buildings include two fine cloisters, the *'Colloquio',* with interesting 16C stained glass, and the *Chapter House,* with another tomb slab by Fr. da Sangallo (of Leonardo Buonafè; 1545) and a good fresco of the Crucifixion by Mariotto Albertinelli. The secluded *GREAT CLOISTER is decorated with 66 majolica tondoes of Saints and Prophets, by And. and Giov. della Robbia. One of the monks' cells may be visited; they each have three rooms, a loggia, and a little garden.

The PALAZZO DEGLI STUDI was begun by Niccolò Acciaiuoli as a meeting place for young Florentines to study the liberal arts (and completed later). It houses a Picture Gallery, dominated by five frescoed *Lunettes of the Passion cycle, by *Pontormo* (1522-25), detached from the Great Cloister. These were painted while he was living in the monastery escaping the plague in Florence in 1522. Also exhibited in the main hall: *Mariotto di Nardo,* Coronation of the Madonna with Saints; *Rid. Ghirlandaio,* SS. Peter Martyr and George; *School of Orcagna,* Tondo of the Madonna and Child; *Jacopo del Casentino,* Madonna and Child (much ruined); and several other paintings by Florentine masters of the 14C and 15C. A Madonna and Child with St John, by *Lucas Cranach* was stolen in 1973 and has still not been recovered. An adjoining room displays 16-17C works.

The country bus ascends the right bank of the Greve.—From (7½ km.) *Le Rose* a long but pleasant walk ascends to L'Impruneta.— 9 km. *Le Tavarnuzze.*—14 km. **L'Impruneta** (274 m), a large village (14,300 inhab.) on a plateau, where the great cattle fair of St Luke is still celebrated (mid-Oct), although it has now become a general fair. The locality is famous for its terracotta. In the large central piazza is the church of *Santa Maria Impruneta,* with a high 13C tower, and an elegant portico of 1634. The interior was restored, after bomb damage in 1944, to its Renaissance aspect. At the entrance to the presbytery are two beautiful tabernacles by *Michelozzo,* with *Terracotta decoration by *Luca della Robbia.* To the r. of the façade are two cloisters, the first of the 15C, and the second, with a pretty garden, dates from the 14C.

D. LASTRA A SIGNA (13 km; bus from Station every ½ hr). About ½ km. beyond the Porta San Frediano (Pl. 5, 9) a road on th left ascends to (10 min.) **Monte Oliveto,** where the Renaissance church of *San Bartolomeo* (for adm. ring at No. 72A) contains two statues of Vestal Virgins (16C and 17C), and, at the high altar, the Entry of Jesus into Jerusalem, by *Santi di Tito.* In the old refectory is a fragment of a fresco of the Last Supper, by *Sodoma.*

Above Monte Oliveto is *Bellosguardo,* a charming hamlet described by Mrs Browning, and containing some fine villas, including *L'Ombrellino,* occupied by Galileo in 1617-31, and *La Torricella,* where Ugo Foscolo lay sick in 1812 (bust). The *Villa di Bellosguardo* was once the home of the tenor Caruso.

Beyond Monte Oliveto the Pisa road passes a number of suburban villages.—5 km. *San Quirico* has a pretty Renaissance church, served by Fra Filippo Lippi in 1442.—8 km. *Casellina.* The church of *San Martino alla Palma* (c. 4 km. S.W.), in a magnificent position, was founded in the 10C, and contains a charming Madonna by a follower of Bernardo Daddi.—About 1 km. beyond (9 km.) *Piscetto,* and 5 min. to the right of the road, is the church of *SS Giuliano e Settimo,* an 8C building, altered in subsequent centuries.—About 2 km. N.W. of (11 km.) *Fornaci* is the BADIA DI SAN SALVATORE A SETTIMO, a 10C abbey, rebuilt for Cistercians in 1236-37, walled and fortified in 1371, and restored since 1944.

The church has an old campanile and a Romanesque façade with a fine round 15C window. In the choir is a marble tabernacle attributed to Giuliano da Maiano, and the chapel on the left has frescoes by *Giov. da San Giovanni* (1629). The interesting remains of the monastery include much of the old fortifications, and the Chapter House and Lay Brothers Hall.

13 km. **Lastra a Signa,** a large village near the confluence of the Vingone and the Arno, preserves its walls of 1380, with three gates. In the Via Carducci is the *Loggia di Sant'Antonio* (1411), formerly the Hospital of the Silk Workers (with polychrome decorations). No. 12 in the adjoining Via dell'Arione is the *Palazzo Pretorio,* with a fine window and the escutcheons of many podestà. The church dates from 1404.

In the hills to the S.W. is the castle of *Malmantile* (1424), an outpost of Castracani against the Florentines, celebrated in a poem by Lorenzo Lippi.—For the continuation of the road to *Signa,* etc., see Rte 45B.

E. POGGIO A CAIANO is reached by bus from the Station. Outside the Porta al Prato the long Via del Ponte alle Mosse (Pl. 1) runs towards Pistoia.—At (6 km.) *Perétola* the autostrada from Florence to the coast diverges on the right. The church contains a *Ciborium by Luca della Robbia (1441), and a stoup by Fr. Ferrucci (1466).—9 km. *Brozzi,* with another ciborium and an interesting font. The church of Sant'Andrea a Brozzi (15C), farther on, contains frescoes by Dom. Ghirlandaio and pupils, and a Crucifix by Giov. di Francesco.—18 km. **Poggio a Caiano,** at the foot of Monte Albano, is famous for its ex-royal *Villa (closed indefinitely for restoration), acquired in 1480 by Lorenzo the Magnificent and rebuilt by *Giul. da Sangallo* (1480-85).

The Villa, beyond the Ombrone, is a rectangular building on a broad terrace (fine view) supported by a colonnade. Of its numerous decorated apartments, the most remarkable is the *SALONE, which is decorated with frescoes (by *Franciabigio, And. del Sarto,* and *Aless. Allori*) of incidents in Roman history paralleled in the history of Cosimo il Vecchio and Lorenzo. The *lunettes, with arresting dream-like figures, are by *Pontormo.* The loggia has a polychrome terracotta frieze, attributed to Giuliano da Sangallo. The garden and park (adm.

daily) are pleasant. Guests were received at the villa before they entered the city, among them Montaigne in 1581.

For the continuation of the road to Prato, Pistoia, etc., see Rte. 45A.

F. VILLA MEDICEA DE CAREGGI, LA PETRAIA, CASTELLO, AND SESTO. FIORENTINO. Bus No. 14 from the Duomo or the Station to Careggi; Bus No. 28 from the Station for La Petraia, Castello, and Sesto. From the Fortezza da Basso (Pl. 2) Via del Romito and its continuation Via F. Corridoni lead N., followed by bus 28 and 14 as far as (3 km.) Piazza Dalmazia in the industrial suburb of *Rifredi*. Here bus 14 diverges right along the broad Viale Morgagni for *Careggi*, the main hospital of Florence. At the top of the hill, beyond the main buildings of the hospital, in in a well-wooded park, is the **Villa Medicea di Careggi,** now used as a nurses' home (adm. only with special permission from the administration of S. Maria Nuova, comp. p. 444).

The Villa, which is heavily machicolated, was acquired by Cosimo il Vecchio in 1417 and enlarged by *Michelozzo* after 1433. It became the literary and artistic centre of the Medicean court, and was the scene of the death of both Cosimo (1464) and Lorenzo (1492). After a period of decay it was redecorated by *Pontormo* and *Bronzino* for Cosimo I (c. 1540) and it was restored in the 19C by Francis Sloan.

A pretty walk (½ hr.) follows the road (l.) beyond the villa, which leads down across the Terzolle to the Villa of *La Quiete*, a convent with some interesting paintings, and along Via di Boldrone to the Villa di Petraia (see below).

From P.za Dalmazia Bus 28 continues viâ Via Santo Stefano in Pane (10-11C church with Della Robbian decoration) along the busy Via Reginaldo Giuliano. Just beyond (5 km.) Il Sodo, a turning on the r. leads up to the **Villa della Petraia** (adm. to park and gardens 9-16.30 or 18.30: to villa, 10-12.30, 14.30-16.30 or 18.30; closed Mon).

Originally a castle of the Brunelleschi, the villa was rebuilt in 1575 for Card. Ferd. Medici by *Buontalenti*. In 1864-70 it was a favourite residence of Victor Emmanuel II, and in 1919 it was presented to the State by Victor Emmanuel III.

A pretty garden and moat precede the villa, which still preserves a tower of the old castle. In the glass-roofed courtyard are frescoes by *Volterrano* (r. and l.) and by *Giov. da San Giovanni;* the rooms contain tapestry, costumes, etc. On the upper terrace of the garden (view) with orange and lemon trees, is a fountain by *Tribolo*, with a *Statue of Venus, by *Giambologna*. The huge ilex (400 years old) lower down was a favourite tree of Victor Emmanuel II (tree-house). A magnificent park extends behind the villa to the E.

At the bottom of Via della Petraia, in front of the Baroque façade of the Villa Corsini, Via di Castello leads shortly to the **Villa di Castello** (now the seat of the Accademia della Crusca; adm. to gardens only, as for La Petraia). This was the favourite residence of the Medici after its acquisition by Lorenzo the Magnificent in 1480.

The villa was sacked during the siege of 1530 but restored under Cosimo I by *Bronzino* and *Pontormo*. Like La Petraia it was presented to the State in 1919.— The typical garden, well laid out by *Tribolo* (c. 1540), contains his *Fountain of Hercules and Cacus, with statues by *Ammannati* and *Pierino da Vinci*. Also, an elaborate grotto full of fantastical animals (with water spouts in the floor), by *Giambologna*. Above, on the terrace, is a colossus rising out of a pool, by *Ammannati*. The huge Orangery should not be missed.

The bus route ends at (9 km.) **Sesto Fiorentino,** a small town (43,700 inhab.) with a 15C Palazzo Pretorio (now the post office) and a church with slight Romanesque remains. Here is the MUSEO DELLE PORCELLANE DI DOCCIA (adm. 9.30-13, 15.30-18.30; closed Mon) with a fine collection relating to the manufacture of Doccia porcelain, founded by Carlo Ginori in 1737. Pietro Bernini, father of Gian Lorenzo, was born in Sesto in 1562.

Other short excursions may be made from Florence to *Bagno a Ripoli* (bus 33); to *Ponte a Ema*, 1 km. E. of the chapel of Santa Caterina dell'Antella, frescoed by Spinello Aretino (bus No. 31 or 32), and *Grássina*, noted for its Good Friday Passion play; to the convent of *La Maddalena* (frescoes by Fra Bartolomeo), 7½ km. along the Faenza road, beyond Le Caldine; etc.

G. THE MUGELLO, to the N.E. of Florence, is best reached by road (bus to Dicomano), making a round tour of 83 km.; railway, viâ Dicomano, to Borgo San Lorenzo in 1 hr. Road (Highway 67) and railway ascend the N. bank of the Arno to 5 km. **Rovezzano,** the home of the sculptor Benedetto da Rovezzano (1474-1552; born near Pistoia). In the church of *Sant'Andrea* is a delightful Madonna from the Della Robbian workshop, and a 13C Madonna of the Florentine school.—7½ km. (r.) The Florence British Military Cemetery, with 1551 graves.—18 km. *Pontassieve,* a centre of the wine trade (16,500 inhab.) stands at the confluence of the Sieve and the Arno.—The road turns N. and ascends the narrow Sieve valley to (26 km.) *Rúfina,* a wine-growing centre.— 35½ km. *Dicomano* has a restored Romanesque church. From here Highway 67 goes on N.E. to Forlì (see p. 406), but this route (N 1) continues to follow the Sieve into the **Mugello,** its upper basin, one of the most characteristic valleys of Tuscany. It is intensely cultivated and is noted for its wine. The many little summer resorts have a temperate summer climate.

44 km. *Vicchio* was the birthplace of Fra Angelico (1387-1455). The Museo Civico has an interesting collection of works of art from churches in the region. At (47 km.) *Vespignano* the house in which Giotto (1266-1336) is thought to have been born has recently been restored and opened to the public (ring for adm.).—At (51 km.) *Borgo San Lorenzo* (buses to Florence), severely damaged by an earthquake in 1919, the road and railway to Faenza (p. 404) diverge on the right.—The road crosses the Sieve at (57 km.) *San Piero a Sieve,* which has a Della Robbia font in its church, and joins the road from Imola (p. 403).—59 km. *Nóvoli,* and from there to (83 km.) *Florence* by Highway 65, see Rte 44A.

44   FROM FLORENCE TO BOLOGNA

A   Viâ La Futa

ROAD, 105½ km.—24 km. *Nóvoli.*—44½ km. *Passo della Futa.*—51½ km. *La Casetta.*—57 km. *Passo della Raticosa.*—62½ km. *Monghidoro.*—70½ km. *Loiano.*—105½ km. **Bologna.**—Buses daily from Florence to Bologna in 4½ hrs; more frequently between Monghidoro and Bologna in 1½ hrs.

Leaving Florence by the Via Cavour (Pl. 3) and Ponte Rosso, this route follows the old Roman Via Bolognese (N 65) through Trespiano, Montórsoli, and Pratolino (here on the right is the magnificent park of the Villa Demidoff, with Giambologna's colossal Appennino). The beautiful but windy road ascends the Carza valley alongside the Faenza railway to (18 km.) *Vaglia.* On the right rises *Montesenario* (817 m), where seven Florentine merchants established the Servite Order in 1231. The church and convent are set in woods full of grottoes and cells, with good views.—At (24½ km.) *Nóvoli* the Bologna road turns left, crosses the Sieve, and ascends above the N. side of the Mugello (see above). Just W. of the road are the *Castello del Trebbio* (adm. by previous appointment only), built by Michelozzo in 1461, where the younger Cosimo spent his youth, and *Cafaggiolo*, the delightful Medici country residence built for Cosimo il Vecchio, also by Michelozzo (1451).— 44½ km. The *Passo della Futa* (903 m) is on the main watershed of the Apennines. The strongest German defences in the 'Gothic Line' were here, but the position was turned by the capture of the Giogo Pass and Firenzuola (p. 403). Beyond the pass the road descends slightly to (46½ km.) *Traversa*, and passes beneath the rocky Sasso di Castro.— 50½ km. *Covigliaio* (874 m) is a little resort.—At (51½ km.) *La Casetta* a steep road to Firenzuola and Imola descends to the right, while this road climbs to (56½ km.) *Pietramala* (851 m), frequented for holidays in summer and winter.—Beyond (57½ km.) the *Passo della Raticosa* (968 m) begins the descent into Emilia (old custom-house at the boundary).—62½ km. *Monghidoro* (841 m) and (70½ km.) *Loiano* are the best known hill-resorts on the N. side of the pass. On the left rise the cliffs of Monte Adone, through which the railway (Rte 44B) tunnels to join this route at (89 km.) *Pianoro* in the Sávena valley.—At (99 km.) *Ponte San Ruffillo* the Bolognese and their allies defeated Bernabò Visconti in 1361.—105½ km. **Bologna,** see Rte 39.

B   Viâ Prato

ROAD, 117 km.—6 km. *Perétola.*—20 km. **Prato.**—43 km. *San Quirico.*—52 km. *Montepiano.*—60½ km. *Castiglione dei Pépoli.*—88½ km. *Vado.*—100½ km. *Sasso Marconi.*—110½ km. *Casalecchio.*—116½ km. **Bologna.** Buses from Florence and from Bologna to Castiglione.

The AUTOSTRADA DEL SOLE (comp. p. 364) diverges from the Pisa autostrada to follow the E. slope of the Monti della Calvana, then, crossing the watershed by spectacular viaducts and tunnels, it joins the line of the Prato-Bologna road beyond Castiglione dei Pépoli.

RAILWAY, 97 km., express trains in 55-80 min., slow trains in 2 hrs. This is part of the 'direttissima' railway route between N. and S. Italy, and is followed by through trains between the Channel Ports, Paris, and German and Austrian cities to Rome, Naples, etc. The line, opened in 1934, is a remarkable engineering feat, and penetrates c. 30 tunnels, including the Grande dell'Appennino, just over 18½ km. long, between the stations of Vernio and San Simplon, and took 10 years to complete. It is followed, beyond San Benedetto, by the *Piandisetta Tunnel* (3¼ km.), and after Vado comes the *Monte Adone Tunnel* (7 km.).

Florence is left by the Porta al Prato (Pl. 1).—At (6 km.) *Perétola,* with the airport of Florence (internal flights to Milan, Rome, etc.), the autostrada begins and this route branches left.—From (12 km.) *Campi Bisenzio* it ascends the Bisenzio, passing beneath the Pisa autostrada.

20 km. **PRATO** (152,400 inhab.) is a rapidly-expanding industrial town, known as the 'Manchester of Tuscany', and long-famous for its woolen industry. It preserves some beautiful monuments within its old walls.

Hotels. Most of the large hotels serve the industrial suburbs; the simpler hotels within the walls are the most convenient for the visitor.

Railway Stations. *Centrale,* E. of the town across the Bisenzio for all main line trains; services on the Florence—Lucca line stop also at *Porta al Serragĺio,* 200 metres N. of the cathedral.

Buses. Frequent services (viâ the autostrada) from Florence (Stazione S.M.N.) by *C.A.P.* (terminal in Piazza Duomo) and *Lazzi* (terminal in P.za S. Francesco).

Parking. The centre is closed to traffic; parking in P.za Mercatale (exc. Mon) or Piazza dei Macelli.

Azienda Autonoma di Turismo, 51 Via Luigi Muzzi (N. of the Duomo). *Information Offices* in Via Cairoli and P.za S.M. delle Carceri.

Theatre. *Teatro Comunale Metastasio,* with a renowned theatre season Oct-April (tickets available also in Florence at No. 7 P.za Ottaviani). Music festival Oct-Dec.—The traditional *Prato Fair* is held in September.

History. Although probably already settled in the Etruscan period, the first recorded mention of Prato is in the 9C. It became a free commune in the 12C and after 1351 came under the influence of Florence. The manufacture of wool in the city had reached European importance by the 13C, and it received further impetus in the following century through the commercial activity of the famous merchant Francesco di Marco Datini. Its textile factories continue to flourish, and it has become the centre of the 'rag-trade' in Europe. As an industrial centre, its population is expanding faster than almost any other city in central Italy.

The approaches from the autostrada and main station reach the walls of the old town at Piazza San Marco. Here has been set up a sculpture (1969-70) by Henry Moore. Viale Piave continues to the *CASTELLO DELL'IMPERATORE (recently restored). It was probably built in 1237-48 for Frederick II and is typical of the Hohenstaufen castles of Southern Italy. The empty interior (adm. 9-12, 16-19 exc. Wed) is of scant interest, except for the walkway around the ramparts which provides a good view of the city and countryside. Concerts and plays are held in the courtyard in summer. In the adjoining piazza stands the church of ***Santa Maria delle Carceri** (closed 12-15.30) built by Giul. da Sangallo, its exterior unfinished. The *Interior (reopened after restoration) constitutes one of the masterpieces of the Renaissance. The frieze and medallions of the Evangelists are from the workshop of *And. della Robbia,* the medallions possibly from a design of *Sansovino.* The stoup is by *Fr. da Sangallo.*

In Via Cairoli, just behind the church, is the *Teatro Comunale Metastasio* (adm. on request at No. 61) with an elegant interior built in 1827-30 by Luigi Cambray Digny. It has a high theatrical reputation.

Farther on is the Romanesque church of *San Francesco,* with a striped marble façade. At the foot of the steps before the high altar is the tomb-slab (covered for protection) of Francesco di Marco Datini, the famous 'Merchant of Prato', by Nic. Lamberti (1409), and above is a wooden crucifix. On the N. wall is the tomb of Gimignano Inghirami (d. 1460), attr. to Bern. Rossellino. From the charming 15C cloister (planted with olive trees) is the entrance to the Chapter House (or *Cappella Migliorati*) whose walls are covered with good frescoes by Niccolò di Pietro Gerini (c. 1395) of the Crucifixion, and Stories from the Life of St Anthony Abbot and St Matthew.—The church of *Spirito Santo* (reached by Via Santa Trínita and, on the right, Via Silvestri), contains a *Presentation in the Temple by Fra Diamante, possibly to a design of Filippo Lippi; a coloured stucco tondo of the Madonna and Child from a design of Bened. da Maiano, and a splendid *Annunciation of the school of Orcagna.

Via Rinaldesca leads from Piazza S. Francesco, off which, in Via Ser Lapo Mazzei, is the *Palazzo Datini.* Part of the decoration and some of the sinopie survive of the exterior mural paintings, attrib. to Niccolò di Pietro Gerini and others, which illustrated the story of the life of Datini (1330-1410; comp. above). His papers and business documents (including over 140,000 letters), all of which were carefully preserved by him, provide a unique record of medieval life; they are housed in an archive in the palace. At the end of Via Ser Lapo Mazzei, Via Guasti leads r. to the fine PIAZZA COMUNE with a statue (1896) of Datini and a fountain by Tacca (1659; original sculptures inside Palazzo Pretorio, comp. below). Here stand the imposing Palazzo Pretorio and the arcaded Palazzo del Comune. The main stone façade of PALAZZO PRETORIO, with its Gothic windows and outside staircase, was added to a medieval core in the early 14C, and the battlements were completed in the 16C. The palace houses the *Galleria Comunale (adm. (9.30-12, 15.30-16.30; Oct-March: 9.30-12, 14-16.30; fest. 9-12; Mon closed).

FIRST FLOOR: frescoed tabernacle by *Filippino Lippi* (1498); Bacchus fountain by *Ferd. Tacca* (1665); copy in the piazza outside. In a small adjacent room are objects and furniture from the old pharmacy of the hospital.—SECOND FLOOR. The MAIN HALL contains the most important *Works in the collection. *Bernardo Daddi*, Story of the Sacred Girdle, Madonna and Saints; *Michele da Firenze*, terracotta tabernacle; *Fra Bartolomeo*, Madonna and Child (fresco fragment); *Giov. di Milano*, Polyptych; *Pietro di Miniato*, Coronation of the Madonna; *Lor. Monaco* (workshop), Madonna enthroned with Saints; *Luca Signorelli* (attrib.), Tondo of the Madonna and Child with Saints; *Filippino Lippi*, Madonna and Child with Saints; *Raffaellino del Garbo*, Tondo of the Madonna and Child with St John; *Andrea di Giusto*, Madonna and Child with Saints; *Filippo Lippi*, Madonna del Ceppo (with Francesco di Marco Datini), Nativity; *Fr. Botticini*, Madonna and Child with Saints; *Zanobi Strozzi*, Predella; *Ridolfo del Ghirlandaio*, Portrait of Baldo Magini; *Piero di Lorenzo Pratese*, Predella; *And. della Robbia*, St Anthony Abbot (lunette). The next two rooms contain later paintings, notably *Battistello*, ('Noli me tangere', and works by *Gasp. Vanvitelli*.
THIRD FLOOR: later paintings, which include *Gian. Dom. Ferritti*, Annunciation, and *Franc. Morandini*, Tobias and the Angel. Here, also, is a collection of sculptures by *Lor. Bartolini* (1777-1850).

In the *Palazzo Comunale* (adm. on request, mornings only), the Sala del Consiglio has a fine ceiling, two 15C frescoes, and a series of portraits (some by *Aless. Allori*) of the grand-dukes of Tuscany.

Via Mazzoni goes on to the spacious PIAZZA DEL DUOMO. The *Duomo has a green and white striped marble façade by *Guidetto da Como*. In the 14C the transepts and apse were added, the design of which is attrib. to *Giov. Pisano*. The top of the fine campanile (early 13C) was added by *Niccolò di Cecco del Mercia* c. 1356. At the S.W. corner projects the *PULPIT OF THE SACRED GIRDLE, designed by *Donatello* and *Michelozzo;* the dancing putti by Donatello (1433-38) have been replaced by casts (the original panels are in the Museo dell'Opera del Duomo, see below). The Holy Girdle is displayed from the pulpit in a traditional ceremony on 1 May, Easter Day, 15 Aug, 8 Sept, and Christmas Day. Over the principal doorway is a *Madonna with SS. Stephen and Lawrence by *And. della Robbia* (1489).

The Romanesque INTERIOR (closed 12-15.30 or 16) has deep arcades decorated in stripes of marble carried on noble green marble columns. Immediately to the left of the entrance is the *CHAPEL OF THE SACRED GIRDLE. The girdle was brought to Prato from the Holy Land in 1141. The good screen was begun by *Maso di Bartolomeo*, and continued by *Ant. di Ser Cola* and *Pasquino di Matteo*. It is entirely frescoed by *Agnolo Gaddi*, and on the altar is a *Madonna and Child by *Giov. Pisano* (1317).—The *PULPIT in the N. aisle is by *Mino da Fiesole* and *Ant. Rossellino*.—In front of the high altar, on which is a bronze crucifix by *Ferd. Tacca* (1653), is a bronze candelabrum by *Maso di Bartolomeo*, similar to that in the Duomo at Pistoia.—The CHOIR is decorated with celebrated *Frescoes by *Filippo Lippi* (helped by *Fra Diamante*). It is one of the most beautiful fresco cycles of the early Renaissance (1452-66), and the monumental figures repay close study (light in chap. to the l.). On the right wall: scenes from the Life of St John the Baptist; the Salome in the *Banquet of Herod is supposed to be a portrait of Lucrezia Buti, Lippi's mistress and later wife. On the left wall: scenes from the Life of St Stephen.—The first chapel on the right has fine 15C frescoes by a follower of *Paolo Uccello* and *And. di Giusto*. In the S. transept are the Death of St Jerome, a painting by *Filippo Lippi* (1452; light in corner on the l.), and a tabernacle (1480) designed by *Giuliano da Maiano*, with a Madonna and Child and a Pietà in bas-relief by his brothers *Benedetto* and *Giovanni*.—In the first chapel to the left of the choir are early 15C frescoes, and in the 2nd chap., the *Tomb of Filippo Inghirami (d. 1480).

The **Museo dell'Opera del Duomo** (entered to the left of the cathedral façade; 9.30-12.30, 15-18.30; fest. 9.30-12.30; closed Tues) has recently been opened and is beautifully arranged in rooms off the old cloister, part of which is a unique survival from the 12C decorated in the marble Florentine style.

ROOM I. *Filippino Lippi*, *St Lucy; *Fra Diamante* (attrib.), Annunciation; *Giov. Toscani*, Two Evangelists; *Niccolò di Tommaso*, SS. John the Baptist and James; *Carlo Dolci*, Guardian angel.—ROOM II. Illuminated 15C anthem books, and an embroidered cope (late 16C).—Off the cloister: Sculpted *Panels of dancing putti by *Donatello* from the Pulpit of the Sacred Girdle (outside the Cathedral, comp. above), here displayed at eye level. *Maestro della Natività di Castello,* Madonna and Child enthroned with Saints (from the church of SS. Giusto e Clemente at Faltugnano); Reliquary for the sacred girdle, an exquisite work by *Maso di Bartolomeo* (1446); *Master of the early 15C* (attrib. to Paolo Uccello), Jacopone da Todi (detached fresco). A treasury contains reliquaries, chalices, thuribles, reliquary busts, and a pax by *Danese Cattaneo.—Tuscan School (14C),* Madonna and Child, Crucifixion, etc.; *School of Botticelli,* Crucifix; *Filippo Lippi* (?), Annunciation; *Caravaggio,* Crowning of thorns (recently attributed to this master, and dated c. 1602-03).

From the Duomo the Largo Carducci leads into Via San Michele where the church of *San Michele* (or *Arciconfraternità di Misericordia*) has an altarpiece of the Assumption by Aless. Allori (1603), and a Romanesque crucifix.

At No. 30 Via del Seminario is the entrance to the church of *San Fabiano* with fragments of a splendid pre-Romanesque pavement on the W. wall, figured with animals, sirens, birds, etc. The other Romanesque details of the church are also notable.

Via Convenevole da Prato leads N.E. to Via della Stufa, off which (l.) opens a piazza with the church of *Sant'Agostino,* erected in 1271, but since considerably altered

The interior contains 16-17C altarpieces. A door in the N. wall leads into the Cloister; from here are reached the Cappella di San Michele with a damaged frieze of saints (14C) and a Madonna and Child, by the School of Ghiberti, and the Chapter House with more 14C frescoes.

From San Michele, Via Convenevole leads back to the church of *San Domenico,* which has an arcaded flank; founded in 1283 it was finished by Giovanni Pisano before 1322. Within (2nd S. altar) is a Crucifix by Niccolò Gerini. In the adjoining convent is a MUSEUM OF MURAL PAINTING (adm. 9.30-12, 15-17.30; fest. 9.30-12; closed Thurs) housing detached frescoes from buildings in the town and surrounding area.

The works include: *Niccolò di Pietro Gerini,* Tabernacolo del Ceppo (with its sinopia); *Maestro delle Madonne* (?), Madonna and Child; *Ant. di Miniato,* Madonna enthroned with Saints (1411); sinopie of the Cappella dell'Assunta in the Duomo, attrib. to Paolo Uccello; graffiti decoration from the Palazzo Vaj of courtly scenes (15C). Also objects from the church Treasury and a charming collection of ex-votoes.

From the S.E. corner of P.za del Duomo, Via Garibaldi leads past the *Madonna del Buon Consiglio* with a Della Robbian lunette (and other works by the Della Robbia in the interior, which is usually locked) to the huge PIAZZA MERCATALE (market on Mondays). Here the modern church of *San Bartolomeo* (the 14C church was destroyed in the war) has a 15C marble tabernacle on the high altar with a painted crucifix of the 14C Pistoian school above. The altarpieces include works by Santi di Tito (Presentation in the Temple) and Leonardo Mascagni (Holy Family). In the crypt is a fine wood Crucifix of the 14C.

The most interesting road from Prato to Pistoia (19½ km.) passes (7½ km.) *Montemurlo,* where the picturesque castle was the scene of the last attempt of the partisans of the Florentine Republic to overthrow the power of the Medici (1537).

The Bologna road ascends the Bisenzio valley, through (31½ km.) the wide upland basin of *Vaiano,* with its 13C campanile. In the hills to the right is *Savignano,* the birthplace of the painter Fra Bart. della Porta (1475-1517) and of the sculptor Lor. Bartolini (1777-1850). Passing (r.) the ruined castle of *Cerbáia,* the road reaches (43 km.) *Vernio San Quírico* (278 m), a substantial village with another castle ruin. The watershed is crossed by an indefinite pass just before (52 km.) *Montepiano* (700 m), a summer resort.—Emilia is entered near (61 km.) *Castiglione dei Pépoli* (691 m), an ancient stronghold of the Pépoli of Bologna, whose castle is now the town hall.—Beyond (72½ km.) *Lagáro* (391 m) the road descends the scantily populated and steep-sided valley of the Setta in company with the Autostrada del Sole. The railway appears on the left, but beyond (89 km.) *Vado* it tunnels through the hills on the right.—Beyond the old railway this route joins Rte 44C at (100½ km.) *Sasso Marconi.*Thence to (117 km.) **Bologna,** see Rte 44C.

C   Viâ Pistoia

ROAD, 133 km. To (35½ km.) *Pistoia,* see Rte 45A.—Highway N64. 54 km. *Passo della Porretta.*—72½ km. **Porretta Terme.**—95 km. *Vergato.*—126½ km. *Casalecchio.*—133 km. **Bologna.**
RAILWAY, 133 km. viâ Prácchia in 2¾-4 hrs, slow trains only; for the express route, see Rte 44B.

From Florence to (35½ km.) *Pistoia,* see Rte 45A. Pistoia is left by Viale Dalmazia and this route soon diverges to the right from the Abetone road to ascend the Valle di Brana, with fine views downhill.—40½ km. *La Cugna.*—At (54 km.) *La Collina* the road reaches the summit-level of the *Passo della Porretta* (or 'della Collina'; 932 m) and enters Emilia. The descent leads into the deep valley of the Limentra.—72½ km. **Porretta Terme** (360 m), long known as *Bagni della Porretta,* is a popular little spa on the Reno, with warm springs of sulphurous and alkaline waters.

An alternative return route to Pistoia (44½ km.) ascends the Reno valley viâ (19½ km.) *Prácchia* (616 m), a summer resort at the mouth of a long railway tunnel, and joins the Abetone road (p. 492) at (24 km.) *Pontepetri.*
The interesting cross-country road leading W. through the Frignano hills from Porretta to Pievepélago (bus to Fanano) passes (20 km.) *Lizzano in Belvedere* and (21½ km.) *Vidiciático* (810 m), two pleasant little hill-resorts.—42½ km. *Fanano* (640 m), with an old church, lies beneath oddly-named *Libro Aperto* (1937 m), which is climbed in c. 6 hrs.—48½ km. *Séstola* (1020 m), a winter and summer resort beneath *Monte Cimone* (2165 m) which is climbed in 4½ hrs (or ascended by cableway in two stages). Sestola is connected by bus with (70 km.) *Pievepélago,* on the Modena-Pistoia road (Rte 38).
Bus services operate from Porretta to Pistoia and Bologna.

At (75 km.) *Silla* the Pievepélago road (see above) bears to the left, and at (85 km.) *Riola* the E. Limentra joins the Reno.—95 km. *Vergato.*—Near (108½ km.) *Marzabotto* is a large Etruscan necropolis of the 6C B.C. (?Misa), still being excavated (adm. 9-12, 14-dusk). At the entrance is the Museo Etrusco Pompeo Aria.—At (116½ km.) *Sasso Marconi,* near the junction of the Setta and the Reno, this route joins the road from Florence viâ Prato (Rte 44B).—121 km. *Pontecchio.*—126½ km. *Casalecchio di Reno,* where the road turns right to cross the Reno, was the scene of a victory of the Visconti over the Bentivoglio in 1402, and of a battle in 1511 between the French under the Sieur de Chaumont and the army of Julius II, known as 'the day of the ass-drivers', because the victorious French knights returned driving asses laden with their booty.—133 km. Bologna (Rte 39) is entered by the Porta Saragozza.

45   FROM FLORENCE TO PISA

A   Viâ Pistoia and Lucca

ROAD, 100 km.; bus in 3 hrs.—6 km. *Perétola.*—16 km. *Póggio a Caiano.*—35½ km. **Pistoia.**—51 km. *Montecatini Terme.*—59 km. *Péscia.*—78 km. **Lucca.**—94½ km. *Bagni San Giuliano.*—100 km. **Pisa.**—The alternative route from Florence to Pistoia viâ Prato (see Rte 44B) is slightly longer.

The AUTOSTRADA (81 km.) from Florence (Perétola) to the Viareggio-Pisa road passes near Pistoia and Lucca and ends 8½ km. N. of Pisa.

RAILWAY, by Viareggio train, 103 km. in 2-2½ hrs, change at Lucca (78 km.). All trains stop at Prato, Pistoia (34 km.), Montecatini, and Péscia.

From Florence to (16 km.) *Poggio a Caiano,* see p. 480. The road traverses a broad vale between Monte Albano (l.) and the Apennines.

35½ km. **PISTOIA** is a lively old Tuscan town (94,800 inhab.) in a pleasant site at the foot of the Apennines and has many fine old buildings whose character recalls its situation between Florence and Pisa. It has an unusual number of beautiful churches with characteristic portals and fine sculptures. It is a good centre for excursions by bus.

Hotels (mostly simple) near the station and church of San Domenico.

Post Office, Via Roma.—*E.P.T.*, 110 Corso Gramsci (information office in Piazza Duomo).

Buses from P.za San Francesco to *Porretta Terme* (1¾ hrs); to *Cutigliano* (1¾ hrs); to *Empoli* (2¼ hrs); to *Florence* (1 hr), and to *Abetone* (2½ hrs); and from Via Gobetti for localities outside the province: Pisa, Forte dei Marmi, La Spezia, Prato, Viareggio, Livorno, Lucca, Montecatini Terme, etc.

Parking. The centre is closed to traffic; parking at the Fortezza.

History. *Pistoria* is first mentioned as the scene of Catiline's defeat in 62 B.C. It was a republic in the 12C but was seized by the Florentines in 1306 and in 1315 by Castruccio Castracani (d. 1328), a military and political adventurer. From 1329 it existed under the protection of Florence, whose fortunes it shared, as the Medici arms on the walls testify. As an ironworking town in medieval times, it gave its name to the pistol (originally a dagger, afterwards a small firearm), and indirectly to the Spanish pistole, so called as smaller than the French crown. Guittone Sinibaldi, called Cino da Pistoia (1270-1337), the friend of Dante, was born here; also Clement IX (Giulio Rospigliosi), Pope in 1667-69.

The approaches from Florence (or from the station) enter the town by the S. gate; from here Via Vannucci and Via Cino lead to Piazza Gavinana. Corso Silvano Fedi, on the right before the piazza, leads to the church of **San Domenico** (late 13C, probably to the design of Fra Sisto and Fra Ristoro, with 14C alterations). Inside is the tomb of Filippo Lazzari (S. wall, near the entrance), by *Bern.* and *Ant. Rossellino,* and (beyond the 3rd S. altar) the notable sculpted tomb effigy of Beato Lorenzo da Ripafratta (d. 1457). In the S. transept are the Rospigliosi tombs.

A door in the S. aisle leads into the Cloister in which is buried, in an unknown spot, the body of Benozzo Gozzoli, who died here in 1497 during the plague. In several rooms of the Domenican convent off the cloister are interesting frescoes

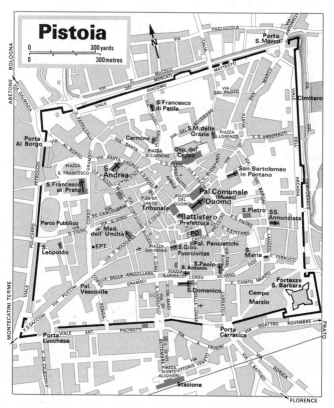

(many detached from the church) shown by a monk (ring at No. 1 P.za San Domenico). The Chapter House has a damaged fresco of the Crucifixion by an unknown master of the mid-13C with its *Sinopia, thought to be the oldest known. The Refectory has more good frescoes from the church. A small museum contains other frescoes, mainly 16C, but including one with the portraits of Dante and Petrarch. Outside the entrance to the Library: Journey of the Magi, attrib. to the school of Benozzo Gozzoli; St Jerome, attrib. to Ant. del Pollaiuolo; and *St Mary Magdalene (14C Sienese). To the S. are remains of a 14C cloister with traces of vault paintings.

On the other side of the Corso S. Fedi is the CHAPEL OF SANT'ANTONIO

ABATE (DEL TAU), restored in 1968 and open 9-14, fest. 9-13, closed Mon. It is entirely covered with *Frescoes by 14-15C artists representing the story of Adam and Eve in the vaults, and, on the walls, various stories from the lives of the saints. They are the work of unknown masters, perhaps including Bonaccorso di Cino and Masolino di Panicale.— Farther along Via Cavour, Via Roma leads left to the spacious PIAZZA 1291-1302. Over the later door are a St Paul between two angels by Iac. di Mazzeo, and (high up on the pinnacle) a figure of St James, attrib. to Orcagna. Inside is a 14C wood Crucifix (left wall).

Via Cavour, leading E. from P.za Gavinana, passes the church of *San Giovanni Fuorcivitas of the 12-14C. The N. side, scarred by war, with a blind arcade surmounted by two blind galleries, serves as a façade. Inside, the *Pulpit is by Fra Gugliemo da Pisa, a follower of Nicola Pisano (1270). Opposite is a white glazed terracotta Visitation attr. to Andrea della Robbia. In the midst of the church is a *Stoup by Giov. Pisano. On the wall to the left of the high altar is a polyptych by Taddeo Gaddi (recently restored). By the W. end of the church, through the entrance to the Cinema Verdi, can be seen the charming cloisters.— Farther along Via Cavour, Via Roma leads left to the spacious PIAZZA DEL DUOMO with its imposing buildings shown off to advantage now that cars are no longer allowed to park here.

The *Duomo has an arcaded Romanesque Pisan façade. The porch was added in 1311, and the high arch in the barrel vault is beautifully decorated by And. della Robbia, as is the *Lunette above the central door. The separate *CAMPANILE was originally a watch tower, and is supposed to have been adapted to its present use in the 14C by the addition of the three tiers of arches.

The INTERIOR (closed 12-15.30) retains traces of 13C and 14C frescoes. On the W. wall are the tomb of St Atho, Bishop of Pistoia, with reliefs of the Sienese school (1337), and a *Font by *Andrea Ferrucci da Fiesole,* on a design of Bened. da Maiano.—In the SOUTH AISLE: *Tomb of Cino da Pistoia, by a Sienese artist (1337). CHAPEL OF ST JAMES (opened by sacristan; fee): silver *Altar of St James, started in 1287 and remodelled and added to during successive generations. The statue of St James is by *Gilio da Pisa* (1349), the nine stories from the Life of St James, on the left flank, by *Leonardo di Giovanni,* and the two half figures on the left side by *Brunelleschi.* Behind the altar is a charming 15C Flemish tapestry. From the Sacristy (r.), a door leads into the MUSEO DIOCESANO ('sagrestia dei belli arredi' recorded by Dante, 'Inferno' XXIV) which has been closed for restoration. It contains precious examples of the goldsmith's art; early vestments; a charming figure of the Madonna by *Ant. Pollaiuolo,* and, at the entrance, a statue of St Michael by *Guido da Como.*—The Chapel to S. of the high altar contains a good painting of SS. Baronto and Desiderio by *Mattia Preti.*—The CHOIR contains colossal statues of SS. James and Zeno by *Vincenzo,* a pupil of Giambologna (1603). To the left of the high altar stands a bronze candelabrum by *Maso di Bartolomeo* (1440), similar to the one in the Duomo at Prato. At the entrance to the CHAPEL OF THE SACRAMENT (N. of the choir) is a fresco fragment of the Madonna. Here, on the S. wall, is a Madonna with SS. John the Baptist and Zeno by *Lor. Credi,* on a design of Andrea del Verrocchio (usually covered), and a *Bust (N. wall) of Abp. Donato de' Medici, by *Ant. Rossellino,* or *Verrocchio.* In the N. aisle, near the entrance, is the tomb of Card. Nic. Forteguerri with two statues of Hope and Faith attrib. to Verrocchio. The figure of Charity was added by *Lorenzetto* in 1515, and the bust and sarcophagus in 1753.—In the Crypt are remains of the former church, and fragments of the 13C pulpit dismantled in the 17C.

Opposite the Duomo is the octagonal *Baptistery (recently reopened after restoration) started in 1338 by *Cellino di Nese* on a design of *Andrea Pisano,* and finished in 1359. Note the capitals and reliefs above the main entrance and the Madonna in the tympanum. On the right is a tiny Gothic pulpit of 1399. In the fine interior, decorating the font, are sculptured slabs of the 13C similar to those existing in several of the Pistoian churches, and possibly originally from the Duomo.

On the W. side of the piazza is the **Palazzo Pretorio,** a Gothic building of 1367 and later, which has a good courtyard, with painted and sculptured armorial bearings of magistrates. On the E. side is the ***Palazzo del Comune,** a fine Italian Gothic building of 1294, with later additions. It now houses the MUSEO CIVICO, to be opened in 1978. The following list includes some of the most important works. *Ridolfo Ghirlandaio* (attr.), Madonna; *Gerino da Pistoia,* Madonna (1509); *Bernardino del Signoraccio,* Madonna. *Agnolo di Paolo di Vetri,* *Bust of Christ; *Beccafumi,* Madonna, Child and St John; *Maestro di Francoforte* (attr.), triptych; *Lorenzo di Credi,* Madonna enthroned; *Raffaellino del Garbo,* Annunciation. School of *Benedetto da Maiano,* sculptured Madonna and Child; *Cosimo Rosselli,* Coronation of the Virgin; *Tommaso Flamberti,* *Marble relief of the Madonna and Child; *Gerino Gerini,* Madonna and Saints; *Lorenzetto,* figure of Card. Forteguerri, from his tomb in the Duomo. School of *Berlinghiero Berlinghieri,* *St Francis and stories from his life; 13C Pistoian school, painted crucifix; school of *Bernardo Daddi,* *Crucifixion; 14C Pistoian school, *Deposition, and Madonna; two lions from the original pulpit in the Duomo (13C); *Lorenzo di Niccolò Gerini,* Madonna; *Mariotto di Nardo* and *Rossello di Jacopo Franchi,* Annunciation and Saints; sculptured fragments after Nicolo and Giov. Pisano; detached fresco of the Madonna, early 12C Tuscan school. Later works by *Carlo Maratta, Sebastiano Ricci,* etc., and a piece of 17C stained glass from the church of San Pietro.

A few minutes' walk to the S.E. is the disused 12C church of *San Pietro,* with a characteristic façade; over the main portal is a relief of Christ giving the keys to St Peter, the Madonna, and the Apostles. To the N. of San Pietro is the church of ***San Bartolomeo in Pantano,** a 12C church, with a relief over the central door, possibly by *Gruamonte* (1167). Inside, good capitals, and a *Pulpit by *Guido da Como* (reassembled from fragments).

Behind the Palazzo Comunale Via Pacini leads N. to the **Ospedale del Ceppo,** founded in the 13-14C, and still in use. The façade is decorated with a famous terracotta *Frieze (1514-25), depicting the seven works of mercy (six by *Santi Buglioni,* the seventh added by *Filippo di Lorenzo Paladini* in 1584-86), and the cardinal and theological virtues by *Giov. della Robbia.* Beneath are medallions with the Annunciation, Visitation, and Assumption and the arms of the hospital, the city, and the Medici, also by *Giov. della Robbia.* To the left of the hospital, above the door of the adjoining church, is a Coronation of the Virgin by *Bened. Buglioni* (1510), the oldest work of the series.

To the E. of the hospital, in P.za San Lorenzo, is the church of *Santa Maria delle Grazie* or *del Letto* (open from 7-10) by Michelozzo, with a good presbytery. The high altar has a fine silver 17C tabernacle, and there is a 17C tomb on the S. wall.

To the W. of the hospital is the church of ***Sant'Andrea,** with a good 12C façade. The relief, of the Journey and Adoration of the Magi, is by *Gruamonte* and his brother *Adeodato,* and is signed (1166). In the long and narrow interior is a 14C font of the Pisan school, and a *Pulpit by *Giov. Pisano,* his masterpiece. In the apse is a statue of St Andrew of the school of Giov. Pisano (formerly on the façade), and in the r. aisle, in a 15C tabernacle, a wood Crucifix by *Giov. Pisano*.

At the end of Via Sant'Andrea is P.za San Francesco, with the church of **San Francesco al Prato**, begun in 1294, with a façade of 1717. The open roofed nave ends in a wide vaulted transept with five E. chapels. Inside, the nave has the damaged remains of frescoes. Behind the high altar (lights to r. and l.) are 14C frescoes showing strong Giottesque influence, possibly the work of a pupil Puccio Capanna. On the altar, Madonna and Saints, a polyptych of the 14C Sienese school has been removed for some years for restoration. In the chapel to the left is a splendid fresco cycle of the *Allegory of the triumph of St Augustine, of the Sienese school. 14C frescoes also decorate the 2nd chap. to the r. of the high altar. In the S. transept are remains of a huge frescoed Crucifixion. A door in this transept leads through the Sacristy to the *Chapter House* (not always open), both of which retain good late 14C frescoes, notably on the E. wall of the latter, the Tree of Life with a Crucifixion. The 14C *Cloister* is beyond.

Via Bozzi and Via Montanara e Curtatone lead back towards the centre of town. To the right, Via della Madonna leads to the 15C church of the **Madonna dell'Umiltà** (still partly in restoration), built by *Ventura Vitoni,* a pupil of Bramante. The dome was added by *Vasari* in 1561; its weight has made necessary the present repairs. The main portal is 17C. The interior is a spacious example of an harmonious Renaissance church. The marble altar, by *Pietro Tacca* (with two of the angels by *Marcacci*), encloses a 14C fresco of the Madonna by *Bart. Cristiani*.

FROM PISTOIA TO ABETONE, 49 km., bus in 2½ hrs. The Bologna road diverges to the right while Highway N66 climbs steeply to (10½ km.) *Cireglio* (fine retrospective view of Pistoia). At (19½ km.) *Pontepetri* is the junction with the road from Pracchia (p. 487). On a higher by-road (r.) are the resorts of *Maresca* and *Gavinana*. The Imperial defeat of the Florentine army at Gavinana in 1530, in which both commanders, Fr. Ferrucci and Philibert, Prince of Orange, were slain, sealed the fate of the Republic.—29 km. *San Marcello Pistoiese* (623 m) is a pleasant summer resort.—Two kilometres beyond (30½ km.) *Mammiano* this route joins Highway 12 from Lucca.—37 km. *Cutigliano* (670 m), to the right of the road, has a fine 14C Palazzo Pretorio. The winter sports facilities include a funicular which mounts to *Doganaccia* (1540 m), another ski resort. A funicular continues to Croce Arcana (1730 m).—Beyond (42 km.) *Pianosinático* (948 m) the road ascends through the splendid forest that still clothes the Tuscan slope of the mountains. *Rivoreto,* 3 km. N. of Pianosinático, has a local Ethnographical Museum.—50 km. The *Passo dell'Abetone* (1388 m) takes its name from a huge fir-tree which has long disappeared. Round the road summit, still on the Tuscan side of the boundary with Emilia, has developed **Abetone**, one of the best-known ski resorts in the Apennines, specially favoured by Florentines. Numerous ski-lifts and chair-lifts ascend to the snow fields. It is also frequented in summer (swimming pools, tennis courts, etc.). Bus services run to Bologna, Florence, Pisa and Ferrara.—From Abetone to *Modena,* see p. 379.

At 'La Verginina', 4 km. N.W. of Pistoia, is a Zoological Garden.

From Pistoia to *Bologna,* see Rte 44C.

The Lucca road and the railway, along with the autostrada, traverse the low pass between the Apennines and Monte Albano on which stands the old fortress of (43 km.) *Serravalle Pistoiese*. At 47 km. the road turns right, leaving on the left the little spa of *Monsummano*, with vapour baths once visited by the wounded Garibaldi. Here was born Gius. Giusti (1809-50), the Tuscan poet; there are plans to restore his birthplace.

51 km. Montecatini Terme, perhaps the best known of Italian spas

(21,400 inhab.) with an international reputation, is frequented for digestive troubles, with warm saline waters used both internally and externally. The town is pleasantly laid out on either side of a fine park. park.

About 500 **Hotels and pensions.**
Spas. *Stabilimento Tettuccio,* with café, music-rooms, etc., the principal rendezvous of the town; *Tamerici, Torretta, Regina, La Salute,* for drinking water; *Terme Leopoldine,* for baths; *Excelsior,* for both, all with pleasant gardens.
Buses to *Lucca, Florence, Pisa, Pistoia,* etc. *Coach Excursions* in the season.

A funicular railway ascends from beyond the spa gardens to *Montecatini Valdiniévole* (or 'Montecatini Alto'), an old hill town (290 m; also reached by road in 5 km.), in a spectacular position, favoured as a residence by Giuseppe Giusti. The Prepositurale of San Pietro has a small museum of vestments, reliquaries, and paintings.

Here the men of Lucca were defeated in 1315 by Uguccione della Faggiola, leader of the Ghibellines of Pisa. The surroundings afford pleasant walks, especially in the Val di Niévole, to the N.

54 km. *Borgo a Buggiano* lies below *Buggiano Castello,* an ancient hill-town with a good Palazzo Pretorio and a church preserving Romanesque details.—59 km. **Péscia** a busy town (19,200 inhab.) is an important horticultural centre particularly noted for asparagus and carnations. The striking flower market (1951) is to be superseded by an even larger one. The *Duomo,* rebuilt in 1693, has a campanile of 1306 and remains of a 13C ambone. *Sant'Antonio* (1361) contains a 13C Deposition group in wood (temporarily removed for restoration). In the 14C church of *San Francesco* are a painting of St Francis, with 6 stories from his life by Bonaventura Berlinghieri (1235). The Cappella Cardini (1451), on the N., is by Buggiano, the adopted son of Brunelleschi. A slightly earlier work by the same artist is *SS Pietro e Paolo.* The *Museo Civico* has Tuscan paintings (14-16C). The handsome *Piazza Mazzini* is the ancient centre of the civic life of the town. In the two valleys of the Pescia river are numerous paper mills.

Collodi, 5 km. W., gave Carlo Lorenzini (1826-90) the pen-name under which he wrote 'Le Avventure di Pinocchio'. The puppet hero is commemorated by a bronze monument (1956), by Emilio Greco; and sculptured tableaux in the museum garden recall episodes from the book. The *Villa Garzoni* (adm. daily 8-20) has beautiful 17C gardens.—Excursions may also be made to *Castelvecchio,* 11 km. N., with a good Romanesque church; and to *Altopascio,* 11 km. S., where Castruccio beat the Florentines in 1325. The Order of the Knights of Altopascio ('del Tau') ran a hospice for pilgrims here in 1084; it has since been famous for its hoteliers.

65 km. Turning for *San Gennaro* (2½ km. r.), where the Romanesque church has an ambone of 1162 by Maestro Filippo.—73 km. *Lunata,* with its tall Romanesque campanile, lies 2 km. S. of *Lámmari,* where the parish church contains a tabernacle, Matteo Civitali's last work.

78 km. **LUCCA,** seat of an archbishop and a provincial capital, remains a quiet and pleasant old town (91,700 inhab.) conserving its magnificent 16-17C ramparts intact; they enclose its still partly Roman street plan. It is especially rich in Romanesque architecture, and many medieval mansions line its narrow streets. The olive oil of Lucca has long been famous.

Post Office, 2 Via Cairoli.—**E.P.T.,** 2 P.za Giudiccioni and 13 Via Vittorio Veneto (information office).

Buses from P.za San Martino for *Abetone, Bagni di Lucca, Florence, Montecatini, Pistoia, Prato, Pisa, Livorno,* etc; and from P.za del Giglio for *Carrara, Viareggio,* etc.

History. The Roman colony of *Luca* was the scene in 56 B.C. of the meeting of Cæsar, Pompey, and Crassus to form the First Triumvirate. The town is reputed to have been the first place in Tuscany to have accepted Christianity and its first bishop was Paulinus, a disciple of St Peter. In 552 the Goths here withstood a prolonged siege by Narses. In the Middle Ages it was an important city under the Lombard marquesses of Tuscany, and later waged constant war with Pisa, Florence and other cities. Under the rule of the adventurer, Castruccio Castracani, in 1316-28, Lucca achieved supremacy in Western Tuscany, but his death was followed by a period of subjection to Pisa (1343-69). Charles IV then gave the Lucchesi a charter of independence, and it maintained its autonomy, often under the suzerainty of noble families, until 1799. In 1805 Napoleon presented the city as a principality to his sister Elisa Baciocchi, and in 1815 it was given to Marie Louise de Bourbon as a duchy. Lucca was a nursery of architecture, and boasts a great sculptor in Matteo Civitali (1435-1501), nearly all of whose works remain in his native place. Pompeo Batoni (1708-87), however, painted his fashionable portraits mainly in Rome. The city is the birthplace also of the musicians Luigi Boccherini (1743-1805) and Giacomo Puccini (1858-1924) whose forbears for four generations had been organists of S. Martino, though he himself was only a chorister at S. Michele.

The PIAZZA NAPOLEONE (with a statue of Marie Louise, by Bartolini) and PIAZZA DEL GIGLIO together may be regarded as the centre of the city. In the former is the **Palazzo Ducale** (*Provinciale*), the old seat of the lords of Lucca, begun by Ammannati in 1578, but many times remodelled.

Most of the works of the PINACOTECA NAZIONALE have been removed from here to the Museo Nazionale Giunigi (see p. 496); those in the three rooms which have remained open are soon to be moved to Palazzo Mansi (p. 495). The most important works still here include: *Andrea del Sarto,* Madonna and Child with St Anne and the young St John; *Luca Giordano,* St Sebastian; *Flemish School,* Annunciation (1414); *Bronzino,* Medici portraits; *Maria Benôit,* Portrait of Elisa Baciocchi; *Sustermans,* Medici portraits; *Tintoretto,* St Mark freeing a slave; *Salvator Rosa,* Four Battle scenes; *Paolo Veronese,* Peter the Hermit before the 'Consiglio Veneto'; *Rosa da Tivoli,* landscapes of the Roman campagna; *Carlo Dolci,* SS. John the Baptist and Anthony Abbot.

Behind the Prefettura stands *San Romano,* a Dominican church containing the tomb of St Romanus by Matteo Civitali (1490).

Beyond P.za del Giglio is P.za San Giovanni, in which rises *San Giovanni* (closed for restoration), a 12C church with a fine portal of 1187 in its rebuilt façade. Off the N. side is the baptistery rebuilt late in the 14C when it was given its sculptured font; the Roman immersion font with tessellated marble surround was uncovered in 1885. In the harmonious P.za San Martino, beyond, stands the ***Cathedral** (*San Martino*), consecrated in 1070 by Pope Alexander II, who had begun the rebuilding while bishop of Lucca.

The upper part of the FAÇADE is by *Guidetto da Como* (1204). Over the left doorway of the portico is a worn relief of a Deposition, and under it an Adoration of the Magi, perhaps early works of *Nicola Pisano*. All the sculpture on the façade is of excellent workmanship. The lower part of the embattled Campanile dates from 1060, the upper from 1261.

The INTERIOR was rebuilt in the 14-15C in a Gothic style, with a polychrome marble floor. Within, on the entrance wall, *St Martin dividing his cloak (13C), from the façade (replaced by a copy). The two stoups are by *Matteo Civitali* (1498). SOUTH AISLE. 2nd altar, *Fed. Zuccari,* Adoration of the Magi; 3rd altar, *Tintoretto,* Last Supper; 4th altar, *Dom. Cresti* (Il Passignano), Crucifixion. The pulpit is by *Matteo*

Civitali. A door admits to the Sacristy with an altarpiece of the Madonna with Saints, by *Dom. Ghirlandaio,* and a detached fresco of the Trinity, attrib. to *Cosimo Rosselli.* The 17C organ is the work of *Dom. Zanobi.*—In the S. transept, tombs of Pietro da Noceto (1472) and Dom. Bertini (1479), both by *Civitali,* who also sculpted the two angels flanking the tabernacle in the Chapel of the Holy Sacrament, and the altar of St Regulus (1484) in front of the high altar. The stained glass is the work of *Pandolfo di Ugolino* of Pisa (1485), and the choir stalls of *Leonardo Marti* (1452).—North transept; altar with figures of the Risen Christ and SS. Peter and Paul, by *Giambologna* (the predella with a view of Lucca is of slightly later date); *Statue of St John the Evangelist by *Iac. della Quercia,* and *Tomb of Ilaria del Carretto Guinigi, his masterpiece (1408). In the Cappella del Santuario, *Virgin and Child enthroned, with saints, by *Fra Bartolomeo* (1509). In the middle of the N. aisle is the octagonal marble *TEMPIETTO, also by *Civitali* (1484), built to house the *Volto Santo, a wooden likeness of Christ, supposed to have been begun by Nicodemus and miraculously completed. The favourite oath of William Rufus is said to have been 'Per Vultum de Lucca'; the effigy could be assigned stylistically to the 11C.

The TREASURY, housed at the Opera del Duomo (No. 5 P.za Antelminelli) has been closed for several years awaiting rearrangement as the Cathedral Museum. It contains some fine examples of medieval silversmiths' work, notably the *Croce dei Pisani, an elaborate crucifix of 1424-39.

From P.za San Giovanni a short road leads N. across Via del Battistero to the 12C church of *San Giusto* (l.), with a good portal. Farther on, across Via Santa Croce, is the 13C church of *San Cristoforo* with a fine interior. It is the burial place of Matt. Civitali (d. 1501) and also serves as a War memorial (the walls are covered with the names of the Dead). In the picturesque Via Fillungo, beyond, are two old towers. Via Roma, in which is *Boccherini's House,* ends on the left in P.za San Michele, with *Palazzo Pretorio* (1492; enlarged 1588), in the portico of which is a statue of Civitali, the architect of the original building. To the right is the magnificent façade of *San Michele in Foro,* typical of the Pisan Romanesque style as developed in Lucca. Begun c. 1143, the building was continued into the next century. The Madonna on the S.W. corner is by Civitali.

In the interior (N. aisle) is a Crucifix painted in the late 12C, and (S. aisle) a Madonna and Child by *And. della robbia.* In the N. transept, SS. Helena, Jerome, Sebastian, and Roch, by *Filippino Lippi;* and a Madonna by *Raff. da Montelupo* (1522), a relief that formed part of the tomb of Sylvester Giles, Bp. of Worcester, who died in Italy in 1521.

Opposite the W. door is the narrow Via di Poggio where (at No. 30) Puccini was born. Via San Paolino continues Via Roma W. to *San Paolino,* by Baccio da Montelupo and Bast. Bertolani (1522-39), which contains a Deposition by Ang. Puccinelli, an early Christian sarcophagus, and a Coronation of the Virgin (15C Florentine school). Nearby, in Via Galli, the *Palazzo Mansi* is being restored to house part of the Pinacoteca Nazionale, to be removed from Palazzo Ducale (comp. above).

Via Calderia leads N. from P.za S. Michele to the church of *San Salvatore,* a 12C church with good sculpture by Biduino above its S. portal. Via del Moro, behind, is lined with medieval mansions. Via Cesare Battisti winds between 17-18C palazzi towards the tall campanile of *San Frediano (1112-47). The much restored mosaic on the façade is possibly the work of Berlinghiero Berlinghieri (13C). The church replaced an earlier basilica and has its apse at the W. end.

In the splendid basilican *INTERIOR is a magnificent *Font, in the form of a fountain covered by a small tempietto, sculpted with reliefs of the story of Moses, the Good Shepherd, and the Apostles. Behind the font is a lunette of the Annunciation by *Andrea della Robbia*. Nearby are two interesting frescoes recently detached from behind the organ on the W. wall. In the 4th chapel of the N. aisle are a Gothic *Altarpiece by *Iac. della Quercia* (1422; assisted by Giov. da Imola) and two pavement tombs by the same artist; facing the altar, *Conception and saints, by Fr. Francia. The 2nd N. chapel is frescoed by *Amico Aspertini* (1508-9).

Just S.W. of the church is the *Palazzo Pfanner* (being restored) with a delightful galleried staircase and 18C garden, near which stands the 14C church of *Sant'Agostino*, its campanile resting on arches of a Roman theatre. Nearby is the little Baroque cupola of one of its chapels, which contains a venerated painting of the Madonna. Farther S.W., the church of *Santa Maria Corteorlandini*, built c. 1187 but exuberantly altered in the 17C, retains part of its 12C structure on the S. side.

The medieval houses of the Via dell'Anfiteatro, on the other side of Via Fillungo, follow the ellipse of the Roman *Amphitheatre,* whose arena forms a remarkable *Piazza. From the N.E. corner a road winds towards *San Pietro Somaldi* a 12C church with a grey and white banded façade of 1248, though the relief above the centre door is by Guido da Como and assistants (1203). Farther on is *San Francesco,* a restored 13C church with memorials to Castracani (d. 1328) and Boccherini (d. 1805), and remains of detached *Frescoes of the 15C Florentine school in the chap. to the right of the high altar. The two lunettes show the Presentation of the Virgin in the temple and the Marriage of the Virgin and they are of remarkably high quality. In the cloister is the tomb of Bonagiunta Tignosini (1274) with a ruined fresco by Deodata Orlandi.

The VILLA GUINIGI (1418) nearby, has been beautifully restored to house the **Museo Nazionale Guinigi** (open 9-14, fest. 9-13, closed Mon) which contains a fine collection of sculpture and paintings from Lucca and its province.

ROOM I. Roman objects found in Lucca including a mosaic pavement (1C A.D.) and a Hellenistic relief of a funerary banquet.—ROOM II. Four Ligurian tombs (reconstructed); Etruscan tomb with gold jewellery and an Attic krater (3C B.C.).—SOUTH PORTICO. Medieval architectural fragments and a tomb slab of a member of the Antelminelli family attrib. to *Iac. della Quercia.*—R. III. Fine examples of Lucchese sculpture (8-14C) including a transenna with a relief of Samson and the lion; fragment of a statue of St Martin (12-13C) from the Duomo; bas-reliefs from the church of S. Jacopo in Altopascio; statuette of the Madonna and Child attrib. to *Biduini.*—R. IV. Virgin annunciate, attrib. to *Nino Pisano;* marble statues by various masters from a polyptych attrib. to Priamo della Quercia (comp. below, R. XII).—R. V. Fine works by *Matteo Civitali.*—R. VII. Weights and measures of Lucca (18-19C).

Stairs lead up to the Pinacoteca. R. X. Inlaid stalls from the Duomo; *Fr. Di Giorgio* (attrib.), Visitation; *Beccafumi,* Scipio; *Pontormo,* *Portrait of Alessandro de' Medici.*—R. XI. Panel paintings including: *Berlinghiero,* Painted Crucifix; *Ugolino Lorenzetti,* Madonna and Child with St John the Evangelist.—R. XII. *Maestro del Bimbo Vispo,* two Saints; *Priamo della Quercia* (attrib.), Polyptych; *Angelo Puccinelli,* Marriage of St Catherine; and other works by the Tuscan school.—R. XIII. *Vecchietta* and *Neroccio,* reliefs in wood; Lucchese works by followers of Filippino Lippi.—R. XIV. Good works by *Fra Bartolomeo* and *Amico Aspertini.*—R. XV. *Il Riccio,* Nativity of the Virgin.—R. XVI, XVII. Church vestments, and paintings by *Giorgio Vasari.*—R. XVIII. *Matteo Civitali,* Ecce Homo; *Guido Reni,* Crucifixion.—R. XX. Three good works by *Pompeo Batoni.*

From P.za S. Francesco Via Fratta (comp. the Plan) leads towards

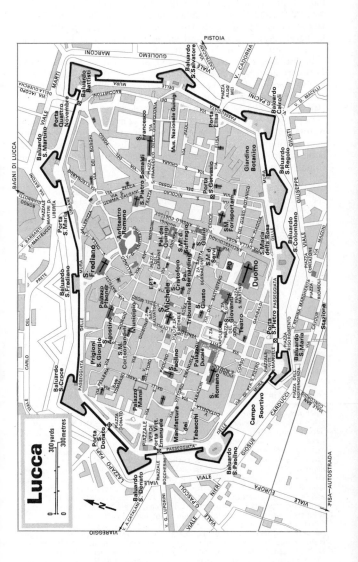

Via Guinigi, a narrow lane dominated by the **Case dei Guinigi,** built in the 14C and remodelled in the 16C. The best preserved houses are Nos. 20, 22, and 29; the last has a picturesque tower (best seen from the neighbouring Via Sant'Andrea) on which trees grow, and another has a medieval loggia. The old chapels of *Sant'Anastasio* and *Sant'Andrea,* reached from Via Sant'Andrea, are interesting.

In Via Santa Croce, beyond and to the left, is ***Santa Maria Forisportam,** another fine church in the 13C Pisan style, named from having been outside the city gates until 1260. It was altered in 1516 by the raising of the nave and transepts. Within are two paintings by *Guercino* (4th S. altar, and N. transept), a font made from an early-Christian sarcophagus, and a painting on a gold ground by *Ang. Puccinelli* (1386; N. transept). Farther E. is the *Porta San Gervasio* (1260), the best of the gates remaining from the second enceinte. Across the 'fosso' in Via Elisa is the church of the *SS Trinità* (key from adjoining convent), which contains a sentimental Madonna della Tosse, by M. Civitali.

In the other direction Via Santa Croce crosses P.za Bernardini, dominated by its 16C palazzo. To the N., in P.za del Suffragio, is the *Oratorio di Santa Giulia* (13-14C), with a painted Crucifixion by the same hand as that in San Michele.

To the S. of Santa Maria Forisportam is the charming little oratory of ***Santa Maria della Rosa,** built in 1309-33 in the Pisan Gothic style, inside which are some traces of the original Roman wall.

An interesting walk may be taken round the **Ramparts,** among the oldest of their kind (1561-1645), built on the system afterwards developed by Vauban, and recalling the ramparts of Berwick-on-Tweed and Verona. Their tree-planted bastions, many of which are adorned with monuments, command good views. The severe *Porta Santa Maria* (1593) on the N. side contrasts with the florid *Porta San Pietro,* by Aless. Resta (1566), leading to the station.

In the foothills, N.E. of Lucca, are the late-17C *Villa Orsetti* (at Márlia, 8 km.), once the home of Elisa Baciocchi (no adm.) where Niccolò Paganini and Metternich stayed; and, at Segromigno (10 km.), the 17C *Villa Mansi* (adm. 9-20), altered by Juvarra, with sumptuous Baroque furnishings and an 'English' garden. From *Vinchiana* (11 km. N. of Lucca on N 12) a by-road winds up through beautiful scenery to (5 km. farther) *San Giorgio di Brancoli,* where the Romanesque church has an *Ambone and a font, both 12C, a St George of the Robbian school, and a 14C painted Crucifixion.

FROM LUCCA TO AULLA, 115 km. by road (bus to Barga in 80 min.); railway (90 km.) in 2 hrs. This route traverses the GARFAGNANA, the valley of the Serchio, well-wooded (famous for its chestnuts) and richly cultivated, lying between the Apennines and the Apuan Alps. There are many marble quarries in the area. From (9 km.) *Ponte a Moriano* the more interesting road follows the W. bank of the Serchio, past (18 km.) *Diécimo* (at the 10th Roman mile from Lucca) with its 13C Romanesque church, and (22 km.) *Borgo a Mozzano,* where the church contains expressive 16C sculpture and a wooden figure of St Bernadine by Matteo Civitali. The Ponte della Maddalena is a remarkable 14C footbridge. Here a road crosses the stream for (29 km.) **Bagni di Lucca** (150 m.), a little spa with warm sulphur and saline waters, somewhat off the main valley on highway N 12. Among its many famous visitors were Shelley, Byron, Browning, and Walter Savage Landor. Here was born Francis Marion Crawford (1854-1909), the novelist, and in the little Protestant cemetery Ouida lies buried. The road, keeping to the E. bank, enters the country of the Castracani family, whose tombs and castle adorn the village of *Ghivizzano* (r.).—From (38 km.) *Fornaci* a road leads to the right for (42 km.) **Barga** (410 m.) above a new town, a characteristic little hill-town (views) with a fine Romanesque *Duomo* containing a sculptured *Pulpit of the late 12C, an early 12C *St Christopher in polychromed wood, and a rich treasury.—56 km. *Castelnuovo di Garfagnana* preserves some remains of its Rocca, or governor's palace, the residence of the poets Ariosto and Fulvio Testi when they were governors of the district. On the road to Pievepélago and Modena (see p. 379) c. 7 km. N. of Castelnuovo, is *Castiglione di Garfagnana,* with 14C walls, where the church of San Michele preserves a Madonna (1389), the only signed work of

Giuliano di Simone of Lucca.—The picturesque road ascends to (82 km.) the *Foce dei Carpinelli* (842 m), beyond which it enters the valley of the Aulella at (92 km.) *Càsola*, and farther on leaves on the left a road to the little spa of *Equi*, 7 km. S.E.— 115 km. *Aulla*, see p. 371.

The old road and the railway to Pisa, hemmed between the two motorway spurs for Viareggio, join the Serchio, passing between the castle of *Nozzano*, a Luccan outpost, and the Pisan castle of Ripafratta; a newer road makes more directly S. for (92 km.) *San Giuliano Terme*, a small spa at the foot of Monte Pisano. A bust and plaque mark the Casa Prinni where Shelley stayed in summer 1820.

100 km. **PISA** (103,500 inhab.), standing on the Arno a few miles from its mouth, is famous among the cities of Italy for its sculpture and architecture. The cathedral, campanile, baptistery, and camposanto (despite irreparable damage to the last) make up a group unrivalled in beauty, a fitting reminder of the ancient greatness of the Pisan Republic. The city also has important manufactures of glass, machinery, and textiles.

Airport, *Galileo Galilei* (San Giusto), 3 km. S. for international services to London, Paris, and Frankfurt; and internal flights to Rome, Verona, and Milan. *Town terminal,* Via Corridoni (Piazza Stazione).

Railway Stations. *Centrale* for all services; *San Rossore,* nearer the cathedral, served by all trains of the Lucca line and a few slow trains on the Spezia line.

Hotels mostly near the main Station; some in the area round the Duomo.

Post Office, P.za Vitt. Emanuele.—**E.P.T.,** 42 Lungarno Mediceo (*Information Office,* 11 P.za del Duomo).

Town Buses from the Station to Piazza Garibaldi and the Duomo, etc.— **Country Buses** from P.za Stazione, P.za Vittorio, or P.za S. Antonio for *Marina di Pisa, Livorno, Lucca; Casciano Terme; Pontedera; San Giuliano Terme; Abetone* and *Pievepèlago,* etc.

History. Pisa was a Roman colony from the 2C B.C., and a naval and commercial port. In the Middle Ages it became a maritime republic, rivalling Genoa, Amalfi, and Venice. Waging incessant war with the Saracens, Pisa deprived them of Corsica, Sardinia, and the Balearic Isles (1050-1100), and at the same time combined war and trade in the East. In 1135, assisting Innocent II against Roger of Sicily, she destroyed Amalfi; but subsequently she joined the Ghibelline party, and remained proudly faithful to it, amid all the Guelph republics surrounding her. In 1284 Pisa was defeated by the Genoese in the naval battle of Meloria and lost her maritime supremacy; thenceforward she had to submit to a succession of lordships, including those of the Gherardesca family (1316-41) and of Gian Galeazzo Visconti (1396-1405). The Florentines gained possession of Pisa in 1405, and after one or two vain efforts at rebellion it became a quiet refuge of scholars and artists, a university having been established there by the Gherardesca c. 1330. When Charles VIII entered Italy in 1494 he was expected to restore her liberty to Pisa, but he broke his promise, and Florence took final possession of the city in 1509. In 1944 the town was bombarded by both German and Allied artillery; the Camposanto and the area near the station suffered worst, and further damage was caused when all the bridges were blown up.—The most illustrious native of Pisa is Galileo Galilei (1564-1642), physicist and astronomer. Pisa was visited by Landor in 1819-21, by Shelley in 1820-22, and by Byron in 1821, and here Browning brought his bride in 1846, before they settled in Florence. Titta Ruffo (1877-1953), the famous baritone, was born in Pisa.

On 28 June takes place the *Giuoco del Ponte,* a sham fight between the people living on either side of the Arno. The combatants wear 16-17C costumes, and the day ends with a procession of both parties.

Art. The Romanesque architecture of Pisa, a remarkable development of the North Italian Romanesque style, had a far-reaching effect on the neighbouring cities, spreading as far afield as Prato and Arezzo, and also into Sardinia, and leaving its imprint on the Gothic buildings that appeared later in the city. Pisan sculpture at the same time was a potent influence in the advance from hieratic formalism, its greatest exponent being Nicola Pisano (c. 1200-c. 1280), probably a native of Apulia established at Pisa. In painting Pisa produced no great master, but

Giunta Pisano (fl. 1202-55) is believed to be the earliest painter whose name is inscribed on any extant work.

The ****Piazza del Duomo,** or *dei Miracoli,* lies well N.W. of the centre. The bright marble buildings are superbly set off by the green lawns between them.

The Duomo and Baptistery are closed from 12.45-15; the Camposanto and Campanile (both with adm. fee) remain open throughout the day, 9-19 (17 in winter).

The ***Duomo,** begun by *Buscheto* in 1063 and continued by *Rainaldo,* is the most important example of the Pisan style and one of the most celebrated Romanesque buildings in Italy. It was restored in 1602-16 after a serious fire in 1595.

The building stands on a white marble pavement and is covered inside and out with black and white marble, toned on the exterior to a delicate grey and russet. The *Façade shows four tiers of columns with open galleries, with a row of seven tall arches below. In the left-hand arch is the tomb of Buscheto. The bronze doors were remodelled after the fire by various sculptors of the school of Giambologna. The usual entrance is the *Portale di San Ranieri,* in the S. transept, with bronze *Doors by Bonanno da Pisa (1180).

The cruciform INTERIOR is over 94½m long and 32m wide (72m across the exceptionally deep transepts). Nearly all the pillars, 68 in number, are antique. The rich ceiling of the NAVE was remodelled after 1596. The *Pulpit, by *Giov. Pisano* (1302-11), removed in 1599 after the fire, was reconstructed in 1926. The columns, on plain bases, resting on lions, or carved into figure sculpture, have statues of sibyls above the capitals, and florid architraves. Above, relief panels representing scenes from the New Testament are separated by figures of prophets. The bronze lamp hanging outside the choir, supposed to have suggested to Galileo the principle of the pendulum, was in fact cast by *Batt. Lorenzi* in 1587, six years after the discovery. The wooden throne and benches opposite the pulpit have good marquetry work. Beneath the dome are remains of a Cosmatesque pavement; another fragment, discovered near the high altar in 1977, may date from the end of the 11C.

In the SOUTH TRANSEPT is the *Tomb of Emp. Henry VII (d. 1313), by *Tino di Camaino.*—The balustrade at the entrance to the CHOIRS bears two bronze angels by Giambologna and assistants (1602). The stalls (15C) were reconstructed in 1616 from what survived the fire. On the entrance piers are a delightful *St Agnes, by *And. del Sarto,* and a Madonna, by *Sogliani.* The lectern and candelabra are by *Matteo Civitali.* On the walls below the cantoria are paintings by *Del Sarto:* *SS. John, Peter, Margaret, and Catherine. The crucifix on the high altar is by *Giambologna;* the angel on the column to the left is by *Stoldo Lorenzi* (1483). Round the APSE, *Sodoma,* Descent from the Cross (1540) and Sacrifice of Abraham (1542); works by *Sogliani,* and *Beccafumi.* In the vault is a fine mosaic, *Our Lord in Glory, a 13C work completed by *Cimabue* in 1302. The *Madonna and Child, a superb work in ivory by *Giov. Pisano,* formerly displayed in the Sacristy, has been removed for safety.—1st chap. l. of high altar: much venerated Madonna (13C; covered).

Outside the E. end of the cathedral rises the ***Campanile,** the famous **Leaning Tower** (splendid *View). It is a superb work, circular in plan and having eight stories of round arches, made up of a blind arcade, six open galleries, and a bell-chamber of smaller diameter. The tower is 54½m high, and leans 4½m. out of the perpendicular.

Begun in 1173, the tower was only 10½ m high when a subsidence of the soil threw it out of the perpendicular. During the 13C the architect in charge appears to have been *Giov. di Simone,* who endeavoured to rectify the inclination as the building proceeded. By 1301 the building had risen as far as the bellchamber, and *Tommaso di Andrea da Pontedera* (c. 1350) completed the tower as it now stands. Galileo made use of it in his famous experiments on the velocity of falling bodies. Despite all efforts to stabilize the structure, the lean is increasing by c. 3.28 mm. each year.

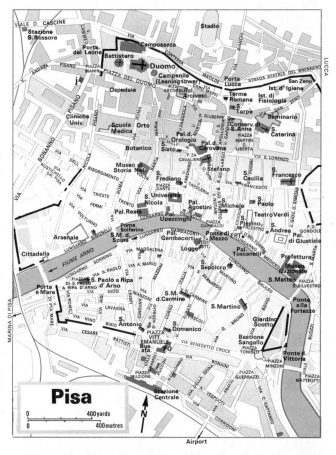

The ***Baptistery,** W. of the Duomo, is a noble circular building begun in 1152 by *Diotisalvi,* and remodelled by *Nicola* and *Giovanni Pisano* (1260-84). The Gothic dome and cusped arches were added in the 14C by *Cellino di Nese.* There are four portals, of which the most elaborate, facing the Duomo, is embellished with foliated columns and a Madonna by *Giov. Pisano* (copy; original in the Museo Nazionale). In the middle of the impressive INTERIOR stands a beautiful octagonal *Font of white marble, carved and inlaid in mosaic, by *Guido da Como* (1246). A statue of St John the Baptist by a local artist, Italo Griselli (1880-1958) stands in the centre on an Arab capital. The *Pulpit, by Nicola Pisano, is signed and dated 1260. Resting on slender pillars bearing figures of the Virtues, it bears panels sculptured in bold relief (Nativity, Adoration of the Magi, Presentation, Crucifixion, Last Judgement). Around the walls are displayed half-figures of Saints and Prophets by *Nicola* and *Giovanni Pisano,* removed from the exterior.

The rectangular **Camposanto,** or cemetery, begun in 1278 by *Giov. di Simone* and completed in the 15C, takes the form of an enclosed cloister lit by graceful traceried windows. Its wealth of frescoes and funeral monuments suffered heavily in 1944.

It is traditionally said that Abp. Lanfranchi (1108-78) brought shiploads of earth from the Holy Land to form a burial-ground here. **Frescoes.** Those that are damaged are gradually being replaced. In some cases only the sinopia remains. The following description starts from the E. corner of the SOUTH WALL: *Benozzo Gozzoli,* Fall of Jericho; Childhood and Youth of Moses; Visit of Queen of Shebah to Solomon; Innocence of Joseph; Joseph at court of Pharaoh; Departure of Abraham and Lot for Palestine; Story of Agar and Abraham; Abraham and the worshippers of Baal; Abraham victorious. *Ant. Veneziano,* Return of St Ranieri. *Andrea Buonaiuti,* St Ranieri in the Holy Land, and his Conversion and Temptations. *Spinello Aretino,* Scenes from the Life of St Ephysius. *Taddeo Gaddi,* Job the alms-giver; with his guests; with his herds; the pact of Satan with God; the first misfortune of Job; his patience; and a landscape.—NORTH WALL: Sinopia of the Cosmograph; Theological Cosmograph; *Piero di Puccio,* The Story of Cain and Abel; Story of Adam, Building of the ark and the flood; (r. of the door) *Benozzo Gozzoli,* Construction of Tower of Babel.

The door gives access to two halls. To the left is the CAPPELLA AMMANNATI with *Frescoes (and some sinopie) of the Triumph of Death, Last Judgement, Stories of the Anchorites, etc. These have been variously attrib. to Orcagna, Fr. Traini, Vitale da Bologna, etc., but are generally held to be by an unknown 14C master named from these frescoes 'The Master of the Triumph of Death'. A bust of Liszt recalls his inspiration from these frescoes which led to the creation of his "Totentanz". The sculptures here include: *Nicolo Pisano,* Madonna and Child, St John the Baptist, and St John the Evangelist; *Nino Pisano,* Madonna and Child; *Tino di Camaino,* Henry VII, with figures; bronze *Griffon, probably 10-11C Egyptian. The adjacent gallery (r.) displays sinopie by *Benozzo Gozzoli.* At the E. corner of the N. wall: *Gozzoli,* Wine harvest and drunkenness of Noah.

Monuments and Sculptures. Most of these have been either destroyed or removed. Of those that remain the most important are: SOUTH WALL (S.E. corner). Inscribed decrees ordaining honours for Gaius and Lucius Cæsar, nephews of Augustus; Roman milestones; Sarcophagi with tritons and nereids; Sarcophagus with the Rape of Proserpine; on this and other sarcophagi (many of which were reused in the Middle Ages), Roman portrait-heads; Tomb of And. Berlinghieri (d. 1826), oculist, by *Thorvaldsen;* Tomb of Fr. Algarotti (d. 1764), physicist; Sarcophagus with the Good Shepherd.—WEST WALL. Harbour chains of the ancient port of Pisa, carried off by the Genoese in 1342; Sarcophagus formed of a bath-tub; Sarcophagus of the 1C.

NORTH WALL. Sarcophagus with a matron and a figure in a toga; Sarcophagus with victories and other figures.—CAPPELLA AULLA, Assumption, by *Giov. della Robbia* (damaged).—Sarcophagus of a married couple; Sarcophagus with Thanatos and Hypnos; Sarcophagi, with Meleager and the Seasons; others, with a battle scene, and with the Good Shepherd; huge Sarcophagus with the Muses.— EAST WALL. Tomb of Fil. Decio (d. 1535), by *Stagio Stagi;* Statue for the tomb of Count Mastiani, by *Lor. Bartolini* (1842); Tomb of the scientist Mossotti (d. 1863), by *Giov. Dupré.*—Near the door are remains of a medieval mosaic.

The dignified Via Santa Maria leads S. from P.za del Duomo towards the centre. On the left Via dei Mille passes (r.) *San Sisto,* an 11C church beautifully restored, to reach the characteristic *PIAZZA DEI CAVALIERI, named from the Knights of St Stephen, an order founded by Cosimo I in 1561 in imitation of the Knights of Malta. *Santo Stefano dei*

Cavalieri, their church, was built to a design of Vasari (1565-69) with a façade by Giovanni de' Medici (1594-1606). It contains banners captured from the infidel and ornaments from the galleys of the knights. The reliquary bust of St Luxorious, in gilded bronze, by Donatello, stolen in 1976, has not yet been returned here since its recovery. To the left is *Palazzo dei Cavalieri,* formerly *della Carovana,* modernized in 1562 by Vasari, with spectacular graffiti decoration. It is now the seat of the Scuola Normale Superiore, a university college of high standing, founded by Napoleon in 1810. Concerts are given here from Dec-May. Outside is a statue of Cosimo I by Francavilla (1596).

The *Palazzo dell'Orologio,* closing the N. side of the square occupies the site the old *Torre dei Gualandi* or *della Muda* (later the Torre della Fame), the 'mews' of the eagles that figure in the Pisan coat-of-arms. Here in 1288 Count Ugolino della Gherardesca, suspected of treachery at the battle of Meloria, and his sons and grandsons were starved to death ('Inferno', XXIII).

Beyond the delightful little P.za Dini the old Via Notari leads on to P.za Garibaldi, a small but animated square opening on the Arno at the N. end of the *Ponte di Mezzo* (scene of the Giuoco del Ponte). Borgo Stretto leads N. again passing (r.) the church of *San Michele in Borgo,* built in 990, with a 14C façade, by Fra Gugl. Agnelli, typical of Pisan Gothic. It has good capitals in the interior. Farther on, Via San Francesco leads right to the church of *Santa Cecilia* (1103) with a façade and campanile decorated with majolica. To the N. across Piazza Martiri (planted with plane trees), stands the church of **Santa Caterina,** built for the Dominicans in the 13C, with a façade in the Pisan Gothic style of 1330. The best of the early tombs in the impressive interior is that, on the left, of Abp. Simone Saltarelli (d. 1342), by *Nino Pisano,* by whom are also the Annunciation figures flanking the high altar. On the left wall, Apotheosis of St Thomas, by *Fr. Traini.*

To the N.E. (comp. the Plan) are vestiges of *Roman Baths,* uncovered in 1942. From Via Cardinale Maffi there is a dramatic view of the Leaning Tower.—In the other direction, Via San Zeno leads N.E. to (c. 400 m) the little romanesque chapel of **San Zeno* (restored; adm. 9-12.30, 15-18) of ancient foundation, showing various architectural styles from the 5C.

Via San Francesco continues E. to the Gothic church of **San Francesco** which has a good campanile. Over the high altar, with a reredos by *Tomaso Pisano,* the vault is painted by *Taddeo Gaddi.* In the flanking chapels: (2nd r.) polyptych of 14C Florentine sch.; (1st l.) St Francis, early 13C Pisan sch., and frescoes (high up) by *Taddeo Gaddi;* (2nd l.), more frescoes and sinopie. In the Sacristy, which has frescoes by *Taddeo di Bartolo,* are displayed interesting sinopie by *Taddeo Gaddi,* recently discovered.

On the S. side of Via San Francesco is P.za San Paolo, where the church of *San Paolo all'Orto* retains a handsome 12C façade. Farther S. is *San Pierino* (1072-1119), which has a large crypt. Via Palestro leads E. to *Sant'Andrea,* another good 12C church.

From San Pierino the Via delle Belle Torri, with 12-13C houses, runs parallel with the river, then curves to join the Lungarno Medíceo. At the corner, on the river, is the 16C *Palazzo Toscanelli* (formerly Lanfranchi), occupied by Byron in 1821-22. Farther on is the *Palazzo de' Medici,* built in the 13-14C and now restored as the *Prefettura.* Beyond, behind the church of *San Matteo* (11-13C, much altered in 17C), are the

Carceri (Prisons), originally the convent of San Matteo and now occupied by the beautifully arranged *Museo Nazionale (adm. 9.30-16; closed Mon).

Only the GROUND FLOOR is open while extensive restoration work is carried out in the Pinacoteca on the first floor. Meanwhile the most important pictures have been brought down and displayed here. They include: *Simone Martini*, Madonna and Child with Saints and *Masaccio*, St Paul. Also temporarily displayed here: *Madonna del Latte, by *Andrea Pisano* (from the church of Santa Maria della Spina).—ENTRANCE HALL, sarcophagus with Good Shepherd (4C).—ROOMS 1-4. Sculptured fragments of 12-13C, including a head of Christ blessing; detached frescoes from San Michele degli Scalzi.—RR. 5-6. *Works by *Giov. Pisano* and his school; 12C fresco of Madonna and Child of the Pisan School; 13C painted crucifix; embroidered cope.—R. 7. Fragments of a pulpit by a follower of Giov. Pisano.—R. 8. Polychromed wooden *Figures by *Andrea Pisano*, and of the Pisan and Sienese schools; painted *Crucifix, signed by *Giunta Pisano*.—RR. 10-11. Bust of the Redeemer in terracotta, by *Verrocchio;* crucifix of Sardo-Catalan school; bas-relief of the Crucifixion by the school of Donatello.—RR. 12-13. Exultets on continuous strips of parchment, 11C and 13C, with illuminations; ivory box (11C Byzantine); *Giov. Pisano*, *Madonna; *Tino di Camaino*, *Madonna, seated. The precious *Cross in rock crystal with miniatures (13C) is not usually displayed; while the *Cintola with five reliefs, enamels, and precious stones has been removed temporarily. Paliotto, embroidered with the Coronation of the Virgin (14C).—R. 17. *Guido Reni*, *Sacred and Profane Love (drawing for the adjacent picture).

The contents of the Pinacoteca on the first floor include the following works (their order is likely to be changed when it is reopened). *'Maestro di San Martino'*, *Madonna and Child; *Deodato Orlandi*, Madonna and Child with saints (1301), including the first appearance in Italy of the cockle-shell of St James. Works by *Giov. di Nicola*, *Turino Vanni*, *Fr. Traini*, and others; tapestries; illuminated psalters. *Fra Angelico*, *The Redeemer; *Masolino* (?), Madonna and Child; *Gentile da Fabriano*, *Madonna and Child; works by *Michele di Matteo*, *Benozzo Gozzoli*, *Bicci di Lorenzo*. Works by *Cecco di Pietro*, *Martino di Bartolomeo,* and *Spinello Aretino*. *Works by *Taddeo di Bartolo* and his school. Further 14C works, including *Giov. da Milano*, *Annunciation. *Ant. Veneziano*, Crucifixion, and St Anthony Abbot; other works of the Florentine, Sienese, and Pisan schools. *Davide Ghirlandaio*, SS. Sebastian and Roch; Woman with a fruit basket (detached fresco); *Dom. Ghirlandaio*, Two Madonnas and saints; *Rosso Fiorentino*, Rebecca and Eliezer at the well; works by *Fr. Francia*, *Botticini*, etc. Later Italian schools, including *G. M. Crespi* and *Bern. Strozzi*. Foreign schools: *Jan Brueghel*, Holy Family; *Lawrence*, George IV; and a small painting of the Crucifixion, attr. to *Henri met des Bles*.

The *Ponte alla Fortezza* (reconstructed in 1958) crosses the Arno to the Lungarno Galilei and the ruined *Palazzo Scotto*. Here Shelley lived in 1820-22, the period of 'Epipsychidion', inspired by the Contessina Emilia Viviani, and of 'Adonais'. The old *Fortezza* is now a public garden.

At No. 7 in Via San Martino, to the W., is a Roman relief called the 'Statue of Chinsica', after a legendary heroine who saved Pisa from the Saracens. The church of *San Martino* preserves remains of the older building (1332) and within, a *Relief of St Martin and the beggar, attr. to And. Pisano (replaced on exterior by a copy).

On the Lungarno Galilei is *San Sepolcro,* an octagonal church of c. 1150, built for the Templars by Diotisalvi. Beyond is P.za Venti Settembre, at the S. end of the Ponte di Mezzo. Here is the 14C *Palazzo Gambacorti*, now the Municipio. To the left in Via di Banchi, is a market-hall of 1603-5, an open portico known as the *Logge di Banchi*.

To the S. opens the Corso Italia, the main street of the city, leading to the church and convent of *San Domenico*. The paintings (by Benozzo Gozzoli and G. B. Tempesti) have been removed from the church during restoration work. To the right, near the church of *Sant'Antonio* (14C; mostly reconstructed), at No. 29 Via Mazzini, is the *Domus Mazziniana*, rebuilt on the foundations of the mansion in which Giuseppe Mazzini died in 1872; it houses a library and museum.

The Lungarno Gambacorti leads on to the church of **Santa Maria della Spina,** a gem of Pisan Gothic architecture, named from a thorn of the Saviour's crown, the gift of a Pisan merchant. It was restored after war damage. The interior is only open at certain hours, but the Madonna and Child by *Nino Pisano,* which was over the altar, has been removed to the Museum (comp. above).—The Lungarno Sonnino leads on past the ex Convent of San Benedetto with good terracotta decoration (restored) to the 11-12C church of **San Paolo a Ripa d'Arno** which has a splendid façade and exterior, recalling that of the Duomo. The solemn bare interior has a handsome Roman sarcophagus, and a fine Romanesque capital (2nd on l.). Behind the church is the curious Romanesque chapel of *Sant'Agata,* a tiny octagonal brick building (12C).

Beyond the 14C Porta a Mare, Ponte della Cittadella crosses the Arno to the Lungarno Simonelli and Lung. ´Pacinotti, which lead back towards the centre. On the left, behind the *Pal. Reale,* built on to an old tower-house, is the church of **San Nicola,** built c. 1150 but much altered. In the 13C **Campanile** is a remarkable spiral staircase (shown on request) on which Bramante (according to Vasari) modelled his Belvedere staircase in the Vatican.

INTERIOR. S. side, 1st chap. *Fr. Traini,* **Madonna and Child;** 4th chap. St Nicholas of Tolentino protecting Pisa (clearly depicted) from the plague, c. 1400.—N. side, 1st chap. **Crucifix,** attrib. to *Giov. Pisano;* 4th chap. **Madonna,** statue in polychrome wood, attrib. to *Nino Pisano.* The Sacristy preserves a wood statue of the Madonna attrib. to the school of Iac. della Quercia.

Farther along the quay are the *Palazzo Upezzinghi* (13-16C) and the *Palazzo Agostini* (early 15C), with terracotta decoration. Between them Via Ventinove Maggio leads past the *University* (courtyard of 1550) to the church of *San Frediano* (11C), preserving good capitals in its altered interior and a 13C Crucifixion on panel. Straight ahead is the Piazza dei Cavalieri, while to the left are the *University Museums* and the *Botanic Garden.*

A favourite excursion from Pisa is to (12 km. S.W.) *Marina di Pisa,* by bus from Piazza Sant'Antonio. This little watering-place, with its dense pinewoods, whose seeds are used for making confectionery, lies near the mouth of the Arno. On the way (6 km.) the road passes close to the church of **San Piero a Grado,** built on the site where St Peter is said to have landed on his journey from Antioch to Rome. It is a Romanesque basilica of the 11C, having a single apse at the W. end and three apses at the E., and a central lateral door. The reused columns with Roman capitals came from an earlier structure of which foundations may be seen at the W. end. The nave is adorned with 13C frescoes.—Between the Arno and the Serchio lies the *Tenuta di San Rossore,* a summer estate of the President of the Republic, with bird and animal sanctuaries. Camels were reintroduced here before the last war, following a tradition begun in the 17C. There is a plan to annexe this area with Migliarino (beyond the Serchio) as a National Park.—On the beach of *Il Gombo,* N. of the mouth of the Arno, Shelley's body was washed ashore in 1822 (comp. p. 112). Allan Ramsay, the painter, was more fortunate and ascaped with his life from a shipwreck here in 1736 on his first journey to Rome.

From Pisa to *Genoa,* see Rte 8; to *Florence* viâ Pontedera (and for the Certosa di Pisa), see below; to *Livorno, Grosseto* and *Rome,* see Rte 50.

B   Viâ Empoli

ROAD, N67, 83 km. 13 km. *Lastra a Signa.*—33 km. **Empoli.**—40 km. *La Scala* (for **San Miniato**).—61 km. **Pontedera.**—66 km. *Fornacette* (for *Livorno,* 93 km.).—83 km. **Pisa.**

RAILWAY, 81 km. in 55-95 min; most of the trains go on to Livorno. This is one of the earliest railways in Italy, projected by Robert Stephenson in 1838-40. Through carriages from Florence to Genoa and Turin run on this line.

From Florence to (13 km.) *Lastra a Signa*, see Rte 43D.—At (15 km.) *Ponte a Signa* an old bridge crosses the Arno to *Signa*, a village noted for straw-plait and terracotta. Road and river enter the *Gonfolina Gorge*, where the Arno cuts through Monte Albano.—25 km. *Montelupo*, at the meeting of the Pesa with the Arno, was fortified by the Florentines in opposition to the now demolished stronghold of *Capraia*, beyond the river; thus the wolf ('lupo') was to devour the goat ('capra'). Baccio d'Agnolo, the sculptor and architect, was born at Montelupo (1460). In the church of San Giovanni (recently restored) is a *Madonna and four saints, of the School of Botticelli.—On the right farther on, is the villa of *L'Ambrogiana* (1587), now an asylum, with angle towers.—30 km. *Pontorme* was the birthplace of Iac. Carucci, called Pontormo (1494-1557), the painter. In the church of San Martino is a statue of the Madonna by Mich. da Firenze.

33 km. **Émpoli,** though of scant architectural interest, is an ancient town (45,800 inhab.), where in 1260 the Ghibelline party held their famous 'parliament' after their victory at Monteaperti; the proposal to raze Florence to the ground was defeated by Farinata degli Uberti, who is honoured for his protest by Dante ('Inferno', x). Iac. Chimenti, the painter, known as L'Empoli (1554-1640) was a native of the town.

In the central P.za Farinata degli Uberti stands the COLLEGIATA (Sant'Andrea); the lower part of the façade dates from 1093, the upper part is 18C imitation. Adjacent is the **Museo della Collegiata** (open 9-13, 15-18; fest. 9-13). In the Baptistery, lectern (1520) of English workmanship.—FIRST FLOOR. R.1. Bicci di Lorenzo, St Nicholas of Tolentino (with contemporary view of the city).—R.2. *Penitent Magdalen, polychromed wooden statue (1455); Lor. Monaco, *Madonna and saints; Lor. di Bicci, Crucifixion; Bicci di Lorenzo, Madonna, *Tabernacle of St Sebastian, painted by Fr. Botticini with sculptures by Ant. Rossellino; Pontormo, two saints.—R.3. *Tabernacle of the Holy Sacrament, by Fr. Botticini, the left part finished by his son Raffaello; painted Madonnas by Lippi and Nicolo di Pietro Gerini; Bern. Rossellino, *Annunciation, marble group; sculptured *Madonnas by Mino da Fiesole and Tino di Camaino.—R.4. Masolino, *Pietà, a superb work, and other pieces of fresco from Santo Stefano; Gherardo Starnina, frescoes; font of the School of Donatello.—LOGGIA, works by And. della Robbia.—Still in the church of **Santo Stefano** is a frescoed *Madonna by Masolino, also a Nativity by Passignano.

On the S.W. slope of Monte Albano, 11 km. N., is **Vinci** (bus), birthplace of Leonardo da Vinci (1452-1519), where the restored 13C Castello houses a small museum (9-12, 15-19 or 14-18; fest. 10-12), containing machines made from his models and a library. The near-by church of *Santa Croce* preserves the font in which Leonardo was baptized. The house at the hamlet of *Anchiano*, higher up the hill, which is believed to be the actual birthplace, was restored in 1952 as a memorial. In the lower town is the *Santissima Annunziata* with an Annunciation attributed to Fra Paolino da Pistoia.—*Cerreto Guidi*, 8 km. N.W. of Empoli, has a *Font by Giov. della Robbia in its church.

The Pisa road, outside the town, passes the church of *Santa Maria a Ripa*, with a St Lucy by And. della Robbia.—At (37½ km.) *Osteria Bianca* the road and railway to Siena diverge on the left, while this road crosses the Elsa.—To the left, above (40 km.) *La Scala*, appears **San Miniato** (23,900 inhab.), a Lombard town that became the seat of the Imperial Vicariate in Tuscany. Here the Countess Matilda was born (1046). Only two towers now remain of the *Rocca* rebuilt by Frederick II, the higher one from which Pier della Vigna killed himself ('Inferno', xiii), and a second one that now serves as the belfry of the *Duomo*. To the left of the Duomo is the MUSEO DIOCESANO (10-12.30, 15.30-19; closed Mon) into which works of art have been collected from churches in the region. Among these are: *Deodato Orlandi,* Crucifixion; remains of a frescoed Maestà by the 'Maestro degli Ordini'; *Neri di Bicci,* Madonna; *Fil. Lippi,* Crucifixion; attr. *Verrocchio,* *Bust of Christ in terracotta; *Madonna of the girdle, attr. to the young *And. del Castagno; Jacopo di Michele,* *Panel painted on both sides (Flagellation, Crucifixion).—The church of *San Domenico* contains a good tomb of 1461, by Bernardo Rossellino.

At (50 km.) *San Romano,* scene of the indecisive battle of 1432 between the Florentines and Sienese, is a good collection of old pharmacy jars.—61 km. **Pontedera** is a busy market town (27,800 inhab.) making motor-scooters.

In the Caldana valley, 16 km. S. (bus), is the little spa of **Casciana** with warm anti-rheumatic waters used for both bathing and drinking.—*Vicopisano,* 8 km. N.W. of Pontedera, preserves many of its old *Fortifications, restored by Brunelleschi, and a plain early-Romanesque church (11C) with a 14C statue of the Baptist and a carved Deposition (12C, much repainted).

At (66 km.) *Fornacette* the Livorno road (N67 bis) bears to the left.— 68 km. *Cáscina,* a centre of the furniture trade, beneath Monte Verruca (536 m), a prominent peak of Monte Pisano, was the scene of a Florentine victory over the Pisans in 1364. The Oratorio di San Giovanni contains a cycle of frescoes by Martino di Bartolomeo (1398) and an altarpiece by Luca di Tommé (temporarily removed to Florence). *Santa Maria is a fine 12C parish church, almost unaltered.—At (71 km.) *San Benedetto,* the church contains a splendid English alabaster (14C).—74 km. *Navacchio.*

To the right is the road to (7 km.) *Calci,* at which are an 11C *Church and the *Certosa di Pisa* (adm. 15-18; winter 14-17; fest. 13.30-or 14-16.30), a charming group of Baroque buildings, with three cloisters.

83 km. **Pisa,** see Rte 45A.

46   FLORENCE TO SIENA

ROAD (Via Cassia: N2), 99 km. 17 km. *San Casciano in Val di Pesa,* where the road diverges right.—32 km. *Montespértoli.*—45 km. *Castelfiorentino.*—54 km. *Certaldo.*—67 km. *San Gimignano.*—73 km. *Poggibonsi,* where the route rejoins N2 (or the Superstrada).—99 km. **Siena.** (The direct road, following N2 all the way viâ the Val di Pesa, is 26 km. shorter.) BUSES to *Siena* 12 times daily in 1¼-2 hrs; to *San Gimignano* 10 times daily via Poggibonsi in 1¼-2 hrs, also viâ *Castelfiorentino* and *Certaldo* 3-4 times daily in 2¼-2½ hrs.

SUPERSTRADA DEL PALIO, 57 km. (no toll), branching from the Autostrada del Sole at Florence (Certosa); 10 km. more, centre to centre.

RAILWAY, viâ Empoli and Poggibonsi, 97 km., c. hourly in 1½-2 hrs. A change is sometimes necessary at Empoli.

An alternative road (N222) runs through the hilly CHIANTI region, world-famous for its wine. Beyond (10 km.) *Grássina* (p. 482) it joins the road from Impruneta and crosses the Passo dei Pecorai (344 m) to the Greve valley.—29 km. *Greve,* a centre of the wine trade, has a monument to Giov. da Verrazzano (d. 1528?), the explorer of the North American coast, who is commemorated also in New York.—46 km. *Castellina in Chianti* preserves its 15C castle and a town gate. The N2 is joined just N. of (68 km.) *Siena.*

The Via Cassia (N2) leaves Florence by the Porta Romana; to (9 km.) *Le Tavarnuzze* just beyond the autostrada junction, see Rte 43C. The road continues for a while in the valley of the Greve; on a hillside across the river is the U.S. Military Cemetery where lie 4403 Americans who fell N. of Rome in 1944-45.—At (13 km.) *Ponte dei Falciani* N2 leaves the river and its attendant by-road to Greve (18 km.; see above), and climbs to (17 km.) *San Casciano in Val di Pesa* (310 m), where the church of the Misericordia contains good Sienese works including a Crucifix by Simone Martini. The main highway continues in the Val di Pesa direct to Poggibonsi (31 km.; see below), viâ Tavarnelle (379 m).

The more interesting road diverges (r.) to (23 km.) *Cerbáia,* where it turns left through (32 km.) *Montespértoli.* The road joins N429 at (45 km.) *Castelfiorentino,* a busy town (17,500 inhab.) largely rebuilt after war damage. The church of Santa Verdiana (18C) has interesting paintings, including a Madonna by Fr. Granacci. San Francesco, begun in 1213, has been closed since 1966 after flood damage.—54 km. **Certaldo,** in the Elsa valley, is an old town (16,000 inhab.) noted for its associations with Boccaccio (1313-75). The author of the 'Decameron' was probably born in Paris, but his father was from Certaldo and the writer spent most of his life and died here. A house in the upper town, which is thought to have belonged to the family, was restored in the last century. Boccaccio was buried in the church of *Santi Michele e Iacopo,* under an inscription written by himself. A later cenotaph (1503) was destroyed in 1783 in disapproval of his writings. The 15C *Palazzo Pretorio* has an attractive courtyard and frescoes by Pier. Fr. Fiorentino. A pretty by-road now climbs into the hills.

67 km. **SAN GIMIGNANO** (324 m), a charming small hill-town of 7570 inhab., has preserved its medieval appearance more completely than any other town in Tuscany. The town is famous for its numerous towers which make it conspicuous from a great distance and provide one of the most famous views in Italy.

The town was long known as 'San Gimignano delle belle Torri' from the noble towers of its palazzi; thirteen still survive out of the seventy-six traditionally thought to have existed. Dante was sent here in 1299 as an ambassador of Florence to attach the smaller town to the Guelph League. The town suffered some war damage.

The entrance to the town is through the *Porta San Giovanni* (1262), finest of the town gates (just outside of which is a large long-term car park). Via San Giovanni continues past the *Palazzo Pratellesi* (14C) to the *Arco dei Becci,* another ancient gate. Beyond it opens the *PIAZZA DELLA CISTERNA,* with its 13-14C buildings, notably the *Palazzo Tortoli* (No. 7). A few paces to the N. is PIAZZA DEL DUOMO.

On the W. side of the piazza a flight of steps mounts to the Romanesque ***Collegiata** (closed 12.30-15), orientated to the W., enlarged in 1466-68 by *Giul. da Maiano.* The interior walls are covered with a series of *Frescoes, scarred by war but mainly well restored. On the W. wall: Last Judgement, by *Taddeo di Bartolo* (1393); Martyrdom of St Sebastian, by *Gozzoli;* here are also two fine statues (painted wood; Madonna and St Gabriel) by *Iac. della Quercia.* South Aisle: *New Testament scenes by *Barna da Siena* (c. 1381) and *Giov. d'Asciano.* North Aisle: Old Testament scenes by *Bartolo di Fredi* (c. 1367). Over the high altar is a ciborium by *Bened. da Maiano* (1475). In the choir are stalls by *Ant. da Colle,* who also wrought the pulpit and lectern. The sacristan shows the **Cappella di Santa Fina,* off the S. aisle (ticket normally includes the Museo Sacro and Museo Civico). Built by *Giul. da Maiano* (1468), with an altar by *Bened. da Maiano,* it has beautiful *Frescoes by *Dom. Ghirlandaio* (helped by *P. F. Fiorentino* and *Mainardi*), depicting the life of the saint.

An archway, surmounted by a statue of San Gimignano (1342), left of the church façade, admits to a courtyard. Here can be seen the

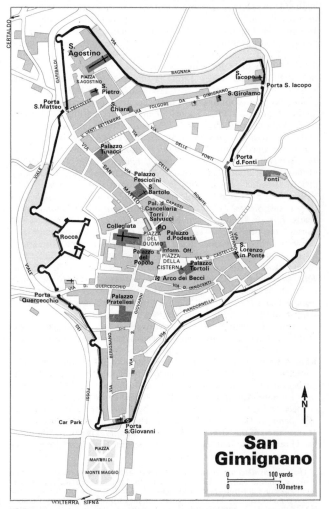

Baptistery loggia with an *Annunciation by *Domenico Ghirlandaio,* and a font of 1378. On the left of the courtyard is the entrance to the MUSEO D'ARTE SACRA (9-12, 15-18), devoted to ecclesiastical works of art, notably 13-15C sculpture, vestments, jewels, and illuminated choirbooks. In the loggia a small Etruscan museum is being arranged.

Behind the cathedral is the ruined *Rocca,* begun in 1353; the surviving tower commands a remarkable *View of the town and countryside.

Across the square the old *Palazzo del Podestà* (1239; enlarged in 1337) is surmounted by the *Torre della Rognosa* (51 m) which rises over a vaulted base and was once appointed the maximum standard of height in order to diminish rivalry in tower-building. On the S. side is the **Palazzo del Popolo** (1288-1323), badly damaged in the war. A passageway leads into a pretty courtyard with fresco fragments (two by Sodoma) and a stairway which mounts to the MUSEO CIVICO (adm. 9.30-12.30, 15.30-18.30; winter 10-13, 14.30-17.30; closed Mon). The Sala del Consiglio, where Dante is supposed to have delivered his appeal, contains a large *Fresco, La Maestà, by *Lippo Memmi* (1317). A small adjoining room displays pharmacy jars and a terracotta bust of Guido Marabottini (15C). Stairs lead up past a room with paintings and a fresco of the Trinity by *Pier Fr. Fiorentino* to the PINACOTECA. Main Hall. *Coppo di Marcovaldo,* *Crucifix; *Guido da Siena,* Madonna and Child enthroned; *Bart. di Giovanni,* Madonna enthroned with Saints; *Benozzo Gozzoli,* Madonna enthroned; *Filippino Lippi,* Two Tondoes of the Annunciation; *Pinturicchio,* Madonna in glory with St Gregory and St Benedict; *Dom. Michelino,* Madonna and Child with four Saints; *Benozzo Gozzoli,* Madonna and Child with Saints.—In the two side-rooms: *Sienese School of 13C,* Crucifix; *Bartolo di Fredi,* Female heads; *Lor. di Niccolò Gerini,* SS. Fina and Gregory, two angels, and stories from their lives.—*Lor. di Niccolò Gerini,* St Bartholomew and stories from his life; *Taddeo di Bartolo,* San Gimignano and stories from his life; *Niccolò Tegliacci,* Madonna in glory with Saints.—In a small room off the stair landing are charming frescoes by *Memmo di Filippuccio* (early 14C). A door gives access to the stairs up to the Tower from which there is a fine view.—The loggia next to the Palazzo del Popolo has a fresco of the Madonna and Child between St John the Baptist and St Michael Archangel by a 14C master.

Beyond the twin *Torri dei Salvucci,* •VIA SAN MATTEO, the most attractive street in the town, lined with medieval buildings, runs towards the *Porta San Matteo* (1262). It passes *Palazzo della Cancelleria,* the Romanesque church of *San Bartolo,* and the 13C Pesciolini tower-house, all grouped outside a double arch from an earlier circuit of walls; farther on is the *Palazzo Tinacci.* Just inside the gate, Via Cellolese leads right for **Sant' Agostino** (1280-98), an aisleless church with three apsidal chapels. Inside (r.) is a marble reredos by *Bened. da Maiano;* 3rd altar left, *Benozzo Gozzoli,* St Sebastian. The high altar is adorned by a *Coronation of the Virgin, by *Piero del Pollaiuolo* (1483), and the choir has *Frescoes (1465) of the Life of St Augustine by *Gozzoli.* Frescoes in the chapel (r.) are by *Bart. di Fredi.*

The *Circonvallazione,* round the 13C walls, affords fine views and access to many picturesque corners. All the churches in the town (and near it) are of interest for architecture or painting (or both): especially noteworthy are *San Girolamo* and *San Iacopo* (reached by Via Venti Settembre), the former with works by Tamagni (1522), the latter, a charming little Pisan-Romanesque building, with a St James, by Pier Fr. Fiorentino. Outside the Porta alle Fonti, just to the S., are the arcaded *Fonti,* a medieval public wellhouse.

The parish church at *Cellole,* 4 km. outside Porta San Matteo, gave Puccini the setting for 'Suor Angelica'.

The road now descends to (73 km.) **Poggibonsi** (116 m), a commercial town of 26,500 inhab. and important road centre, at the foot of its 15C castle. The 13C church of *San Lucchese,* c. 2 km. S., restored after war damage, has frescoes by Bart. di Fredi, and a Della Robbia altarpiece.

About 8 km. S. on N 68 (bus in 15 min., or by branch railway in 18 min.) is **Colle di Val d'Elsa** (223 m; 15,400 inhab.) birthplace of the architect Arnolfo di Cambio (1232-1302). The long main street of the upper town runs along the ridge of the hill to a bridge (views) across which the road passes through the fine *Palazzo Campana* (1539; by Giuliano di Baccio d'Agnolo) into the 'CASTELLO' or old town with many interesting Medieval buildings. The *Duomo* has a pulpit of 1465, the 'Cappella del Chiodo' (r. transept), and a bronze lecturn by Pietro Tacca. The bronze crucifix over the high altar is attrib. to Giambologna. Nearby, at No. 27 Via Castello, the *Palazzo Vescovile* (ring) houses the MUSEO D'ARTE SACRA. In a room with charming frescoes of hunting scenes attrib. to Bartolo di Fredi or Taddeo di Bartolo are a triptych of the Sienese School (late 14C), a Madonna and Child by Luca di Tomé, church vestments, and a chalice of the 12C. The Museum also owns a painting of Christ at the Column by Il Riccio. Beyond, on the r., in the old *Palazzo dei Priori* is the MUSEO CIVICO (in rearrangement) with works by Rutilio Manetti, Seb. Conca, and the school of Mantegna (a Pietà, almost completely ruined). The road continues past more Medieval houses including the tower house of Arnolfo di Cambio. In P.za del Duomo, the ANTIQUARIUM displays the Terrosi collection excavated from a necropolis at Casone, in use from the late Iron Age up to Imperial Roman times. The well-displayed objects include large black-varnished kraters known as 'Malacena' ware. Here also is a fresco of the Madonna and Child by Giacomo Pacchiarotti.

The fine Porta Nuova (probably designed by Giul. da Sangallo) marks the entrance to the town from Volterra. This road runs along a pretty ridge of hills with wide views to (27½ km.) *Volterra* (see p. 560). After c. 1 km. a by-road diverges left for (11 km.) *Casole d'Elsa.* At the beginning of the road an unmade-up track (right) leads to the *Badia a Coneo,* a Sienese Romanesque building of 1125 in a pretty position (the custodian lives next door). The road continues into **Casole d'Elsa** where the *Collegiata* (undergoing painstaking restorations since war damage) has an interesting interior with two monuments by Gano da Siena, a damaged fresco of the Madonna enthroned (School of Duccio), and a terracotta frieze by Giov. della Robbia surrounding reliefs by Cieco da Gambassi. In the adjoining *Canonica* (ring) the paintings include a Madonna and Child attrib. to Duccio, a Madonna and Child with Saints (and a lunette of the Massacre of the Innocents) by And. di Niccolò, and works by Manetti. A choir-book has beautiful illuminations by Lippo Vanni. In the *Palazzo del Comune* is a fresco recently restored and attrib. to Giacomo Pacchiarotti.—At *Mensano,* 7 km. farther S., the Romanesque church has splendid large capitals.

Just beyond Poggibonsi this route joins N 2.—80 km. *Stǎggia* preserves some 14C fortifications and a ruined rocca of 1432. The parish church has a painting by Ant. del Pollaiuolo.—85 km. *Monteriggioni* (l.), standing on a hillock, its 13C *Walls complete with fourteen towers, provides a romantic view from below. It was once a Sienese fortress ('Inferno', xxxi, 41-44). The walls now encircle a tiny Medieval hamlet.

The *Abbadia Isola,* c. 3 km. W., has a church with a basilican interior (restored) with a good altarpiece by Sano di Pietro (1471). A fresco by Taddeo di Bartolo has been detached for restoration. In the priest's house, nearby, is preserved a remarkable painting of the Madonna and Child enthroned, now thought to be an early work by Duccio, and the cover of an Etruscan urn with a fine bas-relief.

99 km. **SIENA,** with 65,200 inhabitants, capital of the Tuscan province of the same name, is second to Florence alone among the cities of Tuscany in its profusion of works of art, preserving its medieval character to a remarkable degree. It stands on a Y-shaped ridge (320 m) and spreads into the adjacent valleys; the streets are consequently often steep, and to pass from one quarter to another it may be necessary to cross a deep valley. For this reason, and also because its treasures are

unusually scattered, an adequate survey of Siena demands four or five days.

Railway Station, below the city and c. 1½ km. N. of it; bus to the centre in 7 min.

Hotels, mostly in N. part of the town near P.za Matteotti; others outside the walls.

Post Office (Pl. 6), P.za Giacomo Matteotti. **Ente Provinciale per il Turismo,** 5 Via di Città. AZIENDA AUTONOMA DI TURISMO, 20 Via Banco di Sotto; *Information Office,* 55 P.za del Campo.

English Church, *St Peter's,* Via Garibaldi, occasional services.

Theatres. *Dei Rinnovati,* Palazzo Pubblico, for opera.—Concerts in the *Accademia Musicale Chigiana,* 82 Via di Città, with international courses in July-Sept.

Parking. The centre has been entirely closed to traffic. Parking areas are clearly indicated at the entrances to the town; best near San Domenico (Pl. 10), the Stadium, Fortezza, and La Lizza.

Palio, see below.

Buses for *Viterbo, Grosseto, Rome, Lucca, Arezzo, Florence,* etc.

History. Siena appears in history as *Sæna Julia,* a Roman colony founded by Augustus. Under Charlemagne the town had its own counts, and about 1125, it became a free republic, which soon entered into rivalry with Florence. The chief of the Lombard League, Pope Alexander III, being a Sienese, the town took his part against Barbarossa, who vainly besieged it (1186); but afterwards, as head of the Tuscan Ghibellines, Siena aided the exiles from Florence and defeated that city at Montaperti (1260). When the Ghibellines were defeated by Charles of Anjou (1270), Siena established a Guelph oligarchy of the middle class ('popolo grosso') ruled by a Council of Nine. In 1348 the town was devastated by plague, and later it was engaged in struggles with Charles IV (1355-69); in 1399 it fell into the power of Gian Galeazzo Visconti, who was scheming to hem in Florence. After his death the city regained its liberty for a while, but Pandolfo Petrucci ('Il Magnifico') made himself autocrat in 1487. Another spell of liberty was marked by a victory over the Florentines and Clement VII (1526), but the Spaniards captured Siena in 1530, and Cosimo I de' Medici, unwilling that Florence should have the spectacle of liberty so close beneath her eyes, entrusted the final suppression of the Sienese to the bloodthirsty Marquis of Marignano, who took the city in 1555 after a disastrous siege of 18 months. Some 700 families, refusing to live beneath the Medicean yoke, migrated to Montalcino, where they maintained a republic until 1559 when that too was handed over to Florence by the treaty of Cateau Cambrésis. Thenceforth Siena shared the history of Florence and Tuscany. On 3 July 1944, French Expeditionary Forces entered Siena unopposed.—The famous natives of Siena (other than painters and sculptors, see below) include Pope Alexander III (d. 1181), St Catherine (Caterina Benincasa; 1347-80), made a Doctor of the Church in 1970, Lelio Sozzini (1525-62) and his nephew Fausto (1539-64), the forerunners of positivism, and Senesino (1680-1750), the castrato.

Since the 13C the city has been divided into three *Terzi:* di Città, di San Martino, and di Camollia. (The three routes below keep only very roughly to their divisions.) Each Terzo is subdivided into wards, or *Contrade*—originally 59, but now reduced to 17. From these, ten are selected to compete in the CORSA DEL PALIO, a horse race which takes place twice a year in the Campo: on 2 July (Visitation) and 16 Aug (the day after the Assumption). The race is preceded by a spectacular parade in costume enlivened by 'sbandierata' (flag-throwing) and culminating in a triumphal chariot drawn by four white oxen. The jockeys (fantini) of the teams, which are named after the Contrade (Aquila, Pantera, Leocorno, Drago, etc.) carry distinctive colours and are dressed in medieval costumes. They race for the *Palio,* or banner, which goes to the winning Contrada, not to an individual. The later, and more important, contest is believed to commemorate the victory of Montaperti; the earlier race was established in 1659.

Art. Sienese ARCHITECTURE, representing a blend of the Gothic style with the Italian spirit, produced the fine Palazzo Comunale, the cathedral, and numerous mansions. The Renaissance was late in influencing Siena (chiefly through Bern. Rossellino and Giul. da Maiano). The architects Lor. Maitani (1275-1330), Fr. di Giorgio Martini (1439-1502), and Baldassare Peruzzi (1481-1537) were natives of the town.—SCULPTURE was represented by Tino di Camaino, Goro di Gregorio, and others of their school in the early 14C; later Iac. della Quercia (1371-1438), gathered round him numerous pupils, and the school renewed its splendour

(c. 1450-1550) in Neroccio di Bartolomeo, Lor. di Pietro (Il Vecchietta), Giov. di Stefano, Fr. Martini (see above), Giac. Cozzarelli, Lor. di Mariano (Il Marrina), and Bart. Neroni (Il Riccio).—In the art of woodcarving Siena held a distinguished place, thanks to Dom. di Nicolò (1363-1450) and Ant. Barili (1453-1516).

Sienese PAINTING, 'arte lieta fra lieto popolo', awoke in Guido da Siena; but it was in Duccio di Buoninsegna (c. 1260-1318), contemporary with Cimabue and surpassing him in grace and feeling, that Sienese painting was emancipated from the spirit of the past. His celebrated 'Maestà' (p. 519) was for a long period the inspiration of the school. The art was carried on by Simone Martini (1283-1344), the friend of Petrarch, and by Lippo Memmi (fl. 1317-47), and it reached maturity in Pietro and Ambrogio Lorenzetti (fl. 1306-50). Later came Taddeo di Bartolo, Dom. di Bartolo, Sano di Pietro, Matteo di Giovanni (the boldest painter of the school), Benvenuto di Giovanni, Lor. di Pietro (see above), Stef. di Giovanni (Sassetta), Fr. Martini (see above), Giov. di Paolo, Bern. Fungai, Giac. Pacchiarotti, and Girol. del Pacchia. The school, from lack of inspiration from without, was exhausted by the end of the 15C. At the beginning of the 16C Sodoma, influenced by the art of Leonardo da Vinci, introduced a new spirit among the artists already mentioned and their immediate successors (Fungai, Dom. Beccafumi. And. Piccinelli, called del Brescianino). In the 19C the town produced the painter Cesare Maccari (1840-1919), and sculptor Giovanni Duprè (1817-82).

The WALLS OF SIENA survive almost entire but, of the original 38 gates, only eight are extant. These are, from the W., clockwise, the *Porta Camollia*, the *Porta Ovile*, the *Porta Pispini*, the *Porta Roma*, the *Porta Tufi*, the *Porta San Marco*, the *Porta Laterina*, and the *Porta Fontebranda*.

The three main streets of Siena, the Banchi di Sopra, the Banchi di Sotto, and the Via di Città, meets at the so-called *Croce del Travaglio* opposite the ***Loggia della Mercanzia** (Pl. 10), now the Circolo degli Uniti and the Provincial Tourist Board. It was begun in 1417 from the plans of Sano di Matteo; the upper story was added in the 17C. The five statues of saints (1456-63) are by *Ant. Federighi* and *Vecchietta*, the former of whom carved the marble bench (r.) beneath the portico. In the Loggia formerly sat what was regarded as the most impartial commercial tribunal, to which even foreign States resorted.

A THE CAMPO AND THE TERZO DI SAN MARTINO

The alleys flanking the Loggia della Mercanzia lead down in steps to the ****Campo,** the main piazza of Siena, and the scene of the Palio. Occupying the site of the Roman forum, it has the form of a fan or scallop-shell and is enclosed by a picturesque medley of mansions and shops. The only survivors of the original 14C buildings are the Palazzo Pubblico, on the flat S.E. side (see below), and the *Palazzo Sansedoni,* dating from 1339, at the N.E. end of the semicircle. The *Fonte Gaia,* at the highest point of the sloping pavement, is a tame reproduction (1868) of the original fountain by Iac. della Quercia (see p. 514). In the middle of the flat S.E. side of the Campo rises the austere but graceful ***Palazzo Pubblico,** in the Gothic style of 1297-1310, with a characteristic Sienese arcade at street level. The lower part is built of stone, the upper part of brick; the top story of the wings was added in 1681. The central section has four stories, and the whole façade is crowned by battlements. On the left rises the slim shaft, in ruddy brown brick, of the * *Torre del Mangia,* built by Muccio and Francesco di Rinaldo of Perugia in 1338-48; the stone cresting is by Agost. di Giovanni. The tower, 102 m high, is named after a former jaquemart and may be ascended (9-12, 14-17; winter 9-14; view). At its base is the *Cappella di Piazza* (1352-76), an open loggia with round arches, beautifully decorated with arabesques; it was built to commemorate the deliverance of the city from the plague of 1348. The chapel was heightened by Ant. Federighi in 1463-68; the dilapidated fresco above the altar is by Sodoma. On a column at the right-hand corner of the palazzo is a bronze she-wolf (part of the arms of Siena, evincing pride in her Roman origin), by Giov. di Turino (1429).

The ground floor, adorned with various works of art (Sodoma, Giov. Pisano, Sano di Pietro, etc.), is used as municipal offices and is difficult of access, but the upper floors may be visited (9-12, 14-17; winter 9-14 entrance on right); they contain numerous works of art, particularly paintings of the Sienese school.

First Floor. In the vestibule, frescoes by *Taddeo di Bartolo,* and a ruined fresco of the Madonna and Child, part of a larger composition by *Ambrogio Lorenzetti* (1340), formerly in the Loggia (see below). The *CAPPELLA DEL CONSIGLIO is closed by an admirable wrought-iron screen (1434), and contains an altarpiece by *Sodoma* (1536), 22 carved *Stalls by *Dom. di Nicolò* (1415-28), frescoes by *Taddeo di Bartolo.*—The SALA DEL MAPPAMONDO, named after a lost painting of the universe ascribed to *A. Lorenzetti,* contains the famous *Maestà by *Simone Martini* (1315; in restoration), a beautiful Madonna seated beneath a baldacchino borne by apostles and surrounded by angels and saints. On the left wall: Victory of the Sienese at Poggio Imperiale, by *Giov. di Cristoforo* and *Fr. Andrea* (1480); Victory at Sinalunga, by *Lippo Vanni;* on the pilasters below, Blessed And. Gallerani and Ambr. Sansedoni, after *Riccio* (17C); St Catherine, by *Vecchietta* (1461); St Bernardine, by *Sano di Pietro* (1460); and (in the angle) Blessed Bern. Tolomei by *Sodoma* (1533). On the adjacent wall: *SS. Victor and Ansanus, by *Sodoma* (1529), the *Virgin and Redeemer, by *Guido da Siena* (second half of 13C but dated 1221); above, *Guidoriccio Fogliani, by *Simone Martini* (1328).—The *SALA DELLA PACE O DEI NOVE was the room of the Nine who ruled Siena after 1270. It is remarkable for its allegorical *Frescoes by *Ambr. Lorenzetti* (1338), forming the most important cycle of secular paintings left from the Middle Ages; the subjects are Good and Evil Government, with their effects. Unfortunately the frescoes have deteriorated.

On the side overlooking the Campo, the SALA DEI PRIORI has frescoes by *Spinello Aretino* (1407-8) telling stories from the Life of Pope Alexander III, a doorway by *Dom. di Nicolò,* and an inlaid wooden seat by Barna di Turino.—The SALA DEL CONCISTORO has a marble doorway by *Bern. Rossellino* (1448); the ceiling frescoes, by *Beccafumi* (1529-35), illustrate heroic deeds of ancient Greece and Rome. Three large Gobelins tapestries represent the elements Earth, Air, and Fire; there are five other tapestries, in the Florentine manner. Above the door, Judgement of Solomon by *Luca Giordano.*—The SALA MONUMENTALE is decorated with frescoes (1886-91) of modern Italian history.

Second Floor. The spacious and airy LOGGIA commands a splendid view of the surrounding country. It has a restored timber ceiling. Here are preserved the remains (partly restored) of the original Fonte Gaia, by *Iac. della Quercia,* once in the Campo (see p. 513). The remains are arranged against the walls in the order they occupied in their original site.

The **Museo Civico** occupies several rooms on the first and second floors of the Palazzo Pubblico, although the collections of antique arms and armour, ceramics, coins, medieval medals and seals, etc. have not been on show for several years. FIRST FLOOR. In the room adjoining the Sala della Pace, objects of historical interest, carved wooden, painted and inlaid coffers, and some paintings.— SECOND FLOOR. Collection of prints. Off the Loggia (see above) is the *Sala Della Signoria,* the seat of the Consiglio Comunale (open to the public only when the Council is in session). The 16C lunettes are decorated with frescoes illustrating events in Sienese history and the walls are hung with 19C paintings.

From the N.E. angle of the Campo a side street leads to the *Palazzo Piccolomini,* a handsome building of the Florentine Renaissance, probably designed by Bern. Rossellino and begun by Porrina in 1469. In the courtyard are good suspended capitals by Marrina (1509). The palazzo contains the ARCHIVIO DI STATO, one of the finest extant collections of archives. The exhibits (open weekdays 11-13) include charters and other manuscripts, autographs, Boccaccio's will, and a unique series of book bindings, among them the *Tavolette di Biccherna*, the painted covers of the municipal account-books, some by the most famous artists of the 13-17C. The study room is open to students from 9-14 on weekdays, Sat 9-13 (closed 15-30 Aug).

Opposite is the *University*, with faculties of medicine and law, founded in 1203. Behind this are *San Vigilio* and the characteristic Via Sallustio Bandini, with 13C houses.

Via Banchi di Sotto leads right. On the right are the elegant *Logge del Papa*, built for Pius II by Federighi (1462), with decorations attr. to Francesco di Giorgio. Farther on in Via di Pantaneto is the church of *San Giorgio*, with an 18C façade and a campanile of 1260. Beyond the church Via dei Pispini leads left. In the piazza which opens on the left, the Renaissance church of *Santo Spirito* has a portal of 1519, the tympanum attrib. to Bald. Peruzzi, and a cupola by Giac. Cozzarelli (1508). It contains paintings and frescoes (1st S. chap.) by Sodoma, statues by Cozzarelli, and (3rd N. chap.) a painted wood Crucifix by Sano di Pietro, and a Madonna enthroned by And. Vanni.

Via dei Pispini ends at the *Porta Pispini* or *San Viene*, above which are the remains of a fresco of the Nativity by Sodoma. To the left of the gate, at an angle of the city walls, is the only surviving bastion of the seven designed by Peruzzi in the 16C to strengthen the earlier defences.—The church of *Santa Eugenia*, outside the gate, has a gentle Madonna, by Matt. di Giovanni.

Vicolo del Sasso opposite the Santo Spirito leads shortly to Via Roma. This leads past the *Palazzo di San Galgano* (No. 47), built in the manner of Giul. da Maiano (1474), to the severe *Porta Romana*, a double fortified gate most likely the work of Ang. di Ventura (1327). At No. 71 Via Roma the premises of the *Società Esecutori di Pie Disposizioni* (adm. 9-12, exc. fest.) contains works by Sodoma, Sano di Pietro, and others. Via Val di Montone leads to **Santa Maria dei Servi** (Pl. 16), a church with a massive brick campanile.

The Renaissance INTERIOR, with nave and aisles, was planned by Peruzzi. SOUTH AISLE. Beyond fragments of 14C frescoes, 2nd Chap. *Madonna del Bordone, by *Coppo di Marcovaldo*, signed and dated 1261, partly repainted by a pupil of Duccio; 5th chap. *Massacre of the Innocents, by *Matt. di Giovanni* (1491). SOUTH TRANSEPT, 14C Crucifix (Sienese school); 2nd chap. r. of high altar, *Massacre of the Innocents, fresco by *Pietro Lorenzetti*. The altarpiece of the *Madonna del Popolo, by *Lippo Memmi* (c. 1317) has been removed; 2nd chap. l. of high altar, Stories from the Life of St John the Baptist, frescoed by *Pietro Lorenzetti*. In a chap. in the N. transept, Madonna del Manto, by *Giov. di Paolo* (1436).

Via San Martino leads back to the Campo past the church of *San Martino*, with a façade by Giov. Fontana (1613); it contains paintings by Guercino, Beccafumi, and Vanni. A rich collection of statuary includes works by Giov. Ant. and Gius. Mazzuoli, also five fine gilded wooden statues, including a *Madonna and Child, formerly thought to have been from the workshop of Iac. della Quercia, but recently attrib. to Ant. Federighi.

B THE CATHEDRAL AND THE TERZO DI CITTÀ

From the opposite side of the Campo the VIA DI CITTÀ, bordered by medieval mansions, winds upward to the S. To the left is the 14C PALAZZO CHIGI-SARACINI, housing the *Accademia Chigiana* (concerts, see p. 512) and containing a rich collection of works of art (by Botticelli, Seb. del Piombo, Sassetta, Vecchietta, Matteo di Giovanni, Neroccio). To the right is *Palazzo Piccolomini delle Papesse* (No. 128), built by Caterina Piccolomini, sister of Pius II, from the plans of Bern. Rossellino (1460-95); it is now occupied by the Bank of Italy. Then comes *Palazzo Marsili* of 1459. In P.za di Postierla, a column (1487) with a fine iron standard-holder is surmounted by a she-wolf. In Via del Capitano (r.) are the 16C *Palazzo Piccolomini Adami* (on the left, at the corner) and the late 13C *Palazzo del Capitano* (No. 15). The street ends in the picturesque P.ZA DEL DUOMO, the cathedral square, just before which is (r.) P.za Iacopo della Quercia.

The ****Cathedral** (Pl. 10; open all day), dedicated to the *Assumption,* is—despite certain Romanesque elements—to be considered the earliest of the great Tuscan Gothic churches. It was begun in 1196 and the main structure was complete by 1215.

Towards the close of the 13C the façade was begun on the plans of *Giov. Pisano,* and in 1339 a scheme was adopted by which an immense nave was to be constructed S. of the original church, which was to become a transept. *Lando di Pietro* and *Giov. di Agostino* began this herculean task, but the plague of 1348 and the political misfortunes of the city compelled its abandonment. The original plan was resumed, leaving the huge unfinished nave to record the ambition of the Sienese. The existing dimensions are 88 m long by 24 m wide (52½ m across the transepts). The apse was completed in 1382. The upper part of the façade, in the style of the cathedral of Orvieto, was added by *Giov. di Cecco* after 1376.

Restoration work, necessitated by the effects of time and weather, was completed in 1951. The famous inlaid pavement was strengthened and cleared; other repairs were carried out to the façade, pinnacles, buttresses, cupola, and roof.

EXTERIOR. Marble steps, flanked by columns bearing the she-wolf of Siena (the originals by Giov. Pisano and Urbano da Cortona are now in the Museo dell'Opera, comp. below), ascend to a plinth of white marble inlaid with black, on which the cathedral stands. The three-pointed *FAÇADE, in polychrome marble, though lacking the perfect proportion of that of Orvieto, is one of the most remarkable creations of Italian architecture. The lower part, having three richly decorated portals of equal height and size, is set off not entirely harmoniously by a great rose window surrounded with sculptural decoration; in the three gables are Venetian mosaics by *Castellani* (1877). The façade is adorned with statues of prophets and philosophers; most of the originals by *Giov. Pisano* and his pupils have been removed to the Opera del Duomo and replaced by copies. On the E. side the CAMPANILE (1313) rises from the transept; its six stories, banded in black and white, are pierced by windows whose openings increase in progression from single to sixfold. A Madonna of the school of Donatello adorns the lunette of the portal in the S. transept.

INTERIOR. The nave and aisles are separated by banded columns of black and white stone, supporting round arches and pointed vaulting. Over the arches in the nave and choir are large terracotta busts of popes (15-16C), with inferior busts of emperors below.

PAVEMENT. The floor of the whole church is ornamented with a remarkable series of 56 historical and other designs, of which the oldest (1369) are in simple 'graffiti' (black outlines on the white marble), while the others are inlaid with black, white, or (1547) colours. Some have been replaced by copies (the originals are in the Opera del Duomo). Those in the nave and aisles are usually uncovered, but the earliest parts are covered by a protective floor and are shown only from c. 7–22 August. More than 40 artists, most of them Sienese, worked at this pavement; among them were *Dom. di Nicolò, Pietro del Minella, Matteo di Giovanni* (Massacre of the Innocents, 1481; N. transept), *Pinturicchio* (Fortune, 1506; 4th bay of nave), *Federighi* (Erythræan sibyl; S. aisle), and *Beccafumi,* the most original and productive (1517–47; 35 pictures).

NAVE. The columns of the main W. door are attributed to *Giov. di Stefano;* the reliefs of the pedestals are by *Urbano da Cortona.* The glass of the rose window represents the Last Supper, after *Perin del Vaga* (1549). The two stoups, near the first pillars, are by *Federighi* (1462). In the S. aisle, statue of Pope Paul V (Camillo Borghese) by *Signorini* (1605). The hexagon of the dome has gilded statues of saints, by *Turapilli* and *Bastiano di Francesco,* and figures of patriarchs and prophets in chiaroscuro, by *Cozzarelli* and others. Farther E. stands the octagonal •PULPIT, the work of *Nicola Pisano,* his son *Giovanni, Arnolfo da Cambio, Lapo* and *Donato Ciuccio di Ciuto* (1265-68). The seven relief panels represent scenes from the New Testament; the elegant staircase was added to a design of *Riccio* in 1570.—In the SOUTH AISLE, above the doorway to the campanile, is the tomb of Bp. Tomaso Piccolomini, by *Neroccio* (1484-85).

In the SOUTH TRANSEPT are statues of Alexander III, by *Raggi* (1663), and of Alexander VII, by *E. Ferrata* (1668). Here the Baroque CAPPELLA CHIGI was built for Alexander VII in 1661 to a design of Bened. Giovannelli to house the Madonna del Voto. It contains several works by *Bernini,* a Visitation by *Maratta,* and the Flight into Egypt, a mosaic after a painting by the same artist. The *Madonna del Voto is attributed to Guido da Siena.

This venerated painting has been the traditional focus of entreaty of the Sienese in time of crisis. On six occasions in their history the inhabitants have placed the keys of their threatened city before it and prayed for deliverance. The first occasion was before the battle of Montaperti; the latest on 18 June 1944, a fortnight before the liberation of Siena.

CHOIR. The high altar is by *Peruzzi* (1532); the huge bronze *Tabernacle by *Vecchietta* (1467-72). At the sides the uppermost angels carrying candles are by *Giov. di Stefano* (1489), the lower two by *Fr. di Giorgio* (1499). The cross and candelabra are to a design of *Riccio* (1570). Eight candelabra stand on brackets in the form of angels, two by Riccio, the rest by *Beccafumi* (1550). The fine *Choir stalls are of varying dates: 1362-97, by several artists under *Fr. del Tonghio;* 1503, by *Giov. da Verona;* and those by *Riccio* and his school, 1567-70. The window in the apse contains *Stained glass (1288) from cartoons by Duccio, the oldest existing glass of Italian manufacture.—To the left of the altar is the entrance to the SACRISTY and CHAPTER HOUSE (sometimes shown by the sacristan), the former with frescoes attrib. to *Dom. di Bartolo, Nicola di Naldo, Gualtieri di Giovanni,* and *Bened. di Bindo.*

Beyond a vestibule with a fine bust of Alexander VII by Melchiorre Caffà, a follower of Bernini, is the Chapter House, with two interesting paintings showing San Bernardino in Siena, by *Sano di Pietro,* and a Madonna with Saints, attrib. to *Giacomo Pacchiarotti.*

In the NORTH TRANSEPT: statues of Pius II, by *Gius. Mazzuoli* (1698). and Pius III, by P. Balestra (1706); *Tomb of Card. Petroni (d. 1313), by *Tino di Camaino;* sepulchral slab (in the pavement) of Bp. Giovanni Pecci, by *Donatello* (c. 1426). The *CAPPELLA DI SAN GIOVANNI BATTISTA, is a graceful Renaissance structure by *Giov. di Stefano* (1482). The elegant portal and railings deserve notice; in the interior are portraits of Alberto Aringhieri, the founder, and paintings of the Life of St John the Baptist, by *Pinturicchio,* statues of St Ansanus, by *Giov. di Stefano,* of St Catherine, by *Neroccio,* and of *St John the Baptist, by *Donatello* (1457); also frescoes by *Pinturicchio* (restored) and decorations in stucco (1596). The stoup is by *Ant. Federighi* (after 1484).

In the NORTH AISLE is the entrance to the *LIBRERIA PICCOLOMINI (open 9-19 every day), one of the most delightful creations of the Renaissance, founded in 1495 by Card. Fr. Piccolomini (afterwards Pius III) to receive the library of his uncle Æneas Silvius Piccolomini (Pius II). Its marble façade is by *Marrina* (1497); in the right-hand niche is a St John the Evangelist by *Vecchietta.*

The interior consists of a hall decorated with *Frescoes by *Pinturicchio* and his pupils (1502-9). They represent ten subjects from the life of Pius II (beginning to the r. of the window): 1. Æneas Silvius goes to the Council of Basle; 2. He presents himself as envoy to James II of Scotland; 3. He is crowned as poet by Frederick III (1442); 4. He is sent by the emperor to Eugenius IV (1445); 5. As Bishop of Siena, he is present at the meeting in 1451 of the Emperor Frederick and his betrothed Eleonora of Portugal outside the Porta Camollia; 6. He is made Cardinal by Calixtus III (1456); 7. He becomes Pope (1458); 8. He proclaims a Crusade at Mantua (1459); 9. He canonizes St Catherine of Siena (1460); 10. He arrives, dying, at Ancona (1464). The vault decoration (recently restored) is also very beautiful.— In the centre is the celebrated antique group of the *Three Graces, a Roman copy of an original by Praxiteles, which served as a model to Pinturicchio, Raphael, and Canova. Around the walls, on benches sculptured by *Barili* (1496), are exhibited the *Choir Books of the cathedral and the Scala hospital, illuminted by Liberale da Verona, Girol. da Cremona, Sano di Pietro, and others.

Farther W. the great *Piccolomini Altar by *And. Bregno* (1485) has statues of SS. Peter, Pius, Gregory, and Paul, documented works of *Michelangelo* (1510-11), who may also have worked on the figure of St Francis begun by *Torrigiani.* The standing Madonna (temporarily removed) is attributed (as an early work) to *Iac. della Quercia,* and the Madonna and Child in the centre (framed by marble reliefs) to *Paolo di Giovanni Fei* (1381). Near the W. end, statue of Marcellus II, by *Cafaggi* (1591).

In the piazza, opposite the cathedral, stands the *Ospedale di Santa Maria della Scala,* which preserves in its Pilgrims' Hall a fine series of 15C frescoes (undergoing restoration); in the adjoining *Church* (1252; enlarged in 1466) are a bronze figure of Christ by Vecchietta and an organ-case by Peruzzi. Along the other side of the piazza is the *Palazzo Reale,* by Buontalenti, now the Prefettura. The unfinished nave of the 'Great Cathedral' (comp. p. 516) gives some idea of the size and beauty of the projected building; its S. aisle has been converted into the **Museo dell'Opera del Duomo** (open 9-13, 14.30-16; winter: 9.30-13, 14.30-16.30; fest. 9-13, 14.30-17).

Ground Floor. SALA DELLE STATUE. Original *Statues and sculptural fragments from the façade of the cathedral, by *Giov. Pisano* and his school, constituting one of the most important groups of Italian Gothic sculpture. In the centre, bas-relief of the Madonna and Child with St Anthony Abbot and Card. Ant. Casini, by *Jacopo della Quercia*. Works by *Urbano da Cortona* (St Peter, St Bernardine in glory); (l. wall) fragments of four symbolic animals sculpted by *Giov. Pisano;* (near the grille), two wolves nursing twins from the columns outside the Duomo (comp. above), one attrib. to *Giov. Pisano*, and the other by *Urbano da Cortona*. In the floor, fragments of the original pavement of the Duomo. At the end. altarpiece of the Baptism of Christ, by *And. del Brescianino* (1524).—In a small room off the entrance hall, kneeling figure of St John the Evangelist, by *Giac. Cozzarelli;* and St John the Baptist, statue in wood by *Fr. di Giorgio Martini* (1464).

First Floor. SALA DI DUCCIO. **La Maestà, by *Duccio di Buoninsegna* (1308-11), a celebrated work painted on both sides, now divided to show both faces: Madonna and Child enthroned and the Story of the Passion. Until 1505 it hung over the high altar in the Cathedral. Also *Birth of the Virgin, by *Pietro Lorenzetti* and *Madonna and Child, an early work by *Duccio* (from the church of S. Cecilia in Crevole).—The other rooms contain illuminated MSS., drawing projects related to the cathedral and P.za del Campo, and a drawing of the pavement of the Cathedral by *Giov. Paciarelli* (1884).

Second Floor. The SALA DEL TESORO contains croziers, reliquaries (including the Reliquary of St Galgano from the end of the 13C); paxes, crucifixes (among which *Christ on the Cross in wood by *Giov. Pisano*), etc. Sculptural works include three busts of Saints, by *Fr. di Valdambrino* in polychrome wood (1409), and 12 statuettes of Saints by *Mazzuoli* (models for the marble statues now in the Brompton Oratory, London).

In a small room (grille usually locked) off the Treasury: works by *Beccafumi*, 3 panels by *Sassetta*, and a detached fresco of the Pietà, by *Vecchietta*.—SALA DELLA MADONNA DAGLI OCCHI GROSSI. In the centre, the *Madonna dagli Occhi Grossi, by an unknown Sienese painter of the 13C. It adorned the high altar before Duccio's Maestà. *Ambr. Lorenzetti,* Four Saints; *Giov. di Paolo,* St Jerome; *Simone Martini,* *Blessed Agostino Novello and Scenes from his life (from the church of Sant'Agostino); *Gregorio di Cecco,* Polyptych; *Matteo di Giovanni,* Madonna and Child; *Sano di Pietro,* Madonna and Child with Saints; *Maestro della Città di Castello,* Madonna and Child.—SALA DEI CONVERSARI. Works by *Matteo di Giovanni; Beccafumi,* *St Paul; *Il Pomerancio,* Madonna and Child with Saints; altar frontals.—The SALA DEI PARATI contains vestments and a marble statue of a child by *Giov. Duprè*. From here is reached the Scala del 'Falciatore', a stair which winds up to the façade of the 'new' cathedral (extensive views of city and countryside).

Beyond a Gothic portal between the incomplete nave and the cathedral, a steep flight of steps descends past the so-called 'Cripta delle Statue' (usually open at the same time as the Museum) with statues from the cathedral by the School of Pisano, and fresco fragments by a follower of Guido da Siena (c. 1270-80; the oldest known frescoes of the Sienese school). At the bottom of the steps is the **Baptistery** (beneath part of the cathedral), with a noble but unfinished façade by *Jacopo di Mino del Pellicciaio* (1382).

The INTERIOR (open 8-13, 14.30-19), finished c. 1325 probably by Camaino and Tino di Camaino, is frescoed in the upper part and vault by Vecchietta and his school. In the middle stands the *FONT designed by *Iac. della Quercia* (1417-30), a hexagonal structure of marble, with bronze panels in relief: Zacharias expelled from the Temple, by *Iac. della Quercia;* Birth of John the Baptist, by *Turino di Sano;* his Preaching, by *Giov. di Turino;* Baptism of Christ and St John in prison, both by *Ghiberti;* *Herod's Feast, by *Donatello*. At the angels are figures of Fortitude, by *Goro di Neroccio;* Justice and Charity, and Prudence, by *Giov. di Turino;* Faith and Hope, by *Donatello*. The statue of St John and five of the figures on the tabernacle rising from the font are by *Iac. della Quercia;* the angels are by *Donatello* and *Giov. di Turino*.

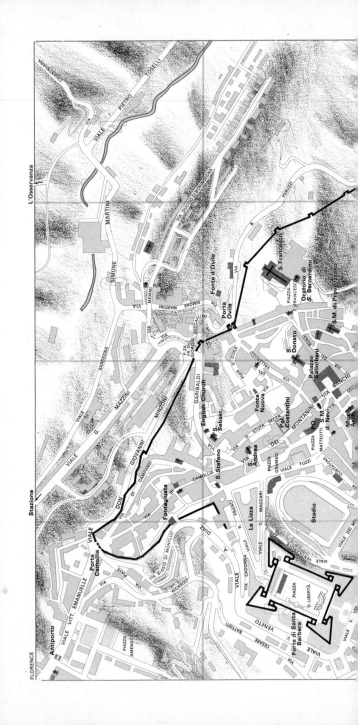

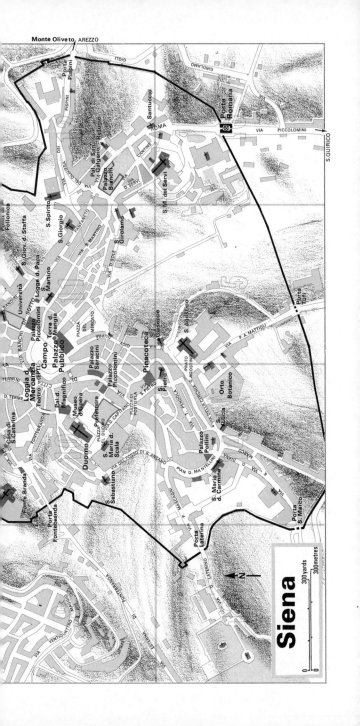

Siena

Monte Oliveto, AREZZO

Porta Pispini

Porta Romana

VIA PICCOLOMINI

S. QUIRICO

VIA PISPINI

Santuccio

ROMA

Pal. di S. Maria Galgano Regugio

Palazzo Bianchi

VIA D. SERVI

S. M. del Servi

VIA DEL GIUSTIZIA

Fonti di Follonica

S. Spirito

VIA DI PANTANETO

VIA DI PANTANETO

VIA DEL MARTINO

Porta Tufi

VIA P. A. MATTIOLI

S. Giov. d. Staffa

S. Giorgio

S. Girolamo

Università

Logge d. Papa

S. Martino

VIA DUPRÈ

VIA DI DUPRÈ

S. Agostino

BANCHI

Palazzo Piccolomini

S. SPIRITO

PIAZZA DEL MERCATO

Pinacoteca

S. Giuseppe

VIA

Torre d. Mangia

Campo

PRATO D. S. AGOSTINO

Loggia di Mercanzia

Teatro

Palazzo Pubblico

Palazzo Saracini

VIA DI STALLOREGGI

Palazzo Piccolomini

VIA

S. Niccolò

Orto Botanico

Pal. d. Magnifico

Museo d'Opera

VIA DI POSTIERLA

S. Pietro

VIA DEL CASATO DI SOTTO

TERMINI

D. TERME

Prefettura

PIAZZA DEL DUOMO

Prefettura

Porta S. Marco

Casa di S. Caterina

VIA FONTEBRANDA

S. Maria d. Scala

Duomo

PIAN D. MATTELLINI

Palazzo Pollini

S. Maria d. Carmine

VIA G. DIANA

VIA S. MARCO

Fonte Branda

VIA DEL COSTO DI S. ANSANO

S. Sebastiano

Porta Laterina

Porta Fontebranda

VIA DI FONTEBRANDA

VIA P. MASCAGNI

VIA VENTIQUATTRO

VIA LATERINO

N

300 yards
300 metres

Immediately E. of the Baptistery is the *Palazzo del Magnifico*, built for Pandolfo Petrucci from the plans of Cozzarelli, who designed also the famous bronze ornaments of the façade (1504-8).

From the cathedral square Via del Capitano leads to P.za di Postierla. Beyond this square extends Via San Pietro, on the left of which is the handsome 14C *Palazzo Buonsignori, restored in 1848. The palazzo houses the **Pinacoteca (Pl. 10), the most important gallery for the study of the great Sienese masters, all of whom are well represented. The works by Sodoma are also important. The gallery is open daily exc. Mon, 9-14; fest. 9-13; the display is chronological.

SECOND FLOOR. ROOM I. *1. Altar frontal, partly in relief, representing Christ blessing between symbols of the Evangelists and six scenes from the Passion, the first securely dated work (1215) of the Sienese school; 597. Crucifix, also with six Passion scenes (first years of 13C); works of the *School of Guido da Siena.*—R. II. *Guido da Siena,* *16. Madonna and Child, dated 1262; 7. Reredos, Madonna and Saints (in restoration). *Guido da Siena and assistants,* 9-13. Scenes from the Life of Christ; and other works of the school of Guido.—R. III. *Duccio di Buoninsegna and Assistants,* *47. Polyptych, Madonna and Saints, a late work; *28. Polyptych, similar subject; *Ugolino di Nerio* 39. Dossal; *34. Crucifixion with St Francis; *Niccolò di Segna,* Madonna della Misericordia (from the church of San Bartolomeo a Vertine in Chianti); *School of Duccio,* Crucifix, from the church of San Polo in Rosso (Gaiole in Chianti).—R. IV. *20. *Duccio,* La Madonna dei Francescani, a tiny work of jewel-like luminosity, considered to be one of his masterpieces (much ruined); 583. *Duccio* (?), Madonna and Child; 40. *Segna di Bonaventura,* Madonna and Saints; 593. *Maestro di Badia a Isola,* Madonna and Child.—R. V. Minor painters of the 14C, including *Bartolo di Fredi* and *Luca di Tommè.*

ROOM VI. *Simone Martini,* Madonna and Child (from the Pieve di San Giovanni Battista in Lucignano d'Arbia), temporarily removed for restoration; 595. *Lippo Memmi,* Madonna.—R. VII. *Paolo di Giovanni Fei,* 116. Nativity of the Virgin, with saints, 300. Polyptych (in restoration); *Pietro Lorenzetti,* Madonna enthroned (from the church of S. Ansano a Dofano, near Monteaperti); 578-9. SS. Agnes and Catherine of Alexandria, two panels from a polyptych; *Ambr. Lorenzetti,* 88. Annunciation, the last dated work by the artist (commissioned in 1344); 70-1. Two views; 65. Madonna between saints and doctors of the church.—R. VIII. 92. *Pietro Lorenzetti,* Allegory of sin and redemption. The first arm of the corridor (R.IX) displays works of the Sienese and Florentine schools, including 119-25. *Spinello Aretino,* Coronation and Dormition of the Virgin, parts of a polyptych. To the right opens Room X, comprising the Chapel, with a good terracotta of St Mary Magdalen attr. to Giac. Cozzarelli, and the Antechapel: *Paolo di Giovanni Fei,* 137. Triptych, Mystical marriage of St Catherine; 146. Diptych.—R. XI. *Taddeo di Bartolo,* 55. Crucifix, *128. Triptych; *131. Annunciation, Dormition, and SS. Cosmas and Damian signed and dated 1409); 133. *Andrea di Bartolo,* Nativity and Resurrection.

Second arm of the Corridor: 60. *Bern. Daddi,* Triptych, dated 1336; 157. *Lorenzo Monaco,* Madonna and saints; *164. *Dom. di Bartolo,* Seated Madonna with angel musicians (dated 1433); 171. *Michelino da Besozzo,* Marriage of St Catherine (the only signed work by this artist). From the chapel end opens R. XII, devoted to *Giovanni di Paolo:* 174-6. Presentation in the Temple, Crucifixion, Flight into Egypt, panels from a predella (1436); 173. St Nicholas of Bari and other saints (signed and dated 1453); *200. Crucifixion (signed and dated 1440).—R. XIII. *Giovanni di Paolo,* 206. Madonna dell'umiltà; 172. Last Judgement. *Sassetta,* 95, 87. Prophets; 168-9. Saints; 167. Last Supper; 166. Temptation of St Anthony (all from an altarpiece painted in 1423-26).—R. XIV. *Neroccio,* 281. Madonna and Child with saints; 282. Similar subject (signed and dated 1476); *Matteo di Giovanni,* *286. Madonna and Child with angels (signed and dated 1470); 280. Similar subject; *Franc. di Giorgio,* 437. Nativity with saints; 277. Annunciation; 293. Madonna with saints.—R. XV. Late 15C works.

RR. XVI–XVIII display works by *Sano di Pietro:* in R. XVI notably 237 and 224. Madonnas; in R. XVII, 227. Assumption with St Thomas receiving the girdle (an early work); 255. Triptych, Madonna and Child amid saints with (above) Christ, and an Annunciation, and (below) scenes from the Life of St Blaise (signed and dated 1449); in R. XVIII, 246. Polyptych, the first securely dated work by the artist (1444); *241. The Madonna appearing to Pope Calixtus III (1456). R.XIX. *Vecchietta,* 210. Madonna and Child with saints, and other works.

First Floor. R. XX. 309. *Girolamo da Cremona,* Annunciation; 581. *Benvenuto di Giovanni,* Noli me tangere.—R. XXI. Recent acquisitions.—R. XXII. Minor 15C painters.—R. XXIII. Umbrian and Umbrian-Sienese schools. 426. *Giac. Pacchiarotti,* Visitation; 149-152. *Unknown 15C Painter,* Triumph of Death; Chastity; Love; Famine; 495. *Pinturicchio,* Holy Family with the young St John; *Girol. Genga,* 333, 334. Ransom of prisoners, and Flight of Aeneas and Anchises from Troy (frescoes from Palazzo del Magnifico).—LOGGIA (R. XXIV). *Fr. Maffei,* Allegorical works from the Palazzo Reale; 633. *Gius. Bazzani* (18C), Deposition.—R. XXV. *Rutilio Manetti,* 626. St Eligius among the plague-stricken; 625. Martyrdom of St Ansanus; 634. *Simondio Salimbeni* (attrib.), St Bernardinus writing the Holy Name of Jesus.

R. XXVI (Belvedere): views of the city). 61. *Rutilio Manetti,* The Vestal demonstrates her innocence (from the Pal. Reale).—R. XXVII. Works of 16C Florentine artists.—R. XXVIII. *Brescianino,* 650-2. Charity; Hope; Fortitude.—R. XXIX. Works of 16C Sienese artists.—R. XXX. 350. *Girolamo del Pacchia,* Madonna and Child; 512. *Sodoma,* Nativity.—R. XXXI. *352. *Sodoma,* Scourging of Christ (fresco from the cloister of San Francesco), a superb work from the period 1511-14.—R. XXXII. 413. *Sodoma,* Deposition.—R. XXXIII. 354. *Sodoma,* Judith; *Beccafumi,* 420. St Catherine receiving the Stigmata; 405. Birth of the Virgin; 307. *Fr. Vanni,* Self portrait.—R. XXXIV is given to works of foreign schools. 501. *Dürer,* St Jerome; works attr. to Rubens.—R. XXXV. 521. *Bern. Strozzi,* St Francis; 454. *Fed. Zuccari* (attr.), Elizabeth I of England.—R. XXXVI. 163. *Lor. Lotto,* Nativity; 456. *Bart. Montagna,* The Virgin, Christ, two fragments of a larger work; 539. *Palma Giovane,* Serpent of Bronze (signed and dated 1598); 544. *Paris Bordone,* Annunciation; 467. *G. B. Moroni,* Portrait.—R. XXXVII. *427. *Beccafumi,* Descent into Hell; *Sodoma,* 401, 443. Descent into Hell, Gethsemane (frescoes).

Beyond the Pinacoteca is the church of *San Pietro alle Scale,* rebuilt in the 18C, with a striking altarpiece, the Flight into Egypt, by Manetti. Also, a polyptych (fragmentary) by Ambr. Lorenzetti, and St Catherine, a fresco fragment by Liberale da Verona. Beyond the *Arco di Sant'Agostino* lies the church of **Sant'Agostino** (Pl. 15), a church dating from 1258 but remodelled in 1749 by L. Vanvitelli. There is a good view from the terrace of the town and countryside beyond.

In the 2nd chapel of the S. aisle is a *Crucifixion by *Perugino.* The Piccolomini Chapel, off the S. side, contains an *Epiphany by *Sodoma,* and a *Massacre of the Innocents, by *Matteo di Giovanni* (1482); in the lunette facing the altar, a fresco of the *Madonna seated among saints, by *Ambr. Lorenzetti.*
From Sant'Agostino Via Sant'Agata, continued by the picturesque Via Giov. Dupré, descends to P.za del Mercato (Pl. 11), from which the Palazzo Pubblico is seen from the rear.—To the S.E. of Sant'Agostino Via Pier Andrea Mattioli leads to the *Porta Tufi* (Pl. 15).

From the Prato Sant'Agostino Via della Cerchia leads S.W. to the church of *Santa Maria del Carmine* (Pl. 14), probably rebuilt by Peruzzi. It contains a *St Michael, by Beccafumi, and the Madonna dei Mantellini (c. 1240) surrounded by figures of Saints by Fr. Vanni. In the apse, behind the altar, is the Madonna del Carmine, a much venerated painting. Opposite is the *Palazzo Pollini* (1537), also by Peruzzi. Pian dei Mantellini, continued by Via del Fosso di Sant'Ansano curves N. past fields planted with olives and vines to *San Sebastiano* (not always open), a small Renaissance church by Domenico Ponsi (1507) with good paintings and a reliquary of 1379 in its attractive interior. Via di Valle Piatta and (l.) Via del Costone, continue to the *Fonte Branda,* a well mentioned as early as 1081 and covered over in 1248 with brick arches by Giov. di Stefano. This marks the entrance to the Terzo di Camollia.

A short distance to the N.E., in Via Benincasa, is the **Casa di Santa Caterina,** or *St Catherine's House* (Pl. 10), the rooms of which were converted into small chapels in 1464. The house is open 9-12, 15.30-17.30.

Caterina Benincasa (1347-80), or Catherine of Siena, was the daughter of a dyer and took the veil at the age of eight. Her visions of the Redeemer, from whom she received the stigmata of His Passion and, like her Alexandrian namesake, a marriage-ring, have been the subject of countless paintings. Her eloquence persuaded Gregory XI to return from Avignon to Rome, and her letters (preserved in the Biblioteca Comunale; see below) are models of style as well as of devotion. She died in Rome, was canonized in 1461, and in 1939 was proclaimed patron saint of Italy. She was made a Doctor of the Church in 1970, the first female Saint, with St Teresa of Avila, to be given this distinction.

The chapels of the interior comprise the ORATORIO DELLA CONTRADA DELL'OCA (in winter open on Sun only 10-11), which was the dyer's workshop, now adorned with statues and paintings, including a polychrome statue of the saint by *Neroccio,* a fresco of St Catherine receiving the stigmata by *Girol. del Pacchia,* and 5 angels by *Sodoma;* the ORATORIO DELLA CAMERA, St Catherine's cell; the ORATORIO DELLA CUCINA, the family kitchen, with an altarpiece by *Fungai,* frescoes by followers of Sodoma, and (W. wall) paintings by *Riccio, Fr. Vanni, Salimbeni,* and others; and the ORATORIO DEL CROCIFISSO, on the site of the saint's orchard, with a Crucifixion (13C Pisan sch.), before which St Catherine received the stigmata at Pisa in 1375.—The charming little LOGGIA was built perhaps by *Peruzzi* but altered by *Pelori* (1533).

Via di Santa Caterina runs W. and E., flanking St Catherine's House. From the house the Via delle Terme leads back to the Croce del Travaglio.

C   THE TERZO DI CAMOLLIA

Via Banchi di Sopra leads N. from the Croce to P.za Tolomei, where from the 11C the Sienese parliament used to assemble. The magistrates of the Republic officiated in the adjoining church of *San Cristoforo,* a Romanesque church much rebuilt in the 18C, with a pretty cupola. It contains a good Madonna with saints by Girol. del Pacchia (1508), a panel of St George and the Dragon (15C Sienese sch.), and a strange 14C wooden Crucifix covered with leather. Opposite stands the *Palazzo Tolomei* (Pl. 10), the oldest private Gothic palace in Siena, begun c. 1205 and restored some 50 years later. Via del Moro, flanking San Cristoforo, leads to Piazza Provenzano Salvani (with a fine view of the city walls), in which the church of *Santa Maria di Provenzano* (1594) contains a much venerated 15C terracotta relief of the Madonna. Farther on, in Piazza San Francesco, is the large Gothic church of **San Francesco** (Pl. 7), built in 1326-1475, all but destroyed in the fire of 1655, and thereafter used as a barracks for a long period. In 1885-92 it was restored; the modern façade is by Mariani and Ceccarelli (1894-1913).

In the choir are portrait-busts of the father and mother of Pius II (Æneas Silvius Piccolomini), sole relics of their tomb by *Fr. Martini.* The first and third chapels in the N. transept contain frescoes by *Pietro* and *Ambr. Lorenzetti* (c. 1331). In the S. transept is a fresco of the Madonna and Child by *Andrea Vanni.* The Renaissance cloisters have been restored to house the Faculty of Political Science of the University.

To the right of the church stands the **Oratorio di San Bernardino** (15C), on the spot where the saint preached (apply to the doorkeeper next door, 10.30-12, 14.30-19.30). The LOWER CHAPEL is painted with frescoes by various artists (17C), representing the saint's life; it contains also a Madonna and saints by *Brescianino* and terracotta statues of SS. Catherine and Bernardine. In the vestibule on the first floor is a standard by *Fr. Vanni,* and a bas-relief signed by *Giov. di Agostino* (1341).—The *UPPER CHAPEL, beautifully decorated by *Ventura Turapilli* (after 1496), contains admirable frescoes, mainly by *Sodoma,* others by *Beccafumi* and *Girol. del Pacchia* (1518-32). Here, also is a *Madonna by *Sano di Pietro.*

To the N. of San Francesco is the 14C *Porta Ovile.* Outside it is the picturesque *Fonte d'Ovile* (1262), while within the walls, in Via Pian d'Ovile, is the brick *Fonte Nuova* of 1293.

From Via Vallerozzi the Via dell'Abbadia passes *San Donato,* a church with a 12C cupola. Via dei Rossi, arched at either end, returns to Via Banchi di Sopra, off which a turning (r.) leads to P.za Salimbeni (Pl. 6). Here are the Gothic *Palazzo Salimbeni* (centre), the *Palazzo Spannocchi* (r.), begun by Giuliano da Maiano (1473) and completed in 1880 by Gius. Partini, and the *Palazzo Tantucci* (l.), by Riccio (1548). These palaces form the seat of the MONTE DEI PASCHI, a banking establishment founded in 1624; this institution owns a good collection of works of art. Farther on, the little oratory of *Sant Maria delle Nevi* (usually locked), an elegant Renaissance building (1471) attrib. to Francesco di Giorgio Martini, contains an *Altarpiece (Our Lady of the Snows) by Matt. di Giovanni (1477).

Via della Sapienza descends S.W. passing the **Biblioteca Comunale** (Pl. 6; open Mon-Sat 9-20). This library contains over 100,000 volumes and 5000 MSS., as well as illuminated missals, breviaries, and books of hours, St Catherine's letters, a 7C papyrus from Ravenna, drawings by Peruzzi and Beccafumi, a work by Dante with illuminations by Botticelli, and fine examples of bookbinding.—Adjoining the library is the *Museo Archeologico Etrusco* (adm. 9-14, fest. 9-13), a collection in 11 rooms of Etruscan and Roman antiquities including the Bargagli Etruscan collection from Sarteano. At the foot of the hill on the Camporegio stands the austere Gothic church of **San Domenico** (Pl. 10), begun in 1226, enlarged, damaged, and altered in successive centuries. The campanile dates from 1340. Internally it is built after the usual Dominican form, with a wide aisleless nave, transepts, and a shallow choir with side chapels. A chapel at the W. end contains the only authentic portrait of St Catherine, by her contemporary and friend, *And. Vanni;* in this chapel she assumed the Dominican habit and several of her miracles occurred. On the S. side opens the CAPPELLA DI SANTA CATERINA, in which are the celebrated *Frescoes by *Sodoma* (1526), representing the saint in ecstasy and swooning, and interceding for the life of a young man brought to repentance. SS. Luke and Jerome are also by *Sodoma,* together with the admirable grotesques on the pilasters; the other frescoes are by *Fr. Vanni* (1593). The tabernacle on the chapel altar, by *Giovanni di Stefano* (1466), encloses a reliquary containing St Catherine's head. Over the high altar is a fine *Tabernacle, with two angels, by *Bened. da Maiano* (c. 1475).

Elsewhere in the church are a Nativity by *Fr. di Giorgio* (S. aisle; at the end) and several paintings by *Matteo di Giovanni.* The huge crypt was begun in the 14C. The

Cloister is being restored; the remains of frescoes by *And. Vanni* and *Lippo Memmi* are to be detached and hung in the church.

From San Domenico the Viale dei Mille leads N.W. towards the modern quarter of the city. On the right it passes the *Stadio Comunale,* Siena's athletic centre, and it ends opposite the **Forte di Santa Barbera,** or *Fortezza Medicea* (Pl. 5), built for Cosimo I de' Medici by Bald. Lanci in 1560. The views hence over the city and the surrounding country are enchanting, especially at sunset. In the vaults of the fortezza is the *Enoteca Italica,* a permanent exhibition of Italian wines. To the N.E. of the fortress extends the LIZZA, a small but attractive public park, with a good statue of Garibaldi (by Romanelli; 1896) flanked by two diverging avenues. From here Via dei Gazzani, passing *Santo Stefano,* a little Romanesque church rebuilt in 1641 (with an altarpiece by And. Vanni and predella by Giov. di Paolo), leads into Via di Camollia, which leads left. Some distance along this street the Vicolo Fontegiusta descends to the little Renaissance church of **Fontegiusta* (1482-84), with an admirable portal by Urbano da Cortona (1489), and, in the interior, a *Tabernacle by Marrina (at the high altar) and a fresco (N. side) by Peruzzi.—Via di Camollia continues past *San Pietro alla Magione* (11C) with a pretty interior and remains of 14C frescoes, to the *Porta Camollia* (1604), inscribed 'Cor magis tibi Sena pandit', to commemorate a visit of the Grand Duke Ferdinand I. A few steps distant is a column recalling the meeting on this spot of Frederick III and Eleanora of Portugal (7 March 1451; comp. p. 518). Beyond the column is the *Antiporto* or barbican (1675), in imitation of the Porta Romana. About 10 min. farther on is the Renaissance *Palazzo dei Diavoli* or *dei Turchi,* by Federighi (1460). From either end of the Via Camollia roads descend to the Piazzale Francesco di Giorgio and the Viale Mazzini, leading to the railway station.

About 2½ km. from the Porta Ovile (Pl. 7) by Via Simone Martini and the 16C *Madonnina Rossa* (beyond the railway crossing), are the convent and church of **L'Osservanza** (adm. 9-13, 16-19), founded in 1423 by St Bernardine with the object of restoring the observance of the original Franciscan rule, relaxed by papal dispensations. The convent was enlarged in 1485, and confiscated by the city in 1874. The church was rebuilt in 1949 after severe war damage to the original design of Fr. di Giorgio and Cozzarelli. The chapels contain (l. to r.) a triptych by the *Maestro dell'Osservanza;* a fine group of the Annunciation by *And. della Robbia;* a *Reliquary by *Francesco di Antonio* (1454); a triptych by *Sano di Pietro;* and (sacristy) a Pietà by *Cozzarelli.* A small Museum includes a Head of Christ by *Lando di Pietro* (1337).

About 8 km. from the Porta Ovile is the *Certosa di Pontignano,* now a university college, with three 14-15C cloisters.

From the Porta San Marco (Pl. 13) Highway N73 (for Massa Marittima and Grosseto; p. 557) passes near (3 km.; l.) the battlemented *Villa di Monastero,* formerly the abbey of Sant'Eugenio (suppressed in 1810). About ½ km. farther on a by-road on the right leads to (5 km. from Siena) the 12C *Castello di Belcaro* (adm. weekdays 14-16, on application), enlarged in the 16C by Peruzzi. In the hills farther W. are the hermitages of *Lecceto* (14C) and *San Leonardo al Lago* (12C).

FROM SIENA TO MONTE OLIVETO, 35 km., bus on weekday afternoons in 1½ hrs, going on to Buonconvento (or by the Chiusi railway to Asciano and bus thence).—This route follows the Arezzo road for 6 km. then bears right through *Taverna d'Arbia.* The main road (comp. p. 532) continues past the site of the battle of Montaperti (1260). The road traverses the dreary mud-covered hills in which is quarried the ochre that yields the well-known pigments 'burnt sienna' and 'raw sienna'.—Two km. off to the right of (21 km.) *Pievina* is the former abbey church of *Rofeno,* now abandoned.—26 km. **Asciano,** with walls built by the Sienese in 1351, is noted for its MUSEO DI ARTE SACRA, adjoining the Romanesque *Collegiata.* Among its pictures are a Nativity of the Virgin by the Maestro dell'Osservanza, a St Michael by Ambr. Lorenzetti, a polyptych by Matteo di Giovanni, a Madonna by Barna, and works by Giov. di Paolo and Taddeo di Bartolo. Finds from the Etruscan necropolis at *Poggio Pinci,* 5 km. E., are displayed in the Museo Etrusco in the ex-church of San Bernardino. The road continues southwards through barren countryside, and soon (35 km.) ***Monte Oliveto Maggiore** comes into view on a richly wooded promontory. Visitors are admitted daily 9.30-12.50, 15-dusk. This famous convent was founded for hermits by Giov. Tolomei di Siena (1313), who assumed the religious name of Bernardo and was beatified. The new 'Olivetan' order, under Benedictine rule, was confirmed by John XXII in 1319. Pius II and Charles V sojourned here, the latter with 2000 followers; the monastery was suppressed by Napoleon in 1810, and after a restoration was made a 'National Monument' in 1866. Some monks remain as caretakers and hospitality is available at the guest-house. From the gateway beneath a great tower (1393) decorated with terracottas by the Della Robbia, a road (and path parallel to the left) wind down to the Monastery through an avenue of cypresses. The GREAT CLOISTER (1426-74) is famous for its 41 *Frescoes from the life of St Benedict, nine of which are by *Signorelli* (1497) and the remainder by *Sodoma* (1505-8); the cycle begins in the E. walk. On the entrance into the vestibule of the church (l.) is a small picture of Christ carrying the Cross by Sodoma. In the vestibule, statue of the Madonna and Child by *Fra Giovanni da Verona*. The façade of the CHURCH is of 1400-17; inside are fine *Choir-stalls by *Giov. da Verona* (1503) and a lectern by *Raff. da Brescia*. From the Middle Cloister is the entrance to the REFECTORY (fresco by Bart. Neroni above the lavabo). The LIBRARY, on the second floor, had 16 of its 20 valuable codexes stolen in 1975; it has notable carving by *Giov. da Verona*. The PHARMACY, with jars, and the CHAPTER HOUSE are also shown.—Beyond Monte Oliveto the road goes on to join N2 at (44 km.) *Buonconvento* (Rte 49).

FROM SIENA TO PERUGIA, c. 110 km. N 326 (the stretch between Val di Chiana and Perugia is now an almost continuous 'superstrada'). N 75 bis. The railway journey (161 km. in c. 3 hrs) involves two changes: at Chiusi and Terontola. The road, at first combined with that to Arezzo, passes S. of the battlefield of *Montaperti* (1260; p. 512), and, at (20½ km.) the Ombrone bridge, leaves the Arezzo road and turns S.E.—27 km. *Rapolano Terme* (334 m), now by-passed, is a medieval town with spa waters and travertine quarries. Also by-passed is (43 km.) **Sinalunga** (364 m), the junction of a branch railway to Arezzo. Here the Sienese defeated the English mercenaries of Nic. da Montefeltro in 1363; here also Garibaldi was arrested in 1867 by Victor Emmanuel II, to prevent an ill-timed descent on Rome. There is a Descent from the Cross by Girol. del Pacchia in the *Collegiata,* and paintings by Benv. di Giovanni, and Cozzarelli (Baptism of Christ) in *San Bernardino,* outside the town. The altarpiece by Sano di Pietro was stolen from here in 1971.—The railway now passes through *Torrita di Siena,* with its nine 16C towers and interesting churches (usually locked) while the road turns E. to cross the Val di Chiana, near the *Abbazia di Farneta* (ring at nearby house), an interesting Romanesque building with a fine crypt. The sacristy has local archæological material.—On the N. shore of Lake Trasimene this route joins the course of N 75 bis; from here to *Perugia,* see Rte 53.

47   FLORENCE TO AREZZO

A   By the Valdarno

ROAD, 86 km. N67 to (18 km.) *Pontassieve;* N69 thence to **Arezzo.** BUSES in 2½ hrs; also direct (once a day) in 1¼ hrs viâ the autostrada (comp below).

A much hillier route to Arezzo (coaches of S.I.T.A. twice daily in 2½ hrs), shorter by 9 km. and followed by the autostrada (see below) leaves Florence by the S. bank of the Arno and Bagno a Ripoli, joining the main route at Incisa. It is interesting for the splendid retrospective views of Florence and for the fine villas around (15 km.) *San Donato in Collina.*

The AUTOSTRADA DEL SOLE (A 1), between Florence (Certosa) and the Arezzo exit (63 km.; 80 km. centre to centre) passes under San Donato in Collina by a tunnel, enters the Valdarno just N. of *Incisa,* follows the E. bank to beyond *Valdarno* (for Montevarchi), then swings away to the S. It commands fine views

RAILWAY, 88 km., in c. 1 hr; a section of the present main line from Milan to Rome (comp. also Rte 48). A new main line to Rome, the 'Direttissima', is nearing completion. Shortening the distance by c. 60 km., it runs more directly between Florence and Incisa, San Giovanni Valdarno, and Chiusi. The first 122 km. between Citta della Pieve (S. of Chiusi) and Rome were opened in 1977, and express trains using this line on the Florence-Rome run reach the capital 15-30 minutes faster.

From Florence by N67 (18 km.) *Pontassieve,* see Rte 43G. Here N69 keeps to the right, still ascending the winding Arno in company with the railway, and shortly leaves on the left the Casentino road (Rte 46B).—23 km. *Sant'Éllero* preserves a castle and a Vallombrosan convent (now a private villa; no adm.). The autostrada passes beneath this road near (36 km.) *Incisa in Valdarno,* so called from the deep chalky cutting made by the river. It was an important stage in the battle for Florence (1944).—41 km. *Figline Valdarno* is a prosperous village with a Collegiata, mainly 16C in appearance, which preserves a Madonna and Child by the 'Maestro di Figline'.—49 km. *San Giovanni Valdarno* (134 m; 20,300 inhab.), with lignite mines and blast furnaces, was the birthplace of the painters Masaccio (Tomaso Guidi, 1401-28) and Giov. da San Giovanni (Giov. Mannozzi, 1592-1636). The basilica of Santa Maria delle Grazie and the medieval Palazzo Pretorio in the main square are worth a visit.

The beautiful *Annunciation in the church of the convent of *Montecarlo,* 2 km. S. beyond the railway, is by Fra Angelico.—An interesting excursion (bus) leads to (15 km. E.) *Loro Ciufenna,* via the little walled 'bastide' of (9 km.) *Terranuova Bracciolini,* founded in 1337. *Grópina,* 2 km. S. of Loro, has a charming Romanesque church.

The road gradually diverges from the Arno.—55 km. *Montevarchi,* an important market-town (23,000 inhab.) with an interesting church and adjacent museum. The Accademia Valdarnese founded by Poggio Bracciolini, has a good collection of fossils (open 16-18, Sun 10-12; closed Mon and in Aug). The road begins to climb and at 66 km. a by-road diverges left to *Laterina* (6 km.) where in 1973 were unearthed long and almost intact stretches of the Via Cassia Vetus. After crossing beneath the autostrada and just before (79 km.) *Indicatore* station the road passes, on the S., *Arezzo British Military Cemetery,* with 1267 graves. The road now descends into the Valdichiana.

86 km. **AREZZO,** pleasantly situated on a hillside (296 m) about 5 km. S. of the Arno, is the ancient and interesting chief town (90,800 inhab.) of the Tuscan province of the same name. It has many artistic attractions, but is above all famous for the fresco cycle painted by Piero della Francesco for the church of San Francesco. Although the plain around the city has been invaded by light industries, the centre has remained remarkably unspoilt.

Hotels on Via Guido Monaco which leads from the station to San Francesco.
Post Office, 34 Via Guido Monaco.—**E.P.T.,** P.za Risorgimento.
Buses from Bus Station in P.za del Popolo. To *Florence,* see above; also frequently to *Sansepolcro,* and *Città di Castello;* many times daily to *Castiglion Fiorentino* and *Cortona;* twice daily to *Siena;* to *Urbino, Fano,* and *Pesaro,* once a day; to *Umbertide* and *Gubbio* 3 times daily; and to *Rimini* in summer.
An *Antiques Fair* is held in P.za Grande on the first Sun of every month.

History. *Arretium,* one of the more important of the twelve cities of the Etruscan Confederation, was originally the foe and later the faithful ally of Rome. It emerged from the Dark Ages as a free republic in the 10C. Generally supporting the Ghibelline party it was frequently at odds with Florence; it shared in the defeat at Campaldino in 1289 and submitted to Florence in 1384.—As a road junction the town had tactical importance in the Second World War. On 16 July 1944, after a day of bitter fighting in the hills to the S., it was entered by the British 6th Armoured Division, who thus secured an administrative base for the assault on the Gothic Line. Nearly every important building was harmed to some extent by bombing.
Ever since the Etruscan period Arezzo has produced notable artists and craftsmen, including the potters who fashioned the 'vasi arretini'. Among its eminent citizens were C. Cilnius Mæcenas (d. 8 B.C.), the friend of Augustus and the patron of Virgil and Horace; Guido d'Arezzo (c. 995-1050), the inventor of the musical scale; Margaritone, the painter (1216-93); Petrarch, the poet (1304-74);

Spinello Aretino, the painter (c. 1350-1410); Aretino (1492-1566), the most outspoken writer of the late Renaissance; and Giorgio Vasari (1512-74), the architect, painter, and historian of art.

Arezzo is noted for its *Giostra del Saracino,* a tournament held annually in the P.za Grande on the 1st Sun in Sept in the late afternoon, with an origin going back to the 13C. Two competitors from each of the four quarters of the town, mounted and armed with lances, charge in turn across the piazza at a pivoting quintain called 'Buratto Re delle Indie' which holds the target in its left hand and in its right

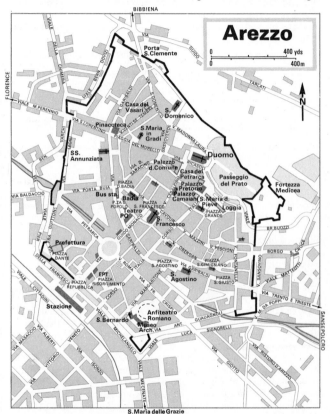

a whip, ending in three wooden balls. Points are awarded (from 1-5) for aim, with bonus points for a broken lance, and penalties if the horseman is struck by the wooden balls as the figure turns on its pivot. Each of the four ancient quarters of the town enters a team under a captain, with standard-bearers, foot-soldiers bowmen, and a band, which plays the 'Saracino hymn'. The four quarters have their own colours: Porta Sant'Andrea, white and green; Porta Crucifera, red and green; Porta del Foro, yellow and crimson; Porta Santo Spirito, yellow and blue. The team (not the individual) scoring the most marks is declared the winner. Tickets for seats (in the shade) are available in advance; standing room only on the day.

In the central PIAZZA SAN FRANCESCO is the church of **San Francesco** (open 7-12.30, 14.30-19.30) built by Fra Giovanni da Pistoia in 1322.

The rose window in the façade wall has stained glass by *Gugl. di Marcillat* (William of Marseille; 1520) showing St Francis and Honorius III. Among the numerous frescoes by local artists on the nave walls (mostly fragments) are an Annunciation by *Spinello Aretino* (towards the E. end of the r. wall). Chapel to right of choir, frescoes by *Spinello:* right, Deeds of St Michael; left, Legend of St Giles. Triptych: Our Lady and St Thomas, by *Nic. di Pietro Gerini.* In the choir is the **LEGEND OF THE TRUE CROSS, by *Piero della Francesca* (c. 1454-66), his masterpiece, and one of the greatest fresco cycles ever produced in Italian painting.

The chronological order of the scenes as they illustrate the story is as follows: RIGHT WALL (top) Death of Adam; the Queen of Sheba recognizes the sacred wood, and she is received by Solomon; (r. of the window) the beam is buried by the order of Solomon; Constantine's Dream; Constantine's victory over Maxentius.— OPPOSITE WALL: (central panel l. of window) Torture of Judas; Discovery and Proof of the Cross by St Helena; Victory of Heraclius over Chosroes; (lunette) Heraclius restores the Cross to Jerusalem.—Also by Piero are the two figures of Prophets on the window wall, and the Annunciation (thought by some scholars to be St Helena receiving the news of her death, and thus connected to the main cycle).

In the chapel l. of the high altar is an Annunciation attrib. to the youth of Luca Signorelli, and a detached fresco of the same subject; (N. side of nave), monument by *Michele da Firenze,* and a 13C Crucifix.

Via Cavour (r.) and Corso Italia (l.) lead to the *Pieve di Santa Maria,* a 12C church replacing an earlier edifice sacked in 1111. The severe yet superbly conceived *FAÇADE (being restored) has a deep central portal flanked by blind arcades which support two deep open arcades and a third colonnade surmounted by an architrave. The 68 diverse pillars include a human figure. The portal bears reliefs of 1216 and the months are illustrated in the intrados. The beautiful *INTERIOR has clustered pillars with good capitals and arches showing the transition to Gothic. In the raised presbytery the *Polyptych by *Pietro Lorenzetti* has been removed for restoration. The crypt below (good capitals) contains a polychrome wood Madonna of the 15C Florentine school. The arcaded apse and the original *Campanile* (1330), with its 40 double openings, are best seen from the steeply-sloping *PIAZZA GRANDE, behind the church. Here stand the Gothic and Renaissance *Palazzo della Fraternità dei Laici,* with a sculpted lunette on the façade by Bern. Rossellino, and the fine *Loggia,* built by Vasari in 1573. The Loggia continues N.W. to Via de' Pileati in which is *Palazzo Camaiani* (16C), with a tower of 1351, now housing the Provincial Archives, and the 14C *Palazzo Pretorio,* bearing on its façade the armorial bearings of many podestà; it is occupied by the Public Library. The road curves up hill to the left, and at No. 1 Via dell'Orto is the *Casa Petrarca* (adm. 10-12, 15-18), reconstructed in 1948 as an academy and library for Petrarchian studies. Visitors are shown the library with MSS. and an autograph letter of the poet (1370). A monument to Petrarch stands in the centre of the *Passeggio del Prato,* a large planted piazza (good views) extending between the cathedral and the 14-16C *Fortezza,* rebuilt by Ant. da Sangallo the Younger and dismantled in 1800.

The **Duomo** was begun in the late 13C and continued until 1510, with a campanile added at the E. end in 1859 and a façade completed in 1914. On the S. side is a good 14C portal. The dark Gothic interior has a nave, tribune, and aisles, clustered columns, pointed arches, and good stained-glass windows by *Gugl. di Marcillat* (1519-23), who painted also the first three vaults of the nave and the first of the N. aisle. In the S. aisle near the entrance is the monument of Gregory X, who died at Arezzo in 1276. Farther along is the canopied recess of the Tarlati Chapel with a frescoed Crucifixion attrib. to a local painter known as the 'Maestro del Vescovado' (mid-14C) and a fine urn of the 4C. Off the N. aisle is a Lady Chapel containing five *Terracottas by *And.* and *Giov. Della Robbia* and the remains of Gregory X; farther on in the same aisle is the *Tomb of Bp. Guido Tarlati, by *Agost. di Giovanni* and *Angiolo da Siena,* with panels representing the warlike life of this zealous Ghibelline (d. 1327). Between the tomb and the sacristy is a beautiful fresco of *St Mary Magdalen, by *Piero della Francesca* (1466). The *High Altar, by many artists including *Giov. di Francesco* and *Betto di Giovanni,* encloses the body of St Donatus (martyred in 361), the patron saint of the city, and its reredos is covered with admirable reliefs. From the sacristy there is access to the MUSEO DIOCESANO (open 10-12, 15-17) with an interesting collection of works (mostly paintings) from the cathedral and diocesan churches.

On the cathedral steps stands a statue of Ferdinand I, by Francavilla after a design of Giambologna. Across P.za della Libertà is the *Palazzo del Comune* of 1333. The old Via Sassoverde leads right from Via Ricasoli to **San Domenico** in a quiet square of lime trees. The church, founded in 1275, has a Romanesque portal with a lunette frescoed by Agnole di Lorentino, and a Gothic campanile. The lively interior, covered with 14-15C frescoes, has a Gothic canopied altar (r.) and a Crucifix by Cimabue in the apse.

Vasari's House (1540-48), No. 55 in Via Venti Settembre is closed for restoration, but is usually open 9.30-15.30 exc. Tues; fest. 9-13. It contains frescoes, paintings, and, among other archives, letters of Michelangelo. The church of *Santa Maria in Gradi* (1592), farther on (l.) has a good altarpiece by And. Della Robbia. At the corner of Via Garibaldi is the **Galleria e Museo Medioevale e Moderno,** housed in the 15C *Palazzo Bruni,* closed for structural repairs, but usually open 9.30-16; fest. 9-13; closed Mon.

Among fragments in the courtyard are capitals and columns from the Pieve, and part of a notable 10C well.—Three rooms to the right contain more medieval fragments, including two Madonnas (14C) from the old gates of the city.
First Floor. R.I. *Margaritone,* St Francis; *School of Guido da Siena,* Madonna; *Iacopo del Casentino,* SS. John the Baptist, John the Evangelist, and Nicholas (parts of a polyptych); *Lor. di Nicolò,* Coronation of the Virgin. Sculpture: 14C *Sienese school,* Head of a warrior; 14C *Pisan school,* Madonna.—R. II. 15C frescoes.—R. III. Frescoes by *Spinello Aretino* and his son, *Parri Spinelli,* among them a Madonna della Misericordia, by the latter.—RR. IV and V. Early Renaissance. The chimneypiece is by *Simone Mosca. Lorentino d'Arezzo,* Madonna and saints; *Bart. della Gatta,* Two paintings of St Roch, the smaller painting including a view of medieval Arezzo; *After Giov. Bellini,* St Sebastian. On tables is a good ivory collection.—R. V. *Signorelli* (?), Madonna and saints (fragment of a fresco); *Nic. Soggi,* Adoration of the Child.
The next five small rooms contain a magnificent *Collection of majolica from Faenza, Gubbio, Deruta, Castel Durante, and Urbino (13-18C), and terracottas by *And. della Robbia* and his followers.
Second Floor. R.I. *Luca Signorelli,* Two paintings of the Madonna and saints; *Dom. Pecori,* Madonna and saints; *Vasari,* Two paintings of St Roch. Excellent collection of glass.—RR. II-IV. *Salvator Rosa,* Two landscapes, Mythological scene; *Gasp. Dughet,* Landscape; *Fr. Gérard,* Portrait of Tommaso Sgricci. The MARIO SALMI BEQUEST occupies two rooms opened in 1963.

On the opposite side of Via Garibaldi is the Renaissance church of the *Santissima Annunziata,* by Bart. della Gatta (1491) and Ant. da Sangallo the Elder (c. 1517). Above the right-hand door is an Annunciation by Spinello Aretino. The harmonious *Interior is adorned with stained glass by Gugl. di Marcillat. To the left, farther on, is the **Badia** or abbey of SS FLORA E LUCILLA, rebuilt by *Vasari,* and containing on the W. wall a *Fresco of St Lawrence, by Bart. della Gatta (1476). In the N. transept is a ciborium exquisitely carved by *Bened. da Maiano.* The high altar was intended by Vasari for his own tomb. The Crucifixion at the end of the right aisle is by *Segna di Bonaventura* (1320). The former monastery preserves a fine 15C cloister.

Via Garibaldi continues S.E., crossing the broad Via Guido Monaco to P.za Sant'Agostino, with a 13C campanile. From here Via Margaritone leads to the *Convento di San Bernardo* whose rebuilt loggie overlook vestiges of a Roman amphitheatre. Here is the **Museo Archeologico Mecenate** (adm. 9–14, fest. 9–13; closed Mon). Other parts of the amphitheatre are visible in the museum rooms.

Ground Floor. RR. I–IV. Etruscan art. Funerary urns, some exquisitely modelled, including one good example from Volterra, with a relief of a funeral combat before the tomb (2–1C B.C.); terracotta memorial statuettes from Chiusi (3–2C).—RR. V–X. Roman mosaics, statues, and bas-reliefs, including a marble altar of the Augustan period, with the legend of Romulus and Remus; portrait of a woman of the Augustan period; portrait of a man (3C A.D.); (R. VII) collection of Aretine coralline vases (B.C. 100–100 A.D.).

Upper Floor. Palæolithic and neolithic collection from the territory of Arezzo.—Etruscan bronzes (7C–2C B.C.).—Collection of grave-goods from the tomb of a young girl from Apulia (1C B.C.). Etruscan jewellery (4C–3C). *Portrait of a man, moulded in gold (Aretine; 3C B.C.) Scent-boxes from Egypt and Asia Minor.—The full collection of Etruscan, Greek, and Roman coins is opened on request.—Another series of rooms contain a curious urn with human head and arms from Chiusi (7C B.C.), and black-figured Attic pottery (7–6C). Three good vases (5C B.C.), with red figures, showing Charioteer, Salute to Warrior, Rape of Hippodamia, the last two by Danae and Meidias (c. 430–420). Large krater attributed to Euphronios (5C B.C.), with Herakles fighting Amazons.

To the S.E. of the station (reached in 10 min. by Viale Michelangelo and Via Mecenate) is the church of **Santa Maria delle Grazie** (1449), with a graceful loggia by *Bened. da Maiano* and a handsome marble and terracotta altar by *And. Della Robbia.*

FROM AREZZO TO SIENA, 64 km., bus in 2¼ hrs. This route leaves Arezzo by N 71 and, after 4 km., joins N 73 on the right.—At (9 km.) *Pieve al Toppo* N 327 branches left for Sinalunga (p. 527).—20 km. *Monte San Savino,* see Rte 48. The road climbs to (27 km.) *Casalino* (533 m), then descends with beautiful views to (39 km.) the Ombrone bridge (p. 527), where it joins N 326.—64 km. *Siena,* see Rte 46.

FROM AREZZO TO SANSEPOLCRO, 38 km.; bus in 1¼ hrs. N 73 climbs S.E. to (8 km.) the *Foce di Scopetone* (526 m) and then descends nearly all the way, following the valley of the Cerfone beyond (12 km.) *Palazzo del Pero* (405 m). At 25 km. this road leaves the Cerfone which descends (r.), accompanied by N 221, to *Monterchi* (3 km.), a fortified frontier village. Below the village, which was the birthplace of the mother of Piero della Francesca, the chapel (the custodian lives next door) of the cemetery contains the *'Madonna del Parto' by him, a detached fresco c. 1445. N 221 continues to Città di Castello (17 km.; p. 582).—At 29 km. a road leads left for **Anghiari** (4 km.; 429 m). This walled village (once *Castrum Angulare*) was the scene in 1440 of a victory of the Florentines under Fr. Sforza over the Visconti of Milan, and in 1796 of a French defeat of the Austrians. The churches of the *Badia* and *S. Agostino* are also interesting; in the latter is a triptych by Matteo di Giovanni. The *Collegiata* contains a charming Last Supper, and Christ washing the disciples' feet, both by Sogliani. In the Renaissance *Palazzo*

Taglieschi is a museum of local art. Highway N 3 (Rte 52) crosses the Tiber short of (38 km.) *Sansepolcro.*

From Arezzo to *Cortona,* see Rte 53.

B By the Casentino

ROAD, 100 km. N 67. At (18 km.) *Pontassieve* bear right then left on N 70 leaving it by the next by-road (r.).—33 km. *Vallombrosa;* the direct road is 9 km. shorter.—43 km. *Consuma.*—62 km. *Poppi.*—67 km. *Bibbiena.*—N 71. 100 km. **Arezzo.**

To (18 km.) *Pontassieve,* see Rte 43G. The Casentino road ascends to the left away from the main Arezzo road (comp. above), and in just over 1 km., at another fork, the direct road again keeps to the left, omitting Vallombrosa. It is better, however, to bear right and ascend through (23 km.) *Pélago* and (27 km.) *Tosi.*

33 km. **Vallombrosa** (958 m) is a summer resort amid pinewoods on the W. slope of the Pratomagno hills.

The famous Monastery was founded by St John Gualberto in 1040, and was the first house of the Vallombrosan Order. The monastery was suppressed in 1866, but re-instated in 1963. The church dates mainly from the 17C, and contains 16C stalls. Milton stayed at the guesthouse of the monastery in 1638 (tablet); the surrounding pine-woods are the "Etrurian shades" of 'Paradise Lost'.

Just under two kilometres from Vallombrosa is **Saltino** (995 m) a summer resort in a more open situation than Vallombrosa, with wide views. It is also frequented by ski-iers, and fine walks may be taken in the *Pratomagno,* to the S.E., among summits 1463 m to 1524 m high.

The road from Vallombrosa towards the Casentino traverses the forest of pine, beech, and oak, ascends the N. side of a little valley, and joins the main road just before (43 km.) *Consuma* a summer and ski resort a few metres below the pass (1023 m) connecting the Pratomagno with the main Apennine chain.

At 53 km. a road on the left diverges for (5 km.) *Pratovecchio* and (6 km.) *Stia,* (441 m) two large villages higher up the **Casentino,** or upper valley of the Arno. This delightful wooded vale was the domain of the Guidi, the Ghibelline family with whom the exiled Dante found a refuge. Their *Castle of *Romena,* dating from the 11C, stands above Pratovecchio; near it (new road) is the fine church of San Pietro with a good Romanesque apse (1152). The church of Stia, likewise Romanesque, contains works by And. Della Robbia and his school. A fine walk of 4 hrs leads N. to the *Source of the Arno* and thence to the summit of *Monte Falterona* (1654 m). The adjacent summit of *Monte Falco,* 4 m higher, is more easily reached from the *Passo la Calla* (1296 m), on the road from Stia into the Romagna viâ the Bidente valley. On its slopes, frequented for skiing, is the Rif. La Burráia (1447 m).

The main road descneds into the Arno valley at (60 km.) the plain of *Campaldino,* where a column marks the battlefield of 1289. Here Dante fought as a young man against the Ghibellines of Arezzo, who were defeated.—62 km. **Poppi,** the birthplace of Mino da Fiesole (1431-84), has a fine *Palazzo Pretorio, built in the 13C as a castle of the Guidi family, which dominates the valley. It also has a delightful arcaded main street.

About 15 km. N.E. is **Camáldoli** (816 m), famous for the monastery of an order founded c. 1012 by St Romuald for hermits living in entire isolation. The main buildings are largely of the 17-18C, but include the charming 16C *Pharmacy. Adjacent is the original Hospice with a cloister and little chapel. Farther up amid the fine forest of firs and pines is the *Eremo* (1104 m), with a group of monastic cells and a Baroque church, on the site of the original hermitage. Hotels provide accommodation for the numerous summer visitors.

67 km. **Bibbiena,** the chief town (10,600 inhab.) of the Casentino, was the birthplace of Bernardo Dovizi, called Cardinal Bibbiena (1470-1520), the friend of Raphael. The early 16C *Palazzo Dovizi,* and the church of *San Lorenzo,* with good Della Robbia terracottas, are interesting. The 12C church of *SS Ippolito e Donato,* lately restored, has a Madonna by Arcangelo di Cola (removed for restoration).

Above *Chiusi della Verna,* 23 km. E. (bus) amid pine-forests, stands the famous monastery of **La Verna** (1129 m), the site of which was given to St Francis in 1213. The principal *Church* contains an Adoration and an *Assumption of the Virgin, by And. Della Robbia; and the *Cappella delle Stimmate,* occupying the spot where St Francis received the Stigmata in 1224, has a grand Crucifixion by the same artist and Renaissance stalls. Many other sites recall the life of St Francis here.

The road descends the Casentino, leaving the Arno at (92 km.) *Borgo a Giovi,* and runs across the plain to (100 km.) **Arezzo.**

48   AREZZO TO ORVIETO AND ROME

AUTOSTRADA DEL SOLE (A1), 218 km. N327 and N326 follow roughly the same course to Chiusi (66 km.), serving the villages on the W. side of the Val di Chiana. For an alternative route (N71), see Rte 53.

RAILWAY from Arezzo to *Rome* direct, 229 km. in 2½-3 hrs (comp. p. 527). As far as *Chiusi-Chianciano Terme* the railway more nearly follows N71, comp. Rte 53; from Chiusi to Rome, 165 km. in c. 2 hrs. At *Orte* the line converges with that from Ancona viâ Foligno and Terni, and branch lines diverge to Capranica-Sutri, and, viâ Attigliano, to Viterbo.

A light railway serves the W. side of the Val di Chiana: from Arezzo to *Sinalunga* in 1 hr; from Sinalunga to *Chiusi* in ½ hr (poor connections).

Leaving Arezzo by the Porta San Lorentino this route joins the Autostrada in just under 11 km. and turns S. in the foothills W. of the Val di Chiana.—24 km. **Monte San Savino** (330 m), 3 km. to the W., was the birthplace of the sculptor And. Contucci, called Sansovino (1460-1529), who is the probable architect of the attractive *Loggia del Mercato.* The *Palazzo Comunale* was designed by Ant. Sangallo the Elder. The church of *Santa Chiara* contains sculptural works by Sansovino and others; *Sant'Agostino,* rebuilt in the 16C, perhaps by Sansovino, contains an altarpiece by Vasari and 14-15C frescoes.

A hilly minor road runs S. to (8 km.) *Lucignano,* a little fortress town, where the Museo Civico has paintings by Luca di Tommè, Ugolino di Nerio, and Luca Signorelli, and a reliquary by Ugolino di Vieri (1350; most of which has been recovered since its theft).—16 km. *Sinalunga* (comp. p. 527) where a slip-road joins the autostrada.

This route passes beneath the Siena-Perugia road just short of (38 km.) the exit named after the VALDICHIANA, the once unhealthy plain lying between the upper basins of the Arno and Tiber. In prehistoric times this valley was the bed of the Arno, which flowed not into the Tyrrhenian Sea but into the Tiber. The marshes left behind when it took its new direction were first drained by the efforts of Cosimo de' Medici; and draining and irrigation operations have gone on almost continuously since. The waters of the valley are carried off N. to the Arno by the *Canale Maestro della Chiana* (begun in 1551), and S. to the Tiber by the much smaller *Chianetta.*

At *Foiano della Chiana* (5 km. N.E.) the churches have attractive Della Robbian groups. *Sinalunga* (comp. above) lies W. of the same exit.

The autostrada commands views (l.) across the Canale Maestro and of the Lago di Montepulciano and Lago di Chiusi, now only marshy pools.—62 km. The exit for Chiusi joins N 146 coming from Chianciano Terme (p. 542), 4 km. W. of the town. **Chiusi,** a drab little town of 9000 inhabitants, stands on a hill to the left of the road.

Chiusi is supposed to have been founded by the Umbrian Cambertes, whence its Etruscan name of *Camars.* One of the twelve cities of the Etruscan Confederation (p. 412) it reached its greatest splendour about the 7C or 6C B.C. Lars Porsena, the *Lucumo* or king, attacked Rome in 508 B.C. (see Macaulay's 'Horatius'), but the town became subject to Rome after 295 B.C. and took the Roman name of *Clusium.* The neighbourhood of the pestilential marshes of the Valdichiana brought decay to Chiusi, but the drainage works begun by Cosimo de' Medici restored some degree of prosperity. Under the streets runs a labyrinth of Etruscan galleries, and a vast Etruscan necropolis surrounds the town.

The Romanesque *Duomo* is built almost entirely of Etruscan and Roman fragments; in the Chapter House are 22 illuminated antiphonals. The campanile is built above a huge antique cistern. In the *Museo Nazionale Etrusco* (adm. 8.30-12.30, fest. 9-13; closed Mon), the most famous of the many notable Etruscan sarcophagi is an alabaster example depicting the deceased, Lars Sentinates. There is also the peculiar Cinerario Gualandi. The church of *San Francesco* dates from the 14C, the ruined *Fortezza* perhaps from the 12C.

The ETRUSCAN *TOMBS in the neighbourhood are well worth a visit. They are approached by pretty country lanes, most of which can be negotiated by car, and the main ones are unlocked by custodians who live nearby. Just outside the town, on the road to Chianciano Terme, Via delle Tombe Etrusche diverges right for the *Tomba della Pellegrina,* with several urns and sarcophagi, the *Tomba della Scimmia* ('of the Ape'), with important wall-paintings, and the *Tomba del Granduca,* with eight cinerary urns remaining on their stone benches.—Another excursion leaves the city beyond the Cimitero Nuovo, and includes the *Tomba Casuccini* with a fine doorway and wall-paintings of sports and games, and the *Tomba delle Tassinaie.*—The *Poggio Gaiella,* a tufa hill 4 km. N., has three stories of passages and galleries; according to tradition, it is the mausoleum of Lars Porsena.

BUSES run from Chiusi station to the town in 5 min., going on to *Chianciano Terme* (½ hr) and *Montepulciano* (1 hr); to *Perugia* in 1¾ hrs; to *Siena* in 3 hrs; and to *Radicófani* in 1 hr, going on to Santa Fiora.—The Radicófani bus passes (12 km.) *Sarteano,* where there are Madonnas by Giacomo di Mino in the churches of San Francesco and San Martino. At *Cetona,* 6 km. S. of Sarteano, are an old castle and, in the Palazzo Terosi, a small Etruscan collection.

Beyond Chiusi the autostrada and the railway follow the same course, crossing into the muddy Páglia valley.—The exit for *Orvieto* is at 102 km. beyond the crossing of N 71 (p. 588), which is soon joined at *Orvieto Scalo* (rly. stn). The town is approached by a winding ascent 5½ km. long.

ORVIETO, built on a precipitous tufa crag (315 m) dominating the valley, is a place of great antiquity, with 23,600 inhabitants, preserving its medieval aspect and renowned for the beauty of its cathedral. Recent building has taken place around the station (*Orvieto Scala*) leaving the old town and the cultivated fields beneath its rock remarkably unchanged. It is the centre of a famed wine-growing area and has notable Etruscan remains. Local crafts include lace and pottery.

Funicular (out of operation for several years but to be reopened; operated by water) from the railway station to (560 m) *Orvieto Città* in 7 min; connecting BUS from the upper station to P.za della Repubblica.

Hotels in the old town (near Corso Cavour and the Duomo) and (in a less pleasant position) in Orvieto Scala, near the station.

Post Office, off Corso Cavour.—**Azienda Autonoma di Turismo,** P.za Duomo.

Buses from P.za San. Domenico and Via Loggia dei Mercanti to *Bolsena;* to *Perugia;* to *Acquapendente;* to *Viterbo,* viâ *Bagnoregio* or viâ *Montefiascone;* to *Rome;* to *Pitigliano;* to *Todi,* etc.

History. Orvieto occupies the site of the ancient *Volsinii* or *Velsina,* one of the chief cities of the Etruscan Confederation. Constantly at war with Rome, the inhabitants suffered disaster in 280 B.C., when the Romans destroyed their city. They fled from their ruined homes and resettled themselves at a spot on the N.E. side of Lake Bolsena which developed into the town of Bolsena. Their original residence became known as *Urbs Vetus* (Old Town), whence the modern name of Orvieto is derived. In the Middle Ages Orvieto was a Guelph stronghold, and many of the popes took refuge here from revolts in Rome. Gregory X here received Edward I of England, on his return from the Crusades. Angelo da Orvieto (14C) and Ascanio Vittozzi (d. 1615), the architects, were natives.

The upper terminus of the funicular from the railway station is on the Piazzale Cahen, where the road from the N. also reaches the town. Conspicuous on the left is the *Fortezza* (1364), the grounds of which are now a public garden commanding fine views of the valley.

A short distance to the N. of the Fortezza is the interesting *Pozzo di San Patrizio* (St Patrick's Well), built by Ant. da Sangallo (1527-37) at the instance of Clement VII, who fled to Orvieto after the sack of Rome. The well, surmounted by a low tower, is 63 m deep, and is encircled by two spiral staircases each of 248 steps and lit by 72 windows. The descent is difficult. A few yards to the W. are the ruins of an Etruscan temple.

From the piazza, Corso Cavour (open to access traffic only) runs through the town from E. to W. At the *Torre del Moro* (12C), Via del Duomo on the left leads to the quiet *P.za del Duomo,* with a quaint row of small houses lining its N. side. At the entrance to the square is a clock tower called *Torre del Maurizio,* surmounted by a bronze figure known as 'Maurizio' (1351) which strikes the hours.

The **Duomo** is one of the most striking buildings of its period in the country. Its construction was ordered by Urban IV to commemorate the miracle of Bolsena (1263; see p. 544). The first stone was laid on 13 Nov 1290, when it was blessed by Nicholas IV. The church was begun to a Romanesque plan, but continued in the newly arrived Gothic taste by *Lor. Maitani,* who took over in 1310. He was followed by his son *Vitale; And. Pisano* (1331-45); *Nino Pisano* (1349); *Andrea di Cecco da Siena* (1356-59); and *And. Orcagna* (1359). *Mich. Sammicheli* became master in 1509-25, and the façade was not completed until the early years of the 17C. The church stands on a plinth of seven steps, alternately red and white. The bold and harmonious exterior has beautiful details.

The *FAÇADE* was designed and begun by *Lor. Maitani.* The *Bas-reliefs* on the lower parts of the pilasters (ascribed to Maitani, his son Vitale, and Nic. and Meo Nuti) depict the story of the Creation to the time of Tubal Cain, the stories of Abraham and David, scenes from the Life of Christ, the Last Judgement, Hell, and Paradise. In the lunette of the main portal is a Madonna by *And. Pisano,* with bronze angels by *Maitani,* who also cast the four lively symbols of the Evangelists. The great rose window is *Orcagna's* work. The mosaics are chiefly reproductions. Of solid bronze, the modern doors (1963-5) were designed by *Emilio Greco.* The Porta di Postierla on the S. side deserves notice. On the N. side are the Porta di Canonica, with a fresco by *And. di Giovanni,* and the Porta del Corporale, surmounted by three statues by *And. Pisano.*

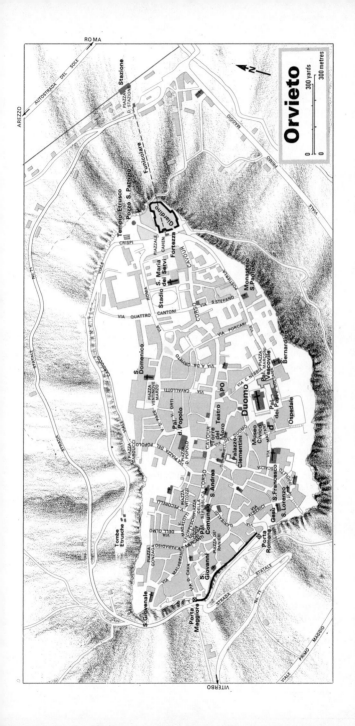

In the uncluttered *INTERIOR (open 7-13, 14.30-19 or 20) the fine architectural lines can be appreciated to the full. The walls are lined with horizontal bands of white and grey. The columns of the nave, with fine capitals, carry round arches, over which a graceful triforium, with a clerestory above it, runs all round the church, except in the transepts.— In the NAVE are a stoup by *Ant. Federighi* (1485) and a font of 1402-7; near the latter is a fresco of the Madonna by *Gentile da Fabriano* (1426; in poor condition). In the N. aisle are three attractive 16C stoups, and in the E. bay of the nave are Baroque statues and groups, most notable of which is the Pietà, by *Ipp. Scalza* (1574), on the N. side. The NORTH TRANSEPT, with a sculptured altarpiece by *Sim. Mosca* and *Raff. da Montelupo* (1542), leads to the *Cappella del Corporale*. On the walls are restored frescoes by *Ugolino di Prete Ilario* (1357-64) and, on the r., a huge panel of the *Madonna dei Raccomandati by Lippo Memmi (1339).

Over the altar incorporated in a large tabernacle, designed by *Nicolò da Siena* (1358) and continued by *Orcagna*, is the *Reliquary of the Corporal, a superb work in silver-gilt with translucent enamels, by the Sienese *Ugolino di Vieri* (1337). This contains the corporal (linen cloth) of the miracle of Bolsena, and is revealed only at Easter and Corpus Domini.

The CHOIR is decorated with frescoes by *Ugolino* and his assistants; the carved and inlaid stalls are the work of *Giov. Ammannati* and other Sienese artists (1331-41). The restored stained glass of the great E. window is by *Giov. di Bonino* (1325-34).—The SOUTH TRANSEPT contains the Altare dei Magi (begun 1514), a good early work of *Sammicheli*, with bas-reliefs by *Raff.* and *Fr. da Montelupo*. At the end is the *Cappella della Madonna di San Brizio, or *Cappella Nuova*, containing the *Frescoes by *Fra Angelico* and *Signorelli* which are the chief treasures of Orvieto.

In 1447 Fra Angelico undertook the painting of the interior of the chapel, and he completed in the same year the two sections of the ceiling which represent the Saviour in Glory (the ninefold hierarchy of angels being by his fellow-worker *Benozzo Gozzoli*) and the prophets. He was recalled to Rome, and it fell to *Luca Signorelli* to complete the work (1499-1504) by painting the walls. He produced one of the most remarkable fresco cycles of the Italian Renaissance. On the Left Wall is the Sermon of Antichrist, with Fra Angelico and Signorelli as two solemn bystanders, and the figure of Dante as one of the crowd; and the Blessed entering Heaven; on the ENTRANCE WALL the Day of Judgement; on the RIGHT WALL the Resurrection of the Body, and the Casting out of the Wicked; on the ALTAR WALL, Angels drive the sinners into Hell and guide the elect to Paradise. On the lower part of the walls are medallion portraits of Homer, Dante, Virgil, Ovid, Horace, Lucan, and Empedocles, and scenes from classical myth and from Dante's 'Divine Comedy'. The Pietà in the recess on the right is also the work of Signorelli. On the Baroque altar is the 13C painting called the Madonna di San Brizio.

In the **Palazzo dei Papi,** immediately S. of the cathedral, begun in 1264 by Urban IV, and continued in 1296-1304, is installed the *MUSEO DELL'OPERA (9-12, 14-16; entrance at the top of the external stairs). In one huge hall is a miscellany of works of art (mostly from the cathedral) displayed in a charming old-fashioned manner. They include: *Statues of the Madonna in marble by *And. Pisano* and his school, by *Nino*

Pisano (1349), and (in wood), by *Giov. Pisano*. Among unfinished works by *Arnolfo di Cambio* are two damaged angels. The wood statue of Christ blessing is attrib. to an assistant of Maitani (1330). The paintings include parts of a fine polyptych by *Simone Martini;* a self-portrait and other works by *Signorelli,* and a Madonna by *Coppo di Marcovaldo* (1268). Outstanding among the metal work is the Reliquary of the Head of San Savino, by *Ugolino di Vieri;* and the collection of vestments is notable. Displayed are two sketches for the façade of the cathedral: as built with three gables (by Maitani), and with only one gable, now thought to be by Arnolfo di Cambio. The colossal figures of the Apostles (16-18C) which formerly lined the nave are stored in a room below not usually open.

In **Palazzo Faina**, to the right, is the *Museo Civico,* with a remarkable collection of Etruscan finds from the area.

GROUND FLOOR. To the left, well-displayed Etruscan antiquities from Orvieto, including a tomb from the necropolis. In the end room, finds from the Belvedere Temple (5C B.C.), and small bronzes.—To the r. of the entrance, finds from excavations in 1960-68 in the cemetery called 'Crocefisso del Tufo' (comp. p. 540). These include a charming collection of vases, terracottas, jewellery, bas-reliefs, etc. The so-called 'Venus of Cannicella' is an Etruscan copy of an Archaic Greek original.—On the TOP FLOOR the *Museo Faina* has an extensive collection of Greek vases of all types found in Etruscan tombs. There are beautiful views of the cathedral and valley from the windows.

Via Maitani leads W. to the church of San *Francesco,* built in the mid-13C. Here, in the presence of Edward I of England, took place the funeral of Prince Henry of Cornwall, murdered at Viterbo in March 1271; here also Boniface VIII canonized St Louis of France.

To the left farther on, in Via Ippolito Scalza, is the 14C church of *San Lorenzo de Arari,* which takes its name from an Etruscan altar beneath the altar-table. Above it is a pretty 12C ciborium. The curious frescoes include four stories from the Life of St Lawrence (1330; restored).

Via Scalza returns to Corso Cavour which leads W. to the church of *Sant'Andrea,* a 12C building with remains of 14C and 15C frescoes, and a fine twelve-sided campanile. Here in 1216 Innocent III proclaimed the Fourth Crusade and in 1281 Martin IV was crowned in the presence of Charles of Anjou. The sacristan (who lives at No. 17 Via Cipriano Manente, through the archway to the S. of the church) will admit to the excavations beneath the church. Here a 6C pavement from the primitive basilica overlies Etruscan and Roman remains. Here, also, are pieces of relief sculpture (8-9C ?) from a choir screen, embedded on the reverse side with Cosmatesque mosaic work (other pieces have been fashioned into a pulpit in the upper church). The Corso ends in P.ZA DELLA REPUBBLICA, the centre of the life of Orvieto. Here is *Palazzo Comunale,* built in 1216, with a façade of c. 1580 by Scalza. Via Loggia dei Mercanti, which leads from here to P.za de' Ranieri, is the most characteristic street of the old city. Beyond P.za della Repubblica, at the N.W. end of the town, is *San Giovenale,* possibly dating from 1004; it contains noteworthy frescoes by local artists (13-16C).

Palazzo del Popolo, in P.za del Popolo, a fine building in tufa, was begun in 1157 and later altered. A small market is held in the piazza. To the N.E. is **San Domenico,** the first church dedicated to St Dominic, built in 1233-64. In its former convent St Thomas Aquinas taught theology. The church has a pretty exterior; in the tall narrow interior are the *Tomb of Card. de Braye (d. 1282), by *Arnolfo di Cambio,* and the

Cappella Petrucci (below the main church, entered from a door in S. wall unlocked by sacristan), an interesting architectural work by *Sammicheli*. It also has various mementoes to St Thomas Aquinas.

Just off the road to the station (1½ km. from the Piazzale Cahen) is an *Etruscan Necropolis* (adm. daily) of the 4C B.C., with small but well-preserved chamber tombs.—The Premonstratensian abbey of *Santi Severo e Martirio*, dating from the 12C, lies S.W. of the city (2½ km. by road or 20 min. by footpath from the Porta Romana). Most interesting of the ruined buildings are the abbot's house, the former refectory (now the Chiesa del Crocifisso), and the original church with its twelve-sided campanile. About 1 km. farther on, at *Settecamini,* is another 4C Etruscan burial-ground.

FROM ORVIETO TO TODI, 48 km.; bus in 2 hrs. Beyond Orvieto station and the Paglia bridge the road bears to the right on N 79 bis, which climbs, at first steeply, to a height of 367 m, and then descends into the Tiber valley. The views are superb; the Tiber is crossed at (43 km.) the old walled village of *Pontecuti.*—48 km. *Todi,* see Rte 52.

About 5 km. farther on the route joins the lower valley of the Tiber, the most famous though not the longest of the rivers of Italy (comp. p. 580).—131 km. *Attigliano.* At *Lugnano in Teverina* (419 m), 10 km. N.E., the charming church, dating from the late 12C but altered in the 15C, contains a triptych by L'Alunno.—143 km. **Orte,** occupying the site of Etrusco-Roman *Horta* on the right bank of the Tiber, has a *Museo d'Arte Sacra* (Key at No. 6 P.za Colonna), occupying the former Romanesque church of San Silvestro (good campanile). The collection includes a Madonna in mosaic (8C, restored) from the old basilica of St Peter in Rome; a Madonna by Taddeo di Bartolo; a 13C panel of St Francis; four panels depicting the life of S. Egidio and a reliquary cross, by Vannuccio di Vivo da Siena (1352).—The road passes over the Nera near its confluence with the Tiber, crosses the main river twice, and at (153 km.) *Magliano Sabina,* with good views w. towards the Monti Cimini, passes beneath the Via Flaminia (Rte 54).

At 186 km. (Exit Roma Nord) a slip road joins the Via Tiberina on the right bank of the Tiber.—218 km. **Rome.**

The autostrada crosses the river for the last time.—At (204 km.) *Settebagni* another slip road joins the Via Salaria on the left bank, affording the most direct approach to the centre of (220 km.) **Rome,** while the autostrada joins the ring road 4 km. farther on.

49   SIENA TO VITERBO AND ROME

ROAD (VIA CASSIA: N 2). 224 km.—43 km. *San Quírico d'Órcia.*—92 km. *Acquapendente.*—112 km. *Bolsena.*—127 km. *Montefiascone.*—143 km. **Viterbo.**—156 km. *Vetralla.*—174 km. *Sutri.*—224 km. **Rome.** Express bus (S.I.T.A.), twice weekly (Mon & Sat) in 4¾ hrs.

RAILWAY, 254 km. in 3¼-4 hrs; a change is usually necessary at *Chiusi.*

The Via Cassia leaves Siena by the Porta Romana.—At (27 km.) *Buonconvento,* on the Ombrone, where the Emp. Henry VII died in 1313, the parish church has an altarpiece by Matteo di Giovanni and a triptych by Sano di Pietro. The small gallery adjoining (undergoing rearrangement) has further notable Sienese paintings. Monte Oliveto (p. 526) lies 9 km. to the left.—At (37 km.) *Torrenieri* the road crosses the Asso and the local railway linking Siena with Grosseto.

*Montalcino, 9 km. S.W., is a beautifully situated little walled town (567 m). It is famed for its wine, the remarkably long-lived Brunello, considered by some experts to be Italy's finest. The last bulwark of Sienese independence, it is crowned by a *Rocca* of 1361. In P.za Cavour the *Museo Civico* contains Sienese paintings (Sano di Pietro, Luca di Tommè, Bartolo di Fredi) and an illuminated bible (12C). The old pharmacy of the neighbouring *Ospedale,* frescoed by Vincenzo Tamagni of San Gimignano, a pupil of Sodoma, houses archæological remains (neolithic to medieval). *Sant'Agostino* has a good rose window and frescoes of the 14C Sienese school; the adjacent seminary houses the *Museo Diocesano* (open daily 9-12, 16-18), with more Sienese primitives, a painted Cross (12-13C), a Crucifixion by Sodoma, and good polychrome wooden statues.—The splendid Benedictine abbey *Church of SANT'ANTIMO (open Sun 9-12, 14-17; other days ask for custodian in the village of Castelnuovo dell'Abate), 8 km. S., lies in a remarkable position enclosed within low hills. It dates mainly from 1118 and preserves two doorways and a crypt of its 9C predecessor, supposedly founded by Charlemagne. The interior (entered at present by a sculptured doorway in the S. Side) is remarkable for its luminous effect, caused by the church having (in part) been built of alabaster. It has fine capitals and pretty apse chapels. The bell-tower, off the N. aisle, has an ingenious dome. In the Sacristy (S. aisle) is a primitive vault and monochrome frescoes. The Crypt has been closed for restoration. In the S. aisle a spiral stair leads up to the Matroneum, fitted up with rooms (15C fireplace, wall-paintings, etc.) from which there is a good view of the church. A Romanesque wooden Crucifixion and Madonna have been removed from here to the church in Castelnuovo dell'Abate. The ruined Refectory and Chapter House now serve as barns.

The road becomes prettier, climbing to (43 km.) **San Quirico d'Órcia** (409 m), which has a splendid Romanesque *Collegiata;* the beautiful S. portal, in the manner of Giov. Pisano, with lions and caryatids, was damaged by shell-fire, as was the Gothic transeptal doorway (1298), but the W. door was unharmed. Inside are a triptych by Sano di Pietro and good stalls of 1502.

FROM SAN QUIRICO D'ORCIA TO CITTÀ DELLA PIEVE, N 146, an important link road (54 km.), well served by buses, between the two main Tuscan highways.—9 km. **Pienza** (491 m) is a charming compact little town, the birthplace in 1405 of Æneas Silvius Piccolomini, afterwards Pius II, who changed its name from *Corsignano* by papal bull (1462) after charging Bernardo Rossellino to make it a centre of art. The *P.za Pio II* is a remarkable example of the 15C Florentine style. The *DUOMO, which has had to be shored up at the E. end, is noteworthy for its fine series of altarpieces painted for the church by Giov. di Paolo, Matt. di Giovanni, Vecchietta, and Sano di Pietro, and for stalls of 1462; in the baptistry below it is a font by Rossellino. The *Palazzo Piccolomini*, on the W. side, begun by Pius II and finished by Pius III, his nephew, is considered Rossellino's masterpiece. The interesting interior may be visited daily, 10-13, 14 or 15-16 or 18. Opposite is the *Palazzo Ammannati,* built by Card. Ammannati of Pavia. In the piazza also are the handsome *Palazzo Comunale* (N. side), the *Palazzo Vescovile* (E. side), and the *Palazzo dei Canonici,* now the MUSEO (open 10-13, 14-16 or 18), containing tapestries, paintings of the Sienese school, an antiphonal illuminated by Sano di Pietro, and the English embroidered *Cope of Pius II. San Francesco,* an early Gothic church behind the Palazzo Piccolomini, and the 12C church of the *Pieve,* S. of the town, are relics of the earlier town of Corsignano.

22 km. **Montepulciano** (14,200 inhab.) is a dignified and interesting town on a hilltop (l.; 665 m) commanding the S.E. part of Tuscany and Umbria. It was the birthplace of and gave its late-Latin name to Politian

(Angelo Ambrogini, 1454-94), the tutor of Lorenzo de'Medici, and perhaps the most original genius among writers of his period. Another distinguished native was Card. Bellarmine (Roberto Bellarmino, 1542-1621), the bogy of British Protestants in James I's days. The town is noted for its wines. Outside the *Porta al Prato* stands the 14C church of *Sant'Agnese.* Inside the gate Via Roma leads up to Via Cavour. Immediately to the left in Via Roma is *Palazzo Tarugi* (No. 82) by Vignola, and, opposite, the handsome *Palazzo Avignonesi* (No. 91), attributed to the same artist. A little farther on the right is *Palazzo Bucelli* (No. 73) with Etruscan urns, reliefs, and inscriptions embedded in its walls. The church of *Sant'Agostino,* farther on (r.) has a good *Façade by Michelozzo, who also carved the high relief over the door. Inside is a Crucifixion by Lor. di Credi (3rd N. altar) and St Bernardine of Siena by Giov. di Paolo (2nd S. altar). Opposite the church is an old tower house with a quaint statue. Via Roma continues to climb steeply to reach the arcaded market; here it joins Via di Voltaia nel Corso which continues left. On the left are the huge *Palazzo Cervini,* begun for Marcellus II before his pontificate, perhaps by Ant. Sangallo the Elder; then (No. 55) *Palazzo Grugni,* with a balconied portal by Vignola; and the church of the *Gesù,* with a Baroque interior by And. del Pozzo. In Via Poliziano, reached by continuing along Via Garibaldi, are the 14C house where Politian was born (No. 5; plaque), and, outside the town wall, the church of *Santa Maria* (13C) containing a small panel of the Madonna and Child (end of N. aisle) attrib. to the school of Duccio, and commanding a good view. The road now skirts the rebuilt *Fortezza* and re-enters the walls by Via della Fortezza to reach the *P.za Grande with a pretty fountain. Here stands the DUOMO (1592-1630).

Inside is a splendid *Triptych at the high altar, by *Taddeo di Bartolo.* The fragments of the tomb of Bart. Aragazzi, secretary to Pope Martin V, by *Michelozzo* (1427-36), include the statue of the defunct (r. of W. door), two bas-reliefs on the first two nave pillars, two statues on either side of the high altar, a statue in a niche on r. of high altar, and a frieze of putti and festoons on the high altar. In 1st chap. in N. aisle, a Della Robbia tabernacle surrounds a bas-relief of the Madonna attrib. to *Bened. da Maiano,* which is flanked by two early statues of prophets, attrib. to *Tino da Camaino.* The font is by *Giov. di Agostino.* In the N. aisle is a Madonna by *Sano di Pietro.*

In the same square are two mansions by Sangallo and (on the W. side) the 14C *Palazzo Comunale* (from the tower of which there is a view). In the characteristic Via Ricci (Renaissance mansions) is the Gothic *Museo Civico* (adm. 10.30-12.30, 16.30-19.30; Mon closed) with a small gallery of paintings of the Tuscan and Umbrian schools. Via del Poggi leads to the church of *Santa Lucia* with a *Madonna by Signorelli in an inconspicuous little chapel to the r. (locked; light switch behind grille operated by a rod). A road decends the hill outside the walls to the church of the *MADONNA DI SAN BIAGIO, approached by a noble cypress avenue. This graceful structure by Ant. da Sangallo the Elder (1518-45), has a beautiful interior. The Canons' House nearby is also by Sangallo.

Montepulciano railway station, on the Siena-Chiusi line, is in the Val di Chiana, 10 km. E. of the town.

The road continues S.E. to the pleasant village of (29 km.) *Chianciano Vecchia* where a Museo d'Arte Sacra has a collection of Sienese and Florentine paintings.—31 km. **Chianciano Terme** (455 m.) is a frequented spa with warm saline and chalybeate waters, and a season lasting from mid-April to the end of October. Numerous hotels and pensions cater for visitors. The place was known to the Romans as *Fontes Clusinae*. The *Acqua Santa* waters are taken internally for liver complaints; the *Sillene* spring is used for baths.—The road goes on over the Autostrada del Sole and, beyond (42 km.) **Chiusi** (Rte 48), passes the railway station of *Chiusi-Chianciano Terme* before joining N 71.—52 km. *Città della Pieve*, see p. 588.

Beyond San Quírico d'Órcia the Via Cassia passes just below (48 km.) *Bagno Vignoni* (r.), a little thermal station, and crosses the Órcia, which farther on is well seen (l.) from a sharp rise.—At 63 km. the main road now keeps right, traversing the watershed between the Órcia and the Páglia by a long tunnel, while the old road rises steeply viâ *Le Conie* to *Radicófani* (783 m; 10 km.), strikingly placed on a basaltic hill. It preserves some remains of a castle built by the English pope Hadrian IV, in which Ghino di Tacco imprisoned the Abbot of Cluny, as related in the 'Decameron'. The church of San Pietro has Della Robbia work, and the Rocca is being restored. Just outside the town, the Palazzo La Posta was used as a hotel by Montaigne, Chateaubriand, and Dickens.

Buses (coming from Chiusi or Siena) run from Radicófani to the summer resorts and winter-sporting centres on the slopes of Monte Amiata, to the W. The main access road leaves the old road at *Le Conie* (see above), passing above the N 2 in its tunnel.—20 km. **Abbadia San Salvatore** (812 m), an ancient little hill-town, takes name from a once powerful Cistercian abbey. It has now been developed as a summer and winter resort. The Romanesque *CHURCH, founded in 743, was rebuilt in 1036 and restored in 16C. It has a 12C Crucifix, frescoes by Giuseppe Nosini, and a huge crypt (8C) with good capitals. The Medieval quarter of the town is of exceptional interest. To the W. rises **Monte Amiata** (1738 m), the highest point in Southern Tuscany, noted for its rich mercury (cinnabar) deposits. The ascent of this extinct tree-clad volcano (wide view) can now be made by a steep road (13 km.); there are refuges for climbers, cableways, and ski-lifts.—24 km. *Piancastagnâio*, amid chestnut groves, has the impressive Palazzo Bourbon del Monte.—36 km. *Santa Fiora* (687 m) has terracottas by And. Della Robbia in its parish church.—Some of the buses go on viâ (43 km.) *Arcidosso* (p. 558) to (47 km.) *Castel del Piano* (632 m), another hill resort, from which Monte Amiata may be approached viâ the Piano di Macinâie, a winter-sporting plateau.

72 km. The old and new roads rejoin in the valley of the Páglia which is now followed and, at 89 km., crossed by the Ponte Gregoriano. A sharp rise brings the road to (92 km.) **Acquapendente** (423 m), an attractive little resort (6000 inhab.), named after its cascades. The 18C *Cathedral* covers an early Romanesque crypt and contains two reliefs by Agost. di Duccio. Hieronymus Fabricius (1537-1619), the master of William Harvey at Padua, was a native of the place.—From (100 km.) *San Lorenzo Nuovo*, situated in the Monti Volsini at the crossing of the road from Orvieto to Pitigliano, N 2 descends to follow the N. shore of Lake Bolsena.

112 km. **Bolsena** (315 m; 4000 inhab.), on the lake shore, was founded by refugees from Volsinii (Orvieto) in 280 B.C.

The town is famous for the miracle of 1263, when a Bohemian priest was convinced of the Real Presence by the dropping of blood from the Host on the altar linen. It was in commemoration of this miracle that Urban IV (1261-64) instituted the feast day of Corpus Domini and ordered the building of the cathedral at Orvieto. The reliquary containing the linen cloth of the miracle is kept in the Cappella del Corporale at Orvieto.

The 11C church of SANTA CRISTINA has an elegant Renaissance façade (1494), flanked on either side by later additions to the church. Two lunettes are filled with reliefs of the Robbian school. Within, to the right of the apse, which has a polyptych by Sano di Pietro, are a chapel with 15C frescoes of the Sienese school, and another adorned with a St Lucy of the Della Robbia school. A good Romanesque door in the N. aisle admits to the *Cappella del Miracolo,* where are preserved the altar stones marked with Christ's blood. Steps descend to a *Grotto* with a good altarpiece, a statue of St Christina by Giov. Della Robbia, and a 9C tabernacle; to the E. are *Catacombs,* to the W. a burial-place of the Lombard period. The *Castle* dates from the 13-14C and houses a small museum of Etruscan and Roman remains.—To the N. of the town are remains of a Roman amphitheatre, affording a splendid view of the lake.

The **Lago di Bolsena** is the classical *Volsiniensis Lacus,* named after the inhabitants of Volsinii or Velsina (see below). The northernmost and the largest of the three volcanic lakes in northern Lazio, it occupies a large crater, in the Monti Volsini, 8½ m. long from N. to S. and 7½ m. across, with a circumference of 28 m. and a maximum depth of 146 metres. In it are two small islands. The *Isola Bisentina* has two buildings attr. to Antonio da Sangallo the Younger: the Palazzo Farnese and the church of SS Giacomo e Cristoforo, with a cupola by Vignola. Some of the Calvary chapels that ascend the hill contain remains of frescoes by a follower of Benozzo Gozzoli. On the *Isola Martana* Amalaswintha, queen of the Ostrogoths, was strangled in 532 by her cousin Theodahad, whom she had chosen to share her throne. The lake abounds in eels and other fish. Dante ('Purgatorio', xxiv) mentions Pope Martin IV, who is believed to have died of a surfeit of eels. A road (60 km.) encircles the lake, serving the villages of Marta, Capodimonte, and Valentano on the S. and W. shores.

A hilly road, climbing 229 m. in 7 km., runs E.N.E. out of Bolsena, joining N71 just S. of (9 km.) *Poggio di Biagio* (p. 589).—22 km. *Orvieto.*

The road continues round the E. shore.—119 km. On the right, between the road and the lake, is *Bolsena British Military Cemetery,* with 600 graves of those who fell in action in June 1944 between Lake Bolsena and Orvieto. The woods near the cemetery later became the Advanced Headquarters of the Allied Armies in Italy.

127 km. **Montefiascone** (12,100 inhab.) stands on a hill (560 m) at the S.E. edge of Lake Bolsena, of which it commands a magnificent view. The town was perhaps originally Etruscan; it became a Roman municipium; as a medieval commune it was involved in the struggles between the papacy and the empire. The Romanesque church of *San Flaviano* is on two levels. The façade (1262) has a Gothic portal. The lower church has splendid capitals and substantial remains of frescoes (15C). To the right of the main entrance is the famous tomb slab of Bishop Fugger of Augsburg, with its strange epitaph: 'Est est est pr(opter) nim(ium) est hic Jo(annes) de Foucris do(minus) meus mortuus est.'

The story is that the prelate used to send his servant in advance to mark with the word 'est' the inns where good wine was to be found; at Montefiascone the servant found such exquisite wine that he wrote 'est, est, est', with the result that his master drank overmuch and died. The wine of the district is called 'Est, est, est' to this day.

In the centre of the town is the *Duomo,* attributed to Sammicheli (1519), but continued and the dome added during the 17C by C. Fontana. James Stuart and Clementina Sobieska were married here in 1719 before taking up residence in Rome. Farther on (r.) is the small Romanesque church of *Sant'Andrea,* with interesting capitals. At the top of the town the ruins of the *Rocca Papale* command a good view of the lake.

This route joins N71, coming from Arezzo (Rte 46), then descends a steep hill to (129km.) *Montefiascone Station,* and follows the railway.

143km. **VITERBO** (325 m), once a rival of Rome as the residence of the popes, is a walled town (57,000 inhab.) with medieval buildings of great interest. The lion, the ancient symbol of the town, recurs frequently as a sculptural motif. The town is justly famous for its many beautiful fountains.

Car Parks in P.za della Rocca and P.za dei Caduti.
Railway Stations. *Porta Fiorentina,* at the N. end of the town, for Orte, and for Rome viâ Capranica-Sutri; *Porta Romana,* an intermediate stop on the latter line; *Nord,* adjoining Porta Fiorentina, for Rome viâ Civita Castellana.
Post Office, Via Ascenzi.—TOURIST OFFICE, 16, P.za dei Caduti.
Buses to *Vetralla, Capránica, Sutri, La Storta,* and *Rome,* see p. 540.—Also to *La Quercia, Bagnaia, Orte,* and *Terni;* viâ Tuscánia to *Cellere,* to *Montalto di Castro,* and to *Valentano;* viâ Montefiascone to *Capodimonte, Valentano, Farnese,* and to *Pitigliano;* also to *Manciano;* viâ Montefiascone to *Bolsena, Acquapendente,* and *Proceno;* viâ Montefiascone and viâ Bagnorégio to *Orvieto;* viâ Vetralla to *Tarquinia* and *Civitavécchia;* viâ Bolsena and Acquapendente to *Siena,* and *Florence.*

History. Viterbo, a minor castle in the 8C, was for centuries in dispute between the papacy and the empire. For a short time, in 1095, it was a free commune; in 1145 it gave refuge to Eugenius III (1145-53); in 1157 it was raised to the dignity of a city; and in 1243 the emperor Frederick II unsuccessfully besieged it. In 1257 Alexander IV chose the city as his residence. Five popes were elected at Viterbo, Martin IV (1281-85) being the last, and four died here. During this short period Viterbo grew in importance at the expense of Rome. The struggle between the two cities lasted some three centuries. After the removal in 1309 of the popes to Avignon, Viterbo fell a prey to faction, became subject to the tyranny of the Di Vico family, and ultimately declined.

In the Second World War Viterbo suffered heavy damage from bombardment.

Via Cassia runs past the *Giardino Pubblico* to *Porta Fiorentina.* Within the gate opens PIAZZA DELLA ROCCA, with a fountain by Raffaele da Montelupo, altered by Vignola. It is dominated by the *Rocca,* or castle of Card. Albornoz (1354), many times altered and enlarged. Via Cairoli leads to the busy P.za dei Caduti, in the centre of which stands the small octagonal oratory of *Santa Maria della Peste* (1494). On the left is the deconsecrated Renaissance church of *San Giovanni Battista* (1515). Via Ascenzi mounts past *Santa Maria della Salute,* a small 14C church built on a centralized plan with a fine sculpted *Portal, then threads an archway into PIAZZA DEL PLEBISCITO, the centre of the town, and the junction of numerous busy roads. On its W. side is the *Palazzo Comunale,* begun in 1460, with a picturesque open courtyard containing a fountain and Etruscan fragments. On the first floor (entered from No. 1 Via Ascenzi; shown on request) are rooms with 15-17C frescoes and a Baroque chapel. On the N. side of the piazza stands the *Palazzo del Podestà* of 1247, with a slender tower of 1487. To the E. is the Romanesque church of *Sant'Angelo,* much altered in the 18C.

Embedded in the façade is a Roman sarcophagus said to contain the body of Galiana, a medieval maiden whose beauty caused a war between Viterbo and Rome, and whose purity was such that, when she drank, the wine was said to be seen passing down her throat.

Off Via San Lorenzo, which runs S. from P.za del Plebiscito, stands (r.) the rambling *Palazzo Chigi,* a fine Renaissance building of the 15C, and, to the S., in an attractive old market square, the Romanesque church of the *Gesù* of the 11C (later restored; kept locked). In this church, in March 1271, Prince Henry of Cornwall, nephew of Henry III of England and son of Richard Plantagenet, king of the Romans, was murdered at the altar by Simon and Gui de Montfort in revenge for the death of their father Simon at the battle of Evesham in 1265. At the end of the street is the shaded P.za della Morte, with a fountain and three bays of a 12C colonnade. To the W. (r.) is the old *Ponte del Duomo*, with visible remains of its Etruscan origins. Beyond the bridge the hospital occupies the restored 15C *Palazzo Farnese*, the supposed birthplace of Paul III (Aless. Farnese). The secluded *PIAZZA SAN LORENZO is a charming survival of the Middle Ages, on the site of the ancient acropolis. On the S. side is the *Casa di Valentino della Pagnotta* (late 13C; reconstructed after war damage). On the N. side rises the ***Palazzo Papale** (c. 1266), used as the episcopal palace since the 15C, with an elegant Gothic loggia.

The large and sombre hall (usually open) at the top of the steps, witnessed the elections of Popes Gregory X (1271), John XXI (1276), and Martin IV (1281). Intrigues protracted the first of these elections for two years, and Raniero Gatti, captain of the people of Viterbo, forced a decision—on the advice of St Bonaventura—by shutting the electors in the palace, then removing the roof of the hall, and finally reducing the food supply. The holes made in the floor for the cardinals' tent-pegs are still visible. It was Gregory X who made the rules under which conclaves are held to this day.—John XXI died of injuries when the ceiling of the new wing collapsed on his head in 1277.

On the W. side of the square is the Romanesque **Cathedral** of *San Lorenzo*, built in 1192, with a façade erected after 1560. The fine campanile dates from late in the 14C. The nave arcades have good capitals. On the interior W. wall is a tomb figure of John XXI; the panel showing Christ blessing, in the left aisle, is attributed to Gerolamo da Cremona. To the left of the high altar a panel representing the Madonna della Carbonara is a good 12C work. The floor retains some 12C mosaic. The font in the right aisle has a basin by Fr. da Ancona (1470). Over the sacristy door is a bust attrib. to Canova. From the sacristy (if closed, apply at the Curia Vescovile in Palazzo Papale) is the entrance to the Chapter House library with the 'Pantheon' of Gottofredo Tignosi, which has 14C miniatures of great interest.

In a small square off Via Cardinale La Fontaine (which runs parallel to Via San Pellegrino, comp. below) stands the church of **Santa Maria Nuova**, one of the finest in the city. It dates from the 12C, and was restored after war damage. The central portal is surmounted by a head of Jupiter, and on the left angle of the façade is a tiny outdoor pulpit from which St Thomas Aquinas preached. The most notable features of the basilican interior are the excellent capitals and a fine *Triptych of Christ with saints, a panel of the 13C. The minute cloister probably dates from the Lombard period.

The Medieval *Contrada traversed by Via San Pellegrino, to the E. of P.za della Morte, affords an almost unspoiled picture of 13C Italy. In PIAZZA SAN PELLEGRINO are the church of *San Pellegrino* and *Palazzo degli Alessandri*, a severe 13C building. Via San Pietro continues S.E. to Porta San Pietro, outside which Via delle Fortezze skirts the city walls. The *Porta Romana*, a busy entrance to the city, was rebuilt in 1653. Just beyond it rises the massive campanile, in part 9C Romanesque, of the church of **San Sisto** (restored). Its fine basilican interior has a splendid raised choir with massive pillars. It contains a high altar composed of

4-5C architectural fragments, to the right of which is a painting by Neri di Bicci. The last column in the N. aisle is interesting.

Outside Porta Romana Via Romana leads shortly to the prison, in the grounds of which (adm. only with special permission) stand the remains of the church of *Santa Maria in Gradi,* destroyed in the war, with the exception of its façade, but still retaining its splendid 13C cloister, built in Gothic style by Roman marble workers.
A second Renaissance cloister has at its centre a fountain of 1480.

Within the walls Via Garibaldi runs to P.za della Fontana Grande where the fountain, the finest and oldest in the city, was begun in 1206 by Bertoldo and Pietro di Giovanni, finished in 1279, and restored by Bened. da Perugia in 1424. To the right of Via Cavour (which leads directly to the centre) is the narrow Via Saffi, in which stands the *Casa Poscia,* a picturesque 14C house. Via della Pace and its continuation lead N.E. to the *Porta della Verità.* Just outside this gate is **Santa Maria della Verità,** a 12C church altered and decorated at later dates. On the W. wall is a damaged detached fresco of the Annunciation (copy of a fresco by Melozzo da Forlì in the Pantheon in Rome) and Saints, attrib. to Lorenzo da Viterbo. The Cappella Mazzatosta is decorated with *Frescoes by *Lorenzo da Viterbo* (1469; restored). The convent on the N. side now houses the **Museo Civico** (8.30-14.30; Oct-April 9-16; fest. 9-13; closed Mon). Rooms leading off the N.E. corner of the splendid *Cloister* (of which three walks date from the 13C and the fourth from the 14C) contain Etruscan antiquities.

ROOM I. Cases of finds from Bisenzio (end of 7C B.C.), pottery, small bronzes, etc.; vases, including Bucchero ware; terracotta votive statues from Bomarzo; finds from Norcia and Ferento.—ROOM II. Terracotta tombs; case of bronze ware and gold jewellery. Other ground-floor rooms are being restored to display Roman works.—FIRST FLOOR. The first rooms contain a marble sphinx by *Pasquale Romano* (signed and dated 1268) and a lion, both from Santa Maria in Gradi; St Bernard, by *Sano di Pietro;* an unglazed terracotta bust of Giov. Batt. Almadiani by *And. Della Robbia* (and a glazed lunette by his school); also a fine bronze ewer in the shape of a lion, an early 13C Sassanian work. In the main room the paintings include: *Antoniazzo Romano,* Madonna and Child, part of a larger work; a 13C Madonna and Child of the Byzantine school; and works by *Giov. Fr. Romanelli.* The most important pieces, however, are in restoration: the superb *Pietà by *Sebastiano del Piombo,* on the back of which are studies from the hand of the master, and a Flagellation attributed to him; and the Incredulity of St Thomas, a youthful work of *Salvator Rosa.*

Viale Raniero Capocci ranges the best preserved sector of the *Walls,* here battlemented and strengthened by towers. Via Mazzini, on the right within Porta della Verità, leads N. to *San Giovanni in Zoccoli,* a much restored 11C church with a rose window and handsome interior with a curious variety of capitals. It contains a primitive episcopal throne and a polyptych by Balletta (1441). The confined Via della Marrocca and Via dell'Orologio Vecchio descend to P.za delle Erbe (fountain of 1621) at the S. end of the long CORSO D'ITALIA, venue of the evening passeggiata.

From the N. end of the Corso the Via di Santa Rosa leads to the right (E.) to the church of *Santa Rosa* (1850), in which is preserved the body of St Rosa (d. 1252), who appeased the strife of the city and inspired it to resist Frederick II. The festival of her translation (3 Sept) is celebrated by a grand procession (traditional since 1663), when a great 'macchina' is carried through the streets. Its design is changed every 5 years (earlier designs displayed in the Museo Civico).

At the N. end of the town stands *San Francesco,* a Gothic church of 1237, restored after war damage. A 15C pulpit built into the façade records the preaching in 1426 of St Bernardine of Siena. Inside are the tombs of Adrian V (d. 1278), attr. to Arnolfo di Cambio, and of Clement IV (d. 1268) by Pietro di Oderisio.

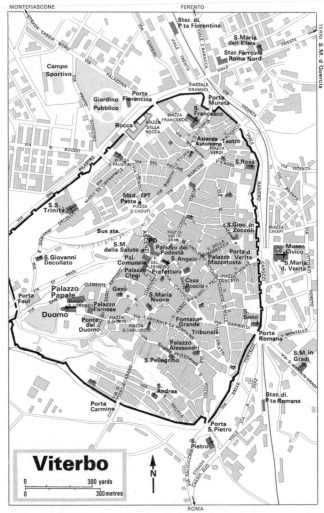

ENVIRONS. The church of Santa Maria della Quercia and the Villa Lante at Bagnáia are both easily reached by a bus which departs from the station every 20 min.—Crossing the railway from the Porta Fiorentina, the straight Viale Trieste runs to (3 km.) *La Quercia,* where the church of ***Santa Maria della Quercia** (closed 12–16) built in 1470–1525, is one of the finest flowerings of the Renaissance. The simple façade is by *Carlo di Mariotto* and *Dom. di Iacopo da Firenzuola* (1509) and the graceful main portal by *Giov. di Bernardino da Viterbo.* The terracotta lunettes above the three doors are by *Andrea della Robbia*. The massive campanile is the work of *Ambrogio da Milano*.

*INTERIOR. The ceiling is by Giov. di Pietro to a design of Ant. da Sangallo (1518-25). The splendid *Tabernacle, by *And. Bregno* (1490), behind the high altar, encloses a tile with a miraculous image of the Madonna. In the apse are fine inlaid stalls (1514) and an altarpiece by *Fra Bartolomeo, Mariotto Albertinelli*, and *Fra Paolino da Pistoia*. In the S. aisle is a Madonna and Child with St Anthony Abbot, by *Monaldo da Viterbo*(1519). From the right of the high altar a door leads to a cloister in two orders: the lower by *Daniele da Viterbo* (1487) was inspired by that of Santa Maria in Gradi, the upper part was added in the 16C. The other conventual buildings, including a second (17C) cloister, and the refectory, constructed by G. B. di Giuliano da Cortona (1519-39) to a design of Ant. da Sangallo the Younger, are now closed.

FROM VITERBO TO CIVITA CASTELLANA, by-roads, 49 km. Railway (45 km.) in 1¼ hrs. Beyond La Quercia (comp. above) N204 continues to (5 km.) *Bagnáia* where the P.za Castello is overlooked by a fine round crenellated tower and has a fountain designed by Vignola. From the piazza several pretty roads mount to the magnificent *Villa Lante, finished to Vignola's designs in 1578. The park, now sadly neglected, is open daily 9.30-12.30, 16-19, while the Italianate gardens are shown only in groups (tours at 10.30, 11.30, 17, and 18). The two pavilions, with frescoes by Tempesta, Raffaellino da Reggio, and G. B. Lombardelli, have been closed indefinitely.—At 9 km. a by-road follows the railway (r.) to (17 km.) *Soriano nel Cimino* (510 m), a small resort, overlooked by a 13C castle of the Orsini, now a prison. The imposing Palazzo Chigi, by Vignola (1562), has a fantastic fountain.

The ascent of the extinct volcano *Monte Cimino* (1053 m) may be made by road (8 km.) from Soriano. Some 45 m below the summit is the curious *Sasso Menicante*, a trachyte block 8½ m long which, ejected by the volcano has been caught by a projecting crag and become a rocking stone.

At the interesting town (27 km.) of *Vignanello* the moated Castello Ruspoli is well preserved; *Vallerano*, just across the railways line, has a fine church of 1609.— Beyond (37 km.) *Fabrica di Roma* the road descends past Falerii Novi to (49 km.) *Civita Castellana*, see Rte 54.

Bomarzo, 19 km. N.E. of Viterbo, off the N 204 (comp. above) shows remains of its Etruscan origins. It is famed for its *PARCO DEI MOSTRI (adm. daily) which contains gigantic sculpted animals and legendary figures, lop-sided buildings, and other exotic fantasies, constructed for Vicino Orsino (mid-16C). Near the entrance is an exquisite little formal temple attr. to Vignola.—*San Martino al Cimino*, 6 km. S. of Viterbo, has a splendid 13C Cistercian abbey church. On the road from Viterbo to Bagnoregio (bus), a by-road to the right by a school 7 km. from the Porta Fiorentina leads in c. 20 min. to the ruins of **Ferentium** (*Férento*). Originally Etruscan, this was a flourishing town in Roman times and the birthplace of the emperor Otho (A.D. 32), but it was destroyed by Viterbo in 1172 for heretically representing Christ on the Cross with open eyes. The most interesting ruins are those of a theatre, and of the church of San Bonifacio (9-10C). Recent excavations have revealed remains of the baths.—27 km. *Bagnoregio* was the birthplace of St Bonaventura (1221-74), the 'doctor seraphicus'. The village, once Balneum Regis, has pictures by Martino di Bartolomeo and Giov. di Paolo in its church. The picturesque old *Civita*, 2 km. E., is being undermined by erosion and is now almost deserted. Here the old cathedral of Bagnoregio has an interesting treasury and a fine Crucifix of the school of Donatello.—The road goes on to (48 km.) *Orvieto*.

FROM VITERBO VIA TUSCANIA TO TARQUINIA, 48 km. Buses from Viterbo to Tuscania and from Tuscania to Tarquinia. Just N. of the town the road forks left off the Via Cassia and gradually descends. At 5 km. a by-road runs S. for the *Bagni di Viterbo*, with spa baths (bus); a fork l. from this road leads to the *Bullicame*, a hot sulphur pool (65°C) mentioned by Dante ('Inferno', xiv, 79). About 5 km. farther S.W. (8 km. from the Porta Faul in Viterbo) is the 15C ruin of *Castel d'Asso*, which preserves the name of *Castellum Axia*, an Etruscan town. Below the castle are some scanty remains of the town and an extensive necropolis, with the two-stored Orioli tomb.—24 km. **Tuscania** (166 m), known until 1911 as *Toscanella*, is an attractively situated little town, retaining its old walls and containing attractive squares, fountains, and medieval buildings, some damaged in 1971 when an earthquake left 18 dead. Within the walls the *Duomo* contains a polyptych by And. di Bartolo, St Bernard with angels, by Sano di Pietro, and figures from a lost 15C altarpiece. In the Largo della Pace a chapel (key at No. 35, near by) contains extensive 15C frescoes. Just outside the Porta San Marco the 15C church of *Santa Maria del Riposo* has a richly decorated portal and an attractive cloister. A new archæological museum is being arranged here. On a hill to the E. of the town stands *San Pietro,* one of the most important churches of its date in Italy. The apse retains externally its 8C appearance, as does much of the interior, though the building was altered in the 12C and given its splendid Cosmatesque *Façade* (in which is embedded an Etruscan figure) in the 13C. The apse frescoes date from the 12C, the ciborium from 1093, and the altar screen and ambone are composed of 7-8C sculpted panels. There are substantial remains of a fine Cosmatesque pavement. The fine crypt has twenty columns of classical date, and a 14C fresco of local saints. The Bishop's Palace houses a small museum of Etruscan finds.—Lower down is the church of *Santa Maria Maggiore,* another fine church begun in the 8C but restyled and reconsecrated in 1207. It has a good sculpted portal of provincial workmanship, and contains a pulpit composed of early and late Romanesque panels, a primitive Gothic ciborium, and a Last Judgement frescoed in the 12C. To the S.W. is the Etruscan *Tomba della Regina.*—The road joins the Via Aurelia 2 km. N. of (48 km.) *Tarquinia* (Rte 50).

———

The VIA CIMINA provides an alternative continuation towards Rome, hilly but most attractive and 5½ km. shorter, across the MONTI CIMINI, rejoining N 2 at Gabelletta (see below). The road climbs continuously for 10 km. to the edge of the crater of *Monte Vénere* whose cone (838 m) rises above the *Lago di Vico.* This, the ancient *Lacus Ciminus,* is a crater-lake 11 m. round with a surface at 507 metres. The road follows the rim, passing above (15 km.) **Caprarola** (3½ km.; l.). The town (510 m; 4560 inhab.) is dominated by the *Villa Farnese* (adm. 8-12, 14-16 or 18), one of the most superb palaces of the Italian Renaissance (1547), built by Vignola on foundations of a castle started by Sangallo. Within is a fine circular courtyard. A magnificent staircase mounts to apartments richly decorated with stuccoes and frescoes by the Zuccari and Tempesta. The figure of St James the Greater, in the chapel, is supposed to be a portrait of Vignola. The vast park with its terraces and fountains is not open to the public without special permission; in it stands the *Palazzina,* the summer residence of the President of the Republic. To the S.W. of the palace stands the early 17C church of *Santa Teresa,* masterpiece of Girolamo Rainaldi.—21 km. **Ronciglione** (441 m; 6400 inhab.), once perhaps an Etruscan settlement, became a duchy of the Farnese family. A picturesque medieval quarter survives near the castle remains. In the P.za del Duomo stands a 16C fountain decorated with unicorn's heads. The churches of *Sant'Andrea* and *Santa Maria della Provvidenza* have good campanili, respectively 15C (by Galasto da Como) and 12-13C. By-roads descend to Capranica and to Sutri (see below), while the Via Cimina runs S.E. to join N 311 from Civita Castellana (comp. p. 607) at 33 km. and N 2 (see below).

From Viterbo the main road runs S. over open uplands.—156 km. **Vetralla** (300 m; 9970 inhab.) contains the Romanesque church of *San Francesco,* with 15-17C frescoes, a Vignolesque Palazzo Comunale, and an 18C cathedral. The church of *Santa Maria Furcassi,* 3 km. N.E., preserves the name of the ancient *Forum Cassii.*

Highway 1 bis crosses the hills westwards to (30 km.) *Tarquinia;* a minor road runs N. to (21 km.) *Tuscania* (comp. above); a by-road, between them, descends N.W. to (10 km.) the Etruscan necropolis of **Norchia,** where the tombs have the appearance of temples, with figured pediments, and where also can be seen romantic remains of medieval houses.

To the S. of Vetralla (reached viâ Cura, see below; bus to Blera) lie areas where, since 1956, the Swedish Institute in Rome, led by King Gustav VI Adolf, has been investigating Etruscan remains in an attempt to discover the origins of the Etruscan people.—12 km. *Blera* is the *Phleva* of the Etruscans. The remains of the ancient town include a necropolis with a conical tomb, two bridges, and a sarcophagus (in the church of Santa Maria).—About 11 km. S., reached by a minor road, is *Civitella Cesi,* c. 3 km. W. of which is the ancient citadel of *San Giovenale,* crowned by the ruins of a medieval castle. Here the Swedes have excavated the oldest Etruscan houses known, and abutments of bridges dating from the 6C B.C.—18 km. *Barbarano Romano,* a picturesque hill-village, is built near the site of an Etruscan township; here in 1963 was unearthed an obelisk, a form of monument not previously associated with the Etruscans.

The Via Cassia passes the Blera turning (comp. above) at (159 km.) *Cura,* just short of *Vetralla Station.*—At (164 km.) *Quércie d'Orlando* the Via Claudia (N493) starts its winding course W. of Lake Bracciano to Rome (77 km.; comp. the 'Blue Guide to Rome').—On the way in to (169 km.) **Capránica** (373 m; 3960 inhab.) the road passes the church of the *Madonna del Piano,* with frescoes attr. to Fr. Cozza or Ant. Carracci. The church of *San Francesco* contains a tomb of two Counts Anguillara attr. to Paolo Romano. The *Ospedale* has a fine Romanesque portal.—174 km. **Sutri** (291 m) is the ancient *Sutrium,* called the 'Gate of Etruria', which was captured by Camillus in 389 B.C. Its cession by the Lombard king Liutprand to Pope Gregory II in 730 marks the beginning of the papal temporal power. The rival popes Gregory VI and Sylvester III were deposed for simony by a synod held here in 1046. Sutri claims to be the birthplace of Pontius Pilate. The *Duomo,* though greatly altered, retains its campanile of 1207. The 18C interior contains remains of Cosmatesque pavement. Above the 2nd altar (l.) is an early 13C mosaic panel in the Byzantine style of Christ blessing. The crypt dates from the Lombard period. The *Municipio* contains a collection of Etruscan antiquities. Besides considerable remains of the walls, of a so-called Palace of Charlemagne, and of an amphitheatre (key at Municipio), there are several Etruscan tombs, one of which, converted into the church of the *Madonna del Parto,* retains fragmentary frescoes.—*Bassano Romano,* where the Palazzo Anguillera has rooms frescoed by Domenichino, is 8 km. S.W.

At (183 km.) *Gabelletta,* by the tiny *Lago Monterosi,* the Via Cimina (see above) comes in on the left. The Via Cassia now by-passes *Monterosi* (276 m; r.), then at (189 km.) *Sette Vene* leaves on the right a road for Lake Bracciano, and undulates across the Monti Sabatini, reaching a summit level of 295 m.—207 km. *Madonna di Bracciano,* the Etruscan *Veii,* 2 km. W., and the road into (224 km.) **Rome** are described in the 'Blue Guide to Rome'.

50   ROME TO PISA

ROAD, N1 (VIA AURELIA), 336km. viâ Grosseto and Livorno (between Tarquinia and Grosseto it is now a 'superstrada').—BUSES of the Lazzi Express from the Via Barberini daily except Sun to *Grosseto* in 3½ hrs; to *Livorno* in 6¼ hrs, going on to *Pisa* in 6¾ hrs.—AUTOSTRADA to Civitavecchia, leaving the Fiumicino road just E. of the airport. It passes under the Via Aurelia to stay inland of it to the junction c. 10km. N. of Civitavecchia.

RAILWAY, generally following the line of the road, to *Pisa Centrale,* 336km. in 3¼-4½ hrs. To *Orbetello,* 150km. in c. 1¾ hrs; to *Grosseto* 188km. in 2-2¼ hrs; to *Livorno Centrale,* 316km. in 3-4 hrs. This important trunk route is followed by the Rome Express and other international trains, with through carriages to Turin, Genoa, Paris, Marseille, etc. The night trains have sleeping-cars.

From Rome to (41km.) *Cerveteri,* see the 'Blue Guide to Rome'. Beyond the turning for Cerveteri the Via Aurelia approaches the sea, crossing the railway. On the right the conical peaks of the Tolfa rise to 430m.—53km. **Santa Severa,** a quiet seaside resort, occupies the site of *Pyrgi,* a Pelasgic town, once the chief port of Caere (Cerveteri).

Pyrgi was famous in antiquity for its Temple of Juno Lucina, sacked by the elder Dionysius of Syracuse in 384 B.C. In the locality are the ruins of a villa said to have been that of Nero's father Cn. Domitius Ahenobarbus (consul A.D. 32). The 14C concentric *Castle* contains, between its second and third wards, the litle 16C church of Santa Severa. On the seaward side of the Castle and connected with it by a wooden bridge, is an imposing cylindrical tower built over the foundations of a Norman fort. In 1957-64 excavations S. of the castle revealed the foundations of two Etruscan temples. The larger (Temple A), of the end of the Archaic period, has a large colonnaded pronaos and three cellae; the second (Temple B), smaller, with a single elongated cella, is older (c. 500 B.C.). Associated painted terracotta reliefs of a Gigantomachia (showing marked Greek influence) have been found; most important, in a small edifice between the temples, were discovered three folded *Sheets of gold leaf, with inscriptions in Phoenician and Etruscan recording the dedication to Astarte (Uni) by Thefarie Velianus, tyrant of Cære. A hoard of Athenian 'owls' and Syracusans coins may have belonged to the sanctuary treasury looted by Dionysius.

The road next passes the *Grottini,* a seaside colony for children, founded by Pius X.—62km. **Santa Marinella** is another attractive seaside resort. It occupies the site of the Roman station of *Ad Punicum* at the end of Cape Linaro. On a promontory E. of the town in 1966 was unearthed a lead plaque bearing one of the longest known Etruscan inscriptions. This came from a sanctuary (6C B.C.) of Minerva. Here also is a 16C *Castle* of the Odescalchi. On the right the summits of the Tolfa range are still visible; prominent, as the road passes the 'Boys' Town' (Villaggio del Fanciullo) founded in 1945, is Monte Paradiso (327m).

72km. **Civitavecchia,** a town of 46,700 inhab., is the modern port of Rome and a base of sea communication with Sardinia. It has been largely rebuilt since the war, and is visited for its renowned fish restaurants.

Railway Stations. *Maríttima,* on the dockside, for trains to Rome for those arriving by sea. Trains to the North pass through the main stn. only.

Buses to *Rome;* also to *Tolfa;* viâ Tarquinia to *Montalto di Castro, Canino,* and *Cellere;* to *Tuscania;* to *Monte Romano, Vetralla,* and *Viterbo;* to *Santa Marinella,* and *Santa Severa.*

Ships of the Soc. Tirrenia daily to *Olbia* and *Cagliari* and *Porto Torres* (Sardinia); also daily to *Golfo Aranci.*—HYDROFOIL to *Olbia.*

History. After the silting up of Ostia and to supplement his new harbour at Porto, Trajan instructed the architect Apollodorus c. 106 to build a new port here, called Centum Cellæ. Among its buildings was a splendid imperial villa, described by the younger Pliny. In 828 the port was destroyed by the Saracens and the inhabitants fled inland. In 855 Pope Leo IV established for them the village of Centocelle, which still exists, 14½ km. N. of the port. Later the population returned to their original home, which they now called *Civitas Vetula*, italianized into *Civitavecchia*. Thenceforth until modern times the city was included in the Papal States. Under the Renaissance popes Civitavecchia became one of the most important of the Mediterranean seaports. Gregory XII kept the pontifical fleet here; Sixtus V built the lighthouse (destroyed in the war); and Alexander VII commissioned Bernini to build the dock basin. Stendhal was consul here (after 1831), and wrote 'The Life of Henri Brulard'—in fact an autobiography.

The **Forte Michelangelo,** on the harbour, begun by Bramante in 1508 and continued by Ant. da Sangallo the Younger, was completed by Michelangelo. The central basin of Trajan's harbour and the docks are still of interest. The *Museo Archeologico Nazionale* (open 8–14 exc. Mon), in Largo Plebiscito, contains a good collection of local archæological finds.

Frescoes in the *Franciscan Church*, by the Japanese artist Hasegawa (1950–54) commemorate the Franciscan missionaries to Japan, who sailed from Civitavecchia and were martyred with many converts at Nagasaki in 1597.

About 4½ km. E., beyond the autostrada entrance, are the ruins of the *Thermæ Taurinæ*, baths built by Hadrian and enlarged by Trajan. The warm sulphur-impregnated waters are still effective in the treatment of rheumatism.

From Civitavecchia a hilly road winds inland to (22 km.) *Tolfa*, built on the ruins of an Etruscan town. Farther on, but just off the road (S.), are (36 km.) the ferruginous *Bagni di Stigliano.—*45 km. *Manziana* is on the Rome-Viterbo railway (viâ Capranica-Sutri).

Beyond Civitavecchia the road bears inland, with the railway now to seaward.—85 km. The road crosses the Mignone, flowing down from the volcanic Tolfa range. At the mouth of the stream is *Torre Bertolda,* or *Sant'Agostino,* supposed to be the spot where St Augustine found the child pouring the water of the sea into a hole in the sand—the image of a finite conception of infinity.

Two km. farther, N 1 bis diverges right viâ (14 km.) *Monte Romano* for (30 km.) *Vetralla* and (43 km.) *Viterbo* (Rte 49).

92 km. **TARQUINIA** stands on a hill (145 m) E. of the Via Aurelia, 3 km. from its railway station, and 5 km. from the sea. The town (13,100 inhab.), called *Corneto* until 1922, is close to the Etruscan *Tarquinii,* which was built on another hill to the E. Its numerous towers give it a characteristic air though its outline is obscured by ugly modern development. The ancient city and its great necropolis have yielded some of the most important Etruscan antiquities yet discovered.

History. *Tarquinii,* cradle of the 'great house of Tarquin', was one of the twelve Etruscan cities and probably the head of the Etruscan Confederation. It is said to have been founded by Tarchon, son or brother of the Lydian prince Tyrrhenus, who is made by Virgil to help Æneas against Turnus. Here sprang from a furrow Tages, son of Hercules, who taught the Etruscans the art of divination. Here also settled Demaratus of Corinth (c. 700 B.C.) whose son Lucius Tarquinius Priscus became the fifth king of Rome. As time went on, Tarquinii became a Roman colony and a municipium, but its fortunes gradually declined. Its ruin was hastened by the inroads of the Lombards and the Saracens. In the 8C or 9C it was deserted by its inhabitants, who founded *Corneto* on the opposite hill. In 1307 the inhabitants of Corneto completed its destruction. In 1489 the first recorded archæological 'dig' in modern times took place here.

At the entrance to the town (P.za Cavour) with the Tourist Office, stands the Gothic-Renaissance *Palazzo Vitelleschi* (1436–39), with a fine courtyard. It contains the ***Museo Nazionale Tarquiniese** (adm. 9-13, 16-19; winter 10-16; Sun 11-16; closed Mon).

In the courtyard are a collection of sarcophagi and sculptured reliefs and, in two rooms leading from this, the *Sarcophagus of Laris Palenas, who holds a scroll on which is an Etruscan inscription; sarcophagus of the so-called Magnate, which retains much of its original polychrome work; and the sarcophagus of the *Obesus, surmounted by a splendid figure of the defunct.—FIRST FLOOR. Room at top of stairs (l.): beautifully displayed polychrome *Group of two winged horses (4-3C), found on the Acropolis.—A room to the r. off the LOGGIA, is the middle one of three containing fine vases. The beautiful GREAT HALL (r.) has 5 cases of superb red-figured vases. *Case* 2. Amphora signed by Phintias (late 6C) with Apollo and Heracles fighting for the tripod, and Dionysus amid satyrs and mænads; *Case* 3. *Kylix, signed by Oltos and Euxitheos, with a meeting of the gods, and Dionysos in a quadriga between satyrs and mænads; Vase, by Charinos, shaped like a woman's head.—The centre room has cases with black- and red-figure vases and jewellery.—In the room to the left are more black-figure vases, with one in *Case* 2, reversed, of a funeral procession; *Case* 6. Amphora of the 'Fikellura' type, decorated with sphinxes, griffins and a hart; Casket in painted terracotta with horses and figures; *Case* 4. Amphora signed by Timotheos.—In the LOGGIA are funerary caskets and Italo-geometric work. Other rooms have been closed indefinitely.

SECOND FLOOR: At the N. end of the loggia (r.) is the tomb of Aurelio Mezzopane (1500), and a short series of rooms containing sculptured remains, and a small collection of paintings, including portraits of Count Nicolò Soderini and Pius VII by Batoni and Camuccini. The second room constitutes the CAPPELLA GENTILIZIA and the third contains a fine painted ceiling, and the remains of 15C *Frescoes. In the large SALONE D'ARMI stand five tombs, the frescoes having been removed from their original sites and re-erected to their original shape, including the *Tomba del Triclinio, most famous of all Tarquinian tombs.

Via Mazzini leads to the *Duomo,* with frescoes (1508) by Ant. da Viterbo, and is continued by Via di Porta Castello to the remains of the Castello in which stands the Romanesque church of *SANTA MARIA DI CASTELLO, begun in 1121 and consecrated in 1208. The façade contains Cosmatesque work signed by Pietro di Ranuccio (1143). The fine interior preserves remains of a Cosmatesque pergamo by Giovanni di Guittone (1208) and two plutei and a ciborium by Giovanni and Guittone, sons of Nicolò Ranucci (1168).—Opposite the Museum, a road leads out of the piazza to reach the church of *San Giovanni,* with a beautiful early-Gothic interior. From Piazza Cavour the main street leads up to Piazza Matteotti with the Post Office. In the picturesque medieval quarter to the N., behind the *Municipio,* are *San Pancrazio,* with a beautiful 13C design (disused), and the neighbouring towers of the *Palazzo dei Priori.* The Via di S. Pancrazio (r. of church) leads up to *San Martino* and SS *Annunziata* (follow signs). Farther up on a promontory with good views is *San Salvatore,* and returning towards the centre, *San Giacomo* (fine rose window).—From Piazza Matteotti, Via di Porta Tarquinia leads S. to the 13C convent and church of *San Francesco.*

The road leads on from San Francesco, through the Porta Tarquinia, to the vast ***Necropolis of Tarquinii** (tours start from the museum at every hour; car essential). The tombs are of immense interest and value for their painted interiors.

The paintings range from the first half of the 6C to the 2C B.C. The various phases are all represented: the Ionic influence of the 6C, the Attic influence of the 5C and, after a static period, the revival of the 4C, with the subsequent slow decadence. Unfortunately the opening of the tombs has, in many instances, hastened their deterioration; in one tomb, opened in 1823, the excavators found a warrior stretched on a bier who crumbled away on the admission of fresh air.

Weather, neglect, and misuse have all contributed to the general ruin. As a rule, the guide will show only the best examples. For a thorough visit special permission must be sought.

There are four main groups of tombs. Outside the Tarquinian gate: *Tomb of the Chase and Fishing* (mid-6C); *Tomb of the Lionesses* (6C); *Tomb of the Pulcella* (Young Girl; mid-5C), with a banqueting scene (damaged in the war); *Tomb of the Festoons* (2C); *Tomb of the Leopards* (early 5C), with banqueting scenes and processions; *Tomb of the Bacchantes* (end of 6C), with a bacchic scene.

Near the modern cemetery: *Tomb of the Dying Man* (end of 6C), with scenes of mourning (damaged); *Tomb of Typhon* (2C), of great size, with a central column, preceded by an altar, on which is a painted figure of a demon; *Tomb of the Shields* (3C), with banqueting scenes; *Tomb of the Cardinal* (3C), the largest of all, with four columns supporting a coffered ceiling; * *Tomb of the Ogre* (first half of 4C), with scenes of the infernal regions. Note the beautiful portrait of a maiden of the Velcha family.

About ½ km. farther on: *Tomb of the Painted Vases* (2nd half of 6C); *Tomb of the Old Man* (end of 6C), with an old man recumbent on a couch.

Last Group: * *Tomb of the Baron* (end of 6C), with figures of men and women standing and of youths on horseback; *Tomb of the Chariots* (early 5C); *Tomb of the Augurs* (mid-6C), with a cruel scene of a blindfold man tortured by the attacks of a fierce dog; * *Tomb of the Bulls* (first half of 6C), in good preservation, with a painting of Achilles lying in wait for Troilus.

The necropolis road reaches in 5 km. the junction with the Monte Romano road (comp. p. 553), where the turning on the left passes long stretches of medieval aqueduct. After a further 5 km. a yellow notice points left towards the so-called ACROPOLIS OF TARQUINII. After 1 km. a path (l.), signposted to the *Ara della Regina,* leads to the huge remains of an altar near to which the Winged Horses, now in the museum, were found. Skirting the hill are tracts of the old town walls.
Lido di Tarquinia, 6 km. S.W. of Tarquinia, has a long sandy beach. To the S. are scanty remains of the Roman Porto Clementino, finally destroyed in 1449, and extensive salt-flats.

110 km. *Montalto di Castro* is connected by bus with its station (2 km. l.). The medieval castle belonged to the Guglielmi.

FROM MONTALTO TO VALENTANO (N 312); 35 km.; bus in 1½ hrs. Some buses go on to Cantioniera Látera and Acquapendente (p. 543), 58 km. in 2½ hrs. The lonely road runs N.E. with arches of an aqueduct on the left, and, after 8 km., leaves on the left the road to the ruins of *Vulci,* one of the important cities of the Etruscans. Its immense *Necropolis* extends for many kilometres and has yielded innumerable vases, bronzes, and other antiquities now scattered in museums all over the world. The necropolis is dominated by the * *Cuccumella,* a gigantic hypogeum surrounded by a wall and containing a maze of passages, walls, and staircases. The city was situated on the river Fiora, the ravine of which is spanned, upstream, by the * *Ponte dell'Abbadia,* one of the most picturesque Etruscan survivals in Italy. The foundations of this steeply hump-backed bridge are late Etruscan, its arch Roman. The so-called *Abbadia,* beside the bridge, is really a small 12C castle. The return to Montalto (11 km.) may be made more directly from the farther side of the bridge.—20 km. *Canino.*—From (35 km.) *Valentano,* with a Farnese castle, a road on the right, skirting the S. shore of the Lago di Bolsena, leads to Viterbo (p. 544). The left branch keeps above the W. side of the lake for Acquapendente.

Beyond Montalto the road crosses the Fiora, and soon afterwards enters Tuscany.—Adjoining (132 km.) *Capalbio Station,* S. of the road, is the *Lago di Burano,* a lagoon 4 km. long. The medieval village of *Capalbio,* 10 km. N.E., is a centre of the Maremma game reserve.— About 3 km. farther on, a flat-topped hill (113 m) comes into view on the left; here stood the city of *Cosa,* founded by the Romans in 273 B.C. and later called *Ansedonia.* Near the beach are hotels and villas.

On top of the hill, surrounded by polygonal walls with 18 towers and three gates, are the remains of the *Capitolium,* a Roman temple with a triple cella (replacing an earlier Etruscan temple), dedicated to Jupiter, Juno, and Minerva. Excavations continue and a small museum has been set up. At the foot of the hill are an ancient outlet of the Lago di Burano and another channel called the Tagliata Etrusca. In the Torre della Tagliata Puccini composed part of 'Tosca'.

The road skirts on the left the extensive Laguna di Orbetello (see below). In the middle of the lagoon, on a sandy isthmus, 4 km. from (143 km.) *Orbetello Scalo* (which has grown up round the station), is **Orbetello,** centre of the fashionable 'Costa Argenta'. This town (14,300 inhab.) was an Etruscan colony and a place of importance in the Middle Ages. It was fortified in 1557 by the Spaniards, who left also the unusual *Polveriera* (powder-works). The *Cathedral,* rebuilt in 1600, preserves a lovely façade of 1376, and an early Romanesque marble altarpiece. The *Antiquarium* displays archaic sculpture in bronze and stone (6C B.C.). On clear mornings there is a wonderful view across the lagoon to Monte Argentario. In 1933 Italo Balbo led a formation flight to Chicago from here.

Monte Argentario (635 m; *View) is an almost circular peninsula joined to the mainland by three narrow strips (tómboli), the outer two, both pine-clad, defining the *Laguna di Orbetello;* the town of Orbetello occupies the central strip. Caravaggio met his end in the lagoon in 1609. On the hill, 5 km. from Orbetello, is the motherhouse of the Passionist Order, founded by St Paul of the Cross in 1720. A road encircles the mountain (26½ km.). On the S.E. side beyond *Póggio Pertuso* is the delightful *Port, Ércole,* a curious, sheltered little port with fortifications of the Spanish period (16C). The *Isola di Giannutri,* 11 m. off shore, has ruins of a Roman villa.

A bus runs from the station viâ Orbetello Città and (12 km.) *Calvello* to (13 km.) *Porta Santo Stefano,* on the N. coast. The rocky bays to the S. afford private beaches to exclusive summer hotels. From the port a motor vessel sails daily in 1 hr (in summer 3 times daily, also by hydrofoil) to the *Isola del Giglio,* 11 m W., with its little grey granite fortress-village.

FROM ORBETELLO TO PITIGLIANO, 62 km.; bus twice daily in 2¼ hrs. This route follows the Via Aurelia N. to (10½ km.) *Albinia,* turning right there on N74 up the Albenga valley, an unfrequented road with good scenery.—14 km. On the left a road leads to Scansano (29 km.; p. 558) viâ *Magliano in Toscana* (11 km.), an ancient walled town with a fine mainly 15C church; another church, outside the S.E. gate, with a Madonna by Neroccio; and, c. ½ hr's walk S.E., near the Romanesque ruin of San Bruzio, extensive remains of an Etruscan necropolis.— N74, passing (23 km.; r.) the Torre della Marsiliana, reaches (43 km.) *Manciano* (443 m), an old Sienese fortress.

From Manciano a secondary road runs N. to (51 km.) *Arcidosso* (p. 558). This route passes (6 km.) *Montemerano,* an old walled town whose church of San Giorgio has 15C frescoes. A Museum is to house the works of art from the church which include a fine pentaptych by Sano di Pietro (1458). 13 km. *Saturnia* has impressive prehistoric walls and medieval ramparts. There is a spa town nearby.

N74 continues.—62 km. **Pitigliano** (313 m), a wine-producing town on Etruscan foundations, was the seat of the Orsini and preserves their palazzo. About 8 km. N. is the half-derelict village of *Sovana,* in the Middle Ages a bishopric and the birthplace of Gregory VII (Hildebrand). Here are an Etruscan necropolis, a Romanesque cathedral, half-abandoned, and the remains of medieval palaces and of a keep of Gregory's family, the Aldobrandeschi. The Romanesque church of Santa Maria has a splendid ciborium (?9C).—Pitigliano is connected by bus with Grosseto (see below), Orvieto viâ Poggio di Biagio (see p. 589), Bolsena and Rome,

Montefiascone and Viterbo, and (not every day) Arcidosso (60 km. N.; p. 558).

Beyond Orbetello road and railway continue to skirt the lagoon. 146 km. *Quattro Strade.*—Beyond (150 km.) *Albinia* the road crosses the river Albenga.—Before (158 km.) *Fonteblanda* it crosses the Osa. A by-road leads left to *Talamone* (4 km.), once an Etruscan city said to have been founded by the Argonaut Telamon c. 1300 B.C. Here the Romans routed the Gauls in 225 B.C. and here Marius landed on his return from Africa in 87 B.C. The sculptured pediments of a temple have been removed to Florence. Here also Garibaldi and the Thousand put in on their way to Sicily in 1860 to collect arms and ammunition and to land a party for a feint attack on the Papal States.

On the left, between the road and the sea, rise the wooded roadless *Monti dell'Uccellina* (415 m) an area of natural beauty which in 1977 was designated a national park (10,000 hectares). Here the *Torre della Bella Marsilia* is the lonely remnant of the castle of Collecchio, home of the Marsili of Siena. In 1543 the castle was destroyed by the corsair Barbarossa and the entire household murdered save for the lovely Margherita, who was carried off to the harem of Sultan Suleiman the Magnificent, soon to become his legitimate sultana and the mother of Selim II. Farther N. are the romantic ruins of the 12C abbey of *San Rabano.*

Beyond the hills the road crosses the Ombrone, the classical Umbro, one of the chief rivers in Etruria.

185 km. **GROSSETO,** with 67,700 inhabitants, is the capital of the province of the same name, one of the nine in Tuscany. It is also the chief town of the *Maremma Toscana,* a district ravaged by malaria throughout the Middle Ages. Reclamation work, started on a considerable scale by the Lorraine grand dukes of Tuscany, has gradually drained the marshes; and a modern 'bonifica' on a large scale has been undertaken since 1930. The town was subject to Siena and later to Florence.

E.P.T., 21 Viale Ximenes.
Buses to *Marina di Grosseto* in ½ hr, going on less frequently to *Castiglione della Pescaia* in 1 hr and to *Follónica* in 2 hrs; to *Alberese* in ½ hr; to *Scansano* in 1½ hrs and *Roccalbegna* in 2½ hrs; to *Pitigliano* in 2½ hrs; to *Rome* in 3½ hrs; to *Siena* in 3-3¼ hrs (see below); to *Florence* in 4 hrs; to *Arezzo* in 6 hrs.—AIRPORT, with flights to Rome and Milan.

The old town is enclosed in a hexagonal *Rampart* of brick, built by the Medici in 1574-93; five of the bastions were laid out as public gardens by Grand Duke Leopold II in 1835; the sixth retains something of its military appearance.

The **Duomo,** founded c. 1190 and consecrated before 1250, is faced with red and white marble (1294); largely rebuilt in the 16C, it was indifferently restored in 1840-45. The campanile dates from 1402. On the S. side of the church are Gothic windows and a sculptured portal. In the interior are a stoup of 1509; a font (1470) by *Ant. di Ghino;* and the altar of the Madonna delle Grazie by the same artist, incorporating an Assumption by *Matt. di Giovanni.* San Francesco has a Crucifix attrib. as an early work to Duccio di Buoninsegna, dating probably from a rededication of the church in 1289. The MUSEO ARCHEOLOGICO E D'ARTE DELLA MAREMMA, (adm. 9.30-13, 16.30-19 exc. Wed; fest. 9.30-13), opened in 1975, contains Etruscan and Roman antiquities from Rusellæ, Vetulonia, and sites in the Maremma, including a black bowl on which is scratched the Etruscan alphabet of 22 letters. On the top floor, the Museo Diocesano displays a Last Judgement of the school of *Guido da Siena,* the Madonna of the Cherries, by *Sassetta,* and works by *Ugolino di Nerio* and *Naddo Ceccarelli.*

In the Etruscan period the plain between Grosseto and the sea was a shallow gulf, above which rose the islets of Vetulonia and Rusellæ. By the time of the Romans the gulf had become a salt lagoon called *Prelius;* by 1380 the lagoon had become a fresh-water lake, the *Lago di Castiglione,* which in turn gave place to malarial swamps, now drained and cultivated (comp. above).—The local seaside resorts are served by N 322, which provides an alternative route to Follónica (46 km.).—13 km. *Marina di Grosseto,* borders a wide sandy beach backed by extensive pinewoods. *Principina a Mare* lies 2 km. S. Farther up the coast stands (24 km.) **Castiglione della Pescaia,** the principal resort of the Maremma, on the site of the Roman *Salebro.* It has a castle and old walls.—27 km. *Riva del Sole,* another resort.—The road now crosses inland of the rocky *Punta Ala* to (46 km.) Follónica (see below).

About 8 km. N.E. of Grosseto, near the little spa of *Roselle Terme,* beside the ruined medieval Torre Moscona, may be traced the walls of **Rusellæ,** probably one of the cities of the Etruscan Confederation. It was pillaged in 935 by the Saracens and soon afterwards disappeared from history. Excavation work is in progress.

FROM GROSSETO TO ARCIDOSSO, 78 km.; bus to Scansano and Roccalbegna. At first the road follows the valley of the Ombrone. At (7 km.) *Istia* it bears E. and then S.E.—From (29 km.) *Scansano* (500 m), roads run S.E. to Montemerano and Manciano (p. 556), and S. to Magliano and Orbetello (p. 556). This road turns N.E.—58 km. *Roccalbegna* (522 m) has a crumbling Rocca and a decayed Romanesque church, from which an admirable painting by Ambr. Lorenzetti has been removed to the canonry.—At (65 km.) *Triana* the road from Manciano (p. 556) is joined.—78 km. *Arcidosso* (500 m) is connected by bus with Pitigliano and with Radicófani. Monte Amiata (p. 543) lies to the E. but is better ascended from the other side.

FROM GROSSETO TO SIENA there are two road routes: the main highway (N 73; bus in 3 hrs), and another viâ Paganico. The main route follows the Via Aurelia N. for 15 km. to the point where N 73 bears right.—35 km. *Roccastrada* (477 m) has a good town belfry. *Roccatederighi,* 13 km. N.W., is a typical old Tuscan hill-village.—At the walled village of (59 km.) *Monticiano* the 13C church of Sant'Agostino has frescoes in its chapter house by Bartolo di Fredi and others. At 63 km. a road on the left diverges for Massa Maríttima, and (73 km.) another to Colle Val d'Elsa.—On the left, 2½ km. towards Massa, is the ruined *Church of SAN GALGANO, built in a French Cistercian Gothic style of singular correctness (1218-88). The abbey, once the chief Cistercian house in Tuscany, was built on the old spot where St Galgano Guidotti made his hermitage in 1180. It fell on evil days in the 16C and was finally dissolved in 1652. It is now roofless and has a grass-grown nave, and is one of the most romantic sites in Tuscany. On the summit of the hill above is the circular Romanesque chapel of *Monte Siepi,* preserving frescoes by Ambr. Lorenzetti.—80 km. *Rosia,* with a Romanesque campanile, is 2 km. N. of the abbey of *Torri,* with its fine three-tiered cloister (11C; open weekdays only 9-12, 15-17).—94 km. *Siena,* see Rte 46.

The other road (N 223) is notable for its views (r.) over the Ombrone valley to Monte Amiata. It passes (25 km.) *Pagánico,* where the town walls were built in 1292-93 by Lando di Pietro and the 14C church contains contemporary Sienese *Frescoes attr. to Bartolo di Fredi; and (48 km.) *Bagni di Petriolo,* a little spa with 15C walls.—77 km. *Siena.*

After leaving Grosseto the modern Via Aurelia runs for a time inland; the Roman road followed the line of the coastal by-roads (see above).— 197 km. Junction of N 73 (comp. above). On a hill to the right stands *Montepescali,* the 'balcony of the Maremma'. The parish church has an altarpiece attrib. to Matteo di Giovanni, and San Niccolò, higher up, has frescoes by a follower of Bartolo di Fredi.—At 206 km. a by-road on the left leads in 5 km. to the hill-top village of *Vetulonia,* on the site of the city of **Vetulonia** or *Vetluna,* one of the most important members of the Etruscan Confederation. Here the Romans defeated the Gauls in 224 B.C. The Romans are said to have borrowed from Vetulonia the insignia of their magistrates—the fasces, curule chair, and toga prætexta—and the use of the brazen trumpet in war. There survive remains of the citadel wall and of a street of houses; the 8C necropolis (guide desirable) extends N.E. beyond the Via Aurelia. There is also a small Antiquarium. The domed Tumulo della Pietera, nearly 3 km. from the village, is the most remarkable tomb.

Among the wooded hills to the left are the iron mines that supply the furnaces of Follónica. The road reaches the sea again on the outskirts of (229 km.) **Follónica,** an expanding town (19,400 inhab.) situated on the gulf of the same name. It has a popular sandy beach and commands views of the island of Elba and of the promontory on which Piombino is situated. From the little *Cala Martina,* to the S., Garibaldi escaped by fishing boat in 1849.

A bus runs from Follónica to (19 km.) **Massa Maríttima** (399 m), birthplace of St Bernadine of Siena (1380-1444). The little town (10,600 inhab.), once an independent republic, preserves its old walls. Among the many dignified 13C buildings are the *Palazzo Comunale,* in which is a *Madonna with angels and saints, by Amb. Lorenzetti (c. 1330), and the *Palazzo del Podestà,* both in the principal piazza of the lower (and older) town. The severe *Cathedral* (San Cerbone), in the Pisan style, was begun c. 1228 and completed in 1287-1314. The story of its patron is sculptured above the main doorway. Within are a splendid font, with reliefs, by Giroldo di Iacopo (1267), and a 15C tabernacle rising from its centre; Lombard reliefs; and a *Madonna della Grazie (1316) by a close follower of Duccio, inspired by the Maestà in Siena. In the undercroft is the tomb of San Cerbone (d. c. 580), with scenes of his life sculptured by Goro di Gregorio (1324), statues by (?) Giov. Pisano, a Crucifixion (restored) painted by Segna di Bonaventura, also remains of 15C frescoes.

In the upper 'new' town are remains of the fortress erected by the Sienese after their conquest of Massa in 1337, and a tower of an older castle (1228); the *Palazzo delle Armi,* housing prehistoric and Etruscan finds; and, beyond the church of *Sant' Agostino* (c. 1300), the *School of Mines,* where a museum illustrates the riches of the metalliferous hills in the vicinity (iron, copper, and lead ores).—The road goes on to Volterra or to Siena (buses to each).

---

246 km. *Venturina* is at an important crossroads. *Campiglia Maríttima,* 4½ km. to the right, is a prosperous agricultural town commanding a wide view. To the left is the road for Campiglia station (2 km.) and for Piombino (14 km.).

Piombino, with 40,400 inhab., is situated at the S. end of the Massoncello promontory, once an island. It is an old seaport now entirely dominated by large and ugly metal works. Buses run from the station to *Porto Vecchio* (for the Elba boats) in 10 min.; to Volterra (2¾ hrs); and to Livorno (2¼ hrs); and a branch railway runs to Campiglia (see above) in 20 min.

At the N. end of the promontory, 15 km. by road from Piombino, is the castellated village preserving the name of **Populonia** (or *Pupluna*)—'sea-girt' in Macaulay's lay—possibly one of the cities of the Etruscan Confederation. Finds in the small *Museo Etrusco* (closed Sun) attest its continuous history from the Iron Age through to the Roman era. It was sacked by Sulla, by Totila, and by the Lombards. Its port and a *Necropolis* of the 9C-3C B.C. are partly occupied by the neighbouring *Porto Baratti,* where the iron ore from Elba was discharged and smelted.

From Piombino a car ferry plies c. 7 times daily, viâ *Cavo* (¾ hr) to *Portoferraio* (1½ hrs) on the N. coast of Elba (c. 18 times daily in June-Sept).—HYDROFOIL (much more expensive) 5 times a day (8 times in high summer).—Another vessel (daily) serves *Porto Azzurro* (1½ hrs) on the E. coast (twice daily in high summer).

ELBA, the Greek *Æthalia* and the Roman *Ilva,* an island 27 km. long and 18 km. across at its broadest, has been famous since ancient times for its iron ore (mentioned by Virgil) and more recently as Napoleon's place of exile in 1814-15. The inhabited part of the island has pretty green and wooded hills while other parts are barren and deserted. It produces a rich red dessert wine, the Vino Aleatico, and is noted for tunny-fishing. It has become fashionable as a summer resort, the climate being mild and sunny.

The chief town is **Portoferraio** (11,000 inhab.), with the great 'Ilva' blast furnaces. It was fortified by Cosimo I de' Medici, and occupied in 1795-97 by the British fleet. The fort still dominates the port, which is otherwise of little distinction. Napoleon's principal residence was the *Villetta dei Mulini,* overlooking the sea; it contains Napoleonic souvenirs.—Buses run to Marciana, to Cavo viâ Porto Azzurro and Rio Marina, to Capolíveri viâ Porto Azzurro, and to Marina di Campo.

A road runs W. from Portoferraio, partly along the N. coast, for Marciana. 8 km. *Biódola,* with a bungalow colony and camping sites amidst rich vegetation overlooking a fine sandy beach, and (11½ km.) *Procchio,* another bathing resort.—From (19 km.) *Marciana Marina* the road runs uphill to (21¼ km.) *Poggio,* the most fashionable resort on the island.—From (27 km.) *Marciana Alta* (cable-car to summit of Monte Capanne, 1018 m) the road goes on to the W. coast with an extension round the coast to Marina di Campo.—A turning on the left, 4½ km. from Portoferraio, leads to the *Villa San Martino,* Napoleon's summer residence, with a collection of modern Tuscan paintings.—Another turning on the left, at Procchio, leads directly to (17 km.) *Marina di Campo,* a bathing resort on the S. coast.—Overlooking a bay of the E. coast, the most beautiful part of the island, is *Porto Azzurro,* formerly *Porto Longone,* with its great Spanish fort of 1602 (now a prison), 15½ km. from Portoferraio. It is connected by road with *Rio Marina,* the chief ore-port, and *Cavo,* to the N.; and with the quaint old hill-village of *Capolíveri,* to the S.W.

Other motor vessels connect Portoferraio with *Livorno* (8¼ hrs; daily in summer, four times a week in winter) viâ Marciana Marina and the mountainous volcanic islets of *Capraia* and *Gorgona;* the low-lying islet of *Pianosa* is now a state prison. It is reached in 5 hrs by boat from Piombino viâ Rio Marina, Porto Azzurro, and Marina di Campo (once a week; permit required).

Via Aurelia regains the coast at (256 km.) *San Vincenzo* a large seaside resort. Just to the S., Riva degli Etruschi is a vast bungalow colony, while to the N. extends a nature reserve. In the hills to the right farther on are the villages of *Castagneto Carducci* and *Bólgheri,* where the poet Carducci spent his childhood (1838-49). Bólgheri is approached from (270 km.) *San Guido* by a splendid long avenue of cypresses, the subject of a poem by Carducci.—281 km. **Cécina** is the junction for Volterra. Buses run in 5 min. to *Cécina Mare.*

FROM CÉCINA TO VOLTERRA (N68), 42 km.; bus in 1¼ hrs; railway also to Saline di Volterra in 35 min; most of the trains come from Pisa.—N68 leaves the Via Aurelia 2 km. N. of Cécina and ascends the pretty valley of the river Cécina.— 32 km. *Saline di Volterra,* named from its salt deposits (which belong to the State), is at the junction of roads to Pomarance and to Pontedera (43 km. N.). There is a fine view of Volterra in the distance surrounded by hills.

42 km. **VOLTERRA** in a magnificent position on a precipitous hill (555 m) with open views in every direction across a splendid landscape of

rolling hills. It is a grim medieval walled town, the successor to an Etruscan city of much greater extent.

Railway Station at *Saline di Volterra,* 10 km. S.W. in the valley (bus connection with trains from P.za Martiri della Libertà), branch line to Cécina with through trains to Pisa.
Parking outside the walls (P.za Martiri della Libertà, Bastione Mediceo, etc); difficult on market days (Sat).
Tourist Office, Via Turazza (at the side of Palazzo dei Priori).
Buses to Pisa, Florence, Massa Marittima, San Gimignano and Siena.

History. *Velathri* was the northernmost of the 12 cities of the Confederation of Etruria Propria and one of the most prominent. In the 3C B.C. it became the Roman *Volaterrae.* It supported the cause of Marius against Sulla and underwent a siege of two years before falling to the troops of the latter. It gained some importance under the Lombards and was for a time the residence of the Lombard kings. After bitter struggles, it was subdued by Florence in 1361. Its natives included the satirist Persius Flaccus (A.D. 34-62), St Linus, the reputed successor of St Peter in the papal chair, and the painter Daniele Ricciarelli da Volterra (1509-66). Almost all the buildings are of a kind of limestone, *panchina,* the matrix of alabaster, which is found here in abundance and is used for making statuettes.

P.za Martiri della Libertà forms the S. entrance to the town. Via Marchesi leads left to *PIAZZA DEI PRIORI,* bordered by mansions medieval or in the medieval style. To the N.E. is the *Palazzo Pretorio* with its *Torre del Porcellino,* while on the S.W. side are the *Bishop's Palace,* originally the town granary, and the austere ***Palazzo dei Priori** (1208-54), now the town hall, the oldest building of its kind in Tuscany. The battlemented tower commands a fine view, but it has been closed for restoration for several years. On the first floor the council chamber has a 14C Florentine fresco (repainted). The floor above contains a charming little PICTURE GALLERY (open 9.30-13, 15-17.30; winter 9-12, 14-16.30; closed Mon). The two rooms are devoted almost entirely to Tuscan masters.

Taddeo di Bartolo, Madonna and saints, a triptych (1411); also two saints from another triptych; *Benvenuto di Giovanni,* *Nativity (1470); *Neri di Bicci,* SS. Sebastian, Bartholomew, and Nicholas of Bari (1478); *Luca Signorelli,* *Annunciation (1491), *Madonna and saints, two charming compositions; *Dom. Ghirlandaio,* Christ in glory, with saints and a donor; *Rosso Fiorentino,* *Descent from the Cross (1521); *Leonardo da Pistoia,* Madonna and saints (1516); *Dan. da Volterra,* Justice (fresco). The Madonna enthroned with four saints is a triptych by the Portuguese painter *Alvaro Pires* (c. 1430).

The **Duomo,** at the back (reached by Via Turazza left of Palazzo dei Priori), is a 12-13C building altered internally in 1584 by Leon. Ricciarelli, and restored after damage in the Second World War. The campanile dates from 1493. The nave and crossing have a 16C coffered ceiling. Beneath the N. arcade is a 13C pulpit considerably restored, and, in the N. aisle, an Annunciation by *Albertinelli* (1497). On the W. wall (l. of door) is a romanesque altar placed beneath a 19C tomb. Above the high altar is a *Ciborium (1471) by *Mino da Fiesole* who also sculpted the two angels on either side on twisted columns (12C). On the altar, silver bust of St Octavian, by *Ant. Pollaiolo* (on the extreme right). The stalls in the apse date from 1404. In the transeptal chapels are a 13C *Deposition group in polychrome wood, and the tomb of St Octavian by *Raff. Cioli* (1522; right-hand angel by *And. Ferrucci*). In the Lady Chapel (entered from the W. end of the N. aisle) is a charming fresco of the Magi by *Benozzo Gozzoli* (in a niche behind a 15C group of the Nativity in terracotta; light on r.).—The octagonal **Baptistery,** by

Giroldo di Iacopo (1283), facing the cathedral, has a font (r. of altar) sculptured by *And. Sansovino* (1502). The altar is surrounded by a fine sculptured arch by *Mino da Fiesole.*

The MUSEO DIOCESANO DI ARTE SACRA (9-13, 15-18), at No. 1 Via Roma, displays good architectural fragments, a bust of St Linus by *And. della Robbia*, a gilded crucifix by *Giambologna*, vestments, and 15C antiphonals.

From Via Marchesi (see above) Via Porta all'Arco descends to the *Arco Etrusco,* a gateway rebuilt in Roman times, with the remains of three colossal Etruscan heads. The little church of *Sant'Alessandro,* mainly 11-12C, is at the foot of the hill.

Via Ricciarelli, forming a picturesque corner (12-13C *Tower-houses) with Via Buomparenti, leads down from the main piazza past the house of Daniele da Volterra (No. 12) to the churches of San Lino (1480-1513) and *San Francesco,* which has a separate chapel of 1315, completely frescoed in 1410 by Cenni di Fr. Cenni.

Outside the 14C *Porta San Francesco* an uninteresting narrow road continues past the ruins of *Santo Stefano* (12C) to (nearly 1 km. from the gate) the imposing church of *San Giusto,* its tall façade (1628) rising above a grassy slope flanked by cypresses. A few hundred metres beyond the road ends at the remains of the *Etruscan Walls,* which are well preserved at many points. They included pastures and springs within their circumference of c. 9 km.—nearly three times that of the medieval walls. From here there is a view of the formidable precipice of the BALZE. where landslips have engulfed the greater part of the earliest necropolis of Volterra, and the remaining area is threatened by further falls. The ruined *Badia* is conspicuous; it is now abandoned but preserves its cloister.

Viale Fr. Ferrucci, outside the medieval walls, runs E. past the *ROMAN THEATRE AND BATHS (no adm. while excavations continue), well seen from the road. Built at the end of the 1C B.C., part of the cavea and scena remain. Within the portico, which was added a century later, are remains of baths with various rooms, one with a mosaic pavement. From Porta Fiorentina Via Guarnacci leads in to the *Casa-Torre Toscano* otherwise reached from the centre by Via Buomparenti and Via Sarti, where the Renaissance *Palazzo Viti* was converted into a theatre in 1819 and is now occupied by a cinema. The church of *San Michele,* opposite the tower-house, has a façade in the Pisan style and, within a Della Robbian Madonna.—At No. 15 Via Don Minzoni, to the S.E., is the *Museo Etrusco Guarnacci* (open 9.30-13, 14.30-18 exc. Mon), founded by Mgr. Mario Guarnacci (1701-85). Nineteen rooms contain more than 600 Etruscan cinerary urns, mostly of the 3C B.C., in alabaster or terracotta; the terracotta urns are probably the oldest. On the lids are generally the recumbent figures of the dead, with the cup of life reversed; many are sculptured with admirable reliefs, including mythological subjects from the Theban or Trojan cycles. A Roman section includes two heads of Augustus from the theatre and mosaics from baths. On the 2nd floor are the city archives and library.—At the end of the street is the massive *Fortezza,* a castle begun by Walter de Brienne, Duke of Athens, in 1343, and completed by Lorenzo the Magnificent in 1472; it has always been used as a prison.

From the near-by *Porta a Selci* a road descends to (1 km.) the 15C church of *San Girolamo,* containing terracottas by Giov. Della Robbia and an *Annunciation by Benv. di Giovanni (1466).

FROM VOLTERRA TO MASSA MARITTIMA, 66 km., bus in 3 hrs. The winding hill-road, with fine views, diverges from N 68 at (9 km.). *Saline di Volterra.*—23 km.

Pomarance, an old walled town with palazzi of the Larderel and other local families, was the birthplace of two painters called Pomarancio, of whom Cristofano Roncalli (1552-1626) was the more famous.—33 km. *Larderello,* on a side road to the left, is noted for the production of boric acid, evaporated from natural vapour-jets (soffioni) which burst forth from the ground.—From the pass of *Aia dei Diavoli* (875 m) the road descends to (66 km.) *Massa.*

Other buses run from Volterra viâ Pontedera to *Pisa* in 2 hrs; and viâ Poggibonsi to *Siena* (2½ hrs) or *Florence* (3 hrs); comp. p. 512.

Beyond Cécina road and railway run close to the shore, leaving on the right at (288 km.) *Vada* the railway to Pisa viâ Colle Salvetti (followed by N 206).—At (293 km.) *Rosignano Solvay* are the factories for processing the soda from the Saline di Volterra. The old town of Rosignano is 4 km. inland.—295 km. *Castiglioncello,* an elegant resort on a promontory, has a small archæological museum. A new tract of the Aurelia has been opened just inland of the old road as far as (305 km.) *Quercianella,* another little seaside resort among pine-woods. The main road runs inland of Antignano and Ardenza, seaside suburbs of Livorno (comp. below) and a motorway by-pass connects with the A 12 autostrada which runs N. from Livorno.

317 km. **LIVORNO** (E.P.T., 6 P.za Cavour) is a busy and flourishing seaport (177,700 inhab.). Beyond the fortifications it preserves few old buildings, especially since the systematic detructions of 1943, but the town is lively and well laid out and the seaboard attractive. The English version of the town's name, **Leghorn,** is now seldom heard.

Though a fortress was contested here between Pisan, Genoese, and Florentine overlords from the early Middle Ages, Livorno dates its rise from 1571, when the new port was begun by decree of Cosimo de' Medici. Ferdinand I (1587-1609) continued the work, and not only began the great mole, but by his proclamation of religious liberty made the town a refuge for persecuted Jews, Greeks who had fled from the Turks, converted Moors expelled from Spain and Portugal under Philip III, and Roman Catholics driven from England under the penal laws. They were joined by many Italians fleeing from the oppression of their own states, and by exiles from Marseilles and Provence. The policy of Ferdinand was pursued by his successors, and Livorno became a great port, second in Italy only to that of Genoa. In 1749 Sir Joshua Reynolds landed here on his only visit to Italy. Pietro Mascagni (1863-1945), composer of 'Cavalleria Rusticana', was born here, as was also Amedeo Modigliani (1884-1920), the painter.

Some 3 m. off Livorno rises the reef of *Meloria,* where the maritime power of Pisa was crushed by the Genoese in 1284; hereabouts also in 1653 an English trading fleet was routed by the Dutch.

The huge Piazza della Repubblica, overlooked by the moated *Fortezza Nuova* (1590), is linked by the Via Grande with the central Piazza Grande. Here stands the *Duomo,* rebuilt in 1954-59, the Doric portico of which still owes something to the original design of Inigo Jones (1605).

Behind the cathedral the Via Cairoli leads past the Post Office (at the back of which is the *Synagogue,* richly decorated with marbles) to the Piazza Cavour. Just S.W. of this is the old English cemetery (closed in 1839), where Tobias Smollett (see below) was buried in 1771. About 1 km. S. in the Piazza Matteotti is the entrance to the park (open 10-20) of the *Villa Fabbricotti* where the MUSEO CIVICO (adm. 10-13, exc. Mon, Thurs also 16-19) has a fine collection of works by the 'Macchiaioli' painters including Giovanni Fattori (1825-1908), a native of the town.

The Via Grande ends at the harbour, where stands the fine *Monument to Ferdinand I,* with his statue by Giovanni Bandini (1595) and four Moorish slaves by P. Tacca (1623-26). Just to the N. is the *Fortezza Vecchia,* built to the design of Ant. da Sangallo in 1521-34, embodying the so-called Matilda Tower (11C) and remains of the Pisan fort of 1377.

The bus (No. 1) along the shore passes the *Aquarium* (10.30-12.30, 15-18; winter 14-17), the *Royal Naval Academy* (founded 1879), and a number of small resorts. Near the Academy is the 17C church of *San Iacopo in Acquaviva,* sited where St James the Great is supposed to have landed on his way to Spain; St Augustine also is said to have stayed here after his baptism.—3 km. *Ardenza* and (4½ km.) *Antignano* are both lively little bathing resorts in the season. By this bus and a funicular railway or directly by bus No. 2 from the P.za Grande, **Montenero** may be reached, where Tobias Smollett (1721-71) spent the last two years of his life. The pilgrimage church contains a miraculous picture of the Madonna, supposed to have sailed by itself in 1345 from the island of Negropont (Euboea) to the shore of Ardenza.

N 1 turns inland, soon leaving N 67 bis (for Pontedera and Florence; Rte 45B) at (325 km.) *Stagno* in the midst of the former marshes of the Arno, drained (c. 1620) by Sir Robert Dudley, and now occupied by a huge oil refinery. Here is the beginning of the A 12 motorway which continues up the coast (comp. Rte 8).—336 km. **Pisa,** see Rte 45A.

VI THE MARCHES AND UMBRIA

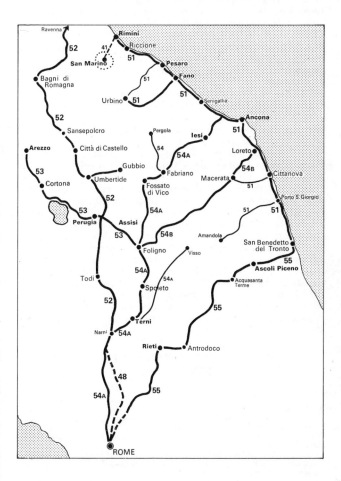

The **Marches** (*Le Marche*) occupy the E. slopes of the Apennines between the rivers Tavullo on the N. and Tronto on the S. They are divided into the provinces of Ancona, Ascoli Piceno, Macerata, and Pesaro e Urbino and have a total area of 9,693,00 sq. km., and a population of 1,390,000.

The Piceni, the earliest known natives, were for many years a thorn in the flesh of Rome, but their district, when subdued, became one of the chief granaries of the empire and was named *Picenum Annonarium* (annona, the year's agricultural produce, esp. grain). Later the district was called *Pentapolis Annonaria* (with part of Romagna, a sub-district of Emilia) and *Pentapolis Picena*. The present name comes from the 11C division of the region into the Marca Anconitana, the Marca Camerinese, and the Marca Fermana. Always, since the 8C, more or less under the jurisdiction of the Pope, the Marches were united to the Church in 1354 by Card. Egidio Albornoz, who offered the inducement of a special constitution. They remained papal territory (except for a brief period after the French Revolution) until the capture of Ancona in 1860 by the Piedmontese army. The region is given up almost entirely to agriculture.

Umbria, an inland region of Italy, perhaps named after the shady forests (umbra) of the Apennines, includes the picturesque middle basin of the Tiber and its tributaries the Chiaggio, Nera, and Paglia. It consists of two provinces—Perugia and the much smaller Terni, making a total area of 8,456,00 sq. km., and a population of 795,200.

Agriculture is the chief industry of the valleys, though there are some lignite mines and stone quarries. Umbria rivals Tuscany for its artistic treasures; as well as Perugia, Assisi, Orvieto, and Spoleto, many lesser cities attract the discriminating traveller. The primitive race of the *Umbri,* regarded by Pliny as the most ancient inhabitants of Italy, originally occupied a territory far more extensive than the modern region. They appear to have yielded ground to the Etruscans and to have fled before them to the mountain fastnesses of the Apennines. In general culture they seem to have been deficient, for they did not evolve an alphabet of their own but borrowed the Etruscan and Latin characters. In 295 B.C. they submitted to the Roman consul Fabius. In the Middle Ages the republican communes and seignories which arose were of but transitory duration, for, from its proximity to Rome, Umbria was always more or less under the sway of the Church, which enjoyed undisputed domination from the 16C until the unification of Italy in 1860.

51   FROM RIMINI TO SAN BENEDETTO DEL TRONTO. URBINO

ROAD, 185 km. N 16, VIA ADRIATICA.—35 km. **Pésaro.**—47 km. *Fano.*—70 km. *Senigállia.*—97 km. **Ancona.**—125 km. *Loreto.*—143 km. *Civitanova Marche.*—186 km. **San Benedetto del Tronto.** For long stretches N. of Ancona the road is badly ribbon-developed and overcrowded. Beyond *Porto Recanati* (127 km.) it skirts the sea and, though it has its picturesque intervals, it is, on the whole, monotonous.

AUTOSTRADA (A 14), a little shorter, roughly parallel but farther inland.

RAILWAY, 177 km. in 2-2½ hrs, closely following the road, with frequent trains. To *Ancona* (92 km.) in 1-1½ hrs.

The **Adriatic Riviera,** an endless succession of fine sandy *Beaches as far as Ancona, is developed almost beyond comfort in the high season, with innumerable hotels. The resorts are liberally supplied with popular entertainments and sports and many have small yacht harbours. The hinterland (Urbino excepted) provides little of the first interest. Beyond Ancona the route gives access to regions remarkable for their historic memories, their magnificent castles, and their austere medieval churches. Many small resorts lie on the coast, with a gently sloping sandy shore, and even some of the most attractive spots are less crowded. The whole coast, however, suffers from the proximity of the busy railway.

From *Rimini* Highway N 16 runs S.E., by-passing (10 km.) *Riccione*
and (18 km.) *Cattólica,* described with Rimini in Rte 41. It crosses the
tiny Tavollo which, emptying into the sea at Cattólica, here marks the
boundary between Romagna and the Marches. The hills now reach the
sea. The walled town of *Gradara,* long visible on its hill (142 m) to the
right, has a fine 14C castle (9-12, 15.30-18 or 19; winter 9-14), the
supposed scene of the tragedy of Francesca da Rimini. About 2 km. E. is
Gradara British Military Cemetery, with 1192 graves.

To seaward lies *Gabicce Mare,* but for the Tavollo an extension of Cattólica,
whence a winding panoramic road follows the cliffs through the ancient village of
Gabicce Monte, affording splendid sea views all the way to (28 km.) *Pésaro.*

35 km. **PÉSARO** occupies the site of the Roman *Pisaurum,* at the
mouth of the Pisaurus, now the Foglia. Formerly one of the cities of the
Maritime Pentapolis, it is the pleasant seaside capital (89,200 inhab.) of
the province of Pésaro e Urbino, one of the four comprising the
Marches, and has a modern holiday quarter.

Hotels on the sea front.
Post Office, P.za del Popolo.—**E.P.T.** 43 Via Rossini.
Buses to *Urbino,* in 1 hr; to *Rimini* in 1 hr; viâ Urbino, Foligno, Spoleto and
Terni to *Rome* in 8 hrs; to *Ancona* in 1½ hrs; viâ Fano to *Cagli* in 1½ hrs; viâ
Fano, Fossombrone, and Urbania to *Lamoli* in 2½ hrs.

History. Pésaro was the seat of a lordship of the Maletestas and the Sforzas, and,
after 1512, of the Della Rovere; and it is the birthplace of the composer Gioacchino
Rossini (1792-1868). The manufacture of majolica here, an industry which still
survives, reached its artistic zenith between the late 15C and early 17C. During the
Second World War its position at the Adriatic end of the Gothic Line attracted
unwelcome interest from both sides; it was bombed and shelled by the Allies and
mined by the Germans.
The **Gothic Line,** never completed by the Germans, but still a formidable
obstacle to the Allied advance in the autumn of 1944, ran across N. Italy from La
Spezia, and passed near Carrara, to the N. of Pistoia, across the Futa Pass, and by
the line of the River Foglia to Pésaro. The assault on the line was begun by the
crossing of the Metauro on 22 Aug 1944. Part of the line was quickly broken but
the Germans, helped by bad weather, reacted with vigour. This stage of the
campaign ended with the capture of Rimini by the 1st Canadian Division on 21
Sept. Thereafter ensued the heartbreaking 'Battle of the Rivers'.

The *Cathedral,* in the Via Rossini, has an early 14C façade,
incomplete and retaining earlier details. This street runs past *Rossini's
House* with a little museum (open 10-12, 16-18; winter 10-12, 14-16; fest,
10-12). Opposite, Via Mazzolari leads to *Palazzo Toschi-Mosca* which
houses the **Musei Civici** (adm. 9.30-12.30, 16-19; winter 8.30-13.30; fest.
9.30-12.30; closed Mon morning), a choice and well-arranged collection
of paintings and majolica.

R.I. *Mariotto di Nardo,* Triptych; *Nicoló di Pietro,* Four saints.—R. II. *Giov.
Bellini,* *Coronation of the Virgin, Crucifixion; *Marco Zoppo,* Pietà.—R. III.
Dom. Beccafumi, Holy Family; *Giov. Bellini,* God the Father.—R. IV.
Sassoferrato, Madonna; *Simone Cantarini,* St Joseph; *Guido Reni,* Fall of the
Giants; *Elisabetta Sirani,* Madonna and St John.—R. V. Works by *Gian And.
Lazzarini* of Pésaro.—The majolica in the other rooms includes a wonderfully
lustrous *Collection by *Mastro Giorgio.*

In Piazza del Popolo is the *Palazzo Ducale* (1450-1510), begun by
Aless. Sforza, with an imposing portico. At the W. corner the Gothic
façade (1395) of the demolished church of *San Domenico* forms the side
wall of the Post Office. Its cloister is a vegetable market. Another
excellent portal (1376-73) is that of *San Francesco,* in the street of the

same name off the S.E. side of the square; that of *Sant'Agostino* (1413), in the Corso Undici Settembre, in the opposite direction, is more richly decorated, and the church has contemporary inlaid stalls. In P.za Olivieri is the *Conservatorio Rossini,* founded by a bequest from the composer. Within are a striking portrait of Rossini by Gustave Doré, his spinet, and the manuscripts of several of his operas (apply to custodian). Mascagni was director here from 1895 to 1905. Behind in Via Mazza, the Palazzo Almerici is the seat of the *Museo Archeologico Oliveriano* (adm. on request) with Etruscan monuments, inscriptions, and bronzes; and a collection of antique coins.

The *Rocca Costanza,* overlooking the seaside quarter, is a regularly planned fort by L. Laurana (1474-1505; used as a prison).—On the hill of San Bártolo (on the road to Cattolica 2 km. N.W. of Pesaro) are the two villas (*Villa Caprile* and *Villa Vittoria*) where Princess Caroline of Wales lived in 1817-19, in each for a little over a year. Here also is the *'Imperiale'* a villa of Aless. Sforza (1469-72), enlarged by Genga for the Della Rovere. Only the Villa Caprile is open (summer 15.30-19).

FROM PÉSARO TO URBINO, N 423, 36 km. bus in 1 hr. This route at first follows N 16 in the direction of Rimini, but at (3½ km.) *Santa Maria* it branches left and ascends the valley of the Foglia.—Before (15 km.) *Montecchio,* on the right of the road, is *Montecchio British Military Cemetery,* with 592 graves. Beyond the village, which was all but destroyed in 1944, the road bears left across the river and ascends. After (31 km.) *Trasanni* (172 m) the rise becomes acute.—36 km. **Urbino,** see below.

47 km. **Fano** (51,300 inhab.) is the ancient *Fanum Fortunæ,* named after its celebrated Temple of Fortune, and lies at the N.E. end of the Via Flaminia (N 3; comp. below). It is justly famous for its sandy beach. The hotel quarter lies N. of the Canale del Porto; the old town, which was mined by the retreating Germans in 1944, to the S.

The main road (by-passed by the Circonvallazione) continues directly into the town as the Corso Matteotti. Beyond its crossing with Via Arco d'Augusto, in P.za Venti Settembre are the *Palazzo della Ragione* (1299), and the *Corte Malatestiana,* part Gothic from the time of Pandolfo III (1413-21) but enlarged in 1544, with a fine courtyard and loggia. Here is housed the CIVICO MUSEO MALATESTIANO (adm. 10-12, 17-19; closed Mon, and Sun & fest. mornings). The Pinacoteca has works by local artists of the 17C including *Pompeo Morganti* and *Fr. Mancini.* The most important paintings include: *Guercino,* Guardian Angel; *Guido Reni,* Annunciation; *Domenichino,* David; and *Mattia Preti,* St Nicholas. Among the earlier paintings: *Giambono,* Polyptych; and *Giov. Santi,* Madonna and Saints. In the numismatic collection are the Malatestian medals (1446), attrib. to *Matteo de' Preti,* and Roman coins from the Fano mint. The paintings and prints of stage designs are by the local artist Giac. Torelli (1608-78).—In *Santa Maria Nuova,* reached by Via de' Pili, are a Visitation, by Giov. Santi, and two *Altarpieces by Perugino (Madonna enthroned, with a Pietà; Annunciation).

From the E. corner of P.za Venti Settembre may be reached the portico of *San Francesco* (church demolished in 1931) with the tombs of Pandolfo III Malatesta (d. 1427) and of his wife, Paola Bianca (d. 1398).

In Via Arco d'Augusto, to the right is *San Domenico,* decorated with frescoes attributed to Ottaviano Nelli, while to the left is the *Duomo* with a restored Romanesque façade. In the Baroque Nolfi chapel in the S. aisle are frescoes by Domenichino (in poor condition after numerous restorations). In the chap. to the r. of the apse, Lod. Carracci, Madonna in glory. The stone pulpit is by Maestro Rainiero, the architect. At the end of the street are the *Logge di San Michele,* a pawnshop of the 15C, constructed partly with material from the neighbouring *Arco di Augusto,* a Roman triumphal arch erected in the 2C A.D. Beyond the arch is the disused church of *San Michele,* with a rich portal by Bern. da Carona (1504-13), which also acquired material from the arch. A fragment of Roman road is visible near by.

Viale della Rimembranza, to the N.W., skirts a fine section of the Augustan *Walls.*

The *Rocca Malatestiana* (1452) occupies the N. corner; the wall adjoining the railway is medieval with an extension beyond P.za Rosselli by Ant. and Luca da Sangallo.

Buses run viâ Fossombrone to (30 km.) *Calmazzo* (comp. below), there bearing off to the S. on N 3 through the *Gola del Furlo* ('forulus'), the narrow ravine of the Candigliano. The road threads a tunnel cut by Vespasian in A.D. 76 to replace an earlier one (still visible) of 220 B.C.—At (42 km.) *Acqualagna* a road runs W. to Città di Castello.—50 km. *Cagli,* with a Renaissance Palazzo Comunale, preserves good Gothic work (14-15C) in three of its churches. The bus-route ends here, but the road goes on to (71 km.) *Scheggia,* and to (84 km.) *Gubbio,* see Rte 52.

FROM FANO TO URBINO, 45 km. bus; railway in c. 70 min. (the trains start from Pésaro). The Via Flaminia (N 3) follows the valley of the Metauro (comp. below), scene of bitter fighting in the assaults on the Gothic Line in Aug 1944.—25 km. **Fossombrone,** a little town of 10,000 inhab. at the foot of a hill, has an elegant 15C *Bishop's Palace* and a Museum occupying a Montefeltro mansion of 1470. Scanty ruins of *Forum Sempronii,* the Roman predecessor of Fossombrone, may be seen at San Martino, 3 km. downstream; but the Roman *Ponte di Diocleziano* (at San Lazzaro), 2 km. upstream, and *Ponte di Traiano* (just S. of Calmazzo) were blown up in the war.—At (30 km.) *Calmazzo,* this route turns right on N 73 bis, and at 38 km. right again.

45 km. **URBINO** (485 m; 16,150 inhab.) in a splendid position set deep amidst rolling hills. The fascinating old city is still contained within its mighty walls. Indelibly associated with the names of Federico da Montefeltro, Raphael, and Bramante, it attracts pilgrims from far and wide, despite its isolated position which makes access difficult from central Italy. Its university dates from 1506. Urbino narrowly escaped destruction in the last War.

Hotels outside the walls (Viale Comandino and Via della Stazione), not convenient for those without a car; simpler hotels in the old city near Piazza della Repubblica.

Station, 2 km. S. of the old town in the valley; served by a branch line from Pésaro and Fano. A bus connects with every train to and from the centre (P.za della Repubblica).

Post Office, 24 Via Bramante.—Azienda di Turismo, P.za Duca Federico.

Car Parking, P.za Mercatale (with underground park).

Buses to *Ancona* in c. 2¼ hrs; to *Cagli* and *Gualdo Tadino* in 2¾ hrs; to *Arezzo* in 2¾ hrs; to *Rimini* in 2 hrs; to *Rome* viâ Foligno and Terni in 5½ hrs.

History. *Urvinum Metaurense* is said to have been founded by the Umbrian leader Metaurus Suassus, and as *Urbinum Hortense* it is mentioned by Pliny as a Roman municipium. The town rose into prominence in the late 12C, when it became subject to the house of Montefeltro. Count Oddantonio da Montefeltro was made the first duke of Urbino in 1443, and he was succeeded in 1444 by his illegitimate half-brother Federico, who was not only a great soldier but a generous patron of art and an enlightened ruler. He received the Garter from Edward IV of

England, and a painting of him in the robes of the order, by Melozzo, is now at Windsor; his marriage with Battista Sforza is commemorated in the picture by Piero della Francesca (1465) in the Uffizi (Florence). His invalid son Guidobaldo I, husband of Elisabetta Gonzaga, was treacherously expelled from his duchy by Cesare Borgia in 1497 but restored after an insurrection. Francesco Maria Della Rovere, nephew of Pope Julius II and of Guidobaldo, who succeeded to the duchy in 1508, proved himself also a brave soldier and a friend of art and learning. He received the Garter from Henry VII, an occasion commemorated by Raphael's painting of St George (1508), now in Leningrad. Francesco Maria II ceded his possessions to the Church in 1626, and in consequence Urbino was despoiled of many treasures. James Stuart, the Old Pretender, was entertained in the palace in 1717-18 and 1722. In the Second World War the city walls were mined, but only those at the S.W. corner went off and the rest were rendered harmless by the British after they had entered the city on 29 Aug 1944. This deliverance was doubly fortunate since Urbino had been chosen as a safe repository for works of art from many places in Italy.

Raphael (Raffaello Sanzio or Santi: 1483-1520), was born at Urbino but, with one exception, no genuine work of his remains in his native city. The artistic movement began at Urbino in the early 15C, with the brothers Salimbeni, Ottaviano Nelli, Antonio da Ferrara, and Luca Della Robbia. Federico's court attracted such artists as the Laurana, Alberti, Baccio Pontelli, Dom. Rosselli, Pisanello, Sperandio, Piero della Francesca, Justus of Ghent, and the Urbinese masters Fra Carnevale and Giov. Santi. Later came the Urbinese Timoteo Viti (1467-1524) and Donato Bramante (1444-1514), from Fermignano. In the 16C Federico Barocci was the chief painter of Urbino. The town was long celebrated for its majolica, whose manufacture was introduced from Castel Durante (c. 1477), and was later perfected by the Fontana family (1520-1605).—Among other natives of Urbino were Polydore Virgil (c. 1470-1555), author of the 'Historia Anglica' and the last collector of Peter's Pence in England, and Clement XI (b. 1649).

The most conspicuous building in Urbino is the *Palazzo Ducale, the masterpiece of *Luciano Laurana*, a Dalmatian who directed the work of building from 1465 to 1474. It is one of the finest ducal palaces in Italy, and marks the beginning of the perfected Renaissance architecture. It is built of creamy Dalmatian limestone, which takes on a polish like that of marble. The front has a loggia between tall flanking towers ending in spires, and the doors, windows, and cornices are covered with arabesques of singular beauty, the work of *Ambr. Barocci*. The top story was completed by *Girol. Genga* c. 1536. It now houses the *Galleria Nazionale delle Marche.

The palace is undergoing a slow restoration; meanwhile all the works of art are on display in a temporary arrangement. The opening times often vary, but at present they are as follows: 1 May-30 Sept, 9-13, 15.30-18.30; winter: 9-14; fest. 9.30-13; closed Mon. In 1975 the three masterpieces from the gallery (Piero della Francesca's Flagellation, and Madonna di Senigallia, and Raphael's Portrait of a lady) were stolen; the news of their recovery in 1976 was greeted by the ringing of all the church bells in the city.

The COURTYARD (1480) is a noble creation. The monumental staircase, with a statue of Duke Federico by Girol. Campagna (1604) ascends to the upper gallery. The rooms are adorned with late 16C stuccoes by *Fr. Ferrucci* and *Fed. Brandani*. RR. I and II. Flemish 17-18C tapestries; note the chimneypieces inscribed 'FE DUX' in R. I, the THRONE ROOM.—R. II. 630. *Marco Basaiti,* Madonna and saints; 646. *Giov. Mansueti,* Pietà.—R. III. 641. *Girol. da Santacroce,* 643. *Giov. Bellini* (attrib.), paintings of the Madonna and saints.—R. IV, with a fine stuccoed ceiling. 635. *Ant. Alberti da Ferrara,* Polyptych: Madonna and saints; above, the Resurrection; 650. *Girol. di Giovanni,* Crucifixion, Virgin and St John.—R. V, with a finely carved doorway, 658, *Giov. Fr. da Rimini,* Head of St Dominic; 664. *Giov. Baronzio,*

Polyptych: Scenes from the Life of Christ.—R. VI. 934. *Ant. Alberti da Ferrara*, Polyptych: Madonna and saints; 676. *Giov. Fr. da Rimini*, Crucifixion (fragments of a polyptych); 679. *Nicola di Maestro Antonio da Ancona*, Annunciation (triptych).—R. VII. *683. *Gentile da Fabriano*, *684. *Allegretto Nuzi*, paintings of the Madonna enthroned. Two superb faldstools of intarsia work inscribed 'Carolus Patri BM' and 'Matri BM'.

From ROOM I is the entrance to R. VIII, the SALA DEGLI ANGELI, with a magnificent chimneypiece by *Dom. Rosselli;* 15-16C Brussels tapestries. 691. *Verrocchio*, Madonna and Child.—R. IX., with two 15C Brussels tapestries, called CAMERA DI LETTO. *692. *Melozzo da Forlì*, Salvator Mundi; 693. *Justus of Ghent*, Last Supper, *694. *Paolo Uccello*, Profanation of the Host; *695. *Pedro Berruguete*, Federico da Montefeltro and Guidobaldo.—R. X. *Piero della Francesca*, *699. Madonna di Senigallia, *700. Flagellation, one of the masterpieces of Italian painting and one of the most discussed for its subject matter and remarkable perspective device. 698. *Fr. di Giorgio Martini* (?), *Ideal City. From here a spiral staircase descends to the tiny CAPPELLA DEL PERDONO (R. XI), rich in marble, with a finely stuccoed ceiling, and to the exquisite little TEMPIETTO DELLE MUSE (R. XII), again with a good ceiling.

R. XIII, DUKE FEDERICO'S STUDY, is celebrated for its walls, entirely composed of splendid *Intarsia work by *Botticelli* and *Baccio Pontelli* (recently beautifully restored); the blue and gold coffered ceiling incorporates the ducal emblems.—R. XIV, the CHAPEL, with marble intarsia work by *Fed. Brandani*. The LOGGIA, in the N.W. tower, commands a noble view.—R. XV. *702. *Raphael*, Portrait of a lady (? Maddalena Doni, called 'La Muta'); *Luca Signorelli*, 707. Crucifixion, 706. Pentecost; *Titian*, 703. Resurrection, 704. Last Supper.—R. XVI. 709-22. *Justus of Ghent* (attrib.), 14 illustrious men (formerly in Duke Federico's Study).—R. XVII. *Giov. Santi*, *742. Tobias and the Angel, and paintings of apostles.—R. XVIII. 4 small paintings by *Santi*, including a Pietà and a female martyr.—R. XIX. 744. *Timoteo Viti*, SS. Martin and Thomas, Abp. Arrivabeni and Guidobaldo.—RR. XX. onwards contain majolica, war-machines, and stained glass designed by *Timoteo Viti*. The sculpture collection includes bas-reliefs by *Ambr. Barocci*, a Madonna and Child, by *Dom. Rosselli; Agostino di Duccio*, Fragment of a Head of the Virgin; works by *Tommaso Flamberti; Lor. Ghiberti*, Madonna and Child (from the church of San Salvatore in Figiano); and *Andrea della Robbia*, *Lunette from San Domenico (see below; removed for restoration).

The 17C paintings displayed on the upper floor include works by *Ann. Carracci, Fed. Zuccari, Il Pomarancio, Seb. Ricci, Carlo Maratti, Seb. Conca*, and numerous paintings by *Fed Barocci*.—In the rooms overlooking the courtyard are detached frescoes from San Francesco in Fermo, by *Giul. da Rimini*, and from other churches in the province.

Opposite the palace is the Romanesque and Gothic church of *San Domenico* (1365), with a Renaissance portal by Maso di Bartolomeo (1449-51). The *Madonna and Saints by Luca della Robbia (1449), formerly in the lunette, is to be displayed in the Palazzo Ducale after its restoration.—The **Duomo,** dating from 1477, was completely rebuilt (consecrated 1801) by *Morigia* after the collapse of the cupola during an earthquake in 1789. The neo-classical interior, by *Gius. Valadier,* contains (S. aisle) *Barocci,* Martyrdom of St Sebastian, and St Cecilia. The chapel to the r. of the high altar, designed by *Carlo Maratti* (with an Assumption by him on the r. wall) has a 14C fresco fragment over the altar. In the main apse is a huge work by *Cristoforo Unterberger.* In the chap. l. of high altar (unlocked by custodian): *Barocci,* *Last Supper; G. B. Urbinelli da Urbino,* Epiphany.

The MUSEO ALBANI DEL DUOMO (open 9-12.30, 14.30-19; in winter on request) contains an interesting collection of works from the sacristy and churches in the diocese, including: frescoes from San Domenico; 17C Casteldurante ceramics; vestments, chalices, etc; bronze lectern of 12C Rhenish work; 14C illuminated MSS. Among the paintings: *And. da Bologna,* Madonna del Latte; *Fed. Barocci,* Saints, Madonna del Gatto; *Gerol. Genga* (?), Madonna della Misericordia; *Aless. Vitali,* St Agnes.—The custodian also shows four underground chapels in the crypt, where a marble statue of the Dead Christ by *Giov. Bandini dell'Opera* has been placed.

Via Garibaldi descends to the church of *San Francesco,* rebuilt in 1740 by Luigi Vanvitelli, but retaining a 14C portico and campanile. To the S.W. Via Barocci leads to the *Oratorio di San Giuseppe* (opened by custodian; ring at No. 3, 9-12.30, 16-19) with a *Nativity by Fed. Brandani, a masterpiece in stucco. The little 14C oratory of *San Giovanni Battista* (opened by the same custodian) contains frescoes by Iac. and Lor. Salimbeni (1416).—From San Francesco Via Raffaello leads N.W. On the left is the *Casa di Raffaello,* the house in which the painter was born, now a small museum (9-13, 15-19; 1 Oct-30 April, 11-17, fest. 9.30-13). The paintings include an Annunciation by Giov. Santi, a Madonna and Child with the young St John, by Giulio Romano, and a predella by Berto di Giovanni, a fine copy of a work by Raphael in Santa Maria Nova in Fano. The fresco of the Madonna and Child, attrib. to Giov. Santi, may possibly be an early work by Raphael himself. The street continues to Piazzale Roma, adorned with a statue of Raphael by L. Belli (1897). The *Walls* of Urbino, almost completely preserved, were begun in 1507 and replace an earlier circumvallation, of which traces survive. The *Fortezza dell'Albornoz,* on the westernmost bastion, has recently been restored and opened to the public.—Outside the walls (20 min. walk W.) is the church of *San Bernardino* (open 9-20), completed before 1472 and attributed to Bramante; here were buried Dukes Federico and Guidobaldo I.

To the S. of Urbino (9 km. by road; 8 min. by railway), on N 73 bis, lies *Fermignano,* birthplace of Bramante. Farther W. (12 km.; 17 km. from Urbino by a direct but hilly road) is *Urbania,* named after Urban VIII (1623-44). Under its previous name of Castel Durante it was noted for its majolica. The little town preserves some fine 15C buildings and a Museum and Art Gallery in the Palazzo Ducale (ring) where the Ducal Library has a large collection of engravings and drawings. The road goes on to Sansepolcro (Rte 52).

Beyond Fano the road crosses the Metauro, the ancient *Metaurus,* where the consuls Claudius Nero and M. Livius Salinator defeated and killed Hasdrubal in 207 B.C. In Aug 1944 the Poles drove the Germans across the Metauro, at the beginning of the assault on the Gothic line (see above).—61 km. *Marotta,* a bathing resort. *Mondavio,* 20 km. S.W. up the Cesano valley, has an imposing fortress begun in 1482 by Fr. di Giorgio Martini.

70 km. **Senigállia,** with 39,900 inhab., a town of ancient foundation, is a seaside resort, with numerous hotels at the mouth of the Misa. It was the birthplace in 1792 of Pius IX.

Azienda Autonoma di Soggiorno, Piazzale Morandi.
Buses to *Ancona, Pergola, Sassoferrato,* etc.
The town of *Sena Gallica* was founded by the Senonian Gauls and colonized by the Romans in 289 B.C. Devastated in the wars between the Guelphs and the Ghibellines, Senigallia attracted the attention of Dante as a typical ruined city. Its famous fair, however, founded in the 13C, survived until the close of the 19C.

The arcaded Via Portici Ercolani, by the river, is the most attractive street. The *Cathedral* dates from 1787. The Gothic *Castle* was restored in 1480, probably by Baccio Pontelli, for Giovanni Della Rovere, nephew of Sixtus IV. Paintings by F. Barocci and Guercino are to be found in the churches of *La Croce* and *San Martino* respectively.—The church of *Santa Maria delle Grazie* 3 km. W. of the town contains a Madonna and saints by Perugino.

Ostra, 15 km. S., and *Corinaldo,* 22 km. S.W. (reached by turnings off the road to Arcevia), have their 15C fortifications.

At (84 km.) *Rocca Priora* the road crosses the Esino near its mouth; here Highway N76 from Jesi and Fabriano (Rte 54) joins N16.—At (86 km.) *Falconara Maríttima,* much disfigured by an oil refinery, the railway to Foligno and Rome diverges inland.—90 km. *Palombina.*

97 km. **ANCONA,** capital of the province of the same name and chief town of the Marches, is splendidly situated in an amphitheatre above the Adriatic and is the only considerable seaport on the E. coast of Italy between Venice and Bari. The town is divided between the 19C quarter with its long broad Viali and spacious squares which extend eastwards to fill the plateau behind the headland, and the more interesting old town on Monte Guasco which overlooks the port. An earthquake in 1972 rendered over half the houses in the historical centre uninhabitable; many of the churches and palaces are still closed for restoration. As a result, the old town is sparsely populated and has a desolate air. The population moved out to new suburbs in the South which have changed the aspect of the city. The population of the commune is 107,400.

Railway Stations. *Centrale,* nearly 2 km. S. of the town; *Maríttima* is now used only by a few slow trains serving Foligno or Rimini.
Hotels are scattered in the modern quarter.
Post Office, P.za Ventiquattro Maggio.—**Ente Provinciale per il Turismo,** Via Marini (Information Office, P.za Rosselli).—**Azienda Autonoma di Turismo,** Via Revel.—*C.I.T.,* 130 Corso Garibaldi (with railway and steamer ticket office).
Buses from the station to Piazza della Repubblica, Piazza Cavour, and Piazza Quattro Novembre; from Piazza Cavour to Piazza Bassi; from Via Castelfidardo (near Piazza Cavour) to *Torrette, Palombina,* and *Falconara,* and *Chiaravalle.*—LOCAL BUSES to *Le Grazie, Valle Miano, Paterno,* viâ Sappanico to *Gallignano* and *Montesicuro,* to *Aspio, Varano,* and *Castelferretti.*—**Country Buses** to *San Benedetto del Tronto* and *Áscoli Piceno;* to *Montacuto;* viâ Castelfidardo to *Recanati* and to *Loreto;* to *Pescara;* viâ Senigallia to *Mondolfo,* to *Pergola,* and to *Sassoferrato;* viâ Falconara to *Jesi* and *Cupramontana;* viâ Jesi to *Fabriano;* viâ Porto Civitanova and viâ Osimo to *Macerata.*
Steamers of the Linee Marittime dell'Adriatico twice a week to Yugoslavia (Zadar, Polo, Split, Dubrovnik), and once a week (with car ferry) to Greece (Pireaus). In summer, cruises, starting in Trieste viâ Venice and Ancona to Yugoslavia. Greek line four times a week to Greece.

History. Ancona is said to have been founded c. 400 B.C. by Syracusan exiles fleeing from the tyranny of Dionysius. Its name, meaning 'an elbow', refers to the curved promontory forming its harbour. It was a flourishing port under the Roman emperors, and was favoured by Trajan. It was one of the cities of the *Maritime Pentapolis,* the others being Fano, Pésaro, and Sinigaglia, and the Emilian city of Rimini; and later it belonged to the exarchs of Ravenna and the States of the Church; Barbarossa twice vainly besieged it. Ancona became a free city in 1177 and, although for a time under the sway of the Malatesta and Albornoz families, it enjoyed its privileges until 1532, when Gonzaga occupied it with papal troops under the crafty pretence of garrisoning it against the Turks. In 1799 it withstood a siege of Russians, Austrians, and Turks; in 1860, after another siege, lasting 11 days, it was united to Italy. On 25 May 1915, during the First World War, the port was bombarded by the Austrian fleet. In the Second World War it was occupied in Sept 1943 by the Germans; between Oct 1943, and its capture by the Polish Corps in July 1944, it underwent a series of bombardments. The populous ancient quarter of the Porto was destroyed. The city and port have recovered steadily, despite setbacks by floods in 1959, and an earthquake in 1972.

The Adriatic Highway makes its approach by the Central Station, just beyond which it bears right to avoid the city. The long Via Marconi continues straight on passing the moated pentagonal *Lazzaretto,* by Vanvitelli, now used as a mooring for the fishing fleet and private boats. Beyond the 18C *Porta Pia* Via Ventinove Settembre continues to Piazza Kennedy. Here is the splendid *Portale di Sant'Agostino* (1460-93), begun by Giorgio Orsini (Juraj Dalmatinac) for the former church of that saint. The adjacent P.za della Repubblica, the business centre, opens on to the harbour.

The modern Corso Garibaldi leads E. through Piazza Roma, on the left side of which is the *Fontana del Calamo* (1560), to the spacious PIAZZA CAVOUR, the modern administrative centre. In it is a statue of Cavour (1810-61). Adjoining is Piazza Ventiquattro Maggio, with the Town Hall and Post Office. From here the broad Viale della Vittoria leads (in over a kilometre) to the *Monumento ai Caduti* (1928), an imposing white circular structure overlooking the sea.

From Piazza della Repubblica Via Gramsci leads N. to the long, narrow Piazza del Plebiscito, commonly 'del Papa' from its statue of Clement XII. It rises picturesquely to the 18C church of *San Domenico* (closed since the earthquake). Nearby, across Via Matteotti, is an archway signed and dated 1221. At the lower end of the piazza is *Palazzo del Governo,* refashioned in the 15C by Fr. di Giorgio (undergoing restoration). From its courtyard Via Pizzecolli climbs up the hill past (No. 17) *Palazzo Bosdari,* the new seat of the small PINACOTECA COMUNALE and GALLERIA DELL' ARTE MODERNA. The palace has a good courtyard and fine ceilings.

ROOM I. *Carlo da Camerino,* Coronation of the Virgin (fresco fragment), Dormition of the Virgin; sculptured heads by the Tuscan school.—R. II. *Carlo Crivelli,* *Madonna and Child, an exquisite tiny work.—R. III. *Neri di Bicci,* Madonna and Child.—R. IV. *Margaritone d'Arezzo,* two reliefs; *Titian,* Virgin and Child, Crucifixion (1562; from the church of San Domenico); *Andrea del Sarto* (and pupils), Madonna and Child with St John; *Carlo Maratta,* Madonna and Child with Saints.—R. V. *Lor. Lotto,* Madonna and Child with Saints.—R. VI. Works by *And. Lilli* (1555-1610).—The upper floor has works by *Fr. Podesti.*— The GALLERIA DELL'ARTE MODERNA includes paintings by *Carlo Levi, Luigi Bartolini,* etc. A spiral staircase gives access to the top of the palace with a dramatic view over the old deserted houses of the city to the port beyond.

The church of *San Francesco delle Scale* has a rich Gothic portal by Giorgio Orsini. Above the high altar is an Assumption by Lor. Lotto (1550). The ruined Renaissance portal to the r. of the façade is all that remains of the convent destroyed in the last War. Farther on are the *Gesù* with a scenographic façade by Vanvitelli (1743; closed for restoration) and *Palazzo Anziani,* incorporating 13C fragments. Here is housed the Faculty of Economics and Commerce of the University of Urbino; it has been moved temporarily to a new building nearby while repair work is carried out. The Gothic arches beneath the piazza, with piles of stone projectiles, are interesting.

The *Palazzo Ferretti,* higher up the street, is occupied by the **Museo Nazionale delle Marche,** arranged on three floors. This has been closed for restoration for several years.

GROUND FLOOR. Mosaics (1-4C A.D.), Roman funerary reliefs; Hellenistic female statue from Fermo.—On the SECOND FLOOR and the floor below is an extensive collection of antiquities, illustrating the civilization of Picenum from prehistoric times to its penetration by the Greeks, the Gauls, and the Romans. In R. 8 are bronzes, grave goods, and cinerary urns showing early Greek influence on the district; also armour in the Etruscan style.—R. 12. Celebrated *Dinos of Amandola,* a masterpiece of Ionic art.—FIRST FLOOR. R. 13. Large Vase decorated with figures of divinities (early 5C B.C.).—R. 14. Bronzes; massive Vase from Numana.—R. 16. Greek art, including a bronze Vase decorated with mermen, fish, and snakes.—RR. 18, 19, 21, and 22. Rich collection of jewellery in the Etruscan style. In R. 21 the bronze Dish with figures of warriors shaped to make handles is noteworthy.—R. 23. Handsome Vase from Numana, slender and with a stem, decorated with the head of a god.—In the *Sala dei Bronzi,* on the ground floor, are a gilded bronze statue of a woman, and fragments of an equestrian statue, both from Cartoceto di Pergola.

To the left of the pretty 13C *Palazzo del Senato* the remains of a Roman amphitheatre have been located. Standing at the top of Monte Guasco and approached by narrow streets or stairs, and commanding a magnificent view of the port, is the *Duomo,* dedicated to St Cyriacus, Bishop of Ancona and a martyr under Julian in 362. This stately church sustained heavy damage in both World Wars, losing its roof in the Second, and after restoration work was completed, it was again shaken by the 1972 earthquake and is closed while repair work proceeds. It is a Romanesque and Byzantine edifice, begun in the 11C, with a handsome façade and porch, both added perhaps by Margaritone d'Arezzo (c. 1270). The campanile dates from before 1314.

The INTERIOR is designed on a greek-cross plan. The 12-sided cupola of the 12C, one of the earliest in Italy, is sustained by four angels in bas relief in the pendentives. The unusual transennæ, decorated with bas reliefs in marble on sandstone, probably dates from the 12C. Some of the columns may have belonged to a Temple of Venus, mentioned by Juvenal as occupying this site, the remains of which have been identified below foundations of a 6C church in the *Crypt.* In the chancel (N. side) is the tomb of Card. Gianelli, by *Giovanni da Traù* (1509), an interesting specimen of the Cinquecento style. The *Museum* (apply to sacristan) contains fragments of 13C reliefs and the fine sarcophagus of Flavius Gorgonius, praetor of Ancona (4C).—In the neighbouring bishop's palace Pope Pius II died in 1464 while trying vainly to start a new crusade.

From the Piazza outside is a fine view of the harbour and docks and the splendid *Arco di Traiano,* on the old N. mole of the harbour, a triumphal arch, erected by Apollodorus (A.D. 115) in honour of Trajan, who had developed the port. Close by is the *Arco Clementino,* by Vanvitelli (18C).

At the bottom of the hill near Palazzo del Governo (comp. the Plan) is the church of *Santa Maria della Piazza,* also closed since 1972. It has a Romanesque façade (1210) adorned with sculptures by 'Master Philippus'. Important remains of mosaics from two earlier churches (5-8C), discovered beneath the present building, may be seen on application to the sacristan.—The *Loggia dei Mercanti,* in the street of

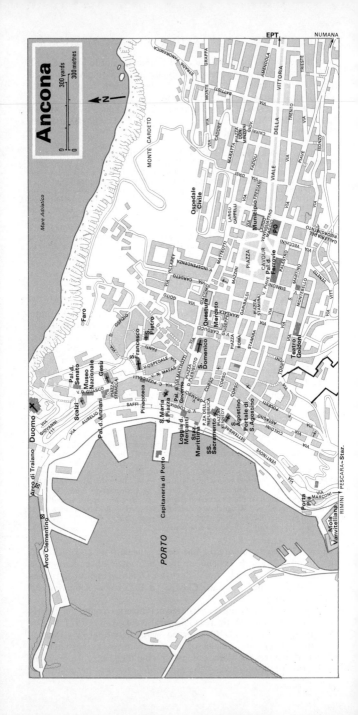

the same name, has a rich façade by Giorgio Orsini (1454-59), most of which has survived (being restored).

About 3 km. S. of Ancona, to the E. of Highway 16, on the road to Verano, is Ancona British Military Cemetery, with 1029 graves.

The hilly coast road to Porto Recanati (32 km.) is interesting, and it traverses the 'Riviera del Cónero' with bathing beaches. At 11 km. a road diverges left for *Santa Maria di Portonovo,* 2 km. E. beside the sea, an unaltered example of a small church of 1034-48.—The road leads round the inland side of *Monte Cónero* (572m; view), on the seaward slopes of which is the former *Abbey of San Pietro* (Camaldulensian), with 11C and 16C buildings, reached by a side road diverging at 18 km.—20 km. *Sirolo,* a little resort with a pine wood.—22 km. *Numana,* reached in summer by steamer from Ancona, has two beaches and the Santuario del Crocifisso, containing a venerated Byzantine Crucifixion (13 or 14C).—32 km. *Porto Recanati,* see p. 578.

From Ancona to *Rome,* see Rte 54.

Beyond Ancona the main road runs inland at first, ascending the hills behind the city to enter the valley of the Áspio. About 2 km. E. of (109 km.) *Áspio Terme,* which has mineral springs, is the market town of *Camerano,* birthplace of the painter Carlo Maratta (1625-1713).—114 km. *Ósimo-Castelfidardo* station.

About 5 km. W. is **Ósimo** (265m), the ancient *Auximium,* the metropolis of Picenum in the 5C. The 13C *Duomo* (restored) has an interesting crypt; the magnificent bronze font in the adjoining baptistery is by the Iacometti (1627). In the church of *San Francesco* is a Madonna and saints by Ant. Solario (1503). In the *Palazzo Comunale* are 12 headless Roman statues and a polyptych (Coronation of the Virgin) by the Vivarini. The *Collegio Campana,* founded 1718, had as pupils Leo XII, Pius VIII, and Aurelio Saffi.—BUSES from the town to *Ancona* viâ Aspio in ½ hr; to *Macerata* in 1 hr. The Macerata road, commanding splendid views, passes the conspicuous castle of Montefiore and (21 km.) *Montecassiano,* a fortified hill-town preserving a town hall and a church (San Marco) by Ant. Lombardo (1467).

The road passes (121 km.) the battlefield of *Castelfidardo* (ossuary) where Gen. Cialdini defeated the papal troops in 1860. The town, 6 km. W. which gave name to the victory, manufactures piano-accordions.

125 km. **LORETO,** a little town of 10,400 inhabitants, stands on a hill (127m) to the right of the road. It is one of the most famous pilgrimage resorts in the world, and, with all the usual characteristics of holy shrines, it is entirely given over to the reception of pilgrims.

According to the legend the house of the Virgin (Casa di Maria or Santa Casa) was transported by angels from Nazareth in Palestine to the hill of Trsat near Rijeka, in 1291, and again, by the same agency, across the Adriatic to the laurel woods which gave name to Loreto, on 10 Dec 1294. Here a church was built over it, which developed into the present sumptuous structure.—Richard Crashaw (? 1613-49) was canon at Loreto and died there.

Station, 2½ km. S.W. of the town on the main Ancona—Foggia line. A bus connects with some trains to outside Porta Romana; otherwise an easy walk leads up steps past the Polish Military cemetery and Via Crucis in c. 20 min. to the town.

The town is surrounded by 16C walls, with curiously shaped battlements; the tall tower of the *Town Hall* is also battlemented. In the centre is the elegant *PIAZZA DELLA MADONNA, with a fountain by Carlo Maderna (being restored). The piazza is closed on two sides by the arcades and loggie of the Palazzo Apostolico; on the third side is the **Santuario della Santa Casa** (open all day 6-20), begun in 1468, continued by Giul. da Maiano, fortified by Baccio Pontelli, completed by Giul. da Sangallo, Fr. Martini, Bramante, And. Sansovino, and Ant. da Sangallo the Younger.

The beautiful façade (1570-87) was built by Sixtus V, whose statue, with fine bas-reliefs by Tiburzio Vergelli and Ant. Calcagni (c. 1589), stands on the steps. To the left is an original campanile by Vanvitelli (1751-54); the great bell cast by Bern. da Rimini in 1516, weighs 22,000 Roman lb. The three magnificent bronze doors of the church bear *Scenes from the Old and New Testaments by various artists (1590-1610). The bronze statue of the Madonna and Child is by Girol. Lombardo (and pupils), 1583.

In the mystic INTERIOR (95 m long) is a *Font by Tib. Vergelli (1600-07). The other side chapels contain copies of works by Guido Reni, Domenichino, Maratta, and others. At the end of the right aisle is the *Sagrestia di San Marco*, with a cupola adorned with *Frescoes by Melozzo da Forlì and his assistants. In the right transept are chapels with modern frescoes (some by Angelica Kauffmann), beyond which is the *Sagrestia di San Giovanni* (light behind door on right) with cupboards attributed to Dom. Indivini da San Severino, a beautiful lavabo by Bened. da Maiano (1484-87), a majolica pavement, and a cupola with frescoes by Luca Signorelli and his assistants (c. 1479). The roofs of the sacristies have been restored since 1944. The APSE frescoes are by Lod. Seitz (1892-1908); on the right is the tomb of Card. Nic. Caetani, by Fr. da Volterra, with a figure designed by G. B. Della Porta.—Off the left transept, which has modern frescoes, are the *Sagrestia di San Matteo* and *Sagrestia di San Luca*, with good terracotta lunettes of the Evangelists, of the Della Robbia school.—The frescoes in the DOME, by Ces. Maccari (1892-1908), portray the various symbols of the Litany of Loreto; they were partly destroyed when a bomb exploded in the drum. Beneath the dome stands the *Santa Casa (closed 13-14.30), concealed by a beautiful marble screen, designed by Bramante, with *Bas-reliefs and *Statues by Sansovino, Raff. da Montelupo, Fr. da Sangallo, Girol. and Aurelio Lombardo, Giov. Battista and Tom. Della Porta, Nic. Tribolo, Dom. de Amis, and Baccio Bandinelli. The interior of the Santa Casa consists of a rectangular chamber with rude walls (traces of Gothic frescoes), divided into two parts by a magnificent bejewelled altar surmounted by a cedar wood image of the Madonna and Child. The altar and statue are restorations after a fire in 1921. From the left transept a corridor gives access to the *Treasury* (closed 13-16), plundered in 1797, with frescoes by Pomarancio.

The PALAZZO APOSTOLICO was begun in 1510 by Bramante; it was continued in 1750, but the third side was never completed. The MUSEO and PINACOTECA inside is open 9-13, 15-18; fest. 9-13; winter 9-13; closed Friday. One room has 8 paintings by *Lor. Lotto*, In the Papal bedroom is a dark Nativity, attrib. to *Ann. Carracci*. There are some fine 17C Brussels tapestries and a splendid collection of majolica from Urbino from the workshop of O. Fontana and Patanazzi.

An archway leads through the palace to a terrace overlooking the plain with a statue of Pope John XXIII, by A. Monteleone (1964).
BUSES run from Loreto to *Ancona* in 1 hr; viâ Recanati to *Macerata* in 1 hr; viâ Appignano to *Tolentino* in 1¾ hrs.

The road now descends to the coast. On the left appears the steep cliffs of the seaward side of Monte Cónero.—128 km. *Porto Recanati* is a seaside resort. Santa Maria di Potenza, an 11C abbey, lies 3 km. S., just inland of *Macerata Mare. Recanati*, 11 km. inland, see Rte 54.—Road and railway now run close to the sea with the autostrada just inland.— 137 km. *Porto Potenza Picena;* the old walled village lies 8 km. inland (bus, going on to Macerata). *Fontespina* is the N. extension of (143 km.) **Civitanova Marche,** a seaside resort, the starting-point of the road and branch-railway to Macerata and Fabriano. A bus runs inland to *Civitanova Alta* (5 km.; 157 m), birthplace of the poet Annibal Caro (1507-66). In the little town is the 16C Palazzo Cesarini.

FROM CIVITANOVA MARCHE TO MACERATA, 27 km.; railway in 35 min. The road ascends the broad valley of the Chienti, passing near the interesting Romanesque churches of *Santa Maria a Pie' di Chienti* (l.; 7 km.), a huge edifice with a fine E. ambulatory (? 9C), and *San Claudio al Chienti* (r.; 17 km.), a tiny church on a Byzantine plan.—At the crossroads of (21 km.) *Pie' di Ripa* this route turns right.—27 km. *Macerata*, see Rte 54B.

The road crosses the Chienti and, beyond (149 km.) *Porto Sant'Elpidio*, the Tenna. *Sant'Elpidio a Mare*, 9 km. inland, is worth a visit for the works by Vitt. Crivelli in its town hall.—*Casabianca* and *Lido di Fermo* are growing resorts.—159 km. **Porto San Giorgio** is an unsophisticated resort with numerous small hotels and a 13C castle, connected by bus with Fermo, Macerata, Áscoli Piceno, etc.

FROM PORTO SAN GIORGIO TO AMÁNDOLA, 56 km.; frequent bus service to Fermo in ½ hr; bus to Fermo and Amándola in 1½ hrs. 7 km. **Fermo** (319 m) is a thriving hill-top town (35,000 inhab.). It was the *Firmum* of Picenum, was a provincial capital in the 10C and afterwards a Guelph commune at war with Áscoli. It was later subject to the Euffreducci and from 1549 to the Church. The *Girone*, or esplanade, on the top of the hill, commands a magnificent *View of the Monti Sibillini and the Gran Sasso. Here is the *Duomo*, rebuilt by Cosimo Morelli in 1789, but retaining an imposing 13-14C façade, and, within considerable remains of a 5C mosaic pavement. In the sacristy is the *Chasuble of St Thomas Becket (presented to a bishop of Fermo), made from a Moorish silk embroidery woven at Almeria in 1116. In the arcaded P.za del Popolo are the *Palazzo degli Studi*, the seat of a university suppressed in 1826, and the *Palazzo del Comune;* this temporarily houses a small picture gallery, including a Nativity by Rubens. Near by are the *Teatro dell'Aquila* (1780) and the church of *San Domenico* (1233), with Gothic stalls and, beneath the former convent, the *Piscina Epuratoria*, dating from A.D. 41-60. Close to the Barriera Marina is *San Francesco* (1240), containing the Euffreducci monument (1527). Towards the Porta Santa Lucia are the churches of *San Zenone*, with a Romanesque portal (1186), and *Sant'Agostino*, partly Romanesque with early frescoes.

The road descends into the wide and fertile valley of the Tenna.—At (30 km.) *Piane di Falerone*, near the river, are the picturesque ruins of the theatre of the ancient *Faleria*. To the N. beyond (4 km.) the village of *Falerone*, is (13 km.) *Massa Fermana*, a walled village with a 14C town-gate, and, in the (recent) parish church a *Triptych by C. Crivelli, representing the Madonna, between SS. John the Baptist, Lawrence, Sylvester, and Francis (signed and dated 1469). Higher up, the church of La Concezione has a painting by Vitt. Crivelli on the same subject, but with St Rufinus taking the place of St John.—55 km. **Amándola** (550 m) was founded in 1248. The church of *Sant'Agostino* has a fine portal by Marino Cedrini of Venice and a graceful campanile. *San Francesco* has a portal of 1423 and contains good frescoes. The town (4200 inhab.), within its ancient walls, lies on Highway 78 at the foot of the MONTI SIBILLINI, the watershed between the Adriatic and Tyrrhenian Seas. The chain, 19 km. long, extends from *Monte Rotondo* (1829 m) on the N. to *Monte Vettore* (2449 m) on the S., and includes many peaks over 1830 m, which offer attractive and picturesque ascents.—BUSES run from Amándola to *Áscoli Piceno* in 2 hrs.

Sarnano, 12 km. N.W. of Amándola, is a spa and summer resort, with isolated hotels below the peaks to the W. Winter sports are practised on Sasso Tetto (1287 m).

Along this prolific coast, fishing boats ('paranze') may be seen in couples, with a net suspended between them. These craft, with their tall, parti-coloured sails on the blue sea, are a favourite subject with artists.— The road crosses the Aso before (169 km.) *Pedaso;* a road ascends the valley for Amándola.—178 km. *Cupramarittima* preserves the name of the goddess Cupra (see below); it is adjoined by a modern resort.— 182 km. **Grottammare,** with a fine sandy beach, was the birthplace in 1521 of Pope Sixtus V. About 1 km. S. is a ruined temple of Cupra, a goddess perhaps of oriental origin.

About 13 km. W. (bus) is *Ripatransone* (494 m), a little town (4900 inhab.) with a notably wide *Panorama. Inhabited perhaps by the same Umbrians that populated Cupra, this town waged continual warfare against Fermo. The walls and gates of the ancient 'urbs' are still extant. The *Duomo*, by Gaspare Guerra (1597), contains a San Carlo by Turchi (?) and wood carvings. In the *Palazzo*

Comunale is a museum containing antiquities from Umbrian tombs, including fibulæ, helmets, and armlets; paintings on panel by Vinc. Pagani and (probably) Vitt. Crivelli; and ceramics, including fragments of an altar by Mattia Della Robbia. The *Palazzo del Podestà* dates from 1304. A road descends to the right, passing many 15-18C houses, to the church of *San Filippo*, with its fine interior (1680-1722) by Lucio Bonomi.—About 20 km. farther W. is *Montalto Marche*, the ancestral home of Sixtus V (see above) and the birthplace of Giuseppe Sacconi (1853-1905), architect of the Victor Emmanuel monument in Rome. Sixtus V founded the beautiful cathedral (1586).

Other buses run from Grottammare to *Áscoli* in 1¼ hrs; to *Ancona* in 2 hrs; to *Macerata*, etc.

186 km. **San Benedetto del Tronto** is an important fishing centre and a pleasant bathing resort, with 46,000 inhabitants. The Promenade is superbly planted with palms and oleanders.

52   RAVENNA TO PERUGIA AND ROME

ROAD, 385 km. N71. 34 km. *Cesena.*—91 km. *Bagno di Romagna.*—N3 bis (being realigned as far as Sansepolcro).—120 km. *Pieve Santo Stefano.*—137 km. **Sansepolcro.**—153 km. *Città di Castello.*—174 km. *Umbértide* (**Gubbio,** 29 km.).—208 km. **Perugia** (by-pass, 4 km. shorter).—253 km. **Todi** (by-pass, 2 km. shorter). [A superstrada continues to join the Terni-Narni road (N3) 8 km. E. of Narni Scalo].—294 km. *Narni Scalo.*—N204. 304 km. *Orte.*—A1. 385 km. **Rome.**

From Ravenna (Rte 40) Via Cesarea (N16) leads out of the town; N71 soon forks right and runs due S. through level fields and orchards. A superstrada is under construction parallel to this route as far as Cesena. The road passes under the A14 autostrada and the main Milan-Rimini railway and crosses the Via Emilia 2½ km. W. of (34 km.) *Cesena* (comp. Rte 41). It now ascends the valley of the Sávio into the Apennines.— 61 km. *Mercato Saraceno.*—69 km. *Sársina,* the birthplace of the comic playwright Plautus (254-184 B.C.), has an interesting museum containing tombs from a Roman cemetery of the Republican and early Empire period. Beyond the artificial lake of *Quarto,* at (87 km.) *San Piero in Bagno,* a road from Forlì comes in from the right.—91 km. *Bagno di Romagna* (491 m) is a small thermal spa in a pleasant wooded vale. From here N71 continues over the Passo dei Mandrioli (1173 m) to Bibbiena (33 km.) in the Tuscan Casentino (Rte 47B). This route however, continues in the Sávio valley where the road, now N3 bis (being realigned as far as Sansepolcro) rises to a summit-level of 853 m at the *Válico di Montecoronaro,* the lowest crossing of the central Apennines. On the descent the road enters Tuscany, joining the infant Tiber, the course of which is now followed all the way to Todi.

The **Tiber,** in Italian *Tévere,* rises on Monte Fumaiolo (1348 m) just to the E. of the road, and flows for 418 km. to the sea. Among its more important tributaries are the Páglia, the Nera, and the Aniene. Flowing through Rome, where it is c. 134 m wide, it divides the city proper from Trastévere and the Vatican City. On leaving Rome it takes a turn to the S.W. to its mouth near Ostia. The Tiber, fed by numerous turbulent mountain streams and sensitive to rainfall, is liable to sudden flooding. Its swift waters are discoloured with yellow mud, even far from its source: hence the epithet *flavus* given to it by Roman poets.

120 km. *Pieve Santo Stefano* was systematically mined in the German retreat, when the Collegiata was left standing almost alone amid ruins. It contains a Della Robbian figure of St Sebastian, a 15C polychrome Madonna, and a 14C wooden Crucifix.

The road on the right here leads to La Verna and Bibbiena (see Rte 47B). A turning on the left along this road leads to the isolated hamlet of *Caprese Michelangelo* (11 km. from Pieve Santo Stefano), where Michelangelo, son of the podestà Leonardo Buonarroti, was born in 1475 in the little 14C town hall, now restored as a Museum. He was christened in the 13C chapel of San Giovanni Battista.

A road from Rimini over the Passo di Viamaggio comes in just before this road reaches (137 km.) **Sansepolcro,** properly *'Borgo Sansepolcro'* (335 m), a small town (15,800 inhab.) on an upland plain growing tobacco. It was the native place of the painters Piero della Francesca (1416-92), Raffaellino del Colle (1490-1566), and Santi di Tito (1538-1603). The art of the crossbow is still practised (contest on 2nd Sun in Sept; comp. p. 583). The PINACOTECA has recently been rearranged in the *Palazzo Comunale* (adm. 10-13, 15-18; winter 10-13, 14-17).

ROOM I. Church vestments and ecclesiastical objects belonging to Bp. Costaguti (18C). On the end wall, Last Supper by *Ant.* and *Remigio Cantagallina* (1604).— ROOM 2. The crown and vestments (mid-14C) used to adorn the Voltio Santo in the cathedral (comp. below).—ROOM 3. *Follower of Pietro Lorenzetti,* Polyptych.—ROOM 4. Tabernacle in terracotta of the Nativity, by the *School of Giovanni della Robbia; Luca Signorelli,* Standard painted on both sides (Crucifixion and Saints); *Gerino da Pistoia,* SS. Peter and Paul.—ROOM 5 contains the masterpieces of the gallery by *Piero della Francesca;* the *Resurrection, a fresco (justly one of his most famous works), Madonna of the Misericordia, polyptych commissioned by the local Confraternity of the Misericordia (1445-62), Bust of a Saint (St Julian ?), and St Louis of Toulouse (both frescoes). The end of the room is devoted to photographs and copies of his other famous works.—ROOM 6. *Giov. Battista Cungi,* Presentation in the Temple; *Raffaelino del Colle,* Assumption (in a beautiful frame), St Leo; *Pontormo,* Martyrdom of San Quintino.—ROOM 7. *Giovanni de' Vecchi,* Presentation of the Virgin in Temple, and Birth of the Virgin; *Santi di Tito,* St Nicholas of Tolentino, Pope St Clement among the faithful, and Pietà.—ROOM 8. *Agost. Ciampelli,* Destruction of the idols; *Leandro Bassano,* Adoration of the Magi.—Stairs mount to two rooms with 14C (detached) frescoes.—The last room has a series of copper plates engraved by *Cherubino Alberti.*

The DUOMO, with an 11C façade, has a Romanesque interior with Gothic elements (restored). South Aisle. *Sienese School,* Fresco of Madonna and Child; *Santi di Tito,* Incredulity of St Thomas; *Bart. della Gatta,* Fresco of the Crucifixion; *Cherubino Alberti,* Crucifixion; *Florentine School (14C),* Madonna and Child, statue in stone; *Raffaele del Colle,* Resurrection of Christ. In the apse are two Della Robbian statues of Saints. In the chapel to the left of the main apse, is a triptych by *Matteo di Giovanni,* the central panel of which, the Baptism of Christ by Piero della Francesca, is now in the National Gallery of London. The large wood Crucifix (the 'Volto Santo') dates in part from the 10C. The painting of the Ascension is now attrib. to Gerino da Pistoia on a cartoon by Perugino. To the l. of the sacristy door is a pretty Della Robbian tabernacle. In the N. aisle, tomb of Simone Graziani, in the manner of Rossellino.

Other churches of interest in the town include *San Francesco* with a high altar of 1304, and *San Lorenzo* with a Deposition by Rosso Fiorentino.

To Arezzo, see Rte 47A.

The road passes into Umbria. At (141 km.) *San Giustino* a mountainous road (N73 bis) climbs N.E. to the *Bocca Trabária* (1049 m), the pass between Umbria and the Marches. From there it descends the Metauro valley to the little old town of *Sant'Angelo in*

Vado (40 km.), going on to Urbania (50 km; p. 572) and Urbino (67 km.; p. 569). This road runs straight across the plain.

153 km. **CITTÀ DI CASTELLO** occupies the site of *Tifernum,* an Umbrian town (36,600 inhab.). In the Middle Ages it gave employment to many artists, among them Raphael, Signorelli, and the Della Robbia. The Vitelli family held the lordship in the 15C. It now has tobacco manufactories. The *Palazzo del Governo,* with a 14C façade, and the *Palazzo Comunale* were built by Angelo da Orvieto (1334-52). The DUOMO, by Elia di Bartolomeo and his assistants (1466-1529), retains parts of an earlier Romanesque building, with a finely carved portal of the 14C and an imposing interior. In the l. transept is a Transfiguration by Rosso Fiorentino. In the Treasury is a silver *Altar-font presented by Celestine II (1143), and the treasury of Canoscio (5-6C). To the S.E. of the cathedral is the church of *San Domenico* with a good side portal and remains of 15C frescoes. In a chap. at the E. end of the nave the two Renaissance altars (1503) formerly held a Crucifixion by Raphael (now in the National Gallery of London; replaced by a copy) and a St Sebastian by Signorelli (now in the Pinacoteca, comp. below). Beyond the church, near the town wall, is the *Palazzo Vitelli,* built by Ant. da Sangallo the Younger (1531-32) with graffiti decoration by Vasari on its garden façade (shown by the custodian). The fine rooms of the palace are now occupied by the PINACOTECA (adm. 9-12.30, 15-17.30; fest. 9-12).

ROOM I. Sienese marble relief of 14C showing the Baptism of Christ; *Ant. Vivarini and Giov. d'Alemagna,* Madonna and Child; *Maestro della Città di Castello,* *Maestà; *Pietro Lorenzetti* or *Spinello Aretino,* Madonna and Child; 15C Florentine reliquary and two statuettes in gilded bronze attrib. to *Lor. Ghiberti; Ant. da Ferrara,* Triptych; *Giorgio di Andrea di Bartolo* (attrib.), Madonna and Child; *Neri di Bicci,* Madonna and Child.—ROOM II. *Luca Signorelli,* *Standard with St John the Baptist, and the Baptism of Christ, *Martyrdom of St Sebastian, and other good works by his School.—ROOM III. *Giusto di Gand* or a follower of Piero della Francesca, Head of the Redeemer; *Dom. Ghirlandaio,* Coronation of the Virgin; *Raphael,* *Standard with the creation of Eve and the Crucifixion of SS. Roch and Sebastian (a beautiful but very damaged work).—ROOM IV. 14-15C frescoes.—From R. V. can be seen the LOGGIA with fine Della Robbian works.—R. VI. 16C paintings.—R. VII. Works by *Raffaellino del Colle,* and a Madonna and Child with two Saints attrib. to *Pontormo.*—R. VIII is decorated with 16C murals.—R. X, the SALONE, is frescoed by *Cola dell' Amatrice* (1537). Here are works by *Pomarancio, Santi di Tito,* and a Madonna and Child with the young St John attrib. to *Dom. Puligo.*
In the church of *San Francesco* is the Vitelli chapel built by Vasari and containing a Coronation of the Virgin by him, and fine intarsia stalls. On the E. side of the town, in another Palazzo Vitelli (P.za Garibaldi), is the Tourist Office and a small archæological collection relating to the Tiber valley.

The road crosses the Tiber twice.—174 km. **Umbértide** (13,900 inhab), though heavily bombed in 1944 is now a busy town with industrial outskirts. The conspicuous church of *Santa Maria della Réggia* has a fine octagonal exterior by Bino Sozi (16C). The crenellated towers (1385) of the *Rocca* survive. On the other side of the railway is the pretty P.za San Francesco with three churches; the first one, *Santa Croce* (being restored in 1977), has a Deposition by Signorelli (temporarily removed).

A pretty road (28 km.) runs from Umbértide through typical Umbrian countryside viâ Castel Rigone to Lake Trasimene and Passignano (comp. p. 589).

On an attractive minor road to Gubbio, c. 4 km. E., is the fine 16C castle of *Civitella Ranieri.* The easier road (N 219) to Gubbio (29 km.) leaves the Perugia road 4 km. S. of Umbértide and passes tobacco fields with their drying houses (identified by their numerous chimneys).

GUBBIO (529 m), a town of 31,800 inhabitants at the foot of Monte Ingino, has preserved to a large degree its medieval character. Its main roads run parallel with each other along the side of the steep hillside.

Post Office, Via Cairoli, *Azienda Autonoma di Turismo,* 6 P.za Oderisi.
Buses from P.za Quaranta Martiri to *Perugia;* to *Scheggia to Fossato di Vico* (nearest rly. station); to *Umbértide* and *Citta di Castello.*

The town grew up beside the ruins of the Umbrian town of *Iguvium* or *Eugubium,* which had a celebrated temple of Jupiter. Gubbio was sacked by the Goths, but retained its independence until 1384, when it was surrendered to the Montefeltro of Urbino. The miniaturist Oderisio (d. 1299?) is considered as the founder of Gubbio's school of painting, which included Guido Palmerucci, Ottaviano Nelli, and Sinibaldo Ibi. The town is famed for its majolica; the chief producer was Giorgio Andreoli da Intra, commonly called Mastro Giorgio, who discovered a peculiar ruby glaze, although hardly any examples of his work survive in the city itself. The picturesque procession of the *Ceri,* which may have a pagan origin, is held yearly on 15 May, the feast day of St Ubaldo (d. 1160), the town's patron saint and bishop who saved it from Barbarossa in 1155. At this ceremony three wax figures of saints, on wooden 'candles', are carried through the streets at the double. On the last Sun in May is held the 'palio dei balestrieri' (crossbowmen), a contest of medieval origin against the citizens of Sansepolcro (p. 581). Many of the old houses of Gubbio (as in other Umbrian towns) have the curious 'Porta del Morto' beside their principal doorway.—Gubbio was the birthplace of Vittoria Accoromboni (1557), original of Webster's heroine in 'The White Devil'.

The entrance to the town from Umbértide passes the extensive remains of a *Roman Theatre* of the 1C A.D., where classical plays are performed in summer, with the remains of a Mausoleum farther S. The town is entered by the Porta degli Ortacci which leads into the large Piazza Quaranta Martiri planted as a public garden, from which there is a good view of all the main monuments of the town climbing the hillside. On the right is the church of *San Francesco* with interesting frescoes in the chapels at the E. end: r. chap., 14C frescoes (recently restored); main chapel, 13C frescoes; l. chap., complete cycle by Ottaviano Nelli of the life of the Madonna. The convent buildings are of interest. The steep Via della Repubblica (off which is the little Romanesque (13C) church of *San Giovanni*) leads up from the square to Via Savelli della Porta. From here cars continue up to the centre by Via Baldassini (l.) and Via dei Consoli (r.), while for those on foot steps mount directly to Via dei Consoli the main street of the city. To the left opens the impressive P.ZA DELLA SIGNORIA with the ***Palazzo dei Consoli,** an admirable building of 1332-46, attributed to *Matteo di Giovannello* of Gubbio, known as Gattapone. On the S.W. side, which rests on a massive vaulting, it is 98 m high. In the interior is the MUSEO E PINACOTECA (open 9 or 9.30-12.30 or 13, 15-17 or 19).

The huge barrel-vaulted hall contains sculptural fragments. In the former chapel, off the hall, with a fresco of the Madonna and Child with Saints by *Palmerucci* are the seven celebrated * *Eugubian Tables.* These are bronze tables found in 1444 near the Roman theatre, bearing inscriptions in the Umbrian language, five in Etruscan, two in Latin characters. They record the rules of a college of priests, and date probably from 250-150 B.C.—A steep flight of stairs leads up to the Pinacoteca. ROOM I is on the extreme left, and contains works by *Palmerucci,* two 14C reliquaries, and a Byzantine diptych.—ROOM II has 15C frescoes.—R. III. 16C doorway, and the Madonna of the Pomegranate attrib. to *Pier Fr. Fiorentino.*—The MAIN HALL has a good brick vault, and the gonfalon of the Confraternity of the Madonna of the Misericordia, a fine work by *Sinibaldo Ibi.*—R. V. Works by *Spagnoletto, Porocaccini,* and the schools of Caravaggio and Leonardo. A door opens on to the Loggia with a splendid view.

Also in the P.za della Signoria is the *Municipio,* formerly the Palazzo Pretorio (1349); in the neighbouring Via dei Consoli the most notable of many fine old houses is the *Palazzo del Bargello,* built for the 13C governors. A narrow archway off the main piazza is sign-posted for pedestrians to the Duomo, also reached by Via Ducale, both of them steep climbs. The *Palazzo Ducale* (by Luciano Laurana, 1475-80) has a fine courtyard (adm. 9-14, fest. 9-13, closed Mon). Opposite is the 13C **Duomo** (open all day) with remarkable stone vaulting and fine works of art in its chapels. Right wall: 1st niche, *Ant. Gherardi,* Adoration of the Magi; 2nd, *Virgilio Nucci,* Madonna of the Consolation. In the presbytery is a fine carved episcopal throne by *Girol. Maffei* (1557). Left wall: 10th niche, *Bened. Nucci,* Sant'Ubaldo; 8th, *Sinibaldo Ibi,* Madonna enthroned with Saints; 7th, *Tim. Viti,* Mary Magdalen (removed for restoration); 6th, Nativity by the school of *Pinturicchio;* 4th, *Dono Doni,* Pietà.—The MUSEUM (reached from the r. side; open 10-17) has been arranged in the Refectory of the old convent which has a ruined fresco of the Crucifixion and Saints attrib. to *Palmerucci.* Here too is displayed the celebrated Flemish *Cope, designed by a disciple of Justus of Ghent and presented by Marcello Cervini (Pope Marcellus II; 1555), and some detached frescoes by *Giacomo di Benedetto di Beda* (13C), from the crypt of the church of Santa Maria dei Laici; and a painting of the Madonna and Child by *Palmerucci.*

Just inside the Porta Romana, at the S.E. end of the town, is the ex 14C church of *Santa Maria Nuova* (10-12, 16-19) containing the *Madonna of the Belvedere, an outstanding work by Nelli (1403). Here too are displayed church vestments, and, on the W. wall are frescoes by the school of Nelli. Outside the gate is *Sant'Agostino,* a 13C church with the triumphal arch and apse entirely frescoed by Ottaviano Nelli and his pupils. On S. side of the nave (5th altar), fresco of Sant'Ubaldo and two Saints, by Nelli, and on N. side of nave (4th altar), Madonna del Soccorso, also by Nelli (restored) and (5th altar), Madonna and Saints, by Fed. Brunori.

A cable-car mounts in 6 min. from the Porta Romana to *Sant'Ubaldo* (827 m; a steep climb by serpentine path from the cathedral) on Monte Ingino, with a superb panorama.

Beyond Umbértide the main road leaves on the left a road to Gubbio (comp. above).—At (198 km.) *Bosco* N 298, coming S. from Gubbio, joins from the left. Two kilometres farther on it branches right again to cross the Tiber at *Ponte Felcino* and form the approach road to (208 km.) **Perugia,** described in Rte 53. Highway 3 bis (c. 4 km. shorter) avoids Perugia by swinging away to the E., for a short distance coincides with the Foligno-Perugia road (Rte 53) for the crossing of the Tiber, and rejoins the old road coming S. from the city at (217 km.) *Osteria dei Cipressi.*—At (223 km.) *Ponte Nuovo* the road crosses back to the left bank of the Tiber.—226 km. *Deruta* (218 m) is famed for its majolica which is still made in great quantity in modern factories in the new town below. In the old town the Palazzo Comunale has a collection of Deruta ware, detached frescoes by local 15C painters, works by l'Alunno, and by Baciccia, and a *Fresco by Fiorenzo di Lorenzo, detached from the church of San Francesco.

253 km. **TODI** (410 m), with 17,300 inhabitants, now by-passed well to the E., stands on a hill just W. of the old road. The ancient Umbrian city of *Tuder,* it preserves many memorials of antiquity. It is the birthplace of Iacopo de' Benedetti (c. 1250-1306), called Iacopone da Todi, poet and mystic, the reputed author of the 'Stabat Mater'. The local carpenters produce good inlay work. An Antiques Fair is held here in spring.

The magnificent central *PIAZZA DEL POPOLO, or Piazza Vittorio Emanuele, is bordered by Gothic and Renaissance buildings, and is spoilt only by the parked cars which are allowed to fill its centre. At the S. end is the battlemented *Palazzo dei Priori* (1293-1337, with 16C additions); on the E. side the PALAZZO COMUNALE occupies the Gothic *Palazzo del Popolo* (1213, with later alterations), likewise battlemented, and the *Palazzo del Capitano* (1290), which is preceded by a monumental flight of steps. The last contains a picture gallery (closed indefinitely for restoration), with a large polyptych by Lo Spagna, a crucifix in bronze attrib. to Giambologna, frescoes, terracottas, and Etruscan bronzes. In the neighbouring P.za Garibaldi is the *Palazzo Atti* (1552). The DUOMO stands at the N. end of the main square, its 13C façade, with a good portal and rose window, also approached by an imposing flight of steps. The fine interior has good Gothic capitals. On the W. wall, Last Judgement by *Ferraù da Faenza.* In the pretty Gothic arcade with 19C local stained glass on the r. side of the nave, are , a 14C altarpiece of the Madonna and Child; remains of a fresco of the Trinity by *Lo Spagna* (1525); and an altarpiece by *Giannicola di Paolo.* On either side of the presbytery, SS. Peter and Paul, small paintings by *Lo Spagna.* A Crucifix of the late 13C hangs in the apse which has inlaid stalls of 1530. On the l. side of the nave are statues of the school of Giov. Pisano.

San Fortunato (1292), on an imposing site a short way S.W. of the main piazza, has an Annunciation, probably by Iac. della Quercia, on its portal. It contains a fresco of the *Madonna and Child by Masolino (4th S. chap.), and 14C frescoes of the life of St Francis (6th S. chap.). At the end of the S. aisle are fresco fragments by Nic. Vannucci da Todi. In the crypt is the tomb of Fra Iacopone. The ruined *Citadel,* at the top of the hill, commands a splendid view. The Mercato Vecchio, S.E. of the P.za del Popolo, preserves four large alcoves from a Roman building; while outside the 13C walls, to the S.W., is * Santa Maria della Consolazione* (1508-24; usually locked), a domed church designed by Cola da Caprarola and completed by Ambr. Barocci and Fr. da Vita, a masterpiece of the Renaissance and close to the art of Bramante.

Of the two railway stations (Ponto Rio and Ponte Naia), the former 2 km. S.E. of the Porta Romana (bus) is the more convenient.—BUSES to *Rome;* daily viâ Massa Martana to *Foligno.*—From Todi to Orvieto, see p. 540.

About 10 km. E., on a by-road near the little fortified town of *Massa Martana,* is the 12C abbey church of Santi Fidenzio e Terenzio.

The by-pass (2 km. shorter) crosses in a tunnel beneath the old road, which it rejoins just short of (265 km.) *San Faustino* station.—272 km. *Acquasparta* (322 m), frequented for its mineral waters, has medieval ramparts and a fine 16C mansion. A few kilometres farther on, a by-road branches left for the remains of Roman CARSULÆ, never rebuilt since its destruction by the Goths. The site, in lovely country, is unenclosed. It was an important Roman station on the Via Flaminia which has been uncovered, together with two temples, an amphitheatre and a theatre. The limit of the town is marked, just over the hill-top, by the Arch of St Damian, near which is a large circular sepulchre. The little church of St Damian was made from Roman materials. The unmade-up road continues to *San Gémini Fonte,* another spa, from which the main road may be rejoined just N. of (282 km.) *San Gémini* (331 m), an old place with interesting architectural details. The road joins the Terni by-pass (comp. Rte 54) near its W. end.

294 km. *Narni Scalo.* **Narni,** on its hill across the Nera, stands on the Via Flaminia, described in the opposite direction (Rte 54), which proceeds to (381 km.) **Rome.**—Alternatively bearing right below the town on N 204, the Nera may be followed to its confluence with the Tiber at (309 km.) *Orte,* where the autostrada (A 1; Rte 48) is joined for (385 km.) **Rome.**

53   AREZZO TO PERUGIA, ASSISI, AND FOLIGNO

ROAD, 123 km. N 71. 28½ km. **Cortona** (5 km. l.).—At (37 km.) *Borghetto* is the junction with the superstrada (N 75 bis) for (78 km.) **Perugia.**—At (92 km.) N 147 diverges l. for (105 km.) **Assisi,** rejoining N 75 just before (116 km.) *Spello.*—123 km. **Foligno.**

RAILWAY, 117 km. in 2-2½ hrs; to *Perugia* (77 km.) in 70-100 min. with a change at *Terontola.*

Beyond Arezzo N 71 skirts the Valdichiana with low hills on the left, some of them planted with olives.—17 km. *Castiglion Fiorentino,* a walled agricultural market-town, stands on a hill to the left. The Collegiata has notable paintings by Bart. della Gatta (1486) and Segna di Bonaventura. In the adjoining Pieve is a fresco of the Deposition by Luca Signorelli. The Pinacoteca, in the Palazzo Comunale, contains a St Francis by Gatta, a 15C silver-gilt and enamel bust of St Ursula, and a Crucifix of the Umbrian school. In the 12C church of San Francesco is a picture of the saint by Margaritone d'Arezzo.—Farther on the road passes close to the castle of *Montécchio Vesponi* conspicuous on a hill to the left with its 13C walls still intact (approached by a rough track; key at neighbouring farm). In the 14C it was given by the grateful Florentines to Sir John Hawkwood, the English-born condottiere.

At (28½ km.) *Cortona-Camucia* station a winding road bears left for 5 km. N.E.; bus) **CORTONA** (22,500 inhab.), built on a long hillside with narrow winding streets covering the steep slopes. One of the most ancient cities in Italy, it is interesting for its Etruscan remains and for its works of art, and commands magnificent views.

History. Cortona, probably one of the twelve cities of the Etruscan Confederation, was already ancient when taken by the Etruscans. It is said to have been originally called *Corythus,* after its founder Corythus, reputed father of Dardanus, the mythical ancestor of the Trojans. Subjugated by Rome about 390 B.C., it sank into insignificance. Its lands were wasted by Hannibal and its territory was three times distributed among Roman soldiers. Fra Angelico lived and worked here c. 1408-18, but most of his paintings have been destroyed; and the city's artistic fame comes chiefly from Luca Signorelli (1441-1523), the great precursor of Michelangelo; another native painter (and architect) was Pietro Berrettini (1596-1669), called Pietro da Cortona. Fr. Laparelli (1521-70), the architect who built Valletta (Malta), was born here. The medieval walls of the town incorporate portions of the Etruscan walls, dating from the 6C or 5C B.C. Many of the old houses have the curious 'Porta del Morto'.

Half-way up to the town is the church of * *Santa Maria del Calcinaio,* a masterpiece of Renaissance architecture by Fr. di Giorgio (1485). The elegant interior with clean architectural lines has a handsome high altar of 1519 by Bernardino Covatti. The stained glass in the rose window is by Guglielmo di Marcillat. In the nave are two paintings by Tommaso Barnabei. A little to the W. is the so-called *Tanella di Pitagora* (ring for custodian), a vaulted Etruscan hypogeum (4C. B.C.), nothing to do with Pythagoras (who lived at Crotone in Southern Italy). Farther down the hill are three chamber tombs of the 7C or 6C. B.C. Near the entrance to the town (closed to traffic; parking near San Domenico) is the early 15C church of *San Domenico* with an ancona of the Coronation of the Virgin by Lor. di Niccolò (1402) in the main apse. In the chap. to the r., Madonna and Saints, an early work by Signorelli. On the left wall of the nave, an Assumption by Bart. della Gatta has been removed for restoration. Also on this wall is a lunette (very ruined; formerly over the portal) of the Madonna frescoed by Fra Angelico and a fresco fragment of St Roch by Bartolomeo della Gatta.

The *Passeggiata* along the hillside behind the church through public gardens commands fine views. Via Santa Margherita leads up to the church of the same name (comp. p. 588) past a Via Crucis in mosaic by Gino Severini (1883-1966), a native of Cortona.

Via Nazionale, popularly 'Rugapiana', the main and only level street, leads to Piazza della Repubblica, the centre of the town. The 13C *Palazzo Comunale* was enlarged in the 16C and extends to P.za Signorelli. Here it adjoins the **Palazzo Pretorio,** a 13C mansion rebuilt in 1608 and restored since 1944, which houses the MUSEO DELL'ACCADEMIA ETRUSCA (adm. 10-13, 15.30-18.30; closed Mon).

In the Main Hall the fine collection of Etruscan antiquities includes bronze statuettes and Bucchero ware, and an elaborately sculptured bronze *Lamp (late 5C B.C.; in the centre case). The small paintings here include: *Luca Signorelli,* Nativity; *Bicci di Lorenzo,* Triptych; *Neri di Bicci,* Pietà and Saints; *Pinturicchio,* Madonna and Child with the young St John (small tondo); *Niccolò di Pietro Gerini,* Saints; *Fr. Signorelli,* Tondo of the Madonna and Saints; *Antoniazzo Romano,* Madonna and Child; *Bart. della Gatta,* Madonna and Child. Also, Byzantine mosaic of the 12C of the Virgin in prayer, and a Roman encaustic tile 'the muse Polimnia' of 1-2C A.D.—Later works include paintings by *Cigoli* and *Piazzetta* and their schools. The other rooms around the courtyard contain an eclectic collection including Egyptian and far Eastern objects, coins, plaques, furniture, etc.

The **Duomo,** to which Via Casali descends, was enlarged in the 16C to designs by Giul. da Sangallo, incorporating earlier elements of the façade, but has been much modified. The Campanile (1566) is by Laparelli. In the interior, behind the main altar by *Fr. Mazzuoli* (1664), are a group of good paintings: (r. to l.) *Cigoli,* Madonna and Saints; *School of Signorelli,* Crucifixion, Incredulity of St Thomas; *Aless. Allori,* Madonna and Saints. At the end of the N. aisle, carved ciborium by *Cuiccio di Nuccio.* The **Museo Diocesano** (adm. 9-12, 15-18), opposite, incorporates the former church of the Gesu (r.) with a fine wooden ceiling by Michelangelo Leggi (1536).

Here are assembled a fine group of paintings: *Luca Signorelli,* Madonna and Saints; Institution of the Eucharist; *Sassetta,* Madonna and Child with Saints; *Pietro Lorenzetti,* Crucifix; *Fra Angelico,* Madonna enthroned with Saints (with a fine predella), *Annunciation (1428-30); *Luca Signorelli,* Nativity, Adoration of the Shepherds, Assumption. The font is by *Ciuccio di Nuccio.*—In a second room: *Luca Signorelli,* Assumption; *Tuscan School of the early 14C,* St Margaret and scenes from her life; *Pietro Lorenzetti,* *Madonna and Child enthroned with angels; *Duccio* (or his School), Madonna and Child; fresco fragments with scenes from the life of Christ (Sienese 14C). The sculptural fragments include a Roman sarcophagus (end of 2C), with combats of Amazons and Centaurs, admired by Donatello and Brunelleschi. Further works by *Signorelli* include the Communion of the Apostles, Madonna and Saints, with *Scenes from the Life of Christ in the predella, and a *Deposition. Besides church vestments, the treasury includes a reliquary by *Giusto da Firenze* (1457).—A room beyond has the cartoons for the mosaics executed by *Gino Severini* for the Via Crucis in Via Santa Margherita (comp. above).—In the lower chapel is a Florentine terracotta Pietà (15C).

From P.za Signorelli Via Dardano leads to the *Porta Colonia,* around which are the most considerable relics of the Etruscan walls, the huge blocks conspicuous below the Roman and Medieval walls above, which stretch away up the hill towards the Fortezza Medicea (comp. below). Outside the gate, in the beautiful countryside below the town, the charming church of *Santa Maria Nuova* (1550-54) is well seen.

Via Santucci mounts through the Palazzo del Popolo to the church of *San Francesco* which preserves a portal of 1245. Inside are the tombs of Bp. Ubertini (1345) and, behind the high altar, of Brother Elias of Cortona, the disciple of St Francis. A Byzantine ivory reliquary of the Holy Cross, kept in a side chapel, is unlocked on request by the sacristan. Luca Signorelli was buried in the crypt below. A steep road leads up past a huge circular water cistern to the pretty church of *San Nicolò* (if closed, ring for custodian). It contains a Standard painted on both sides by Luca Signorelli with a *Deposition (in excellent condition) and a Madonna and Child. On the N. wall is a votive fresco of the Madonna and Saints by the school of Signorelli. The custodian indicates a path up to the top of the hill through the cypress woods which surround the sanctuary of *Santa Margherita,* a 19C church preserving a single rose window of its predecessor. The *Tomb of St Margaret of Laviano (1247-97) is by the native artists Angiolo and Francesco di Pietro (1362). Below the church a Via Crucis descends towards P.za Garibaldi (comp. p. 587) with the stations of the Cross in mosaic by Gino Severini. Just above the church is the *Fortezza Medicea,* recently restored and to be opened to the public. It was built by Laparelli in 1549 and commands a magnificent view. From it can be seen part of the outer circle of walls built by the Etruscans.

BUSES run from Cortona to *Città di Castello* in 1¼ hrs; viâ Teróntola station to *Umbértide* in 2 hrs; to *Perugia* in ¾ hr; etc.

34 km. *Teróntola Station,* on the main line to Rome, where the Perugia branch diverges.—At (37 km.) *Borghetto* this route joins the superstrada (l.) for Perugia.

N 71, the old main road to Orvieto (114 km. from Arezzo) and Rome, continues S., entering Umbria at the N.W. corner of Lake Trasimene (comp. below).— 46 km. *Castiglione del Lago* (304 m), with its castle (splendid view), has a fine situation on a promontory jutting into the lake. The church of the Maddalena has a Madonna and Saints by a follower of Perugino (Sinibaldo Ibi?).—The road turns S.W. to join (64 km.) the road from Siena and Montepulciano 1 km. E. of *Chiusi* station (see p. 535), with a view of the Valdichaina on the right.—72 km. **Città della Pieve** (6450 inhab.), standing on high ground (508 m) 5 km. N.E. of its station, was the birthplace of Pietro Vannucci (1446-1523), called Il Perugino. The church of

Santa Maria dei Bianchi contains his lovely fresco of the Adoration of the Magi (1504), and the *Duomo* has other works by him (recently restored). The road, winding and undulating, passes the large villages of (79 km.) *Monteleone d'Orvieto* and (95 km.) *Ficulle,* then descends into the valley of the Páglia, crossing under the Autostrada del Sole to reach (144 km.) *Orvieto* Station (124 m). **Orvieto,** see Rte 48. Highway N71 continues S.W., winding up to (132 km.) the *Poggio di Biagio* (590 m), whence N74 diverges W. viâ *Pitigliano* (40 km. farther) to reach the coast just N. of Orbetello (83 km.; see Rte 50). This road turns due S., passes into Lazio, and·at (148 km.) *Montefiascone* joins the Via Cassia. From there viâ (164 km.) *Viterbo* to (245 km.) **Rome,** see Rte 49.

The road from Città della Pieve to Perugia (N 220; 43 km.; bus in 1½ hrs starting from Chiusi station) leaves on the left, at 15 km., a road to *Panicale* (7 km.), where the church of San Sebastiano contains frescoes by Perugino. The best view of Lake Trasimene can be enjoyed from the old walls.—From (17 km.) *Tavernelle* is visited the imposing *Santuario della Madonna di Mongiovino,* by Rocco da Vicenza (1513), 2 km. N.—At (21 km.) *Fontignano* (1 km.l.), with its castle, Perugino died of the plague in 1523. The little church of the Annunziata contains his (modern) tomb and a fresco by him.

The road now runs close to Lake Trasimene with fine views of the islands.

Lago Trasimeno, or *Lake Trasimene,* has a circumference of nearly 45 km.; its depth, never more than 7 m, is constantly diminishing because of the formation of peat, and there is some danger of it drying into a marsh. The shores are flat and reedy. The lake, which abounds in fish, has three islands, the largest of which is the *Isola Polvese.* Near the N. shore are the *Isola Maggiore* and the *Isola Minore.* At the S.E. end of the lake is a subterranean outlet built by the Romans and several times reopened. The scene of Hannibal's great victory over the Romans in 217 B.C. is by the N. shore.

43 km. *Tuoro sul Trasimeno.* To the N.W. is the village of *Sanguineto,* whose name ('a name of blood from that day's sanguine rain') commemorates the slaughter by Hannibal of 16,000 Romans after his momentous victory, in the plain below, over the consul Flaminius in 217 B.C.—49 km. *Passignano sul Trasimeno,* with an old fortified quarter on a promontory, is an attractive little lakeside resort with aircraft construction works. A pier on the lake is the starting point for boat excursions to (¼ hr–½ hr) the *Isola Maggiore* (some boats call on the way at Tuoro), with its picturesque lakeside hamlet and the church of San Michele containing paintings by Caporali; also two chapels commemorating a visit of St Francis in 1211. Other boats run to San Feliciano, on the E. shore of the lake, and the *Isola Polvese,* now almost deserted.

Just beyond Passignano a by-road (l.), with fine retrospective views of the lake climbs to (7½ km.) *Castel Rigone,* a little resort, with a pretty Renaissance church (1494) and (28 km.) *Umbértide* (comp. p. 589).

The E. shore juts into the lake at *Monte del Lago,* but the main road now leaves the lake to tunnel under the saddle of (60 km.) *Magione,* which preserves the Badia, a castle of the Knights of Malta, built by Fieravanti c. 1420.

79 km. **PERUGIA** (135,700 inhab.), capital of the province of the same name (6357 sq. km.), which comprises nearly the whole of Umbria, is proudly situated on the top of a hill 494 m above the sea and some 305 m above the Tiber. Its works of art and its historical associations make it one of the most interesting cities in Italy. The special qualities of Perugian art are seen to full advantage in the Sala del Cambio and in the

picture gallery. On a lower scale, Perugia is noted also for its wool, its wrought-iron work, and its chocolate.

Railway Stations. The main station is at *Fontivegge* (Pl. 13), below the city to the S.W., for Foligno (Rome) and Teróntola (Florence); bus, see below.—*Perugia Sant'Anna* (Pl. 11) and *Ponte San Giovanni* (6 km. E.S.E.) are on the branch line to Sansepolcro and Terni.

Car Parking is difficult near the centre which is closed to traffic. Car Parks (with hourly tariff) are indicated on the approaches (P.za Michelotti, Viale Pellini, Via 14 Settembre etc.) Covered Multi-storey Car Park near P.za Matteotti.

Hotels on and near the Corso Vannucci.

Post Office, P.za Matteotti, P.za Partigiani. *Telephone Exchange,* P.za della Repubblica.

Tourist Offices. *Assessorato al Turismo della Regione dell'Umbria,* 30 Corso Vannucci; *Azienda del Turismo,* 21 Via Mazzini (*Information Office,* 9C Corso Vannucci).—**Travel Agents:** *VI.SE.TUR,* 12 P.za Italia, *Tuttoturismo,* 15 Viale Indipendenza.

Buses. No. 1 from the main railway station at Fontivegge to P.za Matteotti; No. **2,** San Marco—Via Fani—Porta San Costanzo—Montebello; No. **5,** P.za 4 Novembre—Sant'Angelo.

Country Buses to *Rome* (once daily on weekdays); to *Assisi;* to *Ponte San Giovanni;* to *Bettona;* viâ *Spello* to *Foligno;* viâ *Foligno* to *Spoleto* (more easily reached by train); to *Gualdo Tadino;* to *Gubbio;* and to *Todi.*

History. *Perusia* was one of the twelve cities of the Etruscan Confederation; and it is to the Etruscans and not to the Umbrians that the city owes its ancient walls and gates. It submitted to the Romans under Q. Fabius in 310 B.C. In the civil war between Octavian (Augustus) and Mark Antony, L. Antonius, brother of the triumvir, was besieged in Perusia in 41-40 B.C. Famine compelled the city's surrender; but one of its citizens, Gaius Cestius, in panic set fire to his own house, and the flames spread, razing all Perusia to the ground. Augustus rebuilt the city and called it *Augusta Perusia*. It is said to have been besieged by Totila in 547, and saved by the wisdom of its bishop, St Herculanus. In 592 it became a Lombard duchy, and after the restoration of the Western Empire its history is one of obscure and intricate wars with neighbouring towns in which it generally took the Guelph side. The first despot was one of the Raspanti ('scratchers'; the nickname of the burghers), named Biondo Michelotti (1393), who murdered two of the noble family of the Baglioni, became leader of the Florentine army, and allied himself with Gian Galeazzo Visconti. The city passed to the latter family, and afterwards to Braccio Fortebraccio (1416-24), the famous 'condottiere' and a wise governor. Perugia was subsequently torn by strife between the rival families of Oddi and Baglioni; and when the latter prevailed they in turn quarrelled, until the day (14 Aug 1500) when all their leaders were massacred as the result of a conspiracy, with the exception of Gian Paolo, who revenged himself upon the murderers. Pope Paul III seized the town in 1535 and, when it rebelled against his salt tax, built a fortress known as the Rocca Paolina on the ruins of the old Baglioni mansions. From then onwards Perugia was ruled by a papal governor. In 1809 it was annexed to the French Empire, and it was called *Pérouse* by the French; in 1815 it was restored to the Church. In 1859 the papal Swiss Guards occupied the city after an indiscriminate masacre, but a year later they were expelled, and a popular insurrection destroyed the Rocca Paolina, the badge of subjection.—The British 8th Army entered Perugia on 20 June 1944.

Art. Perugia was the chief centre of Umbrian painting, which flowered in sweet calm through the storms of civic history. The Umbrian school took its rise in the 12C, but it was only in the 15C that it became independent of Siena and Florence, producing such masters as Gentile da Fabriano, Ottaviano Nelli, Nicolò da Foligno (L'Alunno), Matteo da Gualdo, Bartolomeo Caporali, and Benedetto Bonfigli (c. 1420-96), the first great Perugian painter. His immediate follower was Fiorenzo di Lorenzo (1445-1522), but the greatest renown is that of Pietro Vannucci (1446-1523), born at Città della Pieve, but called *Il Perugino* from his long association with Perugia. Among his numerous disciples of the Umbrian school alone were Bernardino di Betto (Il Pinturicchio or Pintoricchio; 1454-1513), Andrea d'Assisi (L'Ingegno), Tiberio d'Assisi, Fr. Melanzio of Montefalco, Giovanni di Pietro of Spoleto (Lo Spagna), Bern. di Mariotto, Eusebio da San Giorgio, Domenico and Orazio Alfani, and Giannicola di Paolo, with the last-named of whom the school died out.

The approach to Perugia from the W. or from the main station is by Via Venti Settembre, which winds uphill towards the old city. At the Largo Cacciatori degli Alpi, with its monument to Garibaldi by Cesare Zocchi (1887), the road divides. On the right is the *Sant'Anna Station*. Beyond the square the street, now called Via Guglielmo Marconi, continues to climb, and passes through the city walls to join the Corso Cavour, coming from the Porta San Pietro (S.E.)., the entrance from Todi or Assisi.

The street now curves to the left, past (r.) the little Gothic church of *Sant'Ercolano* (1326). On the right the Via Marzia, preserving the name of the Etruscan Porta Marzia, leads into the city. The main road, now called Viale Indipendenza, continues up to traverse the site of the *Rocca Paolina* (comp. below), then almost doubles back on itself as it climbs, passing considerable remains of the Etruscan walls, to reach the PIAZZA ITALIA (Pl. 11), a pleasant square flanked by imposing buildings. On its S. side is the impressive *Prefettura* (1870), whose front bears the Perugian griffin in bronze.

On the S. side of the Prefettura is the charming little terraced *Giardino Carducci* commanding a *View extending from Monte Amiata to the summits of the central Apennines, with Montefalco, Assisi, Spello, Foligno, Spoleto, and other centres.—On the W. side of the Prefettura is the Largo della Libertà.

From the P.za Italia two important streets run N. That on the right is Via Baglioni, leading to Piazza Matteotti. The street on the left is the wide and undulating *CORSO VANNUCCI (totally closed to motor traffic), the finest thoroughfare in Perugia, named in honour of her greatest painter. On the left of the Corso, near its N. end, is the *Collegio del Cambio** (Pl. 6), the hall and chapel of the Bankers' Guild, by *Bart. di Mattiolo* and *Lod. di Antonibo* (1452-57). The hall is decorated with frescoes painted by *Perugino* and his pupils for the merchants, who paid 350 ducats for the work. The Collegio is open on weekdays 9-12.30, 15-17 or 18; Sun & fest. 9-12.30.

INTERIOR. In the vestibule are walnut-wood carvings by *G. Zuccari* (1615-21).—The *Sala dell'Udienza del Cambio* is painted with frescoes by *Perugino* and his pupils (1499-1507). On the left wall are Prudence and Justice, with classical heroes; and Fortitude and Temperance, similarly attended. The elegant and languid figures are in the fashion of the painter's time. On the end wall, Transfiguration and Nativity. On the right wall are the Eternal Father, with Prophets and the Sibyls. This wall and the paintings of Fortitude (see above) are by both tradition and modern criticism attributed to Raphael, then a youth of 17. On the ceiling are liberal arts and pagan divinities, by Perugino's assistants. On the middle pilaster of the left wall is a portrait of Perugino by himself. The splendid carved and inlaid furniture is by *Dom. del Tasso* and *Ant. da Mercatello* (1492, 1508). On the right is a gilded statuette of Justice attrib. to *Bened. da Maiano*.— The good frescoes in the *Cappella di San Giovanni Battista* are mostly by Perugino's disciple, *Giannicola di Paolo*.

Adjacent is the *Palazzo dei Priori** (Pl. 6), now the *Palazzo Comunale* a massive structure by *Giac. di Servadio* and *Giovannello di Benvenuto* (1293-97), afterwards enlarged, and completed in 1443. The whole has been well restored.

The principal façade, overlooking the Corso, has a richly decorated portal; the older façade, overlooking the P.za Quattro Novembre, has a flight of steps and a doorway surmounted by the bronze Perugian griffin and the Guelph lion (temporarily removed), bearing chains, carried off from the gates of Siena by the Perugians after a victory at Torrita in 1358. The latest suggestion about the figures is that the wings of the griffin were added before 1281 to an Etruscan body and the new lion made. To the right are three arches, probably from the church of *San Severo*, destroyed to make room for the palace.

The entrance is from the Corso. On the first floor is the SALA DELLA CONSULTA, with a handsome Renaissance doorway surmounted by a Madonna by *Pinturicchio*. For a long time it was known as the *Sala del Malconsiglio*, from the 'ill-advised' consent of the Perugians to spare the lives of the English soldiers of Sir John Hawkwood, a noted condottiere known in Italy as Giovanni Acuto (d. 1394), by whom they were afterwards defeated in 1366. The *SALA DEI NOTARI (shown by the custodian on the ground floor), on the same floor, is a remarkable vaulted hall with frescoes of Old Testament scenes and fables by a close follower of *Pietro Cavallini* (13C).—On the second floor is the BIBLIOTECA AUGUSTA (weekdays 9-14 and 17-19, Sat 9-12), with a good collection of MSS. and incunabula.

On the third floor (lift) is the *Galleria Nazionale dell'Umbria, the most important collection extant of Umbrian paintings. The gallery is open 9-14 exc. Mon; fest. 9-13.

The SALA MAGGIORE was the hall of the Consiglio Generale del Comune. It contains interesting 13-15C frescoes of the Central Italian schools. ROOMS I and II. Works of the late 13C. R. I. 29. *Duccio di Buoninsegna,* Madonna and angels; 26. *Maestro di San Francesco,* Crucifix, with St Francis in adoration (dated 1272); 32. *Vigoroso da Siena,* Madonna and saints (dated 1269).—R. II. 894-6. *Arnolfo di Cambio,* Statuettes.—R. III. *Meo di Guido da Siena,* 1. Polyptych, 13. Madonna and Child with four saints, 8. Madonna and Child:—R. IV contains 14C Perugian and Sienese works, and a stained glass window (168.) by *Giov. di Bonino.*—R. V. Sienese 14C and early 15C. *Taddeo di Bartolo,* 72. Annunciation, 64. St Peter, 62. Five saints, 66. Madonna and saints (signed and dated 1403), 63. St Paul; *Bartolo di Fredi,* 58. Triptych with the Marriage of St Catherine, saints, Annunciation, 88. Madonna with saints and the prophet Elijah; *59. Lippo Vanni,* Madonna and Child; 116. *Dom. di Bartolo,* Polyptych; 67. *Taddeo di Bartolo,* Pentecost.—R. VI. 79. *Bicci di Lorenzo,* Marriage of St Catherine (with a fine predella); 84. *Pietro di Domenico da Montepulciano,* Madonna between SS. Francis and Anthony Abbot; 129. *Gentile da Fabriano,* Madonna and Child (early work).—RR. VII and VIII. Revival of Umbrian art in the mid-15C.—R. VII. *91-108. Fra Angelico,* Madonna with angels and saints, part of a triptych; in the predella, Miracles and death of St Nicholas; *111-114. Piero° della Francesca,* Madonna with angels and saints, with a beautiful Annunciation above, and, in the predella, Miracles of St Anthony, St Francis, and St Elizabeth; 746. *Fr. di Giorgio Martini,* Scourging of Christ (bronze relief); 124. *Benozzo Gozzoli,* Madonna of Humility and Saints.—R. VIII. *Giov. Boccati,* 437. Pietà 149. Madonna della Misericordia, 150-51. Madonna del Pergolato, 147. Madonna dell'Orchestra; 879. *Fr. di Gentile da Fabriano,* Madonna and Child and Annunciation, processional banner painted on both sides; 169. *L'Alunno,* Gonfalon of the Confraternità dell'Annunziata; 126-8. *Giov. Fr. da Rimini,* Madonna and saints.

R. IX. *Bened. Bonfigli,* 138. Annunciation and St Luke; 140-41. Adoration of the Magi; in the predella, Baptism of Christ, Crucifixion, Miracle of St Nicholas.—R. X. Minor 15C works. *Nicolò ·del Priore,* 204. St Francis receiving the Stigmata, 193-5, 197, 199. Dead Christ and saints; 339-40. Crucifixion; 109. *Antoniazzo Romana,* Madonna; *Perugian School,* 152. Dead Christ, 174. Madonna and Child (fresco); 1054. *Antoniazzo Romano,* Ecce Homo; *Mariano di Antonio,* 117-122. Miracles of SS. Anthony, John the Baptist, and Bernardine; 115. Scenes from the Passion; 236. *Gerolamo da Cremona,* Madonna and angels.—R. XI. Perugian 15C artists. *Fiorenzo di Lorenzo,* 230. Madonna with angels, saints, and donors (probably his earliest work), 235. Painted niche, signed and dated 1487; *Bart. Caporali,* 160-163. Angels with the symbols of the Passion, 221. Pietà (fresco), 166-70. Assumption; above, Eternal Father; 153-4. Angel, St John the Evangelist, St Mary Magdalen, 125. Madonna with angels.— R. XII. *Fiorenzo di Lorenzo,* 231. St Sebastian, 208-19. Madonna and Saints, 178-9. Adoration of the shepherds; 181-2, 206. Triptych of the Madonna and Saints.—*R. XIII. Fiorenzo di Lorenzo,* 177. Madonna with SS. Nicholas of Bari and Catherine (fresco); 435. St Sebastian (fresco); 856. *School of And. della Robbia,* St Francis; *Perugino,* 220. Pietà, 180. Adoration of the Magi (c. 1475); 1056. St Jerome (fresco); 796. *Bened. Buglioni,* Madonna in adoration (terracotta).

R. XIV. *164, 237, 222-9. *Bened. Bonfigli, Pinturicchio, Perugino,* and others, Niche of St Bernardine of Siena (1465 and after); below, Gonfalon of St Bernardine (*Bonfigli*); on the side walls: *Miracles of the saint (*Pinturicchio* and *Perugino*), with remarkable architectural details.—R. XV. *Perugino,* 238, 243, 245, 247, 249-61. Adoration of the shepherds, Baptism of Christ, SS. Jerome and Mary Magdalen, Angel, Eternal Father, in the predella, Adoration of the Magi, Presentation in the Temple, Marriage of Cana, Preaching of St John the Baptist, saints, 270. Madonna della Confraternità della Consolazione, *279. Madonna and Child with four saints (1500; predella in Berlin; in a beautiful frame), 278. Gonfalon of the Confraternità della Giustizia (much restored), 266-9. Transfiguration; in the predella, Annunciation, Nativity, Baptism of Christ; 280. SS. Francis, Jerome, John the Baptist, Sebastian, and Anthony of Padua, *248. Christ in the tomb (1494), 358. Lunette of Adoration of the Shepherds (fresco); *Pinturicchio,* *274. Madonna, SS. Augustine and Jerome; in the predella, St Augustine and the Child, and St Jerome in the desert; above, Annunciation, Christ in the tomb, the Holy Ghost; 276. Gonfalon of St Augustine.

R. XVI (left). 983. *Piero di Cosimo,* Pietà.—R. XVII. *Bern. di Mariotto,* 156. Madonna with St John and two saints, 155. Marriage of St Catherine, 175. Madonna and saints, 157. Coronation of the Virgin; 203. *School of Luca Signorelli,* Madonna with angels and saints; in the predella, St Bernardine, Dream of Innocent III, etc.—R. XVIII. Followers of Perugino. *Giannicola di Paolo,* 323. All Saints' Day, 324. Madonna and St John, 325. Crucifixion (fresco); 273. *Lo Spagna,* Blessed Colomba da Rieti; 271. *Giov. Batt. Caporali,* Madonna and Child enthroned with Saints; *Perugino,* *263-200. Coronation of the Virgin, Crucifixion, painted on both sides.—R. XIX. Pupils of Perugino. *Eusebio da San Giorgio,* 287. Adoration of the Magi, 282. Madonna and saints, 343. Madonna with SS. John the Baptist and Benedict; 347. Three Saints; *Sinibaldo Ibi,* 357. Madonna with four saints, 1005. Standard of St Anthony Abbot; 356. *Sinibaldo Ibi* and *Berto di Giovanni,* Madonna with SS. Augustine and Sebastian; *Berto di Giovanni,* 294. Birth of the Virgin, 295. Presentation of the Virgin, 303. Marriage of the Virgin, 304. Assumption; these four from the predella of *Pinturicchio's* Coronation of the Virgin, now in the Vatican; 309. Coronation of the Virgin, 307-326. St John the Evangelist.

ROOM XX. has ceiling frescoes by *Tom. Bernabei.* The paintings are by 16C followers of Perugino and Raphael. 363. *Pompeo di Anselmo* and *Dom. Alfani,* Holy Family (after Raphael); *Dom. Alfani,* 364. Madonna with SS. Gregory and Nicholas of Bari, 288. Eternal Father (after a drawing by Raphael; originally placed over Raphael's Descent from the Cross, now in the Villa Borghese in Rome), *354. Madonna with angels and saints; 275. *Pompeo Cocchi,* Crucifixion; 414. *Dono Doni,* Birth of the Virgin.—R. XXI. Late Renaissance. 415. *G. B. Naldini,* Presentation in the Temple; 816. Bas relief of Christ routing the merchants from the Temple, by *Vincenzo Danti.*—R. XXII. 733, 763. 14C croziers; *744. Silver-gilt chalice and paten from the church of San Domenico, by *Cataluccio di Pietro da Todi;* *742. Reliquary of gilt metal; 762. Gold reliquary of St Juliana; 868, 317-18. Silver voting chest, used for the election of magistrates; 859. 17C ivory crucifix.—R.XXIII, formerly the Prior's Chapel, with a majolica pavement. *Bonfigli,* Frescoes of the lives of St Ercolano and St Louis of Toulouse, patrons of Perugia (1454-96); stalls by *Gaspare di Iac. da Foligno* and *Paolino da Ascoli* (1452); 720-21. Voting chests.—R. XXIV. 855. *Agost. di Duccio,* Madonna and Child and other sculptural fragments.

From the Sala Maggiore the stair landing is reached and the entrance to Rooms XXVI-XXXVII, recently arranged to display 16C-18C works. Room XXVI, in a fine large hall of the palace, contains works by late 16C painters including *Lattanzio Pagani, Cristoforo Gherardi, Arrigo Fiammingo,* and *Fr. Baldelli;* (on easels): 1084. *Fed. Barocci,* Madonna and Child with the young St John; 1083. *Orazio Gentileschi,* Female Saint at the piano; 1073, 1074. *Valentin,* Noli me tangere, Christ with the Samaritan woman.—R. XXVII. 535. *Pietro da Cortona,* Birth of the Virgin; *Sassoferrato,* 381. Virgin in prayer, 380. Head of the Madonna.—A spiral staircase leads up to R. XXVIII. 614. *Fr. Trevisani,*

Martyrdom of St Andrew; 606. *Benedetto Luti,* Christ in the House of the Pharisee; 379. *Corrado Giaquinto,* Trinity.—R. XXIX. *G. M. Crespi* and the local painters of the 18C.—R. XXX. *Lod. Mazzanti,* St Bernard Tolomei curing the pestilence in Siena in 1348; works by *Seb. Conca* and *Fr. Appiani.*—From R. XXVIII, R. XXXI is entered. Here is a historical topographical display with 16C views of Perugia.—R. XXXII contains wood carvings and Perugian textiles.—R. XXXIII. 18C topographical drawings by *G. B. Wicar.* From here a staircase leads down to the exit.

On the ground floor of the Palazzo dei Priori, entered by the main door (No. 15) in the direction of the P.za Quattro Novembre, is the *Sala di Udienza del Collegio della Mercanzia* (9-13, 15-18; fest. 9-13), with early 15C wood-carving and intarsia work.

The Corso Vannucci ends in the PIAZZA QUATTRO NOVEMBRE (Pl. 7), a square full of character and the most beautiful in Perugia. It has changed its name more than once, having been previously known as the Piazza del Duomo, della Fonte, and del Municipio. On the right, at the corner of the Corso and Piazza Quattro Novembre, is the mutilated *Palazzo del Collegio dei Notari* (15C), with admirable windows. In its centre is the ***Fontana Maggiore,** designed by *Fra Bevignate* (1277-80), with bas-reliefs by *Nicola* and *Giov. Pisano* and three nymphs by Giov. Pisano (formerly attributed to Arnolfo di Cambio). The fountain was carefully restored in 1948-49. To the W. of the piazza is the 13C *Palazzo del Vescovado,* several times rebuilt. Near by is the bell-tower of the cathedral (1606-12), replacing an octagonal Gothic campanile pulled down in 1462. Behind is the little church of the *Maestà delle Volte* (1567-90), named after a fresco of the Sienese School.

On the N. side of the square is the **Cathedral** (Pl. 6; *San Lorenzo;* closed 12.30-16 in summer, 12-15 in winter), a Gothic building of the 15C, orientated towards the W. with an unfinished façade in the Piazza Danti, adjoining on the right. The side facing the Piazza Quattro Novembre is adorned with the elegant *Loggia di Braccio Fortebraccio,* of four arches on octagonal travertine columns, built in 1423. Here, too, is an exterior pulpit built for St Bernardine in 1425 and a bronze statue of Julius III, by Vinc. Danti (1555, the year of the pope's death). The principal doorway of the cathedral, by Galeazzo Alessi (1568), is on the S. flank.

The dark INTERIOR, imposing rather than harmonious, with aisles equal in height to the nave, has columns painted in imitation of impossible marbles. Surrounded by a little altar on a pillar to the right of the nave, the handsome Madonna delle Grazie is attributed to *Giannicola di Paolo.*—The 1st chapel of the right aisle, beyond the tomb of Bp. Baglioni (d. 1451), by *Urbano da Cortona,* is the CAPPELLA DI SAN BERNARDINO, closed by a fine wrought-iron screen (15C). It contains a ***Descent from the Cross by *Barocci* (1569) and a stained-glass window of 1565 designed by *Henri de Malines.* The carved decoration of the Baptistery dates from 1477. In the left aisle are bas-reliefs (*Pietà and Eternal Father) by *Agost. di Duccio;* and (in the first chapel of the aisle) the CAPPELLA DEL SANTO ANELLO, containing the supposed **marriage** ring of the Virgin Mary, piously stolen by the Perugians from Chiusi. It is kept in a chased and gilded reliquary (1498-1511) under the 15 locks and is exhibited only once a year on 30 July. The stalls of the chapel were carved by *G. B. Bastone* (1520-29). In the CHOIR are a bishop's throne of 1520 and stalls of tarsia work by *Giul. da Maiano* and *Dom. del Tasso* (1486-91).

In the SACRISTY, on the right side of the choir, are frescoes of the Life of St Laurence by *Giannant. Pandolfi da Pésaro* (1578) and inlaid cupboards by *Mariotto da Gubbio* (1494-97).—The CANONICAL CLOISTERS have a collection of antique and medieval marbles.—The **Museo dell'Opera** (8-12, 15.30-18), founded in 1923, contains works of art from the cathedral. The paintings include a Madonna, with saints and a donor, by *Signorelli* (1484), the Redeemer and saints, by *Lodivico di Angelo* and works by *Meo di Guido, Caporali, Andrea Vanni,* and others. There is also a valuable collection of illuminated MSS. (breviaries, missals, graduals, and antiphonals), as well as gold and silver reliquaries and other vessels.

From Piazza Danti Via del Sole rises to P.za Michelotti, highest point of the city (494 m), built on the site of the medieval castle, and now surrounded by fine 17C houses. Just below it is Piazza Rossi Scotti, popularly 'Le Prome' with a terrace commanding a fine view to the N. From P.za Michelotti two narrow lanes (Via Mattioli or Via dell'Aquila which begins in a tunnel) descend to the Piazzetta Raffaello, in which is the church of **San Severo** (Pl. 7).

According to tradition in the 11C Camaldulensian monks built here, on the site of a temple of the Sun, a convent and church dedicated to Severus, Bishop of Ravenna. Both were rebuilt in the 15C. In 1748-51 the church was given its present Baroque form. One chapel of the 15C church survives.

In the chapel (closed 12.30-15; ring for custodian) is a celebrated *Fresco by *Raphael* (1505; his earliest work of the kind; recently restored), representing the Holy Trinity with saints. Beneath, in 1512, *Perugino,* already in decline, painted six further saints.

From the P.za Danti the Via Ulisse Rocchi, formerly the Via Vecchia, so called to distinguish it from the parallel Via Nuova, now Via Bartolo, descends steeply N. to the *Arco d'Augusto** (Pl. 7), a noble gateway in which three periods of civilization are represented. The Etruscan lower part dates from the 3-2C B.C.; the upper part, with the inscription *Augusta Perusia,* was added after 40 B.C.; the graceful Renaissance loggia on one of the buttresses in the 16C. In Piazza Fortebraccio beyond the arch is the *Palazzo Gallenga Stuart* (Pl. 6). This 18C palace was given a new wing, in harmony with the old construction, in 1935-37, and is now the seat of the UNIVERSITÀ ITALIANA PER STRANIERI.

This institution was founded in 1921 for the diffusion abroad of the Italian language, literature, and culture. In 1931 it received a gift of $100,000 from the American F. Thorne Rider, for its enlargement. It owns a library (30,000 volumes) of Italian, English, French, and German books. The University is open to students of all nationalities, many of whom attend summer courses here.

From the piazza the Via A. Fabretti leads N.W. to the **University** (Pl. 2), founded in 1307 and transferred in 1811 to its present home, a monastery of Olivetan monks, after their suppression by Napoleon.

From the University the Via F. Innamorati runs W. Out of this street the Via Zeffirino Faina (r.) zigzags up to the *Porta Sant'Angelo,* at the N. end of the city, with a tower of a castle built by Fortebraccio. Near it is the charming church of *Sant'Angelo** (Pl. 2), a round Romanesque building of 5C foundation, said to stand on the site of a temple. Within are 16 antique columns of miscellaneous provenance. Almost opposite is the convent of *Sant'Agnese,* containing frescoes by Perugino and Eusebio da San Giorgio (shown by a sister). Outside the Porta Sant'Angelo is the convent of *Monte Ripido* (Pl. 1), founded in the 13C, with an 18C library.

From the Porta Sant'Angelo Corso Garibaldi returns to the Arco d'Augusto. Near the end of this street, on the left, is *Sant'Agostino* (Pl. 3), with its admirable choir-stalls sculptured and inlaid by Baccio d'Agnolo (1502-32), perhaps from Perugino's designs. In the 1st S. chap. (by Fr. di Guido di Virio da Settignano) is a fresco of the Madonna by Giannicola di Paolo; the 1st N. chap. has a Crucifixion

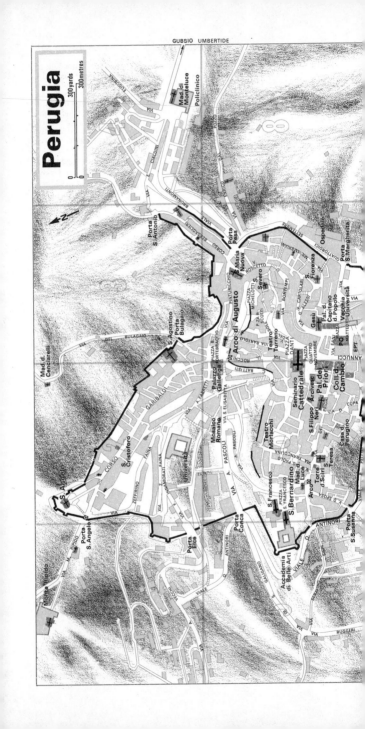

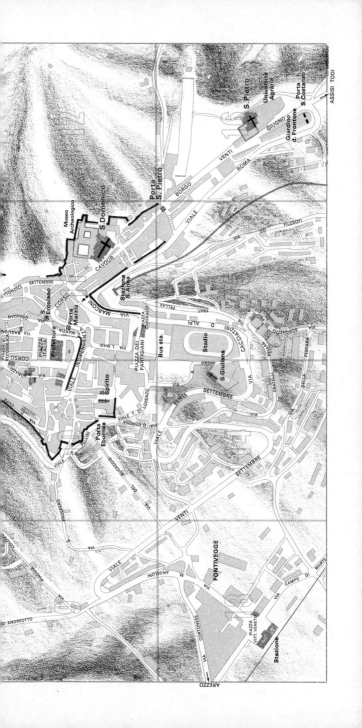

and other fresco fragments by Pellino di Vannuccio (1387). The adjoining 15C *Oratory* (usually closed) has an interior lavishly adorned in the 17C. Beyond the arch Via Pinturicchio leads past (No. 47) the *House of Pinturicchio*. Near the end of the street, also on the right, is the church of *Santa Maria Nuova,* containing good stalls (1476) and a *Gonfalon by Bonfigli (1472), in which the Saviour is darting arrows at the Perugians, with their towers in the background. Near by is the *Porta Pesa,* so called from the weighing of produce brought in from the country. About ½ km. farther on is the *Madonna di Monteluce*(Pl. 4), with a rose window and a double portal (13C) in its façade, and containing a marble tabernacle by Fr. Ferrucci (1487). Adjoining is the *Policlinico*(Ospedali Riuniti di Perugia), whose buildings are spread over the E. part of the Colle di Monteluce.

From the Arco d'Augusto (comp. above) steps lead down beside the University for Foreigners to Via Goldoni which leads into Via Sant'Elisabetta. Here, beyond the span of a bridge, a modern building on the right covers a monochrome *Roman Mosaic* of the 2C, with the story of Orpheus charming the wild beasts (open all day). From here Via Pascoli (left) winds up to the S.W. past fields to Piazza San Francesco. Beyond a little 14C church with a charming bell-tower, the large 13C church of *San Francesco* has been rebuilt since it was ruined by a landslide, but is not yet open. In the adjoining *Cappella della Concezione,* restored in 1928, is another gonfalon by Bonfigli, painted on the occasion of the plague of 1464. At the end of the piazza is the *Oratorio di San Bernardino** (Pl. 6), a building of 1457-61 with a lovely façade decorated with bas-reliefs by *Agostino di Duccio,* and rich in polychrome marbles. A 3C Christian sarcophagus forms the altar. A second Oratory, behind, has a fine wood ceiling of 1558. The adjoining convent is now the seat of the *Accademia di Belle Arti,* a 16C foundation.

To the S.E., beyond the church of the *Madonna della Luce* (Pl. 6), with a graceful Renaissance façade (1512-18) is the pretty old Via dei Priori which climbs back up to Corso Vannucci. Near the beginning of the street are the *Arco di San Luca* (the Gothicized Etruscan Porta Trasimena) and the medieval *Torre degli Sciri*(Pl. 6). Farther on, on the right Via della Cupa affords a fine view of the *Porta Libitana* in the Etruscan walls and leads into Via Deliziosa, in which No. 5 is the *House of Perugino* (Pl. 6). Across Corso Vannucci Via Fani leads into PIAZZA MATTEOTTI (Pl. 7), built in part on the foundations of Etruscan walls. Here are the *Tribunali,* installed in the old University buildings (1453-1515) and in the former *Palazzo del Capitano del Popolo* (1472-81), with a good portal.

From Piazza Matteotti the Via Baglioni leads S. to Piazza Italia. From the N.E. corner of this square Via Marzia skirts the site of the **Rocca Paolina**—'bellissima e inutilissima opera'—built by Ant. Sangallo the Younger in 1540-43 at the command of Paul III, to which end a whole medieval quarter was vaulted over. The Rocca itself was destroyed after 1860. The arch of the Etruscan *Porta Marzia,* re-erected in its present position by Sangallo, gives access (9-12.30, 16-19; closed Mon) to the subterranean Via Bagliona, reopened in 1965 after four centuries. At the end of Via Marzia Corso Cavour descends to the left. On the left is the church of **San Domenico** (Pl. 11), founded in 1305 and rebuilt by Carlo Maderno in 1632. It is the largest church in Perugia (length 122 m).

The fourth chapel of the S. aisle, a relic of the earlier church, has a terracotta frontal by *Agost. di Duccio* (1459); in the right transept is the *Tomb of Benedict

XI (d. 1304), and, in the left, that of Bp. Guidalotti (1429). In the choir are good carved stalls (1498) and an immense 15C stained-glass window, measuring 22½ m by 10 m. The 5th chap. in l. aisle has late 14C Umbrian frescoes. Benedict's robes are preserved in the sacristy.

The convent of San Domenico now houses the *Archivio dello Stato* and the ***Museo Archeologico Nazionale dell'Umbria,** open 9-14; closed Mondays.

The MUSEO ETRUSCO-ROMANO, founded in 1790, was housed in the University from 1812 to 1936; in 1946 the contents were installed at San Domenico. The exhibits are displayed in the portico, the wings of the cloister, and the upper floor of the convent.—*Portico.* Etrusco-Roman inscriptions; sarcophagus with the myth of Meleager; three cippi set up in honour of Augustus when he authorized the rebuilding of Perguia (see p. 590).—Stairs lead up to the *Upper Cloister,* with Etruscan urns and Roman bas-relief fragments. A corridor off the E. walk leads past a colossal head of Claudius from Carsulæ to the SMALL CLOISTER. Here the W. walk has material from recent excavations. The N. walk, with Roman portrait heads, leads to ROOM I (r.). Here is a stele with the representation of two warriors (6C B.C.), and an archaic sphinx from Cetona.—ROOM II contains a large sarcophagus with a victorious return from battle, and a circular cippus with a fine bas-relief.—RR. III & IV contain bronze objects.—RR. V & VI. Finds from the necropoli of Monteluce and Frontone. Beyond a gallery with Greek and Cypriot vases, R. VII has Etruscan mirrors and jewellery. Outside, Cippus in travertine with the celebrated Inscription of Perugia of 151 words, one of the most important monuments of Etruscan epigraphy. R. VIII has a terracotta urn with Medusa.—RR. IX-XI have more local finds. Just outside R. XI is a terracotta statuette of a divinity signed by the artist. R. XII contains small bronzes from Colle Arsiccio.

The MUSEO PREISTORICO, beyond, is one of the most important of its kind. Of particular interest are the discoveries made in 1928-29 at the site of Belverde sul Monte Cetona. In the small cloister are models of cave dwellings of the Iron Age. In the following eight rooms, objects of flint and pottery illustrating the development in Central Italy of civilization from the Palæolithic to the Neolithic Age. The long room around which these rooms are grouped contains material from many other countries. In the Salone, reached by a staircase, are flint axes, daggers and other implements; objects in copper and bronze; discoveries from Belverde (Iron Age): vases, some with geometrical decoration, bone implements, bronze shields and discs, armlets, articles of household use and adornment, and a fine bronze sword.

The Corso Cavour ends at *Porta San Pietro,* by Agost. di Duccio and Polidoro di Stefano (1473).

Borgo Venti Giugno continues to the Benedictine church of ***San Pietro dei Cassinensi** (Pl. 16), i.e. of the monks of Monte Cassino, belonging to a convent (now part of the university) founded by the monk Pietro Vincioli at the end of the 10C. The building (several times remodelled) has a graceful 14C tower. The entrance is by a 16C portal on the left of the convent courtyard. On the left side a Romanesque arch has been laid bare; behind it are 15C frescoes. The interior is basilican, with ancient marble and granite columns. It contains an unusually good collection of paintings. In the NAVE, with a rich ceiling, are eleven large canvases by *L'Aliense* (1592-94), a pupil of Tintoretto. In the S. aisle are the Madonna with SS. Mary Magdalen and Sebastian, by *Eusebio da San Giorgio,* and St Benedict (3rd altar), by the same artist (1492-93); in the N. aisle (just beyond the 1st altar) Pietà, by *Perugino,* an Adoration of the Magi (1508) by *Eusebio,* (in the Cappella Ranieri) *Christ on the Mount, by *Guido Reni,* and (in the Cappella Vibi) a bas-relief by *Mino da Fiesole* (1473).—The SACRISTY (opened on application) contains admirable woodcarvings of 1472, small panels of four *Saints by *Perugino* (1496), a Head of Christ, by *Dosso Dossi,* and a fragment of Deruta majolica pavement (1563). Illuminated choir-books are displayed in a room off the N. aisle (W. end).—In the *CHOIR are stone pulpits with reliefs by *Fr. di Guido,* thrones by *Bened. da Montepulciano* (1555-56), and richly inlaid *Stalls by *Bern. Antonibi, Stef. Zambelli* and others (1526-85).

A *Door at the end of the choir, inlaid by *Fra Damiano* (1536), a brother of Stefano, leads out onto a balcony from which there is a splendid view of Assisi, Spello, etc. The autograph of the poet Carducci (1871) is indicated.—Another fine view, in the direction of Foligno, is obtained from the terrace of the *Giardino del Frontone,* on the other side of the street.—The former convent is now occupied by the Faculty of Agriculture of the University; just beyond is the *Porta Sant Costanzo,* dating from 1587.

Just outside the gateway, to the left, is the church of *San Costanzo* (1143-1205), partly rebuilt and decorated by Leo XIII, who was Bishop of Perugia before his election to the Holy See in 1878.—On the right, outside the Porta San Costanzo, the Viale Roma leads round to the right to the Largo Cacciatori degli Alpi (p. 591). From there roads descend towards the main station, passing (r.) the *Stadio,* Perugia's sports centre, and, farther down, the 13-14C church of *Santa Giuliana* (Pl. 14), with its graceful 14C campanile. The usual entrance is from the courtyard of the military hospital (adm. on application at the gate), which occupies the former convent, including part of a 13C cloister, and the two-storied Great Cloister of the 14C.

About 5 km. from the Porta San Costanzo by the Foligno road, near Ponte San Giovanni (see below; pleasant short cuts for walkers), is the ***Ipogeo dei Volumni** (adm. 9-14; closed Mon), discovered in 1840, one of the finest Etruscan tombs known. Dating from the second half of the 2C B.C., it has the form of a Roman house with atrium, tablinum, and two wings. The walls are adorned with stucco and reliefs. The coffered ceiling has heads hewn out of the rock. In the central chamber nine travertine urns containing the ashes of the Volumnii family show Roman influence (note the urn of Aruns Volumnius); a tenth, in marble, belongs to the 1C A.D. Above the hypogeum, in a modern building, are several urns found in the adjacent cemetery.—To the right beyond the main station, near the little church of San Manno (6 km. from Perugia), is the *Tomb of San Manno,* a spacious vault faced with travertine slabs and having an arched ceiling. The Etruscan inscription states that this tomb belonged to the Precu family.

Bettona, 20 km. S.E. of Perugia viâ Ponte San Giovanni and Torgiano (bus) is the ancient Vettona, and commands a splendid view from its little hill (355 m). It has notable remains of Etruscan walls, and, in the Palazzo del Podestà, a little gallery (if closed apply at the Municipio opposite) of Umbrian paintings (two by Perugino). The church of San Crispolto (the first bishop of Bettona) contains a Nativity by Dono Doni.

The direct road from Perugia to Orvieto (N 317; 77 km.) bears to the right off the road to Todi. It passes (22 km.) *Cerqueto,* where the parish church contains a fresco of St Sebastian, the earliest dated work of Perugino (1478); and (29 km.) *Marsciano,* with remains of a feudal castle.

A winding descent (which passes above the tunnel of the new Perugia by-pass) leaves on the right a road (N 317) to Orvieto, passes the Ipogeo dei Volumni (see above), and from (86 km.) *Ponte San Giovanni* to (90 km.) *Collestrada* briefly coincides with highway N3 bis (Rte 52), crossing the Tiber. Two kilometres farther on N 147 diverges left direct to (105 km.) *Assisi,* while the main road continues directly towards Spello, affording an alternative approach (1 km. longer) viâ Santa Maria degli Angeli (p. 604) and the railway station.

ASSISI (24,500 inhab.), on a commanding spur of Monte Subasio (360-505 m), is a quiet medieval town, imbued with the mystical spirit of one of the most fascinating characters of history. To St Francis of Assisi are due not only the foundation of his Order and the inspiration of his disciple St Clare, but also the artistic movement to which the town owes many of its most beautiful monuments. As one of the most famous shrines in Italy, it is now given over to the reception of its many Italian and foreign visitors.

Railway Station, near Santa Maria degli Angeli, 5 km. S.W. of the town (bus in connection with trains).

Car Parking. Piazza San Francesco (lower church), Largo San Pietro, outside Porta Nuova, P.za Matteotti, etc.

Hotels near the basilica of San Francesco.

Post Office, P.za del Comune.—*Azienda Autonoma di Turismo,* 12 P.za Comune.

Buses from Piazzale Porta San Pietro to *Rome;* to *Perugia* 2-4 times daily in 50 min.; to *Foligno* in ¾ hr; viâ Foligno, Tolentino, Macerata, and San Benedetto del Tronto to *Ascoli Piceno* in 5¾ hrs; to *Gualdo Tadino* in 1¾ hr.—**Coach Excursions** (1 July-30 Sept) to *Gubbio* (3 times a week); to *Spoleto, Montefalco,* and *Bevagna* (once a week); and to *Todi* and *Orvieto* (twice a week).

Annual Festivals connected with St Francis, with processions and liturgical ceremonies are held in Easter Week, 30 April, Ascension Day, Corpus Christi, 22 June, 1-2 August, 11 August, 12 August, 3-4 Oct, and at Christmas.

History. The Umbro-Etruscan and Roman town of *Asisium* was evangelized by St Rufinus, who suffered martyrdom here (238). Later subjected to the dukes of Spoleto, it became a republic in 1184 and engaged in the usual bitter partisanship and frequent wars with neighbour towns. Eventually it passed to the Church. Sextus Propertius (c. 46 B.C.-c. A.D. 14), the elegiac poet, was probably a native of Assisi, though he is claimed also by Spello. St Clare (Chiara), the daughter of a rich family, disciple of St Francis, and foundress of the Poor Clares, was born at Assisi in 1194, and died in her own convent in 1253.

St Francis of Assisi (1182-1226) was the son of a rich merchant, Pietro Bernardone, the husband of Pica (perhaps de Bourlemont, a Provençal). He was baptized as Giovanni, but his father, who at the time was trading in France, called him Francesco. His youth was wild, but at the age of 24 a year's imprisonment at Perugia, followed by an illness, turned his thoughts to the religious life. He began to tend lepers, and to give all he had to the poor. As he was praying in San Damiano a Voice bade him "Rebuild My Church", and in the chapel of Porziuncola he heard the command "Freely ye have received, freely give", which sent him forth the bridegroom of poverty. Although confined as a madman, despoiled by robbers, and ridiculed by his comfortable fellows, he was joined by some "little brethren" who retreated with him to a chapel on Monte Subasio, around which they lived in cells. In May 1209 he obtained from Innocent III the approval of his Order founded on a rule of poverty, chastity, and obedience. He preached his gospel in Italy, in Spain, in Morocco, in Egypt (1219), where the Sultan Melek-el-Kamel received him kindly, and in the Holy Land. In 1221 the Franciscan Rule was sanctioned by Honorius III, and three years later Francis himself retired to La Verna. On 14 Sept 1224, the festival of the Exaltation of the Holy Cross, he had a vision of a seraph with six wings and found in his own body the stigmata or wounds of the Passion. Concealing these from all but a few witnesses, he returned to Assisi, and died at the Porziuncola on 3 Oct 1226, which day is his festival. His love of beasts and birds (who also were his little brethren and little sisters) is well known. St Francis was canonized on 16 July 1228. The Franciscan Order, under its various divisions (Observants, Conventuals, Capuchins, etc.) consisted in the 18C of more than 9000 houses, with 150,000 members. Like the Poor Clares, it has always attracted minds of the sympathetic mystical cast.

The roads ascending to the town converge at the Largo San Pietro. Beyond the 13C *Porta San Francesco* Via Frate Elia leads steeply up to the fine piazza in front of the two-storied ***Basilica of San Francesco,** the principal monument to the memory of St Francis, with its magnificent series of frescoes.

At his death St Francis was interred in the church of San Giorgio. A fund for a memorial church was started in April 1228, and its foundation stone was laid by Gregory IX the day following the canonization ceremony. The lower church was soon ready and on 25 May 1230 the remains were translated to it. The completed church was consecrated by Innocent IV in 1253. The architect may have been *Fil. da Campello, Giov. della Penna,* or *Lapo Lombardo,* but was most likely *Frate*

Elia, Vicar-General of the Franciscans. Early in the 14C the side chapels of the lower church were added. The campanile was completed in 1239.

The church is open all day in summer, but is closed 12.30-14 in winter.—Lights (essential) in each chapel are operated by a 100 l. coin.

The entrance to the LOWER CHURCH is by an admirable Renaissance *Porch of 1487 (very ruined), designed by *Fr. da Pietrasanta,* covering a Gothic *Portal, which leads into the entrance-transept. The cool dim interior, like a huge crypt, is the most impressive part of the building; it contains several 13-14C tombs. In the 1st chapel on the l. are relics of St Francis; outside (r.) is a fresco of the Madonna della Salute, of the school of Ottaviano Nelli (15C). On the right of the transept, in the Cappella di Sant'Antonio, is the entrance to a picturesque cloistered cemetery (14-15C), and at the end of the transept is the Capp. di Santa Caterina, added in 1367, with frescoes by *And. da Bologna.* The nave and its chapels are richly adorned with frescoes, notably the 1st chapel on the left, with the *Story of St Martin, by *Simone Martini* (1322-26), and the 3rd chapel on the right, with the *Life of St Mary Magdalen, most probably by *Giotto* (c. 1314). On the left side of the nave, above the Gothic pulpit, are frescoes by *Giottino.*

On either side of the nave a staircase descends to the CRYPT (restored in 1932), with the stone coffin of St Francis, rendered inaccessible in the 15C as a precaution against Perugian raids, and rediscovered in 1818. Round the tomb are grouped the sarcophagi of the saint's four faithful companions: Fra Leone, Fra Angelo, Fra Masseo, and Fra Ruffino.

In the right transept are the Life of Christ and other beautiful frescoes, of the school of *Giotto;* also a *Madonna enthroned with angels and Saints including St Francis, by *Cimabue,* and a Madonna and two Saints (half-length) ascribed to *Simone Martini.* The Capp. di San Nicola, at the end, is adorned with Giottesque frescoes of c. 1340 illustrating the life of the saint. In the left transept are, on the left, *Frescoes by *Pietro Lorenzetti,* including a fine Crucifixion, the Madonna with SS. John and Francis, and the Descent from the Cross, and, on the right, St Francis receiving the Stigmata from Christ crucified, and scenes from the Passion, and (end chapel of San Giovanni Battista) another *Madonna and saints.

The celebrated *Frescoes (c. 1300) above the high altar (the 'Quattro Vele'), with crowded scenes representing the Mystic Marriage of St Francis with Holy Poverty, Chastity, Obedience, and St Francis in glory, are ascribed either to *Giotto* or to one of his pupils. In the apse are admirable carved stalls of 1471.—Stairs lead up from both transepts to a terrace outside the apse of the upper church overlooking the Cloister of Sixtus IV. Here a door leads into the SALA GOTICA where the **Treasury** is being arranged.

Though several times despoiled it still contains precious treasures. Among the paintings is a Madonna enthroned, by *Spagna* (1516), formerly in the church. Notable among the works of art are the magnificent Flemish *Tapestry of St Francis, presented by Sixtus IV in 1471; the silver gilt *Cup of Nicholas IV (c. 1290), by *Guccio di Mannaie,* with a portrait of the pope in enamel; the altar-frontal of Sixtus IV, perhaps designed by *Ant. del Pollaiuolo,* with figures of the pope and St Francis; a 13C ivory Madonna of French workmanship; a 14C Venetian cross in rock-crystal adorned with enamels; and the illuminated Missal of St Louis of Toulouse (French; mid-13C). Here, too, are displayed sinopie by *Simone Martini,* and recently restored paintings by *Dono Doni.*

The immense **Convent** (now a missionary college; no adm.), with a terrace built on formidable arches, commands splendid views.—Gius. Tartini (1692-1770) composed his 'Devil's Trill' Sonata here (1715) while in hiding from the family of Elisabetta Premazone, whom he had secretly married in Padua.

The well-lighted UPPER CHURCH, in which architecture, frescoes, and glass alike are of the 13C, has a good Gothic portal and rose window in its façade which overlooks a green lawn. The nave has been covered by scaffolding for several years during the summer months while restoration of the frescoes continues. The 32 frescoes above from Old Testament history (many of them sadly damaged) are most likely by *Pietro Cavallini* and his pupils, though ascribed to Cimabue by Vasari. Below is the noble series of 28 *Frescoes from the Life of St Francis (beginning at the right transept), by *Giotto* and his disciples (c. 1290-95). The tiny pulpit dates from c. 1350; in the vaulting are evangelists and doctors. Both transepts are painted by *Cimabue* (although his work also is now sadly much faded)—the *Crucifixion in the left transept is outstanding—and in the choir are frescoes of the Life of the Virgin, also by *Cimabue*, and stalls of 1491-1501 by Dom. Indovini.

Opposite the entrance to the lower church is the graceful Renaissance doorway of the *Oratory of San Bernardino* (1488).

From the upper church of San Francesco, Via San Francesco leads towards the centre of the town past many ancient houses. No. 14 is the *Casa dei Maestri Comacini*. No. 11, the *Oratorio dei Pellegrini*, a relic of a hospital of 1431 where pilgrims used to be lodged, is covered with beautiful frescoes by Mezzastris. The youthful saint to the left of the entrance is attributed to the young Perugino. At No. 3 is the small portico (1267) of the *Monte Frumentario*, beside which is a 16C fountain. An arch marks the beginning of the Via del Seminario, continued by Via Portica, which, after a steep climb, ends at the main square by the *Museo Comunale* (adm. 9-12.30, 15 or 16-18 or 19; fest. 9-12.30; closed Mon). It occupies the crypt of the vanished church of San Nicola and has Roman sculptural fragments. A long corridor gives access to remains of the Roman Forum.

In the beautifully-shaped PIAZZA DEL COMUNE are the *Palazzo del Podestà* and the *Torre Comunale* (both 13C). The *Tempio di Minerva, now the church of *Santa Maria,* has six Corinthian columns and steps of travertine, dating from the time of Augustus. On the S.W. side of the piazza is the *Palazzo Comunale,* or *dei Priori* (1337) containing a collection of Umbrian frescoes (adm. as for Museo Comunale), by the school of Tiberius d'Assisi and Ottaviano Nelli, and a standard painted by Nic. L'Alunno. Just beyond, beneath an archway, a lane descends past a permanent exhibition of local handicrafts to the *Chiesa Nuova* (1615), built on the supposed site of the house in which St Francis was born; an oratory of the 13C in an adjoining alley may be part of the house itself. From the N.E. corner of the piazza Via San Rufino mounts to the **Cathedral** (*San Rufino*), dedicated to the missionary martyr of Assisi. It was rebuilt in 1144 by *Giov. da Gubbio,* and its fine *Façade, with round-headed doors and windows and grotesque carvings of animals, was heightened before the church's consecration in 1253. The campanile stands over a Roman cistern and its base is a relic of the 11C church.

The interior was transformed by *Alessi* in 1571. At the beginning of the r. aisle is the font at which St Francis and St Clare were baptized. The Emperor Frederick

II may also have been baptized here in 1197 (aged 3). In front of the choir are statues of SS. Francis and Clare by *Giov. Dupré* and his daughter (1881-88). The handsome choir-stalls date from 1520. The sacristan shows the small Museo Capitolare (closed 13-15) notable for triptychs by *L'Alunno* (1470), and *Matteo da Gualdo;* the 11C Crypt (outside the church on the right) is also shown.

The lane above the cathedral leads past the remains of a *Roman Theatre* to the *Giardino Pubblico.* Farther N.E., beyond a group of 13C houses, are ruins of a *Roman Amphitheatre* and the *Porta Perlici* (1199). Dominating the town are two citadels, of which the *Rocca Maggiore* (adm. daily) was rebuilt by Card. Albornoz in 1367 (fine view).

From the cathedral a road descends to the red and white Romanesque church of *Santa Chiara* (open 6-20, exc. Chapel of the Sacrament which closes from 12 to 14.30), built in 1257-65. The great flying buttresses that span the road were added at the end of the 14C; the W. front has a fine rose window. In the interior are frescoes of the school of Giotto. The CHAPEL OF THE CRUCIFIX, off the S. side of the nave, contains the painted *Crucifix (late 12C) that spoke to St Francis at San Damiano, and relics of the saint. The adjoining CHAPEL OF THE SACRAMENT has late 14C frescoes of the Annunciation, the Nativity, the Adoration of the Magi, and St George, and a Madonna and saints perhaps by *Giottino*. In the apse hangs a 13C Crucifix by the 'Maestro di Santa Chiara', and in the cross vault are well-preserved Giottesque *Frescoes. In the r. transept, a painting of St Clare with eight stories from her life also attrib. to the 'Maestro di Santa Chiara', and 14C frescoes with scenes from her life. The l. transept has a Nativity by the 14C Umbrian school and a Madonna and Child painted at the end of the 13C. The frescoes high up on the walls here date from the end of the 13C. St Clare is buried in the richly decorated 19C Crypt.

About 1 km. from the *Porta Nuova,* S. of Santa Chiara, is **San Damiano,** where in 1205 St Francis renounced the world, where in 1212 he introduced St Clare into his Order, having "poured the sweetness of Christ into her ears", and where St Clare, holding aloft the Sacrament, repelled an attack of Frederick II's Saracens. The vestibule of the cloister is painted by Eusebio da San Giorgio (1507).—Another excursion may be made to (4 km. E. of the Porta Cappuccini) the secluded little *Eremo delle Carceri,* the forest hermitage of St Francis, with the tree on which the birds perched to receive his blessing, his bed hollowed out in the rock, and a convent founded by St Bernardine.—A new road (un-surfaced) continues up to the summit of *Monte Subasio* (1290 m; *View) which affords pasture for animals.

Via Sant'Agnese returns towards P.za Vescovado where the church of *Santa Maria Maggiore,* with a good wheel-window (1163), occupies the site of a Temple of Apollo and has an interesting crypt. The Via Bernardo da Quintavalle, higher up, retains its medieval character. Farther W. is the Benedictine church of SAN PIETRO, first mentioned in 1029 but dating in its present form from 1268. The triptych by Matteo da Gualdo, which normally hangs in the N. transept, has been temporarily removed for safety.

From the adjoining *Porta San Pietro* (13C) a road descends (or a path in c. 40 min.) past the *British Military Cemetery,* to the conspicuous church of **Santa Maria degli Angeli** (open 6-20; winter 6-12.30, 14.30-18) on the plain below the town. It was designed in 1569 by *Galeazzo Alessi* and others, completed in 1684, and restored by Poletti in 1840 after an earthquake. The façade is by *C. Bazzani* (1928). The church was built to cover the little oratory (*Porziuncola*) founded by hermits from Jerusalem (352), restored by St Benedict (512), and the first centre of the Franciscan order. This was the meeting-place of SS. Francis and

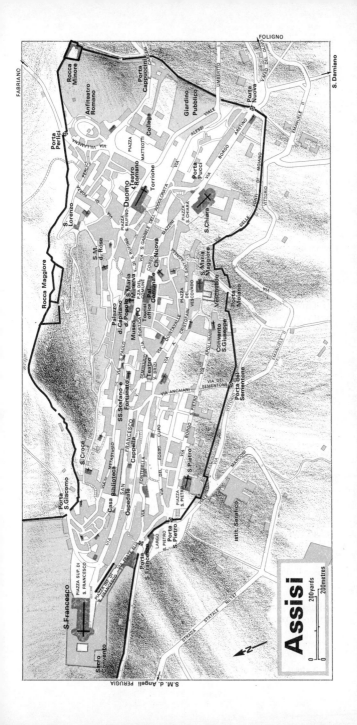

Dominic, and the scene of St Clare's consecration and of St Francis's death.

The CAPPELLA DELLA PORZIUNCOLA stands in the midst of the church, beneath the cupola; over the entrance is a fresco by *Overbeck* (1830) and within is a *Painting, the sole known work of *Ilario da Viterbo* (1393); both depict scenes from the Life of St Francis. The CAPPELLA DEL TRANSITO, at the entrance to the chancel (r.), with frescoes by *Spagna* and a statue of the saint by *And. Della Robbia*, was built over the cell where St Francis died, and contain his heart among its relics. Another fine work by *And. Della Robbia* is the altarpiece in the W. chapel of the N. transept.

From the Sacristy there is access to a portico which leads past a garden of the thornless roses of St Francis which bloom yearly in May (and a bronze statue of the Saint, 1912) to the CAPPELLA DEL ROSETO (named from the roses), built by St Bonaventura over the cave of St Francis, and decorated with frescoes by *Tiberio d'Assisi*, a pupil of Perugino (1506). A corridor leads back to the church past an old pharmacy and the cloisters.—The ANTICO CONVENTO (open 9.30-12.30, 14.30-18.30; closed Wed) has a small collection of paintings including a *Portrait of St Francis, by an unknown master (*'Maestro di San Francesco'*), a *Crucifix by *Giunta Pisano*, another portrait of the saint of the school of *Cimabue*, and a detached fresco of the Madonna enthroned attrib. to *Mezzastris*. There is also a display of church vestments and a delightful missionary museum.—A staircase leads up to the CONVENT OF ST BERNARDINE OF SIENA with his cell. The custodian also shows his chapel and the pulpit from which he preached.

Highway N 147 rejoins the main road in 7 km. at (112 km.) *Passàggio d'Assisi*.—116 km. **Spello,** the Roman *Hispellum*, is an ancient little fortified town (7350 inhab.), picturesquely situated on a hillside (314 m). The main entrance to the town is through the *Porta Consolare* with three Republican statues on its impressive façade. Via Cavour begins a steep and winding ascent up to the centre of the town, passing (l.) the *Cappella Tega* with 15C frescoes. In the first piazza is the church of SANTA MARIA MAGGIORE (12-13C) with a fine portico reworked in 1644 using a Romanesque frieze. At the base of the Romanesque campanile are two Roman columns.

INTERIOR. The two stoups are made from Roman fragments. Off the l. side of the nave the Cappella Baglioni (light on l.) is entirely decorated with *Frescoes by *Pinturicchio*, the Nativity, Annunciation (with a self-portrait near by), the Dispute in the Temple, and four Sibyls in the vault above. Signed and dated 1501, they have recently been beautifully restored. The floor is made of Deruta majolica (1566). The high altar is covered by a fine baldacchino carved by *Rocco da Vicenza* (1515). On the two pilasters flanking the apse are two very late works by *Perugino*. The choir-stalls date from 1512-20. In the l. transept, the Chapel of the Sacrament has a lavabo (on the wall to l. of altar) with an angel frescoed by *Pinturicchio*, and (behind a door near the lavabo) another little chapel has a fine Madonna and Child also by *Pinturicchio*. In the Chapel of the Crucifix, off the r. transept, are two detached frescoes by the school of Pinturicchio. From here there is access to a small MUSEUM (unlocked by the sacristan) from which a painting of the Madonna and Child by Pinturicchio was stolen four years ago, and a precious enamelled cross (1398) has been removed for safety.

Farther up is the church of SANT'ANDREA. Inside, on the r. wall, is a fresco fragment of the Madonna (14C), and, in the r. arm of the crossing, a large altarpiece of the Madonna and Child with Saints (light on r.) by *Pinturicchio* and *Eusebio da San Giorgio*. The pretty high altar has 14C columns. At the beginning of the nave (l.) is a chapel with local 15C frescoes (recently uncovered).

From the piazza, Via Torri di Properzio descends steeply to the Roman *PORTA VENERE, of the Augustan age, the best preserved of the three gateways in the Roman walls.

A short way beyond Sant'Andrea opens Piazza della Repubblica (car

parking). Still higher is the Romanesque church of *San Lorenzo* with a
15C tabernacle. The Via della Torre Belvedere (one-way downhill;
another road is indicated for cars) leads up past the Romanesque church
of *San Martino* to the top of the hill where a single Roman arch marks
the site of the ancient acropolis and a belvedere, near the remains of a
14C Rocca, affords a fine view.

The road below the town passes the ruined *Roman Amphitheatre,* the
Porta Urbica, the *Chiesa Tonda* (1517-39), an attractive work of the
Renaissance, and *San Claudio,* a charming little 12C church.

Beyond Spello the road for (123 km.) **Foligno** (see Rte 54) crosses the
main road and railway.

54   ROME TO SPOLETO, FOLIGNO, AND ANCONA

A   Viâ Fabriano

ROAD, 294 km. N 3 (VIA FLAMINIA). 54 km. *Civita Castellana* (by-pass, 2 km.
shorter).—86 km. **Narni.**—100 km. **Terni** (by-pass).—128 km. **Spoleto** (by-pass
under town).—155 km. **Foligno** (by-pass, 2 km. shorter).—193 km. *Gualdo
Tadino.*—207 km. *Fossato di Vico.*—N 76. 219 km. **Fabriano.**—264 km. **Iesi.**—
294 km. **Ancona.** BUSES from *Rome* (P.za della Repubblica) to *Terni* in 2¼ hrs; to
Foligno in 3¾ hrs.

The AUTOSTRADA DEL SOLE (A 1; see p. 364) affords a faster approach to
Spoleto (6 km. longer). The motorway is left at (76 km.) *Orte,* and N 204, by-
passing both *Narni* and *Terni,* joins N 3 beyond Terni.

RAILWAY, 297 km. 3½-4½ hrs; viâ *Terni* (in 1½ hrs), *Spoleto* (1¾ hrs), *Foligno*
(2¼hrs), *Fabriano* (c. 3 hrs). As far as Orte this route follows the line of the Rome-
Florence railway (p. 527). On slower intermediate trains a change may be necessary
at Orte or at Falconara Marittima.

The VIA FLAMINIA (N 3), at its Roman end reduced in importance since
the completion of the autostrada to Orte, begins at the Porta del Popolo
and, beyond the Tiber, soon diverges right from the Via Cassia. To
(42 km.) *Sant'Oreste* station, see the 'Blue Guide to Rome'. The road
makes a sharp turn left under the railway and runs below Monte Soratte
(r.).

54 km. **Civita Castellana** (148 m) stands on a tufa hill surrounded by
picturesque and precipitous ravines spanned by lofty bridges. The town
(15,400 inhab.) is on the site of the ancient *Falerii,* originally named
Halesus after its founder, a chief of the Auruncans and Oscans. Falerii
was one of the Etruscan lordships and the capital of the Falisci, a tribe
belonging to the Etruscan Confederation but otherwise distinct and
speaking its own language.

The town was taken by Camillus in 394 B.C.; in 241 B.C. the Romans destroyed
it and built *Falerii Novi,* 6 km. W. The new town prospered, but in the 8C and 9C
the population returned to the ancient site, which acquired its present name.

The *Duomo* has a magnificent *Portico and façade by the Cosmati
(1210), and a portion of the choir-screen, with Cosmatesque mosaics, is
preserved in the sacristy; in the crypt are antique columns. The *Rocca,* a
pentagonal fortress begun by Alexander VI and completed for Julius II
by Ant. Sangallo the Elder, contains frescoes in the Borgia state rooms
by the Zuccari. An archæological Museum is being arranged here.

Of **Falerii Vetres,** 1 km. W. on the road to Fabrica di Roma (p. 549), the most
interesting relics are an aqueduct, a ruined Temple of Mercury, and the nucleus of

the necropolis, in which the tombs, cut in the tufa, take the form of an antechamber with a vertical shaft (apparently for the escape of the gases of decomposition) and a sepulchral chamber. Beyond the medieval bridge over the Fosso Maggiore are the ruins of the so-called Temple of Juno Curitis, with a triple cella. Farther along the same road (6km.) stands **Falerii Novi,** the *Walls of which are remarkable. Triangular in plan and c. 2100 m round, they retain 50 of the original 80 towers and two of the nine gates. The Porta di Giove and the Porta del Bove ('Ox Gate') are well preserved. No other ruin gives so complete an idea of a Roman walled town. Within may be recognized the area of the forum and of the theatre. There are also ruins of the 12C Romanesque church of Santa Maria.

Nepi, 13km. S.W. (bus in 20 min.), is another ancient place known for its mineral water, with medieval walls on Etruscan foundations and a fine Rocca; a cathedral preserving a Romanesque portico and crypt; and a fine Baroque town hall. At *Castel Sant'Elia,* 3km. E. of Nepi, the 11C *Church, founded by St Benedict, contains remarkable Romanesque frescoes.

The road turns right in the town and, beyond (62km.) *Civita Castellana-Magliano* station (on the Orte line), crosses the Tiber and the Autostrada del Sole just below the village of Magliano Sabina. On a steep ascent the road enters Umbria. Just before (73km.) *Otrícoli,* it passes (l.) the site of its Umbrian predecessor, Ocriculum, between the road and the Tiber. Remains of the theatre have been unearthed and excavations continue.—At (80km.) *Ponte Sanguinaro* the road forks: the branch on the left is N3 bis, which descends to the Nera valley, joining N 204 and skirting Narni, giving access to the Terni by-pass (to Todi and Perugia, see Rte 52). The old road keeps to the right.

88km. **Narni** is an old hill town (244m) with 20,700 inhabitants, preserving many medieval streets and buildings. Originally called *Nequinum,* it changed its name to *Narnia* (after the river) when it became a Roman colony in 299 B.C. It was the birthplace of the emperor Nerva (A.D. 32), of John XIII (Pope 965-972), and of Erasmo da Narni, called Gattamelata, the condottiere (d. 1443). Virgil, followed by Macaulay ("the pale waves of Nar"), refers to the whitish turbidity of the stream washing the foot of the hill, due to its content of sulphur and lime. The *Duomo,* founded in the 12C, has an outer S. aisle added in the 15C. In this aisle are two white marble pulpits (1490), a wooden statue of St Anthony Abbot, by Vecchietta (1475), and a curious marble screen with very ancient reliefs and Cosmatesque decoration. In the N. aisle is a fresco of the Madonna of the school of Foligno, and throughout the church are good 15C monuments. The *Palazzo Comunale* is adorned with 13-14C sculptures and contains paintings by Benozzo Gozzoli and Dom. Ghirlandaio. The *Loggia dei Priori,* opposite, is attributed to Gattapone. *Santa Maria in Pensole* (1175) has an elegant Romanesque portico. The Via Mazzini, beyond, remains characteristically medieval. *San Francesco* (14C) on the W. flank of the town, and *Sant'Agostino* (15C), on the E., are interesting churches, and the square-towered castle (c. 1370) on the hill-top to the S. commands a good view. Below on the Terni road the 14C *San Girolamo* serves a castellated missionary college.

The road descending towards the station (3 km.; in *Narni Scalo*) crosses the Nera (Nar) near the fine ruined *PONTE D'AUGUSTO which carried the Via Flaminia across the river. From there, passing the *Madonna del Ponte* (rebuilt, after having been blown up along with the medieval road bridge in 1944), it ascends to (12km.) **Amelia,** the ancient *Ameria,* said by Pliny to have been founded three centuries before Rome. It preserves splendid remains of polygonal (Pelasgic) walls, c.8 m high and 3½ m thick, dating from the 6-4C B.C. The campanile of the *Duomo* dates from 1050. In the churches of *San Francesco* and *San Pancrazio* are traces of antique material. Beneath the *Municipio* is a Roman piscina; the *Palazzo Farrattini* contains Roman mosaics.

BUSES run from Amelia to *Terni* and to *Orvieto;* and from Narni to *Rome,* to *Cascia,* and to *Terni.*

100 km. **TERNI** (130 m), a thriving industrial town (111,800 inhab.) making plastics and machinery, is capital of the province of the same name. Badly damaged in the Second World War, it is of predominantly modern appearance, with pleasant residential suburbs.

Post Office, P.za Solferino.—*Ente Provinciale Per Il Turismo,* Viale Cesare Battisti.

Buses to *Marmore, Piediluco* and *La Luce;* to *Sangémini;* viâ Amelia to *Orvieto;* to *Rieti;* to *Perugia;* viâ Narni to *Rome;* viâ Visso to *Tolentino;* to *Spoleto.*

Terni occupies the site of *Interamna Nahars,* so called because it was built between the two streams (inter amnes) Nar and Serra. It is not now considered to be the birthplace of Tacitus the historian, but it is probably that of his fellow-clansman Claudius Tacitus, who was emperor for six months in 275-76. The emperor Gallus was murdered here in 253. The medieval history is insignificant, but in 1798 the French, under Gen. Lemoine, won a victory here over the Neapolitans.

A new bridge over the Nera and the modern Corso del Popolo lead to the central P.za del Popolo, from which the main street continues N. to the station. From the square the Via Cavour runs W. past the 16C *Palazzo Mazzancolli,* beyond which Via Undici Febbraio turns left. In a lane (r.) is the 12C church of *Sant'Alò.* Farther on is the *Duomo,* practically rebuilt in 1653, which retains two early doorways, one Romanesque, the other 14C. Adjacent are the ruins of a Roman *Amphitheatre* dating from A.D. 32. From here Via del Vescovado joins Via Roma, the old main street, which leads left towards the centre. By a medieval tower a turning right crosses the Corso to *San Salvatore,* a church consisting of a 5C rotunda on earlier Roman foundations, and a 12C nave. At the end of Corso del Popolo is the *Palazzo Spada,* the last work of Ant. da Sangallo the Younger (who died here in 1546).

The Corso Vittorio Emanuele continues the old main street through the old quarter to the N.E. In a little square (r.) rises the restored church of *San Pietro* (14C), to the right of which the Palazzo Manassei houses the *Pinacoteca* (closed Mon) with a Marriage of St Catherine, by Benozzo Gozzoli, and a Crucifixion, with SS. Francis and Bernardine, by L'Alunno. The archæological collections of the Museo Civico are temporarily stored in the *Palazzo Carrara* on the far side of the church. *San Lorenzo* and *San Cristoforo,* two 13C churches, are farther N.E., while on the W. side of Corso Tacito is * *San Francesco* (1265, enlarged 1437), with a charming campanile by Angelo da Orvieto (1345). In the Paradisi chapel are restored frescoes of c. 1335 inspired by the Divina Commedia.

The chief attraction in the neighbourhood is an excursion to the * **Cascata delle Marmore,** 6 km. E.S.E.; bus in 25 min. by either the Rieti road (Via Garibaldi) or the Ferentillo road (P.za Dante). These falls (165 m) have been diverted entirely for industrial purposes, but are released to their original channels on Sundays and holidays. In great measure they are the work of man; for Curius Dentatus, conqueror of the Sabines (271 B.C.), was the first to cut a channel by which the river Velinus (Velino) was thrown over a precipice into the River Nar, to prevent floods in the plain of Reate (Rieti). Another channel was cut in 1400 and a third (draining the plain of Rieti without flooding Terni) in 1785. A path leads to the best viewpoint, and it continues to the station of Marmore, on the railway to Rieti.

The abbey of *San Pietro in Valle* is reached by keeping along the lower Marmore road, past (19 km.) *Ferentillo,* to (23 km.) *Macenano* (where the key of the church is kept). Just beyond this hamlet a side turning (l.) leads in c. 1½ km. to the abbey. The domed church, founded in the 8C, preserves its triapsidal plan and contains remarkable though damaged mural paintings of scriptural scenes (c. 1190). The charming two-tiered cloister and the campanile are of 12C workmanship.—Continuation N., see below.

The Rieti road (N 79) continues, skirting the irregular *Lago di Piediluco,* and farther on descends between two smaller lakes, *Lago di Ripa Sottile* (r.) and *Lago Lungo* (l.), into the Plain of Rieti (p. 621).—40 km. *Rieti,* see Rte 55.

FROM TERNI TO VISSO, 72 km. (N 209), following the Nera valley. To (23 km.) *Macenano,* see above.—At (41 km.) *Piedipaterno,* a by-road from Spoleto comes in on the left.—52 km. *Triponzo,* at the confluence of the Nera and the Corno (comp. below).—72 km. *Visso,* a bleak little town (606 m) is a centre for excursions in the Monti Sibillini, to the E. The Gothic church of *Santa Maria,* with a cross by Nic. da Guardiagrele, and several 15-16C palazzi surround the central square.

From Triponzo N 396 follows the Corno to (11 km.) *Serravalle,* junction for **Cáscia** (12 km. S. on N 320), the abode and death-place of St Rita, the 'saint of impossibilities', who was born in 1381 at *Roccaporena,* 5½ km. W. Her sanctuary-church was built in 1937-42.—18 km. **Nórcia** (5020 inhab.), the *frigida Nursia* of Virgil, an old town which has suffered much from earthquakes, was the birthplace of St Benedict (480-543) and of his twin sister St Scholastica. The castle was erected in 1554 by Vignola for Pope Julius III. It houses a Museum with Umbrian paintings and sculptures. The church of *San Benedetto* has a good 14C façade and remains of a late-Roman house in its crypt. Several other churches have good Gothic portals. The *Palazzo Comunale* dates in part from the 13C, while in the Via Umberto is the curious little building called the *Tempietto* (mid-14C).—The road goes on to Tufo, on the Via Salaria (see p. 620).

Beyond Terni the road, joined from the left by the by-pass, climbs the wooded glen of the Tescino between Monte Fionchi (1337 m) on the right and Monte Acetalla (1016 m) on the left, and crosses the Passo della Somma (646 m).

128 km. **SPOLETO** (317 m; 37,100 inhab.) is an interesting old town with some remarkable Roman remains. It lies in a beautiful landscape of high and thickly wooded hills. It is famous for its music and drama festival held in June and July.

Hotels near P.za della Libertà and P.za della Vittoria.

Post Office, Viale Matteotti.—*Azienda Autonoma di Turismo,* P.za della Libertà.

Theatres. *Teatro Nuovo,* Via Vaita Sant'Andrea; *Teatro Caio Melisso,* P.za Duomo.—The FESTIVAL OF TWO WORLDS (June and July) is held in these two theatres, the Roman theatre, and the ex-church and cloister of San Nicolò. Open-air concerts are given in P.za Duomo.

Buses from the station ('Circolare B') ev. 10 min. through the town. Country Buses to *Rome;* to *Urbino;* and to *Florence,* viâ *Perugia* and *Siena.*

Parking. Long term car parks in Viale Giacomo Matteotti and P.za Campello.

The Umbrian *Spoletium* was colonized by the Romans in 242 B.C., and repulsed an attack by Hannibal in 217. It suffered severely in the conflict between Marius and Sulla. In the Middle Ages Spoleto became the seat of a Lombard duchy and a fief of the Countess Matilda. In 1354 it was incorporated in the States of the Church. It was the birthplace of Giovanni di Pietro, known as Lo Spagna (d. 1528).

Viale Matteotti leads to P.za della Libertà, in the upper part of the town, from which is seen the *Roman Theatre* (for adm. apply at the Ufficio Archeologico in the piazza). It has been heavily restored (and was, until recently, covered by other buildings), but retains a remarkable barrel-vaulted passageway beneath the cavea. Behind the scena the apse and conventual buildings of Sant'Agata are conspicuous. Via Brignone leads to the *Arco di Druso* (A.D. 23), which abuts the foundations of the cella of a Roman temple (1C A.D.) and Roman shops (for adm. ring at

Convent). The temple is built in to the walls of the church of *Sant'Ansano,* inside of which further remains of the temple have been exposed around the altar. Steps lead down (lights on left) to the Cappella di Sant'Isacco (the crypt) with primitive (11-12C) frescoes (recently detached and restored). From the neighbouring P.za del Mercato, with a fountain by Costantino Fiaschetti (1746) and a monument to Urban VII by Carlo Maderno (1626; being restored), Via del Municipio leads to *Palazzo Comunale,* which faces a pretty row of old houses. Here is the PINACOTECA (open 10-12.30, 18-20; fest. 10-12.30, 18.30-20; closed Tues).

The collection includes a triptych by *Nic. da Foligno* (*L'Alunno*), a Madonna by *Antonello da Saliba,* frescoes and paintings by *Lo Spagna* and his school, and other Umbrian works; a Mary Magdalen by *Guercino* has been removed for restoration.—The custodian shows also a *Roman House,* supposed to have belonged to Vespasia Polla, the mother of Vespasian, with mosaic floors, an impulvium, etc.

Uphill to the east is P.za Campello (with the 'Fontana del Mascherone'), dominated by the conspicuous *Rocca* (to be opened to the public when the prison is removed to a new building), erected in 1359-64 by Gattapone for Card. Albornoz. To the S. is the *Porta della Rocca.* Outside the gate are further remains of the old walls, and the remarkable aqueduct of the ***Ponte delle Torri,** also probably by Gattapone, but possibly on Roman foundations. It spans a deep ravine amidst ilex groves, and in 230 m long and 80 m high. A path on the far side leads across to the Monteluco road (comp. below). Via Saffi leads back W. to the Palazzo Arcivescovile, in the court of which is the 12C church of *Sant'Eufemia.* The beautiful Romanesque interior has a matroneum, interesting capitals, and some 15C frescoes on the columns. The 15C triptych, behind the 13C cosmatesque altar, has been temporarily removed. From the top of the stepped Via dell'Arringo is a remarkable *View of the cathedral and the countryside beyond. It descends past the apse of Sant'Eufemia and the Renaissance *Palazzo Arroni* (r.) to P.za del Duomo. On the left the *Palazzo della Signoria* contains the MUSEO CIVICO (ring for custodian at the theatre). Here is a good collection of sculpture from the 4C to the 14C; also an inscription of the 3C B.C. forbidding the cutting of timber in a sacred grove. Above the museum is the *Chamber Theatre* (Caio Melisso), resored for the Festival.

The ***Duomo** (closed 13-15), consecrated by Innocent III in 1198, was later much altered. The façade is preceded by an elegant Renaissance portico (1491), by *Ambr. Barocci* and *Pippo Fiorentino,* incorporating two pulpits. Above are eight rose windows, and a mosaic signed *Solsternus* (1207), while the main portal is a fine 12C Romanesque work. The campanile (12C, with additions of 1416 and 1518) incorporates Roman fragments.

The INTERIOR was modernized in 1634-44 for Urban VIII, whose bust, by *Bernini,* surmounts the central door. In the 1st chap. in the S. aisle (unlocked by the custodian) are frescoes by *Pinturicchio* (Madonna and Child with two Saints, and the Eternal Father). In the S. transept are a Madonna and saints by *Ann. Carracci,* the tomb of G. F. Orsini by *Ambr. Barocci* and the ***Tomb of Fra Filippo Lippi,** erected by Florentine artists at the order of Lorenzo de' Medici, with an inscription by Politian. The apse is painted with *Frescoes (damaged) by *Filippo Lippi* (1468-69), finished after his death by *Fra Diamante.* The Cappella delle Reliquie (last chap. in N. aisle) has painted stalls of 1548-54, a Crucifixion by *Sozio* (1187), and a Madonna and Child sculpted in wood (14C).

The Via del Duomo and Via Filitteria lead down to the Teatro Nuovo and the Via Sant'Andrea, and from there to the *Galleria d'Arte*

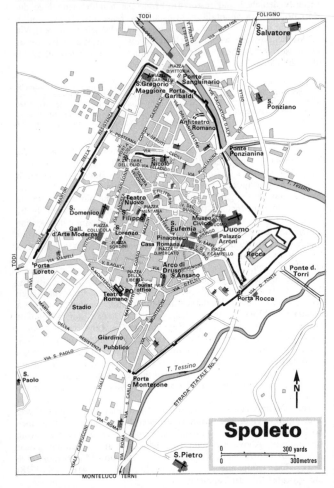

Moderna in the Palazzo Collicola. The 13C church of *San Domenico* has a banded exterior. Inside are fragments of votive frescoes in the nave, and (1st S. altar) the Triumph of St Thomas Aquinas (recently detached and restored) dating from the early 15C. To the r. of the presbytery a barrel-vaulted chapel is entirely covered with frescoes by a 15C artist. On the E. wall of the church (below the windows) are more frescoes and an Umbrian painting of St Peter Martyr. From the chap. to

l. of the presbytery steps (light on left) descend to a crypt with further remains of frescoes. The P.za Torre dell'Olio takes name from the tall medieval tower beyond the *Porta Fuga,* or *di Annibale,* beneath which the Via Porta Fuga descends to join the Corso Garibaldi. Longer but more interesting is the descent by Via Cecili, which affords a view of the best section of the **Walls**—of all periods from the 6C B.C. to the 15C— interrupted by the 14C apse of *San Nicolò.* The ruins of the *Amphitheatre,* farther on, are within the ex-conventual barracks and difficult of access. Via Garibaldi and Via dell'Anfiteatro meet at the P.za Garibaldi, where the 12C church of *San Gregorio* was well restored in 1949. Outside the *Porta Garibaldi,* or Porta Leonina, are the remains of the PONTE SANGUINARIO, a Roman bridge (A.D. 200; apply at Ufficio Imposte e Consumo), abandoned when the river was diverted in the 14C and rediscovered in 1817 when the existing bridge was built.

A short walk to the right, beyond the river, leads to the cemetery and church of *San Salvatore (or Il Crocifisso) combining part of the wall and colonnade of a pagan temple and the façade of a 6C church; within are admirable ancient columns. A little S. is the 12C church of *San Ponziano.*

The EXCURSION TO MONTELUCO (8 km.) may be made by car. From the S. end of the town the Via Roma leads towards the ancient church of **San Pietro** (usually locked), with an admirable Lombard façade, profusely sculptured. Much higher is the 12C church of *San Giuliano,* incorporating fragments of a 6C predecessor. The road climbs through the ilex woods of **Monteluco** (804 m), occupied from the 7C by anchorites, to the convent of *San Francesco* (belvedere). The slopes are now a summer resort.

In the scattered commune of (140 km.) *Campello sul Clitunno* are (r. of the road) the ruins of the little 8C church of Cipriano and Giustina. To the left of the road a green oasis marks the *Fonti del Clitunno,* where the river gushes forth in a sudden flow. This is the classical *Clitumnus,* famed for the white oxen bred on its banks. Its crystal-clear waters have been praised by Byron and Carducci. The road continues to (1 km. farther on) the *Tempietto di Clitunno* (ring for custodian) re-made from antique fragments in the 4C or 5C above a pagan temple which covered another spring (now dry), mentioned by the younger Pliny. The charming little interior has primitive frescoes of SS. Peter and Paul and God the Father (7-8C).—146 km. **Trevi** (6740 inhab.) is conspicuous on a hill (424 m) covered with olive groves, 4 km. E. of its station. Half-way up is the church of the *Madonna delle Lacrime* (if closed, ring at convent) dating from 1487, with a good sculptured portal, and containing an *Adoration of the Magi, by Perugino (r. wall). In the l. transept is a frescoed tabernacle by Lo Spagna. Behind the high altar a detached fresco of the Crucifixion has been placed (removed from the church of San Francesco in the town). In the small picture gallery in the 15C *Municipio* are examples of Spagna and Pinturicchio, *Sant'Amiliano* (12C, restored) has a triple altarpiece by Rocco da Vicenza (1522). The church of *San Martino* (14C), N.E. of the town, has a detached chapel with further work by Spagna.

155 km. **Foligno** (234m) is an industrial town of 51,800 inhabitants, on the River Topino. and the seat of a bishop.

It was the *Fulginia* of the Romans and absorbed the population of *Forum Flaminii,* another Roman town 3½ km. E. Long a free town, latterly under the rule of the Trinci family, it passed to the States of the Church in 1439. Here was born St Angela of Foligno (1248-1309), a noble lady who became a Franciscan tertiary. Its school of painting was largely indebted to Nicolò da Foligno, or Nicolò di Liberatore, sometimes called L'Alunno (c. 1430-1502).

Printing was introduced at Foligno in 1470, only six years after the first book printed in Italy had appeared at Subiaco. Serious damage was done to the town by bombing in 1943-44. Raphael's Madonna di Foligno is now in the Vatican.

The *Palazzo Comunale,* in the P.za della Repubblica, has a 14C tower. In the same square are the Renaissance *Palazzo Orfini* and the *Palazzo Trinci* (1395-1407), with a chapel and a hall containing paintings by Ottaviano Nelli. The Pinacoteca here contains a fresco attrib. to Benozzo Gozzoli from the disused church of San Domenico, paintings by the native artist Pierant. Mezzastris, etc. The much modernized Romanesque **Duomo** (1133-1201) has a magnificent N. façade. In the adjacent Via Gramsci is the graceful *Palazzo Deli* or *Nuti* (16C). The churches of *Santa Maria Infraportas,* a Romanesque basilica with Byzantine and other frescoes, and *San Nicolò,* with two paintings by L'Alunno, deserve a visit. The *Nunziatella,* a chapel in the street of the same name (apply at No. 18) contains a fresco by Perugino.

BUSES to *Montefalco;* to *Bevagna* and *Todi;* to *Perugia* direct and viâ *Assisi;* viâ Tolentino, Macerata, and San Benedetto del Tronto to *Ascoli Piceno;* to *Rome.*

About 5 km. E. of Foligno, on the slopes of Monte Serrone, is the **Abbadia di Sassovivo,** with a beautiful cloister of round arches by a Roman artist (1229).— About 9 km. W., on the road to Todi, is *Bevagna,* a charming little town (4800 inhab.). In the main square, P.za Silvestri, are the Palazzo dei Consoli with Gothic two-light windows (inside is a theatre), and the Romanesque 12C churches of San Silvestro and San Michele (good portals). At the other end of the town, in Via Porta Guelfa, is a Roman mosaic (2C A.D.) with marine figures.—Twelve km. S.W. is **Montefalco** (472 m), named from its lofty position the 'Ringhiera dell'Umbria'. The road enters the town through the Porta Sant'Agostino with a fresco of the Madonna and Saints (14C?) on the inside façade. Via Umberti ascends past *Sant'Agostino,* with numerous frescoes, to the charming circular P.za della Repubblica (car parking) with the *Palazzo Comunale* (view from the tower). Just out of the square (downhill along Via Ringhiera Umbra) is the 14C church of *San Francesco* (which serves as a museum, adm. 9.30-12.30, 15.30-18.30; Sun & fest. 9-12). Here are paintings by Fr. Melanzio, a native artist, Melozzo da Forlì, Antoniazzo Romano, Pier Ant. Mezzastris, and Benozzo Gozzoli (a fresco cycle in the apse of the *Life of St Francis). In the convent church of *Santa Chiara,* on the Spoleto road, the Cappella Santa Croce has 14C Umbrian frescoes, and *Santa Illuminata* has more frescoes by Tiberio d'Assisi, Melanzio, and Mezzastris. In *San Fortunato,* outside the Porta Spoleto, are fragmentary frescoes (including the titular saint) by *Gozzoli.*

Gualdo Cattaneo, 13 km. W. of Montefalco, is a tiny medieval town in a beautiful position.

From Foligno to *Assisi* and *Perugia,* see Rte 53. Both road and railway ascend the valley of the Topino.—178 km. **Nocera Umbra** is a little spa (547 m), with 6320 inhabitants, 3 km. N.E. of its station (396 m). The waters of the *Sorgente Angelica* are bottled and sent all over Italy. Nocera is the *Nuceria Camellaria* of Pliny, and was a lordship of the Trinci family. The former Gothic church of *San Francesco* houses a good collection of paintings, including a 13C Crucifix and a Nativity and Saints, by L'Alunno.—The road undulates sharply and the railway reaches its highest point (483 m) near (185 km.) *Gaifana* on the plateau of the same name.—193 km. *Gualdo Tadino,* 2 km. E. of its station and considerably above it (536 m), stands near the site of the ancient *Tadinum,* where Narses routed the Goths and slew Totila in 552. It is the birthplace of Matteo di Pietro or da Gualdo (fl. 1462-98), some of whose works may be seen in the ex church of San Francesco which now houses the Pinacoteca. Here, too, is a good altarpiece by L'Alunno (1471).

Buses run viâ *Gubbio* to *Città di Castello;* and (once daily) to *Assisi* and *Perugia.*

N76 turns right to pass (202km.) *Fossato di Vico.* From the crossroads N3 goes on viâ Scheggia (17 km.) to Fossombrone (63 km.; p. 569) and from there to the Adriatic coast at Fano. This road passes in a tunnel beneath a ridge marking the boundary of the Marches.

219 km. **Fabriano** (325 m) is a considerable town (28,400 inhab.) noted since the 13C or 14C for its paper mills. The picturesque main square, with a fountain of 1351, is bounded on one side by the 17C *Loggiato San Francesco,* of 19 arches, on the other by the *Bishop's Palace* and *Clock Tower,* and closed at the end by the *Palazzo del Podestà* (1255). The *Pinacoteca* contains paintings of the local school, whose most conspicuous members were Allegretto Nuzi (d. 1374) and his follower Gentile da Fabriano (1370-1427); also good Flemish tapestries. Frescoes by Nuzi adorn the neighbouring *Duomo,* which preserved its 14C apse and cloister through a rebuilding in 1617. The 14-15C church of *Santa Lucia* (often called San Domenico) contains a Madonna by Francescuccio di Cecco (1359).

FROM FABRIANO TO PÉRGOLA, 36 km., bus or railway in 40 min. The route runs through a fertile and well-wooded valley. 18 km. **Sassoferrato,** with 7340 inhab., is the birthplace of G. B. Salvi (1605-85), called Sassoferrato, whose Madonnas are to be seen in numerous Italian churches. The Museo Civico in the Town Hall contains finds from *Sentinum,* where the Romans vanquished the Samnites and Gauls in 295 B.C. (ruins S.W. of town). Spoil from the site was used in the construction of *Santa Croce* (1 km. E.), a 12C church with frescoes and an altarpiece of 1471.—31 km. *Bellisio,* with sulphur mines.—36 km. *Pérgola* is connected by bus with Urbino (2¼ hrs) viâ Bellisio and Cagli; and with Senigallia and Ancona.

About 13 km. N.E. of Sassoferrato is *Arcévia,* where the church of San Medardo contains two good paintings by Signorelli.

The road continues to descend, following the course of the river Esino.—228 km. *Albacina* (284 m) stands above the junction of the railway for Tolentino and Macerata (Rte 54B). In the hills c. 9 km. E. (reached from Poggio San Romualdo) is the abbey of *Val di Castro,* where St Romuald died in 1027. The crypt and chapter-house (11-12C) are the most striking parts of the surviving buildings.

From the junction N256 follows the railway S. viâ (3 km.) *Cerreto d'Esi,* an ancient walled village, to (10 km.) **Matélica** (357 m), a small town (8880 inhab.) whose troublous history is that of its struggle against Camerino. In the church of *San Francesco* are paintings by Marco Palmezzano and Fr. da Fabriano. The *Palazzo Piersanti* has a picture gallery and the main square a pleasant group of old buildings.—The road goes on viâ (18 km.) *Castelraimondo* (comp. Rte 54B) to Camerino, the railway to Macerata and the coast.

235 km. *Genga-San Vittore Terme Station* lies near the junction of the by-road through the *Gola di Frasassi,* a limestone gorge 2 km. long, at the mouth of which stand a small thermal bath and the curious 11C church of *San Vittore delle Chiuse.* The road goes on to *Genga* (9 km.), a little town with a triptych by Ant. da Fabriano in its parish church, and to Sassoferrato (14 km.; see above).—N76 traverses the Gola della Rossa, a gorge in the red limestone, and beyond (242 km.) *Serra San Quírico* the valley opens out. At *Maiolati,* in the hills 8 km. E. of (246 km.) *Gli Angeli,* Gasp. Spontini (1774-1851), the composer, was born and died.

264 km. **Iesi,** a walled town of 41,600 inhabitants, on the Esino, was the Roman *Æsis*. Here were born the emperor Frederick II (1194-1250) and the composer G. B. Pergolesi (1710-36). The Renaissance *Palazzo della Signoria* (1486-98), by Fr. di Giorgio Martini, houses a Museum and Pinacoteca with five admirable *Paintings by Lor. Lotto. The church of *San Marco* has frescoes by the Riminese school. To the S. (24 km.) is *Cíngoli,* an ancient little town famed for its splendid views.—276 km. *Chiaravalle,* a modern-looking town which grew up around a late-12C Cistercian abbey (the plain brick church of which survives), was the birthplace of Maria Montessori (1870-1952), the educationist. *Monte San Vito* and *Morro d'Alba,* 5 km. and 10 km. W., preserve important remains of medieval castles.—At (282 km.) *Rocca Priora* this route joins the coast road from Rimini and turns right across the Esino (the railway crosses the river earlier and joins the coast line at Falconara).—294 km. **Ancona,** see Rte 51.

B   Viâ Macerata

ROAD, 307 km. To (155 km.) *Foligno,* see Rte 54A. N 77. 198 km. *Múccia.*—228 km. **Tolentino.**—246 km. **Macerata.**—270 km. *Recanati.*—277 km. *Loreto.*—N 16. 307 km. **Ancona.**

The road leaves Foligno by the Piazzale Ancona and immediately beyond the railway diverges right into Via Piave (N 77), soon crossing the by-pass. For 16 km. the road winds upwards, in places steeply, with splendid views on the right, to the *Valico Colfiorito* (821 m).—Beyond (165 km.) *Colfiorito* extends a small cultivated plateau on the borders of Umbria and the Marches. To the N. *Monte Pennino* (1571 m) is seen behind Monte Acuto, while to the right of the road rises *Monte Profóglio* (1322 m). On the watershed rises the Chienti, which the road now descends in a deep enclosed valley.—198 km. *Múccia* stands at the junction of a road to Camerino, affording an alternative route by N 256 and N 361 (little difference in distance).

N 256 crosses the *Colle Santa Barbara* (556 m), dips, and rises again to (9 km.) **Camerino,** a cathedral town (6060 inhab.) of Umbrian origin. It possesses a massive castle built by Cæsar Borgia, a university dating from 1727, and a statue of Sixtus V by Vergelli (1586). In the main square are the *Duomo,* with a triptych by Girol. di Giovanni in the sacristy, and the *Museo Diocesano,* with a Madonna by Tiepolo. Near *San Venanzio,* a church with a fine 15C W. door, is the church of the Annunziata (attr. to Rocco da Vicenza). The picture gallery, including an Annunciation by Girol. di Giovanni is temporarily housed in the Municipio. Camerino from c. 1260 to 1539 was a fief of the Varano family, whose castle survives as a picturesque ruin. 7 km. S.E.—At (19 km.) *Castelraimondo* the road joins the railway and the road coming from Fabriano (comp. Rte 54A), then descends the valley of the Potenza by N 361.—31 km. **San Severino Marche** (231 m), with 13,000 inhabitants, is the ancient *Septempeda,* sacked by Totila. It is the birthplace of the anatomist Bart. Eustachi (c. 1500-74), after whom the Eustachian tube is named, and of the painters Lor. Salimbeni (c. 1374-1420) and Lorenzo d'Alessandro (later 15C). The *Palazzo Comunale* houses the Pinacoteca (polyptychs by Nic. da Foligno and Lor. d'Alessandro). The *Duomo Nuovo* has a fine Madonna by Pinturicchio. The Romanesque church of *San Lorenzo* is also in the lower town. In the ancient upper town is the *Duomo Vecchio* (11C and 14C), with notable woodwork by Dom. Indivini and his school (1483-1513), frescoes by the Salimbeni, and a 15C cloister. Tolentino (comp. below) is 11 km. S.E.—The road runs straight in the widening valley, passing (46 km.) the steep turning to *Treia* (4 km. l.), an ancient hill town.—55 km. *Helvia Ricina,* comp. below.

A road diverges right to Triponzo, while this road passes close to the

Rocca di Varano (comp. above), and skirts the Lago di Borgiano.—
225 km. *Le Grazie* is the 'lido' of Tolentino.

228 km. **Tolentino** (228 m), a manufacturing town (17,800 inhab.),
gave its name to the treaty of 1797 whereby Pius VI ceded the Romagna
and Avignon to Napoleon, together with many works of art. The
basilica of SAN NICOLA, with a magnificent portal (1432-35) by Nanni di
Bartolo, has a notable ceiling of 1628. A large detached chapel on the S.
side, frescoed by Romagnole artists of c. 1340, contains the cenotaph
and a statue (by Giorgio da Sebénico) of St Nicholas of Tolentino (d.
1308), who was born at *Sant'Angelo in Pontano*, 30 km. S.E. His tomb is
in the crypt beneath the chapel of the Holy Arms. A charming 13-14C
cloister gives access to a small museum of majolica and the *Museo
Civico*, containing objects from an Umbrian necropolis. The rebuilt
Duomo contains a large 4C sarcophagus. To the S. the Chienti is crossed
by a fortified 13C bridge.—The *Terme di Santa Lucia*, 3 km. N.W., are
frequented for their mineral waters.

The road is joined by the railway from Fabriano. At 233 km. the 14C
castle of *La Rancia* is conspicuous on the right.—240 km. *Urbisaglia*
station. Below the town of Urbisaglia, 8 km. S.W., are some remains of
Roman *Urbs Salvia;* the road to it (N 78) passes the Cistercian abbey
church of *Fiastra,* a well-restored 12C building in brick, with a cloister of
some 200 years later.—At (241 km.) *Sforzacosta* N 77 leaves the Chienti.

245 km. **MACERATA** (315 m) stands 51½ m above its station. It is an
attractive modern town of 44,300 inhabitants situated on the crest of the
hills between the Potenza and the Chienti; the views are charming. First
mentioned in 1022, it came under the rule of the Church in 1445 and
acquired a university in 1543. Macerata was the birthplace of P. Paolo
Floriana (1585-1638), the military engineer, who gave his name to
Floriana in Malta.

Ente Provinciale per il Turismo, 12 P.za Libertà.—*Post Office,* Via Gramsci.
Buses viâ Osimo and viâ Civitanova Marche to *Ancona* in 1½-2 hrs; viâ Porto
Civitanova and Grottammare to *Ascoli Piceno* in 2¾ hrs; viâ Tolentino, Foligno,
and Assisi to *Perugia* in 3¼ hrs; viâ Tolentino to *Camerino* in 1¾ hrs; to *Fermo* in
2 hrs; to *Lereto* in ½ hr; to *Rome* in 5½ hrs.

Broad avenues encircle the old town; the Viale Puccinotti on the S.W.,
between the 14C *Walls* and the *Giardini Diaz,* affords fine views to the
distant Monti Sibillini. The centre of the town is the P.za della Libertà.
On its W. side are the *Palazzo del Comune,* with antiquities from Helvia
Ricina (see below) in its courtyard, and the graceful *Loggia dei
Mercanti,* attributed to Cassiano da Fabriano (1504-5). To the N. the
Prefettura has a portal of 1509. On the E. side stands the church of *San
Paolo* (1655) and the 19C buildings of the *University.*

The Via Don Minzoni leads E. On the right is the *Palazzo Compagnoni- Mare-
foschi,* where on Good Friday 1772 Charles Edward Stuart married Princess
Louise of Stolberg. He signed himself in the chapel register 'Charles III of Great
Britain, France, and Ireland'. His mother, Clementina Sobieska (1702-35), had
been born in the same palace. The *Duomo* is by Cosimo Morelli (1771-90); the
adjacent *Basilica Madre della Misericordia* has an interior by Vanvitelli. In the S.E.
corner of the town stands the huge *Sferisterio,* an arena built in 1821-29. Beyond
lies the modern quarter with the station, c. 1 km. E. of which is the church of *Santa
Maria delle Vergini,* by Galasso Alghisi (1555-73).

Steps descend S. from the centre to *Santa Maria della Porta,* with a

Gothic doorway of c. 1340. To the W. the church of *San Giovanni* contains a Death of the Virgin, by Lanfranco. In the adjoining Library the *Pinacoteca* includes a Madonna by Carlo Crivelli, a self-portrait by Carlo Maratta, and other paintings of the school of the Marches. Below is a carriage museum. In the Corso Matteotti, leading W. from the centre, the *Palazzo Ferri* has diamond-pointed rustication. The *Palazzo Santafiora,* in the Via Garibaldi, farther W., saw Napoleon in 1797 and Murat in 1815.

From Macerata to Civitanova Marche, see p. 578. At *Corridonia* known as Mont'Olmo until 1851, and as Páusula in 1851-1931), nearly 5 km. S. of Pie' di Ripa, the Pinacoteca next to the Collegiata contains a fine triptych by Lor. d'Alessandro (1481), and Madonnas by Andrea da Bologna (1372) and by Carlo Crivelli.

The road descends to the Potenza valley near the extensive ruins of *Helvia Ricina,* a town of dubious origin destroyed in the 5C. The road follows the valley for about 8 km., then branches left to (270 km.) **Recanati** (293 m), an attractive little town (18,000 inhab.) in a commanding position between the Potenza and the Musone. It was the birthplace of Giac. Leopardi (1798-1837), souvenirs of whom may be seen in the *Palazzo Leopardi* (adm. in summer 9-12, 16-19; 15-18 in winter), and of Beniamino Gigli (1890-1957), the tenor, whose tomb recalls the last act of Aida. The *Palazzo Comunale* (9-12, 16-18; fest. 10-12) has paintings by Lorenzo Lotto and a little Gigli museum. The massive 13C *Torre del Borgo,* opposite, bears a bronze relief (1634) by P. P. Iacometti. The church of *San Domenico* has a marble portal of 1481 and a Lotto fresco. The *Museo Diocesano* (apply to sacristan of Duomo) contains a picture gallery.—At (273 km.) *Palazzo Bello* a road descends (r.) directly to the coast at Porto Recanati (8 km.).—277 km. **Loreto,** and from there to (307 km.) **Ancona**, see Rte 51.

55   SAN BENEDETTO DEL TRONTO TO ROME

ROAD, 228 km. N 16, then N 4 (VIA SALARIA). 32 km. **Áscoli Piceno.**—52 km. *Acquasanta Terme.*—123 km.   *Antrodoco.*—137 km.   *Cittaducale.*—147 km. **Rieti.**—228 km.   **Rome.**   BUSES from San Benedetto to Ascoli Piceno (c. every ½ hr) in 50 min.; from Ascoli to Rome, twice daily, in 4½ hrs; more frequently from Rieti to Rome in 2-3½ hrs.

N 16 leads S. and at (4 km.) *Porto d'Áscoli* Via Salaria (N 4) turns right. This ancient and scenically attrative highway follows the railway to Áscoli and the River Tronto on the left.—20 km. *Offida Station.* A bus follows a by-road N. to *Offida* (11 km.; 293 m), a small town with an arcaded Municipio (15C); the 14C brick church of Santa Maria della Rocca has contemporary frescoes in its large crypt.

32 km. **ASCOLI PICENO** (154 m; 56,400 inhab.) is the capital of its province, one of four making up the region of the Marches. Surrounded by greenery, at the confluence of the Tronto and the Castellano, it is a town of medieval aspect built largely of travertine.

Post Office, Via Crispi.—*Ente Provinciale per Il Turismo,* Corso Mazzini.
Buses to *Rome* (see above); to *San Benedetto del Tronto;* also to *Ancona;* to *Téramo;* via San Benedetto del Tronto, Macerata, Tolentino, Foligno and Assisi, to *Perugia;* to *Acquasanta Terme;* and to *Valle Castellana.*

Railway to *San Benedetto del Tronto,* 33 km. in c. 40 min.

Festivals. Carnival with dancing in the streets on Shrove Tues; *Quintana* (first Sun in Aug), costume procession and jousting.

History. *Asculum Picenum,* a Sabine town, at first allied with Rome but afterwards at the head of the Italic League against her, was destroyed in 89 B.C. by Cn. Pompeius Strabo, father of Pompey the Great. An independent commune in 1185, it was taken in 1242 by Frederick II, and in 1504 it put itself under the protection of the Holy See. In 1944 the retreating Germans blew up all the bridges.—About 1486 Carlo Crivelli initiated here an artistic movement which culminated with Nic. Filostesio, generally known as Cola dell'Amatrice, later a follower of Signorelli. Pietro Vannini here brought the goldsmith's art to great perfection, while the art of wood-carving also was cultivated. Áscoli was the birthplace of Girol. Masci (Pope Nicholas IV; c. 1230-92—born at Lisciano, 5 km. S.) and of the poet Fr. Stabili, called Cecco d'Áscoli, burned as an astrologer at Florence in 1327.

From the restored Ponte Maggiore (1373) over the Castellano there is a view of the *Fortezza Malatesta,* enlarged by Sangallo the Younger. On the left, behind the Giardino Pubblico, is the little church of *San Vittore* (10-16C), with 14C frescoes. Farther on are the octagonal 12C **Baptistery,* and the **Duomo** (*Sant'Emidio*), a 12C building reconstructed in 1482, with a magnificent unfinished façade of 1532-39, by Cola dell'Amatrice.

Interior. In a chapel on the right is a beautiful polyptych by *Carlo Crivelli* (1473); on the choir arch is an Assumption by *Ces. Mariani,* by whom are also the frescoes from the Life of Sant'Emidio, in the cupola. The Gothic choir-stalls are by *Paolino d'Áscoli* and *Francesco di Giovanni.* The crypt (restored) dates from the 12C. In the treasury, in the adjoining *Episcopal Palace* (adm. 10-12), are a statue of Sant'Emidio and a silver reliquary by *Pietro Vannini,* a 14C altar-frontal in silver, and a collection of paintings.

In the Via dei Bonaparte, opposite the side portal of the Duomo, is the *Palazzetto Bonaparte* (1507), beautifully adorned.

Beyond the cathedral, in the P.za dell'Arringo, rises the **Palazzo Comunale,** with its Baroque façade by *Gius. Giosafatti* (1683), and the two fine 13C Sale dell'Arringo, on the ground floor. The picture gallery (adm. 10-13, 16.30-18.30; winter, 8-13; fest. 10-12) on the first floor contains works by *Cola* and by *Pietro Alamanno,* triptychs by *Carlo Crivelli,* a St Francis by *Titian* (ruined), an Annunciation by *Guido Reni,* a Death of St Joseph by *Luca Giordano,* St Jerome, by *Aless. Magnasco,* and a famous cope, a very early example of opus anglicanum, given by Nicholas IV to the Duomo in 1288. Palazzo Panichi, opposite, is to house a small archæological collection, notable for finds from the Lombard necropolis of Casteltrosino.—The church of *San Gregorio,* behind the Palazzo Comunale, incorporates a Roman Corinthian prostyle Temple of Vesta.

Via Venti Settembre and Via Trieste lead towards the *PIAZZA DEL POPOLO, picturesque centre of the city. The 13C *Palazzo del Popolo* (restored), in this square, has a portal by Cola dell'Amatrice surmounted by a monument to Paul III (1548). The church of ***San Francesco,** begun in 1262 and completed, except for the roof, in 1464, has beautiful portals, a picturesque apse with seven chapels, and a severe interior. The Great Cloister (1565-1623) is used as a market; the Small Cloister (14C) has been incorporated in a modern building. The elegant *Loggia dei Mercanti* on its right side was designed by Bern. di Pietro of Carona (c. 1600). From there Via Malta (N.) and the Via Cairoli lead to *Santi Vincenzo ed Anastasio* (12C; enlarged in the 14C), with a curious façade of 1389. A little to the N. is the *Ponte di Solestà,* a Roman bridge dating from the early years of the Empire. The Gothic *San Pietro Martire* (14C) stands opposite San Vincenzo. The characteristic Via Soderini leads to the *Casa Longobarda,* with its stark Torre Ercolani, and to the church of *San Giacomo,* restored in the 15C, beyond which is the *Porta Gémina,* with parts of the original Roman walls.

On the way back the road passes the church of *Sant'Agostino,* rebuilt in 1485. It contains a St Francis Xavier, by Baciccia. Opposite are two imposing towers. The Via della Fortezza (r.) mounts the Colle dell'Annunziata (view), in which are large caves, probably substructures of the Roman citadel. On the E. side of the hill is the church of *Sant'Angelo Magno* (1292), while to the W. are remains of a *Roman Theatre.* The road continues through the Parco della Rimembranza to the ex-convent of the *Annunziata.* Steps mount to the *Fortezza Pia,* constructed by Pius IV in 1564.—In the N.E. quarter of the town, among many good 16-17C mansions, the *Palazzo Malaspina* is a bold and original 16C construction, perhaps by Cola.

At (39 km.) *Taverna Piccinini* (209 m), N 78 branches right for Amandola (35 km.; Rte 51) and Macerata (85 km.; Rte 54B).—52 km. Acquasanta Terme (392 m), the Roman *Vicus ad Aquas,* has thermal sulphur springs, which cured Munatius Plancus of rheumatism. The ascent becomes steeper as the river is hemmed in by stratified rocks.— 65 km. *Arquata del Tronto* (719 m) has a castle built by Joan II of Naples. The road continues to climb the Tronto valley between the Monti Sibillini on the right and the Monti della Laga on the left (Pizzo di Sevo, 2419 m).—At (71 km.) *Bivio di Tufo* a difficult mountain road leads W. over the *Forca Canapine* (1541 m) to Norcia (35 km.; p. 610). The road passes from the Marches into Lazio.—At (84 km.) *Ponte della Scandarella* the road divides. The left branch follows the Tronto to Amatrice (4 km.), then descends to L'Aquila (comp. the 'Blue Guide to Southern Italy'). This road climbs steeply above the artificial *Lago della Scandarella,* through *Torrita* to (93 km.) a summit level of 1043 m (good retrospective views). Here is the source of the Velino which the road descends.—109 km. *Posta* (721 m).

Mountain roads go off right to *Leonessa* (19 km.), a remote little place with a notable town-gate and two good Gothic churches; the right-hand road leads to *Montereale* (20 km.), on the road from L'Aquila to Amatrice (comp. above).

The Via Salaria threads the *Gole del Velino,* narrow winding ravines between the Terminillo (2216 m; see below), on the right, and Monte Giano (1820 m) on the left.—123 km. **Antrodoco** (525 m), the ancient *Interocrea,* at the junction of three gorges, is overlooked by a castle of the Vitelli, on a spur of Monte Terminillo. The church of the *Assunta* contains a fine processional cross, perhaps by Nic. da Guardiagrele. Near the exit towards Rieti is the little Romanesque church of *Santa Maria.*

This is the starting-point of N 17, here known as the *Via Sabina,* which runs across the Apennines through L'Aquila to Foggia.

The road runs S.W. with the Sulmona-Terni railway.—131 km. *Terme di Cotilia* uses the sulphur springs of *Cutilia,* where Vespasian died in A.D. 79. Across the railway rise a series of springs which unite to form the *Peschiera,* the second most copious source in Italy (15,456 litres per second).—137 km. **Cittaducale** (481 m) is a medieval fortress on a regular plan, founded in 1309 and named after Robert the Wise, duke of Calabria, afterwards King of Naples.

147 km. **RIETI** (405 m), a provincial capital with 42,100 inhabitants, was the ancient *Reate,* chief town of the Sabines. It was the birthplace of the historian M. Terentius Varro (116-27 B.C.) and the cradle of the imperial Gens Flavia. It has many associations with St Francis of Assisi. The 13C walls and the medieval palaces impart an old-world look to the town.

Post Office, Via Garibaldi.—*Ente Provinciale per Il Turismo* and *Ufficio Informazioni,* P.za Vittorio Emanuele II.

Bus Station, P.za Cavour. Services to *Rome* and to *Ascoli Piceno;* also to *Terminillo,* in ¾ hr; viâ Fonte Colombo to *Greccio,* in ¾ hr; to *Avezzano,* in 3½ hrs; viâ Antrodoco to *Accúmoli* and to *L'Aquila, Pescara,* and *Vasto;* viâ Roccasinibalda to *Cársoli* in 2¼ hrs; to *Terni* in 1¼ hrs.

The *North Wall* of the city stands almost complete except for the breach made by the Piazza Mazzini opposite the railway station. In the square stands *Sant'Agostino,* a 13C church. To the S.W. beyond two more squares, lies Piazza Vittorio Emanuele, site of the ancient forum, where the **Palazzo Comunale** houses a small MUSEO CIVICO (10-13). This displays classical and medieval sculpture; *Antoniazzo Romano, Madonna with SS. Francis and Anthony of Padua* (1464); *Luca di Tommè,* Pentaptych (1370), signed and dated; *Zannino di Pietro,* Triptych (early 15C Venetian school); *Pirro Ligorio*(?), Banner with the Ascension and the Assumption (1546). In the neighbouring P.za Battisti (view) is the **Cathedral,** a Romanesque edifice, largely rebuilt but retaining a crypt of 1109-57. The 4th N. chapel contains a St Barbara designed by Bernini (1657). Here on Whit Sunday 1289 Pope Nicholas IV crowned Charles II of Naples with the empty title of King of Sicily, thus beginning the confusion of the two Sicilies. The *Palazzo Vescovile,* restored in 1928-31, preserves its fine loggia of 1283-88. Within, a plaque records the marriage in Rieti (1185) between the Emp. Henry VI and Constance of Altavilla; in 1234 their son, Frederick II, was received here by Pope Gregory IX, then in need of aid against the rebellious citizens of Rome.

From the centre the Via Roma, passing the church of *San Pietro* (13C doorway) and crossing the Velino river, leads to (5 min.) the *Fonte Cottorella,* a little mineral spring.—From the Porta Romana a road (6 km.) ascends S.W. to the *Cõnvento di Fonte Colombo* (bus, see above), in an ilex grove, where St Francis dictated the rules of his Order in 1223. The *Convento La Foresta,* W. of the town, marks the site of another sojourn of the saint (1225).—To the N. extends the beautiful PLAIN OF RIETI, surrounded by mountains and watered by the Velino; its scenery has been compared with that of the Vale of Tempe in Thessaly. It was drained by Curius Dentatus (p. 609). On the W. side of the plain, 15 km. N.W. of Rieti, is the *Santuario di Greccio* (638 m), where St Francis celebrated Christmas 1223. The present convent, half-way up the hill above the station (on the Terni line), though altered, still preserves an air of Franciscan simplicity. The cave where St Francis slept is still shown. The view of the plain is superb. *Greccio* is 25 min. S. by a pleasant level walk.

FROM RIETI TO TERMINILLO, 21 km.; bus, see above. This mountain road diverges to the left from N4 a little E. of Rieti.—6 km. *Varzia* (579 m).—Beyond (8 km.) *Lisciano* (604 m) the road winds up in sharp curves.

21 km. **Terminillo** (1575-1675 m) is a summer and winter sports resort, with numerous hotels, open in the season only.

Bus from *Rome* viâ Rieti in 3 hrs.

From Terminillo the ascent may be made of **Monte Terminillo** (2216 m; guide available). The summit is reached (c. 4 hrs) Viâ the *Rifugio del Terminilletto* (2205 m). A funicular railway is in operation all the year round.—The descent may be made to Cittaducale (see below).

From Rieti to Terni, see p. 610.

Beyond Rieti the Via Salaria turns due S., ascending into the Sabine Hills. A new road (N4 dir) continues more directly to join the Autostrada del Sole at the Roma Nord Station. At 156 km. the old road (high in the hills to the E.) provides the best access to *Roccasinibalda* (17 km.), where the stately Sforza castle was designed by Bald. Peruzzi (1536), and covered with Michelangelesque frescoes. Also off the old road, beyond *Torricella in Sabina,* is *Monteleone Sabino,* anciently *Trebula Mutusca,* birthplace of L. Mummius, the Roman general, who sacked Corinth in 146 B.C. Its little Romanesque church of Santa Vittoria (12C; 2 km. S.E.) has relics of a much earlier building.—172 km. By-road (r.) for Fara in Sabina (12 km.).

Fara in Sabina, a large village with a 16C church, commands a wide view. The abbey of *Farfa,* 3½ km. N.W., was founded c. 420 by St Lawrence 'the Illuminator' (he restored the sight of many blind persons). The church, rebuilt on new lines by St Thomas of Maurienne in 672, was destroyed after 841 by Barbary pirates, who made the abbey their trading centre. In 1567 (the date of the present church) the Benedictines reoccupied it; and they now manage a school here. Mosaic pavements of both the 7C and the 5C have been preserved in the church.

To the left the Barberini castle of *Nérola* is seen on its hill long before the picturesque old road reaches (184 km.) its approach road.—At (193 km.) *Passo Corese,* the old road joins the main Florence-Rome railway on the left bank of the Tiber, while the new road joins the A1 motorway.—204 km. *Monterotondo Scalo,* and from there to (228 km.) **Rome** (see the 'Blue Guide to Rome').

LIST OF THE
PRINCIPAL ITALIAN ARTISTS

whose works are referred to in the text, with their birthplaces or the schools to which they belonged. — Abbreviations: A. = architect, engr. = engraver, G. = goldsmith, illum. = illuminator, min. = miniaturist, mos. = mosaicist, P. = painter, S. = sculptor, stuc. = stuccoist, W. = woodworker.

ABBREVIATIONS OF CHRISTIAN NAMES

Agost.	= Agostino	Des.	= Desiderio	Ipp.	= Ippolito
Aless.	= Alessandro	Dom.	= Domenico	Laz.	= Lazzaro
Alf.	= Alfonso	Elis.	= Elisabetta	Leon.	= Leonardo
Ambr.	= Ambrogio	Fed.	= Federigo	Lod.	= Lodovico
And.	= Andrea	Fel.	= Felice	Lor.	= Lorenzo
Ang.	= Angelo	Ferd.	= Ferdinando	Mart.	= Martino
Ann.	= Annibale	Fil.	= Filippo	Matt.	= Matteo
Ant.	= Antonio	Fr.	= Francesco	Mich.	= Michele
Baldas.	= Baldassare	G. B.	= Giambattista	Nic.	= Nicola
Bart.	= Bartolomeo	Gasp.	= Gaspare	Pell.	= Pellegrino
Batt.	= Battista	Gaud.	= Gaudenzio	Raff.	= Raffaele
Bened.	= Benedetto	Giac.	= Giacomo	Rid.	= Ridolfo
Benv.	= Benvenuto	Giov.	= Giovanni	Seb.	= Sebastiano
Bern.	= Bernardino	Girol.	= Girolamo	Sim.	= Simone
Cam.	= Camillo	Giul.	= Giuliano	Stef.	= Stefano
Ces.	= Cesare	Gius.	= Giuseppe	Tim.	= Timoteo
Crist.	= Cristoforo	Greg.	= Gregorio	Tom.	= Tomaso
Dan.	= Daniele	Gugl.	= Guglielmo	Vinc.	= Vincenzo
Dav.	= Davide	Iac.	= Iacopo	Vitt.	= Vittorio
Def.	= Defendente	Inn.	= Innocenzo		

ABBREVIATIONS OF THE NAMES OF TOWNS AND PROVINCES

Anc.	= Ancona	Lig.	= Liguria	Pist.	= Pistoia
Are.	= Arezzo	Lomb.	= Lombardy	Rav.	= Ravenna
Ass.	= Assisi	Mant.	= Mantua	Rom.	= Romagna
Berg.	= Bergamo	Mil.	= Milan	Sett.	= Settignano
Bol.	= Bologna	Mod.	= Modena	Trev.	= Treviso
Bres.	= Brescia	Nap.	= Naples	Tur.	= Turin
Crem.	= Cremona	Orv.	= Orvieto	Tusc.	= Tuscany
Emil.	= Emilia	Pad.	= Padua	Umbr.	= Umbria
Faen.	= Faenza	Parm.	= Parma	Urb.	= Urbino
Ferr.	= Ferrara	Pav.	= Pavia	Ven.	= Venice
Fies.	= Fiesole	Per.	= Perugia	Ver.	= Verona
Flor.	= Florence	Piac.	= Piacenza	Vic.	= Vicenza
Gen.	= Genoa	Pied.	= Piedmont		

ABATE, NIC. DELL'(1512-71), P. Mod.—378, 390

ABBONDI, see Scarpagnino

AGNELLI, see Guglielmo

AGNOLO, BACCIO D'(Bartolomeo Baglioni; 1462-1543) A. Flor.—417, 438, 444, 456, 460, 462, 475, 595

AGNOLO, DOM. DI BACCIO D'(1511-after 1552) A. Flor.—444

AGNOLO, GIUL. DI BACCIO D' (Baglioni; 1491-1555), A. Flor.—511

ALAMANNO, PIETRO (de Ghoetbei; late 15C), P. Ascoli.—619

ALBANI, FR. (1578-1660), P. Bol. sch.—54, 159, 380-1, 387, 390-1

ALBERTI, LEON BATT. (1404-72), A.Flor.—15, 16, 204, 206, 208, 408, 416, 440, 443, 446, 455-6, 570

ALBERTINELLI, MARIOTTO (1474-1515), P. Flor. sch.—150, 432, 445, 449, 469, 479, 549, 561

ALBERTONI, GIOV. (1806-87), S. Pied.—50

ALEMAGNA, GIOV. D'(1417-50), P. Ven.—284, 158, 284, 298, 303, 313, 318, 323, 582

ALEOTTI, G. B. (Argenta; 1546-1636), A. Ferr. sch.—359, 370, 404

ALESSANDRO, LOR. D'(?1440-?1503), P. Sanseverino.—616, 618

ALESSI, GALEAZZO (c. 1512-72), A. Per.—95, 99, 102-3, 148-9, 155, 163, 165, 182, 370, 381, 594, 603, 604

ALFANI, DOM. DI PARIDE (c. 1480-1555), P. Per.—358, 590, 593

ALFANI, ORAZIO (son of Dom.; 1510-83), P. Per.—590

623

PALMA VECCHIO (Giac. Negretti; c.
1480-1528), P. Berg. (Ven. sch.).—
94, 150, 158, 176, 180, 263, 274,
285, 298, 301, 306, 316, 356, 378,
432
PALMEZZANO, MARCO (1456-c. 1539),
P. Forli.—158, 262, 301, 399, 404-
5, 469, 615
PANDOLFI, GIANNANT. (fl. 1570-81),
P. Pésaro.—595
PANICALE, see Masolino
PANTEO, MATT. (15C), S. Ver.—216
PAOLINO, FRA, see Pistóia
PAOLO, GIANNICOLA DI (c. 1460-
1544), P. Per.—585, 590-1, 593-5
PAOLO, GIOV. DI (?1403-82), P. &
illum, Siena.—513, 515, 519, 522,
526, 541-2, 549
PAOLO, IAC. DI (1390-1426), P.
Bol.—382-3, 386, 388
PARADISI, NIC. DI PIETRO (fl. 1394-
1430), P. Ven.—303, 410
PARIGI, ALFONSO (father of Giulio;
d. 1590). A. Flor.—426, 463
PARIGI, ALFONSO (son of Giulio; d.
1656), A. Flor.—442, 466
PARIGI, GIULIO (d. 1635), A. & P.
Flor.—438, 442, 466
PARIS, DOM. DI, see Alfani
PARMIGIANINO (Fr. Mazzola; 1503-
40),P. Parm. sch.—18, 19, 368-71,
382, 390, 432
PARODI, DOM. (1668-1740), S. & P.
Gen.—93
PARODI, FIL. (1630-1702), A. & S.
Gen.—22, 103, 314
PARODI, G. B. (son of Fil.; 1674-
1730), P. Gen.—99
PASQUALINO (fl. 1463-1504), P.
Ven.—320
PASSAROTTI, BART. (1529-92), P.
Bol.—388, 390
PASSIGNANO, DOM. (Cresti; 1560-
1638), P. Flor. sch.—424, 449,
494, 506
PASTI, MATT. DE' (fl. 1441-64). A. S.
& P. Ver.—408
PECORARI, FR. (fl. 1336), A. Crem.—
149
PECORI, DOM. (c. 1480-1527), P. Arc.
15-16C), S. Lomb.—202
PELLEGRINI, DOM. (1759-1840), P.
Bassano.—317
PELLEGRINI, GIAN ANT. (1675-1741),
P. Ven.—285
PELLEGRINI, see also Tibaldi
PELLEGRINO, Il, see San Daniele
PELLICCIAIO, JACOPO DI MINO DEL
(d. 1396), P. Siena.—519
PELORI, G. B. (1483-1558), A. & S.
Siena.—524
PENNACCHI, GEROL. DA (the
Younger; 1497-1544), P. S. & A.
Treviso.—328, 404
PENNACCHI, GIROL. (Il Vecchio;
1508-44), S. Ven. sch.—382
PENNACCHI, PIER MARIA (1464-
?1528), P. Trev.—303, 327

PENSABEN, MARCO (1485-1530), P.
Ven.—329
PERUGINO (Pietro Vannucci; 1446-
1523), P. Umbr.—165, 202, 390,
430-31, 437, 445-6, 448-9, 452,
463, 468, 523, 568, 573, 581, 588,
589-93, 595, 598-600, 603, 606,
613-4
PERUZZI, BALDAS. (1481-1537), A. &
P. Siena.—209, 381, 394, 469, 512,
515, 518, 523, 622
PÉSARO, SIM. DA, see Cantarini
PESELLINO, FR. DI STEF. (1422-57),
P. Flor. sch.—179, 428
PIACENTINI, MARCELLO (1881-1960),
A. Rome.—103, 127, 176, 182, 232
PIAZZA, ALBERTINO (15-16C), P.
Lodi.—364-5
PIAZZA, CALLISTO (fl. 1514-62), P.
Lodi.—186, 364
PIAZZETTA, G. B. (1683-1754), P.
Ven.—159, 274, 285, 304, 317-18,
320, 433, 587
PIERMARINI, GIUS. (1734-1808), A.
Foligno.—149, 157, 166, 173, 208
PIETRASANTA, FR. DA (late 15C), A.
& S. Lucca.—602
PIETRO, ANG. & FR. DI, D'ASSISI (fl.
1362), S. in Cortona.—588
PIETRO, BERN. DI (ca Carona; fl.
1500-13), S. Marches.—619
PIETRO, CECCO DI (late 14C), P.
Pisa.—504
PIETRO, LANDO DI (d. 1340), G. &
A. Siena.—516, 526, 558
PIETRO, LOR. DI, see Vecchietta
PIETRO, NIC. DI, see Gerini,
LAMBERTI, and Paradisi
PIETRO, SANO DI (1406-81), P.
Siena.—511, 513, 514, 515, 518,
519, 523, 525-7, 540-2, 544, 547,
550, 556
PIETRO, ZANNINO DI (Giovannino di
Pietro; fl. c. 1407), P. Ven.—621
PILACORTE, GIOV. ANT. (fl. 1484-
1531), S. Carona (Lugano).—334
PINTURICCHIO (Bern. di Betto; c.
1454-1513), P. Per.—510, 517-8,
523, 584, 587, 590, 592-3, 598,
606, 611
PIÒ, ANG. (17C), S. Bol.—389
PIOLA, DOM. (1628-1708), P. Gen.—
21, 94, 99
PIOMBO, SEB. DEL (Luciani; 1485-
1547), P. Ven.—222, 285, 300,
370, 432, 468-9, 516, 547
PISA, BONANNO DA (12C), A. & S.
Pisa.—500
PISA, FRA GUGLIELMO DA (13C), S.
& ?A.—305, 490
PISANELLO (Ant. Pisano; 1377-1455),
P. and medallist, Lomb.—15, 20,
94, 179, 184, 204, 206, 214-15,
217, 219, 223, 284, 437, 570
PISANO, AND. (c. 1270-1348/9), A. &
S. Pontedera.—419-20, 422, 461,
490, 504, 536, 538

NOTES

NOTES

INDEX

Topographical names are printed in **bold** type, names of eminent persons in *italics,* other entries (including the sub-indexes of large towns) in Roman type. The building activities of popes and emperors have generally been ignored.

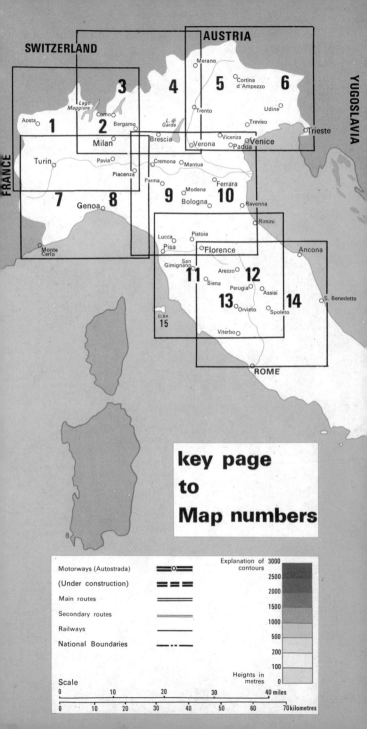

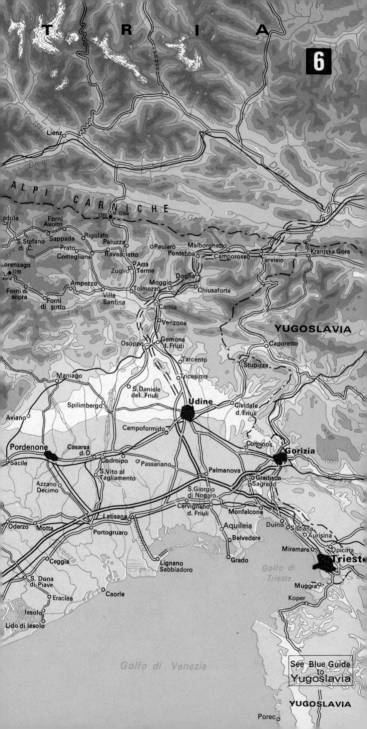

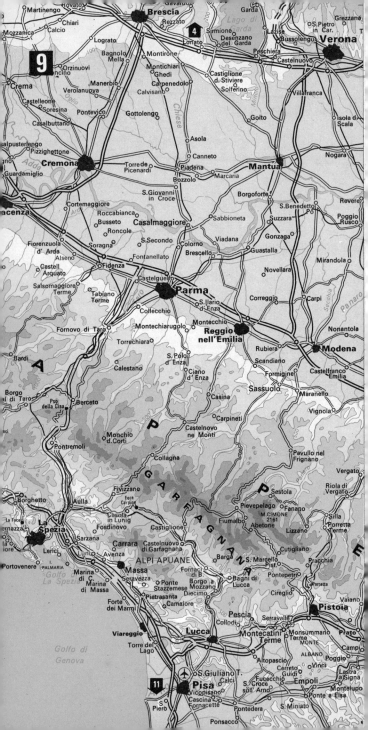

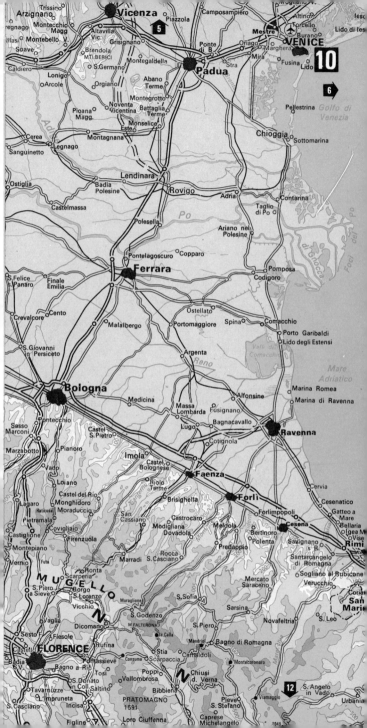

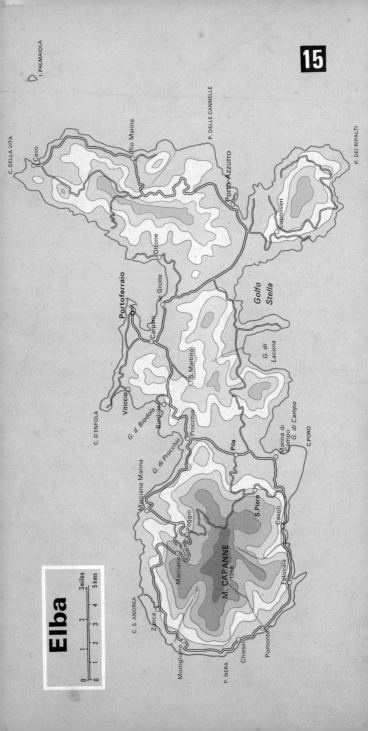

15

Elba

I. PALMAIOLA

C. DELLA VITA

Cavo

Rio Marina

P. DELLE CANNELLE

Porto Azzurro

P. DEI RIPALTI

Ottone

Capoliveri

Portoferraio

le Grotte

Carpani

Golfo Stella

S. Martino

G. di Lacona

C. D'ENFOLA

Viticcio

G. d. Biodola

Biodola

Procchio

Pila

Marina di Campo

G. di Campo

C. PORO

Marciana Marina

G. di Procchio

Poggio

S. Piero

C. S. ANDREA

Marciana

Cavoli

M. CAPANNE
1018

Zanca

Pomonte

P. NERA

Mortigliano

Chiessi

Fetovaia

3 miles
5 kms
0 1 2 3
0 1 2 3 4 5